West's Law School Advisory Board

CONSUMER LAW

CASES AND MATERIALS

Third Edition

By

John A. Spanogle

William Wallace Kirkpatrick Professor of Law
The George Washington University

Ralph J. Rohner

Professor of Law
The Catholic University of America

Dee Pridgen

Associate Dean and Professor of Law
University of Wyoming

Jeff Sovern

Professor of Law
St John's University

AMERICAN CASEBOOK SERIES®

THOMSON

WEST

Mat #40371066

American Casebook Series and West Group are trademarks registered in the U.S. Patent and Trademark Office.

COPYRIGHT © 1979, 1982, 1991 WEST PUBLISHING CO.
© 2007 Thomson/West
    610 Opperman Drive
    P.O. Box 64526
    St. Paul, MN 55164–0526
    1–800–328–9352

Printed in the United States of America

ISBN: 978–0–314–16152–9

 TEXT IS PRINTED ON 10% POST CONSUMER RECYCLED PAPER

To
Pam, Kathy and Sharon,
Monica,
Ken, Keiko and Emmie,
and
Jeri, Melanie, Lindsay and Jesse

*

Preface to the Third Edition

Your authors have allowed sixteen years to pass since the publication of the second edition of this casebook in 1991. Many things have occurred on the consumer law scene, and yet the subject endures. It may be safe to say at this point, over thirty years since consumer protection case books first started to appear and separate courses on consumer law first started to be offered at major law schools across the country, that this is not a fad. There is some kernel of distinction that sets the law affecting consumer transactions apart from other types of commercial law, contracts, torts, etc.

Since the '91 edition, many consumer transactions and the laws governing them have changed dramatically. Concepts that did not get significant attention in the '91 edition—in many cases because they had not yet been conceived—but that now merit inclusion in the book include the internet, predatory lending, telemarketing, identity theft, the rise of mandatory pre-dispute arbitration clauses, spam, phishing, e-commerce, yo-yo sales, shrinkwrap, clickwrap, browsewrap and rolling contracts, credit repair organizations, the sale of consumer information, online privacy, privacy policies, yield-spread premiums, the Boston Fed Study, changes in terms of credit card agreements, PayPal, and payday loans.

The new developments have led to new statutes and regulations, and amendments to existing ones. Thus the Third Edition of the casebook includes such legislative/regulatory developments as CANSPAM, the Gramm-Leach-Bliley Act, FACTA and the 1996 amendments to the Fair Credit Reporting Act, HOEPA, the Telemarketing and Consumer Fraud and Abuse Prevention Act, the Telemarketing Sales Rule and the creation of the "Do Not Call" list," the application of the Fair Debt Collection Practices Act to lawyers engaged in litigation, Check 21, FTC privacy interventions and state statutes governing predatory lending.

The need to include new materials generated significant issues for us in the new edition. Given the time constraints of the standard two or three credit hour law course, authors cannot add to a casebook indefinitely without cutting, so we cut the usury materials sharply because we think usury has become less important in light of federal preemption rules and the exportation doctrine. We also eliminated some of the less important materials on enforcement of consumer rights—though at the same time, we had to add new materials to the enforcement section about mandatory pre-dispute arbitration terms.

Two chapters in the Third Edition are almost completely new: Chapter Nine on predatory lending and Chapter Five on privacy. Some aspects of predatory lending appeared here and there in the '91 edition but given how predatory lending has surfaced as an important area with a new body of law, we thought it best to combine the new rules with the older aspects of predatory lending into a single chapter. The chapter serves several purposes. First, it is a capstone chapter. If Truth in Lending and deceptive trade practices laws worked better, then predatory lending regulation would be less necessary. So the predatory lending chapter picks up where those laws fail. This chapter includes HOEPA (an amendment to TILA focused on predatory lending), the state predatory lending statutes and preemption of state legislation by federal regulators. That last provides a fascinating lesson on preemption, a theme that formerly received a separate chapter but now is integrated with substantive materials at various points in the book. And as you might expect, the predatory lending chapter also builds to some extent on the materials in the credit discrimination section. Thus, the chapter pulls a lot of material together in what is an evolving but fascinating area.

Privacy also gets its own chapter. Privacy is an example of something that consumer law courses formerly gave little or no attention to but that is now so significant in consumer transactions that it merits greater treatment. The chapter takes up three aspects of privacy: first, solicitations, including telemarketing and spam; second, the sale of consumer information, which focuses on the Gramm-Leach-Bliley privacy protections for consumer financial transactions; and finally, online privacy, which involves both solicitations and the sale of consumer information. By organizing it this way, it becomes easier to think about the broad policies which ought to motivate privacy regulation and to see how similar issues are answered differently in different areas: for example: we have a "Do Not Call" list for telemarketing but not a "Do Not Spam" list. Privacy issues surface elsewhere in the book, including, for example, in the materials on debt collection in Chapter Eight—where the book explores the invasion of privacy torts as applied to debt collection, as well as the Fair Debt Collection Practices Act. Privacy also comes up with the chapter on the Fair Credit Reporting Act—which covers, among other things, who can see your credit report and identity theft.

One new coauthor, Jeff Sovern, has joined the team for this Third Edition. Jeff has provided us with the expanded focus on consumer privacy issues, an area that he has written in extensively. He also spearheaded the effort to add a "capstone" type chapter on predatory lending.

Paul Rasor, coauthor on the second edition, chose not to participate in this new edition as he has changed the direction of his career. We nonetheless owe him a debt of thanks for allowing us to build on what he had contributed to the second edition of the book.

We also wish to thank the Consumer Protection classes at the University of Wyoming and St. John's University law schools, who used and commented on draft versions of this new edition. In addition, we wish to thank Mark D. Bauer, Assistant Professor of Law, Stetson University College of Law, and Amy Quester, Adjunct Professor of Law, Washington &

Lee University School of Law, both of whom tested the materials in their classes and made very helpful comments on them.

Ralph Rohner thanks all those colleagues and students whose response to this subject matter and these materials has been so stimulating over the years, especially to co-authors Andy, Dee, and Jeff who have brought to the third edition great patience, insight, energy, and imagination about our favorite area of the law.

Dee Pridgen wishes to thank her research assistants, administrative assistants, library staff and dean and colleagues at the University of Wyoming College of Law, for their support on this project, especially during her sabbatical leave in the fall of 2005. She owes a special thanks to the George Hopper Faculty Research Fund. She also wishes to thank her husband Ken Matsuno and daughters Keiko and Emmie Matsuno, who have endured her preoccupation with this manuscript as it has been brought to fruition.

Jeff Sovern thanks Dean Mary C. Daly, Associate Dean Andrew J. Simons, the librarians (especially Arundhati Satkalmi), his colleagues (particularly Professors John P. Hennigan, Gina M. Calabrese, Ann L. Goldweber, G. Ray Warner, and Linda M. Ryan), his research assistants Tracy Ruhling, Erica A. Coleman, Dana E. Grabiner, Richard Elem, and Elizabeth Daitz as well as Agnieszka Wilewicz at St. John's University School of Law. He is especially grateful for the support of his wife Jeri Gilbert and his children Melanie, Lindsay, and Jesse. Finally, he thanks the many consumer law students who have taught him the things he needed to learn to contribute to this volume.

*

Preface to the Second Edition

> The answers may have changed,
> but the questions remain the same.

In the eleven years since the first edition of this casebook was published, almost every aspect of consumer law has been rewritten. The FTC has taken itself out of the "cutting edge" problems of deceit regulation. A litigation-prone Truth in Lending Act has been replaced by a nearly caseless Truth in Lending Simplification Act. Several approaches to consumer problems which seemed to be promising in 1979 have seemingly not had any great impact. Examples include class actions and the FTC Credit Practices Rule, and other Trade Regulation Rules. "Unconscionability," with only one prominent exception, is used more by corporations than by consumers. Even the federal-state tension and balance which permeated the first edition has shifted—both ways. State usury laws have been "deregulated" and preempted. On the other hand, the use of state "Baby FTC Acts" has grown to fill the gaps left by federal FTC inaction.

—AND YET—

The basic fact patterns analyzed in the Problems of the first edition still exist, with their tension between protecting consumers and allowing creditors and sellers to do business. Thus, a surprising number of the Problems used in the first edition are still useful teaching tools, and have been kept in this second edition. Some of the old scams have disappeared, and some new ones have appeared, and related Problems have been added, amended or deleted as necessary.

It's a different story with the cases and notes. Except for a few classics, or where historical development was needed, most of the cases have been replaced and notes rewritten.

The overall organization of the first edition has been maintained, with its four-Part division into: I. Regulation of Information, II. Regulation of Conduct, III. Regulation of Prices, and IV. Enforcement of all the above. Within those four Parts, there has been some rearrangement. The chapters in Part II relate to three different stages of the consumer transaction: pre-contractual relations (Chapters 3 and 4), obligations during performance (Chapters 5 and 6), and debt collection (Chapters 7, 8 and 9). Part III is broken into chapters on regulation of prices of goods and services (10), state regulation of interest rates (11), federal regulation of interest rates (12), an evaluation of these regulations (13), and the upside-down world of credit insurance (14).

Evaluations of the utility of regulation are attempted at the end of Chapters 2 (information), 4 (credit availability), 6 (cut-off of defenses), 9 (coercive collection) and in all of Chapter 13 (interest rate regulation). We believe that such evaluations are an integral part of any Consumer Law course.

Two new coauthors, Dee Pridgen and Paul Rasor, have joined the team for this second edition. One of the strengths of the first edition was its presentation of the tension between federal and state law in the consumer law area. Since the two original authors are now based in Washington, it seemed appropriate to bring in coauthors who were "outside the Beltway."

Each of the authors thanks all the other coauthors for their feedback, direction and support. Even though we are scattered around the country, overnight mail, the fax machine, the computer and the airplane allowed each of us to participate in the drafting (and redrafting) of all parts of the book. This book may be an example of Tofler's "Third Wave," where geographical boundaries no longer limit what we can do, as long as we can communicate.

We also wish to thank multiple classes of students who read through mimeo versions of earlier drafts of this book, and who helped to improve it by their reactions and constructive comments. It is appropriate that their comments are reflected throughout the book, and their enthusiasm helped us complete it, for they are the ultimate consumers of our effort.

We could not have written this manuscript without the help from each of our schools of our secretarial staffs, librarians, colleagues and deans. To all of them, we give a heartfelt "Thank you." Dee Pridgen especially wishes to acknowledge the financial support she received from the George Hopper Faculty Research Fund.

November, 1990

JOHN A. SPANOGLE
RALPH J. ROHNER
DEE PRIDGEN
PAUL B. RASOR

Preface to the First Edition

Too often, the materials for a consumer protection course start and end with theoretical problems, and have no substance in between. They seem to be based on an assumption that consumer protection laws are either only theoretically possible or some aberrant fluke of legislative madness which will not be repeated.

These materials proceed from a different set of assumptions: (1) Consumer protection statutes and caselaw doctrines are pervasive within the legal structure. (2) They are growing. (3) They are not likely to disappear, but are more likely to increase. (4) Even though they concern widely disparate subject-matter, there are likely to be common doctrinal and practical threads running through them, and it is our job to try to discover these threads.

Another problem with some consumer protection materials is that they rely on long quotations from law review articles, reports and other textual material to present information. There is now sufficient caselaw to provide a core of teaching materials. There are statutes also, in abundance. In many areas, the cases amply set forth both the present practices and the present legal doctrines. However, these cases should be read in the same manner as those for any other course—to evaluate and critique not only the holding of the case, but also its underlying assumptions, statute, and policies.

One pattern running throughout these materials is to compare judge-made law and legislation dealing with the same problem. Thus, where cases are presented, there will usually be discussions of statutory provisions dealing with the same problem.

The authors hope that these materials will enable students to do several things. One is to grasp a reasonable portion of the array of substantive law applicable in consumer transactions, with an appreciation both of its complexity and of its recurrent themes. Another is to appreciate the "hidden" workings of the consumer marketplace—the economic motives and consequences of transaction patterns. An equally important goal is to persuade students—most of whom instinctively applaud anything labeled "consumer protection"—that current statutory and caselaw approaches, and the policy choices underlying them, are not beyond criticism. If iconoclasm is perceived in these materials, it is intended.

For the purposes of this book, "consumer transactions" include those in which individuals enter into consensual arrangements for the purchase of property or services, or for the borrowing of money. These materials treat of the various legal rules designed to protect the consumer's *economic* expectations in those transactions. We therefore do not address such matters as products liability, or the regulation of product safety, or the rights of consumers in landlord-tenant or employment relationships, or other kinds of "transactions" in which consumers engage. Considerable attention is given to credit transactions since those present more, and more complex, legal issues than do cash transactions, and have generated more sweeping statutory controls.

These materials obviously build on concepts and rules treated in basic contracts courses, and in courses on sales, negotiable instruments and secured financing. This book is designed, however, to include ample prefatory and review material so that students need not have taken commercial law courses before taking Consumer Law. Neither of the authors treats those commercial courses as prerequisites, although one of us "recommends" that students take them first. In any event, students may profitably consult a basic commercial law hornbook, such as J. White & R. Summers, Uniform Commercial Code (1972), or R. Braucher & R. Riegert, Introduction to Commercial Transactions (1977).

Each of the authors first acknowledges that the other has contributed more than half the book. It is for this reason that the order of our names on the cover was chosen by coin flip.

To our students, past, present and future, we owe a debt beyond calculation. It is their interest and enthusiasm, their challenges, their critiques and their perceptions, that make this effort worthwhile.

We also acknowledge, with gratitude and affection, the support, encouragement and inspiration provided by two esteemed teachers of the law, Professors Homer Kripke and Fairfax Leary, Jr. In many ways, large and small, they are a part of this book and of the law it portrays.

There are many other people to whom we owe thanks for their help: Professor Jack Ayer, who was kind enough to share his unpublished materials with us, and whose materials furnished a springboard for many of our ideas. Our colleagues, who critiqued parts of the materials, especially Dick Bell, Grace Blumberg, Marjorie Girth, Nils Olsen, George Priest, Jack Schlegal, Paul Spiegelman, and Urban Lester. The mistakes and heresies in the final product, however, are ours, not theirs. And last but not least, our families, who did not tell us too often how absent we were.

April, 1979

JOHN A. SPANOGLE
RALPH J. ROHNER

Summary of Contents

Table of Contents

Page

Table of Cases

The principal cases are in bold type. Cases cited or discussed in the text are roman type. References are to pages. Cases cited in principal cases and within other quoted materials are not included.

Table of Statutes and Regulations

Introduction

What is it that sets consumer law apart from other doctrinal areas that one might study? Is it just that consumer law involves transactions in which individual purchasers or borrowers (for personal, family or household purposes) are interacting with merchants, bankers or financial institutions? Is it simply a different perspective, i.e., one of ostensibly unequal bargaining power between the parties, in recognition of which judges and legislative bodies seek to provide a legal "handicap" to the weaker party? Is it a paternalistic effort to protect the weakest members of society from their own ignorance and vulnerability? Or is it a way of balancing the economic scales, correcting a market imperfection, due to the fact that in many consumer/merchant transactions the assumptions of the perfectly competitive ideal simply do not hold true?

Whatever you may think of consumer law, it is clear that a body of common law, statutes, regulations, and government agency adjudications has proliferated since the rise of the consumer movement in the late 1960s. These various types of law, as they appear related to consumer transactions, are the subject of this casebook. Consumer law can be thought of as the top layer of a pyramid. The common law of contracts and torts, the law of banking and credit, and the Uniform Commercial Code, provide a foundation. The Federal Trade Commission Act pursues unfair and deceptive trade practices under a statutory mandate—whereas the same practices may have been pursued in the past as the tort of fraud, or under the contract doctrine of unconscionability. State unfair and deceptive trade practices acts have the same broad mission. The law of banking and credit has long been with us, but beginning with the Truth in Lending Act of 1968, a specialized area of law pertaining to consumer finance has emerged based on federal and state statutes and has flourished. Article Two of the Uniform Commercial Code lays the groundwork for the law of sales and warranties, and yet the Congress has overlaid this with the Magnuson-Moss Warranty Act and the states have added so-called lemon laws. The common law privacy torts have been supplemented by various statutes aimed at specific types of issues, such as financial privacy and unwanted emails. While this book reviews the bottom layer of the pyramid—because the top layers cannot be understood without reference to the bottom layer on which they rest—most of the book's focus is on rules that apply only to consumer transactions.

The book does not follow the "obvious" organization patterns, such as historical or chronological, because we believe that consumer law does have a set of concepts uniquely its own, and we hope the book will help to analyze them.

A primary level of attack on any perceived pattern of consumer abuse, dealt with in Chapters One and Two, is to regulate the disclosure of information to consumers, both as to accuracy and completeness. Regulation of informational conduct has deep roots and wide acceptance in our society: Truth in Lending is a more modern example, but proscriptions against deceptive advertising have been with us for years and the common law action of deceit is an even more ancient concept. The traditional negative constraints on disclosure (through liability for misrepresentation or breach of express warranty) are compared to the affirmative disclosure requirements embodied in many current laws. These chapters also allow some comparison of alternative legal devices: a common law approach, a generalized statutory standard, such as the Federal Trade Commission's (and its state counterparts') "unfair or deceptive acts or practices," or a detailed and technical statute such as Truth in Lending with its accompanying Regulation Z.

The problem-solver soon learns that disclosure does not eliminate all problems, and that more direct regulation of abuses is necessary in some cases. Thus statutes are passed or judicial decisions are rendered, prohibiting certain described conduct, or prohibiting "unfair" conduct generally, or requiring sellers and creditors to take certain measures for their consumers' protection. Many of these issues arise at the formation of the contract, such as marketing techniques like bait and switch, pyramid schemes, or door-to-door sales. Sometimes the terms of the deal are hidden from the consumer until it is apparently too late—contracts of adhesions are sent with the ordered goods or are buried on the computer screen. Should they be enforced? If so, under what circumstances? These matters form the focus of Chapter Three.

The modern consumer cannot fully participate in the economy without access to credit. And the creditors who serve this need cannot operate without a system for determining which consumers should be considered "credit worthy." Thus in Chapter Four we explore the world of credit reporting, and the increasingly complex regulation surrounding this industry to insure that information about consumers is accurate and is not indiscriminately distributed. The credit reporting system is intricately related to the modern day issue of identity theft, as victims are often left with a tainted credit record. In addition, unfair racial or gender discrimination in the granting of credit can be a problem, and it is also one that is addressed by specific legislation. This aspect of consumer law contains elements of disclosure, direct regulation, federal and state law, and a history of action and reaction in the regulatory arena.

Consumer privacy has emerged as a distinct subject as we enter the 21st century. Chapter Five shows a development that parallels the preceding chapters by starting with a foundation in tort law, and then moving to laws that have been passed in response to marketplace developments, and that exhibit the same complex relationships of disclosure vs. behavioral, broad vs. specific, federal vs. state.

Chapter Six on payment systems, Chapter Seven on warranty limitations and third party financing, and Chapter Eight on debt collection deal with problems consumers may face after their shopping is complete. Payment for consumer goods has evolved from cash or check to credit and debit cards, as well as electronic and internet systems. We begin with a foundation based on the checking system, but the creation of new payment mechanisms has led to different sets of rules, making for a complicated web of regulation. The consumer issues revolve around the marketing of credit cards and other "payment products," changing terms in ongoing accounts with creditors, billing disputes and unauthorized use. For products that exhibit defects, consumers turn to warranties, but too often find that their remedies may be limited. The law responded in an environment based on the Uniform Commercial Code Article Two, but layered by the federal Magnuson-Moss Warranty Act and state lemon laws. Moreover, consumers who have purchased items on credit may face a situation where the seller's duty to make good on its warranty is separate from the consumer's duty to pay the third party creditor. This area of consumer law has been subject to the "tug of war" phenomenon as each new consumer reform is met by a new variation of the issue. Chapter Eight explores what happens when consumers are delinquent in paying their debts. How far can debt collectors go in pursuing payment? Some pre-existing tort protections have been supplemented by the federal statute. This in turn has led to an evolution of interpretations in caselaw, and several rounds of statutory amendments that can make for a fascinating study of how the law may (or may not) keep pace with market developments.

If one were to compare the factual setting of the classic consumer law case of *Williams v. Walker-Thomas Furniture Company,* 350 F.2d 445 (D.C. Cir. 1965), a contracts text favorite used to illustrate the common law doctrine of unconscionability, with some modern situations labeled as "predatory lending," one would find many of the same basic issues. Abusive and overreaching marketing to and enforcement of unfair consumer credit agreements entered into by vulnerable consumers in low income settings have not been eradicated. Chapter Nine on predatory lending is intended as a "capstone" chapter that brings together many of the elements and laws of the preceding chapters and also introduces the approach of direct regulation of the cost of credit.

Finally, in Chapter Ten, we look at the private enforcement of consumer rights. It is a truism that a right is worthless without a remedy. Government enforcement, dealt with in prior chapters, is of course useful, but not sufficient. In the area of consumer rights, there has been an attempt to give consumers access to the courts to obtain justice for injuries that may be relatively small. This has been done through the statutory provision of attorney's fees to the prevailing consumer, class actions, and informal dispute resolution. The latter has proved in more recent times to be a double edged sword: non-court proceedings can be swifter and less expensive than court, but in some manifestations, as in individual commercial-style private arbitration, can be costly and perhaps even impair the ability of consumers to pursue claims.

These materials attempt to take the student through this process of thinking. We hope all of this will engender the type of analysis that creates cross-currents of thought to design non-traditional solutions to traditional problems.

A Note to Our Colleagues in the Chair— Students Should Not Read

We thought that a note on teaching methodology might be helpful. We have tried to present these materials through both cases and formal problems. The casebook seeks not only to familiarize students with the substance of consumer law, but also to provide additional practice with the application of statutes and regulations to factual issues. Consumer law itself is heavily, though not exclusively, statutory, so the course gives students considerable practice at statutory interpretation. The casebook uses problems both to force students to work their way through the statutes and to give students experience in problem-solving. We have tried to design these materials so that they can be used by teachers who prefer to use cases, those who prefer problems, and those in the middle. The problems do not cover exactly the same issues as the cases, and so each can be used to build on the other. The problems serve other goals as well. They are intended to point up flaws in the statutes—such as ambiguous statutory provisions, conflicting statutory provisions, and places where the statutes arguably do not serve their supposed goals. Some of the problems call upon students to consider amending statutes, which brings in policy considerations. The privacy chapter asks students to design privacy policies and notices.

Another principle is to use primary authorities wherever possible, in preference to secondary authority materials. Where we had a choice between presenting a transactional pattern through a law review article versus a case or a problem, we have tried to use the latter, on the ground that the student is likely to read a case more carefully, and a teacher is more likely to discuss a problem in class.

In all chapters, we try to present examples and illustrations of certain overarching themes of consumer law, such as the disclosure of information as a solution versus the use of real limits on behavior; the use of very specific laws and regulations to micromanage consumer transactions versus the use of broad statutes or causes of action that can change with the times; the clash of federal and state law versus the partnership between federal and state law. All of these themes can be seen in most subject areas, including advertising, marketing, credit, warranties, and privacy. Thus, in designing a syllabus, the teacher could pick and choose topics while still touching on most of the major themes of consumer law.

Another theme that has become evident over time is the "tug of war" aspect to consumer law. For example, after consumers won victories with state predatory lending statutes, banking interests found a sympathetic ear with federal regulators who preempted many of these state statutes. Or just as consumer interests appeared to have tamed the "holder-in-due course" monster, it may have been resurrected in the form of shields for assignee liability under TILA or securitization of predatory real estate loans. As business interests stemmed the tide of federal overregulation in the 1980s, a new wave of patchwork state laws arose in areas like state lemon laws and predatory lending. The authors hope these themes of overarching struggles, along with cases, problems and testimony will help students appreciate the drama in a sometimes technical subject.

By the way, if you are a student and have read this section, you have just been part of a demonstration project. Many consumer protection statutes require a legend to appear on consumer contracts or in mailings, which reads something like this:

"Notice to Consumer: Read this before you sign."

Many consumer and industry representatives believe this is a waste of trees used in the paper and a waste of ink as well. Perhaps it would be more effective to require a legend which states:

"Notice to Consumer: You may NOT read this paper before you sign it."

What do you think?

The Statutory Cast of Characters

—or, where do we find the "rules of the game"?

Consumer law is not exclusively statute law, but it is predominantly so. Many of the statutes fall into categories whose names are bandied about by insiders in a manner that is likely to bewilder a stranger. Here is a sort of scorecard calculated to give you brief identifications of the major statutory players.

Beginning with the Third Edition of this casebook, we recommend the use of the accompanying "Statutory Supplement" designed for this edition. It contains all of the major statutory and regulatory provisions that are referred to in the main text. Of course, one would need to consult the original unedited versions of the statutes and regulations for any major research projects related to consumer law. The selections in the supplement are meant for convenient reference by students and professors using the casebook.

A. State Legislation

One could argue that the oldest form of consumer protection against fraud by sellers was not in legislative form, but in the form of common law fraud actions. In this area, the Restatements of Tort and Contract, while not themselves statutes, have had some influence.

The Federal Trade Commission, long a champion of consumer protection on the federal level, built on the state common law to launch a national law of unfair and deceptive trade practices. In the 1960s the FTC urged states to adopt their own versions of the FTC Act, to extend the reach of the federal legislation. These "little FTC Acts," are now in place in all fifty states, and provide state and private causes of action to parallel the FTC's national enforcement authority. No one uniform model law was adopted, but rather the states seem to have followed several different models. Selected state unfair and deceptive trade practice acts are included in the statutory supplement.

In the consumer credit arena, many state statutes parallel or complement the federal law. State usury laws are perhaps the oldest, but these have largely been preempted or fallen into disuse. The Uniform Consumer Credit Code (U3C) is a relatively modern model statute in this sector, but it was published in two forms, one in 1968, and then a revised version in 1974. The U3C was criticized by consumer advocates, and ultimately was adopted in only a few states. Other states enacted hybrids, taking some of the provisions or variations proposed by consumer groups. Virtually every state has some type of consumer credit code, and also small loan licensing statutes. We have used the U3C provisions as a point of reference.

In the 1990s and 2000s, state legislatures have also been active in regulating certain types of abusive loan practices such as "payday" loans (short term, small loans with very high interest rates), and "predatory" loans, i.e., high rate loans typically secured by a residence, which are marred by such practices as frequent refinances (flipping), oppressive terms (such as pre-payment penalties), and are targeted to vulnerable consumers (low-income, minorities, elderly).

Consumer privacy is an area that has come to the forefront of consumer concerns in the 1990s and 2000s. In more recent times, there have been rather specific statutory responses to specific consumer privacy issues. Many of these "sectoral" statutes are federal, such as in the areas of credit reporting, financial privacy, and restrictions on solicitations. But there are various state responses in this area, such as state laws on home and telephone sales and state laws addressing access to consumer credit reports. The interplay between federal and state responses in this area echoes what has occurred in other aspects of consumer law.

In the area of product sales and negotiable instruments, the Uniform Commercial Code (UCC) ought to be the fountainhead of consumer law, but it is not. With only a few exceptions, the UCC does no more than set some outer limits of consumer protection, and provides a foundation for reforms such as state "lemon" laws and the federal Magnuson-Moss Warranty Act. The original drafters of the UCC made a more or less conscious decision to leave the tough consumer questions for another day. This, unfortunately, does not necessarily mean that the UCC is neutral on consumer issues. Instead, by refusing to deal with them, the UCC often treated consumer issues as though they did not exist, and left consumer transactions under the same regulations as merchant-to-merchant transactions. In the 1990s and early 2000s, Articles 2, 2A, 3, 4 and 9 underwent some major revisions, and some consumer protection provisions were added, which will be pointed out in the text. The "pro-consumer" revisions proposed for Article 2 on sales and warranties, however, were stymied by industry opposition, especially from software licensors, and so the subsequently proposed amendments to Article 2 are not as progressive in this respect as some consumer advocates had hoped.

The Uniform Computer Information Transactions Act (UCITA) was one product of the controversy over the revision of Article 2. As its name implies, it applies to software licensing and warranties. While not actually adopted in many states, UCITA has been influential in some cases involving computer information transactions, which are discussed in Chapter Three of the casebook.

The state "lemon" laws, dealing with new car warranties, were overlaid on the framework of the UCC Article 2 warranty law and provide more favorable remedies to consumers who have purchased a vehicle with apparently unfixable defects.

In some areas regulated by state statutes, what uniformity exists has come not from the publication of formal model statutes, but rather from a more ad hoc pattern in which states adopted new statutes to address problems as they came to their attention, and other states followed suit, often mimicking the first law to be enacted. For instance, the state lemon laws were adopted in a wave of enthusiasm in the early 1980s, using the statutes of early adopting states such as Connecticut as a model. The same pattern occurred in the area of anti-predatory lending statutes, with North Carolina serving as a leader in that effort. The ad hoc nature of state legislation in the consumer protection field has often led to countervailing exercises of federal preemption, as has occurred in the area of predatory lending. On the other hand, at times state legislation has responded to a need to expand on or adopt the federal model, as in the "little FTC Acts," or as a way to fill the gaps left by inadequate federal laws, as the state "lemon laws" attempted to improve on not only the UCC but also the federal Magnuson-Moss Warranty Act. This see-saw (or tug-of-war depending on your point of view) between state and federal law constitutes a quintessential aspect of the study of consumer law.

B. Federal Legislation

The Federal Trade Commission Act has, since the 1930s and perhaps earlier, established broad authority for the Commission to act on behalf of consumers in the marketplace. As mentioned above, the mandate is to regulate "unfair and deceptive acts or practices in or affecting commerce," principally under Section 5 of the Act (15 U.S.C. § 45). The Commission is also authorized to issue Trade Regulation Rules which have the full force of law and which in effect add another layer of governmental regulation. FTC rules on door-to-door sales, holder-in-due course, and credit practices are included in the statutory supplement. Perhaps in reaction to the per-ceived over-zealous rulemaking activities engaged in by the FTC in the 1970s, most of the regulations issued by the FTC in the 1990s and 2000s have been specifically authorized by Congressional legislation. These include the Telemarketing Sales Rule (including the popular "Do Not Call" registry), and the regulations implementing the Magnuson-Moss Warranty Act.

In the credit area, Congress enacted the umbrella Consumer Credit Protection Act in 1968 (CCPA, codified starting at 15 U.S.C. § 1601), and has been adding to and revising it ever since. Title I of the CCPA is the Truth in Lending Act (TILA), which requires certain disclosures in con-sumer credit sales and loans, regulates credit advertising, and allows "cooling off" periods and provides other safeguards in certain mortgage transactions. The Truth in Lending title has been amended several times to add new chapters on credit billing practices (the Fair Credit Billing Act), consumer leases (the Consumer Leasing Act), and predatory lending (Home Owners' Equity Protection Act or HOEPA).

The CCPA has also been amended to add new titles dealing with cred-it reporting agencies (Title VI, Fair Credit Reporting Act), discrimination in credit transactions (Title VII, Equal Credit Opportunity Act), collection agency practices (Title VIII, Fair Debt Collection Practices Act), electron-ic fund transfers (Title IX, Electronic Funds Transfer Act), and credit repair (Title IV, Credit Repair Organizations Act). The Fair Credit Report-ing Act (Title VI) was itself amended in 1996 and 2003, mainly in response to concerns about consumer privacy and identity theft. Title VIII on debt collection was also amended in 2006. Thus, this set of federal laws in the consumer credit area appears to provide a framework that can and will be built upon as conditions change in the consumer credit marketplace. The Federal Reserve Board is charged with promulgating regulations under some titles of this statute, and has been quite active in doing so, along with issuing staff commentary. The statutory supplement includes both the statutes and regulations in this important area of federal consumer law.

The Magnuson-Moss Warranty Act, 15 U.S.C. § 2301 et seq., estab-lishes certain minimum requirements for written warranties offered by suppliers of consumer products. The FTC has issued implementing regu-lations.

In the privacy area, in addition to the provisions of the Fair Credit Reporting Act relating to consumer privacy with respect to credit reports, Congress has also passed legislation regulating unsolicited electronic mail (CANSPAM Act, 15 U.S.C. § 7701 et seq.), and consumer financial privacy (Gramm-Leach-Bliley Act, 15 U.S.C. § 6801 et seq.).

As to consumer enforcement, many of the federal statutes referenced above provide private rights of action for consumers, with attorneys' fees and statutory damages for prevailing consumer plaintiffs. However, these provisions aimed at providing better access for consumers to the court-house to enforce their statutorily-created rights have been challenged by another federal law, the Federal Arbitration Act (9 U.S.C. § 1 et seq.), that has undergone somewhat of a renaissance in the 1990s and 2000s as a roadblock to consumer class actions. The issue arises when mandatory arbitration clauses are inserted into the boilerplate of consumer contracts of all types (credit, warranty, etc.), and are then enforced by the courts pursuant to the Federal Arbitration Act.

C. Caveat!

The statutes and regulations mentioned above, exhaustive as they may seem, provide only a partial scorecard. Probably countless bits and pieces of state and federal law impact on consumer transactions; some of these may have broader application while others may be narrow ad hoc consumer protection measures. Also, in the Third Edition, the authors have included some references to consumer protection measures from European Union law, in recognition of the fact that we are now all participants in a global economy.

In the years since consumer protection law has emerged as a "standalone" subject in law schools and legal scholarship, one thing has become clear—no one has a crystal ball that enables us to see the future of consumer law. This book reflects some patterns in the form of a back-and-forth between new developments in the marketplace and legislative responses; between federal legislation, followed by state supplements; and also between early state legislative responses followed by federal legislation and preemption. But the ultimate resolution of these conflicts remains to be seen.

D. Note on editorial style and supplementary materials

In order to conserve space, we have regularly dropped citations from judicial opinions without marking the deletions. We have also frequently omitted footnotes of the court; those footnotes that remain bear the court's numbering.

As noted above, we have published a separate statutory supplement for the Third Edition of the casebook which contains all the major statutory and regulatory provisions cited in the main text.

The matters discussed in this book have also been the subject of considerable commentary elsewhere. For example, two of your authors have published relevant treatises: Dee Pridgen, Consumer Protection and the Law; Dee Pridgen, Consumer Credit and the Law (the latter with Richard M. Alderman since 2007) (both updated annually and, like this casebook, published by Thomson/West); and Ralph Rohner, Truth in Lending (2000) (with Fred H. Miller). The National Consumer Law Center publishes a set of valuable volumes each addressing specific topics in consumer law while Gene A. Marsh's Consumer Protection in a Nutshell (3d ed. 1999) provides a shorter treatment. At least two law journals specialize in consumer issues—the Consumer Finance Law Quarterly Report and the Loyola Consumer Law Review—and the Business Lawyer publishes an annual survey of consumer law developments. Several useful newsletters cover aspects of the field, including the Antitrust and Trade Regulation Report (BNA), Consumer Financial Services Law Report, the Privacy and Security Law Report, Privacy Times, the NCLC Reports, and the Consumer Credit and Truth-in-Lending Compliance Report. While it is not yet clear that blogs will become a permanent feature of the legal landscape, several explore consumer issues, including the Consumer Law and Policy Blog (to which one of your authors is a contributor), located at www.clpblog.org and Credit Slips, at http://www.creditslips.org/creditslips/.

Adam and Brynne: A Cautionary Tale of Two Consumers

[Our years of teaching consumer law have taught us that students sometimes wish a richer roadmap to the course than can be provided in a Table of Contents or even an outline of topics such as we supply above. Accordingly, consider the following story. It provides a brief tour through most of the major topics covered in this volume. How should the law respond to the issues generated by the story? Later you will be able to compare your answers to those produced by our legal system.]

Adam and Brynne Consumer have just graduated from college, married, have good jobs and are setting up a household. They rent, but they need furniture, appliances, and a couple of cars. Neither has ever bought a car before. Someday soon they plan to buy their own house.

Their credit history is mixed, as is usual with students. Both Adam and Brynne have enormous amounts of student loans and credit card debts. Their credit cards, obtained as students when they had very little income, were issued to apparently high-risk holders and the terms are not very favorable. Adam and Brynne would like to replace them with some sort of card with more favorable terms.

When Adam and Brynne began to look at cars, their first difficulty was in obtaining information about the cars. Adam wants to buy a used car; he believes that he is mechanically-adept enough to keep an older car running. But when he is looking at the cars on the lot, how can he tell whether a particular car has been in a serious accident or whether it truly was "owned by a little old lady who only drove it to church on Sundays," as the seller claims?

Brynne, on the other hand, wants none of these problems, so she is looking exclusively at new cars. She believes that she can get all the information she needs from Consumer Reports. Then someone tells her stories of new cars that were driven by the manufacturer's employees with the odometer disconnected, or that had been underwater in a flood, or that fell off the car transporter, and were repaired and sold as new.

Adam and Brynne would like to know whether the seller can deceive them about defects in the cars. They don't think a seller can state a fact that isn't true, but what if the seller only implies it? Or if the seller just stays silent about a fact? What if the seller does not know something; is there a duty on the seller's part to investigate? Or is there a duty on the buyers to investigate? Do the answers to all these questions depend on whether the defect in the car is apparent or latent?

Brynne sees lots of enticing ads for new cars every day, but does not know whether to believe them or not. She knows that the First Amendment to the Constitution protects free speech, but does it also protect false speech about consumer products?

Once Adam and Brynne have decided which car they wish to buy, they will need financing. What information will they need to decide among the various loan offers? How should they get that information? The new car dealership has offered her *either* "0% financing" *or* "$1,000 cash back". Which is more advantageous?

When Adam and Brynne seek new credit cards with better terms, they run into a different problem. Each credit card issuer discloses all its terms, but they cannot understand some of them. The terms are quite complex, with different introductory rates, balance transfer rates, penalty and late fees, over-the-limit fees, and to make matters worse, they cannot decipher the method for calculating the balance on which the rate is charged. Adam and Brynne cannot tell whether the new cards are a "better deal" than the old cards, and so do not know which ones to use.

Next Adam and Brynne go shopping for furniture. They see an ad for "3 rooms of furniture for $2,990," including living room, dining room and bedroom furniture. That amount fits their budget nicely. The pictures in the ad make the furniture look quite attractive, but in the store, the actual furniture looks "tacky." Adam wants to stick to their budget and buy it, but Brynne really wants something better. The salesperson appears and begins to detail all the faults of the advertised furniture, and Adam stops arguing for it.

The salesperson then leads the consumers to a much better-looking set of furniture that is available "for only $6,900." Brynne really likes the new set, but Adam says they can't afford it. The salesperson tries to be helpful, stating that this store uses personal testimonials in its TV advertising. The Consumers could record such a testimonial and would be paid $100.00 each time their ad was seen on TV. If their ad runs three times a week for three months, the better furniture would cost the same as the "tacky" furniture. The Consumers are persuaded that they can afford the more expensive furniture but their testimonial ad ends up being used only twice and then dropped. The Consumers think something is wrong with this transaction, but they do not know what. What, if anything, should be done to help them?

The Consumers ordered a vacuum cleaner online. There were many screens to go through to make that purchase. One screen had a pop-up box with a "click OK to accept terms" button, which they clicked without reading. The machine arrived with three booklets enclosed, each wrapped in plastic. One booklet was labeled "Assembly Instructions," the second was labeled "Operations Manual," and the third was labeled "Important: Please Read." The latter contained seller's terms of the sale contract, including one clause that said the buyers' remedies were limited to repair or replacement of the machine; another clause required dispute resolution exclusively before the American Arbitration Association. The Consumers have decided that they really do not want this machine. What is the effect of the seller's terms of the contract included in the third booklet and in the "click ok" screen?

Meanwhile, after Adam and Brynne had obtained enough information to decide which creditors offered them the best credit terms in their search for new credit cards and car financing, it was time for them to look at their own standing with creditors. They obtained their credit reports at www.annualcreditreport.com (and you should do the same). Adam found several transactions on his credit report he did not remember. He does not know whether this represents gaps in his memory, fraudulent creditors inventing transactions or identity theft. How can he find out and get his record cleared up?

After Brynne decided which creditor was offering her the best deal for the car financing, she filled out an application for credit with it. She was surprised when that creditor stated that Adam would have to co-sign for the loan. Brynne makes as much money as Adam, and wants to have her own, separate credit record because Adam's record has several defects. When Brynne asked why Adam needed to co-sign, she was told "Oh, it is just a standard procedure." But she is convinced that the creditor is afraid that, as a newlywed, she will seek extended maternity leave and default on the loan. Should the law prohibit this? How would she prove her suspicions in court?

Adam loves soccer. He buys every book on soccer that he can find. He shops primarily at one bookstore and uses his credit card to make the purchases. Recently, Adam began receiving telephone calls from companies selling soccer paraphernalia. The first couple of times he was called, Adam reacted enthusiastically and bought something. Since then Adam's enthusiasm has waned, and he wants the calls to stop. He also wants to know how the soccer businesses got his name, and whether his rights have been breached by disclosures to them.

Adam put his name and number on the FTC's "do not call list," but the soccer companies kept calling. They claimed that they had a relationship with Adam before his name went on the list, so they could keep calling. To make matters worse, Adam is now starting to get emails from soccer businesses, including some that are obviously in other countries, and some of them are demanding that he pay for purchases they claim he has made. He does not know whether these represent "phishing expeditions" or a possible identity theft problem. What should Adam do?

For the first year, Brynne was very careful to return every opt-out notice from a financial institution, saying that she did not want her personal information shared with anyone. When the second round of notices came out one year later, she did not bother to respond, because she had already opted out. She also shops on-line a lot, and has never bothered to screen for "cookies." Recently, she has begun receiving a great many emails and "pop-ups" which are very targeted to her situation and show awareness of both her personal finances and her shopping habits. She would like for these to stop. What would you advise her to do?

Adam and Brynne have been receiving mail from credit and debit card companies they have never heard of, promising "Your New Account is Open". Other mail comes from their credit card issuers saying "We are modifying the terms of your credit card contracts." The Consumers do not want the new accounts or the modifications to the existing account terms. Can you do anything to help them?

Adam loaned his credit card to his brother to let him charge the expenses of an evening out. But his brother kept the card and also charged gasoline and food on it. Adam called the credit card issuer and said, "don't let my brother charge anything further on the card." The bank said "Bring us the card." Adam's brother made subsequent purchases on Adam's card—for clothes and car repairs. Adam wants to know two things: (1) How can he avoid liability for any future charges his brother may make? And (2), is he responsible for the purchases his brother has already made?

Brynne set up a PayPal account so she can buy things on EBay. PayPal is charging her for transactions she did not make. First, it drained her bank account and then it added charges to her credit card account. Can she do anything to stop this, or to get her money back?

Meanwhile, Brynne's car has stopped working. It refused to start on cold and snowy mornings. After Brynne endured several mornings of trudging through the snow to public transportation, she called the seller and said she wanted "to give the car back." The seller immediately informed Brynne that they had sold the new car to her "as is," and that all she could rely on was the "standard manufacturer's warranty" that was in the glove box of her car when she purchased it. According to the terms of the manufacturer's warranty, she could bring in the car for repair, but she could not return the car (rescind or revoke her acceptance). The seller says it would be happy to act as the manufacturer's agent, but it has no liability of its own.

Brynne is confused by this. She understands that some kinds of goods can be sold "as is" (with no warranty) but she does not think that that should be possible with new cars. She believes that there should be some law that requires the seller of a new car to stand behind its goods. She also remembers that many of the ads for her new car, including local ads, mentioned a warranty that lasted more than one year. Does Brynne have any rights that can be enforced in a court? Would it be economically feasible to do so?

Brynne had financed the car purchase with a bank loan which had been arranged by the seller. She had the brilliant idea of putting pressure on the seller by refusing to pay the bank. When her first payment was due, she sent no money, but did send a well-written letter explaining why she was not paying. After she missed three payments, the bank sent her a letter stating that if she did not make her payments immediately, its report to the credit reporting agencies would severely damage her credit rating. What can Brynne do now? What should she have done? She believes that she should not have to pay for a car that does not work.

Adam bought the couple's furniture and appliances using his credit card. The furniture seller delivered about half of the furniture and said that the other half was no longer in production, and therefore not available. But the seller charged the entire amount to Adam's credit card, with no reduction for the non-delivered goods. Adam's contract with the seller contains a standard manufacturer's warranty. Does it provide useful relief to Adam? Can Adam get any relief through the bank that issued his credit card? Adam has also discovered that several of the appliances that were delivered do not work or do not operate properly. Should the law provide him any relief?

When Adam refused to pay the charges for the furniture on his credit card bill, his telephone began ringing. At first, it was the credit card issuer, then it was a debt collection agency, and finally it was the debt collection agency's lawyer. Each of them threatened to sue if the debt was not paid. The debt collection agency threatened to repossess the furniture. But nothing happened, so Adam still has not paid. However, the telephone calls keep coming, especially at dinner time, and they are taking a psychological toll. Can they be stopped?

Brynne's car was repossessed in the middle of the night. Brynne heard the repossessors come, so she got out of bed, got in the car, and told the repossessors to go away. They responded that they were only picking the car up to take it back to the seller to repair it. Finally, Brynne was persuaded to get out of the car but she still told the repossessors not to take it away. They did so anyway, once she physically exited the car.

Despite their credit troubles, Adam and Brynne decided to buy a house. They found the perfect house but did not have enough money for a down payment. Most mortgage lenders did not want to make them a loan because of the lack of a down payment and their credit history. One lender, White Point Bank, finally offered them a "nothing down, interest only" loan. They signed dozens of pages of a bewildering stack of papers, but they did get the money and used it to buy their new home.

Later, they learned that White Point had actually made them two loans. One was at an adjustable rate (currently 8%) for 80% of the value of the house, with one balloon payment of the whole principal at the end of five years. The other was a "home improvement loan" for 20% of the value of the house, plus "points" and all the closing costs, at a fixed rate of 36% per year. When they learned the size of the second payment, Adam and Brynne became discouraged.

Black Point Bank offered them a way out. It would consolidate their two loans into one, and would lower their payments substantially. Adam and Brynne readily agreed to this, and signed all the necessary paperwork. Later, they discovered that the principal amount that they had borrowed had increased, and was still increasing further. Black Point explained that it, of course, had to charge significant fees for all its hard work in arranging the new loan and paying off the old loan. Also, since the payments were so low, those payments did not even cover the interest due on the loan, so the principal was growing. However, all that would end after one year, for then the payment schedule would change and the payments would increase enough to cover both the total interest and part of the principal. The Consumers are now terrified of what will happen to them next year. Can anything be done to help them?

Adam and Brynne now have several disputes with sellers and creditors. What is the best way to resolve them? One approach is to complain directly to the merchant or creditor. Would you recommend that?

If they want to go to court, they may have to pay an attorney, and the attorney's fees may be greater than the amount at issue, so court may not be a cost-effective remedy. However, if the statute allows the consumer to recover damages plus attorneys fees, that picture changes. It also changes if the attorney can bring a class action, but that option has its own restrictions.

One major problem is that the Consumers may have signed contracts with clauses that require them to arbitrate and prohibit them from going to court. How effectively can the Consumers vindicate their claims through arbitration? How binding are such clauses?

[If Adam and Brynne were to walk into your law office, would you be able to solve their problems or at least address their questions? Or if you were to represent one or more of the various businesses and creditors with which they dealt, would you have some good legal advice for your client? While your authors would not presume to guarantee that you will, our goal is that through the study of the materials in this book, you will gain a better idea about these matters. Happy reading and enjoy the course.]

*

CONSUMER LAW

CASES AND MATERIALS

Third Edition

*

Chapter 1

REGULATION OF VOLUNTARY DISCLOSURE

SECTION A.   THE COMMON LAW APPROACH—FRAUDULENT MISREPRESENTATIONS, OMISSIONS AND OTHER DEVICES

The consumer's need for reliable information in order to make intelligent purchasing decisions is self-evident. The law has therefore long afforded redress for purchasers who rely to their detriment on seller representations which prove to be false. The formulations of these legal rules have differed, however, depending on the nature of the transaction, the blameworthiness or innocence of the speaker, and the form of remedy sought by the injured buyer. In transactions involving the sale of goods (chattels), sellers are held to any express "warranties" they make as part of the sale, regardless of any intent to deceive or mislead the buyer. Rescission based on mistaken understandings of one or both parties is a traditional equitable remedy. The tort action for deceit, on the other hand, is premised more on seller's fault and buyer's justifiable reliance. The following excerpt from the watershed case of Derry v. Peek, 14 App.Cas. 337, 359, 374–75 (House of Lords, 1889), distinguishes the tort from the equitable remedy:

"This action is one which is commonly called an action of deceit, a mere common-law action." This is the description of it given by Cotton, L.J., in delivering judgment. I think it important that it should be borne in mind that such an action differs essentially from one brought to obtain rescission of a contract on the ground of misrepresentation of a material fact. The principles which govern the two actions differ widely. Where rescission is claimed it is only necessary to prove that there was misrepresentation; then, however honestly it may have been made, however free from blame the person who made it, the contract, having been obtained by misrepresentation, cannot stand. In an action of deceit, on the contrary, it is not enough to establish misrepresentation alone; it is conceded on all hands that something more must be proved to cast liability upon the defendant, though it has been a matter of controversy what

1

additional elements are requisite. I lay stress upon this because observations made by learned judges in actions for rescission have been cited and much relied upon at the bar by counsel for the respondent. Care must obviously be observed in applying the language used in relation to such actions to an action of deceit. * * *

I think the authorities establish the following propositions: First, in order to sustain an action of deceit, there must be proof of fraud, and nothing short of that will suffice. Secondly, fraud is proved when it is shewn that a false representation has been made (1) knowingly, or (2) without belief in its truth, or (3) recklessly, careless whether it be true or false. Although I have treated the second and third as distinct cases, I think the third is but an instance of the second, for one who makes a statement under such circumstances can have no real belief in the truth of what he states. To prevent a false statement being fraudulent, there must, I think, always be an honest belief in its truth. And this probably covers the whole ground, for one who knowingly alleges that which is false, has obviously no such honest belief. Thirdly, if fraud be proved, the motive of the person guilty of it is immaterial. It matters not that there was no intention to cheat or injure the person to whom the statement was made. * * *

In my opinion making a false statement through want of care falls far short of, and is a very different thing from, fraud, and the same may be said of a false representation honestly believed though on insufficient grounds. * * *

Apart from the tort law of deceit or negligence, buyers may be able to recover from sellers on the basis of "warranties" as to the quality of the goods. Historically, the seller's liability for "express" warranties originated as a part of the common law action of assumpsit—i.e., the seller bore responsibility for the represented quality of the goods as a part of his contractual undertaking. For many and varied reasons of policy, later courts and legislatures also found warranty obligations "implied" in the contract. The Uniform Commercial Code states these warranty concepts in sections 2–313, 2–314, and 2–315, available in the statutory supplement. See also James J. White & Robert S. Summers, Uniform Commercial Code, chs. 9–12 (4th Ed., 1995), and Uniform Commercial Code Supplement on Revised Article 1 and Amended Article 2 (2004).

For our purposes, the important points to grasp are the reasons for and consequences of characterizing one form of seller misrepresentation as the *tort* of deceit, and another form of misstatement as a *contractual* breach of warranty. The former rests on the breach of a duty to speak truthfully to those who justifiably rely on the statements, while the latter derives from the notion of a freely assumed (dickered) contractual undertaking. As the contracting process in consumer sales became more formalized, through standardized contract forms and "take it or leave it" attitudes by sellers, open negotiations between sellers and buyers over the quality of goods disappeared. Where contracts shifted the risk of serious injury to consumer buyers, courts responded by imposing quality responsibilities on sellers regardless of their contracts, through the doctrine of strict liability in tort. And in much the same way, the traditional doctrine of deceit has always served as a check on the seller's ability to avoid responsibility for express representations by clever contract gimmicks (such as a "merger" clause triggering the parol evidence rule).

We look more closely at limitations on the seller's freedom to avoid warranty liability in Chapter 7 *infra*. For now students should note that warranty and deceit may sometimes be parallel routes to seller liability, but that each theory has its unique ingredients and limitations. In many cases one theory or the other may be invocable, but not both; at times they may overlap.

The following cases and problems are a summary review of the common law causes of action—particularly the law of fraudulent misrepresentation and omission. The student should be on the lookout for those aspects of deceit which distinguish it from equitable rescission or breach of warranty, and for changing standards of seller responsibility for misstatements. For the basic elements of the common law causes of action, students can refer to Restatement 2d Torts, §§ 525, 551, 552 & 552C, and Restatement 2d Contracts §§ 161–173, available in the statutory supplement.

The common law of misrepresentation has been a known consumer protection device for decades, starting long before any perceived "consumer" movement. It has not, however, been a static doctrine. Many of the "elements" of such a cause of action actually measure society's expectations of the consumer, and the amount of protection he should be afforded—the opinion v. fact dichotomy, reliance, inducement, lack of knowledge of falsity, intention of the deceiver—and was the victim's reliance justifiable? As the following materials show, these standards have changed, and have offered less protection in the past than they do now. The policy question which overrides the technicalities is: What criteria should be used under present societal conditions?

But even with the common law actions still available to modern consumers victimized by fraud or deceit, this approach is limited. The tort actions often require a relatively high burden of proof, especially with regard to the seller's intent. In addition, the buyer's justifiable reliance on the seller's statements, or lack thereof, will also be an issue. Thus, if an innocent consumer were to unknowingly purchase a defective car on the assurance by the dealer that it was in good condition, but without having a written warranty, the common law causes of action would probably not come to that consumer's rescue in most cases (*but see* Carpenter v. Chrysler Corp., *infra*).

As will be developed more fully in this text, consumers now have an array of statutory causes of action to protect them from various forms of seller misrepresentations and to provide disclosures of relevant information. The statutes were developed in part to address the shortcomings of the common law actions discussed here. Among those to be covered in this chapter are the Federal Trade Commission Act, and state unfair and deceptive practices acts. Warranty law and the common law of contracts protect consumers from the injuries inflicted by seller misrepresentation, but special statutes also supplement consumer protection in this area, such as the Magnuson-Moss Warranty Act and state Lemon Laws (protection for breach of new car warranties), to be covered in Chapter 7, *infra*.

1. EXPRESS MISREPRESENTATIONS BY SELLERS

CARPENTER v. CHRYSLER CORPORATION

Missouri Court of Appeals, 1993.
853 S.W.2d 346.

STEPHAN, JUDGE.

Brian and Kendra Carpenter appeal from the judgment of the trial court ordering a new trial in favor of Chrysler Corporation ("Chrysler") and Scott Auto Sales and Finance Company d/b/a Chrysler–Plymouth West ("CPW"). This case arises out of the Carpenters' dissatisfaction with a new 1986 Chrysler LeBaron automobile they purchased at CPW in August 1986. The Carpenters subsequently learned that, prior to their purchase, their car had been driven some distance with a disconnected odometer. The Carpenters then sued Chrysler and CPW.

In their third amended petition, filed January 11, 1991, the Carpenters sought recovery against Chrysler and CPW in five counts. The various counts alleged the following: 1) statutory odometer fraud with damages sought pursuant to Section 407.546, RSMo Cum.Supp.1992 (in effect since 1989), Missouri's odometer altering statute, and pursuant to 15 U.S.C. Section 1981; 2) breach of express warranty under Missouri's New Motor Vehicle Warranties, Nonconformity Act, Sections 407.560–407.579 RSMo 1986 (Missouri's "Lemon Law") seeking rescission of the contract; 3) breach of contract seeking recovery of the full purchase price as damages; 4) entitlement to a declaratory judgment for removal of a lien on the car; and 5) fraudulent misrepresentation.

The trial court directed a verdict in favor of CPW on count one at the close of the Carpenters' opening statement with plaintiffs' consent. The Carpenters withdrew their allegation of odometer fraud in count five against CPW only, not Chrysler. The Carpenters then submitted their action to the jury against Chrysler on their first count for statutory odometer fraud and count five for fraudulent misrepresentation. The jury awarded the Carpenters $3,400 on count one and $3,400 actual and $1.19 million punitive damages on count five against Chrysler.

In the Carpenter's submission to the jury against the car dealer CPW the jury awarded the Carpenters $7,200 for breach of warranty and $3,400 actual and $17,000 punitive damages for fraudulent misrepresentation on count five. The jury also found in favor of the Carpenters on CPW's counterclaim against the Carpenters for nonpayment under the installment sales contract. The Carpenters appeal from the judgment entered by the trial court granting the motions for new trial filed by Chrysler and CPW. We reverse and remand the grant of a new trial in favor of CPW; affirm the grant of a new trial in favor of Chrysler and affirm the denial of judgment notwithstanding the verdict.

* * *

The facts, despite protracted litigation spanning nearly four years and resulting in a voluminous record of more than 1500 pages in the legal file and over 900 pages of transcript, are fairly straightforward. CPW, an automobile dealer in west St. Louis County, Missouri, had received the car at issue here, a 1986 Chrysler LeBaron, from Chrysler's Detroit, Michigan plant in February 1986. In March 1986 CPW discovered a leak in the power steering system of the LeBaron while it was sitting on CPW's sales lot. CPW replaced a seal in the power steering unit and refilled the car's power steering fluid. In April 1986 Chrysler sent CPW a recall notice and repairs kit to correct a wiring harness defect causing intermittent failure to start. However, CPW did not make the repair.

On August 25, 1986, Brian Carpenter ("Carpenter") went to CPW to buy two cars, one for himself and another automobile primarily for the use of his older daughter Kendra, then sixteen, as well as his fifteen year old daughter Kerry. He told the salesman he wanted a reliable car for his daughters. The salesman directed Carpenter's attention to the Chrysler LeBaron stating it was a reliable car. Carpenter did not test-drive the car because it would not start. The salesman attributed the difficulty to a dead battery. Nevertheless, Carpenter signed a sales contract that day to buy the LeBaron. The salesman told him the car would be taken care of and would be ready in two days. Carpenter left.

* * *

Later that same day Carpenter returned to the dealer for his new car. * * *. In order to finance his purchase, Carpenter traded in his Plymouth Reliant for a $2,000 credit and financed the balance of $17,268 under a retail installment contract. * * *

Carpenter began experiencing problems with the car almost immediately after his purchase. He returned the car to CPW on September 1, 1986, complaining of problems with the power steering, ignition, leaky oil and the electronic dash display. CPW replaced the power steering pump and ignition switch. Carpenter picked up the car September 4. He returned it one week later on September 11, 1986, because of persistent oil leaks. CPW replaced seven items.

Carpenter continued to experience problems with the car's power steering, oil leaking and digital dash display. He returned the car a third time to CPW on September 17. CPW removed the transmission and replaced the torque converter with a rebuilt assembly, replaced the oil pump and sent the car again to Firestone for realignment. Carpenter retrieved the car September 25.

The car's digital display gauges remained erratic, the steering "pulled" and, frequently, the car would not start in park, but would have to be started in neutral. On several occasions the car failed to start at all. Carpenter complained repeatedly to CPW and asked that the car be replaced. He took the car in for repairs several times in October and November, but no further work was done by CPW on those occasions.

In November Carpenter received notice of the recall for the defective wiring harness. He took the car to CPW in December for repairs for difficulties with the transmission, the steering, the radio and oil leaking. The car was in the shop from December 1 through December 9. CPW again replaced the torque converter, the speed sensor switch and the entire transaxle. However, CPW did not repair the defective wiring harness.

Despite Carpenter's continued complaints with the car's steering, CPW made no further repairs after those repairs of December 11, 1986, at 4,000 miles. Carpenter's recourse to other dealers provided no satisfaction because they refused to honor the mechanical breakdown protection extended warranty that Carpenter had purchased through CPW. In April 1987 Carpenter notified Mercantile, the assignee of the installment contract on the car, that he intended to make no further car payments because of the car's numerous defects.

In July 1987 Carpenter also received a letter from Lee Iacocca, Chrysler's chairman, informing Carpenter that Carpenter's LeBaron automobile had been utilized in Chrysler's overnight evaluation program while still at the manufacturer's site in Detroit, Michigan, before the car had been shipped to CPW. The Overnight Evaluation Program ("OEP") was a program Chrysler designed to provide an assessment of the function, performance, appearance, safety and quality of its vehicles. A Chrysler employee testified the program had been in effect since at least 1969. Under the program, Chrysler employees drove new Chrysler cars, ready to be shipped, from work to home and back to work in order to evaluate the vehicle's quality. During these test drives the odometers were disconnected. Upon learning of his car's use in the OEP program, Carpenter quit driving the LeBaron sometime in July or August 1987.

* * *

The car was eventually repossessed while sitting in Carpenter's driveway by CPW which had repurchased the installment car contract from Mercantile Bank. CPW resold the car at a wholesale auction to a used car dealer for $2500. Another customer ultimately bought the car in July 1990 for $5200.

After the jury returned its verdicts in favor of Carpenter and against CPW and Chrysler, the trial court permitted Chrysler to introduce certain federal court records offered by Chrysler in mitigation of punitive damages. These records reflected that Chrysler and two of its executives had been indicted; eventually had entered pleas of nolo contendere to criminal charges as a result of the odometer disconnections; and had paid fines of $7.3 million. In a related civil class action involving multi-district litigation, a settlement was reached. The Carpenters had not been involved in that class action suit.

* * *

We begin with a scrutiny of the record on the fraud count. The elements of fraud are: (1) a representation; (2) its falsity; (3) its materiality; (4) the speaker's knowledge of its falsity or his ignorance of its truth; (5) the speaker's intent that it should be acted on by the person and in the manner reasonably contemplated; (6) the hearer's ignorance of the falsity of the representation; (7) the hearer's reliance on the representation being true; (8) his right to rely thereon; and, (9) the hearer's consequent and proximately caused injury.

The Carpenters argue that they produced substantial competent evidence to meet each of these elements to support a finding of fraudulent misrepresentation against both Chrysler and CPW. We first address the Carpenters' fraud claim against Chrysler. The Carpenters claim that by disconnecting the odometer and in failing to tell purchasers about disconnecting the odometer, Chrysler made a representation about the total mileage on the vehicle which was false. At no point does Chrysler deny that it disconnected the LeBaron's odometer. The evidence clearly established the first two elements of the Carpenters' fraud action against Chrysler that Chrysler made a representation that was false.

Chrysler, however, posits there were serious evidentiary shortcomings with the remaining elements of the Carpenters' fraud case against it such as materiality, scienter, reliance and damages. Chrysler highlights its own evidence that it acted with the good faith belief that its OEP benefitted consumers by permitting detection and correction of actual and potential problems and that its operation of OEP was proper and legal. Regardless of Chrysler's motive, such evidence does not contradict that Chrysler knew that certain automobiles it manufactured were driven with disconnected odometers and that Chrysler did not disclose this fact to its car buyers or dealers. Long ago this court held that "a representation with reference to the mileage of an automobile is a representation with reference to a material fact." *Jones v. West Side Buick Auto,* 93 S.W.2d 1083, 1086[2] (Mo.App.1936). The element of materiality was also satisfied, as well as Chrysler's knowledge of the representation's falsity.

Chrysler also attacks evidence of the Carpenters' reliance as too insubstantial to permit submission of the case to the jury. The rule is that, while the plaintiff who complains of the defendant's fraud must show that the false representations made to him by the defendant induced him to act to his prejudice, the fact of his reliance upon such false representations need not invariably be established by direct evidence to that effect, but may be inferred from all the facts and circumstances in the case. *Jones,* 93 S.W.2d at 1087.

Chrysler attempts to distinguish *Jones* from this case. Chrysler observes that in *Jones,* the car buyer testified that he had looked at the odometer to determine the number of miles before he decided to buy the car. The court in *Jones* held that the buyer's act of checking the odometer clearly reflected his reliance on its mileage statement to support a case of fraud. *Id.*

Chrysler emphasizes that the Carpenters, unlike the plaintiff in *Jones,* did not look at the odometer in advance. Chrysler also asserts that the sixteen miles on the LeBaron's odometer had no significance on the Carpenters' decision to buy the car because that same day the Carpenters bought a new Plymouth Turismo which had twenty-five miles on its odometer. Nevertheless, none of this evidence refutes the Carpenters' testimony that they would begin to question a vehicle which displayed forty or more miles on its odometer. More importantly, Carpenter had also testified he would not have bought the car had he known the truth concerning the disconnection of the odometer. This testimony satisfies the element of the Carpenters' reliance on the accuracy of the odometer's reading as an indicia of the car's soundness.

The Carpenters' right to rely has not been questioned by Chrysler. The difference between the Carpenters' and Chrysler's relative positions in their ability to ascertain the truth of the odometer readings sufficiently establishes Carpenters' right to rely.

The final element for a submissible case of fraud against Chrysler requires the Carpenters' proof of damages proximately caused by Chrysler's misrepresentation. Chrysler persuaded the trial court that the Carpenters incurred no damages as a result of the disconnected odometer. Chrysler notes that Carpenter himself testified to his belief that a speedometer malfunction subsequently caused the car's odometer to register mileage incorrectly so that the vehicle had accumulated up to 17,000 more miles than appeared on the odometer. Chrysler concludes that, as a result, the Carpenters would have been forced at any later sale of the car to disclose that its true mileage was unknown, regardless of the car's inclusion within the OEP. Chrysler further states that no evidence established that the car was worth less than the original $16,999.50 purchase price paid by the Carpenters merely because of the car's use within the OEP.

Richard Diklich, the Carpenters' expert witness, calculated a twenty percent reduction in the car's value because of the unknown true mileage, given the type of vehicle, age and condition and mileage. * * *

* * * The car was sold, in fact, for $2,500, to a car dealer. That car dealer, in turn, resold the car as a repossessed auto for $5,200 on July 19, 1990, to a woman interested in buying a used car.

* * * His testimony sufficiently established the element of damages to withstand any challenge to the submissibility of the Carpenters' action against Chrysler for fraudulent misrepresentation for disconnection of the odometer.

[Although the evidence against Chrysler was sufficient to submit to the jury, the appellate court ruled that the trial court had justifiably exercised its discretion to grant a new trial to Chrysler based on a verdict against the weight of the evidence.]

* * *

CPW has also attacked the submissibility of the Carpenters' case against it on claims of breach of warranty and of fraudulent misrepresentation. * * *

The Uniform Commercial Code, in Section.2–313(1)(a), provides that an express warranty is created by an affirmation of fact or promise made by the seller to the buyer which relates to the goods and becomes part of the basis of the bargain. When such a warranty is made, the goods shall conform to the affirmation or promise. *Id.* It is not necessary to the creation of an express warranty that the seller use formal words such as "warrant" or "guarantee". Section.2–313(2). The seller need not have a specific intention to make a warranty. *Id.* An affirmation merely of the value of the goods or a statement purporting to be merely the seller's opinion or commendation of the goods does not create a warranty. *Id.* * * *

The Carpenters submitted to the jury that CPW had represented the LeBaron was reliable and in good, safe and roadworthy condition. CPW contends that the Carpenters failed to show that CPW made any representations of fact, not merely opinions, or that any representations constituted a material factor in the Carpenters' decision to purchase the Chrysler LeBaron automobile. Thus, CPW disputes that the Carpenters established the second and third elements of a prima facie case for breach of warranty.

In detailing his discussions with the car salesman at CPW, Carpenter testified that he had two daughters and that he and his daughters needed two cars in order for them to get to work and to school and that both he and his daughters would need reliable transportation. He was looking for "something that you could count on." Carpenter testified that when the CPW salesman showed him the LeBaron, the salesman said, "it was a good car, reliable, brand new. This might be what you're looking for. This is the kind of car to have." In response to whether the salesman had talked "about success they had had with that type of model of car", Carpenter answered as follows:

> He didn't elaborate on any success; just made the insinuations to me this was a new car, reliable, I can count on it. It was the kind of car I wanted to have for the deal I was trying to make.

When asked what the salesman said about his knowledge of customer satisfaction of other similar cars, Carpenter stated: "Yeah, it was a good car, reliable car, that people were satisfied with it." He testified that he told the salesman he intended the car to be used not only by himself but also by his sixteen year old daughter and, eventually, by his fifteen year old daughter as well. The dealer picked this particular car out for him as suitable, told him it was a new car and that it ran right. The salesman, however, never disclosed that the car had any prior mechanical problems. For example, when the car would not start for the test drive the salesman attributed the problem to a dead battery. Carpenter, instead, only test-drove the other car he purchased for himself. CPW also certified the Missouri Motor Vehicle Inspection Report listing the car's mileage. CPW never mentioned to Carpenter that CPW had repaired a leak in the car's power steering earlier that March or that a recall notice for a wiring harness defect had been sent. This testimony capsulizes the Carpenters' evidence against CPW concerning representations or warranties made by CPW when it sold the LeBaron to the Carpenters.

CPW is correct that a seller may exaggerate the quality or value of goods without becoming liable under a theory of breach of express warranty. A seller may puff his wares or express his opinion about the quality and value of his goods even to the point of exaggeration without incurring warranty obligation. On the other hand, if the representation is a statement of fact, a petition alleging such a misrepresentation may sufficiently state a claim for breach of express warranty or fraudulent misrepresentation. A given representation can be an expression of opinion or a statement of fact depending upon the circumstances surrounding the representation.

We believe that the Carpenters' petition alleged, and their evidence supported, that the representations made by CPW were statements of fact. CPW's salesman referred specifically to this particular car in attesting to its soundness, its reliability. The statements conveyed sufficient definite information about the quality of the LeBaron for that representation to be considered material.

In *Guess v. Lorenz,* 612 S.W.2d 831 (Mo.App.1981), we held the representation that the car was in good condition was an expression of opinion. *Id.* at 833. In *Guess,* the seller of a used car forthrightly pointed out its defects known to her, although her lack of mechanical knowledge was readily apparent. We concluded considering all the circumstances, it would not be reasonable to find that the seller's remarks about the car's condition were statements of fact and not purely opinion. *Id.*

Unlike *Guess* where buyer and seller were on equal footing, the seller here was an experienced car dealer. CPW enjoyed an additional advantage over the Carpenters because they had purchased an automobile from CPW in the past. Through his prior course of dealing with CPW, Carpenter was thereby rendered "disarmed and made credulous" in relying on the salesman's expertise. More importantly, CPW (despite its knowledge to the contrary) failed to disclose that this new car had problems with leaks in its steering system and had already been subject to a recall notice for a wiring harness defect. The evidence sufficiently established that CPW made a material misrepresentation of a statement of fact to the Carpenters to permit submission to the jury of the Carpenters' claim for breach of express warranty.

CPW asserts the same two shortcomings—proof of CPW's making a representation of *fact* and proof that no such representation was *material*—are lacking as elements in the Carpenters' fraud claim. Having analyzed these two elements in our determination whether the Carpenters made a submissible case for breach of express warranty, we need not reiterate our earlier discussion. The same evidence deemed sufficient to establish a material representation of fact to support the Carpenters' claim for breach of express warranty also supports their claim for fraudulent misrepresentation. Satisfied that appellants did make submissible claims against both Chrysler and CPW, we now turn to the merits of the Carpenters' appeal.

[The Missouri Court of Appeals ultimately concluded that the trial court had not abused its discretion to grant a new trial to Chrysler, but that the trial court had erred in granting the car dealer a new trial. The Carpenters waived their verdict for breach of warranty and elected to recover on the fraud count to avoid double recovery. The Supreme Court of Missouri denied cert.]

Notes

1. Do you agree with the jury that Chrysler's Overnight Evaluation Program caused damage to the buyer by driving a new car a few miles with the odometer disconnected? Were the Carpenters justified in relying on the salesman's statement/opinion that the vehicle was reliable?

2. Earlier cases involving consumer claims of fraudulent misrepresentation were more harsh than the *Carpenter* case in applying the fact/opinion dichotomy, and in requiring that the plaintiff's reliance be justifiable. In *Babb v. Bolyard*, 194 Md. 603, 72 A.2d 13 (1950), buyer-plaintiff alleged that a used car seller-defendant had misrepresented that the "dealer's price" of a 1946 Buick was $3000, when in fact it was only $1986. The court directed a verdict for seller on the ground that "a representation as to value is only an expression of opinion, not a statement of fact." Buyer did not have the right "as a person of ordinary prudence to rely upon the alleged misrepresentation."

3. Southern Land Company sold a farm to Saxby, representing it to contain 150 acres of timber, of which about 20 acres had been "burned over," and representing that cordwood would sell for $4 per cord. Saxby bought the property and found there were only 120 acres of timber, of which 60 acres had been burned over; and cordwood sold for a much smaller price than $4 per cord. Saxby sued the seller for fraud. The court ruled against the buyer, saying the seller was "merely expressing his opinion" about the amount of timber and that the price of cordwood in the future was too speculative to support a case for fraudulent misrepresentation. Saxby v. Southern Land Co., 109 Va. 196, 63 S.E. 423 (1909).

4. The principal case listed nine elements of fraud. The elements of the tort of fraudulent misrepresentation (deceit) are also summarized in Restatement 2d, Torts, § 525, as reprinted in the statutory supplement. These elements are subject to slight variations from state to state, and also their

wording has evolved over time. Prosser and Keeton, Torts (5th Ed. 1984), state the elements of the tort cause of action in deceit as follows:

1.   A false representation made by the defendant. In the ordinary case, this representation must be one of fact.

2.   Knowledge or belief on the part of the defendant that the representation is false—or, what is regarded as equivalent, that he has not a sufficient basis of information to make it. This element often is given the technical name of "scienter."

3.   An intention to induce the plaintiff to act or to refrain from action in reliance upon the misrepresentation.

4.   Justifiable reliance upon the representation on the part of the plaintiff, in taking action or refraining from it.

5.   Damage to the plaintiff, resulting from such reliance.

5.   The *Carpenter* case involved an allegation that Chrysler had deliberately operated their new vehicles with an inoperative odometer. Problems with turned-back odometers produced the Federal Motor Vehicle Information and Cost Savings Act, 15 U.S.C.A. §§ 1981–1991, effective in 1973, now codified at 49 U.S.C. §§ 32701–711, which makes it unlawful to alter odometer readings. The Act provides a private cause of action to aggrieved buyers. In addition, Missouri, like all other states, has a Lemon Law, which provides remedies for breach of new car warranties. Lemon Laws will be discussed *infra*, Chapter 7, section B(5). Query—Why didn't the Carpenters just pursue this matter as a Lemon Law case?

6.   The common law misrepresentation approach does not always bring favorable results for consumers, even in modern cases. In a "predatory lending" case the consumer plaintiffs claimed that a mortgage broker misled them regarding the terms of their loan, which contained substantial brokerage fees, a balloon payment, and an interest rate higher than the most favorable one they could obtain. Their common law fraud claim failed, however, since all the terms about which the consumers claimed confusion were disclosed in documents required by the federal Truth in Lending Act. The fact that the consumers admittedly never read the documents precluded them from reasonably relying on the broker's prior representations, according to the court. *See* Mills v. Equicredit Corp., 344 F. Supp. 2d 1071 (E.D. Mich. 2004). Chapter 9, *infra*, will discuss more fully the extent to which the common law failed to stop predatory lending.

Problem 1–1

Carol DePrey received a letter from the Oakwood Shores Resort which stated: "You are called upon to visit our resort, learn about the valuable opportunities available to you in purchasing a time share in our resort property, and then claim one of the Grand Prizes available for good listeners: one brand new BMW automobile, or one certificate entitling you to $10,000 worth of gold bullion. No purchase is required; and Mrs. DePrey, you are guaranteed to be awarded a prize." Carol immediately took the week off from work, jumped into her car, drove 250 miles to Oakwood Shores, listened patiently to its salesman pitch the time share, and then asked for her prize. She was somewhat surprised when the prize proffered was a book about last year's Olympic Games. She refused to accept that book, and asked for "her BMW." Oakwood responded that she did not win a Grand Prize, which was available only to time share purchasers. Instead, as a non-purchaser, she had won only "a prize"—the book.

Carol consults you. Has she a cause of action for common law fraud against Oakwood? What representations were made by Oakwood? Which ones were false? Did Carol justifiably rely on them?

Is it proper to look at the letter as a whole, and ask the court to look at the total effect of all the language rather than specific words or phrases?

How has Carol been hurt? How would her damages be measured? Would you take this case on a contingent fee basis?

2. FAILURE TO DISCLOSE OR FRAUD BY OMISSION

The tort of fraudulent misrepresentation presupposes that there has in fact been a misrepresentation. But what if the seller knows something detrimental about what she is selling but says nothing? The traditional maxim of "caveat emptor" or "buyer beware" is often the rule in such a situation, but there is a growing recognition of fraud by omission under certain circumstances.

JOHNSON v. DAVIS
Supreme Court of Florida, 1985.
480 So.2d 625.

ADKINS, JUSTICE.

* * *

In May of 1982, the Davises entered into a contract to buy for $310,000 the Johnsons' home, which at the time was three years old. The contract required a $5,000 deposit payment, an additional $26,000 deposit payment within five days and a closing by June 21, 1982. The crucial provision of the contract, for the purposes of the case at bar, is Paragraph F which provided:

F. *Roof Inspection:* Prior to closing at Buyer's expense, Buyer shall have the right to obtain a written report from a licensed roofer stating that the roof is in a watertight condition. In the event repairs are required either to correct leaks or to replace damage to facia or soffit, seller shall pay for said repairs which shall be performed by a licensed roofing contractor.

The contract further provided for payment to the "prevailing party" of all costs and reasonable fees in any contract litigation.

Before the Davises made the additional $26,000 deposit payment, Mrs. Davis noticed some buckling and peeling plaster around the corner of a window frame in the family room and stains on the ceilings in the family room and kitchen of the home. Upon inquiring, Mrs. Davis was told by Mr. Johnson that the window had had a minor problem that had long since been corrected and that the stains were wallpaper glue and the result of ceiling beams being moved. There is disagreement among the parties as to whether Mr. Johnson also told Mrs. Davis at this time that there had never been any problems with the roof or ceilings. The Davises thereafter paid the remainder of their deposit and the Johnsons vacated the home. Several days later, following a heavy rain, Mrs. Davis entered the home and discovered water "gushing" in from around the window frame, the ceiling of the family room, the light fixtures, the glass doors, and the stove in the kitchen.

Two roofers hired by the Johnsons' broker concluded that for under $1,000 they could "fix" certain leaks in the roof and by doing so make the roof "watertight." Three roofers hired by the Davises found that the roof was inherently defective, that any repairs would be temporary because the roof was "slipping," and that only a new $15,000 roof could be "watertight."

The Davises filed a complaint alleging breach of contract, fraud and misrepresentation, and sought rescission of the contract and return of their deposit. The Johnsons counterclaimed seeking the deposit as liquidated damages.

* * *

We find that the Johnsons' statements to the Davises regarding the condition of the roof constituted a fraudulent misrepresentation entitling respondents to the return of their $26,000 deposit payment. In the state of Florida, relief for a fraudulent misrepresentation may be granted only when the following elements are present: (1) a false statement concerning a material fact; (2) the representor's knowledge that the representation is false; (3) an intention that the representation induce another to act on it; and, (4) consequent injury by the party acting in reliance on the representation.

The evidence adduced at trial shows that after the buyer and the seller signed the purchase and sales agreement and after receiving the $5,000 initial deposit payment the Johnsons affirmatively repeated to the Davises that there were no problems with the roof. The Johnsons subsequently received the additional $26,000 deposit payment from the Davises. The record reflects that the statement made by the Johnsons was a false representation of material fact, made with knowledge of its falsity, upon which the Davises relied to their detriment as evidenced by the $26,000 paid to the Johnsons.

The doctrine of caveat emptor does not exempt a seller from responsibility for the statements and representations which he makes to induce the buyer to act, when under the circumstances these amount to fraud in the legal sense. To be grounds for relief, the false representations need not have been made at the time of the signing of the purchase and sales agreement in order for the element of reliance to be present.

The fact that the false statements as to the quality of the roof were made after the signing of the purchase and sales agreement does not excuse the seller from liability when the misrepresentations were made prior to the execution of the contract by conveyance of the property. It would be contrary to all notions of fairness and justice for this Court to place its stamp of approval on an affirmative misrepresentation by a wrongdoer just because it was made after the signing of the executory contract when all of the necessary elements for actionable fraud are present. Furthermore, the Davises' reliance on the truth of the Johnsons' representation was justified and is supported by this Court's decision in *Besett v. Basnett,* where we held "that a recipient may rely on the truth of a representation, even though its falsity could have been ascertained had he made an investigation, unless he knows the representation to be false or its falsity is obvious to him."

In determining whether a seller of a home has a duty to disclose latent material defects to a buyer, the established tort law distinction between misfeasance and nonfeasance, action and inaction must carefully be analyzed. The highly individualistic philosophy of the earlier common law consistently imposed liability upon the commission of affirmative acts of harm, but shrank from converting the courts into an institution for forcing men to help one another. This distinction is deeply rooted in our case law. Liability for nonfeasance has therefore been slow to receive recognition in the evolution of tort law.

In theory, the difference between misfeasance and nonfeasance, action and inaction is quite simple and obvious; however, in practice it is not always easy to draw the line and determine whether conduct is active or passive. That is, where failure to disclose a material fact is calculated to induce a false belief, the distinction between concealment and affirmative representations is tenuous. Both proceed from the same motives and are attended with the same consequences; both are violative of the principles of fair dealing and good faith; both are calculated to produce the same result; and, in fact, both essentially have the same effect.

Still there exists in much of our case law the old tort notion that there can be no liability for nonfeasance. The courts in some jurisdictions, including Florida, hold that where the parties are dealing at arms's length and the facts lie equally open to both parties, with equal opportunity of examination, mere nondisclosure does not constitute a fraudulent concealment. The Fourth District affirmed that rule of law in *Banks v. Salina,* and found that although the sellers had sold a home without disclosing the presence of a defective roof and swimming pool of which the sellers had knowledge, "[i]n Florida, there is no duty to disclose when parties are dealing at arms length."

These unappetizing cases are not in tune with the times and do not conform with current notions of justice, equity and fair dealing. One should not be able to stand behind the impervious shield of caveat emptor and take advantage of another's ignorance. Our courts have taken great strides since the days when the judicial emphasis was on rigid rules and ancient precedents. Modern concepts of justice and fair dealing have given our courts the opportunity and latitude to change legal precepts in order to conform to society's needs. Thus, the tendency of the more recent cases has been to restrict rather than extend the doctrine of caveat emptor. The law appears to be working toward the ultimate conclusion that full disclosure of all material facts must be made whenever elementary fair conduct demands it.

* * *

We are of the opinion that the same philosophy regarding the sale of homes should also be the law in the state of Florida. Accordingly, we hold that where the seller of a home knows of facts materially affecting the value of the property which are not readily observable and are not known to the buyer, the seller is under a duty to disclose them to the buyer. This duty is equally applicable to all forms of real property, new and used.

In the case at bar, the evidence shows that the Johnsons knew of and failed to disclose that there had been problems with the roof of the house. Mr. Johnson admitted during his testimony that the Johnsons were aware of roof problems prior to entering into the contract of sale and receiving the $5,000 deposit payment. Thus, we agree with the district court and find that the Johnsons' fraudulent concealment also entitles the Davises to the return of the $5,000 deposit payment plus interest. We further find that the Davises should be awarded costs and fees.

BOYD, CHIEF JUSTICE, dissenting.

I respectfully but strongly dissent to the Court's expansion of the duties of sellers of real property. This ruling will give rise to a flood of litigation and will facilitate unjust outcomes in many cases. If, as a matter of public policy, the well settled law of this state on this question should be changed, the change should come from the legislature. Moreover, I do not find sufficient evidence in the record to justify rescission or a finding of fraud even under present law. I would quash the decision of the district court of appeal.

* * *

I do not agree with the Court's belief that the distinction between nondisclosure and affirmative statement is weak or nonexistent. It is a distinction that we should take special care to emphasize and preserve. Imposition of liability for seller's nondisclosure of the condition of improvements to real property is the first step toward making the seller a guarantor of the good condition of the property. Ultimately this trend will significantly burden the alienability of property because sellers will have to worry about the possibility of catastrophic post-sale judgments for damages sought to pay for repairs. The trend will proceed somewhat as follows. At first, the cause of action will require proof of actual knowledge of the undisclosed defect on the part of the seller. But in many cases the courts will allow it to be shown by circumstantial evidence. Then a rule of constructive knowledge will develop based on the reasoning that if the seller did not know of the defect, he should have known about it before attempting to sell the property. Thus the burden of inspection will shift from the buyer to the seller. Ultimately the courts will be in the position of imposing implied warranties and guaranties on all sellers of real property.

LAYMAN v. BINNS

Supreme Court of Ohio, 1988.
35 Ohio St.3d 176, 519 N.E.2d 642.

The dispute between the parties arises from the sale of a home in January 1978 by the vendors-appellants (Mr. and Mrs. Bradley O. Binns) to the purchasers-appellees (Mr. and Mrs. F. Garry Layman). Purchasers claim that vendors fraudulently concealed a structural defect in the house.

In 1970 or 1971, vendors hired a builder to construct the home. When it was nearly completed, backfilling around the cinder block foundation caused the foundation to give way resulting in a bow in the south basement wall. Steel I-beams were installed to support the bowed wall.

In 1977, vendors listed the home for sale and told their realtor about the basement wall problem and the corrective measures which were taken. The realtor told his sales staff about the defective wall but such information was omitted from the property listings.

The Laymans, with their agent, viewed the Binnses' house in December 1977. Mr. Binns did not accompany purchasers to the basement and he did not mention the bowed wall to the Laymans or their agent. Mr. Layman saw the I-beams but did not question their purpose because he thought they were part of the structure. Mr. Layman did inquire about utility bills and moisture at the east end of the basement. Mr. Binns explained that moisture usually entered the basement during excessive rain in the spring.

The purchase contract, signed by the parties, specified that it was the entire agreement between the parties, that no representations had been made other than those in the contract, and that the purchasers were relying upon their own inspection as to the condition and character of the dwelling. Purchasers paid $75,000 in cash to vendors, and moved into the house in February 1978.

In 1981, a foreclosure action was filed against the purchasers. Later, it was voluntarily dismissed. The purchasers then made an unsuccessful effort to sell the property at private sale. During that time, the defective basement wall was called to their attention by a realtor. Faced with estimates ranging from $32,000 to $49,612 to remedy the defect, they elected to lower their asking price from $125,000 to $75,000. The house still did not sell.

* * *

The trial court (following a bench trial) determined that the structural defect in the wall was known to vendors and "was not apparent upon inspection to inexperienced persons" such as the purchasers. The court found that the vendors had an affirmative duty to call the defect to the purchasers' attention and held that such failure amounted to fraud. The court awarded $40,000 in damages, but declined to assess punitive damages since there was no active concealment of the defect. The court of appeals affirmed.

The cause is before this court pursuant to the allowance of a motion to certify the record.

HERBERT R. BROWN, JUSTICE.

The determinative issue raised on appeal is whether recovery is barred by application of the doctrine of *caveat emptor* (let the buyer beware). We find that it is for the reasons set forth below.

The doctrine of *caveat emptor,* although virtually abolished in the area of personal property, remains a viable rule of law in real estate sales.

* * *

The doctrine of *caveat emptor* is one of long standing. Since problems of varying degree are to be found in most dwellings and buildings, the doctrine performs a function in the real estate market-place. Without the doctrine nearly every sale would invite litigation instituted by a disappointed buyer. Accordingly, we are not disposed to abolish the doctrine of *caveat emptor*. A seller of realty is not obligated to reveal all that he or she knows. A duty falls upon the purchaser to make inquiry and examination.

To make the doctrine operate fairly, courts have established certain conditions upon the rule's application. We summarize and adopt these conditions as follows: (1) the defect must be open to observation or discoverable on reasonable inspection, (2) the purchaser must have an unimpeded opportunity to examine the property and (3) the vendor may not engage in fraud. We measure the case before us against these requirements.

I

The defect here was open to observation. Mr. Layman (one of the purchasers) saw the steel bracing that supported the defective wall. The Laymans contend that Mr. Layman was not an expert and should not be held to have knowledge of the defect simply because he saw a symptom of it. If the issue were the cause of the defect or the remedial effectiveness of the beams, we might agree. However, the test is whether the defect was open to observation. Here, witnesses who viewed the basement detected the bow and steel beams with little effort. The defect was described as obvious and highly visible. The basement wall was bulging.

II

The purchasers had an unhindered opportunity to examine the basement. Mr. Layman saw the steel beams, yet failed to inspect the wall in detail or to ask about the purpose of the beams. The purchasers had a duty to inspect and inquire about the premises in a prudent, diligent manner.

III

This brings us to the final, and pivotal, question. On the facts in this case, did the vendors engage in fraud?

The purchasers admit that no active misrepresentation or misstatement of material fact was made. However, they argue that failure to disclose the bow in the wall constituted fraudulent concealment.

An action for fraud may be grounded upon failure to fully disclose facts of a material nature where there exists a duty to speak. This court has held that a vendor has a duty to disclose material facts which are latent, not readily observable or discoverable through a purchaser's reasonable inspection.

The non-disclosure in this case does not rise to the level of fraud for the reason that the defect here was not latent. It could have been detected by inspection. Thus, the purchasers must show an affirmative misrepresentation or a misstatement of a material fact in order to demonstrate fraud and thereby preclude application of the doctrine of *caveat emptor*. This, they failed to do.

IV

We hold that the doctrine of *caveat emptor* precludes recovery in an action by the purchaser for a structural defect in real estate where (1) the condition complained of is open to observation or discoverable upon reasonable inspection, (2) the purchaser had the full and unimpeded opportunity to examine the premises, and (3) there is no evidence of fraud on the part of the vendor. The judgment of the court of appeals is reversed and final judgment is hereby entered in favor of appellants.

Judgment reversed.

LOCHER, JUSTICE, concurring in part and dissenting in part.

Although I have no quarrel with the law expressed in the syllabus, I cannot concur in its application by the majority to the facts of this case.

In my view, the trial court properly found that the structural defect in the basement wall was not readily apparent upon reasonable inspection by persons inexperienced in such matters, like the Laymans.

* * *

Furthermore, the majority's analysis applies an unreasonably high standard for the purpose of determining whether the Laymans should have observed or discovered the defective wall. In concluding that the defect was open to observation, the majority states that "witnesses who viewed the basement detected the bow and steel beams with little effort." These witnesses were persons with experience in the construction, appraisal and sales of homes. However, the standard by which purchasers of real property should be measured in order to determine whether they should have observed or discovered a structural defect is that of "ordinarily prudent persons of their station and experience confronted with the same or similar circumstances." *Traverse v. Long* (1956), 165 Ohio St. 249, 252, 59 O.O. 325, 326, 135 N.E.2d 256, 259. Because the Laymans have little or no experience in the construction or buying of homes, it is simply unreasonable to compare them to persons with specialized knowledge in the fields of construction and real estate, as opposed to ordinarily prudent persons of like experience. Accordingly, I would affirm the trial court's judgment that persons of the Laymans' experience would not have discovered the defect upon reasonable inspection.

For these reasons, I respectfully dissent.

Notes

1.   Traditionally, courts adhered to a rule of nonliability for mere nondisclosure. The rationale was stated by the Supreme Court of Massachusetts in a 1942 case involving the sale of a house suffering from a termite infestation, which was known to the seller but not disclosed to the buyer:

> If this defendant is liable on this declaration every seller is liable who fails to disclose any nonapparent defect known to him in the subject of the sale which materially reduces its value and which the buyer fails to discover. Similarly it would seem that every buyer would be liable who fails to disclose any nonapparent virtue known to him in the subject of the purchase which materially enhances its value and of which the seller is ignorant. The law has not yet, we believe, reached the point of imposing upon the frailties of human nature a standard so idealistic as this.

Swinton v. Whitinsville Savings Bank, 311 Mass. 677, 42 N.E.2d 808 (1942).

2.   The traditional rule of *caveat emptor* still lives on in modern times in some jurisdictions and in some situations. For instance, in a New York case, an automobile owner traded in a vehicle to a car dealer, knowing that it was titled as a "rebuilt salvage" vehicle, but without disclosing that fact to the dealer. The court dismissed the dealer's claim against the consumer, stating:

> The doctrine of "caveat emptor" is alive and well in the State of New York. It reaches back to 1799 when the Supreme Court of Judicature of New York held that the rule of caveat emptor requires a buyer to examine what is being sold prior to making a purchase and the seller is not responsible for revealing a defect unless the seller practiced fraud or

concealment in order to entrap the buyer. * * * [T]he doctrine of caveat emptor imposes no duty upon a seller to disclose any information in an arm's length transaction unless some conduct on the part of the seller, other than mere silence, rises to the level of active concealment. * * *

Eagle Chevrolet Oldsmobile Cadillac of Johnstown, L.L.C. v. McDuffee, 195 Misc.2d 717, 761 N.Y.S.2d 450 (City Ct., Amsterdam, N.Y. 2003).

3. After *Johnson,* is there any longer a meaningful distinction between misfeasance (deceit by affirmative misrepresentation) and nonfeasance (deceit by silence)? Should there be? Is the dissenting Justice right that this trend will ultimately lead to imposing implied warranties of quality on all sellers of real estate? If it did, would that be a good rule? Would it be in line with current consumer expectations and societal values? Note that the majority in *Johnson* stated that its ruling applied to *all* forms of real property, both new and used. This means that the duty to disclose applies to Mr. & Mrs. Average Homeowner as well as to developers. Is this a good rule? Note also that this rule goes considerably beyond the UCC for personal property, where only professional sellers are held to the implied warranty of merchantability. See UCC § 2–314. Has the court in *Johnson* created an implied warranty of merchantability in real estate sales? The dissenting Justice seems to think so, doesn't he? See *infra* Chapter 7 Section B(6) for a discussion of the implied warranty of habitability as applied to the sale of residential real estate.

4. The history of consumer law, especially in seller-buyer transactions, has in general seen the slow demise of the doctrine of caveat emptor. Presumably, *Johnson* is some proof that this trend continues. Yet the Supreme Court of Ohio in the *Layman* case states that the "doctrine of caveat emptor * * * remains a viable rule of law in real estate sales." Although the results and the rhetoric were different, were the courts in *Johnson* and *Layman* actually applying the same rule to different factual situations?

5. Many state courts have found sellers liable for fraud by omission in situations where, as stated in *Johnson*, the "seller of a home knows of facts materially affecting the value of the property which are not readily observable and are not known to the buyer," and does not disclose. *See, e.g.,* Mitchell v. Christensen, 31 P.3d 572 (Utah 2001) (leaks in swimming pool were not discoverable by reasonable care; sellers who did not disclose were liable for fraudulent nondisclosure); Logue v. Flanagan, 584 S.E.2d 186 (W. Va. 2003) (failure to disclose defective septic system could result in liability for fraud). *See also* Restatement 2d, Torts, § 551, statutory supplement.

6. Where the seller actively conceals a defect, as by filling an automobile's engine cracks with sealer before offering it as a trade-in to a car dealer, he will be liable for fraud. See Lindberg Cadillac Co. v. Aron, 371 S.W.2d 651 (Mo. Ct. App. 1963). Where the sellers concealed a bulging basement wall by placing heavy boxes in front of it, thus impeding the buyers' inspection, the sellers were liable for fraud in a Kentucky case, Flora v. Morris, 2003 WL 21476115 (Ky. Ct. App. 2003). *See also* Restatement 2d, Torts, § 550, statutory supplement.

7. Other courts have followed the lead of *Layman* and deny liability for fraudulent omission where under the facts presented one or more of the

elements is missing. For instance, there was no fraudulent nondisclosure in a case where a leaking kitchen ceiling was wet to the touch and thus readily observable, Havener v. Richardson, 16 F. Supp. 2d 774 (E.D. Mich. 1998) (applying Michigan law), or where the property's location should have put the purchaser on notice of possible water erosion, Stebbins v. Wells, 766 A.2d 369 (R.I. 2001), or where the defendant real estate agent had no knowledge of the alleged water problems and the home was sold under an "as is" contract, Moore v. Prudential Residential Services Limited Partnership, 849 So.2d 914 (Ala. 2002).

8. Many states have adopted real property disclosure statutes that require home sellers to disclose the condition of the house. While the fact that there is such a law does not necessarily supplant the cause of action for common law fraud, *see* Rogers v. Meiser, 68 P.3d 967 (Okla. 2003), where the vendors have made adequate disclosures pursuant to the statute, a claim of fraudulent nondisclosure may fail. *See* Parmely v. Hildebrand, 630 N.W.2d 509 (S.D. 2001).

3. ALTERNATIVES TO COMMON LAW FRAUD

In cases of seller misrepresentation or failure to disclose, aggrieved buyers are not limited to pleading common law fraud or deceit, but may pursue other common law approaches to achieve a remedy. For instance, a contract of sale may be rescinded if it is based on fraud. Also, the law of tort has evolved to recognize additional causes of action, such as negligent misrepresentation or omission and even innocent misrepresentation or omission. The following materials illustrate some of these alternative approaches.

STAMBOVSKY v. ACKLEY

New York Supreme Court, Appellate Division, 1991.
169 A.D.2d 254, 572 N.Y.S.2d 672.

Before MILONAS, J.P., and ROSS, KASSAL, SMITH and RUBIN, JJ.

RUBIN, JUSTICE.

Plaintiff, to his horror, discovered that the house he had recently contracted to purchase was widely reputed to be possessed by poltergeists, reportedly seen by defendant seller and members of her family on numerous occasions over the last nine years. Plaintiff promptly commenced this action seeking rescission of the contract of sale. Supreme Court reluctantly dismissed the complaint, holding that plaintiff has no remedy at law in this jurisdiction.

The unusual facts of this case, as disclosed by the record, clearly warrant a grant of equitable relief to the buyer who, as a resident of New York City, cannot be expected to have any familiarity with the folklore of the Village of Nyack. Not being a "local," plaintiff could not readily learn that the home he had contracted to purchase is haunted. Whether the source of the spectral apparitions seen by defendant seller are parapsychic or psychogenic, having reported their presence in both a national publication ("Readers' Digest") and the local press (in 1977 and

1982, respectively), defendant is estopped to deny their existence and, as a matter of law, the house is haunted. More to the point, however, no divination is required to conclude that it is defendant's promotional efforts in publicizing her close encounters with these spirits which fostered the home's reputation in the community. In 1989, the house was included in a five-home walking tour of Nyack and described in a November 27th newspaper article as "a riverfront Victorian (with ghost)." The impact of the reputation thus created goes to the very essence of the bargain between the parties, greatly impairing both the value of the property and its potential for resale. The extent of this impairment may be presumed for the purpose of reviewing the disposition of this motion to dismiss the cause of action for rescission . . . and represents merely an issue of fact for resolution at trial.

While I agree with Supreme Court that the real estate broker, as agent for the seller, is under no duty to disclose to a potential buyer the phantasmal reputation of the premises and that, in his pursuit of a legal remedy for fraudulent misrepresentation against the seller, plaintiff hasn't a ghost of a chance, I am nevertheless moved by the spirit of equity to allow the buyer to seek rescission of the contract of sale and recovery of his downpayment. New York law fails to recognize any remedy for damages incurred as a result of the seller's mere silence, applying instead the strict rule of caveat emptor. Therefore, the theoretical basis for granting relief, even under the extraordinary facts of this case, is elusive if not ephemeral.

"Pity me not but lend thy serious hearing to what I shall unfold" (William Shakespeare, Hamlet, Act I, Scene V [Ghost]).

From the perspective of a person in the position of plaintiff herein, a very practical problem arises with respect to the discovery of a paranormal phenomenon: "Who you gonna' call?" as the title song to the movie "Ghostbusters" asks. Applying the strict rule of caveat emptor to a contract involving a house possessed by poltergeists conjures up visions of a psychic or medium routinely accompanying the structural engineer and Terminix man on an inspection of every home subject to a contract of sale. It portends that the prudent attorney will establish an escrow account lest the subject of the transaction come back to haunt him and his client—or pray that his malpractice insurance coverage extends to supernatural disasters. In the interest of avoiding such untenable consequences, the notion that a haunting is a condition which can and should be ascertained upon reasonable inspection of the premises is a hobgoblin which should be exorcised from the body of legal precedent and laid quietly to rest.

It has been suggested by a leading authority that the ancient rule which holds that mere non-disclosure does not constitute actionable misrepresentation "finds proper application in cases where the fact undisclosed is patent, or the plaintiff has equal opportunities for obtaining information which he may be expected to utilize, or the defendant has no reason to think that he is acting under any misapprehension"

(Prosser, Law of Torts § 106, at 696 [4th ed., 1971]). However, with respect to transactions in real estate, New York adheres to the doctrine of caveat emptor and imposes no duty upon the vendor to disclose any information concerning the premises unless there is a confidential or fiduciary relationship between the parties or some conduct on the part of the seller which constitutes "active concealment". Normally, some affirmative misrepresentation or partial disclosure is required to impose upon the seller a duty to communicate undisclosed conditions affecting the premises.

Caveat emptor is not so all-encompassing a doctrine of common law as to render every act of non-disclosure immune from redress, whether legal or equitable. "In regard to the necessity of giving information which has not been asked, the rule differs somewhat at law and in equity, and while the law courts would permit no recovery of damages against a vendor, because of mere concealment of facts under certain circumstances, yet if the vendee refused to complete the contract because of the concealment of a material fact on the part of the other, equity would refuse to compel him so to do, because equity only compels the specific performance of a contract which is fair and open, and in regard to which all material matters known to each have been communicated to the other". . . . Where fairness and common sense dictate that an exception should be created, the evolution of the law should not be stifled by rigid application of a legal maxim.

The doctrine of caveat emptor requires that a buyer act prudently to assess the fitness and value of his purchase and operates to bar the purchaser who fails to exercise due care from seeking the equitable remedy of rescission. . . . It should be apparent, however, that the most meticulous inspection and the search would not reveal the presence of poltergeists at the premises or unearth the property's ghoulish reputation in the community. Therefore, there is no sound policy reason to deny plaintiff relief for failing to discover a state of affairs which the most prudent purchaser would not be expected to even contemplate.

Where a condition which has been created by the seller materially impairs the value of the contract and is peculiarly within the knowledge of the seller or unlikely to be discovered by a prudent purchaser exercising due care with respect to the subject transaction, nondisclosure constitutes a basis for rescission as a matter of equity. Any other outcome places upon the buyer not merely the obligation to exercise care in his purchase but rather to be omniscient with respect to any fact which may affect the bargain. No practical purpose is served by imposing such a burden upon a purchaser. To the contrary, it encourages predatory business practice and offends the principle that equity will suffer no wrong to be without a remedy.

Defendant's contention that the contract of sale, particularly the merger or "as is" clause, bars recovery of the buyer's deposit is unavailing. Even an express disclaimer will not be given effect where the facts are peculiarly within the knowledge of the party invoking it. Moreover, a fair reading of the merger clause reveals that it expressly disclaims only representations made with respect to the physical condition of the premises and merely makes general reference to representations concerning "any other matter or things affecting or relating to the aforesaid premises". As broad as this language may be, a reasonable interpretation is that its effect is limited to tangible or physical matters and does not extend to paranormal phenomena. Finally, if the language of the contract is to be construed as broadly as defendant urges to encompass the presence of poltergeists in the house, it cannot be said that she has delivered the premises "vacant" in accordance with her obligation under the provisions of the contract rider.

To the extent New York law may be said to require something more than "mere concealment" to apply even the equitable remedy of rescission, the case of Junius Construction Corporation v. Cohen, 257 N.Y. 393, 178 N.E. 672, while not precisely on point, provides some guidance. In that case, the seller disclosed that an official map indicated two as yet unopened streets which were planned for construction at the edges of the parcel. What was not disclosed was that the same map indicated a third street which, if opened, would divide the plot in half. The court held that, while the seller was under no duty to mention the planned streets at all, having undertaken to disclose two of them, he was obliged to reveal the third .

In the case at bar, defendant seller deliberately fostered the public belief that her home was possessed. Having undertaken to inform the public at large, to whom she has no legal relationship, about the supernatural occurrences on her property, she may be said to owe no less a duty to her contract vendee. It has been remarked that the occasional modern cases which permit a seller to take unfair advantage of a buyer's ignorance so long as he is not actively misled are "singularly unappetizing" (Prosser, Law of Torts § 106, at 696 [4th ed. 1971]). Where, as here, the seller not only takes unfair advantage of the buyer's ignorance but has created and perpetuated a condition about which he is unlikely to even inquire, enforcement of the contract (in whole or in part) is offensive to the court's sense of equity. Application of the remedy of rescission, within the bounds of the narrow exception to the doctrine of caveat emptor set forth herein, is entirely appropriate to relieve the unwitting purchaser from the consequences of a most unnatural bargain.

Accordingly, the judgment of the Supreme Court, which dismissed the complaint pursuant to CPLR 3211(a)(7), should be modified, on the law and the facts and in the exercise of discretion, and the first cause of action seeking rescission of the contract reinstated, without costs.

All concur except MILONAS, J.P. and SMITH, J., who dissent in an opinion by SMITH, J.

SMITH, JUSTICE (dissenting).

I would affirm the dismissal of the complaint by the motion court.

Plaintiff seeks to rescind his contract to purchase defendant Ackley's residential property and recover his down payment. Plaintiff alleges that Ackley and her real estate broker, defendant Ellis Realty, made material misrepresentations of the property in that they failed to disclose that Ackley believed that the house was haunted by poltergeists. Moreover, Ackley shared this belief with her community and the general public through articles published in Reader's Digest (1977) and the local newspaper (1982). In November 1989, approximately two months after the parties entered into the contract of sale but subsequent to the scheduled October 2, 1989 closing, the house was included in a five-house walking tour and again described in the local newspaper as being haunted.

Prior to closing, plaintiff learned of this reputation and unsuccessfully sought to rescind the $650,000 contract of sale and obtain return of his $32,500 down payment without resort to litigation. The plaintiff then commenced this action for that relief and alleged that he would not have entered into the contract had he been so advised and that as a result of the alleged poltergeist activity, the market value and resaleability of the property was greatly diminished. Defendant Ackley has counterclaimed for specific performance.

"It is settled law in New York that the seller of real property is under no duty to speak when the parties deal at arm's length. The mere silence of the seller, without some act or conduct which deceived the purchaser, does not amount to a concealment that is actionable as a fraud. The buyer has the duty to satisfy himself as to the quality of his bargain pursuant to the doctrine of caveat emptor, which in New York State still applies to real estate transactions."

The parties herein were represented by counsel and dealt at arm's length. This is evidenced by the contract of sale which, inter alia, contained various riders and a specific provision that all prior understandings and agreements between the parties were merged into the contract, that the contract completely expressed their full agreement and that neither had relied upon any statement by anyone else not set forth in the contract. There is no allegation that defendants, by some specific act, other than the failure to speak, deceived the plaintiff. Nevertheless, a cause of action may be sufficiently stated where there is a confidential or fiduciary relationship creating a duty to disclose and there was a failure to disclose a material fact, calculated to induce a false belief. However, plaintiff herein has not alleged and there is no basis for concluding that a confidential or fiduciary relationship existed between these parties to an arm's length transaction such as to give rise to a duty to disclose. In addition, there is no allegation that defendants thwarted plaintiff's efforts to fulfill his responsibilities fixed by the doctrine of caveat emptor.

Finally, if the doctrine of caveat emptor is to be discarded, it should be for a reason more substantive than a poltergeist. The existence of a poltergeist is no more binding upon the defendants than it is upon this court.

Based upon the foregoing, the motion court properly dismissed the complaint.

Notes

1. In *Stambovsky*, the New York Appellate Division was willing to recognize a cause of action to rescind a contract to purchase real estate based on the failure to disclose the home's reputation as a haunted house. In a New Jersey case, a builder-developer was found potentially liable under common law fraud (as well as the New Jersey Consumer Fraud Act), for failure to disclose to would-be buyers the presence of a closed toxic waste dump near their housing development. Strawn v. Canuso, 140 N.J. 43, 657 A.2d 420 (1995). This raises the question of how far courts should go in imposing duties on sellers of real property to disclose to buyers conditions that may affect property values. For instance, should sellers have to disclose that a house was (a) the scene of a multiple murder? (b) the home of a dying AIDS patient? Or (c) that a sexual predator lives next door? Many states have passed statutes limiting seller liability for failure to disclose non-physical defects to home buyers. *See* Ronald Benton Brown & Thomas H. Thurlow III, Buyers Beware: Statutes Shield Real Estate Brokers and Sellers Who Do Not Disclose That Properties Are Psychologically Tainted, 49 Okla. L. Rev. 625 (1996).

2. The "economic loss doctrine" is a judicially created doctrine that bars a contracting party from pursuing a tort recovery for purely economic or commercial losses. It was apparently developed to prevent commercial buyers from benefiting from product liability doctrines. See Steven C. Tourek, Thomas H. Boyd, and Charles J. Schoenweter, Bucking the "Trend": The Uniform Commercial Code, the Economic Loss Doctrine, and the Common Law Causes of Action for Fraud and Misrepresentation, 84 Iowa L. Rev 875 (1999).

In a 2004 case, however, a majority of the Wisconsin Supreme Court applied the economic loss doctrine to a consumer case in which a class of buyers was alleging fraudulent nondisclosure of an engine defect in a top-of-the-line Harley–Davidson motorcycle engine, such that the value of the motorcycle was diminished. No personal injury or property damage was alleged. The Wisconsin court said:

> * * * the plaintiffs have warranty remedies for the alleged defects in their motorcycles. In addition, there are contract remedies at law and in equity to the extent that the plaintiffs were fraudulently induced to purchase their motorcycles. A contract fraudulently induced is void or voidable; a party fraudulently induced to enter a contract may affirm the contract and seek damages for breach or pursue the equitable remedy of rescission and seek restitutionary damages, including sums necessary to restore the party fraudulently induced to his position prior to the making of the contract. * * *

In short, we see no reason to recognize an exception to the economic loss doctrine to allow this consumer contract dispute to be remedied as an intentional misrepresentation tort. * * *

Tietsworth v. Harley–Davidson, Inc., 270 Wis.2d 146, 677 N.W.2d 233, 244 (2004).

Will application of the economic loss doctrine to bar common law fraud cases in consumer transactions effectively do away with this approach to remedying seller misrepresentations to consumers? Is it realistic to assume that consumers will be able to adequately protect themselves against fraudulent misrepresentations or failures to disclose as part of the bargaining process? Are contract and equity doctrines and remedies sufficient? Would the economic loss doctrine have changed the result in *Carpenter v. Chrysler*, *supra*, Section A (1)?

3.   Modern common law causes of action also include negligent misrepresentation in addition to fraud or deceit. In this situation, the elements are virtually the same as for fraudulent misrepresentation, except that instead of the seller having knowledge of the falsehood, there is a negligence "should have known" standard. Also, opinions are commonly included, so long as the person speaking has a duty to speak with reasonable care to the intended recipient. This would normally include experts such as real estate brokers, termite inspectors, perhaps even automobile mechanics. The following case is illustrative of how the doctrine of negligent misrepresentation can play out in a consumer transaction. *See generally* Restatement 2d Torts, § 552, statutory supplement.

WARD DEVELOPMENT CO. v. INGRAO

Court of Appeals, Maryland, 1985.
63 Md.App. 645, 493 A.2d 421.

Getty, Judge.

This action arose when thirteen plaintiffs, all homeowners in the Foxhall North Subdivision in Montgomery County, sued three defendants—Ward Development Co., Inc., the developer of the subdivision; Long and Foster Real Estate, Inc., Ward's real estate broker; and William Conrad Behrens, a selling agent with Long & Foster—for fraudulent and negligent misrepresentation. * * * After a three week trial in the Circuit Court for Montgomery County, a jury returned a verdict for the homeowners on the negligent misrepresentation count and assessed damages against the defendants totaling $55,048.00. Appellant Ward now appeals from the judgments entered on the jury verdicts. * * *

Negligent Misrepresentation

The Foxhall North Subdivision is a residential real estate development constructed by Ward Development Co., Inc. On March 2, 1978, Ward employed Long & Foster Real Estate, Inc., to sell thirty-eight homes located in the subdivision. On April 3, 1978, Long & Foster employed William Conrad Behrens to be the selling agent for the homes.

The homes involved in the present suit were sold by Behrens for Long & Foster and Ward between May 27, 1978 and March 6, 1979. As the issue presented here is in the context of a motion for directed verdict (former Rule 552), the evidentiary background will be stated in a light most favorable to the homeowners.

During the bargaining period for the purchase of the homes Behrens told the homeowners that the neighborhood would consist of only 38 or 39 homes and that the road going through the subdivision, Rippling Brook Drive, would dead-end and terminate permanently at the edge of the subdivision. Shortly after the homeowners purchased their homes, however, Rippling Brook Drive was extended and construction was begun on additional homes in the area. In addition, the homeowners' contracts of sale contained the following clause:

> "The estimated cost of deferred water and/or sewer connection charge for which the purchaser is liable is $_____ payable over a period of 35 years."

Each homeowner's contract was filled in with an estimated cost of the sewer and water connection charge; the amounts varied between $250 and $900, "payable over a period of 35 years." When the homeowners received their Montgomery County tax bills for 1979, however, they discovered that their annual sewer and water connection charges were much greater than their contracts had indicated. For example, the contract of one homeowner, Arnold Kaplan, contains an estimate that his deferred water and sewer connection charge would be "$400.00 payable over a period of 35 years" (roughly, an $11.42 annual charge). Kaplan's actual deferred water and sewer connection charge for 1979 was $71.59. The other homeowners testified to similar discrepancies between the sewer and water connection charge as stated in their contracts and the charge which was actually assessed.

In order to explain the reason for the discrepancies, some background information on water and sewer benefit charges in Montgomery County is necessary. Each property owner in Montgomery County is subject to two water and sewer benefit charges. The first charge is termed a "front foot benefit assessment" and is levied to repay bonds sold by the Washington Suburban Sanitary Commission to finance the costs of main water and sewer lines constructed during a given year. The second charge, termed a "house connection charge," is levied to recover the construction costs for connecting water and sewer lines to individual homes. The front foot benefit assessment is an annual charge for 33 years but may also be paid off at any time in one lump sum. The house connection charge is in the nature of a lump sum, but may be deferred and paid off in installments over a 33–year period.

In the instant case the amount Behrens stated in each property owner's contract to be the "sewer and/or water connection charge * * * payable over 35 years" was actually Ward's estimate of a combined total of the property owner's house connection charge plus his front foot benefit assessment for one year (1979).

At the conclusion of the trial, the jury returned verdicts in favor of the homeowners as follows:

(a) No finding of fraud as to any defendant;

(b) $6,006 against all defendants (jointly and severally) for damages incurred as a result of negligent misrepresentation as to the extension of Rippling Brook Drive;

(c) $13,494 against all defendants (jointly and severally) incurred as a result of negligent misrepresentation as to the sewer and water annual assessments;

(d) $41,554 against defendant Ward solely, incurred as a result of negligent misrepresentation as to the sewer and water annual assessments.

Ward now asserts that the trial court erred in denying Ward's motion for directed verdict as to the homeowners' claim for negligent misrepresentation of their sewer and water connection charges. Ward argues that the homeowners' evidence of a negligent misrepresentation was legally deficient in two respects, to-wit:

A. The homeowners failed to show a misrepresentation of a material fact.

B. The homeowners failed to show a misrepresentation as to a past or existing fact.

For the following reasons, we find that the trial court did not err in denying Ward's motion for a directed verdict.

The tort of negligent misrepresentation is one of recent origin in Maryland. The Court of Appeals initially recognized the cause of action in 1938 * * *.

* * * In *Martens Chevrolet v. Seney,* 292 Md. 328, 439 A.2d 534 (1982), the Court * * * outlined the principal elements of negligent misrepresentation as follows:

(1) the defendant, owing a duty of care to the plaintiff, negligently asserts a false statement;

(2) the defendant intends that his statement will be acted upon by the plaintiff;

(3) the defendant has knowledge that the plaintiff will probably rely on the statement, which, if erroneous, will cause loss or injury;

(4) the plaintiff, justifiably, takes action in reliance on the statement; and

(5) the plaintiff suffers damage proximately caused by the defendant's negligence.

The *Martens* Court went on to hold that the buyer of an automobile dealership could bring an action for negligent misrepresentation against the seller for allegedly misinforming the buyer regarding the dealership's financial status.

Turning now to the present case, Ward argues that the trial court erred in denying Ward's motion for a directed verdict because the homeowners failed to prove that the misrepresentation regarding the sewer and water connection charge was a material one. We note first that nowhere in the *Martens* opinion does the Court of Appeals specify that the misrepresentation of a "material fact" is an element of the tort of negligent misrepresentation. An element which is specified, however, is that the plaintiff must justifiably take action in reliance on the misrepresentation. The requirement of justifiable reliance is, by implication, inextricably bound up with the requirement of materiality. An immaterial representation could not, by definition, influence the reasonable man. We conclude, therefore, that for a plaintiff justifiably to take action in reliance on a statement, that statement must be a representation of a material fact.

In defining what is meant by a material fact, Ward quotes the following language from *Babb v. Bolyard,* "[t]he fraud must be material, by which is meant, without it, that the transaction would not have been made." We find a better definition of what constitutes a material fact in Restatement (Second) of Torts, 4057 538 (1977):

> "The matter is material if (a) a reasonable man would attach importance to its existence or non-existence in determining his choice of action in the transaction in question; or (b) the maker of the representation knows or has reason to know that its recipient regards or is likely to regard the matter as important in determining his choice of action, although a reasonable man would not so regard it."

In the instant case, at least one of the homeowners testified that had she known that the actual sewer and water connection charge was as great as it was, she would have contemplated the contract further or at least have done additional comparative shopping. This testimony and the evidence as a whole compels us to conclude that the question of whether the misrepresentation regarding the sewer and water connection charge was one of a material fact was one properly submitted to the jury.

Ward next asserts that the homeowners failed to show that the misrepresentation of the sewer and water connection charge was a representation of a past or existing fact. Ward argues that the statement regarding the charge was merely an estimate and cannot therefore be the basis for a suit for negligent misrepresentation. We disagree. The Court of Appeals has stated that an action for fraudulent misrepresentation will not lie for the unfulfillment of promises or the failure of future events to materialize as predicated.

We recognize the difference between a promise of future events and an estimate by one knowledgeable in a particular field. In the latter situation, redress may be had for representations as to future facts and not merely as to past or existing facts. As stated by the commentators Fleming and Gray, "[i]t is not surprising * * * that courts have been increasingly willing to hold predictive statements material where the circumstances indicate to the addressee that the speaker has a factual basis for his predictions so that the existence of facts is implied by the representations.'' In the instant case, the homeowners relied on Ward and its agents as knowledgeable in the field of real estate. Ward, as the developer of the subdivision, and Behrens, as the real estate selling agent, held themselves out as knowledgeable in matters such as the charge for a sewer and water connection. The homeowners were entitled to rely on that estimate to a reasonable extent. But the charge stated in the contract was so far removed from the actual charge it cannot properly be termed a reasonable estimate and can only be explained as a misrepresentation. Therefore, we hold that the estimate of the sewer and water connection charge was actionable under a theory of negligent misrepresentation.

JUDGMENT AFFIRMED AS TO LIABILITY FOR MISREPRESENTATION AS TO WATER AND SEWER CONNECTION CHARGES. REMANDED FOR NEW TRIAL ON THE ISSUE OF DAMAGES RESULTING THEREFROM.

Notes

1. The rule recognizing potential tort liability for innocent misrepresentation is articulated in the Restatement (Second) of Torts, § 552C:

(1) One who, in a sale, rental or exchange transaction with another, makes a misrepresentation of a material fact for the purpose of inducing the other to act or to refrain from acting in reliance upon it, is subject to liability to the other for pecuniary loss caused to him by his justifiable reliance upon the misrepresentation, even though it is not made fraudulently or negligently.

(2) Damages recoverable under the rule stated in this section are limited to the difference between the value of what the other has parted with and the value of what he has received in the transaction.

What does this formulation do to the common law of deceit? What is the likely rationale for this approach to misrepresentation?

2. Consumer cases involving the tort of innocent misrepresentation are rather scarce, but the cause of action continues to be recognized in a significant number of states. For instance, in an Alabama case, the consumer plaintiff succeeded in overturning summary judgment for the defendant car dealer on an allegation that the dealer had innocently implied that the car he purchased was "new" when in fact it had been subject to prior damage and repair of serious paint problems. The Alabama court stated: "Even though [the plaintiff] presented no evidence that Stephenson Chevrolet knew of any prior damage to the Camaro, Stephenson Chevrolet may be liable for innocent misrepresentation." Dodd v. Nelda Stephenson Chevrolet, Inc., 626 So.2d 1288, 1292 (Ala. 1993).

3. Given the close parallels between the tort of innocent misrepresentation and a claim for breach of express warranty, it appears that courts have been willing to dismiss a claim for innocent misrepresentation on the basis of contract disclaimers, thus limiting the likelihood that a consumer

would be able to prevail. *See, e.g.,* Gibson v. Capano, 241 Conn. 725, 699 A.2d 68 (1997) (seller of home innocently misled buyers regarding the extent of termite damage and the chemical used in prior treatments; state supreme court recognized the applicability of the tort of innocent misrepresentation to this situation, but dismissed the claim due to the presence of an unambiguous disclaimer in the contract to purchase the real estate).

4.   In a few states, courts have held that a seller or real estate agent could be liable for negligent failure to disclose defects they did not actually know about, but which they should have known about. *See, e.g.,* Easton v. Strassburger, 152 Cal.App.3d 90, 199 Cal.Rptr. 383 (1984); Gouveia v. Citicorp Person-to-Person Financial Center, 101 N.M. 572, 686 P.2d 262 (Ct. App. 1984); Secor v. Knight, 716 P.2d 790 (Utah 1986). This might be called a case of "negligent failure to disclose," which would imply a duty of the seller or the agent to inspect the property to be sold in order to discover and disclose the defects. Some states, like California, have enacted statutes codifying the seller/agent's duty to inspect in real estate transactions. Cal. Civil Code §§ 2079–79.5 and 2373.

Problem 1–2

Bill Bones bought a used car from dealer Sam Silver for $3000 cash. Sam made no written or oral representations about the car, and in the contract of sale Sam effectively disclaimed all warranties. One week later Bill discovered that the car had cracks on each side of the engine block, rendering the engine unusable. Sam did not know of the cracked block, as he does not regularly do any mechanical work on the used cars he sells.

Calvin Consumer had sold the car to Sam for $2000 cash some weeks earlier. During the preceding winter the car's engine coolant had frozen, causing the block to crack, and before selling the car to Sam, Calvin had filled the cracks with a "sealer" and covered the filled cracks with a compound which hid them. Calvin had said nothing to Sam.

Does Bill have an action against Sam for deceit? For negligent misrepresentation? What exactly did Sam do or say about the car? Should Sam have inspected the car to discover defects? Does Sam have an action against Calvin for deceit? Cf., Lindberg Cadillac v. Aron, *supra*, Section A(2), n.6. The "representations" (silence about the condition of the engine) are the same in each case. Is the difference in Sam's and Calvin's knowledge critical to the actionability of their conduct? Has Sam suffered any damages as a result of Calvin's silence? Should Sam's ability to recover against Calvin depend upon whether Bill recovered against Sam?

Does Bill have a cause of action directly against Calvin for fraudulent or negligent misrepresentation? Should or could Calvin have foreseen or intended that Bill would be relying on his misrepresentation by silence?

Problem 1–3

Harry and Harriet Hopeful were anxiously seeking a moderately-priced mobile home in which to spend their retirement years in the

Wasatch Mountains, just outside of Salt Lake City, Utah. They visited the sales lot of Comfy Mobile Homes, Inc., and were attracted to a used Victoria two-bedroom model. Concerned about the severe winters in the area, the Hopefuls asked the salesman whether the unit was well-built and heated. The salesman innocently responded that this was a "good solid home, as good as any others on the lot," that it "had a good electric heater," and that they "sold many similar units without complaints" about their heatability. The sales manager of Comfy, who was standing nearby, overheard the discussion but said nothing, even though she was aware that this particular mobile home had been kept in Florida by its prior owners, and was uninsulated. In fact, the lack of insulation explained the very low price being asked for it.

The Hopefuls examined the unit to their heart's content, and agreed to buy it. The contract of sale, which they browsed through while the salesman was doing other paperwork, contained the following clause in 10–point boldface type:

> The purchaser has examined the mobile home agreed to be sold and is familiar with the physical condition thereof. The seller has not made and does not make any representations of any kind as to the physical condition, suitability, or operating costs of said unit, and purchaser acknowledges that no such representations have been made.

> It is understood and agreed that all prior understandings and agreements between the parties are merged in this contract, and that neither party is relying upon any statement or representation not embodied in this contract.

Please assume that the contract also contained an effective disclaimer of all warranties, so that the Hopefuls cannot recover on any cause of action based on a warranty claim.

The following December they became frigidly aware of the lack of insulation, and aware also that they were running up astronomical heating bills trying to keep the place even tolerably warm.

Evaluate Harry and Harriet's chances of recovering from Comfy on a deceit or a negligence cause of action. What, if any, misrepresentations were made by the salesman? By the sales manager? Would the Hopefuls be justified in relying? What would their damages be? Could or should they seek an equitable rescission remedy as in *Stambovsky, supra*? Would they be precluded from recovering in tort under the doctrine of "economic loss"? Would you take this case as a private attorney?

SECTION B.   THE STATUTORY APPROACH— FEDERAL AND STATE

1. FEDERAL REGULATION—THE FTC ACT

a. *Introduction and Overview*

The prior section dealt with the common law standards of informational accuracy available to private parties in private disputes. But the community's distaste for deception is often reflected in broad statutory mandates to public agencies to prohibit marketplace misrepresentation. For example, the Securities & Exchange Commission performs this function for the protection of securities investors.

The dominant agency in the consumer area is the Federal Trade Commission. It is an independent regulatory agency headed by five Commissioners, appointed by the President and confirmed by the Senate, no more than three of whom can be from the same political party. It has enforcement responsibilities in both the competition sector and the consumer protection sector, and has jurisdiction over all U.S. entities except banks, savings and loan institutions, federal credit unions, common carriers and nonprofits, 15 U.S.C. § 46(a).

Section 5(a)(1) of the Federal Trade Commission Act, 15 U.S.C.A. § 45, declares in majestic simplicity:

> Unfair methods of competition in or affecting commerce, and unfair or deceptive acts or practices in or affecting commerce, are hereby declared unlawful.

One particular "unfair or deceptive act or practice" is defined in FTC Act § 12, 15 U.S.C.A. § 52, as the dissemination of "any false advertisement" likely to induce the purchase of food, drugs, devices, or cosmetics. The Act expressly defines "false advertising" in section 15(a)(1) as an advertisement which is "misleading in a material respect." See the full text in the Statutory Supplement.

When the FTC was founded in 1914, its statutory mandate covered only "unfair methods of competition." This was expanded by the Wheeler–Lea amendments of 1938, which added the reference to "unfair or deceptive acts or practices" as well as Section 12 on false advertising. In the 1975 Magnuson–Moss Warranty—FTC Improvement Act, the FTC was given the power to issue industry-wide trade regulation rules, and the authority under Section 13(b) to seek injunctions in federal courts for fraudulent practices.

Not surprisingly, a distinct body of jurisprudence has grown up around the Commission's mandate, much of it dealing with the standards for accuracy of advertising and promotional material. In reading what follows, compare the substantive rules developed by the Commission and the courts to those applied in common law actions in the preceding section.

In the early 1980's, the Commission expanded on the brief wording of the FTC Act in a set of Policy Statements, one defining deceptive trade practices and the other defining unfair trade practices. These policies continue to guide the Commission's consumer protection work, and have also influenced the state unfair and deceptive trade practices acts that are modeled on the FTC Act, discussed *infra* Section B(2).

In this section, we will look briefly at the FTC's traditional stance on deceptive advertising, then we will examine the Deception Policy Statement and its application in modern cases. How the FTC interprets the meaning of advertisements will also be covered. An offshoot of the FTC work in policing deceptive advertising is the Advertising Substantiation doctrine, which requires that advertisers have a reasonable basis for claims prior to disseminating them to the public. The Unfairness Doctrine, which has come to be used in policing advertising practices not otherwise covered by the Deception theory, will be discussed. Finally, we will look briefly at some of the FTC's more innovative remedies for policing advertising, including corrective advertising.

b. *FTC Traditional Approach to Advertising Regulation*

The following excerpt, from the court's opinion in Federal Trade Com'n v. Sterling Drug, Inc., 317 F.2d 669 (2d Cir.1963), summarizes the legal principles traditionally applied by the Commission in advertising cases:

> The legal principles to be applied here are quite clear. The central purpose of the provisions of the Federal Trade Commission Act under discussion is in effect to abolish the rule of *caveat emptor* which traditionally defined rights and responsibilities in the world of commerce. That rule can no longer be relied upon as a means of rewarding fraud and deception, and has been replaced by a rule which gives to the consumer the right to rely upon representations of facts as the truth. In order best to implement the prophylactic purpose of the statute, it has been consistently held that advertising falls within its proscription not only when there is proof of actual deception but also when the representations made have a capacity or tendency to deceive, i.e., when there is a likelihood or fair probability that the reader will be misled. For the same reason, proof of intention to deceive is not requisite to a finding of violation of the statute; since the purpose of the statute is not to punish the wrongdoer but to protect the public, the cardinal factor is the probable effect which the advertiser's handiwork will have upon the eye and mind of the reader. It is therefore necessary in these cases to consider the advertisement in its entirety and not to engage in disputatious dissection. The entire mosaic should be viewed rather than each tile separately. * * *

> Unlike that abiding faith which the law has in the "reasonable man," it has very little faith indeed in the intellectual acuity of the "ordinary purchaser" who is the object of the advertising campaign.

> "The general public has been defined as 'that vast multitude which includes the ignorant, and unthinking and the credulous, who, in making purchases, do not stop to analyze but too often are governed by appearances and general impressions.' The average purchaser has been variously characterized as not 'straight thinking,' subject to 'impressions,' uneducated, and grossly misinformed; he is influenced by prejudice and superstition; and he wishfully believes in miracles, allegedly the result of progress in science * * *. The language of the ordinary purchaser is casual and unaffected. He

is not an 'expert in grammatical construction' or an 'educated analytical reader' and, therefore, he does not normally subject every word in the advertisement to careful study."

1 Callman, Unfair Competition and Trademarks 4057 19.2(a)(1), at 341–44 (1950), and the cases there cited.

It is well established that advertising need not be literally false in order to fall within the proscription of the act. Gone for the most part, fortunately, are the days when the advertiser was so lacking in subtlety as to represent his nostrum as superlative for "arthritis, rheumatism, neuralgia, sciatica, lumbago, gout, coronary thrombosis, brittle bones, bad teeth, malfunctioning glands, infected tonsils, infected appendix, gall stones, neuritis, underweight, constipation, indigestion, lack of energy, lack of vitality, lack of ambition and inability to sleep * * *." See Federal Trade Commission v. National Health Aids, Inc., 108 F.Supp. 340, 342 (D.Md.1952). The courts are no longer content to insist simply upon the "most literal truthfulness," More-trench Corp. v. Federal Trade Commission, 127 F.2d 792 at 795, for we have increasingly come to recognize that "Advertisements as a whole may be completely misleading although every sentence separately considered is literally true. This may be because things are omitted that should be said, or because advertisements are composed or purposefully printed in such way as to mislead." Donaldson v. Read Magazine, 333 U.S. 178, 188, 68 S.Ct. 591, 597, 92 L.Ed. 628 (1948). There are two obvious methods of employing a true statement so as to convey a false impression: one is the half-truth, where the statement is removed from its context and the nondisclosure of its context renders the statement misleading; a second is the ambiguity, where the statement in context has two or more commonly understood meanings, one of which is deceptive.

Problem 1–4

Charles of the Ritz manufactures a cosmetic preparation named "Rejuvenescence Cream." The advertising makes no claims of any kind for this cosmetic, it only repeats the name, and shows the faces of lovely women (with very healthy looking facial skin) in the background. The ads do describe the cream as containing "a vital organic ingredient" and certain "essences and compounds" which bring to the user's skin "the quality and texture of youth." The ads also ask the question: "Don't you want to keep looking young?"

The Commission staff seeks a cease and desist order against this advertising, on the ground that it falsely represented that Rejuvenescence Cream will rejuvenate and restore youth or the appearance of youth to the skin, regardless of the condition of the skin or the age of the user. This claim was deemed false because external applications of cosmetics cannot overcome skin conditions which result from systemic causes or from physiological changes occurring with the passage of time. There is no treatment known to medical science by which changes in the condition of the skin of an individual can be prevented or by which an aged skin can be rejuvenated or restored to a youthful condition.

Two medical experts, one a leading dermatologist, testified for the Commission; and both affirmatively stated that there was nothing known to medical science which could act as a rejuvenating agent and preserve or restore the youthful appearance of the skin. There was no testimony to the contrary; but Charles of the Ritz asserts that, since neither expert had ever used Rejuvenescence Cream or knew what it contained—Charles of the Ritz being unwilling to reveal its secret formula—their testimony was not substantial evidence to support the position of the Commission staff.

Charles of the Ritz also asserts that the use of the name "Rejuvenescence Cream" does not make a representation that the product rejuvenates and restores a youthful appearance to the skin. However, the Commission staff supplies an unabridged Webster's Dictionary which treats "rejuvenescense" as a common word meaning "a renewing of youth", and having "rejuvenation" as a synonym. The Commission's two medical experts both testified that the word meant "restoration of youth" to them.

(a) What exactly is being claimed in the advertisement or by the trade name and how does the FTC try to prove what claim is being made? Is the mere name "Rejuvenescence Cream" a misrepresentation? Is it misleading? What are the criteria for each?

(b) Is anyone being harmed (i.e., actually deceived) by this advertising campaign? Consider whether consumers are being harmed, and also whether competitors are being harmed. If there is harm to either, is it material or significant? If the FTC did nothing, would the market correct itself—because consumers will not continue to purchase a product that doesn't work?

(c) What level of persons should the Commission try to protect? The choices include "the reasonably intelligent consumer," "the average consumer," and "the most naive hypothetical consumer," as well as other points on the spectrum of sophistication. Can the Commission insist upon the most literal truthfulness, such that the ad cannot possibly be misconstrued? Or advertising so clear that, in the words of the prophet Isaiah, "wayfaring men, though fools, shall not err therein"?

(d) Must the Commission staff prove actual deception of the public—or at least some members of the public? The traditional rule is that representations having "a tendency or capacity to deceive" are unlawful. Does that entitle the Commission to speculate about the effect of words and claims on the consuming public? Does the traditional standard require the FTC to put on less proof than the current standard of "likely to mislead consumers acting reasonably under the circumstances"? *See* Cliffdale Associates, *infra* Section B(1)(c).

(e) In determining whether the content of a message is misleading, how relevant are the meanings of individual words obtained from dictionaries? How relevant are "trade meanings"?

Cf. Charles of the Ritz Distributors Corp. v. Federal Trade Commission, 143 F.2d 676 (2d Cir.1944).

Notes

1. Traditionally, the FTC felt obliged to protect the ignorant and the unwary, a la *Charles of the Ritz, supra*. Critics of the early cases refer to this as the "fools test," which "gave the Commission the authority to do just about anything, based largely on its own extreme interpretations of advertising." J. Howard Beales, III, Brightening the Lines: the Use of Policy Statements at the Federal Trade Commission, 72 Antitrust L.J. 1057, 1068 (2005).

2. By the late 1960s, the FTC came in for heavy criticism by both consumer advocates and the more conservative American Bar Association for wasting resources pursuing trivial cases. See both the Nader Report (Cox, Fellmeth & Schultz, The Consumer and the FTC (1969) and the American Bar Association Report (Report of the ABA Commission to Study the FTC (1969). Thirty-five years later, the lead author of the Nader Report appears satisfied with the ultimate effects of this critical investigation: "From a historical perspective, the impact of the Report on the FTC was substantial and lasting. The Report ignited a process that led to both a relatively immediate and an ongoing revitalization of the FTC." Edward F. Cox, Reinvigorating the FTC: The Nader Report and the Rise of Consumer Advocacy, 72 Antitrust L. J. 899, 900 (2005).

3. Under the FTC's Deception Policy adopted in 1983, a deceptive trade practice would include only that which would be "likely to mislead" the "consumer acting reasonably under the circumstances." The new policy and its implications will be discussed in more detail, in the following section.

c. FTC Policy Statement on Deception

In October of 1983, a divided Commission issued a "Policy Statement on Deception," in the form of a letter to Congress. The new policy was used for the first time in the 1984 case of *Cliffdale Associates*. This was an administrative adjudication, in which the staff first tried the case before an Administrative Law Judge employed by the FTC. The ALJ then issued his findings and order, which was then appealed to the Commission. In administrative adjudications, the Commission writes an opinion much like a reviewing court of appeals.

CLIFFDALE ASSOCIATES
Federal Trade Comm., 1984.
103 F.T.C. 110.

OPINION OF THE COMMISSION

By MILLER, CHAIRMAN: Cliffdale Associates, Jean–Claude Koven, and Arthur N. Sussman were charged with unfair methods of competition and unfair or deceptive acts or practices in violation of Section 5 of the Federal Trade Commission Act. Specifically, the complaint charged that respondents misrepresented the value and performance of an automobile engine attachment known as the Ball–Matic Gas Save Valve ("Ball–Matic"). The complaint also charged that respondents lacked a reasonable basis for their performance claims for the Ball–Matic.

Administrative Law Judge Miles J. Brown held that respondents had engaged in false and deceptive advertising and had lacked a reasonable basis for the claims made in their advertisements and promotional materials, in violation of Section 5 of the FTC Act. Both sides appeal from the ALJ's initial decision. We generally agree with the ALJ's findings and conclusions and, except as noted in this opinion, we adopt them as our own.

I. Background

A. The Respondents

1. Cliffdale Associates

Cliffdale is a Connecticut corporation headquartered in Westport, Connecticut. The company is engaged in mail order marketing of different products, including the Ball–Matic. Company sales for the year ending December 31, 1979, were $692,998.

B. The Product

The Ball–Matic was marketed as a gasoline conservation automobile retrofit device. The Ball–Matic is one of a number of "air bleed" devices designed to allow additional air to enter a car's engine in order to improve gasoline mileage.

II. Legal Standard for Deception

The complaint pleads both an unfairness and a deception theory for each alleged violation of Section 5. (Complaint ¶ 6, 7, 8, 11.) However, deception was the standard under which the claims were actually tried, and it is the Commission's view that this was the appropriate approach.

In finding the representations in respondents' advertisements to be deceptive the ALJ accepted complaint counsel's articulation of the standard for deception. He concluded that "any advertising representation that has the tendency and capacity to mislead or deceive a prospective purchaser is an unfair and deceptive practice which violates the Federal Trade Commission Act." We find this approach to deception and violations of Section 5 to be circular and therefore inadequate to provide guidance on how a deception claim should be analyzed. Accordingly, we believe it appropriate for the Commission to articulate a clear and understandable standard for deception.

Consistent with its Policy Statement on Deception, issued on October 14, 1983, the Commission will find an act or practice deceptive if, first, there is a representation, omission, or practice that, second, is likely to mislead consumers acting reasonably under the circumstances, and third, the representation, omission, or practice is material. These elements articulate the factors actually used in most earlier Commission cases identifying whether or not an act or practice was deceptive, even though the language used in those cases was often couched in such terms as "a tendency and capacity to deceive". [see FTC website, www.ftc.gov, for the full text].

The requirement that an act or practice be "likely to mislead", for example, reflects the long established principle that the Commission need not find *actual* deception to hold that a violation of Section 5 has occurred. This concept was explained as early as 1964, when the Commission stated:

> In the application of [the deception] standard to the many different factual patterns that have arisen in cases before the Commission, certain principles have been well established. One is that under Section 5 actual deception of particular consumers need not be shown.

Similarly, the requirement that an act or practice be considered from the perspective of a "consumer acting reasonably in the circumstances" is not new. Virtually all representations, even those that are true, can be misunderstood by some consumers. The Commission has long recognized that the law should not be applied in such a way as to find that honest representations are deceptive simply because they are misunderstood by a few. Thus, the Commission has noted that an advertisement would not be considered deceptive merely because it could be "unreasonably misunderstood by an insignificant and unrepresentative segment of the class of persons to whom the representation is addressed." In recent cases, this concept has been increasingly emphasized by the Commission.

The third element is materiality. As noted in the Commission's policy statement, a material representation, omission, act or practice involves information that is important to consumers and, hence, likely to affect their choice of, or conduct regarding, a product. Consumers thus are likely to suffer injury from a material misrepresentation. A review of past Commission deception cases shows that one of the factors usually considered, either directly or indirectly, is whether or not a claim is material.

Although the ALJ in this case used the phrase "tendency and capacity to deceive" in his initial decision, we find after reviewing the record that his underlying analysis shows that the three elements necessary for a finding of deception are present in this case.

III. *The Question of Liability*

The obvious first step in analyzing whether a claim is deceptive is for the Commission to determine what claim has been made. When the advertisement contains an express claim, the representation itself establishes its meaning. When the claim is implied, the Commission will often be able to determine the meaning through an examination of the representation, including an evaluation of such factors as the entire document, the juxtaposition of various phrases in the document, the nature of the claim, and the nature of the transaction.

In other situations, the Commission will require extrinsic evidence that reasonable consumers interpret the implied claims in a certain way. The evidence can consist of expert opinion, consumer testimony, contests, surveys, or any other reliable evidence of consumer interpretation. In all instances, the Commission will carefully consider any extrinsic evidence that is introduced.

A. Descriptive Claims

a. Were the Claims Made?

[The Commission found that the Ball–Matic device was represented to be an "important new invention," "needed in every car," and would provide "enhanced fuel economy."]

2. Were the Claims Deceptive?

Having determined that respondents made the claims as charged, we must next determine whether the claims were false in a material respect, and thus likely to injure consumers.

a. Ball–Matic as an Important New Invention

The evidence presented at trial amply documented that the Ball–Matic is a simple air-bleed device similar to many other such devices that have been marketed over the years. Clearly the Ball–Matic is not new. In fact, the Commission has already issued cease and desist orders against various marketers of two such devices, the Albano Air Jet and the G.R. Valve, both of which are virtually identical in design to the Ball–Matic. Air-bleed devices have been around a long time and, as the ALJ found, are considered to be of little value by the automobile industry.

The claim that the Ball–Matic was a new invention was expressly made. Having found such a claim to have been made, and that the claim is false, the Commission may infer, within the bounds of reason, that it is material. We therefore conclude that the ALJ was correct in holding that this claim was deceptive.

b. Ball–Matic Needed in Every Vehicle

The ALJ correctly concluded from the evidence presented at trial that most automobiles manufactured after 1974 have carburetors set to perform at such a lean air/fuel mixture that little, if any, fuel economy could be expected by using an air-bleed valve such as the Ball–Matic. There are, therefore, a significant number of consumers as to whom the claim of increased fuel economy is untrue. Accordingly, we agree with the ALJ that the claim that every car and truck needs the Ball–Matic is an express statement contrary to fact.

As with the "new invention" claim, this misrepresentation concerned a material aspect of the product. In the first place the claim was
expressly made, and the Commission may infer materiality. In any event,
the claim that the Ball–Matic is needed on every car would tend to
induce all consumers (including those owning cars for which it has no
utility) to buy the device. Those consumers who cannot in fact profit
from the Ball–Matic will have relied on the representation to their
detriment. Thus, the ALJ was correct in concluding that this claim was
deceptive.

c. *Efficiency Claims*

The ALJ found the representation that the Ball–Matic would significantly improve fuel economy when installed in a typical car and used
under normal driving conditions to be false. We agree. The record
discloses that even under conditions most likely to produce benefits from
the Ball–Matic, the fuel savings do not approach those claimed by
respondents. Respondent's consumer tests and testimonials also fail to
support these claims and, as the ALJ found, are not a recognized way of
testing fuel economy.

Claims about enhanced fuel efficiency resulting from use of the Ball–
Matic are clearly material to consumers. While consumers will not
necessarily expect to achieve the specific fuel economy level represented
in a particular advertisement, the performance claimed in the ads should
be representative of consumers' expected savings from the Ball–Matic. It
was not, and the advertisements were therefore deceptive.

COMMISSIONER PATRICIA P. BAILEY CONCURRING IN THE
RESULT IN PART AND DISSENTING IN PART

* * *

Legal Standard for Deception

This is an uncomplicated case involving a number of advertising
claims, which are clearly false and deceptive, that could have been
addressed with swift and sure justice under existing law. Unfortunately,
a majority of the Commission has chosen to use the case as a vehicle to
set forth a new legal standard which has little to do with the case and
much to do with an ill-advised undertaking to rewrite the law of
deception.

* * *

The second requirement [of the Deception Policy Statement] is that
an act or practice be likely to mislead consumers "acting reasonably
under the circumstances." Of the three newly introduced elements, I
believe this is on its face the most divorced from prior precedent and also
the most likely to produce troubling results.

* * *

* * * I believe the imposition of a "reasonable consumer" test as an element of the legal standard for deception may seriously jeopardize this guiding principle of deception law, which has permitted and encouraged the Commission to spread its protective mantle over the uninformed and credulous, those with understandable but often unreasonable hopes, those with limited reasoning abilities, such as children, and even "average" consumers whose guard may be down or who may behave somewhat carelessly in the face of deceptive conduct.

* * *

[Commissioner Pertschuk filed a similar "dissent".]

Notes

1. Would the claims in the *Cliffdale* case have been held deceptive under the traditional standard? Did the application of the new deception policy make any difference to the outcome of this case?

2. There was some early judicial suggestion that the FTC is applying a more stringent theory of deception. Southwest Sunsites, Inc. v. Federal Trade Com'n, 785 F.2d 1431 (9th Cir.1986): new standard "imposes a greater burden of proof on the FTC to show a violation of Section 5," and the new formulation is "more narrow than, but completely subsumed in, the prior theory."

3. For more in-depth discussions of the 1983 deception policy statement and its possible effects see J. Howard Beales, III, Brightening the Lines: the Use of Policy Statements at the Federal Trade Commission, 72 Antitrust L.J. 1057, 1068 (2005); Jack E. Karns & Alan C. Roline, The Federal Trade Commission's Deception Policy in the Next Millennium: Evaluating the Subjective Impact of Cliffdale Associates, 74 N.D.L. Rev. 441 (1998); Ford & Calfee, Recent Developments in FTC Policy on Deception, 50 J. of Marketing 82 (July 1986); Sullivan, The FTC's Deceptive Advertising Policy: a Legal and Economic Analysis, 64 Or.L.Rev. 593 (1986); Bailey & Pertschuk, The Law of Deception: The Past as Prologue, 33 Am.U.L.Rev. 849 (1984).

4. Do you agree with Commissioner Bailey that the FTC has abandoned its traditional protection of vulnerable consumers? Consider the following problem.

Problem 1–5

A travel agency advertised a meeting as being of special interest to cancer patients. At the meeting, the speaker promoted a trip to the Phillipines that would include an opportunity for travelers to witness and take advantage of "psychic surgery," whereby cancerous tumors are removed without cutting the skin. A film was shown demonstrating psychic surgery. Many terminally ill patients purchased the trip, only to find out that the "surgery" shown on the film was done through sleight of hand techniques, and was a complete fraud.

You are a staff attorney at the FTC. Will you be able to persuade the Commission to issue a complaint in this case under the 1983 Deception

Policy? Was there a misrepresentation being made? Would a reasonable consumer believe in "psychic surgery"? Was this marketing being aimed at "reasonable consumers"? Cf. In re Travel King, 86 F.T.C. 715 (1975).

d. Interpreting the Meaning of the Advertisement

In order to apply its Deception Policy to a particular advertisement, the Commission must interpret the claims being made in the advertisement. Traditionally, the Commission considers the "net impression" of the ad, including visual elements, implied claims and omissions, based on the FTC's own internal expertise. The proper interpretation of an ad was a key issue in the following case.

KRAFT, INC. v. FEDERAL TRADE COMMISSION

United States Court of Appeals, Seventh Circuit, 1992.
970 F.2d 311.

FLAUM, CIRCUIT JUDGE.

Kraft, Inc. ("Kraft") asks us to review an order of the Federal Trade Commission ("FTC" or "Commission") finding that it violated §§ 5 and 12 of the Federal Trade Commission Act ("Act"), 15 U.S.C. §§ 45, 52. The FTC determined that Kraft, in an advertising campaign, had misrepresented information regarding the amount of calcium contained in Kraft Singles American Pasteurized Process Cheese Food ("Singles") relative to the calcium content in five ounces of milk and in imitation cheese slices. The FTC ordered Kraft to cease and desist from making these misrepresentations and Kraft filed this petition for review. We enforce the Commission's order.

I.

Three categories of cheese compete in the individually wrapped process slice market: process cheese food slices, imitation slices, and substitute slices. Process cheese food slices, also known as "dairy slices," must contain at least 51% natural cheese by federal regulation. 21 C.F.R. § 133.173(a)(5). Imitation cheese slices, by contrast, contain little or no natural cheese and consist primarily of water, vegetable oil, flavoring agents, and fortifying agents. While imitation slices are as healthy as process cheese food slices in some nutrient categories, they are as a whole considered "nutritionally inferior" and must carry the label "imitation." Id. at § 101.3(e)(4). Substitute slices fit somewhere in between; they fall short of the natural cheese content of process cheese food slices yet are nutritionally superior to imitation slices. Id. at § 101.3(e)(2). Consistent with FTC usage, we refer to both imitation and substitute slices as "imitation" slices.

Kraft Singles are process cheese food slices. In the early 1980s, Kraft began losing market share to an increasing number of imitation slices that were advertised as both less expensive and equally nutritious as dairy slices like Singles. Kraft responded with a series of advertisements, collectively known as the "Five Ounces of Milk" campaign, designed to inform consumers that Kraft Singles cost more than imitation slices because they are made from five ounces of milk rather than less expensive ingredients. The ads also focused on the calcium content of Kraft Singles in an effort to capitalize on growing consumer interest in adequate calcium consumption.

The FTC filed a complaint against Kraft charging that this advertising campaign materially misrepresented the calcium content and relative calcium benefit of Kraft Singles. The FTC Act makes it unlawful to engage in unfair or deceptive commercial practices, or to induce consumers to purchase certain products through advertising that is misleading in a material respect. Thus, an advertisement is deceptive under the Act if it is likely to mislead consumers, acting reasonably under the circumstances, in a material respect. Cliffdale Assocs., Inc., 103 F.T.C. 110, 164–66 (1984); Federal Trade Commission Policy Statement on Deception, 103 F.T.C. 174 (1984) (appended to Cliffdale Assocs.) [hereinafter "FTC Policy Statement"]. In implementing this standard, the Commission examines the overall net impression of an ad and engages in a three-part inquiry: (1) what claims are conveyed in the ad; (2) are those claims false or misleading; and (3) are those claims material to prospective consumers.

Two facts are critical to understanding the allegations against Kraft. First, although Kraft does use five ounces of milk in making each Kraft Single, roughly 30% of the calcium contained in the milk is lost during processing. Second, the vast majority of imitation slices sold in the United States contain 15% of the U.S. Recommended Daily Allowance (RDA) of calcium per ounce, roughly the same amount contained in Kraft Singles. Specifically then, the FTC complaint alleged that the challenged advertisements made two implied claims, neither of which was true: (1) that a slice of Kraft Singles contains the same amount of calcium as five ounces of milk (the "milk equivalency" claim); and (2) that Kraft Singles contain more calcium than do most imitation cheese slices (the "imitation superiority" claim). The two sets of ads at issue in this case, referred to as the "Skimp" ads and the "Class Picture" ads, ran nationally in print and broadcast media between 1985 and 1987. The Skimp ads were designed to communicate the nutritional benefit of Kraft Singles by referring expressly to their milk and calcium content. The broadcast version of this ad on which the FTC focused contained the following audio copy: Lady (voice over):

> I admit it. I thought of skimping. Could you look into those big blue eyes and skimp on her? So I buy Kraft Singles. Imitation slices use hardly any milk. But Kraft has five ounces per slice. Five ounces. So her little bones get calcium they need to grow. No, she doesn't know what that big Kraft means. Good thing I do. Singers: Kraft Singles. More milk makes 'em ... more milk makes 'em good. Lady (voice over): Skimp on her? No way.

The visual image corresponding to this copy shows, among other things, milk pouring into a glass until it reaches a mark on the glass denoted "five ounces." The commercial also shows milk pouring into a glass which bears the phrase "5 oz. milk slice" and which gradually becomes part of the label on a package of Singles. In January 1986, Kraft revised this ad, changing "Kraft has five ounces per slice" to "Kraft is made from five ounces per slice," Kraft added the disclosure, "one 3/4 ounce slice has 70% of the calcium of five ounces of milk" as a subscript in the television commercial and as a footnote in the print ads.

The Class Picture ads also emphasized the milk and calcium content of Kraft Singles but, unlike the Skimp ads, did not make an express comparison to imitation slices. The version of this ad examined by the FTC depicts a group of school children having their class picture taken, and contains the following audio copy: Announcer (voice over):

> Can you see what's missing in this picture? Well, a government study says that half the school kids in America don't get all the calcium recommended for growing kids. That's why Kraft Singles are important. Kraft is made from five ounces of milk per slice. So they're concentrated with calcium. Calcium the government recommends for strong bones and healthy teeth! Photographer: Say Cheese! Kids: Cheese!

Announcer (voice over):

> "Say Kraft Singles. 'Cause kids love Kraft Singles, right down to their bones." The Class Picture ads also included the subscript disclaimer mentioned above.

After a lengthy trial, the Administrative Law Judge (ALJ) concluded that both the Skimp and Class Picture ads made the milk equivalency claim. Specifically, the ALJ found that the juxtaposition of references to milk and calcium, along with the failure to mention that calcium is lost in processing, implied that each Kraft Single contains the same amount of calcium as five ounces of milk, and that the altered audio copy and subscript disclosure were confusing and inconspicuous and thus insufficient to dispel this impression. Further, the ALJ concluded that both sets of ads falsely conveyed the imitation superiority claim; he determined that reasonable consumers would take away the net impression that Kraft Singles contain more calcium than imitation slices because Kraft Singles contain five ounces of milk and imitation slices have little or no milk. According to the ALJ, both claims were material because they implicated important health concerns. He therefore ordered Kraft to cease and desist from making these claims about any of its individually wrapped slices of process cheese food, imitation cheese, or substitute cheese.

The FTC affirmed the ALJ's decision, with some modifications. In re Kraft, Inc., FTC No. 9208 (Jan. 30, 1991). As to the Skimp ads, the Commission found that four elements conveyed the milk equivalency claim: (1) the use of the word "has" in the phrase "Kraft has five ounces per slice"; (2) repetition of the precise amount of milk in a Kraft Single (five ounces); (3) the use of the word "so" to link the reference to milk with the reference to calcium; and (4) the visual image of milk being poured into a glass up to a five-ounce mark, and the superimposition of that image onto a package of Singles. It also found two additional elements that conveyed the imitation superiority claim: (1) the express reference to imitation slices combined with the use of comparative language ("hardly any," "but"); and (2) the image of a glass containing very little milk during the reference to imitation slices, followed by the image of a glass being filled to the five-ounce mark during the reference to Kraft Singles. The Commission based all of these findings on its own impression of the advertisements and found it unnecessary to resort to extrinsic evidence; it did note, however, that the available extrinsic evidence was consistent with its determinations.

The Commission then examined the Class Picture ads—once again, without resorting to extrinsic evidence—and found that they contained copy substantially similar to the copy in the Skimp ads that conveyed the impression of milk equivalency. It rejected, however, the ALJ's finding that the Class Picture ads made an imitation superiority claim, determining that the ads neither expressly compared Singles to imitation slices, nor contained any visual images to prompt such a comparison, and that available extrinsic evidence did not support the ALJ's finding.

The FTC next found that the claims were material to consumers. It concluded that the milk equivalency claim is a health-related claim that reasonable consumers would find important and that Kraft believed that the claim induced consumers to purchase Singles. The FTC presumed that the imitation superiority claim was material because it found that Kraft intended to make that claim. It also found that the materiality of that claim was demonstrated by evidence that the challenged ads led to increased sales despite a substantially higher price for Singles than for imitation slices.

Finally, the FTC modified the ALJ's cease and desist order by extending its coverage from "individually wrapped slices of cheese, imitation cheese, and substitute cheese" to "any product that is a cheese, related cheese product, imitation cheese, or substitute cheese." The Commission found that the serious, deliberate nature of the violation, combined with the transferability of the violations to other cheese products, justified a broader order. Kraft filed this petition to set-aside the Commission's order or, alternatively, to modify its scope.

* * *

III.

Kraft makes numerous arguments on appeal, but its principal claim is that the FTC erred as a matter of law in not requiring extrinsic evidence of consumer deception. Without such evidence, Kraft claims (1) that the FTC had no objective basis for determining if its ads actually contained the implied claims alleged, and (2) that the FTC's order chills constitutionally protected commercial speech. Alternatively, Kraft contends that substantial evidence does not support the FTC's finding that the Class Picture ads contain the milk equivalency claim. Finally, Kraft maintains that even if it did make the alleged milk equivalency and imitation superiority claims, substantial evidence does not support the FTC's finding that these claims were material to consumers. We address each contention in turn.

A.

1.

In determining what claims are conveyed by a challenged advertisement, the Commission relies on two sources of information: its own viewing of the ad and extrinsic evidence. Its practice is to view the ad first and, if it is unable on its own to determine with confidence what claims are conveyed in a challenged ad, to turn to extrinsic evidence. FTC Policy Statement, 103 F.T.C. at 176. The most convincing extrinsic evidence is a survey "of what consumers thought upon reading the advertisement in question," Thompson Medical, 104 F.T.C. at 788–89, but the Commission also relies on other forms of extrinsic evidence including consumer testimony, expert opinion, and copy tests of ads. FTC Policy Statement, 103 F.T.C. at 176 n. 8.

Kraft has no quarrel with this approach when it comes to determining whether an ad conveys express claims, but contends that the FTC should be required, as a matter of law, to rely on extrinsic evidence rather than its own subjective analysis in all cases involving allegedly implied claims. The basis for this argument is that implied claims, by definition, are not self-evident from the face of an ad. This, combined with the fact that consumer perceptions are shaped by a host of external variables—including their social and educational backgrounds, the environment in which they view the ad, and prior experiences with the product advertised, makes review of implied claims by a five-member commission inherently unreliable. The Commissioners, Kraft argues, are simply incapable of determining what implicit messages consumers are likely to perceive in an ad. Making matters worse, Kraft asserts that the Commissioners are predisposed to find implied claims because the claims have been identified in the complaint, rendering it virtually impossible for them to reflect the perceptions of unbiased consumers.

* * * While this disparity is sometimes justified on grounds of advertising "expertise"—the FTC presumably possesses more of it than courts—Kraft maintains this justification is an illusory one in that the FTC has no special expertise in discerning consumer perceptions. Indeed, proof of the FTC's inexpertise abounds: false advertising cases makes up a small part of the Commission's workload, most commissioners have little prior experience in advertising, and the average tenure of commissioners is very brief. That evidence aside, no amount of expertise in Kraft's view can replace the myriad of external variables affecting consumer perceptions. Here, the Commission found implied claims based solely on its own intuitive reading of the ads (although it did reinforce that conclusion by examining the proffered extrinsic evidence). Had the Commission fully and properly relied on available extrinsic evidence,

Kraft argues it would have conclusively found that consumers do not perceive the milk equivalency and imitation superiority claims in the ads.

While Kraft's arguments may have some force as a matter of policy, they are unavailing as a matter of law. Courts, including the Supreme Court, have uniformly rejected imposing such a requirement on the FTC, and we decline to do so as well. We hold that the Commission may rely on its own reasoned analysis to determine what claims, including implied ones, are conveyed in a challenged advertisement, so long as those claims are reasonably clear from the face of the advertisement.

Kraft's case for a per se rule has two flaws. First, it rests on the faulty premise that implied claims are inescapably subjective and unpredictable. In fact, implied claims fall on a continuum, ranging from the obvious to the barely discernible. The Commission does not have license to go on a fishing expedition to pin liability on advertisers for barely imaginable claims falling at the end of this spectrum. However, when confronted with claims that are implied, yet conspicuous, extrinsic evidence is unnecessary because common sense and administrative experience provide the Commission with adequate tools to make its findings. The implied claims Kraft made are reasonably clear from the face of the advertisements, and hence the Commission was not required to utilize consumer surveys in reaching its decision.

* * * [T]he Commission's expertise in deceptive advertising cases, Kraft's protestations notwithstanding, undoubtedly exceeds that of courts as a general matter. That false advertising cases constitute a small percentage of the FTC's overall workload does not negate the fact that significant resources are devoted to such cases in absolute terms, nor does it account for the institutional expertise the FTC gains through investigations, rulemakings, and consent orders. The Commissioners' personal experiences quite obviously affect their perceptions, but it does not follow that they are incapable of predicting whether a particular claim is likely to be perceived by a reasonable number of consumers.

* * *

Our holding does not diminish the force of Kraft's argument as a policy matter, and, indeed, the extensive body of commentary on the subject makes a compelling argument that reliance on extrinsic evidence should be the rule rather than the exception. Along those lines, the Commission would be well-advised to adopt a consistent position on consumer survey methodology—advertisers and the FTC, it appears, go round and round on this issue—so that any uncertainty is reduced to an absolute minimum.

* * *

V.

For the foregoing reasons, Kraft's petition to set-aside the order is DENIED and the Commission's order is ENFORCED.

MANION, concurring.

While I concur with the opinion of the court, I am concerned that the FTC can avoid extrinsic evidence by simply concluding that a deceptive, implied claim is facially apparent. While the FTC has expertise, consumer surveys provide at least some objective determination of what the purchaser thinks and should be considered since, after all, the consumer is among those we are trying to protect.

Moreover, the FTC's current procedure threatens to chill nonmisleading, protected speech. Although not all commercial speech has constitutional protection, the law has developed since this court decided that the FTC could rely on its own interpretation of ads.... The Supreme Court has recognized that a free flow of information is indispensable to decisionmaking in the free enterprise system. See Virginia State Bd. of Pharmacy v. Virginia Citizens Consumer Council, Inc., 425 U.S. 748, 96 S.Ct. 1817, 48 L.Ed.2d 346 (1976). But the FTC jeopardizes this flow by relying on the FTC commissioners' subjective interpretation to determine whether an ad, while literally true, implies a false message. Advertisers will be unable to predict whether the FTC will find particular ads misleading. Pre-dissemination surveys showing consumers are not misled will be useless since the FTC is free to ignore any such extrinsic evidence and rely on its subjective judgment that consumers may be misled. Advertisers unwilling to gamble with a multi-million dollar ad campaign have essentially two choices: (1) submit every campaign to the FTC in advance or (2) disseminate ads that say little or nothing about a product or service. An advertiser will not want to risk producing comparative ads which the FTC may ultimately find to imply false, unintended messages.

Unfortunately, judicial groping for a distinction between cases where extrinsic evidence is necessary and those where it is not is leaving both advertisers and the FTC uncertain. * * * All this court tells them is that the FTC need not rely on such evidence if the "implied claims [are] reasonably clear from the face of the ads and not unpredictable." Rather than leaving judges to hew the contours of this issue, the FTC would be well-advised to take this court's suggestion—apply its expertise and develop a consumer survey methodology that advertisers can use to ascertain whether their ads contain implied, deceptive messages.

Notes

1. Do you agree with the FTC's interpretation of what this ad is representing to the consumer? What exactly were the challenged claims in the ads? Were the challenged claims true or false? What did Kraft say in their defense? How should the Commission go about interpreting the meaning of advertisements? Should they rely on extrinsic evidence or their net impression? What did the court conclude on this point?

2. Advertisers usually perform elaborate consumer studies, or "copy tests" to determine whether they are conveying the message they want to

convey. Why should five FTC Commissioners in Washington, D.C. feel they have the expertise to determine what consumers are taking from a particular television commercial if even the advertisers themselves don't feel qualified to do this?

See Pitofsky, Beyond Nader: Consumer Protection and the Regulation of Advertising, 90 Harv.L.Rev. 661, 678 (1977). Many commentators have suggested that the FTC be required to use survey evidence in interpreting the meaning of advertisements. See Gellhorn, Proof of Consumer Deception Before the Federal Trade Commission, 17 U.Kan.L.Rev. 559 (1969); Preston, Data–Free at the FTC? How the Federal Trade Commission Decides Whether Extrinsic Evidence of Deceptiveness Is Required, 24 Am.Bus.L.J. 359 (1986).

3.   The Commission itself in a 1984 case declared that if the purported implied claim in an advertisement was not clearly made, it would require complaint counsel to offer extrinsic evidence in the form of consumer surveys, evidence of marketing principles applicable to similar situations, or adequately supported expert opinions. See In re Thompson Medical Co., 104 F.T.C. 648, 789–90 (1984), aff'd 791 F.2d 189 (D.C.Cir.1986), cert. denied, 479 U.S. 1086, 107 S.Ct. 1289, 94 L.Ed.2d 146 (1987).

4.   One author has suggested that the Commission should abandon the impossible task of trying to determine "the" meaning of advertisements, and instead should balance the costs of eliminating any misleading interpretations against the benefits to consumers. See Craswell, Interpreting Deceptive Advertising, 65 B.U.L.Rev. 657 (1985). See also Preston & Richards, Consumer Miscomprehension and Deceptive Advertising: A Response to Professor Craswell, 68 B.U.L.Rev. 431 (1988).

Problem 1–6

The Colgate–Palmolive Company advertises that its shaving cream "Rapid Shave" outshaves them all. Its commercials on television are designed to show that Rapid Shave softens even the toughness of sandpaper so that it can be shaved—a claim which the company has verified in laboratory tests. If real sandpaper were used for the TV demonstration, however, the inadequacies of television transmission make it appear to viewers to be nothing but plain paper—that is, its texture is not visible. The commercials therefore use a simulated prop, or "mock up," made of plexiglass to which sand is applied. The announcer intones the qualities of Rapid Shave and particularly its ability to shave sandpaper, declares "just apply, soak and off in a stroke," and then a razor neatly "shaves" clean the plexiglass mock-up which has been soaked with Rapid Shave.

(a) Is the undisclosed use of a plexiglass substitute a deceptive act subject to FTC prosecution? See FTC v. Colgate–Palmolive Co., 380 U.S. 374, 85 S.Ct. 1035, 13 L.Ed.2d 904 (1965).

(b) What claim or claims are being made in this ad? Which, if any, are deceptive? Are they material?

(c) Would the answer be the same in the case of—

—the use of mashed potatoes to depict ice cream being enjoyed by children, because real ice cream would melt under the TV lights?

—putting marbles in a bowl of soup so that the solid ingredients would be forced to the top and be more visible? See Campbell Soup Co., 77 F.T.C. 664 (1970).

—in an ad focusing on a visual demonstration of pollution reduction for gasoline, showing a county courthouse with a sign reading "Chevron Research Center" (the actual research center was covered in fog on the day of the filming)? Would your answer depend on how important the appearance of the Research Center was to the claims being made in the ad? See Standard Oil Co. of Cal. v. Federal Trade Commission, 577 F.2d 653 (9th Cir. 1978).

—using a reinforced automobile in a re-creation of a "monster truck" exhibition in which all the cars run over by the truck were crushed except the advertised auto? Assume the event actually happened but the auto maker was not there to film the event. See In re Volvo North America Corp., 1992 WL 12011032, 115 F.T.C. 87 (1992).

In each case, what has the manufacturer misrepresented, if anything? Who stands to lose thereby, and what do they stand to lose? Is this sort of policing worth the expenditure of government time, effort and money? Why? What social interest is served thereby?

Problem 1–7

A magazine advertisement for Lean Cuisine frozen entreés showed pictures of some of their products, both prepared and in the package, and of a young man and woman riding on a bicycle. The slogan in large print across the bottom read: ***LEAN ON* LEAN CUISINE.** The text above that tag line read as follows:

> Of all the things we at Stouffer's® pack into our 34 Lean Cuisine® entrees—the freshest ingredients, the ripest vegetables and the perfect blend of herbs and spices—there are some things we skimp on: Calories. Fat. Sodium. With less than 300 calories, controlled fat and always less than 1 gram of sodium* per entrée, we make good sense taste great.

You are an FTC Commissioner. The FTC staff says this ad and others like it are making an implied low sodium claim, which they say is not true because the Lean Cuisine products are not low sodium products under the Food and Drug Administration standards for labeling. The recommended daily limit on sodium for adults is 2400 milligrams, and the FDA defines "low" sodium for an entrée as 240 milligrams or less.

Would you agree with the staff that the ad is making an implied low sodium claim? Why or why not? Is the claim deceptive?

---

* All Lean Cuisine entrees have been re-formulated to contain less than 1 gram (1000 mg.) of sodium.

© 1991 Stouffer Foods Corporation.

Will the "Nutrition Facts" label that appears on every package of Lean Cuisine, showing calories and sodium per serving, as well as the recommended daily allowances of nutrients, among other things, be sufficient to counteract any deceptive impression left by the advertisement?

Notes

1.   In 1990, Congress passed the Nutrition Labeling and Education Act of 1990, which required nutrition information on most food products, and directed the FDA to promulgate implementing regulations. The FDA promulgated its regulations in 1993, which, among other things, instituted the highly readable "Nutrition Facts" disclosures on food products. The FDA labeling regulations attempt to standardize and limit the terms permitted on labels (such as "low fat" or "low sodium"). Although the FTC and the FDA have overlapping jurisdiction in policing food advertising claims, since 1954 the two agencies have informally agreed to concentrate on separate areas, with the FTC assuming primary responsibility for regulating food advertising, and the FDA assuming primary responsibility for regulating food labels. In 1994, the FTC issued an "Enforcement Policy Statement on Food Advertising," which specifically addressed the issue of how to harmonize the FDA's food labeling regulations with the FTC's policies on food advertising. 50 Fed. Reg. 28388 (June 1, 1994). In the FTC statement, the Commission indicated it would give advertisers a bit more leeway in advertising than the FDA allows on labels. For instance, the FTC would permit advertisers to use synonyms for required FDA terminology, and to make certain comparative claims that the FDA would not allow on labels, if the advertisement is properly qualified to avoid misleading consumers.

2.   The advertisement described and quoted in problem 1–7 was one of the ads involved in a suit by the FTC against Stouffer Foods, the makers of "Lean Cuisine" products. One of the major issues at the administrative trial in the Stouffer Foods case was whether or not consumers actually were interpreting the ad as making a low sodium claim. The FTC did one survey of consumers which said the ad did make a low sodium claim; Stouffer Foods did another that contradicted the FTC's findings. The Commission relied on both its own net impression of the ads (in accordance with the holding in *Kraft*), and also on the FTC consumer survey, and ruled against Stouffer Foods. In re Stouffer Foods, FTC docket 9250, Final Order and Opinion of the Commission (Sept. 26, 1994).

e.   Advertising Substantiation

STERLING DRUG, INC. v. FEDERAL TRADE COMMISSION

United States Court of Appeals, Ninth Circuit, 1984.
741 F.2d 1146.

HUG, CIRCUIT JUDGE:

In this appeal from a decision of the Federal Trade Commission, Sterling Drug, Inc. seeks review of a determination that it disseminated false advertising for its nonprescription analgesic products. Sterling contests findings by the Commission that its advertising was deceptive. It contends that the provisions of the cease and desist order are not warranted by the record and that the order applies to more of Sterling's products than is warranted by the record. We uphold the findings and enforce the order.

I

FACTS AND PROCEDURAL HISTORY

Sterling Drug, Inc. ("Sterling") manufactures nonprescription internal analgesic products, including Bayer Aspirin, Bayer Children's Aspirin, Vanquish, Cope, and Midol. In February 1983, the Federal Trade Commission issued an administrative complaint against Sterling in which it was alleged that certain Sterling advertisements violated sections 5 and 12 of the Federal Trade Commission Act, 15 U.S.C. §§ 45 and 52. On the same day, the Commission also charged that two of Sterling's competitors had engaged in deceptive advertising practices. Those complaints named Bristol–Myers Company, which manufactures Bufferin and Excedrin, and American Home Products Corporation, which produces Anacin and Arthritis Pain Formula.

The cases were partially consolidated before an administrative law judge, who held joint hearings on issues common to the three cases. After extensive pretrial discovery, the ALJ held a separate hearing in this case in 1979–80. He heard testimony from forty witnesses, including experts in the fields of medicine, pharmacology, and advertising. He also reviewed hundreds of exhibits and a large volume of scientific publications submitted in conjunction with the testimony of the expert witnesses.

The ALJ found each of the companies liable for violations of the Act and issued broad cease and desist orders barring future violations. Each of the companies appealed to the Commission. In each case, the Commission affirmed the ALJ's decision as modified.

* * *

B. *Discussion*

In its examination of the complaint, the Commission distinguished three distinct types of advertising claims. The first type, establishment claims, suggests that a product's superiority has been scientifically established. An advertiser may make this type of representation through the use of specific language, such as "medically proven," or through the use of visual representations.

The second type of claim is a representation that suggests the product is superior without claiming that superiority has been scientifically established. The claimed superiority may refer to therapeutic efficacy or may describe the product's pharmaceutical attributes, such as freshness, purity, color, and shelf life. The Commission requires that the advertiser have a reasonable basis to support a claim of product superiority.

The third type of claim is puffing. These claims are either vague or highly subjective, *e.g.*, "Bayer works wonders," and therefore no substantiation of the claim is required.

* * *

b. Establishment of Therapeutic Superiority [Bayer Aspirin]

The Commission determined that several advertisements for Bayer Aspirin represented the product to be therapeutically superior and claimed that superiority had been scientifically established. Sterling first contends that those advertisements, read as a whole, merely claimed Bayer's pharmaceutical superiority, not its therapeutic superiority. Its second contention is that there was no establishment claim.

The Commission held it did not need to consider whether Sterling had a reasonable basis to claim Bayer was therapeutically superior, since in every case Sterling had also claimed that Bayer's therapeutic superiority was scientifically established. It concluded that Sterling lacked the substantiation to make these establishment claims. The Commission held that establishment claims could be substantiated only if Sterling relied upon two well-controlled clinical studies that indicated Bayer was superior.

Sterling refutes the conclusion that it made establishment claims, arguing that the text of its advertisements made no explicit assertion that Bayer's therapeutic superiority was established. However, the Commission's conclusions were based upon visual aspects of the advertisements, rather than only on the text. These visual representations included pictures of medical and scientific reports from which consumers could infer that Bayer's effectiveness had been objectively evaluated. The Commission noted that the advertisements conveyed a "serious tone" or a "scientific aura" that also implied scientific approval of the product.

A determination of false advertising can be based upon deceptive visual representations. It is within the Commission's expertise to determine what inferences consumers may draw from such representations. We defer to that expertise and affirm the conclusion that Bayer was advertised to have scientifically established therapeutic superiority.

* * *

b. Establishment of Therapeutic Claims [Cope]

Sterling does not contest the Commission's conclusion that it made therapeutic efficacy claims as to Cope. However, it claims these representations did not include the assertion that Cope's superiority was established.

The Commission based its conclusion on the visual aspects of advertisements for Cope. It cited as an example a television advertisement in which an announcer discussed Cope's efficacy in conjunction with his description of "important studies" on pain relief. The announcer held a copy of the "important studies." In the background were shelves lined with "ponderous books." We agree with the Commission that the combination of the visual and oral representations was apt to convey to consumers a message of proven efficacy.

The Commission found Sterling could not substantiate its claim that Cope's therapeutic efficacy was established. Sterling does not challenge that finding on appeal.

3. Findings Concerning Midol

The complaint charged Sterling with failing to disclose Midol's aspirin content. The Commission held that a mere failure to disclose the presence of aspirin in advertising for aspirin-based analgesics was not misleading. It concluded, however, that it was a deceptive practice to disseminate advertising that implied aspirin-based products did not contain aspirin. It found that certain Midol advertisements did create that impression, and it illustrated its finding with this radio advertisement:

> Midol starts to work fast with an exclusive formula that helps stop periodic pain * * * and its medically approved ingredients give effective relief from headache and low backache. All in all, Midol's unique formula gets you through those days in comfort.

The Commission concluded that the term "exclusive formula" conveyed the message that Midol's analgesic ingredient was not aspirin. It also criticized an advertisement that claimed Midol was made from an "exclusive formula with medication ordinary pain relievers don't give you."

The failure to disclose material information may cause an advertisement to be deceptive, even if it does not state false facts. We must reject Sterling's contention that these advertisements were not intended to suggest that Midol's analgesic ingredient was unique. The illustrative advertisements specifically state that the unique ingredient relieves pain. We agree with the Commission that consumers could easily infer the unique pain reliever was something other than ordinary aspirin.

Notes

1. Why the emphasis in modern FTC advertising cases on advertising substantiation rather than deception? Does this unfairly shift the burden of proof from the Commission to the advertiser?

2. What is the legal basis for the FTC's requirement of prior substantiation for claims made in advertising?

Originally the FTC held that it would be "unfair" for an advertiser to make a product claim without a "reasonable basis." In a 1972 case, the Commission based the requirement on marketplace fairness, pointing to the "imbalance of knowledge and resources between a business enterprise and each of its customers," concluding that "economically it is more rational, and imposes far less cost on society, to require a manufacturer to confirm his affirmative product claims rather than impose a burden upon each individual consumer to test, investigate, or experiment for himself." In re Pfizer, Inc., 81 F.T.C. 23, 62 (1972).

Subsequent cases have based the substantiation requirement on a more limited deception theory. For instance, when Firestone said its tires stop "25% quicker," the FTC said the advertiser was impliedly representing to consumers that the claim was backed by scientific proof. In re Firestone Tire & Rubber Co., 81 F.T.C. 398, 450–51 (1972), aff'd 481 F.2d 246, 250–51 (6th Cir.), cert. denied, 414 U.S. 1112, 94 S.Ct. 841, 38 L.Ed.2d 739 (1973).

3.   The Commission's Policy Statement Regarding Advertising Substantiation, 49 Fed. Reg. 30999 (1984), says that an advertiser must have at least the amount and type of substantiation it claims to have in the ad. Otherwise, the advertiser must have a "reasonable basis." In the Sterling Drug case, for claims that a product's efficacy or superiority is "scientifically established," what level of substantiation was required? How were such claims communicated to the consumer? Was the requirement of two well-controlled clinical studies justified? Would any substantiation be required for mere "puffery"?

Problem 1–8

A nutritional supplement called Weight–Be–Gone, based on traditional herbal medicine, is trying to gain market share. One of the advertisements for Weight–Be–Gone refers to a study published in *Homeopathic News*. The study was not specifically about Weight–Be–Gone, but it did conclude that the main ingredient in Weight–Be–Gone was effective in inducing weight loss without diet or exercise, by speeding up the body's metabolism. If the company wants to use the *Homeopathic News* study in its advertising, would two well-controlled clinical studies be required or could the advertiser simply rely on the article itself for its substantiation? How would the advertiser have to word or otherwise depict its claim in order to satisfy the FTC's ad substantiation requirements?

Notes

1.   In 1994, Congress passed the Dietary Supplement Health and Education Act, which created a class of products known as "dietary supplements" that would no longer have to obtain the FDA's pre-market approval. Pub. L. No. 103–417, 108 Stat. 4325 (codified in scattered sections of 21 U.S.C). The FTC still retains jurisdiction to regulate deceptive advertising of such supplements, however, and has been quite active in this arena.

2.   Since the mid–1990's, the FTC has aggressively pursued deceptive advertising of weight loss products, including weight loss equipment, plans, and dietary supplements, with great success. See FTC Staff, Weight Loss Advertising: An Analysis of Current Trends (2002), available at http://www.ftc.gov/bcp/reports/weightloss.pdf. Typically an FTC case will challenge the ad based on lack of substantiation for performance claims. These ads rely heavily on such techniques as before and after photographs, consumer and celebrity endorsements, and infomercials.

While the standards for the advertiser's substantiation are clear, and have led to many settlements, consent orders and injunctions in favor of the FTC, should there be different standards for the substantiation required for endorsers or product spokespersons? Consider the following case.

FEDERAL TRADE COMMISSION v. GARVEY

United States Court of Appeals, Ninth Circuit (2004).
383 F.3d 891.

Before PREGERSON, McKEOWN, and BYBEE, CIRCUIT JUDGES.

PREGERSON, CIRCUIT JUDGE:

The Federal Trade Commission ("FTC") appeals * * * the ruling, following a bench trial, that Steven Patrick Garvey and Garvey Management Group, Inc. (collectively, the "Garvey defendants") relied on adequate substantiation and therefore are not liable for Garvey's advertising claims for the weight loss product at issue in this case.

For the reasons discussed below, we reverse in part and affirm in part.

BACKGROUND

A. The Enforma System and Its Marketing

This lawsuit arises out of the marketing of a weight loss system sold by Enforma Natural Products, Inc. ("Enforma").[1] Enforma created and marketed two dietary supplements, "Fat Trapper" (or "Fat Trapper Plus") and "Exercise in a Bottle." Together, these two products constitute the "Enforma System." The Fat Trapper product contains chitosan and is a mixture of the shells of certain seafood. It allegedly "surrounds the fat in the food you eat and entraps it," preventing fat absorption. Exercise in a Bottle contains pyruvate, which is found naturally in the body, and allegedly helps enhance one's metabolism.

* * * In conjunction with the marketing of its products, Enforma retained Modern Media, a subsidiary of Media Interactive Technology, Inc., to prepare two thirty-minute infomercials.

Following the advice of Modern Media, Enforma hired Steven Patrick Garvey to star in the infomercials and to be a spokesperson for the Enforma System. Garvey is a retired first baseman for the Los Angeles Dodgers. * * *

Three or four weeks before the filming of the first infomercial, Enforma's Executive Director of Marketing, Michael Ehrman, gave Garvey and his wife a supply of the Enforma System. Between that time and the time of filming, Garvey used the Enforma System and lost approximately eight pounds. Between the filming of the first infomercial and the date the infomercial was broadcast, Garvey's wife used the Enforma

---

1. As discussed further below, Enforma is not a party to this action. The FTC, Enforma, and two of Enforma's principals entered into a stipulated judgment in another case in May 2000.

System and lost approximately twenty-seven pounds. At some point, Garvey also received two booklets produced by Enforma, which provided information about Fat Trapper and Exercise In A Bottle.

* * *

During both infomercials Garvey largely read from the prepared scripts. He and his co-host, Lark Kendall, ad libbed when conducting a demonstration of the Fat Trapper product, but even then, Levine, Richmond, and Grey provided them with a framework for their dialogue. In the infomercials, Garvey made a number of statements regarding the Enforma System, including:

- "Now, if you're tired of trying every new fad diet, if you're tired of trying to work a rigid exercise regime into your busy schedule, if you want to be able to enjoy all those delicious foods that you crave without the guilt while losing weight and keeping it off, call us now...."

- "If you're having trouble losing weight, if you're tired of depriving yourself of all those wonderful and delicious foods that you love, if you find that you don't have the time to exercise as much as you'd like, the Enforma System is the miracle you've been waiting for. It's all natural, it's safe and it works."

- "I love this. So, you can enjoy all these delicious foods like fried chicken, pizza, cheeseburgers, even butter and sour cream, and stop worrying about the weight."

- "The Enforma System has inspired so many to embrace a healthier, more active lifestyle, making good food choices, exercising more and everyone is here to celebrate a system that can end binge dieting forever, because with Enforma you trap the fat from food before it can go to your waistline."

- "[L]ook at all these delicious supposedly forbidden foods; barbecued chicken and ribs, buttered biscuits. Foods you can eat when you crave them without guilt, and it's all because of a few little capsules."

- "Forget all those complicated, expensive diets that deprive you. With all natural Fat Trapper and Exercise in a Bottle—the Enforma System—you simply take Exercise in a Bottle twice a day and Fat Trapper before any meal that contains fat. Then go ahead and enjoy the foods that you love without the fear of fat. It's that easy."

* * * Together, the two infomercials were aired almost 48,000 times throughout the United States from December 1998 through May 2000.

After filming the two infomercials, Garvey made several radio and television appearances to promote the Enforma System. His statements at these appearances were based on script points and guidelines provided by Enforma.

From December 1998 to December 2000, Enforma's sales of Fat Trapper, Fat Trapper Plus, and Exercise in a Bottle exceeded $100 million.

B. *The* Enforma *Action*

The FTC began investigating claims made regarding the Enforma System in 1999. * * *

On April 25, 2000, the FTC filed suit against Enforma, Grey [President and CEO of Enforma], and Zinos [Enforma's Vice President of Sales & Marketing] ("the *Enforma* action"). The FTC's complaint alleged that the defendants, in marketing the Enforma System, undertook deceptive acts or practices and issued false and misleading advertising of a food, drug, device, service, or cosmetic in violation of Sections 5(a) and 12 of the Federal Trade Commission Act ("FTCA"), 15 U.S.C. § § 45(a) and 52. In that action, the FTC sought an injunction to prevent further violations of the FTCA, equitable relief aimed at redressing consumers' injuries, and costs.

A proposed Stipulated Final Order settling the *Enforma* action as to Enforma and Grey (the "Enforma defendants") was filed along with the complaint, and it was entered by Judge J. Spencer Letts on May 11, 2000. This settlement prohibited Enforma and Grey from undertaking specific conduct, such as making certain representations about Enforma's products without reliable scientific support. The settlement also required Enforma and Grey to pay $10 million to the FTC.

C. *The Instant Case*

* * * The FTC filed a complaint against the Garvey defendants, * * * on August 31, 2000. This complaint was similar to that filed in the *Enforma* action; it alleged that the defendants, in marketing the Enforma System, violated Sections 5(a) and 12 of the FTCA.

* * *

The district court held a three-day bench trial on the FTC's claims against the Garvey defendants. On November 25, 2002, the district court issued its findings of fact and conclusions of law and entered judgment in favor of the Garvey defendants. The court concluded that Garvey could not be held liable under a "participant" theory of liability. The court found that Garvey did not have actual knowledge of any material misrepresentations, that he was not recklessly indifferent to the truth or falsity of any representations he made, and that he was neither aware of a high probability that he was making fraudulent representations nor intentionally avoiding the truth with respect to the qualities of the Enforma System. *Cf. FTC v. Publ'g Clearing House, Inc.,* 104 F.3d 1168, 1171 (9th Cir.1997). The district court also found that Garvey could not be held liable as an "endorser" because there was no evidence showing that his statements did not reflect his good faith belief and opinions and there was reasonable substantiation for the statements he made.

The FTC appeals * * * the order and judgment issued after the bench trial.

ANALYSIS

* * *

B. *Bench Trial: The Garvey Defendants*

* * *

2. *Discussion*

The FTC argues that Garvey can be held liable under Sections 5(a) and 12 of the FTCA either as a "direct participant" in the making of false advertising claims or under the principles of "endorser" liability. We discuss each in turn.

a. "Direct Participant" Liability

In *FTC v. Publishing Clearing House, Inc.,* 104 F.3d 1168 (9th Cir.1997), an action brought pursuant to Sections 5 and 13(b) of the FTCA,[9] we held that an individual may be subject to injunctive relief if the FTC can prove that an individual "participated directly" in the acts in question or "had authority to control them." We concluded that, to hold an individual liable for restitution, the FTC must also show that the individual had actual knowledge of the material misrepresentations, was recklessly indifferent to the truth or falsity of a misrepresentation, or had an awareness of a high probability of fraud along with an intentional avoidance of the truth. The district court employed these standards here but did not distinguish between injunctive relief and restitution.[10]

i. "Participant"

The Garvey defendants do not seriously dispute that Garvey was a "participant." Instead, they attempt to short-circuit the FTC's appeal on this issue by arguing that the FTC has failed in meeting its burden of proving the falsity of the claims at issue. They point out that nothing in this case or in the *Enforma* action established that the claims made were false or unsubstantiated. The FTC does not argue that it proved the claims at issue were false and unsubstantiated. Instead, the FTC contends that "settled Commission law" imposes an obligation on an active participant in an advertising campaign to ascertain the existence of substantiation for the claims that the participant makes.

In *Publishing Clearing House,* we put the burden of proving falsity or deception on the FTC. We held that an individual "may be held individually liable for injunctive relief under the [Federal Trade Commis-

9. Section 13(b) is simply the provision that permits the FTC to seek an injunction to stop or prevent a violation of the law. 15 U.S.C. § 53(b).

10. Given the broad language of the Stipulated Final Order, it apparently applies to the Garvey defendants and likely provides the FTC all of the injunctive relief it could get against the Garvey defendants in this case. Therefore, as a practical matter, all the FTC stands to gain from the Garvey defendants here is restitution; the issue of injunctive relief is moot.

sion Act] for corporate practices *if the FTC can prove* [among other things] that the corporation committed misrepresentations or omissions of a kind usually relied on by a reasonably prudent person, resulting in consumer injury...." But in *FTC v. Pantron I Corp.,* 33 F.3d 1088 (9th Cir.1994), a Section 12 case, we presented a somewhat more nuanced picture:

> [T]he Commission has identified two theories on which the government can and often does rely in section 12 cases involving objective product claims. First, the government can assert a so-called "falsity" theory. To prevail on such a theory, the government must carry the burden of proving that the express or implied message conveyed by the ad is false. Alternatively, the government can rely on a so-called "reasonable basis" theory. To prevail on this theory, the government must show that the advertiser lacked a reasonable basis for asserting that the message was true.

The "reasonable basis" theory supports the FTC's argument because it does not require the FTC to prove that the message was false in order to prevail. "In determining whether an advertiser has satisfied the reasonable basis requirement, the Commission or court must first determine what level of substantiation the advertiser is required to have for his advertising claims. Then, the adjudicator must determine whether the advertiser possessed that level of substantiation." *Pantron I,* 33 F.3d at 1096. In this case, the "reasonable basis" theory essentially collapses into the knowledge requirement for restitution. The relevant inquiry in both contexts is, essentially: what did the individual know when making the claims at issue?

ii. The Knowledge Requirement

The district court concluded that Garvey had no actual knowledge of any material misrepresentations regarding the Enforma System. The FTC does not claim that this finding was erroneous. The district court also found the following evidence that provides substantiation for Garvey's advertising claims. First, Garvey himself used the system and lost approximately eight pounds during a three-or four-week period. Second, Garvey's wife, while using the Enforma System, lost approximately twenty-seven pounds between the filming of the first infomercial and the date the program was broadcast to the public. Third, Garvey received and reviewed two booklets containing substantiation materials for Fat Trapper and Exercise In A Bottle. These booklets were produced by Enforma Natural. Fourth, prior to the filming of the second infomercial, Garvey met and spoke with several individuals who had experienced "positive results" using the Enforma System. Fifth, Garvey learned of a pyruvate study published in the American Journal of Clinical Nutrition.

The FTC attempts, unconvincingly, to undercut the significance of this evidence. The FTC argues that Garvey's weight loss was less than the amount by which his weight normally fluctuated during the course of a year. But Garvey clearly stated that his weight had been relatively stable and that, "once I started taking the Enforma System, I saw noticeable weight loss." The FTC also points out that Garvey's wife's weight loss followed childbirth, and she had lost weight after childbirth before. But the relevant testimony provides no indication as to how much she had lost at other times following childbirth or whether the weight loss occurred in a similar time span.

The FTC is also unpersuasive when pointing out flaws in the two booklets that Garvey reviewed. Although they may not conclusively establish the efficacy of the Enforma System, both booklets contain significant, relevant information. In its attack on the Fat Trapper booklet, the FTC states that the booklet does not even mention chitosan. But the Fat Trapper booklet relates information regarding scientific studies and clearly indicates that fiber intake has been found to decrease fat digestibility. Chitosan either is a dietary fiber or is akin to dietary fiber. Even though the booklet may not explicitly mention chitosan, the booklet provides some relevant substantiation for the advertising claims made.

In its attack on the Exercise In A Bottle booklet, the FTC argues that the booklet does not support the contention that pyruvate use has been linked to an increased metabolic rate in humans. But the Exercise In A Bottle booklet points to findings that pyruvate supplementation significantly reduced fat accumulation in rats and pigs and states that pyruvate may cause fat and weight loss through increasing metabolism and fat utilization. It is reasonable for Garvey to have found that this information supported the representations he made.

In sum, we find that the FTC has failed to show that Garvey was recklessly indifferent to the truth of his statements or was aware that fraud was highly probable and intentionally avoided the truth. Garvey had first-hand anecdotal evidence of the efficacy of the Enforma System and had information that purported to present scientific bases for his claims. We find that the substantiation he had was sufficient—at least for someone in Garvey's position[12] to avoid participant liability.

b. "Endorser" Liability

The FTC premises its "endorser" theory of liability on the FTC Guides Concerning Use of Endorsements and Testimonials in Advertising (the "Guides"). According to the Guides, an "endorsement" is "any advertising message ... which message consumers are likely to believe reflects the opinions, beliefs, findings, or experience of a party other than the sponsoring advertiser." 16 C.F.R. § 255.0(b). Among other things, the Guides state that "[e]ndorsements must always reflect the honest

---

12. The Garvey defendants note that there is no settled standard for the level of inquiry to which a commercial spokesperson is held when he or she is hired to participate in a television advertisement. In the context of the knowledge requirement, we find that the fact that the individual is merely a spokesperson is relevant. For instance, the requirement that she be "aware that fraud was highly probable and inten-tionally avoided the truth" clearly turns on subjective knowledge. Likewise, the "reckless indifference" standard implies that an individual's subjective understanding should be taken into account. Indeed, the FTC points out that, in assessing scientific material, Garvey was only required to examine the material from the perspective of a reasonable layperson.

opinions, findings, beliefs, or experience of the endorser. Furthermore, they may not contain any representations which would be deceptive, or could not be substantiated if made directly by the advertiser." 16 C.F.R. § 255.1(a).

The FTC acknowledges that the Guides lack the force of law but contends that they are entitled to deference because of their persuasiveness. * * *

But we decline to decide to what degree of deference the Guides may be entitled or whether the Guides can form an independent basis for spokesperson liability.[14] Such a determination is not necessary to the resolution of this case. Even if the Guides had the full force of law, we would find that Garvey is not liable under them.

The district court found that Garvey did not provide an endorsement as defined in the Guides. Specifically, the district court found that "[t]he Commission has failed to present . . . any facts establishing that consumers are likely to believe that Garvey's statements with respect to the Enforma System reflect the opinions, beliefs, findings and experiences of a party other than Enforma Natural." The district court was presented with evidence from both sides on this issue. For example, the FTC pointed to statements made by Garvey in the infomercials that the Enforma System "works," that he "truly believe[s that it] is the greatest weight loss program in history," that he is "convinced," that he "love[s] this," and that "this is the most amazing system that [he has] ever seen." Further, the FTC offered a rebuttal expert, Dr. Mazis, who testified that Garvey provided an endorsement. The Garvey defendants offered the expert testimony of Dr. Thomas Hollihan, who concluded that Garvey was not an endorser under the Guides.

Under the highly deferential standard of review for findings of fact, we affirm, with the narrow exception described below, the district court's conclusion that Garvey did not provide an endorsement. Because of the conflicting expert testimony and the fact that the statements in the infomercials do not necessarily reflect Garvey's, rather than Enforma's, beliefs, we are not "left with the definite and firm conviction that a mistake has been committed."

But Garvey did make at least a few statements during one appearance on a television show called "Night Talk" (not one of the infomercials) that appear to be clearly an endorsement under the Guides. On that show, the following exchange took place:

MONICA: And I was wondering if you use the product and have you had success with it?

STEVE GARVEY: Yeah. I've endorsed products through the years and we have a family philosophy and that is either we have to take

---

14. Given the tenor of the Guides, they in fact seem aimed at controlling the behavior of the advertisers rather than the endorsers themselves. *See* 16 C.F.R. §§ 255.0– 255.5. In any case, this is an area of law that would benefit from clarification by Congress or the FTC.

the product or it has to be a product that we would be willing to give ou[r] children . . .

I took the product, I was about 195 . . . My normal weight is about 190 and I got down to about 186, so I lost 9 pounds. My wife had just had our second son, Sean Fitzpatrick, and she ended up losing about 28, 29 pounds on the product.

So it worked for both of us and that's why I ended up doing the infomercial because it worked.

As to these particular statements, the district court's findings of fact may have been clearly erroneous.

Nevertheless, we find that the FTC has still failed to meet its burden of proving liability under the Guides. As noted above, the Guides state that "[e]ndorsements must always reflect the honest opinions, findings, beliefs, or experience of the endorser." 16 C.F.R. § 255.1(a). This part of the test for liability is not at issue; Garvey has asserted that all of his statements regarding the Enforma System were statements of his actual beliefs and experiences, and the FTC does not dispute this contention. The next element of endorser liability concerns substantiation. *See* 16 C.F.R. § 255.1 (stating that endorsements "may not contain any representations which would be deceptive, or could not be substantiated if made directly by the advertiser."). On the Night Talk program, Garvey's only statements of endorsement related to his and his wife's weight loss. The Garveys' weight loss is undisputed, and Garvey undoubtedly has first-hand knowledge of those facts. The endorsement claims—that he and his wife lost a certain number of pounds—clearly pass any substantiation requirement for celebrity endorsers.

Therefore, we find that, even if the Guides provided an alternative basis for liability, Garvey would not be liable as an "endorser" under the Guides.

CONCLUSION

For the foregoing reasons, * * * [w]e affirm the district court's judgment in favor of the Garvey defendants.

Notes

1.   Why are celebrity endorsements so popular with advertisers?

2.   In the *Garvey* case, the FTC had two theories of liability involving Garvey: participant liability and endorser liability. What did the FTC have to prove under each of these theories and did they succeed? What differentiates an "endorsement" from an actor reading a script? Did the FTC prove that Garvey actually made an endorsement? Why was this important?

3.   What is the appropriate level of responsibility that a celebrity endorser or spokesperson should bear with regard to the truth of or the substantiation of claims they make for products they are touting? See FTC Guides Concerning Use of Endorsements and Testimonials in Advertising, 16 C.F.R. § 255, in Statutory Supplement.

f. FTC Unfairness Doctrine

The operative language of Section 5 of the FTC Act proscribes *"unfair* or deceptive" conduct. Virtually all of the FTC's advertising activity draws on the deceptiveness term, as well as the specific prohibition of "false" advertising in Section 12. But the disjunctive phrase "unfair *or* deceptive" clearly suggests that the Commission can act independently on unfairness grounds.

The traditional criteria for determining whether a practice was unfair consisted of three prongs:

(1) whether the practice, without necessarily having been previously considered unlawful, offends public policy as it has been established by statutes, the common law, or otherwise—whether, in other words, it is within at least the penumbra of some common-law, statutory, or other established concept of unfairness;

(2) whether it is immoral, unethical, oppressive, or unscrupulous;

(3) whether it causes substantial injury to consumers.

This language was originally used by the Commission in a proposed regulation that would have required a health warning in cigarette advertising, 29 Fed.Reg. 8324, 8355 (1964) (the rule was later superseded by legislation requiring a warning label in ads and on packages for cigarettes, Cigarette Labeling and Advertising Act of 1965, codified at 15 U.S.C.A. §§ 1331–40).

The Commission has occasionally challenged advertising or marketing practices as being "unfair" without also being "deceptive." Of particular interest in this regard was the FTC's 1978 proposal to regulate advertising on TV programs aimed primarily at children. The proposed Rule would have banned or severely limited the kinds of food and toy commercials that dominate the Saturday morning cartoon shows. While these ads were rarely "deceptive" in the conventional sense, the Commission argued that they *unfairly* took advantage of the susceptibilities of the young viewing audience. The proposal was widely criticized, and was aborted in 1980. See generally Sidney M. Milkis, The Federal Trade Commission and Consumer Protection: Regulatory Change and Administrative Pragmatism, 72 Antitrust L.J. 911, 919–927 (2005); William MacLeod, Elizabeth Brunins, and Anna Kertesz, Three Rules and a Constitution: Consumer Protection Finds Its Limits in Competition Policy, 72 Antitrust L.J. 943, 955–964 (2005); J. Howard Beales, III, Advertising to Kids and the FTC: A Regulatory Retrospective that Advises the Present, 12 Geo. Mason L. Rev. 873 (2004).

In the wake of the disastrous attempt in the Children's Advertising rulemaking to use the unfairness prong of the FTC Act, the Commission issued a policy statement on unfairness in 1980 that was intended to fend off legislative restrictions. The 1980 policy places primary emphasis on consumer injury (which must be substantial, not outweighed by countervailing benefits, and must be an injury that consumers could not reasonably avoid). Public policy has become a secondary confirming factor, and public morality has been dropped completely. The policy was codified into the FTC Act in 1994. 15 U.S.C. § 45(n).

Thus, the unfairness doctrine lost its original intuitive meaning based on moral considerations, and has become more of a cost-benefit analysis, with a slant toward consumer sovereignty. See generally Neil W. Averitt, The Meaning of "Unfair Acts or Practices" in Section 5 of the Federal Trade Commission Act, 70 Geo.L.J. 225 (1981). By the late 1990's and early 2000's, the unfairness doctrine was being used to combat unfair practices on the Internet, and theft of personal information, among other things. See Stephen Calkins, FTC Unfairness: An Essay, 46 Wayne L. Rev. 1935 (2000).

The Commission first applied its 1980 Unfairness Policy in a case involving failure to disclose certain information.

IN RE INTERNATIONAL HARVESTER COMPANY

Federal Trade Commission, 1984.
104 F.T.C. 949.

[The complaint charged that Harvester's gasoline-powered tractors were subject to a phenomenon known as fuel geysering, or the forceful ejection of hot fuel through a loosened gas cap. The complaint charged also that fuel geysering could result in serious fires, sometimes involving the tractor operator; that Harvester had been aware of this for many years; that it did not adequately notify its customers of the danger; and that the operators therefore took inadequate measures to protect themselves. The ALJ found all this to be both deceptive and an unfair practice under § 5 of the FTC Act. The Commission reversed the finding of deception, but upheld the finding that this constituted an unfair practice. It also ruled that no corrective order was necessary, since Harvester had already begun issuing adequate warnings.]

BY COMMISSIONER DOUGLAS:

* * *

Unfairness

The Commission's unfairness jurisdiction provides a more general basis for action against acts or practices which cause significant consumer injury. This part of our jurisdiction is broader than that involving deception, and the standards for its exercise are correspondingly more stringent. It requires the complete analysis of a practice which may be harmful to consumers. To put the point another way, unfairness is the set of general principles of which deception is a particularly well-established and streamlined subset.

Over the past four years the Commission has devoted considerable attention to clarifying these general principles. In 1980 we prepared a formal policy statement describing our jurisdiction over unfair practices.

The statement took as its point of departure the familiar language of the *Sperry & Hutchinson* case. It declared that most unfairness cases would be brought under the consumer injury theory identified in that decision. It also systematized the essential elements of that theory. An actionable consumer injury must be: (1) substantial; (2) not outweighed by any offsetting consumer or competitive benefits that the practice produces; and (3) one which consumers could not reasonably have avoided.

The first element to this analysis is that the injury must be substantial. Unlike deception, which focuses on "likely" injury, unfairness cases usually involve actual and completed harms. While in most cases the harm involved is monetary, the policy statement expressly noted the "unwarranted health and safety risks may also support a finding of unfairness."

The second element is that the conduct must be harmful in its net effects. This is simply a recognition of the fact that most conduct creates a mixture of both beneficial and adverse consequences. In analyzing an omission this part of the unfairness analysis requires us to balance against the risks of injury the costs of notification and the costs of determining what the prevailing consumer misconceptions actually are. This inquiry must be made in a level of detail that deception analysis does not contemplate.

Finally, the third element is that the injury be one that consumers could not reasonably have avoided through the exercise of consumer choice. This restriction is necessary in order to keep the FTC Act focused on the economic issues that are its proper concern. The Commission does not ordinarily seek to mandate specific conduct or specific social outcomes, but rather seeks to ensure simply that markets operate freely, so that consumers can make their own decisions.

To accomplish these goals the Commission may require that consumers be given the information that is critical to an informed choice. There is also a need for principled limits on this concept, of course, since virtually any piece of information may be useful to some consumers. While this balance must ultimately be struck in the context of the individual case, the Commission has decided on certain general principles. In most cases it is appropriate to limit mandatory disclosure to those core aspects of a transaction that virtually all consumers would consider essential to an informed decision. These are the same basic characteristics discussed above in connection with common-law merchantability: (1) information bearing on fitness for intended use, and (2) information bearing on significant hidden safety hazards.

* * * In an assessment of unfairness, on the other hand, we conduct a full cost-benefit analysis, in which we weigh the consumer benefits of disclosure against their likely costs, and so there is less risk of an overbroad result. We can therefore take a more inclusive view of the information that must be disclosed under this approach.

In short, an omission may be found unfair even though it is not deceptive. * * *

* * * The unfairness theory, it will be recalled, is the Commission's general law of consumer protection, for which deception is one specific but particularly important application. Unfairness calls for a somewhat more detailed analysis of a challenged practice. This focuses on three criteria: (1) whether the practice creates a serious consumer injury; (2) whether this injury exceeds any offsetting consumer benefits; and (3) whether the injury was one that consumers could not reasonably have avoided. We find that all three criteria are satisfied in the present case.

There clearly has been serious consumer injury. At least one person has been killed and eleven others burned. * * *

The second criterion states the consumer injury must not be outweighed by any countervailing benefits to consumers or to competition that the practice also brings about. This inquiry is particularly important in the case of pure omissions. Since the range of such omissions is potentially infinite, the range of cost-benefit ratios from actions to force disclosure is infinite as well, raising the possibility that a particular action may be ill-advised. We believe that this criterion is also satisfied in the present case, however. The consuming public has realized no benefit from Harvester's non-disclosure that is at all sufficient to offset the human injuries involved.

The principal tradeoff to be considered in this analysis is that involving compliance costs. More information may generally be helpful to consumers, but all such information can be produced only by incurring costs that are ultimately born as higher prices by those same consumers. * * *

Here, however, we have no doubt that such a calculation favors disclosure. Harvester's expenses were not large in relation to the injuries that could have been avoided. Nor do we mean to rule out the possibility that some other, less expensive form of notification—such as a clearly worded warning in the operating manual—would also have been sufficient. We therefore conclude that the costs and benefits in this case satisfy the second unfairness criterion.

Finally, the third unfairness criterion states that the injury must be one that consumers could not reasonably have avoided. Here tractor operators could in fact have avoided their injuries by following a few relatively simple safety rules. If they had refrained from removing the cap from a hot or running tractor—something that both the owner's manuals and common knowledge suggested was a dangerous practice—fuel geysering would have been completely precluded. Harvester therefore argues that one necessary element of unfairness is not present.

Upon full consideration, however, we believe that this element is satisfied as well. The issue here is whether the safety rules for these tractors were adequately disclosed. Whether some consequence is "reasonably avoidable" depends, not just on whether people know the physical steps to take in order to prevent it, but also on whether they understand the necessity of actually taking those steps. We do not believe that this need was fully appreciated here. Farmers may have known that loosening the fuel cap was generally a poor practice, but they did not know from the limited disclosures made, nor could they be expected to know from prior experience, the full consequences that might follow from it. This is therefore not a situation in which the farmers themselves are primarily responsible for their own accidents.

* * *

Since fuel geysering was a risk that they were not aware of, they could not reasonably have avoided it. This is so even though they had been informed of measures to prevent it. Such information was not the same thing as an effective warning:

> [I]mplicit in the duty to warn is the duty to warn with a degree of intensity that would cause a reasonable man to exercise for his own safety the caution commensurate with the potential danger.

Such a warning was not provided in this case. We therefore find that the three elements of unfair conduct are present, and that Harvester's non-disclosures violated Section 5 of the FTC Act.

* * *

CONCLUSION

This case is in most respects a routine dispute over the proper contours of consumer information disclosure. We have resolved that dispute by holding that disclosure was necessary here.

En route to that holding we also had to identify the proper legal framework to use when assessing pure omissions. We have decided that such omissions should be judged as cases of possible unfairness rather than of possible deception. Since pure omissions do not most probably reflect deliberate acts on the part of the sellers, we cannot be confident, without a cost-benefit analysis, that a Commission action would do more good than harm. Yet a cost-benefit analysis is required only under an unfairness and not under a deception approach. We will therefore treat these matters in unfairness terms in order to ensure that such an analysis is made. In so deciding we hope to have added something further to the clarity and rigor of our statute, so that decisions on the merits may henceforth be made and predicted with greater precision.

Notes

1. How did International Harvester's practices fit the FTC's three-prong criteria for an unfair trade practice? Why couldn't the consumers (i.e., farmers using the gasoline tractors) have protected themselves and thereby reasonably avoided the risk of injury?

2. Why did the majority of the Commission in *International Harvester* consider it preferable to deal with the omission of adequate safety information as an unfairness matter, rather than as a deceptive trade practice?

3. Do advertisers have any more concrete guidance from the new policy statement as to what information they must disclose in order to avoid a

charge of unfairness than they did under the old standard? See Craswell, The Identification of Unfair Acts and Practices by the Federal Trade Commission, 1981 Wis.L.Rev. 107 (1981); Rice, Consumer Unfairness at the FTC: Misadventures in Law and Economics, 52 Geo.Wash.L.Rev. 1 (1983).

Problem 1–9

You are one of the five Federal Trade Commissioners. The staff has asked the Commission to issue a complaint against a website operator doing business as "Cupcake Party." The investigation has revealed that Cupcake Party uses domain names that are misspellings of other more popular website domain names, and then makes a change in the copied website which redirects anyone visiting it to other advertising websites, typically for pornography, online gambling, or psychic services. Unwitting computer users who have been redirected in this manner may then try to exit by clicking the "back" button, or the "exit" buttons on their computers, but the copycat website has incapacitated these buttons so that users simply are redirected to other unsavory advertising sites, or subjected to pop-up advertisements in the same vein. Users seem trapped in an endless loop of graphic sexual advertisements. This practice is known as "page-jacking" (copying the legitimate website) and "mouse-trapping" (disabling the "exit" or "back" buttons).

Would you vote in favor of issuing a complaint? Based on deception, unfairness or both? Will the Commission face any special problems due to the fact that they wish to sue someone who is operating in cyberspace? What if it turns out that the originator of the scheme lives in and operates out of Canada? *Cf.*, FTC v. Zuccarini, 2002 WL 1378421 (E.D. Pa. 2002).

g. *FTC Remedies: Corrective Advertising*

The FTC's traditional approach to deceptive or unfair trade advertising would be to go through the administrative process and issue a "cease and desist" order. One of the more creative uses of the cease and desist order is so-called "corrective advertising," in which the advertiser is ordered to cease all advertising unless it also makes a corrective disclosure. The corrective advertising remedy was first approved by the court in 1977, in the following case.

WARNER-LAMBERT CO. v. FEDERAL TRADE COMM.

United States Court of Appeals, District of Columbia Circuit, 1977.
562 F.2d 749.

J. Skelly Wright, Circuit Judge:

[In 1972, the FTC charged Warner–Lambert, the makers of Listerine mouth wash, with deceptively advertising that Listerine would ameliorate, prevent, and cure colds and sore throats. The company had been making these false claims since Listerine was put on the market in 1879. Following a hearing by an administrative law judge, the Commission ordered Warner–Lambert to cease and desist from making the false claims, and to include the following language in the next ten million dollars of Listerine advertising: "Contrary to prior advertising, Listerine will not help prevent colds or sore throats or lessen their severity."

Warner–Lambert appealed the order. The U.S. Court of Appeals for the District of Columbia held that the Commission had the authority under the FTC Act to shape remedies (such as corrective advertising) that go beyond the simple cease and desist order. The court apparently accepted the Commission's argument that corrective advertising was "absolutely necessary to give effect to the prospective cease and desist order; a hundred years of false cold claims have built up a large reservoir of erroneous consumer belief which would persist, unless corrected, long after petitioner ceased making the claims." The court also concluded that the First Amendment protection of commercial speech presented "no obstacle" to corrective advertising orders necessary to regulate false or misleading advertising. Likewise, the novelty of the remedy was not a problem, since the court concluded that the Commission had long had the power to require affirmative disclosures in advertising that would be misleading without it. The court noted that while the label "corrective advertising" may be new, the concept was actually well established.]

IV. The Remedy

Having established that the Commission does have the power to order corrective advertising in appropriate cases, it remains to consider whether use of the remedy against Listerine is warranted and equitable. We have concluded that part 3 of the order should be modified to delete the phrase "Contrary to prior advertising." With that modification, we approve the order.

Our role in reviewing the remedy is limited. The Supreme Court has set forth the standard:

The Commission is the expert body to determine what remedy is necessary to eliminate the unfair or deceptive trade practices which have been disclosed. It has wide latitude for judgment and the courts will not interfere except where the remedy selected has no reasonable relation to the unlawful practices found to exist.

The Commission has adopted the following standard for the imposition of corrective advertising:

[I]f a deceptive advertisement has played a substantial role in creating or reinforcing in the public's mind a false and material belief which lives on after the false advertising ceases, there is clear and continuing injury to competition and to the consuming public as consumers continue to make purchasing decisions based on the false belief. Since this injury cannot be averted by merely requiring respondent to cease disseminating the advertisement, we may appropriately order respondent to take affirmative action designed to terminate the otherwise continuing ill effects of the advertisement.

We think this standard is entirely reasonable. It dictates two factual inquiries: (1) did Listerine's advertisements play a substantial role in creating or reinforcing in the public's mind a false belief about the product? and (2) would this belief linger on after the false advertising ceases? It strikes us that if the answer to both questions is not yes, companies everywhere may be wasting their massive advertising budgets. Indeed, it is more than a little peculiar to hear petitioner assert that its commercials really have no effect on consumer belief.

[T]he Commission adduced survey evidence to support both propositions. We find that the "Product Q" survey data and the expert testimony interpreting them constitute substantial evidence in support of the need for corrective advertising in this case.

We turn next to the specific disclosure required: "Contrary to prior advertising, Listerine will not help prevent colds or sore throats or lessen their severity." Petitioner is ordered to include this statement in every future advertisement for Listerine for a defined period. In printed advertisements it must be displayed in type size at least as large as that in which the principal portion of the text of the advertisement appears and it must be separated from the text so that it can be readily noticed. In television commercials the disclosure must be presented simultaneously in both audio and visual portions. During the audio portion of the disclosure in television and radio advertisements, no other sounds, including music, may occur.

These specifications are well calculated to assure that the disclosure will reach the public. It will necessarily attract the notice of readers, viewers, and listeners, and be plainly conveyed. Given these safeguards, we believe the preamble "Contrary to prior advertising" is not necessary. It can serve only two purposes: either to attract attention that a correction follows or to humiliate the advertiser. The Commission claims only the first purpose for it, and this we think is obviated by the other terms of the order. The second purpose, if it were intended, might be called for in an egregious case of deliberate deception, but this is not one. While we do not decide whether petitioner proffered its cold claims in good faith or bad, the record compiled could support a finding of good faith. On these facts, the confessional preamble to the disclosure is not warranted.

Finally, petitioner challenges the duration of the disclosure requirement. By its terms it continues until respondent has expended on Listerine advertising a sum equal to the average annual Listerine advertising budget for the period April 1962 to March 1972. That is approximately ten million dollars. Thus if petitioner continues to advertise normally the corrective advertising will be required for about one year. We cannot say that is an unreasonably long time in which to correct a hundred years of cold claims. But, to petitioner's distress, the requirement will not expire by mere passage of time. If petitioner cuts back its Listerine advertising, or ceases it altogether, it can only postpone the duty to disclose. The Commission concluded that correction was required and that a duration of a fixed period of time might not accomplish that task, since petitioner could evade the order by choosing not to advertise at all. The formula settled upon by the Commission is reasonably related to the violation it found.

Accordingly, the order, as modified, is affirmed.

[The dissenting opinion of Robb, J., is omitted.]

Notes

1. What is "corrective advertising" and how does it differ from the normal FTC cease and desist order? What was the FTC's rationale for requiring corrective advertising in this case? What criteria does the FTC use to determine if corrective advertising is warranted?

2. How difficult will it be for the Madison Avenue advertising people to bury required "corrective" statements such at the one ordered in *Warner-Lambert* amid music, color or other text? One empirical study showed that at the *end* of the Listerine corrective advertising campaign, 57 percent of Listerine users continued to rate cold and sore throat relief as important in their selection of Listerine as a mouthwash. See Wilkie, McNeill & Mazis, Marketing's "Scarlet Letter": The Theory and Practice of Corrective Advertising, 48 J. of Marketing 11, 26 (Spring 1984).

3. The FTC had not actively pursued corrective advertising orders after the *Warner-Lambert* case until the late 1990's, when the remedy underwent somewhat of a revival. In *Novartis Corp. v. FTC*, 223 F.3d 783 (D.C. Cir. 2000), the Commission ordered the makers of Doan's over-the-counter back pain products to cease making unsubstantiated superiority claims, and to run the following "corrective" disclosure:

> "Although Doan's is an effective pain reliever, there is no evidence that Doan's is more effective than other pain relievers for back pain."

Applying the two-prong test from *Warner-Lambert*, the Commission was satisfied that the evidence showed that the "challenged advertising played a 'substantial role' in creating or reinforcing a false belief;" and that after the campaign ended "a disproportionately high percentage of Doan's users and aware non-users believed that Doan's was more effective than other OTC pain relievers for back pain relief." Thus, the false belief created by the advertisement was likely to linger. The D.C. Circuit Court of Appeals approved the Commission's corrective advertising approach, thus reaffirming the continuing vitality of the *Warner-Lambert* case.

4. Around the same time as the FTC was pursuing its complaint against Doan's Pills, it also targeted an advertising campaign by R.J. Reynolds for Winston No Additives cigarettes. The challenged advertisements contained the following statements:

> "Yours have additives. 94% tobacco. 6% additives. New Winstons don't. 100% true tobacco taste."

> "Winston just got naked. No additives."

> "Thank you for not smoking additives."

"I get enough bull at work. I don't need to smoke it. WINSTON NO ADDITIVES TRUE TASTE."

All of the above ads featured a circular brand containing the words "NO BULL."

Query: Are there any obvious misrepresentations being made in these ads (assuming that the advertised cigarettes in fact contained no additives)? Are there any implied misrepresentations? If so what are they?

The evidence in the FTC case showed there was an unusually extensive nationwide campaign for the "no additives" Winston cigarettes launched in 1997, which continued until March 1999. The ad campaign resulted in an increase in Winston sales of 9%. If the FTC found there was a misrepresentation, would corrective advertising be warranted? For how long? What would you want the corrective message to say? How could you assure the correction would have any impact?

The FTC settled the case with R.J. Reynolds, when the company agreed to include the following disclosure in all Winston ads making a "no additives" claim: "No additives in our tobacco does NOT mean a safer cigarette." In re R.J. Reynolds Tobacco Co., 1999 WL 109621 (F.T.C. 1999), available at www.ftc.gov. Will this become just another white box like the Surgeon General's Warning that no one will pay attention to?

2. STATE REGULATION—"UDAPS" AND "LITTLE FTC ACTS"—REAL REMEDIES FOR REAL PEOPLE

a. Introduction and Overview

The burden of policing deceptive advertising practices does not rest exclusively with the Federal Trade Commission. Today, in every state, there are statutes which parallel and supplement the F.T.C. Act and under which state authorities are often empowered to regulate deceptive advertising and other information practices. In contrast to the FTC Act, which can only be directly enforced by the FTC itself, private rights of action are prevalent under the state statutes. Many of these state laws use the language of § 5 of the F.T.C. Act to describe the conduct subject to regulation. For this reason, they are often known as "little FTC Acts." They are also often referred to as "UDAP" statutes, for "unfair or deceptive acts or practices." For a general discussion see Leafer and Lipson, Consumer Actions Against Unfair or Deceptive Acts or Practices: The Private Uses of Federal Trade Commission Jurisprudence, 48 Geo. Wash.L.Rev. 521 (1980) and Jeff Sovern, Private Actions Under the Deceptive Trade Practices Acts: Reconsidering the FTC Act as Rule Model, 52 Ohio St. L.J. 437 (1991).

These state laws are not uniform; indeed, they vary widely among the states. The majority of the state UDAP statutes trace their origin to the 1967 Uniform Trade Practices and Consumer Protection Law, developed by the Council of State Governments in collaboration with the Federal Trade Commission. This "uniform" law had several alternative formats. One variation uses language patterned directly on the FTC Act, broadly prohibiting "unfair and deceptive acts or practices." Another popular variation enumerates a "laundry list" of prohibited practices, and then adds a "catch-all" prohibition against unfair and deceptive trade practices. The National Conference of Commissioners on Uniform State Laws attempted to unify the differing pieces of state legislation by offering in 1971 the Uniform Consumer Sales Practices Act for enactment by the states. To date, however, the uniform act has been enacted only in Utah, although the Kansas statute is modeled basically on the uniform act. See generally, Dee Pridgen, Consumer Protection and the Law, §§ 3:1–3:8 (Thomson/West 2007). The statutory supplement contains selected sections of representative state statutes from California, Connecticut, New York and Utah.

These "little FTC acts," while mimicking the language of the federal law, have more bite than the parent statute, by providing for enforcement by both state attorneys general and private parties, and affording minimum or multiple damages, as well as attorney fees to the prevailing consumer plaintiff. Despite the lack of uniformity, there are many common elements among the various state statutes. For example, all of them address in some way the overall problem of deception and other unfair practices in consumer transactions. All (or nearly all) of them provide for administrative enforcement by some agency of the state, often the attorney general. Most of them also provide for private actions by consumers, something not available under the federal law. Finally, they all contain penalty provisions of some kind, although these range from injunctive remedies to treble damages or other monetary penalties. Attorney fees are provided to consumer plaintiffs to encourage access to the courts for relatively small claims. Most of the statutes were originally intended to ease the burden of proof on the state or the private plaintiff, as compared to common law fraud, and most look to the body of jurisprudence interpreting the FTC Act for guidance. Over time, this relationship has evolved as both the FTC and the states have changed their general enforcement attitudes regarding consumer protection.

Given the enhanced remedies available to plaintiffs under the "little FTC acts," there has been some contention regarding the scope of these laws. The original intent was to protect consumers who may have suffered from an unequal bargaining position vis-à-vis the merchants. Most of the state UDAP statutes are thus limited in various ways to consumer transactions. But questions have arisen regarding the coverage of professional services, and of businesses as purchasers. Also, given the lower burden of proof and more attractive remedies available under the UDAP statutes, many states have struggled with the question of how to draw the line between the consumer transactions meant to be covered by the state legislature, and isolated contract or business disputes for which the parties should be relegated to their traditional legal remedies, or disputes that are already regulated by another body of law or governmental body, such as the practice of medicine or law.

A thorough compilation and analysis of the various state laws can be found in the National Consumer Law Center publication Unfair and

Deceptive Acts and Practices (2004, 6th Ed.), part of NCLC's Consumer Credit and Sales Legal Practice Series.

The following case provides some useful background on the origins and rationale of the typical state "little FTC act," and also discusses the role of the FTC Act in interpreting these state laws.

MARSHALL v. MILLER

Supreme Court of North Carolina, 1981.
302 N.C. 539, 276 S.E.2d 397.

MEYER, JUSTICE.

Plaintiffs, residents of a mobile home park in Greensboro, North Carolina, bring this action seeking damages from defendants, owners and managers of the park. Each of the plaintiffs seeks damages for certain misrepresentations allegedly made by defendants concerning services which defendants would provide to plaintiffs, lessees of lots in the mobile home park. Plaintiffs offered evidence, and the jury found as fact, that defendants had led plaintiffs to believe that they would be furnished the following services or amenities by the mobile home park: two playgrounds, one basketball court, one swimming pool, adequate garbage facilities and pickup, complete yard care, paved and lighted streets and common facilities. The jury further found that, during the period between 7 October 1974 and the filing of this action on 7 October 1977, defendants had failed to provide any of those facilities or services. Based on these findings of fact by the jury, Judge Alexander determined as a matter of law that certain of defendants' misrepresentations constituted unfair or deceptive acts or practices in or affecting commerce within the meaning of G.S. 75–1.1. * * *

The Court of Appeals found error [in the trial court's statement of the issue] * * * because defendants could be adjudged to have committed unfair or deceptive acts without a showing that they acted in bad faith.

In determining that bad faith was an essential element of plaintiffs' claim, the Court of Appeals recognized that G.S. 75–1.1(a) closely follows the portion of Section 5 of the Federal Trade Commission Act codified at 15 U.S.C. § 45(a)(1) (hereinafter FTC Act). In fact, the language of our statute is identical to that section of the FTC Act. Both acts further provide for government enforcement, our state Act through actions brought by the Attorney General to obtain mandatory orders. (G.S. 75–14). The court may impose civil penalties in suits instituted by the Attorney General in which the defendant is found to have violated G.S. 75–1.1 and the "acts or practices which constituted the violation were, when committed, specifically prohibited by a court order or knowingly violative of a statute." G.S. 75–15.2. Unlike our own statutory scheme, however, the FTC Act confers no private right of action upon an injured party.

Rather, the provisions for private enforcement found in our statute are more closely analogous to Section 4 of the Clayton Act, which provides for private suits with treble damage recovery for violation of federal antitrust laws. 15 U.S.C. § 15 (1976).

It is established by earlier decisions of this Court that federal decisions interpreting the FTC Act may be used as guidance in determining the scope and meaning of G.S. 75–1.1. Federal courts have uniformly held that the FTC may issue a cease and desist order to enforce Section 5 where an act or practice has a capacity to deceive, regardless of the presence or absence of good faith on the part of the offending party. Although recognizing the precedential value of FTC decisions, the Court of Appeals held that, because our state Act provides for a private action, federal decisions to the effect that bad faith was not necessary to show a violation of the FTC Act were not dispositive. Good faith, said the Court of Appeals, may be irrelevant where the Attorney General seeks injunctive relief under G.S. 75–14, a remedy analogous to an FTC cease and desist order, but it should be relevant where a party is potentially liable in a private action for treble damages under G.S. 75–16. Our task is to determine whether the intent of the Legislature will be more fully served if the addition of a private action under our statute brings with it a concomitant requirement that a private party must show bad faith in order to recover treble damages. In resolving that question, we are guided by two other questions: (1) what was this State's unfair and deceptive trade practice act intended to accomplish, and (2) how can the purpose for which the law was passed be most fully realized.

Between the 1960's and the present, North Carolina was one of forty-nine states to adopt consumer protection legislation designed to parallel and supplement the FTC Act. * * *

Such legislation was needed because common law remedies had proved often ineffective. Tort actions for deceit in cases of misrepresentation involved proof of scienter as an essential element and were subject to the defense of "puffing." Proof of actionable fraud involved a heavy burden of proof, including a showing of intent to deceive. Actions alleging breach of express and implied warranties in contract also entailed burdensome elements of proof. A contract action for recision or restitution might be impeded by the parol evidence rule where a form contract disclaimed oral misrepresentations made in the course of a sale. Use of a product after discovery of a defect or misrepresentation might constitute an affirmance of the contract. Any delay in notifying a seller of an intention to rescind might foreclose an action for recision. Against this background, and with the federal act as guidance, North Carolina and all but one of her sister states have adopted unfair and deceptive trade practices statutes.

* * *

As mentioned above, the Court of Appeals felt that, as this was a private action rather than one instituted by the Attorney General, good faith was a proper defense. There is some authority in other jurisdictions for such a distinction. *See, e.g., Bartner v. Carter,* 405 A.2d 194 (Maine 1979) (where "loss of money or property" is an essential element of the claim, private action showing mere proof of capacity to deceive is insufficient).

We reach the contrary result for several reasons. First, nothing in our earlier decisions in *Hardy* and *Johnson* limits the precedential value of FTC jurisprudence to cases or actions brought by the Attorney General. Indeed, both cases actually involved private litigants. Second, unlike statutes enacted by some of our sister states, there is no explicit statutory requirement of a showing of bad faith in G.S. 75–1.1. Finally, as discussed above, under the standards for determining what is unfair and deceptive according to *Johnson,* the intent or good faith belief of the actor is irrelevant.

In an area of law such as this, we would be remiss if we failed to consider also the overall purpose for which this statute was enacted. The commentators agree that state statutes such as ours were enacted to supplement federal legislation, so that local business interests could not proceed with impunity, secure in the knowledge that the dimensions of their transgression would not merit federal action. Given the small dollar amounts often involved in such suits, statutory provision for treble damages found in G.S. 75–16 serves two purposes. First, it makes more economically feasible the bringing of an action where the possible money damages are limited, and thus encourages private enforcement. Second, it increases the incentive for reaching a settlement. Further provision for attorney fees, found in G.S. 75–16.1, also encourages private enforcement in the marketplace. The dissimilarity in language used by our Legislature in G.S. 75–1.1 and G.S. 75–16.1, in that willfulness is specifically mentioned in the latter, was apparently not accidental. The fact that attorney fees may only be awarded upon a specific finding that defendant acted "willfully" indicates, rather clearly we think, that the omission of willfulness, intentional wrongdoing or bad faith as an essential element under G.S. 75–1.1 was deliberate, and supports the result in this case. We further note that G.S. 75–16.1 also provides that an unsuccessful plaintiff may be charged with defendant's attorney fees should the court find that "[t]he party instituting the action knew, or should have known, the action was frivolous and malicious." This is an important counterweight designed to inhibit the bringing of spurious lawsuits which the liberal damages provisions of G.S. 75–16 might otherwise encourage.

Were we to agree with the Court of Appeals, we think we would seriously weaken the effectiveness of G.S. 75–1.1 and circumvent the intent of the Legislature. Except as modified herein, we adopt the opinion of the Court of Appeals.

MODIFIED AND AFFIRMED.

Problem 1–10

Sergeant and Mrs. Bilko went to their local mobile home dealer in Fayetteville, North Carolina to look at a mobile home. They were concerned about the cost of moving the home, since they could be subject to a transfer at any time. They asked the salesman if the army would pay for the moving costs of the home if they had to move, and the salesman assured them (in good faith) that the military would pay. The Bilkos did not check this out with the Base Transportation Office, but went ahead and bought the mobile home on the word of the salesman. Bilko was transferred to California a few months later, and he was informed that the army would pay only $5,000 of the $8,000 cost of moving. The Bilkos could not afford the $3,000 so they left their mobile home in North Carolina and sued the dealer under the North Carolina Unfair and Deceptive Trade Practices Act.

Have the Bilkos stated a cause of action under the UDAP statute? Did the salesman make a false representation? Would good faith be a defense? What about the lack of justifiable reliance—will that be a defense under the state UDAP statute? Would they have prevailed in a common law action for deceit? If the Bilkos prevailed, what damages would they get under the North Carolina law? Would either party get attorney's fees? See Strickland v. A & C Mobile Homes, 70 N.C.App. 768, 321 S.E.2d 16 (1984).

Query: In any state with a UDAP statute like North Carolina's and case law like Marshall v. Miller—no good faith defense, liability measured only by a "tendency to deceive" standard, and treble damages plus attorney's fees—will consumers ever again have to grapple with the components of common law deceit (scienter, materiality, reliance)? Have the state UDAP statutes relegated common law deceit to the history books for consumer transactions? Have the state legislatures and state courts gone too far in protecting consumers from their own foolishness?

Problem 1–11

Re-read Problem 1–3, Section A(3) *supra*. [Harry and Harriet Hopeful bought an uninsulated trailer from Comfy Mobile Homes after Comfy's salesman had innocently made multiple oral statements concerning its quality ("good solid home, as good as any others"), while the informed sales manager stood silently by.] You represent the Hopefuls. Assume you are in the state of Utah.

(a) First, even if you can prove all the above facts, has Comfy violated the state law? Is Comfy's alleged conduct within any of the specific enumerated instances of deception and unconscionable acts, or will you have to fit it into the broad, general language? If the latter, what are the requirements and criteria for finding conduct to be "unconscionable" or "deceptive"? Can FTC decisions be used? Can common law deceit cases be used?

(b) Second, if the Hopefuls prove a violation of the Act, what remedies are they entitled to? In particular, can they have the contract cancelled and get their money back? Can they recover the costs of insulating the mobile home? Can they recover "pain and suffering" damages for shivering through a chilly winter in the mountains? Can they recover attorneys' fees?

(c) Third, after your initial interview with the Hopefuls, how much of the facts will you be aware of? (e.g., the presence of the sales manager? her knowledge?) How solid is your evidence concerning any statements (precise wording?) of the salesman or, the relative quality of the actual trailer? Note that it is after that interview that you will probably decide how seriously you will pursue this case. Does the award of attorneys' fees to the successful consumer make this case look like a sure winner to you now?

b. *Evolving Limits on the State UDAP Statutes*

FREEMAN v. TIME, INC.

United States Court of Appeals, Ninth Circuit, 1995.
68 F.3d 285.

Before: FARRIS and O'SCANNLAIN, CIRCUIT JUDGES, and TASHIMA, DISTRICT JUDGE.

OPINION

TASHIMA, DISTRICT JUDGE:

These are two consolidated appeals from the district court's dismissal of two separate actions alleging that sweepstakes promotional materials were fraudulent and misleading.

FACTS

Plaintiff-appellant Michael Freeman ("Freeman") received two separate mailers for the "Million Dollar Dream Sweepstakes," a promotion of defendant-appellee Time, Inc. ("Time"). The mailers, personalized by computer, are similar in content and format—both contain statements in large type representing that Freeman won the sweepstakes, qualified by language in smaller type indicating that Freeman would win only if he returned a winning prize number. For example, the *Sports Illustrated* promotion states "If you return the grand prize winning number, we'll officially announce that MICHAEL FREEMAN HAS WON $1,666,675.00 AND PAYMENT IS SCHEDULED TO BEGIN." It continues, "If you return the grand prize winning entry, we'll say $1,666,675.00 WINNER MICHAEL FREEMAN OF ENCINO, CALIFORNIA IS OUR LARGEST MAJOR PRIZE WINNER!" The promotion provides, "We are now scheduled to begin payment of the **third and largest prize—the $1,666,675 listed next to the name MICHAEL FREEMAN!** In fact, arrangements have already been made which make it possible to begin payment of the $1,666,675 DIRECTLY to MICHAEL FREEMAN if one of your numbers is the grand prize winner." It concludes that "[i]f you return your entry with the Validation Seal attached and your entry includes the grand prize winning number, MICHAEL FREEMAN IS GUARANTEED TO BE PAID THE ENTIRE $1,666,675.00!"

The mailer includes an "Official Entry Certificate" on which recipient could check a box marked "YES! [Send free gifts and magazine subscription] Also, enter me in the sweepstake and notify me if I'm a winner" or a box marked "NO! [Don't send gifts and subscription] But enter me in the sweepstakes." Separate return envelopes are enclosed for "yes" and "no" entries—printed outside both envelopes is the statement "enter me in the sweepstakes and notify me if I am a millionaire."

The "Million Dollar Dream Sweepstakes Official Rules" provide that random selection of the winner would take place by April 1, 1994 and indicate that "[c]hances of winning are dependent upon the number of entries distributed and received. Distribution of the sweepstakes is estimated not to exceed 900 million." The rules provide an address from which it was possible to obtain a list of major winners, available after August 1994.

Freeman filed a complaint in California Superior Court on April 12, 1993 regarding the *Money* magazine promotion, alleging six causes of action: (1) common law breach of contract; (2) common law fraud; (3) unfair and misleading business practices in violation of California's Unfair Business Practices Act ("UBPA") (Cal.Bus. & Prof.Code § 17200); (4) untrue and misleading advertising in violation of UBPA (Cal.Bus. & Prof.Code § 17500 et seq.); (5) failure to include an "odds of winning" statement in violation of Cal. Bus. & Prof. Code § 17537.1; and (6) unfair and deceptive practices under the California Consumer Legal Remedies Act (Cal.Civ.Code § 1770). On April 27, 1993, plaintiff filed an action alleging identical causes of action with respect to the *Sports Illustrated* promotion. Both actions seek monetary damages, restitution and disgorgement of profits, and injunctive relief. Time removed these two actions to federal court on May 26, 1993 and June 4, 1993, respectively.

Shortly after removal, Time moved to dismiss both complaints pursuant to Fed. R.Civ. P. 12(b)(6) for failure to state a claim upon which relief may be granted. * * * The district court granted both motions * * *. Plaintiff filed notices of appeal * * *. We have jurisdiction under 28 U.S.C. § 1291.

DISCUSSION

Freeman does not challenge the dismissal of his breach of contract and fraud claims. He argues only that the district court erred in dismissing his * * * causes of action for violations of the UBPA and the California Consumer Legal Remedies Act.

* * *

II.   *Unfair Business Practices Act*

* * *

A.   *Likely to be Deceived*

"[T]o state a claim under the [UBPA] one need not plead and prove the elements of a tort. Instead, one need only show that 'members of the public are likely to be deceived.' " Bank of the West, 2 Cal.4th at 1267, 10 Cal.Rptr.2d 538, 833 P.2d 545 (quoting Chern v. Bank of America, 15 Cal.3d 866, 876, 127 Cal.Rptr. 110, 544 P.2d 1310 (1976)). Freeman argues that to demonstrate that "members of the public are likely to be deceived" he need show only that some members of the public, such as the elderly, minors or the mentally disadvantaged, are likely to be deceived. Time argues that the court must consider whether "a person of ordinary intelligence" would be misled.

In a virtually identical case involving the same Time promotion, the district court rejected the plaintiff's proposed "unwary consumer" standard in favor of a "reasonable person" standard. Haskell v. Time. Inc., 857 F.Supp. 1392, 1398 (E.D.Cal.1994) .

* * * Plaintiff admits that "California courts have looked to interpretations of similar provisions in federal law under the Federal Trade Commission Act." *Haskell* noted that "[s]ince 1982 the FTC has interpreted 'deception' in Section 5 of the Federal Trade Commission Act to require a showing of 'potential deception of consumers acting reasonably in the circumstances,' not just any consumers." 857 F.Supp. at 1399 (quoting Southwest Sunsites, Inc. v. FTC, 785 F.2d 1431, 1436 (9th Cir.1986)). *Haskell* further noted that

> the reasonable person standard is well ensconced in the law in a variety of legal contexts in which a claim of deception is brought. It is the standard for false advertising and unfair competition under the Lanham Act, for securities fraud, for deceit and misrepresentation and for common law unfair competition. This list no doubt could be much expanded.

Id. at 1398 (citations omitted). "[B]y explicitly imposing a 'reasonable care' standard on advertisers, § 17500 implicitly adopts such a standard for consumers as well: unless particularly gullible consumers are targeted, a reasonable person may expect others to behave reasonably as well." Id. at 1399. In this case, the mailings were sent to millions of persons and there is no allegation that a particularly vulnerable group was targeted. "[I]n view of the allegations here, the false or misleading advertising and unfair business practices claim must be evaluated from the vantage of a reasonable consumer." Haskell, 857 F.Supp. at 1399.

Freeman argues that his complaint adequately alleges that members of the public would be deceived, since it is likely that the reader will review the large print and ignore the qualifying language in small print. This argument is not persuasive. The promotions expressly and repeatedly state the conditions which must be met in order to win. None of the qualifying language is hidden or unreadably small. The qualifying language appears immediately next to the representations it qualifies and no reasonable reader could ignore it. Any persons who thought that they had won the sweepstakes would be put on notice that this was not guaranteed simply by doing sufficient reading to comply with the instructions for entering the sweepstakes.

Freeman further contends that the qualifying language in the promotion, even if read by the recipient, is ambiguous. He argues, for example, that the statement "If you return the grand prize winning number we'll officially announce that [you have won]" leaves room for the reader to draw an inference that he or she *has* the winning number. Such an inference is unreasonable in the context of the entire document. In dismissing the complaint against Time in *Haskell*, the court noted that such "statements, in context, are not misleading. It is clear from the exemplar that no reasonable addressee could believe that the mailing announced that the addressee was already the winner...." 857 F.Supp. at 1403. We agree. Any ambiguity that Freeman would read into any particular statement is dispelled by the promotion as a whole.

* * *

Freeman failed to state a claim that the promotions violated the UBPA; therefore, the district court's dismissal of such claims is affirmed.

III. Consumers Legal Remedies Act

California's Consumer Legal Remedies Act provides that "[a]ny consumer who suffers any damage as a result of the use or employment by any person of a method, act, or practice declared to be unlawful by Section 1770 may bring an action against such person" for actual damages, injunctive relief, restitution of property, punitive damages, and other relief that the court deems proper. Cal.Civ.Code § 1780(a). Freeman claims that Time violated the prohibition on "[r]epresenting that a transaction confers or involves rights, remedies, or obligations which it does not have or involve, or which are prohibited by law." Cal.Civ.Code § 1770(n). According to Freeman, the promotion falsely represents that the reader has won and thus been conferred certain rights. As discussed above, when read reasonably and in context, the promotion makes no such false representation.[4]

Freeman's complaint does not state a claim under the California Consumer Legal Remedies Act and the district court's dismissal of this claim is also affirmed.

AFFIRMED.

Notes

1. In the *Freeman* case, was it or was it not reasonable for the consumer to assume he had won the prize? Even if the consumer does not believe he has actually won, what other potential consumer deception lies behind the sweepstakes promotions? What is the promoter actually selling?

2. The state attorneys general have succeeded in settling several lawsuits against sweepstakes promoters dating back to at least 1994, aggressive-

---

4. Moreover, it is doubtful that Freeman has "suffer[ed] any damage as a result of" the promotion. The only possible damage is a de minimis 29 cents for postage to mail in his entry.

ly attacking the sweepstakes industry as viciously preying on the unsuspecting elderly population. Why do you suppose the state government officials have been more successful than individual plaintiffs have?

3. At the end of 1999, Congress passed Public Law 106–168, the "Deceptive Mail Prevention and Enforcement Act," which requires disclosures of the odds of winning, that no purchase is necessary to enter a sweepstakes, and that a purchase will not improve a consumer's chances of winning a prize. In addition, in 2000, Publishers Clearing House and Time, Inc. settled with 48 State Attorneys General, agreeing to even more extensive sweepstakes disclosures, and bans on specific misleading practices, such as simulated checks or requesting the recipient's location on prize giveaway day. If you have recently received a sweepstakes promotion in the mail, examine it to see if it provides adequate information to prevent deception. Are the sweepstakes disclosures noticeable? Sufficient? Overbearing? Comprehensible? Not necessary?

4. By adopting the FTC "reasonable consumer" standard in applying California law, is the court bringing the state deceptive practices statute back into the realm of common law deceit and caveat emptor? Or is the court simply applying a "reasonable" standard on an otherwise unfair "strict liability" standard for advertisers? *See* Lavie v. Procter & Gamble Co., 105 Cal.App.4th 496, 129 Cal.Rptr.2d 486 (2003) (confirming that California uses the "ordinary consumer acting reasonably under the circumstances standard, rather than the least sophisticated consumer standard" in applying the state unfair competition and false advertising laws). Many states have adopted the FTC's 1983 Deception Policy in interpreting their little FTC acts, including the reasonable consumer standard. *See* Luskin's, Inc. v. Consumer Protection Division, 353 Md. 335, 726 A.2d 702 (1999); Peabody v. P.J.'s Auto Village, Inc., 153 Vt. 55, 569 A.2d 460 (1989); Caldor, Inc. v. Heslin, 215 Conn. 590, 577 A.2d 1009 (1989). *See also* Karns, Redefining "Deceptive" Advertising Under the Illinois Consumer Fraud and Deceptive Business Practices Act After Cliffdale Associates, 1985 S.Ill.U.L.J. 1.

5. The FTC's 1980 Unfairness Policy, see *supra* Section B(1)(f), was codified into the FTC statute in 1994. 15 U.S.C. § 45(n). As with the FTC deception policy, many states have also adopted the FTC's modified unfairness standards into their interpretation of the state consumer statutes, but some still use the traditional "cigarette rule" standard, that references whether the practice is immoral or unscrupulous. *See* Michael M. Greenfield, Unfairness Under Section 5 of the FTC Act and its Impact on State Law, 46 Wayne L. Rev. 1869 (2000).

6. Given that state little FTC acts were supposed to provide consumers with better legal remedies for unfair or deceptive practices than were available at common law, should there be an exclusion for "puffery"? Some state courts have ruled that mere puffery or opinions by the seller cannot provide a basis for a violation of the state UDAP statute. *See* Lambert v. Downtown Garage, Inc., 262 Va. 707, 553 S.E.2d 714 (2001) (seller's statement that vehicle was in "excellent" condition "is clearly a matter of opinion in the manner of puffing;" seller was not liable for failure to disclose that vehicle had been seriously damaged and would require extensive repairs); Tietsworth v. Harley–Davidson, Inc., 270 Wis.2d 146, 677 N.W.3d 233 (2004)

(claims of manufacturer that its engine was "a masterpiece," of "premium quality," and "filled to the brim with torque and ready to take you thundering down the road," were merely puffery and thus "legally insufficient to support a claim under the statute"). Some states require justifiable reliance to support a claim under the state UDAP statute. *See* Yocca v. Pittsburgh Steelers Sports, Inc., 578 Pa. 479, 854 A.2d 425 (2004) (consumers who purchased option to buy season passes for new stadium were not justified in relying on diagram sketch showing seat locations). In 1994, Professor Thomas Holdych strongly advocated against covering puffery under state UDAP statutes, based on the possible chilling effect on truthful commercial speech. Thomas J. Holdych, Standards for Establishing Deceptive Conduct Under State Deceptive Trade Practices Statutes That Impose Punitive Remedies, 73 Or. L. Rev. 235 (1994). For an argument that puffery should be regulated, *see* Cullen Goretzke, Comment, The Resurgence of Caveat Emptor: Puffery Undermines the Pro–Consumer Trend in Wisconsin's Misrepresentation Doctrine, 2003 Wis. L. Rev. 171 (2003).

Problem 1–12

From their home office in San Bernardino, California, Dick and Jane Smith are engaged in the business of selling vacation certificates over the Internet through mass emails and on their website, "DreamVacations.pff." Their emails state in part:

> "YOU HAVE BEEN SELECTED TO WIN FREE AIRFARE FOR TWO TO HAWAII!!!! Your dream vacation can be yours by filling out the attached form and returning it to DreamVacations.pff within seven days of receiving this message. THANK YOUR LUCKY STARS—THIS IS YOUR DREAM COME TRUE!!!"

Consumers who fill out the form, which asks for personal information, including an email address, find out via a return email that what they have "won" is a vacation "certificate." In order to claim their "free" airfare, the consumer must pay a nonrefundable $15 processing fee, purchase a minimum of seven nights at a designated hotel at non-discounted prices, pay the tax on the airline tickets, and must designate their first, second and third preference for departure dates, no requested date is guaranteed, and all major holidays are excluded.

(a) Fred Freeloader, a resident of San Jose, California, filled out and returned the form, and became incensed when he saw that he would have to pay $15.00 for what he considers a "worthless" vacation certificate. He wants to sue Dick and Jane under the California Unfair Business Practices Act. Will he be able to counteract a defense by Dick and Jane that a "reasonable" consumer would not believe that he had "won" a "free" trip to Hawaii? What damages would Fred be able to prove?

(b) Compare Fred's likelihood of success under the California statute with your previous analysis of Carol DePrey's likelihood of success under common law, in problem 1–1, *supra* Section A(1).

(c) Will it make a difference to the outcome of Fred's suit (under the California law) that the FTC in 1971 adopted a "Guide Concerning Use of the Word 'Free' and Similar Representations," which provides in relevant part: "When making 'Free' or similar offers all the terms, conditions and obligations upon which receipt and retention of the 'Free' item are contingent should be set forth clearly and conspicuously at the outset of the offer so as to leave no reasonable probability that the terms of the offer might be misunderstood." 16 C.F.R. § 251.1 (full text in statutory supplement). *Cf.* Luskin's, Inc. v. Consumer Protection Division, 353 Md. 335, 726 A.2d 702 (1999).

(d) Will the California state Attorney General have a better chance of prevailing against Dick and Jane? Will the state AG be able to obtain a better remedy than Dick and Jane? Will it be a problem that the advertisement was sent "over the Internet"? *See* People ex rel. Vacco v. Lipsitz, 174 Misc.2d 571, 663 N.Y.S.2d 468 (Sup. Ct. 1997).

c. *What Transactions and Parties Are Covered by State UDAP Statutes?*

LY v. NYSTROM

Supreme Court of Minnesota, 2000.
615 N.W.2d 302.

Heard, considered and decided by the court en banc.

OPINION

STRINGER, JUSTICE.

During negotiations between appellant Hoang Minh Ly and respondent Kim Nystrom for the purchase of respondent's restaurant, respondent made misrepresentations to appellant relating to monthly profits and the condition of the restaurant and its inventory. The restaurant never made a profit and discussion between the parties led to a contract cancellation. Appellant then brought suit alleging common law fraud and a violation of Minnesota's Consumer Fraud Act (CFA), Minn.Stat. § 325F.69, subd. 1 (1998), and included a claim for attorney fees under the Private Remedies section of the Attorney General Statute (Private AG Statute), Minn.Stat. § 8.31, subd. 3a (1998). The trial court ruled that respondent defrauded appellant and awarded him a common law fraud damage remedy but denied his motion for attorney fees finding that there was no violation of the CFA because respondent's representations were not made to a large number of consumers. The court of appeals affirmed. *See Ly v. Nystrom,* 602 N.W.2d 644, 647 (Minn.App. 1999). We reverse in part and affirm in part.

In 1981 appellant Hoang Minh Ly came to the United States from Vietnam at the age of 32. When first arriving in the U.S. he worked in various Chinese restaurants as a dishwasher and cook's assistant, positions neither requiring nor providing any business or management experience. In 1989 he met respondent Kim Nystrom while employed as a cook's assistant and she as a waitress at May Ninh restaurant in Maple Grove. Appellant speaks, reads and writes very little English and his formal education ended in Vietnam at the second grade. Respondent is also from Vietnam but speaks and reads English.

A few weeks after the two met respondent left the May Ninh restaurant to work at another restaurant, and between 1990 and 1995 appellant and respondent spoke periodically regarding jobs at various restaurants, including a Shakopee restaurant called Chin Yung, the subject of this litigation. In June of 1996 respondent told appellant she had bought the Chin Yung in 1994 and that she was having trouble hiring people, she wanted to sell the restaurant and encouraged him to consider buying it.

A few days later, on approximately June 14, 1996, appellant visited the restaurant before it opened in the morning. Respondent told appellant "this is a very good place, and it's a good business," and that she would sell the restaurant for $100,000. Appellant called the next day asking respondent to lower the price; she refused, warning him that someone else wanted to buy it so if he was interested he should decide soon. Respondent then represented to appellant that the restaurant's estimated monthly gross revenue was between $25,000 and $30,000 and the monthly profits between $6,000 to $7,000. Respondent told appellant it was a good business and that she would not trick him because they were friends.

The next day, approximately June 15, appellant and his wife went to the restaurant at about 8:00 p.m. The restaurant was not busy and when appellant asked why there were so few patrons respondent replied that customers in Shakopee usually eat and go to sleep earlier because they commute to work. When appellant's wife asked to see the books respondent said that they were not there but a lawyer did not need to review them because she would not lie to appellant. Respondent agreed to lower the purchase price from $100,000 to $90,000 with a cash down payment of $20,000. She also agreed to charge appellant $2,000 a month for rent, $1,200 a month for taxes and a 9% interest rate on the business loan. That night appellant decided to buy the restaurant because he thought $90,000 was a fair price to pay for a restaurant taking in $25,000 to $30,000 a month and because he trusted that respondent would not misrepresent the business.

On June 19, 1996, the parties met again and appellant's wife wrote a check for $5,000, leaving blank the payee designation on the check at respondent's request. The remaining $15,000 was to be paid before June 30. Appellant wanted to show his lawyer the agreement but decided not to do so after respondent assured him that he did not need a lawyer because they were friends and she would not cheat him. When the check was returned to appellant the payee was designated "Anderson Produce."

On June 25, 1996, at around 2:00 p.m. the parties met to sign the lease agreement and promissory note, which respondent prepared, and she again told appellant he did not need a lawyer. Appellant signed the documents without reading them and respondent did not review the documents with him.

* * *

Appellant retained the original menu, the sign and the lunch buffet for a couple of weeks after opening the restaurant but took in only a little over $200 daily. When appellant told respondent that the restaurant was not taking in $700 a day she suggested that he change the sign, menu and buffet. Appellant followed the suggestions and with radio ads and coupons business increased slightly but profits did not increase. The restaurant never made $700 a day and never turned a profit. Appellant estimated his sales per month to be about $6,000 to $7,000, not the $25,000 to $30,000 respondent represented. The physical facilities presented additional problems with the plumbing backed up, the refrigerator and dishwasher not working, the roof leaking, faulty wiring and a parking lot with many potholes. Respondent later told appellant that this may be his fate and to see a fortune teller. She also told him that she would lower his rent but she never did.

Appellant paid respondent about $4,000 in July and August but as his loans increased the amount he could pay decreased-to $3,000 in September, $1,000 in October and $1,000 in November. Respondent refused his offer of a payment of $1,000 for December, warning him that he owed her three months rent and she was going to evict and sue him. In December, respondent called almost every day to ask for payment and told appellant that if he did not give her back the restaurant she would take him to court where he would lose his credit and his home would be seized. During this period appellant was able to keep the restaurant open by running up a $45,000 credit card debt and borrowing approximately $30,000 from friends and family.

On December 22, 1996, an insurance agent went with respondent to the restaurant "with papers * * * declar[ing] the contract null." When appellant said that he wanted his lawyer to evaluate the papers respondent told him that if he did not sign the papers by the next day "the police will come and lock the doors and you cannot bring anything out of the restaurant. And if you try to get in, they will take you away. They will lock you up."

The next day, December 23, 1996, respondent went to appellant's house, again with an insurance agent, and told him that he either had to pay her the full amount he owed or sign a contract stating that all prior contracts were cancelled, and if he did not do either she would take appellant to court because his rent was three months late. Appellant signed the contract declaring all prior contracts "null." Respondent also gave appellant a check for $2,500 to help him pay bills and support his family, but she stopped payment on the check. Respondent sold the restaurant to another purchaser later that day.

Appellant filed a complaint on October 21, 1997 alleging, among other counts, that respondent defrauded appellant and violated the CFA, and requested damages in excess of $50,000, attorney fees and costs pursuant to the Private AG Statute and pre-and post-judgment interest. After a three-day trial the court ruled that respondent defrauded appellant and that the value of the restaurant was $65,000 at the time of the sale. The court applied the damage award formula for common law fraud-the difference between what appellant paid for the restaurant and the fair market value of the restaurant, plus damages resulting from reasonable attempts to mitigate-and reasoned that since appellant bought the restaurant for $90,000 and the fair market value of the restaurant was $65,000, appellant was entitled to judgment for $25,000. The court made no ruling regarding application of the CFA or the Private AG Statute in this order.

On November 9, 1998, appellant moved for costs and attorney fees pursuant to the CFA and the Private AG Statute, claiming $60,920.55. The trial court denied the motion on the basis that appellant's award was based on a common law fraud finding which provided no right to recover attorney fees and the CFA did not apply because respondent's representations were not made to a large number of consumers and did not have the potential to deceive or ensnare any other consumer. With no violation of the CFA, the court ruled that appellant could not recover attorney fees under the Private AG Statute.

The court of appeals affirmed both the finding of common law fraud and the ruling that appellant had no cause of action under the CFA, noting that appellant did not meet the definition of "consumer" because he bought the restaurant with "the intent to produce, manufacture, and resell food, rather than with the intent of direct ownership of the product." *Ly,* 602 N.W.2d at 646–47. As to application of the CFA, the court held that it "only applies in consumer fraud situations and the fraud or misrepresentation must be disseminated to others." *Id.* The court concluded that this was a one-on-one business transaction and that if the court were to adopt appellant's interpretation of the CFA, the CFA would provide remedies for virtually every fraudulent transaction, an expansion of the statute not contemplated by the legislature. *See id.*
* * *

On review here, we address de novo as a matter of statutory interpretation appellant's argument that as a victim of common law fraud he has a cause of action under the CFA and is entitled to attorney fees and costs under the Private AG Statute. We are guided by the principle that the object of all statutory interpretation and construction of law is to ascertain and effectuate the intent of the legislature, *see* Minn.Stat. § 645.16 (1998), and we recognize the broad legislative powers in the passage of laws relating to preserving and protecting the public from mischievous business practices. The CFA and Private AG Statute are legislative enactments of this nature and are generally discussed and applied in concert, but they are separate and distinct in their structure and purpose-thus we analyze them separately.

I. The Consumer Fraud Act

In the late 1950's many state legislatures enacted statutes designed to prohibit deceptive practices and to address the unequal bargaining power often present in consumer transactions. *See* Jeff Sovern, *Private Actions Under the Deceptive Trade Practices Acts: Reconsidering the FTC Act as Role Model,* 52 Ohio St. L.J. 437, 446 (1991). By 1981, every state in the United States had statutes providing for consumer protection enforcement by a state agency-commonly, as in Minnesota, the state attorney general-with broad enforcement authority. *See id.* Minnesota's Consumer Fraud Act was adopted in 1963 to achieve the same purpose and provides the attorney general with authority to seek and obtain injunctive relief to protect consumers from unlawful and fraudulent trade practices in the marketplace. The CFA provides in relevant part:

> The act, use, or employment by any person of any fraud, false pretense, false promise, misrepresentation, misleading statement or deceptive practice, with the intent that others rely thereon in connection with the sale of any merchandise, whether or not any person has in fact been misled, deceived, or damaged thereby, is enjoinable as provided herein.

Minn.Stat. § 325F.69, subd. 1.

The CFA defines "merchandise" as "objects, wares, goods, commodities, intangibles, real estate, loans, or services." Minn.Stat. 325F.68, subd. 2 (1998). The word "consumer" appears nowhere in the CFA, however the statutory purpose of protecting consumers was clear from its inception when it was presented to the legislature in 1963 * * *.

* * *

Respondent contends that the legislature did not intend the CFA to apply to non-consumer commercial transactions, as here, where appellant was a veteran of the restaurant business, had substantial bargaining power in the transaction and clearly purchased the restaurant for commercial, not personal, use. Respondent reads the use of "others" in the CFA language "with the intent that *others* rely thereon" to require the fraud to be perpetrated on others in addition to the plaintiff. Minn.Stat. § 325F.69, subd. 1.

* * * [T]he better reasoning leads to the conclusion that the transaction involving the sale of the Chin Yung restaurant is covered by the CFA. Appellant purchased the restaurant business not for the purpose of reselling it, but rather to sell restaurant services. His status was therefore more that of a consumer of the restaurant business than a buyer of a business for resale. * * * While the CFA does not define "consumer," the legislative history clearly indicates that the CFA was intended to protect a broad, though not limitless, range of individuals from fraudulent and deceptive trade practices, and our decisions have also recognized the breadth of its coverage. Thus, viewing appellant as a "consumer" under the CFA does not push application of the statute onto new ground.

We are also on established ground in holding that even though the unlawful practices respondent engaged in here were in the context of an isolated one-on-one transaction, coverage under the CFA may still be afforded. * * * We attach no importance to the statutory reference to the term "others" in "with the intent that *others* rely thereon," as it most reasonably can only mean that the fraudulent conduct must not have been committed in a vacuum-it must have been intended to deceive someone. *See* Minn.Stat. § 645.08(2) (1998) ("[t]he singular includes the plural; and the plural, the singular"). We conclude that the unlawful practices here, occurring while engaging in a one-on-one transaction for the purchase of a business for operation and not resale, fall within the trade practices prohibited by section 325F.69, subdivision 1.

II. *The Private Attorney General Statute*

The attorney general is provided broad statutory authority under Minn.Stat. § 8.31 to investigate violations of law regarding unlawful business practices barred by a variety of statutory prohibitions including the Consumer Fraud Act, and to seek injunctive relief and civil penalties on behalf of the state. *See* Minn.Stat. § 8.31, subds. 1, 3 (1998). The Private AG Statute, section 8.31, subdivision 3a, further provides that "any person injured by a violation" of the laws entrusted to the attorney general to investigate and enforce may recover damages together with costs and attorney fees* * *.

The sweeping remedies of the Private AG Statute have raised concern about how broadly the legislature intended the statute to be applied, particularly as it relates to common law fraud actions and the recovery of attorney fees. A brief history of the passage of the Private AG Statute sheds light on this issue and reveals the statutory purpose in providing incentives to injured private parties to enforce the unlawful business practices statutes as a substitute for the attorney general. On March 8, 1973, Senator Winston Borden, author of the bill, in a hearing before the Labor and Commerce Committee, stated that its goal was to:

> allow the individual person to bring a civil action for the damages he sustained * * * it's a great means of private enforcement. It's simply impossible for the Attorney General's Office to investigate and prosecute every act of consumer fraud in this state. * * * [And] if a[n] individual could bring an action, he can do some of the prosecuting, he can do some of the enforcing, he can provide some of the protection for himself and others that the Attorney General's Office * * * can not do today * * *.

Similarly, on March 30, 1973, Representative Sieben * * * referred to the importance of providing an incentive to consumers to privately enforce the fraudulent business practices laws: "an operator who can * * * rip off a large number of citizens, and cease operating * * * may likely be able to do so with little threat of legal action. More stringent remedies are therefore needed. * * * [This bill] provides a route for private recovery for the victims of consumer fraud."

The Private AG Statute thus advances the legislature's intent to prevent fraudulent representations and deceptive practices with regard to consumer products by offering an incentive for defrauded consumers to bring claims in lieu of the attorney general. * * *

* * *

The interest of the legislature in creating a supplemental force of private enforcement to address unlawful trade practices is clear from the testimony at committee hearings, but it is equally clear that the sweep of the statute can be no broader than the source of its authority—that of the attorney general—whose duties are to protect *public* rights in the interest of the state. Conversely, it is not the responsibility of the attorney general to protect private or individual interests independent of a public purpose.

We find further support for our holding that public interest must be demonstrated to state a claim under the Private AG Statute based on our conclusion that the legislature could not have intended to sweep every private dispute based on fraud, and falling within the CFA, into a statute where attorney fees and additional costs and expenses would be awarded, because to do so would substantially alter a fundamental principle of law deeply ingrained in our common law jurisprudence-that each party bears his own attorney fees in the absence of a statutory or contractual exception. * * *

Based on these considerations we hold that the Private AG Statute applies only to those claimants who demonstrate that their cause of action benefits the public. * * *

Affirmed in part and reversed in part.

PAGE, JUSTICE (concurring in part, dissenting in part).

I respectfully dissent. I agree with that portion of the court's opinion holding that the Consumer Fraud Act applies to a cause of action brought by a plaintiff who was defrauded in an isolated one-on-one purchase of a restaurant for the purpose of selling restaurant services. I disagree, however, with that part of the opinion holding that Minn.Stat. § 8.31, subd. 3a (1998), does not permit an award of attorney fees in cases arising under the Consumer Fraud Act unless the plaintiff can demonstrate that the cause of action has a public benefit. "[When] the words of a statute are clear and free from ambiguity, we have no right to construe or interpret the statute's language." *Tuma v. Commissioner of Econ. Sec.,* 386 N.W.2d 702, 706 (Minn.1986). "Our duty in such a case is to give effect to the statute's plain meaning." *Id.* The words the legislature used in Minn.Stat. § 8.31, subd. 3a are clear and free from ambiguity. * * *

Had the legislature intended to limit the scope of section 8.31, subdivision 3a, to those causes of action that have a public benefit, it could have easily done so. Whether for good or for ill, by the plain words of the statute, it did not. This court is not authorized nor is it this court's role to read into a statute that which the legislature, by its plain language, has left out.

GILBERT, JUSTICE (concurring in part, dissenting in part).

* * *

The majority holds that although the CFA is intended to protect even the consumer defrauded in an "isolated one-on-one transaction," and even if that same consumer successfully brings suit under the CFA for that unlawful conduct, he is not entitled to reasonable attorney fees under section 8.31, subdivision 3a, because such a transaction does not enhance the public interest generally. That holding is contrary to the purpose of section 8.31, subdivision 3a, which, as the majority acknowledges, was intended to provide incentives for injured consumers to privately enforce the fraudulent business practices laws by eliminating financial barriers to prosecution. When "any person" is injured by a violation of those laws and successfully prosecutes the violator, that consumer has benefited the public by attempting to prevent the fraudulent business conduct of that particular defendant and alleviating, economically and in terms of time and preparation for investigation and litigation, the burden on the attorney general's office to enforce the laws. As we said in *Church of Nativity*, a case involving an individual purchaser involved in a single transaction, "pursuit of a remedy has involved much time and labor; it has been difficult, lengthy and expensive. If there are no attorney fees awarded in this case, [the consumer] will spend virtually all of its damage award paying its attorneys. The private attorney general statute was intended to cover just this type of case." 491 N.W.2d at 8. It creates an unreasonable result to hold that enforcement of the state's laws does not benefit the public generally.

* * *

Notes

1. Do you agree with the Minnesota Supreme Court that the Consumer Fraud Act was meant to cover a commercial transaction involving the purchase of a restaurant? The states are divided as to whether or not their UDAP statutes do or do not cover business transactions. *See* Dee Pridgen, Consumer Protection and the Law (Thomson/West 2007), §§ 4:3–4:4. Why would legislatures want to exclude business transactions from their consumer protection laws?

2. What was the point of including the transaction in the *Ly* case under the state Consumer Fraud Act while denying the prevailing plaintiff his attorney's fees under the related "private attorney general" statute?

3. Several other state courts have imposed a "public interest" requirement onto private plaintiffs seeking relief under their state UDAP statutes. *See, e.g.,* Hangman Ridge Training Stables, Inc. v. Safeco Title Ins. Co., 105 Wash.2d 778, 719 P.2d 531 (1986) (en banc); Zeeman v. Black, 156 Ga.App. 82, 273 S.E.2d 910 (1980); Nelson v. Lusterstone Surfacing Co., 258 Neb.

678, 605 N.W.2d 136 (2000); Noack Enterprises, Inc. v. Country Corner Interiors of Hilton Head Island, Inc., 290 S.C. 475, 351 S.E.2d 347 (Ct. App. 1986); Oswego Laborers; Local 214 Pension Fund v. Marine Midland Bank, 85 N.Y.2d 20, 623 N.Y.S.2d 529, 647 N.E.2d 741 (1995) (conduct must be consumer oriented to come within the scope of the statute). *See generally* Dee Pridgen, Consumer Protection and the Law (Thomson/West 2007), §§ 5:5–5:8. The reasons for reading such a requirement into the statute include: (1) the fact that the FTC Act has a public interest requirement; (2) the desire to eliminate ordinary business disputes from the scope of the consumer protection statute; and (3) to avoid the imposition of stiff penalties on isolated transactions with no potential for repetition.

4.   For an interesting analysis of how state courts have used a philosophy of "Textualism" in interpreting their state UDAP statutes, *see* James P. Nehf, Textualism in the Lower Courts: Lessons from Judges Interpreting Consumer Legislation, 26 Rutgers L.J. 1 (1994). The author concludes that this approach still resulted in considerable leeway for discretion by the judges.

5.   In addition to the issue of whether or not to cover business-to-business transactions under state UDAP statutes, many states have also struggled with whether to cover the "learned professions," i.e., doctors and lawyers. Consider the contrasting approaches in the following two cases.

KARLIN v. IVF AMERICA, INC.

Court of Appeals of New York, 1999.
93 N.Y.2d 282, 690 N.Y.S.2d 495, 712 N.E.2d 662.

Opinion of the Court

Chief Judge Kaye.

In order to ensure an honest marketplace, the General Business Law prohibits all deceptive practices, including false advertising, "in the conduct of any business, trade commerce or in the furnishing of any service in this state" (General Business Law § 349[a]; § 350; * * *. This appeal requires us to determine whether plaintiffs can maintain an action against defendants operating an *in vitro* fertilization (IVF) program for deceptive practices and false advertising under General Business Law § § 349 and 350, or are instead limited to a claim for medical malpractice based on lack of informed consent. We hold that plaintiffs have properly stated causes of action under these consumer protection statutes, and are not precluded from pursuing those claims because the alleged misrepresentations relate to the provision of medical services.

Facts

In 1987, plaintiffs Jayne and Kenneth R. Karlin sought evaluation and treatment from defendants' IVF program. The IVF procedure involves removal of multiple eggs from a woman's ovaries, fertilization of the eggs outside her body and transfer of the fertilized eggs to her uterus in an attempt to impregnate her. Over the course of 2 1/2 years, Mrs.

Karlin completed seven IVF cycles at defendants' clinic but did not become pregnant.

In 1990, the Federal Trade Commission (FTC) charged IVF America and related entities (IVF America) with deceptively advertising and promoting its program, finding the following statements typical of representations in their promotional materials:

"1. 'LIKELY TREATMENT OUTCOMES ... Our experience indicates that when a patient at an IVF [America] Program completes four IVF treatment cycles, the chance of giving birth is about 50%. * * * If *25* women begin a total of *100* IVF cycles ... About *13* (or about 50%) of the women give birth to *18* babies' (emphasis in original) * * *.

"2. '[M]ore than 28% of the couples who complete a cycle of treatment are becoming pregnant' * * *.

"3. '[O]ne out of three couples who complete a cycle of treatment is becoming pregnant.' "

According to the FTC, these statements were misleading because women who participate in IVF America's treatment program "consisting of four IVF cycles have considerably less than a 50 percent chance of giving birth," and women who participate in IVF America's treatment program "consisting of one IVF cycle have considerably less than a 28 to 33 percent chance of becoming pregnant." By consent decree dated December 31, 1990, IVF America agreed to cease and desist from misrepresenting success rates, and also agreed in the future to disclose the basis used for calculating the percentage of patients who have become pregnant or given birth.

In February 1993, however, the ABC News program "20/20" televised an investigative report on the IVF industry in which IVF America employees were shown informing prospective patients that after four to six cycles, IVF America had pregnancy success rates "between 60 to 80 percent." The report also showed an IVF America representative telling a seminar participant that there are "[a]bsolutely not" any long-term effects of the IVF procedure. This report prompted New York City's Department of Consumer Affairs to charge IVF America with violations of the City's Consumer Protection Law. As part of a settlement reached in April 1993, IVF America agreed to refrain both from marketing its services using unsubstantiated pregnancy success rates and from stating that IVF procedures posed no adverse health risks.

The following year, plaintiffs commenced this action alleging that defendants engaged in fraudulent and misleading conduct by disseminating false success rates and misrepresenting health risks associated with IVF. In particular, plaintiffs claim that defendants "exaggerated success rates, excluding certain subsets of failed treatment procedures, emphasizing numerically false and misleading overall success rates and conceal[ing] and misrepresent[ing] significant health risks, high miscarriage rates and excessive neonatal deaths and abnormalities of infants even if a birth resulted from the treatment rendered by defendants."

Supreme Court dismissed all of plaintiffs' causes of action except those alleging unfair and deceptive trade practices in violation of General Business Law § 349, false advertising in violation of General Business Law § 350 and lack of informed consent in violation of Public Health Law § 2805–d. * * * On appeal, the Appellate Division dismissed plaintiffs' General Business Law § § 349 and 350 claims, categorically refusing to apply "the consumer fraud statutes to the providers of medical services" in order to prevent what the court perceived as "a drastic change in basic tort law where the Legislature has not explicitly expressed its intent to effect such a change" (*Karlin v. IVF Am.*, 239 A.D.2d 560, 561, 658 N.Y.S.2d 73). * * *

* * *

ANALYSIS

Pursuant to General Business Law § 349(a), it is unlawful to perform "[d]eceptive acts or practices in the conduct of *any* business, trade or commerce or in the furnishing of *any* service in this state" (emphasis added). The scope of General Business Law § 350 is equally broad, prohibiting the promulgation of "[f]alse advertising in the conduct of *any* business, trade or commerce or in the furnishing of *any* service in this state" (emphasis added). Advertising is "false" if it "is misleading in a material respect" (General Business Law § 350–a [1]).

These statutes on their face apply to virtually all economic activity,* and their application has been correspondingly broad (*see, e.g., People v. Appel,* 258 A.D.2d 957, 685 N.Y.S.2d 504 [editing business]; *Griffin-Amiel v. Terris Orchestras,* 178 Misc.2d 71, 677 N.Y.S.2d 908 [wedding singer]; *Baker v. Burlington Coat Factory Warehouse,* 175 Misc.2d 951, 673 N.Y.S.2d 281 [clothing retailer]; *Perez v. Hempstead Motor Sales,* 173 Misc.2d 710, 662 N.Y.S.2d 184, *affd.* 176 Misc.2d 314, 674 N.Y.S.2d 564 [automobile dealer]; *People v. Lipsitz,* 174 Misc.2d 571, 663 N.Y.S.2d 468 [magazine subscription seller]). The reach of these statutes "provide[s] needed authority to cope with the numerous, ever-changing types of false and deceptive business practices which plague consumers in our State" (N.Y. Dept of Law, Mem to Governor, 1963 N.Y. Legis Ann, at 105).

When section 349 was enacted in 1970, only the Attorney General was empowered to enforce it (General Business Law § 349[b]). It soon became clear, however, that the "broad scope of section 349, combined with the limited resources of the Attorney General, [made] it virtually impossible for the Attorney General to provide more than minimal enforcement" (Mem of Assemblyman Strelzin, L 1980, ch 346, § 1, 1980

---

* A categorical exemption applies to "any television or radio broadcasting station or to any publisher or printer of a newspaper, magazine or other form of printed advertising, who broadcasts, publishes, or prints the advertisement" (General Business Law § 349[e]).

N.Y. Legis Ann, at 146). Accordingly, in 1980 the statute was amended to provide a private right of action (*see*, L 1980, ch 346, § 1). Among the remedies available to private plaintiffs are compensatory damages, limited punitive damages and attorneys' fees (General Business Law § 349[h]).

A blanket exemption for providers of medical services and products is contrary to the plain language of the statutes. Such an exemption is also contrary to legislative history, as supporters of the consumer protection bills recognized that consumers of medical services and products might be particularly vulnerable to unscrupulous business practices. * * *

Indeed, while the question before us is a novel one, General Business Law § § 349 and 350 have long been powerful tools aiding the Attorney General's efforts to combat fraud in the health care and medical services areas. The Attorney General has relied on these provisions to challenge deceptive and fraudulent practices in contexts as diverse as the marketing of AIDS-related products (*People v. Overs Enters.*, Sup Ct, Westchester County, Colabella, J., index No. 16221/92); baldness treatments (*People v. D.J. Carlisi*, Sup Ct, N.Y. County, Ostrau, J., index No. 41189/89); abortion counseling clinics (*People v. Northern Westchester Putnam Assistance to Mother & Unborn Child*, Sup Ct, Dutchess County, Beisner, J., index No. 92–135); hearing aids (*People v. Tolbert*, Sup Ct, Clinton County, Dawson, J., index No. 35678/97); and the therapeutic benefits of adjustable beds and chairs (*People v. Craftmatic/Contour Org.*, Sup Ct, N.Y. County, Friedman, J., index No. 41535/91).

Not only is the categorical exemption crafted by the Appellate Division at odds with the language and history of sections 349 and 350, but also the apparent simplicity of that excision proves elusive when it is necessary to decide who is a "provider of medical services." IVF America, for example, is a publicly traded company engaged in managing and providing services to clinical facilities and physician practices that specialize in infertility treatments; actual patient medical care, however, is furnished by affiliated medical institutions or groups. Thus, it is unclear whether such an entity could itself even be considered as a "provider of medical services."

Despite the scope of General Business Law § § 349 and 350 and the historical use of these statutes to combat fraud in the medical context, defendants argue that plaintiffs' claims must be governed exclusively by New York's informed consent statute, Public Health Law § 2805–d. A suit for medical malpractice based on a lack of informed consent is meant to redress a "failure of the person providing the professional treatment or diagnosis to disclose to the patient such alternatives thereto and the reasonably foreseeable risks and benefits involved as a reasonable medical * * * practitioner under similar circumstances would have disclosed, in a manner permitting the patient to make a knowledgeable evaluation" (Public Health Law § 2805–d [1]). In contrast to the latitude afforded plaintiffs suing for deceptive practices and false advertising, there are numerous restrictions on a plaintiff's ability to sue for malpractice based on a lack of informed consent. Such claims, for example, are limited to certain treatments or diagnostic procedures, require a heightened showing of causation, and are subject to several affirmative defenses and an abbreviated Statute of Limitations (*see,* Public Health Law § 2805–d; CPLR 214–a). These restrictions were enacted in 1975 as part of a bill intended to ensure the ability of physicians to obtain malpractice insurance coverage at reasonable rates.

Notwithstanding defendants' procrustean efforts to cast plaintiffs' deceptive acts and false advertising claims as malpractice claims for lack of informed consent, plaintiffs have clearly alleged conduct beyond the purview of Public Health Law § 2805–d. Plaintiffs do not merely charge that "the person providing the professional treatment" failed to disclose certain pertinent information "to the patient" (Public Health Law § 2805–d [1]). Rather, they claim that defendants' "promotional materials, advertisements, slide presentations * * * and so-called 'educational' seminars" contained misrepresentations that had the effect of "deceiving and misleading members of the public." Nor are plaintiffs' claims limited, as defendants urge, to information provided by defendants "during the course of their medical treatment at the Program." On the contrary, plaintiffs assert that before they started any course of treatment, defendants "deceptively lured" plaintiffs and others, including physicians who refer patients to the IVF America programs, by "deceiving and misleading" them.

Defendants' alleged multi-media dissemination of information to the public is precisely the sort of consumer-oriented conduct that is targeted by General Business Law § § 349 and 350. By alleging that defendants have injured them with consumer-oriented conduct "that is deceptive or misleading in a material way," plaintiffs have stated claims under General Business Law § § 349 and 350 even though the subject of the conduct was *in vitro* fertilization.

* * *

Defendants' concern that allowing plaintiffs to sue doctors for deceptive consumer practices and false advertising may cause a tidal wave of litigation against doctors is misplaced. Because plaintiffs bringing a claim under the consumer protection statutes must demonstrate an impact on consumers at large—something that a physician's treatment of an individual patient typically does not have—these statutes will not supplant traditional medical malpractice actions. Furthermore, as this Court has already observed, the possibility of excessive litigation under the consumer protection statutes is avoided by our "adoption of an objective definition of deceptive acts and practices, whether representations or omissions, limited to those likely to mislead a reasonable consumer acting reasonably under the circumstances" (*Oswego Laborers' Local 214 Pension Fund v. Marine Midland Bank, supra,* 85 N.Y.2d, at 26, 623 N.Y.S.2d 529, 647 N.E.2d 741).

Finally, the interests at stake in an action under the General Business Law are distinctly different from the interests involved in a suit for professional malpractice. Thus, while physicians providing information to their patients in the course of medical treatment may be afforded the benefits of Public Health Law § 2805–d, when they choose to reach out to the consuming public at large in order to promote business—like clothing retailers, automobile dealers and wedding singers who engage in such conduct—they subject themselves to the standards of an honest marketplace secured by General Business Law § § 349 and 350.

* * *

Accordingly, the judgment appealed from and the order of the Appellate Division brought up for review should be modified, with costs to plaintiffs, by denying defendants' motion to dismiss the first and second causes of action and, as so modified, affirmed.

JUDGES BELLACOSA, SMITH, LEVINE, CIPARICK, WESLEY and ROSENBLATT concur.

MACEDO v. DELLO RUSSO

Supreme Court of New Jersey, 2004.
178 N.J. 340, 840 A.2d 238.

PER CURIAM.

Plaintiffs Joseph Macedo and Rosemary Lesky sued Dr. Joseph Dello Russo, the corporate entities he created to perform laser surgery, and Dr. William T. Kellogg alleging, among other things, that defendants violated the Consumer Fraud Act (CFA), *N.J.S.A.* 56:8–1 to–116, when they allowed Kellogg, who was not fully licensed, to treat plaintiffs. Plaintiffs do not allege that their treatment fell below the appropriate medical standard of care or that they suffered any physical injuries as a result thereof, but only that

> through their own words and conduct, the defendants represented to each plaintiff that they would be treated by properly licensed doctors, with no limitations on their licenses, and that Kellogg was a licensed physician with no limitations upon his license, and licensed to provide the care and treatment which he provided to each plaintiff.

Consequently, plaintiffs claim that they suffered "mental anguish," loss of enjoyment of life, medical bills and economic damages for which they seek "compensatory damages, punitive damages, attorneys fees, interest, [and] costs."

The trial court granted defendants' motion to dismiss the CFA count because the allegations underlying it implicate the provision of medical services, a subject outside the purview of the Act. On leave to appeal, the Appellate Division reversed. *Macedo v. Dello Russo,* 359 *N.J.Super.* 78, 819 *A.2d* 5 (2003). In support, the court cited its decision in *Blatterfein v. Larken,* 323 *N.J.Super.* 167, 732 *A.2d* 555 (App.Div.1999) (holding that architect's activity as real estate seller is subject to CFA) and our decision in *Lemelledo v. Beneficial Management Corp.*, 150 *N.J.* 255, 696 *A.*2d 546 (1997) (finding that existence of other regulatory schemes regarding practices of financial institutions presents no limit on applicability of CFA). *Id.* at 81, 83, 819 *A.*2d 5. In reference to *Neveroski v. Blair*, 141 *N.J.Super.* 365, 358 *A.*2d 473 (1976) (concluding real estate broker who negotiates sale of real estate is outside scope of CFA), the court stated:

> To the extent the limiting *dictum* in *Neveroski* ever had a basis in apparent legislative design, subsequent statutory and decisional developments have negated it as a categorical exception to application of the Act. We see no good reason to apply it as a valid, general basis for dismissing claims under the Act as a matter of law.

[*Macedo, supra,* 359 *N.J.Super.* at 83–84, 819 *A.*2d 5.]

We disagree with that analysis as well as with the Appellate Division's reliance on *Blatterfein* and *Lemelledo,* decisions we view as unsupportive of its conclusion. We, therefore, reverse.

In 1960, the Legislature adopted the precursor to the CFA, creating liability in connection with fraud in advertising. *L.* 1960, *c.* 39, p. 137, § 1. The Act obviously was not meant to encompass advertising by physicians because such advertising was not permitted for another two decades. Indeed, it was the 1977 decision of the United States Supreme Court in *Bates v. State Bar of Arizona,* 433 *U.S.* 350, 97 *S.Ct.* 2691, 53 *L.Ed.*2d 810 (1977), that precipitated professional advertising. There, the Court held that although advertisements by attorneys are subject to regulation, they are not subject to "blanket suppression" because they constitute protected speech. *Id.* at 383, 97 *S.Ct.* at 2708–9, 53 *L.Ed.*2d at 835. Thereafter, the Attorney General of New Jersey ruled that a total prohibition against advertising of services by professionals is a First Amendment violation, *U.S. Const.* amend. I., but that reasonable regulation of that advertising is not precluded. The amended physician's advertising rule followed on the heels of those developments.

Since its enactment, the CFA has not been amended to include the advertising of professionals. In fact, the only major substantive change concerning the scope of the CFA came in 1976, when the Act was amended to include the sale of real estate in the definition of "merchandise."

Contemporaneous with that amendment, the first judicial opinion addressing the applicability of the CFA to professionals was rendered, coincidently relating to the sale of real estate. In *Neveroski, supra,* the Appellate Division was faced with the question of whether a real estate broker who deliberately concealed the termite infestation of a home from potential buyers was subject to CFA liability. In ruling that it was not, the court relied on two basic premises. The first was that the CFA had been amended after the acts complained of specifically to include the sale of real estate, thus indicating that the prior version did not encompass that subject. Second, the court stated:

A real estate broker is in a far different category from the purveyors of products or services or other activities. He is in a semi-professional status subject to testing, licensing, regulations, and penalties through other legislative provisions. *See N.J.S.A.* 45:15–1[e]t seq. Although not on the same plane as other professionals such as lawyers, physicians, dentists, accountants or engineers, the nature of his activity is recognized as something beyond the ordinary commercial seller of goods or services—an activity beyond the pale of the act under consideration.

[*Id.* at 379, 358 *A.2d* 473.]

The court went on:

Certainly no one would argue that a member of any of the learned professions is subject to the provisions of the Consumer Fraud Act despite the fact that he renders "services" to the public. And although the literal language may be construed to include professional services, it would be ludicrous to construe the legislation with that broad a sweep in view of the fact that the nature of the services does not fall into the category of consumerism.

[*Ibid.*]

* * *

Since then, no reported New Jersey case has applied the CFA to a representation involving the rendering of services by a learned professional. The Appellate Division here over-read *Blatterfein* in reaching its conclusion to the contrary. In *Blatterfein*, an architect was held subject to the CFA for misrepresentations he made about building materials as part of a real estate merchandising scheme. In other words, although he "happened" to be an architect, he was not functioning in that capacity when he made false representations to induce the purchase of a house. Rather, he was operating as a real estate sales person and that is what subjected him to the CFA. *See also Gilmore v. Berg,* 761 *F.Supp.* 358 (D.N.J.1991) (concluding that lawyer and accountant are answerable under CFA for efforts to "sell" real estate).

Nothing in *Lemelledo* suggests a contrary conclusion. There, in addressing loan-packing, we held that the mere existence of an alternative regulatory scheme by the Department of Banking and Insurance, did not automatically eliminate the applicability of the CFA. Instead, we held that a direct conflict between the schemes would be required in order to conclude that the Legislature did not intend the CFA to apply. *Lemelledo, supra,* 150 *N.J.* at 270, 696 *A.2d* 546. *Lemelledo* would be dispositive here if the issue presented was whether the separate regulatory scheme governing physicians preempts the application of the CFA. It is entirely irrelevant to the threshold question of whether the CFA applies to learned professionals in the first instance.

Thus, today, forty years after the CFA was enacted, our jurisprudence continues to identify learned professionals as beyond the reach of the Act so long as they are operating in their professional capacities. The Legislature is presumed to be aware of that judicial view.

* * *

We therefore must assume that the Legislature approves of the consistent judicial interpretation of the CFA that has been extant for four decades. Under that interpretation, advertisements by learned professionals in respect of the rendering of professional services are insulated from the CFA but subject to comprehensive regulation by the relevant regulatory bodies and to any common-law remedies that otherwise may apply. We consider ourselves bound by that Legislative acquiescence. If we are incorrect in our assumption, we would expect the legislature to take action to amend the statute.

That said, because Dr. Dello Russo's advertising representations were made in his professional capacity regarding his professional services, the trial court correctly dismissed the CFA claim against him. That is not to suggest that Dr. Dello Russo would be insulated from the restraints of the CFA if he acted outside his professional capacity. Like the architect in *Blatterfein,* if Dr. Dello Russo were to engage in the merchandising of a golf course, a vacation time-share or a medical office building, he would be subject, as all merchandisers are, to the CFA.

The judgment of the Appellate Division is reversed.

Notes

1. Which case has the better approach to the question of whether the state UDAP statute should or should not apply to the "learned" professions?

2. The same issue has come up with regard to the application of little FTC acts to lawyers as well. *See* Heslin, Commissioner of Consumer Protection v. Connecticut Law Clinic of Trantolo & Trantolo, 190 Conn. 510, 461 A.2d 938 (1983) (holding that the practice of law in some aspects is covered as part of "trade or commerce," under the Connecticut Unfair Trade Practices Act). The New Hampshire Supreme Court found that the practice of law is exempt as a regulated industry, since admission to the practice of law is regulated by the legislative and judicial branches of state government. See Rousseau v. Eshleman, 128 N.H. 564, 519 A.2d 243 (1986).

3. Are consumers already well protected by the availability of malpractice suits against lawyers or doctors who handle their cases in a negligent manner and by the oversight of state professional conduct committees? Is placing the professions under the jurisdiction of state UDAP statutes a matter of regulatory overkill? Will New York's public interest requirement be sufficient to distinguish those cases meriting UDAP treatment from those that should be relegated to other alternatives, such as malpractice?

4. Some state courts have held that the state's Consumer Protection Act applies to the "entrepreneurial" aspects of legal and medical practice (e.g., billing and advertising), but not to the quality of legal advice and services. See Short v. Demopolis, 103 Wash.2d 52, 691 P.2d 163 (1984); Wright v. Jeckle, 104 Wash.App. 478, 16 P.3d 1268 (2001). *See also* Haynes

v. Yale–New Haven Hospital, 243 Conn. 17, 699 A.2d 964 (1997) and Janusauskas v. Fichman, 264 Conn. 796, 826 A.2d 1066 (2003) (Connecticut Unfair Trade Practices Act applies only to entrepreneurial aspects of medical practice). Is this the proper compromise?

5. The "learned professions" have been held accountable by the FTC under both the antitrust and consumer protection branches of its statutory authority. *See, e.g.,* American Medical Association v. F.T.C., 638 F.2d 443 (1980), *aff'd* 455 U.S. 676, 102 S.Ct. 1744, 71 L.Ed.2d 546 (1982); and In re Wilson Chemical Co., 64 F.T.C. 168 (1964). Should the treatment of the "learned professions" in consumer protection be guided by the treatment of such professions under the antitrust laws? For an illuminating discussion of this question, *see* Mark D. Bauer, The Licensed Professional Exemption in Consumer Protection: At Odds with Antitrust History and Precedent, 73 Tenn. L. Rev. 131 (2006).

6. Should other regulated industries, such as insurance and securities transactions, be exempt from state UDAP statutes? If you were a state legislator, what would you want to know about the regulatory system before determining whether an exemption from the little FTC Act would be appropriate? What are the dangers of UDAP coverage of a regulated industry?

7. Although buying a house is typically one of the largest purchases most consumers make in a lifetime, and one where arguably the consumer is most in need of legal protection, the states are divided on whether or not real estate transactions are included within their state UDAP laws. Often the statutes are limited to acts or practices involving the sale of "goods or services," a phrase which is usually interpreted to exclude real property. A similar issue has arisen with regard to the coverage of deceptive or unfair practices in connection with rental housing. On the other hand, many state UDAP statutes specifically include real estate and rental of residential housing within the definition of consumer transactions. See generally Dee Pridgen, Consumer Protection and the Law (Thomson/West 2007) §§ 4:17–4:20.

Problem 1–13

Review Problem

Jimmy Crane is a 45 year old single man living at home with his mother in Bridgeport, Connecticut. Jimmy has been overweight since he was a child. During his childhood, the other children at school called him "fat boy," or other cruel names. Jimmy has a college degree in computer science. He makes his living working at home, designing Internet web pages for small businesses.

Late one night Jimmy happened to see a half hour television program advertising "Miracle Cream." The advertisement looked like a talk show. A host interviewed several attractive and slender people who said that after using Miracle Cream they lost all their unwanted fat without dieting or exercise. The program showed photographs of these guests showing how fat they looked "before" using Miracle Cream. There was no disclosure that this was an advertisement, and Jimmy did not realize it was a paid advertisement.

Jimmy was very favorably impressed. The next day, he visited a nearby shop selling Miracle Cream. The saleswoman (who worked on commission for Miracle Cream) told Jimmy that most buyers were happy with the product and that the company had not received many complaints. She also told Jimmy that in her opinion, he would be able to get rid of his excess fat within a year by using the cream. She assured Jimmy that dieting and exercise were not necessary to lose weight, if he used the Miracle Cream. Jimmy bought a year's supply of Miracle Cream for $1,200, which was about 1/12 of his yearly income.

Jimmy applied Miracle Cream daily, as the directions on the label said. However, after six months, he was just as overweight as he was before using the cream. He was very disappointed. When he called the company to complain, they said they had a "no refund" policy and refused to do anything.

The Miracle Cream Company has also been investigated by the Federal Trade Commission. Their investigation has found that the "talk show" is really a half hour advertisement, and that the "guests" are actors paid by the Miracle Cream Company. These actors were never overweight, although they did use Miracle Cream for a few weeks before the taping. The "before" photographs were actually different people from those appearing on the advertising show. The FTC also has evidence that no cream currently exists that can cause a person to lose weight without dieting or exercise.

Part A. Jimmy is so angry with the company for taking advantage of him, he wants to know whether he would be able to sue for damages.

(1) Would Jimmy have a good common law fraud case?

(2) Would Jimmy have a good case under the Connecticut Unfair Trade Practices Act?

Part B. The FTC staff wants to convince the Commission to sue the Miracle Cream Company for engaging in a deceptive trade practice in violation of the FTC Act.

1. Will the FTC be likely to bring this case under either their deception or unfairness policy?

2. Will the FTC be likely to bring this case under the FTC's advertising substantiation policy?

3. Will the FTC have to use "extrinsic evidence" to interpret the advertising?

SECTION C. CONSTITUTIONAL LIMITATIONS ON ADVERTISING REGULATION

1. THE EVOLUTION OF THE COMMERCIAL SPEECH DOCTRINE: PROTECTION, BUT AT A LOWER LEVEL?

Before the mid-nineteen seventies it had been axiomatic that "commercial" speech enjoyed no special first amendment protections, and legislatures and agencies were free to regulate advertising and similar marketplace communications at will. The basis for this assumption was an almost offhand opinion of the Supreme Court in the case of Valentine v. Chrestensen, 316 U.S. 52, 62 S.Ct. 920, 86 L.Ed. 1262 (1942), where the Court rejected a free speech challenge to a handbilling ordinance. Under that law Chrestensen was restrained from distributing a double-faced handbill: one side advertised tours of a former Navy submarine he owned; the other side contained a protest against New York City's refusal to allow him the use of a city pier. In sustaining the ordinance, the Court acknowledged that laws could not "unduly burden" free speech in public places, but continued:

> We are equally clear that the Constitution imposes no such restraint on government as respects purely commercial advertising. Whether, and to what extent, one may promote or pursue a gainful occupation in the streets, to what extent such activity shall be adjudged a derogation of the public right of user, are matters for legislative judgment * * *. If the respondent was attempting to use the streets of New York by distributing commercial advertising, the prohibition of the code provision was lawfully invoked against his conduct. 316 U.S. at 54–55, 62 S.Ct. at 921, 86 L.Ed. at 1265.

The constitutional status of commercial speech changed markedly in the 1976 landmark decision in Virginia State Board of Pharmacy v. Virginia Citizens Consumer Council, Inc., 425 U.S. 748, 96 S.Ct. 1817, 48 L.Ed.2d 346 (1976), where the Court rejected as unconstitutional a state statute barring the advertising of prescription drug prices. The opinion acknowledged the purely economic interest of the pharmacist who wants to advertise prices, but stressed the concomitant interests of society as a whole, and of individual consumers, to a free flow of market information:

> Advertising, however tasteless and excessive it sometimes may seem, is nonetheless dissemination of information as to who is producing and selling what product, for what reason, and at what price. So long as we preserve a predominantly free enterprise economy, the allocation of our resources in large measure will be made through numerous private economic decisions. It is a matter of public interest that those decisions, in the aggregate, be intelligent and well informed. To this end, the free flow of commercial information is indispensable.

425 U.S. at 765, 96 S. Ct. at 1827.

Against these considerations, the purported justification for the law—to assure professional standards for pharmacists—carried little weight. The Court summarized the state's interest in banning price advertising for pharmaceutical drugs as seeking to protect consumers against a tendency to choose low cost, low quality pharmacies, thus driving more costly but "professional" pharmacists out of business. To this argument the Court responded:

> There is, of course, an alternative to this highly paternalistic approach. That alternative is to assume that this information is not

in itself harmful, that people will perceive their own best interests if only they are well enough informed, and that the best means to that end is to open the channels of communication rather than to close them.

Va. State Bd. of Pharmacy, 425 U.S. at 770, 96 S. Ct. at 1829.

The Court also distinguished situations where commercial speech was false or misleading, noting that "some forms of commercial speech regulation are surely permissible":

> Nor is there any claim that prescription drug price advertisements are forbidden [under the Virginia statute] because they are false or misleading in any way. Untruthful speech, commercial or otherwise, has never been protected for its own sake. Obviously, much commercial speech is not provably false, or even wholly false, but only deceptive or misleading. We foresee no obstacle to a State's dealing effectively with this problem. The First Amendment, as we construe it today, does not prohibit the State from insuring that the stream of commercial information flow cleanly as well as freely.

Va. State Bd. of Pharmacy, 425 U.S. at 771, 96 S. Ct. at 1830.

A few years later, in Central Hudson Gas & Electric Corp. v. Public Service Commission of New York, 447 U.S. 557, 100 S.Ct. 2343, 65 L.Ed.2d 341 (1980), the Court reviewed a state regulation, emanating from the days of the OPEC oil embargo in 1973, that prohibited electric utilities from advertising to promote the use of electricity. The regulation was sustained in the state courts, but the Supreme Court found that it violated the First Amendment because the complete suppression of speech was more extensive than necessary to further the State's interest in energy conservation. After reviewing its prior holdings, the Court summarized the test to be applied:

> In commercial speech cases, then, a four-part analysis has developed. At the outset, we must determine whether the expression is protected by the First Amendment. For commercial speech to come within that provision, it at least must concern lawful activity and not be misleading. Next we ask whether the asserted governmental interest is substantial. If both inquiries yield positive answers, we must determine whether the regulation directly advances the governmental interest asserted, and whether it is not more extensive than is necessary to serve that interest.

Central Hudson, 447 U.S. at 566, 100 S. Ct. at 2351 .

The "*Central Hudson* formula" was applied in Posadas de Puerto Rico Associates v. Tourism Company of Puerto Rico, 478 U.S. 328, 106 S.Ct. 2968, 92 L.Ed.2d 266 (1986). In an opinion written by (then) Justice Rehnquist, who had dissented in the *Virginia Board of Pharmacy* case, the Court upheld a ban on advertising of casino gambling directed at Puerto Rican residents. After concluding that the reduction of demand for casino gambling by residents was a substantial government interest, the court basically deferred to the legislature in applying the third and fourth prongs of the *Central Hudson* test.

By 1996, the majority of the Supreme Court appeared to take a more protective stance toward commercial speech, while showing less deference toward governmental regulation. While the Justices were somewhat divided, the overall tenor seemed to be that the Court should apply the *Central Hudson* test with more vigor, i.e., that the governmental body seeking to restrict nondeceptive commercial speech would have a heavier burden of justification.

44 LIQUORMART, INC. v. RHODE ISLAND

Supreme Court of the United States, 1996.
517 U.S. 484, 116 S.Ct. 1495, 134 L.Ed.2d 711.

JUSTICE STEVENS delivered the opinion of the Court with respect to Parts I, II, VII, and VIII. JUSTICES KENNEDY, SOUTER, and GINSBURG also joined Parts III and V, JUSTICES KENNEDY and GINSBURG also joined Part IV, and JUSTICES KENNEDY, THOMAS and GINSBURG also joined PART VI.

I

In 1956, the Rhode Island Legislature enacted two separate prohibitions against advertising the retail price of alcoholic beverages. The first applies to vendors licensed in Rhode Island as well as to out-of-state manufacturers, wholesalers, and shippers. It prohibits them from "advertising in any manner whatsoever" the price of any alcoholic beverage offered for sale in the State; the only exception is for price tags or signs displayed with the merchandise within licensed premises and not visible from the street. The second statute applies to the Rhode Island news media. It contains a categorical prohibition against the publication or broadcast of any advertisements—even those referring to sales in other States—that "make reference to the price of any alcoholic beverages."

* * *

II

Petitioners 44 Liquormart, Inc. (44 Liquormart), and Peoples Super Liquor Stores, Inc. (Peoples), are licensed retailers of alcoholic beverages. Petitioner 44 Liquormart operates a store in Rhode Island and petitioner Peoples operates several stores in Massachusetts that are patronized by Rhode Island residents. Peoples uses alcohol price advertising extensively in Massachusetts, where such advertising is permitted, but Rhode Island newspapers and other media outlets have refused to accept such ads.

Complaints from competitors about an advertisement placed by 44 Liquormart in a Rhode Island newspaper in 1991 generated enforcement proceedings that in turn led to the initiation of this litigation. The advertisement did not state the price of any alcoholic beverages. Indeed, it noted that "State law prohibits advertising liquor prices." The ad did, however, state the low prices at which peanuts, potato chips, and Schweppes mixers were being offered, identify various brands of packaged liquor, and include the word "WOW" in large letters next to pictures of vodka and rum bottles. Based on the conclusion that the implied reference to bargain prices for liquor violated the statutory ban on price advertising, the Rhode Island Liquor Control Administrator assessed a $400 fine.

After paying the fine, 44 Liquormart, joined by Peoples, filed this action against the administrator in the Federal District Court seeking a declaratory judgment that the two statutes and the administrator's implementing regulations violate the First Amendment and other provisions of federal law. The Rhode Island Liquor Stores Association was allowed to intervene as a defendant and in due course the State of Rhode Island replaced the administrator as the principal defendant. The parties stipulated that the price advertising ban is vigorously enforced, that Rhode Island permits "all advertising of alcoholic beverages excepting references to price outside the licensed premises," and that petitioners' proposed ads do not concern an illegal activity and presumably would not be false or misleading. The parties disagreed, however, about the impact of the ban on the promotion of temperance in Rhode Island. On that question the District Court heard conflicting expert testimony and reviewed a number of studies.

In his findings of fact, the District Judge first noted that there was a pronounced lack of unanimity among researchers who have studied the impact of advertising on the level of consumption of alcoholic beverages. He referred to a 1985 Federal Trade Commission study that found no evidence that alcohol advertising significantly affects alcohol abuse. Another study indicated that Rhode Island ranks in the upper 30% of States in per capita consumption of alcoholic beverages; alcohol consumption is lower in other States that allow price advertising. After summarizing the testimony of the expert witnesses for both parties, he found "as a fact that Rhode Island's off-premises liquor price advertising ban has no significant impact on levels of alcohol consumption in Rhode Island."

* * * Acknowledging that it might have been reasonable for the state legislature to "assume a correlation between the price advertising ban and reduced consumption," he held that more than a rational basis was required to justify the speech restriction, and that the State had failed to demonstrate a reasonable " 'fit' " between its policy objectives and its chosen means.

The Court of Appeals reversed. It found "inherent merit" in the State's submission that competitive price advertising would lower prices and that lower prices would produce more sales. Moreover, it agreed with the reasoning of the Rhode Island Supreme Court that the Twenty-first Amendment gave the statutes an added presumption of validity.

[The U.S. Supreme Court granted certiorari and reversed the Court of Appeals].

* * *

IV

* * * Rhode Island errs in concluding that all commercial speech regulations are subject to a similar form of constitutional review simply because they target a similar category of expression. The mere fact that messages propose commercial transactions does not in and of itself dictate the constitutional analysis that should apply to decisions to suppress them.

When a State regulates commercial messages to protect consumers from misleading, deceptive, or aggressive sales practices, or requires the disclosure of beneficial consumer information, the purpose of its regulation is consistent with the reasons for according constitutional protection to commercial speech and therefore justifies less than strict review. However, when a State entirely prohibits the dissemination of truthful, nonmisleading commercial messages for reasons unrelated to the preservation of a fair bargaining process, there is far less reason to depart from the rigorous review that the First Amendment generally demands.

* * *

It is the State's interest in protecting consumers from "commercial harms" that provides "the typical reason why commercial speech can be subject to greater governmental regulation than noncommercial speech." Yet bans that target truthful, nonmisleading commercial messages rarely protect consumers from such harms. Instead, such bans often serve only to obscure an "underlying governmental policy" that could be implemented without regulating speech. In this way, these commercial speech bans not only hinder consumer choice, but also impede debate over central issues of public policy.

Precisely because bans against truthful, nonmisleading commercial speech rarely seek to protect consumers from either deception or overreaching, they usually rest solely on the offensive assumption that the public will respond "irrationally" to the truth. The First Amendment directs us to be especially skeptical of regulations that seek to keep people in the dark for what the government perceives to be their own good.

V

* * *

The State argues that the price advertising prohibition should nevertheless be upheld because it directly advances the State's substantial interest in promoting temperance, and because it is no more extensive than necessary. Although there is some confusion as to what Rhode

Island means by temperance, we assume that the State asserts an interest in reducing alcohol consumption.

* * *

We can agree that common sense supports the conclusion that a prohibition against price advertising, like a collusive agreement among competitors to refrain from such advertising, will tend to mitigate competition and maintain prices at a higher level than would prevail in a completely free market. Despite the absence of proof on the point, we can even agree with the State's contention that it is reasonable to assume that demand, and hence consumption throughout the market, is somewhat lower whenever a higher, noncompetitive price level prevails. However, without any findings of fact, or indeed any evidentiary support whatsoever, we cannot agree with the assertion that the price advertising ban will significantly advance the State's interest in promoting temperance.

Although the record suggests that the price advertising ban may have some impact on the purchasing patterns of temperate drinkers of modest means, the State has presented no evidence to suggest that its speech prohibition will significantly reduce marketwide consumption. Indeed, the District Court's considered and uncontradicted finding on this point is directly to the contrary. Moreover, the evidence suggests that the abusive drinker will probably not be deterred by a marginal price increase, and that the true alcoholic may simply reduce his purchases of other necessities.

* * *

The State also cannot satisfy the requirement that its restriction on speech be no more extensive than necessary. It is perfectly obvious that alternative forms of regulation that would not involve any restriction on speech would be more likely to achieve the State's goal of promoting temperance. As the State's own expert conceded, higher prices can be maintained either by direct regulation or by increased taxation. Per capita purchases could be limited as is the case with prescription drugs. Even educational campaigns focused on the problems of excessive, or even moderate, drinking might prove to be more effective.

As a result, even under the less than strict standard that generally applies in commercial speech cases, the State has failed to establish a "reasonable fit" between its abridgment of speech and its temperance goal. It necessarily follows that the price advertising ban cannot survive the more stringent constitutional review that *Central Hudson* itself concluded was appropriate for the complete suppression of truthful, nonmisleading commercial speech.

VI

The State responds by arguing that it merely exercised appropriate "legislative judgment" in determining that a price advertising ban would best promote temperance. Relying on the *Central Hudson* analysis set forth in *Posadas de Puerto Rico Associates* . . ., Rhode Island first argues that, because expert opinions as to the effectiveness of the price advertising ban "go both ways," the Court of Appeals correctly concluded that the ban constituted a "reasonable choice" by the legislature. * * *

* * *

The reasoning in *Posadas* does support the State's argument, but, on reflection, we are now persuaded that *Posadas* erroneously performed the First Amendment analysis. The casino advertising ban was designed to keep truthful, nonmisleading speech from members of the public for fear that they would be more likely to gamble if they received it. * * *

* * *Instead, * * * we conclude that a state legislature does not have the broad discretion to suppress truthful, nonmisleading information for paternalistic purposes that the *Posadas* majority was willing to tolerate. * * *

* * *

VIII

Because Rhode Island has failed to carry its heavy burden of justifying its complete ban on price advertising, we conclude that R.I. Gen. Laws §§ 3–8–7 and 3–8–8.1 (1989), as well as Regulation 32 of the Rhode Island Liquor Control Administration, abridge speech in violation of the First Amendment as made applicable to the States by the Due Process Clause of the Fourteenth Amendment. The judgment of the Court of Appeals is therefore reversed.

It is so ordered.

[JUSTICE SCALIA's concurring opinion is omitted]

JUSTICE THOMAS, concurring in Parts I, II, VI, and VII, and concurring in the judgment.

In cases such as this, in which the government's asserted interest is to keep legal users of a product or service ignorant in order to manipulate their choices in the marketplace, the balancing test adopted in *Central Hudson* should not be applied, in my view. Rather, such an "interest" is *per se* illegitimate and can no more justify regulation of "commercial" speech than it can justify regulation of "noncommercial" speech.

* * *

JUSTICE O'CONNOR, with whom THE CHIEF JUSTICE, JUSTICE SOUTER, and JUSTICE BREYER join, concurring in the judgment.

* * *

Both parties agree that the first two prongs of the *Central Hudson* test are met. Even if we assume, *arguendo*, that Rhode Island's regulation also satisfies the requirement that it directly advance the governmental interest, Rhode Island's regulation fails the final prong; that is, its ban is more extensive than necessary to serve the State's interest.

* * *

Rhode Island offers one, and only one, justification for its ban on price advertising. Rhode Island says that the ban is intended to keep alcohol prices high as a way to keep consumption low. By preventing sellers from informing customers of prices, the regulation prevents competition from driving prices down and requires consumers to spend more time to find the best price for alcohol. The higher cost of obtaining alcohol, Rhode Island argues, will lead to reduced consumption.

The fit between Rhode Island's method and this particular goal is not reasonable. If the target is simply higher prices generally to discourage consumption, the regulation imposes too great, and unnecessary, a prohibition on speech in order to achieve it. The State has other methods at its disposal—methods that would more directly accomplish this stated goal without intruding on sellers' ability to provide truthful, nonmisleading information to customers. Indeed, Rhode Island's own expert conceded that " 'the objective of lowering consumption of alcohol by banning price advertising could be accomplished by establishing minimum prices and/or by increasing sales taxes on alcoholic beverages.' " A tax, for example, is not normally very difficult to administer and would have a far more certain and direct effect on prices, without any restriction on speech. The principal opinion suggests further alternatives, such as limiting per capita purchases or conducting an educational campaign about the dangers of alcohol consumption. The ready availability of such alternatives—at least some of which would far more effectively achieve Rhode Island's only professed goal, at comparatively small additional administrative cost—demonstrates that the fit between ends and means is not narrowly tailored....

* * *

It is true that *Posadas* accepted as reasonable, without further inquiry, Puerto Rico's assertions that the regulations furthered the government's interest and were no more extensive than necessary to serve that interest. Since *Posadas*, however, this Court has examined more searchingly the State's professed goal, and the speech restriction put into place to further it, before accepting a State's claim that the speech restriction satisfies First Amendment scrutiny. In ... these cases we declined to accept at face value the proffered justification for the State's regulation, but examined carefully the relationship between the asserted goal and the speech restriction used to reach that goal. The closer look that we have required since *Posadas* comports better with the purpose of the analysis set out in *Central Hudson*, by requiring the State to show that the speech restriction directly advances its interest and is narrowly tailored. Under such a closer look, Rhode Island's price-advertising ban clearly fails to pass muster.

* * *

Notes

1. For discussions of the evolution of the commercial speech doctrine, *see* Elizabeth Blanks Hindman, The Chickens Have Come Home to Roost: Individualism, Collectivism and Conflict in Commercial Speech Doctrine, 9 Comm. L. & Policy 237 (2004); and Earl M. Maltz, The Strange Career of Commercial Speech, 6 Chapman L. Rev. 161 (2003).

2. The *44 Liquormart* case involved a restriction on so-called "vice" advertising, i.e., advertising of a product that could be considered harmful to consumers. Another "vice" product that has been the subject of various advertising restrictions aimed at reducing consumption is tobacco. The federal Cigarette Labeling and Advertising Act of 1965, and its subsequent iterations, pursued an approach of requiring warnings on tobacco products and in advertisements. 15 U.S.C. §§ 1331–40. In 1998, the major American tobacco companies reached a settlement agreement with 46 state attorneys general. In return for the withdrawal of the state lawsuits against the manufacturers, the companies agreed to a monetary settlement, and also agreed to accept many restrictions on their advertising, including bans on outdoor advertising, bans on the distribution of brand-name merchandise, bans on the use of cartoons in advertising, etc. *See* James P. Nehf, The Advertising and Marketing Mandates of the Attorney General Tobacco Settlement, 7 Consumer L. J. 281 (1999); Gary L. Wilson & Jason A. Gillmer, Minnesota's Tobacco Case: Recovering Damages without Individual Proof of Reliance under Minnesota's Consumer Protection Statute, 25 Wm. Mitchell L. Rev. 567 (1999). A summary of the state settlement is available at the website of the National Association of Attorneys General, <http://www.naag.org/tobac/glance.htm.> Presumably the tobacco manufacturers who agreed to the settlement have waived their First Amendment rights to object to the advertising restrictions.

3. A set of Massachusetts restrictions on the advertising and marketing of tobacco products, including a near-ban on outdoor advertising of these products, was struck down by the Supreme Court in Lorillard Tobacco Co. v. Reilly, 533 U.S. 525, 121 S.Ct. 2404, 150 L.Ed.2d 532 (2001). The ruling was based mostly on federal preemption by the Cigarette Labeling and Advertising Act. Justice O'Connor writing for the Court, however, did apply the *Central Hudson* criteria to restrictions on smokeless tobacco and cigar ads, which are not covered by the federal legislation, and struck them down on First Amendment grounds because they were more restrictive than necessary. In *Lorillard,* the Massachusetts Attorney General had enacted an array of regulations restricting advertising and marketing of tobacco products, all aimed at discouraging use by underage consumers. The Court agreed with the State AG that the state's interest was substantial, and that a ban on outdoor advertising could directly advance that state interest. However, the regulations banning most outdoor advertising of tobacco and severely restricting advertising both inside and outside stores that sell tobacco products, were more extensive than necessary, because they "would constitute nearly a complete ban on the communication of truthful information about [tobacco products] to adult consumers." 533 U.S. at 562, 121 S. Ct. at 2425.

Problem 1–14

Last year the City of Goodberg enacted an ordinance that reads as follows:

> **Alcoholic beverage advertisements**. No person may place any sign, poster, placard, device, graphic display, or any other form of advertising that advertises alcoholic beverages in publicly visible locations. In this section "publicly visible locations" include outdoor billboards, sides of buildings, and free standing signboards.

> This ordinance shall not apply to: any sign placed on the inside or outside of the immediate premises used by licensed sellers of alcohol; any sign on alcohol product packaging; any sign contained on any personal item of clothing or apparel; any sign on any book, magazine, newspaper, or similar publication; any sign on property adjacent to an interstate highway, and any sign in an area zoned for industrial or commercial use.

The City Council took into consideration numerous studies showing that there was a correlation between alcohol advertising and underage drinking, and that drinking is prohibited for persons under the age of twenty-one. The Council also documented the social evils of underage drinking, including deaths, automobile accidents, etc. The ordinance contains an exception for industrial and commercial areas, thus attempting to narrow the ban on outdoor advertising to areas where "minors live, attend school, attend church and engage in recreational activities."

A major beer manufacturer that relies heavily on outdoor advertising to promote its product has challenged the Goodberg ordinance in court. The manufacturer claims the ordinance violates its First Amendment rights and should be struck down. The manufacturer points out that all their ads contain a health warning required by federal law, and that many of their billboards include public service messages, such as "Let's stop underage drinking before it starts."

Which party has the better case on the First Amendment issue, and why?

See Penn Advertising of Baltimore, Inc. v. Mayor and City Council of Baltimore, 101 F.3d 332 (4th Cir. 1996); Anheuser–Busch, Inc. v. Schmoke, 101 F.3d 325 (4th Cir. 1996). *See also* Michael Clisham, Commercial Speech, Federal Preemption, and Tobacco Signage: Obstacles to Eliminating Outdoor Tobacco Advertising, 36 Urban Lawyer 713 (2004).

2. WHAT IS COMMERCIAL SPEECH?

As noted in the preceding subsection, the present status of commercial speech vis-à-vis the First Amendment appears to be that it is protected but to a lesser degree than other forms of speech, such as political commentary. In political debate, even false statements are protected, on the theory that the marketplace of ideas will counteract any harm. However, for commercial speech, based as it is on the consumer interest in the free flow of accurate information in the marketplace for goods and services, there is no protection for deceptive or misleading commercial speech. Nondeceptive commercial speech can be regulated if the restriction is able to pass the now more vigorous *"Central Hudson"* test. Thus there is much at stake in drawing the line between commercial and noncommercial speech. Consider the following case.

BOLGER v. YOUNGS DRUG PRODUCTS CORP.

Supreme Court of the United States, 1983.
463 U.S. 60, 103 S.Ct. 2875, 77 L.Ed.2d 469.

[Youngs engaged in the manufacture, sale and distribution of contraceptives. Youngs publicized its products in part through unsolicited mailings, including information pamphlets discussing the desirability and availability of prophylactics in general or Youngs' products in particular. When informed in 1979 by the Postal Service that its mailings violated a federal law against the mailing of contraceptive advertisements (39 U.S.C. 3001(e)(2)), Youngs brought an action for declaratory and injunctive relief. Since the Postal Service had conceded that the prohibition would not extend to noncommercial speech, it became necessary for the Court to determine whether the informational pamphlets were or were not commercial speech.]

* * *

Most of appellee's mailings fall within the core notion of commercial speech—"speech which does 'no more than propose a commercial transaction.'" *Virginia State Board of Pharmacy v. Virginia Citizens Consumer Council, Inc.*, 425 U.S., at 762, 96 S.Ct., at 1825, quoting *Pittsburgh Press Co. v. Human Relations Comm'n*, 413 U.S. 376, 385, 93 S.Ct. 2553, 2558, 37 L.Ed.2d 669 (1973). Youngs' informational pamphlets, however, cannot be characterized merely as proposals to engage in commercial transactions. Their proper classification as commercial or non-commercial speech thus presents a closer question. The mere fact that these pamphlets are conceded to be advertisements clearly does not compel the conclusion that they are commercial speech. See *New York Times v. Sullivan*, 376 U.S. 254, 265–266, 84 S.Ct. 710, 718–719, 11 L.Ed.2d 686 (1964). Similarly, the reference to a specific product does not by itself render the pamphlets commercial speech.[13] Finally, the fact that Youngs

---

13. One of the informational pamphlets, "Condoms and Human Sexuality," specifically refers to a number of Trojan-brand condoms manufactured by appellee and describes the advantages of each type.

The other informational pamphlet, "Plain Talk about Venereal Disease," repeatedly discusses condoms without any specific reference to those manufactured by appellee. The only reference to appellee's products is contained at the very bottom of the last page, where appellee is identified as the distributor of Trojan-brand prophylactics. That a product is referred to generically does not, however, remove it from the realm of commercial speech. For example, a company with sufficient control of the market for a product may be able to promote the product without reference to its own brand names. Or, a trade association may make statements about a product without reference to specific brand names. See, *e.g.,*

has an economic motivation for mailing the pamphlets would clearly be insufficient by itself to turn the materials into commercial speech.

The combination of *all* these characteristics, however, provides strong support for the District Court's conclusion that the informational pamphlets are properly characterized as commercial speech. The mailings constitute commercial speech notwithstanding the fact that they contain discussions of important public issues such as venereal disease and family planning. We have made clear that advertising which "links a product to a current public debate" is not thereby entitled to the constitutional protection afforded noncommercial speech. *Central Hudson Gas & Electric Corp. v. Public Service Comm'n,* 447 U.S., at 563, n. 5, 100 S.Ct., at 2350, n. 5. A company has the full panoply of protections available to its direct comments on public issues, so there is no reason for providing similar constitutional protection when such statements are made in the context of commercial transactions. See *ibid.* Advertisers should not be permitted to immunize false or misleading product information from government regulation simply by including references to public issues.

We conclude, therefore, that all of the mailings in this case are entitled to the qualified but nonetheless substantial protection accorded to commercial speech.

[Applying the *Central Hudson* formula, the Court then concluded that the challenged statutory provisions were more extensive than necessary to protect the government's interests.]

Notes

1.   What factors did the *Bolger* Court consider relevant to the determination of whether or not the pamphlet was commercial speech? Did the Court hold that all the factors needed to be present for a finding of commercial speech?

2.   Since the *Virginia Pharmacy* case was decided in 1976, the FTC has had to defend its actions against First Amendment challenges by advertisers. Since only deceptive or misleading commercial speech can be prohibited without regard to the *Central Hudson* test, the Commission must in effect show that its remedies will affect only the misleading speech of the commercial advertiser. The Commission has been able to withstand First Amendment challenges to: a ban on a misleading trade name, FTC v. National Commission on Egg Nutrition, 517 F.2d 485 (7th Cir.1975), cert. denied, 426 U.S. 919, 96 S.Ct. 2623, 49 L.Ed.2d 372 (1976); a broad cease and desist order affecting products related to the one that had been deceptively advertised, Kraft v. FTC, 970 F.2d 311 (7th Cir. 1992), *supra* Section B(1)(d); and a corrective advertising order, Novartis Corp. v. FTC, 223 F.3d 783 (D.C. Cir.

National Commission on Egg Nutrition v. FTC, 570 F.2d 157 (CA7 1977) (enforcing in part an FTC order prohibiting false and misleading advertising by an egg industry trade association concerning the relationship between cholesterol, eggs, and heart disease). In this case, Youngs describes itself as "the leader in the manufacture and sale" of contraceptives. Brief for the Appellee at 3.

2000), *supra* Section B(1)(g). The "Do–Not–Call" Telemarketing regulation, promulgated in 2003, was also able to withstand First Amendment scrutiny under the *Central Hudson* test, Mainstream Marketing Services, Inc. v. FTC, 358 F.3d 1228 (10th Cir.), *cert. denied* 543 U.S. 812, 125 S.Ct. 47, 160 L.Ed.2d 16 (2004), *infra* Chapter 5, Section B(1).

3. In 2002, the California Supreme Court considered the definition of commercial speech in Kasky v. Nike, Inc., 27 Cal.4th 939, 119 Cal.Rptr.2d 296, 45 P.3d 243 (2002). In that case, a private plaintiff challenged certain statements made by the Nike Corporation in the course of a public relations campaign. Nike was trying to combat media charges that Nike products (athletic shoes and apparel) were being manufactured in Asian factories where workers were forced to suffer inhumane working conditions. Nike made allegedly deliberately false and misleading statements about the working conditions in these factories in press releases, in letters to newspapers, and in a letter addressed to university presidents and athletic directors. The majority opinion of the California Supreme Court, by Justice Joyce Kennard, first summarized the U.S. Supreme Court's stated rationale for withholding First Amendment protection from false or misleading commercial speech:

(1) "the truth of commercial speech is *more easily verifiable by its disseminator*";

(2) "commercial speech is *hardier* than noncommercial speech in the sense that because they act from a profit motive, are less likely to experience a chilling effect from speech regulation", and

(3) the government has a strong interest in preventing harm to consumers stemming from commercial speech.

45 P.3d at 252–53.

Drawing on the *Bolger* case, the California court articulated its own test for defining commercial speech, concluding that Nike's speech was commercial because there was:

(1) a commercial speaker,

(2) an intended commercial audience (*i.e.,* actual and potential purchasers of Nike products); and

(3) the representations were factual representations of a commercial nature (*i.e.,* statements of fact regarding Nike's own business operations).

45 P.3d at 258. Since the California Supreme Court concluded that Nike had engaged in commercial speech, it was subject to suit under the California Unfair Competition Law. The United States Supreme Court granted certiorari, and heard oral arguments, only to dismiss the case later on the basis that certiorari had been improvidently granted. 539 U.S. 654, 123 S.Ct. 2554, 156 L.Ed.2d 580 (2003).

For an interesting discussion of the history and parties involved in the *Nike* case, *see* Ronald K.L. Collins & David M. Skover, The Landmark Free–Speech Case That Wasn't: The Nike v. Kasky Story, 54 Case Western Reserve L. Rev. 965 (2004). *Compare* Erwin Chemerinsky & Catherine Fisk, What Is Commercial Speech? The Issue Not Decided in Nike v. Kasky, 54 Case Western Reserve L. Rev. 1143 (2004) (supporting the view that Nike had engaged in commercial speech), with Deborah J. La Fetra, Kick It Up a Notch: First Amendment Protection for Commercial Speech, 54 Case Western Reserve L. Rev. 1205 (2004) (supporting Nike's position).

Problem 1–15

The FTC staff wants to seek a cease and desist order against the "Humane" Cosmetic Association. The Association has claimed in press releases, on talk shows and in letters to department stores, that members of the Association subscribe to standards under which cosmetics are produced without "inhumane" animal testing. The products of Association members are labeled with a "Humane" logo, featuring a picture of a cuddly kitten. A local television station has recently broadcast an investigative report claiming that a "Humane" Association testing center in fact uses animal testing for its products in ways that many of its customers would find inhumane. The FTC staff wants the Commission to issue an order requiring the Association to cease using the trade name, "Humane," and to include in their advertising a "corrective" statement to the effect that they have in fact used animal testing to produce their products. The Humane Cosmetic Association asserts that animal testing in the cosmetic industry is a matter of intense national debate and that the FTC staff's proposed order would prevent it from making its case to the public and would clearly subvert the First Amendment. They also assert that although they use animals in testing cosmetics, they do so in what they consider to be a "humane" way.

(a) The FTC staff seeks your analysis of the First Amendment issues. Is this a case involving "commercial speech" under either the *Bolger* test or the *Nike* test? Does it matter? To what extent is this speech protected by the First Amendment?

(b) Does the FTC staff's proposed disclosure go too far? Do the facts meet the prerequisites for corrective advertising set forth in *Warner-Lambert*? Would a ban on the use of the "Humane" logo be considered more extensive than necessary to cure the potential deception?

(c) The Humane Cosmetic Association pays celebrities and experts to appear on talk shows to discuss how cosmetics can be tested on animals in a humane manner. They are not identified as spokespersons for the Association. The Association also pays actors to spend time in the cosmetic sections of department stores and at pet shows talking to members of the public about how they have chosen to use cosmetic products with the "Humane" logo because of their concerns about animal testing. The actors are told never to reveal that they are being paid for these encounters. Would these activities constitute commercial speech? Are they deceptive? *See* FTC Guides on Endorsements, 16 C.F.R. § 255.5.

Sidebar on Charitable Solicitations

Soliciting for charitable causes has become big business, or at least it is an ever present occurrence, as anyone who has a telephone or receives mail can testify. These campaigns are now increasingly directed by professional fundraisers, and the expenses involved may leave very little of the money collected for the actual work of the charitable organization to which people believe they are contributing. Is this activity a potential fraud on the public that can be regulated in the same manner as other commercial speech?

In a series of cases starting in 1980, the Supreme Court has concluded that charitable solicitations are not commercial speech, even when conducted by professional fundraisers. Furthermore, percentage limits on the amount that must go to actual charitable activities, excluding administrative costs and the costs of the solicitation itself, are unconstitutional because such restrictions could limit protected information dissemination and advocacy activities that are tied up in the solicitation itself. See Schaumburg v. Citizens for a Better Environment, 444 U.S. 620, 100 S.Ct. 826, 63 L.Ed.2d 73 (1980); Secretary of State of Maryland v. Joseph H. Munson Co., 467 U.S. 947, 104 S.Ct. 2839, 81 L.Ed.2d 786 (1984).

While the Court has looked rather favorably on required disclosures in the commercial speech area, it struck down a North Carolina statute that would have required professional fundraisers to disclose the percentage of contributions collected during the previous 12 months that were actually turned over to charity. Riley v. National Federation of the Blind of North Carolina, 487 U.S. 781, 108 S.Ct. 2667, 101 L.Ed.2d 669 (1988). The majority concluded that this disclosure would hamper fundraising efforts, particularly for the small or unpopular charities that rely on professionals and receive a relatively small return due to the difficulty of finding donors. The state could deal with fraud by purported charities through more direct measures. Id. Chief Justice Rehnquist, joined by Justice O'Connor, dissenting, asserted that the statute was an economic regulation with an incidental effect on speech, and thus the court should not have applied any type of heightened scrutiny. The required disclosure was deemed by the dissenting justices as equivalent to mandatory disclosure requirements for securities transactions.

The issue of constitutional protection for charitable solicitations surfaced again in response to the FTC's 2003 amended telemarketing regulations, which include some restrictions on telephone solicitations by charitable organizations. Since the FTC does not have jurisdiction over nonprofit organizations, the regulation applies only to professional fundraisers, or "telefunders," not to charities who use their own staff or volunteers to make their phone calls. The amended regulation requires telefunders to restrict their calls to certain hours of the day, to refrain from making "abandoned calls," to disclose promptly they are seeking donations from a named charity, to transmit their name and number to caller identification services, and to refrain from calling again after an individual has so requested (company-specific "do-not-call" rule). 16 C.F.R. § 310. In 2005, a panel of the Fourth Circuit Court of Appeals upheld the FTC's regulation against a First Amendment challenge. National Fed. of the Blind v. FTC, 420 F.3d 331 (4th Cir. 2005). The Court applied the test used in the *Schaumberg, Munson* and *Riley* cases, but noted that the regulations struck down by the U.S. Supreme Court in those prior cases were more restrictive. The Fourth Circuit concluded:

> [T]he FTC was authorized by Congress to promulgate the TSR [Telemarketing Sales Rule], and we find that the rule is consistent with the First Amendment. Since it is "narrowly drawn" to serve the "strong subordinating interest" of protecting residential peace, the TSR embodies a proper compromise between the important speech interests of charities and the equally important need to protect the public from excessive intrusions into the home.

420 F.3d at 351. The Tenth Circuit had previously upheld the Do–Not–Call Registry of the TSR as applied to non-charities under the *Central Hudson* test. *See* Mainstream Marketing Services, Inc. v. FTC, 358 F.3d 1228 (10th Cir.), cert. denied 543 U.S. 812, 125 S.Ct. 47, 160 L.Ed.2d 16 (2004). See *infra* Chapter 5, Section B(1).

Chapter 2

COMPULSORY DISCLOSURE
OF INFORMATION

SECTION A.   INTRODUCTION

1. DISCLOSURE LAWS IN GENERAL

Chapter 1 concerned the regulation of information that may be voluntarily disclosed to a consumer. Beyond this form of regulation, many laws also *require* that suppliers of consumer products provide customers certain information about those products. Some of these laws are of fairly recent origin; others have been on the books for years. They cover a wide array of transactions and they affect all of our day-to-day lives.

Here is one common example: the nutritional labeling on a box of snack crackers. Are they good for you, or not?

Nutrition Facts

Serving Size 6 Crackers (28g)
Servings Per Container About 10

Amount Per Serving
Calories 120   Calories from Fat 35

	% Daily Value*
Total Fat 4g	6%
Saturated Fat 0.5g	3%
Trans Fat 0g	
Polyunsaturated Fat 2g	
Monounsaturated Fat 1g	
Cholesterol 0mg	0%
Sodium 135mg	6%
Total Carbohydrate 20g	7%
Dietary Fiber 3g	13%
Sugars 0g	
Protein 3g	

Vitamin A 0%	•	Vitamin C 0%	
Calcium 0%	•	Iron 8%	

*Percent Daily Values are based on a 2,000 calorie diet. Your daily values may be higher or lower depending on your calorie needs:

	Calories:	2,000	2,500
Total Fat	Less than	65g	80g
Sat Fat	Less than	20g	25g
Cholesterol	Less than	300mg	300mg
Sodium	Less than	2,400mg	2,400mg
Total Carbohydrate		300g	375g
Dietary Fiber		25g	30g

Mandatory disclosure laws are built on the policy premise that the marketplace works best, in economic terms, if the parties have adequate and accurate information about the transactions into which they enter. There is "market failure," say the policy makers and economists, when critical information is not available to one party (here, the consumer), and that party is therefore vulnerable to overreaching by the other. If the law intervenes to require disclosure of critical information to consumers, the theory goes, consumers will be better able to make rational decisions for themselves among competing products and suppliers. Informed consumers can protect themselves, and there is then less need for the law to regulate the substantive content of consumer contracts and transactions.

The federal Truth in Lending Act (TILA), which we examine below, states this policy premise as follows:

The Congress finds that economic stabilization would be enhanced and the competition among the various financial institutions and other firms engaged in the extension of consumer credit would be strengthened by the informed use of credit. The informed use of credit results from an awareness of the cost thereof by consumers. It is the purpose of this [Act] to assure a meaningful disclosure of credit terms so that the consumer will be able to compare more readily the various credit terms available to him and avoid the uninformed use of credit. . . .

TILA § 102(a), 15 U.S.C.A § 1601(a).

There are dozens of federal and state laws that include elements of mandatory disclosure. Some of the oldest are those created by the Federal Food, Drug & Cosmetic Act, 21 U.S.C.A. § 301 et seq., first enacted in 1938. The regulations under this Act contain specifications as to the labeling of contents and ingredients for food, drugs, and cosmetics. See 21 C.F.R. Parts 101 (food), 201 (drugs), and 701 (cosmetics). The cracker box example, above, is pursuant to 21 C.F.R. § 101.9. There are significant disclosure requirements in federal statutes such as the Magnuson–Moss Warranty Act, the Consumer Leasing Act, the Real Estate Settlement Procedures Act—all of which we encounter later in this book. The common questions when evaluating any of these laws are whether the disclosures (1) contain the right information to help consumers understand, (2) are given at times when the disclosures can influence consumer conduct, and (3) are presented in a way that consumers will comprehend and use them.

This Chapter centers on the Truth in Lending Act (TILA), perhaps the most intricate and controversial mandatory disclosure law ever enacted. If the objective is to provide consumers with the "truth" about credit costs, the challenge is daunting.

2. THE INFORMATION PROBLEM IN THE CREDIT MARKET

Credit costs for a product such as a car or major appliance can be as varied as the price of the product itself. Let's say you are in the market for a state-of-the-art wide-screen plasma TV system. You probably expect prices of TVs to vary widely among stores (or internet vendors). If you shop around, you might save hundreds of dollars on the basic price of the TV. You may gather information about the different brands, features, and prices of TVs you are considering, and some of this information may come as disclosures by the manufacturer or dealer about the quality and performance of the goods you want to purchase. We will look at warranty regulation in Chapter 7. But whatever the cash price of the TV you select, you may also need to finance the purchase. You need *credit*. Your quest for information therefore has a dual aspect: one aspect is the goods or services you wish to acquire; the other is the credit you need to pay for those goods or services.

Problem 2–1

You have picked out the TV you want, at a cash price of $5,000. What information do you need or want about the costs of credit to finance your purchase? You may have several sources of credit available to you for the purchase:

1.   You might use a credit card, perhaps a general-purpose Visa or MasterCard. Assume your Visa card carries a daily periodic rate of .041096%, and permits minimum payments of no less than 3% of the outstanding balance. Your Visa card agreement also provides frequent-flyer miles for purchases made with the card.

2.   Or you might use a "private label" credit card issued by a store, like Circuit City or Wal–Mart, in cooperation with a bank, with a $50 annual fee, a monthly carrying charge of 1.5%, and merchandise credits every year in the amount of 1% of all your purchases.

3.   You might go to a bank, finance company, or credit union and apply for a loan to buy the TV:

(a) The bank offers to loan you the $5,000 in exchange for a $50 application fee and your promise to make 36 monthly payments of $180.76.

(b) The finance company will loan you the $5,000 plus $3,000 to consolidate some other debts, if you agree to make 84 monthly payments of $172.86 and give the lender a second mortgage on your home.

(c) The credit union will loan you only $4,000 (requiring you to make a $1,000 down payment), without any application fee, if you agree to make 24 monthly payments of $184.57.

4.   Or the dealer may sell you the TV on an "installment contract" calling for 60 monthly payments of $143.84, and reserving for the seller/creditor a security interest in the TV. The dealer will then sell and assign your contract to a third-party bank or finance company that will collect those monthly payments from you.

5.   You may have a "home equity line of credit" (HELOC) upon which you can draw a check to pay for the TV. This is a revolving (and replenishing) credit line, like your credit card, but secured by a mortgage on your home. Assume the current interest rate is 8.00%, but the rate charged on HELOCs is variable from time to time based on a contractual index, subject to a maximum rate ceiling, or "cap," of 15.00%. And you can usually deduct from your taxable income interest paid on mortgage-secured loans.

6.   There are still other possibilities. The dealer might be willing to *lease* the TV to you, say for twelve months at a monthly rental of $220.00; at the end of the year, you could either return the TV to the dealer, or renew the lease for another year, or buy the TV from the dealer. Or you could acquire the TV in a "rent-to-own" transaction, in which you rent the TV from week to week, and can return it at any time; but if you make a certain number of rent payments, say $90.00 a week for 78 weeks, the TV is yours to keep.

7.   More dramatically, you might refinance your existing home mortgage, and draw out some of the accumulated "equity," sufficient to pay for the new TV and maybe to pay off some medical bills as well. The

refinanced mortgage note will be payable over thirty years at an interest rate of 6.35%.

All of these are variations on a theme. You will pay over time to enjoy the use of the TV now. Relying only on the information given here, and your instincts, *can you begin to analyze and decide which is the better form of financing*?

- Can you tell at a glance which is the *most attractive* of these credit offerings? Is the most attractive necessarily the *cheapest*?

- What information about credit costs is most important to you, and why? For example, is it the *total dollars* you will pay for the credit? Or the *payment schedule*—the amounts and due dates for payments? Or the *interest rate* that accrues over time? Or the inclusion of a *security interest* in the TV, or a *mortgage* on your home?

- Is there any measure for the cost of credit that can reliably be compared across all of these credit offerings (sort of like the "unit cost" figures often displayed for grocery store products)?

- Do you need additional information to make rational choices about the cost of credit? What information? When and how would you like that information presented to you? Are there aspects of these credit arrangements other than strictly the "cost" of the credit that you would like to know about, such as late charges or prepayment fees? How can you possibly make an "informed" decision about this rather bewildering array of credit options?

One obstacle is the difficulty of direct comparison. How do you compare, for example, the relative costs of (1) the credit union installment loan of $4,000 for two years at a cost ("finance charge") of $429.60, with (2) the private-label credit card charge of 1.5% per month on an average daily unpaid balance (which changes constantly), with (3) the seller's five-year installment plan which costs $3,630.40 in finance charge, with (4) a small loan company's offer to pay for your new TV and consolidate $3,000 of your other bills for only $172.86 a month, or a total of $14,520.24 over seven years?

A second obstacle is that creditors may charge different rates to different customers, depending on their credit histories. "Risk-based pricing," they call this. You may not know what rate you will get until after your loan application has been processed. Some creditors may advertise their rates occasionally, but not always. As a result, price comparison for credit costs cannot be done casually, by looking at price tags, but instead requires asking questions of the potential creditor—or carefully reviewing TILA disclosures.

A third obstacle is that you may not know whether a given creditor will consider you to be creditworthy. (Neither, for that matter, may the creditor, at least not without some investigation.) Further, you are unlikely to know the minimum criteria the creditor uses to determine creditworthiness, and you may have heard of examples of creditor rejections which seemed arbitrary to you. Thus, like many consumers, you might end up approaching creditors somewhat "hat in hand," without knowing whether they will even do business with you. In contrast, you normally expect a seller of goods to do business with *any* buyer who offers cash.

As you study the material in this chapter ask whether these information obstacles have been overcome, or at least reduced, by TILA.

3. ALTERNATIVES TO COMPULSORY DISCLOSURE

Mandatory disclosure laws are used in an enormous variety of situations. There are "health" warnings not only on cigarette packages and x-ray machines and toasters and children's toys, but also on consumer credit contracts, see e.g., U3C § 3.203 ["Do not sign this paper before you read it"]. These warnings and other disclosures have larger purposes such as increasing competition, enhancing consumer safety, or preventing financial over-commitment and bankruptcy. But if these are the real goals, why not regulate them directly instead of relying on disclosure laws? *I.e.*, why not simply require low prices or safe toys, rather than merely warn consumers to watch out for high prices and unsafe toys? Is it sufficient response to say we want to preserve a model of "informed" freedom of contract?

Problem 2–2

An industry of "pay day lending" has emerged in recent years. These are short-term loans, usually small or modest in amount, evidenced by the borrower's post-dated check. For example, if a consumer wants a two-week loan of, say, $200, the consumer will write a check for $240.00 to the lender (the extra $40.00 is the lender's fee). If the loan and fee are not otherwise repaid in two weeks (*i.e.*, by the consumer's next pay day), the lender will deposit and collect the check from the consumer's checking account. These loans can be very expensive: a $40 fee to borrow $200 for two weeks equals an annualized interest rate of 520.00%—yes, five hundred twenty percent!

Assume a state legislature, concerned about possible abuses, is determined to regulate pay-day lending. Several ideas have surfaced: (1) Limit the maximum annual interest rate on these loans to 18%; (2) Require more extensive, bold-print disclosure by lenders about the terms and costs of pay day loans; or (3) Flatly prohibit any loan that is evidenced by a post-dated check.

Can you identify the regulatory and policy implications of each of these approaches? I.e., how will they actually work? Which approach is most likely to be effective "consumer protection"? Cf., Christopher Peterson, Truth, Understanding, and High Cost Consumer Credit: The Historical Context of the Truth in Lending Act, 55 Fla. L. Rev. 807 (2003), suggesting that the credit industry will always opt for more disclosure to fend off legal limitations on the pricing of credit products.

Of course there is a fourth option for the legislature, isn't there? That is to do nothing, and let consumers fend for themselves or rely on broad general restraints on "unconscionable" or "deceptive" practices.

4. ANTECEDENTS OF TRUTH IN LENDING

There were some early efforts by the Federal Trade Commission to deal with the problem of credit disclosure, especially the potential for deception caused by the various non-uniform ways of stating interest rates.

FORD MOTOR COMPANY v. FEDERAL TRADE COMMISSION

United States Court of Appeals, Sixth Circuit, 1941.
120 F.2d 175.

HAMILTON, CIRCUIT JUDGE.

This is a petition by the Ford Motor Company to review an order of the Federal Trade Commission requiring it to cease and desist from the use of the word "six percent" or the figure and symbol "6%" in certain forms of advertising in connection with the cost of, or the additional charge for, the use of a deferred or installment payment plan of purchasing automobiles manufactured by it.

The so-called "six percent plan" of financing the retail sale of automobiles was first used in 1935 by the General Motors Corporation, through its wholly-owned subsidiary, the General Motors Acceptance Corporation and was as follows:

"General Motors Acceptance Corporation
"Reduces Time Payment Costs
"On New Cars
"With a new 6% Plan
"Simple as A, B, C

"A—Take Your Unpaid Balance

"B—Add Cost of Insurance

"C—Multiply by 6%—12 Months' plan

"(One-half of one percent per month for periods more or less than 12 months)

"That's your whole financing cost. No extras. No service fees. No other charges.*

" * In some states a small legal documentary fee is required.

"GMAC announces today a new, economical way to buy any new General Motors car from General Motors dealers all over the United States.

"It's the plan you've been waiting for—a plan you can understand at a glance. It is far simpler and more economical than any other automobile time payment arrangement you've ever tried.

"Actually as simple as A, B, C—this new plan provides for convenient time payments of the unpaid balance on your car—including cost of insurance and a financing cost of 6%. This represents a considerable reduction in the cost of financing car purchases. It is not 6% interest, but simply a convenient multiplier anyone can use and understand. Nothing is added in the way of so-called service or carrying charges. There are no extras. Simply a straightforward, easy-to-understand transaction.

"This single step brings the world's finest cars within reach of thousands who have long needed new cars. When you buy a new Cadillac or Buick, Chevrolet or Pontiac, Oldsmobile or LaSalle, on this new plan, you actually save money!"

* * *

General Motors, through its subsidiaries, published many thousands of advertisements featuring this so-called "6% plan," some with the above explanation, others merely referring to a "6%" plan without explanation.

Other leading automobile manufacturing concerns promptly announced similar plans, all featuring the "6%" plan, determined approximately in the same manner as the General Motors, the first to do so being Chrysler, followed by Nash Motors, Reo, Hudson, Graham–Paige, Packard and the petitioner, all appearing in advertisements in newspapers of general and wide circulation and all featuring in a conspicuous manner, the symbol "6%" or the words "six percent," and all determined in the same manner as the plan of petitioner.

* * *

The "6%" plan was computed in actual practice as follows:

On a new car, the purchase price of which is $643 and on which the purchaser makes a down payment of $243, there is an unpaid balance of $400 due and if the dealer furnishes the insurance, its cost on the above transaction would be $15, the total balance to be paid by the purchaser would be $415 and where this amount is paid according to the 6% plan (or ½ of 1% a month) in eighteen consecutive monthly payments of substantially $25 each, the charge of ½ of 1% a month for 18 months, or 9% on $415 would be $37.35, which, added to the original balance of $415, makes a total sum of $452.35.

This same transaction with an unpaid balance of $415 paid in a like manner at $25 a month over a period of eighteen months on a straight 6% simple interest per annum basis, computed on the declining balances as reduced by monthly installments, would amount to $19.34 interest charge or $18.01 less than the charge made pursuant to petitioner's plan. Comparative tables prepared by an expert accountant in evidence in the case indicated that the credit charge under petitioner's "6%" plan amounted to approximately 11½ simple annual interest.

The 6% plans of all of petitioner's competitors were also computed in the above described manner and the average member of the public was under the impression the "6%" plan as advertised by petitioner and the other manufacturers meant 6% simple interest annually on the remaining balance after deducting each successive monthly payment.

The cars manufactured by petitioner at Dearborn, Michigan, and sold through retail dealers to the retail purchasers thereof throughout the United States and in the District of Columbia are in the regular flow of interstate commerce. The Commission found that the statements contained in petitioner's advertising matter with reference to its "6%" plan had the tendency to mislead and deceive, and did mislead and deceive, a substantial part of the purchasing public into the erroneous belief that petitioner's finance plan or method as outlined contemplates a simple 6% interest charge upon the deferred and unpaid balance of the purchase price of cars and tended to cause, and has caused, the public to purchase automobiles from the petitioner through its dealers and agents because of this mistaken belief, when the actual credit charge, computed in accordance with the "6%" plan, amounts to approximately $11\frac{1}{2}\%$ simple annual interest on the unpaid balance of the installments due on cars sold. It also found that these acts and practices of petitioner tended to unfairly divert trade to the petitioner and its dealers from competitors who correctly represented the cost of the credit charges for purchasing cars on the installment or deferred payment plan and a substantial injury had been done by petitioner to competitors in commerce among and between the various states of the United States and the District of Columbia.

* * *

The relevant portion of Section 5 of the Federal Trade Commission Act as it read at the time the present complaint was issued, Act of September 26, 1914, c. 311, 38 Stat. 717, 719, 720, 15 U.S.C.A. 4057 45, is as follows: "That unfair methods of competition in [interstate and foreign] commerce are hereby declared unlawful."

* * *

Unfair methods of competition as used in the Act may consist generally of false advertising of a product, process or method which misleads, or has the capacity or tendency to mislead, the purchasing public into buying such product, process or method in the belief it is acquiring one essentially different. The question does not depend upon the purpose of the advertisement nor upon the good or bad faith of the advertiser. The point for consideration here is whether, under the facts and circumstances in connection with the publication of the advertisement, the language in and of itself, without regard to good or bad faith, is calculated to deceive the buying public into believing it is purchasing petitioner's cars at one price when in fact it is purchasing them at another. A prerequisite to the application of the statute in any case is the unfair interference with interstate trade and such deception of the public as to cause it to buy and pay for something which it is in fact not getting.

Petitioner contends that the method of competition here complained of is not unfair within the meaning of the Act nor of the foregoing general rule, as it long has been the established practice of automobile manufacturers and vendors of merchandise on the deferred payment plan to charge an advance over what would be charged in a cash sale and that it also has been the common practice of banks and small loan companies to advertise loans with a percentage added to the principal payable over fixed periods without calculating interest upon a declining balance. It also charges that the Federal Housing Administration and the Federal Electric Home and Farm Authority, two governmental agencies, use the same plan. It thus argues that the present advertisements were subject to the interpretation only that petitioner was adding a charge to the cash price of its cars because of the extension of credit to the purchaser.

The practices in the automobile industry or those in similar related enterprises are immaterial, if petitioner's advertisements misled the members of the public into purchasing its cars at a higher cost than they otherwise would have paid.

A method inherently unfair does not cease to be so because the falsity of the public representation has become so well known to those engaged in identical or similar enterprises as to no longer deceive them.

The average individual does not make, and often is incapable of making, minute calculations to determine the cost of property purchased on the deferred payment plan. Mechanization, industrialization, and urbanization have transformed the structure of our society and raised to the proportions of a major social problem, the protection of the installment purchaser against his own ignorance and the pressure of his need.

The present advertisement must be considered from the view of the prospective purchasers of petitioner's cars and, in determining its capacity or tendency to mislead, must be judged from its general fabric, not its single threads.

* * *

The primary consideration in carrying out the purpose of the present Act is the promotion and continuance of free enterprise and competition in interstate commerce. Installment credit in varying forms is widely used in this country in the purchase of many types of property and especially affects the manufacturers of automobiles. No one can deny it is in the public interest in the sale on credit of such devices to prevent the use of methods which have a tendency and capacity to mislead the purchasing public and to unfairly damage the manufacturer's present or potential competitors and that such practices may be restrained. * * * When misleading advertisements attract customers by means of deception perpetrated by the advertiser, it is presumed that business is thereby unfairly diverted from a competitor, who truthfully advertises his process, method or goods.

* * *

Cease and desist orders of the Commission should go no further than reasonably necessary to correct the evil complained of and preserve the rights of competitors and the public and we are of the opinion that the order here did not violate this rule, but was necessary to protect the public against the species of deception alleged in the complaint. The Commission's findings are supported by substantial evidence. Petition denied and order of Commission affirmed.

Notes

1. Since the FTC's order was affirmed, shouldn't that have established a sufficient law of deceptive advertising of credit terms? Why didn't it? Would it have been better to have continued the case law approach to these problems (as in *Ford Motor*), rather than the "affirmative action" approach in TILA? For another example of FTC prosecution of deceptive credit marketing, see Tashof v. Federal Trade Commission, 437 F.2d 707 (D.C.Cir. 1970).

2. Ford used an "add-on" formulation in its advertising, and the FTC found it deceptive when compared with "simple annual" interest. Did the FTC find that consumers understood the "6%" ads to state simple interest? If "add-on" computations were commonplace among auto manufacturers, and others, even in the 1930s, how could Ford's use of this formula constitute an unfair method of competition?

3. As the *Ford Motor* case reflects, before the Truth in Lending Act, perhaps the largest problem in the disclosure of credit costs was lack of uniformity. The National Commission on Consumer Finance (NCCF) described the situation as follows in its 1972 report:

Prior to enactment of TIL, information given consumers about their credit arrangements ranged from very little to what TIL now requires. Most consumers were told the amount of their monthly payments and the due dates. Provisions for additional information varied widely among credit grantors, types of credit, and states.

The greatest lack of uniformity was in the quotation of the amount and rate of the finance charge. Some credit grantors provided neither figure, showing only the number and amount of monthly payments and the dollar sum. While many creditors disclosed the dollar amount of the finance charge or provided enough data so that it could be ascertained, they stated the *rate* of charge in a variety of ways.

(1) In some cases no rate of finance charge was quoted.

(2) Retailers, finance companies and some banks often quoted the rate as a dollar add-on—an expression of the dollar amount of the finance charge per annum in relation to the *initial* unpaid balance. For instance, the finance charge on a new car loan might have been stated as $7 per $100 per year, indicating that on a 3–year loan of $2,000 the dollar amount of the finance charge was $420 ($140 × 3 years). The APR on such a contract is 12.83 percent. Prior to the effective date of TIL, add-on rates were heavily advertised.

(3) Commercial and industrial banks often quoted rates on a discount basis—a statement of dollars per $100 of initial unpaid balance on the assumption that the finance charge was deducted from the face amount of the note at the time credit was extended. A charge of $7 per $100 of initial unpaid balance *discounted* for 3 years is equivalent to an APR of 16.01 percent.

(4) Many consumer finance companies, almost all credit unions, and most commercial banks and retailers offering revolving credit accounts stated a monthly rate applied to a defined balance. Banks and retailers often quoted a rate of 1½ percent applied monthly. If applied to daily unpaid balances from the date of credit extension, as in the case of credit unions, the APR was equivalent to 12 times the monthly rate.

(5) A final procedure was to fragment the finance charge so that part appeared as an add-on or discount rate and part as a flat fee or extra charge. For example, industrial loan companies in Georgia charged 8 percent a year discount (to 18 months) plus a flat fee of 8 percent on the first $600 of initial unpaid balance. Thus a 6–month loan of $500 carried a finance charge of $68.14 or an annual rate of 45.33 percent.

National Commission on Consumer Finance, Consumer Credit in the United States 169–70 (1972). Obviously, comparative shopping was difficult or impossible under these conditions.

SECTION B.   DISCLOSURE IN CREDIT TRANSACTIONS: THE TRUTH IN LENDING ACT

1. BACKGROUND

Disclosure of the costs of credit in consumer credit transactions has been through several phases of development. The *Ford Motor* case illustrates one approach—a statute with very generalized standards ("misleading" or "deceptive") to regulate voluntary disclosures by creditors. Of course, this worked only if creditors chose to advertise, and only as long as they were subject to the then limited jurisdiction of the FTC. The Truth in Lending Act, in contrast, represents the other extreme—comprehensive compulsory disclosure through a detailed statute and regulation.

The first draft of truth in lending legislation, introduced in 1960, would have required creditors simply to disclose the interest rate to be charged as a simple annual rate on a declining balance. The reaction of the consumer credit industry was to ask for clarification, rather than to debate whether compulsory disclosure was warranted at all. The debate focused upon what charges should be considered as within "interest," and how to calculate the appropriate rate.

By 1968, it was apparent that a disclosure law could never be drafted to the degree of certainty that the creditors wanted. Instead, the statute could be made relatively clear for most typical transactions, and the Federal Reserve Board would be given the power to issue regulations to clear up remaining problems or uncertainties. This decision made, the Truth in Lending Act was enacted in 1968, to become effective in 1969, 15 U.S.C.A. § 1601 et seq. The Board issued Regulation Z to fill in the statutory gaps, and it continues to amend Regulation Z and to issue explanatory "Commentary" whenever further ambiguities and uncertainties are discovered. For a critical assessment of the TILA drafting process in the late 1960s, see Edward L. Rubin, Legislative Methodology: Some Lessons From the Truth in Lending Act, 80 Geo. L. J. 233 (1991).

All of this was fine in theory, but the actual experience in the beginning was something else. Together, the statute and regulations were technically complex, and difficult to understand. After a few years, a huge body of case law and administrative interpretations had built up. All this led to "disclosure statements" which kept increasing in length and complexity. Creditors found it nearly impossible to comply, and it became great sport among consumer lawyers to nit-pick disclosure statements for arguable violations. Moreover, there was growing evidence that consumers might not understand them anyway.

These problems led to the Truth in Lending Simplification and Reform Act of 1980 (effective 1982), which is basically the present law. The simplification was intended primarily to reduce the amount of information creditors had to disclose to consumers (particularly for closed-end credit transactions), and to reduce creditor liability for violations of the Act. There is some disagreement as to whether the Simplification Act has accomplished all of its goals. But there is no doubt that it is now easier for creditors to comply and harder for consumers to sue for violations. The case law diminished considerably, although TILA litigation remains active. For analysis of the TILA "simplification" effort, see R. Rohner, Truth in Lending "Simplified": Simplified?, 56 N.Y.U.L.Rev. 999 (1981).

In addition to the "simplification" revisions in 1980, the Truth in Lending Act has been amended a number of times. Significant additions include special protections for credit card holders (the Fair Credit Billing Act, 1974), separate disclosures for consumer leases (the Consumer Leasing Act, 1976), new advance disclosures for credit card solicitations (the Fair Credit and Charge Card Disclosure Act, 1988), special disclosures for home-equity lines of credit (the Home Equity Loan Consumer Protection Act, 1988), and disclosures and other restrictions on high-cost mortgage loans (the Home Ownership and Equity Protection Act, 1994). Some TILA provisions range far beyond mere disclosure, and will surface later in this book.

2.   SOME BASIC PARAMETERS OF THE TRUTH IN LENDING ACT

a.   *TILA as Part of CCPA*

The Truth in Lending Act is Title I of the federal Consumer Credit Protection Act (CCPA). The other CCPA titles include the Fair Credit

Reporting Act (CCPA Title VI), the Equal Credit Opportunity Act (CCPA Title VII), the Fair Debt Collection Practices Act (CCPA Title VIII), the Electronic Fund Transfer Act (CCPA Title IX) B all enacted in the 1970s. The most recent expansion is the Credit Repair Organizations Act (CCPA Title IV), added in 1996. Thus, TILA is but a part of a sweeping federal assault on problems in the financial services marketplace. The existence of all this federal legislation creates a degree of friction with state law which historically dominated the field of consumer protection. We will need to ask at numerous points throughout this book: what is the preemptive effect of federal law on state regulation of the same activity?

b. Sources of TILA Guidance

To work at all in the truth in lending area, you must know more than the TIL statute; you must also become familiar with the Federal Reserve Board's Regulation Z, found officially in 12 C.F.R. Part 226. Regulation Z contains the gory details of the disclosures and other rules creditors must follow. Like the statute, Reg. Z was completely rewritten as of 1982. While it is still quite complex, most students find the regulation easier to read than the statute. The Board has also issued (and continually updates) a lengthy Official Staff Commentary on Reg. Z. The official citation is 12 C.F.R. Part 226, Supplement I. This Commentary is essential for practitioners, since it often gives examples and answers operational questions raised by ambiguities in the regulation.

In interpreting TILA, what weight should the courts give to Reg. Z or the Board's Staff Commentary? Courts have always treated administrative interpretations with a certain degree of deference. After all, an agency that specializes in a particular subject matter is likely to have a good deal of useful insight. After the decision of the United States Supreme Court in Ford Motor Credit Co. v. Milhollin, 444 U.S. 555, 100 S.Ct. 790, 63 L.Ed.2d 22 (1980), however, the Federal Reserve Board's positions have taken on even greater significance in TILA matters. In *Milhollin,* the issue was whether acceleration clauses had to be disclosed in closed-end credit transactions. Neither the statute nor the regulation addressed this issue, and the Courts of Appeal had disagreed. The Board staff, however, had taken the position that this disclosure was not required. The Supreme Court ruled that in all TILA cases, the opinions and interpretations by the Board or its staff should be followed unless they are "demonstrably irrational." 444 U.S. at 565, 100 S.Ct. at 796. As a practical matter, this ruling means that the Board's regulations and commentary are the law.

For comprehensive treatises on TILA, see: Ralph J. Rohner & Fred H. Miller (eds), Truth in Lending (Am. Bar Ass'n, 2000), and Supp. (2005); Elizabeth Renuart & Kathleen Keest, Truth in Lending, 5th ed. (Nat'l Cons. L. Ctr., 2003), and Supp. (2005).

c. Scope and Critical Definitions

TILA disclosures are required in all extensions of "*consumer credit*" by a "*creditor.*" TILA then divides the world of consumer credit into two forms: *"open-end"* and *"closed-end."* Open-end credit is basically revolving credit (like your credit card), where new credit is available as you pay back earlier advances. Closed-end credit is anything else, typified by fixed-term installment loans such as for automobile financing and home mortgages. Look carefully at the definitions of each of these terms in Reg. Z § 226.2. The disclosure rules differ for closed-end and open-end credit; in Reg. Z, Subpart B deals with open-end credit, while Subpart C deals with closed-end. The two most important disclosure items in both open-and closed-end credit are the *"Finance Charge"*—the cost of credit as a dollar amount—and the *"Annual Percentage Rate,"* which expresses the cost of credit as an annualized simple-interest percentage.

TILA exempts certain credit transactions, such as those for business or agricultural credit, and securities and commodities accounts. Reg. Z § 226.3(a) and (d). These exclusions are probably consistent with the notion that TILA applies only to consumer credit, *i.e.,* for personal family or household purposes. TILA also excludes credit transactions over $25,000, except for mortgage transactions. This means that while *any* consumer mortgage transaction, regardless of amount, gets TILA disclosures, some consumer loans will fall outside the $25,000 ceiling. This ceiling may have made sense in 1968, but forty years later, when the average cost of a new car is about $27,000, and credit card lines may easily exceed $25,000, many consumer credit agreements technically fall outside the bounds of TILA coverage. *Query*: Does this mean that upscale car buyers and card holders get no TILA disclosures? Should Congress amend TILA to increase this ceiling? To what level should it be increased?

Note that Congress has given the Federal Reserve Board explicit authority to exempt credit transactions involving certain affluent consumers, i.e., those with annual incomes over $200,000 or net assets of $1,000,000. TILA § 105(g), 15 U.S.C.A. § 1604(g). The Board has declined to grant this waiver option to any consumers regardless of income or assets. *Query*: What is the rationale for exempting wealthy consumers from the protections of TILA? Why do you suppose the Board has not acted on it?

By contrast, alert law students will have noticed that TILA also excludes government-guaranteed student loans. Reg. Z § 226.3(f). What is the rationale for that exclusion?

What is *"credit"* and who is a *"creditor"* subject to TILA disclosure responsibilities? Credit is simply "the right to defer payment of debt or to incur debt and defer its payment." Reg. Z § 226.2(a)(14). The consumer's "right" to defer payment derives from the contract with the creditor, who may be the seller of property or services or a lending institution. A "creditor" is anyone who "regularly extends consumer credit. . . ." Reg. Z § 226.2(a)(17). In most cases these definitions will be easy to apply. But consider:

Problem 2–3

Health Club sells annual memberships for $1,200, payable in six monthly installments of $200 each. *I.e.*, the consumer will pay for the full year membership after six months. The Health Club adds no additional charges for these deferred payments, but does impose a late charge of $10.00 if any payment is overdue. Is this an extension of "credit"? Is the Health Club a "creditor"? If both answers are yes, what does the Health Club disclose as the cost of that credit? See Reg. Z § 226.2(a)(14) and (17). And see Mourning v. Family Publications Services, Inc., 411 U.S. 356 (1973), a landmark decision upholding the application of TILA to transactions payable in more than four installments without an explicit finance charge.

Problem 2–4

Mortgage Broker usually acts purely as an intermediary between a consumer borrower and the lender who makes the mortgage loan. Broker arranges thousands of such loans each year working face to face with consumer applicants. Also, on occasion Broker will "speculate" by making a mortgage loan of its own to a consumer who has difficulty qualifying for a mainstream mortgage; Broker usually does this between 5 and 10 times a year. Is the Broker a "creditor" with respect to the thousands of loans it arranges but does not fund? Is Broker a "creditor" with respect to the 5–to–10 loans it does fund each year? See Reg. Z § 226.2(a)(17)(i) fn. 3.

d. Enforcement and Sanctions for Non–Compliance

Various federal agencies are authorized to enforce TILA requirements, including the Federal Trade Commission and the federal bank regulatory agencies. But what gives TILA real teeth as an enforcement device is the availability of private actions by aggrieved consumers. See TILA § 130(a), 15 U.S.C.A. § 1640(a). A consumer who proves a violation of TILA may recover actual damages in all cases, and *statutory* damages (at least $100 and as much as $2,000) for most violations, plus court costs and attorney's fees. This provides consumers a strong incentive to litigate TILA violations. And creditor violations of TILA are likely to be systemic, e.g., printed forms that fail to make the disclosures sufficiently conspicuous, or not properly treating finance charge components. This is ready-made for class actions across the creditor's whole customer base. In other words, the stakes can be very high in TILA litigation.

3. DISCLOSURE FORMAT: SAMPLE DISCLOSURES

a. Closed-end: Retail Installment Contract

The following is a generic adaptation of the front side of a typical closed-end credit contract, including TILA disclosures. If you have recently bought and financed a car, you have signed something like this. Additional contract provisions are likely to fill the reverse side of the form.

FORM 2-A: CLOSED END DISCLOSURES

ACCT. NO. ___1234___   **MARYLAND VEHICLE RETAIL INSTALLMENT CONTRACT**   DATE ___8/28/06___

Buyer (and Co-Buyer) Name and Address (Include County and Zip Code)	**CREDITOR** Seller Name and Address
John & Mary Smith 123 Oak Drive Anywhere, FR 20000	Crossroads Ford, Inc. 987 Main Street Somewhere, FR 20000

You, the Buyer (and Co-Buyer, if any) may buy the vehicle described below for cash or on credit. The cash price is shown below "Cash Price." The credit price is shown below as "Total Sale Price." By signing this contract, you choose to buy the vehicle on credit under the agreements on the front and back of this contract.

New or Used	Year and Make	Series	Body Style	No. Cyl.	If Truck, GVW (lbs.)	Vehicle Identification Number	Use For Which Purchased	
NEW	2006 MERCURY	SABLE	4 DR	6		29G46FP987	☑ Personal ☐ Commercial	☐ Agriculture ☐ _____

INCLUDING:

☑ Radio   Air ☑ Conditioner   Automatic ☑ Transmission   Power ☑ Steering   ☐ _____   ☐ _____

TRADE-IN: ___1999 CHEV.___ $ 2,200 $ _____
Year and Make   Gross Allowance   Amount Owing

ITEMIZATION OF AMOUNT FINANCED

(1) Cash Price		$ 24,800 (1)
(2) Down Payment		
Manufacturer's Rebate Assigned to Creditor	$ _____	
Cash Down Payment	$ 1,000.00	
Pickup Payment Due _____, 19 _____	$ _____	
Trade-In (Description Above)	$ 2,200.00	
Total Down Payment		$ 3,200.00 (2)
(3) Unpaid Balance of Cash Price (1 minus 2)		$ 21,600.00 (3)
(4) Amounts Paid on Your Behalf		
To Public Officials (i) for license, title & registration fees $_____		
(ii) for filing fees $_____		
(iii) for taxes (not in Cash Price) $ _____	$ _____	
To Insurance Companies for		
Vehicle Insurance	$ _____	
Credit Life Insurance	$ 500.00	
Credit Disability Insurance	$ 200.00	
GAP PROTECTION	$ 400.00	
To ABC Co. _____ for SERVICE CONTRACT _____	$ 700.00	
To _____ for _____	$ _____	
To _____ for _____	$ _____	
Total		$ 1,800.00 (4)
(5) Amount Financed (3 plus 4)		$ 23,400.00 (5)

Amount Financed (The amount of credit provided to you or on your behalf).............................	$ 23,400.00
FINANCE CHARGE (The dollar amount the credit will cost you)...	$ 3,757.74
ANNUAL PERCENTAGE RATE (The cost of your credit as a yearly rate)................ ___7.50%___	
Total of Payments (The amount you will have paid when you have made all scheduled payments).............................	$ 27,157.74

Payment Schedule – Your payment schedule will be:

	Number of Payments	Amount of Each Payment	When Payments are Due
☐	47+	$ 565.78	monthly starting
	1 Final	$ 565.80	10-01-06
☐			

Total Sale Price (The total price of your purchase on credit, including your downpayment of $ 3,200.00   ) $ 30,357.74

Prepayment: You may be entitled to a refund of part of the Finance Charge if you pay off your debt early.
Late Payment: You must pay a late charge on the portion of each payment made more than 10 days late. The charge is 7.5 percent of the late amount of $50.00, whichever is less.
Security Interest: You are giving a security interest in the vehicle being purchased.
Contract: Please see this contract for additional information on security interest, nonpayment, default, the right to require repayment of your debt in full before the scheduled date and prepayment refund.

INSURANCE

A. Vehicle Insurance:

You are required to insure the vehicle. If a charge is shown below, the Creditor will try to buy the coverages checked for the term shown. Coverages will be based on the cash value of the vehicle at the time of loss but not more than the limits of the policy.

☐ Comprehensive

☐ Fire-Theft-Combined Additional Coverage

☐ Term _____ Months (Estimate)

☐ ____ Deductible

☐ ____ Towing and Labor

Premium $ _____

VEHICLE INSURANCE MAY BE OBTAINED FROM A PERSON OF YOUR CHOICE
INSURANCE DOES NOT COVER PERSONAL LIABILITY AND PROPERTY DAMAGE CAUSED TO OTHERS

B. Credit and Other Optional Insurance:

CREDIT LIFE, CREDIT DISABILITY AND OTHER OPTIONAL INSURANCE ARE NOT REQUIRED TO OBTAIN CREDIT AND WILL NOT BE PROVIDED UNLESS YOU SIGN AND AGREE TO PAY THE PREMIUM

☑ Credit Life ___Loyal Ins. Co.___   ___John Smith___ $ 500.00   *John Smith*
                Insurer   Insured(s)   Premium   Signature(s)

☑ Credit   ___Loyal Ins. Co.___   ___John Smith___ $ 200.00   *John Smith*
Disability   Insurer   Insured   Premium   Signature(s)
Credit Life and Credit Disability insurance are for the term of the contract. The amount and coverages are shown in a notice or agreement given to you on this date.

☑ GAP PROTECTION   CROSSROADS FORD   48 Mo. $400.00   *John Smith*
     Type of Insurance   Insurer   Term   Premium   Signature(s)

NOTICE TO THE BUYER: Do not sign this contract before you read it or if it contains any blank spaces. You are entitled to an exact copy of the contract you sign. The law of the state of Franklin applies to this contract including Title 12, Subtitle 10 of the Franklin Commercial Law Article.

Buyer acknowledges receipt of a true and completely filled in copy of this contract at the time of signing.

Buyer ___*John Smith*___   (Co) Buyer ___*Mary Smith*___
Signs   Signs

SEE BACK FOR ADDITIONAL AGREEMENTS

By signing below, the Seller accepts this contract

Seller ___*Henry Jones*___   Title ___*Mgr.*___

Assignment: If no other Assignee is named in a separate assignment attached to this contract the Seller assigns it to Firstbank under the Assignment on the back of this contract.

Seller _____ By _____ Title _____

Problem 2–5

(a) On this form, identify each of the disclosures required under Reg. Z § 226.18. From those disclosures, can you gauge whether Mary and John got a good deal on the car, or the financing, or both? Do the disclosures conform to the format requirements in Reg. Z § 226.17?

(b) Is it possible for Mary and Jim to verify the accuracy of the "APR" and "Finance Charge" from the information disclosed on the form? See OEO Training Program Memorandum, infra.

Problem 2–6

Look at the entry in the bottom of the disclosure "box" that reads: **"Security Interest:** You are giving a security interest in the vehicle being purchased." FirstBank, which buys most of dealer's contracts, would like to add, right after that sentence, the following: "Also, if this contract is assigned to Firstbank, Firstbank will have the right of set-off against deposits kept by BUYER in that bank." Firstbank is uncertain whether a right of set-off is technically a security interest or not, but believes it may be useful to alert bank customers that the bank can debit their checking or savings accounts to recover delinquent car payments. Is there any reason why Firstbank should *not* add that extra sentence? See Reg. Z § 226.17(a), commonly known as the "Federal Box" rule. Cf., Goldberg v. Delaware Olds, Inc., 670 F.Supp. 125 (D. Del. 1987).

Problem 2–7

How much flexibility does the Creditor have in designing the "federal box" of TILA disclosures? Could it shrink the type-face? Could it put the items in a different order? Could it use a different color ink instead of bolding certain items? Could it move the disclosures to just above Buyer's signature? Could it put the disclosures on a separate piece of paper? Is there a safe-harbor form that creditors can use with confidence that it satisfies the "clear and conspicuous" standard? See Reg. Z App. H–1; Official Staff Commentary to Apps. G and H ¶ 1; TILA § 130(f).

b.   *Open–End Credit: Solicitation, Account–Opening, and Periodic Statements*

For the most common form of *open-end* account, credit cards, TILA disclosures are required at several different times. The first form below is a mock-up of a typical pre-screened credit card solicitation disclosure, such as all of us receive in the mail on a regular basis. Along with these disclosures come various promotional pieces touting the value and utility of the card, often inviting the consumer to transfer balances from other card accounts to this one. When the consumer responds to the solicitation and a card account is established, another set of disclosures is required as part of the account-opening agreement. (We do not set out a sample of that full agreement, which is often lengthy and includes information beyond credit cost features.) Then, disclosures about account activity are required to accompany each periodic statement. The second form is the face side of a representative periodic statement.

FORM 2-B: CREDIT CARD SOLICITATION DISCLOSURES

FIRSTBANK IMPORTANT DISCLOSURES

ANNUAL PERCENTAGE RATE (APR) for purchases	**7.9%** (0.02164% daily periodic rate)
Other **APRs**	Balance transfer APR: Same as for purchases Cash advance APR: 19.8% (0.05425%) daily periodic rate)
Variable rate information*	Your purchase APR may vary monthly. The rate will be determined by adding 0.9% to the Prime rate. Rate in effect 12/01/05
Grace period for repayment of the balance for purchases	25 days from the date of the periodic statement on new purchases (provided you have paid your previous balance in full by the due date)
Method of computing the balance for purchases	Average daily balance (including new purchases)
Minimum finance charge	For each Billing Period that your Account is subject to a finance charge, a minimum total **FINANCE CHARGE** of $0.50 will be imposed
Membership fee	$0
Miscellaneous fees	Cash advance fee: $3 Late payment fee: $39 Over-the-credit-limit fee: $29 Balance transfer fee: $5 Returned payment fee: $39

Reasons Your Terms Could Change: Variable rates can go up or down when Prime changes. We reserve the right to change the terms of your account, including APRs and fees, at any time for any reason, including changes to competitive or general economic conditions. If we change your terms for reasons other than when Prime changes, we will notify you in writing of your options in advance, including your right to opt out of certain changes.

How Your Credit History Could Affect Your APRs: We do not engage in a practice known as "universal default." Universal default permits a credit card company to increase your APRs *solely* because you fail to make a payment on a loan with another lender or your credit history contains other negative information. If we increase your APRs for any reason disclosed in the above paragraph, we may review your credit history to determine (a) that we should not increase your APRs, or (b) the level of the increase, if any.

* How Your Variable Rate is Calculated: The Prime rate used to determine your APR is the rate published in the "Money Rates" section of *The Wall Street Journal* on the 25th day of each month, or if not published on that date, then as published on the immediately preceding publication date and will take effect with your billing period ending the following month. If the periodic rate(s) and corresponding annual percentage rate(s) increase, the finance charge will increase and your minimum payment may be greater.

Minimum Payment: Your minimum payment will be any amount greater than your revolving credit line, plus 3% of your outstanding balance. If your balance is less than $10, your minimum payment will equal your balance. **Please remember that APR increases and fees, including late and returned check fees, may increase your minimum payment.**

How We Apply Payments: We will apply your payment to pay off lower-rate balances before paying off higher-rate balances.

TERMS AND CONDITIONS

I am applying to Firstbank for a credit card account. To qualify, I understand:

1) This offer is based on an initial assessment that I met Firstbank's initial criteria for creditworthiness.

2) I must be at least 18 years of age and a U.S. citizen or permanent resident alien to qualify for this offer, unless otherwise specified.

3) I may be ineligible if I have been approved for a previous Firstbank offer.

4) Firstbank maintains the right not to open my account if: a) the information provided as part of my application is incomplete, inaccurate or cannot be verified, or if I no longer meet Firstbank's standards for creditworthiness; b) my name and/or mailing address has been altered; c) Firstbank receives my response after the offer has expired. Firstbank may contact me to obtain or confirm application information within 21 days of the receipt of my application. Firstbank's decision to contact me may be based on my creditworthiness.

5) I may receive offers in the future that offer new account terms. If I accept one of these offers, I will be accepting all of the account terms of the new offer, including any fees such as transfer fees.

With respect to this offer, I acknowledge that:

1) I authorize Firstbank to check my credit and employment history and to answer questions about its credit experience with me.

2) If I am applying for a Transfer Request, I authorize Firstbank to bill my approved Firstbank credit card account for the amount(s) listed for transfers.

   I understand that I am applying for a transfer amount up to the total amount listed on my Transfer Request. I understand Firstbank will advise me if it is unable to process my payment request for any reason. In addition, Firstbank will not be responsible for any charges billed to me for the account(s) requested for transfers and Firstbank will process only those Transfer Requests that can be transferred under my assigned credit line.

3) Arbitration: I understand that the Customer Agreement contains an Arbitration Provision that may limit my legal rights, including my right to go to court, to have a jury trial, and to participate in class actions. I will receive the Firstbank Customer Agreement and am bound by its terms and all future revisions. My agreement terms (for example, rates and fees) are subject to change.

4) This offer is nontransferable and void to residents of GU, PR, VI and all other U.S. dependent areas.

5) The terms of this offer may not be applied to existing Firstbank accounts.

6) Firstbank will retain my response form whether or not it is approved.

7) I understand that the amount of my credit line will be determined by Firstbank after review of my application and other information.

8) An applicant, if married, may apply for a separate account.

9) Certain restrictions apply to the card benefits in this offer. Full details will be mailed to you upon approval.

PRESCREEN & OPT–OUT NOTICE: This "prescreened" offer of credit is based on information in your credit report indicating that you meet certain criteria. This offer is not guaranteed if you do not meet our criteria. If you do not want to receive prescreened offers of credit from this and other companies, call the consumer reporting agencies toll free, 1–888–5–OPT-OUT (1–888–567–8688); or write them individually at: Experian Target Marketing, P.O. Box 919, 701 Experian Parkway B2, Allen, TX 75013; Equifax Options, P.O. Box 740123, Atlanta, GA 30374–0123; Trans Union Corporation, Attn: Marketing Opt Out, P.O. Box 505, Woodlyn, PA 19094–0505.

YOUR BILLING RIGHTS

Keep This Notice For Future Use

This notice contains important information about your rights and our responsibilities under the Fair Credit Billing Act.

Notify us in case of errors or questions about your bill. If you think your bill is wrong, or if you need more information about a transaction on your bill, write to us on a separate sheet as soon as possible at the address listed on your bill. We must hear from you no later than 60 days after we sent you the first bill on which the error or problem appeared. You can telephone us, but doing so will not preserve your rights. In your letter, give us the following information:

1. Your name and account number.

2. The dollar amount of the suspected error.

3. Describe the error and explain, if you can, why you believe there is an error.

   If you need more information, describe the item you are not sure about.

If you have authorized us to pay your credit card bill automatically from your savings or checking account, you can stop the payment on any amount you think is wrong. To stop the payment, your letter must reach us three business days before the automatic payment is scheduled to occur.

Your rights and our responsibilities after we receive your written notice. We must acknowledge your letter within 30 days, unless we have corrected the error by then. Within 90 days, we must either correct the error or explain why we believe the bill was correct.

After we receive your letter, we cannot try to collect any amount you question or report you as delinquent. We can continue to bill you for the amount you question, including finance charges, and you will have to make up any missed payments on the questioned amount. In either case, we will send you a statement of the amount you owe and the date that it is due. If you fail to pay the amount that we think you owe, we may report you as delinquent. However, if our explanation does not satisfy you and you write to us within ten days telling us that you still refuse to pay, we must tell anyone we report you to that you have a question about your bill. And, we must tell you the name of anyone we reported you to. We must tell anyone we report you to that the matter has been settled between us when it finally is. If we don't follow these rules, we can't collect the first $50 of the questioned amount, even if your bill was correct.

Special rule for credit card purchases. If you have a problem with the quality of property or services that you purchased with a credit card and you have tried in good faith to correct the problem with the merchant, you may have the right not to pay the remaining amount due on the property or services. There are two limitations on this right:

(a) You must have made the purchase in your home state or, if not within your home state, within 100 miles of your current mailing address; and

(b) The purchase price must have been more than $50.

These limitations do not apply if we own or operate the merchant, or if we mailed you the advertisement for the property or services.

IMPORTANT INFORMATION ABOUT
YOUR CREDIT CARD ACCOUNT

Finance Charge

1. Transactions which are not subject to a grace period are assessed finance charges 1) from the date of the transaction or 2) from the date the transaction is processed to your account or 3) from the first calendar day of the current billing period. Additionally, if you did not pay the "New Balance" from the previous billing period in full, finance charges continue to accrue to your unpaid balance until the unpaid balance is paid in full. This means that you may still owe finance charges, even if you pay the entire New Balance indicated on the front of your statement by the next statement closing date, but did not do so for the previous month. Unpaid finance charges are added to the applicable segment of your Account Cash advances (the cash advance segment) and special transfers (if your account includes a special transfer segment) may not avoid finance charges.

2. **Cash Advance, Purchase/Other Charges and Special Transfer or Special Purchase Segments (If Your Account Includes a Special Transfer of Special Purchase Segment).** Finance charge is calculated by multiplying the daily balance of each segment of your account (e.g., cash advance, purchase, special transfer, and special purchase) by the corresponding daily periodic rate(s) that has been previously disclosed to you. At the end of each day during the billing period, we apply the daily periodic rate for each segment of your account to the daily balance of each segment. Then at the end of the billing period, we add up the results of these daily calculations to arrive at your periodic finance charge for each segment. We add up the results from each segment to arrive at the total periodic finance charge for your account. To get the daily balance for each segment of your account, we take the beginning balance for each segment and add any new transactions and any periodic finance charge calculated on the previous day's balance for that segment. We then subtract any payments or credits posted as of that day that are allocated to that segment. This gives us the separate daily balance for each segment of your account. However, if you paid the New Balance show on your previous statement in full (or if your new balance was zero or a credit amount), new transactions which post to your purchase or special purchase segments are not added to the daily balances.

   To calculate your total finance charge, multiply your average daily balance by the daily periodic rate and by the number of days in the billing period. Due to rounding on a daily basis, there may be a slight variance between this calculation and the amount of finance charge actually assessed.

3. **Determining Daily Periodic Rates.** Divide the corresponding Annual Percentage Rates by 365 and round to the nearest 1/100th of 1%, not to exceed the maximum allowed by applicable law. If the daily periodic rates and corresponding Annual Percentage Rates increase, the Finance Charge will increase and your minimum payment may be greater. Refer to the IMPORTANT DISCLOSURES for daily periodic rates and Annual Percentage Rates.

Other charges

Copying Charge: $3.00 for a copy of a Periodic Statement and $2.00 for a copy of a transaction (fee imposed per copy).

Important information about procedures for applying for or opening a new account

To help the government fight the funding of terrorism and money laundering activities, Federal law requires all financial institutions to obtain, verify and record information that identities each person who opens an account. What this means for you: When you apply for or open an account, we will ask for your name, address, date of birth and other information that will allow us to identify you.

FORM 2-C: OPEN-END PERIODIC STATEMENT

MARY SMITH & JOHN SMITH   **Account Number: 5656 0077 xxxx yyyy**

Your Firstbank Visa® Classic Card

New Balance	$620.18		
Total Credit Line	$3,000.00	Available Credit	$2,590.00
Cash Limit	$3,000.00	Available Cash	$2,800.00
Overlimit Amount	$0.00	Billing Date	10/09/06
Minimum Payment Due	$28.00	Payment Due Date	10/29/06

24-Hour Customer Service	1.800.555-xxxx	Pay online! Visit
For Lost or Stolen Cards	1.800.555-yyyy	**www.firstbank.com**

TransAmerica Airlines Dividend Miles Summary

Dividend Miles Account Number	747zzzz
Miles Earned on Purchases	500
Total Miles Earned This Cycle	500

Transactions   View recent transactions and pay your bill online at www.firstbank.com.

POST. DATE	TRANS. DATE	REF. NO.	DESCRIPTION	AMOUNT CR=CREDIT	
Sep 17	Sep 15	123	Merchant A, Anytown NY		$100.00
Sep 20	Sep20	456	PAYMENT – THANK YOU	CR	$ 90.00
Sep 23	Sep 24	789	Merchant B, Sometown PA		$150.00
Sep 30	Sep 30	010	Cash Advance (Firstbank ATM)		$200.00
Sep 30	Sep 30	111	Cash Advance Fee		$ 3.00
Oct 3	Oct 5	222	Merchant C, Mytown, CT, mdse return	CR	$ 50.00

Account Summary

Previous Balance		$300.00
Purchases	+	$250.00
Cash Advances	+	$200.00
Other Debits	+	$0.00
Credits	-	$ 50.00
FINANCE CHARGE	+	$ 10.18
Payments	-	$ 90.00
New Balance	=	$620.18

Finance Charge Summary

	Corresponding APR	Daily (D)/Monthly (M) Periodic Rate	Average Daily Balance (ADB)	Minimum (M)/ Periodic (P) Charge
Purchases	18.240%	0.04998%v D	$390.00	$5.85 P
Cash	24.240%	0.06642%v D	$ 66.67	$1.33 P

ANNUAL PERCENTAGE RATE 26.75%   v=Variable

IMPORTANT INFORMATION ABOUT YOUR ACCOUNT

FINANCE CHARGE

Annual Percentage Rate (APR)

Refer to the Finance Charge Summary section of your statement for your current rates. A "v" next to a Periodic Rate means the rate may vary.

If your statement has a Cash Advance Fee, the Annual Percentage Rate will look inflated because we annualize the Cash Advance Fee as if it applies each month over a 12-month period. We do this to meet federal disclosure requirements.

Grace Period on New Purchases (at least 20-days)

"Grace Period" means the period of time during a Billing Cycle when you will not accrue Periodic Finance Charges on certain transactions or balances. There is no Grace Period for Cash Advances or Balance Transfers. If you Pay in Full this Statement's New Balance by its Payment Due Date and if you Paid in Full this Statement's Previous Balance by its Payment Due Date, then you will have a Grace Period during the Billing Cycle that began the day after this Statement's Closing Date on the Purchase portion of this Statement's New Balance.

During a 0% promotional APR period: 1) no Periodic Finance Charges accrue on balances with the 0% promotional APR; and 2) you must pay the Total Minimum Payment Due by its Payment Due Date to maintain the 0% promotional APR.

Periodic Finance Charge Calculation Method – Average Daily Balance (Including New Transactions)

For each day in the Billing Cycle, we take your beginning balance, add any new transactions or other debits (including other fees and charges) and subtract any payments or other credits. This gives us that day's Daily Balance. We multiply this Daily Balance by the Daily Periodic Rate to get your Periodic Finance Charge for that day. We add these Periodic Finance Charges to your Daily Balance to get the beginning balance for the next day.

To get your total Periodic Finance Charge for this Billing Cycle, we add all of the Daily Balance charges and round the sum to the next highest cent. This amount is also equal to the Average Daily Balance multiplied by the Daily periodic rate times the number of days in the Billing Cycle rounded to the next highest cent. To determine an Average Daily Balance, we add your Daily Balances and divide by the number of days in the Billing Cycle.

We do this calculation separately for each feature such as Purchases, Cash Advances, Balance Transfers or Promotional Balances. Periodic Finance Charges begin to accrue from the later of the transaction date or the first day of the Billing Cycle in which the transaction appears.

Account Renewal Information for Open Accounts

If your account has an Annual Fee and it is billed on this Statement, we will reverse the fee if you cancel your account and pay off any existing Balance within 30 days of receipt of this Statement otherwise, the Annual Fee is non-refundable. You may continue to use your account during the 30-day period before you cancel. To cancel, write us at the Billing Inquiries address or call us at the phone number on the front.

Your Liability

Our records show that you are liable for any outstanding balance on this account if your name appears on the front of this statement or you otherwise agreed.

Report a Lost or Stolen Card Immediately

Call the 24-hour toll free number 1.800.555.xxxx. Do not use your account after you report a lost or stolen card.

Lost Credit Card Protection Plan

If you have questions about your enrollment or need to file for benefits, please call the applicable toll free number below (Monday-Friday, 7:00 a.m.-10:00 p.m. Central Time):
Cardholder Security Plan- 1.888.555.yyyy; Payment Protection Plan- 1.888.555.0056

Service for International Calling

Dial the AT&T Direct access code for the country you are in and dial 1.888.555.zzzz. For a list of access codes visit www.firstbank.com/contact and select Credit Cards. You may also call us collect at 1.800.555.qqqq.

Service for Hearing-Impaired (TTY/TDD)

Contact our service for the hearing-impaired at 1.800.555.rrrr.

Pay on-line at www.firstbank.com or mail your payment to:
Firstbank, PO BOX xxxx, METROPLOLIS, NJ 07xxx

BILLING RIGHTS SUMMARY

STATEMENT DISCLOSURE:

In Case of Error or Billing Inquiries

If you think your bill is wrong, or if you need more information about a transaction on your bill, *you must write to us (on a separate sheet) at PO Box xxxx, Metropolis, NJ 07xxx as soon as possible to preserve your rights.* We must hear from you no later than 60 days after we sent you the first bill on which the error or problem appeared. In your letter, give us the following information:

- Your name and account number
- The dollar amount of the suspected error
- Describe the error and explain, if you can, why you believe there is an error

You do not have to pay any amount in question while we are investigating, but you are still obligated to pay the parts of your bill that are not in question. While we investigate your questions, we cannot report you as delinquent or take any action to collect the amount you question.

Special Rule for Credit Card Purchases

If you have a problem with the quality of goods or services that you purchased with a credit card, and you have tried in good faith to correct the problem with the merchant, you may not have to pay the remaining amount die on the goods or services. You have this protection only when the purchase price was more than $50 and the purchase was made in your home state or within 100 miles of your mailing address (if we own or operate the merchant, or if we mailed you the advertisement for the property or service, all purchases are covered regardless of the amount or location of purchase).

IMPORTANT CREDIT BUREAU REPORTING INFORMATION REQUIRED BY FEDERAL LAW TO BE DISCLOSED TO YOU

WE MAY REPORT INFORMATION ABOUT YOUR ACCOUNT TO CREDIT BUREAUS. LATE PAYMENTS, MISSED PAYMENTS OR OTHER DEFAULTS ON YOUR ACCOUNT MAY BE REFLECTED IN YOUR CREDIT REPORT.

Problem 2–8

On the "solicitation" form, Form 2–B, identify each of the disclosures required under Reg. Z § 226.5a(b). Then, assuming the consumer accepts the card offer, review the account-opening disclosures the consumer will receive as prescribed in Reg. Z § 226.6. Which of these two sets of disclosures—at the solicitation stage, and again at account opening—is more comprehensive? Will the credit-cost information in the account-opening disclosures always match that in the solicitation disclosures? If *yes*, what is the point of requiring redundant disclosures? If *no*, what is the use of early "solicitation" disclosures if the actual terms of the account may be different?

Problem 2–9

On the periodic statement, Form 2–C, identify each of the disclosures required under Reg. Z § 226.7. To what extent do these disclosures correspond to those made at the solicitation and account-opening stage? To what extent do they differ, and why?

From this statement, answer the following:

1.   Is there a "free ride" or grace period? If so, how long is it? Why would a creditor let customers have a free ride? Is it really free?

2.   What credit shopping purpose is served by the periodic statement?

3.   Do you understand the method used to compute the unpaid balance on the account? How does it work?

4.   How is the finance charge calculated? Does the creditor simply multiply the outstanding balance by the periodic rate? (Which outstanding balance?) Do you think that a stated APR of 18% will always produce the same amount of finance charge?

5.   If the rate is 18% on purchases, and 24% on cash advances, how can the composite APR be 26.75%? See Firstbank's explanation in the "Annual Percentage Rate" section on the second page of the form.

Problem 2–10

Recall that the closed-end disclosures must generally all be contained in a separate "federal box." Are there equivalent requirements for the format of open-end disclosures? Reg. Z § 226.5(a). What explains any differences?

4.   CLOSED–END AND OPEN–END CREDIT DISTINGUISHED

From the forms just reviewed it is clear that there are significant differences between "open-end" and "closed-end" disclosures. The distinction is important, because the form, the content, and the timing of the required disclosures are different for each type. As noted above, the critical definition is that for "open-end credit," Reg. Z § 226.2(a)(20), because "closed-end credit" is defined as any "consumer credit other than open-end credit."

Most types of consumer credit are easy to classify. A closed-end transaction usually involves a single loan or advance of funds, often in a purchase money transaction such as a new car loan or a home mortgage. An open-end transaction, on the other hand, is a revolving account. Here, the parties agree in advance that the borrower may engage in repeated transactions, and may also replenish or increase the amount of credit available by repayment.

Sometimes the line between open-end and closed-end is not so clear:

MYERS v. FIRST TENNESSEE BANK, N.A.

United States District Court, M.D. Alabama, Northern Division, 2001.
136 F.Supp.2d 1225.

ALBRITTON, CHIEF JUDGE.

I.   INTRODUCTION

This cause is before the court on a ... Motion for Summary Judgment filed by First Tennessee on January 31, 2001.

The Plaintiffs, Brenda Myers and Clausezill Myers, . . . claim that Home Cable Concepts of Tennessee, Inc. ("Home Cable") and First Tennessee Bank, N.A. ("First Tennessee") violated the Truth in Lending Act ("TILA"). . . . This court granted a Motion to Dismiss Home Cable from the case without prejudice on February 14, 2000.

* * *

For reasons to be discussed, the Motion for Summary Judgment is due to be DENIED. . . .

III. FACTS

Brenda and Clausezill Myers purchased a satellite dish from Home Cable which was financed by First Tennessee. The sale was solicited by a door-to-door salesman named Jim Campbell who, according to the Plaintiffs, represented that the satellite dish would be paid off in two years at a monthly payment of $59.95. The Plaintiffs were issued a private label credit card. The disclosures given to the Plaintiffs complied with open end financing disclosure requirements under TILA, but not closed end disclosure requirements. The Plaintiffs state that when Brenda Myers received her second bill, she realized that the financing was not as she expected. Brenda Myers states in her deposition that she complained to First Tennessee and that representatives of Home Cable asked her to sign a release of liability, and when she did not, they took her receiver. First Tennessee subsequently credited the full amount charged to the Myers' account and refunded their only payment.

First Tennessee is a national banking association. Home Cable was engaged in the retail sales of satellite television equipment. Home Cable transferred its financing of satellite purchases from Bank One to First Tennessee when the two entered into a Private Label Revolving Credit Plan Agreement. The agreement was not exclusive. Customers could also purchase the satellite systems by paying cash or using other credit cards. The private label revolving credit accounts generally were opened with a credit limit at least $200 higher than the amount of the initial transaction to allow the customer to have additional credit for the next year's programming or maintenance charges.

Randall Hutchinson is a senior vice-president with First Tennessee. Hutchinson oversaw the development of the private label credit card with Home Cable. In his deposition, he states that the additional purchases contemplated by First Tennessee in giving open end credit disclosures in connection with the financing of the satellite dish were programming and service. The Plaintiffs contend that First Tennessee did not reasonably anticipate that these additional purchases would be made on the private label credit card.

IV. DISCUSSION

[T]he Plaintiffs bring a TILA claim. The Plaintiffs contend that First Tennessee violated TILA by characterizing the credit transaction between First Tennessee and the Plaintiffs as an open end credit transaction and providing the disclosures which are required for an open end transaction, when First Tennessee should have provided closed end disclosures.

An open end credit transaction is one in which the creditor reasonably contemplates repeated transactions. Under the defining regulation, Regulation Z, open end credit means credit extended under a plan in which:

> (i) The creditor reasonably contemplates repeated transactions;

> (ii) The creditor may impose a finance charge from time to time on an outstanding unpaid balance; and

> (iii) The amount of credit that may be extended to the consumer during the term of the plan (up to any limit set by the creditor) is generally made available to the extent that any outstanding balance is repaid.

The Official Staff Commentary to this regulation gives further guidance, specifically with regard to the repeated transaction element. The Official Staff Commentary states that "the credit plan must be usable from time to time and the creditor must legitimately expect that there will be repeat business rather than a one-time credit extension." 12 C.F.R. Pt. 226.2(a)(20)–3. Also, the fact that particular consumers do not return for further credit extensions does not prevent a plan from having been properly characterized as open end. The Official Staff Commentary further states that the criterion regarding repeated transactions is a question of fact to be decided in the context of the creditor's type of business and the creditor's relationship with its customers.

The Plaintiffs in this case also point out that there was a proposed amendment to the Official Staff Commentary which was never adopted. Under the proposed commentary, there were five factors to consider including whether the credit line is limited to the purchase of items not likely to be purchased in multiples, whether the credit was established to purchase a designated item, and the amount of the purchase compared to the credit line, the extent to which a creditor reasonably solicits customers with its line of credit to make additional purchases under the credit line, whether the creditor has information on consumers with the credit line showing that consumers have made repeat purchases. *See* 62 Fed. Reg. 64,769, 64,772 (Dec. 7, 1997). An example given of when a creditor was not likely to reasonably assume repeated transactions was where there was a $5,000 credit line to purchase a $4,500 satellite dish. After receiving public comment on the proposed amendment, the Federal Reserve Board expressed criticism of creditors' failing to disclose the finance charge in the "financing of used automobiles and the door-to-door credit sales of satellite dishes, water treatment systems, and home improvement contracts," but withdrew its proposal, stating that it would be infeasible to formulate a clear rule to differentiate between legitimate and illegitimate open end credit programs. See Benion v. Bank One, Dayton, *N.A.*, 144 F.3d 1056, 1059 (7th Cir.1998) (citing 63 Fed. Reg. 16, 669, 16,670 (April 6, 1998)).

There are several cases decided by federal courts which have examined the reasonableness of a creditor's expectation of repeat transactions under facts similar to the facts in this case. One of these cases was decided by another judge in this district. See Perry v. Household Retail Services, 953 F.Supp. 1370 (M.D.Ala.1996), summary judgment granted on other grounds upon reconsideration by, Canaday v. Household Retail Servs., *Inc.,* 119 F.Supp.2d 1258 (M.D.Ala.2000)(De Ment, J.). In *Perry,* the plaintiffs brought a TILA claim challenging the disclosures made with regard to the financing of a satellite dish purchase. The court concluded that a question of fact was raised as to reasonableness which was sufficient to defeat the defendant's motion for summary judgment.

The Seventh Circuit analyzed a case in which Bank One offered a private label credit card to plaintiffs who bought a satellite dish from an authorized dealer. *Benion,* 144 F.3d at 1057. The card had a credit limit a few hundred dollars above the purchase price of the satellite dish and could be used at any of hundreds of authorized retail dealers in the products. The Seventh Circuit reasoned that although the card was issued to purchase a "big ticket" item, the most likely subsequent purchases would be of television sets and programming and would be much less expensive, and the credit limit was set just above the purchase prices of the initial purchase, these and other factors were of marginal relevance and "at worst they could be thought to assume that repeat purchases were expected and to be quibbling merely over the amount of those purchases." The court further rejected the argument that the proposed addition to the Official Staff Commentary was dispositive, stating that "[i]f the Board cannot formulate such a rule in the exercise of its expert administrative discretion, we surely cannot formulate it as a matter of statutory interpretation." The case was before the court on cross motions for summary judgment, and the Seventh Circuit affirmed a grant of summary judgment to the defendant.

The *Benion* decision was followed in a district court in the Seventh Circuit. See Speakman v. Household Retail Services, 1999 WL 515500, No. 97–C–1913 (N.D.Ill. July 14, 1999). In *Speakman,* two married couples who resided in Alabama alleged that the defendant violated TILA by not giving closed end disclosures when they purchased vinyl exterior siding for their homes. The card issued to the plaintiffs could be used at any of the defendant's retail dealers. The court granted summary judgment in favor of the defendant on the reasonableness issue.

In Long v. Fidelity Water Systems, 2000 WL 760328, No. C–97–20118 RMW (N.D.Cal. March 16, 2000), the plaintiffs alleged that the defendant sold water purification systems to homeowners using door-to-door practices which were deceptive because they failed to include the proper TILA disclosures. The court examined the evidence before it, stating that repeat transactions account for 2–3% of the total dollar volume of transactions on the accounts and approximately 1% of the accounts generate a repeat transaction in any month. The court framed the issue before it as whether no rational jury could conclude that it was unreasonable for the defendants to contemplate repeat transactions based on that data. The court also examined the proposed Official Staff Commentary, which specifically refers to the door-to-door sale of water treatment systems as a transaction which concerned the Federal Reserve Board when the total finance charge is not disclosed. The court, relying on *Benion,* determined that no bright line rule distinguishing legitimate open end credit plans from plans which are actually closed end credit plans designed to evade TILA disclosure requirements, can be created as a matter of statutory interpretation based on the number or dollar volume of repeat transactions. Relying in part on the *Perry* decision from this district, the court concluded that summary judgment could not be granted on the reasonableness issue.

First Tennessee relies heavily on the *Benion* and *Speakman* decisions, but does not address the *Long* decision. First Tennessee has argued that it received information from Home Cable that during its arrangement with Bank One, Home Cable had customers who renewed programming with it at a rate of 50% and that the percentage of its customers who financed the additional purchases on the private label credit card was 35%. First Tennessee states, therefore, that there is uncontested evidence that it anticipated repeat customers. Of course, while it may be uncontested that First Tennessee anticipated repeated use of the private label credit card, the inquiry before this court is whether that anticipation was reasonable. Although First Tennessee argues that because the programming obtained at the time of the original purchase would only last one year, it was reasonable to believe that customers would make repeat purchases on the card, that does not necessarily mean that it would be reasonable to conclude that additional programming would be purchased on the First Tennessee revolving credit card.

Under the Official Staff Commentary on TILA regulations, "the criterion regarding repeated transactions is a question of fact to be decided in the context of the creditor's type of business and the creditor's relationship with its customers." 12 C.F.R. Pt. 226.2(a)(20)–3. Questions of fact are generally inappropriate issues for summary disposition. Significantly, the issue in applying the first criterion is an objective reasonableness inquiry, which is generally treated as an issue appropriately resolved by the trier of fact ... The authority for departing from this general rule and making the reasonableness determination as a matter of law is *Speakman,* and to a lesser extent *Benion.* This court will first determine, therefore, whether this case is sufficiently similar to *Speakman* and *Benion* to cause this court to conclude that it must decide the reasonableness issue in First Tennessee's favor as a matter of law.

While First Tennessee contends that the facts of this case are indistinguishable from *Benion* and *Speakman* in any material respect, there are facts in this case which are relevant to a determination of reasonableness which distinguish this case from *Benion* and *Speakman.* For instance, in both *Benion* and *Speakman,* there were retail stores at which the plaintiffs could make additional purchases on the private label credit cards. In fact, the *Benion* court made a point of stating, after citing to the proposed amendment to the Official Staff Commentary cited above, that its case involved the sale of satellite dishes, but not their door-to-door sale. While First Tennessee states that Home Cable had operations in other states, there is no evidence to establish that there were retail stores at which additional programming, or other purchases, could be made. Hutchinson testified in his deposition that Home Cable is the only merchant he is aware of that had done door-to-door sales. Hutchinson Deposition, page 7. Kelly Morrell, the Metro Sales Manager for Middle Tennessee for First Tennessee stated in her deposition that she knew that Home Cable sold satellite dishes door-to-door and did not have a store front or retail business.

Also, the *Speakman* court placed great significance on the fact that the defendants adequately evaluated the likelihood of repeat purchases by looking not only at the past add-on rate of the particular company, but also by looking at other repeat purchase rates at seven other businesses. In this case, the evidence before the court is that First Tennessee only obtained information from Home Cable and did not obtain any information as to past repeat sales from Bank One, which had formerly offered credit for Home Cable purchases, or apparently from other companies engaged in similar credit plans. First Tennessee argues that Bank One would not have shared the information with a competitor. While that may be a factor to be considered in the reasonableness inquiry, the depth of investigative efforts is still a factual difference between this case and *Speakman*.

In addition, the *Benion* court also placed significance on efforts by the lender to promote repeat purchases through advertising. The *Benion* court described the advertising efforts in that case as "an aggressive marketing strategy designed to promote repeat purchases." *Id.* at 1058. While not finding such an aggressive strategy in its case, the *Speakman* court noted that advertising was conducted by the retailer. While First Tennessee says that it pursued an aggressive marketing strategy, it points only to evidence of the terms of its agreement with Home Cable. This court has been pointed to no evidence of advertising in this case, and the Plaintiffs in fact assert that no such advertising was included in monthly statements by First Tennessee.

Considering all of the circumstances of the financing arrangement in this case in the light most favorable to the non-movant, while there are factual similarities between this case and *Speakman* and *Benion*, the court must conclude that the circumstances of this case make it distinguishable from those cases, so that reasonableness cannot be determined as a matter of law.

While there are also factual differences between this case and the *Long* decision, in both *Long* and this case the initial purchase was made from a door-to-door salesperson. Moreover, this court finds the analysis in *Long* persuasive. TILA and its interpretive regulations are ambiguous as to the amount of repeat transactions which are required before it becomes reasonable for a creditor to expect repeat transactions. The court agrees with the *Long* court that the fact, recognized in *Benion,* that the Federal Reserve Board does not feel it appropriate to establish a bright line to distinguish legitimate open end and close end credit plans also means that a court also cannot formulate such a bright line rule. The *Benion* court did not have to decide the issue of whether the absence of a bright line rule should have precluded the district court from granting summary judgment in its case, because the plaintiff in that case did not want to present the issue to a jury. While the *Speakman* court granted summary judgment, this court does not agree with the *Speakman* court that because the court cannot conclude that the defendants acted unreasonably, summary judgment is due to be granted the defendants. Instead, this court agrees with the *Long* and *Perry* courts that where, as here, the evidence could support either a finding of reasonableness or unreasonableness, summary judgment is due to be denied. Accordingly, the court concludes that the circumstances of the credit card plan at issue in this case, which are distinct from the facts in *Benion* and *Speakman* in significant ways, raise a genuine issue of material fact as to reasonableness which precludes summary judgment in this case.

V. CONCLUSION

For the reasons discussed, it is hereby ORDERED as follows:

* * *

... The Motion for Summary Judgment is DENIED.... The case will proceed on the Brenda and Clausezill Myers' statutory and actual damages claims under TILA and on the class members' statutory damages under TILA.

Notes & Questions

1. The issue of "spurious open-end credit" has been around since the beginning of TILA, but surfaced dramatically in a number of cases in the 1990s. As this case indicates, whether a credit arrangement is genuinely open-end or not is a fact question that centers on the reasonableness of the creditor's expectation of repeat business under the credit plan. Since the court here denied summary judgment, that issue remains alive in the case. What evidence is most persuasive on the issue? Can you distinguish this case from *Benion*, where Judge Posner affirmed a grant of summary judgment to the defendant creditor?

2. The forms set out in the prior section show the difference between the disclosures for open-end and closed-end credit. Is either set of disclosures better—more informative—than the other? What information is provided in open-end that is missing in closed-end, and vice versa?

The implication in the *Myers* case is that the open-end disclosures are somehow inferior or less complete. Is that so?

3. As we have seen, the closed-end disclosures are generally given only once, at the inception of the transaction. Open-end credit customers, on the

other hand, may get preliminary disclosures before they apply, another set of disclosures when the account is opened, and then a separate set of disclosures along with each periodic (monthly) statement. Does the accumulation of disclosures in open-end credit make up for any limitations in their content?

Problem 2–11

Geraldine submitted an application to Secondbank to borrow funds to purchase a condominium unit. Secondbank lent Geraldine $100,000 through two separate loans pursuant to the bank's "80–20" loan program. The first loan was a closed-end, thirty-year loan for $80,000 (80% of the condo's value). The second loan was an open-end $20,000 "home equity line of credit." This second loan was initially fully used to cover the other 20% of the purchase price, but would replenish and be reusable as Geraldine paid down the balance. Each loan was secured by a separate mortgage on the condo unit. (The 80–20 loan program was attractive to customers like Geraldine because it avoided the need for expensive private mortgage insurance.) Secondbank gave Geraldine two sets of TILA disclosure forms, closed-end disclosures for the $80,000 loan, and open-end disclosures for the $20,000 line of credit. Geraldine now sues Secondbank, and argues that this arrangement amounts to improper (usurious) "loan splitting," and that the combined loans should be disclosed together so as to state a combined APR for the entire $100,000. How should the court rule? Cf. Rendler v. Corus Bank, N.A., 272 F.3d 992 (7th Cir. 2001).

Problem 2–12

"Credit unions" are financial institutions, like banks, but their customers must share a "common bond" of membership (employment, neighborhood, or other affinity relationship). Assume that University Employees Credit Union offers its members a comprehensive credit "plan" that provides a credit card and also permits the member to borrow for any purpose, including car loans, home improvement loans, and even purchase-money mortgages and home equity lines of credit. The plan is set up as a single open-end account, and open-end disclosures are made accordingly, including periodic statements showing balances outstanding on each sub-account. Is this legitimate, or spurious, open-end credit? See Reg. Z Commentary ¶ 2(a)(20)–3.

QUERY: All of our discussion of TILA disclosures to this point assumes conventional paper documentation. But increasingly merchants and lenders are marketing their credit products on the Internet. Many financial institutions are offering by computer an array of financial services that include loan processing and documentation, as well as periodic account statements accessible through the bank's web site. How should the law assure that the timing and format of electronic TILA disclosures satisfy the rules of Regulation Z, particularly the requirements that disclosures be "clear and conspicuous" and "in a form the customer may keep"? To what extent may a creditor require its customers to accept electronic disclosures? See Reg. Z § 226.36.

Problem 2–13

Firstbank operates a very large credit card program, and chafes every month at the amount it must spend to prepare, print, and mail paper statements to all of its cardholders. The bank would like to encourage its customers to accept monthly billing statements over the Internet. The bank would probably do this by posting all the relevant information on its web page, and customers could access it by entering an appropriate password or PIN. Or the bank might send each cardholder a monthly e-mail statement. The bank asks you to develop a checklist of issues the bank will need to address in shifting from paper to electronic TILA disclosures. For starters, consider the requirements that the disclosures must be "clear and conspicuous" (and "more conspicuous" for the APR and Finance Charge), and "in a form that the consumer may keep." Moreover, TILA requires the card issuer to "furnish" periodic statements; does this allow the bank to shift responsibility to the customer to initiate a monthly inquiry? How should the bank deal with the possibility that the consumer's computer may malfunction, or that the bank's own system may crash or fail? Could the bank go so far as to *require* all of its cardholders to maintain computer access to receive disclosures from the bank? Or at least start charging customers a monthly fee if they insist on receiving paper statements?

5.   TIMING—WHEN MUST DISCLOSURES BE GIVEN?

The Truth in Lending Act's preamble emphasizes that its purpose is "to assure a meaningful disclosure of credit terms so that the consumer will be able to compare more readily the various credit terms available to him and avoid the uninformed use of credit." To accomplish this, it would seem necessary to put the disclosures into the consumer's hands at a time when there is a realistic opportunity to use them for comparative shopping.

In evaluating the materials that follow, consider: (1) when in fact does the TILA require the disclosures to be made; and (2) as of that time, how useful are they to the consumer?

The general rules on timing of TILA disclosures are found in Reg. Z §§ 226.5(b) (for open-end credit) and 226.17(b) (for closed-end credit).

SPEARMAN v. TOM WOOD PONTIAC–GMC, INC.

United States Court of Appeals, Seventh Circuit, 2002.
312 F.3d 848.

ILANA DIAMOND ROVNER, CIRCUIT JUDGE.

Mary Spearman purchased a car from Tom Wood Pontiac–GMC, Inc. ("Tom Wood"), and financed the purchase through the dealership. The Truth in Lending Act ("TILA") requires that certain information be disclosed to a consumer in writing in a form the consumer may keep prior to the consummation of a credit transaction. Spearman concedes that Tom Wood provided the necessary disclosures and that the disclosures were in writing. She sued the dealership, however, asserting that the disclosures were not in a form she could keep and that the disclosures were not made prior to the consummation of the transaction. After considering Spearman's deposition, the sole piece of evidence submitted in cross motions for summary judgment, the district court granted judgment in favor of Tom Wood. We affirm.

I.

In July 1999, Spearman went to the Tom Wood dealership and discussed the purchase of a car with a salesman. Within a few days of August 26, 1999, she executed a "Retail Installment Contract and Security Agreement" ("Contract") in connection with the purchase of a 1997 Chrysler Sebring from Tom Wood. The Contract contained a section dedicated to notices required by TILA. Spearman does not dispute that the section of the Contract titled "Truth in Lending Disclosures" contained all of the disclosures required by TILA. The Tom Wood salesman presented the Contract to Spearman in quadruplicate form, sealed across the top. The pages of the form were not labeled to indicate the intended recipient of each copy. One of the four copies was intended for Spearman, and as soon as she reviewed and signed the Contract, the salesman removed Spearman's copy and handed it to her. He removed the copy by tearing along a perforation at the top of the document. Spearman was unaware that one of the four copies was intended for her to keep until the salesman handed a copy to her. She testified in her deposition that she would have been uncomfortable tearing out a page and keeping it for herself before signing. The Tom Wood salesman did not give Spearman any other copy of the disclosures before presenting her with the Contract in the form we have described. Before Spearman signed the Contract, the Tom Wood salesman told her that he would try to obtain a better financing rate for her and that if he were able to do so, she could simply execute a new Contract. The salesman did not subsequently offer Spearman a lower financing rate. Spearman conceded that she had no intention of shopping around for a better rate herself. However, she later testified that she would not have signed the Contract had she known she would be held to the rate specified in the Contract.

Spearman sued Tom Wood pursuant to 15 U.S.C. § 1601, et seq. and Federal Reserve Board Regulation Z, 12 C.F.R. § 226.17, for failing to provide the necessary TILA disclosures in writing, in a form the consumer may keep, prior to consummation of the transaction. The district court initially granted judgment in favor of Spearman, finding that the deal was consummated the moment Spearman signed the Contract and that the salesman did not give her a copy she could keep until after signing. Tom Wood moved for reconsideration and the district court reversed course, this time granting judgment in favor of Tom Wood. The court determined that providing the disclosure contemporaneously with consummation was sufficient under TILA and Regulation Z, and that there was no meaningful distinction between tearing off a copy before or after the consumer signed the document. The district court also found that Spearman suffered no actual damages as a result of any purported violation of TILA because she conceded she had no intention of shopping around for a better rate. The court found that our decision in *Brown v. Payday Check Advance, Inc.,* 202 F.3d 987 (7th Cir.2000), *cert. denied,* 531 U.S. 820, 121 S.Ct. 61, 148 L.Ed.2d 27 (2000), precluded Spearman from receiving statutory damages for a violation of section 1638(b)(1). The court therefore held that, because she suffered no damages, Spearman could not prevail on her claim even if she proved a violation of TILA and Regulation Z. The court granted judgment in favor of Tom Wood. Spearman appeals.

II.

* * *

The only question is whether Tom Wood's actions conformed to the highly technical requirements of TILA as expressed in Regulation Z.

TILA requires that a creditor disclose certain facts "before the credit is extended." 15 U.S.C. § 1638(b). The Federal Reserve Board has issued regulations implementing this statute (often referred to as "Regulation Z") and has also issued an Official Staff Commentary providing further explanation. *See* 12 C.F.R. §§ 226.17 and Supp. I; . . . The regulations provide, in relevant part:

> The creditor shall make the disclosures required by this subpart clearly and conspicuously in writing, in a form that the consumer may keep.

12 C.F.R. § 226.17(a).

As for the timing of the disclosures, the regulations provide that "[t]he creditor shall make disclosures before consummation of the transaction." 12 C.F.R. § 226.17(b). The Commentary to the regulations clarifies that the disclosures may appear on the same document with the credit contract (as happened here) so long as they are segregated from other information appearing on the form. The Commentary also explains the timing requirement of the statute in greater detail:

> As a general rule, disclosures must be made before "consummation" of the transaction. The disclosure need not be given any particular time before consummation except in certain mortgage transactions[.]

12 C.F.R. § 226, Supp. I, at 17(b). According to the Commentary, state law governs in determining when the deal is consummated. Consummation generally refers to the time when the consumer becomes contractually obliged on the credit arrangement. 12 C.F.R. § 226, Supp. I, at 2(a)(13). The Commentary specifies that a credit transaction is not consummated at the time the underlying sale is final but rather at the time the consumer becomes obligated to accept a particular credit arrangement. *Id.; Janikowski,* 210 F.3d at 767 (TILA disclosures must

be given before the consumer becomes contractually obligated on a credit transaction).

Spearman does not object to the content or placement of the disclosures, claiming only that they were not provided in a form she could keep before consummation of the transaction. In particular, she complains that she did not know she could keep a copy of the disclosures prior to consummation, that she did not feel comfortable tearing off a copy of the unlabeled, bound, multi-page packet, and that Tom Wood did not offer her the single page copy of the disclosures until after she signed the Contract. Spearman objects that the district court opinion places the burden on the consumer to know her rights and affirmatively take steps to assure the creditor's compliance in contravention of the transition in Congressional policy from "Let the buyer beware" to "Let the seller disclose." *Mourning v. Family Publications Service, Inc.,* 411 U.S. 356, 377, 93 S.Ct. 1652, 36 L.Ed.2d 318 (1973). Spearman argues that she was deprived of the opportunity to shop around for a better deal with Tom Wood's deal in hand for comparison.

For the sake of clarity, we will address the two main parts of Spearman's argument separately. Parsing out the requirements of the statute and regulations, the disclosures must be made (1) before consummation and (2) in a form the consumer may keep. As we noted above, the disclosures may be made in the same document as the credit agreement so long as they are properly segregated. Moreover, the disclosure need not be given any particular time before consummation. Thus, the creditor may fulfill the timing requirements of TILA and Regulation Z by providing the consumer with a copy of the contract containing the appropriate disclosures moments before the consumer signs the contract. Tom Wood fulfilled this timing requirement by giving Spearman four copies of the disclosures in the form of the four-part Contract moments before she signed.

Spearman's complaint is that the disclosures were not *in a form she could keep* until after she signed the Contract and her copy was separated out. But a commonsense understanding of the transaction defies this contention. The Tom Wood salesman handed Spearman four copies of the disclosures before consummation of the deal. Spearman testified that she reviewed the Contract before signing it and that no one told her she could not keep it. Indeed, Spearman has presented no evidence that she was not free to keep all or part of the packet the salesman handed her. At that point, she was in physical possession of all four copies and there is no evidence in the record that the salesman would have taken them back. Although Spearman testified that she did not know she could keep this document (or any part of it) and that she felt some discomfort over tearing out a page, the only evidence in the record demonstrates that her reluctance to keep the document given to her was idiosyncratic. TILA does not require a creditor to explain a borrower's rights in this situation. Under Spearman's view of the evidence, the salesman would have been required to hand over the disclosures and then say, for example, "This is yours to keep." TILA imposes no such obligation.

Before signing, the evidence shows only that the entire packet was Spearman's to keep. The subsequent acts of the salesman demonstrated that, after signing, at least one copy of the document was in fact Spearman's to keep. After Spearman signed the Contract, the salesman removed the three copies for the dealership and again handed Spearman her copy of the document. In other words, the Tom Wood salesman gave Spearman the required disclosures and there is no evidence he would have taken them back if she had declined to sign at that time. There was nothing so unusual about the form of the disclosure that an average consumer would not understand he or she could keep the packet, even without signing. The document had been filled out to reflect the buyer, the seller, the specific automobile and all of the financial terms relating to the sale. Once filled out, the form was useless for any transaction other than the one proposed with Spearman. Moreover, the disclosures were not made, for example, on a large sign posted in the dealership's business office or in a bound book or in some other form that an average consumer would be reluctant to keep. Rather, the disclosures were contained on a four-part carbonless form much like forms that consumers encounter every day, when placing an order, for example. The fact that multiple copies were available would, we think, make an average consumer *less* reluctant to take a copy (or even the whole packet) for herself. Spearman herself provides the most likely explanation for why she did not take a copy of the Contract without signing. She had no intention of shopping around for better rates. Tom Wood did all it was required to do when it gave Spearman a copy of the disclosures in a form she could keep before she signed the credit deal.

We might have a different case if Spearman tried to keep the four-part form and the salesman told her she could not, or if the salesman attempted to repossess all or part of the packet. The only evidence in the record, though, indicates that the dealership handed over a document Spearman could keep. Because we find that Tom Wood did not violate TILA or Regulation Z, we need not address Spearman's other argument that she is entitled to statutory damages even though she admittedly suffered no actual damages because she had no intention of shopping for a better deal. We accordingly decline to reconsider our ruling in *Brown v. Payday Check Advance, Inc.*, 202 F.3d 987 (7th Cir.2000).

AFFIRMED.

Notes

1. Is it possible to "consummate" a contract when only one party is bound to it? Isn't that the holding in this case?

2. Suppose that Mary Spearman had spent several hours with the salesman, looking at numerous cars on the lot, taking several for a test drive, negotiating for the price of the car and its accessories, and bargaining for the value of her trade-in. After getting the OK from Mary, and from the sales manager, the salesman printed out the contract and TILA disclosures. Mary looked over the proffered contract and disclosures, and decided she

would like to shop elsewhere for better terms. She picked up the unsigned four-page contract document and turned to leave the dealership. What does your imagination tell you would be the reaction of the salesperson and the sales manager? For a collection of humorous stories about the retail automobile business, written by an experienced practitioner in the field, see Thomas B. Hudson, Car Law (Counselor Library 2006).

3.   Should TILA be amended to require that the disclosures include the statement: **"You may take this document away with you before you sign it."**?

Problem 2–14

(a) Wanda has been shopping for a new car. She finally decided that a new Honda Civic was the "perfect" car for her. At the dealership, she picked out the model and decided on the various special options she wanted included. She bargained with the dealer, and they reached an agreement on the price. At that time, she put down $100 and signed a purchase order, but it had no provisions concerning financing or credit. A few weeks later, Honda delivered the car to the dealership, which in turn called Wanda. When Wanda arrived to pick up her car, the dealer asked her how she wanted to pay for it. Wanda responded that she needed to finance the car, so she filled out a credit application which was approved, signed a purchase money security agreement with the dealer and drove away.

At what point in the transaction must the dealer make the TILA disclosures to Wanda? At that point is Wanda likely to use them for comparison shopping? Are they likely to influence her decision or cause her to change her mind about buying the car? Are they likely to influence her decision or cause her to change her mind about the financing of the car?

(b) Suppose Wanda had executed a complete installment sale contract at the outset, but agreed it was "subject to availability" of the specified model and color from the manufacturer. Dealer left out all the TILA information on the form, and did not sign it. (Dealer would later say he intended to plug in the necessary TILA numbers and sign the contract only when he knew the car was available from the manufacturer and he could use APRs and payment terms prevelant at that time.) Alas, the factory could not supply the particular model, and when Dealer so informed Wanda that the failed condition voided the deal, she was most unhappy. She now sues Dealer for failing to provide the TILA disclosures in the installment sale contract she signed. Dealer argues that since no mutually binding contract ever came into existence, there never was "consummation," and he cannot have violated TILA. Who wins, and why?

Problem 2–15

Velma has also been shopping for a new car, and has picked out exactly the right one, on the dealer's lot and ready for delivery. She signs an installment sale contract which includes TILA disclosures showing, *inter alia*, an APR of 7.5%. She also signs an addendum that provides that the sale is not final until the dealer is able to find a bank or finance company willing to buy Velma's contract at that rate. Dealer cannot get bank or finance company approval on the spot because it is 8:45 on Friday night and those financial institutions are closed (or at least off-line). Velma drives off in the new car, as happy as can be. Four days later Velma gets a call from the Dealer, asking her to stop by at her earliest convenience. When she does, Dealer informs her that "the deal didn't go through" at a 7.5% APR. The best the Dealer could get from any financing source was an APR of 11.3%, which would increase Velma's monthly payment by $50.00. "You have a choice," says Dealer: either rewrite the contract at 11.3% APR, or turn the new car back to the dealer (and pay 25¢ per mile for the mileage she had driven).

What should Velma do? Can Velma insist that Dealer honor the 7.5% APR it "promised" in the TILA disclosures? Has the Dealer violated TILA? Has the Dealer violated any other law you can think of?

Notes

1. *"Spot Delivery."* The dealer practice of delivering cars to customers before the financing is confirmed is called "spot delivery." It helps marketing and is a convenience for customers if the customer is allowed to take delivery of the car before the financing is finalized. In most cases the financing will be approved routinely, and the customer will not have to wait a day or more and then return to the dealership to pick up the car. The practice becomes more ominous, and is referred to as a "yo yo" transaction, when Velma, having once taken delivery, must either surrender the car or agree to higher financing costs.

Read Reg. Z §§ 226.17(b) and 226.2(a)(13). Does TILA determine when "consummation" occurs? Or is this concept dependent upon state contract law? If the latter, will the timing of federally-mandated disclosure vary from state to state?

The Official Commentary to Reg. Z, § 2(a)(13) states:

2(a)(13) "Consummation:

1.   State law governs. When a contractual obligation on the consumer's part is created is a matter to be determined under applicable law; Regulation Z does not make this determination. Consummation does not occur merely because the consumer has made some financial investment in the transaction (for example, by paying a nonrefundable fee) unless, of course, applicable law holds otherwise.

2.   Credit v. sale. Consummation does not occur when the consumer becomes contractually committed to a sale transaction, unless the consumer also becomes legally obligated to accept a particular credit arrangement. For example, when a consumer pays a nonrefundable deposit to purchase an automobile, a purchase contract may be created, but consummation for purposes of the regulation does not occur unless the consumer also contracts for financing at that time.

2. *Credit Card Solicitations.* Increased competition in the credit card market in recent years has led to the widespread use of mass solicitations. Banks and other card issuers mail solicitation brochures to potential customers from prescreened mailing lists. These brochures often tell consumers that they have been "specially selected" and "already approved to enjoy the convenience of a VISA card," and that all they have to do is call the bank at a designated number. When a customer calls, the card and the initial TIL disclosures are typically mailed within a few days.

In the past, these solicitation brochures normally did not contain any of the TIL disclosures, although at times (for example, when the soliciting bank's rates were below those of other banks in the area) they did mention the APR then being charged. Congress thought that consumers should have more information than was typically given to them, so in 1988 it enacted the Fair Credit and Charge Card Disclosure Act. This act added subsections (c) through (g) to TILA § 127, and that law now requires a series of specific disclosures to be made in credit card solicitations. To implement the new law, the Board added a whole new section to Reg. Z, § 226.5a, as well as a couple of new subsections, (e) and (f), to § 226.9.

Problem 2–16

Review the sample solicitation disclosure, Form 2–B, supra. Do you think that the new credit card disclosure rules for solicitations will solve the timing problems? How will they help consumers who take the initiative themselves (rather than responding to a solicitation) when applying for a credit card?

3. Prospective Disclosure of Payoff Periods for Open–End Credit. As we have seen, periodic statements sent to open-end credit customers are largely a reconstruction of account activity during the prior period. But in 2005 Congress amended TILA to add a new, forward-looking disclosure—a "warning" about the dangers of making only minimum payments, and a projection of how many months it would take the consumer to pay off the account balance if the consumer made only minimum payments each month. Bankruptcy Abuse Prevention and Consumer Protection Act, Pub. L. No. 109–8, § 1305 (2005), amending TILA § 127(b), 15 U.S.C. § 1637(b). Consumerists had pressed for this disclosure to help customers understand (and avoid) the long term cost and repayment implications of open-end credit obligations; its inclusion in the bankruptcy "reform" Act was therefore no accident. The new disclosure requirements will take effect only after the Federal Reserve Board has worked out regulations for them, and, at this writing, that regulatory process is still underway.

On the face of it, a heads-up about minimum payments and their consequences *could* be useful to some consumers, if for nothing more than shock value. ["Honey, did you realize it'll take us 66 months to pay off the credit card bill for our new lawn mower?"]. Available data, however, suggests that very few card holders consistently make only the minimum payment (usually 2–3% of the account balance) month after month. How useful is a minimum-payments disclosure to consumers who juggle their repayment pattern from one billing period to the next, or at different times of the year, often quite purposefully? In addition, rather far-fetched estimates are necessary for the disclosure to work; it has to be assumed that the consumer incurs no additional charges on the account, and makes every payment on time with no late fees or other charges. Considering the guesstimate nature of the "unknowns" and "assumptions" that have to go into the disclosure projection, we doubt it will have any measurable deterrent effect on consumer over-extension. Do you agree? If the goal is to prevent consumers from becoming overloaded with long-term credit card debt, wouldn't it be more effective for Congress to increase the portion of the balance that the consumer must pay each month, to, say, 6 or 7%?

6. CREDIT ADVERTISING

The law does not require creditors to advertise prevailing rates or credit terms. But what if creditors do?

When a merchant chooses to advertise credit terms, must the advertising track TILA in terminology and detail? Assuming the ad is accurate, can the merchant tout certain credit features without mentioning others? For example, can an ad promote "6.0% financing," "no money down," or "$250 a month" payment terms?

STATE v. TERRY BUICK, INC.

New York Supreme Court, Dutchess County, 1987.
137 Misc.2d 290, 520 N.Y.S.2d 497.

JAMES D. BENSON, JUSTICE.

This action for an injunction under 15 U.S.C. § 1664 (Truth in Lending Act) General Business Law Article 22–A and CPLR § 6301 enjoining Terry Buick, Inc. from continuing to advertise the terms for credit on vehicles it is selling in an illegal, false and deceptive manner is determined as follows:

In this action, the State of New York sues a retail automobile dealer for a judgment enjoining it from continuing several advertising practices which it claims violate General Business Law §§ 350 and 350—a as well as 15 U.S.C. § 1664(d) and Regulation Z, 12 C.F.R. § 226.24 (Truth in Lending Act). The thrust of the claim is that the defendant did not disclose its payment and financing terms in the sale of automobiles "clearly and conspicuously." At the heart of the controversy are two advertising practices in which the defendant (1) displayed large signs in its showroom window which read "NO MONEY DOWN" "$99 MO" and, (2) the announcement of the actual terms of each sale on 2¼" × ⅜" stickers, legible only upon close inspection, attached to the windshields of vehicles offered for sale.

The proof was clear that the defendant operated an automobile dealership business on Route 9, a very busy public highway in Poughkeepsie. At the time of the events of which the plaintiff complains, the defendant displayed large yellow signs across the street-side face of its building in block letters which read "NO MONEY DOWN INSTANT CREDIT" and in the showroom window beneath it, "$99/MO." The windshields of many of the used cars offered for sale in the yard also bore a large painted sign which read "$99/MO or $199/MO." The record also shows that the defendant attached small stickers to the windshields of each car offered for sale, not legible from the highway, which stated the terms of sale. These announcements showed the stock number of the car, the price, the down payment, the term in months and the average interest rate applied to installment payments. It was not clear whether these stickers were attached before or after the litigation was commenced.

On June 29, 1987, Terry Buick stipulated that it would remove, forthwith, the signs on the building which read "NO MONEY DOWN" and "$99/MO."

The Court viewed the defendant's place of business with the attorneys and examined a number of the windshield stickers. They were legible only upon inspection from a distance of a few feet and set forth the financial details of each offer. Examination of the stickers showed that almost every offering required a down payment to obtain $99 per month financing. Other used cars had only "$99/MO" painted on their windshields. According to the testimony of one witness, the salesman did not know the price of several of such cars. He testified that no cars were offered for sale for $2,000 down and $99 per month.

[TILA] § 1664(d) reads as follows: [Text omitted]

* * *

[NY]   General Business Law § 350 reads:

"False advertising in the conduct of any business, trade or commerce or in the furnishing of any service in this state is hereby declared unlawful."

Section 350–a of that law reads:

"The term "false advertising" means advertising, including labeling, which is misleading in a material respect; and in determining whether any advertising is misleading, there shall be taken into account (among other things) not only representations made by statement, word, design, device, sound or any combination thereof, but also the extent to which the advertising fails to reveal facts material in the light of such representations with respect to the commodity to which the advertising relates under the conditions prescribed in said advertisement, or under such conditions as are customary or usual."

The Court's inspection of the defendant's place of business and its advertising material showed beyond question that the announcement signs were a "come on" designed to lure the eager seeker of a good deal. It also showed that "what you see is not what you get". We have not given the testimony of the undercover agent much weight. It was a contrived tactic practiced upon a relatively guileless salesman by a young woman who pretended to be a purchaser. Her testimony is not necessary, however, to convince the Court that defendant's public announcement of its deals fell far short of the candid display which the law requires. The law requires full disclosure described in the plain language of the statute. A look at the defendant's advertising scheme leads directly to the conclusion that it was designed to attract customers by half truths or falsity. No customer could buy a car on the terms boldly announced on the face of the building. The defendant's intentions did not have to be explained by testimony. No undercover agent was needed to obtain admissions. The message spoke for itself and could not be misread. It was "misleading in a material respect".

Truth in lending laws were not adopted for the canny shopper. They were made for the gullible and those easily led. The Court of Appeals decided in *Guggenheimer v. Ginzburg,* 43 N.Y.2d 268, 273, 401 N.Y.S.2d 182, 372 N.E.2d 17 that, "In weighing a statement's capacity, tendency or effect in deceiving or misleading customers, we do not look to the average customer but to the vast multitude which the statutes were enacted to safeguard, including the ignorant, the unthinking and the credulous who, in making purchases, do not stop to analyze but are governed by appearances and general impressions." The plaintiff was not required to show that anyone had been deceived or that the advertising had injured anyone. It met its burden by showing its misleading effect.

The defendant's violation of Federal and New York State truth in lending laws has been demonstrated.

* * *

The motion for an order granting a preliminary injunction enjoining the defendant Terry Buick, Inc. from continuing to advertise the terms for credit on vehicles it is selling in an illegal, false and deceptive manner is granted.

Notes

1. Under TILA, what is the precise basis for the court's ruling? Did Terry Buick's advertising comply with Reg. Z § 226.24(c)? Note that this section uses the "trigger" concept. That is, certain terms must be disclosed as a complete package if any one of the listed "trigger" terms is advertised. What is the rationale for requiring a package disclosure? Should other terms have been included in the "trigger" list?

2. Why is the New York attorney general the plaintiff in the lawsuit? Could a consumer who had shopped for or purchased a car at Terry Buick have brought a suit? See also Smeyres v. General Motors Corp., 820 F.2d 782 (6th Cir.1987).

3. Do the general format requirements of Reg. Z found in §§ 226.5(a) and 226.17(a) apply to credit advertising? If so, how should they be applied in radio, television, and Internet advertising? May a credit advertiser satisfy TILA standards by having a speed-reader recite the critical credit terms in the last five seconds of the radio ad? Or by having that information crawl— rapidly—across the bottom of the TV screen while the audio/visual ad touts the performance qualities of the car? Or by requiring a keyboard click to

open the triggered information? Are such techniques "clear and conspicuous"?

4. Reconsider the *Ford Motor* case, supra at page 129. There, the F.T.C. attacked credit advertising in general deceptive practice terms, rather than as being in violation of a detailed disclosure statute. At the time, of course, there was no TILA; indeed, federal law looked much like the New York statute involved in Terry Buick. Which approach do you feel provides a better tool for dealing with deceptive advertising?

7. CALCULATING APRS AND FINANCE CHARGES

In the TILA scheme of disclosures, two numbers stand out. These are the "Annual Percentage Rate" and the "Finance Charge." The first states the cost of credit on a comparable, unit-cost, percentage basis, while the second states the cost of credit as dollar amounts. Ultimately, the reliability of TILA depends on the integrity of those two numbers. In part, this is why the APR and Finance Charge must be "more conspicuous" than virtually any of the other disclosures. Reg. Z §§ 226.5(a)(2) and 226.17(a)(2).

a. *Closed–End Rate Calculations*

Truth in Lending uses the term "annual percentage rate," or "APR." It is based on "actuarial" or simple interest calculations. For students (and teachers) who have difficulty mastering the arithmetic of the various methods of computing rates, we supply the following. It is one of the clearer explanations your authors have seen. Although it is dated, the arithmetic has not changed. It is also relevant primarily to closed-end (fixed term) credit.

OEO LEGAL SERVICES TRAINING PROGRAM, MEMORANDUM

(April 1972)*

I. Introduction

[T]he Federal Truth in Lending Act * * * provides a standardized method of computing and disclosing finance charges * * * and an annual percentage rate (APR) * * *. The federal standard [for computing an APR] is computed on an annual basis by the actuarial method while state statutes concerned with imposing maximum rates are inevitably phrased in terms of the add-on or discount method. * * *

The distinction between the different methods is significant. For example, an extension of $100 in credit for one year, payable in 12 monthly regular installments at 8 percent, involves the following Finance Charges and APR's depending upon the method of computing the 8 percent:

* Copyright© by the Legal Services Training Program. Reprinted by permission of the Legal Services Corporation.

Computation Method	Finance Charge	APR
Actuarial	$4.39	8%
Add–On	8.00	14.45%
Discount	8.70	15.68%

* * *

II. COMMON METHODS OF COMPUTING FINANCE CHARGES

A. *Why Simple Math Doesn't Help*

When confronted with the task of computing the unknown of any one of the four key variables in a credit transaction—finance charge (C), amount of credit extended (A), rate (R), or period of time extended in years (T)—the almost instinctive response is to solve for the unknown through the use of the formula: $C = A \times R \times T$. Thus, $8.00 is the finance charge on the $100.00 credit extended at 8% for one year. Right? Yes, if the total debt $(A + C)$ is paid in a single installment at the end of the period. But the formula does not work if any part of the total debt is paid prior to the expiration of the full period. The reason is that the debtor has not had the total use of the amount of the credit for the full period.

When portions of the credit are paid back regularly, at even intervals throughout the full period (as is typical for consumer credit), the departure from the formula is even more extreme. In the case of monthly payments, that portion of the credit which is repaid in the first installment has been enjoyed by the debtor for only one month and has not been properly entered into a formula which contemplates the use of the credit for an entire year. The standard simple formula cannot work, therefore, to solve for any of the variables of consumer credit. For example, in the case of a charge of $8.00 for $100.00 payable in 12 monthly installments, the rate is 14.45 percent when expressed as an APR.

B. *The Actuarial, or Interest on Declining Balances, Method*

This is also referred to as the method to obtain "true" or "simple" interest. And, since it is the method required by Truth in Lending, it is rapidly becoming known as the APR method. This is the classical method, interest having been calculated by this method for at least a couple of thousand years, with the sole exception of consumer credit. By custom, and now by Federal law, the rate is expressed *per year*. For periods less than a year the ratio is constant; at 12% per year the rate per month is 1%, or per quarter, 3%, etc.

The actuarial method is simple and readily adaptable to an open ledger bookkeeping approach of calculation. That is, if you know the APR and the amount of credit, you can compute, by use of the simple formula discussed above $(C = A \times R \times T)$, the amount of each installment allocable to finance charges, the balance going to reduce the amount of credit outstanding. Thus, on $100.00 at an APR of 14.45% payable in monthly installments of $9.00 each:

Installment	Finance Charge	Repayment per Installment	Balance
1	$1.21	$7.79	$92.21
2	1.11	7.89	84.32
3	1.02	7.98	76.34
etc.	etc.	etc.	etc.
12	$8.00	$100.00	

Using this approach you can, in a very backhanded way, analyze a transaction installment-by-installment and check the accuracy of a creditor's disclosures. On a 36 installment transaction this process can become a bit tedious. It only works, however, when approached one installment at a time. There is, unfortunately, no simple algebraic formula for the actuarial method whereby the rate can be conveniently solved for as an unknown (unless you enjoy solving equations which involve unknowns raised to a power equivalent to the number of installments).

* * *

C.   The Add–On Method

This method, generally contemplated by the statutes which regulate installment financing of goods and services, is probably the simplest to calculate. Statutes using the add-on method are typically phrased in terms of dollars per hundred per year. The simple formula can be used to check compliance with a statutory maximum. Merely apply simple multiplication of the add-on rate times the amount of credit extended times the years extended.

As indicated in II A, above, this formula disregards the fact that installments will be paid in monthly. That's the deceptive quality of add-ons. As a result the APR is, roughly usually just a bit less than double the add-on rate. For example, an 8 percent add-on for $100.00 for one year, payable in monthly installments, is the equivalent of 14.45% APR. To solve for the APR when the add-on rate or the finance charge is known to be accurate, you must use a conversion table.

D.   The Discount Method

Traditionally, bankers have used this method of expressing rates, particularly for short term loans. Discount means that something has been subtracted, not added as in the add-on method. That means the finance charge (interest) is taken from the amount of credit extended at the outset, from the top so to speak. Thus, in the case of $100.00 at the 8% discount, for one year, the consumer actually gets only $92.00, not $100.00. Expressing the same transaction in add-on terms, since the debtor is getting only $92.00 and paying $8.00 finance charge, it is an add-on of 8.7%. The APR is 15.7%. The effect of discount rates then is not unlike add-on, except even more exaggerated. For short terms the discount rate will be about one-half of the true APR. At about one year it will start to become less than half and as the time for repayment extends, it will become a smaller and smaller percentage of the true APR. For example, an 8% discount rate is equivalent to 15.7% APR at one year, 17.3% at two years, 18.8% at three years and 22.3% at five. At 10 years of monthly installments, an 8% discount is the equivalent of 49.6% APR!

b. Open–End Rate Calculations

Rates for *open-end* credit are almost always calculated on the basis of a "periodic" rate, which may be daily, monthly or even quarterly, and may be adjustable from time to time according to an external index like the Wall Street Journal prime rate. Most credit card issuers apply daily periodic rates, either to the actual daily balances during the billing cycle, or to the average of daily balances times the number of days in the cycle. The Annual Percentage Rate is determined by multiplying the periodic rate times the number of periods in a year. Thus a monthly periodic rate of 1.5%, times 12 months, becomes an 18% APR. And a daily periodic rate of .049315, times 365 days, likewise becomes an APR of 18%.

Since periodic rates are always applied to balances outstanding from time to time, they are necessarily "actuarial" rates, and are not subject to the skews of add-on or discount calculations.

Note on Calculating the Unpaid Balance

Disclosures in open-end accounts must include a description of the method used to determine the unpaid balance on which the finance charge will be computed. As most creditors know (but most consumers do not), the method a creditor uses can have a significant impact on an individual account. The following material explains the most common methods.

McALISTER AND DESPAIN, CREDIT CARD YIELDS UNDER ALTERNATIVE ASSESSMENT METHODS
2 J. Retail Banking 56, 57–59, 68 (1980)*

Previous Balance. Also known as the "beginning balance." Finance charges are calculated on any beginning unpaid balance shown on the current month's statement before deducting payments or credits received during the billing period and before adding purchases made during the billing period. Thus, the period's credits and debits are treated symmetrically in that both are excluded from the balance upon which the finance charge is assessed. Payments are applied first to any unpaid finance charges and then to principal. If the previous balance is paid in full, no finance charge is assessed. If no payment is made, the unpaid finance charge may become part of the principal balance owed, although the practice varies among creditors.

Adjusted Balance. Finance charges are calculated on the basis of any beginning unpaid balance shown on the current month's billing statement less payments and credits received during the current billing period, but before adding the current month's purchases. The date of payment on an account is irrelevant to the calculation. On the closing date of the account, payments are first applied to any unpaid finance charges and then to principal. If no payment is made, the unpaid finance charge may become part of the new balance owed.

Ending Balance. Finance charges are based on the balance owed at the end of each billing period, including purchases, payments, and credits occurring during the current month. Thus, the period's credits and debits are treated alike in that both are included in the balance on which the finance charge is assessed. Payments are applied first to any unpaid finance charges before application to principal. If no payment is made, the unpaid finance charge may become part of the principal balance owed. Note that no "free ride" is given the customer who pays the account in full unless there is, indeed, no outstanding balance at the end of the month.

Average Daily Balance Including Debits (ADBW). Finance charges are based on the "average" unpaid balance owed during the billing period. This includes all purchases, payments, and credits transacted during the billing period. It is calculated by dividing the sum of the daily unpaid balances, excluding unpaid finance charges, by the number of days in the billing period. Payments are applied first to any unpaid finance charges then to principal. In the event no payment is made on the account, the finance charge is carried forward as a memo balance (i.e., a balance upon which no finance charges are assessed) until a payment sufficient to cover the unpaid finance charge is made. Under this method no finance charge is imposed if the account has a zero balance at the beginning of the billing cycle or if at any time in the billing period the total of payments and other credits equals or exceeds the opening balance.

Average Daily Balance Excluding Debits (ADBX). Sometimes referred to as the "modified" average daily balance, this method calculates finance charges on the basis of an "average" monthly balance, which is computed by dividing the sum of the daily unpaid balances (excluding the sum of the daily debit balances and unpaid finance charges) by the number of days in the billing cycle. Thus, unlike the Adjusted Balance method, the timing of the payment affects the size of the finance charge. Payments usually are applied first to any unpaid finance charge, then to principal. If no payment is made, the unpaid finance charge is carried forward separately, not as part of the principal balance, until payment in sufficient amount to cover the unpaid finance charge is made. No finance charge is imposed if the account has a zero balance at the beginning of the billing period or if the total of payments and credits during the period equals or exceeds the opening balance.

"True" (Actuarial) Average Daily Balance (TADB). Finance charges are based on the "average" unpaid balance during the billing period, including all purchases, payments, and credits on the account during the period. It is calculated in exactly the same way as ADBW except that finance charges are assessed on the average daily balance whether or not the account was paid off during the month (where the sum of credits and payments is equal to or greater than the previous month's balance). Thus, there is no "free ride" under this billing method as there is with ADBW.

* * *

Recent Developments. In recent years a new type of average daily balance system has been initiated by a few firms. ... For purposes of discussion, this newer method will be referred to as ADBR, or simply "retro."

ADBR operates much as an ADBX system insofar as finance charges are not assessed on purchase balances accrued during the current billing cycle of an account. However, if the total of credits and payments in a cycle are less than the previous statement balance (i.e., if the account is not paid off in full), finance charges are assessed *retroactively* in the succeeding month from original date of purchase on the current purchase balance. In other words, no finance charge is assessed during a month on current purchases; but if the account is not paid in full during the following cycle, those same purchases will accrue finance charges from their original date of purchase or date of posting to the account.

Notes

1. As this excerpt suggests, the formulae for calculating the unpaid balance can be very intricate, but it is the balance formula (as much as the nominal APR) that determines the real cost of credit for consumers. How much explanation should the creditor be required to give about the balance formula? In Reg. Z, the Board has waffled a bit on this. In the early solicitation disclosures, the creditor need only provide the name of the method, e.g., "Adjusted Balance." Reg. Z § 226.5a(g). But in the account-opening disclosures and on the periodic statement there must be an "explanation" of the balance computation method. Reg. Z §§ 226.6(a)(3) and 226.7(e). For a case holding that the creditor did not properly disclose the balance assessment method even though it closely tracked a Reg. Z model form, see Schmidt v. Citibank (South Dakota), N.A., 677 F.Supp. 687 (D. Conn. 1987).

2. Ultimately, APRs are "derived" numbers. That is, the APR can be calculated only once the basic terms of the credit—amount borrowed, amount of finance charge, and the payment schedule—are known. The regulatory rules on APR calculation are in Reg. Z §§ 226.14 (for open-end

credit), and 226.22 and Appendix J (for closed-end credit). These rules, along with those on Finance Charges, standardize the mathematical definitions and the iterative process that produces the APR.

c. *Finance Charges*

We turn now to the item that is central to the credit cost disclosure function of TILA—the finance charge. The "finance charge" is probably the most important concept in TILA, so it is worth some effort to understand it. First, if a creditor imposes a finance charge in a consumer transaction, that fact alone brings him within the scope of TILA. See the definition of "creditor" in TILA § 103. Secondly, the finance charge is the figure which translates into the "annual percentage rate" (APR), especially in closed-end transactions. While "finance charge" is expressed in dollars, "APR" is expressed in percentages. Thus, the finance charge tells the consumer the real cost of credit, while the APR tells the comparative cost. It works in the same way as other comparative cost expressions such as cents per pound or dollars per gallon. At this point, you should examine Reg. Z § 226.4 in some detail.

Caveat: TILA "Finance Charges" and State Law Interest Rates

Truth in Lending regulates only the *disclosure* of credit costs; it does not set usury limits or otherwise regulate the permissible amounts of interest or other charges. This function remains basically that of the states, although at this writing the pricing of credit products is largely deregulated; *i.e.*, state usury limits have been raised or repealed or preempted by federal deregulation rules. Still, there remains a hodge-podge of state rate-ceiling laws that set different rate caps for different kinds of transactions, often stating permissible rates as "add-ons," "discounts," monthly carrying charges, and so on and on. State laws may also specifically permit certain additional charges to be imposed beyond the basic "interest" ceiling. There is absolutely no uniformity from state to state with respect to maximum rates or the method of calculating those charges. Thus the uniform disclosure rules of TILA will often produce disclosed "finance charges" and "APRs" quite different from the numerical rate limits set by state law. Students should not be mystified at seeing TILA disclosures that appear a bit high. TILA begins with a half-heartedly inclusive definition of finance charge, and then requires that the APR be stated as a simple-interest percentage. These factors in combination lead to *disclosed* TILA rates that in many cases are numerically higher than (but not in violation of) those state law ceilings that are expressed in non-simple interest terms.

FIRST ACADIANA BANK v. FEDERAL DEPOSIT INSURANCE CORP.

United States Court of Appeals, Fifth Circuit, 1987.
833 F.2d 548.

PATRICK E. HIGGINBOTHAM, CIRCUIT JUDGE:

First Acadiana Bank seeks review of a final administrative order by the Federal Deposit Insurance Corporation. The FDIC found the Bank in violation of the Truth-in-Lending Act and FDIC regulations and ordered the Bank to reimburse certain customers. We affirm.

In 1984, the FDIC notified First Acadiana Bank of Eunice, Louisiana, that it was in violation of the Truth-in-Lending Act and FDIC regulations. Since October 1, 1982, the Bank's policy has been to require each car-loan borrower to employ a bank-approved attorney to prepare a valid chattel mortgage on the car. For two-thirds of such customers, these legal fees were included in the amount financed by the Bank. The amount of the fee was always determined by the attorney and ranged from $55 to $151 per loan.

When the Bank financed such a fee, it did not add it to the "finance charge" listed on the disclosure form presented to the borrower. Nor was the fee included in the computation of the annual percentage rate (APR) listed on the same form. Had these fees been included in the finance charge, the APR in any given loan would have been from half a point to ten points higher than that quoted by the Bank. However, the fees were included in the category "amount financed" and separately disclosed to the borrower.

After the Bank refused to alter its policy pursuant to the compliance examiner's report, the FDIC Board of Review issued a Notice of Charges and of Hearing. An administrative law judge entered an initial decision against the Bank that the FDIC's Board of Directors adopted in whole.

The FDIC order commands the Bank to cease and desist from failing to include the attorneys' fees as part of the finance charge on its disclosure form. The Board also ordered the Bank to identify all consumer automobile loans it made since October 1, 1982, in which the finance charge and annual percentage rate were understated. The Bank must then reimburse each borrower to the extent of the under-statement.

* * *

Under the Act's definition, the attorneys' fees obviously constitute part of the finance charge. Payment of the fees was "incident to the extension of credit," because the Bank would not extend credit otherwise. Likewise, the attorneys' fee to perfect a mortgage is not "of a type payable in a comparable cash transaction," because a cash sale would involve no security interest.

In addition, the fees were "imposed directly or indirectly by the creditor," and thus within the Act's definition. The Bank contends that the fee was imposed not by the Bank but by the attorney perfecting the mortgage insofar as the attorney set the amount of the fee and kept the proceeds. According to the Bank, its policy was simply the practical consequence of Louisiana's strict requirements for a valid chattel mortgage.

We reject the Bank's approach. The Bank has required its borrowers, as a condition to the extension of credit, to pay an avoidable economic cost. Louisiana law does not require the Bank to take a mortgage on a car loan, or to have an attorney complete the mortgage documents. The fact that the precise amount of the fee was set by a third party makes no difference.

We also do not agree that the disputed fees could be finance charges only if the Bank had retained them. Cf. Abbey v. Columbus Dodge, Inc., 607 F.2d 85, 86 (5th Cir.1979) (finance charge includes filing fee only partly retained by lender). Although the Bank retained no fee, it retained a substantial benefit from the attorneys' services: a perfected security interest.

It would be difficult to reconcile any other interpretation with the Act's explicit examples of finance charges, several of which involve payments to third parties. "Finders fees," a "fee for an investigation or credit report," or an insurance premium against the borrower's default all may be set and retained by a party other than the lender.

* * *

Affirmed.

JERRE S. WILLIAMS, CIRCUIT JUDGE, specially concurring:

The opinion for the Court omits a highly significant fact in this case, and as a result reaches a conclusion which extends the definition of "finance charges" under the law beyond reasonable statutory limits. The critical fact is that the Bank recommended two attorneys regularly who were closely associated with the Bank to draft the chattel mortgages which the Bank required. The inclusion of those fees in the "amounts financed" portion of the disclosure form was automatic, and the bank collected the fees and paid the attorneys. Under these circumstances I agree that these fees were finance charges.

At least some of the chattel mortgages were drafted by other attorneys in the community who were not recommended by and had no connection with the Bank. The FDIC takes the position that the fees charged by those attorneys also are finance charges of the Bank but then specifically eschews any attempt to take action against the Bank for failure to include those fees on the ground of pragmatic difficulty.

Since the opinion for the Court does not properly distinguish between a wholly independent action by a lawyer which is necessary and properly required by the Bank before it will issue a loan from the "in house" actions of the Bank in this case, I find it important to dispute this broad interpretation of the statute by the FDIC and by the panel opinion.

I start with the proposition that it is reasonable and sound for a Bank to require that before it gives an automobile loan it will demand a chattel mortgage. It is also reasonable for the Bank to require that the chattel mortgage be drafted by a lawyer. These are simply qualifications which a Bank has a right to make before it will engage in the voluntary act of granting a loan on an automobile. We are not here testing the right of the Bank to demand professional qualifications. Under the reasoning of the panel opinion, if the chattel mortgage had been drafted by the applicant on a standard form sold in the stores or anyone else, the cost of purchasing the form would, under the reasoning of the majority, constitute a "finance charge". If the Bank required that such loan applications be typed, the cost of typing the applications would be a finance charge. If the automobile in question had been purchased at a foreclosure sale, the cost of obtaining the requisite documents to establish clear title from the court clerk would also be a finance charge. I suppose even the ink or pencil used by an individual applicant to fill out an application would be a finance charge.

* * *

Notes

1. Do you agree with the "parade of horribles" raised by the concurring opinion? Under the majority ruling, could the cost of ink really be a finance charge? Are Louisiana creditors hindered in their attempts to take security in car loans?

2. Could a lawyer ethically prepare a security agreement under the circumstances described in the opinion? Who is the client? Who pays the fees? Whose interest would the lawyer understand she is to protect?

3. Examine the list of items in Reg. Z § 226.4(b) and (c) more closely. Notice, for example, that "points" paid by the buyer are included in the Finance Charge, (b)(3), while "points" paid by the seller are not, (c)(5). Why? ("Points" are front-end charges imposed by a lender on a seller or buyer, typically in real estate sales. A "point" equals one per cent of the loan principal.) No matter which party gets charged initially with the points, who eventually pays them?

4. What is the rationale for the exclusions in Reg. Z § 226.4(c)(7)? Wouldn't those items be included in the finance charge but for the special exclusion? Do these exclusions distort the APR disclosed in real estate transactions? Do they reflect the power of the real estate lobby?

5. Students should now appreciate the double significance of determining that a particular charge is within or without the finance charge. If it is in, it increases the numerator of the fraction that becomes the APR. If it is excluded, it not only decreases the numerator by the amount of the charge, it also increases the denominator. Thus, the mathematical effect is compounded, and the APR decreases dramatically. This is so because items excluded from the finance charge are usually (unless prepaid in cash) included in the "amount financed."

Problem 2–17

In the paperwork for his 10–year home improvement loan, Kenneth signed a promissory note for a principal amount of $52,000, including four "points" to be retained by the lender, at a contractual interest rate of 8.00%, payable in 120 installments of $630.90 each. When Kenneth looked at the Truth in Lending disclosures for the loan, however, they showed the same 120–month payment schedule and monthly amount, but the Amount Financed was stated as $50,000 and the APR was 8.90%.

Has Kenneth been ripped off? Are the TILA disclosures erroneous?

Problem 2–18

Firstbank offers home equity lines of credit (HELOCS), which will carry several charges that any given consumer might incur. Assume that the following charges may be imposed under the plan. Which of them are "finance charges" under Reg. Z § 226.4?

A. Charges when the account is opened:

  1. $50 application fee.

  2. $25 "commission" to the employee who personally solicits the consumer's application.

  3. $250 settlement charges (appraisal, credit report, title search, deed preparation and recording, and title insurance premium).

  4. $400 loan origination fee

B. Regular recurring charges:

  1. Interest at a daily periodic rate of .049315 on outstanding balances.

  2. Service charge of $3 for the handling of each draft used to draw on the credit line.

  3. A charge of $3 for each cash advance on the credit card.

  4. Monthly premium for credit life insurance.

  5. Semi-annual premium for property insurance on the consumer's home.

C. Extraordinary charges:

  1. $25 fee for stopping payment on a draft.

  2. $40 fee for sending a monthly payment check that bounces.

  3. $20 charge for a replacement pad of credit-line checks.

  4. Fees for late payment or for exceeding the credit limit.

  5. Attorney's fees and foreclosure costs in the event of default.

HOUSEHOLD CREDIT SERVICES, INC. v. PFENNIG

Supreme Court of the United States, 2004.
541 U.S., 232, 124 S.Ct. 1741, 158 L.Ed.2d 450.

Justice Thomas delivered the opinion of the Court.

Congress enacted the Truth in Lending Act (TILA), 82 Stat. 146, in order to promote the "informed use of credit" by consumers. 15 U.S.C. § 1601(a). To that end, TILA's disclosure provisions seek to ensure "meaningful disclosure of credit terms." Ibid. Further, Congress delegated expansive authority to the Federal Reserve Board (Board) to enact appropriate regulations to advance this purpose. § 1604(a). We granted certiorari, 539 U.S. 957, 123 S.Ct. 2639, 156 L.Ed.2d 654 (2003), to decide whether the Board's Regulation Z, which specifically excludes fees imposed for exceeding a credit limit (over-limit fees) from the definition of "finance charge," is an unreasonable interpretation of § 1605. We conclude that it is not, and, accordingly, we reverse the judgment of the Court of Appeals for the Sixth Circuit.

I.

Respondent, Sharon Pfennig, holds a credit card initially issued by petitioner Household Credit Services, Inc. (Household), but in which petitioner MBNA America Bank, N.A. (MBNA), now holds an interest through the acquisition of Household's credit card portfolio. Although the terms of respondent's credit card agreement set respondent's credit limit at $2,000, respondent was able to make charges exceeding that limit, subject to a $29 "over-limit fee" for each month in which her balance exceeded $2,000.

TILA regulates, inter alia, the substance and form of disclosures that creditors offering "open end consumer credit plans" (a term that includes credit card accounts) must make to consumers, § 1637(a), and provides a civil remedy for consumers who suffer damages as a result of a creditor's failure to comply with TILA's provisions, § 1640. When a creditor and a consumer enter into an open-end consumer credit plan, the creditor is required to provide to the consumer a statement for each billing cycle for which there is an outstanding balance due. § 1637(b). The statement must include the account's outstanding balance at the end of the billing period, § 1637(b)(8), and "[t]he amount of any finance charge added to the account during the period, itemized to show the amounts, if any, due to the application of percentage rates and the amount, if any, imposed as a minimum or fixed charge," § 1637(b)(4). A "finance charge" is an amount "payable directly or indirectly by the person to whom the credit is extended, and imposed directly or indirectly by the creditor as an incident to the extension of credit." § 1605(a). The Board has interpreted this definition to exclude "[c]harges ... for exceeding a credit limit." See 12 CFR § 226.4(c)(2) (2004) (Regulation Z). Thus, although respondent's billing statement disclosed the imposition of an over-limit fee when she exceeded her $2,000 credit limit, consistent with Regulation Z, the amount was not included as part of the "finance charge."

On August 24, 1999, respondent filed a complaint in the United States District Court for the Southern District of Ohio on behalf of a purported nationwide class of all consumers who were charged or assessed over-limit fees by petitioners. Respondent alleged in her complaint that petitioners allowed her and each of the other putative class members to exceed their credit limits, thereby subjecting them to over-limit fees. Petitioners violated TILA, respondent alleged, by failing to classify the over-limit fees as "finance charges" and thereby "misrepresented the true cost of credit" to respondent and the other class members. ... Petitioners moved to dismiss the complaint pursuant to Federal Rule of Civil Procedure 12(b)(6) on the ground that Regulation Z specifically excludes over-limit fees from the definition of "finance charge." 12 CFR § 226.4(c)(2) (2004). The District Court agreed and granted petitioners' motion to dismiss.

On appeal, respondent argued, and the Court of Appeals agreed, that Regulation Z's explicit exclusion of over-limit fees from the definition of "finance charge" conflicts with the plain language of 15 U.S.C. § 1605(a). The Court of Appeals first noted that, as a remedial statute, TILA must be liberally interpreted in favor of consumers. 295 F.3d 522, 528 (C.A.6 2002). The Court of Appeals then concluded that the over-limit fees in this case were imposed "incident to the extension of credit" and therefore fell squarely within § 1605's definition of "finance charge." Id., at 528–529. The Court of Appeals' conclusion turned on the distinction between unilateral acts of default and acts of default resulting from consumers' requests for additional credit, exceeding a predetermined credit limit, that creditors grant. Under the Court of Appeals' reasoning, a penalty imposed due to a unilateral act of default would not constitute a "finance charge." Id., at 530–531. Respondent alleged in her complaint, however, that petitioners "allowed [her] to make charges and/or assessed [her] charges that allowed her balance to exceed her credit limit of two thousand dollars," . . . , putting her actions under the category of acts of default resulting from consumers requests for additional credit, exceeding a predetermined credit limit, that creditors grant. The Court of Appeals held that because petitioners "made an additional extension of credit to [respondent] over and above the alleged 'credit limit,' and charged the over-limit fee as a condition of this additional extension of credit, the over-limit fee clearly and unmistakably fell under the definition of a "finance charge." 295 F.3d, at 530. Based on its reading of respondent's allegations, the Court of Appeals limited its holding to "those instances in which the creditor knowingly permits the credit card holder to exceed his or her credit limit and then imposes a fee incident to the extension of that credit." Id., at 532, n. 5.

Congress has expressly delegated to the Board the authority to prescribe regulations containing "such classifications, differentiations, or other provisions" as, in the judgment of the Board, "are necessary or proper to effectuate the purposes of [TILA], to prevent circumvention or evasion thereof, or to facilitate compliance therewith." § 1604(a). Thus, the Court has previously recognized that "the [Board] has played a pivotal role in 'setting [TILA] in motion . . . .'" Ford Motor Credit Co. v. Milhollin, 444 U.S. 555, 566, 100 S.Ct. 790, 63 L.Ed.2d 22 (1980) (quoting Norwegian Nitrogen Products Co. v. United States, 288 U.S. 294, 315, 53 S.Ct. 350, 77 L.Ed. 796 (1933)). Indeed, "Congress has specifically designated the [Board] and staff as the primary source for interpretation and application of truth-in-lending law." 444 U.S., at 566, 100 S.Ct. 790. As the Court recognized in Ford Motor Credit Co., twice since the passage of TILA, Congress has made this intention clear: first by providing a good-faith defense to creditors who comply with the Board's rules and regulations, 88 Stat. 1518, codified at 15 U.S.C. § 1640(f), and, second, by expanding this good-faith defense to creditors who conform to "any interpretation or approval by an official or employee of the Federal Reserve System duly authorized by the Board to issue such interpretations or approvals," 90 Stat. 197, codified as amended, at § 1640(f).

Respondent does not challenge the Board's authority to issue binding regulations. Thus, in determining whether Regulation Z's interpretation of TILA's text is binding on the courts, we are faced with only two questions. We first ask whether "Congress has directly spoken to the precise question at issue." Chevron U.S.A. Inc. v. Natural Resources Defense Council, Inc., 467 U.S. 837, 842, 104 S.Ct. 2778, 81 L.Ed.2d 694 (1984). If so, courts, as well as the agency, "must give effect to the unambiguously expressed intent of Congress." Id., at 842–843, 104 S.Ct. 2778. However, whenever Congress has "explicitly left a gap for the agency to fill," the agency's regulation is "given controlling weight unless [it is] arbitrary, capricious, or manifestly contrary to the statute." Id., at 843–844, 104 S.Ct. 2778.

TILA itself does not explicitly address whether over-limit fees are included within the definition of "finance charge." Congress defined "finance charge" as "all charges, payable directly or indirectly by the person to whom the credit is extended, and imposed directly or indirectly by the creditor as an incident to the extension of credit." § 1605(a). The Court of Appeals, however, made no attempt to clarify the scope of the critical term "incident to the extension of credit." The Court of Appeals recognized that, " '[i]n ascertaining the plain meaning of the statute, the court must look to the particular statutory language at issue, as well as the language and design of the statute as a whole.' " Id., at 529–530 (quoting K mart Corp. v. Cartier, Inc., 486 U.S. 281, 291, 108 S.Ct. 1811, 100 L.Ed.2d 313 (1988)). However, the Court of Appeals failed to examine TILA's other provisions, or even the surrounding language in § 1605, before reaching its conclusion. Because petitioners would not have imposed the over-limit fee had they not "granted [respondent's] request for additional credit, which resulted in her exceeding her credit limit," the Court of Appeals held that the over-limit fee in this case fell squarely within § 1605(a)'s definition of "finance charge." 295 F.3d, at 528–529. Thus, the Court of Appeals rested its holding primarily on its particular characterization of the transaction that led to the over-limit charge in this case.[1]

The Court of Appeals thus erred in resting its conclusion solely on this particular characterization of the details of credit card transactions, a characterization that is not clearly compelled by the terms and definitions of TILA, and one with which others could reasonably disagree. Certainly, regardless of how the fee is characterized, there is at least some connection between the over-limit fee and an extension of credit. But, this Court has recognized that the phrase "incident to or in

---

1. Because over-limit fees, regardless of a creditor's particular billing practices, are imposed only when a consumer exceeds his credit limit, it is perfectly reasonable to characterize an over-limit fee not as a charge imposed for obtaining an extension of credit over a consumer's credit limit, but rather as a penalty for violating the credit agreement.

conjunction with" implies some necessary connection between the antecedent and its object, although it "does not place beyond rational debate the nature or extent of the required connection." Holly Farms Corp. v. NLRB, 517 U.S. 392, 403, n. 9, 116 S.Ct. 1396, 134 L.Ed.2d 593 (1996) (internal quotation marks omitted). In other words, the phrase "incident to" does not make clear whether a substantial (as opposed to a remote) connection is required. Thus, unlike the Court of Appeals, we cannot conclude that the term "finance charge" unambiguously includes over-limit fees. That term, standing alone, is ambiguous.

The Court of Appeals' characterization of the transaction in this case, however, is not supported even by the facts as set forth in respondent's complaint. Respondent alleged in her complaint that the over-limit fee is imposed for each month in which her balance exceeds the original credit limit. If this were true, however, the over-limit fee would be imposed not as a direct result of an extension of credit for a purchase that caused respondent to exceed her $2,000 limit, but rather as a result of the fact that her charges exceeded her $2,000 limit at the time respondent's monthly charges were officially calculated.

* * *

Moreover, an examination of TILA's related provisions, as well as the full text of § 1605 itself, casts doubt on the Court of Appeals' interpretation of the statute. A consumer holding an open-end credit plan may incur two types of charges—finance charges and "other charges which may be imposed as part of the plan." § 1637(a)(1) (5). TILA does not make clear which charges fall into each category. But TILA's recognition of at least two categories of charges does make clear that Congress did not contemplate that all charges made in connection with an open-end credit plan would be considered "finance charges." And where TILA does explicitly address over-limit fees, it defines them as fees imposed "in connection with an extension of credit," § 1637(c)(1)(B)(iii), rather than "incident to the extension of credit," § 1605(a). Furthermore, none of 1605's specific examples of charges that fall within the definition of "finance charge" includes over-limit or comparable fees. See, e.g., § 1605(a)(2) ("[s]ervice or carrying charge"); § 1605(a)(3) (loan fee or similar charge); § 1605(a)(6) (mortgage broker fees).[2]

As our prior discussion indicates, the best interpretation of the term "finance charge" may exclude over-limit fees. But § 1605(a) is, at best, ambiguous, because neither § 1605(a) nor its surrounding provisions provides a clear answer. While we acknowledge that there may be some fees not explicitly addressed by § 1605(a)'s definition of "finance

2. Additionally, by specifically excepting charges from the term "finance charge" that would otherwise be included under a broad reading of "incident to the extension of credit," see § 1605(a) (charges of a type payable in a comparable cash transaction); ibid. (fees imposed by third-party closing agents); § 1605(d)(1) (fees and charges relating to perfecting security interests); § 1605(e) (fees relating to the extension of credit secured by real property), Congress appears to have excluded such an expansive interpretation of the term.

charge" but which are unambiguously included in or excluded by that definition, over-limit fees are not such fees.

Because § 1605 is ambiguous, the Board's regulation implementing § 1605 "is binding in the courts unless procedurally defective, arbitrary or capricious in substance, or manifestly contrary to the statute." United States v. Mead Corp., 533 U.S. 218, 227, 121 S.Ct. 2164, 150 L.Ed.2d 292 (2001).

Regulation Z's exclusion of over-limit fees from the term "finance charge" is in no way manifestly contrary to § 1605. Regulation Z defines the term "finance charge" as "the cost of consumer credit." 12 CFR § 226.4 (2004). It specifically excludes from the definition of "finance charge" the following:

[THE COURT QUOTES REG. Z § 226.4(c)]

The Board adopted the regulation to emphasize "disclosures that are relevant to credit decisions, as opposed to disclosures related to events occurring after the initial credit choice," because "the primary goals of [TILA] are not particularly enhanced by regulatory provisions relating to changes in terms on outstanding obligations and on the effects of the failure to comply with the terms of the obligation." 45 Fed.Reg. 80649 (1980). The Board's decision to emphasize disclosures that are most relevant to a consumer's initial credit decisions reflects an understanding that "[m]eaningful disclosure does not mean more disclosure," but instead "describes a balance between 'competing considerations of complete disclosure . . . and the need to avoid . . . [informational overload].'" Ford Motor Credit Co., 444 U.S., at 568, 100 S. Ct. 790 (quoting S.Rep. No. 96–73, p. 3 (1979)). Although the fees excluded from the term "finance charge" in Regulation Z (e.g., application charges, late payment charges, and over-limit fees) might be relevant to a consumer's credit decision, the Board rationally concluded that these fees—which are not automatically recurring or are imposed only when a consumer defaults on a credit agreement—are less relevant to determining the true cost of credit. Because over-limit fees, which are imposed only when a consumer breaches the terms of his credit agreement, can reasonably be characterized as a penalty for defaulting on the credit agreement, the Board's decision to exclude them from the term "finance charge" is surely reasonable.

In holding that Regulation Z conflicts with § 1605's definition of the term "finance charge," the Court of Appeals ignored our warning that "judges ought to refrain from substituting their own interstitial lawmaking for that of the [Board]." Ford Motor Credit Co., supra, at 568, 100 S.Ct. 790. Despite the Board's rational decision to adopt a uniform rule excluding from the term "finance charge" all penalties imposed for exceeding the credit limit, the Court of Appeals adopted a case-by-case approach contingent on whether an act of default was "unilateral." Putting aside the lack of textual support for this approach, the Court of Appeals' approach would prove unworkable to creditors and, more importantly, lead to significant confusion for consumers. Under the Court of Appeals' rule, a consumer would be able to decipher if a charge is considered a "finance charge" or an "other charge" each month only by recalling the details of the particular transaction that caused the consumer to exceed his credit limit. In most cases, the consumer would not even know the relevant facts, which are contingent on the nature of the authorization given by the creditor to the merchant. Moreover, the distinction between "unilateral" acts of default and acts of default where a consumer exceeds his credit limit (but has not thereby renegotiated his credit limit and is still subject to the over-limit fee) is based on a fundamental misunderstanding of the workings of the credit card industry. As the Board explained below, a creditor's "authorization" of a particular point-of-sale transaction does not represent a final determination that a particular transaction is within a consumer's credit limit because the authorization system is not suited to identify instantaneously and accurately over-limit transactions. Brief for Board of Governors of Federal Reserve System as Amicus Curiae in No. 00–4213(CA6), pp. 7–9.

Congress has authorized the Board to make "such classifications, differentiations, or other provisions, and [to] provide for such adjustments and exceptions for any class of transactions, as in the judgment of the Board are necessary or proper to effectuate the purposes of [TILA], to prevent circumvention or evasion thereof, or to facilitate compliance therewith." § 1604(a). Here, the Board has accomplished all of these objectives by setting forth a clear, easy to apply (and easy to enforce) rule that highlights the charges the Board determined to be most relevant to a consumer's credit decisions. The judgment of the Court of Appeals is therefore reversed.

It is so ordered.

Notes

1. So, for open-end credit plans, TILA requires that various fees be characterized as either "finance charges" or "other charges." And the dollar amounts of each category must be disclosed on the periodic statement. In *Pfennig*, the bank did just that. Is the whole gist of the case merely whether the bank put the over-limit charge in the right disclosure box?

Not quite. A feature of the open-end rules is the required disclosure of an "historical" APR that reflects all finance charges imposed during the previous billing period. See Reg. Z §§ 226.7(g) and 226.14(c). Assume Sharon Pfennig's balance for the billing period was $2,000, and that the applicable periodic rate was 1.5% per month (corresponding to an 18% APR). That periodic rate would generate a monthly finance charge of $30.00 [$2,000 x .015]. But if the $29.00 over-limit fee were in fact also a finance charge, then the total finance charge for the month would nearly double, to $59.00. [$30.00 from application of the periodic rate, plus the $29.00 over-limit charge]. A $59.00 finance charge imposed on a balance of $2,000 makes the actual rate 2.95% for the monthly billing period, or 35.40% as an annualized figure.

Now you can see what was at stake in *Pfennig*. If the over-limit charge is a finance charge, it skews the retrospective APR dramatically upward for that billing period. Card issuers don't like to disclose 35%—or higher—APRs if they can avoid it!

2. What is the value to consumers of being told what the APR was for last month? How might that affect the consumer's conduct or influence how she handles her credit card account in the future? Probably the most common situation for spikes in the historical APR is when a cardholder uses his card to get a cash advance from an ATM or over the counter at a bank. The cash advance fee is clearly a finance charge, is it not?

Problem 2–19

Thirdbank thinks it has figured a way legitimately to market a "0.00% APR" credit card. It will not impose any periodic *rate* at all. Instead, the bank will charge a set fee each month; the amount of the fee will depend on the balance outstanding. Thus, for balances up to $200, the fee is $2.00; for balances between $200 and $400, the fee is $4.00; for balances from $400 to $800, the fee is $6.00, and so on. Since none of these fees is based on a percentage rate, there is no periodic rate and so no APR either.

Will this work? Advise ThirdBank whether TILA permits it to disclose an APR of 0%.

d. *"Hidden" Finance Charges*

Sometimes your instincts may tell you there *must* be a Finance Charge in the transaction, but you can't quite pin it down. Consider this classic pattern, based on Yazzie v. Reynolds, 623 F.2d 638 (10th Cir. 1980):

Ben's Auto Sales (BAS) was a "buy here, pay here" used car dealer. That is, BAS sold virtually all of its used cars (98%) on installment contracts payable over a number of months; BAS held and collected the contracts itself, and did not sell them to any third-party bank or finance company. BAS offered each car at a single price, whether the customer paid cash or paid in installments. BAS provided TILA disclosures that stated a Finance Charge of $0 and an APR of 0%. The plaintiff buyer in the case argued that the unitary price for each car sold on an installment basis necessarily included costs for the credit extension—paperwork, collections and repossessions, plus the lost opportunity costs of deferring payments. BAS argued in response that any costs attributable to the installment payment arrangements were simply a part of its business overhead, and that it would be impossible to break out a specific portion of the price that represented *credit* costs.

The court denied summary judgment to BAS, saying that "the evidence in the case raises at least a factual issue as to whether these transactions are a ploy ... to avoid the Truth in Lending Act."

Query: If you were plaintiff's counsel, what factual information would you want to produce to prove that there is in fact an identifiable finance charge in these transactions? Cf., In re Stewart, 93 B.R. 878 (Bankr. E.D.Pa. 1988)

Truism: Any merchant who sells goods, services, or other property can always "bury" some of its credit costs in the prices it charges for those products.

VIRACHACK v. UNIVERSITY FORD

U.S. Court of Appeals, Ninth Circuit, 2005.
410 F.3d 579.

NOONAN, CIRCUIT JUDGE:

Malinee B. Virachack and Ritnarone T. Virachack (the Virachacks) appeal the district court's grant of summary judgment to University Ford, a California corporation doing business as Bob Baker Ford, in their action under the Truth In Lending Act (TILA), 15 U.S.C. § 1601 et seq. Holding that Bob Baker Ford did not fail to disclose the total finance charge, we affirm the judgement of the district court.

FACTS

On November 18, 2001, the Virachacks bought a Ford Explorer from Bob Baker Ford. The purchase was partly on credit. Bob Baker Ford made the following statement in the Retail Sales Installment Contract executed by the Virachacks.

FEDERAL TRUTH-IN-LENDING DISCLOSURE

ANNUAL PERCENTAGE RATE	FINANCE CHARGE	Amount Financed	Total of Payments	Total Sale Price
The cost of your credit as a yearly rate	The dollar amount the credit will cost you	The amount of credit provided to you or on your behalf	The amount you will have paid after you have made all payments as schedule	The total cost of your purchase, including your down payment of $4303.14 is
0.90%	$417.47(e)	$22615.33	$23032.80(e)	$27335.94(e)

(e) = estimate

The contract also stated that the Virachacks would make monthly payments of $479.85 for 48 months. The contract also reflected a sales tax of $1,748.47, based on the "cash price" of the vehicle of $23,268.

According to the affidavit of Nathaniel Torres, the finance manager of Bob Baker Ford, on the day the Virachacks bought the Explorer, Ford Motor Company was offering a $2,000 rebate to certain customers buying that model and year vehicle, but was not offering this rebate to customers buying on credit at the 0.9% rate. The availability of the rebate also depended, in part, on the geographical area in which the customer resided. The possibility of the rebate was not mentioned in the "Federal Truth–In–Lending Disclosure" of the contract.

According to Torres, had the Virachacks "desired a factory rebate and financing through Bob Baker Ford, they could have entered into a retail installment contract with Bob Baker Ford at a non-promotional interest rate offered by Ford Motor Credit Company, or they could have entered into a retail installment contract with Bob Baker Ford at whatever interest rate, promotional or not, was offered by any one of the other banks or finance companies to whom we regularly sell contracts."

PROCEEDINGS

* * * The Virachacks alleged that the $2,000 cash rebate they might have received if they had paid cash should have been disclosed as part of the finance charge and that the failure to disclose violated the TILA, 15 U.S.C. § 1638(a)(2),(3), (4), and (5). They sought for themselves and for each member of the plaintiff class damages not to exceed the statutory maximum of the lesser of $500,000 or 1% of the defendant's net worth. *Id.* at § 1640(a)(2)(b).

After discovery, each side moved for summary judgment. Granting summary judgment to Bob Baker Ford, the district court stated:

> The reality of plaintiffs' transaction is that they were given a "discount" on the market interest rate in order to induce them to purchase their vehicle. Indeed, plaintiffs' own separate statement of facts posits that the promotional rate is below the market interest rate. The cash rebate is not a cost of credit imposed upon plaintiffs. Rather, the rebate is an option made available to both cash and credit purchasers in order to induce the purchase of Ford vehicles at a price that would otherwise be unavailable to those consumers. In essence, the promotional interest rate is simply a different form of the cash rebate in that both the rebate and the interest rate are forms of subsidizing the market price of the vehicle offered to consumers in order to generate sales. Thus, the rebate is a "discount" made available to consumers who wish to receive the promotional interest rate but in the form of the reduced APR rather than in cash. Therefore, plaintiffs have received the "discount" made available to cash and other credit purchasers illustrating that the forgone rebate is not a condition of the extension of credit. See 12 C.F.R. Pt. 226, Supp. I, Comment 4(a)(i)(B) (discount available to both cash and credit consumers not a finance charge). Consequently, the record does not support plaintiffs' argument that the forgone rebate is imposed as a condition of the extension of credit or that the rebate is being offered to induce purchases by means other than credit. Therefore, the court concludes that the cash rebate is not part of plaintiffs' cost of credit and need not be disclosed.

Virachack v. Univ. Ford, 259 F.Supp.2d 1089, 1091 (S.D.Cal.2003).

The Virachacks appeal.

ANALYSIS
* * *

The statute defines "finance charge" as "the sum of all charges, payable directly or indirectly by the person to whom the credit is extended, and imposed directly or indirectly by the creditor as an incident to the extension of credit. The finance charge does not include charges of a type payable in a comparable cash transaction." 15 U.S.C. § 1605(a).

The statutory definition does not embrace a rebate that is withheld. A charge is a request for payment. A rebate is a reduction in payment. It is to turn topsy-turvy to contend that a rebate that is not given is a hidden charge.

The Virachaks' case looks less implausible under Regulation Z of the Federal Reserve Bank. This authoritative interpretation of the statute lists among examples of finance charges the following: "Discounts for the purpose of inducing payments by a means other than the use of credit." FRB Regulation Z, 12 C.F.R. § 226.4(b)(9) (2004). How can a discount be a charge? It cannot be. What the Federal Reserve Bank means is that the presence of a discount for a cash transaction is an index that more is being charged for a credit transaction. The Virachacks contend that a rebate for cash on the purchase price is functionally the same as a discount for cash. The rebate is an index that more is being charged for credit. They refer to the Official Staff Commentary on the regulations:

> The seller of land offers individual tracts for $10,000 each. If the purchaser pays cash, the price is $9,000, but if the purchaser finances the tract with the seller the price is $10,000. The $1,000 difference is a finance charge for those who buy the tracts on credit.

Commentary to Fed. Reserve Bd. Reg. Z, 12 C.F.R. part 226 Supp. I 374 para. 4(b)(9)

The preceding example treats the discount as evidence of purpose to induce payment in cash.

The question for decision, then, is whether the $2,000 rebate was offered to induce customers to use means other than credit. The declaration of Nathaniel Torres is that inducement to pay with means other than credit was not the purpose of the offer. Although an employee of Bob Baker Ford, Torres acted as the agent of Ford Motor Company so far as the availability of the rebate was concerned and so may be relied on in his statement that the rebate would have been offered to the Virachacks if they had sought to buy on credit but not at the extraordinarily low rate of 0.9%. If we accept Torres's unchallenged account of the facts, Ford Motor Company denied the rebate only because the manufacturer did not want to offer two incentives to the same customer. According to Torres, the $2,000 rebate is not an index of a hidden credit charge but simply a subsidy from the manufacturer that was available only to those not getting the subsidized interest rate. The element of a purpose to induce a cash payment—the element critical to the Virachacks' case—is absent.

This account is confirmed by two facts also furnished by Torres. Bob Baker Ford did not determine eligibility for the rebate. If a rebate had been offered, the price of the vehicle for sales tax purposes would not have been affected; the tax would have been paid on the price before the rebate. The price is therefore the same on credit or cash terms.

The Virachacks complain that, not being told of the possibility of the rebate in the "Federal Truth–In–Lending Disclosure," they never got to choose; that they, therefore, were not the informed users of credit that the federal law seeks to assure. Compliance with the TILA did not require them to be informed to this extent. They got a good deal. Seeking to get a windfall, they cannot get more than the statute and its regulations afford them.

For the foregoing reasons, the judgment of the district court is AFFIRMED.

B. FLETCHER, CIRCUIT JUDGE, dissenting.

The majority affirms the district court's summary judgment dismissal of the Virachacks' claim under the Truth in Lending Act ("TILA"), concluding their foregone rebate was not a finance charge. I respectfully dissent. A discount or rebate offered to purchasers paying with cash that is not extended to purchasers using credit is a finance charge. See F.R.B. Regulation Z, 12 C.F.R. § 226.4(b)(9) ("Regulation Z").

The Appellants, Malinee B. Virachack and Ritnarone T. Virachack, purchased a Ford Explorer from the Appellee, University Ford d/b/a Bob Baker Ford, the dealer and creditor. The Virachacks purchased the Explorer on a credit plan negotiated with Bob Baker Ford. The credit plan had an Average (sic) Percentage Rate ("APR") of 0.9%. To receive this APR, customers including the Virachacks had to forego a $2,000 manufacturer's rebate offered by Ford Motor Company ("Ford Motor") for the purchase of its Explorer. The $2,000 manufacturer's rebate was offered to all other customers purchasing an Explorer paying either cash or credit. The Virachacks argue the foregone rebate was a finance charge. As such, they argue the $2,000 increase in cost incurred by financing at 0.9% APR should have been disclosed to them under TILA.

A finance charge is defined by TILA "as the sum of all charges, payable directly or indirectly by the person to whom the credit is extended, and imposed directly or indirectly by the creditor as an incident to the extension of credit." 15 U.S.C. § 1605(a). Bob Baker Ford argues the foregone rebate was not a finance charge requiring disclosure under TILA. The district court agreed and the majority opinion affirms.

> As a general matter, discounts to purchasers using cash that are not extended to purchasers using credit are treated as finance charges. See 12 C.F.R. § 226.4(b)(9). Regulation Z specifically lists "Discounts for the purpose of inducing payment by a means other than the use of credit" under examples of finance charges. Id.

* * *

A discount offered to customers that pay in cash but withheld from customers paying with a particular form of credit is considered a finance charge to those customers paying with the particular form of credit. Withholding the rebate from these customers is necessarily a discount for the purpose of inducing payment by other means. This is a legal conclusion. A creditor's testimony on why he or she believes the rebate is withheld from customers paying with a particular form of credit is not pertinent to this consideration. The result of withholding the rebate is a discount to cash paying customers as contrasted to customers paying with the 0.9% APR plan.

The example used in the official staff interpretation of land being sold for $10,000 to purchasers using credit and for $9,000 to purchasers using cash is analogous to the Virachacks' transaction. If the Virachacks had paid cash for their Ford Explorer they would have received the $2,000 rebate. But under the credit plan with 0.9% APR they were denied the rebate and as a result paid $2,000 (plus interest on the $2,000 loaned) more for their car than a cash purchaser. Ford Explorers sold to purchasers paying cash cost at least $2,000 less than the same car sold to purchasers paying with the 0.9% APR credit plan.

The Virachacks are not requesting a "windfall" as the majority opinion suggests. Rather they simply want to be fully informed, as TILA requires, of the full costs of paying with the 0.9% APR credit plan. The credit plan extended to the Virachacks cost them $2,000 (plus interest) more than paying with cash would have cost them.

The district court found the foregone $2,000 rebate was not a finance charge. The district court reasoned that the $2,000 rebate was available to people who paid with either cash or credit. The only group excluded from the $2,000 rebate was composed of people who paid with the 0.9% APR financing. The district court's flawed reasoning was as follows, "Simply put, a consumer may obtain the rebate and still purchase on independently obtained credit. Forgoing the rebate, then, is not a condition of the extension of credit but, instead, is merely a condition of receiving the promotional rate."

The problem with this reasoning is that although forgoing the $2,000 rebate was not a cost for all purchasers using credit, it was a cost for all purchasers using Bob Baker Ford's 0.9% APR financing plan. The official staff interpretation of Regulation Z explains that when determining whether a charge is a finance charge one should look at the particular credit transaction at issue. 12 C.F.R. Pt. 226, Supp. 1 § 226.4–4(a)(1). The staff interpretation states "[c]harges imposed uniformly in cash and credit transactions are not finance charges. In determining whether an item is a finance charge, the creditor should compare the credit transaction in question with a similar cash transaction." Id. (emphasis added). This requires "the credit transaction in question" to be compared with a cash transaction. Id. If one compares the Virachacks' transaction with a cash transaction for a Ford Explorer then the Virachacks paid $2,000 (plus interest) more for their car than a cash purchaser would have paid.

At the time the Virachacks purchased their car, receiving the 0.9% APR credit required a purchaser to forego the $2,000 rebate. This was not a negotiable aspect of the sale. Persons receiving the 0.9% APR forfeited the rebate. Individuals paying cash or with other forms of credit were eligible for the rebate. Thus, in this case, the $2,000 rebate was withheld "as an incident to or as a condition of the extension of credit." 15 U.S.C. § 1605(a); 12 C.F.R. § 226.4(a). Foregoing the $2,000 credit was a cost of receiving Bob Baker Ford's 0.9% APR financing. The district court erred by comparing purchasers using credit as a general group to purchasers using cash. The fact that the Virachacks could seek other financing is irrelevant. When examining the costs of the credit terms offered, the appropriate comparison is between purchasers using the specific type of credit at issue and purchasers paying with cash. In this case, such a comparison reveals that the Virachacks and similarly situated customers paid $2,000 (plus interest) more for their vehicle than a cash purchaser paid for the same vehicle. This price differential for using the 0.9% APR financing was not disclosed to the Virachacks.

The central purpose of TILA is to provide "the informed use of credit" by requiring "meaningful disclosure of credit terms" to consumers. 15 U.S.C. § 1601; Ford Motor Credit Co. v. Milhollin, 444 U.S. 555, 559, 100 S.Ct. 790, 63 L.Ed.2d 22 (1980). If Ford Motor gives a rebate to every Bob Baker Ford customer buying a Ford Explorer but withholds the rebate from those customers financing at 0.9% then the foregone rebate is a cost to the latter group of customers. If 0.9% APR customers are not informed of the $2,000 rebate then they are ignorant of the full cost of the credit. This conflicts with the explicitly stated purpose of TILA:

> It is the purpose of this subchapter [15 U.S.C. § 1601 et seq.] to assure a meaningful disclosure of credit terms so that the consumer will be able to compare more readily the various credit terms available to him and avoid the uninformed use of credit, and to protect the consumer against inaccurate and unfair credit billing and credit card practices.

> 15 U.S.C. § 1601(a).

Not disclosing the $2,000 cost of the 0.9% financing means customers are making uninformed credit decisions. I believe the failure of Bob Baker Ford to disclose the foregone rebate violates TILA. I would reverse.

Notes

1. The "Truth" of Credit Costs in *Virachack*

Can you follow the money in Virachack? Is the incentive arrangement among the dealer (Bob Baker), the finance company (Ford Motor Credit Co.), and the factory (Ford Motor Co.) anything more than a shell game to induce customers to buy? Did the Virachacks really pay $2,000 more than the TILA disclosures revealed?

What if the dealer could prove that Ford Motor Company (the factory) was anxious to reduce its overstocked inventory, and so was willing to sacrifice some of its wholesale revenue by giving rebate checks to some customers and reimbursing FMCC (the finance company) for the lost interest income from other customers. Would this change your sentiment about the case? Suppose, instead, that the Virachacks could prove that the Ford factory simply increased its wholesale prices—what the dealer had to pay—for cars subject to the rebate and low-rate promotions? Now what do you think of the case?

Even if the dissent is correct that the foregone $2,000 rebate appears to be a cost of credit for the Virachacks, which party "imposed" that charge on them? The dealer didn't make an extra nickel on this sale; the cash price of the car was the same whether the buyers took the rebate, or the low rate, or neither. FMCC didn't make any extra money; in fact it collected only a 0.9% finance charge from the buyers and got some reimbursement ("subvention") from the manufacturer. And the Ford factory was either discounting its prices to move inventory or inflating the prices it charged the dealer. In any case, who is the "creditor" here, and how did that party "impose" the $2,000 charge? Review the definition of *creditor* in Reg. Z, particularly § 226.2(a)(17)(i)(B), and *finance charge* in Reg. Z § 226.4(a).

2. Tied-in Sales: The Conundrum of Credit Insurance and Other "Optional" Products

As the "truism" above suggests, a creditor can generate additional revenue for itself by selling the borrower-customer additional products or services, each with its own mark-up or profit. Are the creditors earnings on these "tied" sales finance charges, or not?

The most long-standing example of tied sales is credit life and disability insurance that protects the creditor by paying off the debt if the debtor dies, is disabled, or out of work. The insurance is available through the creditor, but the actual policies or certificates of insurance are issued by third-party insurance companies. The consumer pays a premium for this insurance, and enjoys coverage that may benefit the consumer's family or survivors. At the same time, as the beneficiary of the insurance, the creditor is protected against otherwise uncollectible debts. Moreover, the creditor virtually always receives a portion of the premium as a rebate or commission from the insurance company. In fact, credit insurance, and related products called "debt cancellation agreements" (DCAs), can be enormously profitable for the creditor.

TILA's treatment of credit insurance has been a bit equivocal from the beginning. Credit insurance premiums (and charges for DCAs) **are** *prima facie* finance charges. Reg. Z § 226.4(b)(7) and (10). But those premiums are then excluded from the finance charge if the insurance is voluntary for the customer and the customer signs an election to purchase it after receiving disclosures of its cost. Reg. Z § 226.4(d)(1) and (3). As a practical matter, few creditors will require credit insurance, because that means including the premium in the finance charge and inflating the APR. Instead, creditors make the insurance available on an optional basis, make appropriate disclosures that it is not required, and then try hard to persuade customers to buy it. Critics of credit insurance argue that a phenomenon called "reverse competition'' operates here: creditors are inclined to provide the most expensive insurance coverages, rather than the cheapest, in order to enhance their rebate/commission earnings.

Is the TILA approach a satisfactory accommodation of consumer and creditor expectations about credit insurance? Is it consistent with TILA's quest for "truth" in lending? Is it adequately protective of consumers? Consider:

Problem 2–20

When Wanda went to buy her new car, she bargained with the Dealer over model, color, accessories, and price. She even insisted on knowing what APR would apply to the financing of her purchase. But neither Wanda nor Dealer mentioned credit insurance. When the Dealer prepared the installment sale contract (like the sample earlier in this Chapter), it contained the necessary disclosures that the insurance was optional, and its price. The Dealer put a small "x" at several points on the form, and handed Wanda a pen, implying she was to sign at each point, one of which was the election to buy credit insurance. Wanda looked over the form quickly, and signed at each "x." Later, she read the contract more closely and realized she had purchased $700.00 worth of credit insurance, and that premium was included in the Amount Financed rather than the Finance Charge.

Wanda sues Dealer for violating TILA. She argues that Dealer had implicitly required her to sign up for the credit insurance by indicating where to sign and handing her the pen. She also can prove that 96% of Dealer's customers take the insurance, which, she claims, supports an inference that the insurance is in fact required. Dealer responds that under the parol evidence rule Wanda's signature should be conclusive proof that she elected to buy the insurance. Also, says Dealer, most of his customers are lower income and they buy the credit insurance because they don't have any separate health insurance of their own. Who wins? Cf., USLife Credit Corp. v. FTC, 599 F.2d 1387 (5th Cir. 1979), *reh'g denied*, 604 F.2d 671 (5th Cir. 1979).

Problem 2–21

(a) Suppose, in the prior problem, that the Dealer used a similar technique to get Wanda to purchase an extended warranty on the new car. Dealer obtains the extended warranty contracts from a third-party vendor for an average price of $300.00, and marks them up to about $600.00 for retail customers like Wanda. For each extended warranty sold, Dealer remits $300.00 to the vendor, and keeps the rest. Is this extra income a finance charge? Read Reg. Z § 226.4(a) carefully.

(b) Assume that the extended warranty is not a finance charge, so it can properly be included in the Amount Financed in the transaction. TILA requires creditors to itemize the Amount Financed, including any amounts paid to third parties on the consumer's behalf. Reg. Z § 226.18(c)(1)(iii). May the creditor treat the whole $600.00 extended warranty charge as a third-party payment? Or must the creditor reveal the fact of the $300.00 mark-up that it is retaining? See Reg. Z.

Commentary ¶ 18(c)(1)(iii)–2. And see the regulatory gloss put on this Commentary by Judge Richard Posner in Gibson v. Bob Watson Chevrolet–Geo, Inc., 112 F.3d 283 (7th Cir. 1997). Is Form 2–A, supra, in compliance with TILA on this point?

Problem 2–22

Jane Consumer buys a new compact disc player from Cal's Discount Audio Shop, and pays the $200 price using her Visa card. While Jane will have to repay her bank the $200, Cal got only $192 out of the transaction. This is because the bank charges a 4% "merchant discount" to merchants who honor the cards. The discount covers costs of processing the transaction and advancing credit to the merchant. Jane's monthly statement, however, makes no mention of the 4% merchant discount, nor is that amount computed into the finance charge or APR disclosed to Jane. Has the issuing bank violated TILA? If so, why is it that no card issuer includes information about merchant discounts on its monthly statements?

8.   SPECIAL ISSUES IN MORTGAGE TRANSACTIONS

Transactions involving a mortgage on the consumer's home are likely the largest and most significant credit obligations the consumer incurs in a lifetime. Those transactions get special treatment under TILA, and we look briefly at some of those issues here.

The distinctive TILA treatment of home mortgages includes these elements:

1.   The $25,000 cap on TILA coverage does not apply to transactions "secured by real property, or by personal property used or expected to be used as the principal dwelling of the consumer." Reg. Z § 226.3(b). The "personal property" phrase picks up such items as mobile homes or houseboats.

2.   The definition of "finance charge" specifically excludes certain real-estate related fees, such as title insurance, appraisals, deed preparation, and the like. Reg. Z § 226.4(c)(7).

3.   For "residential mortgages," early estimated disclosures must be given at the time of loan application. Reg. Z § 226.19.

4.   Additional, and lengthy, disclosures are required for "open-end credit plans secured by the consumer's dwelling," i.e., home equity lines of credit, or HELOCs. Reg. Z § 226.5b.

5.   For any variable-rate credit contract "secured by a dwelling," the creditor must include in the contract the maximum interest rate that may be imposed. Reg. Z § 226.30.

6.   Non-purchase money mortgages on the consumer's "principal dwelling" are subject to a three-day right of rescission—a cooling-off period, in effect. Reg. Z §§ 226.15 [open-end credit], 226.23 [closed-end credit]. This includes most second mortgages, including HELOCs, and most refinancings of first mortgages. See Chapter 7, infra.

7. Special disclosures are required for "reverse mortgages," *i.e.*, typically where an elderly consumer draws down the accumulated equity in the home over time. Reg. Z § 226.33.

8. Since the 1994 enactment of the Home Ownership and Equity Protection Act, there are extensive additional disclosures and other limitations on so-called "high cost" mortgages. Reg. Z § 226.32. These provisions are aimed at "predatory lending" practices, and are considered in depth in Chapter 9, infra.

The following case picks up the thread of disclosure concerns in the mortgage context. It also introduces the Real Estate Settlement Procedures Act.

BROPHY v. CHASE MANHATTAN MORT. CO.

U.S. Dist. Ct., E.D. PA., 1996.
947 F.Supp. 879.

ANITA B. BRODY, DISTRICT JUDGE.

Before me is defendants' Motion for Summary Judgment. Plaintiffs Donald Brophy and Joan Brophy ("the Brophys") allege that the defendant Chase Manhattan Mortgage Corporation ("Chase Manhattan") and its agent, defendant William Bowen ("Bowen"), violated the Real Estate Settlement Procedures Act ("RESPA"), 12 U.S.C.A. § 2601 *et seq.,* the Truth in Lending Act ("TILA"), 15 U.S.C.A. § 1601 *et seq.,* the Pennsylvania Unfair Trade Practices and Consumer Protection Law, 73 P.S. § 201–1 *et seq.,* and Pennsylvania tort law by misrepresenting the terms and charges of a Veterans Affairs, fixed rate, thirty (30) year mortgage for the purchase of residential real estate. I will grant defendants' Motion for Summary Judgment with respect to the Brophys' claim under RESPA and TILA, and I will dismiss all remaining claims under state law.

I. FACTS

On June 8, 1995, the Brophys applied for a thirty (30) year fixed-rate mortgage from Chase Manhattan to purchase residential real estate. In connection with their application the Brophys were given two documents, one a "Good Faith Estimate" and the other a Regulation Z Disclosure ("Initial Regulation Z Disclosure"). Under "Items Payable in Connection with Loan," the Good Faith Estimate estimated the Loan Origination Fee would be $886.38, which represented one (1) percent of the loan. The Good Faith Estimate showed a zero ($0.00) figure as the amount for the Loan Discount, indicating that none would be payable. Furthermore, under the section entitled, "Items Required by Lender to be Paid in Advance," the Mortgage Insurance Premium was estimated to be $1,738.[3] Good Faith Estimate dated June 8, 1995. On June 12, 1995,

3. Correspondingly, the Initial Regulation Z Disclosure listed the sum of $886.38 for the item designated "Loan Fee Paid by Buyer" and the sum of $1,738 as a charge for "Private Mortgage Insur-

the Brophys signed the Good Faith Estimate and the Initial Regulation Z Disclosure and returned them to Chase Manhattan.[4]

When the Brophys settled on July 31, 1995, Chase Manhattan gave them a Settlement Statement and a final Regulation Z Disclosure ("Final Regulation Z Disclosure") detailing the actual charges and fees that the Brophys were required to pay. The Settlement Statement listed a Loan Origination Fee of $1,902.02, a Loan Discount of $885.07, and a FA Funding Fee of $2,607. Settlement Statement dated July 31, 1996. In other words, the Loan Origination Fee which was estimated at $886.38 was now $1,902.02; the FA Funding Fee estimated at $1,738 was now $2,607; and the Loan Discount that was estimated at zero ($0.00) was now $885.07.[5] The annual percentage rate, 7.5 percent, did not vary from the time the good faith estimates were made on June 8, 1995, until the time of settlement on July 31, 1995.

II. DISCUSSION

The Brophys claim that Chase Manhattan and Bowen violated RESPA, TILA, the Pennsylvania Unfair Trade and Consumer Protection Act, and state tort law by misrepresenting the charges they would incur at settlement for the mortgage on their home.

A. Real Estate Settlement Procedures Act ("RESPA")

The Brophys contend that the defendants did not comply with the statutory disclosure requirements of RESPA because the defendants failed to provide them with a good faith estimate of the charges that they were likely to incur in connection with the settlement of their mortgage. The Brophys claim that the disclosures they received from the defendants were inaccurate and misleading and thereby violated the requirements of 12 U.S.C.A. § 2604(c) of RESPA[6] and the applicable regulation, Regulation X, 24 C.F.R. § 3500.7(c).[7] The defendants respond that the

---

ance/MIP/VA Funding Fee." Initial Regulation Z Disclosure dated June 8, 1995.

4. The Brophys allege that Bowen, an agent for Chase Manhattan, assured them that the terms of the mortgage were "locked in." Compl. ¶ 18. There is nothing in the evidentiary record, however, to support this.

5. Correspondingly, the Final Regulation Z Disclosure disclosed the sum of $2,787.09 for the "Loan Fee Paid by Buyer" (includes the sum of the Loan Origination Fee and the Loan Discount Fee on the Settlement Statement) and $2,607 for the "Private Mortgage Insurance/MIP/VA Funding Fee." Final Regulation Z Disclosure dated July 31, 1995.

6. Section 2604(c) of RESPA provides:

Each lender shall include with the booklet a good faith estimate of the amount or range of charges for specific settlement services the borrower is likely to incur in con-

nection with the settlement as prescribed by the Secretary. 12 U.S.C. § 2604(c) (West 1989).

7. Regulation X, 24 C.F.R. § 3500.7(c) provides in pertinent part:

Content of good faith estimate. A good faith estimate consists of an estimate, as a dollar amount or range, of each charge which:

* * *

(2) That the borrower will normally pay or incur at or before settlement based upon common practice in the locality of the mortgaged property. Each such estimate must be made in good faith and bear a reasonable relationship to the charge a borrower is likely to be required to pay at settlement, and must be based upon experience in the locality of the mortgaged property ... 24 C.F.R. § 3500.7(c) (West Supp.1996).

Brophys do not state a claim under RESPA because no private right of action exists under § 2604.

The primary source of a private right of action is the text of the statute itself. American Telephone and Telegraph v. M/V Cape Fear, 967 F.2d 864, 866 (3d Cir.1992). Section 2614 of RESPA, the only provision of the Act that provides for a private right of action, states:

> Any action pursuant to the provisions of section 2607 or 2608 of this title may be brought in the United States district court or in any other court of competent jurisdiction ... 12 U.S.C.A. § 2614.

Thus, § 2614 provides for a private right of action for claims brought under § 2607 (prohibits the giving or accepting of fees, kickbacks, or a portion, percentage, or split of the charges for settlement services with others who did not perform those services) and § 2608 (prohibits the seller from requiring the buyer to purchase title insurance from any particular title company) but does not provide for such a right under § 2604, the section the Brophys claim the defendants violated.

* * *

Since the statute specifically provides for a private right of action under specific sections—but not § 2604—a private right of action should not be implied under § 2604. The Honorable Morton A. Brody (no relation to me) in Campbell v. Machias Savings Bank, 865 F.Supp. 26, 32 (D.Maine 1994), is the only other judge found to have spoken on this issue and his holding accords with mine.

The legislative history strengthens my plain meaning interpretation of the statute relating to an implied right of action under § 2604. As originally enacted in December 1974, § 2604(c) required lenders to provide to those who filed an application to borrow money to purchase residential real estate with a booklet to help them better understand the nature and costs of real estate settlement services. It read:

> Each lender [who makes federally related mortgage loans] shall provide the booklet described in such subsection to each person from whom it receives an application to borrow money to finance the purchase of residential real estate. Such booklet shall be provided at the time of receipt of such application.

Real Estate Settlement Procedures Act of 1974, Pub.L. No. 93–533, § 5(c) (amended 1976), 88 Stat. 1725, *reprinted in* 1974 U.S.C.C.A.N. 1984, 1986–87. The original legislation also included § 2605 ("Section 6")—now repealed—which required lenders to provide prospective borrowers with an itemized disclosure of each charge arising in connection with a real estate settlement, or if the exact amount was not available, a good faith estimate of that charge. Section 6 also required lenders to provide these advance disclosures or good faith estimates no later than twelve (12) days prior to settlement. If the lender did not comply with these provisions, Section 6(b) provided for an express private right of action against the lender.

Several months after enacting RESPA, Congress determined that the twelve (12) day advance notice provision under Section 6 only further complicated the settlement process instead of simplifying it. H.R.Rep. No. 667, 94th Cong., 1st Sess. 4 (1975), *reprinted in* 1975 U.S.C.C.A.N. 2448, 2451. As a result, in January 1976, Congress repealed Section 6, including the private right of action against lenders who failed to comply with the advance disclosure/good faith estimate provisions. Still intending to promote the objectives it sought with advance disclosures and good faith estimates, Congress amended § 2604 in January 1976. According to the legislative history, Congress amended § 2604 in order that there would be disclosure of good faith estimates of settlement costs in the special information booklet provided to the borrower at the time a written application for a mortgage loan was made. H.R.Rep. No. 667, 94th Cong., 1st Sess. 2 (1975), *reprinted in* 1975 U.S.C.C.A.N. 2448, 2449. This amendment was codified in § 2604(c), the present form of the statute, and contained no express private right of action for a violation of this good faith estimate requirement.

Furthermore, the legislative history reveals that Congress was well aware that it was eliminating a private right of action by repealing Section 6 and amending § 2604. In opposing the above amendments to RESPA, Representative Leonor K. Sullivan of Missouri warned: "[I]t should be noted that in repealing Section 6, the bill eliminates any penalty whatsoever for failing to give information which is, in fact, a 'good faith' estimate." H.R.Rep. No. 667, 94th Cong., 1st Sess. 18 (1975), *reprinted in* 1975 U.S.C.C.A.N. 2448, 2459. Notwithstanding Representative Sullivan's concern, Congress repealed Section 6, amended § 2604, and as a result, extinguished the private right of action that had initially existed for failure to comply with the advance disclosure/good faith estimate provisions of RESPA. Hence, I conclude that the legislative history indicates that Congress did not intend to create a private right of action under amended § 2604. Therefore, I will grant defendants' Motion for Summary Judgment on the Brophys' claim under RESPA.

B.   Truth in Lending Act ("TILA")

The Brophys allege that the defendants' estimates of the costs associated with their mortgage were not made in good faith in violation of 15 U.S.C.A. § 1638 and Regulation Z, 12 C.F.R. §§ 226.17–.19, because the estimates inaccurately and misleadingly understated the actual costs incurred at settlement. Specifically, at settlement, the Loan Origination Fee that was estimated at $886.38 was $1,902.02; the FA Funding Fee (Mortgage Insurance Premium) that was estimated at $1,738 was $2,607; and the Loan Discount that was estimated at zero ($0.00) was $885.07. Despite these numerical discrepancies, the defendants claim that they have complied with the statutory disclosure requirements under TILA because the statute simply requires them to provide an initial disclosure statement and a final disclosure statement—which they did. Accordingly, defendants assert that the Brophys fail to state a claim under TILA and request summary judgment in their favor.

Section 1638(b)(2) of TILA requires lenders in residential mortgage transactions to provide good faith estimates of the financial disclosures required under § 1638(a).[8] It states:

> In the case of a residential mortgage transaction ... good faith estimates of the disclosures required under subsection (a) of this section shall be made in accordance with regulations of the Board under section 1631(c) of this title before the credit is extended, or shall be delivered or placed in the mail not later than three business days after the creditor receives the consumer's written application, whichever is earlier. If the disclosure statement furnished within three days of the written application contains an annual percentage rate which is subsequently rendered inaccurate within the meaning of subsection 1606(c)[9] of this title, the creditor shall furnish another statement at the time of settlement or consummation.

15 U.S.C.A. § 1638(b)(2) (West 1982). The corresponding regulation, Regulation Z, § 226.19, provides in pertinent part:

> **(a) Residential mortgage transactions subject to RESPA— (1) Time of disclosures.** In a residential mortgage transaction subject to the Real Estate Settlement Procedures Act ... the creditor shall make good faith estimates of the disclosures required by § 226.18 before consummation, or shall deliver or place them in the mail not later than three business days after the creditor receives the consumer's written application, whichever is earlier.

12 C.F.R. § 226.19(a)(1) (West Supp.1996).

Section 1631(c) of TILA authorizes the Board of Governors of the Federal Reserve System, the Board authorized to prescribe regulations under § 1604 of the Act, to allow estimates to satisfy the statutory disclosure requirements of the statute. It states, in pertinent part:

> The Board may provide by regulation that any portion of the information required to be disclosed by this subchapter may be given in the form of estimates where the provider of such information is not in a position to know exact information.

15 U.S.C.A. § 1631(c) (West 1996). The corresponding regulation provides:

> If any information necessary for an accurate disclosure is unknown to the creditor, it shall make the disclosure based on the best information reasonably available and shall state that the disclosure is an estimate.

12 C.F.R. § 226.17(c)(2) (West 1982).

* * *

8. [Quoting TILA § 1638(a)].

9. Section 1606(c) concerns the degree to which the annual percentage rate can vary from the time of disclosure and yet still comply with the Act.

In the present case, the only evidence presented in support of summary judgment was the estimate required under § 1638(b)(2), the settlement statement, and the corresponding Regulation Z disclosures. No depositions, affidavits, or other testimony were submitted by either side. Without more, the Brophys argue that a trier of fact may draw an inference from the disparities between the initial good faith estimates and the final settlement figures that the defendants' initial estimates were not made in good faith. I disagree.

The evidence submitted is uncontradicted: both parties agree that the estimates, settlement statement, and Regulation Z Disclosures are what they claim to be. The dispute centers around the interpretation of the discrepancies within these documents. Although the Brophys assert that the differences between the estimates and the settlement statement stem from the fact that the estimates were not made in good faith, they have proffered no evidence specifically setting forth this claim. In actuality, there are a plethora of possible reasons—not involving defendants' lack of good faith—as to why the estimated figures fluctuated by the time of settlement. While the Brophys insist that an inference of the defendants' lack of good faith can be drawn from the evidence before me sufficient to withstand summary judgment, I cannot take that leap. "The judge's inquiry ... unavoidably asks whether reasonable jurors could find by a preponderance of the evidence that the plaintiff is entitled to a verdict." *Id.* Without depositions, affidavits, or other evidence of that nature detailing specific underlying facts of this dispute, an inference that the defendants estimates were not made in good faith cannot be justifiably drawn. The Brophys have not even submitted an affidavit from a professional in the residential mortgage industry opining on the significance of the disparities between the estimates and the settlement statement and how that might indicate a lack of good faith. Based on the limited evidence before me, a finding by the jury that the defendants' estimates were not made in good faith would be mere speculation.[10]

The statutory framework of TILA also suggests that a discrepancy between the estimates and the final settlement figures—without more—is insufficient to draw an inference that the defendants' estimates were not made in good faith. Under TILA, the nature of the disclosures required in non-residential mortgage transactions fundamentally differs from that of the disclosures required in the residential mortgage context. In non-residential mortgage transactions TILA directs:

[T]he disclosures required under [§ 1638(a)] shall be made before the credit is extended.

15 U.S.C.A. § 1638(b)(1) (West 1982). In contrast, in residential mortgage contexts, TILA requires:

10. If the Brophys' claim were based upon an attack of how the estimates were produced under Regulation Z—although it does not seem to be—then it might survive summary judgment by showing that the defendants failed to base their estimates upon "the best information reasonably available." 12 C.F.R. § 226.17(c)(2). The Brophys, however, have proffered no evidence to show this either.

> In the case of a residential mortgage transaction, . . . good faith estimates of the disclosures required under [§ 1638(a)] shall be made in accordance with [Regulation Z] . . . before the credit is extended.

15 U.S.C.A. § 1638(b)(2) (West 1982). Thus, in residential mortgage contexts, TILA requires estimates—not actual disclosures—of the items listed in § 1638(a). The fact that § 1638(b)(2) only requires estimates of the disclosures presumes that the final figures might change before settlement. In fact, § 1631(c) explicitly states that estimates will be given "where the provider of such information is not in a position to know exact information." 15 U.S.C.A. § 1631(c). Apparently, then, the statute makes allowances for variance between estimates and final disclosures in residential mortgage transactions. Therefore, I cannot draw the inference that the defendants' estimates were not made in good faith solely because the estimates vary from the settlement disclosures.

Along similar lines, the strict liability regime created under the statute also suggests that the Brophys cannot legitimately draw an inference from the discrepancies between the estimates and the settlement statement that the defendants' estimates were not made in good faith. TILA is a strict liability statute liberally construed in favor of consumers. *Smith v. Fidelity Consumer Discount Co.,* 898 F.2d 896, 898 (3d Cir.1990). A creditor who fails to comply with the Act in any respect is liable to the consumer under the statute. *Id.* "[O]nce the court finds a violation, no matter how technical, it has no discretion with respect to [imposing] liability." *Id.* (quoting *Grant v. Imperial Motors,* 539 F.2d 506, 510 (5th Cir.1976)). Therefore, except in the residential mortgage context, any discrepancy between an actual disclosure and what a borrower is later charged ordinarily constitutes a violation under the Act.[11] *See McGowan v. King, Inc.,* 569 F.2d 845, 848 (5th Cir.1978) (understatement of "deferred payment price" by $3.52 constituted violation of TILA); *Grant v. Imperial Motors,* 539 F.2d 506, 510 (5th Cir.1976) (finance charge understated by $16.00 constitutes a violation of TILA). In contrast, in residential mortgage transactions, good faith estimates are required instead of actual disclosures. Estimates are given when a creditor "is not in a position to know exact information," 15 U.S.C.A. § 1631(c), and are "based upon the best information reasonably available." 12 C.F.R. § 226.17(c)(2). Hence, the fact that an estimate fluctuates by the time of settlement does not itself constitute a violation of the Act. Thus, unlike disclosures in non-residential mortgage contexts, the good faith estimates can vary from the time they are revealed until settlement without giving rise to a statutory violation of the Act. Hence, fluctuation of an estimate alone does not invoke liability under the Act. This further supports my conclusion that the necessary inference cannot be drawn that the defendants' estimates failed to be made in good faith on the basis of a change in the estimate alone.

11. Sections 1640(b), (c), (f) enumerate statutory defenses to violations of the Act.

For these reasons, I find that the Brophys' proffer of the documents alone fails to provide the basis for a justifiable inference that the defendants estimates were not made in good faith. Accordingly, I will grant summary judgment in favor of defendants on this claim.

C. Supplemental State Law Claims

The Brophys also allege violations under the Pennsylvania Unfair Trade Practices and Consumer Protection Law, 73 P.S. § 201–1 *et seq.*, and state tort law for the misleading and inaccurate representations concerning the amount and variability of the loan fees. As I am granting defendants' Motion for Summary Judgment on plaintiffs' claims under RESPA and TILA, there are no remaining federal questions before this Court. As a result, I dismiss without prejudice all of plaintiffs' supplemental state law claims.

Note: Home Equity Loans

In recent years, so-called "home equity lines of credit" have become wide-spread. This is sort of a cross between the traditional closed-end second mortgage and the credit card open-end account. Like a credit card account, the consumer is allowed to draw on a pre-established line of credit at varying times and in varying amounts. Like a second mortgage, the lender will take a security interest in the consumer's home to secure the outstanding balance.

When home equity loans first appeared, it seemed clear enough that they were open-end transactions, but the TIL disclosures for open-end transactions were written primarily for credit card accounts. Most credit card accounts are unsecured, but home equity loans are potentially more risky for consumers, because upon default the consumer could lose his or her house. The existing disclosures did not adequately address this problem.

As a result, in 1988 Congress passed the Home Equity Loan Consumer Protection Act of 1988. This act added several new provisions to the Truth in Lending Act. See TILA §§ 127A, 137, and 147, 15 U.S.C. §§ 1637a, 1647, 1665b. In 1989 the Board added corresponding amendments to Reg. Z to implement the new act. For each home equity loan transaction, lenders now must make three sets of disclosures. The first must be made at the time the application is given to the consumer. See Reg. Z § 226.5b(b). The second corresponds to the initial disclosure statement on credit card accounts. Normally, this second set of disclosures will be given at closing, along with the other contract documents. See Reg. Z § 226.6(e). Finally, as in all open-end accounts, a periodic disclosure statement containing the details of the current activity in the account must be provided each month (or other period). Reg. Z § 226.7.

Problem 2–23

Look at the sample suggested by the Board as the HELOC disclosure to be given at the time of application. Reg. Z § 226 App. G–14A. Review it in the light of Reg. Z § 226.5b(d).

(a) Can you follow the disclosures so that you have a basic understanding of the plan? Which pieces of information are most, and least, helpful? In particular, given the volatility of interest rates over time, what is the value of the 15–year "Historical Example"? Does it have any predictive utility?

(b) Are these disclosures too complex and lengthy for an average consumer? Is this an instance of "information overload"? If you think this disclosure is too complex, is that because of the disclosure rules, or is it due to the inherent complexities of HELOC products? If the latter, should the law require simpler, more standardized loan plans, without all the bells and whistles?

Query: The RESPA and TILA "good faith estimates" must be given within three days after the consumer has submitted a written application. Reg. Z § 226.19(a)(1). Even if they precisely state all the relevant mortgage charges, are those "GFEs" likely to affect the consumer's behavior?

Note: *The Gordian Knot of mortgage disclosure*

The *Brophy* case underscores what has become a stalemate of policy-making concerning appropriate disclosure of costs in mortgage transactions. Both RESPA and TILA require "good faith estimates" at the time of application for a mortgage loan. RESPA focuses on charges and disbursements at settlement, i.e., "closing costs." TILA of course addresses the costs of *credit*, including APR and Finance Charge. One issue is whether these sets of disclosures can be synchronized to give consumers the required information in an efficient manner that does not create huge compliance burdens for the mortgage industry. *Brophy* suggests that the responsible agencies, the Department of Housing and Urban Development (for RESPA), and the Federal Reserve Board (for TILA), have made some efforts to coordinate the two sets of disclosures in this regard, within the limits of the respective statutes. The more difficult problem is how to give consumers early information about both closing costs and credit costs that is reliable and firm, and not merely "estimates" subject to dramatic skews between the time of application and mortgage closing, as in *Brophy*.

In the mid–1990s, Congress directed the two agencies, HUD and FRB, to "simplify and improve" TILA and RESPA, by regulation if possible, or by recommending statutory amendments if these were necessary. The agencies together issued a report in 1998, making numerous suggestions for statutory revision of the two statutes: Board of Governors of the Federal Reserve System & Department of Housing and Urban Development, Joint Report to the Congress Concerning Reform of the Truth in Lending Act and the Real Estate Settlement Procedures Act (1998). Regrettably, despite this investment of effort, plus several years of follow-on discussions among interest groups, and intimations by HUD that it would proceed with "reform" on its own, nothing has happened (as of 2007), either in Congress or the agencies.

The "Gordian knot" in this saga is the second issue posed above. One set of voices, on behalf of consumers, claims that early mortgage disclosures, under both RESPA and TILA, are unhelpful and even misleading when they rest on mere "estimates" that do not correspond to the reality of fees, charges, rates, and disbursements that show up in the transaction paperwork at closing. For consumers to make intelligent decisions, they say, the brokers and lenders should be required to commit to the various closing cost fees, and to the rate (APR) and interest (Finance Charge) in the loan itself, within a very short time after the consumer applies for the loan. But, say the brokers and lenders, we cannot realistically commit to specific rates and fees at the start of the application process; we need time to process the application, to consider appraisals, credit reports, and the sundry other assessments that make up the underwriting process. Plus, says the industry, many closing costs are set by third-party suppliers, like appraisers and title insurance companies, and those charges vary with time and circumstance; the best we can do is give you a good-faith estimate. Not necessarily so, is the consumerist rejoinder; closing costs could be ''bundled'' at a disclosable fixed price, and with current technologies interest rates could be quoted that are locked-in in most cases. In the wings, the numerous sub-industries that make up the settlement process—realtors, brokers, inspectors, appraisers, title and casualty insurance companies, courier services, and so on—bridle at suggested intrusions into their businesses.

The debate continues. Perhaps in your (students') lifetimes there will be ''RESPA–TILA reform.'' Meanwhile, your authors are not holding their breaths.

In case we are wrong about RESPA–TILA reform, this space is reserved for appropriate material on that subject.

HENDLEY v. CAMERON–BROWN CO.

United States Court of Appeals, Eleventh Circuit, 1988.
840 F.2d 831.

Vance, Circuit Judge:

The question in this appeal is whether appellee, a mortgage company, properly disclosed the terms of appellants' discounted variable rate loans as required by the Truth In Lending Act, 15 U.S.C. §§ 1601–1693r. Appellants argue that the mortgage company failed to disclose fully the circumstances which would increase the initial interest rate. Finding that appellee was technically in compliance with the regulations and that appellee's good faith effort protected any disclosure inadequacies, the district court for the Middle District of Georgia granted appellee's motion for summary judgment. We reverse.

I.

In the spring of 1984, appellants, the Hendleys and the Blacks, obtained discounted variable rate mortgage loans from appellee to finance the purchase of their homes. One feature of the variable rate loans was the annual adjustment of the interest rate. The annual interest rate was based on an"index plus margin" formula which was determined by adding to the margin, preset at 2.79%, the current index. Appellants claim that they were informed that the interest rate on the loans would adjust annually in the same direction as the index. The Hendleys closed their $69,250 loan on April 30, 1984. On the next day, May 1, 1984, the Blacks closed their $80,025.46 loan. At closing, appellants received a Truth In Lending Disclosure Statement. This disclosure statement identified the mortgage as a variable rate loan and provided that "[t]he interest rate may increase during the term of this transaction if the index increases."

Approximately forty-five days before the end of the loan's first year, appellee informed appellants that the interest rate for the second year would increase from 9.875% to 11.875%. Appellee claims that this increase was based on the "index plus margin" formula provided in the loan agreement checked by the 2% annual cap. Objecting to this increase, appellants filed suit claiming that appellee failed to comply with the disclosure requirements of the Truth In Lending Act. Because the index actually declined in the second year from 10.53% to 9.61%, appellants maintain that the increase is inconsistent with the disclosure statement's language that the interest rate would be adjusted annually in the same direction as the index. Appellants argue that appellee failed to disclose the initial index and that the initial interest rate was discounted or lower than the rate would be if it were calculated by using the "index plus margin" formula. According to appellants these undisclosed facts created other circumstances for an increased interest rate and the failure to disclose this information violated statutory and regulatory disclosure requirements.

The district court ruled that the mortgage company technically complied with the requirements of the Truth In Lending Act and its regulations. The district court found that the initial index information "was not explicitly disclosed" and that the disclosure statement failed to disclose that the initial interest rate was discounted. The court nevertheless held that appellee technically complied with the disclosure requirements due to the lack of specific guidance for discounted variable rate loans. Since the discounted variable rate loan was a new product in early 1984 and the application of Regulation Z, 12 C.F.R. § 226, to these loans was not clear, the court ruled that "any inadequacies are protected by [appellee's] good faith effort at compliance."

II.

Congress enacted the Truth In Lending Act to ensure meaningful disclosures in consumer credit transactions. *See* 15 U.S.C. § 1601(a). The Federal Reserve Board ("Board") promulgated Regulation Z to execute the purposes of the Truth In Lending Act. The Board established the disclosure requirements for variable rate loans in 12 C.F.R. § 226.18(f). This provision provides:

If the annual percentage rate may increase after consummation, the following disclosures [are required]:

(1) The circumstances under which the rate may increase.

* * *

We hold that appellee did not comply with the first requirement by fully disclosing the "circumstances under which the rate may increase." The disclosure statement provided that "the interest rate may increase during the term of this transaction if the index increases." This, however, was not the only circumstance which could cause an increase in the interest rate. As the district court stated, "[t]he problem is that the statement fails to note that the initial interest rate is discounted, creating the possibility of an increase even when the index does not rise." Due to the initial discounted interest rate, the annual interest rate could increase if the index remained constant, or even if the index declined. Absent this information, the disclosure failed to meet regulatory standards.

* * *

Appellee also argues that even if the disclosure were improper, it is insulated from liability under 15 U.S.C. § 1640(f) because it acted in good faith in accordance with the Board's official interpretation of regulation § 226.18(f). * * * Section 1640(f) "does not protect a creditor who *fails* to conform with a regulation or interpretation through an honest, good faith mistake." So a creditor's honest and reasonable but mistaken interpretation is not protected. Appellee's belief that the regulation did not require further disclosure based on its mistaken interpretation of the regulation and reliance on an inapplicable interpretation does not protect it from liability. As a matter of law, the section 1640(f) good faith defense is not available.

III.

Accordingly, we reverse the district court's decision granting summary judgment in favor of appellees and remand for further proceedings consistent with this opinion.

REVERSED and REMANDED.

Notes

1. Variable rates present some formidable problems under the Truth in Lending disclosure scheme, because not only the APR but also the number and amount of payments may change. Do you think that this is an area where consumers are particularly vulnerable and therefore need some additional protection? Why? Read Reg. Z §§ 226.18(f) and 226.19(b). Do these provisions require disclosure of all the important features of variable rate loans? Is there information you would like to see disclosed that is not included? Do they provide consumers with enough information so they can properly analyze and compare the various new types of alternative mortgag-

es such as graduated payment (not variable rate) mortgages, growth equity mortgages, reverse annuity mortgages, etc.? Note that when the transaction in *Hendley* took place, the only guidance on variable rate disclosures was that in Reg. Z § 226.18(f), quoted by the court. But in the late 1980s, the Federal Reserve Board promulgated an expansive new set of required disclosures for variable rate mortgage loans, including a "Consumer Handbook on Adjustable Rate Mortgages," and a dozen other batches of information about the loan. These rules appear in § 226.19(b). How do they deal with the issue in *Hendley*? Is it possible that these rules overdo it, and could cause "information overload"?

2. How on earth can a lender provide a single APR, a total dollar amount of finance charge, and a payment schedule, in a transaction like Hendley's, with a teaser rate at the outset and a variable rate thereafter? See Reg. Z Commentary § 17(c)–10.

3. Consumer spokespersons have argued vigorously for the need for a "worst case" hypothetical example to show the borrower the largest possible increase under the particular variable rate plan. Do current regulations require such a disclosure? See Reg. Z § 226.19(b)(i)(viii). What would be the worst case example for a mortgage with no rate or payment caps?

4. Read Reg. Z § 226.30. This provision was added in 1987 after Congress enacted the Competitive Equality Banking Act of 1987. This provision goes beyond the normal scope of truth in lending and actually imposes a substantive requirement, a "lifetime cap" on the rate which may be imposed. Does it say what the "cap" should be? Are creditors really limited by this rule?

5. Variable rate provisions are not limited to closed-end mortgage credit, and are common in credit card plans and home equity lines of credit (HELOCs) as well. The disclosure rules for variable rate open-end credit generally are in Reg. Z §§ 226.5(b)(1) and 226.6(a)(4) fn. 13. For home equity plans, see Reg. Z §§ 226.5b(d)(12) and 226.6(e)(7).

SECTION C. DISCLOSURE IN OTHER TRANSACTIONS

1. CONSUMER LEASES

During the early 1970s, leasing of automobiles and other durable consumer goods became a popular alternative to buying these items. Because the original TILA did not expressly cover leases, Congress added the Consumer Leasing Act (CLA) to it in 1976. See TILA §§ 181–187, 15 U.S.C.A. § 1667. The CLA requires certain disclosures to be made in lease transactions which exceed four months. Federal Reserve Board Regulation M (16 C.F.R. pt. 213), like its TIL counterpart, Reg. Z, spells out the details.

The following is the "federal box" portion of the model closed-end lease disclosure form approved by the Federal Reserve Board in Regulation M, 12 CFR 213, Appendix A–2. Your authors have inserted numbers to reflect a realistic lease transaction.

FORM 2-D: AUTOMOBILE LEASE DISCLOSURES

Date 8-30-06

Lessor(s) CROSSROADS FORD, INC.   Lessee(s) JOHN & MARY SMITH

Amount Due at Lease Signing or Delivery (Itemized below)* $ 2,511.44	Monthly Payments Your first monthly payment of $ 391.44 is due on 8/30/06, followed by 35 payments of $ 391.44 due on the 1st of each month. The total of your monthly payments is $ 14,091.84	Other Charges (not part of your monthly payment) Disposition fee (if you do not purchase the vehicle) $ 150.00 Total $ 150.00	Total of Payments (The amount you will have paid by the end of the lease) $ 16,361.84

*Itemization of Amount Due at Lease Signing or Delivery	
Amount Due At Lease Signing or Delivery: Capitalized cost reduction $ 2,000.00 First Monthly Payment 391.44 Refundable security deposit Title fees 50.00 Registration fees 70.00 Total $ 2,511.44	**How the Amount Due at Lease Signing or Delivery will be paid:** Net trade-in allowance $ 1,000.00 Rebates and noncash credits Amount to be paid in cash 1,511.44 Total $ 2,511.44

Your monthly payment is determined as shown below:

Gross capitalized cost. The agreed upon value of the vehicle ($ 24,000.00) and any items you pay over the lease term (such as service contracts, insurance, and any outstanding prior credit or lease balance) .... $ 24,700.00

If you want an itemization of this amount, please check this box ☐

Capitalized cost reduction. The amount of any net trade-in allowance, rebate, noncash credit, or cash you pay that reduces the gross capitalized cost	− 2,000.00
Adjusted capitalized cost. The amount used in calculating your base monthly payment	= 22,700.00
Residual value. The value of the vehicle at the end of the lease used in calculating your base monthly payment ..	− 12,500.00
Depreciation and any amortized amounts. The amount charged for the vehicle's decline in value through normal use and for other items paid over the lease term	= 10,200.00
Rent Charge. The amount charged in addition to the depreciation and any amortized amounts	+ 1,000.00
Total of base monthly payments. The depreciation and any amortized amounts plus the rent charge	= 11,200.00
Lease term. The number of months in your lease	36
Base monthly payment	= 372.80
Monthly sales/use tax	+ 18.64 +
Total monthly payment	=$ 391.44

Early termination. You may have to pay a substantial charge if you end this lease early. The charge may be up to several thousand dollars. The actual charge will depend on when the lease is terminated. The earlier you end the lease, the greater this charge is likely to be.

Excessive Wear and Use. You may be charged for excessive wear based on our standards for normal use and for mileage in excess of 12,000 miles per year at the rate of 19¢ per mile.
Purchase Option at End of Lease Term. You have an option to purchase the vehicle at the end of the lease term for $ 12,250.00 and a purchase option fee of $ 250.00
Other Important Terms. See your lease documents for additional information on early termination, purchase options and maintenance responsibilities, warranties, late and default charges, insurance, and any security interest, if applicable.

Problem 2–24

Can you follow the structure and pricing of this motor vehicle lease? Do you understand the terminology: "gross capitalized cost," "capitalized cost reduction," "residual value," etc.? Is this form easier to comprehend than the installment sale form containing Reg. Z credit cost information, Form 2–A, supra? Did the consumer lessee get a good deal here? How do you know?

Notes

1. The federal Consumer Leasing Act has not generated nearly as much litigation as the Truth in Lending Act. Probably the most controversial issue has been the disclosure of early termination charges under Reg. M § 213.4(g). This refers to the amount the consumer will owe if the lease is terminated early, either voluntarily by the consumer or as a result of default.

The various formulas used by lessors are designed to assure that the lessor realizes its full investment in the transaction, which means recovering all the depreciation and profit built into the lease charges over the full term. These formulas can be quite intricate, and tend to require a substantial sum for the consumer to pay off the lease early. Note the shaded disclosure that warns the lessee: **"You may have to pay a substantial charge if you end this lease early."** This was added in the 1997 revision of Regulation M. See: Miller v. Nissan Motor Acceptance Corp., 362 F.3d 209 (3d Cir. 2004).

2. The CLA § 183(b), 15 U.S.C. § 1667b(b), also imposes a substantive restraint on the amount of early termination charges: they must be "reasonable in the light of the anticipated or actual harm caused by the ... early termination." How does one gauge reasonableness in this context? In the *Miller* case just cited, the lessees wanted to terminate the lease, with a monthly rent of $267.00, one month earlier than its scheduled expiration. Believe it or not, the contractual formula in the lease would have required the lessees to pay $5,336.95 for the privilege of paying off 30 days early! [This is because in the lease agreement the lessor had seriously over-estimated the value the car would have at the end of the lease, and the formula was designed to recoup such a shortfall.] The leasing company, however, graciously agreed to accept $267.00 as a payoff. The lower court found the formula in the lease unreasonable, but the Court of Appeals reversed on the ground that the lessees had no standing to challenge the contractual formula since it was not actually applied to them.

3. Aside from the lease disclosures required by federal law, a number of states have enacted motor vehicle leasing laws of their own, usually adopting the federal disclosures by reference and then adding certain substantive restrictions on lease terms and practices. A "Uniform Consumer Leases Act" has been promulgated by the National Conference of Commissioners on Uniform State Laws, but thus far is enacted only in Connecticut. See R. Rohner, Leasing Consumer Goods: The Spotlight Shifts to the Uniform Consumer Leases Act, 35 Conn. L. Rev. 647 (2003).

A more troublesome type of consumer lease is the so-called "rent-to-own" contract. Unlike auto leases, which are typically for terms of years, the typical rent-to-own contract obligates the consumer on a week to week basis. This keeps these contracts out of the reach of the CLA. But are they subject to TILA? Consider the following.

REMCO ENTERPRISES, INC. v. HOUSTON

Kansas Court of Appeals, 1984.
9 Kan.App.2d 296, 677 P.2d 567.

HARRY G. MILLER, JUDGE:

The defendant Alice Houston appeals from the trial court's denial of her two counterclaims against plaintiff Remco Enterprises, Inc. The plaintiff cross-appeals from the trial court's denial of its petition seeking past-due rental payments and possession of a television set which plaintiff had rented to defendant.

The plaintiff is in the business of renting television sets and other appliances. At the time of the trial, the defendant was a 20-year-old single mother of three who had completed only the ninth grade in school and was dependent upon aid to dependent children welfare payments of $320 per month.

On September 11, 1980, plaintiff and defendant entered into a rental agreement with an option to purchase a stereo component set. This agreement provided that if the defendant made 69 weekly payments of $12 each, she would become the owner of the stereo set.

On September 13, 1980, plaintiff and defendant entered into a rental agreement with an option to purchase a console color TV set. This agreement provided that if the defendant made 104 weekly payments of $17 each, she would become the owner of the TV set.

Both agreements were identical but for the number and the amount of payments, and provided that defendant could cancel the agreement at any time by returning the rented property. The agreements also obligated the plaintiff to maintain the equipment.

Defendant complied with the agreement for the stereo set and made the final payment to plaintiff on January 4, 1982. Plaintiff accordingly transferred the ownership of the stereo set to the defendant. On January 23, 1982, with 36 weekly payments remaining on the TV set, defendant made her last payment. On February 1, 1982, plaintiff sued defendant to recover the TV set and past-due rental payments. The defendant counterclaimed alleging that plaintiff had violated the Truth in Lending Act (TILA), 15 U.S.C. § 1601 *et seq.* (1976) and amendments thereto, and the unconscionability provisions of the Kansas Consumer Protection Act, K.S.A. 50–623 *et seq.* and amendments thereto. * * *

In Count I of defendant's counterclaim, the defendant alleged that the "Rental Agreement with Option to Purchase" covering the TV set was in fact a disguised credit sale, and that plaintiff violated the TILA and Regulation Z, 12 C.F.R. § 226 (1980), by failing to disclose the amount of the finance charge and by failing to express the amount of the finance charge in an annual percentage rate. Plaintiff argues that the above disclosures were not required since the agreement was not a "credit sale" within the meaning of the TILA.

* * *

Plaintiff does not contest that defendant had the option to become the owner of the TV set for no additional consideration upon her compliance with her contractual obligations. Nor does plaintiff contest defendant's assertion that the total payments required over the 104 week period, $1,768, was in excess of the aggregate value of the TV set. Rather, plaintiff argues that because the defendant had the right to terminate the agreement at any time after making the first week's payment of $17, she was not contractually obligated to pay any sum substantially equivalent to or in excess of the aggregate value of the TV set which had a retail value of $850.

The rental agreement makes it clear that the defendant had the right to terminate the agreement at the end of any week without penalty in this provision:

"TERMINATION BY RENTER: Renter may terminate this agreement at the end of any rental period by return of the property to owner. Renter is *required* to rent the property for only one rental period."

The agreement also makes it clear that the "rental period" is for one week, and that plaintiff agrees to maintain the TV set in good working order and repair it during defendant's use and possession of it.

* * *

Modified Regulation Z, promulgated by the FRB subsequent to the passage of the Truth in Lending Simplification & Reform Act of 1980, in defining the term "credit sale" specifically excludes a bailment or lease that is terminable without penalty at any time by the consumer. 12 C.F.R. § 226.2(a)(16) (1983). This revised definition reveals the current intent of the FRB that rental agreements such as the one involved herein are not "credit sales" and are not subject to the disclosure requirements of the TILA or Regulation Z.

We therefore conclude that the trial court's ruling that the rental agreement between the plaintiff and the defendant was not a "credit sale" within the meaning of the TILA was not erroneous.

Defendant next contends that the trial court erred in not finding that the excessive price charged by plaintiff and the unfair advantage gained by the plaintiff due to the defendant's poverty and limited education violated the unconscionability provisions of the Kansas Consumer Protection Act, K.S.A. 50–623 *et seq.* and amendments thereto.

* * *

In the present case, the contract called for defendant to pay $1,768 for the set that had a retail value of $850. This allowed plaintiff a profit of $918, or an increase of 108% over the retail price, a near 2:1 ratio. No cases have been cited in which a comparable retail price discrepancy formed the basis for a finding of unconscionability.

The 108% markup in the present case does not shock the conscience of this court when the circumstances surrounding the execution of the contract, including its commercial setting and its purpose and actual effect, are considered.

Although defendant would have had to pay 108% more than a cash customer, defendant received the benefit of not being responsible for service or repairs to the TV set, of not having to undergo a credit check or make a down payment, and of having the option to return the set and cancel the agreement at any time after one week. Most importantly, she received the benefit and use of a TV set which she might not have otherwise had. Although in retrospect it may seem to have been a bad bargain, the price disparity does not rise to the level of unconscionability.

Defendant further argues that the agreement was procedurally unconscionable because of defendant's financial and educational background. The trial court found that defendant knew that she could return the set at any time she desired to terminate the agreement, that she knew how to multiply 104 (weeks) times 17 (dollars), that she was of average intelligence and was not taken advantage of by the seller. Defendant testified that she read the agreement and knew how to multiply. She fully complied with the stereo agreement, and exercised her option to purchase the stereo. The record is devoid of any evidence of any deceptive or oppressive practices, overreaching, intentional misstatements, or concealment of facts by plaintiff.

* * *

The trial court's denial of defendant's counterclaims is affirmed.

Notes

1. The court is correct, is it not, that the current TILA does not cover rent-to-own contracts. Since the CLA does not cover them either, it appears that suppliers of consumer goods under these contracts have carefully structured the transactions so that they fall in the statutory cracks. Does any disclosure law apply to them? Should there be a disclosure law for these transactions? For example, in the Remco contract, the total amount of the rental payments is not disclosed. Is the court's comment that the consumer "knew how to multiply 104 times 17" a sufficient answer?

In an attempt to fill this statutory gap, virtually all states have enacted disclosure laws for rent-to-own and similar contracts. These laws typically require disclosure of the total amount of all payments, the initial payment, other charges, penalties, and the like. See, e.g., Mich.Comp.Laws Ann. §§ 445.951, et seq., in the Statutory Supplement. They do not, however, require the supplier to calculate and disclose the credit sale equivalent of finance charge and APR. Without this, can the consumer truly evaluate the relative merits of the deal?

2. Wasn't it obvious to all parties that Ms. Houston intended to buy the TV set? She had already paid off the stereo, and there was evidence (not discussed by the court) that both parties understood this from the beginning. There was also evidence that Remco's business is directed mainly at low income consumers who cannot get loans but who want to buy TV sets and other items, and that a substantial percentage of "lessees" do in fact pay off and buy the items. If all this is so, isn't the transaction really a secured credit sale? Isn't the distinction between a "lease" and a "sale" completely phony on these facts? See, e.g., Clark v. Rent–It Corp., 685 F.2d 245 (8th Cir.1982), cert. denied, 459 U.S. 1225, 103 S.Ct. 1232, 75 L.Ed.2d 466 (1983). See also Ayer, On the Vacuity of the Sale/Lease Distinction, 68 Iowa L.Rev. 667 (1983).

3. Consider the figures. Ms. Houston was to pay $17 a week for 104 weeks ($1,768) for a TV set worth $850. If this was a credit sale, the entire

$918 mark-up would have to be disclosed as a finance charge, not so? What APR would this have produced? Would you believe approximately 85.00%?! Of course, this was not disclosed. It is unlikely that a court would tolerate this level of return in a credit transaction (indeed, it would be criminal in many states), yet the court said that this did not shock its conscience. Does it shock yours? Does it surprise you? Does it make you reluctant to buy a TV on a rent-to-own basis?

4.   The extremely high rate of return in the Remco lease is typical of rent-to-own agreements; in fact, many produce even higher returns. Usury laws in most states may protect consumers against having to pay such exorbitant rates in loan and credit sale transactions, but usury laws normally do not apply to lease transactions. A few states, however, have recently begun to address the problem of exorbitant rates of return in lease transactions. See: Perez v. Rent–A–Center, Inc., 186 N.J. 188, 892 A.2d 1255 (N.J. 2006) [state retail installment sales act applies to rent-to-own contracts, at least with respect to permissible interest rate ("time price differential") imposed].

2.   OTHER DISCLOSURE LAWS

Compulsory disclosure is not limited to credit transactions. Although there is no general "Truth in Selling" Act, there are other consumer protection statutes which have mandatory disclosure features. There are also disclosure regulations covering other subjects and products from cars to beer. Disclosure in food and drug labeling goes back many decades. The labeling requirements for alcoholic beverages can be found at 27 C.F.R. Parts 4 (wine), 5 (distilled spirits), and 7 (malt beverages). Most early disclosure rules, like the food and drug laws, were concerned primarily with public health and safety. Only relatively recently have disclosure laws been used to address purely economic concerns. This, of course, is the primary emphasis of the TILA.

Other federal laws also require disclosure concerning financial transactions. We have examined a bit of the Real Estate Settlement Procedures Act earlier in this chapter. There is a somewhat parallel set of disclosures required under the Electronic Fund Transfer Act, 15 U.S.C. § 1693–1693r, and Federal Reserve Board Regulation E, 12 C.F.R. Part 205, for consumer use of debit and ATM cards, and other forms of electronic payments. And there is the Truth in Savings Act, 12 U.S.C. 4301 et. seq, and FRB regulation DD, 12 C.F.R. Part 230.

There are also several product disclosure laws relating to automobiles. For example, the Motor Vehicle Information and Cost Savings Act, 15 U.S.C.A. § 1981 et seq., enacted in 1972, requires anyone who sells (or even gives away) a motor vehicle to make a written disclosure of the odometer reading and its accuracy. Used car dealers must put a FTC disclosure form on the window of used cars for sale. See 16 C.F.R. Part 455. The Environmental Protection Agency requires that new vehicles carry stickers which indicate projected fuel economy. See 40 C.F.R. Part 600. There are also labeling rules for tires. See 16 C.F.R. Part 228.

Another important disclosure law is the Interstate Land Sales Full Disclosure Act, 15 U.S.C.A. §§ 1701–20. The ILSFDA was enacted in 1968, the same year as the TILA. It requires that subdivision developers and others who sell or lease 100 or more lots of unimproved land as part of a common promotion file a complex "statement of record" in the Office of Interstate Land Sales Registration. This office is a division of the Department of Housing and Urban Development. The statement is supposed to contain details about both the land and the developer. In addition, when individual lots are sold, the developer must furnish a very detailed property report to the prospective purchaser before any contract is signed. Finally, the purchaser is given a cooling-off period, during which he may rescind the entire transaction. While this rescission right is similar to the right of rescission under TILA, see Chapter 3, Section C, infra, the overall scheme of the ILSFDA more resembles the securities laws than the truth in lending laws.

Another disclosure law is the Magnuson–Moss Warranty Act, 15 U.S.C.A. §§ 2301–12, enacted in 1975, which sets federal standards for written product warranties. We will study this law in more detail in chapter 7, but consider this warm-up:

Problem 2–25

Consider the common situation where Consumer visits a retail store to shop for a television set. Display models are available for inspection, but the Dealer's stock of TVs are all sealed in boxes as they were delivered from the factory. Inside each box, of course, is the brochure that spells out the manufacturer's warranty undertakings. How is Consumer to find out the contents of that warranty before committing to a purchase?

The Federal Trade Commission has issued regulations under the Magnuson–Moss Warranty Act addressing this situation. "Pre–Sale Availability of Written Warranty Terms," 16 C.F.R § 702.3(a) [in the Statutory Supplement]. Is this an adequate response to the customer's need-to-know? Have you ever taken the time to seek out information about manufacturer warranties before you buy?

[To teachers: One of the co-authors makes a field exercise of this issue. Each student is required to go to a retail store selling TVs, and determine how the Dealer satisfies the requirements of the regulation. To a skeptic, the results are not surprising.]

Note: State Disclosure Laws

State law can also provide its share of mandatory disclosure laws. The most visible results of a state mandatory disclosure law are the "unit prices," which many state statutes require grocers to post in their stores, representing the price of a given item by pound, quart, or other standard measure. See, e.g., Mass.Gen.Laws Ann. ch. 94 § 183, N.J. Stat.Ann. 56:8B21, N.Y.Agric. & Mkts.Law § 193–h (McKinney). The purpose of such statutes is to promote comparative food shopping, and they resulted from the perceived failure of different types of disclosures required by the Fair Packaging and Labeling Act (15 U.S.C.A. § 1451, et seq.). See, Schrag, Local Government and Consumer Protection, Consumer Protection Compliance, No. 4, at 8 (1971).

The most ambitious disclosure statute is New York's "Plain Language" Act. The text of this statute is reproduced below.

N.Y.GEN.OBL.LAW (McKINNEY)

§ 5–702.   Requirements for Use of Plain Language in Consumer Transactions

a.   Every written agreement entered into after November first, nineteen hundred seventy-eight, for the lease of space to be occupied for residential purposes, or to which a consumer is a party and the money, property or service which is the subject of the transaction is primarily for personal, family or household purposes must be:

1.   Written in a clear and coherent manner using words with common and every day meanings;

2.   Appropriately divided and captioned by its various sections.

Any creditor, seller or lessor who fails to comply with this subdivision shall be liable to a consumer who is a party to a written agreement governed by this subdivision in an amount equal to any actual damages sustained plus a penalty of fifty dollars. The total class action penalty against any such creditor, seller or lessor shall not exceed ten thousand dollars in any class action or series of class actions arising out of the use by a creditor, seller or lessor of an agreement which fails to comply with this subdivision. No action under this subdivision may be brought after both parties to the agreement have fully performed their obligation under such agreement, nor shall any creditor, seller or lessor who attempts in good faith to comply with this subdivision be liable for such penalties. This subdivision shall not apply to agreements involving amounts in excess of fifty thousand dollars nor prohibit the use of words or phrases or forms of agreement required by state or federal law, rule or regulation or by a governmental instrumentality.

b.   A violation of the provisions of subdivision a. of this section shall not render any such agreement void or voidable nor shall it constitute

1.   A defense to any action or proceeding to enforce such agreement; or

2.   A defense to any action or proceeding for breach of such agreement.

Problem 2–26

Sauce for the Gander.

If you believe that compulsory disclosure of interest rates is a good idea, then you should also decide whether that general concept should be applied to lawyers and their fees.

Under the District of Columbia Rules of Professional Conduct, Rule 1.5 (effective in 1991), lawyers must give to each new client a written statement indicating the "basis or rate" of the lawyer's fee. This statement must be given to the new client "before, or within a reasonable time after, commencing the representation." In the past, many lawyers have advised other lawyers to do so, because it is both a good business practice (avoiding ambiguities and disputes) and good public relations (clients' expectations can then be firm). In D.C. and elsewhere, it was an "ethical recommendation" before it became a "rule".

Would you support making such disclosure mandatory as a "consumer protection" measure? If not, can you articulate why creditors should disclose rates, but lawyers should not? If you cannot articulate such a reason, should we repeal TILA?

SECTION D. AN EVALUATION—EFFECTIVENESS OF MANDATORY DISCLOSURE

What results has Truth in Lending produced? There is uncertainty and much general disagreement on the answer to this question. The following material represents some of the divergent views. After you have read it, you should consider your own position on mandatory disclosure laws. For example, do you think they have accomplished any of their stated goals (discussed below)? Have they made consumer credit contracts more understandable to the average consumer? Are they worth all the trouble and expense? Before you can fairly evaluate these issues, you need to have some idea of just what it was these laws were designed to accomplish in the first place.

Purposes of Disclosure Laws

Disclosure laws like the Truth in Lending Act are obviously intended to inform consumers, but to what ends? And do these laws have purposes other than strictly informational? Consider the following possibilities:

a. *A market function.* Many observers believe that well-informed consumers have a positive effect on the overall consumer market. The theory is that if there are enough well-informed consumers, suppliers of goods and services will compete for their business. The increased competition, in turn, will reduce prices. This may sound like a tall order, but this market function was emphasized by advocates of truth in lending in the very earliest Congressional hearings on the subject. For a more detailed discussion of this idea, see Schwartz and Wilde, Intervening in Markets on the Basis of Imperfect Information: A Legal and Economic Analysis, 127 U.Pa.L.Rev. 630 (1979).

b. *A prescriptive or "best buy" function.* The idea here is that well-informed consumers make better decisions. For example, a consumer who knows that the price of a TV set is lower at store A than store B will probably buy the TV from store A, all other things being equal. If all other things are not equal, however, for example if store A is too far away or store B has a better warranty, the consumer might buy at store

B. The point is that the decision should be made intelligently and with full awareness of the options. See TILA § 102, which reflects this philosophy. The term "best buy" comes from Whitford, The Functions of Disclosure Regulation in Consumer Transactions, 1973 Wis.L.Rev. 400.

c. *A descriptive or "alert" function.* Rather than providing refined shopping information, the basic TIL disclosures might serve merely as warning signals for credit offerings that are far out of line. For example, a consumer might not respond to the difference between APRs of 11.00% and 11.35%, but should react to an APR of 42.00% or even 2.00%. For an elaborate analysis of this "alert" function, see J. Landers and R. Rohner, A Functional Analysis of Truth in Lending, 26 U.C.L.A.L.Rev. 711 (1979).

d. *A "contract synopsis."* Whether used for shopping purposes or not, the TIL disclosures provide an understandable summary of the contract, and may be useful later on when the consumer wants to verify contract terms.

e. *A law reform device.* The need to disclose contract terms clearly and conspicuously may prompt creditors to rethink contract boilerplate that is archaic or unnecessary. It also might stimulate law reform by flushing out harsh terms formerly hidden in the fine print shadows. See 26 U.C.L.A.L.Rev. at 740–45.

f. *A "rough justice" mechanism.* The civil penalty provisions of the TILA permit consumers to use claims of TIL violations for leverage where the real underlying grievance (abusive or deceptive practices) would be hard to prove. See Landers, Some Reflections on Truth in Lending, 1977 U.Ill.L.F. 699.

g. *Long-term consumer education.* Repeated encounters with TIL disclosures, with their standardized terminology, should produce better informed consumers over time. See 26 U.C.L.A.L.Rev. at 737–50.

h. *A "political" function.* This is a cynical view which holds that disclosure laws are not really expected to have any impact. Instead, they are nothing more than political responses to demands for proconsumer legislation. This works because the laws appear to be proconsumer, and because the average consumer is not sophisticated enough to realize that the laws really don't help. See Whitford, supra, 1973 Wis.L.Rev. at 435–39.

Notes

1. Can you think of any other purposes mandatory disclosure laws might serve? Do you think any disclosure law can be expected to accomplish all of this? Might there be harmful side effects? Do you buy the proposition that too much disclosure is counter-productive? See also Grether, Schwartz, & Wilde, The Irrelevance of Information Overload: An Analysis of Search and Disclosure, 59 S.Cal.L.Rev. 277 (1986).

2. How does the purpose of a disclosure law relate to the actual disclosures which should be required? For example, if the purpose is to

increase competition, should the disclosures be limited to cost elements (APR and finance charge)? If the goal is general awareness, should the disclosures be simple rather than detailed? And how is this goal served by making disclosures on a transaction-by-transaction basis? Should information about interest rates be collected and distributed to the public? See TILA § 136, 15 U.S.C. § 1646.

3. Perhaps surprisingly, almost forty years after TILA was enacted, there is relatively little scientific, or empirical, evidence about its effectiveness. There are some behavioral studies that tend generally to show improvements in consumer awareness of credit costs over the TILA years, but it is unclear whether TILA caused or even contributed to that awareness, or if so, how. There is virtually no data that allows one to point to specific TILA-formatted disclosure items and conclude that they work well or poorly. There is a recently published, extensive compilation and assessment of the literature on credit cost disclosure by economists Thomas Durkin & Gregory Elliehausen, Financial Economics of Information Disclosure: Applications of Truth in Lending (Oxford Univ. Press, 2007). In the concluding chapter these authors summarize their observations:

> One message from [the preceding] chapters is clear: it seems the impact of disclosure laws cannot seriously be evaluated absent some careful specification of their goals. If there are multiple goals for a disclosure program, as appears to be the case with many of them, studies of impacts can potentially be ambiguous or even appear conflicting. Research results might well indicate that a program is supremely successful according to one criterion, but it might be a miserable failure based on some other possible objective. This does not mean that the law itself is by any means a failure, although such a finding, as likely as not, is often used as support for suggestions for new or revised disclosures, or even major structural change or repeal.

> Certainly, Truth in Lending fits this description. Despite indications of successes under some criteria, there are almost constant calls for revision of the law, and it has received amendments in most years since inception. There seems to exist for this law a vision that somehow, after enough tinkering, there will arise evidence of a clear impact on some specific, presumably key, aspect of consumers' behavior (like enhanced credit shopping or less credit use). Though cloudy, this vision, the holy grail of disclosures, continues to beckon to reformers and researchers.

4. All sides of the debate over the value and utility of TILA disclosures were aired in an ABA Business Law Section program held in 1997, published in Re–Examining Truth in Lending: Do Borrowers Actually Use Consumer Disclosures?, 52 Cons. Fin. L. Q. Rep. 3 (1998). See also, Payment Cards Center, Federal Reserve Bank of Philadelphia, Federal Consumer Protection Regulation: Disclosures and Beyond, Conference Summary (June 10, 2005) [available at www.philadelphiafed.org/pcc].

5. TILA disclosures—or any disclosures, for that matter—cannot be very effective if consumers lack the educational or formational background to understand them. This is particularly problematic for credit cost disclosures which assume that consumers can grasp the mathematical implications of credit terms. Regrettably, studies of the "financial literacy" of high school

seniors and other young adults have not been encouraging. See, e.g., Lewis Mandell, Financial Literacy: Improving Education, National Jump$tart Coalition, Washington, D.C. (2006). Should the policy-makers focus more attention on educating young adults about consumer financial services, and less on tinkering with TILA details?

6.   The final word: Your authors mostly concur in the following:

Even acknowledging the broad and optimistic statements of congressional purpose in TILA, and the rhetoric of commentators, the realistic objectives of the TILA are quite limited and, given the breadth of consumer protection concerns in the marketplace, quite modest. TILA is meant primarily to assure that accurate, comparable information about credit costs and terms is available to consumers. . . .

Nothing in TILA compels consumers to read, understand and respond to its disclosures. There is no TILA elixir to cure consumer illiteracy, "innumeracy," or plain disinterest. TILA cannot force economic rationality into a consumer's consciousness. About all that can be expected is that adequate amounts of credit cost information are available, at appropriate times, in a more or less understandable format, so that consumers wanting to use it can do so. . . .

TILA cannot be expected to do much more than this. It cannot substitute for usury laws or otherwise control the pricing of credit products. It does not pretend to dictate which credit products may be marketed and which are *verboten*. It cannot save consumers from their own acquisitiveness, financial mismanagement or over-extension. It cannot protect consumers from true fraud or over-reaching. And it certainly cannot fix the economic disabilities of the poor. Nor is it the vehicle for resolving philosophical questions about whether consumer debt is good or evil.

R. Rohner, Whither Truth in Lending, 50 Cons. Fin. L. Q. Rep. 114 (1996).

Chapter 3

ABUSES AT THE FORMATION
OF THE CONTRACT

SECTION A.   THE DEAL THAT IS "TOO GOOD
TO BE TRUE"—BAIT AND SWITCH

STATE v. AMERICAN TV & APPLIANCE
OF MADISON, INC.

Supreme Court of Wisconsin, 1988.
146 Wis.2d 292, 430 N.W.2d 709.

CALLOW, JUSTICE.

This is a review of a published decision of the court of appeals, *State
v. American TV*, 140 Wis.2d 353, 410 N.W.2d 596 (Ct.App.1987). That
decision reversed an order of the circuit court for Dane county, Judge P.
Charles Jones, granting a motion to dismiss the state's complaint for
failure to state a claim in this forfeiture action. We reverse the decision
of the court of appeals because the state cannot prevail, even if the facts
alleged in the complaint are true.

The state filed a complaint against American TV & Appliance of
Madison, Inc., (American) alleging that in January, 1985, American ran
the following radio advertisement one hundred sixty-four times on
twenty-two radio stations:

> There are lots of good quality washers and dryers on the market.
> But when you ask which ones [sic] the best automatic washers and
> dryers, well it's simple. There's Speed Queen, Maytag and all the
> rest. Sears makes good washers and dryers there are lots of other
> good brands. But the best washers and dryers are made by Maytag
> and Speed Queen. And at American we have both of them and
> they're on sale for our January white sale. A clearance sale on the
> finest washers and dryers you can buy. This week a Speed Queen
> washer and dryer set is reduced to 499. This week you can buy the
> finest for less than $500. Both the Speed Queen washer and dryer
> set for 499. Speed Queen, the choice of more commercial laundra-
> mats than any other washer because they last. Because Speed Queen

uses the same transmission in home washes [sic] as they use in commercial washers. When it comes to washers and dryers, there's Maytag, Speed Queen and all the rest. And during American's closeout January white sale you can buy the best like a Speed Queen washer and dryer pair for 499 at American. Why pay more at Sears.

The state contends that this advertisement violated secs. 100.18(1) and (9)(a), Stats. The complaint alleges that American ordered twenty of these $499 Speed Queen sets at a cost of $520 per set. In addition, the complaint alleges that American ordered one hundred thirty-three more expensive washer and dryer sets. Sixty-five of these sets contained more features and were "visually more sophisticated" than the $499 sets. American purchased these for $518. The other sixty-eight sets cost American up to $604 and were of an even higher quality. The complaint states that, although American sold only four of the $499 sets during the sale, the state "believes that a much larger number" of the more expensive sets were sold. In addition, American sold a large number of non-Speed Queen washers and dryers at higher prices.

The complaint also alleges that American employs a commission system under which a salesperson receives commission only on the sale of items at a price greater than the wholesale cost. Since American sold these sets at $21 below cost, the salespersons received no commission on their sale.

The state's complaint alleges that the advertisement is not a bona fide offer to sell the $499 set and that American used the advertisement to induce potential buyers to come to the store where it discouraged the purchase of the $499 set and tried to sell the more expensive unadvertised sets. The state alleges that the following eight indicia reveal American's deceptive intent: (1) the loss of money on sales of the $499 set; (2) the disproportionate number of unadvertised sets purchased for sale; (3) the disproportionate number of unadvertised sets sold; (4) the large expense of advertising a set upon which American would lose money; (5) the plain appearance of the $499 set and the lack of certain features found in more expensive sets, even though the $499 set was advertised as the "best" and "finest"; (6) the commission structure discouraging sales of the $499 set; (7) the training received by sales persons encouraging them to direct customers to the more expensive models; and (8) the fact that American did not permit credit card purchases of the $499 set.

Based upon these allegations, the state, in its complaint, makes two claims for relief. First, it claims that the advertisement is untrue, deceptive or misleading in violation of sec. 100.18(1), Stats. Second, it claims that the advertisement is a part of a plan or scheme, the purpose or effect of which is not to sell the merchandise as advertised, in violation of sec. 100.18(9)(a).[1]

* * *

1. Section 100.18(9)(a), Stats., provides: "It is deemed deceptive advertising, within the meaning of this section, for any person or any agent or employee thereof to make,

II. BAIT AND SWITCH

The state's second claim for relief is based upon sec. 100.18(9)(a), Stats. There are three elements which must be alleged to state a claim under this provision. First, there must be an advertisement. Second, there must be a plan or scheme of which the advertisement is a part. Third, the purpose or effect of this plan must be to not sell the product as advertised.

The state insists that American violated this provision because its advertisement induced customers to visit the stores and then it switched them from the $499 set to more expensive models. The state bases its claim on the eight indicia of intent which, it claims, reveal a purpose not to sell the $499 set as advertised.

Missing from the complaint are allegations tending to prove that, apart from any purpose not to sell the merchandise as advertised, there was a plan or scheme to carry out such a purpose. The state's complaint is more conspicuous by what it does not allege than by what it does allege. It does not allege that the $499 sets were not available to customers. It does not allege that the $499 sets were not sold to customers. To the contrary, it acknowledges four sets *were* sold. It does not allege that the sets displayed were defective. It does not allege that salespersons discouraged any actual customers from buying the $499 model and then switched them to more expensive models. The complaint does not allege any improper overt act.

The complaint does not allege anything except that there were incentives for American to try to sell the more expensive models and that, in fact, it stocked and sold more of those models. All profit motivated retailers recognize these incentives and hope to sell their more profitable items, if possible. Section 100.18(9)(a), Stats., cannot be interpreted to make unlawful such an incentive. The statute requires a plan or scheme which is not demonstrated in this complaint.

Notwithstanding this deficiency in its complaint, the state attempts to rely upon FTC cases and guides for support of its position. It does so to no avail. The cases upon which the state relies do not find the existence of bait and switch merely from the kind of indicia of intent listed by the state. Indeed, the state recognizes that the federal cases often focus on disparagement of the advertised product, and it argues that disparagement occurred in this case. It contends that the $499 set

publish, disseminate, circulate or place before the public in this state in a newspaper or other publication or in the form of book, notice, handbill, poster, bill, circular, pamphlet, letter, sign, placard, card, label or over any radio or television station or in any other way similar or dissimilar to the foregoing, an advertisement, announcement, statement or representation of any kind to the public relating to the purchase, sale, hire, use or lease of real estate, merchandise, securities, service or employment or to the terms or conditions thereof which advertisement, announcement, statement or representation is part of a plan or scheme the purpose or effect of which is not to sell, purchase, hire, use or lease the real estate, merchandise, securities, service or employment as advertised."

was "plain" and lacked many features found in the more expensive models, and thus disparaged itself.

This contention is without merit. The federal cases relied upon by the state, in which the merchandise was found to be self-disparaging, involve defective or poor quality merchandise. In *Household Sewing Machine Co.,* 52 F.T.C. 250, 263–64 (1955), the advertised sewing machine would not perform certain advertised functions and was exceptionally noisy. Similarly, in *Carpets "R" Us, Inc. et al.,* 87 F.T.C. 303, 320–21 (1976), the carpet was of a "poor" quality and appearance. In both cases there was also verbal disparagement by salespersons. By contrast, the state alleges neither verbal disparagement nor defective merchandise. "Plainness" does not constitute defectiveness. The federal cases simply do not support the state's claim.

The state further contends that American disparaged the set by displaying it next to the more sophisticated models. This argument, too, must be rejected. The state points to *Southern States Distributing Co., et al.,* 83 F.T.C. 1126, 1166 (1973), in which swimming pool salespersons induced customers to switch from an economy pool to a deluxe pool by exhibiting two models side by side. However, the FTC's opinion makes it clear that the side-by-side exhibition itself was not the deceptive act. It was that Southern States had constructed the two models in such a way as to misleadingly embellish the expensive model.

The state also relies upon *Carpets "R" Us,* 87 F.T.C. at 320, 321, and *Wilbanks Carpet Specialists, Inc., et al.,* 84 F.T.C. 510, 520 (1974), claiming that side-by-side exhibitions of products disparaged the lower priced items. However, unlike the perfectly functional, albeit plain, washer and dryer set in this case, the lower priced carpets in those cases were of poor quality and disparaged themselves.

Section 100.18(9)(a), Stats., does not require a retailer to display different items in a product line in separate areas of the store out of fear that the less expensive models will compare unfavorably. Side-by-side exhibition, far from being evidence of a bait and switch plan, is helpful to consumers. It enables them to balance price differences with feature differences in order to arrive at the most efficient decision for them, given their tastes and resources.

Failing in its attempt to show disparagement, the state also argues that a showing of disparagement is not needed. Instead, it insists that a finding of bait and switch may be inferred from the advertisement itself and minimal sales resulting from it. It relies upon cases such as *Central Carpet Corp., Inc.,* 85 F.T.C. 1022 (1975), and *Tashof v. Federal Trade Commission,* 437 F.2d 707 (D.C.Cir.1970). What these cases conclude, however, is that, in addition to minimal sales of the product, the court must find bait advertising.

The cases demonstrate that a bait advertisement is one which is false or misleading. In *Tashof,* 437 F.2d at 709, an advertisement offering glasses "complete" for $7.50 was misleading bait advertising because this price applied only to customers who had their own prescriptions. The supposedly "complete" package did not include a free eye examination as some signs and flyers indicated. Similarly, in *Central Carpet,* 85 F.T.C. at 1031, the advertisement itself was deceptive as "the carpeting was not suitable for the uses for which advertised."

The FTC and federal courts have not made a finding of bait and switch simply on the basis of a low number of sales resulting from a *true* advertisement. As we stated above, American's advertisement is not false or misleading and, hence, is not bait advertising. These cases are not applicable to this case.

The FTC Guides in 16 C.F.R. sec. 238.3 (1988) likewise do not support the state's position. As this court noted in *State v. Amoco Oil Co.,* 97 Wis.2d 226, 243, 293 N.W.2d 487 (1980), the Guides are interpretive rules which "do not carry the force and effect of law." [16 C.F.R. § 238 is reprinted in the statutory supplement].

* * *

* * * Only subparagraph (f) [of the FTC Guides], referring to the use of a commission system, applies to this case.

The existence of a commission system is not determinative evidence of a bait and switch plan or scheme. Commission systems merely reflect the general profit motivation which governs all retail operations. Consequently, the federal cases which discuss a commission plan as evidence of bait and switch also rely upon many other evidences of a plan or scheme which are not present in this case. * * * Neither the federal cases nor Guides support the state's position.

* * *

For the reasons set forth, we conclude that the state's complaint fails to state a claim upon which relief can be granted.

The decision of the court of appeals is reversed.

Steinmetz, Justice (dissenting).

* * *

A cause of action based on sec. 100.18(9)(a), Stats., does not require facts to show the defendant's improper overt act. In light of Wisconsin's rules of notice pleading, sec. 100.18(9)(a) only requires that a plaintiff allege facts from which it can be reasonably inferred that such a plan or scheme exists. It is inconceivable that such a plan or scheme cannot be reasonably inferred from the complaint which alleged: (1) American's purchase of only 20 washers while running the advertisement 164 times; (2) American's cost was $21 over the selling price; (3) American's purchase of 133 more expensive washer-dryer sets; (4) American sold only four of the sets in its four stores; and (5) the salesperson's commission structure which provided no commissions on these sets. The majority incorrectly concludes that no plan or scheme could even reasonably be inferred from the complaint.

The majority also mentions that the FTC Guides, 16 C.F.R. sec. 238.3 (1988), aid in determining whether a certain practice is violative of sec. 100.18(9)(a), Stats. The majority concedes that sec. 238.3(f) of the Guides was alleged by the state. However, 238.3(c) provides:

> (c) The failure to have available at all outlets listed in the advertisement a sufficient quantity of the advertised product to meet reasonably anticipated demands, unless the advertisement clearly and adequately discloses that supply is limited and/or the merchandise is available only at designated outlets.

American's advertisement contained no limitation. American ran 164 advertisements on 22 radio stations, yet American ordered only 20 of the advertised sets. The question of whether American ordered a sufficient quantity of the washer-dryer sets to meet reasonably anticipated demands is a matter of proof.

Because the allegations in the complaint do provide sufficient facts from which it could be reasonably inferred that secs. 100.18(1) and 100.18(9)(a), Stats., were violated, I would affirm the court of appeals which reinstated the complaint.

I am authorized to state that CHIEF JUSTICE NATHAN S. HEFFERNAN and JUSTICE SHIRLEY S. ABRAHAMSON join this dissenting opinion.

Query: Would compulsory disclosure of contract terms, as in TILA, have been helpful here? Would a "plain English" statute have any impact? What is it that needs to be disclosed?

Notes

1. What are the critical elements of proof of illegal bait-and-switch? Why is it considered deceptive advertising? In Household Sewing Machine Co., Inc., 76 F.T.C. 207, 239 (1969) the Commission observed:

> The examiner seemed to be saying that since no one "took" the "bait," no one was "switched."

> To define bait and switch in terms of offers or refusals of offers misconceives the essential nature of the practice. Our decisions relating to bait and switch are grounded on a factual determination that the advertised product is not an offer which the seller seriously intends the buyer to accept, but a "come on" which will lead to the sale of a higher priced product. Whether the bait is actually taken or not is of no moment. On the contrary and as the record of this case plainly shows, the assumption of the bait and switch perpetrator is that the bait will probably *not* be "taken" (or at least not swallowed) but will serve as an opening gambit to get the salesman over the doorstep. Insofar as the examiner required proof of actual offers to buy the used machines, and subsequent refusals by respondents to sell, he erred—these factors are not material in establishing an illegal "bait and switch" scheme.

2. In the *American TV* case, what problems of proof did the state AG encounter? What factual allegations supported the state's bait and switch theory? What factors supported the defendant merchant's case? How did the

FTC Guides Against Bait Advertising, 16 C.F.R. Part 238, reprinted in the statutory supplement, figure in? How could the Wisconsin Attorney General's office have bolstered their case?

3. Can an individual consumer challenge a bait and switch practice under state law? If the consumer does not actually purchase anything, what are their damages under a state UDAP statute? See Brashears v. Sight 'N Sound Appliance Centers, Inc., 981 P.2d 1270 (Okla. Ct. Civ. App. 1999).

In a case decided by the Supreme Court of Hawaii, consumers alleged they had been "baited" by a car dealer's advertisement for a "NEW '97 GRAND CHEROKEE LAREDO" priced at "$229 Month, 24 Mos. $0 Cash Down or $20,988." When they arrived at the car dealer's, one of the advertised Jeep Grand Cherokee Laredos was still available, but the salesman pointed to some fine print in the ad that said the "no cash down/$229 month" offer was available only to recent college graduates entitled to a "loyalty rebate." The consumers did not purchase a car but suffered $3–5 damages for gasoline used for the futile trip to the car dealership. The court stated:

> Deception being the evil that consumer fraud statutes seek to rectify, regardless of whether actual purchases have resulted, there is no discernible reason why a consumer should be required to actually purchase any goods or services as a precondition to bringing an action, *inter alia*, for damages that result from injuries caused by false or misleading advertisements. We therefore hold that a consumer who is injured as a result of attempting to purchase goods or services by virtue of an act or practice prohibited by [Hawaii's unfair or deceptive practices act] may recover damages * * *. No actual purchase is necessary.

Zanakis Pico v. Cutter Dodge, Inc., 98 Hawai'i 309, 47 P.3d 1222, 1231–32 (2002). The statute provides for minimum damages in the amount of $1,000, as well as attorney's fees to a prevailing plaintiff. Haw. Rev. Stat. § 480–13(b).

Note on Advertised Specials

Related to bait and switch is the tactic apparently employed by some retail grocers of advertising a special to lure "traffic" into the store without stocking adequate supplies to meet expected demand. A 1967–68 FTC study of grocery stores in the District of Columbia and San Francisco showed an 11% unavailability rate and considerable consumer dissatisfaction with the situation. Thus, in 1971, the FTC promulgated a trade regulation rule requiring grocers to stock an adequate supply to meet the expected demand for advertised specials. 16 C.F.R. Part 424. Defenses were nonexistent unless the grocer maintained records showing the lack of inventory was beyond his control.

In a controversial 1986 report, the FTC staff said that the paperwork and other costs of complying with the advertised specials rule exceeded the benefits by millions of dollars every year. In 1989, the Commission published amendments to the rule. 54 Fed. Reg. 35,456 (Aug. 28, 1989). In the accompanying Statement of Basis and Purpose, the Commission noted that although overall unavailability rates had been reduced by about 50 percent since the original rule's promulgation, surveys indicated that consumers were not much inconvenienced by unavailability and would be willing to tolerate much greater unavailability rates to avoid higher grocery prices. The record also indicated significant costs borne by grocers from overstocking, monitoring, and recordkeeping. The amended rule seeks to reduce these costs while retaining the consumers' benefits by

— allowing broader use of limited availability disclosures in advertising,

— eliminating recordkeeping requirements, and

— allowing food retailers to offer rainchecks or comparable value substitutes if they cannot supply the advertised item.

The Commission majority expressed their faith that the competitive system would provide grocers with ample incentive to avoid disappointing their customers. In the event that some grocers were to take advantage of the new more lenient standards to engage in deliberate understocking without adequate disclosure, however, the Commission asserted that its Bait Advertising Guides (discussed in the *American Television* case, *supra*) would still be applicable.

The current rule on availability of advertised specials, 16 C.F.R. § 424, is reprinted in the statutory supplement.

Problem 3–1

Elder & Johnson Co., a consumer electronics store, advertised a new, wall size, plasma television set for sale at a price of $260, as a "Thursday Only Special." Waldo Nerd saw the ad and immediately hurried downtown to Elder & Johnson's only store in order to buy the advertised TV. He was the third person in the door, but the salesman informed him that the store had only two of the $260 televisions, and he was too late. The salesman also informed him, however, that the store had stocked "hundreds" of "better-quality" big-screen TV's, at "bargain" prices starting at $1750.

Could the Wisconsin Attorney General obtain an injunction against such conduct? Could the FTC obtain a cease and desist order under § 5 of the FTC Act? Do either the FTC's Guides Against Bait Advertising or the Rule on Availability of Advertised Specials apply?

ROSSMAN v. FLEET BANK (R.I.) NATIONAL ASSOCIATION

United States Court of Appeals, Third Circuit, 2002.
280 F.3d 384.

Before: SCIRICA, ALITO and BARRY, CIRCUIT JUDGES.

OPINION OF THE COURT

SCIRICA, CIRCUIT JUDGE.

In this Truth in Lending Act case, we must interpret the "no annual fee" provision of a credit card solicitation. Months after plaintiff Paula

Rossman responded to a solicitation offering this term, defendant Fleet Bank changed the operable credit agreement and imposed an annual fee. Rossman brought this putative class action alleging, *inter alia*, that Fleet violated the TILA by failing to disclose the fee later imposed. The District Court dismissed plaintiff's TILA count for failing to state a claim upon which relief could be granted. We will reverse and remand.

I.

In late 1999, plaintiff Paula Rossman received "Pre–Qualified Invitation" to obtain a credit card from defendant Fleet Bank. The solicitation was for a "Fleet Platinum MasterCard" with a low annual percentage rate and "no annual fee." If interested, the recipient of this offer was to check a box next to which was written, "YES! I want the top card for genuine value and superior savings, the no-annual-fee Platinum MasterCard." An asterisk directed the recipient to a note that stated, "See the TERMS OF PRE QUALIFIED OFFER and CONSUMER INFORMATION for detailed rate and other information."

The enclosure entitled "Consumer Information" contained the "Schumer Box"—the table of basic credit card information that is required under the Truth in Lending Act, 15 U.S.C. § 1601 *et seq.*, as amended by the Fair Credit and Charge Card Disclosure Act of 1988. Within the Schumer Box, there was a column with the heading "Annual Fee"; the box beneath that heading contained only the word "None." On the "Consumer Information" enclosure, but outside the Schumer box, Fleet listed other fees. Also in that location was the statement, "We reserve the right to change the benefit features associated with your Card at any time."

Rossman responded to Fleet's offer, and soon thereafter received her "no-annual-fee Platinum MasterCard." It is unclear from her complaint and the documents in the record exactly when this occurred. It appears, however, that she received her card in December of 1999 or January of 2000. Along with the card, Rossman was sent Fleet's "Cardholder Agreement," which contained the following provision concerning annual fees: "No annual membership fee will be charged to your Account."

The Agreement provided for various applicable annual percentage rates charged on outstanding balances, including the standard rate for purchases (7.99%) and several higher rates that could be triggered by certain acts or omissions on the part of the cardholder. Among these was a rate of 24.99% that Fleet was entitled to impose "upon any closure of [the] Account." The Agreement also contained a change-in-terms provision, which stated:

> We have the right to change any of the terms of this Agreement at any time. You will be given notice of a change as required by applicable law. Any change in terms governs your Account as of the effective date, and will, as permitted by law and at our option, apply both to transactions made on or after such date and to any outstanding Account balance.

In May 2000, Fleet sent a letter to plaintiff announcing its intention to change the terms of the agreement. That letter read, in part:

> Over the past several months, the Federal Reserve has been steadily raising interest rates, making it difficult for credit card issuers to maintain products and services at current rates. While many experts predict that the Federal Reserve will continue to raise interest rates, the regular rate for purchases and balance transfers on your Fleet account remains at a fixed 7.99% APR.

> While this rate remains unchanged, a $35 annual membership fee will apply to your account. Effective with billing cycles closing on or after June 1, 2000, the annual fee will appear beginning with your monthly statement that includes the next anniversary date of your account opening.

Soon thereafter, by letter dated June 20, 2000, Fleet announced a modification of its original change. Claiming the move was necessary in light of still further interest rate hikes by the Federal Reserve, Fleet modified the effective date of the change. Rather than waiting until the anniversary of plaintiff's account opening, Fleet notified Rossman that the annual fee would be imposed almost immediately:

> We are modifying the terms of your Fleet Cardholder Agreement only to correct the timing of the annual membership fee previously disclosed. That fee will first be charged to your Account in your billing cycle that closes in July, 2000, and will be charged in that billing cycle each year thereafter.

A thirty-five-dollar fee was charged to Rossman's account by July 6, 2000, in accordance with the second letter.

Rossman alleges that despite Fleet's protestations that it had been effectively forced to cease offering the card without an annual fee, it continued to solicit other new customers with offers for no-annual-fee credit cards. Thus, she contends, Fleet systematically baited new customers with the no-annual-fee offer, while telling its existing customers that the fee increase was necessitated by changing market conditions. These "no annual fee" offers, Rossman alleges, were made by Fleet with the intention of imposing a fee shortly thereafter.

Rossman filed this putative class action on behalf of herself and "[a]ll persons who received or will receive an offer ... from Fleet ... for a no annual fee credit card, and who accepted that offer and who were then charged, or have been notified they will be charged, an annual fee." She asserts violations of the TILA and Rhode Island law: (1) violation of Rhode Island's Deceptive Trade Practices Act, R.I. Gen. Laws § 6–13.1–1 et seq.; (2) common law fraud; and (3) breach of contract. The essence of plaintiff's TILA claim is that the original solicitations, insofar as they described the credit card as one with no annual fee, violated the TILA's requirement of accurate disclosure.

Fleet moved to dismiss the TILA count, contending Rossman failed to state a proper claim. Granting the motion to dismiss, the District

Court held Rossman's allegations did not state a deficiency in the original disclosures sufficient to constitute a violation under the TILA. Declining to exercise supplemental jurisdiction over the state law claims, the District Court dismissed the suit. Rossman appealed.

* * *

c. Bait-and-Switch Allegations.

Rossman challenges the District Court's dismissal of her TILA claim on the basis of her assertion that Fleet here engaged in a "bait and switch" scheme. Rossman alleges—and we must assume the truth of these allegations for purposes of a 12(b)(6) motion—that Fleet solicited her business with the no-annual-fee offer while intending to change the terms shortly thereafter. Rejecting this claim, the District Court held that the legality of such schemes is outside the TILA's narrow focus on disclosure.

The Federal Trade Commission treats advertising in bait-and-switch schemes as false or misleading. 16 C.F.R. Pt. 238 ("Guides Against Bait Advertising"). Regulation Z also addresses these schemes. *See* 12 C.F.R. § 226.16(a) ("If an advertisement for credit states specific credit terms, it shall state only those terms that actually are or will be arranged or offered by the creditor."); Ralph J. Rohner & Fred H. Miller, *Truth in Lending* 752 (2000) ("This rule is aimed at the ancient but dishonorable practice of 'bait and switch' advertising where the creditor uses the lure of attractive credit terms to induce customers in, but no such favorable terms are in fact available."). Bait advertising, although not necessarily literally false (there is usually a real item described in the advertising), is nonetheless considered deceptive, insofar as it suggests the product advertised is actually offered and intended to be sold, when the real intention is simply to create a contact with the buyer that allows the seller to switch the consumer to a more profitable sale. It is the bait, not the switch, that is deceptive. Hence, the deception occurs at the time of the bait advertisement. Rossman contends Fleet's solicitations contained a deception of this kind, which negates its claim that the disclosures were accurate at the time they were made.

Citing Clark v. Troy & Nichols, Inc., 864 F.2d 1261 (5th Cir.1989), the District Court rejected plaintiff's position. Defendant Troy & Nichols offered to obtain a mortgage for plaintiff Clark on certain terms and the parties entered into an agreement to that effect. Clark was then offered a substantially less advantageous set of terms. Clark refused and the credit arrangement was never consummated.

While accepting that Clark had properly characterized defendants' actions as a bait-and-switch scheme, the Fifth Circuit explicitly rejected bait-and-switch actions under the TILA: "The Truth in Lending Act does not provide a cause of action when a lender engages in 'bait and switch' techniques. It does require that the lender make certain disclosures with respect to the offered terms." *Id.* at 1264. Under this view, the creditor's intention not to offer the originally stated terms is irrelevant to the analysis. So long as the disclosures reflect the stated terms of an agreement, they are accurate under the TILA. And since, in *Clark*, the terms ultimately agreed to were disclosed before the consummation of the loan there at issue, the requirements of the TILA were met. *Cf. Janikowski v. Lynch Ford, Inc.*, 210 F.3d 765, 769 (7th Cir.2000) (holding that "spot delivery" schemes, identical in relevant respects to bait-and-switch schemes, do not violate the TILA).

The District Court here adopted this approach, stating, "Fleet's disclosures in late 1999 were accurate with respect to the terms offered *at that time*; the fact that Fleet allegedly intended to change those terms in the near further did not render the disclosures inaccurate for purposes of the TILA." *Rossman*, 2000 WL 33119419, at *3.

In one sense, the solicitation disclosures here were accurate—the agreement then referred to by the disclosures did not contemplate an annual fee. But in another sense, if Fleet intended to impose an annual fee shortly thereafter, the disclosures were at least misleading. A reasonable consumer would expect that, even if the terms may change, the stated terms are those that the card issuer intends to provide. The disclosures—we assume for these purposes—feigned an intention to provide credit under a set of terms that Fleet did not intend to provide over time. Thus, even if the language of the disclosures did not imply that Fleet was obligated for at least a year, the disclosures were misleading with respect to Fleet's alleged intentions. As the dissent in *Clark* noted, such a deception may, in some ways, be worse than simply inaccurate disclosures:

> The majority concludes that even though the lender never intended to extend credit on the terms disclosed, the accuracy of the disclosures remain untainted. In my view, an intention from the outset not to extend credit on disclosed terms is far more egregious than inaccurate terms. On careful review of the disclosures, one might detect an inconsistency between the interest rate promised and the amortization schedule disclosed. By contrast, there is no way to enter the lender's mind to determine whether he means what he discloses.
>
> Disclosures feigning one's true intention, in my view, are inaccurate.

864 F.2d at 1266 (Thornberry, J., dissenting).

Because the TILA is to be construed strictly against the creditor, *Ramadan*, 156 F.3d at 502, it is at least debatable that the dissent had the better understanding of the accuracy required by the TILA. We need not enter that particular debate, however, because we believe, in any event, this case is distinguishable from *Clark*.

Clark was a classic bait-and-switch case. The plaintiff there was first attracted by a deceptive offer. Having obtained his audience, the lender attempted to switch the offer to a set of terms more favorable to itself and less favorable to the borrower. All of this occurred before the consummation of an agreement. Clark was able to, and chose to, refuse the switch based on accurate disclosures. He was never a party to a credit agreement whose terms were not adequately disclosed.

The disclosures at issue in *Clark* were initial disclosures—disclosures that must be made by a specified time before the consummation of the agreement. With respect to the terms actually offered, disclosure was achieved by the second disclosure statement. The first statement did not accurately reflect the terms of the agreement ultimately offered, but the second statement provided Clark with fully adequate disclosure before an agreement was reached, providing Clark with the opportunity to accept or decline the proposed agreement on the basis of full information. Armed with that information, he chose not to enter into an agreement.

Here, by contrast, the original disclosures were not corrected before Rossman entered into the agreement. These disclosures remained the relevant disclosures of the agreement ultimately reached. But it is essential to the TILA's purposes that consumers be informed of the basic conditions of credit *before* they enter a credit relationship. As the second disclosures in *Clark* did provide adequate information before consummation, these concerns were not implicated there.

This bait-and-switch case, therefore, goes beyond standard bait-and-switch cases such as *Clark*. The switch here did not occur as the result of a sales tactic before the formation of the contract, but by invoking an undisclosed term in an existing contract. Rossman entered the agreement without the benefit of disclosure of what she alleges was Fleet's intended annual fee. To the extent the original disclosures were corrected by the notice of change, this correction happened only after Rossman had used, and been bound by, the agreement for several months. Had Rossman received the notice of the change in the form of an initial notice before opening her account, she would have been subject to a classic bait-and-switch analogous to *Clark*, and would have found herself in a correspondingly less disadvantageous position.

Significantly, it would appear that Rossman was not entirely free, following notice of the pending imposition of the annual fee, to walk away from her credit arrangement in the same way that Clark was upon receiving his second set of disclosures.

Credit card holders may have balances they are unable to pay off within a month. And if Rossman did attempt to cancel the card while carrying a balance, Fleet retained the contractual authority to assess a 24.99% APR on the remaining balance. Therefore, there may have been no way to avoid incurring the obligation to pay the annual fee under the changed contract. As such, the notice of change was correspondingly less valuable than initial disclosure of the annual fee would have been.

Furthermore, Congress has imposed special requirements on credit card solicitations that did not apply to the mortgage in *Clark*. Not only must issuers disclose the basic terms of the agreement prior to consummation ("initial disclosures"), they must *additionally* disclose—clearly, conspicuously, and accurately—many of those terms in the solicitation itself ("solicitation disclosures" or "early disclosures"). These requirements are unique to credit and charge cards. They seek to ensure that consumers have the information needed to make informed choices with respect to credit cards not only before the agreement is consummated, but also at the (generally earlier) point at which they are considering responding to an issuer's solicitation.

Under the approach urged by Fleet, a credit issuer would be able to disclose any terms it wanted to, with no intention ultimately to offer those terms. It could send, together with the card, a new set of disclosures stating the terms it had always actually intended to provide. Fleet's approach would have the potential to render the solicitation disclosure requirements created by the 1988 amendments to the TILA entirely ineffectual. Misleading early disclosures would serve no informative purpose. And worse, the additional disclosure requirement mandated by Congress—for the purpose of encouraging informed consumer choices—could be used for the purpose of deceiving consumers.

The Federal Reserve Board has determined that when a credit card issuer offers rates or fees that are reduced or waived for a limited period of time, the issuer must disclose the applicable rate or fee that will apply indefinitely, and is permitted to disclose introductory rates only if the period of time in which the rate or fee is applicable is also disclosed. 12 C.F.R. Pt. 226, Supp. I, cmt. 5a(b)(1)–5 (introductory rates); cmt. 5a(b)(2)–4 (waived or reduced fees). Thus, as general matter, credit card issuers are required to disclose fees whose imposition will be delayed for a given period of time, such as the annual fee at issue here.

Fleet is apparently of the view that the card issuer's obligation, under this provision, to disclose the temporary nature of the fee in advance arises only when the cardholder agreement, which is ordinarily provided later, will include mention of the fee. Such a rule, however, would permit issuers to readily circumvent the requirement. The common practice of offering cards with low "teaser" rates would effectively be rendered immune from disclosure requirements. From the point of view of the consumer, there is no substantive difference between a card that had a low "fixed" rate that the issuer secretly intends to increase six months later, and a card with a low temporary rate that will similarly increase after half a year. The only purported basis for the difference in disclosure requirements is language in a document that, in most cases, the consumer will not have been provided at the time of the disclosures. Solicitation disclosures are intended to alert the consumer to the basic costs of the credit card he is considering—a purpose unserved where the issuer conceals the temporary nature of a favorable fee or rate in this manner.

Because so many credit solicitations do include introductory rates and fees, it is reasonable to view a solicitation that promises fixed rates and no annual fees as describing an agreement under which the issuer intends to offer those terms until there is a reason to change them. A statement, therefore, that a card has "no annual fee" made by a creditor that intends to impose such a fee shortly thereafter, is misleading. It is an accurate statement only in the narrowest of senses—and not in a sense appropriate to a consumer protection disclosure statute such as the TILA. Fleet's proposed approach would permit the use of required disclosures—intended to protect consumers from hidden costs—to intentionally deceive customers as to the costs of credit. Neither the language of the TILA itself, nor Regulation Z or the Official Staff Interpretations directs such a result.

Rossman has alleged Fleet intentionally and in fact misled her and others with its disclosure of a "no-annual-fee" credit card. If Rossman's allegations are true—which we assume on a motion to dismiss—such misleading statements are inaccurate for purposes of the TILA, and violate its requirements.

CONCLUSION

For the forgoing reasons, we hold that Rossman has stated a claim under the TILA. Accordingly, we will reverse the judgment of the District Court, and remand for proceedings consistent with this opinion.

Notes

1. Why was the credit card solicitation in the *Rossman* case considered a form of "bait and switch"? Is there any relevant difference between what Ms. Rossman alleged and the allegations in the *American TV* case? Which type of bait and switch is more harmful to consumers? Why?

2. Does the Truth in Lending Act prohibit bait advertising? How did the court in *Rossman* distinguish the earlier *Clark* case, decided by the Fifth Circuit Court of Appeals, which stated that "The Truth in Lending Act does not provide a cause of action when a lender engages in 'bait and switch' techniques"? How did the court in *Rossman* reach the conclusion that Fleet's practices, specifically their credit card solicitation disclosures, had violated TILA?

3. Note that in the *Rossman* case, the bank had attempted to use a Change-in-Terms provision to justify its imposition of an annual fee. Why did this argument not prevail? When is a change-in-terms clause valid? Would it have applied if Fleet had waited a year before imposing an annual fee? What if Fleet had tried to add a mandatory arbitration clause? See *infra* Chapter 6, Section C, for a more detailed discussion of change-of-terms provisions in credit accounts.

Problem 3–2

Vader Motors regularly advertises "easy credit, anyone can qualify, drive home your new car today!" Its practice is to quote a price for the vehicle, and an APR, and then offer "spot delivery." Luke, responding to the ad, signed a Purchase Contract, a Retail Installment Sales Contract (RISC) and a "Bailment Agreement for Vehicle Spot Delivery." Luke agreed to pay $20,000 for a new Tiemobile, and was to receive a $5,000 credit for his trade-in. The RISC was contingent on Vader securing third party financing. The Bailment Agreement allowed Luke to take the car without passage of title. Luke also received a TILA disclosure showing a 3% APR. Once these documents were signed, Luke left his trade-in at the dealership and drove home with his new Tiemobile. Three days later, Vader called Luke to notify him that the dealership was not able to obtain the desired financing rates but that Empire Acceptance Corporation (EAC) had offered to finance the loan at a 12% APR. When Luke stated that he would be in the next day to return the Tiemobile and retrieve his trade-in, Vader replied that it had already sold the trade-in. If Luke agrees to the new terms, he would receive a new RISC with a new TILA disclosure, showing the higher APR, etc.

If this type of practice could be proven, would it constitute illegal "bait and switch" marketing of credit? Under the FTC Guides Against Bait Advertising? Under a state UDAP statute similar to Wisconsin's? Under the TILA? Are any other laws potentially being violated in this scenario? How would you rate the harm to the consumer from "yo-yo financing" as compared to the advertising campaign discussed in *American TV* or the credit card solicitation in *Rossman*? What would be an appropriate remedy for the consumer, if any? *Cf.* Bragg v. Bill Heard Chevrolet, Inc., 374 F.3d 1060 (11th Cir. 2004).

Note on Negative Option Plans by Internet Service Providers

In the early 1970's, the FTC promulgated its "Negative Option" rule to address problems consumers had with "book of the month club" arrangements. 16 C.F.R. § 425. A negative option plan is one in which the consumer is automatically shipped and billed for an item (like a book or CD) unless he/she takes some affirmative action to cancel. Specifically, the FTC regulation defines "negative option plan" as:

> A contractual plan or arrangement under which a seller periodically sends to subscribers an announcement which identifies merchandise (other than annual supplements to previously acquired merchandise) it proposes to send to subscribers to such plan, and the subscribers thereafter receive and are billed for the merchandise identified in each such announcement, unless by a date or within a time specified by the seller with respect to each such announcement the subscribers, in conformity with the provisions of such plan, instruct the seller not to send the identified merchandise.

Consumer advocates objected that this marketing method takes advantage of the human tendency to procrastinate and do nothing. The FTC regulation requires such plans to make disclosures in the promotional materials and in the announcement of the selections of the consumer's need to cancel to avoid being billed, and of the method required to do so. 16 C.F.R. § 425(a). The rule also contains requirements for crediting consumers for merchandise they have returned, prompt shipping of promised bonus merchandise, and adequate notification to the consumer to allow him/her to exercise their option to cancel before merchandise is shipped. *Id.* at § 425(b). *See generally* Dennis D. Lamont, Comment, Negative Option Offers in Consumer Service Contracts: A Principled Reconciliation of Commerce and

Consumer Protection, 42 U.C.L.A. L. Rev. 1315 (1995). (The author discusses the FTC Negative Option regulation and its history at 1369–1383).

"Free trial offer" marketing plans, used in the late 1990's by three of the largest Internet service providers in the U.S., America Online, Inc., CompuServe, Inc., and Prodigy Services Corp., present another type of "negative option" for consumers. These free trial offers for Internet service typically involved direct mailing of a disk and instructional materials. The promotion usually emphasized a certain number of free hours of Internet access, say 600, which could be used during the first 30 days. Like the "book of the month club," however, the consumer had to take affirmative steps to cancel to avoid being charged after the time period for the free hours of access had expired. A consumer who did nothing might end up being billed for more than they had counted on.

The FTC staff alleged that the companies did not disclose to consumers in the promotional material that they would incur charges unless they took steps to cancel their membership during the trial period. Furthermore, if consumers did not cancel, they were automatically enrolled and charged monthly membership fees. The FTC also charged the companies with electronically debiting consumers' accounts without proper authorization. In re America Online, Inc., 1997 WL 220352 (F.T.C.); In re CompuServe, Inc., 1997 WL 220351 (F.T.C.); In re Prodigy Services Corp., 1997 WL 220350 (F.T.C.). Some consumers complained that although it was very easy to sign up online for the free trial offer, the cancellation was more cumbersome and had to take place by regular mail or telephone during business hours.

Would these marketing practices be covered by the FTC Negative Option rule? By the FTC Act Section Five (15 U.S.C. § 45)? If you were an FTC staff attorney negotiating a settlement, what provisions would you advocate and why? If you were working for America Online, how would you defend the free trial offer promotion as a legitimate marketing tool?

See 72 Antitrust & Trade Regulation Reports 458 (May 8, 1997) for a summary of the FTC complaints and settlement terms.

Problem 3–3

Waldo Nerd was shopping for a telephone with an answering machine. He went back to Elder & Johnson Co. and saw two products that met his needs. One was priced at $100 with a $30 rebate. The second was priced at $80. Waldo decided to purchase the more expensive product on the theory that he would soon be getting a $30 rebate. Once Waldo installed the new telephone and answering machine, however, he discovered that the requirements for obtaining the rebate were fairly onerous, including filling out a form, submitting the "rebate receipt" and cutting out and sending in the bar code from the packaging. He never got around to sending it in, and thus ended up paying $100 for what he thought would be a $70 product.

Would E&J's rebate offer constitute an illegal bait and switch or a "negative option" under relevant FTC law? What if the store knew from past experience that only 20% of its customers ever successfully complete the rebate application, yet they emphasize the "after rebate" price in the store and in their advertising? What if the store never pays the rebates unless the customer who sent in the rebate follows up with another inquiry? Would any of these variation raise state UDAP issues? Common law fraud issues? Should the FTC or the State AG require better disclosures in rebate offers—i.e., disclose that only 20% ever actually get the rebate? Disclose the conditions for obtaining the rebate and the length of time it will take?

SECTION B.   THE DEAL THAT CONTEMPLATES FINDING OTHER SUCKERS—PYRAMID SCHEMES AND REFERRAL SALES

The pyramid scheme is an enduring consumer scam that originated in revival style motivational meetings, and continues to find victims worldwide via internet web pages and emails. The lure is a chance to earn easy money simply by recruiting others to join the operation. As the name suggests, the technique involves the selling of the right to sell, indefinitely, in an inverted pyramid fashion. The "genius" at pyramid selling was Glenn Turner whose Koscot (cosmetics) and Dare-to-be-Great (self-improvement course) pyramids earned him (1) a great deal of money; (2) prosecutions by countless federal, state and local officials; and (3) eventual bankruptcy and dismemberment of his corporate empire.

Turner's selling scheme utilized high pressure group sessions (Golden Opportunity, or GO meetings) replete with flashing $100 bills, exuberant salesmen, and promises of vast annual incomes. In the Koscot plan, consumers could purchase the right to sell cosmetics; but, more importantly, they could purchase the right to sell distributorships (or sub-franchises) to others who in turn could sell cosmetics or new distributorships. Each such sale would earn an override commission for the original enrollee, larger of course, for sales of distributorships than for actual sales of cosmetics products. Dare-to-be-Great was similar, the actual product consisting of nothing more than a cassette tape extolling Turner's own philosophy of success. The pyramid scheme obviously suffers from mathematical impossibility—several rounds of distributorship sales would exhaust the population of the world.

Turner, and other pyramid marketers, have been successfully prosecuted on numerous grounds: fraudulent sales practices, postal fraud, sales of unregistered securities, antitrust violations, and others. *See, e.g.,* Kugler v. Koscot Interplanetary, Inc., 120 N.J.Super. 216, 293 A.2d 682 (1972); Webster v. Omnitrition Internat'l, Inc., 79 F.3d 776 (9th Cir. 1996); U.S. v. Gold Unlimited, Inc., 177 F.3d 472 (6th Cir. 1999). Modern variations are now popping up on the Internet and in developing countries. Ironically, the participants sometimes blame the prosecutors for stopping their scheme, still believing that they would have made money if only they had been allowed to keep it going. Consider the following case, which illustrates a "classic" type of pyramid scheme.

NIELSEN v. MYERS

Court of Appeals of Oregon, 2004.
193 Or.App. 388, 90 P.3d 628.

Before HASELTON, PRESIDING JUDGE, and LINDER and WOLLHEIM, JUDGES.

LINDER, J.

Plaintiffs in this case participated in a "gifting club" in which they and others paid cash—either $2,000 or $6,000—to obtain a position on a pyramid-shaped "board" in the hope that they might eventually move to the top of the board and receive a large return (more than $13,000) on their investment. Their success in reaching the top depended on a sufficient number of additional individuals being recruited to also make a cash "gift" to participate. The Oregon Attorney General concluded that the club was an illegal pyramid scheme and took steps to halt it. In response, plaintiffs brought this declaratory judgment action seeking to have their activities declared lawful and to enjoin the Attorney General from further efforts to force them to cease involvement with the club. On cross-motions for summary judgment, the trial court concluded that the gifting club was an unlawful pyramid club under the Oregon Unlawful Trade Practices Act (UTPA) and entered a declaration accordingly. *See* ORS 646.608(1)(r). Following a further evidentiary proceeding, the court imposed a $25,000 civil penalty against plaintiff Ray Sweat. See ORS 646.642(1). Plaintiffs appeal, and we affirm.

The gifting club that gave rise to this case was named, inscrutably, the Northwest Family Reunion (NWFR). As explained to the participants, the NWFR gifting club used a board called the "Pit Stop Report," which consisted of four levels and a total of 15 positions for participants. NWFR invoked a race car analogy to denominate positions on different levels of the board, with the first level positions (*i.e.*, lowest) termed "pit crew," the second-level positions termed "mechanics," the third-level positions termed "pace cars," and the top-level position termed the "lead driver." By committing to pay $2,000 in cash to NWFR, a participant obtained a "pit crew" position on the first level. Once the first level, consisting of eight positions, was filled, the newly joining participants "gifted" their $2,000 to the person at the top of the board. The actual exchange of money took place at a so-called gifting meeting or ceremony. Because of acknowledged uncertainty about the legality of the activities in Oregon, the actual giftings were held in Washington. After the gifting to the person at the top of the board, the board split into two new boards, and each participant moved up one level. The sequence then would begin anew. That is, a new group of participants would be recruited to fill the first level; when the first level was fully filled, the new participants would gift their $2,000 participation fee to the top person on the board; and the board would then split into two boards. The sequence was to continue *ad infinitum,* with new members continually being recruited to join with the hope of reaching the top of the board.

Pursuant to the NWFR rules, an investor could pay $2,000 to name another person to a position on a board, but names listed on boards could not be changed without approval. One NWFR participant, Pemberton, explained that he paid to obtain positions for his wife and aunt, who were unaware that they he had placed their names on boards. NWFR rules prohibited participants from taking part in more four boards at a time. Anyone could solicit people to join NWFR and could otherwise talk about and tell others about the gifting scheme. But given the structure of the scheme, only those named on boards stood to gain by recruiting new participants—in doing so, they improved their chances of reaching the top of the pyramid and receiving a windfall, one that NWFR represented would be tax free.

NWFR was introduced to the Klamath Falls area in 1999 by plaintiff Micka, who learned about the gifting activities from NWFR organizers in Washington. Micka, in turn, told plaintiffs about NWFR and encouraged them to participate. Plaintiffs paid to obtain positions on boards for themselves, and each induced at least one other person to participate in NWFR. Plaintiffs also organized NWFR in the Klamath Falls area. Word of NWFR's activities passed among family members, friends, work associates, and even casual acquaintances. Those interested in NWFR attended meetings where the rules of the club were explained, as was the prospect for making a significant return on their money. People who invested $2,000 in NWFR in fact were drawn by the possibility—which they understood not to be a promise or guarantee—that they potentially would reap a much larger amount of tax-free cash.

In late July 1999, the Oregon Attorney General issued a press release, which was published in the Klamath Falls newspaper, announcing the Attorney General's legal opinion that NWFR was a pyramid club in violation of the UTPA and warning that participants could face fines of up to $25,000 for each attempt to recruit a new participant. At that point, all of the plaintiffs save one—Ray Sweat—ceased their involvement with NWFR. After the press release was published in the Klamath Falls newspaper, Sweat invited Ritchie, a previous NWFR participant, to attend two giftings, but Ritchie declined.

In the two months following the press release, the Attorney General's Office served each plaintiff with an investigative demand, a notice of unlawful trade practices, and a proposed assurance of voluntary compliance (AVC). *See* ORS 646.632. Plaintiffs refused to sign the AVCs and instead filed an action against the state in Klamath County, seeking a declaration from the trial court that NWFR is legal under the UTPA and requesting injunctive relief against the state. The state counterclaimed, seeking a declaration that plaintiffs had engaged in an unlawful trade practice under ORS 646.608(1)(r), an injunction to prohibit plaintiffs from further involvement with NWFR, a penalty of $25,000 for each willful violation of the UTPA, and attorney fees.

Both parties moved for summary judgment. The trial court granted the state's motion and denied that of plaintiffs, concluding that NWFR was a "cash-for-cash pyramid club" in violation of the UTPA. *See* ORS 646.609 (defining "pyramid club"). The trial court also permanently enjoined plaintiffs from becoming involved in pyramid clubs in the future. After a trial on the issue of penalties, the trial court assessed a $25,000 penalty against Ray Sweat, finding that he willfully violated the UTPA by inviting Ritchie to two giftings after the Attorney General's press release had been published in the local newspaper. *See* ORS 646.642(3). Plaintiffs moved for a new trial, which the court denied, and this appeal followed.

On appeal, we address only plaintiffs' claim that the trial court, in granting summary judgment in favor of the state, erroneously concluded that NWFR legally qualifies as a pyramid club under ORS 646.609. We therefore begin with an overview of the portions of the UTPA relevant to that issue.

Oregon's UTPA is a comprehensive statute for the protection of consumers, one that provides for both public and private enforcement. ORS 646.608(1) sets forth a nonexclusive but extensive list of practices that are unlawful when done in the course of a person's business, vocation, or occupation. Relevant here is paragraph (1)(r), which prohibits organizing, inducing, or attempting to induce membership in a pyramid club. The term "pyramid club" is defined in ORS 646.609, as pertinent here, as

> a sales device whereby a person, upon condition that the person make an investment, is granted a license or right to solicit or recruit for economic gain one or more additional persons who are also granted such license or right upon condition of making an investment and who may further perpetuate the chain of persons who are granted such license or right upon such condition.

Drawing from that definition, plaintiffs advance several theories in support of their argument that, as a matter of law, the NWFR gifting club did not legally qualify as a pyramid club. We consider each argument in turn.

First, plaintiffs insist that their activities did not violate ORS 646.608(1)(r) because NWFR did not require a $2,000 investment as a condition to the right to solicit or recruit additional participants. In particular, plaintiffs rely on repeated representations by NWFR organizers and participants that anyone could talk about NWFR's activities and anyone could encourage, solicit, or recruit others to participate in NWFR. Said another way, no one had to be a participant in the gifting club or pay for a position on one of NWFR's boards to be able to encourage others to participate in NWFR's investment scheme.

We agree with the state, however, that the text of the statute readily answers plaintiffs' argument in that regard. The vice to which the statute is directed is not the granting of a license or right to solicit or recruit, without more. Rather, the statute describes the right as a "license or right to solicit or recruit *for economic gain*." ORS 646.609 (emphasis added). The record establishes, as plaintiffs contend, that anyone could talk about and encourage participation in NWFR's gifting scheme. But the record also establishes that the only persons who stood to gain economically from doing so were persons who were participants on the boards. The factual evidence is undisputed that the only way to be a participant was to make an investment of $2,000 in exchange for a place on the board. *A fortiori,* to solicit or recruit *for economic gain,* a person had to invest money in NWFR. Thus, as the definition requires, NWFR in fact conditioned the right or license to solicit or recruit *for economic gain* on making an investment.

That analysis invites two further questions, however: Who has to make the investment? And who has to acquire the right to solicit for economic gain? Plaintiffs argue that ORS 646.609 requires that the person who makes the investment—that is, who tenders the $2,000—be the same person who possesses the right to solicit for economic gain. That proposition leads plaintiffs to their second theory for why the NWFR gifting club did not legally qualify as a pyramid club-*viz.,* under NWFR's rules, an investor could place anyone's name on a board; the name did not have to be the investor's own. In fact, the record establishes that at least one investor, as earlier noted, secured two positions and then placed his wife's and aunt's names on boards without their knowledge. According to plaintiffs, the fact that the economic gain could be realized by someone other than the investor defeats a conclusion that NWFR's gifting club is a pyramid club within the meaning of ORS 646.609.

* * *

Assuming, without deciding, that ORS 646.609 requires that the investor be the same person who acquires the right to solicit or recruit new members for economic gain, NWFR's practice of permitting investors to name other people to positions on boards satisfies that requirement. On these facts, at least initially, the investor *is* the person who holds the right to solicit for economic gain. The record is clear that, as a condition of placing one's own name—or someone else's—on a board, a person must either tender or commit to tendering $2,000 in cash. Once that is done, that person may place his or her name, or anyone else's name, on a board. At the moment of tender, the person making the investment is in full and unilateral control over who will be the named participant on the board. Thus, the investor *acquires* the right to solicit or recruit for economic gain, even if the investor chooses not to retain that right. By placing another name on the board, the investor effectively assigns or transfers the right acquired to another person. In the interim, however, the right was acquired by the investor in exchange for the investment. That is enough to satisfy the statute.

Plaintiff's final theory for why the NWFR gifting scheme did not legally qualify as a pyramid club is that the reference in ORS 646.609 to a "sales device" requires some form of deception, trick, or misrepresentation in the inducement to participate in the scheme. * * *

* * *

We further agree with the state that, to the extent that ORS 646.609 requires deception, it contemplates only the deception that is inherent in the kind of investment scheme that the statute itself describes. The pyramid scheme involved in this case is a classic one; only the nomenclature and analogies distinguish it. This one was based on car racing, with positions denominated pit crew, mechanics, and so on. Nearly identical pyramid schemes have been devised using, for example, "airplane" analogies (with passenger, crew, copilot, and pilot positions on the boards)[10] or corporate organizational models (with positions for founders, vice-presidents, presidents, and a CEO on the boards).[11] All operate in essentially the same way. At the bottom of the pyramid are new investors, who pay for the right to place a name on the board. When the bottom layer is filled, the new investment money is given to the person in the topmost position, the board splits in two, and new investors must be recruited for the participants to continue to move up through the levels to reach the top position, which is the only point at which those participants will, if ever, receive an economic gain.

As other courts have observed, such schemes are "inherently deceptive." *Kugler v. Koscot Interplanetary, Inc.*, 120 N.J.Super. 216, 232, 293 A.2d 682, 690 (1972). Nothing in this record suggests that participants in NWFR had any awareness of the number of participants necessary to perpetuate the gifting cycle given the exponential increase in the number of boards every time a board "splits." Nor did they know how long the boards had been in existence or to what degree the pool of potential participants had been exhausted. That lack of awareness, which is commonplace, is the "core deception" of the pyramid scheme. Eric Witiw, *Selling the Right to Sell the Same Right to Sell: Applying the Consumer Fraud Act, the Uniform Securities Law, and the Criminal Code to Pyramid Schemes*, 26 Seton Hall L. Rev. 1635, 1637 (1996).

The reality is that, after a "relatively small number of progressions and divisions, a pool of multi millions of persons would be required to provide this voracious amoeba-like pyramid with the number of [new participants] necessary for it to continue to divide and exist." *Pacurib v. Villacruz*, 183 Misc.2d 850, 855, 705 N.Y.S.2d 819, 823 (N.Y. Cir. Ct. 1999). As explained in *Pacurib*, which involved a scheme that used a corporate organizational analogy:

> "For the original [eight] investing founders to reach the apex of the pyramid * * *, the board must progress three levels and 48 new

---

10. See, *e.g., State ex rel Mays v. Ridenhour,* 248 Kan. 919, 811 P.2d 1220 (1991).

11. See, *e.g., Pacurib v. Villacruz,* 183 Misc.2d 850, 705 N.Y.S.2d 819 (N.Y. Cir. Ct. 1999).

founders must join making a total of 56 participants. Moreover, in order for these [eight] investing founders to retire and be paid, the board must progress another level and 64 new founders must join the eight boards headed by these [eight] CEOs. At this level, a total of 120 paying founders will have participated. Although sufficient possible recruits are available at these early stages of the program, the pool of available people rapidly dissipates as the program progresses. As the chart demonstrates,[12] at the 20th level 4,194,304 new investing founders would be required in order for all previous CEOs to be paid and retire; and at that level a total of 8,388,600 investing founders will have participated. Just to advance one additional level, these 20th level founders would require an additional 8,388,608 new founders, thus making a total of 16,777,208 participating founders. In addition, consider the staggering number of new recruits which would be necessary for all of these 20th level founders to advance to the CEO position. Obviously, such a pool of persons would more than exhaust even the largest of the population centers in the United States."

Id. at 856, 705 N.Y.S.2d at 824 (emphasis omitted).

In short, we do not agree with plaintiffs that the legislature, in defining a pyramid club as a sales device of a particular kind, imposed a requirement that the scheme involve overt deception or misrepresentation in inducing investors to invest. To the contrary, the legislature specifically qualified the prohibited sales device as one "whereby" an investor, rather than purchasing a right to a product or service, buys only the right to recruit other investors for economic gain, who then, in chain-link fashion, purchase the same right. The legislature undoubtedly did so in recognition that such a pyramid scheme is inherently deceptive. Thus, merely qualifying as an investment scheme of the type that the statute describes, as NWFR's gifting club did in this case, is enough to bring the scheme within the statutory prohibition. The trial court therefore correctly granted summary judgment for the state and declared the gifting club activities to be unlawful under the UTPA.

Affirmed.

12. To illustrate the mathematical computations and geometric progressions involved, we borrow from a chart set forth by the court in *Pacurib,* 183 Misc.2d at 854 n. 3, 705 N.Y.S.2d at 823 n. 3:

Levels of Progression	New Participants Necessary For Each Newly Created Board To Split and Continue	Total Paying Founders
0	7	0
1	8	8
2	16	24
3	32	56
4	64	120
5	128	248
6	256	504
7	512	1,016
8	1,024	2,040
9	2,048	4,088
10	4,096	8,184
11	8,192	16,376
12	16,384	32,760
13	32,768	65,528
14	65,536	131,064
15	131,072	262,136
16	262,144	524,280
17	524,288	1,048,568
18	1,048576	2,097,144
19	2,097,152	4,194,296
20	4,194,304	8,388,600

Notes

1. The court in the *Nielson* case, in the course of applying the state statute to the facts presented, also made the point that all pyramid schemes are "inherently deceptive." Why?

2. Many states, like Oregon, have enacted specific legislation banning pyramid or "multi-level" sales plans as defined in the statute. See summary in U.S. v. Gold Unlimited, Inc., 177 F.3d 472, 483 (6th Cir. 1999). For example, Illinois defines a prohibited pyramid sales scheme as follows:

> [A]ny plan or operation whereby a person in exchange for money or other thing of value acquires the opportunity to receive a benefit or thing of value, which is primarily based upon the inducement of additional persons, by himself or others, regardless of number, to participate in the same plan or operation and is not primarily contingent on the volume or quantity of goods, services, or other property sold or distributed or to be sold or distributed to persons for purposes of resale to consumers.

Ill.Rev.Stat. Ch. 121 ½ par. 261(g).

State attorneys general and other plaintiffs relying on such statutes have had mixed results. *Compare* People ex rel. Hartigan v. Dynasty System Corp., 128 Ill.App.3d 874, 83 Ill.Dec. 937, 471 N.E.2d 236 (1984); State ex rel. Edmisten v. Challenge, 54 N.C.App. 513, 284 S.E.2d 333 (1981); Love v. Durastill of Richmond, Inc., 242 Va. 186, 408 S.E.2d 892 (1991) (defendants' conduct fell within statutory definition of pyramid sales); with State ex rel. Miller v. American Professional Marketing, 382 N.W.2d 117 (Iowa 1986); Whole Living, Inc., v. Tolman, 344 F. Supp. 2d 739 (D. Utah 2004) (defendants' sales plan was a legitimate multilevel distributing plan, and did not fall within the prohibited category defined in the statute).

3. The FTC has used its general authority to prohibit unfair and deceptive trade practices under FTC Act Section Five in combating pyramid schemes. See Stone & Steiner, The Federal Trade Commission and Pyramid Sales Schemes, 15 Pac. L.J. 879 (1984). However, the FTC early on articulated a test for determining what constitutes a deceptive pyramid scheme:

> [Pyramid schemes] are characterized by the payment by participants of money to the company in return for which they receive (1) the right to sell a product *and* (2) the right to receive in return for recruiting other participants into the program rewards which are unrelated to sale of the product to ultimate users.

In re Koscot Interplanetary, Inc., 86 F.T.C. 1106, 1181 (1975), aff'd mem. Sub nom., Turner v. F.T.C., 580 F.2d 701 (D.C. Cir. 1978).

Conversely, the FTC has found that certain types of multi-level marketing plans are not illegal pyramid schemes, such as plans that have stringent policies to prevent inventory loading, avoid market saturation, and encourage actual retail sales of a product. *See* In re Amway Corp., 93 F.T.C. 618 (1979).

4. Can you articulate what it is that distinguishes a deceptive or unfair pyramid scheme from the Avon lady?

Problem 3–4

The State of Illinois has brought a case against a company called Ultramax, which operates the Ultramax Buyers' Service and the Ultramax Matrix, a multi-level marketing plan. For a payment of $36 a month, subscribers to the Buyer's Service may purchase products and services at a discount from various suppliers who have agreements with Ultramax. Subscribers are also entitled for no extra fee to become Matrix "marketers" by signing an agreement with the company and undergoing some modest training. All 10,874 subscribers to the Buyers' Service have also signed marketer agreements, although only 10% of these are "active," i.e., up to date on their fee payments.

A marketer earns commissions on the $36 monthly subscription fees paid by new subscribers he sponsors, and also earns commissions on the fees paid by new subscribers sponsored by the original subscribers, and so on up to the ninth level. Each marketer must recruit at least three new subscribers. A marketer's monthly commission check increases according to a schedule on each of the nine levels. At Level 1, he earns a commission of 1% of the $36 fee paid by each of his subscribers at that level ($1.08 a month, assuming three subscribers). However, at Level 9, the marketer would have 19,683 subscribers in his down-line organization, and his commission at this level is 6% of each $36 fee, or $42,515.28 per month.

The State's complaint alleged that the Ultramax marketing plan violates the Illinois Consumer Fraud and Deceptive Business Practices Act, Ill.Rev.Stat. ch. 121½ ¶ 261(g) (quoted in the preceding notes). On these facts, Ultramax has filed a motion to dismiss. What arguments would you make on behalf of Ultramax? The State Attorney General? How should the trial court rule on the motion? Does the specificity of the statutory language help or hurt the state's case? Does it help or hurt the marketer's case? See People ex rel. Hartigan v. Unimax Inc., 168 Ill.App.3d 718, 119 Ill.Dec. 558, 523 N.E.2d 26 (1988).

Problem 3–5

An FTC investigation has uncovered a massive worldwide multi-level marketing operation, StarBiz.com, that appears to have some aspects of an illegal pyramid scheme. The promoters have a website and offer in-person sales presentations promoting the opportunity to earn thousands of dollars per week by recruiting new Associates into the StarBiz program. The company sells CD–Roms, computer disks, videos and books on the StarBiz program, as well as a canned PowerPoint presentation that Associates may use to recruit others. The fee to participate in the StarBiz program is $100 per year plus a fee of $25 to purchase an "e-Commerce Web Pak" that provides two websites, one for recruitment and one for personal use. Virtually all the StarBiz Associates purchase the Web Pak, and all use the recruiting website but few use the personal website. One favorite claim made by StarBiz enthusiasts is that the system was put together by a gentleman who was able to retire on $400,000 per month within six months of joining StarBiz, and now lives in a luxury home in the Bahamas. Associates who pay to participate in the StarBiz program can earn compensation from a "downline" consisting of all the people directly or indirectly sponsored by that Associate.

You are an FTC Consumer Protection Bureau staff attorney. Given these facts, what violations would you charge in your complaint against StarBiz? Would you use an administrative proceeding or try for an injunction in federal court under Section 53(b)? What problems might you encounter in tracking down the main perpetrators? What if you learn that the assets of StarBiz are being moved to "offshore" banks, such as in the West Indies? What if the victims who might be entitled to redress are scattered around the world? Can you frame a plan of prosecution that would satisfy the FTC Commissioners that it will be feasible to pursue this case and provide meaningful remedies to consumers?

See FTC v. SkyBiz.com, Inc., Civ. Action 01CV0396, N.D. Okla., Stipulated Final Judgment 01/28/03, available on http://www. FTC.gov; FTC v. Fortuna Alliance, L.L.C., Civ. No. C96–799M, W.D. Wash., Stipulated Final Judgment 2/24/97, available on http:// www.FTC.gov; FTC v. Five–Star Auto Club, Inc., 97 F. Supp. 2d 502 (S.D.N.Y. 2000).

Note on Referral Sales

Related to the pyramid scheme is the so-called "referral sale," where customers are induced to buy a product or service through promises of commissions, rebates or other credits for supplying the names of other potential customers. In most of these cases the basic purchase price the consumer agrees to pay is highly inflated, and the promises of referral commissions prove illusory.

The Uniform Consumer Credit Code contains a provision banning referral sales, reprinted in the statutory supplement. Here is what the drafters had to say about this practice in their commentary to U.C.C.C. 3.309:

1. The typical referral sale scheme which would be barred by this section is one in which the seller, before closing the sale, offers to reduce the price by $25 for every name of a person the buyer supplies who will agree to buy from the seller. The seller may be able to make an inflated price tag much more palatable to a buyer if he can convince the buyer that the referral plan will greatly reduce the amount he will actually have to pay. The buyer may not realize until later that his friends whose names he submitted are not as gullible as he and that he is bound to pay the original balance of the contract price.

2. The evil this section is aimed at is the raising of expectations in a buyer of benefits to accrue to him from events which are to occur in the future. This provision has no effect on a seller's agreement to reduce at the time of the sale the price of an item in exchange for the buyer's giving the seller a list of prospective purchasers or assisting in other ways if the price reduction is not contingent on whether the purchasers do in fact buy or on whether other events occur in the future.

3. The misuse of the referral sale scheme has been so pervasive in some segments of vendor credit that this provision, in an effort to halt these practices, not only makes agreements in violation of this section unenforceable but also allows the buyer to retain the goods sold or the benefit of services rendered with no obligation to pay for them. Alternatively, the buyer may rescind the agreement, return the goods, and

recover any payment. Use of a referral scheme subjects the offending seller or lessor to a penalty under Section 5.201. Creditors cannot evade this section by the use of credit cards or consumer loans.

Problem 3–6

Same facts as Problem 1–1, Chapter 1, Section A(1). Carol DePrey visits Oakwood Shores Resort and listens to a sales pitch for the Resort's time shares. However, this time assume Carol decides to purchase a time share for $6,800 based on the sales representative's promise that she will receive either a $50 check, a reduction of maintenance fees, or a bonus week, for each person referred to Oakwood Shores. For Carol to obtain the benefit, the referred individual is required to attend a similar sales presentation to the one Carol attended.

Assume the following state statute is in effect in the relevant jurisdiction:

> No seller or lessor may use any referral selling plan to make a consumer sale unless the seller or lessor first pays the buyer or lessee the full amount of potential compensation offered to that buyer or lessee under that plan.

> "Referral selling plan" means any method of sale where the seller or lessor, as an inducement for a consumer sale, offers compensation to a prospective buyer or lessee either for a) names of other prospective buyers or lessees, or b) otherwise aiding the seller or lessor in making consumer sales.

The statute provides for private remedies, including damages and attorney's fees. Has Oakwood Shores violated the statute quoted above? If Carol were to sue Oakwood Shores under these provisions, would she have to prove she provided names to Oakwood and was due compensation? Should she be able to rescind the time-share sale?

See Pliss v. Peppertree Resort Villas, Inc., 264 Wis.2d 735, 663 N.W.2d 851 (Ct. App. 2003). See also Uniform Consumer Credit Code § 3.309.

Problem 3–7

Crafty Siders, Inc., a purveyor of home siding, makes the following statements to selected potential customers: "We are using a new method of advertising. We are not going to pay newspapers, TV, or radio anymore, for they already make enough money. Instead we are going to pay our customers to advertise for us, and let you use those payments from us to practically pay for your new siding. If you buy from us, we will offer you $25 per month to let us erect a sign in your front yard saying that your home has our siding." Of course, the sign remains in the customer's front yard only so long as it is effective—i.e., only so long as it or the customer produces new sales, but the customer does not know that, yet. Is this actionable as a referral sale, or under any other principle, under the case-law, or the U3C § 3.309? Would it make a difference if the customer knew from the beginning that the term of the sign placement depended upon continuously generating new sales?

SECTION C. IN–HOME SOLICITATIONS AND THE "COOLING OFF" PERIOD

Sellers may choose among many ways of soliciting consumers to buy their wares. Some means of soliciting sales are relatively impersonal: radio and television advertising, or the internet, for example. This section focuses one particular type of more personalized sales pitch, in-home solicitation. If a contract is concluded in the consumer's home, is there more of a chance that the sale was the result of high-pressure or overreaching tactics by the salesperson? Is there a need for a special type of consumer protection in this setting?

Problem 3–8

A state attorney general has brought an action for injunctive and restitutionary relief, under a statute authorizing such actions against any "unfair, deceptive, fraudulent or unconscionable sales practices." You are the trial court judge in the case, and the following evidence has been presented before you. Without proof of overt misrepresentations by the seller, is there a basis for your court to enjoin these sales practices? Does the fact that the sales pitch was made in the consumer's home make any difference? See Kugler v. Romain, 58 N.J. 522, 279 A.2d 640 (1971), from which the following facts are drawn.

[Defendant, Educational Services Company] was engaged in the installment sale of so-called educational books and related materials * * * Sales solicitations were made exclusively through house-to-house canvass by defendant's employees. No advance appointments were made. The solicitors simply descended upon a selected section of a municipality and undertook by house-to-house calls to sell a package of books which was described in large type on the contract presented to the prospective customers as "A Complete Ten Year Educational Program." * * * near-by was the plea "Give your child its chance." In engaging his sales personnel, defendant sought persons who were "sales oriented" and extroverted. * * *

The geographical areas to be the subject of sales solicitation were primarily * * * urban centers * * * chosen by defendant who was familiar with them and the class of people to be sought out by his sales force. Within these target areas, the sales solicitations were consciously directed toward minority group consumers and consumers of limited education and economic means. Persons with incomes of less than $5000 a year were favored; some buyers were welfare recipients. Sales among these people were thought to be "easier." Although the canvassing was door-to-door, ordinances in the municipalities involved in this case which required licensing or registration were ignored. * * *

The printed contract form marked "Retail Installment Obligation," which was presented to the customer for signature, consisted of a single sheet covered with printed matter on both sides. The cash and time sale prices were printed on the face of the contract, the former at $249.50, and the latter at $279.95, less a $9 down payment which was obtained whenever possible. Apparently no one paid the cash price. Also printed on the face in small print was the statement: "This order is not subject to cancellation and set is not returnable." * * *

[T]he wholesale price for the basic package, including the bonus items, was $35 to $40. Thus the cash sale price was six or seven times the wholesale price. * * * The Attorney General offered uncontradicted expert evidence that in view of industry-wide practices the maximum retail price which should have been charged for the entire package was approximately $108–$110. * * * [He] offered persuasive evidence that the books had little or no educational value for the children in the age group and socioeconomic position the defendant represented would be benefited by them.

The testimony showed that as to the New Achievement Library, three of the five volumes dealing with Nature, Science and Civilization, represented "very poor, watered-down articles which cover the * * * areas very superficially." They were of "extremely little use" or value as a means of raising the educational level of the children they were supposed to help. Another volume entitled "Getting Acquainted with Your Opportunities in Education" was extremely poor both in quality and content. Although the volume required a tenth grade reading level, it contained articles which the witness characterized as obsolete at the time it was being sold and irrelevant to 98% of its intended readers. * * * As to "High School Self Taught," the four volumes were useless for * * * basic education for any individual. They might have some value for refreshment purposes for a person who has been through high school, "but for one to self teach, it is just impossible." Similar comments were made about other books in the package. Taken as a whole, the witness said that, in his judgment, the books "will serve no purpose in improving the intellectual level of these children. . . ."

Defendant offered no contradictory proof on this subject.

The Attorney General produced 24 consumers who testified concerning their own experiences with defendant's sales personnel which led to the execution of the printed form purchase contracts. In no case was there any real explanation of the obligation being assumed upon signing the contract. Many buyers, relying on the representations of defendant's agents, did not read the form being signed.

Query: Would compulsory disclosure of contract terms, as in TILA, have been helpful here? Would the New York Clear Language Act have any impact? What is it that needs to be disclosed?

A Radical Departure—Restructuring the Transaction

Although Attorney General Kugler was successful in his efforts to enjoin the particular door-to-door selling scheme depicted in the problem above, it was with great difficulty, for he had not only to litigate both at the trial and appellate levels, but also to litigate very difficult fact issues at the trial. This enormous investment of attorney resources was required because his only weapon was a general-language consumer fraud statute; it will not happen very often. The problem therefore raises the question whether there might be a better legal response to this kind of imposition, one which does not make the outcome depend on post-contract litigation over the existence of fraud in the transaction?

Note that controls on disclosure, through fraud doctrines or legislation like TILA have an obvious limitation. They still permit the seller or creditor to construct the transaction and its terms however he chooses, and to hold the consumer to his signed obligation, so long as pertinent information is disclosed accurately before the magic moment of contract consummation. The consumer has little or no real chance to reflect on the sales pitch, the disclosures or the contract document before becoming legally obligated.

One way of breaking this Gordian knot is to restructure the transaction pattern in such a way that consumers *do* have an opportunity for reflection, for second-thoughts, and for careful reading of disclosures and other documents—an opportunity, in other words, to "cool off." Because of situations like those in Problem 7, *supra*, this cooling-off notion has gotten particular acceptance in legislation dealing with door-to-door sales. The usual format of these statutes is to provide that consumers will have a specified period after signing a contract within which they may disavow, or cancel, it without penalty by notifying the seller of their election to do so. The seller or creditor is required to inform the consumer of this right, and to provide the consumer with written cancellation forms to be returned if the consumer elects to cancel. Often the seller is prohibited from delivering goods or otherwise performing the contract until the period has expired.

The rationale for such substantive interference with the parties' freedom of contract is succinctly stated in an opinion of the Arizona Supreme Court sustaining the constitutionality of a home-solicitation "cooling off" statute. Arizona v. Direct Sellers Ass'n, 108 Ariz. 165, 494 P.2d 361 (1972). Quoting from a legislative committee report, the court stated:

> Although, without doubt, unethical sales techniques are employed in all methods of retailing, * * * this bill [is limited] to direct selling. This is partially because * * * a disproportionate number of door-to-door sales involve misleading or high pressure sales tactics, and partially because of certain of the unique characteristics of direct selling which seem to leave the consumer particularly vulnerable: The buyer has not made a conscious decision, as by entering a store, to expose himself to a sales pitch. * * * The buyer has no way of screening the type of salesman who comes to his door, as he does in choosing the stores in which he shops. The buyer may feel intimidated into making a purchase from a salesman within the

home, for there is no place to which he or she can readily escape. The buyer * * * has no opportunity for comparing value. And finally, the selling company does not have the same opportunity to police the conduct of its salesmen and their representations in the buyer's home, as it does when they operate within a store.

In addition, door-to-door sellers commonly work on commission, and are often well-trained. And, as Problem 3–8 above suggests, door-to-door sellers can pick their neighborhoods on the basis of income, ethnic makeup, or other demographic factors, to maximize their chances of success.

Notes

1. Recurrent abuses in door-to-door selling have prompted legislative responses other than cooling-off period requirements. One is the prohibition of "referral" sales, discussed in the preceding section. Another is the imposition of licensing or registration requirements on door-to-door sellers. Do you think these techniques work better than cooling-off periods? On the other hand, home selling has never been banned in this country. Are there any advantages to the consumer and/or to the seller from in-home sales? Do they offset the potential abuses? Why do you suppose the cooling—off period became such a popular legislative approach in the area of door-to-door sales?

2. The idea of cooling-off legislation first gained currency not in this country, but in England, where it was embodied in the Hire–Purchase Act of 1964. Individual states in the United States began adopting cooling-off statutes in the middle 1960's. See Sher, The Cooling–Off Period in Door-to-Door Sales, 15 U.C.L.A. L. Rev. 717 (1968). The U3C provides for a cooling off period in home solicitation sales. See U3C §§ 3.501–3.505. Except for New Mexico, every state has now adopted a cooling-off statute. See Dee Pridgen and Richard M. Alderman, Consumer Credit and the Law App. 15A (2007). The various state laws on the subject are varied, and they do not all operate under the same conditions or in the same types of transactions. In 1972, the FTC promulgated a trade regulation rule, codified at 16 C.F.R. § 429.0 et seq., requiring a cooling-off period in all door-to-door sales, whether for cash or on credit.

3. The federal Truth in Lending Act also provides a cooling-off period in certain transactions in which a security interest is retained in the consumer's home. See TILA 15 U.S.C. § 1635; Reg. 12 C.F.R. §§ 226.15 (open-end transactions) and 226.23 (closed-end transactions). Unlike the FTC rule and the state statutes, there is no requirement of a door-to-door sale. However, home improvement contractors, the primary target of the TILA provision, often use door-to-door sales methods, and then take a second mortgage in the consumer's home to secure the debt. As a result, the criteria which trigger both provisions may be met in many transactions. See, for example, the *Cole* case immediately below.

4. Despite the prevalence of cooling-off period statutes and rules, little empirical evidence is available to establish that consumers benefit from them. A study of a statute enacted in Connecticut that provided consumers one day to rescind contracts found that the provision "benefits consumers

very little." Note, A Case Study of the Impact of Consumer Legislation: The Elimination of Negotiability and the Cooling–Off Period, 78 Yale L.J. 618, 628 (1969). Whether that is also true of three-day cooling-off periods is unclear. Some evidence suggests that consumers will not often avail themselves of cooling-off periods. Thus, psychologists have observed that many consumers are reluctant to part with possessions, including possessions held only briefly. This tendency, dubbed the endowment effect, is illustrated by an experiment reported in Jack Knetsch, The Endowment Effect and Evidence of Nonreversible Indifference Curves, in Choices, Values, and Frames 171, 172–73 (2000) (Daniel Kahneman & Amos Tversky, eds.). When individuals were given a coffee mug and invited to trade it for a candy bar, 89% refused to make the exchange. When a different group was provided with candy bars and invited to exchange them for mugs, 90% declined the offer. Consequently, Jon D. Hanson and Douglas A. Kysar have argued, sellers can persuade consumers to go through with a purchase if they can get the item to be purchased into the buyer's possession even for a short time. Jon D. Hanson and Douglas A. Kysar, Taking Behavioralism Seriously: The Problem of Market Manipulation, 74 N.Y.U.L.Rev. 630, 734 (1999). If it is true that consumers do not take advantage of cooling-off periods, is there any point in requiring merchants to provide them?

5. Cooling-off periods have been widely adopted in Europe for a wide variety of consumer transactions. For an interesting summary of cooling-off laws in Europe and an economic analysis of their provisions, *see* Pamaria Rekaiti and Roger Van den Bergh, Cooling–Off Periods in the Consumer Laws of the EC Member States: A Comparative Law and Economics Approach, 23 J. of Consumer Policy 371 (2000).

6. One important policy issue raised by these different provisions is to decide which transactions need a cooling-off period and which do not. For example, is it possible to identify the characteristics of those transactions for which cooling-off periods have been provided? Are there others which should be included?

COLE v. LOVETT

United States District Court, Southern District of Mississippi, 1987.
672 F.Supp. 947, aff'd, 833 F.2d 1008 (5th Cir.).

TOM S. LEE, DISTRICT JUDGE

* * *

On Tuesday, November 9, 1982, at approximately six o'clock p.m., plaintiffs Norman and Judy Cole were visited by two representatives of Capitol Roofing, Tony Stepp and Ken Smith. After describing the siding proposed to be sold to the Coles and installed on their home, Stepp estimated the cost of covering the Cole home at $4900. This sales call resulted in plaintiffs', on the same evening, signing a contract for the installation of vinyl siding on their home. During this transaction, Stepp presented a number of documents to the Coles for their signatures, including a work order contract, home improvement retail installment contract security agreement and disclosure statement (disclosure statement), loan application, notice of right to cancel, and deed of trust. Although all of the documents were signed by plaintiffs, they both testified that the only document they actually saw was the work order contract. Stepp had represented to them that the papers they were signing included a work order, credit application and insurance papers. According to the Coles, the papers were arranged one on top of the other, with the contract being the top paper. As Stepp presented the papers for their signature, he lifted only so much of a document as was necessary to obtain their signatures at the bottom of each page. When the transaction was completed, the Coles were given a single carbon copy of the work order contract and a copy of the disclosure statement. According to the Coles' testimony, which the court credits, they received no copies of the remaining documents.

Shortly after Stepp and Smith left the home, plaintiffs discussed the matter and decided to hold off on the transaction with Capitol Roofing. They wished to obtain more estimates and have time to decide if they really wanted the siding. Early the next morning, Judy Cole called Capitol Roofing and informed Stepp that she and her husband had decided to wait, to which Stepp replied that the papers had been processed, the workers would be out at the end of the week, and there was nothing he could do.[2]

Frustrated and not knowing what else to do, Mrs. Cole accepted Stepp's explanation. Upon returning home from work that day, she discovered the Capitol Roofing installation crew putting siding on the home. She did not tell them to leave because she believed that she and her husband were bound since they had signed the contract. Subsequently, on November 27, after the job was completed, plaintiffs signed a completion certificate acknowledging their satisfaction with the work which had been done. Immediately upon completion of the paperwork, including the completion certificate, Capitol Roofing assigned the contract to defendant UCM.[3] At trial, there was testimony from two UCM employees, John Nowell and Marvin Murray, regarding UCM's normal procedure for handling the purchase of a retail installment contract from Capitol Roofing. According to their testimony, once an application for a potential customer was approved, Capitol Roofing would furnish UCM

---

2. Stepp, at trial, admitted having received a phone call from Judy Cole early on the morning following the consummation of the transaction, but claimed that she had called him to discuss the color of the siding to be applied. Stepp's explanation of the call was inconsistent with an earlier version related by J.L. Lovett on the telephone to Charles Ramberg, attorney for plaintiffs. Lovett told Ramberg that Mrs. Cole had called on November 10 to demand that the work begin immediately. This discrepancy leads the court to credit the testimony of Judy Cole regarding her conversation with Stepp on November 10.

3. United Companies Mortgage, as Capitol Roofing's assignee, became subject to all of the Coles' claims and defenses against Capitol Roofing by virtue of a provision in the contract that, "[a]ny holder of this consumer credit contract is subject to all claims and defenses which the debtor could assert against the seller of goods or services obtained pursuant hereto or with the proceeds hereof. Recovery hereunder by the debtor shall not exceed amounts paid by the debtor hereunder." This provision was contained in the contract pursuant to the Federal Trade Commission Holder in Due Course Rule, 16 C.F.R. § 433.2 (1986).

with the disclosure statement and notice of right to rescind. The UCM employees would communicate with the customer to verify that the customer had received the required forms, and that they understood the terms and knew with whom they were dealing. Although it was established at trial that this was UCM's normal procedure, the Coles firmly denied having been contacted by anyone from UCM and the court so finds.

Despite continuing problems with the siding and repeated unsuccessful calls by Judy Cole to Capitol Roofing requesting that the problems be remedied, plaintiffs made monthly payments to UCM. However, after having made eleven payments, the Coles became totally frustrated and discontinued further payment. They subsequently retained counsel who, by letter dated December 19, 1984, informed both J.L. Lovett and UCM that the Coles desired to exercise their right of rescission under the Truth–In–Lending Act (TILA), 15 U.S.C. §§ 1601–1693 (1982), and their right of cancellation pursuant to the Mississippi Home Sales Solicitation Act (MHSSA), Miss. Code Ann. §§ 75–66–1–11 (Supp.1986). Upon receiving no response from defendants, plaintiffs instituted this action on November 7, 1985, seeking to enforce their right of rescission and alleging breach of express and implied warranties by defendants. UCM counterclaimed alleging the Coles' default under the contract.

Truth In Lending Act

The TILA and its implementing Regulation Z require that prior to the consummation of a consumer credit sale, the creditor make certain disclosures to the obligor and give the obligor notice of his right to rescind the transaction. The consumer has until midnight of the third business day following consummation of the transaction or delivery of notice of the right to rescind, or delivery of all material disclosures, whichever occurs last, to rescind the transaction. If the required notice or material disclosures are not delivered, the right to rescission extends for three years following consummation of the transaction.

* * *

The plaintiffs next charge that Capitol Roofing failed to furnish them with notice of their right to rescind as required by TILA. TILA and Regulation Z expressly require the creditor in a consumer credit transaction, in which a security interest is being conveyed in the property used by the consumers as their principal dwelling, to provide each consumer who own[s] an interest in the property two copies of a notice of the right to rescind. At trial, Stepp testified that he verbally informed the Coles of their right to rescind the transaction and gave them each two copies of a notice of right to cancel form which contained the required information. Capitol Roofing introduced a document entitled "notice of right to cancel" with an acknowledgement of receipt of form signed by both plaintiffs and dated November 9, 1982. However, the Coles claimed that they had never seen the notice of right to cancel and that, despite their having signed the acknowledgement portion of the document, neither of them ever received copies of the notice form. Moreover, both testified that Stepp never explained the right of rescission and, in fact, after her discussion with Stepp on November 10, Judy Cole was under the impression that she and her husband were bound by having signed the contract. The effect of the Coles' signatures on the acknowledgement is governed by 15 D.S.C. § 1635(c) which provides that a written acknowledgement of receipt of disclosures by a TILA creditor "does no more than create a rebuttable presumption of delivery thereof." As it appears from the testimony that the Coles were unaware of any right of recission and did not learn of their right until much later upon consulting with an attorney, the court is of the opinion that the Coles have effectively rebutted the presumption of delivery. The court finds that plaintiffs were not informed of their right to rescind and that, notwithstanding their signing an acknowledgement of receipt of forms, they never received copies of the notice. The failure by Capitol Roofing to provide each of the plaintiffs with the required notice constituted a violation of TILA and entitled them to rescind the transaction. As they were never given proper notice of their right to rescind, they timely exercised this right, having notified defendants of their rescission within three years following consummation of the transaction. *See* 15 U.S.C. § 1635(f).[5]

* * *

As a result of Capitol Roofing's violations of TILA, plaintiffs were entitled to rescind the transaction. After the Coles served notice on defendants of their election to cancel the transaction, defendants were required to "return to the [Coles] any money or property given as earnest money, down payment, or otherwise, and [were required to] take any action necessary or appropriate to reflect the termination of any security interest created under the transaction." 15 U.S.C. § 1635(b); 12 C.F.R. § 226.23(d)(2). Plaintiffs' attempt at cancellation was met with total inaction by defendants. Consequently, the Coles are entitled to the cancellation of the finance charges in their transaction, and to have the security interest in their home voided.

MISSISSIPPI HOME SOLICITATION SALES ACT

In addition to their TILA claims, plaintiffs have alleged violations of the MHSSA. Like TILA, the MHSSA imposes notice and disclosure requirements upon a seller in a transaction which is a "home solicitation sale." A home solicitation sale is defined as "a consumer credit sale of goods or services in which the seller * * * engages in a personal solicitation of the sale at a residence of the buyer and the buyer's agreement or offer to purchase is there given to the seller...." Miss.

---

5. While TILA provides for the assessment of civil penalty damages against creditors for noncompliance with the Act, an action to recover such damages must be brought within one year from the date of the violation. 15 U.S.C. § 1640(a) and (c). Because the Coles did not file their lawsuit until more than one year following the consummation of their transaction, no penalty damages lie under the Act.

Code Ann. § 75–66–1. This section excludes from coverage sales which are initiated by the buyer.

* * *

As the court has concluded that plaintiffs have established violations of both TILA and MHSSA, and that under MHSSA the Coles have no obligation to pay for the siding on their home, this court need not consider the breach of warranty claims alleged by plaintiffs. Further, plaintiffs are entitled to cancellation of the transaction under both MHSSA and TILA, and UCM is entitled to no relief on its counterclaim for damages as a result of plaintiffs' default on the underlying contract. Defendants are also required, pursuant to Miss.Code Ann. § 75–66–7(3), to return to the Coles the sum of $1703.57, representing the total of payments made by the Coles. * * *

Notes

1.   Truth in Lending extends the right to rescind for up to three years if the initial (material) disclosures or disclosure of the right to rescind are not given properly. 12 C.F.R. §§ 226.15(a)(3) & .23(a)(3). Cases in which the consumer successfully exercises the right to cancel within the initial three days virtually never get to court. Thus, the vast majority of reported TILA rescission cases will involve the stickier issues that come up when the right to cancel is invoked long after the transaction was concluded. See generally Ralph J. Rohner & Fred H. Miller, The Law of Truth in Lending ¶ 8.01[4][b], at 601 (2000). See also Dee Pridgen, Truth in Lending's Right of Rescission: The Well Has Not Run Dry, 43 Cons.Fin.L.Q. 49 (1989).

2.   In the principal case, why did the three day cooling-off period fail to work for the Coles?

3.   In the *Cole* case, Capitol Roofing left a paper trail attempting to show compliance with Truth in Lending, which was contradicted by the testimony of the consumers. Would their tactics have worked in a court less inclined to believe the testimony of the consumer plaintiffs? Were the consumers negligent in not reading the papers they signed? Was the remedy too harsh on the creditor?

4.   In 1988 the FTC affirmed the continuing need for its door-to-door sales rule, but it granted an exemption for sales at public car auctions and at arts and crafts fairs. See 53 Fed. Reg. 45,455, effective December 12, 1988. Is there a relevant distinction between these types of situations and the scenario involving the Coles?

Problem 3–9

Ima Victim, a homeowner, called repairman Sam Slick, reported that her air conditioner was not operating properly and asked Sam to come to her home and repair it. Sam arrived, inspected the unit and reported that Ima needed a new condenser, which Sam would obtain and install for her. Sam also reported that the house seemed to be very dry— a condition which could be cured by installing a humidifier—and that he could obtain and install one of those also. Ima agreed to both the new condenser and the humidifier. Sam wrote up an installment contract for both, but did not give any notices relating to a three-day cooling-off period.

(a) Are rescission notices required by the FTC Door-to-Door Sales Rule in this case? See 16 C.F.R. § 429.0, reproduced in the Supplement. Is this a door-to-door sale? Did the buyer initiate the contact in such a manner as to preclude application of the rule? Note that it may be possible to treat the air conditioner and the humidifier separately from a policy standpoint, but would it make any sense to have different legal requirements for each?

(b) Are rescission notices required under Regulation Z, 12 C.F.R. § 226.23? Note that Sam will undoubtedly acquire a "mechanic's lien" on Ima's real estate for his service and labor. See Reg. Z § 226.2(a)(25).

(c) If both TILA and the FTC Rule require such notices, with which must Sam comply? See FTC Rule, 429.0(a)(2).

(d) What recourse would Ima have if Sam did not provide her with a required notice?

(e) Would it make any difference if Ima's house was not her residence, but instead was a rental house she owned? See Louis Luskin and Sons Inc. v. Samovitz, 166 Cal.App.2d 533, 166 Cal.App.3d 533, 212 Cal.Rptr. 612 (1985).

(f) Suppose Sam's attorney concludes that Ima does not have a right to rescind but Ima's attorney insists that she does. What should Sam's attorney recommend? See New Maine Nat. Bank v. Gendron, 780 F.Supp. 52 (D.Me.1991).

(g) Suppose Sam is willing to accept Ima's rescission and make the required tender but is worried that Ima no longer has the property to return and doesn't have enough savings to pay Sam its value. What would you advise Sam? See Riopta v. Amresco Residential Mortg. Corp., 101 F.Supp.2d 1326 (D. Haw. 1999); Elwin Griffith, Truth in Lending— The Right of Rescission, Disclosure of the Finance Charge, and Itemization of the Amount Financed in Closed–End Transactions, 6 Geo. Mason L. Rev. 191 (1998).

Notes

1. Burke v. Yingling, 446 Pa.Super. 16, 666 A.2d 288 (1995), involved a contract for the sale and installation of a customized $21,533.82 audio-visual system. Installation took several months during which Buyer became dissatisfied and sent Seller written notice that Buyer wished to cancel. When Seller sued for the unpaid portion of the price, Buyer counterclaimed for failure to comply with the Pennsylvania statute requiring notice of a right to rescind. The trial court granted summary judgment for the Seller on the counterclaim explaining that because "Buyer is a sophisticated consumer who himself initiated contact with Seller and who conducted lengthy negotiations over the purchase of a very expensive product, Buyer is simply not the

type of consumer" the statute is intended to protect. The Superior Court "reluctantly" reversed, noting that

> It is unfortunate, but this legislative language clearly provides a right to cancel to all buyers even if the buyer is sophisticated, in no way deceived or pressured by the Seller, and takes adequate time to reflect before agreeing to the transaction. * * * There is no evidence that Buyer was compelled to purchase the audio visual system because of high pressure sales tactics. . . .

Is the result in *Burke* troublesome, or is it simply the byproduct of a rule which usually yields the right result? Can the statutes and rules which provide for a cooling-off period be amended to avoid the *Burke* result? How?

2. The power to rescind under the Truth in Lending Act expires after three years. 15 U.S.C. § 1635(f). When a debt collector brings a collection action more than three years after consummation of the transaction, may the borrower assert the right to rescind as an affirmative defense? The Supreme Court answered in the negative in Beach v. Ocwen Federal Bank, 523 U.S. 410, 118 S.Ct. 1408, 140 L.Ed.2d 566 (1998).

Note on "Emergency Repairs"

The FTC Rule, the U3C and Reg. Z each provide (in slightly different language) that their three day cooling-off provisions do not apply in emergencies if the consumer requests the goods or services be furnished without delay. FTC Rule 16 C.F.R. § 429.0(a)(3), U3C § 3.502(5); Reg. Z 12 C.F.R. § 226.23(e). Why are emergency waivers included in these laws? What is the scope of the problem perceived? Does this exception provide a device for evading the statute? Consider the following problem.

Problem 3–10

The Flaky Furnace Co. establishes the following sales technique: "Heating engineers" are sent to homes, where they gain the permission of the owner to dismantle the furnace for a free inspection. The result of many inspections is an assertion that the furnace needs repairs and is so dangerous that it cannot be reassembled and operated safely, or at least that Flaky's employees would not want to guarantee its safety if the owner insisted upon reassembly without repair. When the owner agrees to repair the furnace, both he and Flaky's employee go to a notary public, where the owner makes an affidavit that he requests the repairs without delay because of an emergency. Has the owner a cause of action against Flaky under the U3C "home solicitation sales" provisions? Has he a cause of action under TILA?

Could the FTC obtain a cease and desist order against this conduct? Before promulgating its Door-to-Door Sales Rule the FTC had repeatedly attempted to regulate similar conduct, apparently without lasting effect. See Holland Furnace Co. v. Federal Trade Com'n, 295 F.2d 302 (7th Cir.1961). Why did it then *design* a Trade Regulation Rule with a potential loophole built in?

SECTION D.   WHAT ARE THE TERMS OF THE DEAL?—HEREIN OF SHRINKWRAP, CLICKWRAP, BROWSEWRAP AND "ROLLING" CONTRACTS

Standardized forms, or contracts of adhesion, are commonplace in consumer contracts and have been for some time. They provide an efficient way for merchants and consumers to do business in mass transactions. Yet there is always the risk that a standard term may be unduly favorable to the author of the contract, the merchant. A new twist on this theme emerged in the mid–1990's, and is especially prevalent in the sale of computers, software, and information or communication services. In the past, courts clung to the fiction that the consumer "agreed" to all the boilerplate terms in a standard form contract because they at least had the contract in front of them and had an opportunity to read it before indicating agreement by signing. The "shrinkwrap" phenomenon consists of terms and conditions that the consumer does not see until they purchase the product, typically software, or until they open the shipping package for items purchased by telephone. Once the consumer is confronted with standard terms, such as warranty limitations or an agreement to arbitrate all disputes, they are deemed to have agreed to them by virtue of either breaking the shrinkwrap and using the software, or by not returning the item to the seller. "Clickwrap" agreements appear on a seller's website or on a software installation CD. In the clickwrap scenario a box pops up on the computer screen directing the user to click "I agree" to certain terms and conditions, usually available on a long scroll down, in order to be able to use the product. "Browsewrap" agreement refers to terms and conditions appearing on a link on the seller's website that the user does not have to "click through" at all. *See generally* Robert A. Hillman & Jeffrey J. Rachlinski, Standard–Form Contracting in the Electronic Age, 77 N.Y.U.L. Rev. 429 (2002).

These methods of adding terms to standardized consumer contracts have been controversial but appear to be gaining widespread acceptance in the courts. The wellspring for the shrinkwrap cases originated in the Seventh Circuit Court of Appeals, in two cases in which Judge Frank Easterbrook wrote the opinions. The *Pro CD* case is referenced within the *Hill v. Gateway 2000* case.

HILL v. GATEWAY 2000, INC.

United States Court of Appeals, Seventh Circuit, 1997.
105 F.3d 1147.

Before CUMMINGS, WOOD, JR., and EASTERBROOK, CIRCUIT JUDGES.

EASTERBROOK, CIRCUIT JUDGE.

A customer picks up the phone, orders a computer, and gives a credit card number. Presently a box arrives, containing the computer and a list of terms, said to govern unless the customer returns the computer within 30 days. Are these terms effective as the parties' contract, or is the contract term-free because the order-taker did not read any terms over the phone and elicit the customer's assent?

One of the terms in the box containing a Gateway 2000 system was an arbitration clause. Rich and Enza Hill, the customers, kept the computer more than 30 days before complaining about its components and performance. They filed suit in federal court arguing, among other things, that the product's shortcomings make Gateway a racketeer (mail and wire fraud are said to be the predicate offenses), leading to treble damages under RICO for the Hills and a class of all other purchasers. Gateway asked the district court to enforce the arbitration clause; the judge refused, writing that "[t]he present record is insufficient to support a finding of a valid arbitration agreement between the parties or that the plaintiffs were given adequate notice of the arbitration clause." Gateway took an immediate appeal, as is its right. 9 U.S.C. § 16(a)(1)(A).

The Hills say that the arbitration clause did not stand out: they concede noticing the statement of terms but deny reading it closely enough to discover the agreement to arbitrate, and they ask us to conclude that they therefore may go to court. Yet an agreement to arbitrate must be enforced "save upon such grounds as exist at law or in equity for the revocation of any contract." 9 U.S.C. § 2. Doctor's Associates, Inc. v. Casarotto, 517U.S. 681, 116 S.Ct. 1652, 134 L.Ed.2d 902 (1996), holds that this provision of the Federal Arbitration Act is inconsistent with any requirement that an arbitration clause be prominent. A contract need not be read to be effective; people who accept take the risk that the unread terms may in retrospect prove unwelcome. Terms inside Gateway's box stand or fall together. If they constitute the parties' contract because the Hills had an opportunity to return the computer after reading them, then all must be enforced.

ProCD, Inc. v. Zeidenberg, 86 F.3d 1447 (7th Cir.1996), holds that terms inside a box of software bind consumers who use the software after an opportunity to read the terms and to reject them by returning the product. Likewise, Carnival Cruise Lines, Inc. v. Shute, 499 U.S. 585, 111 S.Ct. 1522, 113 L.Ed.2d 622 (1991), enforces a forum-selection clause that was included among three pages of terms attached to a cruise ship ticket. ProCD and Carnival Cruise Lines exemplify the many commercial transactions in which people pay for products with terms to follow; ProCD discusses others. 86 F.3d at 1451–52. The district court concluded in ProCD that the contract is formed when the consumer pays for the software; as a result, the court held, only terms known to the consumer at that moment are part of the contract, and provisos inside the box do not count. Although this is one way a contract could be formed, it is not the only way: "A vendor, as master of the offer, may invite acceptance by conduct, and may propose limitations on the kind of conduct that constitutes acceptance. A buyer may accept by performing the acts the vendor proposes to treat as acceptance." Id. at 1452. Gateway shipped computers with the same sort of accept-or-return offer ProCD made to users of its software. ProCD relied on the Uniform Commercial Code rather than any peculiarities of Wisconsin law; both Illinois and South Dakota, the two states whose law might govern relations between Gateway and the Hills, have adopted the UCC; neither side has pointed us to any atypical doctrines in those states that might be pertinent; ProCD therefore applies to this dispute.

Plaintiffs ask us to limit ProCD to software, but where's the sense in that? ProCD is about the law of contract, not the law of software. Payment preceding the revelation of full terms is common for air transportation, insurance, and many other endeavors. Practical considerations support allowing vendors to enclose the full legal terms with their products. Cashiers cannot be expected to read legal documents to customers before ringing up sales. If the staff at the other end of the phone for direct-sales operations such as Gateway's had to read the four-page statement of terms before taking the buyer's credit card number, the droning voice would anesthetize rather than enlighten many potential buyers. Others would hang up in a rage over the waste of their time. And oral recitation would not avoid customers' assertions (whether true or feigned) that the clerk did not read term X to them, or that they did not remember or understand it. Writing provides benefits for both sides of commercial transactions. Customers as a group are better off when vendors skip costly and ineffectual steps such as telephonic recitation, and use instead a simple approve-or-return device. Competent adults are bound by such documents, read or unread. For what little it is worth, we add that the box from Gateway was crammed with software. The computer came with an operating system, without which it was useful only as a boat anchor. Gateway also included many application programs. So the Hills' effort to limit ProCD to software would not avail them factually, even if it were sound legally—which it is not.

For their second sally, the Hills contend that ProCD should be limited to executory contracts (to licenses in particular), and therefore does not apply because both parties' performance of this contract was complete when the box arrived at their home. This is legally and factually wrong: legally because the question at hand concerns the formation of the contract rather than its performance, and factually because both contracts were incompletely performed. ProCD did not depend on the fact that the seller characterized the transaction as a license rather than as a contract; we treated it as a contract for the sale of goods and reserved the question whether for other purposes a "license" characterization might be preferable. 86 F.3d at 1450. All debates about characterization to one side, the transaction in ProCD was no more executory than the one here: Zeidenberg paid for the software and walked out of the store with a box under his arm, so if arrival of the box with the product ends the time for revelation of contractual terms, then the time ended in ProCD before Zeidenberg opened the box. But of course ProCD had not completed performance with delivery of the box, and neither had Gateway. One element of the transaction was the warranty, which obliges sellers to fix defects in their products. The Hills have invoked Gateway's warranty and are not satisfied with its response, so they are not well positioned to say that Gateway's obligations were fulfilled when the motor carrier unloaded the box. What is more, both ProCD and Gateway promised to help customers to use their products. Long-term service and information obligations are common in the computer business, on both hardware and software sides. Gateway offers "lifetime service" and has a round-the-clock telephone hotline to fulfil this promise. Some vendors spend more money helping customers use their products than on developing and manufacturing them. The document in Gateway's box includes promises of future performance that some consumers value highly; these promises bind Gateway just as the arbitration clause binds the Hills.

Next the Hills insist that ProCD is irrelevant because Zeidenberg was a "merchant" and they are not. Section 2–207(2) of the UCC, the infamous battle-of-the-forms section, states that "additional terms [following acceptance of an offer] are to be construed as proposals for addition to a contract. Between merchants such terms become part of the contract unless ...". Plaintiffs tell us that ProCD came out as it did only because Zeidenberg was a "merchant" and the terms inside ProCD's box were not excluded by the "unless" clause. This argument pays scant attention to the opinion in ProCD, which concluded that, when there is only one form, "sec. 2–207 is irrelevant." 86 F.3d at 1452. The question in ProCD was not whether terms were added to a contract after its formation, but how and when the contract was formed—in particular, whether a vendor may propose that a contract of sale be formed, not in the store (or over the phone) with the payment of money or a general "send me the product," but after the customer has had a chance to inspect both the item and the terms. ProCD answers "yes," for merchants and consumers alike. Yet again, for what little it is worth we observe that the Hills misunderstand the setting of ProCD. A "merchant" under the UCC "means a person who deals in goods of the kind or otherwise by his occupation holds himself out as having knowledge or skill peculiar to the practices or goods involved in the transaction", § 2–104(1). Zeidenberg bought the product at a retail store, an uncommon place for merchants to acquire inventory. His corporation put ProCD's database on the Internet for anyone to browse, which led to the litigation but did not make Zeidenberg a software merchant.

At oral argument the Hills propounded still another distinction: the box containing ProCD's software displayed a notice that additional terms were within, while the box containing Gateway's computer did not. The difference is functional, not legal. Consumers browsing the aisles of a store can look at the box, and if they are unwilling to deal with the prospect of additional terms can leave the box alone, avoiding the transactions costs of returning the package after reviewing its contents. Gateway's box, by contrast, is just a shipping carton; it is not on display anywhere. Its function is to protect the product during transit, and the information on its sides is for the use of handlers rather than would-be purchasers.

Perhaps the Hills would have had a better argument if they were first alerted to the bundling of hardware and legal-ware after opening the box and wanted to return the computer in order to avoid disagreeable terms, but were dissuaded by the expense of shipping. What the remedy would be in such a case—could it exceed the shipping charges?—is an interesting question, but one that need not detain us because the Hills knew before they ordered the computer that the carton would include some important terms, and they did not seek to discover these in advance. Gateway's ads state that their products come with limited warranties and lifetime support. How limited was the warranty—30 days, with service contingent on shipping the computer back, or five years, with free onsite service? What sort of support was offered? Shoppers have three principal ways to discover these things. First, they can ask the vendor to send a copy before deciding whether to buy. The Magnuson–Moss Warranty Act requires firms to distribute their warranty terms on request, 15 U.S.C. § 2302(b)(1)(A); the Hills do not contend that Gateway would have refused to enclose the remaining terms too. Concealment would be bad for business, scaring some customers away and leading to excess returns from others. Second, shoppers can consult public sources (computer magazines, the Web sites of vendors) that may contain this information. Third, they may inspect the documents after the product's delivery. Like Zeidenberg, the Hills took the third option. By keeping the computer beyond 30 days, the Hills accepted Gateway's offer, including the arbitration clause.

* * * Whatever may be said pro and con about the cost and efficacy of arbitration (which the Hills disparage) is for Congress and the contracting parties to consider. Claims based on RICO are no less arbitrable than those founded on the contract or the law of torts. The decision of the district court is vacated, and this case is remanded with instructions to compel the Hills to submit their dispute to arbitration.

Notes

1. The holding in *Gateway* has been heavily criticized by academics. *See, e.g.,* Shubba Ghosh, Where's the Sense in *Hill v. Gateway 2000*?: Reflections on the Visible Hand of Norm Creation, 16 Touro L. Rev. 1125 (2000); Roger C. Bern, "Terms Later" Contracting: Bad Economics, Bad Morals, and a Bad Idea for a Uniform Law, Judge Easterbrook Notwithstanding, 12 J. Law & Policy 641 (2004); William H. Lawrence, Rolling Contracts Rolling Over Contract Law, 41 San Diego L. Rev. 1099 (2004).

2. Most courts have followed the *Gateway* holding, however, and have enforced terms in consumer contracts that were not revealed to the consumer until sometime after purchase and delivery. For examples involving merchant/consumer transactions, see O'Quin v. Verizon Wireless, 256 F. Supp. 2d 512 (M.D. La. 2003) (telephone handsets and cellphone service); Bischoff v. DirecTV, Inc., 180 F. Supp. 2d 1097 (C.D. Cal. 2002) (satellite television subscription); Lozano v. AT & T Wireless, 216 F. Supp. 2d 1071 (C.D. Cal. 2002) (cellular phone service); Stenzel v. Dell, Inc., 2004 WL

1433657 (Me. Super. Ct. 2004) (computer). A few post-*Gateway* decisions have refused to enforce terms in the box or shrinkwrap agreements, on the basis that these should be considered "additional terms" that would require express consumer agreement under UCC 2–207 (unamended). See Klocek v. Gateway, Inc., 104 F. Supp. 2d 1332 (D. Kan. 2000).

3. Is a "rolling contract" or the use of shrinkwrap terms actually a deceptive or unfair practice under the FTC Act? Consider the following:

> The economics of bait and switch are very similar to those of delayed disclosure until after consumers have paid and taken delivery. Both practices thwart consumers' ability to be smart shoppers by researching the best deal before initiating a purchase. In a bait and switch, a customer who responds to an advertisement for low-price goods by going to the store does not have to make a purchase of higher priced goods when the goods advertised are unavailable. But, the customer has wasted the time and costs involved in going to the store unless she makes a purchase. Shopping is therefore burdened. Similarly, when a merchant delays disclosure of material terms until after payment and delivery, but tries to compensate for that by giving a right of return to customers who choose to reject terms once they are disclosed, the merchant inhibits shopping. The right of return does not compensate for the wasted time involved in searching for the transaction, deciding upon it, then reversing it, and starting over to find another deal.

Jean Braucher, Delayed Disclosure in Consumer E–Commerce as an Unfair and Deceptive Practice, 46 Wayne L. Rev. 1805 (2000).

4. Does the packaging of the terms with the product unnecessarily raise transaction costs to the consumer, resulting in consumers not having the information they need to make informed decisions? According to one of the textbook authors,

> * * * [t]he requirement that consumers unhappy with the terms of the contract go to the effort of repacking and returning the computer— rather than just withdrawing from the contract before the computer was sent—increases the likelihood that even a consumer who learned of the binding arbitration in time to object to it would not bother to rescind the deal.

Jeff Sovern, Towards a New Model of Consumer Protection: The Problem of Inflated Transaction Costs, 47 Wm. & Mary L. Rev. 1635 (2006).

In the *Gateway* case, Judge Easterbrook suggests that consumers could consult the web sites of vendors if they wish to determine the terms of the contract prior to shipping. How easy is it to find such information on manufacturer websites? An interesting experiment can be done by trying to locate arbitration and/or warranty clauses on websites—are they readily available? Does the consumer have to make a special effort to find such information?

5. On the other hand, are shrinkwrap or rolling contracts essentially a benign practice that can result in efficient mass transactions? Do they simply reflect the reality that most consumers do not read standard terms whether they are presented before or after purchase, and that the courts will protect them from unconscionable terms?

In sum, rolling contracts, * * * should be treated no differently than other form contracts. Existing law's presumption of "blanket assent" and policing of seller misconduct allows for an efficient and fair presentation of terms in both traditional and rolling contract settings.

The only difference between rolling contracts and paradigm standard-form transactions is whether consumers have the opportunity to read the terms before or after payment and delivery of the goods. A good argument can be made that, if anything, the opportunity to read the terms at home creates more of a reason to enforce standard terms in the rolling contract context. But, if consumers generally do not read standard terms under any circumstances, the particular time at which they could have read them should not control their legal treatment. Consumers will purchase Gateway computers and ignore the terms regardless of whether they have the opportunity to see the terms before or after the computer is delivered.

Robert A. Hillman, Rolling Contracts, 71 Fordham L. Rev. 743, 756–57 (2002). See also Clayton P. Gillette, Rolling Contracts as an Agency Problem, 2004 Wis. L. Rev. 679 (2004).

6.   Many have argued that the Hills and Gateway formed a contract when the Hills completed their telephonic order, citing (unamended) UCC §§ 2–204, and 2–206(1)(b), thus making the terms in the box merely proposals for additional terms or for contract modification, under § 2–209. What would have happened if Gateway had accepted payment for the computer but had not shipped the goods? Would the Hills have a good case for breach of contract? Yet Judge Easterbrook's ruling seems to say no contract was formed until 30 days after the package was received, when the terms and conditions were accepted by virtue of inaction by the consumers.

The 2003 proposed amendment of Article 2 contains a significant revision of § 2–207, stating that if a contract is formed by conduct, the terms include "(a) terms that appear in the records of both parties; (b) terms, whether in a record or not, to which both parties agree; and (c) terms supplied or incorporated under any provision of this Act." The official comment states that the section is not limited to contracts where there has been a "battle of the forms." UCC § 2–207, Comment 1. The commentary goes on to state that "the section omits any specific treatment of terms attached to the goods, or in or on the container in which the goods are delivered," thus attempting to maintain neutrality in the debate over the holding in *Hill v. Gateway*. UCC § 2–207, Comment 5. Section 2–313A (as stated in 2003 proposed amendment), however, makes it clear that the manufacturer will be obligated by warranties included in the box, and will also be able to modify or limit warranties by terms in the box sent to a "remote purchaser." See infra, chapter 7, Section B(3).

7.   In the "clickwrap" situation, where the consumer has the opportunity to scroll through and read the terms of the contract and must click an "I agree" button on the computer screen prior to being bound, the necessary assent to the terms seems more apparent than in the shrinkwrap situation where the consumer's inaction is implied assent to the terms. Clickwrap agreements have usually been upheld as enforceable. See Caspi v. Microsoft Network, L.L.C., 323 N.J.Super. 118, 732 A.2d 528 (1999); Forrest v. Verizon

Communications, Inc., 805 A.2d 1007 (D.C. Ct. App. 2002). See also Amended UCC § 2–204.

Problem 3–11

Gavin Geek purchased a home computer from DVader.Computers.com by ordering from their website. He started at the homepage, then clicked on the link to desktop pc's, selected a model he liked at a price that was acceptable, and then clicked a button to place this item into his virtual shopping cart. The terms and conditions of all sales of DVader products were available by clicking on a hyperlink entitled "Legal Stuff," which was visible by scrolling down to the bottom of the homepage. Gavin did not notice this link. He then proceeded to the virtual check-out where he typed in some personal information, including his name, address, and credit card number. After selecting the shipping method and reviewing the model, price and delivery options, he pressed a "submit order" button. A few days later, a computer arrived in a box that had the DVader logo on the outside, return address, and Gavin's address but nothing else.

Upon opening the box and taking out the computer, a document floated out. Gavin ignored it and set up the computer. After experiencing repeated problems with the computer and getting no coherent response from the DVader customer service department, Gavin wants to sue for breach of warranty. At this point, he looks at the document that came with the computer, which bears the title Terms and Conditions of Agreement. Among its sixteen paragraphs is paragraph 10, which reads: "All disputes shall be resolved by arbitration in the state of Nasturcia under Nasturcian law." The Terms and Conditions document, which is identical to the one linked to the website homepage, contains a "total satisfaction policy," whereby the consumer may return the computer for a refund within 5 days if not satisfied. The Agreement does not state any specific deadline or procedure for return or cancellation if the consumer does not wish to accept the Terms and Conditions.

If Gavin were to take DVader Computers to court, would the company be able to enforce Paragraph 10 and compel arbitration under Nasturcian law in Nasturcia?

Cf. Defontes v. Dell Computers Corp., 2004 WL 253560 (R.I. Super. Ct. 2004).

SPECHT v. NETSCAPE COMMUNICATIONS CORPORATION

United States Court of Appeals, Second Circuit, 2002.
306 F.3d 17.

Before McLAUGHLIN, LEVAL, and SOTOMAYOR, CIRCUIT JUDGES.

SOTOMAYOR, CIRCUIT JUDGE.

This is an appeal from a judgment of the Southern District of New York denying a motion by defendants-appellants Netscape Communications Corporation and its corporate parent, America Online, Inc. (collectively, "defendants" or "Netscape"), to compel arbitration and to stay court proceedings. In order to resolve the central question of arbitrability presented here, we must address issues of contract formation in cyberspace. Principally, we are asked to determine whether plaintiffs-appellees ("plaintiffs"), by acting upon defendants' invitation to download free software made available on defendants' webpage, agreed to be bound by the software's license terms (which included the arbitration clause at issue), even though plaintiffs could not have learned of the existence of those terms unless, prior to executing the download, they had scrolled down the webpage to a screen located below the download button. We agree with the district court that a reasonably prudent Internet user in circumstances such as these would not have known or learned of the existence of the license terms before responding to defendants' invitation to download the free software, and that defendants therefore did not provide reasonable notice of the license terms. In consequence, plaintiffs' bare act of downloading the software did not unambiguously manifest assent to the arbitration provision contained in the license terms.

* * *

We therefore affirm the district court's denial of defendants' motion to compel arbitration and to stay court proceedings.

BACKGROUND

I. Facts

In three related putative class actions, plaintiffs alleged that, unknown to them, their use of SmartDownload transmitted to defendants private information about plaintiffs' downloading of files from the Internet, thereby effecting an electronic surveillance of their online activities in violation of two federal statutes, the Electronic Communications Privacy Act, 18 U.S.C. § § 2510 *et seq.,* and the Computer Fraud and Abuse Act, 18 U.S.C. § 1030.

Specifically, plaintiffs alleged that when they first used Netscape's Communicator—a software program that permits Internet browsing—the program created and stored on each of their computer hard drives a small text file known as a "cookie" that functioned "as a kind of electronic identification tag for future communications" between their computers and Netscape. Plaintiffs further alleged that when they installed SmartDownload—a separate software "plug-in"[2] that served to enhance Communicator's browsing capabilities—SmartDownload created and stored on their computer hard drives another string of characters,

---

2. Netscape's website defines "plug-ins" as "software programs that extend the capabilities of the Netscape Browser in a specific way—giving you, for example, the ability to play audio samples or view video movies from within your browser." (http://wp.netscape.com/plugins/) SmartDownload purportedly made it easier for users of browser programs like Communicator to download files from the Internet without losing their progress when they paused to engage in some other task, or if their Internet connection was severed. *See Specht,* 150 F.Supp.2d at 587.

known as a "Key," which similarly functioned as an identification tag in future communications with Netscape. According to the complaints in this case, each time a computer user employed Communicator to download a file from the Internet, SmartDownload "assume[d] from Communicator the task of downloading" the file and transmitted to Netscape the address of the file being downloaded together with the cookie created by Communicator and the Key created by SmartDownload. These processes, plaintiffs claim, constituted unlawful "eavesdropping" on users of Netscape's software products as well as on Internet websites from which users employing SmartDownload downloaded files.

In the time period relevant to this litigation, Netscape offered on its website various software programs, including Communicator and Smart-Download, which visitors to the site were invited to obtain free of charge. It is undisputed that five of the six named plaintiffs—Michael Fagan, John Gibson, Mark Gruber, Sean Kelly, and Sherry Weindorf—downloaded Communicator from the Netscape website. These plaintiffs acknowledge that when they proceeded to initiate installation[3] of Communicator, they were automatically shown a scrollable text of that program's license agreement and were not permitted to complete the installation until they had clicked on a "Yes" button to indicate that they accepted all the license terms.[4] If a user attempted to install Communicator without clicking "Yes," the installation would be aborted. All five named user plaintiffs expressly agreed to Communicator's license terms by clicking "Yes." The Communicator license agreement that these plaintiffs saw made no mention of SmartDownload or other plug-in programs, and stated that "[t]hese terms apply to Netscape Communicator and Netscape Navigator" and that "all disputes relating to this Agreement (excepting any dispute relating to intellectual property rights)" are subject to "binding arbitration in Santa Clara County, California."

Although Communicator could be obtained independently of Smart-Download, all the named user plaintiffs, except Fagan, downloaded and installed Communicator in connection with downloading SmartDown-

---

3. There is a difference between downloading and installing a software program. When a user downloads a program from the Internet to his or her computer, the program file is stored on the user's hard drive but typically is not operable until the user installs or executes it, usually by double-clicking on the file and causing the program to run.

4. This kind of online software license agreement has come to be known as "click-wrap" (by analogy to "shrinkwrap," used in the licensing of tangible forms of software sold in packages) because it "presents the user with a message on his or her computer screen, requiring that the user manifest his or her assent to the terms of the license agreement by clicking on an icon. The product cannot be obtained or used unless and until the icon is clicked." *Specht,* 150 F.Supp.2d at 593–94 (footnote omitted). Just as breaking the shrinkwrap seal and using the enclosed computer program after encountering notice of the existence of governing license terms has been deemed by some courts to constitute assent to those terms in the context of tangible software, *see, e.g., ProCD, Inc. v. Zeidenberg,* 86 F.3d 1447, 1451 (7th Cir.1996), so clicking on a webpage's clickwrap button after receiving notice of the existence of license terms has been held by some courts to manifest an Internet user's assent to terms governing the use of downloadable intangible software, *see, e.g., Hotmail Corp. v. Van$ Money Pie Inc.,* 47 U.S.P.Q.2d 1020, 1025 (N.D.Cal.1998).

load. Each of these plaintiffs allegedly arrived at a Netscape webpage captioned "SmartDownload Communicator" that urged them to "Download With Confidence Using SmartDownload!" At or near the bottom of the screen facing plaintiffs was the prompt "Start Download" and a tinted button labeled "Download." By clicking on the button, plaintiffs initiated the download of SmartDownload. Once that process was complete, SmartDownload, as its first plug-in task, permitted plaintiffs to proceed with downloading and installing Communicator, an operation that was accompanied by the clickwrap display of Communicator's license terms described above.

The signal difference between downloading Communicator and downloading SmartDownload was that no clickwrap presentation accompanied the latter operation. Instead, once plaintiffs Gibson, Gruber, Kelly, and Weindorf had clicked on the "Download" button located at or near the bottom of their screen, and the downloading of SmartDownload was complete, these plaintiffs encountered no further information about the plug-in program or the existence of license terms governing its use. The sole reference to SmartDownload's license terms on the "Smart-Download Communicator" webpage was located in text that would have become visible to plaintiffs only if they had scrolled down to the next screen.

Had plaintiffs scrolled down instead of acting on defendants' invitation to click on the "Download" button, they would have encountered the following invitation: "Please review and agree to the terms of the *Netscape SmartDownload software license agreement* before downloading and using the software." Plaintiffs Gibson, Gruber, Kelly, and Weindorf averred in their affidavits that they never saw this reference to the SmartDownload license agreement when they clicked on the "Download" button. * * *

In sum, plaintiffs Gibson, Gruber, Kelly, and Weindorf allege that the process of obtaining SmartDownload contrasted sharply with that of obtaining Communicator. Having selected SmartDownload, they were required neither to express unambiguous assent to that program's license agreement nor even to view the license terms or become aware of their existence before proceeding with the invited download of the free plug-in program. Moreover, once these plaintiffs had initiated the download, the existence of SmartDownload's license terms was not mentioned while the software was running or at any later point in plaintiffs' experience of the product.

Even for a user who, unlike plaintiffs, did happen to scroll down past the download button, SmartDownload's license terms would not have been immediately displayed in the manner of Communicator's clickwrapped terms. Instead, if such a user had seen the notice of SmartDownload's terms and then clicked on the underlined invitation to review and agree to the terms, a hypertext link would have taken the user to a separate webpage entitled "License & Support Agreements." The first paragraph on this page read, in pertinent part:

The use of each Netscape software product is governed by a license agreement. You must read and agree to the license agreement terms BEFORE acquiring a product. Please click on the appropriate link below to review the current license agreement for the product of interest to you before acquisition. For products available for download, you must read and agree to the license agreement terms BEFORE you install the software. If you do not agree to the license terms, do not download, install or use the software.

Below this paragraph appeared a list of license agreements, the first of which was *"License Agreement for Netscape Navigator and Netscape Communicator Product Family* (Netscape Navigator, Netscape Communicator and Netscape SmartDownload)." If the user clicked on that link, he or she would be taken to yet another webpage that contained the full text of a license agreement that was identical in every respect to the Communicator license agreement except that it stated that its "terms apply to Netscape Communicator, Netscape Navigator, and Netscape SmartDownload." The license agreement granted the user a nonexclusive license to use and reproduce the software, subject to certain terms:

BY CLICKING THE ACCEPTANCE BUTTON OR INSTALLING OR USING NETSCAPE COMMUNICATOR, NETSCAPE NAVIGATOR, OR NETSCAPE SMARTDOWNLOAD SOFTWARE (THE "PRODUCT"), THE INDIVIDUAL OR ENTITY LICENSING THE PRODUCT ("LICENSEE") IS CONSENTING TO BE BOUND BY AND IS BECOMING A PARTY TO THIS AGREEMENT. IF LICENSEE DOES NOT AGREE TO ALL OF THE TERMS OF THIS AGREEMENT, THE BUTTON INDICATING NON–ACCEPTANCE MUST BE SELECTED, AND LICENSEE MUST NOT INSTALL OR USE THE SOFTWARE.

Among the license terms was a provision requiring virtually all disputes relating to the agreement to be submitted to arbitration:

Unless otherwise agreed in writing, all disputes relating to this Agreement (excepting any dispute relating to intellectual property rights) shall be subject to final and binding arbitration in Santa Clara County, California, under the auspices of JAMS/EndDispute, with the losing party paying all costs of arbitration.

* * *

DISCUSSION

* * *

*III.　Whether the User Plaintiffs Had Reasonable Notice
of and Manifested Assent to the SmartDownload
License Agreement*

Whether governed by the common law or by Article 2 of the Uniform Commercial Code ("UCC"), a transaction, in order to be a contract, requires a manifestation of agreement between the parties.[13] Mutual manifestation of assent, whether by written or spoken word or by conduct, is the touchstone of contract. Although an onlooker observing the disputed transactions in this case would have seen each of the user plaintiffs click on the SmartDownload "Download" button, a consumer's clicking on a download button does not communicate assent to contractual terms if the offer did not make clear to the consumer that clicking on the download button would signify assent to those terms. California's common law is clear that "an offeree, regardless of apparent manifestation of his consent, is not bound by inconspicuous contractual provisions of which he is unaware, contained in a document whose contractual nature is not obvious."

13. The district court concluded that the SmartDownload transactions here should be governed by "California law as it relates to the sale of goods, including the Uniform Commercial Code in effect in California." *Specht,* 150 F.Supp.2d at 591. It is not obvious, however, that UCC Article 2 ("sales of goods") applies to the licensing of software that is downloadable from the Internet. *Cf. Advent Sys. Ltd. v. Unisys Corp.,* 925 F.2d 670, 675 (3d Cir.1991) ("The increasing frequency of computer products as subjects of commercial litigation has led to controversy over whether software is a 'good' or intellectual property. The [UCC] does not specifically mention software."); Lorin Brennan, *Why Article 2 Cannot Apply to Software Transactions,* PLI Patents, Copyrights, Trademarks, & Literary Property Course Handbook Series (Feb.-Mar. 2001) (demonstrating the trend in case law away from application of UCC provisions to software sales and licensing and toward application of intellectual property principles). There is no doubt that a sale of tangible goods over the Internet is governed by Article 2 of the UCC. *See, e.g., Butler v. Beer Across Am.,* 83 F.Supp.2d 1261, 1263–64 & n. 6 (N.D.Ala.2000) (applying Article 2 to an Internet sale of bottles of beer). Some courts have also applied Article 2, occasionally with misgivings, to sales of off-the-shelf software in tangible, packaged formats. *See, e.g., ProCD,* 86 F.3d at 1450 ("[W]e treat the [database] licenses as ordinary contracts accompanying the sale of products, and therefore as governed by the common law of contracts and the Uniform Commercial Code. Whether there are legal differences between 'contracts' and 'licenses' (which may matter under the copyright doctrine of first sale) is a subject for another day."); *I.Lan Sys., Inc. v. Nextpoint Networks, Inc.,* 183 F.Supp.2d 328, 332 (D.Mass.2002) (stating, in the context of a dispute between business parties, that "Article 2 technically does not, and certainly will not in the future, govern software licenses, but for the time being, the Court will assume that it does").

Downloadable software, however, is scarcely a "tangible" good, and, in part because software may be obtained, copied, or transferred effortlessly at the stroke of a computer key, licensing of such Internet products has assumed a vast importance in recent years. Recognizing that "a body of law based on images of Downloadable software, however, is scarcely a "tangible" good, and, in part because software may be obtained, copied, or transferred effortlessly at the stroke of a computer key, licensing of such Internet products has assumed a vast importance in recent years. Recognizing that "a body of law based on images of the sale of manufactured goods ill fits licenses and other transactions in computer information," the National Conference of Commissioners on Uniform State Laws has promulgated the Uniform Computer Information Transactions Act ("UCITA"), a code resembling UCC Article 2 in many respects but drafted to reflect emergent practices in the sale and licensing of computer information. UCITA, prefatory note (rev. ed. Aug. 23, 2001) (available at www.ucitaonline.com/ucita.html). UCITA—originally intended as a new Article 2B to supplement Articles 2 and 2A of the UCC but later proposed as an independent code—has been adopted by two states, Maryland and Virginia. *See* Md.Code Ann. Com. Law §§ 22–101 *et seq.;* Va.Code Ann. §§ 59.1–501.1 *et seq.*

We need not decide today whether UCC Article 2 applies to Internet transactions in downloadable products. The district court's analysis and the parties' arguments on appeal show that, for present purposes, there is no essential difference between UCC Article 2 and the common law of contracts. We therefore apply the common law, with exceptions as noted.

Arbitration agreements are no exception to the requirement of manifestation of assent. "This principle of knowing consent applies with particular force to provisions for arbitration." Clarity and conspicuousness of arbitration terms are important in securing informed assent. "If a party wishes to bind in writing another to an agreement to arbitrate future disputes, such purpose should be accomplished in a way that each party to the arrangement will fully and clearly comprehend that the agreement to arbitrate exists and binds the parties thereto." Thus, California contract law measures assent by an objective standard that takes into account both what the offeree said, wrote, or did and the transactional context in which the offeree verbalized or acted.

A. *The Reasonably Prudent Offeree of Downloadable Software*

Defendants argue that plaintiffs must be held to a standard of reasonable prudence and that, because notice of the existence of Smart-Download license terms was on the next scrollable screen, plaintiffs were on "inquiry notice" of those terms. We disagree with the proposition that a reasonably prudent offeree in plaintiffs' position would necessarily have known or learned of the existence of the SmartDownload license agreement prior to acting, so that plaintiffs may be held to have assented to that agreement with constructive notice of its terms. It is true that "[a] party cannot avoid the terms of a contract on the ground that he or she failed to read it before signing." But courts are quick to add: "An exception to this general rule exists when the writing does not appear to be a contract and the terms are not called to the attention of the recipient. In such a case, no contract is formed with respect to the undisclosed term."

* * * [R]eceipt of a physical document containing contract terms or notice thereof is frequently deemed, in the world of paper transactions, a sufficient circumstance to place the offeree on inquiry notice of those terms. These principles apply equally to the emergent world of online product delivery, pop-up screens, hyperlinked pages, clickwrap licensing, scrollable documents, and urgent admonitions to "Download Now!". What plaintiffs saw when they were being invited by defendants to download this fast, free plug-in called SmartDownload was a screen containing praise for the product and, at the very bottom of the screen, a "Download" button. Defendants argue that under the principles set forth in the cases cited above, a "fair and prudent person using ordinary care" would have been on inquiry notice of SmartDownload's license terms.

We are not persuaded that a reasonably prudent offeree in these circumstances would have known of the existence of license terms. Plaintiffs were responding to an offer that did not carry an immediately visible notice of the existence of license terms or require unambiguous manifestation of assent to those terms. Thus, plaintiffs' "apparent manifestation of ... consent" was to terms "contained in a document whose contractual nature [was] not obvious." Moreover, the fact that, given the position of the scroll bar on their computer screens, plaintiffs may have been aware that an unexplored portion of the Netscape webpage remained below the download button does not mean that they reasonably should have concluded that this portion contained a notice of license terms. In their deposition testimony, plaintiffs variously stated that they used the scroll bar "[o]nly if there is something that I feel I need to see that is on—that is off the page," or that the elevated position of the scroll bar suggested the presence of "mere[ ] formalities, standard lower banner links" or "that the page is bigger than what I can see." Plaintiffs testified, and defendants did not refute, that plaintiffs were in fact unaware that defendants intended to attach license terms to the use of SmartDownload.

We conclude that in circumstances such as these, where consumers are urged to download free software at the immediate click of a button, a reference to the existence of license terms on a submerged screen is not sufficient to place consumers on inquiry or constructive notice of those terms. The SmartDownload webpage screen was "printed in such a manner that it tended to conceal the fact that it was an express acceptance of [Netscape's] rules and regulations." Internet users may have, as defendants put it, "as much time as they need[ ]" to scroll through multiple screens on a webpage, but there is no reason to assume that viewers will scroll down to subsequent screens simply because screens are there. When products are "free" and users are invited to download them in the absence of reasonably conspicuous notice that they are about to bind themselves to contract terms, the transactional circumstances cannot be fully analogized to those in the paper world of arm's-length bargaining. In the next two sections, we discuss case law and other legal authorities that have addressed the circumstances of computer sales, software licensing, and online transacting. Those authorities tend strongly to support our conclusion that plaintiffs did not manifest assent to SmartDownload's license terms.

B.   Shrinkwrap Licensing and Related Practices

Defendants cite certain well-known cases involving shrinkwrap licensing and related commercial practices in support of their contention that plaintiffs became bound by the SmartDownload license terms by virtue of inquiry notice. For example, in *Hill v. Gateway 2000, Inc.,* 105 F.3d 1147 (7th Cir.1997), the Seventh Circuit held that where a purchaser had ordered a computer over the telephone, received the order in a shipped box containing the computer along with printed contract terms, and did not return the computer within the thirty days required by the terms, the purchaser was bound by the contract. *Id.* at 1148–49. In *ProCD, Inc. v. Zeidenberg,* the same court held that where an individual purchased software in a box containing license terms which were displayed on the computer screen every time the user executed the software program, the user had sufficient opportunity to review the terms and to return the software, and so was contractually bound after retaining the product. *ProCD,* 86 F.3d at 1452.

These cases do not help defendants. To the extent that they hold that the purchaser of a computer or tangible software is contractually bound after failing to object to printed license terms provided with the product, *Hill* and *Brower* do not differ markedly from the cases involving traditional paper contracting discussed in the previous section. Insofar as the purchaser in *ProCD* was confronted with conspicuous, mandatory license terms every time he ran the software on his computer, that case actually undermines defendants' contention that downloading in the absence of conspicuous terms is an act that binds plaintiffs to those terms. In *Mortenson,* the full text of license terms was printed on each sealed diskette envelope inside the software box, printed again on the inside cover of the user manual, and notice of the terms appeared on the computer screen every time the purchaser executed the program. *Mortenson,* 970 P.2d at 806. In sum, the foregoing cases are clearly distinguishable from the facts of the present action.

C. Online Transactions

Cases in which courts have found contracts arising from Internet use do not assist defendants, because in those circumstances there was much clearer notice than in the present case that a user's act would manifest assent to contract terms. *See, e.g.,* * * * *Caspi v. Microsoft Network, L.L.C.,* 323 N.J.Super. 118, 732 A.2d 528, 530, 532–33 (N.J.Super.Ct.App.Div.1999) (upholding forum selection clause where subscribers to online software were required to review license terms in scrollable window and to click "I Agree" or "I Don't Agree") * * *.[17]

* * *

17. Although the parties here do not refer to it, California's consumer fraud statute, Cal. Bus. & Prof.Code § 17538, is one of the few state statutes to regulate online transactions in goods or services. The statute provides that in disclosing information regarding return and refund policies and other vital consumer information, online vendors must legibly display the information either:

(i) [on] the first screen displayed when the vendor's electronic site is accessed, (ii) on the screen on which goods or services are first offered, (iii) on the screen on which a buyer may place the order for goods or services, (iv) on the screen on which the buyer may enter payment information, such as a credit card account number, or (v) for nonbrowser-based technologies, in a manner that gives the user a reasonable opportunity to review that information.

Id. § 17538(d)(2)(A). The statute's clear purpose is to ensure that consumers engaging in online transactions have relevant information before they can be bound. Although consumer fraud as such is not alleged in the present action, and § 17538 protects only California residents, we note that the statute is consistent with the principle of conspicuous notice of the existence of contract terms that is also found in California's common law of contracts.

In addition, the model code, UCITA, discussed above, generally recognizes the importance of conspicuous notice and unambiguous manifestation of assent in online sales and licensing of computer information. For example, § 112, which addresses manifestation of assent, provides that a user's opportunity to review online contract terms exists if a "record" (or electronic writing) of the contract terms is "made available in a manner that ought to call it to the attention of a reasonable person and permit review." UCITA, § 112(e)(1) Section 112 also provides, in pertinent part, that "[a] person manifests assent to a record or term if the person, acting with knowledge of, or after having an opportunity to review the record or term or a copy of it ... intentionally engages in conduct or makes statements with reason to know that the other party or its electronic agent may infer from the conduct or statement that the

CONCLUSION

For the foregoing reasons, we affirm the district court's denial of defendants' motion to compel arbitration and to stay court proceedings.

Notes

1. In the setup described in the *Netscape* case, how exactly did the defendants contend that the consumer plaintiffs had agreed to the terms in the software license? How were consumers able to access these terms? Was there any affirmative manifestation of assent by the users? How does this differ from "clickwrap"? How does it differ from "shrinkwrap" as discussed in *Hill v. Gateway* and *Pro-CD*?

2. Amended UCC Article Two, Section 2–204, explicitly states that a contract may be formed through the interaction of an electronic agent and an individual. Also, amended sections 2–211–213 adopt provisions of the Uniform Electronic Transactions Act (UETA), designed to make electronic forms of contracting enforceable. However, as noted in the principal case in Footnote 13, it is not obvious that UCC Article 2 should apply to the licensing of software, as opposed to goods.

3. The National Conference of Commissioners on Uniform State Laws (NCCUSL) promulgated the controversial Uniform Computer Information

person assents to the record or term." *Id.* § 112(a)(2). In the case of a "mass-market license," a party adopts the terms of the license only by manifesting assent "before or during the party's initial performance or use of or access to the information." *Id.* § 209(a).

UCITA § 211 sets forth a number of guidelines for "internet-type" transactions involving the supply of information or software. For example, a licensor should make standard terms "available for review" prior to delivery or obligation to pay (1) by "displaying prominently and in close proximity to a description of the computer information, or to instructions or steps for acquiring it, the standard terms or a reference to an electronic location from which they can be readily obtained," or (2) by "disclosing the availability of the standard terms in a prominent place on the site from which the computer information is offered and promptly furnishing a copy of the standard terms on request before the transfer of the computer information." *Id.* § 211(1)(A–B). The commentary to § 211 adds: "The intent of the close proximity standard is that the terms or the reference to them would be called to the attention of an ordinary reasonable person." *Id.* § 211 cmt. 3. The commentary also approves of prominent hypertext links that draw attention to the existence of a standard agreement and allow users to view the terms of the license. *Id.*

After reviewing the California common law and other relevant legal authority, we conclude that under the circumstances here, plaintiffs' downloading of Smart-Download did not constitute acceptance of defendants' license terms. Reasonably conspicuous notice of the existence of contract terms and unambiguous manifestation of assent to those terms by consumers are essential if electronic bargaining is to have integrity and credibility. We hold that a reasonably prudent offeree in plaintiffs' position would not have known or learned, prior to acting on the invitation to download, of the reference to SmartDownload's license terms hidden below the "Download" button on the next screen. We affirm the district court's conclusion that the user plaintiffs, including Fagan, are not bound by the arbitration clause contained in those terms.

We hasten to point out that UCITA, which has been enacted into law only in Maryland and Virginia, does not govern the parties' transactions in the present case, but we nevertheless find that UCITA's provisions offer insight into the evolving online "circumstances" that defendants argue placed plaintiffs on inquiry notice of the existence of the SmartDownload license terms. UCITA has been controversial as a result of the perceived breadth of some of its provisions. * * *

Transactions Act (UCITA), specifically to deal with software licensing. Thus far, it has been adopted only in two states, Maryland and Virginia, and appears to have stalled in its present form. Nonetheless, as demonstrated by the *Specht* case, footnote 17, UCITA has provided some guidance to courts struggling to deal with electronic contracting. As noted by the court in *Specht*, UCITA Section 112(e) (now section 113(a)), provides that in order to manifest assent, the contract terms should be "made available in a manner that ought to call it to the attention of a reasonable person and permit review." UCITA also has a provision on mass-market software licenses, Section 209, that provides for both "opportunity to review" before assent, and for post payment and delivery disclosure of terms, as long as there is a right to return if the consumer does not wish to assent. UCITA critic Professor Jean Braucher says of this provision:

> At the point that a customer has paid, taken delivery, and is about to access or use a product, the customer already will have made a decision to acquire. The customer has sunk decision costs and is psychologically committed. Inertia will have set in, which makes it highly unlikely the customer will reverse course. Furthermore, to continue to shop, the customer would have to go to the trouble of undoing the first transaction (returning the product for a refund) and then looking for another, better one, without prior access to terms.

Jean Braucher, The Failed Promise of the UCITA Mass–Market Concept and Its Lessons for Policing of Standard Form Contracts, 7 J. Small & Emerging Bus. L. 393, 404 (2003).

4.   E-commerce of course implicates global markets. So if a consumer in White Plains, New York purchases a product from Nokia, will she be required to submit disputes to an arbitrator in Finland? Will the European customers of U.S. e-businesses be able to take advantage of the European Union's more restrictive laws on consumer contracts? For instance, the EU has a Distance Selling Directive requiring sellers to provide certain pre-transaction disclosures, and also has a right to cancel. The EU also has an Unfair Terms Directive that is intended to protect consumers from one-sided or unfair contract clauses in merchant/consumer contracts. These EU directives tend to be more specific and more pro-consumer than the U.S. broad ban on unconscionable contract terms. See Michael L. Rustad, Punitive Damages in Cyberspace: Where in the World Is the Consumer?, 7 Chap. L. Rev. 39, 85–92 (2004).

Problem 3–12

Your client runs an e-business that offers both free information and also sells related products directly to consumers. The client wants to ban commercial copying and distribution of the free information from the web site, but also wants to sell products and bind the consumer to settling disputes through arbitration. How can they do it in a way that does not detract from their website marketing while still maintaining enforceability of the various restrictions? Based on the caselaw and using the relevant UCITA provisions as "guidance"—what kind of advice would you give the client? Should they use clickwrap, browsewrap, shrinkwrap or some combination? What principles should they keep in mind in terms of placing these items on the website? What substantive consumer protection limits would apply to the types of "e-boilerplate" clauses that can be used? What if the client intends to sell to customers in Europe or other countries? Can you identify a sample of commercial websites illustrating the application of your principles, or illustrating standard form clauses that may not be enforced?

Chapter 4

ASSURING ACCESS TO THE MARKET

Consumers may never experience the benefits (or frustrations) of certain consumer transactions, such as borrowing money, if they are arbitrarily denied the opportunity to engage in them at all: the door is shut to them from the start. Even consumers who are able to obtain credit may find that their credit costs have been set arbitrarily high. A merchant's or creditor's refusal to deal with otherwise eligible consumers or to charge those consumers a fair price may be due to many things. The materials in this chapter examine two causes: (1) misinformation about the consumer's qualifications and (2) discrimination, again chiefly in the credit market.

SECTION A. CREDIT REPORTING

1. FOUNDATION

Imagine that you are a bank contemplating lending a substantial sum to a consumer. You would probably be unwilling to do so unless you were fairly confident that the consumer would repay the loan. If the consumer had a history of repaying such loans, you would undoubtedly be more comfortable making the loan, and you might even be willing to do so on favorable terms. During the nineteenth century, consumer reporting agencies, or credit bureaus as they are commonly known, came into existence to provide information lenders needed to determine the creditworthiness of consumers. Evan Hendricks, Credit Scores & Credit Reports 177 (2d ed. 2005). Today the industry is dominated by three large national institutions, Experian, Equifax, and TransUnion, which maintain databases on consumers throughout the country. Hundreds of resellers of credit information also provide information to subscribers. When a consumer applies for a loan, the lender typically obtains a credit report from one of these credit bureaus. The credit report and the accompanying credit score are likely to play a key role in determining both whether the lender grants the loan and its terms.

The gathering and distribution of credit information has progressed considerably since the nineteenth century. Today, credit bureaus obtain their information from a variety of sources. Some information derives from public records, such as court records of judgments or bankruptcies, but much of the information supplied by credit bureaus comes from creditors themselves, which report their experiences with particular consumers electronically. The big three credit bureaus each reportedly receive more than 24 billion items of information annually. Robert B. Avery, Paul S. Calem, & Glenn B. Canner, Credit Report Accuracy and Access to Credit, Federal Reserve Bulletin, Summer 2004 at 297, 298. The following excerpt describes the contents of credit files:

DEE PRIDGEN, CONSUMER CREDIT AND THE LAW

§ 2.1 (2006).

An individual credit history (also referred to as a credit report, or file), normally contains:

(1) identifying information, including name, address, social security number, date of birth, previous address and telephone number;

(2) description of accounts, including mortgages, auto and other installment loans, credit cards, and department store cards and collection accounts, and the date opened, balance due, date of last payment, and credit limit, among other things;

(3) account payment history, which usually features codes classifying consumers on how timely they pay their bills, and whether there are any defaults;

(4) inquiries, showing companies that accessed the report;

(5) public record information, such as arrests and convictions, lawsuits, and bankruptcies; and

(6) some reports, known as investigative reports, also contain more personal information gleaned from interviews, such as the subject's lifestyle, marital problems, drinking habits, etc.

———

Accurate credit reports benefit both lenders and consumers with good credit records. Inaccurate credit reports can be extremely damaging, however, to consumers with good credit histories if the inaccuracies prevent the consumers from obtaining credit. Accordingly, the remainder of this subsection as well as Subsection Two will explore the causes and consequences of errors in credit records. Later in the chapter, Subsection Three treats the privacy issue of who can see a credit report (privacy issues will receive further attention in Chapter Five) while Subsection Four explores the scope of federal protection for consumer reports. Finally, Subsection Five will introduce you to credit repair organizations.

Neither the marketplace nor the common law created a reliable mechanism for correcting inaccurate credit reports. Consumers who sued in defamation were rarely successful because nearly all jurisdictions applied the doctrine of qualified privilege to reporting agencies. This meant that before plaintiffs could recover, they had to show malice, something that is nearly impossible to do. Credit reporting agencies simply gather and report information in what, for them, are routine business transactions. They almost never know personally any of the people they report on, and they are not likely to act with malice toward a particular consumer. As a result, the qualified privilege operated almost as a grant of absolute immunity. See, e.g., Dun & Bradstreet, Inc. v. Robinson, 233 Ark. 168, 345 S.W.2d 34 (1961). The creditor who may have caused the confusion by reporting the erroneous information in the first place was also able to take advantage of the privilege.

Accordingly, in 1970, Congress enacted the federal Fair Credit Reporting Act (FCRA) to deal with the issues raised by the flow of information into and out of credit reporting agencies. The FCRA regulates many aspects of credit bureau practices and provides remedies to individuals when certain of these statutory mandates are not followed. Several states have enacted similar statutes, a list of which can be found at Dee Pridgen, Consumer Credit and the Law App. 2A (Thompson/West 2006), but many of the state laws substantially resemble the federal statute. This chapter will focus on the FCRA. The FCRA, reprinted in the Statutory Supplement, is codified at 15 U.S.C.A. § 1681 et seq., and is Title VI of the omnibus Consumer Credit Protection Act (CCPA).

Much of this section will address the legal consequences when the credit reporting system breaks down—just as many law school courses focus largely on transactions in which things go wrong. But you should also understand that the significance of the FCRA derives in part from its role in validating the credit reporting system and increasing the reliability of that system. The information exchanges that the FCRA authorizes have contributed to making our consumer credit markets strong and accessible, especially compared to other countries without the information freedom the FCRA gives the United States.

The causes of inaccuracies in credit reports have varied over time. Until some time in the 1990s, most errors in credit records were apparently inadvertent—though even inadvertent errors can create significant problems for consumers. Opinions differed about the number of such errors and the extent to which the FCRA was able to address them; in any event, Congress enacted significant amendments to the FCRA in 1996. Even as amended, however, the FCRA was not enough to deal with the identity theft epidemic that started in the 1990's. The testimony immediately following demonstrates some of the reasons. Though much of this section focuses on identity theft, many of the provisions of the FCRA were enacted before identity theft became a problem and apply to other situations as well, such as when a loan is declined because of errors in a report that were not caused by identity theft.

TESTIMONY OF JOHN M. HARRISON, ROCKY HILL, CONNECTICUT AT HEARINGS ON "THE GROWING PROBLEM OF IDENTITY THEFT AND ITS RELATIONSHIP TO THE FAIR CREDIT REPORTING ACT" BEFORE THE SENATE BANKING COMMITTEE

(June 19, 2003).

My introduction to the crime of identity theft began on November 5, 2001. On that day I was contacted by a detective from Beaumont, Texas who was investigating a Harley–Davidson motorcycle which had been purchased in my name and SSN. He tracked me down through my credit report. From that same credit report, the detective realized I was a victim of identity theft and he explained to me that someone had been using my name and SSN to open credit accounts and he pointed me in the right direction.

On that very same day, I reported my identity stolen to the FTC through their website. I also contacted all three repositories [credit bureaus], ordered my credit reports, initiated fraud alerts and began contacting creditors immediately. Once I received my credit reports, I filed a police report with Army's Criminal Investigation Division which luckily had a branch near Hartford, Connecticut. Just one month later, on Dec. 12, 2001, Jerry Wayne Phillips was arrested in Burke County, North Carolina during [a] traffic stop. He was riding the Harley–Davidson motorcycle the police officer in Texas was investigating. Phillips was indicted on federal charges in Texas, pled guilty to one count of identity theft, and is currently serving a 41–month sentence at a Federal Prison in Minnesota.

What I've learned since November 5, 2001 is that Phillips gained control of my identity on July 27, 2001 when army officials on Fort Bragg, NC issued him an active duty military ID card in my name and social security number. In a taped interview, Phillips claimed the ID was easy to get. That occurred about 1–½ years after my retirement as an Army Captain.

DAMAGES:

The military ID combined with my once excellent credit history allowed Phillips to go on an unhindered spending spree lasting just four months. From July to December 2001, Phillips had acquired goods, services, and cash in my name valued at over $260,000. None of the accounts were opened in my home state of Connecticut. He opened accounts as far south as Florida, as far North as Virginia and as far West as Texas. I've identified more than 60 fraudulent accounts of all types: credit accounts; personal and auto loans; checking and savings accounts; and utility accounts.

He purchased two trucks through Ford Credit valued at over $85,000. A Harley–Davidson motorcycle for $25,000. He rented a house in Virginia and purchased a time-share in Hilton Head, South Carolina. One of the accounts opened by Phillips was with the Army & Air Force Exchange Service (AAFES). He also wrote bad checks in these exchanges. I originally disputed this account in March 2002 when AAFES attempted to garnish my military retirement pay. I was able to stop the garnishment by providing supporting documentation to AAFES. They made a second attempt to garnish my retirement in January 2003 for the same debt. Unfortunately, my letter to AAFES went ignored the second time and the garnishment began the end of January. Eventually and with the assistance of Congressman Larson's office, the garnishment was stopped in March 2003 and AAFES refunded the money that had been taken from my retirement pay. I have always been somewhat distressed at the military's involvement in the theft of my identity. They issued the fraudulent ID card that allowed Phillips to open all these accounts and quite obviously, someone was very negligent in their duties. The garnishment greatly added to that distress.

FCRA RELATIONSHIP:

While Phillips made creditors, banks, and willing merchants the monetary victims of this crime, it has been those same creditors and credit reporting agencies that made me a victim. I have struggled with the repositories, creditors, and debt collectors for 20 straight months now and still have many accounts and debts incorrectly reported in my name and SSN. My imposter has been in jail for 19 of those 20 months and no accounts have been opened in my name since his incarceration at the end of 2001. I have overwhelming documentation to verify I did not open any of these accounts and I've willingly provided those documents to all creditors I've found as well as the credit bureaus. I've discovered it's more cost effective for creditors to write the debt off in the victim's name than go after the real criminal, even after you tell them who and where the real criminal is. Credit bureaus hide behind the fact that they are only reporting what creditors tell them while at the same time, victims are repeatedly sending affidavits, police reports and detailed dispute letters proving the creditors are wrong. That is why it takes identity theft victims years instead of months to recover from this crime.

From that first day in November 2001, I have been very aggressive about restoring the damage done in my name. I have sought out the fraudulent accounts and in most cases; I've contacted them before they've contacted me. I've disputed all accounts directly with the creditors following that up by disputing the accounts through the repositories. I've encountered a great many difficulties. While two of the repositories have done what I consider to be a fair job assisting me and responding to my disputes, one of them, Equifax has failed to meet nearly all the provisions of the FCRA. It took eleven months and three dispute letters to get a second report from Equifax. Further, I found the report they sent to me was not the same report they were sending to creditors. Both reports that Equifax has in their system still contain as many as fifteen fraudulent accounts.

I also found that when I disputed accounts to any of the repositories, whether the results of the re-investigation come back with deleted or verified accounts, the accounts were rarely resolved. Creditors were either not accepting my dispute through the repositories or the dispute was not being sent to them. In either event, the majority of creditors continue to seek me out directly or through a debt collector. In some instances, I've had accounts deleted from one repository only to have it show up with another one. I've also encountered creditors that after I have initiated contact with them to dispute an account, sold the debt to or hired debt collectors that seek me out at a later time. I've also had difficulties with accounts that return months after I have successfully disputed them, like AAFES. Lastly, there have also been accounts that I've contacted and could find no record of a debt in my name and then months later their debt collectors are calling my home or showing up on my credit reports. It has been and continues to be a nightmare.

I've accounted for over 100 bad checks drafted from four different fraudulent checking accounts. Phillips wrote bad checks in eight different states and they account for nearly $60,000 of the total debt. Unfortunately, the checking accounts have created significantly more complications for me than the credit accounts. While creditors have just three reporting agencies to choose from, banks and vendors that accept checks have a multitude of reporting agencies. Additionally, the majority of those reporting agencies, which maintain both positive and negative information on consumers, do not provide consumer reports nor are there systems in place to dispute negative information. I've spent a great deal of time trying to understand the checking situation to learn how to properly dispute each bad check that was written. My conclusion is, there is no system in place to assist an identity theft victim when banking accounts are opened in your name and SSN, but are completely removed and unrelated to your own banking accounts. This industry is well behind the progress that has been made in the credit industry.

PERSONAL IMPACT:

There is a still misconception by some that creditors, merchants, banks and others that sustain monetary losses are the only victims of identity theft. So often when speaking to someone about my situation the comment is made, "At least you're not responsible to pay these fraudulent debts". Somehow, that makes my situation seem less tenuous. I've invested over 1100 hours of my time defending myself and working to restore my credit and banking histories. I've filled eight notebooks with over 1500 pages of documentation. I can account for about $1500 in out of pocket expenses directly related to my identity theft. Higher interest rates have cost me over $4000. I've been unknowingly sued by at least one of the creditors. I've had my military retirement garnished. I'm not credit worthy enough to open any new accounts and bad checks reported in my name prevent me from opening any deposit accounts with banks.

It was also during January 2003 that my own creditors began taking adverse actions against me as a result of the negative information contained in my credit reports. I lost $25,000 in available credit as my creditors closed accounts with zero balances or lowered my credit limit to existing balances. I had been with some of those creditors over ten years, but my history of always paying on time did not influence their decisions.

EMOTIONAL IMPACT:

I've always considered myself to be a very strong individual. During the twenty years I spent in the military, I was often singled out as someone that worked extremely well under stress. The length of time it takes to resolve a stolen identity, the frustration in dealing with companies that don't understand the crime or its impact and don't take the correct actions, repeatedly having to clear up the same accounts, the constant phone calls and letters from debt collectors is enough to cause anyone emotional distress.

In September 2002, eleven months into my struggle, I began to have difficulties with anxiety and insomnia and my physician prescribed a mild anti-depressant. In January 2003, the problems with my identity were causing serious distractions for my work as a salesperson. I spoke with my supervisor about the problems and began weekly therapy in February 2003 through our Employee Assistance Program. I was diagnosed with Post Traumatic Stress Disorder. As the doctor put it, my fight or flight instincts were stuck on "fight". Those problems eventually led to my termination at the end of April 2003. I was given no notice of the termination nor was there a severance offered. I simply had the rug pulled from underneath me. At present I find myself unemployed for the first time since I was 14 years old, being treated for what now has become depression, in the worst job market in 9 years, and still dealing with the same situation that got me here in the first place. Sadly, even as I look back over the last twenty months and re-trace my steps, I can't identify a single thing I could have done differently that may have prevented the situation I'm currently in.

Notes

1. See also Jeff Sovern, The Jewel of Their Souls: Preventing Identity Theft Through Loss Allocation Rules, 64 U. Pitt. L. Rev. 343, 345 (2003):

> Many victims have been charged with crimes committed by their impersonators. Indeed, one survey found that 15% of identity theft victims had acquired criminal records because of the actions of imposters. Victims in such circumstances may spend time in jail, lose their jobs, and be denied driver's licenses and the right to vote.

2. Would it have mattered if the inaccuracies in Mr. Harrison's credit records were the result of negligence rather than identity theft? As you read through the materials that follow, ask yourself if the FCRA provides differ-

ent treatment for those who have been victimized by identity thieves or those whose credit reports contain inadvertent errors? Should it?

3. Identity theft occurs when someone uses someone else's identity to obtain access to goods, credit, or other services, as happened to John Harrison. On average, every ten seconds, another American is victimized by identity thieves. Gary Rivlin, Purloined Lives; Identity Theft is Increasing, Bringing a Lifetime of Worry for Many, N. Y. Times, March 17, 2005, at C1, C8. Indeed, more consumers complain to the Federal Trade Commission about identity theft than any other consumer problem. A 2003 Report to the FTC estimated that identity theft costs the nation $50 billion per year and that the average victimized consumer spent $500 and 30 hours dealing with the theft. Synovate, Federal Trade Commission, Identity Theft Survey Report (2003), available at http://www.ftc.gov/os/2003/09/synovatereport.pdf. Though thieves have stolen the identity of others for such varied purposes as obtaining employment, purchasing guns, obtaining government documents or benefits (e.g., a driver's license or Social Security card), securing telephone or utility services, opening bank accounts, having surgery performed, and even having children, we will focus largely on the use of identity theft to obtain credit.

———

Until 1998, no federal laws specifically addressed identity theft. Victims of identity theft were relegated to whatever remedies they could find in the Fair Credit Reporting Act and at common law (discussed below). In 1998, Congress enacted the Identity Theft and Assumption Deterrence Act, codified at 18 U.S.C. § 1028(a)(7). This statute and many similar state statutes made identity theft a crime, but unfortunately identity theft became still more prevalent. Consequently, in 2003, Congress passed the Fair and Accurate Credit Transactions Act (FAC-TA), Pub. L. 108–159, 117 Stat. 1952, amending the FCRA and adding new safeguards for identity theft victims. Perhaps the most significant of FACTA's safeguards is the right it confers upon consumers to obtain a free copy of their credit report annually, FCRA §§ 1681g, 1681j(a)(1), though Consumer Reports has complained that the website which consumers can visit to obtain the report is "devilishly difficult to use." Credit Scores; What You Don't Know Can Be Held Against You, Consumer Rep., Aug., 2005 at 16. In addition, identity theft victims who meet certain requirements can have information resulting from the identity theft blocked from their credit reports. FCRA § 1681c–2. Some other FACTA safeguards will be considered in connection with the problems below.

Unfortunately, the FCRA is a complex statute that is difficult to decipher. One reason for that is that the statute imposes different requirements on three groups: credit bureaus, furnishers of data to credit bureaus, and users of the reports provided by the bureaus. While the last two groups overlap, a creditor's obligations in a particular transaction depends on whether it is supplying information to or obtaining information from the credit bureau. The statute creates a complicated system—explored in the next subsection—intended to enable consumers to discover errors and obtain their correction. To make matters even more troublesome, consumers may bring private claims to enforce some obligations under the statute but other provisions may be enforced only by public agencies. As you explore the statute, ask yourself why consumers should be able to enforce some provisions but not others.

The FTC, the agency charged with enforcement of the FCRA, has recently published a number of regulations implementing and interpreting FCRA provisions. The Commission has also, over the years, written interpretations and advisory letters on many aspects of the FCRA. In addition, in 1990, the FTC issued an Official Commentary to the FCRA which consolidated and updated the various policy statements and interpretations the FTC had previously produced. See 16 C.F.R. Part 600. Because the FCRA has undergone significant revisions since the FTC last amended the Commentary, the Commentary is chiefly useful in interpreting older provisions of the statute.

2. REGULATION OF AGENCY FILES—CLEANING UP INACCURATE INFORMATION

Follow carefully the scenario called for under the FCRA. If the user of a consumer report bases an adverse action—which includes a denial of credit—on information contained in a consumer report, the user must provide the consumer with the contact information of the consumer reporting agency, together with other information, including a statement that the consumer has a right to obtain a free copy of the report from the consumer reporting agency and to dispute the accuracy or completeness of information in the report. § 1681m. The consumer can then obtain the information in the report from the consumer reporting agency. § 1681g. If the consumer disputes any of the information, the agency must conduct a reasonable investigation and delete inaccurate or unverified information or accept a "brief statement" of the consumer's dispute. Reporting agencies must maintain "reasonable procedures to assure maximum possible accuracy." § 1681e(b). The statute also requires furnishers of information (typically creditors) which have received notice that an item is disputed to conduct an investigation and correct an error. § 1681s–2(b). With some exceptions, liability attaches to negligent and willful non-compliance with the statute. §§ 1681n, 1681o. Are the obligations imposed by the FCRA on reporting agencies and furnishers of information, respectively, to maintain accuracy, investigate claims of error, and correct errors different? If so, what accounts for the differences? Do these requirements strike you as clear? Adequate? The following problems and cases explore these provisions more fully.

Problem 4–1

For years, Darnay has been paying his bills on time to preserve his credit rating for when he needed it. A year ago Darnay contracted to buy a house, paid a deposit of $10,000, and applied to CCC for a mortgage. CCC asked Credit Bureau for a report on Darnay. The report showed that Darnay had defaulted on numerous credit obligations and so CCC wishes to deny Darnay's application. What, if anything, must CCC tell Darnay? See FCRA § 1681m. Would CCC have had to tell Darnay anything about the credit report if it had made the loan on favorable terms?

If Darnay then gets in touch with Credit Bureau "to straighten things out," what must it tell him? See FCRA §§ 1681g, 1681j(b). Must Credit Bureau tell Darnay exactly what caused CCC to turn down the loan? Must Credit Bureau tell Darnay its sources of information? Would CCC's or Credit Bureau's disclosure obligations be different if Darnay had not in fact defaulted on his credit obligations but the reports of default were the product of inadvertent errors or, alternatively, identity theft?

Notes

1. While the FCRA does not require the lender to inform the consumer of the reason for a rejection, the Equal Credit Opportunity Act, to be explored in the next section, does. 15 U.S.C. § 1691(d). Consequently, when the requirements of the two statutes are combined, the effect is to require a lender taking an "adverse action" based on information contained in a consumer report to notify the consumer of the reason for the decision as well as the fact that the decision was founded on data in the consumer report. The meaning of the phrase "adverse action" will be discussed in the next section, but note that in 2003 Congress extended the definition of adverse action under the FCRA to include many situations in which, based at least in part on the credit report, the creditor offers to loan money on materially less favorable terms than it offers to a substantial portion of its borrowers. § 1681m(h); see also 12 C.F.R. § 202.2(c). In other words, if the creditor offers to make a loan on unfavorable terms—such as a higher interest rate— it may have engaged in an adverse action, thereby triggering disclosures under the FCRA. Apparently not wanting consumers to bring a private claim when creditors failed to comply with this so-called "risk-based pricing" subsection, Congress also added a new subsection, § 1681m(h)(8), which provides that "this section" may be enforced exclusively by administrative agencies. This created a further issue, however: § 1681m also imposes on creditors a number of other obligations, including the obligation to provide various notices—such as the notice of an adverse action—to consumers who have been turned down for a loan because of information in a consumer report. Before the 2003 FACTA Act, consumers could bring a private claim to enforce those obligations, but did § 1681m(h)(8) take that private claim away? Most courts have concluded that consumers may no longer bring a private claim to enforce any portion of § 1681m, see, e.g., Murray v. GMAC Mortg. Corp., 434 F.3d 948 (7th Cir. 2006), but Barnette v. Brook Road, Inc., 429 F.Supp.2d 741 (E.D.Va. 2006), found the change to be a "scrivener's error" and ruled that the private claim survives.

2. Must a consumer consent before a credit bureau can maintain a file on her?

Problem 4–2

When Darnay examined his credit record, he discovered that it contained numerous entries reflecting defaults on credit charges that he had not incurred but that had nevertheless been reported by lenders. He believes that he has been a victim of identity theft. He immediately wrote to Credit Bureau and asked it to delete the erroneous entries. What should CB do? See FCRA §§ 1681i, 1681c–2, 1681a(q)(4). Would it matter if the erroneous entries were not the work of an identity thief? If CB concludes that the entries are correct, what can Darnay do? Assuming that the information is correct, how long can CB keep the information in its files? See FCRA § 605(a). Would Darnay have a claim against CB for reporting erroneous entries to CCC? See Polzer v. TRW; Richardson v. Fleet Bank; Sarver v. Experian Information Solutions; FCRA §§ 1681e(b), 1681h(e).

POLZER v. TRW, INC.

New York Supreme Court, Appellate Division, First Department, 1998.
256 A.D.2d 248, 682 N.Y.S.2d 194.

[The facts do not appear in the opinion, but according to David E. Worsley, Fair Credit Reporting Cases Illustrate Risks for Credit Reporting Agencies, Creditor, and Lawyers 56 Consumer Fin. L.Q. Rep. 68 (2002) were as follows:

> the plaintiffs alleged that they were the victims of identity theft and that the defendants facilitated and exacerbated the harm plaintiffs suffered.... The plaintiffs believed that their identities were stolen ... by an imposter, who ... armed with the plaintiffs' personal identification information, as well as all of their legitimate credit account numbers, quickly went to work changing their address at the plaintiffs' banks and at credit reporting agencies.... That change apparently was accepted by defendants without serious inquiry or requiring any proof that the plaintiffs had actually moved. The "fraud address" was then spread by the three major credit reporting agencies, which sold their names and new addresses to other banks seeking to offer them pre-approved credit cards. Those offers were sent to the imposter at the fraud address and the imposter had more than enough information to complete the applications and obtain the credit cards. The imposter ran up $100,000 in fraudulent charges.

This appeal involved plaintiffs' claims against credit card issuers Bank of New York and Mobil for issuing credit cards to the imposter.]

MEMORANDUM DECISION. Order, Supreme Court, New York County (Beatrice Shainswit, J.), entered on or about May 19, 1997, which, *inter alia,* granted defendant Bank of New York (Delaware) ("BNY") summary judgment dismissing plaintiffs' 40th through 43rd causes of action and granted defendant Mobil Oil Credit Corporation

("Mobil") summary judgment dismissing plaintiffs' 50th through 53rd causes of action, unanimously affirmed, without costs. * * *

Substantively, the motion court properly determined that New York does not recognize a cause of action for "negligent enablement of impostor fraud", and that plaintiffs otherwise failed to state a cause of action in negligence, because BNY and Mobil had no special relationship either with the impostor who stole the plaintiffs' credit information and fraudulently obtained credit cards, or with plaintiffs, with whom they stood simply in a creditor/debtor relationship.

To the extent that plaintiffs pleaded causes of action based on intentional or negligent infliction of emotional distress or prima facie tort, the motion court properly granted summary judgment dismissing those claims as well, because there was no evidence of ill will, malice or extreme outrageous conduct, or of actual physical injury or apprehension of physical harm, and because there was no special duty owed plaintiffs by Mobil and BNY, and finally because plaintiffs failed to allege, much less offer proof of, special damages.

The motion court, in addition, properly granted summary judgment dismissing plaintiffs' statutory claims brought under the Deceptive Acts & Practices Act (General Business Law § 349). Assuming arguendo that plaintiffs' complaints are consumer-oriented, and that the complained of action or inaction by BNY or Mobil was somehow improper, plaintiffs failed to make the requisite showing that the complained of conduct was deceptive or misleading to them. An action does not compensate for "frustration" and, as noted, plaintiffs have failed to demonstrate any damages or actual loss. In addition, because the alleged offensive acts or omissions ceased several years before the commencement of this action, the motion court properly determined that there was no basis for an injunction.

In dismissing plaintiffs' statutory claims, the motion court also properly determined that the acts or omissions that are alleged to have violated General Business Law § 349 were protected by the qualified immunity granted pursuant to the Federal Fair Credit Reporting Act (15 USC § 1681h [e]), since General Business Law § 349[d] provides that it is a complete defense if the alleged act or practice complies with the rules and regulations of, and the statutes administered by, *inter alia,* the Federal Trade Commission. Finally, the motion court properly determined that plaintiffs failed to demonstrate, even to the extent necessary to avoid summary judgment, that BNY and Mobil were liable pursuant to General Business Law § 703 *et seq.*

Notes

1. In Garay v. U.S. Bancorp, 303 F.Supp.2d 299 (E.D.N.Y. 2004), the court held that there is no private right of action under the Identity Theft and Assumption Deterrence Act of 1998.

2. The principal case is criticized in Heather M. Howard, Note, The Negligent Enablement of Imposter Fraud: A Common–Sense Common Law

Claim, 54 Duke L.J. 1263 (2005). Should courts create such a common law tort?

RICHARDSON v. FLEET BANK

United States District Court for the District of Massachusetts, 2001.
190 F.Supp.2d 81.

FREEDMAN, Senior District Judge.

Introduction

In this action, the plaintiffs, Denise M. Richardson and Robert L. Richardson ("plaintiffs") allege that the defendant, Equifax Credit Information Services ("Equifax") violated the Fair Credit Reporting Act ("FCRA") * * * and the Massachusetts Consumer Credit Reporting Act ("MCCRA").* * *

II.   Background

In April 1988, the plaintiffs obtained a $50,000 equity loan from Shawmut Bank of Hampshire County ("Shawmut"). Over the next four years, they attempted to pay down the principal by including additional money with their minimum monthly obligations. But in 1992, during an attempted refinancing, the plaintiffs discovered that Shawmut had not credited their accounts with the extra payments. Subsequently, the plaintiffs initiated a lawsuit against Shawmut over its allegedly inaccurate accounting methods, and settled the case in December 1994. In consideration of the plaintiffs' release of their claims, Shawmut released them from the remaining $20,000 on the loan, and agreed that no derogatory information about them or their claim against the bank would be reported to any credit reporting agency. However, Shawmut classified the lost $20,000 as a "charge-off," and its debt collectors attempted to collect the unpaid balance approximately one year after settling the case. After the plaintiffs complained to Shawmut, the bank issued a letter to the plaintiffs on December 1, 1995 stating that it would notify the appropriate credit reporting agencies of its error, and that the comments regarding their account, No. 700170000015362 ("700 account"), would thereafter read "paid as agreed."

After Shawmut was acquired by Fleet Bank ("Fleet") in January 1996, Denise Richardson ordered copies of credit reports to confirm that Shawmut had removed any derogatory information. Instead, she learned that Fleet was reporting the discharged Shawmut mortgage as a charge-off. In May 1996, the plaintiffs contacted Fleet, whose agent John Wasik ("Wasik") acknowledged the error and assured them that the erroneous information would be removed and all credit reporting agencies notified of the error. Wasik forwarded a Universal Data Form ("UDF") to the plaintiffs, indicating that a request was made to the relevant credit agencies to change the plaintiffs' account regarding the Shawmut mortgage to "paid as agreed." It is standard practice at Fleet to send UDF forms to three major credit reporting agencies: Equifax, TRW/Experian, and Trans Union. The UDF, however, contained inaccurate data regarding the dates of origin and termination of the plaintiffs' account, as well as its "source code."

In March 1997, the plaintiffs obtained an Equifax credit report and learned that Fleet had not only continued to report their "700 account" as charged-off through October 1996, but also had reported the account a second time under a different account number, No. 56700170000015362 ("567 account"). In May 1997, the plaintiffs again reported the dispute to Fleet. To correct this problem, Wasik issued two additional UDFs, one in the name of each plaintiff, to Equifax requesting a change in the plaintiffs' credit histories to read "paid as agreed." Both UDFs issued in May 1997 refer only to the plaintiffs' "700 account". Equifax, however, has no record of receiving any UDFs from Wasik.

On August 27, 1997, the plaintiffs received letters indicating that their applications for credit card accounts with BP Oil had been denied. The letters stated the "primary reason" for the denial as "derogatory information on credit file," and named Equifax as the credit reporting agency responsible for providing the plaintiffs' credit history. On October 15, 1997, the plaintiffs received an Equifax credit report, reflecting their "700 account" as "transferred or sold" and reporting their "567 account" as "charged-off." On November 4, 1997, the plaintiffs sent a letter to Equifax requesting an investigation of the Fleet account. On November 15, 1997, Equifax reported to the plaintiffs that Fleet had verified the accuracy of the two accounts. The plaintiffs attempted to use these letters from Equifax to notify Fleet of its erroneous reporting. However, Fleet never responded, as it had already sold the account to Portfolio Recovery Assets ("PRA"), a debt collection agency.

In September 1999, after receiving a letter from PRA attempting to collect an alleged outstanding balance of more than $20,000, the plaintiffs again ordered automated disclosures of their Equifax files. The credit reports contained three charge-offs: the "567 account" on Denise Richardson's report, and the "700 account" and "567 account" on Robert Richardson's report. The plaintiffs subsequently called Equifax directly to dispute these items. After completing its investigation, Equifax deleted the "567 accounts" from both files and verified, through Fleet, the remaining charge-off on Robert Richardson's file.

On April 1, 1999, the plaintiffs filed the instant action in the Massachusetts Hampshire County Superior Court, charging Equifax with violations of the FCRA and MCCRA, as well as Mass.Gen.Laws ch. 93A ("chapter 93A"), and the common law torts of defamation and intentional infliction of emotional distress. The defendant joined in a notice of removal to the federal court, and now moves for summary judgment. * * *

IV. Discussion

A. *Fair Credit Reporting Act*

The plaintiffs claim that Equifax violated the FCRA and MCCRA by failing to follow reasonable procedures to ensure the maximum possible accuracy of information when preparing credit reports. *See* 15 U.S.C. § 1681e(b) ("section 1681e(b)"); Mass.Gen.Laws ch. 93, § 54(b). In addition, the plaintiffs allege that Equifax violated the FCRA and MCCRA by failing to make reasonable and timely efforts to reinvestigate the accuracy of information that they disputed. *See* 15 U.S.C. § 1681i ("section 1681i"); Mass.Gen.Laws ch. 93, § 58(a). A negligent violation of either of these sections subjects the credit reporting agency to liability for actual damages sustained as a result of a violation, together with the costs of the action and a reasonable attorney's fee. 15 U.S.C. § 1681o; Mass.Gen.Laws § 64. A willful violation of either section subjects the agency to liability for punitive damages. 15 U.S.C. § 1681n; Mass.Gen. Laws ch. 93, § 63. * * *

2. *Section 1681e(b) Claim*

Under the FCRA, a consumer reporting agency must follow "reasonable procedures to assure maximum possible accuracy" regarding the information contained in a consumer's credit report. 15 U.S.C. § 1681e(b). A claim of noncompliance with section 1681e(b) "consists of four elements: (1) inaccurate information was included in a consumer's credit report; (2) the inaccuracy was due to defendant's failure to follow reasonable procedures to assure maximum possible accuracy; (3) the consumer suffered injury; and (4) the consumer's injury was caused by the inclusion of the inaccurate entry." *Philbin v. Trans Union Corp.,* 101 F.3d 957, 962 (3d Cir.1996). In this case, Equifax apparently does not dispute that inaccurate information was placed in reports it prepared regarding the plaintiffs' credit history. However, Equifax does challenge the plaintiffs' ability to demonstrate the remaining three elements of a section 1681e(b) claim. The Court will address each disputed element in turn.

a. Reasonable Procedures

Equifax contends that it maintains reasonable procedures as a matter of law because it transcribed, stored, and communicated consumer information from Fleet, a source that it believed to be reliable and credible on its face. In addition, it argues that the plaintiffs cannot produce any proof that they caused Equifax to be notified that their credit history was being erroneously reported.

Section 1681e(b) mandates that agencies follow reasonable procedures in preparing consumer reports but "does not impose strict liability for inaccurate entries in consumer reports; the preparer is held only to a duty of reasonable care. The exercise of reasonable care is determined by reference to what a reasonably prudent person would do under the circumstances." *Spence v. TRW, Inc.,* 92 F.3d 380, 383 (6th Cir.1996) (citations omitted). In evaluating whether procedures are reasonable, courts also balance "the potential harm from inaccuracy against the burden of safeguarding against such inaccuracy." *Stewart v. Credit Bureau, Inc.,* 734 F.2d 47, 50 (D.C.Cir.1984).

The Court declines to say that relying on creditors for accurate credit information constitutes a reasonable procedure as a matter of law where, as here, the credit reporting agency had reason to know of the dispute between the plaintiffs and Equifax. *See Bryant v. TRW,* 689 F.2d 72, 77 (6th Cir.1982) (where agency knew of dispute between consumer and creditors, confirming consumer's credit information with creditors constituted unreasonable procedure); *Barron v. Trans Union Corp.,* 82 F.Supp.2d at 1295–96. A credit reporting agency is initially entitled to rely on information contained in the reports issued by credit grantors, because it would be unduly burdensome and inefficient to require an agency to look beyond the face of every credit report. However, once notified that a consumer disputes the information contained in such records, exclusive reliance on such information is neither reasonable or justified. *See Henson v. CSC Credit Servs.,* 29 F.3d 280, 285 (7th Cir.1994) (credit reporting agency entitled to rely on court dockets to correctly recite consumer's credit history absent notice that information is flawed); *Gill v. Kostroff,* Civ. A. 98–930–T17A, 2000 WL 141258, at *6 (M.D.Fla.2000). Thus, "[a] credit reporting agency that has been notified of potentially inaccurate information in a consumer's credit report is in a very different position than one who has no such notice." *Henson,* 29 F.3d at 286.

In this case, the exhibits and affidavits show that the plaintiffs caused notices to be sent to Equifax regarding errors in their credit history on at least three occasions before Equifax prepared their credit report for BP Oil. Despite the communication of these notices, Equifax continued to rely exclusively on Fleet's version of the plaintiffs' credit history. In the Court's view, there exists a genuine issue of material fact as to whether it was reasonable for Equifax to rely exclusively on the information provided by Fleet, given that Equifax knew or should have known that this information was unreliable or inaccurate. *See Gill,* 2000 WL 141258, at *7 (genuine issue of material fact exists as to whether defendant maintained reasonable procedures where plaintiff sent several notices to defendant, but defendant failed to correct reported errors).

Equifax contends that the plaintiffs have produced no evidence that it received the correction notices purportedly sent by Shawmut and Fleet. However, the plaintiffs have proffered letters from both Shawmut and Fleet indicating that they would inform the relevant credit reporting agencies, including Equifax, of the errors regarding the plaintiffs' Shawmut account. In addition, it was standard business practice at Fleet to send UDF notices to Equifax. Although the affidavit of Janet Mullins, Senior Manager in the Office of Consumer Affairs for Equifax, states that Equifax has no record of receiving the UDFs sent by Fleet, her statement is silent on whether Equifax has a record of receiving the Shawmut notice. Moreover, even if Equifax had categorically denied ever receiving all three correction statements from Shawmut and Fleet, this assertion merely creates a classic dispute of material fact that is susceptible of resolution only by the finder of fact at trial.

* * *

b. Damages

Equifax also challenges the sufficiency of the plaintiffs' evidence regarding damages on the ground that damages under the FCRA "cannot be recovered without a showing of actual loss." Defendant's Motion for Summary Judgment at 10. To the contrary, courts have consistently held that "actual damages may include humiliation and mental distress, even in the absence of out-of-pocket expenses." *Casella v. Equifax Credit Info. Servs.*, 56 F.3d 469, 474 (2d Cir.1995), *cert. denied,* 517 U.S. 1150, 116 S.Ct. 1452, 134 L.Ed.2d 571 (1996); *see Cousin v. Trans Union Corp.*, 246 F.3d 359, 369 n. 15 (5th Cir.2001) (emotional distress damages compensable under FCRA); *Philbin,* 101 F.3d at 962 & n. 3 (same); *Guimond,* 45 F.3d at 1333 (same). Here, the plaintiffs allege that they have suffered emotional distress upon learning that Equifax has reported incorrect credit information to prospective creditors, and resulting from the denial of credit by BP Oil, as well as their lengthy effort to correct their credit reports. *See, e.g., Stevenson v. TRW, Inc.*, 987 F.2d 288, 296–97 (5th Cir.1993) (affirming award of damages for pain and suffering where consumer experienced humiliation resulting from three credit and lengthy dealings with credit reporting agency). Thus, the Court cannot say that the plaintiffs fail to state a genuine issue of material fact on the question of damages. * * *

3. Section 1681i

Section 1681i(a)(1)(A) of the FCRA provides, in pertinent part, that where a consumer notifies a credit reporting agency that information contained in his or her report may be inaccurate, "the agency shall reinvestigate free of charge and record the current status of the disputed information, or delete the item from the file...." Equifax argues that the statute requires a credit reporting agency only to confirm the accuracy of the information with the original source of information, but imposes no mandate on the agency to take additional steps to confirm the accuracy of the disputed information. However, the majority of courts hold that section 1681i(a) requires a credit reporting agency, in certain circumstances, to verify the accuracy of its initial source of information. *See, e.g., Cushman v. Trans Union Corp.*, 115 F.3d 220, 225 (3d Cir.1997); *Henson,* 29 F.3d at 286–87; *Stevenson,* 987 F.2d at 293. "Whether the credit reporting agency has a duty to go beyond the original source will depend, in part, on whether the consumer has alerted the reporting agency to the possibility that the source may be unreliable or the reporting agency itself knows or should know that the source is unreliable." *Henson,* 29 F.3d at 286. Moreover, the courts have determined in this context that "[w]hether a reasonable investigation has been conducted is generally a question for the jury." *Bruce v. First U.S.A. Bank, Nat'l Ass'n,* 103 F.Supp.2d 1135, 1143 (E.D.Mo.2000).

Viewing the record in the light most favorable to the plaintiffs, the Court concludes that the plaintiffs' section 1681i claim survives Equifax's motion for summary judgment. The plaintiffs submit copies of four separate written communications to Equifax in which they dispute the accuracy of their credit history. In addition, one of these letters includes a copy of the discharged Shawmut mortgage. Despite the plaintiffs' repeated complaints, Equifax continued to rely solely upon the information provided by Fleet when it investigated the plaintiffs' complaints in November 1997 and September 1999. Thus, genuine issues of material fact exist as to whether Equifax fulfilled its duty to reinvestigate pursuant to section 1681i. *See Cushman,* 115 F.3d at 226 (denying defendant's motion for summary judgment in claim for failure to reinvestigate where it merely verified negative information with credit grantors despite consumer's warning that information was inaccurate); *Stevenson,* 987 F.2d at 293 (same); *cf. Pinner v. Schmidt,* 805 F.2d 1258, 1262 (5th Cir.1986) (denying defendant's motion for new trial for failure to reinvestigate where consumer informed reporting agency of his personal dispute with credit grantor, yet reporting agency relied solely on credit grantor for information during investigation), *cert. denied,* 483 U.S. 1022, 107 S.Ct. 3267, 97 L.Ed.2d 766 (1987) and *cert. denied sub nom. Credit Bureau Services–New Orleans v. Pinner,* 483 U.S. 1032, 107 S.Ct. 3276, 97 L.Ed.2d 780 (1987). "In a reinvestigation of the accuracy of credit reports, a credit bureau must bear some responsibility for evaluating the accuracy of information obtained from subscribers." *Stevenson,* 987 F.2d at 293. * * *

V. CONCLUSION

Accordingly * * * Equifax's motion is DENIED with regard to the plaintiffs' claims that Equifax breached its duties to maintain reasonable procedures and to reinvestigate under the FCRA (Count XIII) and MCCRA (Count XII).

SARVER v. EXPERIAN INFORMATION SOLUTIONS

United States Court of Appeals for the Seventh Circuit, 2004.
390 F.3d 969.

TERRENCE T. EVANS, CIRCUIT JUDGE.

Lloyd Sarver appeals from an order granting summary judgment to Experian Information Solutions, Inc., a credit reporting company, on his claim under the Fair Credit Reporting Act (FCRA), 15 U.S.C. §§ 1681 *et seq.*

Experian reported inaccurate information on Sarver's credit report, which on August 2, 2002, caused the Monogram Bank of Georgia to deny him credit. Monogram cited the Experian credit report and particularly a reference to a bankruptcy which appeared on the report. Both before and after Monogram denied him credit, Sarver asked for a copy of his credit report. He received copies both times and both reports showed that accounts with Cross Country Bank were listed as having been "involved in bankruptcy." No other accounts had that notation, although other accounts had significant problems. A Bank One installment account had a balance past due 180 days, and another company, Providian, had written off $3,099 on a revolving account. On August 29, 2002, Sarver wrote Experian informing it that the bankruptcy notation was inaccurate[1] and asking that it be removed from his report. * * *

We turn to Sarver's claim under § 1681e(b), which requires that a credit reporting agency follow "reasonable procedures to assure maximum possible accuracy" when it prepares a credit report. The reasonableness of a reporting agency's procedures is normally a question for trial unless the reasonableness or unreasonableness of the procedures is beyond question. *Crabill,* 259 F.3d at 663. However, to state a claim under the statute, a consumer must sufficiently allege "that a credit reporting agency prepared a report containing 'inaccurate' information." *Cahlin v. General Motors Acceptance Corp.,* 936 F.2d 1151, 1156 (11th Cir.1991). However, the credit reporting agency is not automatically liable even if the consumer proves that it prepared an inaccurate credit report because the FCRA "does not make reporting agencies strictly liable for all inaccuracies." *Id.* A credit reporting agency is not liable under the FCRA if it followed "reasonable procedures to assure maximum possible accuracy," but nonetheless reported inaccurate information in the consumer's credit report. *Henson,* 29 F.3d at 284. The Commentary of the Federal Trade Commission to the FCRA, 16 C.F.R. pt. 600, app., section 607 at 3.A, states that the section does not hold a reporting agency responsible where an item of information, received from a source that it reasonably believes is reputable, turns out to be inaccurate unless the agency receives notice of systemic problems with its procedures.

Experian has provided an account of its procedures. The affidavit of David Browne, Experian's compliance manager, explains that the company gathers credit information originated by approximately 40,000 sources. The information is stored in a complex system of national databases, containing approximately 200 million names and addresses and some 2.6 billion trade lines, which include information about consumer accounts, judgments, etc. The company processes over 50 million updates to trade information each day. Lenders report millions of accounts to Experian daily; they provide identifying information, including address, social security number, and date of birth. The identifying information is used to link the credit items to the appropriate consumer. Mr. Browne also notes that Experian's computer system does not store complete credit reports, but rather stores the individual items of credit information linked to identifying information. The credit report is generated at the time an inquiry for it is received.

One can easily see how, even with safeguards in place, mistakes can happen. But given the complexity of the system and the volume of information involved, a mistake does not render the procedures unreasonable. In his attempt to show that Experian's procedures are unreasonable, Sarver argues that someone should have noticed that only the Cross Country accounts were shown to have been involved in bankrupt-

---

1. Although no one disputes that our Lloyd Sarver never filed for bankruptcy, a "Lloyd Sarver" did so in 1997 in the United States Bankruptcy Court for the Middle District of Pennsylvania.

cy. That anomaly should have alerted Experian, Sarver says, to the fact that the report was inaccurate. What Sarver is asking, then, is that each computer-generated report be examined for anomalous information and, if it is found, an investigation be launched. In the absence of notice of prevalent unreliable information from a reporting lender, which would put Experian on notice that problems exist, we cannot find that such a requirement to investigate would be reasonable given the enormous volume of information Experian processes daily.

We found in *Henson* that a consumer reporting agency was not liable, as a matter of law, for reporting information from a judgment docket unless there was prior notice from the consumer that the information might be inaccurate. We said that a contrary rule of law would require credit reporting agencies to go beyond the face of numerous court records to determine whether they correctly report the outcome of the underlying action. Such a rule would also require credit reporting agencies to engage in background research which would substantially increase the cost of their services. In turn, they would be forced to pass on the increased costs to their customers and ultimately to the individual consumer. *Henson,* 29 F.3d at 285. The same could be said for records from financial institutions. As we said, in his affidavit Mr. Browne proclaims, and there is nothing in the record to make us doubt his statement, that lenders report many millions of accounts to Experian daily. Sarver's report, dated August 26, 2002, contains entries from six different lenders. The increased cost to Experian to examine each of these entries individually would be enormous. We find that as a matter of law there is nothing in this record to show that Experian's procedures are unreasonable.

Accordingly, we AFFIRM the judgment of the district court.

Notes

1. Should credit bureaus have an obligation to know what is in their files? How comfortable would a lawyer be arguing that a client need not be aware of the contents of its files? Would it be possible for credit bureaus to develop software that would search for anomalies such as the one in *Sarver* and flag them for human attention? Would doing so substantially increase the cost of the services provided by credit bureaus, the fear that appeared to motivate the *Sarver* court? Would it be relevant if credit bureaus already have software that searches for other anomalies, such as apparent attempts to take out car loans by six-year olds? Are consumers better served by bearing the increased costs the *Sarver* court fears, or by increasing the likelihood that errors in credit records are caught?

2. The FCRA did not abolish common law defamation actions for false information in consumer reports, but it did codify the qualified privilege. See FCRA § 1681h(e). In addition, in Thornton v. Equifax, Inc., 619 F.2d 700 (8th Cir.), cert. denied, 449 U.S. 835, 101 S.Ct. 108, 66 L.Ed.2d 41 (1980), the court held that a federal standard, not a state standard, was to be used under this section to determine whether sufficient malice had been estab-

lished to get past the privilege. The appropriate federal standard was held to be that used in the famous case of New York Times Co. v. Sullivan, 376 U.S. 254, 84 S.Ct. 710, 11 L.Ed.2d 686 (1964): knowledge that the report was false or reckless disregard of whether it was false. Since common law actions were invariably unsuccessful even before the FCRA, perhaps consumers haven't lost much by this provision. For further discussion of these issues, see Maurer, Common Law Defamation and the Fair Credit Reporting Act, 72 Georgetown L.J. 95 (1983).

3. Credit bureau processes for handling disputes with consumers are reportedly highly automated. According to one commentator, employees typically are able to devote only a few minutes to each disputed item. When a consumer disputes an item, an employee will often submit the dispute to the creditor electronically; the creditor's computer then determines if the disputed entry is identical to the information in the creditor's records, and if it is, the creditor reports to the credit bureau that the information has been verified. Evan Hendricks, Credit Scores & Credit Reports 161–63 (2d ed. 2005). Does this procedure satisfy the FCRA? Would you counsel consumers to request in their complaint letter that a human being personally review the matter?

4. The Consumer Data Industry Association ("CDIA"), an industry trade association, provided information to the General Accounting Office on dispute reinvestigations by the three major credit bureaus during various periods in 2002. According to the CDIA, the original item was verified as reported in 46% of the disputes, while the item was modified, updated or deleted in accordance with the furnisher's instructions in 37.5% of the disputes. U.S. GAO, Consumer Credit: Limited Information Exists on Extent of Credit Report Errors and Their Implications for Consumers 8 (2003).

5. As the title of the GAO Report referred to in the preceding note suggests, the GAO concluded that available information is not sufficient to provide a comprehensive assessment of overall credit report accuracy. Perhaps not surprisingly, industry and consumer organizations differ about the frequency of errors in consumer reports. Industry representatives told the GAO that "an extremely small percentage of people" to whom credit reports were disclosed identified an error in the reports. Id. at 6. By contrast, a Consumer Reports evaluation of 63 credit reports found serious inaccuracies in more than half. Your Money; Credit Reports, Consumer Rep. July 2000 at 52. Another study of credit reports concluded that "tens of millions of consumers are at risk of being penalized for incorrect information in their credit report[s] * * *. Almost one in ten consumers runs the risk of being excluded from the credit marketplace altogether because of incomplete records, duplicate reports, and mixed files." Consumer Federation of America & National Credit Reporting Association, Credit Score Accuracy and Implications for Consumers 37, 39 (2002). See also Robert Avery, Paul Calem, Glenn Canner & Raphael Bostic, An Overview of Consumer Data and Reporting, Federal Res. Bull. 47, 71 (Feb. 2003) (about 70% of reports omitted at least one credit limit); US PIRG, Mistakes Do Happen: A Look at Errors in Consumer Credit Reports 4 (June 2004) (25% of credit reports reviewed in study contained serious errors).

6. Errors creep into credit reports for a variety of reasons. One common reason is that information about one person is incorrectly attributed to another. For example, in Sheffer v. Experian Information Solutions, 249 F.Supp.2d 560 (E.D.Pa. 2003), the plaintiff's credit report erroneously reported his death after his file was merged with the file of a deceased consumer. Repeated complaints to the credit bureau—including some by the supposedly-deceased plaintiff himself—elicited the response that the credit bureau had reinvestigated the matter and that the creditor had verified the report of the plaintiff's death. Such errors may occur because of similarities in names or other identifying information. Under what circumstances would such a mix-up violate the FCRA?

7. Do credit reports that are technically accurate but could nevertheless be misleading pass muster under the FCRA? For example, in Koropoulos v. Credit Bureau, Inc., 734 F.2d 37 (D.C. Cir. 1984), plaintiff paid off a loan after having defaulted on it. The credit bureau's code on plaintiff's credit report could have been interpreted both to mean that the plaintiff had paid off the debt and that he had not. The Court of Appeals found that there was a genuine issue of fact as to whether the report was too misleading to satisfy the statutory requirement of "maximum possible accuracy." On the other hand, other courts have found that technically accurate information was sufficient. See, e.g. Heupel v. Trans Union LLC, 193 F.Supp.2d 1234 (N.D.Ala. 2002). Should the standard differ from that for deception under the FTC Act? Why or why not?

8. In Wantz v. Experian Information Solutions, 386 F.3d 829 (7th Cir. 2004), plaintiff complained of errors in his credit file but could not show that the credit bureau he sued (as opposed to some other credit bureau) had issued a report containing the error. In affirming a grant of summary judgment for the credit bureau, the court wrote:

> [W]ithout a consumer report, there is no duty under the Act to follow reasonable procedures. * * * [W]here there is no evidence of disclosure to a third party, the plaintiff cannot establish the existence of a consumer report. Without such a report, there could be no duty to follow reasonable procedures regarding the report, nor could damages flow from a breach of that duty.

If the consumer's files contains inaccurate data but the credit bureau does not issue an inaccurate report, is the consumer damaged?

9. The following problem picks up on two themes of this section. First, notice that the problem deals with the obligations of a furnisher of information (typically, a creditor) rather than a credit reporting agency. Do the obligations of these two different types of entities differ? One explanation for any differences may stem from the fact that until the 1996 amendments to the FCRA, Congress had imposed few obligations on furnishers of information. As for the second theme, does the statute give consumers a private claim to enforce all the provisions illustrated in the problem? Both themes are also apparent in the *Johnson* case.

Problem 4–3

(a) Darnay followed up his actions in the preceding problem by writing to some of the creditors which had reported that he had defaulted on credit obligations and requesting an investigation. Darnay stated in his letters that he had not incurred the charges attributed to him. Some of these creditors initially reviewed only their credit card records without comparing Darnay's signature to the signature on the receipts, and concluded that the charges were in fact Darnay's. Does Darnay have a claim against the lenders whose investigation was limited to reviewing their credit card records? See FCRA § 1681s–2(b); Johnson v. MBNA America Bank.

(b) Darnay also asked the creditors to furnish him with copies of the credit applications they claimed he had submitted to them. Some creditors complied, but others did not. Does Darnay have a claim against the lenders who refused to turn over the credit applications to him? See FCRA § 1681g(e).

JOHNSON v. MBNA AMERICA BANK

United States Court of Appeals for the Fourth Circuit, 2004.
357 F.3d 426.

WILLIAM W. WILKINS, Chief Judge. MBNA America Bank, N.A. (MBNA) appeals a judgment entered against it following a jury verdict in favor of Linda Johnson in her action alleging that MBNA violated a provision of the Fair Credit Reporting Act (FCRA), *see* 15 U.S.C.A. § 1681s–2(b)(1) (West 1998) (amended Dec. 4, 2003), by failing to conduct a reasonable investigation of Johnson's dispute concerning an MBNA account appearing on her credit report. Finding no reversible error, we affirm.

I.

The account at issue, an MBNA MasterCard account, was opened in November 1987. The parties disagree regarding who applied for this account and therefore who was legally obligated to pay amounts owed on it. It is undisputed that one of the applicants was Edward N. Slater, whom Johnson married in March 1991. MBNA contends that Johnson was a co-applicant with Slater, and thus a co-obligor on the account. Johnson claims, however, that she was merely an authorized user and not a co-applicant. In December 2000, Slater filed for bankruptcy, and MBNA promptly removed his name from the account. That same month, MBNA contacted Johnson and informed her that she was responsible for the approximately $17,000 balance on the account. After obtaining copies of her credit report from the three major credit reporting agencies— Experian, Equifax, and Trans Union—Johnson disputed the MBNA account with each of the credit reporting agencies. In response, each credit reporting agency sent to MBNA an automated consumer dispute verification (ACDV). The ACDVs that Experian and Trans Union sent to MBNA specifically indicated that Johnson was disputing that she was a co-obligor on the account. *See* J.A. 278 (Experian) ("CONSUMER STATES BELONGS TO HUSBAND ONLY"); *id.* at 283 (Trans Union) ("WAS NEVER A SIGNER ON ACCOUNT. WAS AN AUTHORIZED

USER"). The ACDV that Equifax sent to MBNA stated that Johnson disputed the account balance.

In response to each of these ACDVs, MBNA agents reviewed the account information contained in MBNA's computerized Customer Information System (CIS) and, based on the results of that review, notified the credit reporting agencies that MBNA had verified that the disputed information was correct. Based on MBNA's responses to the ACDVs, the credit reporting agencies continued reporting the MBNA account on Johnson's credit report.

Johnson subsequently sued MBNA, claiming, *inter alia,* that it had violated the FCRA by failing to conduct a proper investigation of her dispute. *See* 15 U.S.C.A. § 1681s–2(b)(1). A jury trial was held, and, following the presentation of Johnson's case, MBNA moved for judgment as a matter of law. That motion was denied. After the close of the evidence, the jury found that MBNA had negligently failed to comply with the FCRA, and it awarded Johnson $90,300 in actual damages. MBNA renewed its motion for judgment as a matter of law, asserting that § 1681s–2(b)(1) only required MBNA to conduct a cursory review of its records to verify the disputed information. Alternatively, MBNA argued that even if it were required to conduct a reasonable investigation of Johnson's dispute, the evidence showed that MBNA had met that obligation. The district court again denied MBNA's motion, concluding that § 1681s–2(b)(1) required MBNA to conduct a reasonable investigation and that there was sufficient evidence from which the jury could conclude that MBNA had failed to do so.

II.

MBNA first maintains that the district court erred in ruling that § 1681s–2(b)(1) requires furnishers of credit information to conduct a reasonable investigation of consumer disputes. Section 1681s–2(b)(1) imposes certain duties on a creditor who has been notified by a credit reporting agency that a consumer has disputed information furnished by that creditor:

> After receiving notice pursuant to section 1681i(a)(2) of this title of a dispute with regard to the completeness or accuracy of any information provided by a person to a consumer reporting agency, the person shall—
>
> > (A) conduct an investigation with respect to the disputed information;
> >
> > (B) review all relevant information provided by the consumer reporting agency . . . ;
> >
> > (C) report the results of the investigation to the consumer reporting agency; and
> >
> > (D) if the investigation finds that the information is incomplete or inaccurate, report those results to all other consumer reporting agencies to which the person furnished the informa-

tion and that compile and maintain files on consumers on a nationwide basis.

We recognize that the FCRA applies not only to those that furnish and report consumer credit information but also to those that furnish and report certain other types of information regarding consumers. *See* 15 U.S.C.A. § 1681a(d)(1) (West 1998 & Supp.2003). Thus, consistent with other provisions of the FCRA, § 1681s–2(b) uses the general terms "furnisher[ ] of information" and "consumer reporting agency." However, because of the specific nature of this case, and for ease of reference, in this opinion we use the terms "creditor" and "credit reporting agency." Nonetheless, our discussion of § 1681s–2(b)(1) and other FCRA provisions applies equally to those who furnish other types of consumer information.

MBNA argues that the language of § 1681s–2(b)(1)(A), requiring furnishers of credit information to "conduct an investigation" regarding disputed information, imposes only a minimal duty on creditors to briefly review their records to determine whether the disputed information is correct. Stated differently, MBNA contends that this provision does not contain any qualitative component that would allow courts or juries to assess whether the creditor's investigation was reasonable. By contrast, Johnson asserts that § 1681s–2(b)(1)(A) requires creditors to conduct a reasonable investigation. * * *

The key term at issue here, "investigation," is defined as "[a] detailed inquiry or systematic examination." *Am. Heritage Dictionary* 920 (4th ed.2000); *see Webster's Third New Int'l Dictionary* 1189 (1981) (defining "investigation" as "a searching inquiry"). Thus, the plain meaning of "investigation" clearly requires some degree of careful inquiry by creditors. Further, § 1681s–2(b)(1)(A) uses the term "investigation" in the context of articulating a creditor's duties in the consumer dispute process outlined by the FCRA. It would make little sense to conclude that, in creating a system intended to give consumers a means to dispute—and, ultimately, correct—inaccurate information on their credit reports, Congress used the term "investigation" to include superficial, *un* reasonable inquiries by creditors. *Cf. Cahlin v. Gen. Motors Acceptance Corp.,* 936 F.2d 1151, 1160 (11th Cir.1991) (interpreting analogous statute governing reinvestigations of consumer disputes by credit reporting agencies to require reasonable investigations); *Pinner v. Schmidt,* 805 F.2d 1258, 1262 (5th Cir.1986) (same). We therefore hold that § 1681s–2(b)(1) requires creditors, after receiving notice of a consumer dispute from a credit reporting agency, to conduct a reasonable investigation of their records to determine whether the disputed information can be verified.

III.

MBNA next contends that even if § 1681s–2(b)(1) requires creditors to conduct reasonable investigations of consumer disputes, no evidence here supports a determination by the jury that MBNA's investigation of

Johnson's dispute was unreasonable. We review the denial of MBNA's motion for judgment as a matter of law de novo. *See Baynard v. Malone,* 268 F.3d 228, 234 (4th Cir.2001). We must view the evidence in the light most favorable to Johnson, the nonmovant, and draw all reasonable inferences in her favor without weighing the evidence or assessing the witnesses' credibility. *See id.* at 234–35. "The question is whether a jury, viewing the evidence in the light most favorable to [Johnson], could have properly reached the conclusion reached by this jury." *Id.* at 235 (internal quotation marks omitted). We must reverse if a reasonable jury could only rule in favor of MBNA; if reasonable minds could differ, we must affirm.

As explained above, MBNA was notified of the specific nature of Johnson's dispute—namely, her assertion that she was not a co-obligor on the account. Yet MBNA's agents testified that their investigation was primarily limited to (1) confirming that the name and address listed on the ACDVs were the same as the name and address contained in the CIS,[3] and (2) noting that the CIS contained a code indicating that Johnson was the sole responsible party on the account. The MBNA agents also testified that, in investigating consumer disputes generally, they do not look beyond the information contained in the CIS and never consult underlying documents such as account applications. Based on this evidence, a jury could reasonably conclude that MBNA acted unreasonably in failing to verify the accuracy of the information contained in the CIS.

MBNA argues that other information contained in the CIS compels the conclusion that its investigation was reasonable. For example, in support of its alleged belief that Johnson was a co-applicant, MBNA presented evidence that Johnson's last name had been changed on the account following her marriage to Slater and that Johnson's name was listed on the billing statements. But this evidence is equally consistent with Johnson's contention that she was only an authorized user on Slater's account and that, to the extent MBNA's records listed her as a co-obligor, those records were incorrect. MBNA also points to evidence indicating that, during her conversations with MBNA following Slater's bankruptcy filing, Johnson attempted to set up a reduced payment plan and changed the address on the account to her business address. However, a jury could reasonably conclude that this evidence showed only that Johnson had tried to make payment arrangements even though she had no legal obligation to do so. Indeed, Johnson testified that, during her conversations with MBNA, she had consistently maintained that she was not responsible for paying the account.

Additionally, MBNA argues that Johnson failed to establish that MBNA's allegedly inadequate investigation was the proximate cause of her damages because there were no other records MBNA could have

3. Under MBNA's procedures, agents are only required to confirm two out of four pieces of information contained in the CIS—name, address, social security num- ber, and date of birth—in order to verify an account holder's identity. Johnson's social security number and date of birth were not listed on the CIS summary screen.

examined that would have changed the results of its investigation. In particular, MBNA relies on testimony that, pursuant to its five-year document retention policy, the original account application was no longer in MBNA's possession. Even accepting this testimony, however, a jury could reasonably conclude that if the MBNA agents had investigated the matter further and determined that MBNA no longer had the application, they could have at least informed the credit reporting agencies that MBNA could not conclusively verify that Johnson was a co-obligor. *See* 15 U.S.C.A. § 1681i(a)(5)(A) (West 1998) (providing that if disputed information "cannot be verified, the consumer reporting agency shall promptly delete that item of information from the consumer's file or modify that item of information, as appropriate, based on the results of the reinvestigation") (amended Dec. 4, 2003).

IV.

MBNA next asserts that the district court improperly instructed the jury regarding the standards for determining liability. * * *

A.

MBNA first argues that the district court erred in instructing the jury that, in determining whether MBNA's investigation was reasonable, it should consider "the cost of verifying the accuracy of the information versus the possible harm of reporting inaccurate information." J.A. 767–68. MBNA apparently contends that the balancing test described in this instruction is inapplicable here because it is derived from cases involving the reasonableness of a *credit reporting agency's* reinvestigation, *see, e.g., Cushman v. Trans Union Corp.,* 115 F.3d 220, 225 (3d Cir.1997); *Henson v. CSC Credit Servs.,* 29 F.3d 280, 287 (7th Cir.1994). We recognize that creditors and credit reporting agencies have different roles and duties in investigating consumer disputes under the FCRA. Nevertheless, we believe that the general balancing test articulated by the district court—weighing the cost of verifying disputed information against the possible harm to the consumer—logically applies in determining whether the steps taken (and not taken) by a creditor in investigating a dispute constitute a reasonable investigation. The district court therefore did not abuse its discretion in giving this instruction.

B.

MBNA also contends that, after instructing the jury that the FCRA "does not require that credit card account records, including original applications, be kept in any particular form," J.A. 770, the district court erred in further instructing the jury that "the law does prohibit MBNA from maintaining its record[s] in such manner as to consciously avoid knowing that information it is reporting is [in]accurate," *id.* MBNA claims that this instruction improperly permitted the jury to assess the adequacy of MBNA's record keeping system. However, the other detailed instructions given by the district court made clear that Johnson's claim was based on MBNA's failure to conduct a reasonable investigation of its records, not on the inadequacy of those records. And, it appears that the brief instruction challenged by MBNA, which the district court gave near the end of its jury instructions, was simply intended to clarify the legal effect of MBNA not maintaining the original account application—not to invite the jury to independently assess MBNA's record keeping practices.

MBNA further claims that the challenged instruction improperly incorporated a legal standard from another provision of § 1681s–2, relating to the accuracy of information that creditors provide to credit reporting agencies. *See* 15 U.S.C.A. § 1681s–2(a)(1)(A) (West 1998) (prohibiting creditors from furnishing consumer information to a credit reporting agency "if the [creditor] knows or consciously avoids knowing that the information is inaccurate") (amended Dec. 4, 2003). MBNA emphasizes that this provision is enforceable only by government agencies and officials, not by consumers. *See* 15 U.S.C.A. § 1681s–2(d) (West 1998) (amended Dec. 4, 2003). Again, however, the extensive instructions by the district court made clear that Johnson's claim was based on MBNA's duty to investigate consumer disputes, not its duty to provide accurate information. Indeed, the district court instructed the jury that the damages recoverable by Johnson "may not include any damages that were caused by the inaccuracy of the information itself." J.A. 768. We therefore conclude that the instruction given by the district court did not mislead the jury or otherwise prejudice MBNA.

V.

For the reasons set forth above, we affirm the judgment of the district court.

Notes

1. How did Congress determine which rights given consumers by the FCRA can be privately enforced and which should not be?

2. Plaintiff in Farren v. RJM Acquisition Funding, LLC, 2005 WL 1799413 (E.D.Pa. 2005), claimed that RJM, a furnisher of credit information, had not conducted a reasonable investigation. The court found as a matter of law that the furnisher's procedures did indeed satisfy the statutory mandate. The court described the procedures as follows:

> (1) the RJM representative writes the RJM account number that corresponds with the account referenced in the CDV on the top right hand corner of the CDV; (2) RJM's representative compares all of the identity factors provided in the CDV to the identity factors in RJM's data file; (3) RJM's representative reviews the reason for the dispute indicated by the Debtor on the CDV; (4) RJM's representative reviews the activity on the account to determine whether the collector notes contained anything that would indicate that the information RJM had received from Fingerhut when the account was acquired was not accurate; and (5) a RJM supervisor reviews the work of the representative to ensure the representative had verified the Account Information as RJM reports it.

Plaintiff argued that RJM should have checked with the plaintiff, obtained more information from a credit bureau, verified the plaintiff's address and date of birth, or examined information outside its own database. The court rejected this argument, explaining that "The statute does not require RJM or any data furnisher to take extraordinary means to investigate and *discover* disputed information but rather calls for a more passive investigation where the data furnisher is determining only that the information provided to it matches the information in its records."

Problem 4–4

Darnay has now carefully reviewed several credit applications made in his name that were sent to him by creditors. As Darnay suspected, the applications were submitted by identity thieves. One application was made to an Illinois car dealership. Darnay has never been to Illinois. The application gave two different addresses for Darnay—both erroneous— stating in one place that he lived on North First Street and in another that he lived on South First Street. It also said that his telephone number was in the 300 area code even though no such area code exists in the continental United States. Finally, Darnay's last name was misspelled on the credit application. The dealership granted the loan and later reported that Darnay had defaulted on it. Does Darnay have a claim against the Illinois dealership for attributing damaging information to him? See FCRA §§ 1681s–2(a)(1)(A), 1681s–2(c), (d); Gorman v. Wolpoff & Abramson, LLP, 370 F.Supp.2d 1005 (N.D.Cal. 2005). If not, could the state in which he lives sue on his behalf and obtain damages for him? If he could show that the dealer had acted maliciously in reporting his default, would he be able to bring an action under the state common law of defamation? See §§ 1681h(e); 1681t(b)(1)(F).

Note

The FCRA accuracy requirements for furnishers of information contrast sharply with the accuracy requirements for credit bureaus, both in their complexity and content. Under § 1681s–2(a)(1)(A), a furnisher may not supply information to a consumer reporting agency that it knows or has reasonable cause to believe is inaccurate. Subsection (a)(1)(D) defines reasonable cause to believe information is inaccurate as meaning "specific knowledge, other than solely allegations by the consumer, that would cause a reasonable person to have substantial doubts about the accuracy of the information." So far, so good. But subsection (a)(1)(C) has an exception: furnishers of information are not held to the standards of (a)(1)(A) if they clearly and conspicuously provide consumers an address consumers can use to report inaccuracies. Finally, subsection (a)(1)(B) provides that if a consumer has notified the furnisher of a genuine error at the address the furnisher has identified for such notices, the furnisher may not report the erroneous information. This last requirement applies regardless of whether the furnisher fits within the (a)(1)(C) exception and does not provide for an exception in situations in which the furnisher reasonably believes the information to be accurate. Would you advise a furnisher of information to take advantage of the (a)(1)(C) exception? If so, how would you advise it to provide "clear and conspicuous" notice to consumers of its address for receiving reports of errors? Would Congress have done better to require that furnishers of information use "reasonable procedures to assure maximum possible accuracy" as it did for credit bureaus? Why do you suppose it did not? To make matters even more complex, do consumers have a private claim to enforce the provisions of the statute against furnishers of information? How easy would it be for an unassisted consumer to navigate through these provisions?

Problem 4–5

After putting in a considerable amount of time and money, Darnay persuaded each creditor listed on the credit report that he did not incur the debts run up by the identity thieves. Recently, however, Darnay noticed that several of the erroneous entries previously deleted from his credit record have reappeared. Does Darnay have a claim against the credit reporting agencies or creditors for reporting previously-deleted erroneous information? See FCRA § 1681i(a)(5)(B), (C).

Problem 4–6

Should the lenders have notified Darnay that they had sent damaging information about him to the credit bureau? See FCRA § 1681s–2(a)(7)(A)(ii). Would a lender have to notify Darnay if it secured a credit report on Darnay? See FCRA § 1681s–2(a)(7)(G)(i).

Problem 4–7

Darnay asked the credit bureaus to place a fraud alert in his credit report; initially one credit bureau balked at the request, but ultimately it and the others agreed. Does Darnay have a right to have a fraud alert placed in his credit report? See FCRA § 1681c–1(a)(1). What types of fraud alerts are available? How long do they last? What does Darnay have to do to get a fraud alert? Under what circumstances would you advise a client to ask for a fraud alert?

Problem 4–8

Notwithstanding the fraud alert, several new and damaging entries have appeared in Darnay's credit report. Apparently identity thieves have continued to obtain credit in Darnay's name. Does Darnay have a claim against the lenders who lent after the fraud alert appeared on his credit report? See FCRA § 1681c-1(h)(1)(B)(i).

Note

Consumers are not the only ones who are hurt by identity theft. When a lender loans to an identity thief, it cannot recover the money from the impersonated consumer and usually cannot obtain it from the thief either, sometimes because the thief cannot be located and other times because the thief has no assets. Accordingly, lenders have a considerable stake in reducing identity theft. In that light, why was it necessary for Congress to enact the FACTA safeguards? For example, wouldn't it have been in the interest of the financial industry to create and respect fraud alerts without legislative intervention?

Note on Data Protection

Identity thieves need a certain amount of information to impersonate their victims. Names and Social Security numbers are of particular value. Sometimes the thieves obtain the consumer's information directly from the consumer or from papers discarded by consumers (so-called "dumpster diving"). But other times thieves obtain the information from sources to which the victim provided the information in the normal course of business, as in the *Andrews* case below. The thief may, for example, hack into a merchant's computer system or purchase the information from a faithless employee of an enterprise.

This matter has drawn more attention since 2003 when a California statute took effect. The statute obliges merchants that conduct business in California to disclose security breaches of computerized data systems that result in an unauthorized person acquiring the unencrypted personal data of California residents. Cal.Civ.Code § 1798.82. See also Cal.Civ.Code § 1798.81.5(b) ("A business that owns or licenses personal information about a California resident shall implement and maintain reasonable security procedures and practices appropriate to the nature of the information * * *."). What advice would you give a consumer who received notice that her data had been compromised? Would you counsel a company that had experienced such a security breach to notify only its California customers (and customers in other states that have enacted a California-like statute), or to notify its non-California customers as well? Would you advise a California company to disclose that it had suffered a security breach if the breach involved access to paper files rather than to a computerized data system? Why should the California statute treat paper files differently from computerized files? See Thomas H. Skinner, California's Database Breach Notification Security Act: The First State Breach Notification Law is Not Yet a Suitable Template for National Identity Theft Legislation, 10 Richmond J.L. & Tech. 1 (2003). Compare N.C. Gen. Stat. § 75–65 (extending coverage to paper records).

In the wake of the California statute, many other states adopted similar legislation while numerous enterprises—including, ironically, the FTC—have reported that outsiders had obtained access to personal information in their possession. Of perhaps immediate interest to law students will be the fact that some university records have been compromised, See Thieves, Hackers Gain Access to University Files, Consumer Fin.Serv.L.Rept., Apr. 20, 2005 at 18, but in fact the information of tens of millions of consumers may have been obtained by outsiders.

Is the California statute wise policy? One study estimated that the benefits of providing notice to those whose data have been compromised ranges between $7.50 and $10 per person and that the costs of notification programs are likely to exceed that amount. Thomas M. Lenard & Paul H. Rubin, An Economic Analysis of Notification Requirements for Data Security Breaches 3, 16 (2005). See also Ponemon Institute, Lost Customer Information : What Does a Data Breach Cost Companies 2 (2005) (survey concludes that cost of recovering from data breach—including opportunity costs caused by lost customers—averages $140 per lost customer record). In light of evidence suggesting that few breaches result in harmful misuse of data, see Fred H. Cate, Information Security Breaches and the Threat to Consumers 4 (2005), are consumers better off if companies notify them of the breaches? Would you want to know if your data had been compromised? Is this an area better left to state legislation for the time being, or is federal regulation more appropriate? For a proposed solution to the problem, see Daniel J. Solove & Chris Jay Hoofnagle, A Model Regime of Privacy Protection, 2006 Ill. L. Rev. 357 (2006).

Would a consumer who had been victimized by an identity thief have a claim against the source of the identity thief's information? On what theory? Compare Vincent R. Johnson, Cybersecurity, Identity Theft, and the Limits of Tort Liability, 57 S.C.L. Rev. 255 (2005) (arguing that courts should create common law tort claim and suggesting that a private claim could be based on some state data protection statutes) with Guin v. Brazos Higher Educ. Service Corp., Inc., 2006 WL 288483 (D.Minn. 2006) (granting summary judgment in favor of firm in negligence claim when a laptop containing unencrypted consumer information was stolen from an employee's home and there was no evidence that plaintiff had been a victim of identity theft or that plaintiff's personal information had been accessed). If the source had adopted a privacy policy promising to maintain the security of the information, the consumer might have a claim based on breach of that promise, but what if the source had not adopted such a policy? Two developments shed light on the issue. The first is Bell v. Michigan Council 25, 2005 WL 356306 (Mich. App.), appeal denied, 474 Mich. 989, 707 N.W.2d 597 (Mich. 2005). The plaintiffs, union members, sued the union after the daughter of the union's treasurer stole their identities. Both the treasurer and her daughter had brought union records home from the union's office. The court, over a dissent, concluded that a "special relationship" existed between the union and its members which required the union to adopt safeguards to protect the security of information about the members which could be used to appropriate their identity.

The second development is a series of data security cases brought by the FTC using its unfairness power. In one such case, In re B.J.'s Wholesale Club, Inc., 2005 WL 2395788 (F.T.C. 2005), the FTC charged that B.J's failure to take appropriate security measures enabled unauthorized persons to obtain access to customer information and use that information to make fraudulent purchases. The matter terminated in a consent decree under which B.J.'s agreed to establish a comprehensive security program. B.J's and cases like it demonstrate that the FTC believes that a company's failure to take adequate steps to safeguard customer information constitutes an unfair practice, at least in some circumstances, even when the company has not made any promises about privacy to the public. That in turn may have some significance for private claims under state UDAP statutes. Of course, the FTC may also use its deception power to proceed against companies that make deceptive claims about the security they provide for consumer information. Summaries of FTC cases and consent decrees based upon a deception theory may be found at Anne P. Forntey & Lisa C. DeLessio, Federal Laws Applicable to Consumer Data Security Breaches, 59 Consumer Fin. L.Q. Rep. 229 (2005).

Several federal statutes and regulations are also relevant. As will be discussed in the next subsection, the FCRA limits access to consumer reports. FACTA added to the FCRA a provision on disposal of consumer records. See § 1681w. Regulations implementing the provision can be found at 16 C.F.R. Part 682. The Gramm–Leach–Bliley Act, to be discussed in Chapter Five, also imposes on financial institutions obligations to keep certain consumer information confidential. Pursuant to the authority granted by that statute, a number of federal agencies banded together to promulgate a Rule imposing obligations on financial institutions to protect consumer information. This Rule, codified at various C.F.R. provisions, may be found at 66 Fed. Reg. 8616 (Feb. 1, 2001). An FTC Safeguards Rule also appears at 16 C.F.R. Part 314. Federal agencies have stated that financial institutions should notify affected customers upon discovering that information has or may have been misused. See Dept. of Treasury, Fed.Res.Sys., Fed. Deposit Ins. Corp., Interagency Guidance on Response Programs for Unauthorized Access to Customer Information and Customer Notice, 70 Fed. Reg. 15,736 (2005). The FTC has also urged financial institutions to consider notifying customers of breaches. See FTC, Financial Institutions and Customer Data: Complying with the Safeguards Rule, available at http://www.ftc.gov/bcp/conline/pubs/buspubs/safeguards.htm.

Problem 4–9

There are two guys from Syracuse named James Andrew O'Brian and James Andre O'Brian. James Andrew is a lawyer who continuously over estimates his future income. He bought a BMW, but could not keep up the payments, and it was repossessed. He bought a ritzy townhouse — same story. He now has $9,000 in unpaid entertainment bills on his American Express card.

James Andre, on the other hand, has no blemishes on his credit record at all. He just graduated from plumber school, and wants to take a well-earned motoring vacation out West. He applied to Amoco, Exxon–Mobil and Texaco for credit cards. All three companies ask for credit reports from the Credit Bureau Co. (CBC) on "James A. O'Brian", because this is how James Andre filled in their application forms. Exxon and Texaco receive reports from CBC on James Andre's credit record, and promptly issue credit cards to him. Amoco, however, receives from CBC a report on James Andrew's credit record, and promptly denied the credit card application, giving a proper notice as required by FCRA.

If James Andre inquires of CBC, will he learn about the information Amoco received, or only what is in *his* file? See FCRA § 1681g(a). Since all the information in his file is correct, there seems to be no perceptible problem. However, one piece of information will be *missing* from James Andre's file: there is no record in it of CBC furnishing a report to Amoco. How likely is he to notice that? Note that his attorney should note the discrepancy and pursue it. Does that give you a better appreciation of the reasons for FCRA § 1681g(a)(3)? If CBC's mistake is discovered, can James Andre force it to send a new report to Amoco? Would James Andre have a claim against either CBC or Amoco?

3. INVASIONS OF PRIVACY: WHO CAN SEE YOUR REPORT?

Problem 4–10

In Problem 4–4 above, would Darnay have a claim against the credit reporting agencies for providing Darnay's credit report to the lenders to whom the imposter applied for credit? See FCRA § 1681b(a)(3)(A); Andrews v. TRW.

ANDREWS v. TRW, INC.

United States Court of Appeals for the Ninth Circuit, 2000.
225 F.3d 1063, reversed on other grounds, sub nom. TRW Inc. v. Andrews,
534 U.S. 19, 122 S.Ct. 441, 151 L.Ed.2d 339 (2001).

NOONAN, CIRCUIT JUDGE:

Adelaide Andrews (Andrews) appeals the judgment by the district court in her suit against TRW, Inc. The case involves the rights under the Fair Credit Reporting Act, 15 U.S.C. §§ 1681–1681u (1994 & Supp. II) (FCRA), and Cal. Bus. & Prof.Code § 17200 et. seq. (1996), of a person claiming to be damaged by the disclosure of inaccurate credit information by a consumer credit reporting agency such as TRW.

We hold that Andrews's suit was not barred by § 1681p. We further hold that it was not a question of law but a question to be resolved by the jury as to whether TRW had reason to believe that it was furnishing information in connection with a consumer transaction involving Andrews. For these reasons we reverse the partial summary judgments awarded TRW on the first of Andrews's claims. As to the claims that did go to trial and ended in judgment against her after trial, we find no harmful error and affirm.

FACTS

In June 1993, Andrea Andrews (hereafter the Imposter) obtained the social security number and California driver's license number of Adelaide Andrews (hereafter the Plaintiff). The Imposter did so simply by misusing her position as a doctor's receptionist and copying the information that the Plaintiff, as a patient in that office, supplied to the doctor.

In 1994–1995 the Imposter applied for credit to four companies subscribing to TRW's credit reports. For example, on July 25, 1994, to First Consumers National Bank (FCNB), the Imposter applied as Andrea A. Andrews, 3993–1/2 Harvard Blvd., Los Angeles, CA, 90062, phone 213–312–0605, employed at Spensor Robbyns Products, Los Angeles. The Imposter gave the birth date and social security number of the Plaintiff. In this application the only misinformation was the Imposter's use of the Plaintiff's social security number and date of birth. On October 28, 1994 to Express Department Stores the Imposter made a comparable credit application, using her own identity except for the Plaintiff's social security number. Again, in January 1995, to Commercial Credit the Imposter applied for credit, using her own identity, except for Plaintiff's social security number and a clumsy misspelling of her first name as "Adeliade."

TRW responded to the credit inquiries of the three companies by treating the applications as made by the Plaintiff. TRW furnished the information in its file on the Plaintiff and added the three inquiries to the Plaintiff's file.

Each of the credit applications applied for by the Imposter was turned down by the company getting the TRW report. In addition, the Imposter applied for cable service to a public utility, Prime Cable of Las Vegas, which was required by law to provide cable services but nonetheless asked for a TRW report. The Imposter applied as Andrea Andrews, 4201 S. Decatur #2202, Las Vegas, NV, 89103, Phone 248–6352. The Imposter used the social security number of the Plaintiff, which was the only stolen item of identity provided. This account became delinquent and was referred to a collection agency.

The Plaintiff, however, became aware of the Imposter only on May 31, 1995 when she sought to refinance the mortgage on her home. The bank from which the financing was sought received a report from Chase Credit Research, not a party to this case, whose report combined information from TRW and two other credit reporting agencies. Now aware of the fraud, Andrews contacted TRW and requested deletion from her file of all reference to the Imposter's fraudulent activities. TRW complied.

PROCEEDINGS

On October 21, 1996, the Plaintiff filed this suit in the district court. In her first claim she alleged that TRW had furnished credit reports without "reasonable grounds for believing" that she was the consumer whom the credit applications involved, contrary to 15 U.S.C. §§ 1681b and 1681e(a), and that as a consequence she had suffered damages including an expenditure of time and money and "commercial impairment, inconvenience, embarrassment, humiliation, and emotional distress including physical manifestations." In her second claim, she alleged that TRW had violated § 1681e by not maintaining the "reasonable procedures" required by that statute in order "to assure maximum possible accuracy of the information concerning the individual about whom the report relates." 15 U.S.C. § 1681e(b). She alleged the same damages. She asserted that both violations were willful and that both also violated Cal. Bus. & Prof.Code § 17200 et. seq. She sought actual and punitive damages and an injunction requiring TRW to comply with the Fair Credit Reporting Act by "requiring a sufficient number of corresponding points of reference" before disseminating an individual's credit history or attributing information to an individual's credit file.

On May 28, 1998, the district court granted partial summary judgment to TRW. The court held that the two year statute of limitations provided by § 1681p began to run at the time the alleged wrongful disclosures of credit information were made to the requesting companies.

By this test the complaint was too late as to the disclosures made to FCNB and to Prime Cable. As to the disclosures made to Express and Commercial, the court ruled that they were made for a purpose permissible under § 1681b(a)(3)(A), because the Plaintiff, even against her will, was "involved" in the credit transaction initiated by the Imposter. Any other rule, the court said, would place "too heavy a burden on credit reporting agencies." In addition, the court ruled that TRW had used the "reasonable procedures" required by § 1681e(a) to limit disclosures to permissible purposes. For these several reasons, the court granted summary judgment to TRW on the Plaintiff's first claim.

The court also struck Plaintiff's claim for punitive damages on both her first and second causes of action. The court ruled that the Plaintiff had produced no evidence of TRW's conscious disregard of reasonable procedures. In so ruling, the court did not consider the testimony of Dr. Douglas Stott Parker, the Plaintiff's expert on computers or the testimony of Evan Hendricks, the Plaintiff's expert on the prevalence of identity theft. TRW then moved in limine to bar from testifying at trial the Plaintiff's witness Douglas Stott Parker, offered as an expert on the Plaintiff's second claim that TRW's procedures were not reasonable in assuring maximum possible accuracy. Relying in part on its earlier rulings, the district court ordered that Parker not testify as to procedures leading to inaccuracy in TRW disclosing the Plaintiff's information upon the Impostor's applications.

The case proceeded to trial on the Plaintiff's second and third claims. The jury returned a verdict for TRW. The Plaintiff appeals the consequent judgment on all her claims.

ANALYSIS

[The court's discussion of the statute of limitations issue, which was subsequently overturned by the Supreme Court, is omitted. The limitations provision was later amended by Congress in FACTA.]

Disclosure Without Reasonable Belief. Under § 1681b. TRW could only furnish a report on a consumer to a customer which it had "reason to believe" intended to use the information in connection with "a credit transaction involving the consumer on whom the information is to be furnished." 15 U.S.C. § 1681b(a)(3). Did TRW have a reasonable belief that the Plaintiff was the consumer involved in the credit transactions as to which the four companies sought a report from TRW? As the district court observed, there are 250,000,000 persons in the United States (not all of them having Social Security numbers) and 1,000,000,000 possibilities as to what any one Social Security number may be. The random chance of anyone matching a name to a number is very small. If TRW could assume that only such chance matching would occur, it was reasonable as a matter of law in releasing the Plaintiff's file when an application matched her last name and the number. But we do not live in a world in which such matches are made only by chance.

We take judicial notice that in many ways persons are required to make their social security numbers available so that they are no longer private or confidential but open to scrutiny and copying. Not least of these ways is on applications for credit, as TRW had reason to know. In a world where names are disseminated with the numbers attached and dishonest persons exist, the matching of a name to a number is not a random matter. It is quintessentially a job for a jury to decide whether identity theft has been common enough for it to be reasonable for a credit reporting agency to disclose credit information merely because a last name matches a social security number on file.

In making that determination the jury would be helped by expert opinion on the prevalence of identity theft, as the district court would have been helped if it had given consideration to the Plaintiff's witnesses on this point before giving summary judgment. The reasonableness of TRW's responses should also have been assessed by a jury with reference to the information TRW had indicating that the Imposter was not the Plaintiff. TRW argues that people do use nicknames and change addresses. But how many people misspell their first name? How many people mistake their date of birth? No rule of law answers these questions. A jury will have to say how reasonable a belief is that let a social security number trump all evidence of dissimilarity between the Plaintiff and the Imposter.

The district court held that the Plaintiff was involved in the transaction because her number was used. The statutory phrase is "a credit transaction involving the consumer." 15 U.S.C. § 1681b(a)(3)(A). "Involve" has two dictionary meanings that are relevant: (1) "to draw in as a participant" or (2) "to oblige to become associated." The district court understood the word in the second sense. We are reluctant to conclude that Congress meant to harness any consumer to any transaction where any crook chose to use his or her number. The first meaning of the statutory term must be preferred here. In that sense the Plaintiff was not involved.

Another consideration for the district court was that a different rule would impose too heavy a cost on TRW. The statute, however, has already made the determination as to what is a bearable cost for a credit reporting agency. The cost is what it takes to have a reasonable belief. In this case that belief needed determination by a jury not a judge. We reinstate the Plaintiff's first claim together with her request for punitive damages based upon it. * * *

Note

California has enacted a statute which provides that credit bureaus cannot furnish information to retail sellers unless the credit bureau matches "with a reasonable degree of certainty," at least three "categories of identifying information" within the credit bureau's file on the consumer to information provided to the credit reporting agency by the seller. Cal.Civ. Code § 1785.14(a)(1). Identifying information can include the consumer's name, date of birth, driver's license number, place of employment, current residence address, previous residence address, or social security number. Subsection (a)(2) of the statute also requires credit applicants appearing in person to submit a photo identification to the seller.

Problem 4–11

Dirk and Payne, attorneys, represented opposing parties in a case filed by Payne's client. In an attempt to impugn Payne's integrity, Dirk, who also owns a retail business in connection with which he extends credit, procured Payne's credit report from Credit Bureau and submitted it to the court. Does Payne have a valid claim under the FCRA against Dirk and Credit Bureau? See FCRA 1681a(d), 1681b, 1681e, 1681n, 1681q; Klapper v. Shapiro, 154 Misc.2d 459, 586 N.Y.S.2d 846 (N.Y.Sup. 1992).

Dirk defends by arguing that the FCRA simply does not apply to this report. Under the definition in FCRA 1681a(d), Dirk argues, a report is a "consumer report" only if it is issued for credit, insurance, employment, or "other purposes authorized under section 1681b." Since this report was not issued for any of the listed purposes, it is outside the scope of the FCRA, and Payne has no remedy. As Payne's counsel, how do you respond?

Problem 4–12

Nott's Used Cars routinely obtains the credit reports of anyone who walks into its showroom inquiring about its cars. Nott's uses the information to steer consumers to cars likely to be within their price range. Is anything wrong with this practice?

Notes

1. The FCRA permits credit bureaus to supply lenders with lists of consumers who meet certain criteria specified by the lender so that the lender may send the consumers solicitations for loans. If you have received a credit card solicitation in the mail, chances are that it is the result of such "prescreening." Prescreening will be covered more fully in Chapter Six.

2. Under the FCRA, must a consumer consent before a creditor obtains a report from a credit bureau? A number of states have enacted statutes permitting consumers to bar access to their credit reports unless the consumer gives permission. Some, like the California statute, Cal.Civ.Code § 1785.11.2, extend to all consumers, while others, like the Texas statute, Tx.Bus. & Com. §§ 20.034—20.039, may only be used by identity theft victims. This procedure, called a security freeze was conceived as an anti-identity theft measure. A model state statute, titled "The CLEAN Credit and Identity Theft Protection Act: Model State Laws," which includes a security freeze provision, as well as others, was produced by Public Interest Research Groups & Consumers Union in 2005.

3. A consumer sues a creditor because of inaccuracies in his credit report about a closed account. The creditor obtains the credit report to

evaluate the validity of the consumer's claim. Did the creditor violate the FCRA? See Hinton v. USA Funds, 2005 WL 730963 (N.D.Ill. 2005).

4.   Privacy issues will also be discussed in Chapter Five.

4.   MORE ON THE DEFINITIONS OF CONSUMER REPORT AND CONSUMER REPORTING AGENCY

Most of the provisions of the FCRA apply only to consumer reports issued by consumer reporting agencies. Consequently, the definitions of those phrases are important to determining the applicability of the statute. The definitions are interdependent: to be a consumer report, a report must be issued by a consumer reporting agency, while to be a consumer reporting agency, one must issue consumer reports. Notice that the statute refers to "consumer reports," not the more commonly used "credit report."

Problem 4–13

Klinger has just moved out of an apartment he rented from Potter. Potter claims Klinger owes him $150 for repairs and cleaning, but Klinger disputes that he owes any money to Potter.

Potter is a member of RentCheck, an association of local landlords which maintains files on all local tenants. All of the information in RentCheck's files comes from those landlords. Potter reports to Rent-Check that Klinger is a "messy tenant who did not properly clean the premises at the end of the rental term when he left."

Klinger now goes to several other landlords seeking to rent an apartment. Each landlord checks with RentCheck to determine whether there is a file on Klinger and what it says. After hearing what was in the file, each landlord turned Klinger down, but said nothing about Rent-Check or its files to Klinger.

Has anyone violated the FCRA? Note that the information on Klinger had nothing to do with his *creditworthiness*. Does that matter? See FCRA 1681a(d), (f), (k), 1681b, 1681m; Cotto v. Jenney, 721 F.Supp. 5 (D.Mass. 1989).

Problem 4–14

If a Law School reports to employers that a student has been charged with Honor Code violations, is the School a credit reporting agency and is the information a consumer report?

Notes

1.   The definition of consumer report excludes reports containing only information about transactions between the consumer and the provider of the information itself. As a result, a report by a lender solely on its own experiences with its borrowers would not qualify as a consumer report. Accordingly, a lender which furnished only such reports would not be a consumer reporting agency. See, e.g., DiGianni v. Stern's, 26 F.3d 346 (2d Cir. 1994).

2. Trans Union Corp. v. FTC, 245 F.3d 809 (D.C.Cir. 2001), cert. denied, 536 U.S. 915, 122 S.Ct. 2386, 153 L.Ed.2d 199 (2002), involved target marketing lists sold by a credit bureau. The lists consisted of names and addresses of consumers who met specified criteria, such as having taken out particular loans or having credit cards. The FTC determined that the lists were consumer reports because purchasers of a list would know that those on it met the criteria. The Commission ordered the credit bureau to cease selling the lists because target marketing is not a permitted use for a consumer report under the FCRA. The court denied the credit bureau's petition for review. Does it make sense that a list of names and addresses would qualify as a consumer report? If so, would a telephone directory also be a consumer report?

Note on Preemption Under the FCRA

Preemption under the FCRA is just as complicated as any other aspect of the statute, as Problem 4–4 *supra* suggests. See FCRA § 1681t. The general preemption provision appears in subsection (a) and resembles many other preemption provisions: it precludes application only of state laws that are inconsistent with the FCRA. But § 1681t(b) also preempts any state law that regulates any subject matter pertaining to many of the specific provisions of the FCRA, including the duties of furnishers of information used in consumer reports and prescreening. Finally, the section also exempts from its provisions a number of cited state statutes that might otherwise be preempted. For discussion of the scope of FCRA preemption, see Gail Hillebrand, After the FACTA: State Power to Prevent Identity Theft, 17 Loy. Consumer L. Rep. 53 (2004); Ann P. Fortney, Uniform National Standards for a Nationwide Industry—FCRA Preemption of State Laws Under the FACT Act, 58 Consumer Fin. L.Q.Rept.259 (2004).

Note on Constitutional Implications of Credit Reporting

In Chapter One, we considered the impact of the First Amendment's limited protection of commercial speech on the ability of the FTC and other government agencies to regulate advertising practices. While it may seem less immediately obvious, these same First Amendment issues are raised in the credit reporting context. After all, what is a credit report if not commercial speech? This raises the possibility that regulation of credit reporting practices, through the FCRA or otherwise, might be unconstitutional. In fact, in Equifax Services, Inc. v. Cohen, 420 A.2d 189 (Me. 1980), the Supreme Judicial Court of Maine held portions of the Maine credit reporting statute unconstitutional on these very grounds. The FCRA has fared better, however; Trans Union Corp. v. FTC, 245 F.3d 809, 818 (D.C.Cir. 2001), *cert. denied*, 536 U.S. 915, 122 S.Ct. 2386, 153 L.Ed.2d 199 (2002), upheld the statute against a First Amendment challenge, finding a substantial governmental interest in protecting the privacy of consumer credit information. The Court also rejected application of the strict scrutiny standard, given that individual credit reports address matters "solely of interest to the company and its business customers" instead of matters "of public concern."

5. CREDIT REPAIR ORGANIZATIONS

FEDERAL TRADE COMMISSION v. GILL

United States Court of Appeals, Ninth Circuit, 2001.
265 F.3d 944.

PAEZ, CIRCUIT JUDGE.

It has been said that bad credit is like a "Scarlet Letter." As Americans' reliance on credit has increased, so-called "credit repair clinics" have emerged, preying on individuals desperate to improve their credit records. These organizations typically promise they can have any negative information removed permanently from any credit report ... for a fee. On September 30, 1996, Congress enacted the Credit Repair Organizations Act ("CRO Act"), 15 U.S.C. §§ 1679–1679j, to ensure that the clinics provide potential customers with the information needed to decide whether to employ the services of such an organization and "to protect the public from unfair or deceptive advertising and business practices by credit repair organizations." 15 U.S.C. § 1679(b).

The Federal Trade Commission ("FTC" or "Commission") filed the instant action for injunctive and other equitable relief on March 2, 1998, against Defendants Keith H. Gill and Richard Murkey for alleged violations of the CRO Act and the Federal Trade Commission Act, 15 U.S.C. § 45(a). Defendants have, since 1995, offered services to remove any type of negative information from consumers' credit reports. Defendants promised a "free consultation," then demanded advance payment for their services.

The district court granted the FTC's motion for summary judgment, permanently enjoined Defendants from participating in the credit repair business, and ordered them to pay $1,335,912.14 as equitable monetary relief (consumer redress, restitution and/or disgorgement). Defendant Murkey raises several arguments on appeal: (1) triable issues of fact exist regarding the alleged false representations and acceptance of payment before services were rendered; * * * Defendant Gill similarly maintains that triable issues of fact exist regarding his alleged violations of the CRO Act and the FTC Act. * * *

We have jurisdiction under 28 U.S.C. § 1291, and we affirm.

RELEVANT STATUTES

A. Fair Credit Reporting Act

The FCRA limits the length of time that a CRA is permitted to report an adverse item of information. Generally, bankruptcies may be reported for ten years; all other negative information can remain on a report for up to seven years. 15 U.S.C. § 1681c(a). Older items are referred to as "obsolete."

The FCRA sets forth a procedure for disputing the completeness or accuracy of an item and obtaining a reinvestigation. When a consumer notifies a CRA of a disputed item, that agency has 30 days to "reinvestigate free of charge and record the current status of the disputed information, or delete the item from the file in accordance with paragraph (5), before the end of the 30–day period [.]" 15 U.S.C. § 1681i(a)(1)(A). * * *

B.   The Credit Repair Organizations Act

Enter the credit repair clinic. Congress had recognized the abuses by many of the newly emerging credit repair clinics well before it finally enacted the CRO Act in 1996. In 1988, Representative Frank Annunzio described these businesses as "kin to 'get rich quick' schemes. They promise fast results and newfound wealth in the form of available credit." 134 CONG. REC. H6707–06 (daily ed. August 9, 1988) (statement of Rep. Annunzio), 1988 WL 175220. The House Report on the Consumer Reporting Reform Act of 1994, the immediate predecessor to the Act passed in 1996, explained further:

> [T]hese credit repair businesses, through advertisements and oral representations, lead consumers to believe that adverse information in their consumer reports can be deleted or modified regardless of its accuracy ... however, accurate, adverse information may be reported for 7 years, or in the case of bankruptcy, 10 years. Therefore, such representations by credit repair clinics are often misleading. . . .

> Where credit repair clinics do succeed, however, they often do so through abuse of the reinvestigation procedures ... consumer reporting agencies must generally delete information that cannot be verified within 30 days of receiving notice of the dispute. Credit repair clinics take advantage of this provision by inundating consumer reporting agencies with so many challenges to consumer reports that the reinvestigation system breaks down, and the adverse, but accurate, information is deleted.

H.R. Rep. NO. 103–486 (1994), 1994 WL 164513. Thus, the CRO Act's express purposes are twofold: "(1) to ensure that prospective buyers of the services of credit repair organizations are provided with the information necessary to make an informed decision regarding the purchase of such services; and (2) to protect the public from unfair or deceptive advertising and business practices by credit repair organizations." 15 U.S.C. § 1679(b).

The CRO Act became effective on April 1, 1997. Of the prohibited practices listed in the CRO Act, three are involved in the instant appeal: Sections 1679b(a)(1), 1679b(a)(3), and 1679b(b). Section 1679b(a)(1) prohibits any person from mak[ing] any statement, or counsel[ing] or advis[ing] any consumer to make any statement, which is untrue or misleading (or which, upon the exercise of reasonable care, should be known by the credit repair organization, officer, employee, agent, or other person to be untrue or misleading) with respect to any consumer's credit worthiness [sic], credit standing, or credit capacity to (A) any consumer reporting agency.... 15 U.S.C. § 1679b(a)(1). Section 1679b(a)(3) prohibits any person from "mak[ing] or us[ing] any untrue or misleading representation of the services of the credit repair organization[.]" Finally, Section 1679b(b) provides that "[n]o credit repair organization may charge or receive any money or other valuable consideration for the performance of any service which the credit repair organization has agreed to perform for any consumer before such service is *fully* performed." 15 U.S.C. § 1679b(b) (emphasis added).

A violation of the CRO Act is to be treated as a violation of the FTC Act. 15 U.S.C. § 1679h(b).* * *

FACTUAL AND PROCEDURAL BACKGROUND

Defendant Keith H. Gill is licensed to practice law in California and works as a sole practitioner as the Law Offices of Keith Gill. In addition to a general legal practice, beginning in 1995, Gill has offered credit repair services to consumers, ostensibly through his law office, but in reality through defendant Richard Murkey. Defendants have used telephones, the U.S. Mail, and radio to advertise their credit repair services to consumers. Under the CRO Act, the Law Offices of Keith Gill qualifies as a "credit repair organization."

Most consumers signed contracts with Gill's law office, and both Gill and Murkey testified that they considered every consumer who signs a retainer agreement with the Gill law office to be Gill's client. Gill testified that his relationship with Murkey is governed by a written contract between the two.

From at least 1995 to 1999, Defendant Richard Murkey operated a credit repair business under the auspices and out of the offices of Defendant Gill's law offices in Woodland Hills, California.[4] Murkey never registered his credit repair business with the State of California or posted a bond, as required by California Civil Code § 1789.12(b)(5), ostensibly because he operated out of Gill's offices (attorneys are exempt from the registration requirement).

To reach potential credit repair clients, Defendants used radio broadcasts, newspaper ads, telephone conversations, and personal meetings throughout the United States. During 1997 and 1998, Murkey appeared regularly on a radio talk program broadcast throughout most of Southern California, discussing credit restoration. The format resembled a talk show, and when Murkey was not available, stations replayed the tapes, rather like a radio infomercial. He told consumers that any sort of negative information, including accurate and not obsolete information, could legally be removed from a consumer's credit report, notably, through the use of Defendants' services. Murkey repeated the telephone and facsimile numbers and encouraged consumers to call for a

---

4. Until 1990, Murkey practiced law. He resigned from the State Bar of California pending disbarment proceedings, including allegations that he had practiced law while under suspension and had committed multiple acts of misappropriation of client funds.

free credit evaluation or further information. Examples of claims made during the broadcasts include:

> "There literally is nothing a consumer can possibly have on a credit report that we cannot remove and we can remove it legally."

> "There [are] many legal ways under the Federal Fair Credit Reporting Act to fix credit, no matter what type of negative it is, including foreclosure and or bankruptcy, judgments, tax liens . . . even if those [items] are not paid off." * * *

> "It doesn't make a difference what type of negative [information] you have: We have files in our offices verifying that we can legally remove bankruptcies, foreclosures, what they call short pays in the real estate community, judgments, tax liens, surrenders, repossessions, defaulted student loans, charge-offs, settlements, collections and even late accounts for child support. . . . It does not make a difference if that item was legally put on there or not and to us it doesn't make a difference if you still owe money." * * *

> "Most likely, in our offices, we can clean your credit in six weeks to two months."

* * * Murkey and those working for him made similar representations to consumers via telephone. * * *

Murkey's face-to-face representations were no different. Consumers were told that for a nominal fee, based on the number and type of negative items, the negative information would be removed from their credit report in a matter of weeks or a few months.[6] Defendants deliberately did not ask, however, whether a negative item on a consumer's credit report was accurate or complete.

Murkey generally handled the initial consultation with prospective clients and made the payment arrangements. He explained the manner in which he could assist them in having negative information removed from a credit report, offered to show them results he had obtained for others, and explained the costs for his services. Although no services were performed during the initial "free" consultation, Defendants sought advanced payment of between 25 and 50% of the estimated costs of the services. Defendants generally gave consumers a written estimate based on a "fee schedule," with each negative item listed separately. At that point, Murkey would negotiate the "real" fee. After consumers

---

6. Murkey promoted Defendants' credit repair business through public appearances, including presentations to mortgage brokers and a bar association. He told one group of mortgage brokers that "99.9 percent of the time everything we take off stays off forever . . . we tell our clients this, and we put it in writing, if anything comes back on the credit report at all we'll take it off again for free." He added, "on average of all of our clients, at least half the nega-tives will be gone in the first six-week period." When a member of the audience asked how realistic it was for a client whose Chapter 7 bankruptcy had been discharged just six months ago to expect to have the bankruptcy removed from the credit report, Murkey responded "it's very realistic." He reassured the audience: "We do this 100 percent legally so your clients can sleep at night and so can I."

made the down payment, Defendants billed them on a regular basis, regardless of whether the services had been completed.

In fact, Defendants' "legal" process for "removing" negative information from their clients' credit reports was premised on the obligation of credit reporting agencies ("CRAs") to respond to all consumer disputes within 30 days. As set forth above, CRAs must remove any legitimately challenged item that they cannot verify within the 30 day period. If the CRA does verify the item, even after 30 days have passed, it can (and generally will) restore the item to the credit report.

Defendants' credit repair services consisted almost exclusively of inundating the credit reporting agencies with dispute letters, sent in the *consumer's* name, which falsely alleged that various items on the credit report were incorrect or that a particular account did not belong to the consumer. Consumers did not review or approve any of these letters and have stated that they did not authorize Defendants to provide false information to the CRAs. Defendants' letters did generate large volumes of correspondence from CRAs to the clients, however, which created the impression that Defendants were performing as promised. Many of the clients did not discover right away that Defendants' efforts failed to produce the promised results, however, in part because Defendants had instructed their clients to forward these communications directly to Defendants. When the clients learned that their credit report problems had not been resolved, they tried contacting Murkey, who rarely responded. Murkey nevertheless continued to bill the consumers.* * *

The FTC filed this action against Gill and Murkey on March 2, 1998, in the U.S. District Court for the Central District of California, seeking a permanent injunction and consumer redress. The Commission asserted three claims: (1) violation of the CRO Act by charging clients for services that were not fully performed; (2) violation of the CRO Act by making untrue or misleading statements to induce consumers to purchase their services; and (3) violation of the FTC Act by making untrue or misleading statements to induce consumers to purchase services. * * *

The FTC moved for summary judgment on August 30, 1999 * * *

After hearing argument on October 7, 1999, the district court granted the FTC's motion in its entirety on November 3, 1999. The court entered a permanent injunction prohibiting Defendants from participating in any aspect of the credit repair business, making certain representations to consumers regarding Defendants' credit repair services, reporting false or misleading information to a credit reporting agency, and otherwise violating the CRO Act. *Id.* at 1049–50. The court ordered Defendants to return payments received for any credit repair services performed pursuant to contracts entered before March 4, 1998, notably, for any consumer who did not sign a new retainer agreement following entry of the preliminary injunction. The district court ordered Defendants jointly and severally to pay the sum of $1,335,912.14 to the FTC as equitable monetary relief, including without limitation consumer redress, restitution and/or disgorgement. *Id.* at 1050. * * *

DISCUSSION

A. Genuine Issues of Triable Fact [Murkey and Gill]

Defendants both maintain that disputes exist regarding their purported false representation and acceptance of payment before rendering services. As the district court found, no such disputes exist.

1. False Representations

As a preliminary matter, violation of the CRO Act's prohibition against making or using any untrue or misleading representation of the services of the credit repair organization is not only a violation of the CRO Act, 15 U.S.C. § 1679b(a)(3), but also an unfair or deceptive act or practice in commerce in violation of section 5(a) of the FTC Act, 15 U.S.C. § 45(a). 15 U.S.C. § 1679h(b)(1). As the district court correctly observed, "liability attaches even if the representation made by the credit repair organization is not made 'for the purpose of induc[ing]' consumers to purchase a particular service or good." *FTC v. Gill,* 71 F.Supp.2d at 1038. All the FTC must show to establish violations of both acts, then, is an untrue or misleading statement regarding the services of the CRO.

* * *

In sum, Murkey fails to counter the FTC's substantial showing that he made statements and created an overall "net impression" that he could legally and permanently get negative information removed from consumers' credit reports, even if the information was accurate, complete, and not obsolete. These representations were false and constitute violations of both the CRO Act and the FTC Act.

2. Acceptance of Money

The CRO Act prohibits acceptance of *any* payment before fully performing all services (even assuming Murkey could and did do what he represented he would do). * * * In sum, we agree with the district court's finding that Murkey violated the CRO Act by accepting payment before he had fully performed the services.

Notes

1. Section 1681i(a)(3) of the FCRA permits credit bureaus to decline to conduct a reinvestigation of a consumer dispute if the credit bureau reasonably determines that the dispute is frivolous. Similarly, creditors may disregard disputes submitted by credit repair organizations under § 1681s–2(a)(8)(g).

2. The CROA, reprinted in the Statutory Supplement, is codified as Title IV of the Consumer Credit Protection Act at 15 U.S.C. § 1679 et seq. In addition to the provisions referred to in *Gill,* the CROA contains disclosure requirements designed to reduce the likelihood that credit repair entities can deceive consumers. Thus, § 1679c requires that credit repair agencies provide consumers with a written statement explaining, among

other things, their rights under the FCRA and CROA. CROA also requires credit repair organizations to provide consumers with a written contract and to allow consumers to cancel the contract within three days, under §§ 1679d, 1679e. The statute provides for enforcement by the FTC, states, or by private actions under §§ 1679g, 1679h. Many states have also passed similar statutes. Why did Congress regulate credit repair organizations instead of simply banning them? Given that, as *Gill* notes, misrepresentations by credit repair agencies already violate the FTC Act (and presumably UDAP statutes as well), why wasn't existing law good enough?

3.   Supporters of credit repair organizations claim that consumers need representatives to help deal with credit reporting agencies and the confusing maze of credit reports and the FCRA. Would you advise a friend who had credit problems to use one of these organizations? Can it do anything that your friend could not do for herself? Is your friend likely to understand all of her rights under the FCRA?

4.   Why did the court in *Gill* note that the defendants did not ask their clients whether negative items in the consumer's credit report were accurate or complete? See CROA § 1679b(a)(1).

5.   After *Gill*, would you advise an attorney to charge a client in advance for securing corrections in the client's credit report? See § 1679b(b).

SECTION B.   CREDIT DISCRIMINATION

1.   FOUNDATION: THE PRE–ECOA PROBLEM—DISCRIMINATION BY CREDITORS AND ITS EFFECTS ON THE AVAILABILITY OF CREDIT

Many consumer transactions offer little opportunity to discriminate. In the typical retail transaction, for example, prices are clearly marked and the seller cannot easily raise its prices for particular customers. But some merchants do have the power to discriminate. Automobile prices, for example, are often set through bargaining, and some evidence indicates that car dealers vary prices according to ethnicity and gender. See, e.g, Ian Ayres, Fair Driving: Gender and Race Discrimination in Retail Car Negotiations, 104 Harv. L. Rev. 817 (1991) ("white women had to pay forty percent higher markups than white men; black men had to pay more than twice the markup, and black women had to pay more than three times the markup of white male[s]."). Similarly, online merchants have been known to charge different prices to different consumers. See Janet Adamy, E–Tailers Can Target Prices Based on Customer Data, Lexington Herald–Leader (KY), Sept.16, 2000, at B1; Joseph Turow, Lauren Feldman, & Kimberly Meltzer, Open to Exploitation : American Shoppers Online and Offline 11 (2005). And of course, universities do not charge everyone the same price—they just call their discounts "scholarships."

Credit transactions also provide an opportunity for discrimination. Indeed, it is the very nature of a credit transaction for the creditor to be "discriminating" in its choice of customers: the creditor will want assurances that the borrower will be able (and disposed) to repay the credit as scheduled. The desire for this assurance prompts creditors to obtain credit reports and otherwise to evaluate the creditworthiness of the prospective borrower.

The process of determining creditworthiness has, in the past, been a very private and proprietary matter for most creditors. That is, they rarely advertise or publicize the details of their credit granting criteria, with the result that consumers often must apply for credit as supplicants, hopeful of the creditor's beneficence, and fearful that their qualifications should be found wanting in some unknown aspect. From the creditor's point of view, since it takes the risk of non-payment, it is entitled to set the qualifying standards.

This state of affairs might not give rise to concern were it not for three considerations. First, the judgments of loan officers or creditor actuaries are not infallible. Second, credit is no longer either a luxury to be dispensed by whim nor an opiate for the groveling poor—it has become a virtual necessity for most consumers, to purchase homes, automobiles, and the quality of lifestyle our society promises. Third, considerable evidence suggested that in deciding on loan applications, some lenders formerly (and, some would say, still do) took into account criteria such as the applicant's marital status, race, ethnicity, and gender. In this setting it becomes understandable that lawmakers should take an interest in assuring the fairest policies in credit granting and seek to bar discrimination on the basis of criteria seen as inappropriate.

Before the ECOA was enacted in 1974, there was much evidence of widespread discriminatory lending practices. The following material summarizes some of the evidence.

NATIONAL COMMISSION ON CONSUMER FINANCE, CONSUMER CREDIT IN THE UNITED STATES

152–54 (1972).

With respect to sex discrimination in the field of consumer credit, testimony presented at the hearings can be summarized as follows:

1. Single women have more trouble obtaining credit than single men. (This appeared to be more characteristic of mortgage credit than of consumer credit.)

2. Creditors generally require a woman upon marriage to reapply for credit, usually in her husband's name. Similar reapplication is not asked of men when they marry. * * *

3. Creditors are often unwilling to extend credit to a married woman in her own name. * * *

4. Creditors are often unwilling to count the wife's income when a married couple applies for credit. * * *

5. Women who are divorced or widowed have trouble reestablishing credit. Women who are separated have a particularly difficult time, since the accounts may still be in the husband's name.

The anecdotal evidence was supplemented by a survey of 23 commercial banks conducted by the St. Paul Department of Human Rights. A man and a woman with virtually identical qualifications applied for a $600 loan to finance a used car without the signature of the other spouse. Each applicant was the wage earner, and the spouse was in school. Eleven of the banks visited by the woman "either strictly required the husband's signature or stated it was their preference although they would accept an application and possibly make an exception to the general policy." When the same banks, plus two additional banks that would make no commitment to the female applicant, were visited by the male interviewer, six said that they would prefer both signatures but would make an exception for him; one insisted on both signatures; and six "told the male interviewer that he, as a married man, could obtain the loan without his wife's signature." * * *

RACIAL DISCRIMINATION

Historically, minority groups have faced discrimination in the nation's economic and social structures. * * *

Frederick D. Sturdivant, alone and in collaboration with Walter T. Wilhelm, narrowed exploration of a nationwide problem to the Los Angeles area. In "Poverty, Minorities and Consumer Exploitation," Sturdivant and Wilhelm found that credit charges were frequently used by merchants in ghetto areas of Los Angeles as a vehicle to practice economic, racial and ethnic discrimination against installment buyers. Their study indicated that economic discrimination was a feature of any type of ghetto marketplace, and that within those marketplaces price or credit discrimination might be practiced against other minorities who went outside their own area to shop in another ghetto business district. * * *

2. REGULATION OF OVERT DISCRIMINATION—THE BASIC ECOA SCHEME

In 1974, Congress responded to the findings of the National Commission on Consumer Finance and to other evidence of lending discrimination by enacting the Equal Credit Opportunity Act (ECOA), CCPA § 701 et seq., 15 U.S.C.A. § 1691 et seq. In its original form, ECOA prohibited discrimination only on the basis of sex and marital status. In 1976, however, it was broadened considerably, and ECOA now also prohibits discrimination on the basis of race, color, religion, national origin, age, receipt of public assistance benefits, and the good faith exercise of rights under the CCPA.

As with the Truth in Lending Act, the Federal Reserve Board has issued a set of implementing regulations and an official staff commentary interpreting ECOA. The regulations are known as Regulation B and are found at 12 C.F.R. Part 202. Both ECOA and Regulation B appear in the Statutory Supplement.

Problem 4–15

Dan Jones, recently divorced, and Dorie Smith, a single 24 year old assistant librarian, cohabit and apply jointly to First Federal Savings & Loan Association for a purchase money mortgage loan. Their application describes the $122,000 home they intend to purchase and notes Dan's salary of $37,000 and Dorie's of $25,600. Their respective credit histories, verified by First Federal, are flawless. Nonetheless, Dan and Dorie are turned down for their mortgage. Together they visit First Federal where the loan officer explains that its action is based on a corporate policy that it will not deal with people who are "living in sin," because it wishes to discourage such conduct.

Under any of the statutory or caselaw material we have seen thus far, do Dan and Dorie have any rights against First Federal? Would they have any rights under the Equal Credit Opportunity Act, discussed below? See ECOA § 701(a), 15 U.S.C. § 1691(a); Reg. B, 12 C.F.R. § 202.6(b)(8).

Problem 4–16

Dan and Dorie then apply to Second Federal Savings and Loan Association for a purchase money mortgage. Again, they are turned down. When they visit Second Federal, the accommodating loan officer explains that the association's action is based on an analysis of all of its mortgages over the past ten years. According to that analysis, single and recently divorced men are more likely to default than married men; and women in Dorie's age bracket tend to leave the work force after a few years to become mothers and housewives. In addition, the loan officer says, married couples are statistically much more stable obligors than unmarried co-applicants. All in all, he concludes, there is too much risk for the association in their application.

The association's required income for the mortgage Dan and Dorie seek is $62,000, which makes them a border-line case in any event. The association's 10–year analysis of its mortgages shows that, in over 10% of the instances involving employed women in Dorie's age bracket where the woman's income was necessary to meet the association's required income level, it soon ceased and the borrowers defaulted on their loans. Second Association discounted Dorie's income by 10%, as an experience factor, and therefore Dan and Dorie do not meet the income requirements.

Is there unlawful "discrimination" in this case? Is it unlawful in the constitutional sense of a deprivation of civil liberties under color of law, or only in an economic sense of an unfair application of criteria? If the latter, in what sense is it unfair?

Problem 4–17

Suppose, in Problem 4–15, that Dan and Dorie are both men. Their house costs the same as in Problem 4–15, their income figures are the same as for Dan and Dorie in Problem 4–15, and they are turned down for the same reason, and First refused to pool their incomes, so they did not meet First's income guidelines. Do Dan and Dorie have a claim under ECOA? Would it matter if Dan and Dorie were married or parties to a civil union?

Problem 4–18

Lucas Rosa, a biological male, applied for a loan at Park West Bank wearing traditionally feminine attire. A bank employee stated that she would not provide Rosa a loan application until Rosa "went home and changed." Does Rosa have a claim under ECOA? See Rosa v. Park West Bank & Trust Co., 214 F.3d 213 (1st Cir. 2000).

Notes

1. A number of state credit discrimination statutes prohibit discrimination on the basis of sexual orientation. See, e.g., N.Y. Exec. L. § 296–a(1)(a); Wis. Stat. § 224.77(1)(*o*).

2. How would you answer the creditor's argument in Problem 4–16 that it was simply concerned about the continuity of the plaintiffs' income? After all, isn't that something a creditor ought to be worried about?

MILLER v. AMERICAN EXPRESS CO.

United States Court of Appeals, Ninth Circuit, 1982.
688 F.2d 1235.

BOOCHEVER, CIRCUIT JUDGE:

Virginia Miller brought an action in district court alleging a violation of the Equal Credit Opportunity Act (ECOA), 15 U.S.C. §§ 1691 *et seq.,* after her American Express card was cancelled following the death of her husband. * * *

Maurice Miller, plaintiff's late husband, applied for and received an American Express credit card in 1966. His account was denominated a Basic Card Account. Later in 1966, plaintiff Virginia Miller applied for and was granted a supplementary card. Her application was signed by her husband as the basic cardholder and by her. Mrs. Miller agreed to be personally liable for all charges made on her supplementary card. Her card bore a different account number from her husband's card, was issued in her own name, required a separate annual fee, and bore a different expiration date from Mr. Miller's card. The Millers used their American Express cards until Mr. Miller passed away in May, 1979. Two months after her husband's death, Mrs. Miller attempted to use her card during a shopping trip and was informed by the store clerk that her account had been cancelled. This was the first notice she received of the cancellation. Subsequently, Amex informed her that her account had been cancelled pursuant to a policy of automatically terminating the account of a supplementary cardholder upon the death of a basic cardholder. Amex invited her to apply for a basic account. Her application for a new account consisted merely of filling out a short form, entitled "Request to Change Membership status from Supplementary to

Basic Card member,'' which did not require any financial or credit history data. Amex issued Mrs. Miller a new card, apparently on the basis of her thirteen year credit history in the use of the card it had just cancelled. Mrs. Miller brought suit against Amex for violation of the ECOA.

* * * The court awarded summary judgment to Amex without specifying its reasons.

ANALYSIS

The issues on this appeal are whether Amex's policy of cancelling a spouse's supplementary account upon the death of the basic cardholder violates the ECOA and whether a plaintiff must always show discriminatory intent or effect to establish an ECOA violation. The facts are undisputed, therefore, we must decide whether the substantive law was correctly applied. We hold that there has been credit discrimination within the meaning of the ECOA and that partial summary judgment on the issue of liability should have been granted to Mrs. Miller, rather than to Amex.

The ECOA makes it unlawful for any creditor to discriminate with respect to any credit transaction on the basis of marital status. 15 U.S.C. § 1691(a)(1). It also authorizes the Board of Governors of the Federal Reserve System (Board) to prescribe regulations, and creates a private right of action for declaratory and equitable relief and for actual and punitive damages.

In order to carry out the purposes of the ECOA, the Board promulgated the regulations codified at 12 C.F.R. §§ 201.1 *et seq.* Section 202.7(c)(1) provides that a creditor shall not terminate the account of a person who is contractually liable on an existing open end account on the basis of a change in marital status in the absence of evidence of inability or unwillingness to repay. Under certain circumstances, a creditor may require a reapplication after a change in the applicant's marital status. 12 C.F.R. § 202.7(c)(2).

Mrs. Miller's Amex card was cancelled after her marital status changed from married to widowed. Under § 202.7(c)(2), Amex could have asked her to reapply for credit, but instead it first terminated her card and then invited reapplication. There was no contention or evidence that her widowhood rendered Mrs. Miller unable or unwilling to pay, indeed, Amex's prompt issuance of a new card to her indicates that she was considered creditworthy.

Amex has argued that there was no violation of the ECOA for three reasons: that Section 202.7(c) was beyond the scope of the Board's authority, that Mrs. Miller was not "contractually liable on an existing open end account" within the meaning of § 202.7(c), and that the termination did not constitute discrimination on the basis of marital status because it occurred pursuant to a policy of automatic cancellation of all supplementary cardholders whether they were widow, widower, sibling, or child of the basic cardholder. We hold that § 202.7(c) was within the scope of the Board's authority under the ECOA, and that Mrs. Miller was within the protection of the regulation.

I

AUTHORITY FOR SECTION 202.7(c)

* * * Section 2.207(c) is directly addressed to one of the evils that the ECOA was designed to prevent: loss of credit because of widowhood. It was therefore within the discretion allowed the Board to define termination of credit as a result of the death of a spouse as credit discrimination.

II

APPLICATION OF SECTION 202.7(c)

A. Coverage of the Regulation: Contractual Liability on an Open End Account

By its terms, § 202.7(c) reaches only terminations of existing open end accounts on which the creditholder is contractually liable. * * * "Contractually liable" means "expressly obligated to repay all debts arising on an account by reason of an agreement to that effect." 12 C.F.R. § 202.2(i). Amex has argued that the reference to persons "contractually liable" was meant to exclude spouses who are only "users" of accounts. The Federal Reserve Board's comments, made when the "contractually liable" phrase was added in 1975, indicate that the phrase was designed to exclude a "user" who might be liable for a specific debt charged to a spouse's account, *"but [who] is not liable on the contract creating the account."* 40 Fed.Reg. 49,298 (1975) (emphasis added).

Mrs. Miller was not, however, merely a user of her husband's basic account. She was personally liable under the contract creating her supplementary account for all debts charged on her card by any person. For example, Mrs. Miller would have been personally liable for even charges made on her supplementary card by her husband, the basic cardholder.

Amex's cardholder agreement provides that "by either signing, using or accepting the Card, you will be agreeing with us to everything written here" and that "[i]f you are a Supplementary Cardmember, you are liable to us for all Charges made in connection with the Card issued to you * * *." This language made Mrs. Miller "contractually liable" for all debts on her supplementary account.

* * * [In] *Anderson v. United Finance Co.,* 666 F.2d 1274, 1277 (9th Cir.1982), * * * we held that there was credit "discrimination" within the meaning of the ECOA when a regulation promulgated under the ECOA was violated. No showing of any specific intent to discriminate was required. As another court has noted, not requiring proof of discriminatory intent is especially appropriate in analysis of ECOA violations because "discrimination in credit transactions is more likely to be of the unintentional, rather than the intentional, variety." *Cherry v. Amoco Oil Co.*, 490 F.Supp. 1026, 1030 (N.D.Ga.1980).

If specific intent is not proved, we nevertheless do not think that a statistical showing of an adverse impact on women is always necessary to the plaintiff's case. The ECOA's history refers by analogy to the disparate treatment and adverse impact tests for discrimination which are used in employment discrimination cases under Title VII. * * * Read in full, the Senate Report allows but does not limit proof of credit discrimination to the two traditional Title VII tests for employment discrimination. It also expressly recognizes that a creditor's conduct in an individual transaction may be considered to determine the existence of credit discrimination, quite apart from intent or from a statistical showing of adverse impact.

The conduct here was squarely within that prohibited by § 202.7(c). Mrs. Miller's account was terminated in response to her husband's death and without reference to or even inquiry regarding her creditworthiness. It is undisputed that the death of her husband was the sole reason for Amex's termination of Mrs. Miller's credit. Amex contends that its automatic cancellation policy was necessary to protect it from noncreditworthy supplementary cardholders. The regulations, however, prohibit termination based on a spouse's death in the absence of evidence of inability or unwillingness to repay. Amex has never contended in this action that the death of her husband rendered Mrs. Miller unable or unwilling to pay charges made on her card. The fact that the cancellation policy could also result in the termination of a supplemental cardholder who was not protected by the ECOA, such as a sibling or friend of the basic cardholder, does not change the essential fact that Mrs. Miller's account was terminated solely because of her husband's death. The interruption of Mrs. Miller's credit on the basis of the change in her marital status is precisely the type of occurrence that the ECOA and regulations thereunder are designed to prevent.

We hold that the undisputed facts show, as a matter of law, that Amex violated the ECOA and regulations thereunder in its termination of Mrs. Miller's supplementary card. For this reason, we reverse the district court's grant of summary judgment for Amex and instruct that partial summary judgment should be awarded to Mrs. Miller on the issue of liability. The case is remanded for further proceedings consistent with this opinion.

POOLE, CIRCUIT JUDGE, dissenting.

The majority today holds in effect that a credit practice need not be discriminatory to violate the Equal Credit Opportunity Act (the Act). Because this holding is contrary to the clear language and purpose of the Act, I respectfully dissent.

Applicability of § 202.7(c)

The majority correctly finds that the liabilities imposed upon supplementary cardholders are inconsistent with mere "authorized user" status.

Violation of § 202.7(c)

It is a fact that American Express cancelled appellant's supplementary card after the death of her husband. Section 202.7(c), however, does not prohibit the termination of an account after a change in an applicant's marital status; it prohibits only the termination of an account "on the basis of" such a change. Since the change in appellant's marital status was not the basis for American Express's decision to cancel her supplementary card, there has been no violation of § 202.7(c).

Notes

1. What damages did Virginia Miller suffer as a result of American Express' action?

2. The court refers to the "disparate treatment" and "disparate impact" tests for proving employment discrimination under Title VII. Here, the court holds that the discrimination in this case is so open that no such fact development is needed. Note that ECOA § 701(a), 15 U.S.C. § 1691(a), is stated in terms of a direct prohibition which does not require such indirect proof. However, not all discrimination will be so open. Where the discrimination is more disguised, courts have indeed used the disparate treatment and disparate impact tests which are treated later in this section.

Problem 4–19

Jane applied for an individual loan from Ace Finance. All credit checks and other verifications were done solely in Jane's name. Ace agreed to make the loan if she would put up her sailboat as security. The sailboat was jointly owned by Jane and her husband, Dick. As a result, Ace has asked you to advise it whether it can require the signature of both Jane and Dick on the security agreement without violating ECOA. If Ace also wanted Dick to sign the underlying promissory note, would your answer be the same? Secured credit issues are governed by Reg. B, 12 C.F.R. § 202.7(d)(4). Does that provision decide issues concerning both the security agreement and the note?

Problem 4–20

Dagwood and Blondie are separated, and divorce proceedings are pending. Blondie wants to buy her own home, and applied to Ace Savings and Loan for a home mortgage loan. Ace believes that Blondie's income is sufficient to support the amount of the mortgage, but it would also rely on the security of the mortgage interest in the house. It does not fully understand the impact of Dagwood's current relationship on that mortgage interest. Thus, it wants Dagwood to co-sign the mortgage and wants you to advise it whether a demand for Dagwood's signature would violate ECOA. See Reg. B, 12 C.F.R. § 202.7.

Problem 4–21

Susan, who receives a small amount of welfare to supplement her wages, recently applied to lease a car at Bull Motors so that she could commute to her job. Upon learning Susan's ethnicity, Bull sneered, "We don't lease to people of that sort or to welfare queens," and denied Susan's application. Does Susan have a claim under ECOA? See ECOA § 701a(d), 15 U.S.C. § 1691a(d); Brothers v. First Leasing, 724 F.2d 789 (9th Cir. 1984); Liberty Leasing Co. v. Machamer, 6 F.Supp.2d 714 (S.D.Ohio 1998). Would it matter if the lease were for a home? See Laramore v. Ritchie Realty Management Co., 397 F.3d 544 (7th Cir. 2005).

Notification of Adverse Action

Like the FCRA, the ECOA requires a creditor who has taken "adverse action" to send a notice to the credit applicant. See ECOA § 701(d), 15 U.S.C. § 1691(d) and Reg. B, 12 C.F.R. §§ 202.2 and 202.9. Failure to provide the notice violates ECOA even in the absence of discrimination. See Costa v. Mauro Chevrolet, Inc., 390 F. Supp. 2d 720 (N.D.Ill. 2005). Just what sort of notice must the creditor give?

Problem 4–22

Suppose that in Problem 3–2 in Chapter Three, after Vader called Luke to tell him that EAC was willing to finance the loan at 12%, Luke declined and Vader demanded return of the car. When Luke brought the car in the following day, Vader returned to him the value of the trade-in, less a deduction for the mileage Luke had driven the Tiemobile. Luke has not had any other communications from Vader in the six months since and has never heard from EAC. He asks you if he has an ECOA claim against Vader or EAC. Does he? Is Vader a creditor? See ECOA § 701(d), 15 U.S.C. § 1691(d); Reg. B, 12 C.F.R. §§ 202.2(c), 202.9(a) Bayard v. Behlmann Automotive Services, Inc., 292 F.Supp.2d 1181 (E.D.Mo. 2003).

Notes

1. The definition of "adverse action" under the FCRA in § 1681a(k) is broader than the ECOA definition. The FCRA definition incorporates the ECOA definition, but goes beyond it to include denials in connection with transactions to which ECOA would not normally apply, such as insurance, employment, and government benefits. The FCRA definition also contains a catch-all in § 1681a(k)(1)(iv): "an action taken or determination that is—(I) made in connection with an application that was made by, or a transaction that was initiated by, any consumer * * * and (II) adverse to the interests of the consumer." Does the catch-all extend to credit transactions, given that the ECOA definition incorporated into the FCRA definition would already include such transactions? If so, what credit transactions, if any, would be included within the FCRA definition that are not included within the ECOA definition? Notice that the catch-all does not require a denial, but rather

extends to an "action taken or determination." Why would Congress have wanted a broader definition for adverse action under the FCRA (which imposes an obligation to disclose that the adverse action was based on information contained in a credit report) than under ECOA (which imposes an obligation to disclose the reasons for an adverse action)? The 2003 FACTA Act added § 1681m(h) to the FCRA obliging lenders to notify consumers when credit is offered on "terms that are materially less favorable than the most favorable terms available to a substantial proportion of consumers." Is there a comparable requirement under ECOA?

2. The Fed's Commentary offers the following guidance on the definition of creditor in ¶ 202.2(*l*)–2:

> For certain purposes, the term creditor includes persons such as real estate brokers, automobile dealers, home builders, and home-improvement contractors who do not participate in credit decisions but who only accept applications and refer applicants to creditors, or select or offer to select creditors to whom credit requests can be made. These persons must comply with § 202.4(a), the general rule prohibiting discrimination, and with § 202.4(b), the general rule against discouraging applications.

When the Fed revised Reg. B and the comment to their current version in 2003, it provided the following explanation:

> Comment 2(*l*)–2 is intended to clarify that where the only role a person plays is accepting and referring applications for credit, or selecting creditors to whom applications will be made, the person meets the definition of creditor, but only for purposes of the prohibitions against discrimination and discouragement. For example, an automobile dealer may merely accept and refer applications for credit, or it may accept applications, perform underwriting, and make a decision whether to extend credit. Where the automobile dealer only accepts applications for credit and refers those applications to another creditor who makes the credit decision—for example, where the dealer does not participate in setting the terms of the credit or making the credit decision—the dealer is subject only to §§ 202.4(a) and (b) for purposes of compliance with Regulation B.

FISCHL v. GENERAL MOTORS ACCEPTANCE CORP.

United States Court of Appeals, Fifth Circuit, 1983.
708 F.2d 143.

POLITZ, CIRCUIT JUDGE:

Terry Fischl sued General Motors Acceptance Corporation (GMAC), alleging that its failure to furnish specific reasons for denying him credit, and to disclose that this denial was predicated in whole or part on information derived from a credit reporting agency, violated the Equal Credit Opportunity Act (ECOA), 15 U.S.C. § 1691 *et seq.*, Regulation B promulgated thereunder, 12 C.F.R. § 202, and the Fair Credit Reporting Act (FCRA), 15 U.S.C. § 1681 *et seq.* Following a bench trial, the district court entered judgment for GMAC. We reverse and remand.

FACTUAL AND PROCEDURAL BACKGROUND

On September 27, 1980, Fischl applied in writing to O.E. Harring, Inc., a New Orleans automobile dealership, for credit covering $12,000 of the $15,000 purchase price of a 1980 BMW automobile. A Harring salesman referred Fischl's credit application to GMAC, communicating the information by telephone. After transcribing this information on an application form, GMAC employees contacted Credit Bureau Services, a local credit reporting service, and obtained a consumer report on Fischl.

Both the application and the consumer report reflected that Fischl, a 27 year-old single homeowner, made mortgage payments of $564.80 per month. Although he held two sales jobs and earned a total monthly income of approximately $4,000, the credit report erroneously referred to one position as past employment. Credit references listed on the application were VISA, MasterCharge, Diner's Club and General Electric Credit Corporation. The credit report disclosed that Fischl had achieved an A–1 credit rating on current accounts with two area retailers, the New Orleans Public Service, First Homestead, and VISA or MasterCharge. An account in good standing with Sears, Roebuck and Company was mistakenly described in the report as a credit inquiry.

After reviewing the application and report, Robert Bell, GMAC's credit supervisor, determined that Fischl's credit background was deficient in terms of duration and extent; specifically, there were no sustained monthly payments of an amount comparable to that required to finance the purchase of the BMW. Based on these factors, Bell decided that credit at the level requested should not be extended, a decision approved by Lester Robinson, Bell's immediate superior.

On October 3, 1980, Fischl received a form letter from GMAC advising that his application had been rejected and noting, as the reason therefor, that "credit references are insufficient." The portion of the form letter designed to disclose the creditor's use of information from outside sources was marked "disclosure inapplicable." That same day, Fischl secured a copy of his credit report from Credit Bureau Services which reflected GMAC's inquiry. In subsequent telephone conversations with Bell and Robinson, both of which he initiated, Fischl learned that GMAC had received a consumer report from a credit reporting service. During these conversations, more specific reasons for the denial of credit were advanced and the name and address of the credit bureau were given. Shortly thereafter, Fischl secured a $12,000 loan from an area bank at a lower rate of interest than that offered by GMAC.

EQUAL CREDIT OPPORTUNITY ACT

The district court found that GMAC's adverse determination letter adequately informed Fischl of the basis for rejection of his credit application and, because the reason assigned therein was similar to one proposed in the Federal Reserve Board's (Board) model checklist, 12 C.F.R. § 202.9(b)(2), that the creditor was insulated from liability under 15 U.S.C. § 1691e(e). Fischl contends that the district court erred in holding that GMAC provided him with the specific reasons for credit denial mandated by 15 U.S.C. §§ 1691(b)(2) and (3) and Regulation B, 12 C.F.R. § 202.9. He argues that the reason cited in GMAC's adverse determination letter, "credit references are insufficient," does not afford notice of the actual grounds for the denial, to-wit, the brevity of his credit history and the excessiveness of the amount he wished to finance when measured against the size of his current credit obligations.

* * * [A] creditor electing to provide a statement of reasons for denial or termination of credit in accordance with § 1691(d)(2)(A) must apprise the applicant in writing of the specific reasons for its adverse action. Section 202.9(b)(2) reiterates the specificity requirement set forth in § 1691(d)(3), dictates the inclusion of the "principal" reasons for adverse action, and advises creditors that completion of the model form contained therein assures compliance with § 202.9(a)(2)(i). * * * With respect to the proper use of the sample form outlined in § 202.9(b)(2), the Board emphasized:

> The sample form is illustrative and may not be appropriate for all creditors. It was designed to disclose those factors which creditors most commonly consider. Some of the reasons listed on the form could be misleading when compared to the factors actually scored. In such cases, it is improper to complete the form by simply checking the closest identifiable factor listed. For example, a creditor that considers only bank references (and disregards finance company references altogether) should disclose "insufficient bank references" (not "insufficient credit references"). Similarly, a creditor that considers bank references and other credit references as separate factors should treat the two factors separately in disclosing reasons. The creditor should either add those other factors to the form or check "other" and include the appropriate explanation. In providing reasons for adverse action, creditors need not describe how or why a factor adversely affected an applicant. For example, the notice may say "length of residence" rather than "too short a period of residence."

12 C.F.R. § 202.901(f).

After considering the notice transmitted in light of the congressional language and purpose of § 1691(d), we find that GMAC's perfunctory reliance on the Board's sample checklist was manifestly inappropriate. While it resembles the category of "insufficient credit references" deemed acceptable by the Board, § 202.9(b)(2), the reason for refusal of credit noted by GMAC, "credit references are insufficient," arguably communicates a different meaning. The Board's statement connotes quantitative inadequacy; that of GMAC implies some qualitative deficiency in Fischl's credit status. GMAC's statement does not signal the nature of that deficiency and, since the name and address of the credit bureau was not supplied, did not provide the mandated opportunity for the applicant to correct erroneous information.

Assuming, *arguendo,* that GMAC's phrase "credit references are insufficient" conveys substantially the same message as its regulatory counterpart, the notice provided in this case fails to satisfy the informative purposes of the ECOA. Upon receipt of GMAC's adverse determination letter, Fischl found himself in the dilemma described by one commentator:

> The "insufficient credit references" reason has been severely criticized by rejected applicants because it fails to tell them how they can meet the creditor's requirements. The statement only raises the question of what "sufficient" is, and without further explanation, an applicant is left to speculate as to what will meet the creditor's standards.

Given that a combination of factors contributed to GMAC's adverse credit determination, the reason articulated was misleading, or at best excessively vague. *See Carroll v. Exxon Co., U.S.A.,* 434 F.Supp. 557 (E.D.La.1977). A GMAC employee acknowledged at trial that "many things can come under the definition of 'credit references are insufficient'." Being unaware of the creditor's minimum standards of creditworthiness, Fischl was unable to translate this reason into concrete criteria. He could neither improve his credit application, correct any misinformation in his credit record, or guard against discrimination, thus thwarting both the educational and protective objectives of the ECOA. GMAC's subsequent oral clarification of the factors which actually motivated its adverse decision did not remedy this omission. Consistent with the Board's recent admonition that the protection of § 1691e(e) may not be invoked where factors delineated in the sample checklist are misleading by comparison to those actually weighed, or do not coincide with those in fact relied upon, *see* 12 C.F.R. § 202.901(f), we conclude that GMAC's conduct fell squarely within that proscribed by § 1691(d) and Regulation B.

FAIR CREDIT REPORTING ACT

Fischl next argues that the district court erred in finding, first, that credit was not denied in whole or part on the basis of information contained in the consumer report issued by Credit Bureau Services, within the meaning of 15 U.S.C. § 1681m(a) and, second, that GMAC's oral disclosure of the name and address of the agency in response to Fischl's inquiry complied with the statute. Credit was not refused, in the district court's estimation, "because of information *in* the report; nothing adverse was there * * * [rather, Fischl] was denied credit, in a sense, for what was *not* in the report: there was not sufficient evidence * * * of his ability to sustain high monthly payments." (emphasis by the trial court.)

Section 1681m(a)'s disclosure requirement is triggered "[w]henever credit * * * for personal * * * purposes * * * is denied * * * either wholly or partly because of information contained in the consumer report from a consumer reporting agency * * *." * * * The purpose of the notification provision is to enable the subject of a consumer report to request disclosure from the reporting agency of the nature and scope of the information in his file.

Disclosure is not conditioned upon the creditor's consideration of derogatory or negative information in a consumer report in arriving at an adverse decision, so long as that decision is attributable wholly or in part to information in the report.

* * * Thus a creditor could, upon obtaining a consumer report, discover that a prospective borrower had established an excellent credit record over a period of years, yet determine that qualifications revealed in the report did not meet its own standards of creditworthiness. Under these circumstances, disclosure would be mandated.

Such is the case herein. Fischl's application for credit was denied in part because of information in a report prepared by a credit reporting service. This information was incomplete and misleading. The details of his credit history set forth in the report, when evaluated under GMAC's judgmental criteria, did not furnish a sufficient guarantee of financial responsibility to support an extension of credit in the amount sought. GMAC concluded that the record of Fischl's current obligations did not justify a prediction that he could successfully undertake the monthly payments contemplated.

Despite its reliance on data contained in the credit report, when reporting to Fischl via the form letter of October 3, 1980, GMAC did not disclose this information, advising instead that disclosure was inapplicable. This action did not comport with § 1681m(a). Similarly, GMAC's subsequent oral response to Fischl's inquiry, noting the name and address of the credit bureau, did not suffice under the statute. We need not and do not decide whether the notice required by § 1681m(a) must be written, nor do we decide the mandated timing for the notice. Those questions remain for another day.

REVERSED and REMANDED for further proceedings consistent herewith.

Note

1. Did Terry Fischl suffer any damages? Was he required to show any discrimination? Is the notice requirement just another of those "technical" rules that increases costs in credit transactions? What purpose does it serve? Does it have anything to do with discrimination?

2. Suppose that Haring had decided Fischl's application would not meet GMAC's standards for a loan and never forwarded the application to GMAC. Because GMAC never received the application, it had no obligation to send Fischl an adverse action letter. But would Haring have such an obligation? See Treadway v. Gateway Chevrolet Oldsmobile Inc., 362 F.3d 971 (7th Cir. 2004).

Problem 4–23

The Ace County Community Organization operates a small loan program for residents of Ace County and their family members. Decisions on whether to grant loans are made by Ace's treasurer, Buck N. Ham, a retired banker, according to his own "gut feeling" about the applicant. Ham has many years' experience at making such judgments, both at the bank and Ace and his "uncollectables" are low. In addition, Ham takes the usual data on applicants (income, length of time on the job, etc.), but this is not what he relies upon in "close cases."

Fleur D. Lee, a recent graduate with a promised $120,000/year job at Dewey, Cheatham, and Howe, applied to Ace for a $30,000 loan to buy a new BMW. Ham talked with her for about 10 minutes. During that time, he called her "girl" about a dozen times. The last time he did that, Fleur interrupted him and told him that that was an inappropriate and demeaning form of reference. The interview ended soon thereafter. Fleur has a spotless credit record, and her salary would meet Ace's requirements for a $30,000 loan.

Buck has a negative "gut feeling" about Fleur's application, and wants to decline it. He knows that, under ECOA, he will have to send her an "adverse action letter." He asks your advice as to what to say in the letter is the reason for denying the application.

(a) Would you advise Buck to state that Fleur's credit application was denied due to "short length of employment history" and "currently unemployed"? See Reg. B, 12 C.F.R. § 202.9, Reg. B Appendix C, and *Fischl*.

(b) Would you advise Buck to state that he has a "negative gut feeling" about the likelihood of repayment of this loan? See ECOA, 15 U.S.C. § 1691(a).

(c) Would you advise Buck not to state a specific reason for denial, but instead under Reg. B, 12 C.F.R. § 202.9(a)(2)(ii) to notify Fleur of her right to request a statement of specific reasons? Is this likely to solve Buck's problem, or only delay its resolution?

(d) Would you advise Buck to ignore his "gut feeling" and approve the credit application?

(e) Would you give none of the above as advice, and advance an alternative?

(f) Having made whatever advice you chose under (a)-(e), did it assist the policies underlying ECOA?

3. MODERN (POST–ECOA) CREDIT GRANTING SYSTEMS

Traditionally, creditors used their own subjective judgment as the "system" to evaluate the creditworthiness of their applicants. Credit officers in lending institutions relied on their past experience and perhaps on institutional guidelines in making their decisions. Such "judgmental systems" have been criticized, however. For example, critics charge that credit officials often have a poor or a distorted recollection of past experiences. Another potential problem is that institutional guidelines may be outdated and may not reflect large-scale changes in the applicant pool over time. Often these problems lead to inadvertent discrimination. See generally, Hsia, Credit Scoring and the Equal Opportunity Act, 30 Hastings L.J. 371 (1978).

More recently, the credit industry has developed new systems of evaluating credit applicants known as "credit scoring" and its descendant, automated underwriting. Fair Isaac Corporation is undoubtedly the leader in the credit scoring field. Its precise algorithms for calculating credit scores are proprietary and closely-held secrets, but some information is available. According to Fair Isaac's web site (www.myfico.com), about 35% of the credit score is determined by the consumer's credit history; about 30% by how much the consumer already owes; about 15% by the length of the consumer's credit history; and about 10% each by new credit entries (e.g., the number of recently opened accounts and recent credit inquiries) and the type of credit the applicant uses (e.g., credit cards and mortgages). Fair Isaac reportedly uses about two dozen characteristics in its credit scoring systems and has several different models that vary according to the type of credit sought, among other things. See Evan Hendricks, Credit Scores & Credit Reports 26–27 (2d ed. 2005). Different systems can produce different scores for the same individual, with obvious consequences for the individual's ability to obtain credit. See Consumer Federation of America & Nat'l Credit Reporting Ass'n, Credit Score Accuracy and Implications for Consumers 22 (2002). The three major credit bureaus all use slightly different credit scoring systems—though all three were designed by Fair Isaac—and some lenders also use their own systems. In addition the three major credit bureaus are developing their own system for calculating credit scores, to be called VantageScore. VantageScore's credit scores reportedly depend on payment history (32% of the score), utilization (23%) balances (15%), length of credit history (13%), recent credit (10%), and available credit (7%). See Damon Darlin, The Credit Game is Getting a Second Scorekeeper, N.Y. Times, July 8, 2006 at C6. How should a consumer behave if the same conduct raises her Fair Isaac score but lowers her VantageScore?

The description of credit scoring systems in the following article would undoubtedly seem primitive to today's credit granting industry. Though it is no longer an accurate portrayal of credit scoring, it still serves to illustrate how these systems are created and used.

NOEL CAPON, CREDIT SCORING SYSTEMS: A CRITICAL ANALYSIS

46 J. Marketing 82, 83–86 (1982).*

The basic procedure for developing credit scoring systems involves the selection of samples of goods and bads from the creditor's files. Upwards of 50, and as many as 300 * * * potential predictor characteristics are obtained from the application blank. A multivariate statistical technique such as regression or discriminant analysis * * * is employed, frequently in a stepwise manner, to identify those predictor characteristics, typically from eight to twelve, which contribute most to separation of the two groups. These selected characteristics, determined in part by the initial set of characteristics available from the application blank and in part by the data, and their point values are unique to an individual system. An example of a regionally based system of a major national retailer is shown in Table 1.

An applicant for credit is evaluated in a credit scoring system by simply summing the points received on the various application characteristics to arrive at a total score. This score may be treated in a number of ways depending on the system design. In the single cut-off method, the applicant's total score is compared to a single cut-off point score. If this score exceeds the cut-off, credit is granted; otherwise the applicant is rejected. * * *

TABLE 1

Major National Retailer's Final Scoring Table for Application Characteristics

Zip Code		Time at Present Address	
Zip Codes A	60	Less than 6 months	39
Zip Codes B	48	6 months–1 year 5 months	30
Zip Codes C	41	1 year 6 months–3 years 5 months	27
Zip Codes D	37	3 years 6 months–7 years 5	30
Not answered	53	7 years 6 months–12 years 5 months	39
Bank Reference		12 years 6 months or longer	50
Checking only	0	Not answered	36
Savings only	0		
Checking & Savings	15	Time with Employer	
Bank name or loan only	0	Less than 6 months	31
No bank reference	7	6 months–5 years 5 months	24
Not answered	7	5 years 6 months–8 years 5 months	26
Type of Housing		8 years 6 months–15 years 5 months	31
Own/buying	44	15 years 6 months or longer	39
Rents	35	Homemakers	39
All other	41	Retired	31
Not answered	39	Unemployed	29
Occupation		Not answered	29
Clergy	46		
Creative	41	Finance Company Reference	
Driver	33	Yes	0
Executive	62	Other references only	25
Guard	46	No	25
Homemaker	50	Not answered	15
Labor	33		
Manager	46	Other Department Store/Oil Card/ Major Credit Card	
Military enlisted	46	Department store only	12
Military officer	62	Oil Card only	12
Officer staff	46	Major credit card only	17
Outside	33	Department store and oil card	17
Production	41	Department store and credit card	31
Professional	62	Major credit card and oil card	31

Retired	62	All three	31
Sales	46	Other references only	0
Semi-professional	50	No credit	0
Service	41	Not answered	12
Student	46		
Teacher	41		
Unemployed	33		
All other	46		
Not answered	47		

The creditor sets his/her cut-off values on the basis of the probabilities of repayment and nonpayment associated with the various point scores and the tradeoffs between type I and type II errors. The higher an acceptance cut-off is set, the lower the type I error (accepting applicants who fail to repay), while the lower a rejection cut-off value, the lower the type II error (failing to accept applicants who would have repaid).

The critical distinction between extant credit scoring systems and other methods of credit evaluation is the absence, in credit scoring, of an explanatory model. While judgmental systems are based, however imperfectly, upon a credit evaluator's explanatory model of credit performance, credit scoring systems are concerned solely with statistical predictability. Since prediction is the sole criterion for acceptability, any individual characteristic that can be scored, other than obviously illegal characteristics, has potential for inclusion in a credit scoring system. A partial list of characteristics used by creditors in the development of their systems is presented in Table 2.

TABLE 2

Partial List of Factors Used to Develop Credit Scoring Systems

Telephone at home
Own/rent living accommodations
Age
Time at home address
Industry in which employed
Time with employer
Time with previous employer
Type of employment
Number of dependents
Types of credit reference
Income
Savings and loan references
Trade union membership
Age difference between man and wife
Telephone at work
Length of product being purchased

First letter of last name
Bank savings account
Bank checking account
Zip code of residence
Age of automobile
Make and model of automobile
Geographic area of U.S.
Finance company reference
Debt to income ratio
Monthly rent/mortgage payment
Family size
Telephone area code
Location of relatives
Number of children
Number of other dependents
Ownership of life insurance
Width of product being purchased

Few of these variables bear an explanatory relationship to credit performance. At best they might be statistical predictors whose relationship to payment performance can exist only through a complex chain of intervening variables. The overwhelming concern of creditors for prediction and a total unconcern for other issues was perhaps most tellingly demonstrated in the exchange between Senator Carl Levin (D., Michigan) and William Fair, chairman of Fair, Isaac and Company, the leading developer of credit scoring systems, at the Senate hearings on S15. Senator Levin asked Mr. Fair whether he *should be allowed* to use certain characteristics in the development of credit scoring systems (*Credit Card Redlining* 1979, p. 221):

> **Senator Levin:** "You feel that you should be allowed to consider *race?*" (emphasis added)
>
> **Mr. Fair:** "That is correct."
>
> **Senator Levin:** "Would the same thing be true with *religion?*"
>
> **Mr. Fair:** "Yes."
>
> **Senator Levin:** "Would the same thing be true with *sex?*"
>
> **Mr. Fair:** "Yes."
>
> **Senator Levin:** "Would the same thing be true with *age?*"
>
> **Mr. Fair:** "Yes."
>
> **Senator Levin:** "The same thing be true with *marital status?*"
>
> **Mr. Fair:** "Yes."
>
> **Senator Levin:** "*Ethnic origin?*"
>
> **Mr. Fair:** "Yes."

This exchange demonstrates very clearly that in the development of credit scoring systems, for Fair, Isaac and Company at least, no issue other than statistical predictability is of any consequence. Although professing a commitment to obey the law, Fair, Isaac and Company, if statistical predictability were found and it were so able, would provide its customers with credit scoring systems that discriminated on the basis of *race, religion, sex, age, marital status* and *ethnic origin*.

Notes

1.   In a footnote, the author of the above article noted:

A logical extension of Mr. Fair's position would allow the inclusion of such characteristics as color of hair (if any), left or right-handedness, wear eyeglasses, height, weight, early morning drink preference (tea, coffee, milk, other), first digit of social security number, last digit of social security number, sexual preference (none, same, different, both), educational level, sports preference (football, baseball, tennis, soccer, golf, other), and favorite movie star (select from list), if it could be shown that they were statistically related to payment performance.

Is he correct? Assuming a creditor did use some of these factors in its evaluation system, would that violate the ECOA or Reg. B? Is there a requirement that factors used in a scoring table be intuitively related to creditworthiness? See Reg. B, 12 C.F.R. § 202.6(a).

2.   Does Table 1 make sense to you? Answer the following questions:

a.   In the "occupation" category, how would you score a law professor? A Congressman?

b.   Which factor carries the greatest weight? Why? How are relative weights determined?

c.   How many points do you get for a good credit history or a high income?

d.   How much does long-term stability in your job or your residence count?

e.   Is whether the table makes sense to you even relevant under the ECOA?

3.   Notice that the ECOA imposes certain limitations on the types of information a creditor can gather. See Reg. B, 12 C.F.R. § 202.5(c) and (d). Why restrict a creditor's access to information? Are any of the characteristics listed in these provisions relevant to a credit decision? Which ones? Under what circumstances?

4.   Could a credit scoring system have a built-in bias? Evaluate the following argument: "The computer scoring system is discriminatory * * * because major values in the system are assigned to characteristics (industry employing and type of employment) which have a significant correlation with sex." Shuman v. Standard Oil of California, 453 F.Supp. 1150, 1156 (N.D.Cal.1978). Does this argument seem to hold with the scoring system described above? Does Fair Isaac's weighting of factors to determine its credit score, described *supra*, seem like a sensible weighting? If not, does it matter as long as the weighting is predictive of defaults? Could it result in protected groups receiving lower credit scores than other groups? If so, would that be acceptable if the lower scores are based on factors that have been proved empirically to predict the likelihood of default?

5.   Can scoring systems be justified on a cost-benefit analysis? Supporters of credit scoring claim that they reduce the time needed to consider loan applications, reduce mortgage processing costs, and more accurately predict creditworthiness than judgmental systems. See Freddie Mac, Making Mortgage Lending Simpler and Fairer for America's Families (1996). One prominent economist has suggested that "[d]iscrimination is largely a matter of basing decisions on incomplete information: generalizing from a person's race or sex to his or her character or ability." Richard Posner, The Economics of Justice 345 (1981). Do you agree? Professor (now Judge) Posner also suggests that the cost of information is a major factor in processes such as hiring or credit granting. It is easier and cheaper to follow a flat rule against hiring former criminals, for example, than it is to investigate the individual circumstances in each case. Do you agree? Does this sort of analysis help explain the use of scoring systems?

6.   Critics of credit scoring point to a well-publicized incident involving Lawrence Lindsey, a member of the Federal Reserve Board, who was denied a credit card by Toys 'R' Us despite having good credit and earning $123,100 per year. See Douglas Armstrong, Merits, Mistakes of Credit Scoring Fuel Debate; Some Say System Helps Lenders and Borrowers; Others Call it Terrifying, Milwaukee J. Sentinel, Nov. 16, 1997 at Bus. 1. The credit scoring program rejected Lindsey because a number of lenders had recently

requested his credit record. Critics have also complained that credit scoring does not take into account how people may improve their "credit behavior." See Snigdha Prakash, Credit Scoring, Used Alone, Seen Promoting Loan Bias, Am. Banker, Sept. 21, 1995, at 10.

7. When a creditor uses a scoring system, how should it state the reasons for adverse action? Can it simply disclose the fact that the applicant did not receive a high enough score? How will the lender even know the actual reason for the action if the computer merely manipulates a bunch of numbers? The Federal Reserve Board has issued the following Official Staff Commentary, ¶ 202.9(b)(2)–4, 5, which addresses this problem. Does it help?

> 4. *Credit scoring system.* If a creditor bases the denial or other adverse action on a credit scoring system, the reasons disclosed must relate only to those factors actually scored in the system. Moreover, no factor that was a principal reason for adverse action may be excluded from disclosure. The creditor must disclose the actual reasons for denial (for example, "age of automobile") even if the relationship of that factor to predicting creditworthiness may not be clear to the applicant.

> 5. *Credit scoring—method for selecting reasons.* The regulation does not require that any one method be used for selecting reasons for a credit denial or other adverse action that is based on a credit scoring system. Various methods will meet the requirements of the regulation. One method is to identify the factors for which the applicant's score fell furthest below the average score for each of those factors achieved by applicants whose total score was at or slightly above the minimum passing score. Another method is to identify the factors for which the applicant's score fell furthest below the average score for each of those factors achieved by all applicants. These average scores could be calculated during the development or use of the system. Any other method that produces results substantially similar to either of these methods is also acceptable under the regulation.

The Commentary also states that "The regulation does not mandate that a specific number of reasons be disclosed, but disclosure of more than four reasons is not likely to be helpful to the applicant." ¶ 202.9(b)(2)–1. What should a creditor do when it has five reasons for denial?

8. The development of a secondary market in mortgages has also contributed to the increase in use of credit scores. Often the original mortgage lender sells the mortgage to another in the secondary market. A good credit score facilitates such a sale. See Evan Hendricks, Credit Scores & Credit Reports 40–42 (2d ed. 2005).

9. The FACTA Act gives consumers a right to obtain their credit scores upon payment of a fee. See 15 U.S.C. § 1681g(f).

Problem 4–24

Nationwide Retailers Co. has just adopted a credit scoring system. In fact, it adopted the exact scoring system described in Table 1 of the Capon article, above. It requires a score of at least 225 to grant any loan. For example, a secretary, with a new rental address in Zip Code C and a new employer, and with only an oil company credit card and both a checking and a savings account at her bank, and no finance company reference, will score 244.

Constance Baker is a teacher who took a new job, and also rented a furnished apartment in Zip Code C, one year ago. She has a checking account at her bank, but has an account with a mutual money market fund, rather than a bank savings account. She has credit cards from oil companies and from other department stores. She once got a loan from a finance company and pre-paid it.

At the end of her first year in her new job, Constance decided to move to a better apartment, which was not furnished. She did, however, find the perfect furniture for the new apartment at Nationwide.

She then applied to Nationwide for its credit card. However, as Table 1 demonstrates, she scored only 188 on its scoring system (Zip Code: 41; Bank Ref.: 0; Housing: 35; Occupation: 41; Time at Address: 30; Time with Employer: 24; Fin. Co.: 0; Credit Card: 17). Nationwide asks you what it should say as a "statement of specific reasons" for its denial of credit. What is your advice? Is the Official Staff commentary, above, helpful?

Note that the factors for which her score fell furthest below the averages may be the Bank and Finance Co. References. Should Nationwide tell Constance to 1) open a savings account (even though that is financially counterproductive) and 2) don't tell us about your finance company loan? Or, should it tell her that her score is below average (the secretary new to town) in seven different categories?

If you were Constance, what would *you* want to be told, and why? Is that likely to be disclosed under ECOA?

4. PROVING DISCRIMINATION

In some ECOA cases, proof of discrimination is not difficult. For example, no additional proof of discrimination would be required if a creditor were to insist that an applicant's spouse sign a note even though the applicant herself qualified for credit, see Anderson v. United Finance Co., 666 F.2d 1274 (9th Cir. 1982), or a lender were to state that members of a particular racial group would not be eligible for a loan, see Moore v. United States Dep't of Agric. on Behalf of Farmers Home Admin., 55 F.3d 991 (5th Cir. 1995) (no whites can qualify). But many ECOA cases do not present such overt evidence of disparate treatment of protected and unprotected groups. Consequently, courts have approved two other methods for proving discrimination, methods which are not easy to use or even articulate or understand. The most highly developed body of case law under any federal discrimination statute is no doubt that applying the Equal Employment Opportunity Act (EEOA, not to be confused with the ECOA), Title VII of the Civil Rights Act of 1964, 42 U.S.C.A. § 2000e et seq. Under Title VII, the courts have applied two separate legal theories to determine whether discrimination exists in individual cases. These are (1) comparative evidence of disparate treatment, and (2) evidence of disparate impact or effects. You may think of these tests as devices to help focus the court's inquiry and evaluate the difficult issues of evidence and proof which are inevitable in discrimination cases. When faced with questions of proof under ECOA, courts initially transplanted these tests to the problem of credit discrimination. Consequently, you should have some understanding of how they work.

We begin with the disparate treatment test. Here, the plaintiff normally alleges that an employer or creditor treated her less favorably than other people in her position, and that the difference in treatment was due to her race or sex or some other improper characteristic, rather than her qualifications. To win a case under this test, the plaintiff must prove that the discrimination, or disparate treatment, was intentional. Proving subjective intent is always difficult; defendants are not likely to testify that "our policy is simple; we don't hire blacks." Recognizing this, the courts have articulated a series of burden-shifting mechanisms which make the proof issues somewhat more objective. These mechanisms have been articulated in various forms, but, in general, the plaintiff can establish a prima facie case by showing, as the court put it in Ring v. First Interstate Mortgage, Inc., 984 F.2d 924 (8th Cir. 1993), "(1) that he was a member of a protected class; (2) that he applied for and qualified for a loan from Defendants; (3) that the loan was rejected despite his qualifications; and (4) that Defendants continued to approve loans for applicants with qualifications similar to those of Plaintiff." The burden of going forward then shifts to the defendant-creditor. It may rebut the plaintiff's case by showing that there was a legitimate, non-discriminatory reason for its decision. If the defendant can do this, the plaintiff gets one final shot. She may still prevail if she can show that the so-called legitimate reason offered by the defendant was merely a pretext for discrimination. See, e.g., Mercado–Garcia v. Ponce Federal Bank, 979 F.2d 890 (1st Cir. 1992). As you might imagine, it is sometimes hard to keep track of all these shifting burdens. To make matters even more complicated, one Circuit has now abandoned the disparate treatment test, in the *Latimore* case *infra*.

The disparate impact test, or "effects" test as it is often called, is quite different. To start, the plaintiff does not have to prove that the discrimination was intentional. Instead, the operative idea is that employment or credit practices which appear to be neutral might nevertheless create disparities among groups, especially to the disadvantage of groups the law wishes to protect such as minorities or women. Further, this might happen quite irrespective of the employer's or creditor's intent. Thus, a plaintiff who relies on this theory must prove the existence and extent of these disparities, and must also prove that the disparities were caused by the specific practice being challenged.

In disparate impact cases, it is important to remember that the court is looking for evidence of disparities among entire groups, and not simply individual instances of discrimination. As a result, the evidence is likely to be highly statistical and quite complex. It will probably include elaborate information about applicant pools, percentages of employees or credit recipients from various groups, and other statistical data. If the evidence shows that the effect of the challenged practice is to create a "statistically significant" disparity in treatment among the various groups (an issue over which the experts are sure to disagree), the plaintiff has established a prima facie case. As in the disparate treatment cases, the burden then shifts to the defendant. It may escape liability if it can demonstrate that the challenged practice is nevertheless legitimate, despite its adverse impact on the protected group. Normally this involves a showing that the practice has a manifest relationship to job performance or creditworthiness, or was otherwise justified by business necessity.

A.B. & S. AUTO SERVICE, INC. v. SOUTH SHORE BANK OF CHICAGO

United States District Court, Northern District of Illinois, 1997.
962 F.Supp. 1056.

ANN CLAIRE WILLIAMS, DISTRICT JUDGE.

Plaintiffs AB & S Auto Service, Inc. and Jerry L. Bonner bring this action under the Equal Credit Opportunity Act, 15 U.S.C. § 1691 et seq., against defendant South Shore Bank of Chicago. Both parties' cross-motions for summary judgment are presently before the court. For the following reasons the court denies plaintiffs' motion for summary judgment and grants defendant's motion for summary judgment.

BACKGROUND

A.B. & S. Auto Service, Inc. ("AB & S") is an automobile repair shop located in Chicago. Jerry L. Bonner ("Bonner") is AB & S's president and he is an African–American. South Shore Bank (the "bank") is a commercial bank with its main office located at 71st and Jeffery Boulevard, in Chicago's South Shore neighborhood. * * * The bank participates in the loan guarantee program sponsored by the Small Business Administration ("SBA"). The SBA requires all SBA loan applicants to complete an SBA Form 912 Statement of Personal History. The SBA Form 912 asks applicants if they have ever been charged with or arrested or convicted for any criminal offense other than a minor motor vehicle violation and asks applicants to provide details. In addition form 912 states: "The fact that you have an arrest or conviction record will not necessarily disqualify you." Before submitting a business loan guarantee request to the SBA for approval, the bank is expected to make an independent judgment concerning an applicant's criminal record in evaluating the applicant's character and other relevant factors.

In February 1995, AB & S applied for a $230,000 business loan from the bank after having a similar SBA loan request rejected by LaSalle Bank Lakeview. On December 27, 1994, Bonner submitted to the bank the completed SBA form 912. In response to form 912's question about arrests and convictions, Bonner listed five incidents in which he was arrested and charged, but not convicted: 1) "domestic matters (husband/wife)" sometime between 1982 and 1984; 2) possession of a controlled substance in 1985; 3) disorderly conduct between 1985 and 1990; 4) possession of a controlled substance in May 1990; and 5) possession of a stolen car in September 1994. Bonner did not deny engaging in any of the conduct for which he was arrested. Bonner also listed one conviction for aggravated battery for stabbing and seriously injuring a man in 1983. He maintains that he acted in defense of himself and his wife who were assaulted by a number of assailants.

The bank reviews applications through a loan committee process. Ms. Leslie Davis, an African–American Vice President at the bank, reviewed the application of Bonner and recommended it for approval. However, at the loan committee meeting, Jim Bringley and Dick Turner agreed that Bonner's loan request should be denied. * * * Concern was expressed about Bonner's criminal record as set forth in the SBA Form 912. They found the criminal record to reflect poorly on Bonner's judgment and character. The bank decided not to make the $230,000 SBA loan to AB & S. Bonner's criminal record was a motivating factor in the bank's decision not to make the loan. However, the bank does not automatically reject business loan applications made by people with criminal records. The bank's general practice in evaluating business loan applications is to consider an applicant's criminal history and the surrounding facts on a case-by-case basis and to utilize that information in evaluating the applicant's character and judgment which, in turn, is used in assessing the ability and willingness of the applicant to repay the loan.

During the last 15 years, the bank has considered thousands of business loan applications. There is no evidence that the bank has denied any loan requests because of an applicant's criminal history other than AB & S's $230,000 loan request. The bank does not keep records of rejected business loan applicants; specifically, the bank does not keep records of applicants who were rejected on the basis of a criminal record. The bank does not keep records that indicate the race of a rejected loan applicant. The bank has made at least three business loans to applicants with criminal records. One of these three applicants was African–American.

Dr. Jaslin U. Salmon testified as an expert witness for plaintiffs in this case. He is a professor at Triton College and has researched and reviewed various statistics in order to give an opinion in this case. He opines that any kind of decision that is based on arrest records would militate against people of color. He indicated that some studies have suggested that although a higher percentage of blacks are arrested for and convicted of crimes, those figures do not necessarily reflect that a higher percentage of blacks actually commit crimes. He suggests that, based on his research, that there are many cases in which the black applicant is qualified, credit worthy, but was not given the loan for other reasons and among those reasons, arrest records had been taken into consideration. However, the bank disputes this point because Dr. Salmon was unable to identify a single study showing that consideration of arrest records has a disproportionate impact on African–American applicants for any type of credit, much less any study addressing the impact on business loan applicants.

Plaintiffs initiated this action under * * * the Equal Credit Opportunity Act ("ECOA"), 15 U.S.C. § 1691 et seq. Plaintiffs allege that the bank's practice of considering an applicant's criminal record in making business loan decisions has an unlawful disparate impact on African–American men. On December 13, 1995, plaintiffs voluntarily dismissed the § 1981 claim, leaving only the ECOA claim. Now pursuant to Fed.R.Civ.P. 56(c), defendant moves this court for summary judgment because plaintiffs cannot establish a prima facie under the ECOA. According to defendant, even if plaintiff could establish the prima facie case, the bank is still entitled to summary judgment because consideration of an applicant's criminal record in evaluating SBA loan requests is justified as relevant to creditworthiness and the bank's obligation to do so as an SBA-approved lender. Plaintiffs also move this court for summary judgment on the grounds that considering an applicant's criminal record, without relating it to creditworthiness, discriminates against blacks and is unjustified. * * *

ANALYSIS

The court must determine whether South Shore Bank's policy of inquiring about a credit applicant's criminal record, in compliance with the SBA's requirements, violates the ECOA. * * * A credit applicant can prove discrimination under the ECOA by using any one of the following three different approaches used in the employment discrimination context: 1) direct evidence of discrimination;[5] 2) disparate impact analysis, also called the "effects" test; or 3) disparate treatment analysis. * * *

In order to prove discrimination under the disparate impact analysis or "effects" test,[7] an applicant must show how "a policy, procedure, or practice specifically identified by the [applicant] has a significantly

---

5. To prove discrimination in violation of the ECOA with direct evidence, an applicant must offer direct evidence that the decision to deny credit was based on an impermissible factor. *See Saldana v. Citibank, Federal Savings Bank,* No. 93 C 4164, 1996 WL 332451 *2 (N.D.Ill. June 13, 1996); See Charlotte E. Thomas, *Defending a Free Standing Equal Credit Opportunity Act Claim,* 114 Banking Law Journal 108, 109 (1997) (" 'Direct evidence' of discrimination may be established through explicit and unambiguous statements of hostility toward persons protected by ECOA, which prove discrimination without inference or presumption.")

7. In June 1995, the Board of Governors of the Federal Reserve System ("FRB") promulgated its final version of its amendments to Regulation B which implements the ECOA. 60 Fed.Reg. 29965 (June 7, 1995). These amendments covered a variety of issues; however, most importantly it touched on the disparate impact approach. Specifically, section 202.6(a) provides:

> Except as otherwise provided in the act and this regulation, a creditor may consider any information obtained, so long as the information is not used to discriminate against an applicant on a prohibited basis.[footnote 2]

[Footnote 2 reads:] The legislative history of the act indicates that the Congress intended an "effects test" concept, as outlined in the employment field by the Supreme Court in the cases of *Griggs v. Duke Power Co.* 401 U.S. 424, 91 S.Ct. 849, 28 L.Ed.2d 158 (1971) and *Albemarle Paper Co. v. Moody,* 422 U.S. 405, 95 S.Ct. 2362, 45 L.Ed.2d 280 (1975), to be applicable to a creditor's determination of creditworthiness.

12 C.F.R. § 202.6(a) (West 1997).

greater discriminatory impact on members of a protected class." *Saldana,* No. 93 C 4164, 1996 WL 332451, at *4 * * *; *See also Sayers,* 522 F.Supp. at 839 (To make out the prima facie case, plaintiff must show that the defendant's requirements for accepting credit applications result in the acceptance of credit applicants in a pattern significantly different from that of the general pool of applicants.) Plaintiffs traditionally establish this prima facie case by making "a statistical comparison of the representation of the protected class in the applicant pool with representation in the group actually accepted from the pool." *Id.* "If the statistical disparity is significant, then plaintiff is deemed to have made out a prima facie case." *Cherry,* 490 F.Supp. at 1030. However, courts have found that "proof of disparate impact need not be shown by statistics in every case nor need it be shown by proof of actual disproportionate exclusion from the applicant pool." *Id.* at 1031. The *Cherry* court commented that some Title VII cases have permitted reference to the general population on the assumption that the applicant pool would possess approximately the same characteristics. But this assumption is not valid in every case. Plaintiff must demonstrate why the use of general population statistics would be valid.

Once the plaintiff has made the prima facie case, the defendant-lender must demonstrate that any policy, procedure, or practice has a manifest relationship to the creditworthiness of the applicant. * * * In other words, the onus is on the defendant to show that the particular practice makes defendant's credit evaluation system more predictive than it would be otherwise.

I. *Prima Facie Case*

Courts have held that the use of general population statistics is insufficient to make out a prima facie case under the ECOA. In *Saldana,* the plaintiff, loan-applicant, sued Citibank claiming it denied her loan based on its policy of redlining. *Saldana,* No. 93 C 4164, 1996 WL 332451 at *1. Saldana tried to make her case under the disparate impact theory. Specifically, she claimed that Citibank had an unwritten policy that set the minimum amount for a rehab loan at $100,000. This policy, she claims, disproportionately impacted the African–American community because few African–Americans could meet this financial test based on their income and net-worth. Saldana offered statistical evidence regarding 1) the bank's loan approval rate for loans over $100,000 in the Austin area; 2) the bank's loan rejection rate for white and African–American applicants in comparison with their representation in the greater Chicago community; and 3) the bank's average refinancing approval and average rejection rate in Austin in comparison to the City of Chicago's average approval and rejection rates. While the court found that this last set of statistics successfully presented some statistical evidence comparing the Austin community to the greater Chicago community, the court still found that "these statistics are of a very general nature and do not relate specifically to the policy identified as having a discriminatory impact. Thus, Saldana has failed to establish her claim under a disparate impact analysis."

Similarly, in *Cherry,* the credit-card applicant sued Amoco Oil Company, alleging that Amoco's use of zip code ratings in Atlanta, which assigned low-ratings to those zip code areas where Amoco had unfavorable delinquency experience, adversely effected black applicants disproportionately. *Cherry,* 490 F.Supp. at 1027–28. The plaintiff's witness testified that he compiled statistics that proved that there is a significant correlation between acceptance rate/percentage of white population or conversely rejection rate/percentage of non-white population. Following the guidance of *Griggs,* 401 U.S. 424, 91 S.Ct. 849, 28 L.Ed.2d 158 (1971), the court held that this statistical evidence did not make out a prima facie case. Specifically, plaintiff did not demonstrate why the court should assume that the applicant pool possessed approximately the same characteristics as the general population surveyed. * * *

Plaintiffs claim that South Shore Bank's practice of considering an applicant's criminal record in making commercial lending decisions has a disparate impact on African–Americans. To make the prima facie case plaintiffs offer the testimony of Dr. Jaslin U. Salmon. Dr. Salmon testified that any decision that is based on arrest records would militate against people of color. He suggests that, based on his research, there are many cases in which the black applicant is qualified, credit worthy, but was not given the loan for other reasons and among those reasons, arrest records had been taken into consideration. However, the bank disputes this point because Dr. Salmon was unable to identify a single study showing that consideration of arrest records has a disproportionate impact on African–American applicants for any type of credit, much less any study addressing the impact on business loan applicants.[10]

In addition to Dr. Salmon's testimony, plaintiffs offer the general population statistics of arrest rates by race in 1990. Considering these general population statistics, the court finds that, like both the *Mat-*

---

10. Specifically, Dr. Salmon was asked the following questions:

Q: Assuming putting aside the question of arrest or convictions, just taking the fact that the black applicant is qualified to begin with, that is but for the arrest or conviction, the black would be eligible for credit or a loan, are you aware of any statistics regarding the impact of arrest or convictions on that black applicant who is otherwise qualified for a loan and is otherwise credit worthy?

A: Yes, I am telling you that what I know is that there are many cases in which the black applicant is qualified, credit worthy, but was not given the loans for other reasons and among those reasons, things like arrests and things like their job situation have been taken into consideration.

Q: Have you used those statistics in forming any of your opinions?

A: Yes, because based on what I know of the way blacks have been treated and based on my own understanding of how the institutions work, yes, I recognize that blacks and other minorities have been disproportionately affected.

Q: Where would I go to find these statistics you say that is where blacks are otherwise qualified for loans or credit worthy, if I wanted to see them myself?

A: Again, I am telling you that I cannot offhand at this point tell you what those sources are, but some of it may have been from newspapers, some it [sic] of it from magazines, and I can't reference those very particularly right now, but I can certainly find those for you at a later date.

thews, Hill, Cherry, and *Saldana* courts found, these statistics are insufficient to make out a prima facie case under the ECOA. The court recognizes that the ECOA prohibits creditors from inquiring into the race, sex or marital status of an applicant. This in turn places plaintiffs in a difficult position of trying to prove disproportionate impact without any access to a creditor's statistical lending profile. However, as the *Cherry* court held, plaintiffs can refer to the general population as long as plaintiffs clearly demonstrate that the applicant pool would posses [sic] approximately the same characteristics. Considering the statistical proof and the testimony of Dr. Salmon, the court finds that plaintiffs have not made this showing that the applicant pool possesses approximately the same characteristics as the general population.

Both the statistics and Dr. Salmon's supporting testimony do not answer the following questions raised in *Carolina Freight Carriers Corp.* and *Hill:* 1) how many African–Americans with convictions or arrests are otherwise qualified for the loan; and 2) how many African–Americans are deterred from applying because of the bank's practice. Plaintiffs' evidence is further undermined, as it was in *Hill,* by the fact that the bank's practice of considering an applicant's criminal record was not consistently applied to disqualify applicants with criminal records. Rather, the bank has made at least three business loans to applicants with criminal records. One of these three applicants with criminal records is African–American.

Plaintiffs urge this court to consider several EEOC decisions, specifically EEOC decision 6357, which cites to *Gregory v. Litton Systems, Inc.,* 316 F.Supp. 401, 403 (C.D.Cal.1970), *modified by,* 472 F.2d 631 (1972). The court recognizes that the *Gregory* court held that the policy of automatically rejecting an applicant because of his significant arrest record is illegal because it has been shown to eliminate black applicants at a higher rate than white applicants and it is usually irrelevant as a predictor of job performance. * * * However, the facts of this case, as in both *Smith* and *Hill,* are distinct from the facts in *Gregory* because South Shore Bank does not have a blanket policy of excluding applicants with criminal records. Therefore, the holding of *Gregory* does not apply to this case.

II. Manifest Relationship to Creditworthiness

Generally when the plaintiff has failed to make out a prima facie case, courts do not require the defendant-lender to show that the practice has a manifest relationship to creditworthiness. In the present case, assuming, arguendo, that plaintiff did set forth enough evidence to make out the prima facie case, the court must then determine whether South Shore Bank has demonstrated that its practice of considering an applicant's criminal record is legitimately related to the extension of credit.

South Shore Bank's practice of inquiring into a credit applicant's criminal history is legitimately related to its extension of credit for two reasons. First, the regulations require the SBA, in evaluating a loan guarantee application, to consider "the character, reputation, and credit history of the applicant, its associates, and guarantors." 13 C.F.R. § 120.150. As a participant in the SBA loan guarantee program, South Shore Bank is obligated to consider an applicant's criminal record provided on SBA Form 912 in its evaluation of a loan applicant's character. Following the guidance of *Cragin,* the court finds that, because the bank's practice of considering criminal record information is required by the SBA to participate in the SBA loan guarantee program, the practice is legitimately related to the extension of credit and, therefore, permissible.

Secondly, the bank's inquiry into an applicant's criminal record provides relevant information about an applicant's creditworthiness, particularly his judgment and character. Plaintiff Bonner admits that several of the incidents described in his completed SBA Form 912: possession of a controlled substance, domestic abuse, and disorderly conduct, reflected negatively on his judgment and character. Specifically, Bonner admits that these incidents involved an exercise of bad judgment. Therefore, because an applicant's judgment and character may legitimately be considered in making commercial lending decisions, South Shore Bank's practice of considering criminal history as it relates to character and judgment bears a legitimate and manifest relationship to the extension of credit. Therefore, the court finds that the bank has successfully demonstrated that its practice of inquiring into a credit applicant's criminal record is legitimately related to the extension of credit.

Plaintiffs have failed to make out a prima facie case of discrimination in violation of the ECOA under the disparate impact theory. Despite the fact that plaintiffs have not made their prima facie case, defendant, on the other hand, has demonstrated that its practice has a manifest relationship to the extension of credit.

CONCLUSION

For the foregoing reasons, the court grants defendant South Shore Bank's motion for summary judgment and denies plaintiff Bonner and AB & S's motion for summary judgment.

Notes

1. Why wasn't it enough for plaintiff to show the general population statistics of arrest rates by race?

2. Was the bank helped by its failure to keep statistics on the criminal records of unsuccessful applicants? After this case, would you counsel banks to maintain information about rejected applications?

3. Is it fair that the bank disqualified Bonner based on arrests for which he was not convicted? If not, does it matter under ECOA?

4. Bonner was applying for a business loan. Are business loans within the scope of the ECOA?

5. A 2005 Supreme Court decision in which five Justices approved the use of the disparate impact test in cases arising under the Age Discrimination in Employment Act (ADEA) has sparked new questions about whether and how the disparate impact test is to be used under ECOA. Justice Stevens, writing for a plurality that included Justices Souter, Ginsburg, and Breyer in Smith v. City of Jackson, 544 U.S. 228, 125 S.Ct. 1536, 161 L.Ed.2d 410 (2005), based his conclusion in part on the text of the ADEA, which prohibits conduct that "adversely affects" employment status. ECOA does not include that language. It could be argued that omission of similar words from ECOA meant that Congress did not intend ECOA to reach conduct that has an unintentionally adverse effect on credit decisions involving protected classes. On the other hand, the plurality's decision was also based on administrative interpretations applying the disparate impact test to ADEA cases, and the relevant administrative agency—the Federal Reserve Board—takes the position that the disparate impact test can be used under ECOA. This last point would probably persuade Justice Scalia, who agreed with the plurality that disparate impact cases can be brought under the ADEA on the ground that the Court should defer to the administrative agencies' reasonable interpretations. *Smith* also concluded that it was not enough for the plaintiffs merely to show that a protected class is being treated less favorably; the plaintiffs must also identify a particular practice that caused the alleged disparate impact. Finally, *Smith* hearkened back to an earlier Title VII employment discrimination decision, Wards Cove Packing Co. v. Atonio, 490 U.S. 642, 109 S.Ct. 2115, 104 L.Ed.2d 733 (1989). *Wards Cove* had taken a narrow approach to disparate impact cases, but Congress had overturned it as to Title VII cases in 1991. See Civil Rights Act of 1991, § 2, 105 Stat. 1071. Because the 1991 statute did not similarly amend the ADEA, the *Smith* Court concluded that *Wards Cove* governs the legitimate business justification in ADEA cases. Accordingly, even though the employer in *Smith* might have been able to accomplish its goals in other reasonable ways—ways that did not have a disparate impact on a protected class—the employer could nevertheless avoid liability by showing that the method it had selected to serve its purpose was "not unreasonable." The 1991 statute did not amend ECOA either, and so by parity of reasoning, *Wards Cove* and the "not unreasonable" test probably apply to ECOA claims as well. See generally Peter N. Cubita & Michelle Hartmann, The ECOA Discrimination Proscription and Disparate Impact—Interpreting the Meaning of the Words That Actually Are There, 61 Bus. Law. 829 (2006).

6. Are anti-discrimination laws doomed to fail? Evaluate the following argument:

> [Assume that] blacks are discriminated against in credit and employment because (for whatever reason) their performance in these areas is on average poorer than whites'. Some states and the federal government pass laws to prevent discrimination against blacks. Barred from using race as proxy for employment suitability and creditworthiness, employers and lenders cast about for other proxies and settle on arrest records, conviction records, bankruptcies, judgments, and the like. They do this not because they are trying to discriminate against blacks but because they want to screen out (or into lower wage or higher interest-rate categories) people who do not meet their qualification at normal prices.

If, however, race is a reasonably close proxy for the underlying characteristics in which the employer and creditor are interested, and if the substitute proxies are also reasonably accurate, then the substitute proxies will have almost the same effect on the racial composition of employees and borrowers as explicit use of the racial proxy had. The ban on discrimination will have little impact.*

R. Posner, The Economics of Justice 302 (1981). Is the use of proxies illegal under the ECOA?

7. The problem of proving discrimination statistically may be exacerbated by the fact that race may play a role in some applications but not others. For example, one study concluded that race was not a significant factor in weighing applications by strong credit candidates, but was an important factor for marginal candidates. William C. Hunter & Mary Beth Walker, The Cultural Affinity Hypothesis and Mortgage Lending Decisions, 13 J. Real Estate & Econ. 57 (1996).

8. In addition to the ECOA, other federal laws prohibit discriminatory practices in certain housing transactions, and are discussed in the following materials. See, e.g. § 805 of the Fair Housing Act, 42 U.S.C.A. § 3605 and 42 U.S.C.A. § 1982, part of the Civil Rights Act of 1866, both of which are reprinted in the Statutory Supplement.

Problem 4–25

A small loan company in New York has studied the ECOA and Regulation B carefully, and wants to avoid any consideration of prohibited bases under that law. It therefore analyzes all its credit files for the past twenty years, and finds that type of employment and place of residence both are good predictors of creditworthiness. Based on that analysis, the company determines it will make no further loans to persons who work as domestics, bartenders, busboys or cab drivers, nor to persons who live in certain neighborhoods in Brooklyn. Is the company safe from an ECOA challenge? Is it important that demographic studies would place large numbers of African–Americans, Jews, Latinos, Latinas, and women in those jobs and those neighborhoods?

LATIMORE v. CITIBANK FEDERAL SAVINGS BANK

United States Court of Appeals, Seventh Circuit, 1998.
151 F.3d 712.

POSNER, CHIEF JUDGE.

Helen Latimore, a black woman, brought a suit charging racial discrimination in real estate lending by Citibank and two of its employees, in violation of an assortment of federal civil rights laws including the Equal Credit Opportunity Act, 15 U.S.C. § 1691(a)(1), and the Fair Housing Act, 42 U.S.C. §§ 3605(a), (b). The district court granted summary judgment for the defendants. Latimore's appeal requires us to

---

* Reprinted with permission of the publisher from THE ECONOMICS OF JUSTICE by Richard A. Posner, p. 306, Cambridge, Mass.; Harvard University Press, Copyright © 1981, 1983 by the President and Fellows of Harvard College.

consider what the prima facie case of credit discrimination is, that is, how much evidence a plaintiff must submit in order to withstand a motion for summary judgment. There is no reason to think that the answer will be different depending on the particular civil rights statute sued under.

Owner of a home in a largely black neighborhood on the south side of Chicago, Latimore applied to Citibank for a $51,000 loan secured by the home. She satisfied Citibank's standards for creditworthiness, but the bank's rules also required that the ratio of the appraised value of the security (Latimore's home) to the amount of the loan not exceed 75 percent. The bank's appraiser, defendant Kernbauer, appraised the property at only $45,000, yielding a loan-to-value ratio of 113 percent. When defendant Lundberg, the account executive handling Latimore's application, informed her that the appraised value of the home was too low to support a loan in the amount sought, Latimore told Lundberg that the house had been appraised less than a year earlier for $82,000. Lundberg asked Latimore for the appraisal report, and when Lundberg received it she sent it together with Kernbauer's report to the bank's appraisal review department. The department declined to overrule Kernbauer's appraisal, on the ground that the comparable sales on which the $82,000 appraisal had been based weren't really comparable, because they involved property more than six blocks from Latimore's home. And so Latimore did not receive the loan. Some months later she applied for a loan from another bank, which appraised her home at $79,000 and made her the loan, though for a smaller amount than she had sought from Citibank ($46,000 instead of $51,000) and at a one percent higher interest rate. The damages sought are the additional interest plus certain consequential damages.

In most discrimination cases, the plaintiff can establish a prima facie case either by presenting evidence of having been actually discriminated against on some forbidden ground such as race or by satisfying the *McDonnell Douglas* standard. * * * Under that standard, in a typical case of employment discrimination, involving say the denial of a promotion to a black employee, the plaintiff would have to show only that he was qualified for the promotion and that a white got it instead, and the burden would then be on the employer to come forth with a noninvidious reason for why the white rather than the black got the promotion. Although the *McDonnell Douglas* standard originated and evolved in cases involving racial discrimination in employment, it has been extended to all sorts of other discrimination not even limited to the employment setting. * * * So numerous are these extensions that we were not surprised when the bank's counsel invited us to use *McDonnell Douglas* as a template in credit discrimination cases as well.

But wholesale transposition of the *McDonnell Douglas* standard to the credit discrimination context would display insensitivity to the thinking behind the standard. Normally the burden of producing evidence of each element of the plaintiff's claim is on the plaintiff. There has to be a reason for shifting the burden to the defendant. It is not reason enough that essential evidence is in the defendant's possession and would be difficult for the plaintiff, even with the aid of modern pretrial discovery, to dig out of the defendant. Before the defendant may be put to the burden of producing evidence, the plaintiff has to show that there is some ground for suspecting that the defendant has indeed violated the plaintiff's rights. Otherwise we would have a regime of precomplaint discovery. Anyone could put anyone else to the burden of producing evidence without having anything better than a hope and a prayer that the evidence would establish a violation. Cf. Bruce L. Hay, "Allocating the Burden of Proof," 72 *Ind. L.J.* 651 (1997).

The fact that a qualified black is passed over for promotion in favor of a white has been thought sufficiently suspicious to place on the defendant the minimum burden of presenting a noninvidious reason why the black lost out. But it is the competitive situation—the black facing off as it were against the white—that creates the (minimal) suspicion, and there is no comparable competitive situation in the usual allegation of credit discrimination. Latimore was not competing with a white person for a $51,000 loan. A bank does not announce, "We are making a $51,000 real estate loan today; please submit your applications, and we'll choose the application that we like best and give that applicant the loan." If a bank did that, and a black and a white each submitted an application, and the black's application satisfied the bank's criteria of creditworthiness and value-to-loan ratio yet the white received the loan, we would have a situation roughly parallel to that of a *McDonnell Douglas* case. And when we have an approximation to such a situation, a variant of the *McDonnell Douglas* standard may apply, as we shall see. But such cases are rare, and this is not one of them. The Supreme Court has reminded us that *McDonnell Douglas* was not intended to be a straitjacket into which every discrimination case must be forced kicking and screaming. * * *

The reason the bank—the (principal) defendant—urges adoption of the standard is that it construes it to require that Latimore show not only that she was creditworthy by the bank's standards, which she was, but also that she satisfied the bank's appraiser, which she did not, about the value of her house. There is no question that to be a qualified borrower—the counterpart to a worker who is performing to his employer's satisfaction in the employment discrimination context * * *—the plaintiff has to meet the lender's requirements for collateral as well as to establish personal creditworthiness. But Citibank does not require that the borrower satisfy *its* appraiser; it requires only that the appraised value bear a specified relation to the amount of the loan sought, and the opinion of its own appraiser is not conclusive evidence of that value. The bank is willing to consider evidence from other sources and to overrule its own appraiser. The bank's appraisal review department could have overruled Kernbauer; that's why the bank has an appraisal *review* department.

Latimore argues, in her own variant of *McDonnell Douglas* (so strong is the magnetic field of that opinion), that all she had to show in order to withstand summary judgment was that her house was in a minority neighborhood, an appraisal (but not necessarily the defendant's) estimated the value of the house to be at least as great as the loan, the plaintiff was creditworthy, yet the loan was rejected. This cannot be right either, and not only because creditors rarely lend up to the value of the collateral and because there is nothing remotely suspicious about the bank's 75 percent rule. Appraisals are fallible, and if banks reposed automatic, unthinking trust in all third-party appraisals they would not employ their own appraisers, as Citibank does. No reasonable suspicion of racial discrimination can arise from the mere fact of a discrepancy between an appraisal conducted by another bank and the appraisal made by Citibank's employee.

Latimore's proposed prima facie case, like the bank's, lacks any comparison between the treatment of blacks and the treatment of whites. At the heart of *McDonnell Douglas* is the idea that if the black is treated worse than the white in a situation in which there is no *obvious* reason for the difference in treatment (such as that the black lacks an essential qualification for the promotion), there is *something* for the employer to explain; and although the competitive situation which invites and facilitates comparison is usually missing from credit discrimination cases, sometimes there will be another basis for comparison. Suppose, for example, that Latimore and Eromital (who is white), apply at roughly the same time for roughly the same-sized loan from the same Citibank office. The two prospective borrowers are equally creditworthy and the collateral they offer to put up is appraised at the same amount. Both applications are forwarded to Ms. Lundberg and she turns down Latimore's application and approves Eromital's. The similarity in the situations of the white and the black would be sufficient to impose on Citibank a duty of explaining why the white was treated better. No effort at making such a comparison was attempted here.

So neither *McDonnell Douglas* nor the kind of *McDonnell Douglas* knock off which we have just sketched * * * is available here. But that does not end the case. It is always open to a plaintiff in a discrimination case to try to show in a conventional way, without relying on any special doctrines of burden-shifting, that there is enough evidence, direct or circumstantial, of discrimination to create a triable issue. * * * And Latimore has tried to do that. She hired an expert to conduct a retrospective appraisal, that is, an appraisal of the value of her home at the time that Citibank appraised it. The expert came in with an appraisal of $62,000. But this gets her nowhere. Under the bank's 75 percent rule, which Latimore doesn't claim to be racially discriminatory, a $62,000 appraisal would not support a $51,000 loan; 75 percent of $62,000 is $46,500 (almost exactly what she got from the other bank, but at a higher interest rate). Real estate appraisal is not an exact science, moreover, and so the fact that Citibank's appraisal was lower than someone else's does not create an inference of discrimination. For all that appears, Citibank uses conservative appraisal methods—perhaps in order to keep interest rates low, for remember that while Latimore did succeed eventually in obtaining a loan on her house, she had to pay a higher interest rate and on a smaller loan than she wanted.

Latimore argues that Citibank exhibited favoritism toward white would-be borrowers. The specific contention is that these white borrowers were similarly situated to Latimore in the sense of wanting loans of the same amount secured by property having the same appraised value, but that Lundberg went out of her way to help them raise the appraised value of their property and she didn't go out of her way to help Latimore. Specifically, when she reported to a white borrower that the appraised value of his property was too low to support the loan he was seeking, she would encourage him to find additional "comparables" (comparable sales) of which the bank's appraiser might not have known, in order to justify an increase in the appraised value. But remember that when Lundberg informed Latimore of the results of Kernbauer's appraisal, Latimore told her about the other appraisal, and Lundberg urged her to send that in. The fact that Latimore had gotten a higher appraisal implied additional comparables, since appraisals of residential real estate are based on comparable sales. By asking for the higher appraisal, Lundberg was in effect encouraging Latimore to submit additional comparables. It was not Lundberg's fault that they turned out not to satisfy the bank's definition of comparability. She did for Latimore what she did for white people in Latimore's position. * * *

Taking all the evidence as favorably to the plaintiff as the record permits, no reasonable jury could find that she was turned down because of her race; and so the grant of summary judgment to the defendants must be affirmed.

COOLEY v. STERLING BANK

United States District Court, Middle District of Alabama, 2003.
280 F.Supp.2d 1331, aff'd, 116 Fed. Appx. 242 (Table),
2004 WL 1737138 (11th Cir. 2004).

Albritton, Chief Judge.

I. Introduction

This cause is before the court on a Motion for Summary Judgment and a Motion to Strike filed by Defendants Sterling Bank and Synovus Financial Corporation of Alabama, and two Motions to Strike filed by Plaintiff Nash Cooley.

The Plaintiff filed his original Complaint in this case against Sterling Bank on September 17, 2002. The Plaintiff filed an Amended Complaint on January 31, 2003, in which the Plaintiff added Synovus Financial Corporation of Alabama * * *. In the Complaint, the Plaintiff brings claims under 42 U.S.C. § 1981, the Equal Credit Opportunity Act, 15 U.S.C. § 1691 *et seq.,* and the Fair Housing Act, 42 U.S.C. § 3601 *et seq.,* alleging that the Defendants denied his application for a $100,000 unsecured line of credit because of his race. The Defendants responded by filing a motion for Motion for Summary Judgment on June 9, 2003.

For the reasons to be discussed, the Defendants' Motion for Summary Judgment is due to be GRANTED, the Defendants' Motion to Strike is due to be GRANTED in part, and the Plaintiff's Motions to Strike are DENIED. * * *

III. FACTS

The submissions of the parties establish the following facts, construed in a light most favorable to the nonmovant:

The Plaintiff is a sixty-six year old African–American male who lives in Montgomery, Alabama. Since the mid–1980s, the Plaintiff's primary source of income has come from his ownership of residential rental properties in the Montgomery area. The Plaintiff currently owns approximately fifteen apartment units and twenty-four houses.

In order to have the financial flexibility to invest in new real estate ventures, the Plaintiff has maintained active lines of credit with various financial institutions. * * *

By the summer of 2000, the Plaintiff had $100,000 unsecured lines of credit at two separate banks. The Plaintiff ultimately hoped to establish five $100,000 lines of credit in order to complete a real estate project that he began in 1992. To meet his financial goals, the Plaintiff approached Sterling Bank ("Sterling") in September 2000 about another $100,000 unsecured line of credit. The Plaintiff chose Sterling because he had a prior business relationship with Kenny Hill, the Branch Manager of Sterling's Taylor Road Branch, when Hill worked at Colonial Bank. * * *

In September 2000, the Plaintiff met with Hill to apply for a $100,000 unsecured line of credit with Sterling. * * * On September 15, 2000, Hill conducted a credit check on the Plaintiff that revealed a "Beacon Score" of 749. Although this score was commensurate with an "excellent credit rating," Hill became concerned about the Plaintiff's income level after reviewing the remainder of the Plaintiff's financial information. Specifically, the Plaintiff's most recent tax return indicated that the Plaintiff and his wife had a joint pre-tax income of $106,214. Of this amount, Hill calculated that the income attributable to the Plaintiff was $51,483. Because the Plaintiff was applying for an unsecured line of credit in his name only, Hill was worried that the Plaintiff's income level was insufficient for him to obtain a $100,000 line of credit. Additionally, Hill was apprehensive about approving the Plaintiff's request with knowledge that the Plaintiff had two existing $100,000 lines of credit.

After Hill compiled the Plaintiff's loan materials, he presented them to Bob Ramsey, Sterling's Executive Vice President in charge of lending. Because Hill did not have the authority to approve a loan in excess of $50,000, he met with Ramsey to discuss the Plaintiff's loan application. * * * Hill expressed his concerns about the Plaintiff's financial situation and Ramsey concurred. In short, Ramsey concluded that the Plaintiff's "individual income of $51,464 simply did not justify adding another $100,000 unsecured debt on top of the two existing lines of credit at other banks totaling $200,000." Instead of denying the Plaintiff's request outright, Ramsey suggested making either a secured loan in the same amount or an unsecured loan for $25,000. After Ramsey and Hill agreed that a counteroffer was the best solution, Hill informed Ramsey that the Plaintiff was "African American and might claim racism." In response, Ramsey suggested discussing the matter with Alan Worrell, Sterling's Chief Executive Officer. Worrell agreed with Hill and Ramsey's assessment of the Plaintiff's financial situation and indicated his preference to find an alternative way to establish a credit relationship with the Plaintiff.

On September 18, 2000, Hill informed the Plaintiff of Sterling's decision and gave him a document entitled "Notice of Action Taken." The document explained that Sterling could not provide the Plaintiff with a $100,000 unsecured line of credit, but was willing to offer "a $25,000 unsecured line of credit or a larger secured line." In response, the Plaintiff immediately requested a list of the individuals on Sterling's Board of Directors so he could contact them about his loan denial. The Plaintiff also expressed his belief that Sterling was discriminating against him on the basis of race.

After learning of the Plaintiff's reaction, Worrell requested that Hill arrange a meeting between the Plaintiff and Worrell. During their meeting, the Plaintiff explained to Worrell that he wanted a line of credit from Sterling in order to "purchase a home and do bigger projects." Knowing of the Plaintiff's two existing lines, Worrell asked the Plaintiff why he needed a third line. The Plaintiff found this question "really insulting" because no banker had ever insinuated to him that he had enough money to accomplish his projects. Worrell informed the Plaintiff that he had "good credit," but expressed concerns about the Plaintiff's financial ability, given his income level and existing lines of credit, to "service that much debt if those loans were drawn upon." At the conclusion of the meeting, Worrell emphasized that he wanted to do business with the Plaintiff and hoped the Plaintiff would consider Sterling's counteroffer.

During Sterling's Board of Directors meeting on September 20, 2000, Worrell informed the Board of the Plaintiff's stated intent to contact individual Board members about his loan application. Worrell explained to the Board that the Plaintiff was accusing Sterling of discrimination because Sterling proposed a counteroffer rather than approve the Plaintiff's loan application on his terms. Additionally, Worrell provided each Board member with a memorandum prepared by Hill that explained the reasons behind Sterling's decision. The memorandum states that based on the Plaintiff's "income level, amount of outstanding debt, and open lines of credit," Hill, Worrell and Ramsey made a "group decision" to offer the Plaintiff "a $25,000 unsecured line of credit or the option to discuss a larger line on a secured basis."

According to Greg Calhoun, an African–American member of Sterling's Board of Directors, individual Board members began discussing the Plaintiff's application during the meeting. Calhoun stated in his deposition that the Board "didn't think [the Plaintiff] could qualify for a hundred thousand dollar line of credit being ... that he was a retired school teacher." Moreover, Board members "jok[ed] about [the Plaintiff's application]" and "laughed about the Plaintiff." In response, Calhoun told the other Board members that he believed they were putting the Plaintiff down. Calhoun then "told them they was [sic] all Republicans, and they're all members of the Montgomery Country Club. And there's no way that a black man can come in here and get money from the bank." Following this statement, Calhoun informed the Board that he was resigning. In Calhoun's opinion, Sterling denied the Plaintiff's loan application "because of [the Plaintiff's] skin color."

* * *

Additionally, Hill stated that "this credit decision was a bank decision (in which I was involved) and did not involve the Board."

IV. DISCUSSION

In his Second Amended Complaint, the Plaintiff contends that the Defendants, Sterling Bank and Synovus Financial Corporation of Alabama ("Synovus"), violated 42 U.S.C. § 1981, the Equal Credit Opportunity Act ("ECOA"), 15 U.S.C. § 1691 et seq., and the Fair Housing Act ("FHA"), 42 U.S.C. § 3601 et seq., by denying his application for a $100,000 unsecured line of credit because of his race. Section 1981 provides that "[a]ll persons ... shall have the same right in every State and Territory to make and enforce contracts ... as is enjoyed by white citizens." 42 U.S.C. § 1981. Section 1981 applies to this case because the Plaintiff contends that Sterling prevented him from signing a loan contract because of his race. * * *

Before delving into the factual merits of these claims, the court must first address a legal dispute between the parties regarding the Plaintiff's burden of proof. Because section 1981, the ECOA and the FHA are anti-discrimination statutes, the Defendants contend that the court's analysis should be governed by the methods of analysis developed for use in cases under Title VII of the Civil Rights Act of 1964. According to this approach, the Plaintiff must present either direct evidence of discriminatory intent, or use the factors set forth in burden-shifting analysis developed by the Supreme Court in *McDonnell Douglas Corp. v. Green,* 411 U.S. 792, 93 S.Ct. 1817, 36 L.Ed.2d 668 (1973), to raise, by indirect or circumstantial evidence, an inference of discrimination. In contrast, the Plaintiff relies exclusively on a decision from the United States Court of Appeals for the Seventh Circuit in which that court rejected the *McDonnell Douglas* burden-shifting model for credit discrimination claims brought under the ECOA and FHA. *See Latimore v. Citibank Fed. Sav. Bank* * * *

Although the Seventh Circuit's approach to credit discrimination claims is interesting, this court is bound to follow the precedent set forth by the Eleventh Circuit. With respect to claims brought under section

1981 and the FHA, the Eleventh Circuit has expressly held that Title VII's method of analysis governs. *See Wright v. Southland Corp.*, 187 F.3d 1287, 1298 n. 12 (11th Cir.1999) (stating that "[c]laims under 1981 are analyzed in the same manner as claims under Title VII"); *Secretary, United States Dep't of Hous. and Urban Dev. v. Blackwell*, 908 F.2d 864, 870 (11th Cir.1990) (holding that the "the legal framework developed by the federal courts in discrimination cases brought under . . . Title VII of the Civil Rights Act" applies in FHA cases). As for the Eleventh Circuit's stance on ECOA claims, the court notes that it has been unable to locate a case in which the Eleventh Circuit applied Title VII's framework to a claim brought pursuant to 15 U.S.C. § 1691(a). Nevertheless, this court concludes that Title VII's analytical approach applies to ECOA discrimination claims. The court rejects the approach take by the Seventh Circuit for two reasons. First, all circuits that have addressed the issue, other than the Seventh, have applied Title VII's framework to ECOA claims. * * * Second, the Eleventh Circuit has unflinchingly applied Title VII's analytical framework to a host of anti-discrimination statutes, thus this court does not find any reason to suspect that the Eleventh Circuit would take a different approach to the ECOA. * * *

Having concluded that Title VII's analytical framework will govern the Plaintiff's section 1981, FHA and ECOA claims, the court will now address the merits of these claims. As discussed above, Title VII's framework permits a plaintiff in a discrimination case to proceed by one of two means: 1) circumstantial evidence under *McDonnell Douglas* burden shifting, or 2) direct evidence. *See Damon v. Fleming Supermarkets*, 196 F.3d 1354, 1359 (11th Cir.1999). "Direct evidence is evidence that establishes the existence of discriminatory intent behind the employment decision without any inference or presumption. Therefore, remarks by non-decisionmakers or remarks unrelated to the decision making process itself are not direct evidence of discrimination." *Standard v. A.B.E.L. Servs., Inc.*, 161 F.3d 1318, 1330 (11th Cir.1998) (citations omitted). As the Eleventh Circuit has explained, "only the most blatant remarks, whose intent could be nothing other than to discriminate on the protected classification are direct evidence of discrimination." *Id.* (internal quotations omitted); *see Gullatte v. Westpoint Stevens, Inc.*, 100 F.Supp.2d 1315, 1318 (M.D.Ala.2000) (explaining that "the paradigm example of direct evidence would be a statement such as 'Fire Earley—he is too old'."). In this case, none of the statements regarding the Plaintiff's race outlined above meet the standards of direct evidence of race discrimination, thus the court's analysis will be guided by the three-step framework established in *McDonnell Douglas Corp. v. Green*, 411 U.S. 792, 93 S.Ct. 1817, 36 L.Ed.2d 668 (1973).

Under the *McDonnell Douglas* analysis, the plaintiff must first establish a prima facie case of race discrimination. At the second stage, the burden of production is placed upon the defendant to articulate a legitimate non-discriminatory reason for its adverse action. Once the defendant satisfies its burden of production, the plaintiff then has the burden of persuading the court that the proffered reason for the defendant's action is a pretext for discrimination. The plaintiff may satisfy this burden either directly, by persuading the court that a discriminatory reason more likely motivated the employer, or indirectly, by showing that the employer's proffered explanation is unworthy of belief. A plaintiff's prima facie case, combined with sufficient evidence to find that the defendant's asserted justification is false, may permit the trier of fact to conclude that the defendant unlawfully discriminated against the plaintiff.

* * * In the credit discrimination context, a plaintiff can establish a prima facie case of discrimination by offering evidence showing: 1) that the plaintiff is a member of a protected class; 2) that the plaintiff applied for and was qualified for a loan from the defendant; 3) that the loan was rejected despite the plaintiff's qualifications; and 4) that the defendant continued to approve loans for applicants outside of the plaintiff's protected class with similar qualifications.

In this case, the parties do not dispute the existence of the first and third elements, as the Plaintiff is an African–American who applied for a line of credit and Sterling rejected his application despite his qualifications. Therefore, the only contested aspects of the Plaintiff's prima facie case are whether the Plaintiff was "qualified" for a $100,000 unsecured line of credit, and whether Sterling continued to approve loans for white applicants with "similar qualifications." Even assuming the Plaintiff could establish that he was qualified for the line of credit he requested, the court concludes that the Plaintiff has not presented sufficient evidence to establish that Sterling approved loans for white applicants with similar qualifications.

* * * [T]he Plaintiff must present evidence that he was "similarly situated in all relevant aspects" to the non-minority applicants who received loans from Sterling. In other words, a comparator's credit qualifications and loan details must be "nearly identical" to the Plaintiff's in order to prevent this court from second guessing the bank's business decision "and confusing apples with oranges." *Id.; see* Sallion, 87 F.Supp.2d at 1331 ("[A plaintiff] does not have to find an exact match between her application and applicants outside the protected classes who received loans, but comparator loan files must be significantly parallel in every material respect.").

In support of his position that Sterling approved loans for non-minority applicants with similar qualifications, the Plaintiff has introduced into evidence credit files of twenty Caucasian credit applicants who sought unsecured loans of $100,000 or more between January 2000 and April 2002. Additionally, the Plaintiff has submitted an affidavit from Charles L. "Rusty" Williams, an expert in banking and loan decision making, that analyzes this data. Although Williams concedes that "not all of the files produced are comparator loan files," he has highlighted three specific files that he believes "significantly parallel" the Plaintiff's loan file. Williams directs the court's attention to the loan files identified by the parties as numbers 17, 19, and 29.

After considering the factual specifics of these files against the Plaintiff's file, the court concludes that they are neither "nearly identical" nor "similarly situated in all relevant aspects." This conclusion is warranted for several reasons. First, unlike the three comparators, the Plaintiff was the only person who had active unsecured lines of credit at other financial institutions at the time he applied for his loan. Second, the undisputed evidence establishes that the Plaintiff's annual income was approximately $51,000. By comparison, "loan 17" earned $145,000, "loan 19" earned $300,000, and "loan 29" earned $148,000. Stated differently, the closest comparator to the Plaintiff earned approximately three times as much money as he did. Third, the Plaintiff was applying for his first line of credit with Sterling, thus he did not have an established credit relationship. In contrast, "loan 17" had been renewed 3 times, "loan 19" had been renewed twice, and "loan 29" had been renewed 5 times. Taken together, the Plaintiff has not directed the court to any evidence to suggest that an applicant similarly situated to the Plaintiff in terms of a prior credit relationship, existing lines of credit, and annual income received a loan from Sterling. Each of these factors is a "relevant aspect" of a bank's decision to extend or deny credit, thus the court concludes that the Plaintiff has not established the requisite degree of similarity to meet his burden at the prima facie stage.

Although the Plaintiff has directed the court to areas of his credit history which are similar to the three comparator loans—for example, total assets and Beacon Score—the areas discussed above are sufficiently dissimilar to destroy any presumption of discrimination that could arise from a comparison of the loan files. As stated by the Eleventh Circuit, a "valid prima facie case creates a presumption that discrimination has occurred." *Walker v. Mortham,* 158 F.3d 1177, 1183 (11th Cir.1998). The "similarly situated" prong of the prima facie test is important because no presumption of discrimination arises the fact that a defendant treated dissimilar persons differently. The present case illustrates this principle, as the Plaintiff has failed to show that Sterling approved a loan for a non-minority applicant "similarly situated" to the Plaintiff "in all relevant aspects." Because the Plaintiff has failed to establish a prima facie case of discrimination, summary judgment is due to be granted in favor of the Defendants.

Even assuming, however, that the Plaintiff could establish a prima facie case, the court concludes that the Plaintiff's claims would fail at the pretext stage of the *McDonnell Douglas* analysis. With respect to Sterling's legitimate, non-discriminatory reason for its decision, Sterling denied the Plaintiff's loan request due to the Plaintiff's "heavy debt to income ratio." Specifically, the Plaintiff had an individual income of $51,484 and his financial statement showed a debt of $265,000 and unsecured lines of credit totaling an additional $200,000. As Hill stated in his October 27, 2000 letter to the Plaintiff: "Bottom line, with a potential debt load of $465,000 on income of $51,484," Sterling was not prepared to offer a $100,000 unsecured line of credit.

Because Sterling articulated a non-discriminatory reason for its decision, the burden shifts back to the Plaintiff to offer sufficient evidence for a reasonable factfinder to conclude that Sterling's proffered reason was not the true reasons for its decision to deny the Plaintiff's credit application, but a pretext for discrimination. * * * The Plaintiff can accomplish this task "(1) by showing that the legitimate nondiscriminatory reasons should not be believed; or (2) by showing that, in light of all of the evidence, discriminatory reasons more likely motivated the decision than the proffered reasons." *See Standard,* 161 F.3d at 1332. The Plaintiff's evidence of pretext comes in three forms. First, Plaintiff points to Greg Calhoun's testimony as evidence of Sterling's racial discrimination. Second, the Plaintiff argues that Sterling's reasons are unworthy of belief because his application should have been accepted due to his superior credit rating and substantial net worth. Third, the Plaintiff contends that Sterling's failure to follow its own lending policies is evidence of pretext.

When viewed in a light most favorable to the Plaintiff, Greg Calhoun's testimony establishes that members of Sterling's Board of Directors laughed and joked after Worrell informed the Board that the Plaintiff may be contacting them about the decision to deny his loan. According to the Eleventh Circuit, however, "comments by non-decisionmakers do not raise an inference of discrimination, especially if those comments are ambiguous." *Mitchell v. USBI Co.,* 186 F.3d 1352, 1355 (11th Cir.1999). In the present case, the undisputed evidence establishes that Hill, Ramsey, and Worrell made a "group decision" to deny the Plaintiff's loan request prior to the September Board meeting, thus the Board was not a decisionmaker in this process. Only Ramsey, Worrell, or Sterling's loan committee had the requisite authority to approve a loan request. * * * Furthermore, the laughter that Calhoun says he heard most certainly qualifies as an ambiguous statement that does not necessarily reflect discriminatory intent. * * * There is no evidence to suggest that the Board made any racially derogatory jokes or comments. *Compare Busby v. City of Orlando,* 931 F.2d 764, 781–82 (11th Cir.1991) (concluding that racially derogatory jokes are evidence of discriminatory intent). Consequently, the Plaintiff cannot rely on Calhoun's deposition testimony as evidence of pretext.

The Plaintiff also contends that he has undermined the truthfulness of Sterling's reasons by producing evidence of his excellent credit credentials. For example, the Plaintiff states that he "was worth $2.6 million when he applied for the loan, he had an unblemished financial history, his beacon score was very high, he had over half a million dollars in liquid assets, he had over $100,000.00 in Sterling Bank and he was close friends with [Kenny Hill,] the Vice President of Sterling Bank." The central problem with this line of argument is that it fails to recognize that proving pretext requires more than showing that a bank was wrong in its assessment of the underlying facts or was otherwise lacking in wisdom in its decision not to extend credit. Federal courts do not sit as a court of appeals that reexamines a bank's business decisions. *See Elrod v. Sears, Roebuck & Co.*, 939 F.2d 1466, 1470 (11th Cir.1991). Instead, the court's inquiry at the pretext stage is limited to whether the bank "gave an honest explanation of its behavior." *Id*. Therefore, to establish pretext, the Plaintiff must meet the bank's non-discriminatory "reason head on and rebut it," rather than simply present evidence of his positive credentials and ask the court to substitute its business judgment for that of the bank.

The Plaintiff relies heavily on the expert analysis of Charles "Rusty" Williams to establish pretext, however, Williams's affidavit merely provides a thorough recitation of the Plaintiff's positive credentials and does not cast doubt on Sterling's assertion that the Plaintiff's individual annual income was insufficient relative to his current debt level to support another $100,000 unsecured line of credit. Although Williams states that the "assertion that [the Plaintiff's] income was not sufficient to support $300,000 of unsecured loans is unfounded[,]" Williams's only supporting evidence is the Plaintiff's "large number of liquid assets" and positive credit report. This evidence is insufficient to establish pretext because Williams completely ignores the fact that Sterling did not deny the Plaintiff's loan application because of insufficient liquid assets or a poor credit rating. Sterling rejected the Plaintiff's loan request because his annual income could not shoulder an additional $100,000 worth of debt. Rather than undermine Sterling's non-discriminatory reason "head on," Williams has "side-stepped" the issue by pointing to evidence of the Plaintiff's positive credentials, which, as the court previously explained, cannot establish pretext.

Finally, the Plaintiff attempts to establish pretext by arguing that Sterling has failed to follow its own banking policies. According to Williams, Sterling did not adhere to its loan policies "when granting loans to various Caucasian individuals." Nevertheless, Williams fails to direct the court to any specific loan policy provisions that Sterling violated. In his brief, the Plaintiff contends that Sterling "failed to calculate debt service coverage ratios on all but one of the twenty loan files." Even assuming that this fact is true, it is not enough to establish pretext. Although "[d]epartures from normal procedures may be suggestive of discrimination," *Morrison v. Booth*, 763 F.2d 1366, 1374 (11th Cir.1985), "the mere fact that [a bank] failed to follow its own internal procedures does not necessarily suggest that [the bank] was motivated by illegal discriminatory intent." *See Randle v. City of Aurora*, 69 F.3d 441, 454 (10th Cir.1995). Here, the court concludes that Sterling's failure to calculate debt service coverage ratios in some of its loan files neither undermines its non-discriminatory reasons for denying the Plaintiff's loan nor provides a basis from which a reasonable jury could conclude that Sterling was more likely motivated by a discriminatory reason.

V. Conclusion and Order

For the reasons stated above, the court concludes that the Plaintiff has not proven a prima facie case of credit discrimination due to the absence of sufficient evidence to establish that Sterling approved loans for applicants outside of the plaintiff's protected class with similar loan qualifications. Even if the Plaintiff could prove his prima facie case, however, the court finds that the evidence submitted is insufficient to establish that Sterling's non-discriminatory reasons for its loan decision are pretextual. Accordingly, Sterling's Motion for Summary Judgment is due to be GRANTED * * *

Notes

1. After *Latimore*, how can a plaintiff prove discrimination in the Seventh Circuit? Will the disparate treatment test work? What about the disparate effects test?

2. Is *Latimore* correct that the Title VII model is inappropriate in credit discrimination cases because individuals rarely compete for loans as they do for jobs? If so, why does the Court use its "Eromital" example that presents just such a competition? See Mane Hajdin, The McDonnell Douglas Standard in Lending–Discrimination Cases: A Circuit Split? 33 McGeorge L. Rev. 1, 14–15 (2001–2002). Other than Eleventh Circuit precedent, what arguments does *Cooley* make for using the disparate treatment test? Are there other arguments to be made? Other cases appearing to continue reliance on the Title VII burden-shifting model and therefore rejecting Latimore in credit discrimination cases include Mays v. Buckeye Rural Elect. Coop., 277 F.3d 873 (6th Cir. 2002); Rosa v. Park West Bank, 214 F.3d 213 (1st Cir. 2000); Sallion v. SunTrust Bank, 87 F.Supp.2d 1323 (N.D. Ga. 2000).

3. Assume that Hill, Ramsey, and Worrell had joked about the plaintiff's application and laughed at the plaintiff at the time they made the decision to deny his application in the form he had requested. Would this be sufficient to establish a prima facie case under the disparate treatment test? What if all of the legitimate reasons cited by the court for denying the loan were still present? How should the test be applied if the lender's motives in denying the loan were mixed, that is, based partly on proper criteria (past performance on other loans) and partly on improper criteria (sexual stereotypes)? Cf. Price Waterhouse v. Hopkins, 490 U.S. 228, 109 S.Ct. 1775, 104 L.Ed.2d 268 (1989), superseded by statute in employment law, 42 U.S.C.A. § 2000e–2(m).

Problem 4–26

Willie Acton grew up in an African–American ghetto in a large city. His athletic ability made him a basketball star in high school, but not quite good enough for college scholarship offers. There was also the matter of several juvenile arrests and convictions, one for assault and one for vandalism. After high school Willie joined the army and spent several years at various bases in the southwest. He got an honorable discharge and, as he put it, "I got my head on straight." He went to work as an apprentice electrician (hoping to develop skills learned in the service) for a company in Tucson, Arizona. Six months later he transferred to the company's Memphis, Tennessee, offices. A year after that he moved back to the city where he grew up, partly to be close to his sister, but also to take what he thought would be a better job. The job did not work out well—Willie's lack of seniority precluded promotion to jobs for which he thought he was qualified—so he moved to another minority-run company in the same city.

About this same time he married, and the couple rented a larger apartment closer to Willie's job in the inner city area. Willie's sense of frugality led him to maintain a modest savings account in a nearby savings and loan association.

About a year and a half later Willie and his wife thought it was time they bought a house. Both of them agreed they wanted to stay in the downtown area, and they located a home for sale in Willie's old neighborhood. The house was about forty years old; it needed paint and a new roof, but it was spacious and the Actons could see all kinds of possibilities for renovating and redecorating it themselves.

But when the Actons applied to their savings and loan association for mortgage credit, they were turned down, politely but firmly. The loan officer told Willie that he didn't qualify on several grounds: (1) his prior criminal record; (2) his frequent job changes; (3) the unsuitability of the home as mortgage collateral, it being in a borderline area with generally deteriorating property values, and almost exclusively blue collar workers living there.

The Actons have hired your firm to represent them. What theories might you develop on their behalf? Be prepared to suggest what additional information would be needed to support your theories, and how you could obtain that information.

Problem 4–27

Larry's Bank has an arrangement with several car dealers. When a consumer wishes to buy a car on credit but does not have a lender lined up, Larry's uses its credit scoring model—which is carefully formulated to avoid discriminating against any protected group—to calculate the minimum interest rate it would charge that consumer (called the "buy rate" because it is the rate at which Larry's is willing to buy the consumer's loan from the dealer). Larry's then notifies the dealer of the buy rate. The dealer then negotiates the loan with the consumer, and is permitted to add up to 3% to the buy rate (called the "markup"). After the dealer makes the loan, it sells it to Larry's. If the loan includes a markup, Larry's rebates a portion of the markup to the dealer and retains a portion. Larry's would like to know whether this arrangement exposes it to any risks. If a dealer charges a higher markup to groups protected under ECOA, would Larry's be liable? Advise Larry's. See ECOA, 15 U.S.C. § 1691a(e); Reg B, 12 C.F.R. § 202.2(*l*); Coleman v. General Motors Accept. Corp., 196 F.R.D. 315 (M.D.Tn. 2000), *order granting class certification vacated*, 296 F.3d 443 (6th Cir. 2002). The Official Staff Commentary on Regulation B provides in ¶ 2(*l*)(1) that "creditor" "may include an assignee or a potential purchaser of the obligation who influences the credit decision by indicating whether or not it will purchase the obligation if the transaction is consummated."

5. REDLINING—DISCRIMINATION IN HOME MORTGAGE LENDING

The term "redlining" apparently derives from the practices of the Home Owners' Loan Corporation (HOLC), a Depression-era government-sponsored program that institutionalized standardized appraisal practices as part of the mortgage-granting process. HOLC appraisers used a color-coded rating system to evaluate the risks of lending within specific neighborhoods; one supposed "risk" was racial integration. Red was the worst grade. See Charles L. Nier, III, Perpetuation of Segregation: Toward a New Historical and Legal Interpretation of Redlining Under the Fair Housing Act, 32 J. Marshall L. Rev. 617, 620–24 (1999). Though HOLC itself seemingly was willing to lend to red areas, over time the word redlining came to refer to the practice of rejecting mortgage and home improvement loan applications from certain neighborhoods, generally because of their racial composition. More recently, the phrase "reverse-redlining," has come to signify the targeting of redlined communities for the offering of credit on expensive terms.

As explained in Note, Attacking the Urban Redlining Problem, 56 B.U.L.Rev. 989, 989–90, 996–97 (1976):*

> Redlining can have a considerable impact upon an urban community. Neighborhood vitality bears a direct relationship to the adequate availability of mortgage credit. Because of the enormous costs involved, very few individuals can afford to buy or even repair a home with their savings alone. Thus, to a large extent, institutional lenders determine the futures of individual urban neighborhoods. Those neighborhoods that receive adequate funding will remain viable while those that do not are likely to decay. As a result, redlining can often be a self-fulfilling prophecy; frequently, a lender's fear that an area is on the decline ultimately causes that decline to occur.

Not only does redlining deprive neighborhoods of needed development, but it can also pull money out of communities. When banks maintain branches in neighborhoods but do not lend in those neighborhoods, the effect is to use the savings of one neighborhood to develop others. Congress responded to this problem by enacting the Community Reinvestment Act of 1977, 12 U.S.C.A. § 2901 et seq. The CRA and its implementing regulations require regulatory agencies to consider whether financial institutions are meeting the credit needs of the entire community, including low-and moderate-income neighborhoods. The CRA does not provide for a private cause of action, see Hicks v. Resolution Trust Corp., 970 F.2d 378 (7th Cir.1992), but it has been a potent weapon when banks seek a merger. Federally-chartered financial institutions require approval from their federal supervisory agencies for certain activities, including merging with another institution or opening a new branch. On a number of occasions, local groups have threatened to file with banking agencies CRA-based objections to a merger. The ensuing negotiations have frequently produced commitments to increase lending to minority communities. See Marianne Lavelle, Advocates for Poor Pounce When Banks Plan Mergers; In an Effort to Ward Off Problems With Regulators, Banks are Pledging to Invest Millions in Inner–City Communities, Nat'l L.J., Feb. 12, 1996, at B1. Regulatory enforcement of CRA has been uneven: while regulators denied few requests on CRA grounds before 1991, for a time afterwards they enforced the statute somewhat more aggressively. See Richard D. Marsico, Shedding Some Light on Lending: The Effect of Expanded Disclosure Laws on Home Mortgage Marketing Lending and Discrimination in the New York Metropolitan Area, 27 Fordham Urb. L.J. 481, 507–09 (1999).

Supporters of CRA claim that it has increased lending to low-income areas that might otherwise remain blighted. See e.g., Editorial, A 20–Year Antidote to Red–Lining, St. Louis Post–Dispatch, Oct. 12, 1997 at O2B ("CRA is credited with encouraging banks and thrifts to make $175 billion in loan commitments to low-and moderate-income consumers in the past four years."). Critics of CRA complain that it forces banks to lend to higher-risk borrowers and interferes with normal market forces. See Joseph J. Norton, "Fair Lending" Requirements: The Intervention of a Governmental Social Agenda into Bank Supervision and Regulation, 49 Consumer Fin. L. Q. 17, 27–28 (1995). They claim that CRA imposes significant compliance costs on institutions and charge that it discourages lenders from opening branches in low-income neighborhoods while penalizing lenders that already have such branches by requiring them to make loans they might otherwise not be able to justify making. See Jonathan R. Macey & Geoffrey P. Miler, The Community Reinvestment Act: An Economic Analysis, 79 Va. L. Rev. 291 (1993). Critics also claim that banks do in fact meet the credit needs of low-income areas. See Jeffrey M. Lacker, Neighborhoods and Banking, Fed. Reserve Bank of Richmond Econ. Q. Spring 1995 at 13. Finally, they contend that whatever merit CRA might have had when first enacted, changes in the mortgage industry—an influx of mortgage companies eager to serve the needs of CRA-eligible borrowers—have made it unnecessary. Jeffery W. Gunther, Kelly Klemme and Kenneth J. Robinson, Redlining or Red Herring, Southwest Econ., May/June 1999.

Empirical study has found that CRA-type lending has increased faster than lending in other markets. Robert E. Litan, Nicholas P. Retsinas, Eric S. Belsky & Susan White Haag, The Community Reinvestment Act After Financial Modernization: A Baseline Report (U.S. Treasury Dept. 2000). Similarly, a study by the Fed found that when banks consolidate, they "generally increased the proportion of loans [they] extend[]" to lower-income and minority communities. Robert B. Avery, Raphael W. Bostic, Paul S. Calem & Glenn B. Cannor, Trends in Home Purchase Lending: Consolidation and the Community Reinvestment Act, 85 Fed. Res. Bull. 81, 82 (1999). While some have concluded that the

CRA has had an impact, see Joint Center for Housing Studies, Harvard University, The 25th Anniversary of the Community Reinvestment Act: Access to Capital in an Evolving Financial Services System 58 (2002) ("CRA lenders originate a higher proportion of CRA-eligible loans than they would if CRA did not exist"); Eric Belsky, Michael Schill & Anthony Yezer, The Effect of the Community Reinvestment Act on Bank and Thrift Home Purchase Mortgage Lending (Harvard University Joint Center for Housing Studies 2001) ("the most comprehensive evidence on lending patterns thus far analyzed is consistent with the proposition that CRA does have a positive effect on low and moderate income lending by depository institutions."); Michael S. Barr, Credit Where It Counts: The Community Reinvestment Act and Its Critics, 80 N.Y.U.L. Rev. 513, 580 (2005) ("CRA appears to increase lending to low-and moderate-income communities and minority borrowers more than one would predict based on market forces and other factors."), others attribute the increases in lending to deregulation and new technologies, see Jeffrey W. Gunther, Should CRA Stand for "Community Redundancy Act"? Regulation at 56 (2000).

Additional empirical evidence sheds some light on whether the increase in lending to low-and moderate-income communities has come at too dear a cost. In 2000 the Federal Reserve Board surveyed banks about the profitability of CRA-related loans. Report by the Board of Governors of the Federal Reserve System, The Performance and Profitability of CRA–Related Lending (2000). The Fed invited the largest 500 retail banking institutions to participate, but only 143 did, raising questions about how typical the respondents' experiences are of banking generally. In any event, more than half of those who responded indicated that CRA-related lending was about as profitable as non-CRA home purchase and refinancing lending, while 19% reported that it was less profitable and 25% stated that it was somewhat less profitable. The Fed also noted that "More than two-thirds of the respondents report that their CRA-related lending has led to new, profitable opportunities." *Id.* at xii. Another survey—this one conducted by a banking trade association of its members—found that small banks spent an average of $84,445 annually to comply with CRA while larger banks spent $115,270. Grant Thornton, Independent Community Bankers of America, The High Cost of Community Bank CRA Compliance: Comparison of "Large" and "Small" Community Banks *vi*.

CARTWRIGHT v. AMERICAN SAVINGS & LOAN ASSOC.

United States Court of Appeals, Seventh Circuit, 1989.
880 F.2d 912.

COFFEY, CIRCUIT JUDGE

The plaintiffs-appellants Mary Cartwright and the Northwest Indiana Open Housing Center commenced a suit alleging that the defendant-appellee American Savings & Loan Association ("American

Savings") refused to approve an application for a home construction loan in 1980 because of Mary Cartwright's race and sex and engaged in "redlining" in the neighborhood where Mrs. Cartwright intended to build, in violation of the Fair Housing Act (42 U.S.C. §§ 3604 and 3605), the Equal Credit Opportunity Act (15 U.S.C. § 1691) and civil rights statutes (42 U.S.C. §§ 1981 and 1982). American Savings moved for involuntary dismissal pursuant to Fed.R.Civ.P. 41(b), arguing that the facts and the law presented during the court trial failed to establish a right to relief. The district judge agreed. We affirm.

I.

On August 24, 1965, the plaintiff-appellant Mary Cartwright, a black female, and her first husband, Shishmon Bailey, obtained a mortgage loan from the defendant-appellee American Savings for a single-family residence at 5901 Columbia Avenue, Hammond, Indiana. Some twelve years later, on December 5, 1977, American Savings approved a second mortgage on the same real estate at 5901 Columbia in the amount of $15,000.

On or about July 10, 1980, Mary Cartwright and her second husband, Lawrence Cartwright, purchased lots 29 through 33 at 1112 Merrill Street in the East Hammond (Indiana) urban renewal area. * * *

On August 28, 1980, Mary and Lawrence Cartwright applied for a $90,000 home mortgage loan from American Savings to finance the construction of a home on the Merrill Street property. * * * Louis Green, vice-president of American Savings charged with mortgage loan responsibility, accepted the Cartwrights' application on August 28, 1980. * * *

[The district court found that the bank was not able to consider the 1980 application.]

Both Green and Mary Cartwright testified that Green advised the appellant during the May 28, 1982, meeting that interest rates were extremely high (17 1/2 percent) at the time and that it would be more economically advantageous for her to sell her home rather than offer it for rent and apply the sale proceeds toward the construction costs of her proposed new Merrill Street residence. Green also reiterated that Mrs. Cartwright could apply for Indiana Housing Authority bond money through the Lake Mortgage Company. The appellant testified that Green also told her during this meeting that she should sell her Columbia Avenue home because "being a woman you can't take care of two properties." Although Green and Cartwright arranged the May 28, 1982, meeting so Cartwright could file a new loan application, she chose not to complete an application at that time but did file a new loan application in early October 1982, which American Savings approved on November 22, 1982. Mary Cartwright had no contact with Green or American Savings between the May 28, 1982, meeting and the commencement of this suit on August 27, 1982.

The trial court * * * found as follows:

"At all times relevant hereto, Mary Cartwright was a creditworthy individual and her credit history with American Savings was considered good. She had been a customer of American Savings since at least August of 1965. Mrs. Cartwright was and is an articulate and intelligent person.

* * *

American Savings did not reject or otherwise turn down or deny the loan application of Mary and Lawrence Cartwright. * * *American Savings' treatment of Mary and Lawrence Cartwrights' 1980 loan application was not based upon the race of Mary and/or Lawrence Cartwright and the racial character of the community in which they intended to build. American Savings' treatment of Mary Cartwright's loan inquiries in 1982 was not based upon Cartwright's race and/or sex or the racial character of the community in which she intended to build. American Savings has not engaged in the practice of 'redlining' in the central Hammond area, and has in fact provided a significant number of mortgage loans in this area."

In its conclusions of law, the trial court stated that the appellants failed to make out a prima facie case under § 3605 of the Fair Housing Act (42 U.S.C. § 3601 *et seq.*), captioned "Discrimination in financing of housing," initially stating:

"There is no evidence indicating that American Savings rejected or otherwise denied the August 1980 application. This application, because of lack of communication, inconsistent positions taken by Mrs. Cartwright, and total misunderstanding, went into abeyance and into limbo. Therefore, the plaintiffs have not proved that the loan was rejected . . . ,"

as § 3605 requires. The court also concluded that American Savings did not discriminate against Mary Cartwright. * * * Lastly, the court concluded that American Savings did not engage in "redlining" within the meaning of § 3605 because

"[T]he plaintiffs' evidence fails to offer a comparison between American Savings and other lending institutions; the relevant amount of total mortgage activity in all relevant areas; the number of mortgage applications received by American Savings, and the number of those applications rejected or withdrawn; or a relationship of comparable transactions from areas other than the area where the Cartwrights intended to build. This raw data does not establish that American Savings has engaged in any form of redlining."

* * * With respect to the appellants' claims under the Equal Credit Opportunity Act (15 U.S.C. § 1691), the court found no violation, stating:

"With respect to the August 1980 application, there was no evidence of discrimination by the defendant. As discussed previously, the application went into abeyance because of the total lack of consistent communication and understanding between Mrs. Cartwright and Mr. Green. Such lack of communication does not amount to discriminatory conduct by American Savings. Also, the application was not rejected and therefore no adverse action was taken with respect to the loan. With respect to the 1982 transaction, there has also not been a violation of the Equal Credit Opportunity Act. There is no evidence of race or sex discrimination regarding this transaction. Mrs. Cartwright never applied for a mortgage in early 1982 from American Savings."

The district court also denied relief under 42 U.S.C. §§ 1981 and 1982 because the appellants failed to establish to the court's satisfaction that American Savings intentionally discriminated against Mary Cartwright. * * *

II.

The plaintiffs-appellants challenge certain findings of fact and conclusions of law relating to each of the causes of action contained in their complaint.

§ 3605 of the Fair Housing Act

* * * The appellants also challenge several findings of fact relating to their claim under § 3605. The appellants allege, contrary to the court's findings, that American Savings * * * engaged in credit discrimination, or "redlining," based on the racial character of the community in which the Cartwrights intended to build. * * *

The trial court also found that the documentary evidence fails to support the appellants' allegation that American Savings engaged in redlining in violation of § 3605 of the Fair Housing Act. The appellants argue in their plethora of unsupported claims of error that the statistical as well as the testimonial evidence supports their redlining allegation.

The plaintiffs-appellants' statistical evidence of redlining from our review seems to rest upon two trial exhibits they prepared from information American Savings supplied revealing that American Savings granted two residential mortgage loans from January 1980 through January 1984 in the substantially black, urban area of Hammond containing Mary Cartwright's Merrill Street property ("census tract" number 207). In contrast, American Savings granted, during the same period, thirty six residential mortgage loans in census tract number 427, and twenty-five residential mortgage loans in census tract number 404, both of which, according to the 1980 census, have a zero to one percent black population. The appellants maintain that the disparity in the number of the residential loans American Savings granted in a minority area as opposed to a non-minority area constitutes proof of redlining.

The obvious flaw in the appellants' "disparity" argument is their failure to identify any relevant statistical evidence of the number of residential loan applications American Savings received from financially qualified borrowers in any particular census tract or geographical area, and how many of those applications it rejected. Such proof lies at the very heart of any redlining allegation, as it is absurd to allege a discriminatory refusal to approve loan applications in a particular area without proof that qualified borrowers actually applied and were rejected. We are unmoved by the fact that American Savings granted "only" two loan applications between January 1980 and January 1984 in census tract 207, because the appellants failed to present evidence of the number of applications American Savings received in that time frame for property located in that tract. It may be (for all we can determine from the record before us) that American Savings received only two loan applications for housing purchases in census tract 207, and granted them both. This evidence of a violation of § 3605 falls far short of establishing redlining.

Moreover, Louis Green's testimony supports the conclusion that the number of residential loan applications granted in census tract 207 was low because applications were few and far between, and not because American Savings practiced credit discrimination. Green (who served on American Savings' loan committee) testified that to his knowledge American Savings did not reject a single residential loan application from 1978 through the time of trial relating to property located in census tract 207. In addition, Green testified that American Savings did not receive any loan applications for construction in the East Hammond urban renewal area (part of census tract 207) prior to the time the Cartwrights applied for their loan in August 1980, and that the number of mortgage loan applications was generally low in 1979 and 1980 probably or possibly due to extremely high interest rates. We fail to understand how American Savings can be considered as responsible for redlining a particular geographical area if in fact as the testimony reveals it granted every application submitted to it for homes located therein, and the appellants failed to demonstrate that that is not, in fact, what occurred.

At oral argument, the appellants' counsel conceded that there is no "raw data" in the record establishing the number of residential loan applications American Savings received and rejected in "census tract" number 207. However, counsel contended and speculated that—based on Louis Green's treatment of Mary Cartwright during their May 28, 1982, meeting—that American Savings has a policy of "discouraging" loan applications for property located in minority neighborhoods. As we discuss *infra*, Louis Green did not "discourage" Mary Cartwright from filing a new loan application in May 1982. Rather, Green provided information regarding the record high 17 1/2 percent interest rate and the availability of low interest loans through another institution participating in the Indiana Housing Authority's bond program. We find no evidence in the record that would tend to suggest much less establish that Green offered the information with a racially discriminatory motive. We therefore reject the appellants' contention that American Savings had a policy of discouraging mortgage loan applications for property located in substantially or predominantly black neighborhoods.

The appellants also contend that their claim of redlining finds support in Mary and Lawrence Cartwrights' testimony that Louis Green told them during the initial August 28, 1980, meeting that the East Hammond urban renewal area could not "support" or "afford" a house as large as the one the Cartwrights wanted to build, but that other communities could support it. We note that the district court's findings of fact are silent as to whether Louis Green actually told the Cartwrights that the urban renewal area could not "afford" their proposed home, and this court refuses to assume facts unsupported as findings in the district court record. Even assuming that Green told the Cartwrights that the urban renewal area could not "afford" their proposed residence, we are not persuaded that the evidence establishes redlining.

The Fair Housing Act's prohibition against denying a loan based upon the location of the dwelling does not require that a lender disregard its legitimate business interests or make an investment that is not economically sound. It seems obvious that a lender must be concerned, for example, about financing a new, $90,000 home in a residential area comprised of homes valued at $60,000 or less. If the borrower defaults on the loan, the lender must foreclose and may be unable to recoup its investment, as potential buyers might be reluctant to pay $90,000 for the home (and other lenders may be unwilling to finance the purchase) in light of the surrounding property values. The regulations implementing the Fair Housing Act address this type of concern, stating lenders may legitimately consider "the present market value of the property offered as security . . . and the likelihood that the property will retain an adequate value over the term of the loan." 12 C.F.R. § 31.8(c)(7). *See also Thomas v. First Fed. Sav. Bank of Indiana*, 653 F.Supp. 1330, 1340 (N.D.Ind.1987) ("there is nothing in the Board's regulations or in the Board's policies which mandates an association to make a bad loan as long as the criteria they use for making the loan are legitimate business criteria. . . ." *Id.* (quoting *Laufman v. Oakley Bldg. & Loan Co.*, 408 F.Supp. 489, 501 (S.D.Oh.1976))).

If Louis Green told the Cartwrights that the East Hammond urban renewal area could not "afford" their proposed home, we believe the comment reflected American Savings' legitimate financial concern regarding (in the language of the regulation) "the present market value of the [Cartwrights'] property" and "the likelihood that the property [would] retain an adequate value over the term of the loan." In fact, Louis Green testified that his principal concern was that the Cartwrights' property and proposed residence would not retain an adequate value over the term of the loan, thereby putting American Savings at risk:

"Q: Mr. Green, when the Cartwrights came to see you in August of 1980, were you generally familiar with the urban renewal section in which they were proposing to build the house?

A: Generally familiar.

Q: What, if any, concern did you have about their plans to construct a $95,000 or $100,000 home in that area?

A: I assume that my concern was that there may not be—it might be an over-improvement for the area.

Q: What do you mean by an over-improvement to the area?

A: Well, an area, let's say comprised of $60,000 homes would have a—assuming you're going to build a $100,000 home in that particular area, as a lender we would obviously have a problem should we get that particular property back in a year or two or three or five.

* * *

Q: Now, when you either met with the Cartwrights or talked to Mrs. Cartwright concerning information about other construction or pending construction or plans, why did you ask the Cartwrights to give you that information?

* * *

A: Because to my way of thinking, that would be—it could very well be without any comparable homes, it would effectively be a depreciating influence, thereby endanger—increasing our risk as lender."

Neither Mary nor Lawrence Cartwright, nor Green's testimony, permits an inference that American Savings refused to invest in the East Hammond urban renewal area. The evidence demonstrates nothing more than that American Savings was concerned about financing a large, relatively expensive home in an area lacking other homes of comparable market value and sound economic judgment of this nature cannot be considered as a violation of the Fair Housing Act. As the lending institution, American Savings certainly has a real and substantial, legitimate interest in recouping its investment in the event the Cartwrights defaulted on their loan. Moreover, there is nothing in the record which leads us to believe that American Savings would have been concerned about the location of the Cartwrights' property had they intended to build a home of comparable value to others in the area. We affirm the district court's conclusion that American Savings did not engage in redlining in violation of § 3605 of the Fair Housing Act. * * *

The Equal Credit Opportunity Act Claims

The appellants also challenge the district court's rejection of their claims under the Equal Credit Opportunity Act, * * *

Finally, the appellants argue that Louis Green's statements to Mary Cartwright during their May 28, 1982, meeting establish a violation of § 1691(a)(1) of the Equal Credit Opportunity Act. Green told Mrs. Cartwright during the May 28, 1982, meeting that interest rates were at an all time record high level of 17 1/2 percent industry-wide; that it was financially advisable for her to sell her Columbia Avenue residence and use the proceeds as a downpayment on the loan needed for construction on her Merrill Street property; furthermore, that low interest loans were available to certain qualified borrowers through the Indiana Housing Authority's bond program and that another financial institution, Lake Mortgage Company, was a participant in the bond program.[18] The appellants, grasping for straws, and again venturing into the hazardous valley of speculation, claim that Green's advice was designed to discourage Mary Cartwright from applying for a home loan because of her race and her sex, and because American Savings did not want to invest in the East Hammond urban renewal area.

Our review of the record convinces us that Green did not discourage much less prevent Mary Cartwright from filing a loan application in May 1982. In our view, Louis Green offered Mrs. Cartwright valuable, sound financially reasoned, well-intentioned advice, for which she should have been appreciative, in advising her that the 17 1/2 percent interest rates were at an all time high, that there were advantages in selling her Columbia Avenue home and that low interest financing was available through another institution. Lenders should be commended, rather than sued, for advising borrowers of their various options and the economic realities of the day. We fail to understand how Mrs. Cartwright could have interpreted Green's comments during the May 28 meeting to mean that American Savings did not want to do business with her. From our review, the record evidence demonstrates that American Savings was only too happy to accommodate Mrs. Cartwright, as well as to assist her in her desire to live in the East Hammond urban renewal area. American Savings and Mary Cartwright had been doing business together since 1965, and American Savings had approved a first and second mortgage on Cartwright's Columbia Avenue property, which the district court found (and the appellants do not dispute) is located in the same "census tract" as the Merrill Street property at issue in this case. If for seventeen years American Savings saw no reason to discriminate against Mary Cartwright because of her race, sex or the location of her property, it is specious to allege that it would discriminate against her in 1982. Indeed, when Mary Cartwright finally did fill out a new loan application with American Savings in October 1982 for her Merrill Street home, American Savings granted the application the following month. Therefore, we also affirm the district court's conclusion that American Savings did not violate § 1691(a)(1) of the Equal Credit Opportunity Act in connection with Mary Cartwright's 1982 loan inquiry.

We also feel compelled at this juncture to express our belief that this case is yet another product of our overly litigious society, where lawsuits result from every real or imagined slight. The evidence demonstrates

---

18. Mary Cartwright testified that Louis Green also told her during the May 28, 1982, meeting that she should sell her Columbia Avenue home because "being a woman you can't take care of two properties." However, the district court did not make a finding of fact that Green made the comment to Mrs. Cartwright and thus im- plicitly rejected the testimony. Moreover, even assuming Green made the remark, we are convinced, viewing the record in its entirety, that the district court did not commit error in finding that American Savings did not discriminate against Mary Cartwright because of her sex.

that American Savings had a long, mutually satisfactory relationship with the appellant; that American Savings had on previous occasions granted first and second mortgages on the appellant's property located in the very same area she alleges American Savings redlined; that American Savings never denied the 1980 loan application that lies at the heart of the appellant's case; that the appellant effectively advised American Savings not to take any action on that application until she worked out her "personal problems"; and that in 1982 when the appellant was ready to pursue the loan, American Savings granted her new application—but the appellant decided to take her business elsewhere. These facts simply do not warrant the expense and diversion of private, public and judicial resources this suit has occasioned. * * *

III.

We hold that the trial court's findings of fact, based on its consideration of the documentary evidence and the credibility of the witnesses, are not clearly erroneous. We also concur with the court's conclusions of law. * * *The judgment of the district court is AFFIRMED.

CUDAHY, CIRCUIT JUDGE, concurring:

I concur in the result and in the analysis because the issues primarily involve questions of fact and the district court's fact-finding is not clearly erroneous. I should prefer, however, not to address the general question who is the more deserving or meritorious litigant. This is a question we have neither the capability nor the obligation to answer.

Notes

1.   Why didn't the plaintiff sue under the CRA? Do ECOA or the FHA even mention redlining?

2.   Do you agree that this case is an example of our overly-litigious society?

3.   How might the plaintiff have proved her redlining claim? One critic of *Cartwright* has written:

> After considering the enormous number of hours needed to compile such daunting statistics and the plaintiff's need to rely on the allegedly discriminatory lending institution to supply much of this data, it appears unlikely that the Cartwright decision and the judicial standard for Fair Housing Act and Equal Credit Opportunity Act claims would allow plaintiffs to bring viable causes of action, even when discrimination clearly exists. The amount of statistical data on mortgage lenders needed to satisfy FHA and ECOA claims is unjustly overwhelming.

Michael S. Little, Note, A Citizen's Guide to Attacking Mortgage Discrimination: The Lack of Judicial Relief, 15 B.C. Third World L.J. 323 (1995). Do you agree?

4.   The court stated that "the number of residential loan applications granted in census tract 207 was low because applications were few and far between." Does the lender have any responsibility to increase the number of

applications from tract 207? If not, should it? What if the lender contributed to the paucity of such applications? See Charles L. Nier, III, Perpetuation of Segregation: Toward a New Historical and Legal Interpretation of Redlining Under the Fair Housing Act, 32 J. Marshall L. Rev. 617, 646–67 (1999) (few applications might be made to a bank that is "effective at the practice of redlining"). Plaintiff apparently tried to suggest as much by arguing that the bank discouraged her from applying for a loan. What evidence would have persuaded the court that the bank did indeed attempt to discourage her from applying? Would it have made a difference if the court concluded that the bank had attempted to dissuade her from applying?

5. The court approves the practice of taking into account the value of the surrounding homes in considering the loan. How is that different from redlining?

6. A number of states have enacted anti-redlining statutes. For example, Mass. Gen. Laws Ann. Ch. 183, § 64 provides: "No mortgagee shall discriminate, on a basis that is arbitrary or unsupported by a reasonable analysis of the lending risks associated with a residential mortgage transaction * * * on the basis such property is located in a specific neighborhood or geographical area." Would that statute have been helpful to the Cartwrights?

7. One commentator has concluded:

Federal and state courts are financially unequipped and overburdened: therefore, they are ineffective and impractical arenas for resolving a wave of highly intricate and emotionally charged disputes involving mortgage redlining * * * [courts] are likely to practice race and gender discrimination themselves.

Willy E. Rice, Race, Gender, "Redlining," and the Discriminatory Access to Loans, Credit, and Insurance: An Historical and Empirical Analysis of Consumers Who Sued Lenders and Insurers in Federal and State Courts, 1950–1995, 33 San Diego L. Rev. 583, 597–98 (1996). After reading the cases in this chapter, would you agree?

8. Another scholar has suggested that financial institutions should be able to fulfill their CRA obligations by making a substantial investment in community development banks and other qualifying investments. Peter P. Swire, Safe Harbors and a Proposal to Improve the Community Reinvestment Act, 79 Va. L. Rev. 349 (1993). Would this be a more effective way of addressing redlining?

9. Why should mortgage lenders have an obligation to serve their entire community? Has Congress imposed such an obligation on any other enterprise? See Lawrence J. White, The Community Reinvestment Act: Good Intentions Headed in the Wrong Direction, 20 Fordham. Urb. L.J. 281 (1993).

10. Race continued to play a role in appraisals decades after the Depression. See Hanson v. Veterans Admin., 800 F.2d 1381 (5th Cir. 1986) ("Appellants introduced proof that a widely used appraisal text, *The Appraisal of Real Estate,* instructed appraisers until 1977 that the value of the property being appraised should be adjusted downward if the ethnic composition of the neighborhood to which it belonged was not homogeneous.").

Underappraisals can be an effective way to redline because they both make it harder for the buyer to obtain a loan and reduce the value of other homes in the area. As *Cartwright* demonstrates, the value of homes is affected by the value of neighboring real estate—thus making the underappraisal a self-fulfilling reality. See Steptoe v. Savings of America, 800 F.Supp. 1542, 1547 (N.D. Ohio 1992) (plaintiffs made out prima facie case that alleged underappraisal had racially discriminatory effect on plaintiffs themselves and "possibly, all other potential borrowers who wished to purchase homes in the" neighborhood.). Federal regulations state that a lender may not rely on an appraisal which it knows or should know "is discriminatory on the basis of the age or location of the dwelling." 12 C.F.R. § 528.2a(a). Would this have helped in *Cartwright*? A 1991 amendment to ECOA gives applicants the right to a copy of the appraisal. See 15 U.S.C. § 1691(e). Other federal regulations address other practices which lend themselves to redlining, such as advertising. See 12 C.F.R. Parts 338 and 528.

11.   What are the differences between ECOA, the FHA, and § 1982?

12.   Neighborhood groups also complain about housing insurance redlining. Because lenders typically will not provide a mortgage to an uninsured house, consumers who cannot obtain insurance cannot obtain a mortgage, and so will be unable to buy a house in the redlined neighborhood. Is insurance redlining prohibited by any of the federal laws we have studied in this chapter? See National Assoc. for the Advancement of Colored People v. Am. Fam. Mut. Ins. Co., 978 F.2d 287 (7th Cir. 1992), *cert. denied* 508 U.S. 907, 113 S.Ct. 2335, 124 L.Ed.2d 247 (1993) (insurance redlining violates § 3604 of FHA).

Note on Data About Discrimination

Another statute directed at lending discrimination is the Home Mortgage Disclosure Act of 1975 (HMDA), 12 U.S.C.A. § 2801 et seq. HMDA requires all depository lending institutions to compile and make available to the public the number and total dollar amount of all mortgage loans for each fiscal year, grouped according to census tract or zip code area. The theory is that individuals and groups, by analyzing the data, will be able to discover redlining practices and use public pressure, deposit withdrawals, or other means to attack offensive practices. The current version of the implementing regulations requires lenders to record and make available to the public the ethnicity, race, and sex of applicants for housing loans whether the loan was granted or not, 12 C.F.R. §§ 203.4(a)(10), 203.5, information which might have been helpful in *Cartwright*. HMDA data can be useful in proving or disproving discrimination in connection with housing lending, but such data tends not to be available for other types of loans; indeed, ECOA bars lenders from inquiring about such things as ethnicity, subject to certain exceptions. Reg. B, 12 C.F.R. § 202.5(b).

While HMDA requires only the collection and publication of data, it may have had an effect on mortgage lending. One commentator found that after amendments in HMDA increased the amount of data to be disclosed, "the market share of applications from and loans to African–Americans, Latinos, [low and moderate income] applicants increased" in the area studied. Richard D. Marsico, Shedding Some Light on Lending: The Effect of Expanded

Disclosure Laws on Home Mortgage Marketing Lending and Discrimination in the New York Metropolitan Area, 27 Fordham Urb. L.J. 481, 528 (1999) (hereinafter "Marsico Study"). But perhaps HMDA's greatest impact has come from the data it made available indicating that people of color were two or three times more likely to be denied mortgage loans than whites. See, e.g., Binyamin Appelbaum & Ted Mellnik, The Hard Truth in Lending, Charlotte Observer, Aug. 28, 2005 (in 2004, "the nation's 10 largest banks still denied black applicants twice as often as whites. On average they made only 5 percent of their home loans to blacks."). Similarly, Census data consistently reports that a far higher percentage of non-Hispanic whites own their own homes than African–Americans, among others. See U.S. Census Bureau, Homeownership Rates by Race and Ethnicity of Householder: 1994 to 2004, available at http://www.census.gov/hhes/www/housing/hvs/annual04/ ann04t20.html (as of 2004, 72.8% of whites owned their home while 49.1% of African–Americans did). Nevertheless, this data left unanswered an important question: were the different rates because of discrimination or more neutral reasons, such as weaker applications? In 1992, a study, later published as Alicia H. Munnell, Geoffrey M.B. Tootell, Lynn E. Browne & James McEneaney, Mortgage Lending In Boston: Interpreting HMDA Data, 86 Amer. Econ. Rev. 25 (1996), and commonly called the Boston Fed Study, attempted to answer that question. The authors, who were able to obtain additional data from Boston-area lenders, concluded that "white applicants with the same property and personal characteristics as minorities would have experienced a rejection rate of 20 percent rather than the minority rate of 28 percent." Id. at 26. According to the Boston Fed Study, the data suggested that "given the same property and personal characteristics, white applicants may enjoy a general presumption of creditworthiness that black and Hispanic applicants do not." Id.

Not surprisingly, the Boston Fed Study proved exceedingly controversial and sparked numerous critical responses. See e.g., Mark Zandi, Boston Fed's Bias Study Was Deeply Flawed, Am. Banker, Aug. 19, 1993 at 13 (arguing that the Boston Fed Study failed to take into account the state of the economy and housing markets, omitted key variables, and made data encoding errors); Gary S. Becker, The Evidence Against Banks Doesn't Prove Bias, Bus Wk., Apr. 19, 1993, at 18 (arguing that the Boston Fed Study focused on the wrong data); Peter Brinelow & Leslie Spencer, The Hidden Clue, Forbes, Jan. 4, 1993, at 48 (criticizing the Boston Fed Study for failing to take into account default rates). Other commentators, though noting some errors in the Boston Fed Study, were supportive of its conclusions. See e.g., James H. Carr & Isaac F. Megbolugbe, The Federal Reserve Bank of Boston Study on Mortgage Lending Revisited, 4 J. Housing Res. 277 (1993); Dennis Glennon & Mitchell Stengel, An Evaluation of the Federal Reserve Bank of Boston's Study of Racial Discrimination in Mortgage Lending, Office of the Comptroller of the Currency, Economic & Policy Anal. Working Paper 94–2 (1994). Much of the data and the comments on it are summarized and criticized in turn in a book-length study, Stephen Ross & Ross Yinger, The Color of Credit (2002), which agrees with many, but not all, of the findings of the Boston Fed Study. One commentator summed up the debate: "A skeptic with a strong prior belief in the ability of market forces to restrain unprofitable discrimination could easily remain unconvinced by the Boston Fed

Study. On the other hand, critics with a strong prior belief in the prevalence of discrimination will find striking confirmation in the Boston Fed Study. Between these extremes lies a range of reasonable assessments." Jeffrey M. Lacker, Neighborhoods and Banking, Fed. Reserve Bank of Richmond Econ. Q. Spring 1995 at 13. Later studies may shed additional light on the problem of mortgage discrimination. See, e.g., Gary A. Dynski, Is Discrimination Disappearing? Residential Credit Market Evidence, 1992–98, 28 Int'l J. Social Econ. 1025, 1043 (2001) ("White applicants were found to have a statistically significant advantage. . . .").

Around the same time that the Boston Fed Study became public, federal enforcement authorities commenced a number of actions against various banks. Most of these cases terminated in settlements, and so did not produce reported decisions. See generally U.S. General Accounting Office, Fair Lending: Federal Oversight and Enforcement Improved but Some Challenges Remain 42–47 (1996). One issue that some of the cases raised is presented in the following problem:

Problem 4–28

Turalow Bank operates in a highly segregated metropolitan area, with some predominantly white counties and some predominantly African–American counties. White applicants to Turalow have the same loan acceptance rate as non-white applicants, but Turalow receives many more applications from whites than from non-whites. Turalow is confident that in deciding on loan applications it has never discriminated against a single applicant on a prohibited basis, nor does it treat applicants differently depending on their neighborhood. Nevertheless, Turalow markets its loans more aggressively in white communities than minority communities. All but three of Turalow's branches are located in census tracts in which a majority of residents are white; of the remaining three, two branches were acquired as part of a merger with another bank while the third was first opened at a time when the census tract was white. Turalow rarely uses newspapers, radio stations, or other media outlets that target minority communities. Most of its loan originators are white and obtain business from white-owned and operated businesses with whom the originators have longstanding relationships. Turalow would like to know if it is taking any risks under the CRA, ECOA, or the FHA. Advise Turalow. See Cartwright v. American Savings & Loan Assoc.

Notes

1. The Marsico Study cited above concludes at p. 529 that "marketing is a very effective way to increase lending."

2. Do anti-discrimination laws have any implications for lenders that engage in prescreening (prescreening, discussed more fully in Chapter Six, is a process in which credit bureaus provide lenders with a list of consumers who meet criteria established by the lenders; the lenders then send the consumers mail solicitations, typically for credit cards)? See Timothy C. Lambert, Fair Marketing: Challenging Pre–Application Practices, 87 Geo. L.

J. 2181 (1999). Given that people of color are less likely to have access to the internet than whites, see U.S. Dept. of Commerce, Econ. & Statistics Admin. & Nat'l Telecomm. & Info. Admin., A Nation Online: How Americans are Expanding Their Use of the Internet (2002), is a lender that offers special terms for online applications engaged in a form of redlining? See Internet–Only Products, Services May Spark Claims of "Weblining," 71 U.S.L.W. 2390 (Dec. 17, 2002).

3. In an attempt to give guidance to lenders about what enforcement agencies will consider in determining if lending discrimination exists and to provide for uniform policies, nine regulatory agencies banded together to produce a Policy Statement on Discrimination in Lending, 59 Fed. Reg. 18,266 (Apr. 15, 1994).

4. Scholars have studied other aspects of lending discrimination as well. Thus, a study of markups over buy rates (that is, the minimum interest rate a lender will charge a particular borrower; see Problem 4–27, *supra*) at one mortgage lender found that blacks and Hispanics have higher incidences of markups and higher markups than whites. See Harold A. Black, Thomas P. Boehm & Ramon P. DeGennaro, Is There Discrimination in Mortgage Pricing? The Case of Overages, 27 J. Banking & Fin. 1139, 1147 (2003). Another study found that "Conventional loan interest rates, while varying markedly between individuals, are largely race-neutral." Gordon W. Crawford & Eric Rosenblatt, Differences in the Cost of Mortgage Credit Implications for Discrimination, 19 J. Real Est. Fin. & Econ. 147 (1999). The same study noted that government credit models showed differences of about $1.80 per month on loans to some groups, an amount that was statistically significant.

Question

As a result of the Boston Fed Study, many expressions of outrage and calls for investigation have been voiced by civil rights advocates and politicians. What do you think should be done about all this? If you were counsel for a Congressional committee looking into the problem, what would you recommend? Should the law be amended? How? (Is the problem one of law?) Congress has enacted at least five relevant statutes, several of which have been amended over the years. Is another statute the answer? If you were counsel for a bank or other mortgage lender, what would you recommend, if anything, as a response to the reports cited above?

MATTHEWS v. NEW CENTURY MORTGAGE CORP.

United States District Court, Southern District of Ohio, Eastern Division, 2002.
185 F.Supp.2d 874.

CHATIGNY, DISTRICT JUDGE.

I. INTRODUCTION

This matter is before the Court on the Defendant's Motion to Dismiss the Plaintiffs' Second Amended Complaint. Jurisdiction is proper under 28 U.S.C. § 1331. Based on the following analysis, the Court

GRANTS the Defendant's Motion in part and **DENIES** the Defendant's Motion in part.

II. Facts

A. *Ruth Morgan*

Plaintiff Ruth Morgan, then an 87-year-old single woman, was contacted in October 1997 by an employee of Century 21 Home Improvement and Incredible Exteriors, Inc. ("Century 21"). The Century 21 employee told Ms. Morgan that the siding on her home had to be replaced because it was dirty and not up to code. Approximately one week later, Ms. Morgan signed a contract with Century 21 for new siding costing $17,325 after assurances by a different Century 21 employee, Antonio Barrett, that Ms. Morgan could obtain a loan to finance her new siding. Mr. Barrett also indicated that the loan would finance other home repairs and a used car.

On November 7, 1997, Mike Lewis, an employee of Century Mortgage, Inc. ("Century Mortgage"), met with Ms. Morgan in her home regarding her loan, although Ms. Morgan had neither contacted Central Mortgage, nor sought Central Mortgage's services in any way. Mr. Lewis brought to the meeting papers for Ms. Morgan to sign regarding what she believed was an application for a home-improvement loan to cover the cost of her new siding. Ms. Morgan signed numerous papers, but did not receive copies of what she signed. At that meeting, Ms. Morgan was not informed of her right to cancel her loan application.

On November 24, 1997, Mr. Mark Hanna, then the manager of Southeast Equity Title Agency ("Southeast Equity"), met with Ms. Morgan and Mr. Barrett at Ms. Morgan's home so that she could sign closing papers for her loan. According to Ms. Morgan, she had no opportunity to review the loan documents before she signed them, nor did she receive copies of the loan documents for review either prior to or at closing. Nonetheless, she felt obligated to agree to the terms of the loan, as the siding had already been removed from her house.[2] Ms. Morgan was not informed at this meeting of her three-day right to cancellation. Ms. Morgan's closing statement listed the Defendant, New Century Mortgage Corp. ("New Century"), as the lender of a $49,000 loan.

In December 1997, Ms. Morgan received, at her request, copies of the paperwork that Mr. Hanna had brought to her house. The copies, however, were not signed by Ms. Morgan. The paperwork included a "Notice of Right to Cancel" that was neither filled out nor signed. The documents did not include a Truth-in-Lending statement, a Loan Agreement Contract with the lender, employment verification forms, or Final Uniform Residential Loan Application.

---

2. Since that time, Ms. Morgan's siding has been replaced. She alleges, however, that the work was done so poorly that it must be taken down and replaced again.

Along with the paperwork, Southeast Equity sent a check payable to Ms. Morgan in the amount of $2345.07. Ms. Morgan cashed the check, and then gave it to Mr. Barrett, who had informed her that he would use the money to take care of her home repairs, other than the siding, and to buy her a used car. Ms. Morgan, however, has not had contact with Mr. Barrett since she gave him that money, and she never received either the promised home repairs or the used car.

In January 1998, Ms. Morgan began making monthly payments on the loan in the amount of $459.97. Shortly thereafter, Ms. Morgan received notice that the amount of her monthly payments would increase. Then, in December 1998 and January 1999, New Century returned Ms. Morgan's payment checks, stating that $459.97 did not represent the total amount due. In March 1999, New Century, through its trustee, U.S. Bank Trust National Association, filed a complaint against Ms. Morgan for foreclosure of her home. Despite her prior efforts, Ms. Morgan did not learn the actual terms of the loan she had obtained from New Century until it filed for foreclosure. Thus, she learned that the loan that she had believed was intended only to finance her home repairs for $17,325.00 was actually for the refinancing of her home for $49,000.00. It was also at this time that she learned for the first time that her occupation had been listed as "quilt-maker" on the loan application forms, and that a business card stating that Ms. Morgan was a quilt-maker with American Quilts was a part of her mortgage file. In actuality, Ms. Morgan was never involved in a quilt-making business, nor did she have business cards to that effect. Finally, Ms. Morgan learned that her monthly income had been stated as $1500.00 on the loan application form, with quilt-making as her source of income, when, in actuality, her total monthly income was $713.00 in social security benefits.

The Plaintiffs allege, based on the foregoing facts, that Ms. Morgan relied on the Defendant's representations that she was receiving a home improvement loan that would result in lower monthly bill payments when, in fact, she paid high rates and fees for a loan that depleted the equity she had in her home. They contend that, as a result of the foreclosure proceedings, Ms. Morgan suffered extreme emotional and physical distress.

[The court described similar allegations by plaintiffs Hazel Jean Matthews, Marie I. Summerall, and Ella Mae Arnold.]

* * * Subsequently, on May 18, 2001, the Plaintiffs filed a Second Amended Complaint, which is the subject of New Century's Motion to Dismiss, now before this Court. * * * Plaintiffs allege that Central Mortgage referred a number of "stated income loans," high risk loans with high interest rates, to New Century. Numerous such loan packages referred to New Century contained false and fraudulently obtained information. The Plaintiffs contend that New Century obtained such loans with respect to each of the Plaintiffs.

The Plaintiffs allege, furthermore, that Rebecca Blankenship, the former president of Central Mortgage, had close personal ties with various employees at New Century (including her brothers and her husband, Kevin Blankenship, Jeff Snyder, and Robert Banhagel). They claim that, in the course and scope of their employment, Kevin Blankenship, Jeff Snyder, and Robert Banhagel all processed loans for New Century that had been referred to them by Central Mortgage. The Plaintiffs contend that New Century's relationships with Central Mortgage, Equibanc Mortgage, and K & R Equity constituted associations which engaged in a common, on-going course of conduct to induce borrowers to enter into highly inflated loans with their common motivation being profit. The Plaintiffs contend that each of the Defendant mortgage brokers was acting in concert with New Century, and that all of the Defendants engaged in a pattern or practice of targeting single, elderly females for unfair loan practices. Finally, the Plaintiffs allege that the Defendants knew or should have known that the Plaintiffs' monthly incomes were insufficient to take on the debt obligations that were effectively forced upon them by the Defendants' fraudulent conduct, and that New Century, specifically, made the loans to the Plaintiffs despite the fact that New Century knew or should have known that the Plaintiffs had no ability to repay the loans.

Based on the foregoing, the Plaintiffs asserted against New Century claims under or of: (1) the Federal Fair Housing Act; (2) the Equal Credit Opportunity Act; (3) the Truth-in-Lending Act; (4) Ohio Rev.Code § 4112.02; (5) civil conspiracy; (6) common law fraud; (7) Ohio Rev.Code § 2923.31 *et seq.*, the Ohio RICO statute; and (8) unconscionability. Defendant New Century has filed a Motion to Dismiss all of the Plaintiffs' claims against it pursuant to Fed.R.Civ.P. 12(b)(6), for failure to state a claim. * * *

IV. ANALYSIS

* * *

B. *Fair Housing Act*

The Plaintiffs allege that New Century's conduct in connection with their mortgages constitutes discrimination on the basis of gender, age, and marital status in violation of sections 804(b) and 805 of the FHA, 42 U.S.C. §§ 3604(b), 3605. New Century contends that the Plaintiffs have failed to state a claim against it under either of these provisions of the FHA.

1. 42 U.S.C. § 3604(b)

Section 804(b) of the FHA states, in pertinent part:

[I]t shall be unlawful—

(b) To discriminate against any person in the terms, conditions, or privileges of sale or rental of a dwelling, or in the provision of services or facilities in connection therewith, because of ... sex ... [or] familial status ....

42 U.S.C. § 3604.

The Plaintiffs assert that their Complaint states a valid claim under this provision because the Defendant's actions, though not amounting to a literal "sale or rental," nonetheless relate to the sale or rental of a dwelling. The Court finds the Plaintiffs' argument to be without merit.

Section 804 of the FHA, 42 U.S.C. § 3604, is to be read liberally, so that its terms reach transactions that fall beyond the literal scope of selling or renting housing. * * * Despite the breadth of the provision, however, it does not reach the particular transactions at issue in this case. To the contrary, this Court has specifically stated that transactions such as these, involving financial assistance requested for the purpose of improving, repairing, or maintaining a dwelling that the owner had previously acquired, fall outside the scope of § 3604. *Laufman v. Oakley Bldg. & Loan Co.,* 408 F.Supp. 489, 492 (S.D.Ohio 1976); *see also Eva,* 143 F.Supp.2d at 886 (stating that it is clear that § 3604 covers transactions related to acquiring a home, as opposed to § 3605, which covers "the making or purchasing of loans or providing other financial assistance for maintaining a dwelling previously acquired").

As the transactions at issue in this case relate to the allegedly discriminatory provision of mortgages on homes that were previously acquired by the Plaintiffs, the Court finds that 42 U.S.C. § 3604(b) does not apply, and **GRANTS** the Defendant's Motion to Dismiss this claim.

2. *42 U.S.C. § 3605*

The Plaintiffs have also alleged that New Century violated § 805 of the FHA, 42 U.S.C. § 3605. That provision reads, in relevant part:

(a) In general

It shall be unlawful for any person or other entity whose business includes engaging in residential real estate-related transactions to discriminate against any person in making available such a transaction, or in the terms or conditions of such a transaction, because of ... sex ... [or] familial status ....

(b) "Residential real estate-related transaction" defined

As used in this section, the term "residential real estate-related transaction" means ... (1) The making or purchasing of loans or providing other financial assistance-(A) for purchasing, constructing, improving, repairing, or maintaining a dwelling ....

The Plaintiffs' claim brought under this provision essentially amounts to a claim that New Century engaged in "reverse redlining." "Reverse redlining" is the situation in which a lender unlawfully discriminates by extending credit to a neighborhood or class of people (typically living in the same neighborhood) on terms less favorable than would have been extended to people outside the particular class at issue. *See* Frank Lopez, *Using the Fair Housing Act to Combat Predatory Lending,* 6 Geo. J. Pov. L. & Pol'yY 73, 77 (1999). In like fashion, the Plaintiffs in this case allege that New Century violated the FHA by granting them a loan on grossly unfavorable terms based on their age, sex, and marital status, and that such terms would not have been extended to credit applicants who were not elderly, unmarried women.

Although the issue has not been directly addressed by the Sixth Circuit, other courts have held that reverse redlining claims are cognizable under the FHA. *See, e.g., Honorable v. Easy Life Real Estate System,* 100 F.Supp.2d 885, 892 (N.D.Ill.2000) (citing *NAACP v. American Family Mut. Ins. Co.,* 978 F.2d 287, 301 (7th Cir.1992)); *Hargraves v. Capital City Mortgage Corp.,* 140 F.Supp.2d 7, 20 (D.D.C.2000) (recognizing that predatory loan practices can make housing unavailable by putting borrowers at risk of losing the real property that secures their loans). The elements of a reverse redlining claim brought under the FHA, 42 U.S.C. § 3605, are a variation of the elements that typically must be shown for a claim of discrimination under § 3605. A plaintiff invoking § 3605 must demonstrate the same factors that she would have to demonstrate for a Title VII claim. *See Babin,* 18 F.3d at 346 (finding that the plaintiffs must show: (1) that they were members of a protected class; (2) that they attempted to engage in a "real estate-related transaction" with the defendant and met all relevant qualifications for doing so; (3) that defendant lender refused to transact business with the plaintiffs despite their qualifications; and (4) that the defendant lender continued to engage in that type of transaction with other parties with similar qualifications).

To set forth a cognizable reverse redlining claim under § 3605, essentially the same elements must be established, except that the plaintiff need not show that the lender refused to transact business, but only that the lender refused to transact business *on fair terms.* Specifically, to establish a *prima facie* case of discrimination in violation of § 3605 based on reverse redlining, the plaintiff must show: (1) that she is a member of a protected class; (2) that she applied for and was qualified for loans; (3) that the loans were given on grossly unfavorable terms; and (4) that the lender continues to provide loans to other applicants with similar qualifications, but on significantly more favorable terms. In the alternative, if the plaintiff presents direct evidence that the lender intentionally targeted her for unfair loans on the basis of sex and marital status, the plaintiff need not also show that the lender makes loans on more favorable terms to others. *See Hargraves,* 140 F.Supp.2d at 20 (finding that such a requirement would allow an injustice to continue so long as it was visited exclusively on one class of people).

This Court finds that the Plaintiffs have alleged sufficient facts to survive the motion to dismiss their claim under § 3605. First, the Plaintiffs clearly are members of a protected class. Second, they applied for and were qualified for loans. Third, the Plaintiffs have alleged that New Century gave them their loans on grossly unfavorable terms. Finally, while the Defendant is correct that the Plaintiffs have not alleged that other similarly situated people were given loans on more favorable terms, the Plaintiffs have nonetheless presented a cognizable claim, as they allege and may be able to show directly that New Century intentionally targeted them for unfair loans on the basis of their sex and marital status, thus eliminating the necessity of proving the fourth element of the *prima facie* case.

Therefore, the Court **DENIES** the Defendant's Motion to Dismiss the Plaintiffs' claim for violation of 42 U.S.C. § 3605.

C.   Equal Credit Opportunity Act

[F]or the Plaintiffs to establish a *prima facie* case for violation of ECOA, they must show: (1) that they are members of a protected class; (2) that they applied for credit from the Defendant; (3) that they were qualified for the credit; and (4) that their credit applications were denied despite their qualifications.

The elements for a *prima facie* case under ECOA can be adapted to the Plaintiffs' reverse redlining claims. *See Hargraves v. Capital City Mortgage Corp.*, 140 F.Supp.2d 7, 23 (D.D.C.2000) (finding that the plain language of the statutory provision indicates that it is not limited to loan applicants who were rejected). The plain language of the statute indicates that it applies to discrimination with respect to "any aspect of a credit transaction." A "credit transaction" has been deemed to include not only the extension of credit itself, but also terms of credit, along with various other matters. *See* 12 C.F.R. § 202.2(m). Thus, to survive the Defendant's Motion to Dismiss, the Plaintiffs need not allege that they were denied credit, so long as they allege that they were discriminated against in the terms of their credit based on the sex, marital status, or age.

It is undisputed that the Plaintiffs allege that they are members of a protected class who applied for and were qualified for credit. The Court finds that the Plaintiffs have also alleged that, although they were not denied credit, they were discriminated against in the terms of the loans they were granted on the basis of their sex, marital status, or age.

Therefore, the Court **DENIES** the Defendant's Motion to Dismiss the Plaintiffs' ECOA claims.

D.   Truth-in-Lending Act

The Plaintiffs' Complaint asserts that New Century violated "various provisions" of the Truth-in-Lending Act ("TILA"), 15 U.S.C. § 1601, *et seq.* New Century, however, asserts that the TILA claim must fail because the Plaintiffs have failed to plead it with the specificity that is necessary to give notice of the claim that is being asserted.

TILA was designed to increase the information available to consumers in credit transactions. *Cornist v. B.J.T. Auto Sales, Inc.*, 272 F.3d 322, 326 (6th Cir.2001). * * * Among the information that must be available to a consumer in a credit transaction is the consumer's right to rescind.

The failure of a creditor to provide the consumer with notice of this right to rescind is actionable under the statute. * * *

Both Ms. Morgan and Ms. Summerall specifically allege that they were not given notice of their three-day right to cancel the loan agreement. Similarly, Ms. Matthews and Ms. Arnold allege that they did not receive copies of their loan documents (which would include notice of the right to rescind) prior to closing. Thus, the Court finds that each of the Plaintiffs has properly alleged an actionable TILA violation against New Century.

Therefore, the Court **DENIES** the Defendant's Motion to Dismiss the Plaintiffs' TILA claims.

* * *

F. Civil Conspiracy

* * *

The Court finds that the Plaintiffs have adequately set forth a claim for civil conspiracy against New Century. First, the Complaint sets forth facts tending to show that New Century, or some of its employees, maliciously combined with various mortgage brokers to commit fraud upon the Plaintiffs in a way that resulted in actual damages. * * *

Therefore, the Court **DENIES** the Defendant's Motion to Dismiss the Plaintiffs' civil conspiracy claim.

G. Common Law Fraud

* * *

New Century argues that the Plaintiffs' fraud claim must fail because the Plaintiffs have failed to allege either that New Century made an affirmative misrepresentation or that New Century concealed a material fact while under a duty to disclose that fact to the Plaintiffs. Their argument hinges primarily on the fact that the only alleged material misrepresentations or concealments of fact, the falsification of the Plaintiffs' income and employment status on their loan applications, were attributed to the individual brokers, not New Century, the lender. * * *

* * * [T]he Court finds that the Plaintiffs have also properly set forth a claim of fraud against New Century. As the Court finds that the Plaintiffs have properly asserted a civil conspiracy claim against New Century, the Court also concludes that New Century can be held liable for any acts committed by its co-conspirators in furtherance of their conspiracy. Thus, because the Plaintiffs have properly alleged that the individual mortgage brokers engaged in fraudulent acts, New Century itself can be liable for those actions if the Plaintiffs succeed in proving a conspiracy existed between New Century and the mortgage brokers.

Therefore, the Court **DENIES** the Defendant's Motion to Dismiss the Plaintiffs' common law fraud claim.

H. *Ohio Pattern of Corrupt Activities Act*

The Plaintiffs have alleged a claim against New Century for violation of the Ohio Pattern of Corrupt Activities Act ("PCA"), Ohio Rev.Code § 2923.31, *et seq.,* which is patterned after the Federal Racketeering Influenced and Corrupt Organizations Act ("RICO"), 18 U.S.C. § 1961, *et seq.* * * *.

* * *

As the Court finds that the Plaintiffs have alleged each of the elements of a PCA violation with the specificity necessary to give New Century notice of the claim brought against it, the Court **DENIES** the Defendant's Motion to Dismiss this claim.

I. *Unconscionability*

The Plaintiffs claim that the loan agreements involved here are unconscionable, and should be declared null and void by this Court. New Century moves to dismiss this claim on the ground that the Plaintiffs have failed to allege the facts necessary to support a claim of unconscionability.

* * *

The Court finds that the Plaintiffs have sufficiently pled facts necessary to withstand the Defendant's Motion to Dismiss their unconscionability claim. First, the Plaintiffs' Complaint asserts, as the facts as set forth therein indicate, that the terms of the contracts involved in these transactions were so one-sided in favor of New Century as to be unlawful. Second, the Plaintiffs properly allege that the contracts also were procedurally unconscionable, in that the individual mortgage brokers had significantly greater bargaining power, business acumen, and experience than the Plaintiffs. The mortgage brokers presented to the Plaintiffs contracts that they or their employers had drafted, which they apparently did not even allow the Plaintiffs to read before signing. While the Court recognizes that New Century did not directly participate in the negotiating process with the Plaintiffs, New Century cannot escape liability on that basis. As the Court finds that the Plaintiffs have properly alleged a claim of civil conspiracy against New Century, New Century may be found liable for the alleged unconscionability of its co-conspirators.

Because the Court finds that the Plaintiffs have properly alleged claims of substantive and procedural unconscionability, the Court **DENIES** the Defendant's Motion to Dismiss this claim.

* * *

Notes

1. The loan application misrepresented the plaintiff as a quilt-maker and inflated her income. Presumably the plaintiff signed the loan applica-

tion. Should that have an impact on her claim? Would it matter in a case in which the lender and the broker lacked the close ties found in this case?

2.   Though the reverse-redlining in the principal case took the form of lending to single elderly women, reverse redliners also target members of minority groups. One commentator refers to this as "racialized predatory lending" and has called for criminal sanctions against those who engage in it. See Cecil J. Hunt, In the Racial Crosshairs: Reconsidering Racially Targeted Predatory Lending Under a New Theory of Economic Hate Crime, 35 U. Tol. L. Rev. 211 (2003).

SECTION C.   PERSPECTIVES: AN EVALUATION OF THE COSTS AND BENEFITS OF REGULATION OF ACCESS TO THE MARKET

This chapter brings together two separate areas of the law—credit reporting and discrimination in the granting of credit—that have in common both an attempt to facilitate consumer access to credit and the fact that they have frequently drawn legislative attention. Credit discrimination is regulated by no fewer than five federal statutes. Congress made substantial revisions to the FCRA in both 1996 and 2003, and has also enacted other statutes directed solely at identity theft. State legislatures have also weighed in. Yet it appears that the problems of inaccurate credit reports and credit discrimination are still with us. Your editors anticipate that Congress and state legislatures will continue tinkering with these areas. Identity theft, in particular, seems likely to generate additional legislation. If the state statutes regulating data protection and mandating credit freezes succeed in reducing the incidence of identity theft, more states will probably adopt them, and perhaps Congress will as well. Regulatory initiatives are also likely: for example, beginning in 2004, federal regulators adopted new regulations, codified at various points in 12 C.F.R., that have the effect of reducing CRA scrutiny for many financial institutions. The changes are assessed in Richard D. Marsico, The 2004–2005 Amendments to the Community Reinvestment Act Regulations: For Communities, One Step Forward and Three Steps Back, 39 Clearinghouse Rev. J. Poverty L. & Pol'y 534 (2006).

Proposals to amend legislation and regulations in the credit arena invariably raise questions about the cost of the proposal. The credibility of cost projections can be informed by the history of past cost predictions. Before the amendment of ECOA to require disclosure of reasons for adverse action, Congress was treated to the following estimate of the cost of giving reasons for adverse action:

Sears Roebuck and Company stated that its annual estimated cost for such compliance would be approximately $5 per letter. * * * Even if all creditors could operate as efficiently as Sears, the aggregate annual cost of this requirement could easily amount to hundreds of millions of dollars. The requirement is staggeringly inflationary.

Testimony of National Retail Merchants Association, Hearings on S. 483, S. 1900, S. 1927, S. 1961, and H.R. 6516, Subcommittee on Consumer Affairs, U.S. Senate Committee on Banking, Housing and Urban Affairs 399 (1975).

After enactment, the Federal Reserve Board surveyed large creditors to determine the actual costs of furnishing rejected applicants with statements of reasons for adverse action under Reg. B § 202.9. Board of Governors of the Federal Reserve System, Exercise of Consumer Rights Under the Equal Credit Opportunity and Fair Credit Billing Acts, 64 Fed.Res.Bull. 363 (1978). Sears reported that the average cost of providing rejected credit applicants with the reasons for rejection was 59 cents. A number of creditors, unlike Sears, took advantage of the ECOA provision permitting them to furnish the reasons to rejected applicants only upon request; because most rejected applicants did not request the reasons, this offered a further opportunity to reduce the cost per rejected applicant. The Board also noted that "Many of the rejected credit applicants who were initially given reasons for credit denial supplied additional information, and a high proportion of those were then granted credit."

Notes

1. What would account for the wide difference between the $5.00 estimate and the 59 cent actual cost to Sears of an adverse action letter? Before you assume that there was any intentional misrepresentation, consider the difference in the quality of thinking about cost minimization by a Sears attorney before enactment of the legislation and the thinking about cost minimization by professional managers after enactment.

2. Whatever the reason for the differences between cost estimates and actual costs, what is the likely effect upon Sears's credibility before future legislative or agency hearings?

Attempting a Cost-benefit Analysis

The previous materials have analyzed only the costs related to the applicable regulations, and that is but one-half of the equation involved in a cost-benefit analysis.

Problem 4–29

Can you compare the costs and benefits of adverse action notices? If not what data, if any, would permit you to do so? How do you value, in dollar terms, the ability to obtain credit—especially after a denial? It may be a blessing to most, but a disaster to some. What is the worth, in dollar terms, to a rejected person of being given reasons for denial of their credit application? In purely economic terms, that may depend upon whether the reasons can be overcome or not, but surely that analysis does not measure psychological factors. Are the people who receive the benefit of the adverse action notice the people who pay for the adverse action notice? If not, does that matter? Is any attempt to compare costs and benefits of regulation likely to depend ultimately upon some evaluation of subjective, non-economic factors?

Chapter 5

PRIVACY AND CONSUMER TRANSACTIONS: SOLICITATIONS AND THE COLLECTION OF INFORMATION ABOUT CONSUMERS

SECTION A. FOUNDATION

Privacy is a theme that runs throughout consumer law. Privacy issues have already surfaced in Chapter Three's treatment of door-to-door sales and Chapter Four's coverage of who can see a credit report. Privacy issues will also receive attention in Chapter Eight when we explore the rights of consumer-debtors to be free from unwelcome pressure from creditors. This chapter will focus largely on two related privacy concerns: first, to what extent does the mode in which a solicitation is made (as opposed to the content of the solicitation) affect the rights of merchants and consumers; and second, to what extent do consumers have the right to keep information about their transactions private, or conversely, do businesses have the right to share consumer information with others.

Many students will already be familiar with privacy issues in two contexts. First, constitutional law classes frequently cover the constitutional right to privacy, most notably in connection with abortion. Constitutional privacy concepts will not generally be relevant to the privacy issues addressed in this chapter, except to the extent that they reinforce the existence of a general right (albeit one that is limited) to be let alone. See Samuel D. Warren & Louis D. Brandeis, The Right to Privacy, 4 Harv. L. Rev. 193 (1890). Second, Students may have encountered the invasion of privacy torts famously cataloged by Dean Prosser: (1) intrusion upon the plaintiff's seclusion or solitude; (2) public disclosure of embarrassing private facts; (3) publicity which places the plaintiff in a false light; and (4) appropriation, for the defendant's advantage, of the plaintiff's name or likeness. See William L. Prosser, Privacy, 48 Cal. L. Rev. 383 (1960). These torts too, are often unhelpful to consumers facing the issues dealt with in this chapter, either because courts have generally found them inapplicable or because, as in the credit reporting context, legislatures have preempted their application. Instead, consumers seeking legal protection must look elsewhere. Can you think of any rules that you have seen thus far in this course that might be helpful to consumers?

Consumer privacy law in the United States is sometimes described as sectoral, in that different sectors of the economy are subject to varying degrees of privacy regulation. Some consumer transactions are confidential; others are largely unfettered by privacy regulations; still other transactions can be disclosed under certain circumstances. Rather than reviewing all the consumer privacy laws, this chapter will focus on some of the privacy laws which are of greatest significance to consumers, in an attempt to expose students to different approaches to privacy regulation.

Problem 5–1

Lindsay Video Rentals and the Melanie Bookstore wish to enter into an agreement and seek your advice. Many books are made into movies while numerous movies inspire novelizations. Under the proposed agreement, Lindsay will provide Melanie with the names and rentals of customers who have rented videos and Melanie in turn will supply Lindsay with the names and purchases of customers who have bought books. Each will then solicit the other's customers. Would this arrangement be lawful? See 18 U.S.C. § 2710 in the Statutory Supplement; Dwyer v. American Express. Would it matter if Melanie provided Lindsay with the name of a customer who had bought a book titled "Living with HIV/AIDS"?

DWYER v. AMERICAN EXPRESS CO.

Appellate Court of Illinois, First District.
273 Ill.App.3d 742, 210 Ill.Dec. 375, 652 N.E.2d 1351 (1995), petition for leave
to appeal denied, 165 Ill.2d 549, 662 N.E.2d 423, 214 Ill.Dec. 857 (1996).

JUSTICE BUCKLEY delivered the opinion of the court:

Plaintiffs, American Express cardholders, appeal the circuit court's dismissal of their claims for invasion of privacy and consumer fraud against defendants, American Express Company, American Express Credit Corporation, and American Express Travel Related Services Company, for their practice of renting information regarding cardholder spending habits.

On May 13, 1992, the New York Attorney General released a press statement describing an agreement it had entered into with defendants. The following day, newspapers reported defendants' actions which gave rise to this agreement. According to the news articles, defendants categorize and rank their cardholders into six tiers based on spending habits and then rent this information to participating merchants as part of a targeted joint-marketing and sales program. For example, a cardholder may be characterized as "Rodeo Drive Chic" or "Value Oriented." In order to characterize its cardholders, defendants analyze where they shop and how much they spend, and also consider behavioral characteristics and spending histories. Defendants then offer to create a list of cardholders who would most likely shop in a particular store and rent that list to the merchant.

Defendants also offer to create lists which target cardholders who purchase specific types of items, such as fine jewelry. The merchants using the defendants' service can also target shoppers in categories such as mail-order apparel buyers, home-improvement shoppers, electronics shoppers, luxury lodgers, card members with children, skiers, frequent business travelers, resort users, Asian/European travelers, luxury European car owners, or recent movers. Finally, defendants offer joint-marketing ventures to merchants who generate substantial sales through the American Express card. Defendants mail special promotions devised by the merchants to its cardholders and share the profits generated by these advertisements.

On May 14, 1992, Patrick E. Dwyer filed a class action against defendants. His complaint alleges that defendants intruded into their cardholders' seclusion, commercially appropriated their cardholders' personal spending habits, and violated the Illinois consumer fraud statute and consumer fraud statutes in other jurisdictions. Plaintiffs moved to certify the class, add parties, and file an amended, consolidated complaint. Defendants moved to dismiss the claims. After hearing argument on the motion to dismiss, the circuit court granted that motion and denied plaintiffs' motions as moot. Plaintiffs appeal the circuit court order.

Plaintiffs have alleged that defendants' practices constitute an invasion of their privacy and violate the Illinois Consumer Fraud and Deceptive Business Practices Act (Act or Consumer Fraud Act) (Ill.Rev. Stat.1991, ch. 121 1/2 , par. 261 *et seq.* (now 815 ILCS 505/1 *et seq.* (West 1992))). For the reasons discussed below, we find that plaintiffs have not stated a cause of action under either of these theories.

INVASION OF PRIVACY

There are four branches of the privacy invasion tort identified by the Restatement (Second) of Torts. These are: (1) an unreasonable intrusion upon the seclusion of another; (2) an appropriation of another's name or likeness; (3) a public disclosure of private facts; and (4) publicity which reasonably places another in a false light before the public. (Restatement (Second) of Torts §§ 652B, 652C, 652D, 652E, at 378–94 (1977)). Plaintiffs' complaint includes claims under the first and second branches.

As a preliminary matter, we note that a cause of action for intrusion into seclusion has never been recognized explicitly by the Illinois Supreme Court. * * * The third district recognized the intrusion tort in *Melvin v. Burling* (1986), 141 Ill.App.3d 786, 95 Ill.Dec. 919, 490 N.E.2d 1011. In *Melvin,* the court set out four elements which must be alleged in order to state a cause of action: (1) an unauthorized intrusion or prying into the plaintiff's seclusion; (2) an intrusion which is offensive or objectionable to a reasonable man; (3) the matter upon which the intrusion occurs is private; and (4) the intrusion causes anguish and suffering. Since the third district set out the four elements in *Melvin,* this district has applied these elements without directly addressing the issue of whether the cause of action exists in this State.

Plaintiffs' allegations fail to satisfy the first element, an unauthorized intrusion or prying into the plaintiffs' seclusion. The alleged wrongful actions involve the defendants' practice of renting lists that they have compiled from information contained in their own records. By using the American Express card, a cardholder is voluntarily, and necessarily, giving information to defendants that, if analyzed, will reveal a cardholder's spending habits and shopping preferences. We cannot hold that a defendant has committed an unauthorized intrusion by compiling the information voluntarily given to it and then renting its compilation.

Plaintiffs claim that because defendants rented lists based on this compiled information, this case involves the disclosure of private financial information and most closely resembles cases involving intrusion into private financial dealings, such as bank account transactions. Plaintiffs cite several cases in which courts have recognized the right to privacy surrounding financial transactions. See *Zimmermann v. Wilson* (3d Cir.1936), 81 F.2d 847 (holding examination of information in taxpayers' bank books would violate the taxpayers' privacy rights); *Brex v. Smith* (1929), 104 N.J.Eq. 386, 146 A. 34 (upholding claim for unauthorized intrusion into the plaintiff's bank account); *Hickson v. Home Federal* (N.D.Ga.1992), 805 F.Supp. 1567 (finding bank disclosure to credit bureau of borrower's loan payment delinquency could violate borrower's right to privacy); *Suburban Trust Co. v. Waller* (1979), 44 Md.App. 335, 408 A.2d 758 (holding bank cannot reveal information about customers' account or transaction unless compelled by legal process); *Mason v. Williams Discount Center, Inc.* (Mo.1982), 639 S.W.2d 836 (finding store's posting of names of bad check risks invades plaintiff's privacy).

However, we find that this case more closely resembles the sale of magazine subscription lists, which was at issue in *Shibley v. Time, Inc.* (1975), 45 Ohio App.2d 69, 341 N.E.2d 337. In *Shibley,* the plaintiffs claimed that the defendant's practice of selling and renting magazine subscription lists without the subscribers' prior consent "constitut[ed] an invasion of privacy because it amount[ed] to a sale of individual 'personality profiles,' which subjects the subscribers to solicitations from direct mail advertisers." (*Shibley,* 45 Ohio App.2d at 71, 341 N.E.2d at 339.) The plaintiffs also claimed that the lists amounted to a tortious appropriation of their names and "personality profiles." The trial court dismissed the plaintiffs' complaint and the Court of Appeals of Ohio affirmed. *Shibley,* 45 Ohio App.2d at 71, 341 N.E.2d at 339.

The *Shibley* court found that an Ohio statute, which permitted the sale of names and addresses of registrants of motor vehicles, indicated that the defendant's activity was not an invasion of privacy. The court considered a Federal district court case from New York, *Lamont v. Commissioner of Motor Vehicles* (S.D.N.Y.1967), 269 F.Supp. 880, *aff'd* (2d Cir.1967) 386 F.2d 449 *cert. denied* (1968), 391 U.S. 915, 88 S.Ct. 1811, 20 L.Ed.2d 654, to be insightful. In *Lamont,* the plaintiff claimed an invasion of privacy arising from the State's sale of its list of names and addresses of registered motor-vehicle owners to mail-order advertisers. The *Lamont* court held that however "noxious" advertising by mail might be, the burden was acceptable as far as the Constitution is concerned. (*Lamont,* 269 F.Supp. at 883.) The *Shibley* court followed the reasoning in *Lamont* and held:

> "The right to privacy does not extend to the mailbox and therefore it is constitutionally permissible to sell subscription lists to direct mail advertisers. It necessarily follows that the practice complained of here does not constitute an invasion of privacy even if appellants' unsupported assertion that this amounts to the sale of 'personality profiles' is taken as true because these profiles are only used to determine what type of advertisement is to be sent." *Shibley,* 45 Ohio App.2d at 73, 341 N.E.2d at 339–40.

Defendants rent names and addresses after they create a list of cardholders who have certain shopping tendencies; they are not disclosing financial information about particular cardholders. These lists are being used solely for the purpose of determining what type of advertising should be sent to whom. We also note that the Illinois Vehicle Code authorizes the Secretary of State to sell lists of names and addresses of licensed drivers and registered motor-vehicle owners. (625 ILCS 5/2—123 (West 1992).) Thus, we hold that the alleged actions here do not constitute an unreasonable intrusion into the seclusion of another. We so hold without expressing a view as to the appellate court conflict regarding the recognition of this cause of action.

Considering plaintiffs' appropriation claim, the elements of the tort are: an appropriation, without consent, of one's name or likeness for another's use or benefit. (Restatement (Second) of Torts § 652C (1977)). This branch of the privacy doctrine is designed to protect a person from having his name or image used for commercial purposes without consent. (See *Douglass v. Hustler Magazine* (7th Cir.1985), 769 F.2d 1128, *cert. denied* (1986), 475 U.S. 1094, 106 S.Ct. 1489, 89 L.Ed.2d 892 (finding defendant appropriated the value of model's likeness when it published nude pictures of her without consent).) According to the Restatement, the purpose of this tort is to protect the "interest of the individual in the exclusive use of his own identity, in so far as it is represented by his name or likeness." (Restatement (Second) of Torts § 652C, Comment *a* (1977).) Illustrations of this tort provided by the Restatement include the publication of a person's photograph without consent in an advertisement; operating a corporation named after a prominent public figure without the person's consent; impersonating a man to obtain information regarding the affairs of the man's wife; and filing a lawsuit in the name of another without the other's consent. Restatement (Second) of Torts § 652C, Comment *b* (1965).

Plaintiffs claim that defendants appropriate information about cardholders' personalities, including their names and perceived lifestyles, without their consent. Defendants argue that their practice does not adversely affect the interest of a cardholder in the "exclusive use of his own identity," using the language of the Restatement. Defendants also argue that the cardholders' names lack value and that the lists that defendants create are valuable because "they identify a useful aggregate of potential customers to whom offers may be sent."

Defendants cite *Cox v. Hatch* (Utah 1988), 761 P.2d 556, to support their argument. In *Cox,* the supreme court of Utah held that there had been no wrongful appropriation of plaintiffs' images through use of their pictures in campaign advertisements because the plaintiffs did not allege that their images had any intrinsic value or that they enjoyed any particular fame or notoriety. (*Cox,* 761 P.2d at 564.) Even more persuasive is *Shibley v. Time, Inc.* (1975), 45 Ohio App.2d 69, 341 N.E.2d 337, discussed above, wherein the Court of Appeals of Ohio found that merely placing a person's name on a "personality profile" list and providing that list to a third party, did not constitute tortious appropriation. *Shibley,* 45 Ohio App.2d at 71, 341 N.E.2d at 339.

To counter defendants' argument, plaintiffs point out that the tort of appropriation is not limited to strictly commercial situations. See *Annerino v. Dell Publishing Co.* (1958), 17 Ill.App.2d 205, 208, 149 N.E.2d 761 (implying that the holding of *Eick v. Perk Dog Food Co.* (1952), 347 Ill.App. 293, 106 N.E.2d 742, was being expanded beyond strictly commercial situations), and *Douglass v. Hustler Magazine* (7th Cir.1985), 769 F.2d 1128, 1138 (recognizing a good appropriation claim under Illinois law for commercial nonadvertising use of photographs); see also *Zacchini v. Scripps–Howard Broadcasting Co.* (1976), 47 Ohio St.2d 224, 351 N.E.2d 454, *rev'd on other grounds* (1977), 433 U.S. 562, 97 S.Ct. 2849, 53 L.Ed.2d 965, (holding that Ohio law does not limit appropriation claims to commercial appropriation).

Nonetheless, we again follow the reasoning in *Shibley* and find that plaintiffs have not stated a claim for tortious appropriation because they have failed to allege the first element. Undeniably, each cardholder's name is valuable to defendants. The more names included on a list, the more that list will be worth. However, a single, random cardholder's name has little or no intrinsic value to defendants (or a merchant). Rather, an individual name has value only when it is associated with one of defendants' lists. Defendants create value by categorizing and aggregating these names. Furthermore, defendants' practices do not deprive any of the cardholders of any value their individual names may possess.

Consumer Fraud Act

Plaintiffs' complaint also includes a claim under the Illinois Consumer Fraud Act. (Ill.Rev.Stat.1991, ch. 121 1/2 , par. 261 *et seq.* (now

815 ILCS 505/1 *et seq.* (West 1992)).) To establish a deceptive practice claim, a plaintiff must allege and prove (1) the misrepresentation or concealment of a material fact, (2) an intent by defendant that plaintiff rely on the misrepresentation or concealment, and (3) the deception occurred in the course of conduct involving a trade or commerce. Ill.Rev.Stat.1991, ch. 121 1/2, par. 262 (now 815 ILCS 505/2 (West 1992)).

According to the plaintiffs, defendants conducted a survey which showed that 80% of Americans do not think companies should release personal information to other companies. Plaintiffs have alleged that defendants did disclose that it would use information provided in the credit card application, but this disclosure did not inform the cardholders that information about their card usage would be used. It is highly possible that some customers would have refrained from using the American Express Card if they had known that defendants were analyzing their spending habits. Therefore, plaintiffs have sufficiently alleged that the undisclosed practices of defendants are material and deceptive.

As to the second element, the Act only requires defendants' intent that plaintiffs rely on the deceptive practice. Actual reliance is not required "A party is considered to intend the necessary consequences of his own acts or conduct." (*Warren v. LeMay* (1986), 142 Ill.App.3d 550, 566, 96 Ill.Dec. 418, 428, 491 N.E.2d 464, 474.) When considering whether this element is met, good or bad faith is not important and innocent misrepresentations may be actionable. (*Warren,* 142 Ill.App.3d at 566, 96 Ill.Dec. at 428, 491 N.E.2d at 474.) Defendants had a strong incentive to keep their practice a secret because disclosure would have resulted in fewer cardholders using their card. Thus, plaintiffs have sufficiently alleged that defendants intended for plaintiff's [sic] to rely on the nondisclosure of their practice.

The third element is not at issue in this case. However, defendants argue that plaintiffs have failed to allege facts that might establish that they suffered any damages. The Illinois Consumer Fraud Act provides a private cause of action for damages to "[a]ny person who suffers damage as a result of a violation of th[e] Act." (Ill.Rev.Stat.1991, ch. 121 1/2, par. 270a (now 815 ILCS 505/10a(a) (West 1992)).) Defendants contend, and we agree, that the only damage plaintiffs could have suffered was a surfeit of unwanted mail. We reject plaintiffs' assertion that the damages in this case arise from the disclosure of personal financial matters. Defendants only disclose which of their cardholders might be interested in purchasing items from a particular merchant based on card usage. Defendants' practice does not amount to a disclosure of personal financial matters. Plaintiffs have failed to allege how they were damaged by defendants' practice of selecting cardholders for mailings likely to be of interest to them.

Plaintiffs argue that the consumer fraud statutes of other States allow recovery of mental anguish even if no other damages are pled or proved. Apparently, plaintiffs would like this court to assume that a third party's knowledge of a cardholder's interest in their goods or services causes mental anguish to cardholders. Such an assumption without any supporting allegations would be wholly unfounded in this case. Therefore, we hold that plaintiffs have failed to allege facts that might establish that they have suffered any damages as a result of defendants' practices.

Accordingly, for the reasons set forth above, we affirm the order of the circuit court of Cook County.

Notes

In the *Lamont* case, cited in *Dwyer*, Judge Frankel wrote:

The short, though regular, journey from mail box to trash can—for the contents of which the State chooses to pay the freight when it facilitates the distribution of trash—is an acceptable burden, at least so far as the Constitution is concerned. And the bells at the door and on the telephone, though their ring is a more imperious nuisance than the mailman's tidings, accomplish more peripheral assaults than the blare of an inescapable radio.

2.   Since the *Lamont* case was decided, Congress enacted the Driver's Privacy Protection Act governing access to state motor vehicle information. The Act permits states to sell information about individuals for "marketing or solicitations if the State has obtained the express consent of the person to whom such personal information pertains." 18 U.S.C. § 2721(b)(12).

3.   Congress enacted 18 U.S.C. § 2710 after a newspaper printed the video rental records of Supreme Court nominee Robert Bork. What do you think Congress would have done had the media publicized Bork's book purchases?

4.   Weld v. CVS Pharmacy, Inc., 1999 WL 494114 (Mass. Super. Ct. 1999), involved a pharmacy that had arranged for targeted mailings to be sent to its customers who took specific medications or had particular conditions. The mailings—which were financed by drug manufacturers—urged the customers to refill prescriptions or discuss health issues with their physicians; some provided information about medications the customers were not then taking, presumably to persuade the customers to try the medications. At least one consumer who had received the mailing brought suit based on common law invasion of privacy theories and a Massachusetts statute (Mass.Gen.L.Ann. 214 § 1B) forbidding "unreasonable, substantial or serious interference with ... privacy," among other theories. Noting that the "the use of plaintiffs' private information for the defendants' financial gain" fell within the scope of the appropriation invasion of privacy tort, the court denied defendants' motion for summary judgment, distinguishing *Shibley* and *Dwyer* on the ground that consumers "arguably possess a greater expectation of privacy as to the use of their names in connection with their prescription and medical information than in connection with an individual's spending and reading habits." The court noted, however, that the common law privacy claims might be preempted by the Massachusetts statute, and gave as an additional reason for denying summary judgment that the record needed additional development. The court also denied

summary judgment on plaintiffs' unfairness claim. For an argument that the appropriation invasion of privacy tort lies against merchants who collect and sell an extensive consumer data profile, see Andrew J. McClurg, A Thousand Words are Worth a Picture: A Privacy Tort Response to Consumer Data Profiling, 98 Nw.L.Rev. 63 (2003). Health care privacy is now regulated by regulations adopted pursuant to the Health Insurance Portability and Accountability Act of 1996 ("HIPAA"), Pub. L. No. 141–191, 110 Stat. 1936 (1996). See Standards for Privacy of Individually Identifiable Health Information, 65 Fed. Reg. 82,462 (Dec. 28, 2000), codified at 45 C.F.R. pts. 160, 164.

5.   Remsburg v. Docusearch, Inc., 149 N.H. 148, 816 A.2d 1001 (2003), arose after a stalker obtained a woman's Social Security number and work address from an internet-based investigation service. The stalker then drove to the woman's workplace and killed her. The service had obtained the work address through a subcontractor who had made a "pretexting" call—that is, a call in which the caller lied about who she was and the purpose of the call to secure the information sought. The administrator of the victim's estate sued the service on various theories, including invasion of privacy and violation of a state UDAP statute. The court ruled that people do not have a reasonable expectation of privacy in their work address, and so an action for intrusion of seclusion would not lie for that disclosure. Similarly, the court held that the appropriation privacy tort was not applicable. On the other hand, the court concluded that people do have an expectation of privacy in their Social Security numbers, and so an action for intrusion into seclusion would be permitted if the fact-finder determined that the intrusion would have been offensive to a person of ordinary sensibilities. The court also found that an investigator has a duty to exercise reasonable care before disclosing a third person's information to a client. Finally, the court ruled that the pretexting call had violated the state UDAP statute. The Gramm–Leach–Bliley Act, discussed more fully *infra* in Section C, prohibits the use of pretexting to obtain customer information from financial institution. 15 U.S.C. § 6821. In addition, late in 2006, in the wake of a corporate pretexting scandal, Congress enacted 18 U.S.C. § 1039, which bars obtaining or attempting to obtain confidential phone records by pretexting or via the Internet without the permission of the consumer to whom the record pertains, as well as selling, purchasing, or receiving confidential phone records without the permission of the affected consumer. Should federal law bar the use of pretexting to obtain other consumer information?

6.   Would regulatory restraints on the transfer of accurate information about consumers violate the First Amendment? For different answers, see Eugene Volokh, Freedom of Speech and Information Privacy: The Troubling Implications of a Right to Stop People From Speaking About You, 52 Stan. L. Rev. 1049 (2000); Daniel J. Solove, The Virtues of Knowing Less: Justifying Privacy Protections Against Disclosure, 53 Duke L. J. 967 (2003).

7.   A number of state constitutions protect individual privacy. For example, California's Constitution describes pursuing and obtaining privacy as an "inalienable right." Cal. Const. Art. 1, § 1. Do these constitutional provisions have any bearing on the problems raised by this chapter?

8. Are the invasion of privacy torts, the FTC Act, and UDAP statutes appropriate vehicles for addressing the sale of consumer information and the use of consumer information to solicit transactions? See Joel R. Reidenberg, Privacy Wrongs in Search of Remedies, 54 Hastings L. J. 877 (2003). Does the equitable doctrine of unjust enrichment offer any aid to aggrieved consumers? See James P. Nehf, Recognizing the Societal Value in Information Privacy, 78 Wash. L. Rev. 1, 31–32 (2003). If not, would society be better off by enacting broad laws to protect consumer privacy, continuing its practice of sectoral privacy regulation, or abandoning efforts to protect consumer privacy?

SECTION B.   PERSONALIZED SOLICITATIONS

Sellers may choose among many ways of soliciting consumers to buy their wares. Some means of soliciting sales are relatively impersonal, such as radio and television advertising. This section focuses on more targeted sales pitches. Door-to-door sales—perhaps the most intrusive personalized sales solicitation—were addressed in Chapter Three. This Section explores two other forms of targeted sales pitches. Subsection One treats telemarketing while Subsection Two addresses unsolicited commercial electronic mail, more commonly known as spam. Among the questions raised by this section is the extent to which the regulation of solicitations should vary depending on the method of soliciting.

1.   TELEPHONE SALES

Telemarketers face a number of legal restraints. First, the FTC maintains a "Do–Not–Call" list which includes more than 100 million phone numbers. Second, telemarketers must comply with an additional set of rules as to calls they are permitted to make, either to those who are not on the Do–Not–Call list, or because the call is within an exception to the calls barred by the Do–Not–Call list regulations. Finally, federal law bars the sending of unsolicited faxes and the use of recorded phone solicitations. Each of these is discussed in this subsection. Relevant statutes and regulations appear in the Statutory Supplement.

The case below addresses a challenge to the constitutionality of the Do–Not–Call list. In light of the materials you read in Chapter One on constitutional limitations on solicitations, would you expect the Do–Not–Call list to survive the challenge? Why or why not? The case also explains the developments leading to creation of the Do–Not–Call list.

MAINSTREAM MARKETING SERVICES v. FEDERAL TRADE COMMISSION
United States Court of Appeals, Tenth Circuit, 2004.
358 F.3d 1228, certiorari denied, 543 U.S. 812,
125 S.Ct. 47, 160 L.Ed.2d 16 (2004).

EBEL, CIRCUIT JUDGE.

The four cases consolidated in this appeal involve challenges to the national do-not-call registry, which allows individuals to register their phone numbers on a national "do-not-call list" and prohibits most commercial telemarketers from calling the numbers on that list. The primary issue in this case is whether the First Amendment prevents the government from establishing an opt-in telemarketing regulation that provides a mechanism for consumers to restrict commercial sales calls but does not provide a similar mechanism to limit charitable or political calls.[1] We hold that the do-not-call registry is a valid commercial speech regulation because it directly advances the government's important interests in safeguarding personal privacy and reducing the danger of telemarketing abuse without burdening an excessive amount of speech. In other words, there is a reasonable fit between the do-not-call regulations and the government's reasons for enacting them.

As we discuss below in greater detail, four key aspects of the do-not-call registry convince us that it is consistent with First Amendment requirements. First, the list restricts only core commercial speech—i.e., commercial sales calls.[2] Second, the do-not-call registry targets speech that invades the privacy of the home, a personal sanctuary that enjoys a unique status in our constitutional jurisprudence. *See Frisby v. Schultz,* 487 U.S. 474, 484, 108 S.Ct. 2495, 101 L.Ed.2d 420 (1988). Third, the do-not-call registry is an opt-in program that puts the choice of whether or not to restrict commercial calls entirely in the hands of consumers. Fourth, the do-not-call registry materially furthers the government's interests in combating the danger of abusive telemarketing and preventing the invasion of consumer privacy, blocking a significant number of the calls that cause these problems. Under these circumstances, we conclude that the requirements of the First Amendment are satisfied.

A number of additional features of the national do-not-call registry, although not dispositive, further demonstrate that the list is consistent with the First Amendment rights of commercial speakers. The challenged regulations do not hinder any business' ability to contact consumers by other means, such as through direct mailings or other forms of advertising. Moreover, they give consumers a number of different options to avoid calls they do not want to receive. Namely, consumers who wish to restrict some but not all commercial sales calls can do so by using company-specific do-not-call lists or by granting some businesses express permission to call. In addition, the government chose to offer consumers broader options to restrict commercial sales calls than charitable and political calls after finding that commercial calls were more intrusive and posed a greater danger of consumer abuse. The government also had evidence that the less restrictive company-specific do-not-call list did not solve the problems caused by commercial telemarketing,

---

1. The telemarketers also marshal attacks on the fees they must pay to access the national do-not-call registry and to the regulations' exception for commercial callers who have an established business relationship with the consumer. We address those alternative arguments in parts IV(A) and IV(B) below. Finally, in part IV(C), we discuss the FTC's statutory authority to enact its national do-not-call regulations.

2. We express no opinion as to whether the do-not-call registry would be constitutional if it applied to political and charitable callers.

but it had no comparable evidence with respect to charitable and political fundraising.

The national do-not-call registry offers consumers a tool with which they can protect their homes against intrusions that Congress has determined to be particularly invasive. Just as a consumer can avoid door-to-door peddlers by placing a "No Solicitation" sign in his or her front yard, the do-not-call registry lets consumers avoid unwanted sales pitches that invade the home via telephone, if they choose to do so. We are convinced that the First Amendment does not prevent the government from giving consumers this option.

I. BACKGROUND

In 2003, two federal agencies—the Federal Trade Commission (FTC) and the Federal Communications Commission (FCC)—promulgated rules that together created the national do-not-call registry. *See* 16 C.F.R. § 310.4(b)(1)(iii)(B) (FTC rule); 47 C.F.R. § 64.1200(c)(2) (FCC rule). The national do-not-call registry is a list containing the personal telephone numbers of telephone subscribers who have voluntarily indicated that they do not wish to receive unsolicited calls from commercial telemarketers. Commercial telemarketers are generally prohibited from calling phone numbers that have been placed on the do-not-call registry, and they must pay an annual fee to access the numbers on the registry so that they can delete those numbers from their telephone solicitation lists. So far, consumers have registered more than 50 million phone numbers on the national do-not-call registry.

The national do-not-call registry's restrictions apply only to telemarketing calls made by or on behalf of sellers of goods or services, and not to charitable or political fundraising calls. 16 C.F.R. §§ 310.4(b)(1)(iii)(B), 310.6(a); 47 C.F.R. §§ 64.1200(c)(2), 64.1200(f)(9).[6] Additionally, a seller may call consumers who have signed up for the national registry if it has an established business relationship with the consumer or if the consumer has given that seller express written permission to call. 16 C.F.R. § 310.4(b)(1)(iii)(B)(i-ii); 47 C.F.R. § 64.1200(f)(9)(i-ii).[7] Telemarketers generally have three months from

---

6. There has been some confusion throughout this litigation with respect to how to define the term "telemarketing." *Compare* Telemarketing and Consumer Fraud and Abuse Prevention Act of 1994, Pub.L. No. 103–297, 108 Stat. 1545 at §§ 7 (1994) ("Telemarketing Act") (defining "telemarketing" as calls "conducted to induce purchases of goods or services") *with Mainstream Mktg. Servs., Inc. v. FTC,* 283 F.Supp.2d 1151, 1154 (D.Colo.2003) (describing "telemarketing" as the practice of "soliciting sales and donations" conducted by businesses, charities, political organizations, and others). Unless otherwise indicated, we use the term "telemarketing" to refer to commercial sales calls made to in-

duce purchases of goods or services (not charitable or political fundraising) consistent with Congress' definition in the Telemarketing Act.

7. The "established business relationship" exception allows businesses to call customers with whom they have conducted a financial transaction or to whom they have sold, rented, or leased goods or services within 18 months of the telephone call. 47 C.F.R. § 64.1200(f)(3); Telemarketing Sales Rule, Statement of Basis and Purpose, 68 Fed.Reg. 4580, 4591 (Jan. 29, 2003). Additionally, sellers can call consumers on the national do-not-call registry within three months after the consumer

the date on which a consumer signs up for the registry to remove the consumer's phone number from their call lists. 16 C.F.R. § 310.4(b)(3)(iv); 47 C.F.R. § 64.1200(c)(2)(i)(D). Consumer registrations remain valid for five years, and phone numbers that are disconnected or reassigned will be periodically removed from the registry. 47 C.F.R § 64.1200(c)(2); Telemarketing Sales Rule, Statement of Basis and Purpose, 68 Fed.Reg. 4580, 4640 (Jan. 29, 2003).

The national do-not-call registry is the product of a regulatory effort dating back to 1991 aimed at protecting the privacy rights of consumers and curbing the risk of telemarketing abuse. *See generally FTC v. Mainstream Mktg. Servs., Inc.,* 345 F.3d 850, 857–58 (10th Cir.2003). In the Telephone Consumer Protection Act of 1991 ("TCPA")—under which the FCC enacted its do-not-call rules—Congress found that for many consumers telemarketing sales calls constitute an intrusive invasion of privacy. *See* Pub.L. No. 102–243, 105 Stat. 2394 at § 2 (1991). Moreover, the TCPA's legislative history cited statistical data indicating that "most unwanted telephone solicitations are commercial in nature" and that "unwanted commercial calls are a far bigger problem than unsolicited calls from political or charitable organizations." H.R.Rep. No. 102–317 at 16 (1991). The TCPA therefore authorized the FCC to establish a national database of consumers who object to receiving "telephone solicitations," which the act defined as commercial sales calls. Pub.L. No. 102–243, 105 Stat. 2394 at § 3.[8]

Furthermore, in the Telemarketing and Consumer Fraud and Abuse Prevention Act of 1994 ("Telemarketing Act")—under which the FTC enacted its do-not-call rules—Congress found that consumers lose an estimated $40 billion each year due to telemarketing fraud. *See* Pub.L. No. 103–297, 108 Stat. 1545 at § 2 (1994). Therefore, Congress authorized the FTC to prohibit sales calls that a reasonable consumer would consider coercive or abusive of his or her right to privacy. *Id.* at § 3.

The FCC and FTC initially sought to accomplish the goals of the TCPA and the Telemarketing Act by adopting company-specific do-not-call lists, requiring sellers to maintain lists of consumers who have requested not to be called by that particular solicitor, and requiring telemarketers to honor those requests. *See* Rules and Regulations Implementing the Telephone Consumer Protection Act of 1991, Report and Order, 7 FCC Rcd. 8752 at ¶ 23–24 (Sept. 17, 1992); Telemarketing Sales Rule, Statement of Basis and Purpose, 60 Fed.Reg. 43842, 43854–55 (Aug. 23, 1995). Yet in enacting the national do-not-call registry, the agencies concluded that the company-specific lists had failed to achieve Congress' objectives. *See* Telemarketing Sales Rule, Statement of Basis

---

makes an inquiry or application. 47 C.F.R § 64.1200(f)(3). A seller who has an established business relationship with a consumer is still bound to comply with the company-specific rules if the consumer requests not to be called. *Id.* at § 64.1200(f)(3)(i).

8. The TCPA defines a "telephone solicitation" as a "telephone call or message for the purpose of encouraging the purchase or rental of, or investment in, property, goods, or services," excluding, inter alia, calls from tax exempt nonprofit organizations. Pub.L. No. 103–297, 108 Stat. 1545 at § 3.

and Purpose, 68 Fed Reg. 4580, 4629, 4631 (Jan. 29, 2003); Rules and Regulations Implementing the Telephone Consumer Protection Act (TCPA) of 1991, 68 Fed.Reg. 44144, 44144–45 (July 25, 2003). Among other shortfalls, the agencies explained that the large number of possible telephone solicitors made it burdensome for consumers to assert their rights under the company-specific rules, and that commercial telemarketers often ignored consumers' requests not to be called. 68 Fed.Reg. at 4629. Accordingly, the agencies decided to keep the company-specific rules as an option available to consumers, but to supplement them with the national do-not-call registry. *Id.;* 68 Fed.Reg. at 44144.

In this appeal we have consolidated four cases challenging various aspects of the national do-not-call registry. Cases Nos. 03–1429, 03–6258 and 03–9571 involve First Amendment attacks on the do-not-call list and its registry fees. We address these issues in parts III and IV(A) respectively. * * * Finally, in part IV(C), we address the alternative argument that the FTC lacked statutory authority to enact its do-not-call regulations, an argument that the district court relied upon in case No. 03–6258. We conclude that all of the telemarketers' challenges lack merit and we uphold the do-not-call list in its entirety. * * *

III.   First Amendment Analysis

The national do-not-call registry's telemarketing restrictions apply only to commercial speech. Like most commercial speech regulations, the do-not-call rules draw a line between commercial and non-commercial speech on the basis of content. * * *

Central Hudson established a three-part test governing First Amendment challenges to regulations restricting non-misleading commercial speech that relates to lawful activity. First, the government must assert a substantial interest to be achieved by the regulation. Second, the regulation must directly advance that governmental interest, meaning that it must do more than provide "only ineffective or remote support for the government's purpose." Third, although the regulation need not be the least restrictive measure available, it must be narrowly tailored not to restrict more speech than necessary. Together, these final two factors require that there be a reasonable fit between the government's objectives and the means it chooses to accomplish those ends. *United States v. Edge Broad. Co.,* 509 U.S. 418, 427–28, 113 S.Ct. 2696, 125 L.Ed.2d 345 (1993).

* * *

A.   Governmental Interests

The government asserts that the do-not-call regulations are justified by its interests in 1) protecting the privacy of individuals in their homes, and 2) protecting consumers against the risk of fraudulent and abusive solicitation. *See* 68 Fed.Reg. 44144; 68 Fed.Reg. at 4635. Both of these justifications are undisputedly substantial governmental interests.

In *Rowan v. United States Post Office Dep't,* the Supreme Court upheld the right of a homeowner to restrict material that could be mailed to his or her house. 397 U.S. 728, 90 S.Ct. 1484, 25 L.Ed.2d 736 (1970). The Court emphasized the importance of individual privacy, particularly in the context of the home, stating that "the ancient concept that 'a man's home is his castle' into which 'not even the king may enter' has lost none of its vitality." In *Frisby v. Schultz,* the Court again stressed the unique nature of the home and recognized that "the State's interest in protecting the well-being, tranquility, and privacy of the home is certainly of the highest order in a free and civilized society." 487 U.S. 474, 484, 108 S.Ct. 2495, 101 L.Ed.2d 420 (1988) (quoting *Carey v. Brown,* 447 U.S. 455, 471, 100 S.Ct. 2286, 65 L.Ed.2d 263 (1980)). As the Court held in *Frisby:*

> One important aspect of residential privacy is protection of the unwilling listener.... [A] special benefit of the privacy all citizens enjoy within their own walls, which the State may legislate to protect, is an ability to avoid intrusions. Thus, we have repeatedly held that individuals are not required to welcome unwanted speech into their own homes and that the government may protect this freedom.

Id. at 484–85, 108 S.Ct. 2495 (citations omitted). Likewise, in *Hill v. Colorado,* the Court called the unwilling listener's interest in avoiding unwanted communication part of the broader right to be let alone that Justice Brandeis described as "the right most valued by civilized men." 530 U.S. 703, 716–17, 120 S.Ct. 2480, 147 L.Ed.2d 597 (2000) (quoting *Olmstead v. United States,* 277 U.S. 438, 478, 48 S.Ct. 564, 72 L.Ed. 944 (1928) (Brandeis, J., dissenting)). The Court added that the right to avoid unwanted speech has special force in the context of the home. *Id.; see also FCC v. Pacifica Found.,* 438 U.S. 726, 748, 98 S.Ct. 3026, 57 L.Ed.2d 1073 (1978) ("[I]n the privacy of the home ... the individual's right to be left alone plainly outweighs the First Amendment rights of an intruder.").

Additionally, the Supreme Court has recognized that the government has a substantial interest in preventing abusive and coercive sales practices. *Edenfield v. Fane,* 507 U.S. 761, 768–69, 113 S.Ct. 1792, 123 L.Ed.2d 543 (1993) ("[T]he First Amendment ... does not prohibit the State from insuring that the stream of commercial information flow[s] cleanly as well as freely.") (quoting *Virginia State Bd. of Pharmacy v. Virginia Citizens Consumer Council, Inc.,* 425 U.S. 748, 771–72, 96 S.Ct. 1817, 48 L.Ed.2d 346 (1976)).

B. *Reasonable Fit*

A reasonable fit exists between the do-not-call rules and the government's privacy and consumer protection interests if the regulation directly advances those interests and is narrowly tailored. *See Central Hudson,* 447 U.S. at 564–65, 100 S.Ct. 2343. In this context, the "narrowly tailored" standard does not require that the government's response to protect substantial interests be the least restrictive measure available. All that is required is a proportional response. *Board of Trs. of State Univ. of N.Y. v. Fox,* 492 U.S. 469, 480, 109 S.Ct. 3028, 106 L.Ed.2d 388 (1989).

In other words, the national do-not-call registry is valid if it is designed to provide effective support for the government's purposes and if the government did not suppress an excessive amount of speech when substantially narrower restrictions would have worked just as well. *See Central Hudson,* 447 U.S. at 564–65, 100 S.Ct. 2343. These criteria are plainly established in this case. The do-not-call registry directly advances the government's interests by effectively blocking a significant number of the calls that cause the problems the government sought to redress. It is narrowly tailored because its opt-in character ensures that it does not inhibit any speech directed at the home of a willing listener.

1. *Effectiveness*

The telemarketers assert that the do-not-call registry is unconstitutionally underinclusive because it does not apply to charitable and political callers. First Amendment challenges based on underinclusiveness face an uphill battle in the commercial speech context. As a general rule, the First Amendment does not require that the government regulate all aspects of a problem before it can make progress on any front. * * *

As discussed above, the national do-not-call registry is designed to reduce intrusions into personal privacy and the risk of telemarketing fraud and abuse that accompany unwanted telephone solicitation. The registry directly advances those goals. So far, more than 50 million telephone numbers have been registered on the do-not-call list, and the do-not-call regulations protect these households from receiving most unwanted telemarketing calls. According to the telemarketers' own estimate, 2.64 telemarketing calls per week—or more than 137 calls annually—were directed at an average consumer before the do-not-call list came into effect. *Cf.* 68 Fed.Reg. at 44152 (discussing the five-fold increase in the total number of telemarketing calls between 1991 and 2003). Accordingly, absent the do-not-call registry, telemarketers would call those consumers who have already signed up for the registry an estimated total of 6.85 *billion* times each year.

To be sure, the do-not-call list will not block all of these calls. Nevertheless, it will prohibit a substantial number of them, making it difficult to fathom how the registry could be called an "ineffective" means of stopping invasive or abusive calls, or a regulation that "furnish[es] only speculative or marginal support" for the government's interests. *See also id.* (noting the effectiveness of state do-not-call lists in reducing unwanted telemarketing calls).

* * *

Finally, the type of unsolicited calls that the do-not-call list does prohibit—commercial sales calls—is the type that Congress, the FTC and the FCC have all determined to be most to blame for the problems the government is seeking to redress. According to the legislative history accompanying the TCPA, "[c]omplaint statistics show that unwanted commercial calls are a far bigger problem than unsolicited calls from political or charitable organizations." H.R.Rep. No. 102–317, at 16 (1991) (noting that non-commercial calls were less intrusive to consumers' privacy because they are more expected and because there is a lower volume of such calls); *see also* 68 Fed.Reg. at 44153. Similarly, the FCC determined that calls from solicitors with an established business relationship with the recipient are less problematic than other commercial calls. 68 Fed.Reg. at 44154 ("Consumers are more likely to anticipate contacts from companies with whom they have an existing relationship and the volume of such calls will most likely be lower.").

Additionally, the FTC has found that commercial callers are more likely than non-commercial callers to engage in deceptive and abusive practices. 68 Fed.Reg. at 4637 ("When a pure commercial transaction is at stake, callers have an incentive to engage in all the things that telemarketers are hated for. But non-commercial speech is a different matter."). Specifically, the FTC concluded that in charitable and political calls, a significant purpose of the call is to sell a cause, not merely to receive a donation, and that non-commercial callers thus have stronger incentives not to alienate the people they call or to engage in abusive and deceptive practices. *Id.; cf. Village of Schaumburg v. Citizens for a Better Env't*, 444 U.S. 620, 632, 100 S.Ct. 826, 63 L.Ed.2d 73 (1980) ("[B]ecause charitable solicitation does more than inform private economic decisions and is not primarily concerned with providing information about the characteristics and costs of goods and services, it is not dealt with as a variety of purely commercial speech."). The speech regulated by the do-not-call list is therefore the speech most likely to cause the problems the government sought to alleviate in enacting that list, further demonstrating that the regulation directly advances the government's interests.

In sum, the do-not-call list directly advances the government's interests—reducing intrusions upon consumer privacy and the risk of fraud or abuse—by restricting a substantial number (and also a substantial percentage) of the calls that cause these problems. * * *

2. Narrow Tailoring

Although the least restrictive means test is not the test to be used in the commercial speech context, commercial speech regulations do at least have to be "narrowly tailored" and provide a "reasonable fit" between the problem and the solution. Whether or not there are "numerous and obvious less-burdensome alternatives" is a relevant consideration in our narrow tailoring analysis. *Went For It*, 515 U.S. at 632, 115 S.Ct. 2371. A law is narrowly tailored if it "promotes a substantial government interest that would be achieved less effectively absent the regulation." *Ward v. Rock Against Racism*, 491 U.S. 781, 799, 109 S.Ct. 2746, 105 L.Ed.2d 661 (1989). Accordingly, we consider whether there are numerous and obvious alternatives that would restrict less speech and would serve the government's interest as effectively as the challenged law.

We hold that the national do-not-call registry is narrowly tailored because it does not over-regulate protected speech; rather, it restricts only calls that are targeted at unwilling recipients. *Cf. Frisby v. Schultz,* 487 U.S. 474, 485, 108 S.Ct. 2495, 101 L.Ed.2d 420 (1988) ("There simply is no right to force speech into the home of an unwilling listener."); *Rowan v. United States Post Office Dep't,* 397 U.S. 728, 738, 90 S.Ct. 1484, 25 L.Ed.2d 736 (1970) ("We therefore categorically reject the argument that a vendor has a right under the Constitution or otherwise to send unwanted material into the home of another."). The do-not-call registry prohibits only telemarketing calls aimed at consumers who have affirmatively indicated that they do not want to receive such calls and for whom such calls would constitute an invasion of privacy. *See Hill v. Colorado,* 530 U.S. 703, 716–17, 120 S.Ct. 2480, 147 L.Ed.2d 597 (2000) (the right of privacy includes an unwilling listener's interest in avoiding unwanted communication). The Supreme Court has repeatedly held that speech restrictions based on private choice (i.e.—an opt-in feature) are less restrictive than laws that prohibit speech directly. In *Rowan,* for example, the Court approved a law under which an individual could require a mailer to stop all future mailings if he or she received advertisements that he or she believed to be erotically arousing or sexually provocative. 397 U.S. at 729–30, 738, 90 S.Ct. 1484. Although it was the government that empowered individuals to avoid materials they considered provocative, the Court emphasized that the mailer's right to communicate was circumscribed only by an affirmative act of a householder. *Id.* at 738, 90 S.Ct. 1484. "Congress has erected a wall—or more accurately permits a citizen to erect a wall—that no advertiser may penetrate without his acquiescence.... The asserted right of a mailer, we repeat, stops at the outer boundary of every person's domain." *Id.*

* * *

Like the do-not-mail regulation approved in *Rowan,* the national do-not-call registry does not itself prohibit any speech. Instead, it merely "permits a citizen to erect a wall ... that no advertiser may penetrate without his acquiescence." *See Rowan,* 397 U.S. at 738, 90 S.Ct. 1484. Almost by definition, the do-not-call regulations only block calls that would constitute unwanted intrusions into the privacy of consumers who have signed up for the list. Moreover, it allows consumers who feel susceptible to telephone fraud or abuse to ensure that most commercial callers will not have an opportunity to victimize them. Under the circumstances we address in this case, we conclude that the do-not-call registry's opt-in feature renders it a narrowly tailored commercial speech regulation.

* * *

From the consumer's perspective, the do-not-call rules provide a number of different options allowing consumers to dictate what telemarketing calls they wish to receive and what calls they wish to avoid. Consumers who would like to receive some commercial sales calls but not others can sign up for the national do-not-call registry but give written permission to call to those businesses from whom they wish to receive offers. *See* 16 C.F.R. § 310.4(b)(1)(iii)(B)(*i*); 47 C.F.R. § 64.1200(f)(9)(i). Alternatively, they may decline to sign up on the national registry but make company-specific do-not-call requests with those particular businesses from whom they do not wish to receive calls. *See* 16 C.F.R. § 310.4(b)(1)(iii)(A); 47 C.F.R. § 64.1200(d)(3). Therefore, under the current regulations, consumers choose between two default rules—either that telemarketers may call or that they may not. Then, consumers may make company-specific modifications to either of these default rules as they see fit, either granting particular sellers permission to call or blocking calls from certain sellers. Finally, none of the telemarketers' proposed alternatives would serve the government's interests as effectively as the national do-not-call list. Primarily, the telemarketers suggest that company-specific rules effectively protected consumers. Yet as the FTC found, "[t]he record in this matter overwhelmingly shows the contrary ... it shows that the company-specific approach is seriously inadequate to protect consumers' privacy from an abusive pattern of calls placed by a seller or telemarketer." 68 Fed.Reg. at 4631.

First, the company-specific approach proved to be extremely burdensome to consumers, who had to repeat their do-not-call requests to every solicitor who called. *Id.* at 4629. In effect, this system gave solicitors one free chance to call each consumer, although many consumers find even an initial unsolicited sales call abusive and invasive of privacy. * * * Second, the government's experience under the company-specific rules demonstrated that commercial solicitors often ignored consumers' requests to be placed on their company-specific lists. 68 Fed.Reg. at 4629. Third, consumers have no way to verify whether their numbers have been removed from a solicitor's calling list in response to a company-specific do-not-call request. *Id.* Finally, company-specific rules are difficult to enforce because they require consumers to bear the evidentiary burden of keeping lists detailing which telemarketers have called them and what do-not-call requests they have made. *Id.*

* * *

Finally, the telemarketers argue that it would have been less restrictive to let consumers rely on technological alternatives—such as caller ID, call rejection services, and electronic devices designed to block unwanted calls. Each of these alternatives puts the cost of avoiding unwanted telemarketing calls on consumers. Furthermore, as the FCC found, "[a]lthough technology has improved to assist consumers in blocking unwanted calls, it has also evolved in such a way as to assist telemarketers in making greater numbers of calls and even circumventing such blocking technologies." 68 Fed.Reg. at 44147. Forcing consumers to compete in a technological arms race with the telemarketing industry is not an equally effective alternative to the do-not-call registry.

In sum, the do-not-call registry is narrowly tailored to restrict only speech that contributes to the problems the government seeks to redress, namely the intrusion into personal privacy and the risk of fraud and abuse caused by telephone calls that consumers do not welcome into their homes. No calls are restricted unless the recipient has affirmatively declared that he or she does not wish to receive them. Moreover, telemarketers still have the ability to contact consumers in other ways, and consumers have a number of different options in determining what telemarketing calls they will receive. Finally, there are not numerous and obvious less-burdensome alternatives that would restrict less speech while accomplishing the government's objectives equally as well. * * *

D. Summary

For the reasons discussed above, the government has asserted substantial interests to be served by the do-not-call registry (privacy and consumer protection), the do-not-call registry will directly advance those interests by banning a substantial amount of unwanted telemarketing calls, and the regulation is narrowly tailored because its opt-in feature ensures that it does not restrict any speech directed at a willing listener. In other words, the do-not-call registry bears a reasonable fit with the purposes the government sought to advance. Therefore, it is consistent with the limits the First Amendment imposes on laws restricting commercial speech.

IV. OTHER ISSUES

The telemarketers also challenge various other aspects of the do-not-call registry. In turn, we consider 1) whether the fees telemarketers must pay to access the registry are constitutional, 2) whether it was arbitrary and capricious for the FCC to approve the established business relationship exception, and 3) whether the FTC had statutory authority to enact its do-not-call rules.

A. The Do–Not–Call Registry Fees

To obtain the phone numbers of consumers who have signed up for the national do-not-call registry, telemarketers must pay a modest annual access fee determined by the FTC. * * * The telemarketers argue that this fee unconstitutionally imposes a revenue tax on protected speech. We disagree.

* * *

C. The FTC's Statutory Authority

In case No. 03–6258, the district court held that the FTC lacked statutory authority to enact the do-not-call registry. In the Telemarketing Act, Congress authorized the FTC to "prescribe rules prohibiting deceptive telemarketing acts or practices and other abusive telemarketing acts or practices." Pub.L. 103–297, 108 Stat. 1545 at § 3. More specifically, Congress directed the FTC to include "a requirement that telemarketers may not undertake a pattern of unsolicited telephone calls which the reasonable consumer would consider coercive or abusive of such consumer's right to privacy." *Id.* The FTC's conclusion that this language authorized it to enact the national do-not-call registry is entitled to deference under the familiar test outlined in *Chevron, U.S.A., Inc. v. Natural Resources Defense Council*, 467 U.S. 837, 842–43, 104 S.Ct. 2778, 81 L.Ed.2d 694 (1984). In light of this deference, we conclude that the FTC did have statutory authority to promulgate its do-not-call regulations because the agency's view that the Telemarketing Act authorized it to enact those rules is at least a permissible construction of that statute.

Moreover, even if some doubt once existed, Congress erased it through subsequent legislation. * * * In the Do–Not–Call Implementation Act, Congress directed the FCC and FTC to maximize consistency between their respective do-not-call rules and authorized the FTC to collect do-not-call registry fees to offset the administrative costs of the regulations. Pub.L. 108–10, 117 Stat. 557 at §§ 2–3. Furthermore, in response to the district court's decision in case No. 03–6258, Congress expressly ratified the FTC's do-not-call regulations. An Act to Ratify the Authority of the Federal Trade Commission to Establish a Do–Not–Call Registry, Pub.L. 108–82, 117 Stat 1006 (2003). The FTC's statutory authority is now unmistakably clear.

V. Conclusion

We hold that 1) the do-not-call list is a valid commercial speech regulation under *Central Hudson* because it directly advances substantial governmental interests and is narrowly tailored; 2) the registry fees telemarketers must pay to access the list are a permissible measure designed to defray the cost of legitimate government regulation; 3) it was not arbitrary and capricious for the FCC to adopt the established business relationship exception; and 4) the FTC has statutory authority to establish and implement the national do-not-call registry.

Notes

1.   Why would consumers not add their numbers to the Do–Not–Call List? Do some people want to receive telemarketing calls?

2.   The Do–Not–Call list is the only list operated by the federal government barring solicitors from communicating with consumers. As discussed in the next section, the FTC recommended against establishing a similar list for people who do not want to receive unsolicited commercial email. The Direct Marketing Association maintains a list (called the "Mail Preference Service" or "MPS") of consumers who do not wish to receive direct mail. Members of the DMA are required to remove the consumers on the MPS list from their mailing lists. Many direct mail senders are not members of the DMA and are thus under no obligation to use the MPS, though the DMA makes it

available to non-members of the DMA. Should Congress create a "Do–Not–Mail" list similar to the Do–Not–Call List? If so, would it be constitutional? How are telephone solicitations different from direct mail solicitations?

3.   The USA PATRIOT Act, enacted in 2001, amended the definition of telemarketing in the Telemarketing Act to extend the statute's application to charitable fundraising. See 15 U.S.C. § 6106(4). Because the FTC lacks jurisdiction over nonprofits, however, the FTC has interpreted its power as limited to fundraising conducted by for-profit telemarketers (so-called, "tele-funders") on behalf of charities; that is, when a charity pays a for-profit telemarketer to make fundraising calls. 68 Fed.Reg. 4580 at 4584–85. (Jan. 30, 2002). That interpretation, and the resulting amendments to the Tele-marketing Sales Rule, were upheld over a dissent in National Federation of the Blind v. FTC, 420 F.3d 331 (4th Cir. 2005), cert. denied, ___ U.S. ___, 126 S.Ct. 2058, 164 L.Ed.2d 779 (2006). To what extent should nonprofit organizations seeking contributions be covered by the Do–Not–Call list? The sale of lists of donors can be extremely lucrative for nonprofits. In response, commentators have urged the establishment of a Do–Not–Share list barring nonprofits from providing contact information for donors on the list. See Ely R. Levy & Norman I. Silber, Nonprofit Fundraising and Consumer Protec-tion: A Donor's Right to Privacy, 15 Stan. L. & Pol'y Rev. 519 (2004).

4.   Other commentators have suggested that a better alternative to the Do–Not–Call list would be a system in which consumers could charge telemarketers for their calls. Consumers would thus be compensated for their time, and if they demanded excessive prices, telemarketers would not call them. See Ian Ayres & Mathew Funk, Marketing Privacy, 20 Yale J. on Reg. 77 (2003).

5.   For an interesting account of the story behind the Do–Not–Call list, see Sidney M. Malkis, The Federal Trade Commission and Consumer Protec-tion: Regulatory Change and Administrative Pragmatism, 72 Antitrust L.J. 911 (2005).

6.   Though the Do–Not–Call list appears to have reduced the number of telemarketing calls received by those listed on it, it has not stopped them completely, as demonstrated by a report that Delaware Governor Ruth Ann Minner still received occasional telemarketing calls on her "secret homeland defense hotline" to the Department of Homeland Security despite the fact that it was listed on the Do–Not–Call list. See In Brief, Hotline 'Junk' Calls, Privacy Times, June 23, 2006 at 9.

Problem 5–2

Jesse works for a for-profit telemarketing business which has been retained to make phone calls urging people to donate to The Frobisher Center, a non-profit enterprise. May he call people on the FTC's Do–Not–Call List? May he call people who have previously requested that they not receive fundraising calls for The Frobisher Center? See 16 C.F.R. § 310.4(b) in the Statutory Supplement.

Problem 5–3

Angus visited the web site of Rophos, Inc. a company that sells DVD's. Angus became interested in a particular DVD and noticed that the web site permitted him to watch a preview of the DVD if he completed an online "Application to Watch Previews," a process that included providing his telephone number. Angus filled out the form, but after watching the preview, decided against purchasing the DVD. A day later, Angus received a call from a Rophos telemarketer offering products for sale even though Angus had previously listed himself on the FTC's Do–Not–Call List. Angus asks you whether Rophos has violated the TSR. See 16 C.F.R. §§ 310.2(n), 310.4(b); Michael P. Considine, Comment, User Registration Websites: Possible E–Loopholes to the National Do–Not–Call Registry, 53 Emory L. J. 1951 (2004).

Problem 5–4

Vic Video recently got a telephone call from a representative of Software Unlimited, who wanted to sell him a subscription to a monthly video game service for his home computer. The salesperson asserted that the games were the top of the line, were compatible with all makes of computer, and would cost "only pennies a day." Vic orally agreed to subscribe. Three days later he received his first set of games and a bill in the mail for $32 for the first month. The games were of poor quality and would not work properly on Vic's computer. Would the FTC Door-to-Door Sales Rule apply to Vic's problem? See § 429.0(a)(4). If not, does the FTC's Telemarketing Sales Rule ("TSR") provide for a cooling-off period? If not, does the TSR offer Vic any other aid? See § 310.3(a)(4). What if instead of Software Unlimited calling Vic, Vic had visited their website and purchased the software online. Vic connects to the internet through his telephone lines. Must the seller provide a cooling-off period?

Note

Many states have enacted cooling-off periods for telephone sales. See, e.g., N.Y. Pers. Prop. L. § 440 *et seq.* The statutes are summarized in Dee Pridgen, Consumer Credit and the Law App. 15A (2006). Courts have also interpreted state door-to-door sales statutes as applicable to telemarketing sales. See People v. Toomey, 157 Cal.App.3d 1, 13–14, 203 Cal.Rptr. 642, 650 (1st Dist. 1984); Brown v. Martinelli, 66 Ohio St.2d 45, 20 Ohio Op. 3d 38, 419 N.E.2d 1081 (1981). Does the rationale for a cooling-off period for sales in the home apply to telephone sales? If not, why should telephone sales be subject to cooling-off periods?

Problem 5–5

Kacey, a telemarketer, called Danny and persuaded Danny to invest $75,000 in gemstones by describing the investment as a "sure thing." In fact, the gems are worthless and Danny lost his investment. After selling the gems to Danny, Kacey sold a list of her customers to Ethan. Ethan then called Danny to say that for a small fee paid in advance he would be able to recover for Danny the amount Danny lost to Kacey. Danny paid the fee but never heard from Ethan again. Have Kacey or Ethan violated the TSR? See 16 C.F.R. §§ 310.3(a)(2)(vi), 310.4(a)(3). Would it matter if Ethan were an attorney? Who enforces the TSR? See §§ 6102, 6103, 6104.

Problem 5–6

Kimmy, a small town merchant with a good credit record is approached by Sasha, a telemarketer in need of credit services. Sasha asks Kimmy to submit Sasha's credit card slips to VISA or Mastercard in return for a fee. What advice would you give Kimmy? See 16 C.F.R. §§ 310.3(c).

Problem 5–7

Arabella was just sitting down to dinner one night when the phone rang. The caller explained that he was conducting a marketing survey about reading habits. After ten minutes, the caller offered Arabella membership in a book club, an offer she declined. Did the caller violate the TSR? See 16 C.F.R. § 310.4(d).

Problem 5–8

Jim has a bad credit record and has been unable to obtain a credit card. One evening Jim received a telephone call from a telemarketer, Avery, who claimed he could arrange for Jim to get a "Gold" credit card that could be used to make purchases while helping Jim build up a good credit record. Avery sent a runner to pick up the $50 fee from Jim. When Jim later obtained the card, he discovered that it must be "secured" by having a sufficient amount on deposit with the sponsoring bank to cover any purchases, and purchases can only be made from a special catalog. Did Avery violate the TSR? See 16 C.F.R. §§ 310.3(a)(1)(ii), (2)(ii); 310.4(a)(4); 310.2(h), (i); People v. Financial Services Network, 930 F.Supp. 865 (W.D.N.Y. 1996). Would it matter if Avery had explained from the beginning that the card must be secured by a deposit?

Problem 5–9

Avery's telemarketing business is barely profitable, and so Avery would like to find a way to reduce the time his telemarketers spend waiting to be connected to the next consumer. Avery wishes to buy a computer system that will dial several numbers simultaneously and then connect available telemarketers to the first line that answers, while disconnecting any lines telemarketers are not available for. Avery anticipates that this will result in ten percent of his calls being abandoned. Would that violate the TSR? See 16 C.F. R. § 310.4(b)(1)(iv), (b)(4).

Note on Unsolicited Commercial Faxes and Recorded Solicitations

The Telephone Consumer Protection Act, 47 U.S.C. § 227, prohibits, with some exceptions, merchants from sending faxes consisting of unsolicited advertisements or making phone calls using recorded voices (which would include advertisements). The statute permits consumers to bring a private claim in state court for an injunction and the greater of actual monetary losses or $500 per violation "if otherwise permitted by the laws or rules of court of a State." Willful or knowing violations of the statute or implementing regulations may be punishable by treble damages in the court's discretion. The statute may also be enforced by the Federal Communications Commission and state officials. The FCC's regulations implementing the statute appear at 47 C.F.R. § 64.1200.

Students who have not themselves received recorded telephone solicitations may be puzzled by the decision to ban them altogether while permitting telemarketers to call those who are not listed on the Do–Not–Call List. The court in Moser v. FCC, 46 F.3d 970 (9th Cir.), cert. denied, 515 U.S. 1161, 115 S.Ct. 2615, 132 L.Ed.2d 857 (1995), offered the following explanation for Congress's action:

> By the fall of 1991, more than 180,000 solicitors were using automated machines to telephone 7 million people each day. [citing Senate Report No. 102–178, 102d Cong., 1st Sess. (1991), *reprinted in* 1991 U.S.C.C.A.N. 1968, 1970.] In addition to the sheer volume of automated calls, Congress determined that such calls were "more of a nuisance and a greater invasion of privacy than calls placed by 'live' persons" because such calls "cannot interact with the customer except in preprogrammed ways" and "do not allow the caller to feel the frustration of the called party...." *Id.* at 1972. Customers who wanted to remove their names from calling lists were forced to wait until the end of taped messages to hear the callers' identifying information. Prerecorded messages cluttered answering machines, and automated devices did not disconnect immediately after a hang up. *Id.* at 1972.

Moser upheld the prohibition on recorded solicitations against constitutional challenge. See also Margulis v. P & M Consulting, Inc., 121 S.W.3d 246 (Mo.App. 2003). Among the cases upholding the constitutionality of the ban on unsolicited faxes are Missouri ex rel. Nixon v. American Blast Fax, Inc., 323 F.3d 649 (8th Cir. 2003), cert. denied, 540 U.S. 1104, 124 S.Ct. 1043, 157 L.Ed.2d 888 (2004); Destination Ventures, Ltd. v. F.C.C., 46 F.3d 54 (9th Cir. 1995); Rudgayzer & Gratt v. Enine, Inc., 4 Misc.3d 4,, 779 N.Y.S.2d 882 (N.Y. Sup.2004); Kaufman v. ACS Systems, Inc., 110 Cal.App.4th 886, 2 Cal.Rptr.3d 296 (2003).

Why should Congress treat faxes differently from telemarketing solicitations or (as we will see in the next section) unsolicited commercial email? If Congress had imposed an outright ban on telemarketing, instead of using a Do–Not–Call list, would the ban have been constitutional?

2. UNSOLICITED COMMERCIAL EMAIL

Most advertising is expensive. Ads on television, radio, and in newspapers are all costly. Direct mail advertisers must pay for postage, printing costs and often the cost of acquiring mailing lists while telemarketers incur expenses for labor and telephone lines. Such solicitations do not make sense unless they are likely to generate enough sales to offset their cost. But spam is different. Once the spammer has a list of email addresses, the cost of sending spam is trivial. Consequently, spammers find it profitable to use spam to solicit sales even for products that generate few sales per solicitation. The result is a flood of offers for products few consumers want and that are not usually advertised in other media. Ironically, while spam is inexpensive for its senders, it can be costly for others. As the court explained in White Buffalo Ventures, LLC v. University of Texas at Austin, 2004 WL 1854168 (W.D.Tex. 2004), aff'd in part, 420 F.3d 366 (5th Cir. 2005), *cert. denied*, ___ U.S. ___, 126 S.Ct. 1039, 163 L.Ed.2d 856 (2006):

> Spam imposes significant economic burdens on ISPs, consumers, and businesses. Left unchecked at its present rate of increase, spam may soon undermine the usefulness and efficiency of e-mail as a communications tool. Massive volumes of spam can clog a computer network, slowing Internet service for those who share that network. ISPs must respond to rising volumes of spam by investing in new equipment to increase capacity and customer service personnel to deal with increased subscriber complaints. ISPs also face high costs maintaining e-mail filtering systems and other anti-spam technology on their networks to reduce the deluge of spam. Increasingly, ISPs are also undertaking extensive investigative and legal efforts to track down and prosecute those who send the most spam, in some cases spending over a million dollars to find and sue a single, heavy-volume spammer.

> Though major service providers tend to disagree about the overall monetary impact spam has had on their respective networks, anti-spam initiatives cost providers time and money, and those expenses typically have been passed on as increased charges to consumers. A 2001 European Union study found that spam cost Internet subscribers worldwide $9.4 billion each year, and USA Today reported in April that research organizations estimate that fighting spam adds an average of $2 per month to an individual's Internet bill. Additionally, some observers expect that free e-mail services (often used by students and employees who obtain free Internet access) will be downsized as the costs of spam increase, which may result in consumers facing significant "switching costs" as they are forced to migrate to subscription-based services. As reported by the Boston Globe, industry analysts are concerned that this trend could influence millions of consumers to abandon the use of e-mail messaging as a viable means of communication.

* * *

In addition to the costs to ISPs and consumers, recent industry research has focused on the impact of spam's growth on businesses and e-commerce. Ferris Research currently estimates that costs to United States businesses from spam in lost productivity, network system upgrades, unrecoverable data, and increased personnel costs, combined, will top $10 billion in 2003. Of that total, Ferris estimates that employee productivity losses from sifting through and deleting spam accounts for nearly $4 billion alone. Recent press reports also indicate that large companies with corporate networks typically spend between $1 to $2 per user each month to prevent spam, which is currently estimated to make up 24 percent of such corporations' inbound e-mail. At current growth rates, however, spam could account for nearly 50 percent of all inbound e-mail to large corporations by 2004. Ferris reports that corporate costs of fighting spam today represent a 300 percent increase from 2 years ago, and the Yankee Group estimates that costs to corporations could reach $12 billion globally within the next 18 months. Based on current spam growth rates, the Radicati Group estimates that, on a worldwide basis, spam could cost corporations over $113 billion by 2007.

Congress responded by enacting CANSPAM, which appears in the Statutory Supplement. Rather than banning spam, CANSPAM regulates it. It obliges spammers both to include in unsolicited commercial emails a mechanism spam recipients can use to opt-out of additional emails from that sender and to honor such opt-outs. It also prohibits certain deceptive practices and contains provisions designed to make it difficult for spammers to evade CANSPAM. These provisions and others are explored in the following problems.

Problem 5–10

Your clients, Fred and George Wiley, want to make a quick buck selling joke magic tricks. They recently bought a list containing the email addresses of 10,000 people whom they believe might be good customers for their products. They want to know whether the CAN-SPAM Act will prevent them from soliciting customers via email.

Problem 5–11

The Wileys would like to send the people on their list repeated emails offering other products. Assuming that they can lawfully use the email list, the Wileys would like to know whether they have to make it possible for recipients of their emails to let the Wileys know that they do not want to receive any more email, and if people do so, whether the Wileys have to respect that request. See 15 U.S.C. § 7704(a)(3), (4).

Problem 5–12

The Wileys have obtained a list of consumers' birthdays and would like to know if they can combine their advertisement with a cordial birthday greeting. They would use as their subject line the phrase "Happy Birthday." See 15 U.S.C. § 7704(a)(1), (2), (5). Alternatively, they would like to know if they would run afoul of CANSPAM if they misrepresented the virtues of their products in the body of their email messages, but the message was otherwise truthful.

Problem 5–13

The Wileys wonder if they can avoid application of CANSPAM by sending their spam as instant messages (sometimes called "spim"), rather than conventional spam. See 15 U.S.C. §§ 7702(2), 7704. What if they send their spam in the form of text messages to cell phones? Joffe v. Acacia Mortg. Corp., 211 Ariz. 325, 121 P.3d 831 (Ariz.App. 2005).

Problem 5–14

The Wileys have concluded that no one will read their emails or buy their products if they comply with CANSPAM. Accordingly, they are contemplating actions to avoid following the statute. They have several questions.

A. First, they would like to know what risks they run if they simply ignore the statute. See 15 U.S.C. § 7706.

B. Second, the Wileys know of some unscrupulous spammers whom the Wileys could get to send their email for them, and the Wileys would like to know if that would expose them to any risks. See 15 U.S.C. § 7705.

C. Third, they have acquired technology that permits them to take over the computer of anyone connected to the internet in such a way that they could send their emails to people through that person's computer without that person being aware of what the Wileys have done. Doing so would make it more difficult for enforcement agencies to track the Wileys down. They would like to know if the statute bars such activity. See 18 U.S.C. § 1037.

D. Finally, because the Wileys live in England, they wonder if they can simply avoid application of the statute by virtue of being outside the US. In answering this question, consider 18 U.S.C. § 1030(e)(2)(B), which provides that "the term 'protected computer' means a computer ... which is used in interstate or foreign commerce or communication, including a computer located outside the United States that is used in a manner that affects interstate or foreign commerce or communication of the United States...."

FEDERAL TRADE COMMISSION
v. PHOENIX AVATAR, LLC

United States District Court, N.D. Illinois.
2004 WL 1746698, 2004–2 Trade Cases P 74,507 (2004).

HOLDERMAN, J.

Before this court is the Federal Trade Commission's ("FTC") request for a preliminary injunction to be entered against defendants Daniel J. Lin, Mark M. Sadek, James Lin, and Christopher Chung. A Temporary Restraining Order ("TRO") against these defendants was entered on April 23, 2004 and has continued by consent pending this ruling. Defendants Phoenix Avatar, LLC and DJL, LLC have failed to appear and a preliminary injunction was entered against these defendants on May 6, 2004. The request for a preliminary injunction against remaining defendants Daniel Lin, Mark Sadek, James Lin, and Christopher Chung is based on purported violations of the Controlling the Assault of Non–Solicited Pornography and Marketing Act of 2003 ("CAN–SPAM"), 15 U.S.C. § 7701 *et seq.* and 15 U.S.C. §§ 45(a),

52(a)("FTC Act"). For the following reasons, the request for a preliminary injunction is granted. * * *

FINDINGS OF FACT

Based on the evidence presented in the record, the court makes the following factual findings.

I.   Background; FTC's Preliminary Investigation Which Led to Avatar

Theresa J. Bresnahan ("Bresnahan"), paralegal specialist with the FTC, presented most of the FTC's evidence in support of a preliminary injunction. Bresnahan testified that an e-mail consists of two parts, a header and a body. Among other things, the header usually contains identifying information fields such as the intended recipient, the sender of the e-mail, the date, and a subject line. Oftentimes, the e-mail body will contain a hyperlink, which is a link to a specific Web site on the Internet. When a user "clicks" on a hyperlink, that user's Internet browser opens up on the specified Web site. A domain name, which is usually purchased by a user, is a unique name that identifies a Web site. For example, *www.xyz.com*. A sub-page designation identifies subsequent Web pages within the main Web site. For example, "info" is the sub-page designation in *www.xyz.com/info*, and clicking on this as a hyperlink would take the user to the "info" sub-page within the *www.xyz.com* Web site.

* * *

II.   Undercover Purchases

For purposes of investigating the Avatar domain names, Bresnahan posed as a consumer, using an alias and undercover information, including a shipping address, telephone line, e-mail address and a VISA credit card account. Bresnahan made four purchases from Web sites with Avatar domain names, two of which are relevant to the instant request for a preliminary injunction. Bresnahan linked to these Web sites by clicking on hyperlinks contained in spam received from the spam database or commercial Internet news groups.

* * *

STANDARD OF REVIEW

This court reviews the FTC's request for an injunction pursuant to 15 U.S.C. § 53(b) under the "public interest" test, which requires that this court to (1) determine the FTC's likelihood of success on the merits, and (2) balance the equities. * * *

ANALYSIS

I.   FTC's Likelihood of Success on the Merits

To establish a likelihood of success on the merits, the FTC must show a violation of the law that the defendants committed. The two statutes allegedly violated by the defendants are the FTC Act and CAN–SPAM. The court will first address whether these statutes have been violated and then, evaluating all of the evidence, the court will analyze the FTC's likelihood of success in establishing the defendants' liability at a trial on the merits.

A. *Violations of the FTC Act and CAN–SPAM*

(i) *FTC Act*

This court rules that the FTC has a better than negligible chance of success on the merits of its claim that the representations regarding the Premium Diet Patch ("diet patch") are deceptive. The Web sites and packaging of the diet patch made express claims that the diet patch would cause weight loss by suppressing appetite and boosting metabolism. The packaging represented that the diet patch was a "weight loss formula," and that using the diet patch would "safely stimulate your metabolism, causing your body to use and absorb food more efficiently and to burn fat rather than store it." The two Web sites that the FTC utilized to purchase the product contained similar representations, describing the diet patch as "a highly effective weight loss patch."

The evidence presented at the hearing showed that these representations were false. In sum, Dr. Jensen testified that there is no scientific evidence relied upon by the medical community that would suggest that the diet patch the defendants sold or advertised on the two Web sites would cause any weight loss, increase metabolism, or decrease appetite. The evidence submitted by the defendants to the contrary does not detract from Dr. Jensen's conclusions, and certainly does not provide substantiation for the defendants' contention that the diet patch representations are not deceptive. * * *

(ii) *Violations of CAN–SPAM*

On January 1, 2004, the Controlling the Assault of Non-solicited Pornography and Marketing Act of 2003 ("CAN–SPAM") went into effect. In this legislation, Congress made the finding that electronic mail had not only "become an extremely important and popular means of communication, relied on by millions of Americans on a daily basis," but that it also served an important role "for the development of frictionless commerce." 15 U.S.C. § 7701(a)(1). These great benefits for society and economy are, however, "threatened by the extremely rapid growth in the volume of unsolicited commercial electronic mail." § 7701(a)(2). According to Congress, unsolicited commercial electronic mail, or spam, "account[s] for over half of all electronic mail traffic, up from an estimated 7 percent in 2001." § 7701(a)(2). The prevalence of spam significantly detracts from the efficiency and convenience of electronic mail. *See* §§ 7701(a)(3), (a)(4), (a)(5), (a)(6). Congress specifically listed what it considered to be the evils of spam: that its source and purpose for being sent are often disguised, §§ 7701(a)(7), (a)(8); that senders of spam often do not provide its recipients with the ability "to reject (or "opt-out" of) receipt" of the spam, § 7701(a)(9); and that senders of spam are able "to gather large numbers of electronic mail address on an automated basis from Internet websites ... where users must post their addresses in order to make full use of the website or service." § 7701(a)(10).

Based upon these findings, Congress determined that:

> (1) there is a substantial government interest in regulation of commercial electronic mail on a nationwide basis;

> (2) senders of commercial electronic mail should not mislead recipients as to the source or content of such mail; and

> (3) recipients of commercial electronic mail have a right to decline to receive additional commercial electronic mail from the same source.

§ 7701(b). Finally, CAN–SPAM specifically notes that "[i]t is the sense of Congress that ... Spam has become the method of choice for those who distribute pornography, perpetrate fraudulent schemes, and introduce viruses, worms, and Trojan horses into personal and business computer systems." § 7703(c). * * *

There is no dispute that the e-mails in question violate CAN–SPAM. These e-mails, in fact, violate most, if not all, of CAN–SPAM's major provisions. Both of the technical experts testified at the preliminary injunction hearing that the e-mail messages marketing the two Web sites countupandlookaway.com and keepyourmatehappy.biz concealed the identify of the sender, violating section 7704(a)(1)'s requirement that e-mail messages shall not contain "header information that is materially false or materially misleading." Furthermore, the e-mails do contain neither a conspicuous notice of the ability to "opt-out," nor the sender's physical postal address, nor a clear notice that the e-mails are commercial solicitations. All of these omissions violate CAN–SPAM. § 7704(a)(5)(A).

While defendants have not disputed that the e-mails violate CAN–SPAM, they have attempted to mount a constitutional challenge to CAN–SPAM itself. According to the defendants, CAN–SPAM "prohibits various e-mail messages which omit certain information, and accordingly, is a content-based Internet restriction, which is presumed invalid." Defendants support this conclusory statement with a quote from the Supreme Court's recent decision in *Ashcroft v. American Civil Liberties Union,* 542 U.S. 656, 124 S.Ct. 2783, 159 L.Ed.2d 690 (2004), in which the Supreme Court held that the Child Online Protection Act ("COPA"), 47 U.S.C. § 231, was an invalid content based restriction. This court will only consider the single constitutional argument raised by defendants. Defendants contention that a prohibition on e-mails omitting certain information—or a requirement of disclosures—amounts to content-based restrictions on speech is rejected because it "overlooks material differences between disclosure requirements and outright prohibitions on speech." *Zauderer v. Office of Disciplinary Counsel of the Supreme Court of Ohio,* 471 U.S. 626, 105 S.Ct. 2265, 2281, 85 L.Ed.2d 652 (1985). In short, requiring disclosure of information does not amount to a content-based restriction. *See Id.* Accordingly, defendants constitutional claim fails.

B. *Defendants' Responsibility for Violations of the FTC Act and CAN–SPAM*

The evidence connects the defendants to the entities selling the diet patches from the two Web sites countupandlookaway.com and keepyourmatehappy.biz and also establishes that the money spent purchasing the diet patches ended up in the defendants' possession.

Phoenix Avatar, LLC was listed by MyPaySystems as the vendor selling diet patches from countupandlookaway.com, and AIT Herbal Marketing was listed on the invoice from this purchase, and AIT Herbal Marketing appeared on the FTC's credit card statement for the second purchase. Thus, the evidence establishes that Phoenix Avatar, LLC, and AIT Herbal Marketing were selling the diet patches marketed on the Web sites countupandlookaway.com and keepyourmatehappy.biz.

The fact that these entities used these Web sites to sell their products establishes that they are likely responsible for the content of the Web sites. Similarly, the entities are likely responsible for the offending spam, which functioned as advertisements for the Web sites. The offending spam contained hyperlinks to these Web sites and also contained advertisements such as "Amazing patch makes you shed the pounds!" which directed recipients of the spam to the Web sites. Accordingly, it is quite likely that the entities utilizing the Web sites to sell diet patches initiated the transmission of the spam advertising the Web sites.

This conclusion is not undermined by the absence of technical evidence tracing the spam in this case back to its source. Both experts testified to the difficulties of determining the source of spam, due to the fact that those who send spam go to great lengths to hide their identities. And both experts testified that the e-mails in this case contain misleading information inserted for the purpose of obfuscating their true source. The FTC's expert also testified that no technical method existed to determine the source of the e-mails because of the use of open proxies. Technical evidence connecting a person or an entity to spam would certainly be persuasive. However, it is not necessary to prove a violation of CAN–SPAM, as the definition of "initiate" in CAN–SPAM makes clear. Liability is not limited to those who physically cause spam to be transmitted, but also extends to those who "procure the origination" of offending spam. 15 U.S.C. § 7702(9). The technical evidence attested to by defendants' expert Howell could not establish who "procure[d] the origination" of spam. Therefore, the statute necessarily contemplates the use of nontechnical evidence to prove the source of offending spam.

Finally, the evidence connects the defendants to these two entities that are likely responsible for the deceptive practices and CAN–SPAM violations described above. Defendant James Lin, utilizing his bank account 884282030 jointly controlled with defendants Daniel Lin and Mark Sadek, paid the fee required to form Phoenix Avatar, LLC. The record also establishes that defendant Christopher Chung registered the

Fictitious Business Name AIT Herbal Marketing, which was listed on the invoice the FTC received from its first undercover purchase. AIT Herbal Marketing, through M. Sadek, applied for the P.O. Box 251570, from which both undercover purchases were shipped. The FTC's undercover credit card was billed by AIT Herbal Marketing for the second undercover purchase. The evidence establishes that credits to AIT Herbal Marketing's merchant account with a credit card processor were deposited into bank account 884282030. The FTC has shown that the defendants are likely the individuals acting through the entities Phoenix Avatar, LLC and AIT Herbal Marketing.

At this stage of the litigation, the court is also not swayed by defendants mere assertion that the FTC has failed to offer evidence of the defendants' "actual knowledge and/or participation in what the FTC claims to be deceptive acts and practices." (Defs.' Closing at 18.) *See FTC v. Amy Travel Service, Inc.*, 875 F.2d 564, 573–74 (7th Cir.1989). This standard applies when determining which individuals to hold liable after corporate liability is established. *Id.* However, AIT Herbal Marketing, the entity purporting to sell both diet patches is not a corporation. It is simply a fictitious business name, and the evidence introduced by the FTC shows that the individuals using and profiting from this name are the defendants. Finally, the FTC has shown the defendants "active involvement in [the] business affairs" of Phoenix Avatar, LLC, which is "probative of [their] knowledge" of that company's deceptive acts and practices. *Id.* at 574.

Accordingly, this court finds that the FTC has a better than negligible chance of success in showing that the individual defendants are responsible for the violations of the FTC Act and CAN–SPAM. * * *

Considering the equities, this court finds that the balance of equities favors the FTC because the defendants have not demonstrated any significant, much less irreparable injury to them from the FTC's requested preliminary injunction. This conclusion is strengthened when the court factors into the balance the FTC's likelihood of success. For purposes of applying the sliding scale analysis, this court finds the FTC's likelihood of success on the merits as greater than a mere better than negligible chance. The FTC has amassed a persuasive chain of evidence connecting the defendants to violations of the FTC Act and CAN–SPAM. This evidence is sufficient to support by a preponderance of the evidence the finding sought by the FTC against the defendants. This strong showing, coupled with the presumption that public equities receive far greater weight than private equities, establishes that the balance of equities favors the FTC in this case.

Conclusion

Accordingly, the request for a preliminary injunction against defendants Daniel J. Lin, Mark M. Sadek, James Lin, and Christopher Chung is granted. . . .

Notes

1. *Phoenix Avatar* demonstrates the difficulty both of tracing spam back to a particular sender and of proving that the sender originated the spam. Given the resources required to do so, is CANSPAM a good solution to the problem of spam?

2. Many states have also enacted anti-spam laws. Virginia enacted the first statute to provide for criminal penalties, Va. Code Ann. § 18.2–152.3:1. The statute applies to spammers who intentionally falsify or forge electronic mail transmission information or other routing information if they meet certain requirements for the number of spam sent or revenue derived from spam. Because the Virginia law applies not only to spam sent to Virginians, but also to spam sent through Virginia-based ISP's, which includes America Online, the Virginia statute is particularly significant. The statute was upheld against constitutional challenge in Virginia v. Jaynes, 2004 WL 2085359 (Va. Cir. Ct. 2004). See also Beyond Systems, Inc. v. Keynetics, Inc., 422 F.Supp.2d 523 (D.Md. 2006) (Maryland statute). One issue that arises in connection with state spam statutes is that senders of spam may not know where the recipients of their spam are located; many email addresses do not indicate the location of the recipient. See State v. Heckel, 122 Wash.App. 60, 93 P.3d 189 (2004), review denied 153 Wash.2d 1021, 108 P.3d 1229 (2005) (rejecting e-mailer's defense that he didn't know his emails were directed to Washington residents when he sent more than 100,000 email messages per week and state had advised him that Washington residents were receiving his emails).

3. In 15 U.S.C. § 7708, Congress directed the FTC to report on the feasibility of establishing a Do–Not–Email registry, similar to the Do–Not–Call telemarketing registry. The FTC determined that spammers would use such a registry as a source for email addresses and that until authentication mechanisms improved, it would be impossible to identify those who misused the registry. Accordingly, the FTC recommended against establishment of such a registry, but called for improving authentication methods. FTC, National Do Not Email Registry: A Report to Congress (June 2004), available at http://www.ftc.gov/reports/dneregistry/report.pdf. Nevertheless, some states have enacted statutes, designed to protect children from inappropriate advertisements, that establish lists of protected "contact points" of minors, including email addresses. See 2003 MI S.B. 1025 (SN); Utah Code Ann. § 13–39–101 et seq.

4. Does spam serve a legitimate purpose? One study found that four percent of spam recipients purchased something advertised through spam in a 12–month period, representing 4.7 million purchasers. Rockbridge Assoc., Summary Report of the 2004 National Technology Readiness Survey (2004) ("NTRS"), available at http://www.smith.umd.edu/ntrs/NTRS_2004.pdf. Another study concluded that 1.2 million households had bought something advertised to them in spam. Net Threat Rising, Consumer Rep., Sept. 2005, at 13. Still another study found that spam urging investors to buy stock is followed by an increase in trading activity in the stock and positive cumulative abnormal returns for the stock. Rainer Böhme & Thorsten Holz, The

Effect of Stock Spam on Financial Markets (2006), available at SSRN:http://ssrn.com/abstract=897431.

5.   Considerable sentiment exists to the effect that CANSPAM has been a failure. Some estimates claim that spam now represents 80% of all e-mail sent. See Tom Zeller Jr., Law Barring Junk E–Mail Allows a Flood Instead, N.Y. Times, Feb. 1, 2004. A 2004 study by MX Logic found that only three percent of spam complies with CANSPAM. See MX Logic Finds That Only 3 Percent Of Unsolicited Commercial Email Complies With CAN–SPAM Law, available at http://www.mxlogic.com/news_events/CAN–SPAM.2_10_04.html. Is the problem one of enforcement? The FTC reportedly added only one person to its enforcement staff after enactment of CANSPAM. See Net Threat Rising, Consumer Rep., Sept. 2005, at 15. On the other hand, legitimate "etailers" seem to be complying with the statute. An FTC study found that 89% of the top 100 etailers complied with opt-out requests made by FTC staff testers. See FTC, Top Etailers' Compliance With CAN–SPAM's Opt–Out Provisions (2005). Another FTC report concluded that CANSPAM has been effective in causing legitimate online marketers to adopt commercial email "best practices" and in providing law enforcement agencies another tool to use against spammers. See FTC, Effectiveness and Enforcement of the CAN–SPAM Act (2005).

6.   Is spam actionable under the common law doctrine of trespass to chattels? Compare CompuServe Inc. v. Cyber Promotions, Inc., 962 F.Supp. 1015 (S.D. Ohio 1997) (granting preliminary injunction to Internet service provider on ground that spam is trespass to chattel) with Intel Corp. v. Hamidi, 30 Cal.4th 1342, 1347, 1 Cal.Rptr.3d 32, 71 P.3d 296, 300 (2003) ("under California law the tort does not encompass, and should not be extended to encompass, an electronic communication that neither damages the recipient computer system nor impairs its functioning."). Does the common law of nuisance offer aid? See Adam Mossoff, Spam—Oy, What a Nuisance!, 19 Berkeley Tech. L. J. 625 (2004). If so, would these claims be preempted by CANSPAM? See 15 U.S.C. § 7707(b).

7.   Is the best answer to the problem of spam a legal solution, or to wait for a technical solution? Is it appropriate to impose criminal penalties on the senders of spam? Would Congress have done better simply to prohibit the sending of unsolicited commercial email? Does spam require a global solution? Efforts at a global solution are underway: the Organization for Economic Cooperation and Development (OECD) has held multiple workshops on spam. Late in 2006, Congress enacted the U.S. SAFE WEB Act of 2006, Pub. L. No. 109–455, to facilitate cooperation between the FTC and its international counterparts in addressing spam and other global internet problems like spyware.

8.   A problem related to spam is "pop-up" ads, ads that appear on a computer user's screen while the user is browsing a web site. Does CAN-SPAM apply to pop up ads? Cf. Riddle v. Celebrity Cruises, Inc., 105 P.3d 970, 974 (Utah App. 2004) (In ruling that a since-repealed Utah anti-spam statute does not apply to pop-up ads, the court explained that "Pop-ups . . . are not sent to specifically predefined destinations. The host website produces the pop-up by directing the browser to open another window and display particular content."). See generally Emily Woodward Deutsch, Too

Many Open Windows? Exploring the Privacy Implications of Pop–Up Ads, 2 Univ. Ottawa L. & Tech. J. 397 (2005) (exploring theories on which pop-ups may be attacked).

9.   CANSPAM and its implementing regulations also regulate sexually explicit spam. See 16 C.F.R. § 316.4 (sexually-oriented spam must include the phrase "SEXUALLY–EXPLICIT" in capital letters at the beginning of the subject line).

10.   Does CANSPAM apply to political spam? Should it? See Vivek Arora, The CAN–SPAM Act: An Inadequate Attempt to Deal with a Growing Problem, 39 Colum J.L & Soc. Prob. 299 (2006).

Problem 5–15

You represent Big Bank. Recently, a number of your customers have received emails purporting to be from Big Bank and requesting that the recipients verify their account data. In fact, the Bank had nothing to do with the emails; customers who responded to the email provided their data to thieves who then used the data to impersonate the customers. Big Bank wishes to know first, whether it is liable to any consumers who were victimized by these so-called "phishing" scams; and second, what steps it can take to protect its customers from future phishing attempts.

Problem 5–16

You have been elected to your state legislature and would like to propose legislation to allow your constituents to bring a private claim against the senders of spam. Would such a state statute run into any problems under CANSPAM? See 15 U.S.C. § 7707(b). What if the state statute were limited to spam that contained false statements? See Cal. Bus. & Professions § 17529.5.

Notes

1.   Some state anti-spam statutes required (in provisions that have since been preempted by CANSPAM) that the subject lines for spam contain letters such as "ADV" which would alert consumers and spam filters that the message was an unsolicited commercial email. See e.g., Ariz. Rev. Stat. Ann. § 44–1372.01(B)(1). Is CANSPAM an improvement on that requirement? The FTC, by a four-to-one vote, opined that such subject line labeling requirements were not helpful to consumers. Federal Trade Commission, Subject Line Labeling As a Weapon Against Spam; A CAN–SPAM Act Report to Congress (June 2005). The Commission concluded that neither the state laws (before they were preempted) nor similar requirements in other countries had reduced the incidence of spam and that spam filters were more effective in blocking spam.

2.   Is spam better suited to nationwide regulation—which would justify preemption of state laws—or state regulation? Why?

3.   A number of states, in now-preempted statutes, also adopted an "opt-in" approach to spam. Delaware, for example, made it a crime to send bulk unsolicited commercial email unless the recipient either consented to the spam or had a prior business relationship with the sender. 11 Del. Code

§ 937. The European Union has also adopted an opt-in approach. See Art. 13 of Directive 2002/58/EC, available at http://europa.eu.int/eur-lex/pri/en/oj/dat/2002/L_201/L_20120020731en00370047.pdf (July 12, 2002). Is such an approach preferable to CANSPAM?

4. Quite a few states have enacted anti-phishing statutes. See, e.g., RCWA 19.190.010(2) making it unlawful "to solicit, request, or take any action to induce a person to provide personally identifying information by means of a web page, electronic mail message, or otherwise using the internet by representing oneself, either directly or by implication, to be another person, without the authority or approval of such other person." Is that statute preempted by CANSPAM?

5. One telephone survey found that 49% of United States adults cannot distinguish phishing from legitimate emails. Joseph Turow, Lauren Feldman, & Kimberly Meltzer, Open to Exploitation : American Shoppers Online and Offline 3 (2005). Six percent of the respondents to another survey had provided personal information to phishers, but only 0.5 percent had suffered losses—though the losses averaged $400. Net Threat Rising, Consumer Rep., Sept. 2005, at 13.

SECTION C.   SALE OF CONSUMER INFORMATION

Before merchants can solicit consumers to buy their wares, they need consumer contact information. Many businesses compile lists of consumers based on their own transactions with customers. But many also buy and sell customer information. As mentioned in Section A, regulation of the transfer of information about consumers is sectoral. Many businesses can share information about consumers without any restraint at all while others are subject to regulation. This Section will explore the rules governing one sector of the economy—financial institutions—that has drawn attention from regulators and consumers in recent years and that offers interesting lessons for the regulation of privacy.

Consumers traditionally have used financial institutions as places to invest, borrow, deposit money, and make payments (through checking accounts and credit cards, and the like). The privacy of consumer credit transactions has long been regulated by the Fair Credit Reporting Act and its state counterparts, discussed in Chapter Four, but what about the privacy of other financial transactions? Until 1999, bank depositors in the United States were largely unprotected by privacy regulation, something most consumers probably did not realize. In the late nineties, state regulators sued a number of banks for disclosing customer information to third-party marketers, including telemarketers. See Minnesota v. Fleet Mortg. Corp., 158 F. Supp. 2d 962 (D. Minn. 2001); David W. Roderer, Tentative Steps Toward Financial Privacy, 4 N.C. Banking Inst. 209, 210–11 (2000); Elizabeth K. Brill, Privacy and Financial Institutions: Current Developments Concerning the Gramm–Leach–Bliley Act of 1999, 21 Ann. Rev. Banking L. 167, 176 (2002). The cases produced a clamor for statutory protections, and Congress responded by enacting the Gramm–Leach–Bliley Act ("GLB"), relevant parts of which are reproduced in the Statutory Supplement together with implementing regulations.

GLB permits financial institutions to disclose information about consumers provided the institution notifies consumers of their right to keep the information confidential. If you have a bank account or a credit card, you have probably received a notice informing you of your right to "opt-out" of the disclosure of your information. Did you opt-out? Did you read the privacy notice? Do you remember receiving such a notice? The statute requires that the notices be clear and conspicuous, § 6802(b)(1)(A). The regulations define that phrase as requiring that the notice be "reasonably understandable and designed to call attention to the nature and significance of the information in the notice." § 313.3(b)(1). In examples in (b)(2), the regulations elaborate: something is reasonably understandable if it is presented in "clear concise sentences, paragraphs, and sections;" uses "short explanatory sentences," and definite, concrete, everyday words;" avoids "multiple negatives" and legal and business terminology. A writing is designed to call attention if it uses plain-language headings and an easy-to-read typeface and type size.

Problem 5–17

You are counsel to Grin's Bank. Grin's wishes to sell information about its depositors to telemarketers, a trade which has been very lucrative for the bank in the past. Because the telemarketers pay a fee for each depositor whose information they purchase, Grin's hopes that as few depositors as possible opt out of the sale. Grin's asks you to prepare a notice to its depositors that complies with GLB. In preparing the notice:

  A. How specifically would you refer to the telemarketers? See 16 C.F.R. §§ 313.6(c)(3), 313.7(a)(2)(i)(A).

  B. Would you rather the notice be long or short? How comprehensible would you want to make the notice? What constraints do the statute and regulations impose? See GLB § 6802(b)(1)(A), 16 C.F.R. § 313.3(b)

  C. Would you advise your client to print the notice in four colors or one? Would you advise your client to distribute the notice together with depositors' bank statements and colorful promotional materials, or in a separate mailing?

  D. After reviewing the notice you drafted, some Grin's officials question whether you have interpreted the statute too aggressively. What would the consequences be if your notice violates the statute?

Notes

1. Critics charge that the notices are unreadable. See John Schwartz, Privacy Policy Notices are Called Too Common and Too Confusing, N.Y. Times, May 7, 2001 at A1; Mark Hochhauser, Lost in the Fine Print: Readability of Financial Privacy Notices (2001) (available at http://www.privacyrights.org/ar/GLB–Reading.htm). On the other hand, an American Bankers Association telephone survey reported that two-thirds of the consumers who said they had received the notices claimed to have read them. See W.A. Lee, Opt–Out Notices Give No One A Thrill, 166 American Banker Issue 131, at 1 (July 10, 2001). According to a Securities Industry Association survey, of the people surveyed, 60% recalled receiving the notices; of the group who remembered receiving the notices, two-thirds claimed to have read them; and of the people who read the notices, 84% believed they understood them. In Brief: SIA Survey Finds Privacy Notices Work, American Banker, Aug. 14, 2001, at 5. Here is an excerpt from Capital One's notice, as reported by John Schwartz, *supra*:

> We may share the information described on Page 1 under "information we may collect" with companies in the Capital One family or with business partners such as financial service providers (including credit bureaus, mortgage bankers, securities broker-dealers and insurance agents); nonfinancial companies (including retailers, online and offline advertisers, membership list vendors, direct marketers, airlines and publishers); companies that perform marketing services on our behalf, or other financial institutions with which we have joint marketing agreements; and others, such as non-profit organizations and third parties that you direct us to share information about you.

Does the notice satisfy the regulations? Will consumers find the paragraph meaningful? Are they likely to read it? Do financial institutions want consumers to read the notices? Consider the following excerpt from a January 12, 2005 speech by Julie Williams, Acting Comptroller of the Currency, available at http://www.occ.treas.gov/ftp/release/2005–1a.pdf:

> [W]hen presented with the prospect of lessening burden and saving costs by providing a streamlined, short form privacy notice containing only certain key information—some in the industry seem to balk. Marketing departments get uneasy because simple and straightforward disclosure of a bank's information sharing policies and an easy means for customers to opt out of that sharing might mean–*that customers will actually understand those policies—and decide to opt out!* The tension here is that shorter, focused consumer disclosures can meaningfully reduce regulatory burden, but, if they are done well, they will also empower consumers to make some decisions that a particular bank may not like.

2. Financial institutions complain that the cost of drafting and sending notices to all their customers has been staggering. According to the Lee article cited in the preceding note, financial institutions had already sent out more than a billion notices to consumers by 2001. A survey conducted by America's Community Bankers and published as a supplement to the Wash. Perspective, Dec. 3, 2001 (ACB Survey") found that compliance costs for

institutions were about $1.37 per customer. Part of the problem is that different types of customers (e.g., depositors, credit cardholders, other borrowers, investors in securities) require different notices. Many consumers who use more than one financial institution receive many different notices, which may add to the confusion.

3.   Financial institutions continue to provide information about their customers to others. The ACB Survey reported that about half the financial institutions with assets exceeding $1 billion share consumer information with non-affiliated third parties while the "great majority" of smaller institutions do not provide customer information to third parties.

4.   GLB does not provide for a private cause of action for failure to comply with its provisions. See, e.g., Borinski v. Williamson, 2004 WL 433746 (N.D. Tex. 2004). Financial institutions are examined by regulators for compliance with a variety of laws, including GLB. Financial institutions have some power to choose their regulator by, for example, incorporating under state or federal law. All other things being equal, would you expect a financial institution to select a regulator which was more or less aggressive in enforcing GLB? If a financial institution violated its written privacy policy, would it be liable under a state UDAP statute or for common law fraud or breach of contract? In Smith v. Chase Manhattan Bank, 293 A.D.2d 598, 741 N.Y.S.2d 100 (2d Dept. 2002), credit card holders and borrowers claimed that the defendant bank had sold information to non-affiliated third parties in violation of its written confidentiality commitment. The court dismissed plaintiffs' UDAP claim on the ground that the complaint failed to allege actual injury. The court explained: "the 'harm' at the heart of this purported class action, is that class members were merely offered products and services which they were free to decline. This does not qualify as actual harm." Could a violation of GLB give rise to a claim founded on negligence *per se*? See Anthony E. White, Comment, The Recognition of a Negligence Cause of Action for Victims of Identity Theft: Someone Stole My Identity, Now Who is Going to Pay for It? 88 Marq. L. Rev. 847 (2005).

5.   How effective has GLB been? What data is publicly available suggests that few consumers have opted out. See Testimony of John C. Dugan, Partner at Covington and Burling on behalf of the Financial Services Coordinating Council, Before the U.S. Sen. Com. On Banking, Housing and Urban Affairs, Sept. 19, 2002 ("opt-out rates have generally been low, and in nearly all cases under 10 percent."); W.A. Lee, Opt–Out Notices Give No One A Thrill, 166 American Banker Issue 131, at 1 (July 10, 2001) ("5% opt-out rate . . . has been circulating as the unofficial industry figure. . . ."); ACB Survey (60% of financial institutions report that less than one percent of customers opted out). Is the best measure of the effectiveness of GLB the percentage of consumers who have opted out?

Problem 5–18

You are a member of Congress serving on the committee having jurisdiction over GLB. What would you do about the GLB privacy provisions? Would you:

A.   Vote to repeal them, perhaps on the ground that they have been ineffective in protecting consumer privacy, or alternatively on the theory that if few consumers have directed their financial institutions not to disclose information about them, consumers must not care very much about financial privacy?

B.   Leave them alone?

C.   Vote to amend them to increase the likelihood that consumers would receive meaningful notice or would otherwise receive more protection? How would you accomplish that?

Notes

1.   California bars financial institutions from disclosing consumer information in most instances unless the consumer affirmatively consents to the disclosure; i.e., unless the consumer opts in. See 2003 Cal. Legis. Serv. Ch. 241 (S.B. 1), codified at Cal. Fin. Code §§ 4050–59. The portion of the statute dealing with the sharing of information among affiliated companies was found to be preempted at least in part by the Fair Credit Report Act in American Bankers Ass'n. v. Gould, 412 F.3d 1081 (9th Cir. 2005), and on remand the district court enjoined California from enforcing the affiliate-sharing provisions. American Bankers Ass'n v. Lockyer, 2005 WL 2452798 (E.D.Cal. 2005). Several other states have enacted opt-in systems, and the FTC has opined that some of these are not preempted by GLB. See, e.g. N.D. Cent. Code § 6–08.1–01 et seq.; the June 28, 2001 FTC opinion that it is not preempted may be found at http://www.ftc.gov/os/2001/06/northdakotaletter. htm. Similarly, the constitutionality of Vermont's opt-in system was upheld in American Council of Life Insurers v. Vermont, 2004 WL 578737 (Vt. Super. Ct. 2004). If few consumers opt in, so that financial institutions lose a stream of revenue, what impact will that have on the pricing of financial products?

2.   How might consumers and companies behave differently under an opt-in regime, as opposed to an opt-out regime? As for consumers, some evidence suggests that many consumers choose the course of least resistance. An unintentional experiment in automobile insurance in New Jersey and Pennsylvania illustrates the point. Pennsylvania policies provided that consumers could bring a certain claim, but offered them the choice of paying lower rates in exchange for foregoing the right to bring the claim. Approximately 75% decided to keep the right to sue. By contrast, New Jersey policies did not permit drivers to bring the claim, but offered them the right to do so if they paid higher rates. About 20% agreed to pay the higher rates. In other words, most motorists did not deviate from the default choice. Eric J. Johnson, John Hershey, Jacqueline Meszaros, & Howard Kunreuther, Framing, Probability Distortions, and Insurance Decisions *in* Choices, Values, and Frames 224, 238 (2000) (Daniel Kahneman & Amos Tversky, eds.). As for companies, see Jeff Sovern, Opting In, Opting Out, or No Options At All: The Fight for Control of Personal Information, 74 Wash. L. Rev. 1033, 1102 (1999):

After the FCC ruled that phone companies seeking to use phone-calling patterns for marketing purposes must first obtain the consumer's permission, the telephone company in my area attempted to secure that permission. Its representatives called and sent mailings to subscribers.

The company also set up a toll-free number for consumers with questions. The mailing I received was brief, printed in different colors, and written in plain English. It also promised, in words which were underlined, that "we'll never share this information with any outside company." A postage-paid envelope and a printed form were included for consumers to respond. Consumers who accept the offer need only check a box, sign and date the form, and print their name. The company also offered consumers incentives to sign up—such as a five-dollar check, two free movie tickets, or a ten-dollar certificate from certain retailers—thus increasing the likelihood that consumers will pay attention to the information.

Some commentators have concluded that in the online environment, whether privacy choices are a matter of opting in or opting out makes no difference because web site designers can design questions and use defaults in such a way as to secure the consent of nearly all visitors to a web site. See Steven Bellman, Eric J. Johnson & Gerald L. Lohse, To Opt–In or Opt–Out? It Depends on the Question, Association for Computing Machinery, Communications of the ACM, Feb. 2001, at 25.

3. How expensive would an opt-in system be? U.S. West reported that when it attempted to obtain permission from its customers to use their calling patterns, reaching a live respondent with the authority to grant consent required 4.8 dialing attempts. Every positive response cost $20.66. Direct mail elicited a response rate of less than 11% for residential customers while the cost per positive response was $29.32 plus any incentives offered. Letter from Kathryn Marie Krause, U.S. West Senior Attorney to William F. Caton, Acting Secretary, FCC, dated Sept. 9, 1997. See also Michael E. Staten & Fred H. Cate, The Adverse Impact of Opt–In Privacy Rules on Consumers: A Case Study of Retail Credit (2002).

4. In 2006, Congress added Subsection (e) to § 6803 directing Federal regulators to develop a model privacy disclosure form. The hope is that the model form will be both brief and comprehensible. Financial institutions using the model form would be deemed to be in compliance with the statute. Would consumers be more likely to read a shorter form? Would you? See also Kleimann Communication Group, Inc., Evolution of a Prototype Financial Privacy Notice: A Report on the Form Development Project (2006) available at http://ftc.gov/privacy/privacyinitiatives/ftcfinalreport060228.pdf (project— conducted under the aegis of six federal agencies that enforce GLB— developed and tested on consumers form that seems relatively simple to read and understand).

5. How broadly should GLB apply? Should attorneys have to comply with its provisions? The court in American Bar Assoc. v. FTC, 430 F.3d 457 (D.C. Cir. 2005) held that GLB does not apply to lawyers engaged in practice of law. Note, however, that attorneys representing financial institutions may have obligations under GLB. Should credit reporting agencies, already regulated by the Fair Credit Reporting Act, also be subject to GLB? See Trans Union LLC v. FTC, 295 F.3d 42 (D.C. Cir. 2002) (upholding FTC determination that credit reporting agencies are "financial institutions" within scope of GLB). The court also rebuffed Trans Union's challenge to FTC regulations defining "personally identifiable financial information" as including

"header information;" that is, a consumer's name, address, telephone number, and Social Security number. Should GLB apply to credit counseling services? See FTC v. AmeriDebt, Inc., 343 F. Supp. 2d 451 (D.Md. 2004) (upholding FTC regulation giving affirmative answer).

6. Must non-financial businesses (i.e., businesses that are not subject to GLB) that collect consumer information honor a consumer's request not to disclose that information to others? If not, should GLB be amended to require such businesses to honor such requests? California has taken a different approach. It requires certain businesses that share the personal information of consumers with a third party for purposes of direct marketing to disclose to consumers upon request the type of information provided the third party and the names of the recipients of the information. Cal. Civil Code § 1798.83. The statute applies to businesses with more than twenty employees. Under subsection (b)(1)(3), the business has no obligation to reveal information as to disclosures made about specific consumers; in other words, the business seemingly complies with the statute if it makes standardized disclosures like "We disclosed X facts about our customers to Y Company." As an alternative to making the disclosure, businesses comply with the statute if they adopt an opt-in approach to the disclosure of consumer information and so notify consumers, under subsection (c)(2).

Problem 5–19

Molly has a credit card from Grin's Bank. Recently she applied for life insurance from the Dragon Insurance Company. Dragon and Grin's are owned by the same holding company, and Grin's furnishes Molly's credit card records to Dragon. Dragon denies Molly's application because her credit card records indicate she is a skydiving enthusiast. Do Grin's or Dragon face any restraints in sharing information this way? Would it make a difference if Molly had previously directed Grin's not to disclose her financial records to others? Does GLB address this issue? See 15 U.S.C. §§ 6802(a), 6803, 16 C.F.R. § 313.3(a), FCRA §§ 1681a(d)(2), 1681s–3. Would a state statute that provided for an opt-in approach to information sharing among affiliates be preempted? FCRA § 1681t(b)(2).

Problem 5–20

Percy has filed a class action suit against Grin's Bank, claiming that Grin's violated various provisions of the Truth in Lending Act and Equal Credit Opportunity Act. During the discovery phase of the suit, Percy served Grin's with a request for documents pertaining to other Grin's customers. Grin's moved for a protective order denying the requested discovery, claiming that because Percy sought nonpublic personal information, was not affiliated with Grin's, and did not come within the opt-out notices Grin's had supplied its customers, Grin's was precluded by GLB from disclosing the information. Grin's concedes that the information sought is relevant and that it has no basis for objecting to the discovery other than GLB. How should the motion be resolved? See 15 U.S.C. § 6802(e)(8); Marks v. Global Mortgage Group, 218 F.R.D. 492 (S.D. W. Va. 2003).

Note

Do consumers ever benefit from the trade in their personal information? Private investigators sometimes use such information to reunite families. See Tom Zeller Jr., Investigators Argue for Access to Private Data, N.Y. Times, March 21, 2005 at C1.

SECTION D. ONLINE PRIVACY

IN RE DOUBLE–CLICK INC. PRIVACY LITIGATION

United States District Court for the Southern District of New York, 2001.
154 F.Supp.2d 497.

* * *

DOUBLECLICK'S TECHNOLOGY AND SERVICES

DoubleClick provides the Internet's largest advertising service. Commercial Web sites often rent-out online advertising "space" to other Web sites. In the simplest type of arrangement, the host Web site (e.g., Lycos.com) rents space on its webpages to another Web site (e.g., TheGlobe.com) to place a "hotlink" banner advertisement ("banner advertisement"). When a user on the host Web site "clicks" on the banner advertisement, he is automatically connected to the advertiser's designated Web site.

DoubleClick acts as an intermediary between host Web sites and Web sites seeking to place banner advertisements. It promises client Web sites that it will place their banner advertisements in front of viewers who match their demographic target. For example, DoubleClick might try to place banner advertisements for a Web site that sells golfclubs in front of high-income people who follow golf and have a track record of making expensive online purchases. DoubleClick creates value for its customers in large part by building detailed profiles of Internet users.[7] and using them to target clients' advertisements.

DoubleClick compiles user profiles utilizing its proprietary technologies and analyses in cooperation with its affiliated Web sites. Double-Click is affiliated with over 11,000 Web sites for which and on which it provides targeted banner advertisements. A select group of over 1,500 of these Web sites form the "DoubleClick Network" and are among "the most highly trafficked and branded sites on the Web." In addition, DoubleClick owns and operates two Web sites through which it also collects user data: (1) the Internet Address Finder ("IAF"); and (2) NetDeals.com.

---

7. It is important to note that the term "user" actually refers to a particular computer, not a particular person. DoubleClick collects information based upon the computer's Web activity, regardless of whether one person or one hundred people happen to use that computer. In the same vein, if one person uses multiple computers, DoubleClick would be unable to identify and aggregate the person's activity on different computers.

When users visit any of these DoubleClick-affiliated Web sites, a "cookie" is placed on their hard drives. Cookies are computer programs commonly used by Web sites to store useful information such as user-names, passwords, and preferences, making it easier for users to access Web pages in an efficient manner. However, Plaintiffs allege that Doub-leClick's cookies collect "information that Web users, including plaintiffs and the Class, consider to be personal and private, such as names, e-mail addresses, home and business addresses, telephone numbers, searches performed on the Internet, Web pages or sites visited on the Internet and other communications and information that users would not ordi-narily expect advertisers to be able to collect." Amended Complaint at ¶ 38. DoubleClick's cookies store this personal information on users' hard drives until DoubleClick electronically accesses the cookies and uploads the data.

How DoubleClick targets banner advertisements and utilizes cookies to collect user information is crucial to our analysis under the three statutes. Therefore, we examine both processes in greater detail.

A. Targeting Banner Advertisements

DoubleClick's advertising targeting process involves three partici-pants and four steps. The three participants are: (1) the user; (2) the DoubleClick-affiliated Web site; (3) the DoubleClick server. For the purposes of this discussion, we assume that a DoubleClick cookie already sits on the user's computer with the identification number "#0001."

In Step One, a user seeks to access a DoubleClick-affiliated Web site such as Lycos.com. The user's browser sends a communication to Ly-cos.com (technically, to Lycos.com's server) saying, in essence, "Send me your homepage." * * * This communication may contain data submitted as part of the request, such as a query string or field information.

In Step Two, Lycos.com receives the request, processes it, and returns a communication to the user saying "Here is the Web page you requested." The communication has two parts. The first part is a copy of the Lycos.com homepage, essentially the collection [of] article summar-ies, pictures and hotlinks a user sees on his screen when Lycos.com appears. The only objects missing are the banner advertisements; in their places lie blank spaces. * * * The second part of the communica-tion is an IP-address link to the DoubleClick server. * * * This link instructs the user's computer to send a communication automatically to DoubleClick's server.

In Step Three, as per the IP-address instruction, the user's comput-er sends a communication to the DoubleClick server saying "I am cookie #0001, send me banner advertisements to fill the blank spaces in the Lycos.com Web page." This communication contains information includ-ing the cookie identification number, the name of the DoubleClick-affiliated Web site the user requested, and the user's browser-type. * * *

Finally, in Step Four, the DoubleClick server identifies the user's profile by the cookie identification number and runs a complex set of algorithms based, in part, on the user's profile, to determine which advertisements it will present to the user. * * * It then sends a communication to the user with banner advertisements saying "Here are the targeted banner advertisements for the Lycos.com homepage." Meanwhile, it also updates the user's profile with the information from the request. * * *

DoubleClick's targeted advertising process is invisible to the user. His experience consists simply of requesting the Lycos.com homepage and, several moments later, receiving it complete with banner advertisements.

B. Cookie Information Collection

DoubleClick's cookies only collect information from one step of the above process: Step One. The cookies capture certain parts of the communications that users send to DoubleClick-affiliated Web sites. They collect this information in three ways: (1) "GET" submissions, (2) "POST" submissions, and (3) "GIF" submissions.

GET information is submitted as part of a Web site's address or "URL," in what is known as a "query string." For example, a request for a hypothetical online record store's selection of Bon Jovi albums might read: *http://recordstore.hypothetical.com/search?terms=bonjovi.* The URL query string begins with the "?" character meaning the cookie would record that the user requested information about Bon Jovi.

Users submit POST information when they fill-in multiple blank fields on a webpage. For example, if a user signed-up for an online discussion group, he might have to fill-in fields with his name, address, email address, phone number and discussion group alias. The cookie would capture this submitted POST information.

Finally, DoubleClick places GIF tags on its affiliated Web sites. GIF tags are the size of a single pixel and are invisible to users. Unseen, they record the users' movements throughout the affiliated Web site, enabling DoubleClick to learn what information the user sought and viewed.

Although the information collected by DoubleClick's cookies is allegedly voluminous and detailed, it is important to note three clearly defined parameters. First, DoubleClick's cookies *only* collect information concerning users' activities *on DoubleClick-affiliated Web sites*. Thus, if a user visits an unaffiliated Web site, the DoubleClick cookie captures no information. Second, plaintiff does not allege that DoubleClick ever attempted to collect *any* information other than the GET, POST, and GIF information submitted by users. DoubleClick is never alleged to have accessed files, programs or other information on users' hard drives. Third, DoubleClick will not collect information from any user who takes simple steps to prevent DoubleClick's tracking. As plaintiffs' counsel demonstrated at oral argument, users can easily and at no cost prevent DoubleClick from collecting information from them. They may do this in two ways: (1) visiting the DoubleClick Web site and requesting an "opt-out" cookie; and (2) configuring their browsers to block any cookies from being deposited. * * *

Once DoubleClick collects information from the cookies on users' hard drives, it aggregates and compiles the information to build demographic profiles of users. Plaintiffs allege that DoubleClick has more than 100 million user profiles in its database. Exploiting its proprietary Dynamic Advertising Reporting & Targeting ("DART") technology, DoubleClick and its licensees target banner advertisements using these demographic profiles.

ABACUS ACQUISITION AND FTC INVESTIGATION

In June 1999, DoubleClick purchased Abacus Direct Corp. ("Abacus") for more than one billion dollars. Abacus was a direct-marketing services company that maintained a database of names, addresses, telephone numbers, retail purchasing habits and other personal information on approximately ninety percent of American households, which it sold to direct marketing companies. Plaintiffs allege that DoubleClick planned to combine its database of online profiles with Abacus' database of offline customer profiles in order to create a super-database capable of matching users' online activities with their names and addresses.

In furtherance of this effort, DoubleClick created the Abacus Online Alliance ("Abacus Alliance") and amended its privacy policy. The Abacus Alliance is purportedly a confidential group of online marketers and publishers who secretly contribute their compiled customer data to a cooperative database managed by DoubleClick. In return for their contributions, Abacus Alliance members gain access to exclusive DoubleClick products and services. In mid–1999, shortly after acquiring Abacus, DoubleClick amended its privacy policy by removing its assurance that information gathered from users online would not be associated with their personally identifiable information.

Not long after the Abacus acquisition, the Federal Trade Commission ("FTC") launched an investigation into whether DoubleClick's collection, compilation and use of consumer information constituted unfair or deceptive trade practices in violation of Section 5 of the Federal Trade Commission Act.[14] On March 2, 2000, Kevin O'Connor, DoubleClick's CEO and Chairman of the Board, announced that he had made a "mistake" by planning to merge DoubleClick's and Abacus' databases and stated that DoubleClick would undertake no such merger until it reached an agreement with the United States government and Internet

---

14. Specifically, "[t]he primary purposes of the inquiry were: 1) whether [DoubleClick] used or disclosed consumers' PII [personal identifying information] for purposes other than those disclosed in, or in contravention of, its privacy policy, including in particular, whether it combined PII from Abacus Direct (an offline direct marketing company that it had acquired) with non-PII clickstream data that DoubleClick had collected; and 2) whether [DoubleClick] used or disclosed sensitive information about consumers in contravention of its stated privacy policy." Letter from Joel Winston, Acting Associate Director, Division of Financial Practices, FTC, to Christine Varney, Esq., Hogan & Hartson, Outside Counsel for DoubleClick, January 22, 2001 ("FTC January 22, 2001 Letter.").

industry regarding privacy standards. It is unclear whether DoubleClick had already merged any of the information.

The FTC concluded its investigation on January 22, 2001. In a letter to DoubleClick's outside counsel, the FTC announced that it was ending its investigation with no finding that DoubleClick had engaged in unfair or deceptive trade practices. It summarized its conclusions:

> Based on this investigation, it appears to staff that DoubleClick never used or disclosed consumers' PII [personal identifiable information] for purposes other than those disclosed in its privacy policy. Specifically, it appears that DoubleClick did not combine PII from Abacus Direct with clickstream collected on client Web sites. In addition, it appears that DoubleClick has not used sensitive data for any online preference marketing product, in contravention of its stated online policy. We understand that DoubleClick's Boomerang product takes user data from one site to target advertising to the same user on other sites. However, the user profiles DoubleClick creates for its Boomerang clients for this targeting contains only non-PII. Furthermore, we understand that for all new Boomerang clients, DoubleClick requires by contract that the site disclose in its privacy policy that it uses DoubleClick's services to target advertising to consumers, and DoubleClick will not implement Boomerang on a site until such disclosures are posted.

The letter also noted several commitments DoubleClick made to modifying its privacy policy to "enhance its effectiveness," including allowing a user to request an "opt out" cookie that would prevent DoubleClick from collecting information from that user. * * *

Notes

1. The plaintiffs in *DoubleClick* had asserted claims arising under Title II of the Electronic Communications Privacy Act, 18 U.S.C. § 2701 et seq., the Federal Wiretap Act, 18 U.S.C. § 2510 et seq., the Computer Fraud and Abuse Act, 18 U.S.C. § 1030, et seq., and various state laws. The court dismissed the federal claims and declined to exercise supplemental jurisdiction over the state claims. The case was later settled. What do you think the state law claims were?

2. Assuming that the combining of information from Abacus and DoubleClick had not violated any previously-stated commitments, would it be objectionable on other grounds? Is there anything troublesome about DoubleClick's practices?

3. What regulations, if any are appropriate in the online arena? Should regulators refrain from action on the theory that technological solutions will be developed? For the view that technology is unlikely to solve online privacy problems, see James P. Nehf, Incomparability and the Passive Virtues of Ad Hoc Privacy Policy, 76 Univ. Colo. L. Rev. 1, 26–27 (2005).

4. Probably Congress's most significant effort to date in connection with online privacy is the 1998 Children's Online Privacy Protection Act

("COPPA"), 15 U.S.C. § 6501 et seq. COPPA was presaged by the FTC's consent decree in In re Geocities, 127 F.T.C. 94 (1999), in which the FTC claimed that the respondent sold information collected on its web site from children. COPPA applies to three types of web sites that collect personal information: first, sites targeted to children (defined as children under the age of 13); second, sites which have actual knowledge that they are collecting personal information from a child; and third general commercial web sites which have a section targeted to children, in which case COPPA applies only to the children's area. Web sites within COPPA's purview are obliged to post a privacy policy and, in most instances, to obtain permission from a child's parent or guardian before collecting information from the child. COPPA also authorizes the FTC to approve private "safe-harbor" programs under which industry groups can adopt self-regulatory guidelines; web sites which adhere to the guidelines are considered in compliance with COPPA. The FTC has approved a number of these safe-harbor programs. COPPA provides for enforcement by the states and various federal agencies, including the FTC. For more on COPPA, see Nancy L. Savitt, A Synopsis of the Children's Online Privacy Protection Act, 16 St. John's J. Leg. Comment. 631 (2002). If you have children who surf the web, have you granted permission to a web site to collect information from your children?

5. Protection of the online privacy of adults at the federal level has fallen largely to the FTC. The FTC has for the most part confined its formal efforts to enforcing the promises companies have made in their privacy policies, bringing an occasional action against a web site operator. For example, after Toysmart.com promised never to disclose personal information it collected, it attempted to sell its customer list and the FTC intervened. The FTC later settled with Toysmart (a copy of the consent agreement can be found at http://www.ftc.gov/os/2000/07/toysmartconsent.htm) and the list was ultimately destroyed.

6. Federal law does not require web sites not directed to children to post a privacy policy, just as it does not normally require offline businesses to make a privacy policy available to the public (financial institutions covered by GLB being a notable exception). A few states have enacted legislation protecting privacy on the internet. California requires operators of commercial web sites or online services that collect personally-identifiable information about California residents to post a privacy policy conspicuously on their web site. West's Ann.Cal.Bus. & Prof.Code § 22575. The privacy policy must identify the categories of information the operator collects and the categories of third-parties to whom the information may be provided; describe any process the operator provides for consumers to review and request changes in their information; and describe the process by which the operator will notify consumers who visit the site of changes in the privacy policy. Note that the California statute applies to web site operators based outside of California as long as the web site collects information about California residents. Minnesota bars internet service providers ("ISP's") from knowingly disclosing personally identifiable information about their customers, with some exceptions. Minn. Stat. § 325M.02. The statute defines ISP's as enterprises that provide consumers with access to the web; in other words, the statute does not apply to web site operators generally. Minn. Stat. 325M.01.3. Would you advise a client that did no business with residents of a

state that requires posting of a privacy policy to post a privacy policy anyway? Why or why not? How might Congress react if few companies post privacy policies? See James P. Nehf, Shopping for Privacy Online: Consumer Decision–Making Strategies and the Emerging Market for Information Privacy, 2005 U. Ill. J.L. Tech. & Pol'y 1.

7. Does your school post a privacy policy? Should it? One survey of top-ranked colleges and universities found that "nearly all of these institutions engage in some practices online that pose a potential privacy risk." Mary J. Culnan, Thomas J. Carlin, & Traci A. Logan, Bentley–Watchfire® Survey of Online Privacy Practices in Higher Education Final Report 9 (2006).

8. Online privacy is unusual in that it instantaneously combines the gathering of information about consumers (the subject of the preceding section) and solicitations (the subject of Section B).

Problem 5–21

Melanie, a large offline bookseller located on the East Coast, is in the process of establishing a web site which will permit customers to order books online. Though Melanie has never shared information about its customers with others and has no plans to do so, it is not enthusiastic about making an ironclad commitment to maintain that policy. Because most of its customers use a Melanie affinity card (which entitles customers to a discount on purchases), the bookstore already possesses a considerable amount of information about its customers' book-buying habits. Melanie does not currently nor has it in the past provided a privacy policy to its customers. Melanie has no plans to collect personal information about children or to direct its web site to children. Melanie asks you to advise it as to the following:

A. Should Melanie post a privacy policy on its web site at all? Would your advice be different if Melanie expected to sell to Californians, or was not sure if it would sell to Californians? What about if it expected to sell to those outside the United States?

B. If Melanie does post such a policy, what should it state? For example, should Melanie promise not to disclose customer information; state that it does not currently disclose customer information but reserves the right to do so in the future; or simply state that Melanie may disclose customer information? Would you recommend stating that consumers have the right to obtain access to information about them in the company's possession?

C. Assuming Melanie posts a privacy policy on its web site, how prominently should Melanie display the policy? Should it expend extra effort to make it easy to understand?

D. Should Melanie post on its web site or otherwise make available a privacy policy relating to information collected in offline transactions, and if so, what should that policy be? If not, should the privacy policy distinguish between online and offline transactions?

E. Are there any questions that you would discourage Melanie from asking on its web site?

Notes

1. A 2005 telephone survey found that 75% of American adult users of the internet believe that the fact that a web site has a privacy policy means that the site will not make their information available to other websites and companies. Joseph Turow, Lauren Feldman, & Kimberly Meltzer, Open to Exploitation: American Shoppers Online and Offline 3 (2005). The authors suggest that companies should be obliged to use the label "Using Your Information" instead of "Privacy Policy." Should regulators specify the content of privacy policies? See James P. Nehf, Shopping for Privacy Online: Consumer Decision–Making Strategies and the Emerging Market for Information Privacy, 2005 U. Ill. J.L. Tech. & Pol'y 1, 3–4:

> [Privacy p]olicies might disclose how data is collected and how it will be transferred, sold, or traded, but often the message is that information will be collected in whatever way the Web site can obtain it, and the site reserves the right to share or sell it with impunity. * * * [C]onsumers' privacy interests may in fact be no better protected today than they were ten years ago. * * * [T]here may be little incentive for online businesses to adopt and adhere to strong privacy policies. It is the appearance of privacy that seems to matter most.

2. Some operators of web sites have voluntarily agreed to privacy standards imposed by a private organization, such as TrustE. Would you advise a client to assume such an obligation? Why or why not?

3. The European Union's Article 29 Data Protection Working Party issued a document titled "Opinion on More Harmonised Information Provisions" on November 25, 2004 addressing the use of shorter privacy notices. Examples of a short privacy notice, and a slightly longer "condensed" privacy notice, can be found at http://europa.eu.int/comm/justice_home/fsj/privacy/docs/wpdocs/2004/wp100a_en.pdf. Under what circumstances would you counsel clients to use a short privacy notice? Would consumers be better served by short notices?

F.T.C. v. SEISMIC ENTERTAINMENT PRODUCTIONS, INC.

United States District Court for the District of New Hampshire, 2004.
2004 WL 2403124.

DiClerico, J.

The Federal Trade Commission ("FTC") brings an action against Sanford Wallace, Seismic Entertainment Productions, Inc., and Smart-Bot.Net, Inc., under the Federal Trade Commission Act, seeking an injunction to stop the defendants from engaging in certain internet marketing practices. The FTC contends that the defendants' marketing practices are unfair practices affecting commerce and seeks injunctive and related relief under the Federal Trade Commission Act ("FTCA").

Currently before the court is the FTC's motion for a temporary restraining order ("TRO") and other equitable relief.

The defendants were served with and filed an objection to the TRO motion. * * *

BACKGROUND

The FTC seeks temporary injunctive relief to restrict the defendants' activities pending resolution of their request for a preliminary injunction. Specifically, the FTC asks that the defendants, along with individuals acting with them or on their behalf, be required to remove software script that exploits the web browser security vulnerabilities referenced in Microsoft Bulletins MS03–032 and MS03–040 or any other web browser security vulnerabilities that allow the defendants to install, download, or deposit any software code, program, or content onto a computer without the computer user's knowledge or authorization. * * *

In support of their motion, the FTC represents that the defendants have reconfigured consumers' computers by installing a software code, without the consumers' knowledge or authorization, that gives the defendants access to those computers for purposes of advertising. The FTC has submitted a declaration by Steven D. Gribble, Ph.D., an assistant professor of Computer Science and Engineering at the University of Washington, who tested and evaluated the effects of the defendants' activities. The FTC has also submitted the declarations of Sallie S. Schools, an investigator in Bureau of Consumer Protection of the FTC, and of individuals who have been affected by the defendants' actions and practices.

Dr. Gribble explains that "spyware" is software that gathers information about a computer's use and transmits that information to someone else, appropriates the computer's resources, or alters the functions of existing applications on the computer, all without the computer user's knowledge or consent. A type of "spyware" that uses collected information to display targeted advertisements is called "adware." Dr. Gribble found that the defendants exploit known security vulnerabilities in certain web browsers to gain access to computers, without their users' knowledge or consent, through web sites controlled by the defendants. The defendants' web sites instruct vulnerable web browsers to display pop-up advertisements and content from other pages of the network of web sites. The web sites use "exploit code" to change the computer user's homepage, override search functions on the browser, and download and install spyware and other programs. These activities are all done without the computer user's knowledge or authorization.

The defendants use the pop-up advertisements to market their own "anti-spyware" products along with others' products. The defendants' actions have caused affected computers to slow, malfunction, or crash completely. Consumers whose computers have been affected by the defendants' activities have spent considerable time, and in some cases money, to fix the problems caused by the defendants.

The defendants do not deny that they engage in the activities described by the FTC. Instead, they object to the FTC's negative characterization of their activities. The defendants argue that at least some of their activities are widely accepted internet practices and should not be prohibited. The defendants also do not contest that their activities have generated substantial revenue, through sales of their own products and advertising commissions on sales made by others.

The court notes that the issues presented here apparently raise a matter of first impression. Similar activities, however, have not been seen as acceptable practices by affected consumers. *See Brown v. Erie Ins. Exch.,* 2004 WL 318888 (Cal.Ct.App. Feb.20, 2004) (discussing class action against similar activities in context of insurance coverage dispute).

DISCUSSION

When, as here, the FTC seeks temporary injunctive relief pending further proceedings on the complaint for a permanent injunction, the court does not use the traditional TRO standard but instead applies the more lenient "public interest" standard. *World Travel,* 861 F.2d at 1029. Under the public interest standard, the FTC need not prove irreparable harm, but instead the court considers the likelihood that the FTC will succeed on the merits and balances the equities implicated by the challenged activities. * * * Although the court may consider the private concerns raised by the proposed relief in balancing the equities, the public interest is entitled to greater weight. *World Travel,* 861 F.2d at 1029.

A. *Likelihood of Success*

To show a likelihood of success, the FTC must demonstrate that the defendants' activities are unfair or deceptive within the meaning of the FTCA. * * * The defendants' activities in the new arena of internet advertising do not necessarily fit easily into the traditional concepts of unfair and deceptive acts and practices under the FTCA. Nevertheless, the declarations of the computer users who have been affected by the defendants' activities amply support the likelihood that the FTC will be able to prove violations of the FTCA and that consumers have experienced substantial injury without countervailing benefits. The declarants' experiences include unauthorized changes of their home pages, difficulty using their computers, and infusions of pop-up ads, including pornographic ads and ads for anti-spyware software. The affected users were not notified of the defendants' activities and did not know what had caused the problems with their computers, making the defendants' activities both deceptive and unfair.

One declaration states that 200 computers in the Atlanta office of a national company were affected by the defendants' practices for a period of two weeks. During that time, the computers did not function properly, worked slowly, froze, lost data, and crashed. The problems required a significant amount of time by technical specialists to remove the defendants' programs and software from the affected computers.

The vice president of an internet advertising company discovered that advertising from defendant Seismic Entertainment Productions caused problems with the company's computers and that a supposedly revised and clean version of the ad also generated similar problems and complaints and was then cancelled. A school district in Michigan had affected computers that required a significant amount of time by the computer specialist to clear the problems created by the defendants.

Individual users report that they bought the anti-spyware offered for sale by the defendants to "fix" the problems the defendants had caused. They also attempted to solve the problems by resetting their computers, exiting and rebooting, running anti-virus software, and getting help from experts. One user said that she was unable to fix her computer, even with help from computer science graduate students, and after two and a half weeks the hard drive failed, requiring her to buy a new computer. All of the users who submitted declarations experienced significant interruptions in their computer use.

The defendants have offered no contrary evidence or explanations of any kind and do not dispute that they engage in the activities charged by the FTC. Instead, counsel for the defendants argues that at least some of their activities are accepted marketing practices used by reputable companies. Although the defendants insist that they need time to investigate the FTC's charges, they have not offered any explanation of their activities to counter the FTC's well-supported claims.

Based on the present record, the FTC is likely to succeed in showing that the defendants' activities are unfair and deceptive practices within the meaning of the FTCA. Those activities cause and will continue to cause substantial injury to consumers by negatively affecting the performance of their computers and requiring significant time and expense to remedy the problems the defendants cause. Consumers are not able to avoid these problems because the defendants access their computers, install software and programs, and make changes without the user's knowledge or consent. The defendants have offered no countervailing benefit from their activities to consumers or competition, and the court perceives no such benefits from the present record. Therefore, at this early stage, the FTC appears to be likely to succeed on the merits of the claim that the defendants are violating, and continue to violate, the FTCA.

B. Balance of the Equities

For similar reasons, the balance of the equities favors granting temporary injunctive relief. * * *

CONCLUSION

For the foregoing reasons, the FTC's motion for a temporary restraining order ... is granted in part as is set forth in the accompanying order. * * *

Notes

1.   Can spyware be challenged under any other theories? See Sotelo v. DirectRevenue, LLC, 384 F.Supp.2d 1219 (N.D.Ill. 2005) (denying motion to dismiss claims in trespass to chattel, negligence, and based on state computer crime statute but granting motion to dismiss unjust enrichment claim); Michael D. Lane, Spies Among Us: Can New Legislation Stop Spyware from Bugging Your Computer? 17 Loy. Consumer L.Rev. 283 (2005) (discussing application of Consumer Fraud and Abuse Act, 18 U.S.C. § 1030, to spyware). Probably most spyware ends up on a computer when the computer's operator unwittingly consents to the spyware, by for example, clicking "I consent" on an agreement to download software the consumer wants, but which also includes the spyware. Could a consumer prevail in a lawsuit challenging spyware if the consumer consented to have the spyware on the computer in such circumstances? See Wayne R. Barnes, Rethinking Spyware: Questioning the Propriety of Contractual Consent to Online Surveillance, 39 U.C. Davis L. Rev. 1545 (2006) (arguing that the consent given for spyware should be invalid as unconscionable and against public policy). Compare the page-jacking problem in Chapter One. Is spyware best dealt with under the FTC Act and state UDAP statutes, or would it be preferable to enact statutes directed at the problem of spyware? In 2004, Utah became the first state to enact spyware legislation when it passed the Spyware Control Act, U.C.A. 1953 § 13–40–101. After the statute was found unconstitutional in an unreported decision in WhenU.com v. Utah, Utah Dist.Ct. No. 040907578 (June 28, 2004), on the ground that internet advertising involves interstate commerce, Utah amended the statute to require those who would deposit spyware onto a user's computer to first ask the user's state of residence; if the user replies that he or she resides in Utah, the statute bars the download. 2005 Utah Laws Ch. 169. Several other states have also enacted spyware legislation. See e.g., Cal. Bus. & Prof. Code § 22947 et seq.; Ariz. Rev. Stat. 44–8101. Is spyware best addressed at the state level or the federal level? See Peter S. Menell, Regulating "Spyware": The Limitations of State "Laboratories" and the Case for Federal Preemption of State Unfair Competition Laws, 20 Berkeley Tech. L.J. 1363 (2005). Is the problem of spyware susceptible to a solution rooted in rules? See Susan P. Crawford, First Do No Harm: The Problem of Spyware, 20 Berkeley Tech. L.J. 1433 (2005).

2.   Half the respondents to one survey of more than 3,200 households with internet access reported that they had experienced a spyware infection in the preceding six months; 18 percent found it necessary to erase their hard drives. Net Threat Rising, Consumer Rep., Sept. 2005, at 12.

3.   The F.T.C. later obtained default judgments in the principal case.

SECTION E.   PERSPECTIVES

The preceding sections have demonstrated a broad array of regulatory approaches to the gathering of information about and solicitation of consumers. Regulatory responses include doing nothing (e.g., the book store example in Section A); an outright ban on a practice (e.g., unsolicited commercial faxes and recorded telephone solicitations); allowing consumers some control (e.g., permitting consumers to add their telephone numbers to the "Do–Not–Call" list or to limit the trade in their financial information under GLB); requiring merchants to refrain from deception (e.g., CAN–SPAM), and allowing consumers to rescind a transaction (e.g., door-to-door sales in Chapter Three). What considerations underlie these different approaches to the problem?

Law-makers have also chosen other ways to deal with the gathering of consumer information. Two more approaches merit attention. The first of these can be found in the much-quoted Report of the Secretary's Advisory Committee on Automated Personal Data Systems, Records, Computers and the Rights of Citizens (1973), which called for establishment of a Code of Fair Information Practices based on the following:

- There must be no personal data record keeping systems whose very existence is secret.

- There must be a way for an individual to find out what information about him is in a record and how it is used.

- There must be a way for an individual to prevent information about him that was obtained for one purpose from being used or made available for other purposes without his consent.

- There must be a way for an individual to correct or amend a record of identifiable information about him.

- Any organization creating, maintaining, using, or disseminating records of identifiable personal data must assure the reliability of the data for their intended use and must take precautions to prevent misuse of the data.

In the more than three decades since that report was issued, how close have we come to adopting its proposals?

The second approach worth discussion can be found overseas. The European Union has taken a very protective stance towards consumer privacy issues in Directive 95/46/EC (Oct. 24, 1995). Article Seven of the EU Directive bars the disclosure of personal information in most circumstances unless the consumer to whom the data pertains has consented to the disclosure. Article 12 gives consumers a right of access to data about them and to be told what is being done with it. The European Union approach also has consequences for Americans because the EU Data Protection Directive bars the transfer of personal data to third countries unless the country "ensures an adequate level of protection." Art. 25. This has created problems for, among others, American companies with operations in Europe that wish to transfer data to offices in the United States. Article 26 of the Directive permits the transfer of data in such circumstances if the firms involved enter into agreements providing for protection of the data; the European Union has also agreed with the FTC on a Safe Harbor program for the transfer of data. To participate in the Safe Harbor program, a company must, among other requirements, sign up with the United States Department of Commerce and certify each year that it is in compliance with certain privacy principles.

The future of consumer privacy in the United States remains less clear than the EU Directive. Will privacy protections in the United States remain sectoral in nature, and represent ad hoc responses to particular problems, or will the United States adopt an across-the-board approach as the European Union has? Not only will the law continue to wrestle with existing issues, but technological developments can be expected to generate new privacy problems. One such technological development is likely to be the Radio Frequency Identification Device (RFID). RFIDs are analogous to bar codes, except that they broadcast radio signals that can be detected by RFID readers which can determine the location and movements of the RFID. RFIDs can be attached to consumer goods so that merchants can track inventory, for example. But they could also be used to track the movements of people. In the movie "Minority Report," characters walking through public places were greeted by personalized advertisements that addressed them by name. RFIDs may someday make that possible. What consumer privacy issues do RFIDs raise? Should consumers have any rights to control the data generated by RFIDs that pertain to them? Should firms have the right to sell that data? See Darren Handler, The Wild, Wild West: A Privacy Showdown on the Radio Frequency Identification (RFID) Systems Technological Frontier, 32 W. St. U.L. Rev. 199 (2005); Katherine Delaney, Privacy Year in Review: America's Privacy Laws Fall Short with RFID Regulation, 1 ISJLP 543 (2005); Laura Hildner, Defusing the Threat of RFID: Protecting Consumer Privacy Through Technology–Specific Legislation at the State Level, 41 Harv. C.R.-C.L.L. Rev. 133 (2006). An attempt under the aegis of the Center for Democracy and Technology to formulate guidelines for the use of RFIDs may be found at http://www.cdt.org/privacy/20060501rfid-best-practices.php.

Chapter 6

CONSUMER ACCOUNTS: CREDIT AND DEBIT CARDS, AND MORE

SECTION A. OVERVIEW

Most of the material in the prior chapters pertains to activity at the *beginning* of a consumer transaction, where the legal concerns are to protect the consumer from vulnerability to deceptive advertising, mis-disclosure, or high-pressure selling, for examples. One theme of this Chapter, by contrast, is to look at issues arising during the *performance* phase of consumer transactions, particularly where there are ongoing "account" arrangements in place, and the concerns are to protect consumers from abuses and risks in that context.

A second theme in this chapter is to examine consumer protections in the "payments system." Most consumer accounts involve financial services, like a checking account, or credit or debit card accounts. Even though a checking account represents the consumer's funds on deposit, while a credit card represents a line of credit to the card holder, the common characteristic of these accounts is that they are routinely used by consumers to make payments for goods or services they have pur-chased. The proliferation of consumer payment systems over recent decades includes, of course, the old stand-bys, cash and checks. But increasingly consumers rely on other forms of payment or financial exchange, usually rested on "accounts" with merchants or financial institutions, and implemented by a credit or debit card or other electron-ic medium. Newer forms of payment arrangements that are becoming commonplace include internet banking, stored-value cards, and internet purchase exchanges like PayPal and others. Even the conventional check system is being revolutionized by "check conversion" arrangements and by the introduction of "substitute checks" under the federal Check 21 Act of 2003 (formally the Check Clearing for the 21st Century Act, Pub. L. No. 108–100).

Probably the only certainty about the development of these systems in the years ahead is that they will be driven by technology and economics—toward more streamlined, convenient, and efficient payments. In this dynamic payments environment, there is law in place to address *some* of the problems that consumers face in their relationships with various account holders; some of that law dates back to the 1970s when credit and debit cards were young. Other legal guidelines are more recent, and yet others will emerge with time.

This Chapter examines where the law is, and where it may be going, with respect to the marketing of payment services, the fluidity, content, and pricing of the account features, account management and error resolution responsibilities, and liability for unauthorized use.

SECTION B.   MARKETING CREDIT CARDS AND OTHER PAYMENT SERVICES

The days are long gone when almost every retail store offered its own credit card, or charge card, plan. The same is true of the days when almost every bank was a credit card issuer. Now, the bulk of all credit cards are issued by a handful of large banks operating nationwide, and retailers are happy to sell on credit to customers proffering Visa or MasterCards. In this highly competitive market for credit (and deposit) customers, banks and other institutions invest millions of dollars to market their accounts by ubiquitous mailings and (at least before "do-not-call" restrictions) telemarketing.

How much legal freedom do the credit-card marketers have in this regard? From what do consumers need protections? What protections are appropriate?

MUNOZ v. SEVENTH AVENUE, INC.

U.S. District Court, Northern District of Illinois, 2004.
2004 WL 1593906.

Hart, J.

In this putative class action, plaintiff Gloria Munoz alleges that defendant Seventh Avenue, Inc. violated a provision of the Truth in Lending Act ("TILA"), 15 U.S.C. § 1642, which provides in part: "No credit card shall be issued except in response to a request or application therefor." Plaintiff contends that a Seventh Avenue catalog that she received contained an unsolicited credit card. Defendant contends it was an offer of credit that did not constitute a credit card as that term is used in § 1642. Presently pending is defendant's motion ... to dismiss the complaint for failing to state a claim upon which relief may be granted.

* * *

Plaintiff has alleged that a credit card was sent to her. However, she also attached to the complaint a copy of the page of the catalog that she contends included the credit card. Attached to defendant's motion to dismiss are additional pages of the catalog. These additional pages may be considered because the document is central to plaintiff's allegations. Plaintiff does not object to consideration of the additional pages nor contend that the copy is inaccurate. To the extent the catalog itself shows that no credit card was included, that must be taken as true instead of plaintiff's conclusory allegation that a credit card was sent.

Plaintiff contends that a page of the Seventh Avenue catalog that was sent to her includes a credit card. That page is reproduced on the next page of this opinion.

The order form provided with the catalog also contains the account number, the statement that "YOUR ACCOUNT IS PRE–APPROVED!," and that plaintiff could charge up to $1000.00 and pay only $35 a month. The order form provides three payment options when ordering: (1) pay by a general credit or debit card; (2) enclose a check or money order; or (3) "CHOOSE 'N CHARGE—Bill me monthly according to the easy payment plan terms and conditions on the back of this order form." There is also an "express order form" that only permits charging to the Choose 'N Charge account and again contains the account number, that the account is pre-approved, and references to making no payment now and being billed monthly.

The reverse side of the order form contains terms that are customary for credit card accounts. It also contains the following statement, which is not highlighted in any way. "All credit orders are subject to credit approval. Terms of The Offer: Information contained in a consumer report on you received from a credit reporting agency was used by us in connection with this offer of credit. This offer was made because that report indicated you satisfied the criteria for credit-worthiness used to select consumers for this offer. You may receive an account with a credit line ranging from a minimum of $50.00 up to the amount stated in this offer, or a higher amount specified by us."

Section 1642, which is part of TILA, prohibits the issuance of a credit card absent a prior request or application from the consumer.... Under the Fair Credit Reporting Act ("FCRA"), a credit reporting agency may provide a creditor with a list of unsolicited consumers who meet certain credit criteria and the creditor may send firm offers of credit that are conditional on the consumer satisfying certain criteria....

SEVENTH AVENUE

1112 Seventh Avenue • Monroe, Wisconsin

YOUR ACCOUNT IS NOW OPEN!

Welcome!

Here's your new Spring Catalog—full of exciting discoveries in home furnishings and decoratives, gifts, apparel, jewelry and accessories, collectibles, and much, much more!

Your CHOOSE 'N CHARGE account makes it so easy. Just place your order, and your payments could be as little as $20 a month! And, if you're adding to your outstanding account, your payments may not increase at all. The complete terms of your convenient credit are on the back of the center order form.

Discover the fun of shopping from your new Seventh Avenue catalog! Just send either order form, give us a call, or go to our web site for this easy payment plan. Let us know which "discoveries" you want, and we'll do all the rest!

Sincerely,

Kate Kirby

P.S.
YOUR ACCOUNT
IS PRE-APPROVED!

YOU CAN CHARGE

UP TO $1,000.00

AND PAY
ONLY $35 a month

(See credit terms on back of center order form.)

MONTHLY PAYMENT PLAN

Order now and pay later

Pay as little as $20 a month.

Order again, and your payments may not increase.

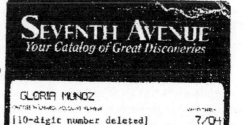

SEVENTH AVENUE
Your Catalog of Great Discoveries

GLORIA MUNOZ

CHOOSE 'N CHARGE ACCOUNT NUMBER

[10-digit number deleted]

GOOD THRU

7/04

NON-TRANSFERABLE

www.SeventhAvenue.com

Chrome-plated cooking grate

Steel mesh safety screen

SA
EXCLUSIVE

Look for this symbol throughout your catalog. It means you've discovered a Seventh Avenue Exclusive available only here.

©2004 Seventh Avenue, Inc.

Defendant contends its offer constituted a firm offer of credit and plaintiff does not argue otherwise, only noting that whether the mailing constituted a firm offer of credit is irrelevant. Plaintiff is correct. No provision of the FCRA permits firm offers of credit to an unsolicited consumer to be accompanied by the issuance of a credit card. Nor does TILA contain any such exception to § 1642. Thus, even if defendant's mailing qualified as a firm offer of credit under the FCRA, § 1642 was violated if that firm offer was accompanied by the issuance of a credit card. Thus, the issue as to the merits of plaintiff's § 1642 claim is whether the form with an account number that was included in the catalog was an issued credit card as that term is used in TILA.

The statute defines a "credit card" as meaning "any card, plate, coupon book or other credit device existing for the purpose of obtaining money, property, labor, or services on credit." 15 U.S.C. § 1602(k). The term "credit device" is not further defined. Regulation Z defines "credit card" as meaning "any card, plate, coupon book, or other single credit device that may be used from time to time to obtain credit." 12 C.F.R. § 226.2(a)(15).

Defendant argues that the piece of paper that is claimed to be a credit card in this case does not qualify as such because it does not meet the standards for a credit card as defined by the American National Standards Institute (ANSI) and International Organization for Standardization (ISO), including standards as to thickness, having a magnetic strip, and using a 16–digit account number. The statutory definition of credit card, however, is broader than the ANSI and ISO standards. The statutory definition refers to "any card," not just a specific type of card. Moreover, the statutory definition is not limited to a card; it also includes any plate, coupon book, or credit device as long as it is used to obtain cash, property, or services on credit. The particular shape or format of the device is of little import.

* * *

Section 1602(k) contains a broad definition of "credit card" which encompasses items that are not within the common understanding of the term credit card, such as a "coupon book" or "other credit device." The form with an account number that was printed on the previously reproduced page of the Seventh Avenue catalog was a device that could be used to purchase property on credit. It is in the shape of a card, but apparently was not perforated or otherwise readily separated from the entire page of the catalog. But even if it was not "any card" as that term is used in § 1602(k), the form and account number provided certainly would qualify as a credit device as that term is used in § 1602(k). Additionally, the Choose 'N Charge terms contained on the reverse side of the order form of the catalog are fully consistent with this being a credit card account. Since an account number already existed, and plaintiff did not have to complete any application, the credit card must be considered an issued credit card.

By sending out a pre-approved account number, defendant's catalog went beyond containing merely a firm offer of credit. On the factual allegations presently before the court, the catalog also contained an issued credit device, which constitutes a credit card as that term is used in § 1642 and defined in § 1602(k). The motion to dismiss will be denied.

* * *

Notes and Questions

1. The TILA provision prohibiting the unsolicited mailing of credit cards dates to 1970. Why would Congress, at that rather early stage in the development of credit cards, prohibit an "unsolicited" marketing practice? Don't consumers get samples of all kinds of products sent to them in the mail? How could consumers be harmed by this practice? After all, if they don't want the credit card or other product, all they need to do is throw it away. For the background of the ban on unsolicited issuance of credit cards, see R. Rohner & F. Miller, Truth in Lending § 10.02 (ABA, 2000).

2. Do you agree with the court that this catalog page information is a "credit card" subject to the statutory prohibition against unsolicited issuance? What makes it so? Would a customer have to cut out the catalog page, and "present" it to the store to get credit? How would you advise Seventh Avenue, Inc. to market its pre-approved catalog credit line in the future?

Problem 6–1

Thirdbank and Telecom, Inc. have agreed to collaborate in issuing a card that functions as a long-distance calling card for telephone services provided by Telecom but also can be activated to operate as a standard credit card. To activate the credit card function, the consumer would have to call a toll-free number and confirm the consumer's desire to use the card as a credit card. Thirdbank and Telecom send these cards to thousands of consumers, including to Sylvester, who immediately files suit claiming that this constitutes a violation of TILA, particularly the ban on unsolicited issuance in Reg. Z § 226.12(a). Thirdbank and Telecom defend by arguing that, while the card physically resembles a credit card, it cannot be so used until the consumer initiates the toll-free call and activates the card's credit function. What outcome? If it is a TILA violation, who is liable: Thirdbank, Telecom, or both? Swift v. First USA Bank, 1999 WL 1212561 (N.D.Ill. 1999).

Problem 6–2

Firstbank asks your advice on whether it can send to its existing customers what are called "convenience checks" or "cash-advance checks," on an unsolicited basis. Convenience checks are regular-looking blank checks that the consumer can use to draw on the credit card account, for example to pay the store for a new TV. Cash-advance checks, on the other hand, are checks issued by the bank or merchant payable to the consumer; if the consumer cashes or deposits the check, the amount of the check is added to the balance owing on the consumer's account. What do you say to Firstbank? If it is appropriate to bar unsolicited issuance of the plastic card itself, wouldn't it be consistent to bar unsolicited issuance of these other devices that encourage consumers to run up their credit card debt?

Problem 6–3

Firstbank also wants to put a "check card" into the hands of as many of its deposit customers as it can. (This is a card that is used to withdraw funds from the customer's deposit account, either at an ATM or through point-of-sale transactions.) So Firstbank adopts the same marketing technique as in Problem 6–1. *I.e.*, it mails plastic cards to its customers and to prospective depositors along with promotional material. The cards are fully functional when sent, but Firstbank's system will not allow them to be used until the customer calls the bank's toll-free number to validate the card.

Electronic "access devices" such as this are regulated by the Electronic Fund Transfer Act, 15 U.S.C. § 1693, and the Federal Reserve Board's Regulation E, 12 C.F.R. Part 205. Is Firstbank permitted to distribute the cards in this fashion? See Regulation E § 205.5(b). Are there distinctions between credit cards and check cards that would justify different rules on unsolicited issuance?

Note on Pre-screening

We have all received credit card solicitations from banks we've never dealt with, that pronounce that we are pre-approved to receive their super-duper card. How does the card issuer know enough about us to consider us creditworthy at this point? The answer often lies in the practice called "pre-screening." Typically the bank or other entity that wants to market the cards will give a list of its credit criteria for prospective customers to a credit bureau (a "consumer reporting agency"), and ask the bureau to generate from its massive databases the names and addresses of people who meet those criteria. In other words, the bank will know that each person on the pre-screened list appears qualified, but the bank will not have a full credit report showing all the details of each person's credit history.

The court in the *Munoz* case, supra, alludes to this practice, and notes that it is regulated by the Fair Credit Reporting Act (FCRA), 15 U.S.C. § 1681 et seq., which we considered in the prior chapter. As we saw, that Act generally does not permit credit bureaus to release to banks or other merchants detailed information about a consumer unless the consumer consents or there is a legitimate credit transaction between the consumer and the bank or other merchant. In the context of pre-screening, this means that the bank or merchant as the "user" of the pre-screened list must make a "firm offer of credit" to every person on the pre-screened list. 15 U.S.C. § 1681b(c)(1)(B). The consumer must also be informed that he or she has been pre-screened, and given the opportunity to opt out of future solicitations.

The banks and merchants insisted that they needed to reserve an opportunity, once a consumer responded to the solicitation, to then get a full, detailed credit report on that individual, and reassess or verify the consumer's eligibility for the credit. The FCRA accommodates this "back side" verification process. 15 U.S.C. § 1681a(*l*). Thus banks or other card issuers can use credit bureau data to pre-approve their marketing targets and then send out completely unsolicited "firm offers" of credit, yet retain the right to second-guess whether the consumer actually gets the promised credit or not.

Are there opportunities for abuse in all of this?

PERRY v. FIRST NATIONAL BANK

U.S. Court of Appeals, Seventh Circuit, 2006.
459 F.3d 816.

Before FLAUM, CHIEF JUDGE, BAUER and EVANS, CIRCUIT JUDGES.

FLAUM, Chief Judge. Plaintiff–Appellant Thelma Perry filed a class action suit against Defendant–Appellee First National Bank, d/b/a First National Credit Card ("First National") under the Fair Credit Reporting Act ("FCRA" or "Act"), 15 U.S.C. § 1681 *et seq.* Perry alleged that the company violated 15 U.S.C. § 1681m(d) by failing to include a clear and conspicuous statement of certain disclosures required under the FCRA.

Perry sought to amend her complaint to allege that First National's offer of credit was a sham, not a firm offer of credit, and that, pursuant to 15 U.S.C. § 1681b(c)(1)(B)(i), First National was prohibited from accessing her consumer credit report. The district court denied Perry's motion to amend, finding that the credit offer was a firm offer and that amending the complaint would be futile.

Perry appeals the . . . denial of her motion to amend. For the following reasons, we affirm.

I. BACKGROUND

Perry received a credit solicitation mailing from First National, dated February 14, 2005, offering her a pre-approved Visa credit card with a $250 limit. The mailing contained a letter as well as a brochure setting forth the terms and conditions of the offer. One paragraph of the brochure, titled, "Fair Credit Report Act Notice" ("Notice") advised recipients in bold letters that "the credit bureau gave us your name and address and indicated that you met our minimum credit criteria," and that "you can tell credit bureaus to stop using your credit information for this purpose." The solicitation letter itself does not specifically refer to the Notice.

Perry did not authorize First National to access her consumer credit report. She alleges that First National accessed her consumer report and used a consumer reporting agency to target certain people, e.g., individuals with poor credit or individuals who recently obtained bankruptcy discharges, for sub-prime credit offers.

Perry alleged in her complaint that First National violated 15 U.S.C. § 1681m(d) by failing to include a "clear and conspicuous" statement of certain disclosures required by the FCRA. Perry tried to introduce the report of Timothy Shanahan ("Shanahan report"), a professor of education at the University of Illinois at Chicago, to support her argument that the Notice was not "clear and conspicuous ." The Shanahan report included a "legibility analysis."

The district court found that Perry did not have a statutory right to bring a private cause of action under § 1681m(d), due to a 2003 amendment to the FCRA that eliminated the right to bring such actions. The district court therefore granted summary judgment for First National. The district court also granted First National's motion to strike Shanahan's report, explaining that "[b]ecause no private right of action exists under § 1681m, an evaluation of the Notice is not relevant to the instant case."

Perry also argued that even if her claim under § 1681m(d) could not succeed, she should be allowed to amend her complaint to plead a violation of 15 U.S.C. § 1681b(c)(1)(B)(i). Section 1681b(c)(1)(B)(i) permits a consumer credit agency to furnish a consumer report even though the consumer has not initiated or authorized the release only if the credit or insurance provider is extending the consumer a "firm offer of credit." Perry contends that the credit solicitation was not a firm offer of credit because it was for such a small amount of credit that it was virtually worthless. The district court disagreed and found that Perry could not state a claim under § 1681b(c)(1)(B)(i), because First National's credit offer was a "firm offer of credit." The district court denied Perry's motion to amend, finding that although the minimum amount of credit that First National offered was small, the interest rate was clear, approval was guaranteed, and the credit card did not contain usage limitations.

II. Discussion

* * *

[*Eds.:* The court determined that plaintiff had no private cause of action with respect to the pre-screening disclosures.]

B. *Firm Offer of Credit Under 15 U.S.C. § 1681b(c)(1)(B)(i)*

Perry argued before the district court that she should be allowed to amend her complaint to allege that First National's credit solicitation was not a firm offer of credit and thus that First National was prohibited by 15 U.S.C. § 1681b(c)(1)(B)(i) from obtaining her credit information to make the solicitation. The district court denied the motion to amend, finding that the credit solicitation was a firm offer and that it would be futile for Perry to amend her complaint. According to the district court, Perry's allegations were distinguishable from those made by the plaintiff in Cole v. U.S. Capital, 389 F.3d 719 (7th Cir.2004), in which we reversed a grant of summary judgment for defendants on a similar FCRA claim. The district court reasoned that although First National's credit solicitation offered a small minimum amount of credit, Perry failed to allege that the credit card's interest rate was unclear, that approval was not guaranteed, or that there were any usage limitations on the credit line.

Under 15 U.S.C. § 1681b(c), a credit or insurance provider can obtain a consumer's credit information from a credit agency without the consumer's permission only if the provider is making a "firm offer of credit" to the consumer. 15 U.S.C. § 1681b(c)(1)(B)(i). "Firm offer of credit" is defined by statute as "any offer of credit or insurance to a consumer that will be honored if the consumer is determined, based on information in a consumer report on the consumer, to meet the specific criteria used to select the consumer for the offer, except that the offer may be further conditioned on one or more of" several conditions that are not relevant to this appeal. 15 U.S.C. § 1681a(*l*).

In determining "whether the offer of credit comports with the statutory definition, a court must consider the *entire* offer and the effect of all the material conditions that comprise the credit product in question. If, after examining the entire context, the court determines that the 'offer' was a guise for solicitation rather than a legitimate credit product, the communication cannot be considered a firm offer of credit." *Cole,* 389 F.3d at 727–28; *see also Murray,* 434 F.3d at 955–56.

Perry relies on *Cole* to argue essentially that First National's credit solicitation was a sham, not a firm offer of credit, because it offered only a small amount of credit and required payment of comparatively large fees. Perry alleged:

> The solicitation offers a minimum credit line of $250. However, if the offer is accepted, the consumer is charged a processing fee of $9.00 (which is due with the application), an "acceptance" fee of $119.00, an annual membership fee of $50.00, and a "participation" fee of $72.00 per year (charged at a rate of $6.00 per month), for a total of $184.00 in fees for the opening of a credit card account, with $175.00 appearing on the first bill that the cardholder would receive. This means that the effective amount of credit being granted with the card is $75.00, with an outstanding balance of $175.00 that is subject to an annual percentage rate of 18.9%. The amount of credit being offered is therefore virtually worthless, and does not constitute a firm offer of credit.

We agree with the district court that First National's credit solicitation constituted a firm offer of credit. In *Cole,* we identified three factors supporting the appellant's argument that the defendant's solicitation was not a firm offer: 1) it was not clear that credit approval was guaranteed; 2) the precise rate of credit and other material terms were not included in the solicitation; and 3) the credit card limit, $300, was relatively small in relation to the known limitations of the card, which could be used only toward a vehicle purchase at a particular car dealership. *Cole,* 389 F.3d at 728. The *Cole* Court found that the appellant's pleadings reasonably supported the appellant's claim that the defendant's offer was a sham, made only to justify accessing consumer credit reports and solicit buyers for the car dealership. *Id.* The credit solicitation expressly stated that "[g]auranteed approval is neither express nor implied," which "create[d] a question whether the offer of credit w[ould] be honored." *Id.* Additionally, "the relatively small amount of credit combined with the known limitations of the offer—that it must be used to purchase a vehicle—raise[d] a question of whether the offer ha[d] value to the consumer." *Id.* The Court also found that the missing material terms from the credit solicitation "render[ed] it impossible for the court to determine from the pleadings whether the offer ha [d] value." *Id.*

The credit solicitation at issue in this case does not present the same problems as the solicitation in *Cole.* First, it is clear from the face of First National's solicitation that recipients are preapproved. The solicitation states, "Your good standing has been found creditworthy by Legacy Visa and that qualifies you for a new Visa account." Perry does not argue that she or any class member was denied credit upon responding to the solicitation. Second, the interest rate for the credit card is stated in the terms and conditions brochure sent with the credit solicitation, and is set at 18.9 percent.

Third, although the credit limit is quite low, the card can be used to purchase any products or services for which Visa is accepted. This is in stark contrast to the credit offered in *Cole,* which could be used only toward the purchase of a vehicle at a particular car dealership. In *Cole,* the cost of purchasing a vehicle dwarfed the value of the credit offer. According to Perry, the credit line she was offered actually was much worse than the one at issue in that case, because *Cole* concerned a $300 credit line, whereas she was offered only "$75 in effective credit." Perry's argument is somewhat misleading. $75 would be the available credit limit in the first month the credit card was used. The processing fee ($9) and acceptance fee ($119) are one-time charges. Once these are paid, the credit recipient would be required to pay $6 per month for the participation fee and $50 the following year for the yearly membership fee.

We recognize that First National's credit solicitation requires card holders to pay a significant amount of money in fees, which are quite high in relation to the credit line offered. We realize that this is not an attractive deal for the great majority of consumers. However, the card is not without value. If the credit card holder paid off the card each month, the card would allow him or her to make almost $3000 in purchases in one year. The credit card holder would also build up a credit rating, which is useful to individuals who are trying to establish credit for the first time or to reestablish good credit. Additionally, First National's offer was not a "guise for solicitation," *Cole,* 389 F.3d at 728, or "a sham offer used to pitch a product rather than extend credit," *Murray,* 434 F.3d at 955. The only product First National offered was a credit line. Taking these factors together, we find that the district court did not err by denying Perry's request to amend her complaint to add her claim under 15 U.S.C. § 1681b(c)(1)(B)(i).[2]

Additionally, we affirm the district court's ruling to deny Perry's request to obtain discovery on the percentage of consumers who responded to First National's solicitation, the percentage that received credit cards, and the amount of money First National earns in interest as compared to the amount in earns in fees from credit cards like the one offered to Perry. Perry has not demonstrated that this evidence is relevant to our inquiry. As Perry admits, most consumers who receive credit solicitations do not apply for the offered credit card, regardless of how attractive the terms of the offer are. Also, Perry does not suggest that many consumers applied for First National's credit cards and were rejected. Finally, Perry does not explain why the district court should have let it obtain information on the amount of money First National earns in interest versus in fees. For instance, what ratio of interest charges versus fees would demonstrate that a credit offer was not a "firm offer"? The fact that First National may earn a significant portion of its revenues from fees charged for credit cards like those offered to Perry does not make its credit solicitation a sham—the focus of our inquiry is whether the credit solicitation offers value to the consumer, and in this case we have determined that it does.

III. CONCLUSION

For the foregoing reasons, we AFFIRM the district court in full.

EVANS, CIRCUIT JUDGE, dissenting. I respectfully dissent, because I do not agree that the solicitation First National sent to Perry can reasonably be considered a "firm offer of credit."

True, the solicitation in this case does not present the exact same problems as the one at issue in *Cole v. U.S. Capital,* 389 F.3d 719 (7th Cir.2004). In this case, recipients are "preapproved," the interest rate and other terms are disclosed, and the card can be used to do more than simply buy a car at a particular dealership. If those narrow factors were all that *Cole* required for a "firm offer of credit," I would gladly join the majority opinion.

---

2. In reaching this conclusion, we have considered our dissenting colleague's unease that First National's credit offer will be accepted only by those consumers who do not fully understand the offer's terms or by those who cannot obtain credit on more favorable terms, such as individuals with very poor credit histories or who are emerging from bankruptcy. However, as the dissent acknowledges, the FCRA is designed to protect the privacy of consumers' credit histories, not to prevent consumers from making unwise financial choices even when they are provided with all the material terms necessary to make informed decisions. Additionally, we are concerned that accepting our colleague's position may have the unintended consequence of precluding consumers with past financial problems from obtaining credit at all, and thus make it even more difficult for them to receive loans and mortgages. We are understanding of the plight of consumers who must choose between having no credit and having credit on less than favorable terms, but we also recognize that a company like First National will not offer credit to consumers on terms that will not allow it to earn a return.

But *Cole* emphasizes that under the FCRA, a firm offer of credit must have "sufficient value for the consumer," 389 F.3d at 726. The majority opinion, I believe, glosses over this larger point. As we explained, "A definition of 'firm offer of credit' that does not incorporate the concept of value to the consumer upsets the balance Congress carefully struck between a consumer's interest in privacy and the benefit of a firm offer of credit for all those chosen through the pre-screening process." *Id.* at 726–27. The three factors discussed by the majority are not the entire analysis. In *Cole* we recognized more broadly that the "terms of an offer . . . may be so onerous as to deprive the offer of any appreciable value." *Id.* at 728. To determine whether an offer meets the standards of the FCRA,

> a court must consider the *entire* offer and the effect of *all* the material conditions that comprise the credit product in question. If, after examining the entire context, the court determines that the "offer" was a guise for solicitation rather than a legitimate credit product, the communication cannot be considered a firm offer of credit.

Id.

I am troubled when I imagine the consumer for whom First National's product—with its $9 "processing fee," $119 "acceptance fee," $50 "annual membership fee," and $72 annual "participation fee," all coming out of a mere $250 line of credit—would be considered to carry appreciable value. Credit card companies employ savvy marketing analysts and sophisticated algorithms to target their offers toward particular niches of consumers. For anyone who understands credit card marketing schemes, it is difficult not to conclude that First National is using its privileged access to financial data simply to extract one creative fee on top of another from consumers who are either naive, desperate, or both.

The majority, echoing a point made by First National's counsel at oral argument, explains that the card is, in theory, "not without value" because a card holder who paid off her entire balance every month would have almost $3,000 in purchasing power (albeit in small revolving increments) each year. Of course, a consumer who has the cash flow to pay her bills in full every month has no actual need for credit. She would be better off with a bank account debit card, for which she would not be required to enrich First National by $250 the first year and $122 each year thereafter.

Thus, the only person for whom First National's product objectively might have some utility is the consumer whose financial history is so catastrophic that a card encumbered by usurious fees, along with 18.9% interest, is the only option for rehabilitating a credit rating. Even so, before I could accept assurances about the card's theoretical value for such a consumer, I would need to know how many such card holders—who dutifully avoid late payments and maxed-out balances—actually are among First National's customers or within its target market for this particular product. I suspect not many, because they'd have better options.

Even if the FCRA is intended only to protect consumers' privacy, not to safeguard them against predatory credit practices and their own poor financial judgment, I conclude that First National's offer is not a "legitimate credit product," *id.*, which is distinguishable from a "sales pitch[ ]," *id.* at 727. In *Cole,* the sales pitch was for a car; in this case, it is for an unconscionably one-sided financial deal that defies a reasonable concept of sufficient value. On my reading of the relevant statute and our precedent, "[s]uch importuning simply—and understandably—is not among the permissible reasons for which a credit agency may disclose a consumer's credit information. Defining a firm offer of credit as merely any offer that will be honored elevates form over substance" and deprives the FCRA "of all serious purpose." *Id.* (citations omitted). For these reasons, I cannot join the majority opinion.

Query: Is the majority correct in its fn. 2 that the FCRA is not designed to "prevent consumers from making unwise financial choices?" At least with respect to pre-screening, what **is** FCRA designed to do?

Problem 6–4

Jewelry Store (Jeweler) gets a pre-screened list of potential customers from Credit Bureau, using credit eligibility criteria that are very low; as a result many of the names on the list have weak or blemished credit histories. Jeweler then mails flyers to all the people on the list, announcing a big clearance sale and assuring:

> You are pre-approved for credit for any purchase you make. Up to $2,500 of credit to qualifying customers, and everyone qualifies!

When Zachary receives the flyer he goes to Jeweler to buy his wife a new ring that costs $5,000. Jeweler tells Zachary, however, that he only qualifies for $100.00 of credit from the store, and must finance the remaining $4,900.00 on his own. Zachary sues Jeweler for violating the Fair Credit Reporting Act, claiming specifically that Jeweler was not making a genuine "firm offer of credit" to the pre-screened list. In discovery Jeweler concedes that in fact 90% of the customers who responded to Jeweler's flyer were extended credit of less than $200.00, and only a handful received credit over $2,000.00.

a. On Zachary's motion for summary judgment, how should the judge rule? See the *Perry* court's discussion of Cole v. U.S. Capital, Inc., 389 F.3d 719 (7th Cir. 2004).

b. Assume Jeweler's flyer is considered a "firm offer of credit" for pre-screening purposes. Could the Federal Trade Commission nonetheless prosecute Jeweler for false or deceptive advertising? See FCRA, 15 U.S.C. § 1681m(d)(4).

SECTION C. THE "ACCOUNT" PARADIGM: CHANGES IN TERMS; FEES AND MORE FEES

It seems to be generally taken for granted that where a merchant and customer maintain a financial account relationship, like a credit or debit card plan, or a bank deposit account, the terms of that relationship may change from time to time with the agreement of the parties.

But how does this play out in the consumer markets? For example, may a credit card issuer simply notify its customers that the applicable Annual Percentage Rate will double next month, and treat the customer's acquiescence or continued use of the card as acceptance of the new rate? May the card issuer add entirely new terms, on the same basis?

GARBER v. HARRIS TRUST & SAVINGS BANK

Appellate Court of Illinois, First District, Third Division, 1982.
104 Ill.App.3d 675, 60 Ill.Dec. 410, 432 N.E.2d 1309.

WHITE, P. J.

Plaintiffs, Gary L. Blank and Sheldon Garber, purporting to represent a class of credit cardholders, brought this action in chancery against defendants Harris Trust and Savings Bank (Harris Trust), Sears Roebuck and Co. (Sears), J. C. Penney Co., Inc. (Penney), and First National Bank of Chicago (FNB). The amended complaint alleges that Blank is the holder of credit cards issued by the defendants Sears, Penney and FNB. It also alleges that Garber is the holder of Master Charge credit cards issued by Harris Trust. In essence, the amended complaint asserts that each defendant had breached the provisions of its "cardholder agreement" document by changing the terms on which that defendant would offer to extend credit and that the alleged changes in the cardholder agreements were void for lack of consideration. These cardholder agreements are alleged to be contracts. In their prayer for relief, plaintiffs sought injunctive relief against the changes, money damages, and other relief. Defendants moved to dismiss the amended complaint. After hearing oral argument, the circuit court entered an order granting the motions to dismiss and dismissing the cause of action with prejudice. Plaintiffs appeal from this order.

The alleged modifications of the cardholder agreements at issue are as follows. In spring 1980, FNB announced that, effective July 1, 1980, it would begin charging a $20 annual fee for its VISA cards and would increase the minimum monthly payment from four% to five% on the outstanding balance in any VISA account. The changed terms only became effective if cardholders used their cards after June 30, 1980. Penney allegedly breached its cardholder agreement by initiating a policy whereby finance charges on future purchases would be assessed against a cardholder from the date of each purchase, regardless of the date on which he was billed. This policy allegedly modified provisions of the original Penney cardholder agreement which provided that a finance charge would be assessed against a cardholder from the date on which he was billed. The alleged modifications by Sears arose out of two notices which Sears sent to its cardholders. The first notice was sent to cardholders in January 1980, and it advised them of a change in the method of computing finance charges which took effect in March 1980. Pursuant to this change, purchases, payments and credits to a cardholder's account during the current monthly billing period would be included in the computation of each day's average daily balance, a figure used to compute finance charges. The notice gave the cardholder the options of discontinuing the use of his Sears credit privileges after the effective date of the change or of continuing to use his card, thereby accepting the proposed change. The second notice, sent to Sears cardholders in May 1980, advised them of a change (increase) in the minimum monthly payment schedule which took effect in July, 1980. This notice gave the cardholder similar options. The new schedule of minimum payments would apply to previous balances as well as to future purchases, if the card was used after this modification. The alleged modification complained of with respect to Harris Trust was that Harris had notified its cardholders that after May 1980, Harris would impose an annual fee upon the use of its card. This notice also informed cardholders that the changes announced would become effective after June 4, 1980, assuming that the cardholder uses his account on or after that date.

Plaintiffs assert that the cardholder agreements between the defendant credit card issuers and the plaintiff credit cardholders are binding contracts to continue to extend credit on the same terms and that there was no consideration to support the alleged modifications since a promise to do something which one is already obligated to do, i.e., to extend credit, does not constitute a valid consideration. Plaintiffs find the existence of a contract in the following manner. The applications and brochures, displayed and advertised by defendants, are invitations for an offer. The credit application submitted by a potential cardholder to one of the defendant credit card issuers constitutes an offer. Acceptance of this offer occurs when the issuer issues a credit card to the cardholder. A cardholder furnishes consideration to the issuer by providing the issuer with requested credit information and by allowing the issuer to commence a credit check prior to the issuance of the card.

Conversely, the card issuers argue that the issuance of a card constitutes an offer to extend credit, and that offer is accepted by use of the card. Upon such use, the cardholder agrees to all provisions in the cardholder agreement, and the agreement becomes a binding contract between the cardholder and the issuer. In other words, each use of the credit card constitutes a separate contract between the parties.

For the reasons stated below, we conclude that a contract was not formed at the time of the issuance of the credit card; that a separate contract is created each time the card is used according to the terms of the cardholder agreement at the time of such use; that the cardholder agreements were subject to modification at will; and that in any event, consideration was given for the modifications.

Although the parties do not refer us to any Illinois cases to support the position that cardholder agreements are standing offers to extend credit, support for this position is found in the case law of other jurisdictions. In City Stores Co. v. Henderson (1967), 116 Ga. App. 114, 156 S.E.2d 818, plaintiffs brought an action for tortuous misconduct based upon an alleged refusal, without prior notice of credit revocation, of defendant's clerk to extend further credit to one of the plaintiffs when she sought to charge purchases made at its store. In discussing the nature of the relationship between a cardholder and the issuer of the card, the court stated:

> "The issuance of a credit card is but an offer to extend a line of open account credit. It is unilateral and supported by no consideration. The offer may be withdrawn at any time, without prior notice, for any reason or, indeed, for no reason at all, and its withdrawal breaches no duty—for there is no duty to continue it—and violates no rights. Acceptance or use of the card by the offeree makes a contract between the parties according to its terms, but we have seen none which prevents a termination of the arrangement at any time by either party." (116 Ga. App. 114, 120–21, 156 S.E.2d 818, 823.)

This language was quoted with approval in Novack v. Cities Service Oil Co. (1977), 149 N.J.Super. 542, 548, 374 A.2d 89, 92, affirmed (1978), 159 N.J.Super. 400, 388 A.2d 264.... In Novack, the plaintiff's complaint alleged, in part, a cause of action grounded in contract for the allegedly wrongful termination of his Cities Service credit card. His argument was that defendant, by cancelling plaintiff's credit card without notice and contrary to established intercompany procedures, breached an express term of the contract between them. In finding as a matter of law that no contractual relationship was created by the issuance and receipt of the credit card, the court stated:

> "The conclusion that the issuance of a credit card does not create a contract includes an analysis of the concept of consideration. It is well settled that to be enforceable a contract must be supported by valuable consideration. [Citations.] Consideration involves a detriment incurred by the promisee or a benefit received by the promisor, at the promisor's request. In the credit card relationship, neither status is created. The holder of the card (promisee) is free to cancel or not use it, and has gratuitously received an opportunity to purchase without incurring any detriment. Additionally, there does not appear to be any benefit bargained for or received by the issuing company (promisor). Lacking consideration, the credit card account is, as stated in City Stores, a continuing offer to purchase which may be withdrawn by either party at any time." 149 N.J. Super. 542, 548–49, 374 A.2d 89, 92.

Thus the prevailing view in this country is that the issuance of a credit card is only an offer to extend credit. There is no persuasive reason, under the circumstances presented in the instant appeal, for swaying from the accepted position that the issuance of a credit card does not create a contract.

We therefore conclude that defendant credit card issuers could terminate or modify the terms of their offers to extend credit as to future transactions. Once a credit card issuer withdraws its offer, a cardholder cannot compel it to extend credit to him in accordance with the terms of that offer.

* * *

[*Eds.:* Omitted is the courts' discussion of several alternative grounds for finding the change in terms permissible.]

Assuming again that the cardholder agreements themselves constitute a contract between card issuer and cardholder, we conclude that the cardholder agreements were terminable at will by virtue of their cancellation provisions, and therefore, that the agreements could be modified at any time as to future transactions. . . .

"Parties to a contract may cancel it at any time by mutual consent, and there is no reason why they may not agree in advance that the contract made by them shall cease to be binding at any time, at the option of either or both of them, if there is, in fact, a valid contract made by them." (353 Ill. 541, 545.)

Thus, the cardholder agreements in question were terminable at the will of the card issuer. Following the reasoning above with respect to contracts of indefinite duration, we conclude that the cardholder agreements of FNB, Harris Trust and Penney, if contracts, could be modified at any time by the card issuers as a condition of continuance.

The cardholder agreements of FNB and Penney discussed under this point, as noted, also contained "change of terms" provisions. These provisions merely express what the card issuer has the right to by virtue of the agreement being terminable at will. We see no good reason why such provisions should not be enforced according to their terms, assuming the existence of a valid contract.

Furthermore, assuming that the cardholder agreements are contracts, we conclude that the modifications of those agreements by these credit card issuers were supported by valid consideration. Since the cardholder agreements are terminable at will, the card issuers were under no obligation to extend credit in the future. "Any act or promise which is of benefit to one party or disadvantage to the other is a sufficient consideration to support a contract." (Steinberg v. Chicago Medical School (1977), 69 Ill. 2d 320, 330, 371 N.E.2d 634.) By extending credit on new terms, the card issuers gave consideration for the modified agreements.

The modifications made by FNB and Sears may have a retroactive impact on previously vested credit balances of cardholders, depending upon whether or not the cardholder uses his card after the effective date of the modification. The modifications only took effect if the cardholder used his card after that date. As noted above, case law from other jurisdictions provides that use of the card by the cardholder makes a contract between the cardholder and the issuer. Thus, any retroactive impact of these modifications on previous vested credit balances would affect valid contracts between the parties. However, the extension of credit after the effective date of the change would be consideration for such modification.

Beck v. First National Bank (Minn. 1978), 270 N.W.2d 281, is instructive. That case involved an action for usury under the National Bank Act. The plaintiff and the defendant bank were parties to a "checking-plus" agreement. Pursuant to that agreement, the bank authorized the plaintiff to create overdrafts in his checking accounts, and the overdrafts were to be treated as loans. Subsequently, the bank sent the plaintiff a notice which informed "checking-plus" customers that on a specified date the interest rate would be increased. Plaintiff had the choices of continuing his use of the checking plus plan at the increased rate or of discontinuing the plan. After the effective date of the change, the plaintiff continued to write checks in excess of his checking account balance, and the new rate was applied to his new advances, as well as his past balances. In analyzing these facts, the court stated;

> "The checking-plus agreement between plaintiff and the Bank provided that it could be terminated by either party at any time by 'giving written notice to that effect to the other party.' The Bank's September notice to plaintiff was in effect a notice of termination of the checking-plus agreement coupled with an offer to continue the present service at a new rate, * * *. By writing new overdrafts, plaintiff accepted this offer and thus refinanced his existing balance under the new arrangement and the new law." (270 N.W.2d 281, 287.) We follow Beck, and find that plaintiff cardholders accepted the modification if they used their credit cards after the modifications.

Plaintiffs rely on Board of Education v. Barracks (1924), 235 Ill. App. 35, in arguing that consideration for an original contract does not attach to and support subsequent modifications. That case, quoting from other cases, stated that "doing or undertaking to do only that which one is already under a legal obligation to do by his contract is no consideration for another's agreement." (235 Ill. App. 35, 45.) This principle is inapplicable here. Either the cardholder agreements constituted offers to extend credit which could be withdrawn at any time, or if they constituted contracts, those contracts were terminable at will. Thus, the card issuers here had no pre-existing duty to furnish credit forever on fixed terms. Significantly, Barracks did not involve a contract terminable at will.

Plaintiffs also argue that they have not accepted the modifications. Most of the modifications had prospective effects only, but, as discussed above, some had retroactive effects. We feel that Beck disposes of this argument. They also rely on People ex rel. Sterba v. Blaser (1975), 33 Ill. App. 3d 1, 337 N.E.2d 410, which stated "that no contract can be modified or amended in an ex parte fashion by one of the contracting parties without the knowledge and consent of the remaining party to the agreement." (33 Ill. App. 3d 1, 9.) The case at bar, however, involves at most a contract terminable at will, and the law is clear that such a contract can be modified at any time as a condition of its continuance.

* * *

For the aforementioned reasons, the judgment of the circuit court of Cook County is affirmed.

Notes and Questions

1.   The *Garber* court's view of the revocability or changeability of account terms is recognized generally in 1–2 Corbin on Contracts § 2.33 (Supp. 2006):

> There is one sort of case in which the offer is not made irrevocable either by part performance or by an express notice of acceptance. This is the case in which an offer has been made in such terms as to create a power to make a series of separate contracts by a series of separate acceptances. The closing of one of these separate contracts by one acceptance leaves the offer still revocable as to any subsequent acceptance. * * *

> The typical credit card fits the mold of an offer by the issuer to a series of unilateral contracts.

Some courts have treated the financial institution's ability to change terms as merely a freedom-of-contract matter—*i.e.*, assuming the original account agreement is a good and binding contract, the creditor may change terms because the "contract" permits it. Indeed, this is an alternative ground in *Garber*. There are also a number of state statutes that specifically permit card issuers to change terms. Cf., Uniform Consumer Credit Code § 3.205 (1974).

2.   Probably no one argues that account terms, once established, should be frozen for all time. Open-end account relationships, whether rested on the *Garber* analysis or otherwise, would lose their attractiveness and functionality if the card issuer could not adjust account terms from time to time to reflect operating costs and competitive pressures. But even Corbin recognizes there may be limits on the freedom of a card issuer to re-write the account provisions unilaterally, such as where the card holder pays an annual fee, or where a particular account arrangement might give rise to an "implied promise of good faith and fair dealing, nothing less, but also nothing more." Corbin on Contracts, supra note 1. The "good faith and fair dealing" argument was attempted, unsuccessfully, in Edelist v. MBNA America Bank, 790 A.2d 1249 (Del. Super. Ct. 2001).

3. Recall the *Rossman* case in Chapter 3, where the card issuer promoted "no annual fee," but then changed terms to impose such a fee. Is the *Rossman* courts' view of the contract formation process consistent with *Garber*, just above?

Problem 6–5

Friendly Bank's card holder agreement with Sandra contained a change-in-terms provision that said:

> "We [bank] may change any term, condition, service, or feature of your Account at any time. We will provide you with notice of the change to the extent required by law."

Some time later the Bank sent Sandra her regular monthly statement. Included in the envelope was a single-page "stuffer," captioned "Important Change in Terms Notice." The notice stated that henceforth any and all disputes arising in connection with the account would be resolved by binding arbitration, and that the card holder would therefore have no right to a jury trial and could not pursue any claim as a class action. Sandra discarded the stuffer without reading it.

Sandra and the Bank later had a dispute about the amount owing on the account. Sandra filed suit, and the Bank moved for dismissal on the ground that the arbitration provision was binding on her. Sandra argued in return that the change-in-term provision in the account agreement permitted only changes or modifications to *existing* terms, such as the APR, but did not contemplate wholly new terms such as the arbitration provision. Moreover, she argued, the Bank should not be able to deprive her of her constitutional right to jury trial, or her ability to bring a class action, by a casual change-in-terms notice stuffed in with her periodic statement.

a. What outcome? See Badie v. Bank of America, 67 Cal.App.4th 779, 79 Cal.Rptr.2d 273 (1998): "[P]ermitting the bank to exercise its unilateral rights under the change of terms provision, without any limitation on the substantive nature of the change permitted, would open the door to a claim that the agreements are illusory."

b. Would your answer change if the original agreement had clearly disclosed that the bank could unilaterally change *or add* terms? Cf., Mandel v. Household Bank (Nev.), N.A., 129 Cal.Rptr.2d 380 (Cal. Ct. App. 4th Dist. 2005)[applying Nevada law].

c. Could Sandra argue that, even if the changed or new term is permissible as a matter of contract formation, the resulting term is unconscionable? On what grounds? Challenges to arbitration clauses on the ground of unconscionability are discussed further in Chapter 10.

Problem 6–6

Left Bank's credit card account agreements originally contained a generic change-in-terms provision that permitted the Bank "to change the rates, fees, and terms, at any time and for any reason." Bank later notified its credit card customers that it was changing that change-in-terms provision to add this qualification:

> "These reasons may be based on information in your credit report, such as your failure to make payments to another creditor when due, amounts owed to other creditors, the number of credit accounts outstanding, or the number of credit inquiries."

Sebastian received this notice, wasn't sure what it meant, and continued to use his credit card as he had always done. Sebastian was meticulous in making timely payments on his credit card account with Left Bank, and on all his credit obligations. He was therefore stunned to receive a notice from Left Bank advising that the rate on his credit card was being increased from 12% APR to 23% APR, and he demanded an explanation from Left Bank. The bank told Sebastian that there had been a number of requests for credit reports on him from other creditors, and that these inquiries changed the Bank's credit profile on him to a higher risk category.

Sebastian thinks it is preposterous that the bank can almost double his interest rate when he has a perfect payment record on all his debts, and the inquiries by other creditors were the result of his shopping around to a number of lenders for the best rates on a new home equity credit line.

Is there anything legally wrong with the Bank's practice here? Is the problem with the change-in-terms provision itself, or with the nature of the change being made?

Notes

1. The practice involved in the preceding problem is called "universal default," connoting that the creditor may treat as a default under its customer agreement any delinquency, default, or change in risk profile under any other credit account of that customer, or under the customer's credit report as a whole. (Note that creditors are allowed to get credit reports on existing customers in order to monitor their overall credit worthiness, Fair Credit Reporting Act, 15 U.S.C. § 1681b(a)(3)(F)(ii).) Creditors that use this universal-default technique believe it is a sound actuarial practice that permits them to differentiate fairly among their customers, and impose higher costs or fees only on those customers who are statistically predictable to be more prone to default. Those who dislike universal default argue that it is unfair and somehow discriminatory to make a customer pay a premium to Creditor A because of a delinquency to Creditor B. Others, some from each side, believe that universal default is terrible customer relations, whether lawful or not.

2. The Truth in Lending Act imposes an advance notice requirement when card issuers change certain terms. Reg. Z § 226.9(c). Would that requirement have applied in the *Garber* case, supra? Would it apply in the Problem 6–5 cases, supra, where the changed term was the addition of a mandatory arbitration provision? Would it apply in Problem 6–6, supra, where the change was to adopt a universal default policy? Does the TILA

disclosure regarding changes in terms add anything of value for the consumer? That is, if the bank wants to change a contractual term, doesn't the bank have to communicate that new term (as an "offer," under *Garber*) to the consumer?

3. What is the consumer to do, on receipt of a change-in-terms notice, if the consumer does not wish to accept the changed term? Can the consumer simply write back to the bank and say: "Thanks for offering to increase my APR from 12 to 23%, but I decline your offer. I prefer to continue using my card at the old rate."? Both by state law, and widespread industry practice, change-in-terms notices give consumers the right to opt out or refuse the new or modified term. But to do so, the customer must destroy or return the card, or at least discontinue using it. How realistic is it for a consumer to do this, if the consumer has been relying on the card as a source of credit and has no other credit cards or other supply of funds?

4. Are there comparable change-in-terms issues in closed-end credit, like auto loans or home mortgages? The answer is, in part, no, because there is no way for a closed-end creditor to impose a changed term on the consumer who can stand on the terms of the agreement originally made. But the answer is also partially yes, because the creditor can structure the closed-end transaction to have variable, or adjustable, price terms. This is common for variable-rate mortgages (where the interest rate fluctuates with an index), or mortgages with adjustable payment amounts. Provisions such as prepayment penalties, due-on-sale clauses, assumption fees, or "payable on demand" features, also allow the creditor to recoup some extra revenue if those trigger events occur. The difference, of course, is that these cost variants are included in the credit agreement from the outset (and presumably disclosed), rather than foisted on the consumer through a change-in-terms notice months or years later.

Problem 6–7

Same facts as Problem 6–6, except that Left Bank's change-in-terms notice applied to fees imposed in its customers' checking accounts, rather than their credit card accounts. Is there anything about a deposit account agreement that makes it more, or less, susceptible to unilateral change-in-terms notices? See Perdue v. Crocker National Bank, 38 Cal.3d 913, 216 Cal.Rptr. 345, 702 P.2d 503 (1985) [changes in fees for overdrawn checks].

Note: Fees and More Fees

1. Over recent years financial institutions have been "unbundling" the pricing of their financial products and services. They charge an ever-wider variety of fees in connection with credit and debit card plans, checking accounts, and other payment and deposit services. And those fees and charges seem to be getting larger and larger. Some of these fees are "delinquency" charges, such as for late payments, sending a payment check that bounces, exceeding a credit limit, or drawing overdrafts on a checking account, not to mention substantial charges for collection, including attorney's fees. Other fees are attributable to "service" features on the account, such as for copies of cancelled checks, or pads of new checks, or per-item fees

for checks the consumer writes, or international currency exchange fees for advancing funds through ATMs overseas. Another category can also include fees for services or products that are "optional" additions to the account, such as for expediting a customer's payment to meet a deadline, or for credit insurance or "debt cancellation agreements" that relieve the consumer from certain payment responsibilities. Sometimes a "fee" may be small and virtually invisible but no less real. Consider Berenson v. National Financial Services, LLC, 403 F.Supp.2d 133 (D.Mass 2005): Consumer had entered into an electronic bill payment arrangement ("BillPay") with defendant, in which defendant would debit the customer's account several days before actually transmitting the funds to the designated payees. Customer argued that the several days of lost interest on those debited funds should be disclosed as a "fee" under the EFTA. The court agreed that there was enough to the argument to let it go to trial, and denied defendant's motion for summary judgment.

In isolation, each of these fees may be no worse than a mild irritation. But in the aggregate, or when the fees are collected again and again over time, the grievance effect—and the financial cost—multiplies. A question worth asking, then, is to what extent does the law protect consumers from a broad proliferation of account-related fees, or from fees that seem arbitrary, inflated, or otherwise unreasonable. The answer, we submit, is not very much.

2. Historically, in credit transactions, the permissibility of various fees was closely related to the issue of usury. That is, if the fee was not independently justifiable, it would be treated as part of the cost of the credit and might well push the effective rate of interest over the legal line. The case excerpt that follows is a typical judicial response to a challenge to late fees and "extension" fees. The broader aspects of usury are discussed in Chapter 9.

HAYES v. FIRST NAT'L BANK OF MEMPHIS

Supreme Court of Arkansas, 1974.
256 Ark. 328, 507 S.W.2d 701.

[*Eds.*: The plaintiffs asserted that two fees applied to their closed-end mobile home loan made the loan usurious: (1) a $5 charge imposed on several payments that came in late, and (2) an extension charge of $41 for pushing back (deferring) the remaining payment schedule for 60 days.]

FOGELMAN, JUSTICE.

The question presented by this appeal is whether "late charges" made on an installment purchase contract and a charge made for an extension agreement voided the entire debt for usury. We conclude that they did not.

* * *

We have held that a "late charge" is in the nature of a penalty for delinquency and does not render the transaction usurious, even when provided for in the instrument evidencing it. The rationale of these cases and others like them is that agreements for penalties to induce prompt payment are free from usury, because the buyer has it in his power to avoid the penalty by discharging the debt when it is due. This is not to say that an agreement of this sort will not be declared usurious if it is shown to be mere contrivance to avoid usury and the real intention is a loan or forbearance of money and the taking of more than legal interest. But such an intention must first be made manifest from the agreement itself or from extraneous proof. * * *

The payment for the extension is a different matter. There can be no doubt that it is a charge for the forbearance of money, which simply means that the person to whom it is due foregoes payment in cash and waits for all or part of his money until a later date. We have not attempted to apply the test mathematically, however, because, even if the extension agreement was usurious, the original contract is not tainted by it, because the facts and circumstances existing at the time that contract was entered into, rather than the subsequent actions of the parties, determine whether it is usurious. * * *

Notes

1. Many state laws specifically authorize certain fees over and above the usury limits for interest, or "finance charge," imposed in credit transactions. E.g., U3C § 2.501. State laws also commonly limit the amount of late payment or deferral charges. Cf. U3C §§ 2.502, 2.503. And the FTC Credit Practices Rule, 16 C.F.R. § 444.4, makes it an unfair practice to "pyramid" late charges, i.e., to impose a late charge "when the only delinquency is attributable to late fee(s) or delinquency charge(s) assessed on earlier installment(s)."

2. One kind of extra credit charge may have bitten the dust in recent years. This is so-called "non-filing insurance," which (theoretically) protects a creditor from loss resulting from failure to file a UCC financing statement to perfect its security interest in debtor's collateral. See, e.g., Regulation Z § 226.4(e)(3), excluding non-filing insurance from the finance charge for TILA disclosure purposes. The U3C also treats non-filing insurance as "official fees," permitted as "additional charges." U3C §§ 2.501(1)(a); 1.301(27)(b). The courts have recognized that the actual risk from not filing a financing statement is almost non-existent, and that creditors were using non-filing insurance in fact as default insurance, i.e., to cover losses from debtors who filed bankruptcy, skipped town, or otherwise just couldn't pay. See Adams v. Plaza Finance Co., Inc., 168 F.3d 932 (7th Cir. 1999).

Problem 6–8

Buck N. Hamm borrowed $4,000 from Fleur D. Lee, and was obligated to pay it back at a rate of $100 per month due on the first of each month. The contract also provided that Fleur could assess a late charge of $5 for any payment more than 20 days late. The January, February, and March payments were on time. The April payment was three weeks late (it was tax time). The May, June, and July payments were all paid on time. Fleur's computer assessed Buck a $5 late charge in April, applied $5 of the May payment to the April late charge; this made the May payment short, so the computer assessed another $5 for May, applied $5 of the June payment to cover it, and will continue doing this forever. Is this permissible under the U3C and FTC rules cited in Note 1 above?

Suppose Buck had missed the April payment completely, but then made the May, June, and subsequent payments on time. Can Fleur allocate the May payment to April, and the June payment to May, and so on, technically making each of those subsequent payments late, and then impose a new $5 late charge each month? Or could Fleur simply impose a new $5 late charge for each month the April payment remains outstanding?

Problem 6–9

Suppose Buck's loan from Fleur is an open-end credit plan, like a credit card or home-equity line of credit. If a payment is late, interest of course continues to accrue on the unpaid amount, doesn't it? Should a creditor be able to recover both that accrued interest plus a late charge of, say, $39?

Notes: Banks' "Exporting" of Interest Rates and Fees, and Preemption of State Limits on Non–Interest Fees and Charges

1.   State law restraints on fees and charges imposed by banks in credit transactions are largely moot. This is because federal law allows banks to "export" the interest rates and fees permissible in the bank's home state. Banks engaged in national marketing of credit cards or other credit products therefore tend to locate themselves in states where rates and fees are deregulated. We will look more extensively at this exporting phenomenon in Chapter 9. The Comptroller of the Currency confirms the rates-and-fees privilege for national (i.e., federally chartered) banks in 12 C.F.R. § 7.4001, defining exportable "interest" to include:

> the following fees connected with credit extension or availability: numerical periodic rates, late fees, creditor-imposed not sufficient funds (NSF) fees charged when a borrower tenders payment on a debt with a check drawn on insufficient funds, overlimit fees, annual fees, cash advance fees, and membership fees. * * *

Thus, national banks can export not only explicit interest rates, but most other credit fees as well, so long as those fees are allowed by the bank's home state.

2.   Federal law creates a similar preemptive effect on state laws regulating non-interest fees and charges imposed by banks in connection with checking, savings, and similar deposit accounts. A companion regulation of the OCC, 12 C.F.R. § 7.4002, puts it this way:

> (a) *Authority to impose charges and fees.* A national bank may charge its customers non-interest charges and fees, including deposit account service charges.

(b) *Considerations.* (1) All charges and fees should be arrived at by each bank on a competitive basis and not on the basis of any agreement, arrangement, undertaking, understanding, or discussion with other banks or their officers. (2) The establishment of non-interest charges and fees, their amounts, and the method of calculating them are business decisions to be made by each bank, in its discretion, according to sound banking judgment and safe and sound banking principles. A national bank establishes non-interest charges and fees in accordance with safe and sound banking principles if the bank employs a decision-making process through which it considers the following factors, among others:

(1) The cost incurred by the bank in providing the service;

(2) The deterrence of misuse by customers of banking services;

(3) The enhancement of the competitive position of the bank in accordance with the bank's business plan and marketing strategy; and

(4) The maintenance of the safety and soundness of the institution.

* * *

(d) *State law.* The OCC applies preemption principles derived from the United States Constitution, as interpreted through judicial precedent, when determining whether State laws apply that purport to limit or prohibit charges and fees described in this section. * * *

Query: Is the thrust of this regulation to protect consumers from being gouged, or to encourage banks to make money from fee revenues?

Problem 6–10

Firstbank (a national bank) imposes a fee of $49.00 on any customer who deposits a check into an account at Firstbank if that check is dishonored and returned by the bank on which it was drawn. Lemuel is a customer of Firstbank who has been stuck with such a charge. He has developed reliable data that the actual cost to the bank of handling such returned checks is no more than $5.00 per item; this includes personnel time involved in processing the charge-back to the customer's account, and postage to return the bounced check to the customer. Lemuel contacts the OCC to complain that this fee is unfair, on two grounds: (1) the fee is grossly disproportionate to any costs incurred by the bank in handling returned checks, and so represents windfall profits, and (2) it is unconscionable to penalize Lemuel when the bounced check was not his fault—it was issued by someone else who didn't keep a sufficient balance in his account.

What reception is Lemuel's complaint likely to receive from the OCC? From a court?

Notes

1. A government study, done at the request of a congressional committee, has acknowledged the "un-bundling" pattern, finding that, indeed,

credit card fees and charges have mushroomed, while the underlying interest rates have flattened or decreased:

> Since about 1990, the pricing structures of credit cards have evolved to encompass a greater variety of interest rates and fees that can increase cardholder's costs; however, cardholders generally are assessed lower interest rates than those that prevailed in the past, and most have not been assessed penalty fees. For many years after being introduced, credit cards generally charged fixed single rates of interest of around 20 percent, had few fees, and were offered only to consumers with high credit standing. After 1990, card issuers began to introduce cards with a greater variety of interest rates and fees, and the amounts that cardholders can be charged have been growing. For example, our analysis of 28 popular cards and other information indicates that cardholders could be charged

> - up to three different interest rates for different transactions, such as one rate for purchases and another for cash advances, with rates for purchases that ranged from about 8 percent to about 19 percent;
>
> - penalty fees for certain cardholder actions, such as making a late payment (an average of almost $34 in 2005, up from an average of about $13 in 1995) or exceeding a credit limit (an average of about $31 in 2005, up from about $13 in 1995); and
>
> - a higher interest rate—some charging over 30 percent—as a penalty for exhibiting riskier behavior, such as paying late.

U.S. Government Accountability Office, Report: Credit Cards: Increased Complexity in Rates and Fees Heightens Need for More Effective Disclosures to Consumers 4–5 (September 2006).

2. But what to do about this proliferation of fees phenomenon? The GAO Report suggests (rather meekly, we believe) that the "Federal Reserve should ensure that [credit card] disclosures more clearly emphasize those terms that can significantly affect cardholder costs, such as the actions that can cause default or other penalty pricing rates to be imposed." *Id.* at 79. Recall the material in Chapter 2 on TILA disclosures. Is it as simple as the GAO seems to assume to layer new "clearly emphasize[d]" disclosures on top of the existing disclosure requirements? What of the barriers of information overload, and consumer financial illiteracy?

3. Another approach could be to cut away the complexity of credit card fee structures by prohibiting certain potentially unfair terms or fees altogether, or requiring a certain standardization of credit card plans for those terms that remain, or both. Ronald J. Mann, Contracting for Credit, 104 Mich. L. Rev. 899 (2006). Professor Mann notes that standardized contracts prevail in the mortgage markets, at least for mortgages eligible for purchase by Fannie Mae (FNMA). *Id.* at 927–28.

4. Yet another approach might be to set a broad norm that prohibits pricing practices that are unduly inflated and so generate unnecessary transaction costs for consumers. This could be applied not just to credit card fees, but to all consumer transactions. Jeff Sovern, Toward a New Model of Consumer Protection: The Problem of Inflated Transaction Costs, 47 Wm. &

Mary L. Rev. 1635 (2006). Is this a precise enough standard to be applied by courts? By legislatures?

SECTION D.   BILLING DISPUTES: ACCOUNT (MIS)MANAGEMENT

Many different kinds of problems can arise in the course of consumer account relationships, problems that often defy solution under conventional contract principles. The materials that follow address some of these recurring problems, both for credit cards and debit cards. The legal system traditionally drew a sharp distinction between debit and credit, and the rules you will study in this section reflect this. As you work your way through the materials, you should consider whether the legal system has responded adequately to the growing tendency in the consumer finance industry to blur this traditional distinction.

Note on Source Materials

Most of the rules regulating the consumer credit card relationship are found in the Truth in Lending Act, especially in chapter 4 of the TILA (enacted separately in 1974 as the "Fair Credit Billing Act," or FCBA), §§ 161–171, 15 USC §§ 1666–1666j. The Reg. Z counterparts can be found generally in §§ 226.12 and 226.13.

For debit cards, another federal statute applies. This is the Electronic Fund Transfer Act of 1978, 15 U.S.C.A. §§ 1693–1693r. The EFTA was codified as Title IX of the federal Consumer Credit Protection Act. It, too, carries with it a Federal Reserve Board regulation, Reg. E, 12 C.F.R. Part 205. Both the EFTA and Reg. E appear in the statutory supplement.

Problem 6–11

Joachim McGillicuddy receives his monthly MasterCard billing statement from Big Bank, the bank which issued Joachim's card. The statement contains a charge for $43 for "lingerie" purchased from a store in Reno, Nevada. Joachim thinks to himself, "I'm no transvestite, and besides, I've never even been to Reno. There must be some mistake." He writes a careful letter to Big Bank, explaining that there must be another Joachim McGillicuddy somewhere whose charge was erroneously put on his statement. Joachim gets no reply, but next month gets another statement. He writes again. No answer. He calls. And calls. Finally he sends a collect telegram. Six months after Joachim received the first erroneous statement, Big writes to Joachim, saying it has checked the sales slip and believes it is in fact his signature. Big therefore "regrets" it could not respond more promptly, but flatly refuses to credit Joachim with either the $43 or the $4.02 in finance charges that accrued over the six months.

(a) Do any of the disclosure or regulatory rules we have encountered thus far provide Joachim with any usable rights against Big Bank? Is there any way Joachim could force Big to adjust his account promptly? (Couldn't he just cancel his card?)

(b) It was largely in response to stories like this one that Congress enacted the Fair Credit Billing Act (cited above in Note on Source Materials). What are the rights and duties of Joachim and Big Bank under the FCBA? See Reg. Z § 226.13.

Notes

1. What is a "billing error" that triggers the FCBA error-resolution provisions? In Problem 6–11, for example, could Joachim invoke these provisions if his monthly statement reflected a charge for carpeting which he in fact had purchased, but which was never delivered by the store? Suppose the carpet was delivered and installed, but Joachim later discovered defects in it? See Reg. Z § 226.13(a). We will consider the question of the card issuer's potential liability for defective goods in Chapter 7.

2. Once a billing error procedure is initiated by the consumer, the card issuer must conduct a "reasonable investigation" of the claim. Reg. Z § 226.13(f). What does this require the issuer to do? For example, Joachim may claim that he does not remember making any purchase from a boutique in Reno. Big Bank may have received only an electronic transmission of transaction data through the MasterCard network; i.e., it may not have an actual copy of the sales slip submitted by the store. Must it contact the store to verify the transaction, such as by getting a copy of the sales slip (if one still exists)? See Reg. Z § 226.13(f) fn. 31. Could Big satisfy its duty by simply reviewing its own internal records? Many merchants now get customer signatures on an electronic pad. Should the card issuer be expected at least to retrieve the electronic signature when the customer disputes the charge? (Do such signatures look much like the customer's regular signature?)

3. Suppose Big Bank investigates promptly and reports to Joachim that it remains convinced of the genuineness of his signature on the Reno sales slip. What can Joachim do now? See Reg. Z § 226.13(h). Can Big cancel Joachim's card, or sue to recover the disputed $43? If it does, can it also report its actions to the local credit bureau?

4. How is a card holder supposed to know what to do in order to exercise his rights under the FCBA? For that matter, how is he supposed to know that he even has any rights? See Reg. Z §§ 226.6(d) and 226.7(k). Suppose that on the day after Joachim received the statement showing the disputed lingerie charge, he called Big Bank and told it of the alleged error, and then sent a photocopy of the statement with a circle around the disputed item. Would this be sufficient to trigger the FCBA procedures?

5. A related problem is that of the "shrinking billing period." Most credit card plans contain a "free ride" period, that is, they permit the cardholder to avoid finance charges on purchases by paying the entire balance within a certain period. Sometimes this period is stated in actual time, such as "within 25 days"; other times it is measured by reference to a stated due date. But what happens if the card issuer takes its time about getting the statement to the consumer? If the end of the free ride period is,

say, October 10, but the consumer doesn't get the statement until October 5, the benefit of the grace period is all but lost. Consumers complained about this problem, too, and Congress responded by including TILA § 163 in the Fair Credit Billing chapter of TILA. This section is clearly a compromise, is it not? Is it fair to consumers? To card issuers?

6. During the 1980s there was a shift from "country club" billing to "descriptive" billing systems. Creditors now give the consumer a monthly statement with brief, computer-generated descriptions of transactions during the billing period. Under "country club" billing, they had sent actual copies of the sales slips signed at the point of sale. In descriptive billing systems, the merchant's bank captures the payment and other information about the transaction, and then "truncates," or destroys, the sales slips. The information is then routed electronically to the card issuing bank. Naturally, this system is cheaper and more efficient to operate than the old paper-based "country club" systems. And, the less information required to be sent, the quicker and cheaper it is. But at some point, doesn't the terseness of the description make it difficult or impossible for the consumer to verify the statement?

What should be the limits of brevity in descriptive billing? Review the detailed provisions of Reg. Z § 226.8. If you use your VISA card to purchase half a dozen different items of cosmetics at a drugstore, what will your monthly statement "identify"? Would it be sufficient merely to say, for example, "Rexall #78, Ashtabula"? Would the description be any different if you used the drug store's own credit card? Should it be?

7. Are there any error resolution procedures for closed-end credit accounts? Should there be? Are consumers as likely to get into disputes with their closed-end creditors as with their credit card issuers? If they do get into disputes, should they have fewer rights? See Bailey v. Capitol Motors, Inc., 307 Md. 343, 513 A.2d 912 (1986); Jacobs v. Marine Midland Bank, N.A., 124 Misc.2d 162, 475 N.Y.S.2d 1003 (Sup.Ct.1984).

Problem 6–12

Paul Porter sought to withdraw $100 from his checking account at First Bank via the automated teller machine. When no money was dispensed, he reported the problem to a bank official (whose name he can no longer remember) and was told the matter would be investigated. A few weeks later, he tried to withdraw $200 through the ATM, and again no money appeared although he had pushed all the necessary buttons. He repeated the process a second time, to no avail. He again reported the problem to the bank management. To his dismay, his next bank statement showed one withdrawal of $100 and two of $200 which he never actually received. The next day, Porter comes to your office seeking legal advice on whether he can recover the $500. What will you tell him? See EFTA § 908 and Reg. E § 205.11. See also Porter v. Citibank, N.A., 123 Misc.2d 28, 472 N.Y.S.2d 582 (N.Y.City Civ.Ct.1984).

Notes

1. Are the error resolution procedures under the EFTA for debit cards comparable to those under the FCBA for credit cards? If not, how do they differ? Are there important transactional differences which justify different procedures? Don't forget that if a consumer disputes an item on a credit card bill, he can always refuse to pay until the dispute gets resolved. But if the bank charged the consumer's deposit account for an erroneous electronic debit, the consumer will lose the use of those funds while the dispute is pending unless the account is recredited during the interim. (People who live from paycheck to paycheck will understand the importance of this issue.) Is the bank required to recredit the consumer's account? See EFTA § 908(a) and (c); Reg. E § 205.11(c).

2. In disputes like the one illustrated in Problem 6–12, isn't the allocation of the burden of proof decisive? Who should have the burden of proof? Which party has access to the records which are most likely to reveal the truth? (Are *any* records likely to reveal the truth?) If the burden of proof is on the bank, isn't there a danger that consumers will make false claims? If so, is the danger any greater in consumer banking transactions than in other areas?

3. Why should error resolution procedures be limited to credit card and EFT accounts? Why shouldn't they apply as well to ordinary checking accounts? (They don't, do they? See the definition of "electronic fund transfer" in EFTA § 903(6).) Many checking accounts have EFT features as well; that is, consumers may write checks or use their debit cards against the same account. Normally, the consumer receives a single monthly statement showing all activity, both electronic and paper-based. If the statement contained some mistakes, would the error resolution procedures apply only to the EFT items, but not to the check items? Does this make sense?

4. Some observers have suggested that the statutory dispute-resolution procedures for credit and debit cards are preferable to handling disputes through the judicial process, precisely because they permit expeditious, low-cost, technology-based handling, even though the statutory procedures do not afford consumers all the components of traditional "due process." See Andrew P. Morriss & Jason Korosec, Private Dispute Resolution in the Card Context: Structure, Reputation, and Incentives, 1 Geo. Mason J. of Law, Economics & Policy 393 (2005). Do you agree?

Problem 6–13

Beulah has returned to Merchant some clothing she bought with her Visa card, and the Merchant has duly reported a credit to the card-issuing Bank. Since her Visa account was otherwise fully paid, this resulted in a credit balance for Beulah. If Beulah then doesn't use the card for several months, what obligation does the bank have with respect to that credit balance? Reg. Z § 226.11.

Assume Beulah made some purchases during the next month, so that some finance charge would accrue. Beulah now argues that this credit balance should be factored into any subsequent calculation of the "average daily balance" in the account. That is, overpayments or credits should be treated as negative entries that should be subtracted from any purchases or advances she makes, thus lowering her "average" balance and reducing the resulting finance charge amount. The bank responds that there is nothing in the law or the customer agreement that requires it to pay interest on credit balances (which would be the effect of such subtraction). What do you think? At very least, Beulah argues further, the Bank's disclosure of an "average daily balance" method for balance calculations is erroneous under Reg. Z § 226.6(a)(3) because the Bank does not calculate a real arithmetic "average." Cf., Hale v. MBNA America Bank, N.A., 2000 WL 1346812 (S.D. N.Y., 2000).

GALE v. HYDE PARK BANK

U.S. Court of Appeals, Seventh Circuit, 2004.
384 F.3d 451.

EASTERBROOK, CIRCUIT JUDGE.

In April 2002 Andrew Gale overdrew his checking account at Hyde Park Bank. He blamed the Bank, asserting that its delay in posting to his account a transaction in December 2001 with his debit card led him to think that the account contained a greater balance. He sued under the Electronic Funds Transfer Act, contending that the delay in posting the debit-card transaction violated 15 U.S.C. § 1693h(a)(1), which requires banks to make electronic fund transfers in a "timely manner". He also contended that the Bank had failed to provide him with information required by 15 U.S.C. § 1693f. The district court dismissed the complaint under Fed.R.Civ.P. 12(b)(6) for failure to state a claim on which relief may be granted. The district court wrote that the Bank had posted the transaction within 48 hours of its arrival through the interbank network, and that the merchant (or perhaps the network) rather than the Bank had been responsible for the delay.

The court's assumption that 48 hours was "timely" may be tenable, though both the statute and the implementing regulations leave that word undefined. See Donald I. Baker & Roland E. Brandel, *The Law of Electronic Fund Transfer Systems: Legal and Strategic Planning* ¶ 17.03[3][a] (2004 ed.). But in supposing that the Bank acted promptly after notification, the court relied on a view of the facts adverse to the plaintiff, which Rule 12(b)(6) does not permit. See *Hishon v. King & Spalding,* 467 U.S. 69, 104 S.Ct. 2229, 81 L.Ed.2d 59 (1984). It is not as if Gale had himself pleaded that the debit did not find its way to the Bank for four months after the retail transaction. This is the Bank's view of matters, not Gale's. That the Bank said the same thing to Gale in email messages that Gale attached to the complaint does not amount to a concession; the plaintiff may tell the court what his adversary has said without throwing in the towel. See *Carroll v. Yates,* 362 F.3d 984, 986 (7th Cir.2004). Anyway, attributing significance to the emails should have led the judge to convert the Bank's motion to one for summary judgment, as Rule 12(b) itself provides. What actually happened should be resolved by summary judgment or trial, not by decision on the pleadings.

Still, the district court's disposition was at least partly correct. To recover under § 1693h the plaintiff must show that a violation of the law led to injury, and Gale has pleaded himself out of court on that subject by demonstrating that his errors rather than the Bank's caused all loss. (The only loss appears to be the fee for overdrawing the account.) Gale's complaint shows that his failure to keep the account adequately funded is the root of the problem. Had the debit been posted in December 2001, and everything else remained the same, Gale still would have overdrawn the account in April 2002.

Using a debit card is like writing a check: Gale's contract with the Bank required him to record all transactions and ensure that the balance supports each new one, even if transactions are not yet posted (just as some checks may not be cashed immediately). The Bank sent Gale statements showing that his purchase in December 2001 had yet to be deducted from his account. Gale needed to keep on hand funds to cover all outstanding transactions; he failed to do this and cannot shift responsibility to the Bank.

The timeliness requirement is principally for the benefit of the person entitled to receipt of the funds. In other words, transferees are in the zone of interests protected by this aspect of the statute. Cf. *National Credit Union Administration v. First National Bank & Trust Co.,* 522 U.S. 479, 118 S. Ct. 927, 140 L.Ed.2d 1 (1998). Transferors usually are not, as delay gives them the benefit of the float. One can imagine an injury that transferors could suffer: if the merchant noticed the delay in payment and took steps that deprived the transferor of the benefit of the bargain, or adversely affected his credit rating, then there could be a compensable injury. Gale does not allege such events, however; his complaint and appellate brief show that his sole concern is ending up with an overdrawn account in April 2002. Failure to keep the account in funds cannot be a source of damages under § 1693h(a).

This leaves the claim based on § 1693f, which both the district court and the Bank's appellate brief let pass in silence. It is not so easily disposed of, because violations of that section (unlike violations of § 1693h) can lead to statutory damages even in the absence of injury. Compare 15 U.S.C. § 1693m(a)(2)(A) with § 1693h(c).

Section 1693f(a) provides that after a customer reports that an error has occurred, the financial institution must "investigate the alleged error, determine whether an error has occurred, and report or mail the results of such investigation and determination to the consumer within ten business days." Gale contends that he did not receive a timely report of "the results"; instead the Bank rejected his claim without much explanation. In other words, Gale contends, he got a "determination" but not "the results of such investigation" or the supporting documentation. See § 1693f(d) ("If the financial institution determines after its investigation pursuant to subsection (a) . . . that an error did not occur, it shall deliver or mail to the consumer an explanation of its findings within 3 business days after the conclusion of its investigation, and upon request of the consumer promptly deliver or mail to the consumer reproductions of all documents which the financial institution relied on to conclude that such error did not occur. The financial institution shall include notice of the right to request reproductions with the explanation of its findings.'').

Moreover, implementing regulations require financial institutions to provide customers with details of their error-resolution procedures and update these notices at least annually. 12 C.F.R. §§ 205.7(b)(10), 205.8(b). Gale's complaint can be read to allege that the Bank failed to give him this required information. Likewise it can be read to allege a violation of 12 C.F.R. § 205.11(a), which requires financial institutions to provide customers on request with ''additional information or clarification concerning an electronic fund transfer, including a request the consumer makes to determine whether an error exists''. Although the complaint did not cite these regulations, it did not have to. Complaints plead *claims,* not legal theories. See *Bartholet v. Reishauer A.G. (Zurich),* 953 F.2d 1073 (7th Cir.1992). All a complaint need do is narrate a claim for relief. See Fed.R.Civ.P. 8; *Swierkiewicz v. Sorema N.A.,* 534 U.S. 506, 122 S.Ct. 992, 152 L.Ed.2d 1 (2002). Gale's complaint met this standard. He is entitled to judicial resolution of that grievance.

The judgment is vacated, and the case is remanded for further proceedings on Gale's claim under § 1693f and the corresponding regulations.

Notes

1.   The court has little sympathy for Mr. Gale who can't keep track of the balance in his checking account. On the other hand, perhaps we can commiserate with him for overlooking a transaction from four months ago that has not been posted (i.e., charged) to the account. Still, why should the bank be exposed to litigation for a debit card processing delay that was not its fault?

2.   The court cites the EFTA, in particular15 U.S.C. § 1693h(a)(1), for the responsibility of a financial institution to make an electronic funds transfer in a ''timely manner.'' This requirement clearly applies to the customer's bank when the customer instructs it directly to make an electronic payment, such as through an Internet banking service. But does it apply to the merchant who accepts (and fails to transmit) a debit card payment instruction, or to the network through which the transfer is processed? Should it?

Prefatory Note: ''Wrongful Dishonor.'' What if the dispute escalates to the point that the card issuer cancels the card? Or, what if the card is simply ''wrongfully dishonored,'' even without a pre-existing dispute? There certainly is a dispute after the dishonor.

Problem 6–14

Following the advice he heard on TV, Fred Consumer never leaves home without his American Express card. He has embarked on a two-week vacation to Hawaii, and when he arrives at the hotel, he proffers his card to pay for his room. The clerk consults by phone with the American Express authorization service, and then tells Fred: "American Express says you are delinquent on your account. Your card is cancelled as of now, and I am instructed to keep it." Fred does not have enough cash or other credit cards to cover his hotel bill, and so has to cancel his vacation. Does he have a cause of action against American Express? Does the answer depend on whether American Express is correct or mistaken about Fred's delinquency?

GRAY v. AMERICAN EXPRESS CO.

U.S. Court of Appeals, District of Columbia Circuit, 1984.
743 F.2d 10.

MIKVA, CIRCUIT JUDGE.

We are called upon to determine what rights, if any, appellant Oscar Gray has against American Express arising from the circumstances under which it cancelled his American Express credit card. The District Court granted summary judgment to American Express; we vacate that judgment and remand for further proceedings.

I. BACKGROUND

Gray had been a cardholder since 1964. In 1981, following some complicated billings arising out of deferred travel charges incurred by Gray, disputes arose about the amount due American Express. After considerable correspondence, the pertinence and timeliness of which we will detail below, American Express decided to cancel Gray's card. No notification of this cancellation was communicated to Gray until the night of April 8, 1982, when he offered his American Express card to pay for a wedding anniversary dinner he and his wife already had consumed in a Washington restaurant. The restaurant informed Gray that American Express had refused to accept the charges for the meal and had instructed the restaurant to confiscate and destroy his card. Gray spoke to the American Express employee on the telephone at the restaurant who informed him, "Your account is cancelled as of now."

The cancellation prompted Gray to file a lengthy complaint in District Court, stating claims under both diversity and federal question jurisdiction. He alleged that the actions of American Express violated the contract between them, known as the "Cardmember Agreement," as well as the Fair Credit Billing Act (the "Act"), 15 U.S.C. §§ 1666–1666j, Pub.L. 93–495, Tit. III, 88 Stat. 1511 (1974). The District Court granted summary judgment for American Express and dismissed the complaint.

The surge in the use of credit cards, the "plastic money" of our society, has been so quick that the law has had difficulty keeping pace. It was not until 1974 that Congress passed the Act, first making a serious effort to regulate the relationship between a credit cardholder and the issuing company. We hold that the District Court was too swift to conclude that the Act offers no protection to Gray and further hold that longstanding principles of contract law afford Gray substantial rights. We thus vacate the District Court's judgment and remand.

II. Discussion

A. The Statutory Claim

Fair Credit Billing Act seeks to prescribe an orderly procedure for identifying and resolving disputes between a cardholder and a card issuer as to the amount due at any given time.

* * *

1. The Billing Error

The billing dispute in issue arose after Gray used his credit card to purchase airline tickets costing $9312. American Express agreed that Gray could pay for the tickets in 12 equal installments over 12 months. In January and February of 1981, Gray made substantial prepayments of $3500 and $1156 respectively. He so advised American Express by letter of February 8, 1981. There is no dispute about these payments, nor about Gray's handling of them. At this point the numbers become confusing because American Express, apparently in error, converted the deferred payment plan to a current charge on the March bill. American Express thereafter began to show Gray as delinquent, due at least in part to the dispute as to how and why the deferred billing had been converted to a current charge.

The District Court held that Gray failed to trigger the protection of the Act because he neglected to notify American Express in writing within 60 days after he first received an erroneous billing. Gray insists that his first letter to American Express on April 22, 1981, well within the 60 day period set forth in the statute, identified the dispute as it first appeared in the March, 1981 billing. According to Gray's complaint, the dispute continued to simmer for over a year because American Express never fulfilled its investigative and other obligations under the Act.

The District Court made no mention of the April 22, 1981 letter, deeming instead a September, 1981 letter as the first notification from Gray as to the existence of a dispute. We conclude that the District Court erred in overlooking the April letter.

Gray's April 22, 1981 letter complained specifically about the March bill and the miscrediting of the prepayments. Whatever the import and impact of other correspondence and actions of the parties, we hold that, through this earlier letter, Gray triggered the procedural protections of the Act. The letter enabled the card issuer to identify the name and account number, indicated that the cardholder believed that an error existed in a particular amount and set forth the cardholder's reasons why he believed an error had been made. The later correspondence and activities may be treated as evidentiary in nature—sufficient perhaps to show that American Express fulfilled all of its obligations under the Act, but not pertinent to the question of whether the Act was triggered in the first place.

2. *Reporting and Collection Efforts*

Gray alleged in count III that, notwithstanding his having given notice of dispute under § 1666 through his letters, American Express nevertheless turned over his account for collection to a bill collection agency. The District Judge dismissed this count (misdesignating it as count IV) by concluding that it failed to state a claim for relief. The District Court erred. *See* 15 U.S.C. §§ 1640(a), 1666a. We think that count III states an independent cause of action under § 1666a because Gray's April 22, 1981 correspondence brought the dispute within the Act's coverage. The question of American Express' compliance with the reporting and collection requirements of the Act also warrants consideration on remand.

3. *The Act and the Cardmember Agreement*

As we have indicated above, the District Court summarily resolved Gray's statutory claims by wrongly concluding that the Act did not apply. On appeal, American Express also urges that, even if the Act is otherwise pertinent, Gray was bound by the terms of the Cardmember Agreement which empowered American Express to cancel the credit card without notice and without cause. The contract between Gray and American Express provides:

> [W]e can revoke your right to use [the card] at any time. We can do this with or without cause and without giving you notice.

American Express concludes from this language that the cancellation was not of the kind prohibited by the Act, even though the Act regulates other aspects of the relationship between the cardholder and the card issuer.

Section 1666(d) of the Act states that, during the pendency of a disputed billing, the card issuer, until it fulfills its other obligations under § 1666(a)(B)(ii), shall not cause the cardholder's account to be restricted or closed because of the failure of the obligor to pay the amount in dispute. *See also* 12 C.F.R. § 226.14(d). American Express seems to argue that, despite that provision, it can exercise its right to cancellation for cause unrelated to the disputed amount, or for no cause, thus bringing itself out from under the statute. At the very least, the argument is audacious. American Express would restrict the efficacy of the statute to those situations where the parties had not agreed to a "without cause, without notice" cancellation clause, or to those cases where the cardholder can prove that the sole reason for cancellation was the amount in dispute. We doubt that Congress painted with such a faint brush.

The effect of American Express's argument is to allow the equivalent of a "waiver" of coverage of the Act simply by allowing the parties to contract it away. Congress usually is not so tepid in its approach to consumer problems. See 118 Cong.Rec. 14,835 (1972) (remarks by Sen.

Proxmire, principal proponent of the Act, concerning a technical amendment to a predecessor bill later carried over into the Act; its purpose was to prevent "possible evasion" by precluding the creditor from including a pre-dispute waiver provision in the card agreement); 119 Cong.Rec. 25,400 (1973) (remarks by Sen. Proxmire on S. 2101, another predecessor: "The legislation seeks to establish a system for insuring that billing disputes or inquiries are resolved in a fair and timely manner.") (emphasis added).

Moreover, the consumer-oriented statutes that Congress has enacted in recent years belie the unrestrained reading that American Express gives to the Act in light of its contract. Waiver of statutory rights, particularly by a contract of adhesion, is hardly consistent with the legislature's purpose. The rationale of consumer protection legislation is to even out the inequalities that consumers normally bring to the bargain. To allow such protection to be waived by boiler plate language of the contract puts the legislative process to a foolish and unproductive task. A court ought not impute such nonsense to a Congress intent on correcting abuses in the market place.

* * *

Thus we hold that the Act's notice provision was met by Gray's April 22, 1981 letter and remand the case to the District Court for trial of Gray's statutory cause of action. American Express will be obliged to justify its conduct in this case as fully satisfying its obligations under the Act.

* * *

C. *Discovery*

Because the case is to be remanded for further proceedings, we think it appropriate to comment on the appellee's extraordinary use of interrogatories below. It appears to be of some significance to this case that Gray is a lawyer, because only a lawyer, tenacious even beyond the professional custom, would have been able to withstand the expenses and excesses of this litigation. Perhaps the presence of a lawyer-plaintiff caused American Express particular concern that occasioned their plethora of interrogatories; perhaps it was the shorter, but nonetheless substantial, set of interrogatories that plaintiff served on defendant. Whoever was the instigator and whatever the reason, the various sets of interrogatories and their answers are in the hundreds of pages. They run as far afield as inquiring the name of every law firm that plaintiff had been affiliated with since 1951 to asking all of the "professional credentials" that he had acquired in his lifetime; from psychiatrists consulted since 1978 to meals eaten at the fated restaurant since the suit was filed. The length, scope and detail of the interrogatories propounded by American Express suggest a strategy of attrition rather than a legitimate discovery of the facts needed to resolve a dispute over the account.

* * *

On remand, we think the trial court should take the quantity and relevance of the discovery into account in setting the case for trial and in determining what, if any, further discovery should be allowed, and in deciding whether sanctions for abusive litigation practices are appropriate.

The size of the record and the vigor with which the defenses have been pursued make it apparent that only a stubborn professional could seek to avail himself of the protection guaranteed by statute and the common law. The courts must exercise control so that access to justice is not foreclosed by such tactics at the preliminary stages of suit. Deep pockets and stubbornness ought not be prerequisites to bringing a case like this one to issue.

Conclusion

The District Court's order of summary judgment and dismissal is hereby vacated. The case is remanded for further proceedings consistent with this opinion.

So Ordered.

Problem 6–15

Caroline has arranged with her Bank to receive her paycheck by electronic deposit each month. She also has arranged with the Bank for electronic bill payment of certain of her recurring obligations, including payment of premiums on her home-owner's casualty insurance policy. At the end of August, the Bank's system malfunctions and fails to credit Caroline's deposit account with her paycheck. As a result, there are insufficient funds in the account to cover her insurance payment. Caroline is unaware of these problems because she has embarked on a month-long business trip. Because of the lack of funds, the Bank does not pay the insurance premium, While Caroline is gone, a hurricane sweeps her city, substantially damaging her home. The insurance company refuses to cover the loss, claiming the policy lapsed for non-payment of premiums. Does Caroline have a claim against Bank? See EFTA § 910.

SECTION E.   UNAUTHORIZED USE

The three most likely forms of consumer payment (other than cash) are personal check, credit card, and debit card. The most familiar to most of us is probably the check. There is a well-developed body of law concerning liability for forged or unauthorized checks. The bank may not charge its customer's account for any check which is not "properly payable." See Uniform Commercial Code (UCC) § 4–401. Further, any unauthorized signature is "ineffective" to bind a customer. UCC § 3–403(a). As a result, a consumer whose check book is stolen and whose signature is forged is not responsible for payment of the forged checks. If the bank has charged its customer's account for these checks, it must reimburse the customer, unless the bank can demonstrate that the customer has ratified the payment or that the customer's negligence contributed to the forgery. See UCC §§ 3–403, 3–406, 4–406.

Does this approach make sense in the credit card or debit card context? Whether it does or not, Congress took a different approach. In fact, Congress took different approaches for credit cards and for debit cards, and neither approach matches that for checks. As you read the following materials, you should consider whether it makes any sense to have different rules for allocating losses due to forgeries and other frauds for each type of payment. After all, why should a consumer's risk vary according to which piece of plastic he pulls out of his pocket? Or, to be more precise, why should the risk vary according to which piece of plastic the thief pulls out of the consumer's stolen wallet?

Problem 6–16

As noted, the UCC generally puts the risk of forged checks on the drawee bank, and gives the customer up to a year to report such forgeries. UCC §§ 4–401, 4–406. UCC § 4–103(a) also provides that a bank cannot disclaim its obligations of good faith and ordinary care, although the bank may by agreement with its customer, set "the standards by which the bank's responsibility is to be measured if those standards are not manifestly unreasonable."

Secondbank asks your advice on whether it can include the following in its signature-card customer agreements:

Customer agrees that bank is not responsible for any fraudulently signed or altered check if the check is forged or altered so cleverly that such fraud could not reasonably be detected. In any case, the bank will not be liable unless customer reports the fraud to the bank within 30 days after the bank sends to customer a statement covering the fraudulent check.

What is your advice?

Problem 6–17

Robin Hood steals Sam Tudent's wallet with his MasterCard in it. Sam never notifies the issuing bank of the theft. During the next 30 days, Hood charges $1500 worth of goods and services on Sam's Master-Card, each charge being less than $50. What must the issuing bank plead and prove before it can recover anything from Sam? If it does plead and prove all those things, how much is it entitled to recover? How many "unauthorized uses" occurred?

Problem 6–18

Sam Tudent has used his Visa credit card for a year now, and it is about to expire. The Bank that issued the card sends him a replacement credit card, but Sam is so irritated at Bank because of the way it has handled his account that he throws both the new and the old credit cards in the trash. Someone retrieved the new Visa card and purchased goods worth $1000 with it.

Was this an "unauthorized use" of the Visa credit card? See TILA § 133. Was the replacement card an "accepted" credit card? (Was it "accepted" by Sam?) See TILA § 103(l) and Reg. Z § 226.12(a) and footnote 21. If the credit card is an "accepted credit card" under the TILA, what effect does that have on whether the purchaser is an "authorized user" of the credit card or not? Would the answer or the analysis change if the new card required an "activation" call from the card holder's home number?

Problem 6–19

Sally Tudent has used her Visa debit card to access funds in her deposit account for a year now, and it is about to expire. Bank sends her a replacement Visa debit card. However, Sally doesn't like either the ATMs or the debit cards, so she throws both the new and the old debit cards in the trash. From then on, she plans to access the funds in her account only by checks. Someone retrieves the new debit card and immediately takes it to First Bank's nearest ATM and uses it to withdraw $100 in cash.

Is this an "unauthorized transfer" under the EFTA? See EFTA § 903(1). Is there any reason to treat this situation differently from the situation in Problem 6–18? Please consider not only the language of the statutes and regulations, but also the various risks to the parties involved in each situation.

Courts have applied common law agency principles to interpret questions involving unauthorized signatures on negotiable instruments. See UCC §§ 3–403 and 3–404. Can this approach be used successfully in other payment systems? What about in credit card transactions? See TILA § 103(o), and Walker Bank & Trust Co. v. Jones, infra. How about in debit card transactions? See EFTA § 903(11). Are the terms "actual, implied or apparent authority" any more clearly defined than they are in the UCC? Is the definition found in EFTA § 903(11) a step towards more clear boundaries for liability, or is it more confusing than the application of common law principles? Do we need the definitions to be clearer?

WALKER BANK & TRUST CO. v. JONES

Supreme Court of Utah, 1983.
672 P.2d 73, cert. denied 466 U.S. 937, 104 S.Ct. 1911, 80 L.Ed.2d 460 (1984).

HALL, CHIEF JUSTICE:

At issue in these consolidated cases is the liability of defendants to plaintiff Walker Bank for expenses allegedly incurred by defendants' separated spouses upon credit card accounts established by the plaintiff bank in the names of the defendants. Defendants appeal from adverse summary judgment orders on the grounds that their rights under the Federal Truth in Lending Act were violated.

A. DEFENDANT BETTY JONES

In 1977, Defendant Jones established VISA and Master Charge accounts with plaintiff Walker Bank (hereinafter "Bank"). Upon her request, credit cards were issued on those accounts to herself and her husband in each of their names.

On or about November 11, 1977, defendant Jones informed the Bank, by two separate letters, that she would no longer honor charges made by her husband on the two accounts, whereupon the Bank immediately revoked both accounts and requested the return of the credit cards. Despite numerous notices of revocation and requests for surrender of the cards, both defendant Jones and her husband retained their cards and continued to make charges against the accounts.

It was not until March 9, 1978, that defendant Jones finally relinquished her credit cards to the Bank, and then only after a persuasive visit to her place of employment by a Bank employee. At the time she surrendered her cards, the balance owing on the combined accounts (VISA and Master Charge) was $2,685.70. Her refusal to pay this balance prompted the Bank's institution of this suit to recover the same.

B. DEFENDANT GLORIA HARLAN

In July, 1979, defendant Harlan, who was prior to that time a VISA cardholder at plaintiff Bank, requested that her husband, John Harlan, be added to the account as an authorized user. The Bank honored this request and issued a card to Mr. Harlan. Shortly thereafter, at some point between July and the end of 1979, the Harlans separated and defendant (Mrs.) Harlan informed the Bank by letter that she either wanted the account closed or wanted the Bank to deny further extensions of credit to her husband.

Notwithstanding the explicit requirement in the account agreement that all outstanding credit cards be returned to the Bank in order to close the account, defendant Harlan did not tender either her card or her husband's at the time she made the aforementioned request. As to her card, she informed the Bank that she could not return it because it had been destroyed in the Bank's automated teller. Notwithstanding, however, she returned the card to the Bank some three months later (March, 1980).

In the interim period, i.e., after defendant's correspondence with the Bank regarding the exclusion of her husband from her account and prior to the relinquishment of her card, several charges were made (purportedly by Mr. Harlan) on the account for which the Bank now seeks recovery. The Bank has sued only Mrs. Harlan, as owner of the account.

Defendants' sole contention on appeal is that the Federal Truth in Lending Act (hereinafter "TILA") limits their liability, for the unauthorized use of the credit cards by their husbands, to a maximum of $50. The specific section of the Act upon which this contention rests is 15 U.S.C. § 1643.

* * *

The Bank's rejoinder is that § 1643 does not apply, inasmuch as defendants' husbands' use of the credit cards was at no time "unauthorized use" within the meaning of the statute. Whether such use was "unauthorized," as that term is contemplated by the statute, is the pivotal question in this case.

* * *

Defendants' [sic] aver that the effect of their notification to the Bank stating that they would no longer be responsible for charges made against their accounts by their husbands was to render any subsequent use (by their husbands) of the cards unauthorized. This notification, defendants maintain, was all that was necessary to revoke the authority they had once created in their husbands and thereby invoke the § 1643 limitations on cardholder liability.

The Bank's position is that unauthorized use within the meaning of § 1643 is precisely what the statutory definition (§ 1602(*o*) *supra*) says it is, to wit: "[U]se * * * by a person * * * who does not have actual, implied, or apparent authority * * *," and that notification to the card issuer has no bearing whatsoever on whether the use is unauthorized, so as to entitle a cardholder to the statutory limitation of liability. We agree with this position.

* * *

The Bank maintains that defendants' husbands clearly had "apparent" authority to use the cards, inasmuch as their signatures were the same as the signatures on the cards, and their names, the same as those imprinted upon the cards. Accordingly, it contends that no unauthorized use was made of the cards, and that defendants therefore cannot invoke the limitations on liability provided by the TILA.

Again, we find the Bank's position to be meritorious. Apparent authority exists:

> [W]here a person has created such an appearance of things that it causes a third party reasonably and prudently to believe that a second party has the power to act on behalf of the first person * * *[5]

As previously pointed out, at defendants' request their husbands were issued cards bearing the husbands' own names and signatures. These cards were, therefore, a representation to the merchants (third parties) to whom they were presented that defendants' husbands (second parties—cardbearers) were authorized to make charges upon the defendants' (first parties—cardholders) accounts. This apparent authority conferred upon defendants' husbands by reason of the credit cards thus precluded the application of the TILA.

In view of our determination that the TILA has no application to the present case, we hold that liability for defendants' husbands' use of the cards is governed by their contracts with the Bank. The contractual agreements between defendants and the Bank provided clearly and

---

5. *Wynn v. McMahon Ford Co.,* Mo. App., 414 S.W.2d 330, 336 (1967).

unequivocally that *all* cards issued upon the accounts be returned to the Bank in order to terminate defendants' liability. Accordingly, defendants' refusal to relinquish either their cards or their husbands', at the time they notified the Bank that they no longer accepted liability for their husbands' charges, justified the Bank's disregard of that notification and refusal to terminate defendants' liability at that time.

The dissent expresses concern that the decision of the Court imposes an unreasonable burden on the cardholder. We disagree because in our opinion justice is better served by placing the responsibility for the credit escapades of an errant spouse (or son, daughter, mother, father, etc.) on the cardholder rather than the Bank. The cardholder is not left powerless to protect against misuse of the card. He or she need only surrender the cards and close the account, just as the defendants in the instant case were requested by the Bank to do.

Affirmed. No costs awarded.

DURHAM, JUSTICE (dissenting):

I dissent from the majority opinion because I believe that the federal statute and the specific cardholder agreements in question relieve the defendants of liability for the unauthorized use of their credit cards by their spouses.

* * *

First, the result of the majority opinion runs counter to the purpose of § 1643 of the TILA, which has been described as follows:

> The federal credit card statute reflects a policy decision that it is preferable for the issuer to bear fraud losses arising from credit card use.
>
> * * *[I]ssuers are in a better position to control the occurrence of these losses. They not only select the merchants who may accept the card and the holders who may use it, but also design the security systems for card distribution, user identification, and loss notification. Hence, *the statutory choice of issuer liability assures that the problem of credit card loss is the responsibility of the party most likely to take efficient steps in its resolution.*

Weistart, *Consumer Protection in the Credit Card Industry: Federal Legislative Controls,* 70 Mich.L.Rev. 1475, 1509–10 (1972) (citations omitted) (emphasis added).

Under the present circumstances, I acknowledge that the burden or risk of liability should initially fall on the cardholder because use of the credit card by a spouse is, and remains, authorized until notice is given to the card issuer that the authority to use the credit card is revoked. However, once the cardholder notifies the card issuer of the revocation of that authority, it is clear that the card issuer is in the best position to protect itself, the cardholder and third parties. The card issuer can protect both itself and the cardholder by refusing to pay any charges on the account, and it can protect third parties by listing the credit card in the regional warning bulletins. The issuer need only terminate the existing account, transfer all existing charges to a new number, and issue a new card to the cardholder. * * * Thus, in conformance with the purpose of § 1643 of the TILA, the better holding in this case, as a policy matter, is that, after notification to the card issuer, the cardholder should be relieved of all liability for the unauthorized use of the credit card by an estranged spouse.

Second, the language of § 1643 and the law of agency require that the defendants be relieved of liability. As the majority opinion recognizes, state law determines the question of whether the defendants' husbands are clothed with "apparent authority." * * * Under Utah law, a husband or wife may terminate an agency created in the spouse in the same manner as any other agency. The majority opinion holds that the defendants' husbands' use was authorized because the husbands had "apparent authority." This is apparently a reference to the relationship between the husband and third-party merchants who rely on the husband's possession of a credit card with his name and matching signature on it. It cannot refer to the existence of apparent authority vis-a-vis the Bank, because the Bank has been *expressly notified* of the revocation of all authority. I fail to see why the existence of "apparent authority" as to third-party merchants should govern the liability of a cardholder whose spouse "steals" a card in the context of marital difficulties, any more than it would govern in the case of a cardholder whose card is stolen before delivery and bears a "matching signature" forged thereon by a thief.

It is well recognized that apparent authority exists only to the extent that the *principal* represents to a third person that another is one's agent. In the present case, with respect to the Bank, the husbands' authority, actual, implied and apparent, was specifically terminated by the defendants (the principals) when the Bank was notified that the husbands' authority to use the defendants' credit cards was revoked. Thus, after notification, the husbands' use was unauthorized and both § 1643 and the provisions of the cardholder agreements relieved the defendants of all liability for charges incurred by their husbands subsequent to that notification.

* * *

Finally, the majority opinion ignores the impracticality of imposing the burden on a cardholder of obtaining a credit card from an estranged spouse in order to return it to the Bank. It is unrealistic to think that estranged spouses will be cooperative. Moreover, it is extremely unwise to arm one spouse with a weapon which permits virtually unlimited spending at the expense of the other. As is illustrated by the facts of these cases, where the whereabouts of the unauthorized spouse are unknown, the cardholder may be powerless to acquire possession of his or her card and return it to the Bank, which, according to the majority opinion, is the only way to limit liability. One result of the majority opinion will surely be to encourage the "theft" by divorcing spouses of credit cards they were authorized to use during the marriage and the liberal use of those cards at the other spouse's expense.

* * *

Notes

1. In Stieger v. Chevy Chase Savings Bank, F.S.B., 666 A.2d 479 (D.C.App.1995), Paul Stieger entrusted his card to a "Ms. Garrett" to make several specified purchases. Instead, Ms. Garrett ran up a substantial amount of charges on the card. Apparently Paul's signature had worn off on the back of the card, and Ms. Garrett had signed "P. Stieger" in that spot, so that her (forged) signature on card receipts matched that on the card. The court found that this conveyed apparent authority, and Stieger was therefore responsible for all of the charges. Is this consistent with *Walker Bank*, above? How could the wrongdoer's forgery on the card operate to bind the card holder?

Compare Young v. Bank of America National Trust & Savings Association, 141 Cal.App.3d 108, 190 Cal.Rptr. 122 (1983): under California law, where card holder authorized a friend to use her card only for a specific purchase, but the friend kept the card and ran up substantial charges, this was a "stolen" card and the friend's use was unauthorized. Is this consistent with *Walker Bank*?

2. The TILA rules on unauthorized credit card use apply to business credit cards as well as those held by individual consumers. TILA § 135, 15 U.S.C. § 1645. Issues of apparent authority get tricky when the wrongdoer is an employee of the card holder. In Mastercard v. Town of Newport, 133 Wis.2d 328, 396 N.W.2d 345 (App.1986), the city had established a corporate MasterCard account for use by the city clerk for certain official purposes. When the clerk exceeded her authority and made several personal charges, the court held the city liable for all of them. The court said that the $50 limit was intended to apply only if the card was lost or stolen. But, "when, as here, a credit cardholder authorizes another to use the card for a specific purpose, and the other person uses it for another purpose, such a use is not an 'unauthorized use' within the meaning of [the TILA]." 396 N.W.2d at 348. See also: DBI Architects v. American Express Travel Related Services, 388 F.3d 886 (D.C.Cir. 2004); Minskoff v. American Express Travel Related Services, 98 F.3d 703 (2d Cir. 1996). In each of these cases the wrongdoer-employee fraudulently acquired and used a business credit card, and covered the fraud trail by writing company checks to pay the monthly card bill. The court found apparent authority sufficient to bind the employer based on the employer's negligent failure to review the monthly statements. Does it make sense to base liability for credit card fraud losses on a legal doctrine as slippery as state agency law? Compare the treatment of debit card losses, below.

3. As the dissent in *Walker Bank* points out, a cardholder who wants to terminate the authority of a former spouse to use the account has something of a dilemma. What action would you recommend be taken? Is there an equivalent dilemma for the bank? If the *Young* view is correct, what can the bank do to protect itself and its participating merchants from unauthorized

card charges? How do you think the holdings in *Walker Bank* or *Stieger* will affect bank policies?

4. The authorized user practice raises other issues. As described in the *Walker Bank* case, an account is often opened in the name of one person, and other named persons (often spouses or children) are authorized to use the account. Separate cards, embossed in the names of the other persons, may be issued. These users are not contractually liable to the card issuer for charges they incur on the account; instead, the issuer normally relies on the credit standing of the primary account holder. But if the authorized user incurs charges for himself (or his children whom he has an obligation to support), might the issuer be able to recover directly from the user under a theory of quasi- or implied contract or family "necessaries"? See Sears Roebuck & Co. v. Ragucci, 203 N.J.Super. 82, 495 A.2d 923 (1985).

5. If the most a credit card issuer can recover from its victim-customer is $50, is it worthwhile for the issuer to pursue such a claim? Many card issuers have adopted a policy of imposing *no* liability for unauthorized use, not even $50. (Why would they do that?) At the same time, some card issuers and other vendors peddle to card holders "lost credit card" insurance, making good profits in the bargain. Is it deceptive to market such insurance without disclosing the limits on liability both by federal law and industry practice?

6. While consumers may have once thought of credit card fraud in relatively small terms—$100 or so at a time, for example—banks and law enforcement agencies have a different perspective, and consumers themselves are bombarded in the press and elsewhere with warnings and alerts about possible security breaches with respect to their financial accounts. Fraud involving consumer accounts, whether instigated by credit card, debit card, or conventional check, is big business, even if it is only a piece of broader concerns about identity theft and information-security.

Problem 6-20

Father entrusts his son Prodigal with his debit card and personal identification number (PIN) so that Prodigal can get $50 from a nearby automated teller machine for his Saturday night date. Instead, Prodigal drops out of sight and begins withdrawing $100 a week from Father's account. Father, hoping that Prodigal will return and beg forgiveness, does not notify the bank. When total withdrawals reach $2,000 and it becomes apparent that Prodigal has no plans to return, Father demands that the bank reimburse his account.

(a) Must the bank do so? In what amount? See EFTA §§ 903(11) and 909; Reg. E § 205.6.

(b) Would the result be different if Prodigal had taken the card and PIN from Father's wallet without permission?

OGNIBENE v. CITIBANK, N.A.

Civil Court of the City of New York, New York County, Small Claims Part, 1981.
112 Misc.2d 219, 446 N.Y.S.2d 845.

Mara T. Thorpe, Judge:

Plaintiff seeks to recover $400.00 withdrawn from his account at the defendant bank by an unauthorized person using an automated teller machine. The court has concluded that plaintiff was the victim of a scam which defendant has been aware of for some time.

Defendant's witness, an assistant manager of one of its branches, described how the scam works: A customer enters the automated teller machine (ATM) area for the purpose of using a machine for the transaction of business with the bank. At the time that he enters, a person is using the customer service telephone located between the two automated teller machines and appears to be telling customer service that one of the machines is malfunctioning. This person is the perpetrator of the scam and his conversation with customer service is only simulated. He observes the customer press his personal identification code into one of the two machines. Having learned the code, the perpetrator then tells the customer that customer service has advised him to ask the customer to insert his Citicard into the allegedly malfunctioning machine to check whether it will work with a card other than the perpetrator's. When a good samaritan customer accedes to the request, the other machine is activated. The perpetrator then presses a code into the machine, which the customer does not realize is his own code which the perpetrator has just observed. After continuing the simulated conversation on the telephone, the perpetrator advises the customer that customer services has asked if he would try his Citicard in the allegedly malfunctioning machine once more. A second insertion of the cards permits cash to be released by the machine, and if the customer does as requested, the thief has effectuated a cash withdrawal from the unwary customer's account.

Plaintiff testified that on August 16, 1981, he went to the ATM area at one of defendant's branches and activated one of the machines with his Citibank card, pressed in his personal identification code and withdrew $20.00. While he did this a person who was using the telephone between plaintiff's machine and the adjoining machine said into the telephone, "I'll see if his card works in my machine." Thereupon he asked plaintiff if he could use his card to see if the other machine was working. Plaintiff handed it to him and saw him insert it into the adjoining machine at least two times while stating into the telephone, "Yes, it seems to be working."

Defendant's computer records in evidence show that two withdrawals of $200.00 each from plaintiff's account were made on August 16, 1981, on the machine adjoining the one plaintiff used for his $20.00 withdrawal. The two $200.00 withdrawals were made at 5:42 p.m. and 5:43 p.m. respectively; plaintiff's own $20.00 withdrawal was made at 5:41 p.m. At the time, plaintiff was unaware that any withdrawals from his account were being made on the adjoining machine.

The only fair and reasonable inferences to be drawn from all of the evidence are that the person who appeared to be conversing on the telephone observed the plaintiff enter his personal identification code into the machine from which he withdrew $20.00 and that he entered it into the adjoining machine while simulating a conversation with customer service about that machine's malfunctioning. It is conceded in the testimony of defendant's assistant branch manager that it would have been possible for a person who was positioned so as to appear to be speaking on the telephone physically to observe the code being entered into the machine by plaintiff. Although plaintiff is not certain that his card was inserted in the adjoining machine more than twice, the circumstances indicate that it was inserted four times. No issue of fraud by plaintiff or anyone acting in concert with him has been raised by defendant. Having observed plaintiff's demeanor, the court found him to be a credible witness and is of the opinion that no such issues exist in this case.

The basic rights, liabilities and responsibilities of the banks which offer electronic money transfer services and the consumers who use them have been established by the federal legislation contained in 15 U.S.C.A. 1693 et seq., commonly called the Electronic Fund Transfers Act (EFT). Although the EFT Act preempts state law only to the extent of any inconsistency (15 U.S.C.A. 1693q), to date New York State has not enacted legislation which governs the resolution of the issues herein. Therefore, the EFT Act is applicable.

The EFT Act places various limits on a consumer's liability for electronic fund transfers from his account if they are "unauthorized." Insofar as is relevant here, a transfer is "unauthorized" if 1) it is initiated by a person other than the consumer and without actual authority to initiate such transfer, 2) the consumer receives no benefit from it, and 3) the consumer did not furnish such person "with the card, code or other means of access" to his account. 15 U.S.C.A. 1693a(11).

In an action involving a consumer's liability for an electronic fund transfer, such as the one at bar, the burden of going forward to show an "unauthorized" transfer from his account is on the consumer. The EFT Act places upon the bank, however, the burden of proof of any consumer liability for the transfer. 15 U.S.C.A. 1693g(b). To establish full liability on the part of the consumer, the bank must prove that the transfer was authorized. To be entitled to even the limited liability imposed by the statute on the consumer, the bank must prove that certain conditions of consumer liability, set forth in 15 U.S.C.A. 1693g(a) have been met and that certain disclosures mandated by 15 U.S.C.A. 1693c(a)(1) and (2) have been made.

Plaintiff herein met his burden of going forward. He did not initiate the withdrawals in question, did not authorize the person in the ATM area to make them, and did not benefit from them.

However, defendant's position is, in essence, that although plaintiff was duped, the bank's burden of proof on the issue of authorization has been met by plaintiff's testimony that he permitted his card to be used in the adjoining machine by the other person. The court does not agree.

The EFT Act requires that the consumer have furnished to a person initiating the transfer the "card, code, or other means of access" to his account to be ineligible for the limitations on liability afforded by the Act when transfers are "unauthorized." The evidence establishes that in order to obtain access to an account via an automated teller machine, both the card and the personal identification code must be used. Thus, by merely giving his card to the person initiating the transfer, a consumer does not furnish the "means of access" to his account. To do so, he would have to furnish the personal identification code as well. See 12 C.F.R. 205.2(a)(*l*), the regulation promulgated under the EFT Act which defines "access device" as "a card, code or other means of access to [an] * * * account *or any combination thereof* (emphasis added).

The court finds that plaintiff did not furnish his personal identification code to the person initiating the $400.00 transfer within the meaning of the EFT Act. There is no evidence that he deliberately or even negligently did so. On the contrary, the unauthorized person was able to obtain the code because of defendant's own negligence. Since the bank had knowledge of the scam and its operational details (including the central role of the customer service telephone), it was negligent in failing to provide plaintiff-customer with information sufficient to alert him to the danger when he found himself in the position of a potential victim. Although in June, 1981, after the scam came to defendant's attention, it posted signs in its ATM areas containing a red circle approximately inches in diameter in which is written "Do Not Let Your Citicard Be Used For Any Transaction But Your Own", the court finds that this printed admonition is not a sufficient security measure since it fails to state the reason why one should not do so. Since a customer of defendant's electronic fund transfer service must employ both the card and the personal identification code in order to withdraw money from his account, the danger of loaning his card briefly for the purpose of checking the functioning of an adjoining automated teller machine would not be immediately apparent to one who has not divulged his personal identification number and who is unaware that it has been revealed merely by virtue of his own transaction with the machine.

Since the bank established the electronic fund transfer service and has the ability to tighten its security characteristics, the responsibility for the fact that plaintiffs code, one of the two necessary components of the "access device" or "means of access" to his account, was observed and utilized as it was must rest with the bank.

For the foregoing reasons and in view of the fact that the primary purpose of the EFT Act and the regulation promulgated thereunder is the protection of individual consumers (12 C.F.R. 205. l(b)), the court concludes that plaintiff did not furnish his code to anyone within the meaning of the Act. Accordingly, since the person who obtained it did not have actual authority to initiate the transfer, the transfer qualifies as an "unauthorized" one under 15 U.S.C.A. 1693a(11) and the bank cannot hold plaintiff fully liable for the $400.00 withdrawal.

To avail itself of the limited liability imposed by the Act upon a consumer in the event of an "unauthorized" transfer, the bank must demonstrate 1) that the means of access utilized for the transfer was "accepted" and 2) that the bank has provided a way which the user of the means of access can be identified as the person authorized to use it. 15 U.S.C.A. 1693g(a) and (b). One definition of "accepted" under the Act is that the consumer has used the means of access. 15 U.S.C.A. 1693a(*l*). Both of the foregoing conditions of liability have been met here since plaintiff used the means of access to his account to withdraw the $20.00 and had been given a personal identification code.

Additionally, the bank must prove that it disclosed to the consumer his liability for unauthorized electronic fund transfers and certain information pertaining to notification of the bank in the event the consumer believes that an unauthorized transfer has been or may be effected. 15 U.S.C.A. 1693c(a)(*l*) and (2) and 1693g(b). Defendant did not establish that it made such disclosures to plaintiff. Accordingly, it is not entitled to avail itself of the benefit of the limited liability for unauthorized transfers imposed upon consumers by the Act.

For the foregoing reasons, judgment shall be for plaintiff in the sum of $400.00.

Notes

1. The New York Attorney General also brought a case against Citibank based on the ATM problems and won injunctive relief, damages, and restitution. Citibank agreed to pay nearly $500,000 to customers who had been victims of the scam discussed in the preceding case. Afterwards, Citibank changed its software, and now uses polarized glass which makes it impossible to read ATM screens from an angle.

2. In *Ognibene*, why wasn't the customer responsible for $50 of the $400 loss? Did the bank's lawyer make a mistake somewhere?

3. When an unauthorized transfer is alleged, EFTA § 909(b) places the burden of proof squarely upon "the financial institution" to show authorization. Can the burden be met simply by presenting the record of the payment order, and alleging that a PIN is necessary to access the computer? Consider the following excerpt from Judd v. Citibank, 107 Misc.2d 526, 435 N.Y.S.2d 210 (N.Y.City Ct.1980), decided under pre-EFTA concepts:

From the testimony adduced at trial it appears that the funds in question were withdrawn from plaintiff's account on February 26, 1980 between 2:13 and 2:14 P.M., and on March 28, 1980 between 2:30 and 2:32 P.M. Plaintiff testified and produced a letter from her employer to the effect that she was at work on both occasions and could not have made the said withdrawals. Citibank produced computer printouts documenting the withdrawals in issue, which printouts were explained (translated) by the bank's witness, the branch manager. Defendant asserts that the funds in question were and could have been withdrawn from the Judd account by use of a validated Citicard at a Citibank electronic teller, coupled with entry of the correct [PIN]. Citibank has submitted a statement in support of its contention that it has effected stringent security measures to prevent the unauthorized use of Citicards. Plaintiff testified that not only did she not let anyone else use her Citicard but that she never told anyone her [PIN] and never wrote it down.

The question presented is a basic one, of evidence, burdens and credibility: Has plaintiff proven her case by a fair preponderance of the credible evidence? In this case we are met with a credible witness on the one hand and a computer printout on the other. It is evident that there was no opportunity to cross examine the computer or the printout it produced. * * *

* * * [T]his court is not prepared to go so far as to rule that where a credible witness is faced with the adverse "testimony" of a machine, he is as a matter of law faced also with an unmeetable burden of proof. It is too commonplace in our society that when faced with the choice of man or machine we readily accept the "word" of the machine everytime. This, despite the tales of computer malfunctions that we hear daily. Defendant's own witness testified to physical malfunctions of the very system in issue.

This court, as trier of the fact, finds that plaintiff has proven her case by a fair preponderance of the credible evidence. * * *

4.   Congress established the National Commission on Electronic Fund Transfers in 1974. This commission issued a final report three years later, and the report formed much of the basis for the EFTA. The commission had recommended that losses should fall on the customer if the customer was negligent. This rule would have followed the UCC's treatment of fraud losses for forged checks. As finally enacted, however, the EFTA contains no reference to negligence. Does that mean that the customer loss limits apply even if the customer wrote his PIN on his card?

5.   What happens if a state law is different? Michigan followed the UCC model in its EFT law, and imposes liability on the customer if the bank can prove "that the customer's negligence substantially contributed to the unauthorized use." Mich.Comp.Laws Ann. § 488.14. Does this mean debit cardholders in Michigan must be more careful than cardholders in Kansas? Is EFTA § 919 relevant?

Problem 6–21

Late at night you are confronted on the street by a robber who demands "your money or your life." You have no cash, but the robber spots your plastic Firstbank debit card. At gunpoint, you are marched to the bank's 24–hour teller machine and instructed to withdraw $1000. After deliberating (a la Jack Benny), you do so, and give the money to the robber, who disappears. Can you insist that Firstbank recredit your account?

Problem 6–22

An employee in the computer department at Firstbank has devised a way to steal money from customer accounts without using any card or personal identification number. His scheme involves manipulating the computer program in such a way that electronic transfers are made from customer accounts to an account in the employee's name. When the thefts are discovered, you realize that he has "hit" your account to the tune of $500. Must the bank reimburse you? Was this an "unauthorized" transfer within the meaning of the EFTA? If not, does that make them "authorized" and binding on you?

Note: Where Do Fraud Losses Go?

The federal laws we have been looking at—TILA, 15 U.S.C. § 1643 (for credit cards) and EFTA, 15 U.S.C. § 1693g (for debit cards)—clearly allocate unauthorized-use liability between card issuers and consumers, with the larger share of the loss allocated to the issuer bank. But is that the end of the matter? May the bank shunt fraud losses back to the merchant who honored the card by delivering goods or services to the crook? Consider the following case.

THOMAS D. MANGELSEN, INC. v. HEARTLAND PAYMENT SYSTEMS, INC.

United States District Court, District of Nebraska, 2005.
2005 WL 2076421.

SMITH CAMP, J. [*Eds.: docket references omitted.*]

This matter is before the Court on a Motion to Dismiss under Fed. R. Civ. Pro. 12(b)(6) filed by Defendant, Bank of America, Inc. ("BOA"), based on an alleged failure to state a claim upon which relief can be granted; and a Motion to Dismiss filed by Defendant, Heartland Payment Systems, Inc. ("Heartland"), based on the Court's alleged lack of personal jurisdiction over Heartland and improper venue. The issues have been fully briefed. The Complaint alleges that BOA violated 15 U.S.C. § 1643 by wrongfully charging back credit card transactions that were allegedly authorized by BOA cardholder, Michael Persky. The Complaint further alleges that Heartland breached a merchant processing agreement between Heartland and Plaintiff, Thomas D. Mangelsen, Inc. ("Mangelsen"), by failing or refusing to reverse chargebacks for the Persky transactions. * * * For the reasons discussed below, the Court finds Mangelsen has failed to state a claim for which relief can be granted against BOA; therefore, BOA's 12(b)(6) Motion to Dismiss will be granted. The Court further finds that Mangelsen's pendent breach-of-contract claim against Heartland should be dismissed without prejudice because the Court declines to exercise supplemental jurisdiction pursuant to 28 U.S.C. § 1367(c)(3). * * *

BACKGROUND

Mangelsen is a corporation organized and existing under the laws of the State of Nebraska, with its principal place of business in Omaha, Nebraska. Mangelsen sells limited-edition photographs, posters, and prints, and provides custom framing services. Heartland is a corporation organized and existing under the laws of the State of Delaware, with its principal place of business in Princeton, New Jersey. Heartland provides bankcard transaction processing services to merchants. BOA is a corporation organized and existing under the laws of Delaware, with its principal place of business in Charlotte, North Carolina. BOA issues bankcards to consumers and businesses for credit purchases. Mangelsen and Heartland entered into a merchant processing agreement (the "Agreement"), whereby Heartland agreed to provide bankcard transaction processing services to Mangelsen in exchange for a fee. * * *

On September 17, 2004, Michael Persky, a BOA cardholder, visited Mangelsen's gallery in the Denver International Airport. Persky indicated he would like to make a purchase from Mangelsen, not exceeding $18,000, which was his BOA credit limit. The Complaint alleges that three days later, Persky and/or Mike Jones, an allegedly authorized user of Persky's BOA bankcard, placed an $18,000 order over the telephone for Mangelsen's artwork. This order was placed on Persky's BOA bankcard. Heartland verified the availability of funds on Persky's BOA bankcard and processed the transaction. Mangelsen then prepared and shipped the artwork to Persky's place of business in Ventura, California. On November 12, 2004, Heartland informed Mangelsen that BOA had charged back the $18,000 Persky transaction as a fraudulent transaction. Pursuant to the Agreement, Heartland requested that Mangelsen provide Heartland proof of delivery of the artwork in order to reverse the chargebacks. Mangelsen sent Heartland proof of delivery; however, Heartland failed or refused to reverse the chargebacks. Similarly, BOA failed or refused to reverse the chargebacks. Mangelsen claims BOA wrongfully charged back the $18,000 Persky transaction, in violation of 15 U.S.C. § 1643, which establishes liability limits for unauthorized use of credit cards. Mangelsen further alleges that Heartland breached the Agreement with Mangelsen by failing or refusing to reverse the chargebacks. BOA filed a motion to dismiss under 12(b)(6), claiming Mangelsen failed to state a claim for which relief can be granted, claiming the Truth in Lending Act, 15 U.S.C. § 1601, *et seq.*, ("TILA") affords no rights or remedies to Mangelsen. Heartland filed a motion to dismiss for improper venue and lack of personal jurisdiction, citing the forum selection provision in the Agreement and claiming the Court lacks subject matter jurisdiction.

Discussion

Truth in Lending Act. TILA, along with 12 C.F.R. § 226 *et. seq.* ("Regulation Z"), was enacted to promote "the informed use of credit" by consumers and to protect consumers from inaccurate and unfair credit card practices. 15 U.S.C. 1601(a); see Household Credit Services, Inc. v. Pfennig, 541 U.S. 232, 235, 124 S.Ct. 1741, 158 L.Ed.2d 450 (2004).... Section 1643, titled "Liability of holder of credit card," sets forth the circumstances under which a cardholder may be liable for the unauthorized use of his or her bankcard and places caps on the cardholder's liability. 15 U.S.C. § 1643. Section 1643(b) addresses actions between a card issuer and a cardholder, placing the burden of proof on the card issuer to show charges on a credit card were authorized. § 1643(b).

However, § 1643 does not recognize merchants' rights against card issuers or cardholders. As BOA and Heartland point out, various federal courts of appeals and federal district courts have determined that § 1643 of TILA applies to consumers. See e.g. American Airlines, Inc. v. Remis Industries, Inc., 494 F.2d 196, 202 (2d Cir.1974) (holding § 1643(a) applies to all credit card holders); accord Martin v. American Express, Inc., 361 So.2d 597, 600 (Ala.App.1978) (stating Congress intended § 1643 to protect the consumer against unauthorized use). Additionally, legislative history of TILA indicates that Congress enacted TILA in part to give aggrieved debtors the right to institute civil actions against creditors who failed to comply with TILA's requirements. *See* H.R.Rep. No. 90–1040 (1968), reprinted in 1968 U.S.C.C.A.N.1962, 1976.... Mangelsen has failed to cite any authority which supports its contention that TILA, and more specifically § 1643, provides relief to merchants. Based on the language of § 1643 and other provisions of TILA, as well as TILA's legislative history, I find that Mangelsen is not among the persons or entities Congress intended to protect when it enacted TILA. Section 1643 does not apply to Mangelsen because he is neither a cardholder nor a card issuer. The Court finds that Mangelsen has failed to state a claim for which relief can be granted; therefore, BOA's Motion to Dismiss is granted.

SUPPLEMENTAL JURISDICTION

The breach-of-contract claim against Heartland is before the Court pursuant to 28 U.S.C. § 1367, which grants supplemental jurisdiction to a district court over all claims so related to the claim over which the district court has original jurisdiction that they form part of the same case or controversy. Gregoire v. Class, 236 F.3d 413, 419 (8th Cir.2000). However, once a district court dismisses the claims over which it has original jurisdiction, the court has discretion whether to exercise supplemental jurisdiction. 28 U.S.C. § 1367(c)(3).... Because this matter is in the early stages of litigation, and the statute of limitations has not run on Mangelsen's breach-of-contract claim against Heartland, the Court declines to exercise supplemental jurisdiction. Mangelsen's breach-of-contract claim against Heartland is dismissed without prejudice.

* * *

Queries:

1. The court is clearly correct, isn't it, that TILA addresses its unauthorized-use liability rule at card *issuers*, and not at merchants who honor the card? But by what authority is the card issuer (BOA) then able to "charge back" the $18,000 purchase amount to Mangelsen (the merchant)? Whatever the source of the chargeback "right," is it consistent with the statutory loss allocation rules to permit the card issuer to dump the entire loss on someone else?

2. Part of the rationale for the existing statutory loss allocation rule was to encourage card issuers, who were promoting card use hither

and yon, to design their systems with maximum security against unauthorized use. See the dissenting opinion in the *Walker Bank* case, supra this Chapter. But if card issuers can routinely charge back fraud losses to the merchant, what incentives are there for the banks to be security conscious in building and operating their card programs?

3. Who determines whether the purchase transaction was legitimate or "unauthorized"? If it is the bank alone, how do we know that the bank has diligently assessed whether the card use was proper or fraudulent? Maybe the bank just gave in to a persistent customer, and now wants to shift the loss to the merchant, like Mangelsen, who seems as much a victim as Persky (the card holder). How can Mangelsen influence the bank's decision on handling this matter?

4. How many $18,000 hits like this can Mangelsen's picture gallery take and stay in business? How many $18,000 hits like this can Bank of America take and stay in business? (The last two questions are unfair, aren't they?) What are the chances that Mangelsen will be able to recover the $18,000 from the fraudulent buyer?

SECTION F. EMERGING PAYMENT SYSTEMS AND ISSUES

This Section sketches some of the new payment patterns, and probes for consumer issues likely to be imbedded in them. Some of the issues previously discussed for credit and debit cards are likely to recur. And there certainly will be new ones. One common issue for all new payment systems is: *What law applies*? State common law? The Uniform Commercial Code, Federal Reserve Board regulations, like Reg. Z for credit transactions, Reg. E for electronic fund transfer, Reg. CC for check collections, Reg. DD for deposit accounts, and so on.

There are comparable developments in "payments law" around the world, and in many countries the changeover from cash to electronic payments is proceeding even faster than in the U.S. Cf., Arnold S. Rosenberg, Better Than Cash? Global Proliferation of Payment Cards and Consumer Protection Policy, 44 Colum. J. of Transnational Law 520 (2006).

1. CHECK TRUNCATION

The banking and financial communities have been trying for half a century to find ways to eliminate the physical transfer and handling of the 50 billion or so checks issued in the U.S. each year. A significant break-through occurred in 2003 with the enactment of the Check Clearing for the 21st Century Act (referred to generally as "Check 21"), Pub. L. No. 108–100. 117 Stat. 1177, codified at 12 U.S.C. §§ 5001–5018. The Federal Reserve has issued regulations for Check 21 as Subpart D of its Reg. CC, 12 C.F.R. Part 229. Pertinent sections of Reg. CC are in the statutory supplement.

The gist of Check 21 is that banks need no longer send the original check all the way through banking channels to the drawee for payment, but instead may send an electronic image of that original check, so long as it is capable of being re-converted to paper form at the demand of the transferee. Such a re-converted item is called a "substitute check." The original check might therefore be "truncated" at the bank of first deposit, and an electronic image forwarded for collection. If the drawee bank, or the drawer/consumer, wants to require production of a paper check, the substitute check would suffice for that purpose. Since Check 21 applies to all checks, not just consumer items, the full details of Check 21 are best left to Payment Systems courses. But we can pose several questions. Cf. Mark E. Budnitz, The Check 21 Challenge: Will Banks Take Advantage of Consumers?, 58 Cons. Fin. L. Q. Rep. 369 (2004).

Problem 6–23

Harriet, a frugal senior citizen living on a fixed income, will only keep her checking account at a bank that returns the paper checks along with her statement at the end of the month. Flower Bank has been providing Harriet that service for years. With the advent of Check 21, however, Flower Bank wants to accept electronic-image presentment of checks, but will then re-convert the images into substitute checks and return those items to customers like Harriet. Harriet is concerned that the substitute checks will not allow her to verify signatures on the checks (including endorsements), and will not suffice as proof of payment if she has a dispute with a merchant or needs such proof for tax purposes. Advise Harriet: Should she change banks, or stick with Flower Bank? See Reg. CC §§ 229.2(aaa); 229.51.

Problem 6–24

(a) Harriet sends a check for $500 to Merchant. When Merchant receives Harriet's check, Merchant promptly deposits it at Secondbank. Secondbank sends an electronic image forward for collection, and puts the original check in temporary storage pending destruction. Thief steals the stored check from Secondbank and cashes it at a local store. Both the electronic version and the paper original are processed through to Flower Bank and are paid and charged to Harriet's account. When Harriet sees both the original and "substitute" check and realizes that her account has been debited twice for the same item, she frantically asks your advice. What rights does she have under Check 21? See Reg. CC §§ 229.52, 229.54. Under other law?

(b) The same thief does the same thing to another check, this one written by Ismelda to Merchant and deposited at Secondbank. After Secondbank forwards an electronic image for collection, thief steals and cashes the original check which is presented and paid, resulting in a double charge to Ismelda's account. Ismelda, however, does not get "substitute checks" at the end of the month; for her, Flower Bank merely provides a computer print-out showing paid checks by check number and amount. What are Ismelda's rights under Check 21? [Note that no substitute check was ever created in this case.] Under any other law?

2. ELECTRONIC CHECK CONVERSION

Another form of check truncation has emerged without the need for explicit legislation like Check 21. This is called "electronic check conversion," or "ECK" for short.

> You may have noticed changes in your bank statement lately. You don't find the canceled check for the $700 you paid the credit card company. Instead the debits section of the statement has the cryptic entry "$700 Electronic/ACH Debit Ace Credit Card acct pymt 115." You ask your banker about this. He yawns dismissively and says this is merely "lockbox check conversion." Your check has been converted into a debit transaction.

James H. Johnston, Why Is Your Canceled Check No Longer in the Mail, Legal Times, June 7, 2004, at 17. This writer goes on to assert: "Although both the Federal Reserve Board and the Federal Trade Commission approve, check conversion is a bad idea." *Id.* Why should that be so? What does ECK really mean?

In one version of ECK, when the consumer tenders a check to a merchant at the point of sale (thus, a "POS" ECK), the merchant swipes it through a reader which captures the critical information from the magnetic numerals on the check, and the merchant enters the amount. This electronic information is then forwarded to the customer's bank through electronic switches overseen by the National Automated Clearing House Association (NACHA). The original paper check is either returned to the customer at the point of sale or retained and destroyed by the merchant.

The other ECK version is called "accounts receivable check conversion," or "ARC." This is what the writer above describes. Consumer sends a check by mail to a creditor. Creditor electronically captures the essential information from the check, and sends it, through the automated clearing house network, to the consumer's bank for payment. Creditor destroys the original check. Both this version, and the POS version, are based on the consumer's consent to ECK handling of the item; this consent is imputed to the consumer from notices posted at the point of sale or contained in the consumer's billing statement from the creditor.

In both these patterns, the paper check is "truncated" by the payee, and there is no need for physical check handling through the Federal Reserve system or otherwise. As a result, merchants collect payments more quickly than in the conventional check system, and conversely consumers lose the "float" they used to enjoy while the paper checks were in the collection pipeline. And of course the consumer will not receive a canceled check at the end of the month because the payee creditor has retained it.

Even though the consumer actually executes and delivers a paper check to initiate an ECK transaction, the Federal Reserve has now affirmed that Regulation E applies to both POS and ARC versions of electronic check conversion. Regulation E § 205.3(b)(2). In addition:

- the merchant receiving the check must give notice that "the transaction will or may be" processed as an EFT. Reg. E § 205.3(b)(2)(ii);

- the consumer must authorize ECK handling, and does so "when the consumer receives notice and goes forward with the transaction," *id.*; and

- the notice must also alert the consumer that ECK will speed up the debit to the consumer's account, and that the actual check will not be returned to the consumer, Reg. E § 205.3(b)(2)(iii).

ECK payments seem to be increasingly common, though it remains to be seen whether ECK will flourish or languish in light of Check 21. (Your authors' hunch is that it will be the former, since ECK essentially bypasses the Check 21 and other legal restraints in the check collection process under Regulation CC.)

Problem 6–25

As was his custom, Germaine mailed a check on the first of the month to pay his telephone bill. (He had not noticed the ECK notices (described *supra*) included with his bill.) When Germaine got his checking account statement for that month, he realized that, while he had written the phone-bill check for $50, it was posted as a $500 ACH charge to his account. Plus there was an additional $10 charge described as "late charge/Phone Co." (Later investigation will determine that Phone Company had erroneously entered the wrong amount when it converted the check to an electronic debit item, and then had added on $10 because the payment was in fact overdue. Germaine is irritated, and wants the matter fixed, ASAP. What are Germaine's rights? Against whom—his bank, the phone company, both, or neither? For example, can he invoke the error resolution procedures of Reg. E § 205.11 against the Phone Company? Can he invoke those procedures against his Bank, and if so how can he prove that the check was written for only $50 (the Phone Company kept it)? If the Bank recredits Germaine for the overcharge, can Bank recover the money from Phone Company? On what authority—UCC check-presentment warranties, perhaps? Cf., UCC § 4–208.

Problem 6–26

The Reg. E provisions discussed above bring ECK transactions under that regulation only if they are "one-time" transfers. Thus the consumer must receive a separate notice each time the merchant/payee wishes to convert a check to an electronic debit. Credit Card Bank thinks it is silly to have to include the Reg. E notices in every single monthly statement it sends—a waste of time and money, plus, the Bank says, their cardholders don't read the notices anyhow. Bank asks you whether it could provide its customers a change-in-terms notice indicating that henceforth all monthly payment checks would be converted to ECK. Is that allowable? Is Reg. E § 205.10 relevant?

3. STORED–VALUE CARDS

If the general objective of these payment system innovations is to reduce the burdens of processing billions of paper checks, why not go all the way and eliminate the checks altogether. One way to do this would be to replace checks (and much cash, as well) with plastic cards that carry electronically-accessible value. Here is one observer's overview of this development:

> Prepaid cards, also commonly referred to as "stored value cards," include a wide variety of products, including gift cards, phone cards, teen cards, government benefit cards, travel cards, flexible spending account cards, subway system cards, employee incentive cards, and payroll cards. Despite the broad array of prepaid cards, they are all plastic, credit-card sized cards with a magnetic stripe, bar code, or embedded chip that permits the holders of the cards to access funds for the purchase of goods or services. And while they look a lot like credit cards and debit cards, they neither involve credit nor are they tied to a cardholder's demand deposit account.

> Just [a few] years ago, most lawyers probably had only a passing awareness of the existence of prepaid cards, and likely had little or no understanding of the laws applicable to them. Since that time, prepaid cards have exploded, both in numbers and in uses. Indeed, while still a small part of aggregate retail payments, prepaid cards counted for over 1.9 billion transactions in 2002, totaling $54.6 billion. Since that time these figures have grown annually at double-digit rates. So it is not surprising that today most everyone is familiar with at least some forms of prepaid cards. What may be surprising, however, is that even for those who keep abreast of these issues, there is still great uncertainty as to the laws applicable to prepaid cards.

Christopher B. Woods, Stored Value Cards, 59 Cons. Fin. L. Q. Rep. 211 (2005).

The balance of the article just quoted is a useful canvass of pertinent laws, from money-transmitter laws to state escheat laws. There is a smattering of state laws emerging on "consumer issues" such as:

a. Dormancy fees—Some issuers impose charges when the card has not been used within some stated period, thus eating away at its redeemable value.

b. Expiration dates—The same effect occurs if the card has an expiration date, after which the card is useless.

c. Lost or stolen cards—Should the consumer be entitled to a replacement card, or refund, if the original stored-value card is lost or stolen?

d. Payroll card fees—Should payroll cards (discussed below) be subject to fees imposed by the issuer or other financial institutions, which have the effect of reducing the employee's take-home pay?

e. FDIC insurance—Should payroll cards, or other prepaid cards, be considered "accounts" for purposes of Federal Deposit Insurance Corporation protection of bank account balances?

As a general proposition, stored-value cards are <u>not</u> covered by the EFTA and Reg. E, even though they involve electronic storage and transfers of value. This exclusion is because the coverage rules of EFTA require that there be an electronic credit or debit *to a consumer's asset account*, and stored-value cards have not been understood to represent such an account of the consumer. Think of the $25 gift card that you buy at Wal–Mart for your nephew's birthday; you don't think of yourself, or your nephew, as having an "account" with the retailer, do you?

In 2006, however, the Federal Reserve Board acted to expand Reg. E to cover "payroll cards." The Board explained:

> Payroll cards have become increasingly popular with some employers, financial institutions, and payroll service providers as a means of providing a consumer's wages or other recurring compensation payments—assets that the consumer is able to access and spend via an access device that provides functionality comparable to that of a debit card. Typically, an employer, in conjunction with a bank, will provide the employee with a plastic card with a magnetic stripe; this card accesses an account (or subaccount) assigned to an individual employee. Each payday, the employer credits this account for the amount of the employee's compensation instead of providing the employee with a paper check or making a direct deposit of salary to the employee's checking account. The employee-consumer can use the payroll card to withdraw his or her funds at an ATM, and to make purchases at POS (and possibly get cash back). Some payroll cards may offer features such as convenience checks and electronic bill payment. Payroll cards are often marketed to employers as an effective means of providing wages to employees who lack a traditional banking relationship. For "unbanked" consumers, payroll card products can serve as substitutes for traditional transaction accounts at a financial institution.

Federal Reserve Board, Regulation E Interim Final Rule: Supplementary Information, 71 Fed. Reg. 1473 (2006). Earlier background on this rulemaking can be found in Mark E. Budnitz, Stored Value Cards and the Consumer: The Need for Regulation, 46 Amer. U. L. Rev. 1027 (1997).

Under the 2006 rule, payroll card accounts are defined as "accounts" for purposes of coverage under Reg. E. See Reg. E § 205.2(b)(2). The major question that remained was whether payroll card accounts should be subject to the general rules in Reg. E concerning periodic statements about account activity. Having lost his checkbook, is the employee now going to lose his monthly statement as well? The Board took a tentative position (thus the "interim" nature of the rule), embodied in a new Reg. E section, § 205.18, that gives financial institutions some flexibility in the way they provide account information to payroll card holders.

In issuing the new rule, the Board described how it used focus groups to help determine what account information approaches worked best. 71 Fed. Reg. 1473, 1476 (2006).

Problem 6–27

How often and how closely do you look at your *checking account* monthly statement to verify transactions and to reconcile your account balance? With a copy of your checking account statement in hand, review the "alternative to periodic statement" provision in Reg. E § 205.18(b). If you had a payroll card, would you be more or less likely to check your account status, transactions, and balances than for your checking account? Why? Is there any information about the payroll card account that you would want to have but is not provided, either under the basic periodic statement rule, § 205.9, or the new alternative, § 205.18?

If you find the § 205.18 alternative satisfactory, should the law (UCC?) permit the same alternative for regular checking accounts?

Problem 6–28

Employer thinks these developments are great, and so announces a company-wide policy that henceforth all employee compensation will be disbursed through payroll cards. Some employees complain to the Boss that they prefer to receive old-fashioned paper paychecks. Some other employees complain that they prefer to have their pay electronically transferred to their regular checking accounts. Boss says to both groups: "My way, or the highway," *i.e.*, take your pay by payroll card or work elsewhere. Can Employer do this? See EFTA § 913, 15 U.S.C. § 1693k.

4. INTERNET PAYMENT SERVICES

It is probably not surprising that the explosion of selling and buying on the Internet has spawned its own electronic payment mechanisms. These mechanisms usually act as intermediaries to facilitate and transfer credits and debits between participating sellers and buyers, thus permitting Internet transactions to be concluded more speedily and reliably than if the parties had to work out their own payment arrangements. The following case excerpt describes one of those services and suggests the kinds of problems consumers may encounter with it, especially in its start-up phase.

COMB v. PAYPAL, INC.

U.S. District Court, Northern District, California, 2002.
218 F. Supp. 2d 1165.

ORDER DENYING MOTIONS TO COMPEL INDIVIDUAL ARBITRATION

FOGEL, DISTRICT JUDGE.

Plaintiffs seek injunctive relief and related remedies on behalf of a purported nationwide class for alleged violations of state and federal law by Defendant PayPal, Inc. ("PayPal"). PayPal moves to compel individual arbitration pursuant to the arbitration clause contained in its standard User Agreement and the Federal Arbitration Act ("FAA"), 9 U.S.C. § 1, *et seq*. The Court has read and considered the moving, responding and supplemental papers as well as the oral arguments presented by counsel on August 12, 2002. For the reasons set forth below, the motions will be denied.

I. BACKGROUND

A. *Customer Complaints*

PayPal is an online payment service that allows a business or private individual to send and receive payments via the Internet. A PayPal account holder sends money by informing Paypal of the intended recipient's e-mail address and the amount to be sent and by designating a funding source such as a credit card, bank account or separate PayPal account. PayPal accesses the funds and immediately makes them available to the intended recipient. If an intended recipient does not have a PayPal account, the recipient must open an account to access the payment by following a link that is included in the payment notification e-mail. PayPal generates revenues from transaction fees and the interest it derives from holding funds until they are sent.

As of January 1, 2001, approximately 10,000 account holders had registered with PayPal. PayPal thereafter experienced a sudden and dramatic increase in its popularity, attracting one million customers over the next five months and 10.6 million accounts (of which 8.5 million were held by private individuals) by September 30, 2001. Currently, PayPal provides services to twelve million accounts, and approximately 18,000 new accounts are opened each day. Plaintiffs allege that while PayPal has experienced a seven-fold increase in revenues and a thirteen-fold increase in users, it only has doubled the number of service representatives available to address customer concerns.

Plaintiffs contend that because PayPal's customer base has exceeded its operational capacity, PayPal has been and continues to be unable to maintain and manage accounts in the manner required by applicable state and federal legislation. Plaintiffs allege in particular that when PayPal investigates a customer's complaint of fraud, it freezes the customer's access to his or her account until the investigation is completed, but at the same time keeps the account open for deposits, a practice which allows PayPal to derive economic benefit from the deposits while preventing customers from accessing even undisputed funds while the investigation is pending. Plaintiffs further allege that PayPal does not provide a toll-free customer service telephone number, does not effectively publish the customer service telephone number it does provide, requires customers to report erroneous transactions by e-mail while not providing a specific e-mail address for that purpose, requires customers to provide numerous and burdensome personal documents before it undertakes an investigation, responds to e-mail inquiries with form letters, refuses to provide details or explanations with respect to its investigations, and provides no procedure by which a customer can appeal the results of an investigation. Plaintiffs also allege that when customers are able to contact PayPal representatives, the representatives are combative and rude, refuse to answer specific questions, hang up in the middle of phone calls, provide "canned" responses to individualized problems, require customers to fax information while providing inoperative fax numbers, and refuse to allow customers to speak to managers.

Newspaper articles have reported that disgruntled customers who have been unable to contact anyone at PayPal to resolve their disputes have created their own website providing consumers with difficult-to-find customer service numbers and reporting their own frustrations with PayPal's service. According to these accounts, PayPal has a backlog of over 100,000 unanswered customer complaints, a fact that has led the Better Business Bureau to revoke its seal of approval. Plaintiffs allege that PayPal profits from its alleged acts and omissions because customers either abandon their efforts to recover their money or, in cases in which funds actually are returned, because it retains the interest collected on the funds it has held during the investigation process.

1. Craig Comb

Plaintiff Craig Comb ("Comb"), who is not a PayPal customer, alleges the following: On February 15, 2002, without his knowledge, consent or authorization, PayPal removed the sums of $110.00 and $450.00 from his bank account. Comb allegedly had difficulty contacting PayPal with respect to the erroneous transfer and finally reached a PayPal representative on February 18, 2002 to report the alleged error. PayPal acknowledged the error and returned the entire $560.00 to Comb's account on February 25, 2002.

PayPal's transfers, however, caused Comb's bank account to have insufficient funds, and the bank charged Comb $208.50 for failing to maintain his required balance. Comb contacted PayPal and requested reimbursement for the insufficient fund penalty and any interest his funds accrued while in PayPal's possession. PayPal allegedly refused to pay either amount, disputing Comb's figures but failing to provide Comb its own figures or documentation of its investigation.

2. Roberta Toher

Plaintiff Roberta Toher ("Toher") alleges the following: Toher opened a PayPal account sometime in 2000. PayPal failed to provide her with the name, address, and telephone number of a person she should notify in the event of an unauthorized electronic transfer. On February 24, 2002, Toher discovered that PayPal had transferred funds from her checking account to four individuals without her knowledge, consent or authorization. Toher had difficulty locating any telephone number for contacting PayPal. Once she found a telephone number, which was not toll-free, she was placed on hold for a lengthy period of time, and no one answered her call. Toher then located PayPal's e-mail address and reported the error by e-mail.

On or about February 25, 2002, PayPal responded to Toher by e-mail and instructed her to report the erroneous transaction by sending her complaint to either of two e-mail addresses it provided. Toher sent her complaint to one e-mail address, from which it was returned undeliverable, and then to the other address. She also attempted again to contact PayPal by telephone. After Toher again was placed on hold for a lengthy period of time, a PayPal representative instructed her to change her password and report the error by telephone to a different department. Toher called that department's telephone number and spoke with a service representative who informed her that he had verified that the transaction had not been initiated by Toher and that PayPal would send Toher a letter explaining how to report the transaction in writing. During this time, the recipients who erroneously had received the funds e-mailed Toher and inquired as to the reason for the payment.

On or about February 27, 2002, before her complaint had been investigated or resolved, PayPal informed Toher that it intended to take money from her checking account because her bank had declined a different, unrelated transaction. Toher called PayPal and explained that she had filed a claim with respect to the erroneous withdrawal and instructed PayPal to stop removing funds from the checking account. PayPal explained that there was nothing it could do to stop the latter transaction, and Toher was forced to pay a $27.00 fee to her bank to decline all subsequent electronic transactions related to PayPal. Toher contacted PayPal to request for a second time the letter explaining how to report her original claim. PayPal subsequently informed Toher that it would begin processing her claim once she completed and returned a notarized affidavit by mail.

On March 6, 2002, PayPal sent Toher a series of e-mails explaining that because her bank had declined its attempted transfers, PayPal intended to transfer funds from her credit card account. Toher in turn closed and reopened her credit card account to prevent PayPal from accessing her funds. As of the date the instant suit was filed, PayPal had not acknowledged that Toher had reported an erroneous withdrawal or that an error had occurred, nor had it undertaken any investigation with respect to Toher's complaint.

3. Jeffrey Resnick

Plaintiff Jeffrey Resnick ("Resnick") alleges the following: Resnick registered an account with PayPal and linked his e-mail address *resnickjeff@hotmail.com* (with two "f"s) to that account. He used the account to sell comic books on eBay, an Internet auction service. On January 29, 2002, a third party appropriated Resnick's PayPal user name and password and linked an e-mail account resnickjefff@hotmail. com (with three "f"s) to Resnick's PayPal account. The third party sold two Apple Computers on eBay, and the buyers deposited their payment into the fraudulent account. When the buyers did not receive their product, they filed a complaint with PayPal, which without notice or explanation then restricted Resnick's legitimate account.

In late January or early February 2002, Resnick learned that his account had been restricted and contacted PayPal to inquire as to the reason. Once informed of the circumstances, Resnick explained that he had not sold the computers and stated that because the fraudulent account's e-mail address contained three "f"'s rather than two, someone must have appropriated his account information. At the time he filed the instant suit, although more than forty-five days had elapsed since he informed PayPal of its error, he had not received any information or documentation with respect to the status of PayPal's investigation, and PayPal had not unrestricted or credited his account.

B. User Agreement

PayPal customers open an account by completing an online application for a personal, premier, or business account. A prospective customer clicks a box at the bottom of the application page that reads, "[you] have read and agree to the User Agreement and [PayPal's] privacy policy." A link to the text of the User Agreement is located at the bottom of the application. The link need not be opened for the application to be processed. The User Agreement is lengthy, consisting of twenty-five printed pages and eleven sections, each containing a number of subparagraphs enumerating the parties' respective obligations and duties.

PayPal admonishes every customer to read the User Agreement carefully, informs him or her that the Agreement forms a binding contract, and advises the customer to retain a copy of the User Agreement. The User Agreement is a "clickwrap contract," formed when the customer "click[s] 'I Agree,' 'I Accept,' or by submitting payment information through the Service ..." User Agreement, ¶ 2.

The User Agreement contains the following arbitration clause:

> **Arbitration.** Any controversy or claim arising out of or relating to this Agreement or the provision of Services shall be settled by binding arbitration in accordance with the commercial arbitration rules of the American Arbitration Association. Any such controversy or claim shall be arbitrated on an individual basis, and shall not be consolidated in any arbitration with any claim or controversy of any other party. The arbitration shall be conducted in Santa Clara County, California, and judgment on the arbitration award may be entered in any court having jurisdiction thereof. Either you or PayPal may seek any interim or preliminary relief from a court of competent jurisdiction in Santa Clara County, California necessary to protect the rights or property of you or PayPal, Inc. (or its agents, suppliers, and subcontractors) pending the completion of arbitration.

User Agreement, Section II (19).

[Eds.: Omitted here is the court's discussion of the challenges to the validity of the arbitration clause. That issue is addressed further in Chapter 10.]

* * *

III. DISPOSITION

Having considered the terms of the User Agreement generally and the arbitration clause in particular, as well as the totality of the circumstances, the Court concludes that the User Agreement and arbitration clause are substantively unconscionable under California law and that arbitration cannot be compelled herein. Good cause therefor appearing, IT IS HEREBY ORDERED that the motions to compel individual arbitration are DENIED.

[*Eds.*: In light of this disposition, the court does not address whether any of PayPal's conduct was unlawful under specific federal or state laws. In their complaint, 2002 WL 32961681, plaintiffs claimed violations of the federal EFTA, and state law counts of unfair practices, conversion, money had and received, unjust enrichment, and negligence.]

Problem 6–29

What legal protections do consumers need in systems like PayPal? Are those protections sufficiently provided by existing laws, and if so, which laws? The most likely relevant existing law is the federal EFTA with its implementing Regulation E.

• Does the EFTA apply to PayPal? Reg. E §§ 205.3 [coverage], 205.14 [applicability to EFT providers that do not hold the customer's account].

• For each of the three plaintiffs in the *Comb* case, which provisions of EFTA or Reg. E apply to their specific grievances? Consider Reg. E §§ 205.6 [liability for unauthorized transfers]; 205.8(b) [error resolution notice]; 205.11 [error resolution procedures].

• Suppose Crook (mis)uses PayPal to charge several purchases to Victim's credit card account without authorization. Which unauthorized-use and error-resolution rules apply—those of Reg. Z for credit cards, or those of Reg. E for electronic fund transfers? Cf. Reg. E § 205.12(a).

• Recall the material in Chapter 3, Section D, on "clickwrap" contracting. Is it relevant here as well?

Chapter 7

CUTTING OFF CONSUMER CLAIMS AND DEFENSES: CONSUMER PRODUCT WARRANTIES AND THIRD PARTY FINANCING

SECTION A.   INTRODUCTION

Traditional legal doctrines impose substantial responsibilities on sellers for the honesty, quality and safety of their performance. A dissatisfied customer may recover damages upon proof of seller's negligence, or breach of implied or express warranties. A buyer may recover damages or rescind if there was fraud in the transaction, or misrepresentation by the seller.

Also, by traditional rules, a third party who purchased the seller's contractual right to payment took those rights subject to the consumer's defenses against the seller. Thus the fact that a consumer's obligation was assigned to a bank or other financer did not, alone, diminish the consumer's rights.

But for all these conventional principles there were equally well-established bypasses which sellers and creditors could use to reduce or eliminate their exposure to liability. In the setting of contractual warranties, which were perceived to arise from the contractual agreement of the parties, the parties—at least the *dominant* party—were free to contract away those responsibilities. And for third party financers the law supplied the doctrine of "negotiability" of commercial paper with its resultant protection for bona fide purchasers of such paper ("holders in due course").

The Uniform Commercial Code, as originally promulgated, retained most of the conventional wisdom. As between seller and buyer, any affirmation of fact, promise, description or sample creates an express warranty that the goods will conform, if such representation is a part of the "basis of the bargain." UCC § 2–313. In addition, merchant sellers warrant the "merchantability" of their wares, i.e., their fitness for ordinary use. UCC § 2–314. Sellers may also impliedly warrant that their goods are suitable for particular purposes. UCC § 2–315. Against these warranties, however, stand the "disclaimer" rules of UCC § 2–316 through which warranties may be avoided by specific and conspicuous language, by buyer's failure to see patent defects, or even by use of shorthand phrases like "as is." Thus, with only the UCC as a benchmark, a seller can reduce his duty to merely delivering something that meets the basic contract description ("one RCA portable TV"). And under the parol evidence rule inclusion of a "merger" clause would avoid liability for seller's oral statements (or mis-statements), UCC § 2–202. Finally, even if seller gave a warranty, he could scale down buyer's remedy. UCC § 2–719.

As for the protection of third party assignees, the UCC was equally solicitous. If a bank or finance company purchased from a dealer a "negotiable instrument" (UCC § 3–104) under circumstances where it qualified as a "holder in due course" (UCC § 3–302), the creditor could enforce the instrument free from all consumer defenses except a small number of "real" defenses (UCC § 3–305). Alternatively, the third party may acquire virtually identical protection by having the dealer insert a "waiver of defense" clause in the underlying consumer obligation. Furthermore, such a clause is implied into any secured sale involving a negotiable note. See UCC § 9–206(1) (now 9–403).

In a process that began in the early 1990's and culminated in 2003, Article Two of the UCC, pertaining to sale of goods, underwent a revision process. Some early versions contained significant consumer protection reforms. One was a proposed requirement of express consumer agreement to any disclaimer of the implied warranty of merchantability. Another was a proposed treatment of standard form contracts that would have provided for a type of blanket assent to standardized terms, but with a provision that enforcement of terms that would not have been reasonably expected would not be allowed in consumer contracts. This draft was withdrawn from consideration by the leadership of the National Conference of Commissioners on Uniform State Laws (NCCUSL) on the basis that it would not have been enactable in the states. In the end, the NCCUSL and ALI agreed to a much more modest "amendment" of Article Two, which was promulgated in 2003. The enactment process has been slow to get started, with no states yet adopting the amended version of Article 2 as of 2006. Nonetheless, the changes affecting consumer warranties will be noted in these materials on the assumption that they will eventually be enacted by the states.

Article 9, on the other hand, was substantially revised in 1999, and the revised version was quickly adopted by the state legislatures. Sections 9–403 and –404 provide significant protection for consumers seeking to raise claims against assignees of consumer contracts.

For consumer transactions, the implications of the **traditional** UCC rules and sub-rules are easy to see. Sellers and creditors, who could be expected to be in a position to dictate the form and content of their mass-produced consumer contracts, did just that. Warranty "disclaimers" became boilerplate. Negotiable promissory notes (or their functional twins, "waiver of defense" clauses) became standard formalities in credit transactions. Consumers were left with little more than ownership rights in cars that would not run, furniture that fell apart, and appliances that defied repair. *See, e.g., First Nat'l Bank of Elgin v. Husted,* 57 Ill.App.2d 227, 205 N.E.2d 780 (1965).

The materials that follow trace the law's response to this state of consumer disability. First through the courts, and then through the legislatures, the law with respect to consumer claims and defenses has been turned virtually upside down. Sweeping "reforms" were instituted in the latter half of the 20th century. These materials explore two of the developing streams:

> (1) the attack on warranty disclaimers and remedy limitations; and

> (2) the elimination of holder in due course protections.

SECTION B. CONSUMER PRODUCT WARRANTIES: THE QUEST FOR AN EFFECTIVE REMEDY

1. RETURN OF DEFECTIVE GOODS UNDER THE UCC: CONSUMER SALVATION OR CONSUMER NIGHTMARE?

The Uniform Commercial Code is the foundation of all modern warranty law. It applies to both consumer and business transactions. The UCC is premised on the notion that the parties to a transaction are equals who can agree or not agree to anything they please.

Article Two pertains to the law of sales, including warranties, as described in the preceding section. The standard remedies for breach of warranty under the UCC include damages, UCC § 2–714, rejection of goods that do not conform to the warranty, § 2–601, and revocation of acceptance and return of the defective goods leading to a refund of the purchase price, § 2–608. Most consumers are not in a position to resell defective goods, so they normally do not want the remedy of keeping the goods and claiming damages for the loss in value caused by the breach. Also, rejection of goods is available in theory to consumers, but must be done relatively quickly. UCC § 2–602. In the typical consumer case, the consumer will have kept the product for a period of time while trying to obtain a repair or refund from the immediate seller, so that rejection is no longer an available alternative.

Thus, the "ideal" remedy for an individual who has purchased a defective product (assuming that it has not caused physical injury but only economic loss) would be to return the product and obtain a refund of the purchase price. Obviously, an effective warranty disclaimer may preclude this remedy. UCC § 2–316. And even if the warranty has not been disclaimed, moreover, a limitation of remedy clause may pose another obstacle facing the consumer. UCC § 2–719. A new car buyer whose remedy for breach of warranty is limited to repair or replacement of defective parts may soon get frustrated when he finds he must take the car back to the garage again and again. Also, the consumer will likely want a remedy against the "deep pocket" manufacturer, but lack of privity may also be a problem under the UCC. *See infra* subsections 2 & 3.

Yet despite all this, the consumer does have the possibility of claiming the right to revoke acceptance and return defective goods. UCC § 2–608. Courts have become more inclined to uphold this right in consumer cases in modern times. This is not to say there is a yellow brick road that will inevitably lead the consumer to the desired goal, however.

Note the various land mines awaiting the unwary consumer-buyer on her path to the desired goal of return and refund. To revoke acceptance under § 2–608 the consumer must:

— show substantial impairment of value,

— show that non-discovery of the defect was "induced either by difficulty of discovery before acceptance or by the seller's assurances,"

— revoke acceptance within a "reasonable time after the buyer * * * should have discovered [the defects]" and "before any substantial change,"

— properly notify the seller of the alleged breach, and

— refrain from further use of the goods.

Despite these difficulties, revocation of acceptance and return of defective goods has been called "the consumer buyer's most important remedy under Article 2." B. Clark & C. Smith, The Law of Product Warranties 7–15 (1984).

McCULLOUGH v. BILL SWAD CHRYSLER–PLYMOUTH

Ohio Supreme Court, 1983.
5 Ohio St.3d 181, 449 N.E.2d 1289.

On May 23, 1978, appellee, Deborah A. McCullough (then Deborah Miller), purchased a 1978 Chrysler LeBaron from appellant, Bill Swad Chrysler–Plymouth, Inc. (now Bill Swad Datsun, Inc.). The automobile was protected by both a limited warranty and a Vehicle Service Contract (extended warranty). Following delivery of the vehicle, appellee and her (then) fiance informed appellant's sales agent of problems they had noted with the car's brakes, lack of rustproofing, paint job and seat panels. Other problems were noted by appellee as to the car's transmission and air conditioning. The next day, the brakes failed, and appellee returned the car to appellant for the necessary repairs.

When again in possession of the car, appellee discovered that the brakes had not been fixed properly and that none of the cosmetic work was done. Problems were also noted with respect to the car's steering mechanism. Again, the car was returned for repair and again new problems appeared, this time as to the windshield post, the vinyl top and the paint job. Only two weeks later, appellant was unable to eliminate a noise appellee complained of that had developed in the car's rear end.

On June 26, 1978, appellee returned the car to appellant for correction both of the still unremedied defects and of other flaws that had surfaced since the last failed repair effort. Appellant retained possession of the vehicle for over three weeks in order to service it, but even then many of the former problems persisted. Moreover, appellant's workmanship had apparently caused new defects to arise affecting the car's stereo system, landau top and exterior. Appellee also experienced difficulties with vibrations, the horn, and the brakes.

The following month, while appellee was on a short trip away from her home, the automobile's engine abruptly shut off. The car eventually had to be towed to appellant's service shop for repair. A few days later, when appellee and her husband were embarked on an extensive honeymoon vacation, the brakes again failed. Upon returning from their excursion, the newlyweds, who had prepared a list of thirty-two of the automobile's defects, submitted the list to appellant and again requested their correction. By the end of October 1978, few of the enumerated problems had been remedied.

In early November 1978, appellee contacted appellant's successor, Chrysler–Plymouth East ("East"), regarding further servicing of the vehicle. East was not able to undertake the requested repairs until January 1979. Despite the additional work which East performed, the vehicle continued to malfunction. After May 1979, East refused to perform any additional work on the automobile, claiming that the vehicle was in satisfactory condition, appellee's assertions to the contrary notwithstanding.

On January 8, 1979, appellee, by letter addressed to appellant, called for the rescission of the purchase agreement, demanded a refund of the entire purchase price and expenses incurred, and offered to return the automobile to appellant upon receipt of shipping instructions. Appellant did not respond to appellee's letter, and appellee continued to operate the car.

On January 12, 1979, appellee filed suit against appellant, East, Chrysler Corporation, and City National Bank & Trust Co., seeking rescission of the sales agreement and incidental and consequential damages. By the time of trial, June 25, 1980, the subject vehicle had been driven nearly 35,000 miles, approximately 23,000 of which were logged after appellee mailed her notice of revocation. The trial court dismissed the action as to East, the bank and Chrysler Corporation, but entered judgment for appellee against appellant in the amount of $9,376.82, and ordered the return of the automobile to appellant. The court of appeals subsequently affirmed, determining that appellee had properly revoked her acceptance of the automobile despite her continued use of the vehicle, which use the appellate court found reasonable.

The cause is now before this court pursuant to the allowance of a motion to certify the record.

LOCHER, JUSTICE.

The case at bar essentially poses but a single question: Whether appellee, by continuing to operate the vehicle she had purchased from appellant after notifying the latter of her intent to rescind the purchase agreement, waived her right to revoke her initial acceptance. After having thoroughly reviewed both the relevant facts in the present cause and the applicable law, we find that appellee, despite her extensive use of the car following her revocation, in no way forfeited such right.

* * *

Although the legal question presented in appellant's first objection is a novel one for this bench, other state courts which have addressed the issue have held that whether continued use of goods after notification of revocation of their acceptance vitiates such revocation is solely dependent upon whether such use was reasonable. Moreover, whether such use was reasonable is a question to be determined by the trier of fact.

The genesis of the "reasonable use" test lies in the recognition that frequently a buyer, after revoking his earlier acceptance of a good, is constrained by exogenous circumstances—many of which the seller controls—to continue using the good until a suitable replacement may realistically be secured. Clearly, to penalize the buyer for a predicament not of his own creation would be patently unjust. As the court stated in *Richardson v. Messina* (1960), 361 Mich. 364, 369, 105 N.W.2d 153, 156:

> * * * It does not lie in the seller's mouth to demand the utmost in nicety between permissible and impermissible use, for the perilous situation in which the purchaser finds himself arises from the imperfections of that furnished, for a consideration, by the seller himself. * * *

In ascertaining whether a buyer's continued use of an item after revocation of its acceptance was reasonable, the trier of fact should pose and divine the answers to the following queries: (1) Upon being apprised of the buyer's revocation of his acceptance, what instructions, if any, did the seller tender the buyer concerning return of the now rejected goods? (2) Did the buyer's business needs or personal circumstances compel the continued use? (3) During the period of such use, did the seller persist in assuring the buyer that all nonconformities would be cured or that provisions would otherwise be made to recompense the latter for the dissatisfaction and inconvenience which the defects caused him? (4) Did the seller act in good faith? (5) Was the seller unduly prejudiced by the buyer's continued use?

It is manifest that, upon consideration of the aforementioned criteria, appellee acted reasonably in continuing to operate her motor vehicle even after revocation of acceptance. First, the failure of the seller to advise the buyer, after the latter has revoked his acceptance of the goods, how the goods were to be returned entitles the buyer to retain possession of them. Appellant, in the case at bar, did not respond to appellee's request for instructions regarding the disposition of the vehicle. Failing to have done so, appellant can hardly be heard now to complain of appellee's continued use of the automobile.

Secondly, appellee, a young clerical secretary of limited financial resources, was scarcely in position to return the defective automobile and obtain a second in order to meet her business and personal needs. A most unreasonable obligation would be imposed upon appellee were she to be required, in effect, to secure a loan to purchase a second car while remaining liable for repayment of the first car loan.

Additionally, appellant's successor (East), by attempting to repair the appellee's vehicle even after she tendered her notice of revocation, provided both express and tacit assurances that the automobile's defects were remediable, thereby, inducing her to retain possession. Moreover, whether appellant acted in good faith throughout this episode is highly problematic, especially given the fact that whenever repair of the car was undertaken, new defects often miraculously arose while previous ones frequently went uncorrected. Both appellant's and East's refusal to honor the warranties before their expiration also evidences less than fair dealing.

* * *

Appellant maintains, however, that even if appellee's continued operation of the automobile after revocation was reasonable, such use is "*prima facie* evidence" that the vehicle's nonconformities did not substantially impair its value to appellee, thus precluding availability of the remedy of revocation. Such an inference, though, may not be drawn. As stated earlier, external conditions beyond the buyer's immediate control often mandate continued use of an item even after revocation of its acceptance. Thus, it cannot seriously be contended that appellee, by continuing to operate the defective vehicle, intimated that its nonconformities did not substantially diminish its worth in her eyes.

* * *

Whether a complained of nonconformity substantially impairs an item's worth to the buyer is a determination exclusively within the purview of the factfinder and must be based on objective evidence of the buyer's idiosyncratic tastes and needs. Any defect that shakes the buyer's faith or undermines his confidence in the reliability and integrity of the purchased item is deemed to work a substantial impairment of the item's value and to provide a basis for revocation of the underlying sales agreement. Clearly, no error was committed in finding that the fears occasioned by the recurrent brake failings, steering malfunctions and other mechanical difficulties, as well as the utter frustration caused by the seemingly endless array of cosmetic flaws, constituted nonconformities giving rise to the remedy of revocation.

* * *

On the basis of the foregoing analysis, we affirm the judgment of the court of appeals.

Judgment affirmed.

HOLMES, JUSTICE, dissenting in part and concurring in part.

I concur in the syllabus law as set forth in this case, but would remand to the trial court for a determination of the amount due the dealer from the buyer as a setoff due to the buyer's use of the goods after revocation. Both the court of appeals and this court state that Swad should be entitled to such an offset against the judgment for the reasonable value of the use of the automobile after the revocation. However, both courts summarily dispense with such an offset by stating that Swad introduced no evidence to establish the reasonable value of the automobile's use.

The need for any such evidence when the appellant was asserting that the buyer had waived any right to revoke acceptance would, from the standpoint of trial procedure, have been highly questionable. The seller should be given an opportunity to present evidence of the reasonable value of such use, or the trial court should take judicial notice of the fair market value of the use of such an automobile.

GASQUE v. MOOERS MOTOR CAR CO., INC.

Supreme Court of Virginia, 1984.
227 Va. 154, 313 S.E.2d 384.

RUSSELL, JUSTICE. * * *

In accordance with established standards of appellate review, we must view the evidence in the light most favorable to the parties prevailing below. The buyers took delivery of a new Fiat from Mooers on February 21, 1979. At various subsequent times, they reported to Mooers that they had experienced a water leak, a loose gearshift lever, difficulty shifting into second and third gear, heater malfunction, an inoperative clock and interior light, a loose wire under the dash, blown fuses, a piece missing from a front door, automatic choke problems, difficulty starting, fast idling, difficulty closing the rear door on the driver's side, difficulty opening the rear door on the passenger's side, excessive oil consumption, loud vibrations, and various other noises and rattles. In addition, they claimed that the reclining front seat broke, and that they experienced repeated difficulty with the foot-long plastic extension to the gearshift lever, which pulled loose.

The buyers returned the car to Mooers on March 13, March 23, an unspecified date in May, June 22, June 27, July 20, and August 6, 1979, for service. On each occasion, Mooers repaired the items complained of, without charge, although Mooers could find no evidence of some of the problems described by the buyers. Mooers conceded that the car experienced a recurring problem with the gearshift extension and testified that this defect affected three out of seventy cars of this model which it had recently sold. Mooers' service manager testified that the gearshift extension would come off only if used improperly by pulling it upward and that the car was still operable without the extension. The car was in fact driven for thousands of miles while subject to this defect. Although Mooers thought a permanent repair of this problem could be accomplished, the difficulty continued up to the time of trial.

The buyers consulted counsel, who, on September 19, 1979, wrote to Mooers and to Fiat demanding "a full refund including interests and expenses for the times that the vehicle was in the shop or, in the alternative, the replacement of said automobile."

The buyers continued to drive the Fiat, except when it was left with Mooers for service. When the car was last in Mooers' shop for repairs on August 6, it had 4,543 miles on the odometer. When buyers' counsel wrote to Mooers on September 19, he stated that the car had been driven 5,400 miles. At the time of trial on May 21, 1980, the car had been driven over 8,000 miles. The buyers testified that they purchased a used Volkswagen in November 1979, and permanently parked the Fiat, which by then had been driven 8,000 miles, in their driveway.

* * *

A buyer's right to revoke acceptance does not arise from every breach of warranty, notwithstanding the availability of damages for the breach; it arises only where the value of the goods to the buyer is substantially impaired. The test of such impairment is not, however, a diminution in value of the goods on the open market, or to the average buyer, but rather a substantial impairment of value to the particular buyer involved.

* * *

How may this be shown? Undoubtedly, there may be a purchaser of an automobile who wants it for an unusual and special purpose, such as display in a collection of antique vehicles. But the burden would be on the buyer to show such a special need. In the absence of such a showing, the fact-finder is entitled to infer that the goods are needed by the buyer for their customary and ordinary purpose—simple transportation in the case of an automobile. In the instant case, there was persuasive evidence that the Fiat in question substantially fulfilled that purpose. It had been driven 5,400 miles by the time the buyers sought to revoke acceptance and an additional 2,600 miles thereafter. The trial court applied a standard of "driveability" as the test of whether the car's value to the buyers was substantially impaired. While such a standard would not be of universal application, we cannot say that it was erroneous where the buyers failed to prove any need for the car beyond ordinary transportation. Accordingly, the trial court's finding in this respect was supported by evidence and will not be disturbed on appeal.

* * * Revocation of acceptance must be made promptly, or within a reasonable time after acceptance, and the buyer may not use the goods to a material degree and then attempt to revoke. * * * But after giving notice of revocation, the buyer holds the goods as bailee for the seller. The buyer cannot continue to use them as his own and still have the benefit of rescission; his continued use becomes wrongful against the seller, unless induced by the seller's instructions or promises.

Exceptions have been made to the rule in mobile home cases, where departure from the home before resolving the litigation would cause undue hardship to the buyer and where the buyer's continued occupancy might be the best means of safeguarding the property for a seller who refuses to take it back. But this reasoning has no application to the continuing use of an automobile, which ordinarily depreciates in value with every mile it is driven.

Applying these principles to the case at bar, the buyers' delay, at least until after August 6, was reasonable in light of the seller's continuing efforts to effect repairs, which were only partially successful. But it is equally clear that the buyers' continued use of the car after giving notice of revocation of acceptance on September 19, during which time they drove it 2,600 miles, was entirely inconsistent with their position as a bailee, maintaining custody only to safeguard the car for the seller. Such personal use of what they contended to be the seller's property does not meet the standard of commercial reasonableness, and the trial court correctly so held.

The trial court correctly struck the evidence against Fiat. The remedy of revocation of acceptance was the sole relief available to the buyers under their bill of complaint, as noted above. This remedy lies only against a seller of goods, not against a remote manufacturer. This is so because the remedy, where successful, cancels a contract of sale, restores both title to and possession of the goods to the seller, restores the purchase price to the buyer, and as fairly as possible, returns the contracting parties to the *status quo ante*. The remote manufacturer, having no part in the sale transaction, has no role to play in such a restoration of former positions.

The buyers argue that this limitation on revocation revivifies the "archaic doctrine of privity." We disagree. A remote manufacturer is liable to a buyer for damages arising from negligence or from breach of warranty, and the defense of lack of privity has been abolished as to such cases. Code § 8.2–318. But the remedy of revocation of acceptance under Code § 8.2–608 is conceptually inapplicable to any persons other than the parties to the contract of sale sought to be rescinded.

For these reasons, the decree will be

Affirmed.

Notes

1. Under UCC § 2–608, the buyer is not supposed to exercise ownership rights over the product after revocation of acceptance, as discussed in

Gasque. Yet in *McCullough*, the court held that the consumer could continue to use the car after revocation of acceptance. Which approach is better? Many courts in addition to *McCullough* have ruled that continued use after revocation does not act as an acceptance as long as the use is reasonable. See North River Homes, Inc. v. Bosarge, 594 So.2d 1153 (Miss. 1992); Cuesta v. Classic Wheels, Inc., 358 N.J.Super. 512, 818 A.2d 448 (2003). What factors led the court in *McCullough* to conclude that continued use was reasonable? Should it make any difference whether the product is a car, a mobile home, or something else?

2.   Justice Holmes, dissenting and concurring in *McCullough,* suggested the seller be awarded a setoff for the value of the buyer's use after revocation. This principle is now accepted in case law. See Carolyn F. Lazaris, Note, Article 2: Revocation of Acceptance—Should a Seller Be Granted Setoff for the Buyer's Use of the Goods?, 30 New Eng. L. Rev. 1073 (1996). The principle of reasonable use after revocation with a right of seller setoff is also incorporated into the amended version of Article 2. UCC § 2–608(4) (as amended 2003).

3.   Substantial impairment of value is one of the prerequisites for revocation of acceptance and return of defective goods. Why was the value of the car deemed substantially impaired in the *McCullough* case but not in *Gasque*? Which approach to substantial impairment is more relevant in consumer cases, the "shaken faith" test alluded to in *McCullough* or the "driveability" test applied in *Gasque?* Is the test for substantial impairment of value in UCC § 2–608 objective or subjective? Does the Code language itself provide a clue? *See* Jorgensen v. Pressnall, 274 Or. 285, 545 P.2d 1382 (1976).

4.   In *Gasque*, the court ruled that the consumer could have no revocation remedy against Fiat, the remote manufacturer. Do you agree? What happens if the dealer is in bankruptcy or goes out of business or has successfully disclaimed all warranties? Does the ruling in *Gasque* mean that revocation is no longer available as a consumer remedy?

Consider the following case.

FODE v. CAPITAL RV CENTER, INC.

Supreme Court of North Dakota, 1998.
575 N.W.2d 682.

SANDSTROM, JUSTICE.

Coachmen Recreational Vehicle Co. and Capital RV Center, Inc., (defendants) appealed from a judgment entered upon a jury verdict granting Albert and Birdie Fode revocation of their acceptance of a motor home, finding Coachmen breached its warranty to Fodes, and awarding Fodes damages, and from an order denying the defendants' motion for judgment as a matter of law or for a new trial. Fodes cross-appealed from the judgment. We hold Fodes were entitled to revoke acceptance of the motor home against both defendants, and the jury verdict is supported by substantial evidence. We also hold the trial court abused its discretion in awarding Fodes attorney fees without affording the defendants an opportunity to be heard. We affirm the judgment, reverse the award of attorney fees, and remand for reconsideration of the amount of the attorney fee award.

I

In January 1992, Capital sold Fodes a motor home manufactured by Coachmen. Capital's sales contract with Fodes said the motor home was "sold new with sportscoach" manufacturer warranty and, in bold print, included language stating Capital disclaimed all warranties:

> MANUFACTURER'S WARRANTY: ANY WARRANTY ON ANY NEW VEHICLE OR USED VEHICLE STILL SUBJECT TO A MANUFACTURER'S WARRANTY IS THAT MADE BY THE MANUFACTURER ONLY. THE SELLER HEREBY DISCLAIMS ALL WARRANTIES, EITHER EXPRESS OR IMPLIED, INCLUDING ANY IMPLIED WARRANTY OF MERCHANTABILITY OR FITNESS FOR A PARTICULAR PURPOSE, ANY STATEMENT CONTAINED HEREIN DOES NOT APPLY WHERE PROHIBITED BY LAW.

Coachmen's "new recreational vehicle limited warranty" for the motor home said:

COVERAGE PROVIDED

Coachmen Recreational Vehicle Company will, for one year from the retail purchase date, or for the first 15,000 miles of use, whichever comes first, make repairs which are necessary because of defects in material or workmanship. We will repair or replace any defective part at no cost to you. Because of design changes and improvements, we may substitute parts or components of substantially equal quality. This warranty covers you, as the first retail purchaser of our new product, from an authorized Coachmen dealer.

TO OBTAIN SERVICE

For warranty service, take the product, at your expense, to an authorized Coachmen dealer or service center.

* * *

WE SHALL NOT BE LIABLE FOR INCIDENTAL OR CONSEQUENTIAL DAMAGES, such as expenses for transportation, lodging, loss or damage to person property, loss of use of your product, inconvenience, or loss of income. Some states do not allow exclusion or limitation of incidental or consequential damages, so the above limitation or exclusion may not apply to you.

* * *

IMPLIED WARRANTIES, INCLUDING ANY WARRANTY OF MERCHANTABILITY OR FITNESS FOR A PARTICULAR PURPOSE, ARE LIMITED IN DURATION TO THE TERM OF THIS

WRITTEN WARRANTY. Some states do not allow limitations on how long an implied warranty lasts, so the above limitation may not apply to you.

This warranty gives you specific legal rights, and you may also have other rights which vary from state to state.

Albert Fode and Capital signed a "warranty registration," which said the motor home was warranted in the name of Capital as the dealer and certified "all warranties [had been] clearly explained." Fodes, however, testified Coachmen's warranty was not delivered to them.

According to Fodes, they experienced numerous problems with the motor home, including several malfunctions of the electrical system, defective shocks and equalizer bar, and insufficient power to drive the vehicle faster than 65 miles per hour. They testified those problems effectively precluded them from using the motor home for their intended purpose. Finally, in January 1993, Fodes were unable to start the motor home for several days, and they requested revocation of their acceptance. The defendants refused Fodes' request.

Fodes sued Capital and Coachmen for revocation of acceptance and breach of warranty. The trial court granted Capital summary judgment on Fodes' breach of warranty claim against it. In Fodes' revocation of acceptance claim, a jury awarded them $9,600 plus interest from Capital and $20,000 plus interest from Coachmen. In Fodes' breach of warranty claim against Coachmen, the jury awarded them $5,000 plus $1,500 in incidental and $5,000 in consequential damages. The jury also decided Fodes were entitled to attorney fees on their breach of warranty claim against Coachmen.

* * *

II

The defendants contend Fodes were not, as a matter of law, entitled to revoke acceptance against Coachmen. The defendants argue Coachmen is not a "seller" under the Uniform Commercial Code (N.D.C.C. Title 41), and a buyer generally may revoke acceptance of goods only against an immediate seller under N.D.C.C. § 41–02–71 (U.C.C. § 2–608).

* * *

Under those U.C.C. provisions, a buyer generally may revoke acceptance of goods only against its own seller.

Under different formulations of an exception to the general rule, however, some courts have allowed a buyer to revoke acceptance against a non-privity manufacturer if the manufacturer has expressly warranted goods to the ultimate buyer.

* * *

In *Troutman v. Pierce, Inc.*, 402 N.W.2d 920 (N.D.1987), buyers of a mobile home sued the seller and the manufacturer for revocation of acceptance, and the seller cross-claimed against the manufacturer for contribution or indemnity. A jury found the manufacturer, but not the seller, had breached express and implied warranties; there were no substantial defects in the mobile home which were the responsibility of the seller; and there were substantial defects in the mobile home which were the responsibility of the manufacturer. The judgment decreed the buyers had validly revoked their acceptance of the mobile home, allowed the buyers to recover their damages, and ordered the manufacturer to indemnify the seller.

On appeal, the manufacturer argued the trial court erred in ruling the buyers had validly revoked acceptance of the mobile home because the jury found the seller was not responsible for any of the unremedied defects. This Court ruled:

> The buyer's right of revocation is not conditioned upon whether it is the seller or the manufacturer that is responsible for the nonconformity. Under § 41–02–71 (2–608), N.D.C.C., a buyer is entitled to revoke his acceptance of a unit if a 'nonconformity substantially impairs its value to him,' regardless of whether it is the seller or the manufacturer that is responsible for the nonconformity. The jury found that there were substantial defects in the mobile home that substantially impaired its value to the [buyers] and constituted breaches of express and implied warranties. The jury also found that [manufacturer] and [seller] were given reasonable notice of the defects and a reasonable opportunity to remedy the defects. Thus, the trial court did not err in determining that the [buyers] had validly revoked their acceptance of the mobile home.

Troutman at 922–23. *Troutman* affirmed a judgment allowing the buyer to revoke acceptance against a non-privity manufacturer; however, the parties did not specifically argue whether the buyer could revoke acceptance against the non-privity manufacturer, and this Court did not decide that issue.

* * *

The defendants argue *Troutman* appears to adopt the minority position that privity is not required to maintain a revocation of acceptance claim against a manufacturer. *See* Gary L. Monserud, Judgment Against a Non-breaching Seller: The Cost of Outrunning the Law to do Justice under Section 2–608 of the Uniform Commercial Code, 70 N.D.L.Rev. 809, 812 n. 20 (1994). * * *

In *Durfee* [*v. Rod Baxter Imports, Inc.*, 262 N.W.2d 349 at 357 (Minn. 1977)], the Minnesota Supreme Court considered a distributor's argument it was not liable to a buyer for revocation of acceptance because it had no direct contractual relationship with the buyer:

> Although the relevant sections of Article 2 of the Uniform Commercial Code seem to require a buyer-seller relationship, [the

distributor] does not escape liability on this ground in these circumstances.

"The existence and comprehensiveness of a warranty undoubtedly are significant factors in a consumer's decision to purchase a particular automobile. [The distributor] evidently warrants its automobiles to increase retail sales and indirectly its own sales of Saab automobiles. When the exclusive remedy found in the warranty fails of its essential purpose and when the remaining defects are substantial enough to justify revocation of acceptance, we think the buyer is entitled to look to the warrantor for relief. If plaintiff had sued [the distributor] for breach of either express warranty or implied warranty, the absence of privity would not bar the suit despite the language of the pertinent Code sections.... We see no reason why the result should differ merely because plaintiff has chosen to revoke his acceptance instead of suing for breach of warranty. The remedies of the Code are to be liberally administered...."

In [*Volkswagen, Inc. v. Novak,* 418 So. 2d 801, at 803 (Miss. 1982)], the purchasers of a new car revoked acceptance against a manufacturer who had extended a limited warranty to the purchasers. In affirming revocation against the manufacturer, the Mississippi Supreme Court concluded the manufacturer was a "seller":

[T]he retailer[']s sales contract [and] the manufacturer's warranty, are so closely linked both in time of delivery and subject matter, that they blended into a single unit at the time of sale. We are fortified in this statement by the general observance that sales are usually made, not only upon the make and model of the automobile, but also upon the assurance of the manufacturer, through its warranty, that the vehicle will conform to the standards of merchantability.

Novak at 804.

Here, Capital's sales contract with Fodes expressly said the motor home was "sold new with sportscoach" manufacturer warranty. In a provision disclaiming Capital's warranty liability, Capital's sales contract with Fodes specified "MANUFACTURER'S WARRANTY: ANY WARRANTY ON ANY NEW VEHICLE ... IS THAT MADE BY THE MANUFACTURER ONLY." Coachmen's "new recreational vehicle limited warranty" directed the buyer to take the product to "an authorized Coachmen dealer or service center" for warranty service, and Albert Fode signed a "warranty registration," which said the mobile home was warranted in the name of Capital as the dealer. These documents unambiguously passed Coachmen's warranty to Fodes and specified the product was warranted in the name of Capital as the dealer. Capital's sales contract with Fodes and Coachmen's warranty are "so closely linked both in time of delivery and subject matter, that they blended into a single unit at the time of sale." *Novak* at 804.

In proceedings before the trial court, Coachmen asserted the general rule precluded revocation of acceptance against a non-privity manufacturer, and Fodes contended revocation against Coachmen was authorized under an exception to the general rule. In instructing the jury revocation of acceptance applied to Coachmen, the trial court, as a matter of law, effectively ruled revocation against a manufacturer was available under the exception. We conclude reasonable persons could not disagree about the application of the exception to this case. Coachmen, therefore, is a seller for purposes of Fodes' revocation of acceptance claim. We hold Coachmen was not entitled to a judgment as a matter of law on the revocation of acceptance claim, and the trial court did not err in instructing the jury Fodes' revocation of acceptance claim applied to Coachmen.

* * *

VIII

We affirm the judgment, reverse the award of attorney fees and remand for reconsideration of the amount of attorney fees.

VANDE WALLE, C.J., and MESCHKE, NEUMANN and MARING, JJ., concur.

Notes

1.   On what basis did the court in *Fode* make its ruling that buyers of a defective mobile home could revoke acceptance vis-à-vis the remote manufacturer? Do you agree that courts should make such an exception, especially in consumer cases?

2.   While the view expressed in the *Fode* case has its adherents, it appears that the majority of courts considering this issue follow the holding in *Gasque*, to the effect that a buyer may not revoke acceptance against a remote manufacturer under UCC § 2–608. The most persuasive reasoning for not allowing revocation against a remote manufacturer is that the remedy does not "fit" the relationship. Revocation seeks to put the parties back into their pre-sale status, but since the consumer never paid the manufacturer directly and did not obtain the product from the manufacturer, essentially these parties have nothing to return to each other. Courts have also used textual analysis of the wording of UCC § 2–608 and related sections to reach this conclusion. *See* Hines v. Mercedes–Benz USA, LLC, 358 F. Supp. 2d 1222 (N.D. Ga. 2005); Griffith v. Latham Motors, Inc., 128 Idaho 356, 913 P.2d 572 (1996); Hardy v. Winnebago Industries, Inc., 120 Md.App. 261, 706 A.2d 1086 (1998); Neal v. SMC Corp., 99 S.W.2d 813 (Tex. Ct. App. 2003). *See also* cases discussed in Harry M. Flechtner, Enforcing Manufacturers' Warranties, "Pass Through" Warranties, and the Like: Can the Buyer Get a Refund?, 50 Rutgers L. Rev. 397 (1998).

3.   The amended UCC Article Two added Sections 2–313A and 2–313B to extend a manufacturer's obligations with regard to new goods to remote purchasers. Do these new sections create a right to revoke acceptance directly from a remote manufacturer in scenario's like those in *Gasque* and *Fode*? Why or why not?

4.   As will be discussed in the subsection on state Lemon Laws, *infra* Section B(5), in the case of new automobiles under warranty, there is usually

no need to attempt to revoke acceptance against a distant manufacturer because that remedy is already included in the Lemon Law.

2. THE ASSAULT ON WARRANTY DISCLAIMERS AND LIMITATIONS ON REMEDIES

This section presumes that students have at least passing familiarity with the UCC provisions on warranties, disclaimers, and remedy limitations. UCC §§ 2–313 to 2–316, and 2–719. See generally J. White and R. Summers, Uniform Commercial Code, Chapters 9–12 (4th Ed. 1995). Our focus here is primarily on the consumer's claim for *economic loss,* rather than on the broader questions involving the doctrine of strict liability in tort under Restatement (Third) Torts: Products Liability.

Problem 7–1

Robbin Hood bought a used car on credit from Alan Dale, doing business as Dale Auto Center. The contract of sale conspicuously stated that the car was sold "as is" and "with all faults." Hood drove the car off the lot and used it for 30 days. Then the car became inoperable, and Dale refused to repair, replace or refund. Does Hood have a successful cause of action against Dale under the UCC? See UCC § 2–316(2), (3) and UCC § 2–302; Basselen v. General Motors Corp., 341 Ill.App.3d 278, 275 Ill.Dec. 267, 792 N.E.2d 498, 507–508 (2003).

Note that since the mid–1980's, the FTC used car rule, 16 C.F.R. § 455, requires a window sticker emphasizing and explaining the meaning of "as is" and encouraging consumers to get all promises in writing and seek the opinion of an independent mechanic on the car's condition before buying.

Problem 7–2

Hood bought a used car from Dale on credit. The contract of sale contained an express warranty with a one-year duration. After 30 days the car became inoperable. Can Hood safely stop making payments on the car? See UCC §§ 2–607(1), 2–717.

This may seem like an academic question in this simple transaction; presumably if seller sues buyer for the price buyer will defend and seek a set-off under UCC § 2–714 for breach of warranty. The issue becomes less academic, however, when we include the very real possibility of default judgments, and the effects of security interests and garnishments.

At the least, remember that there is a major distinction between buyer's ability to go to court and sue for breach of warranty, and buyer's ability to use self-help in the form of withholding payments. The right to exercise self-help seems deeply imbedded in our folklore; many dissatisfied consumers instinctively react by withholding payments, often with sad results. In reality self-help under the UCC is very limited, for UCC § 2–717 requires some moderately intricate "dance steps" as conditions to its use. The buyer must *notify* the seller of his intention to deduct damages from the payments, and may deduct only the damages caused by the breach of warranty—not the entire price. How likely is it that an unadvised consumer will adhere to these restrictions?

The judicial assault on warranty disclaimers began with the landmark case of Henningsen v. Bloomfield Motors, Inc., 32 N.J. 358, 161 A.2d 69 (1960). Ten days after her husband had purchased a new Plymouth, Helen Henningsen was injured when the car's steering mechanism failed. The sale contract had included a limited warranty against defective parts, and a remedy limited to replacement of such parts. In a long and rambling decision, Judge Francis denied effect to the disclaimer and limitation of remedy provisions, both as against Bloomfield Motors and against the Chrysler Corporation, citing the "gross inequality of bargaining position occupied by the consumer" and the "public policy" of protecting "the ordinary man against the loss of important rights."

Even in the context of purely economic loss, courts have often found ways within the parameters of the UCC to help the consumer get around warranty disclaimers and remedy limitations. Consider the following.

GIARRATANO v. MIDAS MUFFLER

City Court, City of Yonkers, Westchester County, New York, 1995.
166 Misc.2d 390, 630 N.Y.S.2d 656.

Thomas A. Dickerson, Judge.

On May 5, 1993 the plaintiff drove her vehicle, a 1990 Honda Civic, to the defendant, a Midas Muffler shop located at 400 South Broadway, Tarrytown, New York ["Midas"] to have her brakes serviced. A Midas mechanic inspected the Honda and replaced the front brake pads, resurfaced the right and left front rotors, replaced the shims and relined the rear brakes.

Seeking to avoid the high cost of a future "brake job" the plaintiff decided to buy a Midas Warranty Certificate sold by defendant which provided:

WARRANTY PERIOD

Your Midas brake shoes or disc brake pads are warranted by Midas to you, the original purchaser, for as long as you own the vehicle on which the brake shoes and/or disc brake pads were originally installed.

WHAT IS COVERED

If your Midas brake shoes and/or disc brake pads become damaged, defective or worn out ... Midas will install replacement warranted brake shoes or disc brake pads. You will not be charged for the brake shoes or disc brake pads or the labor required to install them. The brake shoes and/or disc brake pads will be considered worn out when the lining's minimum wearable thickness is less than manufacture's specifications....

WHAT IS NOT COVERED

This warranty does not cover the cost of additional components and labor required to restore the brake system to its proper operation. The Midas shop must restore the entire brake system to its proper operation. If you do not authorize this service, you will receive non-installed, non-warranted brake shoes and/or disc brake pads....

On December 15, 1994 the plaintiff's brakes were screeching once again. The plaintiff returned her vehicle to Midas for servicing. Plaintiff presented her Warranty Certificate and requested that defendant inspect the front wheels and replace worn brake pads, free of charge.

Midas's mechanic removed the Honda's front wheels, found that the right front inner brake pads were worn and invited plaintiff to inspect. Plaintiff observed the worn pads and requested that defendant replace them. Midas's mechanic, however, refused to replace the worn brake pads unless plaintiff allowed him to (1) inspect the entire brake system, front and rear, and (2) replace any and all parts which Midas determined to be needed to restore the entire brake system to its proper operation. Plaintiff would, of course, be required to pay all of the costs [labor and parts] generated during this restoration process.

The plaintiff refused to permit Midas to inspect the entire brake system and make repairs as it deemed necessary. Midas's manager not only failed to replace plaintiff's worn brake pads but also failed to give her "non-installed, non-warranted brake shoes and/or disc brake pads". The plaintiff took possession of her vehicle and drove to a service station located in Irvington, New York, where she purchased new brake pads and had them installed for $128.10.

At trial Midas's manager's only explanation for why it was necessary to inspect the entire brake system and make repairs deemed necessary and proper by Midas was to protect Midas from exposure to consumer lawsuits arising from accidents traceable to that part of the brake system that had not been inspected.

DISCUSSION

The plaintiff seeks damages of $128.10, the amount she paid to another repair shop to remove and replace her worn right front brake pads. Plaintiff reasonably expected Midas to honor its Warranty Certificate and provide the new brake pads which she had already paid for but was forced to purchase a second time elsewhere.

Based upon a review of the facts the Court finds that plaintiff has asserted the following cognizable causes of action against the defendant: (1) violation of U.C.C. § 2–316(1) (exclusion or modification of warranties), (2) violation of U.C.C. § 2–719(2) (contractual modification or limitation of remedy), (3) violation of General Business Law § 617(2)(a) (motor vehicle parts warranty), (4) breach of warranty and (5) violation of General Business Law § 349 (unfair, deceptive and misleading business practices).

The Auto Repair Business

Generally, car and truck owners know precious little about how their vehicles operate. When a problem arises they must rely upon repair shops that on occasion may be operated by unscrupulous people

Extended and New Parts Warranties

The extended warranty and new parts warranty business generates extraordinary profits for the retailers of cars, trucks and automotive parts and for repair shops. It has been estimated that no more than 20% of the people who buy warranties ever use them. Of the 20% that actually try to use their warranties, as did the plaintiff, they soon discover that the real costs can easily exceed the initial cost of the Warranty Certificate. Stated, simply, selling Warranty Certificates is a gold mine for Midas.

The Midas Warranty Certificate

Consumers that use the Midas Warranty Certificate believe it to be similar to an insurance policy where in return for the consumer's payment Midas assumes the risk of worn brake pads and undertakes to indemnify the consumer against such loss by replacing them free of charge. This expectation is reasonable, can be derived from the express language in the Warranty Certificate ["If your Midas ... brake pads become ... worn out ... Midas will install replacement warranted ... brake pads. You will not be charged for the brake ... pads or the labor required to install them ..."] and has been the subject of nationwide advertising for decades, see e.g., *Parthenopoulos v. Maddox*, 629 S.W.2d 563 (Mo.App.1981) (Midas customer charged $140.00 for guaranteed brake job); *Brooks v. Midas–International Corp.*, 47 Ill.App.3d 266, 270, 5 Ill.Dec. 492, 494, 361 N.E.2d 815, 817 (1977) ("plaintiff ... alleged ... that (Midas) misrepresented its guarantee for the purpose of creating the impression in consumer's minds that no charges would be assessed other than an installation charge ... (Midas's) purpose was to induce (consumers) to purchase from (Midas) instead of its competitors").

The Condition Precedent

From Midas's standpoint the Warranty Certificate is not insurance at all but a clever marketing device used to lure consumers back to Midas repair shops for simple repairs which can be done by others. Once in the shop Midas personnel refuse to honor the Warranty Certificate unless the consumer complies with a condition precedent, i.e., Midas personnel *must* be given an opportunity to find other "problems" in the brake system and *must* correct those problems at the consumer's expense. With the exception of selling warranties that are never used, Midas does not make money unless it is selling parts and charging for labor. It is a near certainty that once a consumer's vehicle is up on the Midas garage rack that "problems" will be found and expensive solutions required.

Violation Of U.C.C. § 2–316(1)

U.C.C. § 2–316(1) provides that "Words or conduct ... (creating) ... an express warranty and words or conduct tending to negate or limit warranty shall be construed wherever reasonable as consistent with each other ...". The Midas Warranty Certificate has two operative clauses which conflict with each other.

> First, "WHAT IS COVERED ... Midas will install replacement warranted brake ... pads. You will not be charged for the brake ... pads or the labor required to install them".

> Second, "WHAT IS NOT COVERED. This warranty does not cover the cost of additional components and labor required to restore the brake system to its proper operation. The Midas shop must restore the entire brake system to its proper operation ...".

The second operative clause is unclear and ambiguous and as such should be construed against Midas and in favor of the plaintiff, see e.g., *Stream v. Sportscar Salon, Ltd.*, 91 Misc.2d 99, 102–103, 397 N.Y.S.2d 677, 680–681 (1977); *Walsh v. Ford Motor Company*, 59 Misc.2d 241, 242, 298 N.Y.S.2d 538, 540 (1969). In addition, the second clause violates U.C.C. § 2–316(1) since it negates and emasculates the first clause. The two clauses can not be reconciled and as such the first clause, "WHAT IS COVERED," must prevail over the second clause, "WHAT IS NOT COVERED".

Violation Of U.C.C. § 2–719(2)

U.C.C. § 2–719(2) provides that "Where circumstances cause an exclusive or limited remedy to fail of its essential purpose, remedy may be had as provided in this Act". Plaintiff purchased the Midas Warranty Certificate for a specific purpose, i.e., to have the brake pads on her vehicle replaced and installed without cost should the pads become worn. Requiring plaintiff to spend substantial sums to make repairs to her entire brake system as Midas deems appropriate and necessary is to deprive plaintiff of the substantial benefit of the new parts warranty which she purchased. As such the Warranty Certificate as interpreted by Midas fails of its essential purpose and violates U.C.C. § 2–719(2).

* * *

Violation Of G.B.L. § 349

General Business Law § 349 ("G.B.L. § 349") prohibits unfair and deceptive business practices and applies to automobile warranties.

G.B.L. § 349 is a broad, remedial statute directed towards giving consumers a powerful remedy. The elements of a violation of G.B.L. § 349 are (1) proof that the practice was deceptive or misleading in a material respect and (2) proof that plaintiff was injured. There is no requirement under G.B.L. § 349 that plaintiff prove that defendant's practices or acts were intentional, fraudulent or even reckless. Nor does plaintiff have to prove reliance upon defendant's deceptive practices.

In this case the Midas Warranty Certificate was misleading and deceptive in that it promised the replacement of worn brake pads free of charge and then emasculated that promise by requiring plaintiff to pay for additional brake system repairs which Midas would deem necessary and proper. Defendant has violated G.B.L. § 349 and is responsible for all appropriate damages thereunder.

Damages

The plaintiff shall be awarded the following damages:

First, damages will include $128.10 representing the cost of purchasing and installing new brake pads which Midas refused to install;

Second, pursuant to G.B.L. § 349(h) the Court finds that Midas wilfully violated G.B.L. § 349. The Court trebles plaintiff's actual damages to $384.30;

Third, pursuant to G.B.L. § 349(h) the Court awards plaintiff's attorney legal fees of $100.00.

Notes

1. What type of warranty was given in the Midas Warranty Certificate? Was Midas able to disclaim the warranty or limit the remedy for breach? Did Midas violate any relevant consumer protection law? How did the non-UCC aspects of the case affect the consumer's potential remedies? Would this case have been attractive to private attorneys in the absence of special consumer protection statutes?

2. As to implied warranties, other courts have held that in some situations, attempted disclaimers of the implied warranty of merchantability were invalid because not written in the proper language, or not sufficiently conspicuous. *See* Christopher v. Larson Ford Sales, 557 P.2d 1009 (Utah 1976); Blankenship v. Northtown Ford, Inc., 95 Ill.App.3d 303, 50 Ill.Dec. 850, 420 N.E.2d 167 (1981); Stream v. Sportscar Salon, Ltd., 91 Misc.2d 99, 397 N.Y.S.2d 677 (N.Y. City Civ. Ct. 1977). *But see* Hornberger v. General Motors Corp., 929 F.Supp. 884 (E.D. Pa. 1996) (warranty disclaimers were sufficiently conspicuous and limited warranty did not fail of its essential purpose).

3. The amended versions of UCC § 2–316(2) and (3) contain some special safeguards applicable in consumer contracts. For instance, to disclaim the implied warranty of merchantability in a consumer contract under 2–316(2),

the language must be in a record, be conspicuous, and state "The seller undertakes no responsibility for the quality of the goods except as otherwise provided in this contract."

UCC § 2–316(2) (amended 2003).

The implied warranty of merchantability in consumer contracts may also be disclaimed under 2–316(3) through the use of expressions such as "as is, and "with all faults," but in the case of a consumer contract the disclaimer "must be evidenced by a record" and must be "set forth conspicuously in the record." UCC § 2–316(3) (as amended 2003).

Do these changes sufficiently protect the consumer from unwittingly purchasing a product that carries no implied warranty of merchantability?

4.   Consumers have also been relatively successful under the Code in arguing that an exclusive remedy—free repair—has "failed of its essential purpose." UCC § 2–719(1)(b). In most cases, if the vehicle or other product still does not operate as it should after the seller has been given a reasonable chance to repair, the limited remedy has failed of its essential purpose, and the buyer can invoke other remedies. Numerous cases follow this pattern. *See, e.g.*, Pierce v. Catalina Yachts, Inc., 2 P.3d 618 (Alaska 2000); Volkswagen of America, Inc. v. Harrell, 431 So.2d 156 (Ala.1983); Ford Motor Co. v. Mayes, 575 S.W.2d 480 (Ky.App.1978); McCullough v. Bill Swad Chrysler–Plymouth, Inc., *supra* Section B(1), Osburn v. Bendix Home Systems, Inc., 613 P.2d 445 (Okl.1980), Jacobs v. Rosemount Dodge–Winnebago South, 310 N.W.2d 71 (Minn.1981).

5.   Once the consumer overcomes the warranty disclaimer and remedy limitation, he may still have to satisfy UCC § 2–608 to revoke acceptance, return the defective goods, and obtain a refund. State lemon laws, discussed *infra* Section B(5), streamline this procedure by permitting consumers to obtain revocation and refund (or a replacement vehicle) directly from the manufacturer, without having to prove failure of essential purpose or substantial impairment of value.

Problem 7–3

Robbin Hood bought a new car from Dale on credit. Dale passed on a manufacturer's warranty, which contained the following language:

> Manufacturer warrants this car to be free from defects in material and workmanship for 12 months or 12,000 miles, whichever comes first. Manufacturer makes no other EXPRESS WARRANTY, and NO IMPLIED WARRANTIES of MERCHANTABILITY OR FITNESS. Manufacturer's obligation under this warranty is limited to repair or replacement of defective parts without charge to Buyer.

Thirty days after the sale, as Hood was driving on the expressway, a cotter pin in the steering mechanism broke. Hood could not control the car, and it crashed into a bridge abutment. Hood was injured and the car was totally destroyed. The manufacturer is willing to stipulate that the cotter pin was defective, and is willing to give Hood a replacement cotter pin, but is not willing to offer more. If Hood sues Dale and/or the manufacturer under the UCC, how would this case be decided? See not only UCC § 2–316, but also § 2–719. Which would be more applicable to the last quoted clause in the contract? Section 2–719(3) may determine the effect of the clause on the part of the suit concerning physical injury, but Hood is also concerned with economic loss—i.e. the cost of repairing or replacing the car. How much does the UCC help Hood in obtaining redress for the loss of the car? Even if Hood were able to get around the warranty disclaimer and remedy limitation, would he be able to revoke acceptance? Against Dale? Against the manufacturer?

Problem 7–4

Gavin Geek purchased a "zip drive" from DVader Corporation for $100.00. A "zip drive" is a device that stores large amounts of data for personal computers. One week after taking home the DVader zip drive, breaking the shrink wrap, installing the required software from a CD and using the drive to store data, Gavin discovered that the DVader zip drive suffered from a defect known as the "Click of Death." The drive defect rendered the data stored on the disk unreadable and when Gavin attempted to use another drive to read the data from the affected disk, the defect was transferred to that drive, causing further damage. At this point, Gavin discovered DVader's "Limited Warranty," which expressly warranted against defects in the product. The warranty was included inside the zip drive's packaging, and provided for a right of return within three days if the consumer did not agree to the terms. The document limited remedies for defective products to free replacement of the defective zip drive and also stated that "DVader shall not be liable for incidental or consequential damages (such as but not limited to, loss of data or damage to disk drives or removable magnet media storage disks)."

Gavin is not so interested in a free replacement zip drive, although he would like to get his money back and wants to be compensated for the collateral damage suffered as a result of the "Click of Death" defect. Can Gavin challenge the warranty disclaimer and limitation of remedies clauses under UCC §§ 2–719 or 2–302 under either version of UCC Article 2? What if Gavin had ordered the zip drive online from DVader's website, and the relevant terms were in a "clickwrap" agreement (i.e., terms are available in scroll down form, buyer must click "I agree" in order to buy the product)? *See supra*, Chapter 3, problem 3–11. Would that make a difference in the outcome?

See Hill v. Gateway, *supra* Chapter 3, Section C; and Rinaldi v. Iomega Corp., 1999 WL 1442014 (Del. Super. Ct. 1999). See UCITA §§ 112, 113, 209 and 406. See also Jane M. Rolling, The UCC Under Wraps: Exposing the Need for More Notice to Consumers of Computer Software with Shrinkwrapped Licenses, 104 Comm. L.J. 197 (1999).

3. LIABILITY OF THE MANUFACTURER: THE PRIVITY BARRIER AND THE UCC

As demonstrated in the *Midas Muffler* case, it is possible for a consumer to find some remedies within the confines of the UCC (with some assistance from the state UDAP statute). The questions remain whether the risk of defective products should be removed altogether from the contracting power of the parties and whether the policy reflected in *Henningsen* applies with equal force to economic loss as well as to personal injuries.

Where the manufacturer issues an express warranty that is "passed through" to the ultimate consumer, or where the manufacturer engages in mass media advertising in which it makes specific performance claims or other promises, many courts have applied the UCC law of warranty and held the remote seller liable for breach. See, e.g., Cipollone v. Liggett Group, Inc., 893 F.2d 541 (3d Cir. 1990), aff'd in part and rev'd in part, 505 U.S. 504, 112 S.Ct. 2608, 120 L.Ed.2d 407 (1992). See also Curtis R. Reitz, Manufacturers' Warranties of Consumer Goods, 75 Wash. U.L.Q. 357 (1997); Donald F. Clifford, Express Warranty Liability of Remote Sellers: One Purchase, Two Relationships, 75 Wash. U.L.Q. 413 (1997). A minority, such as *Fode v. Capital RV Center, Inc., supra* Section B(1), will also permit the consumer to revoke acceptance, return the defective goods and obtain a refund under UCC § 2–608 from a remote manufacturer.

The amended UCC Article 2 specifically provides for an "obligation" to be created from a manufacturer to a remote purchaser, by including either a description or a remedial promise in a record furnished to the remote purchaser, UCC § 2–313A (as amended 2003), or by virtue of an advertisement to the public in which the manufacturer makes an affirmation of fact regarding the product or a remedial promise, UCC § 2–313B (as amended 2003). Both of these new sections permit the remote seller to modify or limit remedies available to the remote purchaser.

Whether or not the remote purchaser can hold the manufacturer liable for breach of the implied warranty of merchantability, as opposed to an express warranty, presents a more difficult question. Manufacturer liability to remote purchasers is common for physical injuries caused by defective products under the tort of strict liability, see Restatement of Torts (3d): Product Liability, but it has been called "exceedingly rare" in cases where the consumer seeks recovery purely for economic loss. See Curtis R. Reitz, Manufacturers' Warranties of Consumer Goods, 75 Wash. U.L.Q. 357, 374 (1997). Some states have eliminated the privity barrier for economic loss in consumer cases through special legislation. The following case may demonstrate a turning point in the direction of eliminating the privity barrier for claims of economic loss.

HYUNDAI MOTOR AMERICA, INC. v. GOODIN

Supreme Court of Indiana, 2005.
822 N.E.2d 947.

BOEHM, JUSTICE.

We hold that a consumer may sue a manufacturer for economic loss based on breach of the implied warranty of merchantability even if the consumer purchased the product from an intermediary in the distribution chain. There is no requirement of "vertical" privity for such a claim.

FACTS AND PROCEDURAL BACKGROUND

On November 18, 2000, Sandra Goodin test drove a Hyundai Sonata at AutoChoice Hyundai in Evansville, Indiana. The car was represented as new and showed nineteen miles on the odometer. Goodin testified that when she applied the brakes in the course of the test drive she experienced a "shimmy, shake, pulsating type feel." The AutoChoice salesperson told her that this was caused by flat spots on the tires from extended inactivity and offered to have the tires rotated and inspected. After this explanation, Goodin purchased the Sonata for $22,710.00.

The manufacturer, Hyundai, provided three limited warranties: 1 year/12,000 miles on "wear items;" 5 years/60,000 miles "bumper to bumper;" and 10 years/100,000 miles on the powertrain.[1] Hyundai concedes that brake rotors, brake calipers, and brake caliper slides were subject to the 5 year/60,000 mile warranty covering "[r]epair or replacement of any component originally manufactured or installed by [Hyundai] that is found to be defective in material or workmanship under normal use and maintenance." To claim under this warranty, a vehicle must be serviced by an authorized Hyundai dealer who is then reimbursed by Hyundai for any necessary parts or labor.

Three days after the car was purchased, Goodin's husband, Steven Hicks, took it back to AutoChoice for the promised tire work. Goodin testified that she continued to feel the shimmy but did nothing further for a month. On December 22, she took the car to a different Hyundai dealer, Bales Auto Mall, in Jeffersonville, Indiana, for an unrelated problem and also made an appointment six days later for Bales to inspect the brakes. Bales serviced the brake rotors for warping, but on May 1, 2001, Goodin returned to Bales complaining that the vehicle continued to vibrate when the brakes were applied. Bales found the rotors to be out of tolerance and machined them. Eighteen days later Goodin again returned to Bales, reporting that she still felt vibrations and for the first time also heard a "popping" noise. Goodin told the service advisor at Bales that she thought there may be a problem with the suspension, and Bales changed and lubed the strut assembly. Eleven days later Goodin once more brought the car to Bales reporting continued shimmy and also a "bed spring type" noise originating from the brakes. The Bales mechanic was unable to duplicate the brake problem, but balanced and rotated the tires as Goodin had requested. One week later Goodin returned to Bales where she and Jerry Hawes, Bales's Service Manager, test drove the Sonata. The brake problem did not occur during the test drive, but Hawes identified a noise from the direction of the left front tire and repaired the rubber mounting bracket.

---

1. On the "Buyers Order," AutoChoice Hyundai included the following preprinted language in capital letters:

ALL WARRANTIES, IF ANY, BY A MANUFACTURER OR SUPPLIER OTHER THAN DEALER ARE THEIRS, NOT DEALER'S, AND ONLY SUCH MANUFACTURER OR OTHER SUPPLIER SHALL BE LIABLE FOR PERFORMANCE UNDER SUCH WARRANTIES, UNLESS DEALER FURNISHES BUYER WITH A SEPARATE WRITTEN WARRANTY MADE BY DEALER ON ITS OWN BEHALF. DEALER HEREBY DISCLAIMS ALL WARRANTIES, EXPRESS OR IMPLIED, INCLUDING ANY IMPLIED WARRANTIES OF MERCHANTABILITY OR FITNESS FOR A PARTICULAR PURPOSE, ON ALL GOODS AND SERVICES SOLD BY DEALER. . . .

Goodin told Hawes that the brake problem had occurred about seventy percent of the time. The problem was worse when it was wet or cool, was consistently occurring when she drove down a steep hill near her home, and was less frequent when a passenger's weight was added. Goodin made arrangements to leave the car with Hawes at Bales, but, according to Hawes, over a several day period he could not duplicate the symptoms Goodin reported.

On August 24, 2001, Goodin took her car back to her original dealer, AutoChoice, reporting that the brakes "squeak and grind when applied." Goodin left the car with AutoChoice where the left front rotor was machined and loose bolts on the front upper control arm were tightened. Goodin testified that after this five-day procedure the brakes began to make the same noises and vibrations even before she arrived home.

In October 2001 Goodin hired an attorney who faxed a letter to Hyundai Motor America giving notice of her complaint and requesting a refund of the purchase price. On November 13, 2001, Goodin filed a complaint against Hyundai Motor America, Inc. alleging claims under the Magnuson–Moss Warranty Act, 15 U.S.C. § § 2301–2312, for breach of express warranty, breach of implied warranty, and revocation of acceptance. * * *

At the conclusion of a two day trial, the jury was instructed on all claims. Over defendants' objection, the instructions on implied warranties made no reference to a privity requirement. The jury returned a verdict for Hyundai on Goodin's breach of express warranty claim, but found in favor of Goodin on her claim for breach of implied warranty of merchantability. Damages of $3,000.00 were assessed and Goodin's counsel was later awarded attorneys' fees of $19,237.50 pursuant to the fee shifting provisions of the Magnuson–Moss Warranty Act.

* * *

Hyundai appealed, asserting: (1) it was not estopped from asserting a defense of lack of privity; and (2) lack of vertical privity barred Goodin's recovery for breach of implied warranty of merchantability. The Court of Appeals agreed on both points, holding that Hyundai was not estopped from asserting that privity was an element of Goodin's prima facia case, and, because privity was lacking, Goodin did not prove her case. *Hyundai Motor Am., Inc. v. Goodin,* 804 N.E.2d 775, 781 (Ind.Ct.App.2004). The Magnuson–Moss Warranty Act looks to state law for the contours of implied warranties. The Court of Appeals was "not unsympathetic" to Goodin's claims but regarded itself as bound by a footnote in *Martin Rispens & Son v. Hall Farms, Inc.,* 621 N.E.2d 1078, 1084 n. 2 (Ind.1993), where this Court stated: "In Indiana, privity between the seller and the buyer is required to maintain a cause of action on the implied warranties of merchantability." *Id.* at 784. We granted transfer.

VERTICAL PRIVITY

A. *The Relationship Between Federal and State Law in Claims Based on Implied Warranty of Merchantability*

This case is brought under a federal statute. The Magnuson–Moss Warranty Act, 15 U.S.C. §§ 2301–2312 (2000), provides a federal right of action for consumers to enforce written or implied warranties where they claim to be damaged by the failure of a supplier, warrantor, or service contractor to comply with any obligation under that statute or under a written warranty, implied warranty, or service contract. The Act also limits the extent to which manufacturers who give express warranties may disclaim or modify implied warranties, but looks to state law as the source of any express or implied warranty. As the Seventh Circuit recently put it: "Because § § 2308 and 2304(a) do not modify, or discuss in any way, a state's ability to establish a privity requirement, whether privity is a prerequisite to a claim for breach of implied warranty under the Magnuson–Moss Act therefore hinges entirely on the applicable state law." *Voelker v. Porsche Cars N. Am., Inc.,* 353 F.3d 516, 525 (7th Cir.2003).

Goodin's claim is for breach of the implied warranty of merchantability, not for violation of any substantive provision of the federal statute. Accordingly, her claim lives or dies on the resolution of an issue of state law, specifically whether Indiana requires privity between buyer and manufacturer for a claim of breach of implied warranty.

* * *

C. *Origins of Privity*

Indiana has adopted the Uniform Commercial Code, notably its provision that: "A warranty that the goods shall be merchantable is implied in a contract for their sale if the seller is a merchant with respect to goods of that kind...." Ind.Code § 26–1–2–314(1) (2004). Hyundai asserts, and the Court of Appeals found, Indiana law requires vertical privity between manufacturer and consumer when economic damages are sought. Goodin argues that traditional privity of contract between the consumer and manufacturer is not required for a claim against a manufacturer for breach of the implied warranty of merchantability, especially if the manufacturer provides a Magnuson–Moss express warranty with the product.

Privity originated as a doctrine limiting tort relief for breach of warranties. The lack of privity defense was first recognized in *Winterbottom v. Wright,* 10 M. & W. 109, 152 Eng Rep 402 (Ex. 1842). 2 *Hawkland, UCC Series,* § 2–318:1 at 771 (2001). In that case, the court sustained a demurrer to a suit by an injured coachman for breach of warranty by a third party who contracted with the owner to maintain the coach. In this century, however, *MacPherson v. Buick Motor Co.,* 217 N.Y. 382, 111 N.E. 1050 (1916), and *Henningsen v. Bloomfield Motors, Inc.,* 32 N.J. 358, 161 A.2d 69 (1960), established that lack of privity between an automobile manufacturer and a consumer would not preclude the consumer's action for personal injuries and property damage caused by the negligent manufacture of an automobile. "Vertical" privity typically becomes an issue when a purchaser files a breach of warranty action against a vendor in the purchaser's distribution chain who is not the purchaser's immediate seller. *Hawkland, supra,* at 771. Simply put, vertical privity exists only between immediate links in a distribution chain. A buyer in the same chain who did not purchase directly from a seller is "remote" as to that seller. *Id.* "Horizontal" privity, in contrast, refers to claims by nonpurchasers, typically someone who did not purchase the product but who was injured while using it. 1 *James J. White & Robert S. Summers, Uniform Commercial Code* 585 (4th ed.1995). Goodin purchased her car from a dealership and is thus remote from the manufacturer and lacks "vertical" privity with Hyundai.

"Although warranty liability originated as a tort doctrine, it was assimilated by the law of contracts and ultimately became part of the law of sales." *Hawkland, supra,* at 771. But "privity is more than an accident of history. It permitted manufacturers and distributors to control in some measure their risks of doing business." Richard W. Duesenberg, *The Manufacturer's Last Stand: The Disclaimer,* 20 Bus. Law 159, 161 (1964). Because vertical privity involves a claim by a purchaser who voluntarily acquired the goods, it enjoys a stronger claim to justification on the basis of freedom of contract or consensual relationship. It nevertheless has come under criticism in recent years, and this is the first opportunity for this Court to give full consideration to this issue.

* * *

F. *Privity as an Obsolete Requirement as Applied to Consumer Goods*

* * *

Courts that have abolished vertical privity have cited a variety of reasons. Principal among these is the view that, in today's economy, manufactured products typically reach the consuming public through one or more intermediaries. As a result, any loss from an unmerchantable product is likely to be identified only after the product is attempted to be used or consumed. * * * Yet others have focused on the point that if implied warranties are effective against remote sellers it produces a chain of lawsuits or crossclaims against those up the distribution chain. * * * And some focus on the reality in today's world that manufacturers focus on the consumer in communications promoting the product. * * *

Finally, some jurisdictions have abolished privity in warranty actions where only economic losses were sought based on the notion that there is "no reason to distinguish between recovery for personal and property injury, on the one hand, and economic loss on the other." *Hiles Co. v. Johnston Pump Co.,* 93 Nev. 73, 560 P.2d 154, 157 (1977). A variance on this theme is the view that abolishing privity "simply recognizes that economic loss is potentially devastating to the buyer of an unmerchantable product and that it is unjust to preclude any recovery from the manufacturer for such loss because of a lack of privity, when the slightest physical injury can give rise to strict liability under the same circumstances." *Groppel,* 616 S.W.2d at 59. One court preserving the privity requirement expressed the view that "there may be cases where the plaintiff may be unfairly prejudiced by the operation of the economic loss rule in combination with the privity requirement." *Ramerth v. Hart,* 133 Idaho 194, 983 P.2d 848, 852 (1999).

In Indiana, the economic loss rule applies to bar recovery in tort "where a negligence claim is based upon the failure of a product to perform as expected and the plaintiff suffers only economic damages." *Martin Rispens,* 621 N.E.2d at 1089. Possibly because of the economic loss rule, Goodin did not raise a negligence claim here. Furthermore, at oral argument Goodin's attorney pointed to the warranty disclaimer in the Buyer's Order as a bar to Goodin's ability to sue her direct seller, AutoChoice, which could then have sued Hyundai for reimbursement. This disclaimer, Goodin contends, precluded a chain of claims ultimately reaching the manufacturer. Therefore, Goodin claims that if this Court does not abolish the vertical privity requirement she will be left without a remedy for Hyundai's breach of its implied warranty of merchantability, and Hyundai's implied warranty becomes nonexistent in practical terms.

The basis for the privity requirement in a contract claim is essentially the idea that the parties to a sale of goods are free to bargain for themselves and thus allocation of risk of failure of a product is best left to the private sector. Otherwise stated, the law should not impose a contract the parties do not wish to make. The Court of Appeals summarized this view well:

> Generally privity extends to the parties to the contract of sale. It relates to the bargained for expectations of the buyer and seller. Accordingly, when the cause of action arises out of economic loss related to the loss of the bargain or profits and consequential damages related thereto, the bargained for expectations of buyer and seller are relevant and privity between them is still required. Implied warranties of merchantability and fitness for a particular use, as they relate to economic loss from the bargain, cannot then ordinarily be sustained between the buyer and a remote manufacturer.

Richards, 179 Ind.App. at 112, 384 N.E.2d at 1092 (citations omitted). We think that this rationale has eroded to the point of invisibility as applied to many types of consumer goods in today's economy. The UCC recognizes an implied warranty of merchantability if "goods" are sold to "consumers" by one who ordinarily deals in this product. Warranties are often explicitly promoted as marketing tools, as was true in this case of the Hyundai warranties. Consumer expectations are framed by these legal developments to the point where technically advanced consumer goods are virtually always sold under express warranties, which, as a matter of federal law run to the consumer without regard to privity. 15 U.S.C. § 2310. Magnuson–Moss precludes a disclaimer of the implied warranty of merchantability as to consumer goods where an express warranty is given. 15 U.S.C. § 2308. Given this framework, we think ordinary consumers are entitled to, and do, expect that a consumer product sold under a warranty is merchantable, at least at the modest level of merchantability set by UCC section 2–314, where hazards common to the type of product do not render the product unfit for normal use.

Even if one party to the contract—the manufacturer—intends to extend an implied warranty only to the immediate purchaser, in a consumer setting, doing away with the privity requirement for a product subject to the Magnuson–Moss Warranty Act, rather than rewriting the deal, simply gives the consumer the contract the consumer expected. The manufacturer, on the other hand is encouraged to build quality into its products. To the extent there is a cost of adding uniform or standard quality in all products, the risk of a lemon is passed to all buyers in the form of pricing and not randomly distributed among those unfortunate enough to have acquired one of the lemons. Moreover, elimination of privity requirement gives consumers such as Goodin the value of their expected bargain, but will rarely do more than duplicate the Products Liability Act as to other consequential damages. The remedy for breach of implied warranty of merchantability is in most cases, including this one, the difference between "the value of the goods accepted and the value they would have had if they had been as warranted." I.C. § 26–1–2–714(2). This gives the buyer the benefit of the bargain. In most cases, however, if any additional damages are available under the UCC as the result of abolishing privity, Indiana law would award the same damages under the Products Liability Act as personal injury or damage to "other property" from a "defective" product.

For the reasons given above we conclude that Indiana law does not require vertical privity between a consumer and a manufacturer as a condition to a claim by the consumer against the manufacturer for breach of the manufacturer's implied warranty of merchantability.

CONCLUSION

The judgment of the trial court is affirmed.

Notes

1.   Why do you suppose this case was brought under the Magnuson Moss Warranty Act? How does the federal MMWA define or interpret the implied warranties of merchantability being enforced? Does it address the privity issue? Does it help the consumer with regard to warranty disclaimers?

2.   What rationale did the Indiana Supreme Court give for abolishing the vertical privity requirement with regard to consumer goods? Does their reasoning take account of the parties' freedom of contract?

3. The process of eliminating the vertical privity requirement for economic loss cases in consumer transactions has been slow indeed. In a much earlier case, Morrow v. New Moon Homes, Inc., 548 P.2d 279 (Alaska 1976), the Alaska Supreme Court, holding a remote manufacturer liable to the ultimate consumer for breach of the implied warranty of merchantability, stated: "[T]here is no satisfactory justification for a remedial scheme which extends the warranty action to a consumer suffering personal injury or property damage but denies similar relief to the consumer 'fortunate' enough to suffer only direct economic loss."

Note on Non–Uniform Amendment to the UCC and Other Statutory Limits on Vertical Privity

The provision set out below represents a direct legislative attack on warranty disclaimers and remedy limitations. Which is preferable, this statutory approach, or continued caselaw development? Does this statute affect both personal injury and economic loss cases? Does it moot the other issues raised in *Goodin?* Would enactment of this statute induce manufacturers to discontinue using language in their contracts similar to that in Problem 7–3, *supra?*

MARYLAND COMMERCIAL CODE

Section 2–316.1: Limitation of Exclusion or Modification of Warranties.

(1) The provisions of § 2–316 shall not apply to sales of consumer goods, as defined by § 9–109, services or both.

(2) Any oral or written language used by a seller of consumer goods and services, which attempts to exclude or modify any implied warranties of merchantability and fitness for a particular purpose or to exclude or modify the consumer's remedies for breach of those warranties, is unenforceable. However, the seller may recover from the manufacturer any damages resulting from breach of the [above-described] warranty. * * *

(3) Any oral or written language used by a manufacturer of consumer goods, which attempts to limit or modify a consumer's remedies for breach of the manufacturer's express warranties, is unenforceable, unless the manufacturer provides reasonable and expeditious means of performing the warranty obligations.

This is a non-uniform amendment to the UCC, as enacted in Maryland. Connecticut, the District of Columbia, Maine, Massachusetts, and Vermont have enacted similar provisions. See also Kan.Stat.Ann. 50–639, Mass. G.L. c. 106, § 2–316A, and W.Va. Code, 46A–6–107. See also Jacobs v. Yamaha Motor Corp., U.S.A., 649 N.E.2d 758 (Mass. 1995).

Some, but not all, of these statutes eliminate the requirement of vertical privity as well. Mississippi prohibits the limitation of remedies for breach of the implied warranty, Miss.Code § 75–2–719(4), and by virtue of having repealed UCC § 2–316, prohibited the exclusion or modification of the implied warranty of merchantability as well. See Beck Enterprises, Inc. v. Hester, 512 So.2d 672 (Miss.1987).

Under the Song–Beverly Act, California prohibits disclaimers of implied warranties of merchantability in the sale of consumer goods when the seller provides an express warranty. Cal. Civ. Code § 1793.

For an excellent summary and analysis of these state laws, see National Consumer Law Center, Consumer Warranty Law: Lemon Law, Magnuson–Moss, UCC, Mobile Home, and Other Warranty Statutes § 5.4 (2001 with 2004 Cumulative Supplement).

Problem 7–5

(a) Sam Tudent bought a car from Muck Motors in Maryland. After the sale, and after he had paid cash for the car, Sam realized that he had received a "standard warranty" exactly like that in Problem 7–3, *supra*. Before any defect in the car has appeared, he consults you. What, if anything, can he do?

(b) Same transaction as in (a) except that a month after the sale the car becomes inoperable. What can Sam do?

(c) Would you have any additional suggestions for Sam using his state "little FTC Act?" Are there any advantages to pleading the case as an unfair or deceptive trade practice, rather than a simple breach of warranty? Any disadvantages?

4. THE MAGNUSON–MOSS WARRANTY ACT

Overview

The Magnuson–Moss Warranty Act (MMWA), 15 U.S.C.A. §§ 2301–11, was enacted in 1975. Both the statute and the accompanying FTC regulations can be found in the statutory supplement. In this legislation, Congress attempted to address some common consumer problems with warranties, namely:

> (1) complex language that rendered warranty terms incomprehensible to most people,

> (2) warranties that appeared to give meaningful warranty protection but turned out to be much less than expected, and

> (3) lack of meaningful access to the courts to enforce consumers' rights under their warranties.

The MMWA was hailed as a major piece of consumer protection legislation, but it also has many limitations.

The Magnuson–Moss Warranty Act is primarily a detailed disclosure law. The MMWA does not require the issuance of a warranty, nor does it regulate the substance of most warranty terms. Just as Truth in Lending is based on the theory that informed comparison shopping for credit would improve competition in the consumer credit market, so too the MMWA assumes that better informed consumers would select products with better warranties. This in turn would induce manufacturers to compete on warranty terms. Competition on warranties could ultimately lead to better quality products, since strong warranties normally will not accompany weak products. See generally C. Reitz, Consumer Protection under the Magnuson–Moss Warranty Act (2d ed. 1987).

Following are the basic features of the MMWA.

The Act requires disclosures of the terms of warranties in *simple and readily understood language*. This has proven to be difficult to achieve in practice. MMWA, 15 U.S.C. § 2302; 16 C.F.R. Part 700 (Hereafter Rule 700, 701, etc.)

The Act requires *pre-sale availability,* i.e., the exact text of the written warranty must be available to consumers before they buy. MMWA, 15 U.S.C. § 2302(b)(1)(A) and Rule 702. This permits consumers to comparison shop for the best warranty, if they so desire. However, the retailer retains considerable flexibility on the manner in which the text of the warranty is to be made available. Thus, a retailer may simply make warranties available on request, provided he posts a sign to that effect. Rule 702.3.

The Act requires *standard terminology* for warranties. Written warranties on consumer goods must be called either "full" or "limited." "Full" warranties must meet certain standards. MMWA, 15 U.S.C. §§ 2303, 2304 and 2305, and Rule 700. All other written warranties must be called "limited."

The Act imposes *limits on disclaimers of implied warranties*. Sellers who offer written warranties on consumer products *may not* disclaim entirely any implied warranty that arises under state law, although they may limit the duration of the implied warranty. MMWA, 15 U.S.C. § 2308. This very important provision gives consumers a method to avoid warranty disclaimers in their contracts.

The Act provides a *private right of action* for aggrieved consumers. The Act gives consumers the right to enforce the warranty provisions of *their own individual contracts* or to sue for damages for violations of the Act. MMWA, 15 U.S.C. § 2310(d). Unlike the Truth in Lending Act, however, the MMWA Act does not provide for minimum statutory penalties. The consumer is limited to proven damages, and may be awarded costs and attorney's fees.

The Act permits suit in either federal or state court. A consumer can sue in state court for ordinary breach of warranty under MMWA and thereby be awarded attorney's fees. See, e.g., Hyundai Motor America, Inc. v. Goodin, supra, Section B(3). Federal actions are more limited. The jurisdictional amount for a federal action is $50,000, and there must be at least 100 individuals for a class action. Cf. Seybold v. Francis P. Dean, Inc., 628 F.Supp. 912 (W.D.Pa.1986).

Finally, the Act attempts to facilitate the establishment of *informal dispute resolution* procedures for resolving warranty disputes. MMWA 15 U.S.C. § 2310(a) and Rule 703. This aspect of the law did not have much impact at first. As states passed lemon laws in the 1980s that incorporate by reference the FTC/MMWA rule on informal dispute resolution, however, many automobile manufacturers established such procedures.

The FTC's Rule 703 for informal dispute mechanisms contains significant safeguards for consumers. Notably, there is a provision stating that even though the consumer may have to exhaust this remedy prior to going to court, a decision by a Rule 703 mechanism is not binding on the consumer, and thus does not preclude a later legal action. 16 C.F.R. § 703.5(j). In the 1990's and 2000's, however, most courts have ruled that a binding arbitration clause in a consumer product warranty contract is enforceable, despite the fact that the consumer may lose his or her option to go to court under MMWA. See Davis v. Southern Energy Homes, Inc., 305 F.3d 1268 (11th Cir. 2002); Walton v. Rose Mobile Homes LLC, 298 F.3d 470 (5th Cir. 2002). The basis for these opinions is the presumption in favor of enforcing arbitration clauses contained in the Federal Arbitration Act, 9 U.S.C. § 1. See discussion of arbitration in consumer transactions, *infra*, Chapter 10, Section C(2).

As is the case for most consumer protection legislation, the MMWA is *limited in scope* to warranties on "consumer" products. Unlike some other statutes, however, the MMWA uses an "objective" test, i.e., whether the product is "normally used for personal, family or household purposes," rather than the particular buyer's subjective purpose. MMWA 15 U.S.C. § 2301(1). Thus, a business that purchased a car for deliveries may be able to argue its warranty is within the coverage of the Act because cars are normally used for family or personal purposes. See Business Modeling Techniques, Inc. v. General Motors Corp., 474 N.Y.S. 258 (N.Y. Sup. Ct. 1984) (automobile); Najran Co. v. Fleetwood Enterprises, Inc., 659 F.Supp. 1081 (S.D. Ga. 1986) (mobile home). On the other hand, a flat bed truck or an airplane used for personal reasons would not come within the scope of MMWA because it is normally a commercial vehicle. See Crume v. Ford Motor Co., 60 Or.App. 224, 653 P.2d 564 (1982); CAT Aircraft Leasing, Inc. v. Cessna Aircraft Co., 1991–1 Trade Cas. ¶ 69299, 1990 WL 171010 (D. Kan. 1990) ("the protections afforded by [the] Magnuson–Moss Act are not designed to encompass the purchase of a $3,000,000 jet"); Cinquegrani v. Sandel Avionics, 2001 WL 649488 (N.D. Ill. 2001).

The operative portions of the MMWA are also limited to "written warranties," as defined in the Act, 15 U.S.C. § 2301(6). How does this term differ from express or implied warranties in the UCC or warranties enforceable under the common law of contracts?

On the question of how the MMWA defines "written warranty" and whether the MMWA has real utility for the lemon-buying consumer, consider the following case.

VENTURA v. FORD MOTOR CORP.

Superior Court of New Jersey, Appellate Division, 1981.
180 N.J.Super. 45, 433 A.2d 801.

[When his new car proved seriously defective, and unrepairable, Ventura sued Marino Auto Sales (the dealer) and Ford (the manufacturer) for breach of warranty. Marino cross-claimed against Ford for indemnification. The trial court awarded Ventura rescission and damages against Marino Auto Sales, and allowed Marino to recover over against Ford. The lower court also awarded Ventura $5,165 in attorney's fees against Ford, but denied Ventura's claim for punitive and treble damages. Ford appeals.]

[W]e affirm plaintiff's recovery. We conclude that, despite Marino Auto's attempted disclaimer of all warranties, plaintiff can recover from Marino Auto for the breach of implied warranty of merchantability. We also uphold the award of counsel fees against Ford pursuant to the Magnuson–Moss Warranty Act.

The contract of sale between Marino Auto and plaintiff conspicuously contained the following legend on its face:

> The seller, MARINO AUTO SALES, Inc., hereby expressly disclaims all warranties, either expressed or implied, including any implied warranty of merchantability or fitness for a particular purpose, and MARINO AUTO SALES, Inc., neither assumes nor authorizes another person to assume for it any liability in connection with the sale of the vehicle.

On the back of this sales order-contract were the following terms which were made part of the contract:

> 7. It is expressly agreed that there are no warranties, express or implied, made by either the selling dealer or the manufacturer on the motor vehicle, chassis or parts furnished hereunder except, in the case of a new motor vehicle the warranty expressly given to the purchaser upon the delivery of such motor vehicle or chassis.

> The selling dealer also agrees to promptly perform and fulfill all terms and conditions of the owner service policy.

For the purpose of this opinion we will assume that the disclaimer of implied warranties of merchantability and fitness was effective under the Uniform Commercial Code, N.J.S.A. 12A:2–316. Since the dealer passed on to the purchaser a warranty from the manufacturer, we will not consider whether the attempted disclaimer by Marino Auto should be voided as unconscionable and contrary to public policy under N.J.S.A. 12A:2–302, even though such disclaimer could foreclose rescission or other remedies against the dealer and, without privity between buyer and manufacturer, rescission has been held ordinarily unavailable, under the Code against the manufacturer. * * * It may be argued that the dealer's conduct in transmitting Ford's warranty to plaintiff, the reference to such warranty in paragraph 7 on the back of the purchaser order-contract, and the undertaking "to promptly perform and fulfill all terms and conditions of the owner service policy," are inconsistent with a disclaimer of all warranties and that such a disclaimer is an unreasonable construction. The contract in the *Henningsen* case contained the identical obligation to perform all terms and conditions of the owner service policy. The combination of the dealer's undertaking and the automobile manufacturer's warranty was interpreted in *Henningsen* to rebut the disclaimer of implied warranty of merchantability by the dealer. The court held that the attempt to limit liability to the replacement of defective parts was contrary to public policy and void with respect to a claim for personal injuries resulting from an accident caused by defects in an automobile. However, we need not explore these issues further because the Magnuson–Moss Warranty Act has solved many of the problems posed by the intricacies confronting consumers under the preexisting law of sales.

The Magnuson–Moss Warranty–Federal Trade Commission Improvement Act, supra, was adopted on January 4, 1975, 88 Stat. 2183. Its purpose was to make "warranties on consumer products more readily understandable and enforceable." Note, 7 Rutgers–Camden L.J. 379 (1976). The act enhances the consumer's position by allowing recovery under a warranty without regard to privity of contract between the consumer and warrantor, by prohibiting the disclaimer of implied warranties in a written warranty, and by enlarging the remedies available to a consumer for breach of warranty, including the award of attorneys' fees. * * *

* * *

We will first consider the application of this act to the dealer, Marino Auto. As quoted above, paragraph 7 of the purchase order contract provides that there are no warranties, express or implied, made by the selling dealer or manufacturer except, in the case of a new motor vehicle, "the warranty expressly given to the purchaser upon delivery of such motor vehicle * * *." This section also provides: "The selling dealer also agrees to promptly perform and fulfill all terms and conditions of the owner service policy." Ford contended in the trial court that Marino Auto had "a duty" to properly diagnose and make repairs, that such duty was "fixed both by the express warranty * * * which they passed on * * * and by the terms of [paragraph 7 of the contract with plaintiff]" by which Marino Auto expressly undertook "to perform its obligations under the owner service policy." See 15 U.S.C.A. § 2310(f); 16 C.F.R. § 700.4 (1980). The provision in paragraph 7 in these circumstances is a "written warranty" within the meaning of § 2301(6)(B) since it constitutes an undertaking in connection with the sale to take "remedial action with respect to such product in the event that such product fails to meet the specifications set forth in the undertaking * * *." In our view the specifications of the undertaking include, at the least, the provisions of the limited warranty furnished by Ford, namely:

LIMITED WARRANTY (12 MONTHS OR 12,000 MILES/19,312 KILOMETRES) 1978 NEW CAR AND LIGHT TRUCK

Ford warrants for its 1978 model cars and light trucks that the Selling Dealer will repair or replace free any parts, except tires, found under normal use in the U.S. or Canada to be defective in factory materials or workmanship within the earlier of 12 months or 12,000 miles/19,312 km from either first use or retail delivery. All we require is that you properly operate and maintain your vehicle and that you return for warranty service to your Selling Dealer or any Ford or Lincoln–Mercury Dealer if you are traveling, have moved a long distance or need emergency repairs. Warranty repairs will be made with Ford Authorized Service or Remanufactured Parts.

THERE IS NO OTHER EXPRESS WARRANTY ON THIS VEHICLE.[4]

The record does not contain a written description of the "owner service policy" which the dealer agreed to perform. Nevertheless, since Ford is the appellant here, we take its contentions at trial and documents in the record to establish the dealer's obligation to Ford and to plaintiff to make the warranty repairs on behalf of Ford (subject to the right of reimbursement or other terms that may be contained in their agreement). For the purpose of this appeal we are satisfied that the dealer's undertaking in paragraph 7 constitutes a written warranty within the meaning of 15 U.S.C.A. § 2301(6)(B). Accordingly, having furnished a written warranty to the consumer, the dealer as a supplier may not "disclaim or modify [except to limit in duration] any implied warranty to a consumer * * *." The result of this analysis is to invalidate the attempted disclaimer by the dealer of the implied warranties of merchantability and fitness.[5] Being bound by those implied warranties arising under state law, N.J.S.A. 12A:2–314 and 315, Marino Auto was liable to plaintiff for the breach thereof as found by the trial judge, and plaintiff could timely revoke his acceptance of the automobile and claim a refund of his purchase price. N.J.S.A. 12A:2–608 and N.J.S.A. 12A:2–711. Zabriskie Chevrolet, Inc. v. Smith, 99 N.J.Super. 441, 240 A.2d 195 (Law Div.1968). In this connection we note that the trial judge found

---

4. The warranty also provided:

TO THE EXTENT ALLOWED BY LAW:

1. ANY IMPLIED WARRANTY OF MERCHANTABILITY OR FITNESS IS LIMITED TO THE 12 MONTH OR 12,000–MILE/19,312–KM DURATION OF THIS WRITTEN WARRANTY.

2. NEITHER FORD NOR THE SELLING DEALER SHALL HAVE ANY RESPONSIBILITY FOR LOSS OF USE OF THE VEHICLE, LOSS OF TIME, INCONVENIENCE, COMMERCIAL LOSS OR CONSEQUENTIAL DAMAGES.

Some states do not allow limitations on how long an implied warranty lasts or the exclusion or limitation of incidental or consequential damages, so the above limitations may not apply to you.

This warranty gives you specific legal rights, and you also may have other rights which vary from state to state.

5. The same holding would apply if the undertaking by Marino Auto to perform the "owner service policy" is construed as a "service contract." 15 U.S.C.A. § 2308(a), supra.

that plaintiff's attempted revocation of acceptance was made in timely fashion, and that finding has adequate support in the evidence.

As the trial judge noted, 15 U.S.C.A. § 2310(d)(1) provides that a consumer who is damaged by the failure of a warrantor to comply with any obligation under the act, or under a written warranty or implied warranty or service contract, may bring suit "for damages and other legal and equitable relief * * *." Although the remedy of refund of the purchase price is expressly provided by the Magnuson–Moss Warranty Act for breach of a full warranty, granting this remedy under state law for breach of a limited warranty is not barred by or inconsistent with the act. 15 U.S.C.A. § 2311(b)(1) provides that nothing in the act restricts "any right or remedy of any consumer under State law or other Federal law." See also 15 U.S.C.A. § 2311(c)(2). Thus, for breach of the implied warranty of merchantability, plaintiff was entitled to revoke acceptance against Marino Auto, and a judgment for the purchase price less an allowance for the use of the vehicle was properly entered against Marino Auto. N.J.S.A. 12A:2–608 and 711. Cf. 15 U.S.C.A. § 2301(12) which defines "refund" as the return of the purchase price "less reasonable depreciation based on actual use where permitted" by regulations.

[The court also held that Ventura also could have recovered against Ford for Ford's breach of its limited warranty.]

Notes

1. Would the dealer's disclaimer of all warranties express or implied have been effective under the UCC (pre-2003 amendment)? Would you have taken this case before the MMWA was passed? How exactly did the MMWA help the consumer to overcome the dealer's warranty disclaimer? *See* 15 U.S.C. §§ 2301(6)(B) and 2308. *See also* GMAC v. Jankowitz, 216 N.J.Super. 313, 523 A.2d 695 (1987); and Johnson v. Earnhardt's Gilbert Dodge, Inc., 210 Ariz. 375, 111 P.3d 417 (2005) (although used car dealer had sold vehicle "as is," it had given a "written warranty" under MMWA by virtue of providing a service contract, and thus was unable to completely disclaim the implied warranty of merchantability).

2. What remedy did the buyer obtain from the dealer? What remedy did the buyer obtain from Ford?

3. In the more common situation where the dealer disclaims all warranties and simply carries out repairs under the manufacturer's warranty, however, the dealer is not likely to be liable under the MMWA for breach of the implied warranty. See Pratt v. Colonial–Sales–Lease Rental, Inc., 799 F.Supp. 1132 (N.D. Ala. 1992); Frank Griffin Volkswagen, Inc. v. Smith, 610 So.2d 597 (Fla. Dist. Ct. App. 1992); Fode v. Capital RV Center, *supra* Section B(1).

4. As discussed in Hyundai Motor America, Inc. v. Goodin, *supra* Section B(3), the MMWA "limits the extent to which manufacturers who give express warranties may disclaim or modify implied warranties, but looks to state law as the source of any express or implied warranty." *See also* 15 U.S.C. § 2301(7), Schimmer v. Jaguar Cars, Inc., 384 F.3d 402 (7th Cir.

2004). The Illinois Supreme Court in a 1986 case held that the MMWA can itself establish privity between the consumer and a distant seller who offers an express written warranty to consumers. *See* Szajna v. General Motors Corp., 115 Ill.2d 294, 104 Ill.Dec. 898, 503 N.E.2d 760 (1986). Most federal courts now agree, however, that if state law requires privity for a breach of implied warranty, then the implied warranty cannot be enforced against that distant seller under MMWA. *See, e.g.*, Voelker v. Porsche Cars N. Am., Inc., 353 F.3d 516, 525–26 (7th Cir. 2003); Abraham v. Volkswagen of Am., Inc., 795 F.2d 238 (2d Cir. 1986). As one early federal case put it, "If state law requires vertical privity to enforce an implied warranty and there is none, then, like the yeastless soufflé, the warranty does not 'arise.' " Feinstein v. Firestone Tire & Rubber Co., 535 F.Supp. 595, n. 13 (S.D.N.Y. 1982). As further noted in the *Goodin* case, however, the number of states that still require vertical privity for breach of the implied warranty in consumer cases is growing smaller.

5. If applicable, most state lemon laws will also help consumers break the privity barrier and obtain a remedy directly from the manufacturer. See *infra*, Section B(5).

6. Consumer leasing of automobiles, as opposed to buying them on credit, has grown in popularity since the 1980's. Typically these are new vehicles that are still under a manufacturer's warranty. When problems are encountered under these warranties, the question has arisen whether or not the MMWA applies to the lease of consumer products. Consider the following.

Problem 7–6

In January, Dapper Dan leased a new SUV for three years from Local Car Dealer. As part of the lease agreement, Local Dealer provided Dan with a "New Car Limited Warranty," which required the manufacturer to "repair or replace any factory-installed part that was defective in material or workmanship under normal use." The warranty was effective for three years or 36,000 miles, and was to begin "on the date the car was first delivered to the first retail purchaser, or the date it was first used as a demonstrator, lease or company car, whichever came first." Soon after Dan accepted delivery, the SUV suffered numerous problems, including "pulling" to the right, problems with the automatic transmission not shifting properly, stalling out at traffic lights, and water leaks. Dan took the SUV to Local on seven occasions during the first six months of the lease, but the defects persisted. At that time, Dan informed Local that he wished to terminate the lease or be given another comparable vehicle. Local refused. Dan then notified the manufacturer that he was revoking acceptance. When the manufacturer refused as well, Dan commenced a legal action against the manufacturer alleging breach of a written warranty under the MMWA.

The manufacturer has moved to dismiss the complaint on the basis that the MMWA does not apply to leases, but only to purchased products. Write a brief memorandum or make an oral presentation arguing for Dapper Dan that the MMWA does apply to leases. In the alternative, write a brief memorandum or make an oral presentation arguing for

Manufacturer that the MMWA does not apply to leases. The relevant sections of the statute are 15 U.S.C. § 2301(3) & (6), and § 2310(d).

(a) Consider how the courts would interpret these sections with regard to the question of lease coverage. Should they use a "plain language" approach? Examine legislative history? The purpose of the statute? Other analogous pieces of consumer legislation? Will these different approaches make a difference in the outcome?

(b) Would it make a difference whether the leased car is first sold with a warranty to a finance company who actually leases it to the consumer and assigns the warranty to the lessee?

(c) Why would this issue of MMWA coverage of leases be an important issue to both consumer lessees and to the manufacturers or lessors?

Problem 7–7

The Avis Skewer Company has always sold its barbecue skewers on a "satisfaction guaranteed" basis, giving dissatisfied customers either a refund or a replacement. This guarantee is good for ten days, and Avis specifically limits its liability to refund or replacement by excluding responsibility for consequential damages.

The Hertz Skewer Company has always given a lifetime guarantee that "Our skewer will withstand trampling by herds of elephants forever. If it doesn't, we will repair or replace it for free." Hertz also excludes responsibility for consequential damages.

The National Skewer Company offers a ten year warranty against all defects, with guaranteed repair or replacement upon payment of a $5 handling charge. It also limits all implied warranties of merchantability or fitness to the same ten year period.

The Budget Skewer Company has always sold its skewers "as is".

Under the Magnuson–Moss Warranty Act, how must each company describe its guarantees in the future? Which description is likely to sound better in an advertising campaign? Which, in fact, is the best warranty? Is the average consumer likely to understand correctly what each type of guarantee really means? See Magnuson–Moss Warranty Act, §§ 2303, 2304.

Problem 7–8

With the MMWA in mind, reexamine the form contract recited in Problem 7–3, *supra*. If you were to review this contract as a legal advisor to the manufacturer, what wording, if any, would you advise the manufacturer to change? Does MMWA § 2308 create any problem? How must the contract be designated? See MMWA §§ 2303–2304. Would all written warranties have to meet the "federal minimum standards for warranty" set forth in § 2304? Why or why not?

5. LEMON LAWS

Overview

Beginning in the early 1980's, all fifty states passed so-called "lemon laws" to address perceived inadequacies in the UCC and the MMWA.

The main issue dealt with in the state lemon laws is to provide an adequate remedy for breach of warranty to the average purchaser of a new automobile exhibiting serious defects. No model or uniform law exists, so these state laws have many variations, but they also have many common elements. Typically, the lemon law functions as a supplement to both the UCC and the MMWA in automobile warranty cases, and a lemon law count is often pled in tandem with other statutory causes of action. The Ohio Lemon Law, Ohio R.C. tit. 13, Ch. 1345.71–.78, available in the statutory supplement, contains most of the features of a typical state lemon law, and can serve as a prototype. Following is a summary of the basic features of state lemon laws, with references to the Ohio statute.

1. All lemon laws provide the consumer with a direct remedy from the manufacturer, thus eliminating the "privity" barrier. Ohio R.C. § 1345.72(B).

2. All lemon laws basically overcome the remedy limitations in warranties by providing consumers with the right to a refund of the purchase price or a replacement vehicle from the manufacturer if the vehicle is not repaired after a reasonable number of attempts. The statutory remedies supersede any remedy limitation in the contract. Ohio R.C. § 1345.72(B).

3. The lemon law eliminates the uncertainty of the UCC "failure of essential purpose" approach, UCC § 2–719(2), by establishing a presumption that a certain number of repair attempts or days out of service will constitute a "reasonable" opportunity to repair. Ohio R.C. § 1345.73.

4. The lemon law encourages the less expensive and faster procedure of informal dispute resolution, usually keyed to standards set forth in the MMWA regulation 16 C.F.R. § 703. Ohio R.C. § 1345.77. Typically, the consumer would have to exhaust their remedies under a conforming dispute resolution system before going to court.

5. If the consumer goes to court to enforce their lemon law remedies, they would be entitled to recover attorney's fees and court costs if they prevail. Ohio R.C. § 1345.75(A).

6. Most state lemon laws provide for a disclosure or "title branding" of the status of vehicles that have been returned to the manufacturer as lemons and then are resold to the public. Ohio R.C. § 1345.76.

7. Some lemon laws, such as Ohio's, require a disclosure to consumers at purchase regarding their lemon law rights. Ohio R.C. § 1345.74.

8. All lemon laws are limited in scope, typically to new passenger cars under express warranty. Many lemon laws now cover leased vehicles as well. Ohio R.C. § 1345.71(A), (C) & (D).

See Dee Pridgen, Consumer Protection and the Law, Appendices 15A and 15B (Thomson/West 2007) for current citations and summaries of the state lemon laws. See also Philip R. Nowicki, State Lemon Law

Coverage Terms: Dissecting the Differences, 11 Loyola Cons. L. Rev. 39 (1998) for a summary of the differences among state lemon laws.

The following two cases illustrate some of the continuing legal issues in lemon law litigation.

CHMILL v. FRIENDLY FORD–MERCURY OF JANESVILLE, INC.

Court of Appeals of Wisconsin, 1988.
144 Wis.2d 796, 424 N.W.2d 747.

SUNDBY, JUDGE.

This case requires an interpretation of sec. 218.015, Stats. (1983–84), Wisconsin's Lemon Law. Friendly Ford–Mercury of Janesville, Inc., and Ford Motor Company appeal a judgment under the law requiring them to replace the Chmills' Ford Tempo with a comparable new motor vehicle. We affirm.

I.

BACKGROUND OF THE CASE

On November 26, 1983, the Chmills purchased a demonstrator 1984 Ford Tempo, from Friendly Ford–Mercury of Janesville, Inc. Friendly Ford gave the Chmills a new-car warranty which expired May 4, 1984 when the Chmills had driven the vehicle 12,000 miles.

The trial court found that between the date of purchase and April 2, 1984, the Chmills on at least five occasions had reported a "pulling" problem to Friendly Ford and had left the vehicle with it to be repaired. In December 1984, the Chmills received a recall notice from Ford concerning a rear wheel alignment problem. On December 10, 1984 the Chmills presented the vehicle to Friendly Ford for repair pursuant to the recall notice. The rear wheels were realigned to attempt to correct the alignment and tire wear problems.

On December 8, 1984 the Chmills sought relief from the Ford Consumer Appeals Board. Friendly Ford's service manager responded that recent road tests had shown that the allegation of a "pulling" problem was unfounded. However, he agreed that a tie rod was defective and it was replaced. According to the Chmills the pulling problem continued. They commenced this action July 15, 1985. The defendants established that as of the final day of trial, June 27, 1986, the Chmills had driven the vehicle 78,000 miles.

* * *

The trial court made a finding of fact and a conclusion of law that the pulling problem constituted a nonconformity which substantially impaired the use, value and safety of the vehicle. [Under the Wisconsin statute, if such a nonconformity remains unrepaired after a reasonable attempt, the manufacturer must, at the consumer's option, either replace the vehicle with a comparable new one, or refund the purchase price.]

"Nonconformity" is defined in sec. 218.015(1)(f), Stats., which pro vides:

"Nonconformity" means a condition or defect which substantially impairs the use, value or safety of a motor vehicle, and is covered by an express warranty applicable to the motor vehicle, but does not include a condition or defect which is the result of abuse, neglect or unauthorized modification or alteration of the motor vehicle by a consumer.

* * *

IV.

SUBSTANTIAL IMPAIRMENT

The defendants argue that because the Chmills drove the vehicle 78,000 miles, it does not have a substantial impairment as a matter of law. They rely on cases decided under the Uniform Commercial Code: *Gasque v. Mooers Motor Car Co., Inc.,* 227 Va. 154, 313 S.E.2d 384 (1984).

Cases decided under the U.C.C. are inapposite because nonconformity thereunder is determined solely under a value standard. Uniform Commercial Code sec. 2–608(1) (sec. 402.608(1), Stats.) permits a buyer to revoke his acceptance of a commercial unit whose "nonconformity substantially impairs its value to him." This is a far different standard from the sec. 218.015(1)(f), Stats., standard which defines a nonconformity in terms of use and safety as well as value.

In *Gasque,* 313 S.E.2d at 389, the fact that the vehicle had substantially fulfilled its primary purpose—simple transportation—was held to satisfy the requirements of the code. However, that a vehicle has served its primary purpose of providing "simple transportation" does not satisfy the use, value and safety standard of sec. 218.015(1)(f), Stats. We therefore reject the defendant's argument that because the Chmills drove the defective vehicle for 78,000 miles, there was, as a matter of law, no substantial impairment within the meaning of sec. 218.015(1)(f). Each case must be examined on its facts under the standard of sec. 218.015(1)(f).

The trial court found that, on her way home from the dealership, Mrs. Chmill discovered that the vehicle pulled to the left. The pulling problem continued and the vehicle was returned to Friendly Ford in December, 1983 for repair. Thereafter, through April of 1984 and no less than once each month, Mrs. Chmill returned the vehicle to Friendly Ford for repair of the pulling problem. The Chmills testified that Friendly Ford's service manager told them the vehicle should be replaced or repurchased since it was defective and could not be repaired. This testimony was unchallenged. An experienced car salesman and buyer for a Buick–Pontiac dealership testified that because of the pulling defect, the value of the vehicle was substantially less than the price paid by the Chmills. From these facts and testimony the trial court found that the pulling problem substantially impaired the use, value and safety of the vehicle. That finding is not clearly erroneous. We affirm the trial court's determination that the facts in this case fulfill the legal standard of "substantial impairment."

V.

ATTEMPTS TO REPAIR

We consider next the defendants' claim that there were not four attempts to repair the vehicle as required by sec. 218.015(1)(h)1, Stats.

To be entitled to recovery under sec. 218.015(2)(b), Stats., a consumer must establish that "after a reasonable attempt to repair the nonconformity [it] cannot be repaired." Section 218.015(1)(h) provides in part:

"Reasonable attempt to repair" means any of the following occurring within the term of an express warranty applicable to a new motor vehicle or within one year after first delivery of the motor vehicle to a consumer, whichever is sooner:

1. The same nonconformity with the warranty is subject to repair by the manufacturer or any of its authorized motor vehicle dealers at least 4 times and the nonconformity continues.

The defendants "vigorously dispute" the trial court's finding of fact that between the date of purchase of the vehicle and April 2, 1984, Mrs. Chmill had on at least five occasions left the vehicle with Friendly Ford to correct the pulling defect. However, they accept that finding for decision-making purposes. They suggest that a vehicle is not "subject to repair" unless the dealer has attempted to repair it. The defendants argue that the record shows that Friendly Ford did not attempt to repair the vehicle four times within the warranty period because the defective condition could not be verified by it.

The construction of the statute urged by the defendants would lead to an unreasonable result. If an acknowledged defect cannot be diagnosed by the service agency no matter how many times the consumer presents the vehicle for repair, the consumer is without recourse. Remedial statutes should be construed to suppress the mischief and advance the remedy which the statute intended to afford. We reject the defendant's hypertechnical construction of the statute as unreasonable. We conclude that the Chmills complied with the statute when on at least four occasions within the warranty period they presented the vehicle to Friendly Ford to be repaired.

* * *

Judgment affirmed, and cause remanded for further proceedings consistent with this opinion.

Notes

1. Like Wisconsin, many state lemon laws require that a "nonconformity" "substantially impair" the use, safety or value of the vehicle before such a defect will qualify for lemon law relief. Depending on the wording of the statute, this standard can be considered objective, subjective or both. *See, e.g.,* General Motors Corp. v. Dohmann, 247 Conn. 274, 722 A.2d 1205 (1998) (Connecticut lemon law uses a mixed subjective/objective standard for interpreting "substantial impairment"); Jolovitz v. Alfa Romeo Distributors of N. Am., 760 A.2d 625 (Me. 2000) (applying objective standard for "substantial impairment"); Schonscheck v. Paccar, Inc., 261 Wis.2d 769, 661 N.W.2d 476 (2003) (driveability of vehicle does not preclude finding of substantial impairment, citing *Chmill*).

2. Typically under a state lemon law, the consumer is not required to prove the cause of a particular defect, but simply that the defect was not successfully repaired after a reasonable number of attempts. *See, e.g.,* Taylor v. Volvo N. Am. Corp., 339 N.C. 238, 451 S.E.2d 618 (1994); Oregel v. Am. Isuzu Motors, Inc., 90 Cal.App.4th 1094, 109 Cal.Rptr.2d 583 (2001).

ROYSTER v. TOYOTA MOTOR SALES, U.S.A., INC.

Supreme Court of Ohio, 2001.
92 Ohio St.3d 327, 750 N.E.2d 531.

PFEIFER, J.

In this case, we address Ohio's Lemon Law, specifically the portion of R.C. 1345.73 that addresses whether a manufacturer has had a reasonable opportunity to repair a defective automobile. We hold that a consumer enjoys a presumption of recovery under R.C. 1345.73(B) if his or her vehicle is out of service by reason of repair for a cumulative total of thirty or more calendar days in the first year of ownership regardless of whether the vehicle was successfully repaired at some point beyond that thirty-day period.

FACTUAL AND PROCEDURAL BACKGROUND

The facts here are not in dispute. On February 3, 1996, appellant Kimberly G. Royster leased a new 1996 Toyota 4–Runner at the Toyota on the Heights dealership in Cleveland Heights, Ohio. The vehicle was warranted by appellee, Toyota Motor Sales U.S.A., Inc. ("Toyota"). Toyota issued Royster a three-year/thirty-six-thousand-mile warranty on the vehicle. Approximately nine months after gaining possession of the vehicle, on November 7, 1996, Royster noticed that it was leaking a red fluid. The vehicle was towed to the dealership that day. At that time it had an odometer reading of approximately 10,129 miles.

The dealership determined that the 4–Runner had a leaking head gasket that needed to be replaced. However, the dealership had difficulty locating the correct part. Thus, the dealership did not complete the repair until December 31, 1996, after the vehicle had been unavailable to

Royster for fifty-five days. Toyota on the Heights had provided Royster with a used Toyota Camry as a loaner at no charge beginning on November 15, 1996.

On January 6, 1997, Royster returned the vehicle to the dealership to correct problems with the paint on a door and with the brakes. The brakes required resurfacing due to disuse during the extended repair period. The repairs were made, and Royster picked up her vehicle. After that, Royster experienced no further mechanical difficulties with the 4–Runner.

On May 30, 1997, Royster filed a Lemon Law claim against Toyota. Both parties filed motions for summary judgment. On June 9, 1998, the trial court granted Royster's motion. The court held that Royster had demonstrated her right to recovery based upon the Lemon Law's presumption in favor of recovery if a vehicle is "out of service by reason of repair for a cumulative total of thirty or more calendar days" in the first year of ownership. The court awarded her and her lienholder $38,565.54 and also entered an additional $7,649 judgment against Toyota for Royster's attorney fees. Toyota appealed the ruling.

The Eighth District Court of Appeals overturned the trial court's decision. The court held that the trial court had erred in finding that the car's fifty-five days out of service created a presumption of recovery for Royster under the Lemon Law. The appellate court held that the dealership made a reasonable number of attempts to repair the vehicle and was ultimately successful in conforming the car to its warranty. The court reasoned that Royster would have had a valid Lemon Law claim only if the vehicle had not conformed to its warranty after the dealership's "reasonable number of repair attempts." The cause is before this court upon the allowance of a discretionary appeal.

LAW AND ANALYSIS

The car-buying experience may be the most complicated mating dance in all of the animal world. It seems a given that both parties must engage in half-truths ("I don't know if I can afford this"), double meanings ("Let's see if we can make the numbers work"), semantic gymnastics ("Priced below invoice"), expressions of powerlessness ("Let me talk to my manager"/"Let me talk to my spouse"), and white lies ("I'm talking to someone at another dealership") before the relationship finally culminates in a deal. Once the deal for a new automobile is complete, however, the clear language of the General Assembly takes over, without any hidden meanings or purposely confusing wordplay.

Ohio's Lemon Law is designed to protect consumers from chronically defective new automobiles. It requires new vehicles to live up to warranties given by manufacturers. The Lemon Law attaches a clear duty to sellers, and provides a clear remedy to buyers should the seller breach its duty.

Pursuant to R.C. 1345.72(A), a vehicle must abide by its warranty, and if the condition of the automobile does not meet what is warranted, the seller must repair it * * * [see statutory supplement for language of statute].

While R.C. 1345.72(A) attaches a clear duty on sellers and gives them the opportunity to preclude recovery by making prompt repairs, R.C. 1345.72(B) provides consumers a swift and simple remedy should the car not be made right within a reasonable number of attempts. * * * [see statutory supplement for language of statute].

Thus, if a manufacturer cannot repair a new automobile after a reasonable number of attempts, a buyer may request a refund or a replacement. Lest there be a doubt, and subsequent exhaustive litigation, as to what constitutes "a reasonable number of repair attempts," R.C. 1345.73 sets limits. * * * [see statutory supplement for language of statute].

R.C. 1345.73 is at the heart of this case. The appellate court held that R.C. 1345.73(B) does not create a presumption of recovery "but rather a presumption that a reasonable number of attempts to conform the vehicle to warranty have been made." According to the appellate court, the buyer must further show that after that "reasonable number of attempts" the vehicle still does not conform to its warranty. Because Royster had failed to prove that the 4–Runner remained defective after Toyota's nearly two-month repair attempt, the court ordered judgment in Toyota's favor.

We disagree with the appellate court's interpretation. The Lemon Law recognizes that occasionally new cars do have problems, but if those problems keep happening, or cannot be repaired in a reasonable amount of time, then the consumer did not get what he or she bargained for. R.C. 1345.73 is the "enough is enough" portion of the statute. That section makes the amount of repair activity on the vehicle define whether the vehicle is a lemon. R.C. 1345.73 is a kind of statute of limitations—it sets in well-defined terms the limit of frustration a consumer must endure.

R.C. 1345.73 sets the cutoff point of reasonableness. Under R.C. 1345.73(A), (C), and (D), respectively, a manufacturer gets three tries to repair a particular nonconformity, eight tries to correct any combination of nonconformities that substantially impair the use and value of the vehicle, and one try to repair a nonconformity that results in a condition that makes the vehicle extremely dangerous to drive. The statute does its best to avoid leaving reasonableness open to interpretation, instead defining what is reasonable in strict terms.

The subsection applicable in this case, R.C. 1345.73(B), marks as thirty days the limit that a consumer need tolerate having his or her vehicle out of service in the first year of ownership. Whether the vehicle is driveable after those thirty days is irrelevant. Indeed, the statute speaks in terms of a *cumulative* thirty days out of service. Thus, the vehicle could have entered the shop on numerous occasions and been repaired each time. The *unavailability* of the new car is the key element. The fact that a consumer cannot drive a newly purchased vehicle for a full month in the first year of ownership defines the vehicle as a lemon. The General Assembly struck thirty days as the balance between what a consumer must endure and the time a manufacturer needs to make necessary repairs. Nothing beyond thirty days is statutorily reasonable. Once the boundaries of reasonableness have been passed, the vehicle at that point becomes, legally, a lemon.

By leaving little room for interpretation, R.C. 1345.73 leaves little room for litigation. As a consumer-protection law, the Lemon Law must be simple and must have teeth in order to be effective. The law is designed for self-help without protracted litigation. To work well, the statute needs a harsh remedy at a time certain. Ohio's Lemon Law does that better than most states' laws:

> "Ohio's standards for 'reasonable number of attempts' are among the most stringent in the nation in that the number of repair attempts before liability attaches is low. * * * Under the lemon law, the consumer need only show that his automobile has been unsuccessfully repaired the requisite number of times and the Act takes effect. Unless the manufacturer can show that the defects were not substantial or were the fault of the consumer, the manufacturer will be forced to replace the car or refund the purchase price." Comment, Ohio's Lemon Law: Ohio Joins the Rest of the Nation in Waging War Against the Automobile Limited Warranty (1989), 57 U.Cin.L.J. 1015, 1032.

Despite its pucker-inducing remedy, the Lemon Law does have protections for manufacturers. The law does not create remedies for buyers who have soured on their new vehicle for cosmetic or other trivial reasons. The vehicle's problem must "substantially impai[r] the use, safety, or value of the motor vehicle to the consumer." Besides the requirement of a major defect and the right of the manufacturer to preclude recovery by prompt repair, the Lemon Law also provides defenses to manufacturers. A consumer cannot recover under the Lemon Law if the nonconformity is "the result of abuse, neglect, or the unauthorized modification or alteration of a motor vehicle by anyone other than the manufacturer, its agent, or its authorized dealer." R.C. 1345.75.

Still, the Lemon Law remains a powerful tool for consumers. A tangential effect of a tough Lemon Law may be to persuade manufacturers to be hyper-vigilant when new car buyers bring their vehicles in for repair. In most cases, the threat of a remedy may be enough to achieve a positive result with which both parties can be happy. Unfortunately, that did not happen in this case.

We agree with the trial court in this case that a leaking head gasket "certainly maintains the look, feel, and potential expense of a disaster" and meets the statutory definition of a substantial impairment. Toyota obviously failed to repair the problem within thirty days, and failed to assert that any of the statutory affirmative defenses were applicable. The appellate court seemed to consider the dealership's providing of a loaner car a *de facto* affirmative defense. While an admirable gesture, lending a car to a consumer with a Lemon Law claim provides no statutory defense. The true focus of the Lemon Law is on the *automobile*. In enacting the Lemon Law, the General Assembly defines for consumers when an automobile becomes a lemon, not when a dealer is not being considerate enough.

Royster demonstrated that she enjoyed a presumption of recovery under R.C. 1345.73(B). Toyota had no defenses available. Accordingly, we reverse the judgment of the court of appeals and reinstate the judgment of the trial court. Further, we grant appellant's motion to remand the cause to the trial court for a determination of additional attorney fees incurred on appeal.

Judgment reversed and cause remanded.

[Opinion by COOK, J., concurring in part and dissenting in part, omitted].

* * *

LUNDBERG STRATTON, J., dissenting.

I respectfully dissent from the majority decision that a thirty-day delay in a repair creates a virtually irrebuttable presumption of recovery.

The purpose and spirit of the Lemon Law is to provide a remedy to a consumer who has lost confidence in the operation of his or her new vehicle due to a significant or persistent defect that cannot be repaired at all or cannot be repaired in a reasonable number of attempts. Consequently, a Lemon Law claim arises only where the manufacturer is unable to repair a defect that "substantially impairs the use, safety, or value" of the vehicle or alternatively is unable to repair the defect in a reasonable number of attempts. R.C. 1345.72(B). As the majority recognizes, "[t]he Lemon Law recognizes that occasionally new cars do have problems, but if those problems keep happening, or cannot be repaired in a reasonable amount of time, then the consumer did not get what he or she bargained for."

In this case, the engine was subject to a single repair, which completely corrected the defect. The majority opinion focuses on the thirty-day presumption in R.C. 1345.73(B) and holds that if a vehicle is out of service for a cumulative of thirty days, the owner enjoys a presumption of recovery. I agree with Justice Cook's dissent to the extent that R.C. 1345.73(B) does not provide a presumption of *recovery*, but merely a presumption that the manufacturer has undertaken a reasonable number of attempts to repair the vehicle, which is only one element of a Lemon Law claim. However, I also believe that, contrary to the import of the majority's opinion, the presumption in R.C. 1345.73(B) is rebuttable and in fact has been rebutted in this case.

* * *

It is undisputed that the 4–Runner was unavailable to Royster for more than thirty days. However, the reason for the delay was not an inability by Toyota to promptly diagnose or repair the defect. Rather, the delay was due to the unavailability of the replacement head gasket. But for the delay in receiving the replacement head gasket, the 4–Runner would have been in the shop for less than thirty days and the presumption under R.C. 1345.73(B) would never have arisen. I do not believe that a delay in acquiring a part deprives the consumer of what he or she bargained for, because it does not lessen the consumer's confidence in the *operation* of the vehicle. I believe that the presumption set out in R.C. 1345.73(B), that the manufacturer has undertaken a "reasonable number of attempts to repair," is rebutted where the sole reason for the delay was a back-ordered part. Thus, I believe that Toyota has rebutted the presumption that it had undertaken a reasonable number of attempts to repair Royster's 4–Runner. Therefore, Royster's complaint would fail because she cannot prove an essential element of the Lemon Law statute.

I do not intend to trivialize losing the use of a vehicle for almost two months. However, Toyota provided Royster a loaner vehicle to use free of charge while the 4–Runner was in the shop.

The majority's holding distorts the spirit and purpose of the Lemon Law and opens the floodgates for consumers to return new vehicles that are not genuine lemons as envisioned by the Lemon Law to the unjustified financial detriment of auto manufacturers. Accordingly, I respectfully dissent and would affirm the court of appeals' judgment.

Notes

1. Which judge has the better argument in the *Royster* case? Did the majority in fact create an irrebuttable presumption not intended by the legislature? Or did the legislature indeed intend to mandate recovery for the consumer in this type of situation? If so, is it fair to the manufacturer?

2. The Ninth Circuit Court of Appeals, applying Nevada law, held in a 2005 case that days out of service due to the unavailability of a part are counted in the presumption of reasonable opportunity to repair. The court pointed out that the consumer "had no control over the ordering of the parts, nor was she in a position to know how long the necessary parts would take to arrive." Milicevic v. Fletcher Jones Imports, Ltd., 402 F.3d 912 (9th Cir. 2005).

3. Other courts have ruled that a consumer need not prove that a defect is still in existence or unrepaired at the time of trial or arbitration, so long as it was still unrepaired after the presumptively reasonable number of unsuccessful repair attempts. *See* Krasnow v. Mercedes–Benz of North America, Inc., 1998 WL 437339 (Conn. Super. Ct. 1998); DiVigenze v. Chrysler Corp., 345 N.J.Super. 314, 785 A.2d 37 (2001); DaimlerChrysler Corp. v. Spitzer, 6 Misc.3d 228, 782 N.Y.S.2d 610 (2004) (requiring that the defect remain unrepaired "would induce consumers to stop trying to repair their vehicles after the fourth unsuccessful repair attempt and either drive defective vehicles or let them sit idle in order to be entitled to the repair

presumption * * *. This is something few consumers can afford to do. Nor is this a reasonable result.'').

4. When is a new car "new" for purposes of the lemon law? There is a split in the state courts regarding whether a vehicle that is sold to another consumer during the initial warranty period would still be considered "new" under the state lemon law. Some state statutes have been interpreted to cover cars with significant mileage so long as they are still covered by the original manufacturer warranty when purchased. See Britton v. Bill Anselmi Pontiac–Buick–GMC, Inc., 786 P.2d 855 (Wyo. 1990); Chrysler Motors Corp. v. Flowers, 116 Wash.2d 208, 803 P.2d 314 (1991); Subaru of America, Inc. v. Peters, 256 Va. 43, 500 S.E.2d 803 (1998). Other state courts have refused to apply their state lemon law to vehicles with significant mileage. See American Motors Sales Corp. v. Brown, 152 A.D.2d 343, 548 N.Y.S.2d 791 (N.Y. App. Div. 1989); Schey v. Chrysler Corp., 228 Wis.2d 483, 597 N.W.2d 457 (1999); Day v. Beau Townsend Ford, 129 Ohio App.3d 265, 717 N.E.2d 769 (1998).

5. The remedy of a refund, available under most state lemon laws, may sound attractive, but it comes with qualifications. In most states, there is a mileage setoff to cover the reasonable value of use by the consumer prior to the refund. In Ohio, the State Supreme Court held that a mileage setoff accepted by the consumer as part of an arbitration award was valid, even though the statute does not specifically provide for such a setoff. Maitland v. Ford Motor Co., 103 Ohio St.3d 463, 816 N.E.2d 1061 (2004).

Many lemon owners have traded in another vehicle when they purchased their lemon. If the dealer inflated the trade in value, however, in a situation where the consumer owed more on the trade-in than its retail value, there may be "negative equity" involved. In a Florida case, the court used the actual retail value of the trade-in minus the debt owed on the trade-in that was paid by the dealer, to calculate the refund, so that the consumer's refund on the lemon was less than they bargained for. See Holzhauer–Mosher v. Ford Motor Co., 772 So.2d 7 (Fla. Dist. Ct. App. 2000).

6. Lemon laws are specifically aimed at automotive vehicles. Do we need similar legislation for other types of products/purchases? What about computers? Pets? Other products? Why did the state legislatures in the 1980's feel the need to pass lemon laws, which basically streamline the process of providing desired remedies for consumers with breach of warranty issues on their new vehicles, when Congress had already passed the MMWA to deal with warranty issues on a much wider range of consumer products?

Problem 7–9

Robbin Hood bought a new Dodge station wagon for $20,000 from Dale Dodge in Akron, Ohio. The car came with an express warranty which states in full:

LIMITED WARRANTY

The manufacturer warrants this car to be free from defects in material and workmanship for 36 months or 36,000 miles, whichever comes first. Manufacturer makes no other express warranty, and any implied warranty of merchantability or fitness is limited to the

36 month or 36,000 mile duration of this written warranty. The buyer's exclusive remedy under this warranty is repair or replacement of defective parts, which will be done without charge to the buyer, at any designated Dodge dealership.

Dale Dodge furnished a separate document to Hood, which stated in pertinent part:

The selling dealer agrees to perform all repairs required under this warranty as an agent of the manufacturer but makes absolutely NO EXPRESS OR IMPLIED WARRANTY OF MERCHANTABILITY OR FITNESS.

The automatic transmission has broken down four times since Hood purchased the car and each time the repair failed to correct the problem. Dale now says he will replace the transmission.

It is 9 months since Hood bought the car, and the odometer reads 10,220 miles. Hood comes to you for legal advice. He confides that the car is really too expensive for him so he would prefer to get his money back and rescind the whole transaction.

(a) Is Hood in a better position under the Ohio lemon law than he would be with only the UCC or with the UCC and the MMWA (i.e., will he have an easier time getting his preferred remedy of returning the car and getting a refund)? What type of remedy will Hood get if he is successful under the lemon law? Will the remedy limitation in the warranty be a problem? Will Hood have to litigate the issue of how many attempts to repair or how many days out of service is reasonable? Will he have to worry about privity of contract? What if the car were still "driveable"—will that bar Hood's recovery under the lemon law? What if the problem with the transmission was actually fixed on the fourth try? Will Hood get attorneys' fees under the lemon law?

(b) What does Hood give up to get these lemon law remedies? Does he get a full refund or will there be some deductions? Will he automatically get a refund or will he have to accept a replacement vehicle? What if the manufacturer has instituted an informal dispute resolution system? What if there is a binding arbitration clause in the warranty?

Problem 7–10

A new Jeep Cherokee was sold to Abigail and Adam Fleck in the State of Ohio. The Flecks complained of multiple water leaks and returned the Jeep to Chrysler, which repurchased it under the state lemon law. Chrysler repaired the vehicle and sold it at auction to Gigantic Auto Mall in Cleveland, Ohio. At that time, Gigantic was furnished a disclosure notice that the vehicle had been repurchased as a settlement of a Customer Arbitration Board case, and that it had experienced water leaks. The Belzers purchased the same Jeep from Gigantic but the dealer failed to pass on the disclosure notice to them. At the time of their purchase, the Jeep had 10,000 miles on the odometer. The Belzers experienced repeated problems with water leaks, some of which were repaired by Gigantic at no cost to them. When they sought to trade-in the Jeep at another dealership, they learned that it was a lemon buyback. The Belzers are outraged, because they say they never would have bought a lemon, or at least that they would not have been willing to pay as much for it as they did, had they known it was repurchased by the manufacturer under the lemon law. What remedies, if any, do the Belzers have under the Ohio Lemon Law against the dealer for failing to disclose the Jeep's buyback status? Do they have any remedies against Chrysler? Will they need to look beyond the lemon law for a remedy?

See Ohio R.C. 1345.76 and .78; and Pearn v. DaimlerChrysler Corp., 148 Ohio App.3d 228, 772 N.E.2d 712 (2002); Carter v. Chrysler Corp., 743 So.2d 456 (Ala. Ct. Civ. App. 1999); Alexander v. DaimlerChrysler Corp., 2004 WL 179369 (N.C. Super. Ct. 2004). *See also* Johnson v. Ford Motor Co., 35 Cal.4th 1191, 29 Cal.Rptr.3d 401, 113 P.3d 82 (2005) (punitive damages awarded against manufacturer based on practice of issuing "Owner Appreciation Certificates" good for credits of up to $5,000 on trade-ins for new Ford vehicles when customers complained of defects; court held that this practice was an end-run around the title-branding requirements of California law that would have applied had the vehicles been reacquired as lemons).

6. REAL ESTATE

Thus, far, we have said nothing about warranties in the sale of real estate. The law of warranties in realty sales may be just about one hundred years behind that of personal property warranties. Neither the UCC nor the MMWA are applicable.

ALBRECHT v. CLIFFORD

Supreme Judicial Court of Massachusetts, 2002.
436 Mass. 706, 767 N.E.2d 42.

CORDY, J.

In 1993, Peter L. Albrecht and Margaret Page Albrecht bought a newly constructed single-family home with nine fireplaces from Alfred G. Clifford, an architect and general contractor. Several years later, the Albrechts learned that there were defects in the fireplaces and chimneys in another house that Clifford had built in their neighborhood. Consequently, they retained an inspector who found similar defects in the Albrechts' home. The Albrechts filed a complaint in the Superior Court asserting claims against Clifford for breach of contract (Counts I and II), breach of an implied warranty that the residence was constructed in a good and workmanlike manner (Count III), fraud and deceit (Count IV), negligent misrepresentation (Count V), and violation of G.L. c. 93A (Count VI). A judge in the Superior Court allowed Clifford's motion for summary judgment on all the Albrechts' claims. They appealed. We transferred the appeal to this court on our own motion to consider whether an implied warranty arises out of a contract for the sale of a newly constructed residence by a builder-vendor. We conclude that there is such a warranty but affirm the entry of summary judgment for the defendant on statute of limitations grounds. We affirm the judge's summary judgment rulings on the Albrechts' contract claims on other grounds.

1. *Background.* In March, 1992, Clifford began construction of a single-family home on property he owned in Newbury (residence). In September, 1993, the Albrechts decided to buy the residence, and with the assistance of experienced and capable counsel, negotiated the terms of the sale with Clifford, including certain express warranties. On September 16, 1993, the Albrechts and Clifford executed a standard form purchase and sale agreement (agreement). Exhibit A to the agreement set forth the express warranties that Clifford and the Albrechts agreed would survive the delivery of the deed for one year, including: "all systems, e.g., plumbing, electrical, heating, fireplaces and chimneys etc., will work properly"; "the entire premises is built according to municipal and state regulations, including building, zoning, health, safety, electrical and plumbing codes"; and "the premises have been constructed in a good and workmanlike manner." However, this express warranty provision required the Albrechts to give Clifford written notice of any defects within one year of the delivery of the deed. On October 26, 1993, the Albrechts bought the residence from Clifford for $595,000. They moved in on December 23, 1993, but never used any of the fireplaces.

In December, 1996, the Albrechts were told by a neighbor that the fireplaces and chimneys in their home, also built by Clifford, were defective. The Albrechts hired a mason whose inspection of the home led him to conclude that the Albrechts' fireplaces and chimneys were also defective. The Albrechts sent two letters to Clifford asking him to repair the defects, but Clifford and the Albrechts were unable to agree on a solution. On February 6, 1998, the Albrechts filed this lawsuit. During the litigation that ensued, the Albrechts retained an expert who concluded that the chimneys, fireboxes, dampers, flues, and smoke chambers were "not constructed in a good and workmanlike manner" and did not comply with the State building code.

2. *Implied warranty of habitability.* In 1964, the Supreme Court of Colorado was the first court in the country to abandon the doctrine of caveat emptor and hold that a builder-vendor of a completed residential home impliedly warrants that it complies with applicable building code requirements, is built in a workmanlike manner, and is suitable for habitation. *Carpenter v. Donohoe,* 154 Colo. 78, 83–84, 388 P.2d 399 (1964). Since the decision in *Carpenter,* the majority of jurisdictions have similarly abandoned the doctrine of caveat emptor, and adopted implied warranties of habitability or good workmanlike quality in the sale of newly constructed houses. Although we have abandoned the doctrine of caveat emptor in the context of residential leases and held that such leases carry with them an implied warranty of habitability, until today, we have not adopted such a warranty in the sale of new homes.

There are a number of important policy considerations that have led other jurisdictions to adopt the type of implied warranty urged on us in this case. An implied warranty assures that consumers receive that for which they have bargained, an objectively habitable home, see *Miller v. Cannon Hill Estates, Ltd.,* 2 K.B. 113, 120–121, 1931 WL 26626 (1931); it protects purchasers from structural defects that are nearly impossible to ascertain by inspection after the home is built, see *Christensen v. R.D. Sell Constr. Co.,* 774 S.W.2d 535, 538 (Mo.Ct.App.1989); and it imposes the burden of repairing latent defects on the person who has the opportunity to notice, avoid, or correct them during the construction process, see *Duncan v. Schuster–Graham Homes, Inc.,* 194 Colo. 441, 444, 578 P.2d 637 (1978).

These sound policy reasons lead us to adopt an implied warranty of habitability that attaches to the sale of new homes by builder-vendors in the Commonwealth.[9] The adoption of such a warranty is also consistent with the protections that our law affords consumers in other contexts. See *Boston Hous. Auth. v. Hemingway,* 363 Mass. 184, 293 N.E.2d 831 (1973) (implied warranty of habitability in residential leases); *George v. Goldman,* 333 Mass. 496, 131 N.E.2d 772 (1956) (implied warranty in construction contracts to do workmanlike job and use reasonable skill). See also G.L. c. 106, § 2–314 (implied warranty of merchantability for goods). Its purpose is to protect a purchaser of a new home from latent defects that create substantial questions of safety and habitability. While the scope of this warranty must be left largely to case-by-case determination, a home that is unsafe because it deviates from fundamental aspects of the applicable building codes, or is structurally unsound, or fails to keep out the elements because of defects of construction, would breach the implied warranty we adopt today.

This implied warranty is independent and collateral to the covenant to convey, and survives the passing of title to and taking possession of the real estate. It cannot be waived or disclaimed, because to permit the disclaimer of a warranty protecting a purchaser from the consequences of latent defects would defeat the very purpose of the warranty.[10]

This implied warranty does not make the builder an insurer against any and all defects in a home, impose on the builder an obligation to deliver a perfect house, or protect against mere defects in workmanship, minor or procedural violations of the applicable building codes, or defects that are trivial or aesthetic. Its adoption is not intended to affect a buyer's ability to inspect a house before purchase, to condition the purchase on a satisfactory inspection result, or to negotiate additional express warranties.

To establish a breach of the implied warranty of habitability a plaintiff will have to demonstrate that (1) he purchased a new house from the defendant-builder-vendor; (2) the house contained a latent

9. We are not called on here to decide whether a second or subsequent purchaser may state a claim for breach of this implied warranty against the builder within the applicable statute of limitations.

10. The implied warranty that we establish here does not apply to the purchase or sale of unfinished homes, where the parties may choose to waive or disclaim all warranties.

defect; (3) the defect manifested itself only after its purchase; (4) the defect was caused by the builder's improper design, material, or workmanship; and (5) the defect created a substantial question of safety or made the house unfit for human habitation. In addition, the claim must be brought within the three-year statute of limitations and the six-year statute of repose set forth in G.L. c. 260, § 2B.[11]

The motion judge concluded that the Albrechts' claim for relief under a theory of implied warranty failed because no such cause of action had been recognized in Massachusetts. Having recognized such a warranty, we now apply the principles just announced to the record on summary judgment.

The Albrechts are purchasers of a newly constructed home from a builder-vendor, and the defects about which they complain were discovered after they purchased the residence. In addition, based on their expert's affidavit, the Albrechts have adequately demonstrated, for purposes of summary judgment, that there are genuine issues of disputed fact about whether the defects were caused by the builder's improper design and workmanship, and whether they created a substantial question of safety.

Whether the Albrechts can adequately demonstrate that the defects were "latent" is more questionable. Latent defects are conditions that are hidden or concealed, and are not discoverable by reasonable and customary observation or inspection. Black's Law Dictionary 429, 887 (7th ed. 1999). The defects in this case, however, were in some measure readily observable. In concluding that the fireplaces and chimneys were defective, the Albrechts' expert did not have to dismantle them or any other part of the residence. He merely made observations and measurements of the materials and components (e.g., hearths, fireplace boxes, dampers, flues, smoke chambers) that were readily accessible.[14] Admittedly, some of the observations (e.g., smoke chambers, flues, and chimney interiors) were more difficult than others (hearths, fireplace boxes, and dampers), and were made with the assistance of video equipment. Whether the discovery and correction of the obvious defects would have led to the discovery of those which were more difficult to observe is a close question on summary judgment, but is one that we need not

---

11.   General Laws c. 260, § 2B, provides: "Action of tort for damages arising out of any deficiency or neglect in the design, planning, construction or general administration of an improvement to real property ... shall be commenced only within three years next after the cause of action accrues; provided, however, that in no event shall such actions be commenced more than six years after the earlier of the dates of (1) the opening of the improvement to use; or (2) substantial completion of the improvement and the taking of possession for occupancy by the owner." This statute is appropriately applied to an implied warranty of habitabil-

ity because such a warranty is an obligation imposed by law and is "imposed apart from and independent of promises made and therefore apart from any manifested intention of parties to a contract." W.L. Prosser & W.P. Keeton, Torts § 92, at 656 (5th ed. 1984). * * *

14.   The expert concluded, among other things, that the combined depths of the fireboxes and hearths were too small, the dampers were too small, the flue liners were too small, and the walls around these components were not thick enough, all in violation of the State building code.

resolve. We conclude, as the motion judge did, that even assuming a cause of action for the violation of an implied warranty, the Albrechts were barred from pursuing this claim because of their failure to raise it within the three-year statute of limitations.

3. *Statute of limitations.* The Albrechts bought the residence on October 26, 1993, moved in on December 23, 1993, and filed their complaint on February 6, 1998, more than four years later. The motion judge concluded that, absent tolling of the applicable statutes of limitations, the claims for fraud and deceit (Count IV), negligent misrepresentation (Count V), and G.L. c. 93A (Count VI) were time barred.[15] He also concluded that the statutes were not tolled in the circumstances of this case. We agree.

To defeat Clifford's motion for summary judgment, the Albrechts sought to invoke the discovery rule. "The rule, which operates to toll a limitations period until a prospective plaintiff learns or should have learned that he has been injured, may arise in three circumstances: where a misrepresentation concerns a fact that was 'inherently unknowable' to the injured party, where a wrongdoer breached some duty of disclosure, or where a wrongdoer concealed the existence of a cause of action through some affirmative act done with the intent to deceive." *Patsos v. First Albany Corp.*, 433 Mass. 323, 328, 741 N.E.2d 841 (2001), citing *Protective Life Ins. Co. v. Sullivan,* 425 Mass. 615, 631–632, 682 N.E.2d 624 (1997).

* * *

The Albrechts claim that the purported defects were inherently unknowable and that they did not have any reason to suspect that there was a problem until December, 1996, when neighbors told them about their own problems with their fireplaces and chimneys. The motion judge concluded from the undisputed facts that the Albrechts' claims were not "inherently unknowable":

> [T]he defects alleged were readily seen on an inspection conducted sometime after December of 1996. Such an inspection equally as well could have been conducted in 1993 when the Albrechts moved in. Similarly, the mere use of at least some of the nine fireplaces should have signalled a problem, if there was one. And perhaps most obviously, charges that the hearths were the wrong size or the fireboxes not deep enough presented situations that were in plain sight and discoverable by simple measurements.

Whether the defects were inherently unknowable or not, we conclude that on the record of undisputed facts, the Albrechts cannot meet their burden of demonstrating that "in the exercise of reasonable diligence, they should not have known" of them. It was not reasonable as a

---

15. The judge applied the three-year statute of limitations in G.L. c. 260, § § 2A, 2B, to Counts IV and V and the four-year statute of limitations in G.L. c. 260, § 5A, to Count VI.

matter of law for the Albrechts neither to inspect[16] nor to use the fireplaces when they knew the express warranty on the fireplaces and chimneys, which they had negotiated, lasted only one year. This conclusion is also implicit in the judge's conclusion that the defects were not "inherently unknowable" in the circumstances of this case. The statutes of limitations were therefore not tolled and the Albrechts' claims for fraud and deceit, negligent misrepresentation, and violation of G.L. c. 93A were filed after the applicable statutes of limitations had expired. For the same reason, the three-year statute of limitations provided in G.L. c. 260, § 2B, expired on the claim for breach of the implied warranty of habitability announced in today's decision.

Judgment affirmed.

Problem 7–11

Hovel Homes constructed a new home for Jack and Jill Hill. Two years later, Hill was transferred to another state and the Hills sold their home to Humpty Dumpty. Several months after he moved in, Dumpty gradually became aware that the electrical wiring was defective and dangerous. He determined that it would cost $4,000 to have the wiring brought up to standard. He wants to sue Hovel for breach of the implied warranty of habitability. Thus far his state has only recognized an implied warranty for the benefit of the original purchaser. Should the implied warranty extend to Humpty Dumpty? What are the arguments on each side? Compare Nichols v. R.R. Beaufort & Assoc., Inc., 727 A.2d 174 (R.I. 1999) with VonHoldt v. Barba & Barba Construc., Inc., 677 N.E.2d 836 (Ill. 1997).

Problem 7–12

Harry Hovel, President of Hovel Homes, would like to get into the business of building quickie condominium developments for retired persons. His jurisdiction has enacted the Uniform Condominium Act (UCA), which Hovel has heard will impose special warranty standards on residential condominium sales. He wants to disclaim all such warranties. He asks you whether an "as is" clause will accomplish his goal. Will it? If not, what can you put in his contract which will be effective? See UCA § 4–115(b) in the statutory supplement.

Notes

1. By 2005, every state except Utah had recognized, through judicial decisions or statute, an implied warranty of habitability running from the builder/seller to the original buyer. National Consumer Law Center, Consumer Warranty Law: Lemon Law, Magnuson–Moss, UCC, Mobile Home, and Other Warranty Statutes § 16.3.1 (2d ed. 2001, and 2005 supplement).

---

16. The Albrechts contracted for a pre-purchase inspection of the residence that was limited to "readily accessible areas of the building" and "to visual observations only." The inspection report specifically stated that: "The report is not a compliance inspection or certification for past or present governmental codes or regulations of any kind." The inspection did not require the inspector to ignite a solid fuel fire or observe the interior of the fireplaces or flues.

A few states have legislated an implied warranty of habitability for new homes. *See, e.g.,* Md. Real Prop. Code Ann. 10–201(b)-(c); Conn.Gen.Stat. Ann. 4057 47–118(a), Minn.Stat. 327A.02, subd. 1; N.J.Stat.Ann. 46:3B–3(b); Va. Code 55–70.1. *See generally,* Jeff Sovern, Toward a Theory of Warranties in Sales of New Homes: Housing the Implied Warranty Advocates, Law and Economics Mavens, and Consumer Psychologists under One Roof, 1993 Wis. L. Rev. 13 (1993) (advocating disclosure of standardized warranties in housing, with enhanced enforcement of consumers' warranty rights).

2. One of the earlier cases to recognize an implied warranty of habitability stated the rationale this way:

> Since World War II homes have been built in tremendous numbers. There have come into being developer-builders operating on a large scale. Many firms and persons, large and small operators, hold themselves out as skilled in home construction and are in the business of building and selling to individual owners. Developers contract with builders to construct for resale. Building construction by modern methods is complex and intertwined with governmental codes and regulations. The ordinary home buyer is not in a position, by skill or training, to discover defects lurking in the plumbing, the electrical wiring, the structure itself, all of which is usually covered up and not open for inspection.

> A home buyer should be able to place reliance on the builder or developer who sells him a new house. The improved real estate the average family buys gives it thoughtful pause not only because of the base price but the interest involved over a long period of time. This is usually the largest single purchase a family makes for a lifetime. * * *

Tavares v. Horstman, 542 P.2d 1275 (Wyo. 1975).

3. By 2005 only 18 states had extended liability for defects from the builder to subsequent purchasers, and some of these are based on a negligence theory, not warranty. See Dee Pridgen, Consumer Protection and the Law, Appendix 18B (Thomson/West 2007). Other states have held firm on the idea that the warranty does not go farther than the first buyer. See Ellis v. Robert C. Morris, Inc., 128 N.H. 358, 513 A.2d 951 (1986).

4. No state implies a warranty of habitability from the seller of a used home who was not the original builder (although some states have real estate disclosure laws that may be applicable). A disappointed buyer in this type of transaction would be relegated to common law fraud remedies, or a state "little FTC act," if applicable. *See, e.g.,* Johnson v. Davis, *supra* Chapter 1, Section A(2), and Layman v. Binns, *supra* Chapter 1, Section A(2).

5. Unlike the situation for new homes, it is much more common for states to have enacted legislation mandating express and implied warranties to be given by developers of condominiums or other types of common-ownership residential or recreational property. About one-third of the states have passed such laws, many of them derived from either the 1977 or 1980 Uniform Condominium Act or the 1982 Uniform Common Interest Ownership Act. How clear are the standards of the warranty stated in UCA § 4–

114? Would it be better or worse to rely on common law development of warranties for condominiums?

6. Should warranty legislation be developed for mobile home purchasers? Are mobile homes covered by the UCC? Seventeen states have enacted laws mandating some type of warranty on new mobile homes, usually a one year warranty against defects. See Dee Pridgen, Consumer Protection and the Law, Appendix 17A (Thomson/West 2007). A proposed FTC regulation that would have addressed problems of poor warranty performance in the mobile home industry was withdrawn in 1986.

7. Similar warranty notions are commonly applied with respect to apartments and other rental property. Some of the landmarks in this important area of landlord-tenant law are: Javins v. First National Realty Corp., 428 F.2d 1071 (D.C.Cir.1970); Boston Housing Authority v. Hemingway, 363 Mass. 184, 293 N.E.2d 831 (1973). Many states have passed landlord/tenant legislation to protect the interest of tenants. *See, e.g.,* Arthur R. Gaudio, Wyoming's Residential Rental Property Act—A Critical Review, 35 Land & Water L. Rev. 455 (2000), providing a brief history of landlord tenant law and critiquing Wyoming's state statute.

SECTION C.   THE DEMISE (AND REBIRTH?) OF SPECIAL PROTECTION TO THIRD–PARTY LENDERS (HOLDERS IN DUE COURSE)

1. INTRODUCTION

In this section, we will examine the long and complex saga of how consumers' claims and defenses may be cut off due to special protections for third-party lenders, or so-called "holders in due course." This phenomenon was quite prevalent in the mid–20th century and was based on a long-standing commercial doctrine protecting the "holder in due course" from liability for problems underlying certain "negotiable instruments." This ancient doctrine was and remains codified in the Uniform Commercial Code, Article 3–302. The application of the doctrine to consumer transactions became a focus of criticism. This concern was summed up by Grant Gilmore in 1954:

> It is hard, and it becomes each year harder, for counsel to explain convincingly why "the law" requires that a hard-pressed wage-earner who has been bilked by a now-insolvent seller into buying junk masquerading as a television set or a washing machine must pay the full price to a bank or finance company whose own relationship with the fraudulent seller has been intimate, long-continued and profitable.

Grant Gilmore, The Commercial Doctrine of Good Faith Purchase, 63 Yale L.J. 1057, 1098 (1954).

The first major milestone in the battle against the holder in due course doctrine in consumer credit was the passage in 1975 of the FTC's "Holder Rule." This rule, 16 C.F.R. § 433, reprinted in the statutory supplement, requires sellers to insert a "notice" into consumer credit contracts that allows consumers to assert their claims and defenses against the holder of the contract. The lead up to the regulation and its aftermath will be covered in some detail in this section. In the 1990's and 2000's, the courts have focused on interpreting the limits on the FTC Holder Rule, such as whether and to what extent consumers can use the FTC "notice" as a basis for affirmative recovery against a creditor, rather than simply as a defense against further payments.

Under a 1980 amendment to the TILA, assignee liability for TILA violations, other than those apparent on the face of the credit documents, has been eliminated, even in cases where the FTC notice is contained in the contract. However, creditors in certain high cost mortgage loans, as defined under the HOEPA amendment to TILA, do not enjoy this protection. Also, where residential mortgage loans are pooled through so-called "securitization" into publicly traded investment vehicles, the traditional holder in due course protections apparently still prevail, even in cases of predatory lending, because the FTC rule is not applicable.

The 1999 revision of UCC Article 9, which was quickly enacted by the state legislatures, contains some significant tie-ins with the FTC Holder Rule. Sections 9–403(d) and 9–404(d) (text in the statutory supplement), basically render waiver of defense clauses ineffective in consumer transactions, and provide the consumer debtor with a right to recover from an assignee on the same terms as the FTC Holder Rule would require. Section 3–302(g), as amended, also acknowledges that the UCC's Holder in Due Course section is "subject to any law limiting status as a holder in due course in particular classes of transactions."

Since the FTC Holder rule was promulgated in 1975, consumer credit has moved away from closed end installment type credit and more toward the use of credit cards or open end credit as a means of purchasing household goods other than automobiles. While the FTC regulation does not apply to open end credit, the TILA does contain a provision allowing consumers to raise their claims and defenses based on merchant misconduct against the credit card issuer.

In sum, the FTC rule was a major achievement for consumer protection, but it did not completely solve the basic issue of the unfairness of separating the seller's duty to perform from the consumer's obligation to pay. There are significant limits on the efficacy of the FTC Holder Rule and it is not applicable at all in certain major areas, such as non-apparent TILA violations. Thus, as the market changes, and as the law evolves, the battle to maintain consumers' claims and defenses will continue to be waged. As Ralph Rohner said in a "prognosis" that is as true today as it was when written in 1975:

> Holder in due course is not dead, even in its historical sense, so long as different jurisdictions treat it differently in their courts and legislatures and so long as it is not abolished root and branch in all consumer transactions—from home improvements to auto sales to

credit card purchases. In fact, to prolong the metaphor, holder in due course is not a single organism slayable in a single blow. It is a collection of legal traditions and rules and commercial practices which merge into a single result: the insulation of financers from consumer claims. No assault on the doctrine can therefore succeed unless it is both comprehensive and uniform, and the impetus for such an attack may need to come from the federal level.

Ralph J. Rohner, Holder in Due Course in Consumer Transactions: Requiem, Revival, or Reformation?, 60 Cornell L. Rev. 503, 566–67 (1975).

2. ANNALS OF CONSUMER LAW: THE FTC ASSAULT ON HOLDER IN DUE COURSE

In 1975, the Federal Trade Commission determined that "[I]t constitutes an unfair and deceptive practice to use contractual boilerplate to separate a buyer's duty to pay from a seller's duty to perform." Preservation of Consumer's Claims and Defenses, Statement of Basis and Purpose, 40 Fed. Reg. 53,506, at 53,524 (1975).

Various legal devices were used to accomplish this result. First, the consumer might be required to execute a negotiable promissory note, separate from the sales agreement, which was then sold to a third party, such as a finance company. That third party then became a "holder in due course" who took the note free of most claims and defenses that the consumer might have against the original seller.

The same result could also be achieved by including in the consumer contract a standard term in which the consumer "agrees" to assert any claim or defense only against the seller, and not against the assignee. This is known as a "waiver of defense" clause.

Finally, the consumer could obtain a direct loan from a lender, and then use those proceeds to purchase goods or services. In this situation, it appears that the lender is independent from the seller, and thus should not be answerable for the seller's legal transgressions vis-à-vis the consumer. Yet in many cases the purportedly independent lender was in fact connected to the seller by common ownership, agreement, or a long course of dealing. At times the seller might not only recommend a particular lender, but might also transport the consumer to the lender's office. The FTC Holder Rule attempts to address all three of these situations.

The FTC rule was preceded by both court cases and state statutes seeking to mitigate the effect of the Holder in Due Course doctrine as applied to consumer transactions. The court cases used principles of public policy, unconscionability and close-connectedness between the seller and the holder, to defeat holder in due course status for the creditor. State legislatures passed a patchwork of legislation to the same end. In some states, the use of negotiable instruments, waiver of defense clauses and "holder in due course" principles were prohibited in consumer sales. See, e.g., Uniform Consumer Credit Code §§ 3.307 and

3.404. Others allowed the consumer to raise claims and defenses during a certain complaint period. Many of the state laws limited consumers to raising their claims as defenses or recoupment in a creditor's suit. Despite these inroads against the Holder in Due Course doctrine in consumer transactions, the Commission concluded that federal action was necessary. Federal Trade Commission, Preservation of Consumers' Claims and Defenses, Statement of Basis and Purpose, 40 Fed. Reg. 53,506, 53,508 (Nov. 18, 1975).

The Commission articulated an economically oriented rationale when it adopted the Holder in Due Course Rule:

> Our primary concern, in the course of these proceedings, has been the distribution or allocation of costs occasioned by seller misconduct in credit sale transactions. These costs arise from breaches of contract, breaches of warranty, misrepresentation, and even fraud. The current commercial system which enables sellers and creditors to divorce a consumer's obligation to pay for goods and services from the seller's obligation to perform as promised, allocates all of these costs to the consumer/buyer. Consumers are generally not in a position to evaluate the likelihood of seller misconduct in a particular transaction. Misconduct costs are not incorporated in the price of the goods or services, nor are they reflected in any deferred payment price or unpaid balance of a sales-related loan. Seller misconduct costs are thus externalized in a way that renders many sales finance transactions inherently deceptive and misleading. In addition, to the extent that consumers are also compelled to bear the costs occasioned by the misconduct of another, while the "guilty" party avoids all liability, we believe that reliance on contractual foreclosures of equities in consumer transactions constitutes an unfair practice under Section Five of the F.T.C. Act.

* * *

> This rule approaches these problems by reallocating the costs of seller misconduct in the consumer market. It would, we believe, reduce these costs to the minimum level obtainable in an imperfect system and internalize those that remain. As a practical matter, the creditor is always in a better position than the buyer to return seller misconduct costs to sellers, the guilty party. This is the real location desired, a return of costs to the party who generates them. The creditor financing the transaction is in a better position to do this than the consumer, because (1) he engages in many transactions where consumers deal infrequently; (2) he has access to a variety of information systems which are unavailable to consumers; (3) he has recourse to contractual devices which render the routine return of seller misconduct costs to sellers relatively cheap and automatic; and (4) the creditor possesses the means to initiate a lawsuit and prosecute it to judgment where recourse to the legal system is necessary.

We believe that a rule which compels creditors to either absorb seller misconduct costs or return them to sellers, by denying sellers access to cut-off devices, will discourage many of the predatory practices and schemes discussed above * * *. Creditors will simply not accept the risks generated by the truly unscrupulous merchant. The market will be policed in this fashion and all parties will benefit accordingly. * * * The creditor may also look to a "reserve" or "recourse" arrangement or account with the seller for reimbursement. In such cases, the price of financing will more accurately reflect the actual costs of sales finance.

Federal Trade Commission, Preservation of Consumers' Claims and Defenses, Statement of Basis and Purpose, 40 Fed. Reg. 53,506, 53,522–23 (Nov. 18, 1975).

The Holder in Due Course Rule abrogated the use of the holder in due course doctrine in consumer credit transactions by requiring sellers to include a notice in all consumer credit sales instruments stating that any subsequent holder is subject to all claims and defenses that could be asserted against the seller. The notice, set forth in 16 C.F.R. Part 433.2, states as follows:

NOTICE

ANY HOLDER OF THIS CONSUMER CREDIT CONTRACT IS SUBJECT TO ALL CLAIMS AND DEFENSES WHICH THE DEBTOR COULD ASSERT AGAINST THE SELLER OF GOODS OR SERVICES OBTAINED PURSUANT HERETO OR WITH THE PROCEEDS HEREOF. RECOVERY HEREUNDER BY THE DEBTOR SHALL NOT EXCEED AMOUNTS PAID BY THE DEBTOR HEREUNDER.

Problem 7–13

(a) Hood bought a used car from Dale on credit. Hood also purchased from Dale a one-year service contract that was supposed to pay for 100% of the parts and service for any repairs required for defects not caused by consumer abuse or normal wear and tear. It also contained a clause:

"I (We) will settle all claims of any kind against SELLER directly with SELLER and if SELLER assigns this note I (we) will not use any such claim as a defense, setoff or counterclaim against any effort by the holder to enforce this instrument."

The contract does not contain the FTC Holder Notice. Dale assigned the credit contract to Nottingham Bank. After 30 days the car became inoperable, and Dale refuses to repair, replace or refund. If Hood refuses to pay because the car is inoperable, does Bank have a successful cause of action against Hood? See UCC § 9–403(d).

(b) Same facts as (a), except that this time Hood signs a negotiable promissory note which is then purchased by Nottingham Bank. When the car becomes inoperable, Hood refuses to pay. Does Bank have a successful cause of action against Hood? See UCC §§ 9–403(d), 3–305.

(c) Can Hood sue Dale for not including the FTC Holder Notice? Under the FTC Act? Under state law? If so, what type of state law would be most productive? *See* Martin B. White, Coping with Violations of the Federal Trade Commission's Holder in Due Course Rule, 66 Temple L. Rev. 661 (1993).

(d) Can the FTC enforce its Holder Rule against Dale? Against the Bank for accepting a consumer credit contract without the required notice? See 53 Fed. Reg. 44,456 (Nov. 3, 1988); 57 Fed. Reg. 28,814 (June 29, 1992).

Problem 7–14

Hood bought a used car from Dale based on the salesman's claims that the vehicle was in good working condition and had never been in a major accident. After Hood took possession of the car, it soon developed problems and Hood later found out that the car had in fact been involved in a major collision. Hood paid $2,000 on the credit contract before Dale went out of business. Hood still owes $10,000 to Nottingham Bank, based on the consumer credit contract that had been assigned from Dale to Bank. The preprinted contract contained the FTC notice. Can Hood safely stop making payments to Bank? If sued by the Bank for the balance due, can Hood prove Dale's fraud as a defense? Could Hood get punitive damages from Bank for Dale's fraud? Can Hood obtain revocation of acceptance under UCC 2–608 and recover the $2,000 already paid to Nottingham Bank? *See* Tinker v. De Maria Porsche Audi, Inc., 459 So.2d 487 (Fla. Ct. App. 1984); Mount v. LaSalle Bank Lake View, 926 F.Supp. 759 (N.D. Ill. 1996); Gaddy v. Galarza Motor Sport, Ltd., 2000 WL 1364451 (N.D. Ill. 2000).

Problem 7–15

Robbin Hood bought a used car from William Scarlet, doing business as "Scarlet's Auto Sales, the Home of Guaranteed Credit," under the following circumstances: Hood visited Scarlet's lot seeking a used car for $1000. Scarlet showed him several $1000 cars, but also told him of their known and suspected defects, and said he could not give a warranty with any of them. Hood decided he did not want any of them. Then Hood saw just the car—for $10,000. Scarlet said it was "a beautiful car" and that he could give a 30–day limited warranty on it.

Unfortunately Hood didn't have $10,000. Scarlet offered to help. Scarlet said he had a friend, John Little, who ran the Little Finance Co., which might make a loan to Hood as a "special favor" to Scarlet. Actually, Scarlet had an agreement with Little that Little would lend to all of Scarlet's customers if Scarlet would bring *all* of his credit customers to Little. The agreement was crucial to Scarlet who operated on a shoestring and could not have guaranteed financing through any bank— and all of his customers needed financing. The deal was profitable to

Little because many of Scarlet's customers were low credit risks, and he got them all, not just the high risk ones.

So, Scarlet drove Hood to see Little. Little went through all the motions of running a credit check, just enough to make Hood nervous, and then approved the loan. Hood borrowed $10,000 from Little, and executed a promissory note promising to repay the principal and $2,000 interest in 48 monthly payments of $250 each. None of the contract documents contained the FTC notice. Little then gave Hood a check for $10,000 payable to "Robbin Hood and William Scarlet." Hood endorsed the check and gave it to Scarlet. Scarlet delivered the car keys to Hood, who drove it away. Three days later, the automatic transmission failed, making it quite difficult to shift into reverse gear. Scarlet claims the transmission is not covered by the warranty, and refuses to fix it for free. In fact, Scarlet is on the verge of bankruptcy.

(a) What are Scarlet's obligations under the FTC Rule? What are Little's obligations? What rights does Hood have against Little under the FTC Rule? See 16 C.F.R. §§ 433.1(d) and 433.2(b).

(b) What rights does Hood have against Little under the U3C? See § 3.405.

Also consider the following case.

ASSOCIATES HOME EQUITY SERVICES, INC. v. TROUP

Superior Court of New Jersey, Appellate Division (2001).
778 A.2d 529.

HAVEY, P.J.A.D.

This is a foreclosure action. Defendants Beatrice and Curtis Troup, African–Americans, obtained a mortgage loan from third-party defendant East Coast Mortgage Corp. (ECM) to pay for repairs on their Newark home made by third-party defendants Gary Wishnia, General Builders Supply, Inc. and Property Redevelopment Center, Inc. (collectively Wishnia). The mortgage and note were assigned by ECM to Associates Home Equity Services, Inc. (Associates). When the Troups defaulted, Associates instituted this foreclosure proceeding. The Troups filed a counterclaim against Associates and a third-party complaint against Wishnia and ECM, claiming violations of the Consumer Fraud Act (CFA), *N.J.S.A.* 56:8–1 to –106, the Law Against Discrimination (LAD), *N.J.S.A.* 10:5–1 to –49, the Fair Housing Act (FHA), 42 *U.S.C.A.* § § 3601 to 3631, the Civil Rights Act (CRA), 42 *U.S.C.A.* § 1981, and the Truth–In–Lending Act (TILA), 15 *U.S.C.A.* § 1635. The trial court granted summary judgment dismissing all of the Troups' claims against Associates and ECM, and entered a judgment of foreclosure in favor of Associates. The court found that the terms of ECM's construction loan were not unconscionable and that the Troups' affirmative claims under the applicable state and federal laws were barred by the governing statute of limitations. We granted the Troups' motion for leave to appeal.

We affirm in part and reverse in part. We conclude that it was premature to dismiss the Troups' claim that Associates engaged in predatory lending activities. The Troups are entitled to discovery on this claim. Further, although the Troups' affirmative claims against Associates under the governing statutes are time-barred, they may be considered in support of the affirmative defense of equitable recoupment. *See R.* 4:5–4 (if a party mistakenly designates an affirmative defense as a counterclaim, the court may in the interest of justice, treat the pleading "as if there had been a proper designation"). We further conclude that genuine issues of material fact exist respecting whether the "Holder Rule," 16 *C.F.R.* § 433, applies in this case, subjecting ECM to liability for the wrongdoings of Wishnia, the home repair contractor. Fact issues also exist as to whether defendants engaged in unconscionable business practices under the CFA.

Considering the evidentiary material in a light most favorable to the Troups, these are the facts. Beatrice Troup, a seventy-four year old African American, has lived at 62 Vanderpool Street in Newark for approximately forty years. Following a telephone solicitation by Gary Wishnia, an agent for General Builders Supply, Inc., Beatrice and her son Curtis executed a contract for exterior home repairs with General on September 1, 1995. The contract price was $38,500, payable "$479.75 for 240 months." Beatrice claims that Wishnia told her "not to worry, he would get me financing." An amended contract was executed on November 16, 1995, for additional interior home repairs, increasing the contract price to $49,990. The agreement provided that "[payments] are to be made beginning January 1, 1996 payable to Property Redevelopment Center, Inc. until permanent financing is obtained."[1]

Some time before September 14, 1995, Jeffrey Ahrens, ECM's representative, prepared the Troups' loan application. A credit search was conducted. According to Beatrice, the Troups had no personal dealings with ECM. She and her son Curtis dealt directly with Wishnia who arranged a limousine to transport the Troups to ECM's office to close the loan. Also, Wishnia did the "leg work" in processing the loan and obtained all income documentation required by ECM.

The Troups' loan application, dated September 14, 1995, but not signed by them until the closing date of April 27, 1996, provided for a $46,500 loan at an annual interest rate of 11.65 percent, adjustable after six months. The Truth–In–Lending disclosure form signed by the Troups at closing stated that the loan was a "balloon" type, payable in fifteen years, with the last payment being $41,603.58. The Troups were also charged four points, or four percent of the total loan amount. At the closing, Beatrice was required to execute a deed conveying the property to herself and her son.

At some point after April 27, 1996, ECM assigned the mortgage and note to Associates. On May 11, 1998, Associates filed a foreclosure complaint alleging that the Troups had failed to make the required

---

1. Property Redevelopment Center was a separate enterprise operated by Wishnia.

payments under the mortgage and note. The Troups filed an answer, counterclaim and third-party complaint consisting of fifteen counts against the Wishnia defendants, ECM and Associates. Pertinent here are the counts charging Wishnia with "unconscionably poor" workmanship, and that Wishnia had conspired with ECM to place the mortgage financing with ECM and "to reap profits by subjecting the Troups to unconscionable, illegal and fraudulent home repair and financing transactions." The Troups charged Associates and third-party defendants with unconscionable and deceptive conduct in violation of the CFA. They further allege that ECM violated the TILA by failing to provide them with a "clear and conspicuous notice" of the expiration date of their right to rescind, failing to make proper disclosures, and materially understating the finance charges. Finally, the Troups asserted that Associates "participated in, authorized and/or ratified and/or had constructive knowledge of" the deceptive unconscionable acts of ECM and engaged in predatory lending practices in violation of the FHA, the CRA, and the LAD.

In dismissing all of the Troups' claims against ECM and Associates, and entering a judgment of foreclosure in Associates' favor, the trial court found that the terms of the mortgage loan given to the Troups were not "unconscionable when looked at in its entirety," given the fact that, although a 6.6 percent rate was available to "prime borrowers," the Troups "did not appear to be AAA rating." The claims against ECM based on Wishnia's deceptive and unconscionable conduct and workmanship were dismissed because, according to the court, ECM could not be held accountable for Wishnia's conduct. The court also determined that all of the Troups' claims against ECM and Associates were barred by the governing statutes of limitations under the LAD, the FHA and the CFA. Finally, the court dismissed the Troups' demand for rescission under the TILA, concluding that "there was conspicuous notice given" of the right to rescind.

* * *

[The court held that dismissal of the Troups' predatory lending claim against Associates was premature because the Troups did not have an opportunity for meaningful discovery. The court also held that although their other claims for damages under various federal and state statutes were barred by the statute of limitations, these claims could be cognizable under a theory of equitable recoupment.]

II

The Troups and *amicus* argue that the trial court erred in dismissing the Troups' claims against ECM and Ahrens based on the so-called "Holder Rule."

16 *C.F.R.* § 433.2 (2001) provides that, in connection with any sale of goods or services to consumers, affecting commerce, it is an unfair or deceptive act or practice within the meaning of § 5 of the Federal Trade

Commission Act for a seller to accept as full or partial payment for the services rendered:

> the proceeds of any purchase money loan (as purchase money loan is defined herein), unless any consumer credit contract made in connection with such purchase money loan contains the following provision in at least ten point, bold face, type:

> ### NOTICE

> ANY HOLDER OF THIS CONSUMER CREDIT CONTRACT IS SUBJECT TO ALL CLAIMS AND DEFENSES WHICH THE DEBTOR COULD ASSERT AGAINST THE SELLER OF GOODS OR SERVICES OBTAINED WITH THE PROCEEDS HEREOF. RECOVERY HEREUNDER BY THE DEBTOR SHALL NOT EXCEED AMOUNTS PAID BY THE DEBTOR HEREUNDER.

[*Id.* at § 433.2(a).]

* * *

Essentially, the Holder Rule strips the ultimate holder of the paper of its traditional status as a holder-in-due-course and subjects it to any potential defenses which the purchaser might have against the seller. The Federal Trade Commission has included within the reach of the Holder Rule those sellers and creditors who "employ procedures in the course of arranging the financing of a consumer sale which separate the buyer's duty to pay for goods or services rendered from the seller's reciprocal duty to perform as promised." 40 *F.Reg.* 53,506, 53,522 (1975). The agency has recognized this practice as "dragging the body," wherein:

> a merchant, desiring to circumvent restrictions upon the holder in due course doctrine, arranges for a consumer purchase to be financed by a cooperating financing agency. The resultant financial transaction has the appearance of a direct cash loan, payment of which can be enforced by the loan company without reference to the underlying transaction.

[40 *F.Reg., supra,* at 53,514.]

Consequently, the Holder Rule expressly incorporates "purchase money loan[s]" within the scope of the rule. *See* 16 *C.F.R.* § 433.2(b). A "[p]urchase money loan" is defined as "[a] cash advance which is received by a consumer" which is applied "in whole or substantial part, to a purchase of goods or services from a seller who (1) refers consumers to the creditor or (2) is affiliated with the creditor by common control, contract or business arrangement." 16 *C.F.R.* § 431.1(d).

Here, there is at the very least a fact issue concerning whether ECM's note constituted a "purchase money loan." ECM's financing provided the Troups with a "cash advance" totaling $49,990 which was applied in "substantial part" to pay for the improvements made to the home by Wishnia. *Ibid*. There is also evidence that Wishnia "refers consumers" to ECM. *Ibid*. Indeed, in this case Wishnia made all the arrangements for the loan and had the Troups chauffeured to ECM's offices to close. A reasonable jury could also conclude that Wishnia was "affiliated with" ECM by "business arrangement." *Ibid*. The Troups presented evidence that Wishnia and ECM had mutually arranged at least six other home improvement or equity loans to other customers living in the City of Newark or the Newark area.

Nevertheless, ECM argues that the Holder Rule is inapplicable for three reasons. First, it claims that it did not "purchase" a "consumer credit contract" because initially the Troups paid Wishnia's affiliated companies monthly payments on the home repair contracts before the loan was made by ECM. This argument ignores the undisputed evidence that, before the Troups signed the first contract, Wishnia told Beatrice "not to worry, he would get [her] financing." Further, the second contract provides that "[payments] are to be made beginning January 1, 1996 payable to Property Redevelopment Center, Inc. *until permanent financing is obtained*." (Emphasis added). Indeed, after the contract was executed, Wishnia promptly arranged the loan with ECM, with whom he had placed other home repair contracts on behalf of other borrowers. In our view, reasonable minds could conclude that Wishnia and ECM contemplated from the outset that the loan to finance Wishnia's contracting work would be placed by ECM. We agree with the Troups that, under these circumstances, Wishnia and ECM should not be permitted to circumvent the consequences of the Holder Rule simply because Wishnia arranged for temporary financing with his affiliated companies.

Second, ECM argues that the Holder Rule is inapplicable because the bold-typed notice required by 16 *C.F.R.* 433.2 was never placed on the relevant documents. We reject that argument. Although it is true that the documents did not contain the requisite notice, it is inconceivable to us that ECM and Ahrens may evade the remedial reach of the Holder Rule simply because of that omission. It was their responsibility to insert the notice. Indeed, as a financing institution, ECM must be charged with notice of the requirement. Moreover, the bold-typed notice is required by New Jersey law. *N.J.A.C.* 13:45A–16.2(a)(13)ii, states:

> No home improvement contract shall require or entail the execution of any note, unless such note shall have conspicuously printed thereon the disclosures required by ... Federal law (16 C.F.R. section 433.2) concerning the preservation of buyers' claims and defenses.

"[T]he law is a silent factor in every contract." *Silverstein v. Keane*, 19 *N.J.* 1, 13, 115 *A*.2d 1 (1955) (citation and quotation marks omitted). Moreover, equity looks to substance rather than form. These well-settled maxims should apply here to effectuate New Jersey's regulatory goal by "reading into" the pertinent documents the notice required by 16 *C.F.R.* § 433.2 and *N.J.A.C.* 13:45A–16.2(a)(13)ii.

Third, ECM claims that the Holder Rule is inapplicable because it has assigned the note to Associates.[8] We reject that argument as well. The clear and unambiguous language of the Rule "notifies *all potential holders* that, if they accept an assignment of the contract, they will be 'stepping into the seller's shoes.' " *Lozada v. Dale Baker Oldsmobile, Inc.,* 91 *F.Supp.*2d 1087, 1094 (W.D.Mich.2000) (quoting *Oxford Fin. Cos., Inc. v. Velez,* 807 *S.W.*2d 460, 463 (Tex.Ct.App.1991) (emphasis added)). Thus, the creditor-assignee becomes " 'subject to' *any* claims or defenses the debtor can assert against the seller." *Oxford Fin., supra,* 807 *S.W.*2d at 463. Here, ECM, as "a potential holder" had notice that if it procured the purchase money loan arranged by Wishnia, it may be stepping into Wishnia's shoes. We cannot accept the proposition that the FTC contemplated that such result would not attach simply because of a subsequent assignment of the loan, especially when, as here, it is claimed that ECM actively participated with Wishnia, the seller, in placing the loan with the Troups.[9] We conclude that fact issues exist respecting ECM's liability under the Holder Rule. Summary judgment dismissing the Troups' claims is therefore reversed. * * *

* * *

[The court reversed summary judgment in favor of Associates on the consumer fraud claim, but affirmed the trial court's dismissal of the Troups' demand for rescission under the TILA].

Affirmed in part, reversed and remanded in part.

Notes

1. On what basis did the court hold that ECM was answerable to the consumer debtors for the transgressions of the seller, even though the FTC notice was not actually contained in the loan documents?

2. How likely is it that the Troups will be able to succeed in their affirmative claims against the assignee, ECM, based on the misbehavior of the home improvement contractor?

3. Why do you suppose the Troups did not seek to hold Associates liable under the Holder Rule?

8. The Troups do not argue that the Holder Rule applies to Associates.

9. There is some debate respecting the level of recovery under the Holder Rule when the consumer asserts an affirmative claim against the creditor. In this appeal, we are called upon only to decide whether the Holder Rule applies, not to define the extent of the Troups' remedy, if it applies. Suffice it to say that, as we understand the Troups' claim, they seek to assert their rights under the Holder Rule by compelling ECM to pay their debt owed to Associates, in the event the Troups do not prevail against Associates. In addition, the Troups seek an award of counsel fees under the CFA.

3. HOLDER IN DUE COURSE REVIVED?—LIMITS ON THE FTC HOLDER RULE

a. Limits on "Affirmative" Recovery

Problem 7–16

Same facts as problem 7–14, *supra*, Section C(2), except this time instead of being sued by the bank, Hood is suing both the car dealer and the financing bank for fraud, based on the misrepresentation regarding the prior accident. The bank argues that the FTC Holder Notice can only be used affirmatively against an assignee of a consumer credit contract in situations where the seller's conduct or breach has rendered the vehicle essentially worthless to the consumer, so that a rescission of the contract is appropriate. The bank bases its theory on the FTC's Statement of Basis and Purpose that accompanied the promulgation of the rule, to the effect that the rule was mainly aimed at allowing a consumer to defend against a creditor suit for payment by raising a claim against the seller as a set-off. The Statement said an affirmative action against the creditor for a return of monies based on the seller's breach, would be limited to situations where the "seller's breach is so substantial that a court is persuaded that rescission and restitution are justified." 40 Fed. Reg. at 53,524. The Statement went on to say that "[c]onsumers will not be in a position to obtain an affirmative recovery from a creditor, unless they have actually commenced payments and received little or nothing of value from the seller." Id. at 53,527. Hood argues that the only limitation on affirmative relief contained in the FTC Notice and in the actual rule is that the affirmative relief against the creditor may not exceed what the consumer has paid. Hood says the court should not add additional limits that are not in the language of the rule.

(a) Which party has the better argument? Does the consumer have to prove a claim against the seller serious enough to warrant rescission to assert an affirmative claim against the holder? Compare Comer v. Person Auto Sales, Inc., 368 F. Supp. 2d 478 (M.D. N.C. 2005) with Lozada v. Dale Baker Oldsmobile, Inc., 91 F. Supp. 2d 1087 (W.D. Mich. 2000).

(b) The defendant bank moves for summary judgment, asserting that the FTC Holder Notice cannot be used affirmatively against an assignee, but only defensively in a suit for nonpayment, based on a state law subjecting an assignee of a consumer credit contract to all of the consumer's claims and defenses against the seller arising from the sale, but also limiting the consumer's rights to defensive or set-off claims against the assignee. Can such a state law serve to limit Hood's right to assert an affirmative claim against an assignee under the FTC Holder Rule? Compare LaBarre v. Credit Acceptance Corp., 175 F.3d 640 (8th Cir. 1999) (Minnesota law limiting consumer to defensive claims applies) with Eachen v. Scott Housing Systems, Inc., 630 F.Supp. 162 (M.D. Ala. 1986) (Alabama law limiting consumer recovery against assignee to defensive claims cannot be used to effectively rescind the FTC regulation).

b. *Limited Liability for Assignees under TILA*

RAMADAN v. CHASE MANHATTAN CORPORATION

United States Court of Appeals, Third Circuit. 2000.
229 F.3d 194.

SCIRICA, CIRCUIT JUDGE.

This appeal requires us to apply the Truth in Lending Act's assignee liability provisions in light of contract language required by regulatory fiat and to determine the parameters of assignee liability under the TILA. Asserting a violation of the Truth in Lending Act, plaintiff alleges she was harmed by deceptive lending practices of a dealer from whom she purchased an automobile. Plaintiff seeks to recover against Hyundai Motor Finance Co., the assignee of her finance agreement, rather than against the automobile dealer. Three Circuit Courts of Appeals have encountered nearly identical TILA claims and all have concluded plaintiffs could not state a claim.[1] Following those courts, the District Court granted Hyundai's motion to dismiss under Federal Rule of Civil Procedure 12(b)(6). We will affirm.

I.

* * *

II.

As noted by the District Court, the facts in this case are uncomplicated. Ramadan purchased a used Hyundai for $4,238.50 from automobile dealer Bob Ciasulli, Inc. Plaintiff also purchased an extended warranty contract for $998.00. Because she purchased on credit, the sale was achieved through a Retail Installment Contract ("RIC"). Hyundai provided the RIC form to the dealer. Contemporaneous with its execution, the RIC was assigned to Hyundai Motor Finance Corp.

* * *

The RIC contained a provision which itemized "Other Charges Including Amounts Paid to Others on Your Behalf" and stated $998.00 had been paid for a service contract. Ramadan alleges an undisclosed amount of that figure was retained by the dealer without her knowledge in violation of the TILA. Given the nature of review of a motion made under Fed.R.Civ.P. 12(b)(6), we must accept plaintiff's assertion as true.

Central to this case are two provisions—TILA's assignee liability rule and a Holder Notice required by Federal Trade Commission regulations. The TILA section which governs assignee liability provides:

> Except as otherwise provided in this subchapter, any civil action for a violation of this subchapter ... which may be brought against a creditor may be maintained against any assignee of such creditor

---

1. *See Green v. Levis Motors, Inc.,* 179 F.3d 286 (5th Cir.1999); *Ellis v. GMAC,* 160 F.3d 703 (11th Cir.1998); *Taylor v. Quality Hyundai, Inc.,* 150 F.3d 689 (7th Cir.1998).

only if the violation for which such action or proceeding is brought *is apparent on the face of the disclosure statement,* ... 15 U.S.C. § 1641 (a) [emphasis added by the court].

In accord with FTC rules, the RIC also contained a Holder Notice [see text in statutory supplement, subjecting the holder of the consumer credit contract to "all" claims and defenses which the debtor could assert against the seller].

The proper understanding of these two provisions lies at the heart of this case. * * *

III.

Ramadan contends § 1641(a) encompasses her claim that the TILA violation here was apparent on the face of the disclosure statement as that concept is statutorily defined. She also asserts Hyundai is liable because it expressly assumed assignee liability by including the Holder Notice clause in the RIC.

A.

* * *

[Judge Scirica rejected plaintiff's argument that the TILA violation was "apparent on the face" of the disclosure statement].

B.

Ramadan also contends the District Court erred in granting Hyundai's motion to dismiss because of Hyundai's express assumption of assignee liability. As noted, the FTC-required Holder Notice included in the RIC provides for assignee liability with regard to "all claims and defenses which the debtor could assert against the seller. . . ." In light of this provision, plaintiff asserts the RIC should be enforced as written.

The same argument has been made to, and rejected by, other courts that have examined assignee liability under TILA. *See, e.g., Green,* 179 F.3d at 296; *Ellis,* 160 F.3d at 709; *Taylor,* 150 F.3d at 693. The *Taylor* Court noted that, by FTC regulation, the RIC must contain the Holder Notice. *See Taylor,* 150 F.3d at 692 (citing 16 C.F.R. § 433.2). Because of that requirement, the Taylor Court concluded

The Holder Notice, even though contained within the contract, was not the subject of bargaining between the parties, and indeed could not have been. It is part of the contract by force of law, and it must be read in light of other laws that modify its reach.

Id. at 693. In the opinion of the *Taylor* Court, § 1641(a) "limited one set of claims [the Holder Notice] may carry through to the assignee. . . ." *Id.* The Eleventh Circuit similarly concluded the Holder Notice language "required by the FTC regulation standing alone does not suffice to subject [assignee] to liability." *Ellis,* 160 F.3d at 709. The notice could not have such an effect because inclusion of required language did not result from "bargaining or agreement by the parties to reflect [ ] a voluntary and intentional assumption of liability." *Id.* In fact, every federal court that has considered the Holder Notice argument since the *Taylor* decision, including the District Court here, followed *Taylor's* reasoning and concluded inclusion of the Holder Notice cannot trump the assignee liability rules in § 1641(a).

Plaintiff challenges the soundness of the *Taylor, Ellis* and *Green* decisions and contests whether Hyundai's inclusion of the Holder Notice was truly involuntary. According to plaintiff, Hyundai could have carved out an exception to TILA liability in the Holder Notice. Given that option, Ramadan asserts inclusion of the unaltered Holder Notice reflects Hyundai's intent to assume greater liability than that created by § 1641(a).

That argument misses the point. The FTC rule requiring the Holder Notice is explicit regarding its inclusion:

> In connection with any sale or lease of goods or services to consumers . . . it is an unfair or deceptive act or practice . . . for a seller, directly or indirectly, to:
>
> > (a) Take or receive a consumer credit contract which fails to contain the [Holder Notice] provision in at least ten point, bold face type. . . .

16 C.F.R. § 433.2. By its terms, the FTC regulation is mandatory; it does not contemplate deviations or modifications. Because regulations cannot trump statutory mandates, the FTC mandated language must be understood in light of any statutory limitations.

Plaintiff also takes issue with the involuntariness argument central to the *Taylor-Ellis* analysis contending it is inconsistent with the standard of review on a motion to dismiss. There is, however, no allegation the Holder Notice was included voluntarily by Hyundai. In fact, plaintiff's complaint recognizes the Holder Notice was included in the RIC in compliance with 16 C.F.R. § 422.3. *See* Compl. at ¶ 41. Given the regulatory requirement, it is reasonable to assume the Holder Notice was not voluntarily included and therefore does not manifest Hyundai's intent to contract around § 1641(a).

* * *

As the dissent notes, parties to a contract may "waive statutory protections and assume liabilities not required by law." *Ellis,* 160 F.3d at 709. But like the court in *Ellis,* we believe the defendant has not done so here. There is no allegation or evidence that Hyundai waived its statutory rights or agreed to assume liability beyond that set forth in § 1641(a). Hyundai's failure to include with the Holder Notice a warning or disclaimer does not constitute the type of intentional relinquishment necessary to give rise to a waiver of statutory rights. Without some evidence the parties bargained for and Hyundai waived its statutory rights, there is no basis to impose waiver or estoppel.

IV.

For the foregoing reasons, we will affirm the District Court's judgment dismissing plaintiff's complaint under Fed.R.Civ.P. 12(b)(6).

POLLAK, DISTRICT JUDGE [sitting by designation], dissenting.

I agree with the court's conclusion, in Part III(A) of its opinion, that the case at bar is not one in which the alleged violation of the TILA "is apparent on the face of the disclosure statement" and hence could have been the basis for Ms. Ramadan's suit "against [Hyundai Motor Finance (hereinafter "Hyundai") as] assignee of[a] creditor." 15 U.S.C. § 1641(a). But I disagree with the court's conclusion, in Part III(B) of its opinion, that the language of the Holder Notice, which was contained in Ms. Ramadan's automobile finance agreement and which advised Ms. Ramadan that "ANY HOLDER OF THIS CONSUMER CREDIT CON-TRACT IS SUBJECT TO ALL CLAIMS ... WHICH THE DEBTOR COULD ASSERT AGAINST THE SELLER," did not provide a basis for Ms. Ramadan's suit against Hyundai.

As I understand the court's opinion, its determination that the Holder Notice is nugatory is the product of the following syllogism: (1) The Holder Notice appeared in Ms. Ramadan's finance agreement (and, one must suppose, hundreds of thousands of other finance agreements) not as a provision voluntarily acquiesced in by the seller and the assignee finance company, but in compliance with a regulation of the Federal Trade Commission making it "an unfair and deceptive trade act or practice ... for a seller, directly or indirectly, to ... [t]ake or receive a consumer credit contract which fails to contain the [Holder Notice] provision...." 16 C.F.R. § 433.2.(2) In determining the scope of civil liability for violations of the TILA, Congress has limited the liability of an assignee of a finance agreement to violations "apparent on the face of the disclosure statement, except where the assignment was involuntary." 15 U.S.C. § 1641(a). (3) Since the Holder Notice's inclusion in the Ramadan finance agreement was, in the court's view, coerced by the FTC; and since the Holder Notice, as prescribed by the FTC regulation, is in the court's view, in "irreconcilable conflict" with the TILA; and since "regulations cannot trump statutory mandates," the Holder Notice must give way.

The syllogism has, unquestionably, a straightforward simplicity which makes it quite compelling. The difficulty with the syllogism is that its focus is confined to the respective interests of Congress, the FTC, and Hyundai. Ms. Ramadan is, it appears, outside the terms of debate. But it is the Ramadans of the world to whom the Holder Notice is addressed. It is the Ramadans of the world who can be taken to have relied on what the Hyundais of the world have, by accepting assignment of finance agreements, said to them. Granted that Congress has authority to negate the FTC directive that the Holder Notice be incorporated in every "consumer credit contract." That appears to be what Congress meant to do when, in 1980, it amended TILA in a fashion that substantially narrowed the assignee liability that the FTC had established by regulation several years before. But if, after 1980, a finance company continued to accept (or, if new to the financial marketplace, commenced accepting) finance agreements which contained the Holder Notice, why—as between the finance company and the purchaser-borrower—shouldn't the finance company be held to the representation of holder liability contained in the finance agreement?

The court's answer, so it would appear, is that the Holder Notice was never bargained for—that in its inception it was placed in finance agreements by virtue of FTC ukase. And presumably the court is also of the view that it is the enduring *in terrorem*ness of the FTC's authority that accounts for the continuing presence of the Holder Notice in finance agreements entered into (and sometimes litigated about) a decade, or even two decades, after Congress amended the TILA and, by hypothesis, exercised its authority to deflate the FTC regulation. I will not argue (although I think the argument could plausibly be made) that by now the Holder Notices that remain in place are there because finance companies, well aware that Congress in 1980 relieved them of any administratively mandated liability, have decided to accept liability as a contractual matter. To the contrary, I am prepared to accept, *arguendo*, that the Holder Notice remains an unbargained-for ingredient of the standard finance agreement. But it seems to me that a finance company, feeling that the Holder Notice is in place via *force majeure* and intending to defend against its applicability in any litigation that may arise, should, before accepting assignment of a finance agreement, insist that the Holder Notice be garlanded with *caveat emptors* that warn the purchaser-borrower of the finance company's view that the 1980 TILA amendment robs the Holder Notice of substantive effect. A finance company has no ground for supposing that more than one in tens of thousands of purchaser-borrowers (the Ramadans of the world) will be conversant with the interplay between the FTC regulation and TILA. Given the disparity in the possession of crucial information, I would conclude that an assignee finance company that failed to insist on inclusion of an appropriate warning adjacent to the Holder Notice should be estopped from invoking the Holder Notice in litigation.

Requiring an assignee finance company that wishes to protect against TILA liability to add the type of warning described above would avoid the difficulty of frustrating a purchaser-borrower's expectations. It would also avoid the consequences the court appears to be concerned about. Finance companies would no longer have grounds for feeling that they were being pushed by the FTC to give up rights guaranteed by Congress. Finance companies would have the choice to construct a contract that assigned TILA liability or to construct a contract that did not do so. Purchaser-borrowers' reasonable expectations, and finance companies' freedom to avoid assignee liability (as they are entitled to do under 15 U.S.C. § 1641(a)), would thus be preserved.

This approach is possible because the conflict between the statutory and regulatory provisions is not, as the court states, "irreconcilable." As was recognized in *Ellis v. General Motors Acceptance Corp.*, 160 F.3d

703, 709 (11th Cir.1998), "[i]t is certainly true that parties can waive statutory protections and assume liabilities not required by law." And while Hyundai is required by the FTC to include the Holder Notice as written, the FTC regulation does not prohibit additional language preserving the finance companies' rights under 15 U.S.C. § 1641(a). Nor could the FTC prohibit the inclusion of such language, for the very reason that animates the court's opinion: the FTC's regulations cannot trump congressional statutes.

* * *

For these reasons, I respectfully dissent.

Notes

1. Do you agree with the majority that the TILA limits on assignee liability were meant by Congress to "trump" the effect of the FTC Holder notice appearing in a consumer credit contract? Or do you agree with dissenting Judge Pollack that an assignee must disclose its limited liability under TILA to avoid being liable under the FTC Holder Rule? Should Congress or the FTC deal with this issue?

2. As noted by Judge Scirica in his majority opinion in Ramadan, most courts that have considered this issue agree that an assignee retains its TILA limits on liability for non-apparent TILA violations, even if the credit contract contains the FTC Holder notice. But should this principle apply to shield assignees from non-TILA claims that could be raised against the seller, such as fraud? Consider the following:

Problem 7–17

Same facts as problem 7–16, supra Section C(3)(a), i.e., Hood brings suit against dealer and credit assignee, alleging fraudulent misrepresentations about prior accidents involving the vehicle being sold. Assignee argues it is not liable for the dealer's fraud, despite the presence of the FTC Holder notice in the contract, because there are no apparent violations of any kind on the face of the loan documents, citing TILA, 15 U.S.C. § 1641(a). Which side has the better argument? *See* Jackson v. South Holland Dodge, Inc., 197 Ill.2d 39, 258 Ill.Dec. 79, 755 N.E.2d 462 (2001); Costa v. Mauro Chevrolet, Inc., 390 F. Supp. 2d 720 (N.D. Ill. 2005); Eromon v. Grand Auto Sales, Inc., 333 F. Supp. 2d 702 (N.D. Ill. 2004). *But see* Green v. Levis Motors, Inc., 179 F.3d 286 (5th Cir. 1999) ("§ 1641(a) limits assignee liability on only one set of claims (i.e., the specified TILA claims)").

c. The Special Case of HOEPA Loans

Congress in the 1994 amendments to TILA known as the Home Owners Equity Protection Act (HOEPA), see discussion *infra* chapter 9, provided special consumer protections for certain high cost mortgages, and appears to have resurrected the idea behind the FTC Holder Rule for loans covered by HOEPA. Read 15 U.S.C. § 1641(d) and consider the following case:

BRYANT v. MORTGAGE CAPITAL
RESOURCE CORP.

United States District Court, N.D. Georgia, 2002.
197 F. Supp. 2d 1357.

MARTIN, DISTRICT JUDGE.

* * *

I. BACKGROUND

A. *Factual Background*

Plaintiffs bring this action stating that they are members of a putative class seeking relief against their mortgage lender, Mortgage Capital Resource ("MCR"). Plaintiffs allege MCR engaged in predatory lending practices in violation of state and federal law. Defendants Residential Funding Corporation ("RFC") and Chase Manhattan Bank (as Indenture Trustee in care of RFC) purchased and otherwise acquired a large number of MCR-originated high cost, high interest loans thereby, allegedly, incurring liability as assignees under TILA (as amended by the Home Ownership and Equity Protection Act of 1994 ("HOEPA")). *See* 15 U.S.C. § 1641(d)(1).

1. *MCR's Alleged Fraudulent Scheme*

Plaintiffs assert that MCR engaged in a predatory lending scheme by issuing HOEPA loans [as defined in 15 U.S.C. § 1602(aa)(1), in statutory supplement], to consumers with good overall credit without complying with the disclosures provisions laid out in TILA. These high cost second mortgage loans permitted homeowners to borrow money against the equity in their homes under a closed-end credit transaction characterized by unusually high interest rates and/or up-front transaction fees. Because they typically yield a high return and involve little risk to the holder of the loan, HOEPA loans are easily transferrable in the secondary market.

To attract potential borrowers, plaintiffs allege that MCR contacted homeowners by mail with brochures promoting low cost, low interest loans. Plaintiffs contend that MCR targeted consumers with positive credit and encouraged them to complete loan applications over the phone. Plaintiffs further contend MCR would thereafter execute a "bait and switch" whereby MCR would hurry borrowers through the closing and substitute high cost, high interest loans for the more favorable loans originally applied for by plaintiffs. Plaintiffs assert that MCR's practices violate HOEPA insofar as the company failed to timely disclose information required under the Act. In particular, plaintiffs submit that, by hurrying loan applicants through the closing process, MCR violated 15 U.S.C. § 1639(b)(1), which mandates that disclosures under HOEPA "shall not be given less than 3 business days prior to consummation of the transaction." According to plaintiffs, such disclosure was not provided until the time of closing.

In addition, plaintiffs allege that, in an attempt to conceal its wrongdoing, MCR falsified closing documents so as to reflect that the mandatory disclosures were timely provided to plaintiffs. Plaintiffs contend that MCR's scheme denied plaintiffs the protections provided by TILA, including the mandatory "cooling off" period designed to enable unsuspecting consumers to recognize and avoid the predatory features of high cost, high interest loans.

2. Assignee Defendants: RFC & Chase Manhattan

RFC's involvement in the present action is tied to its purchase and acquisition of a large number of the MCR-originated HOEPA loans. Under the federal truth-in-lending laws, civil actions brought against a creditor may, with limited exceptions, be maintained against an assignee. 15 U.S.C. § 1641(d)(1). Relying on this provision and the alleged violations committed by MCR, plaintiffs seek to impose liability upon RFC based solely upon its acquisition of MCR's high cost mortgages in the secondary market.

B. Procedural Background

[Mortgage Capital Resource, the originator of the loans, and the entity responsible for the HOEPA disclosures, went bankrupt during the course of the litigation].

II. DISCUSSION

A. Motion to Dismiss

* * *

2. Truth-in-Lending Act

* * *

b. Section 1641(d)(1)

The court must next address whether, as plaintiffs assert, 15 U.S.C. § 1641(d)(1) renders assignees jointly and severally liable for a creditor's independent violations of state law [see statutory supplement for text]. Plaintiffs, in Counts II and III of their Complaint, *inter alia,* that MCR engaged in common law fraud and other unlawful practices in violation state RICO laws. Plaintiffs further contend that, as an assignee of HOEPA loans, RFC is jointly and severally liable with MCR under 15 U.S.C. § 1641(d)(1) because RFC knowingly and voluntarily stepped into the shoes of MCR upon acquiring MCR-originated HOEPA loans. Plaintiffs further aver that section 1641(d)(1) provides them with the affirmative right to assert claims against RFC based solely upon MCR's independent and allegedly unlawful conduct in connection with the issuance of plaintiffs' loans. RFC counters that section 1641(d)(1) merely eliminates an assignee's ability to assert the holder-in-due-course defense.

Based on the plain language of the statute, however, it is clear that Congress intended to subject assignees of HOEPA loans to a more expansive standard of liability than is normally applied under TILA.[22] Support for this conclusion can also be drawn from the legislative history of HOEPA, which reveals that, through the enactment of HOEPA, Congress intended to force the "High Cost Mortgage" market to police itself. *See* S.Rep. No. 103–169, at 28 (1994), *reprinted in* 1994 U.S.C.C.A.N. 1881, 1912. To that end, Congress eliminated the holder-in-due-course defense to assignees of high cost mortgages and rendered them subject to "all claims and defenses, whether under [TILA] or other law, that could [otherwise] be raised against the original lender." *See id.* A review of the legislative history further indicates that section 1641(d)(1) was intended to mirror the "Holder Rule" promulgated by the Federal Trade Commission ("FTC") relating to "consumer install-ment" loans, *see id.*, which provides, in part, that "[a]ny holder of [a] consumer credit contract is subject to all claims and defenses which the debtor could assert against the seller of goods or services . . . ." 16 C.F.R. § 433.2. Through the adoption of this rule, the FTC abrogated the holder-in-due-course principle in much the same fashion as Congress abrogated the rule through the enactment of HOEPA. The courts in this circuit having considered the question have held that section 433.2 preserves a consumer's independent claims and defenses against assign-ees of HOEPA loans. *See, e.g., Eachen v. Scott Housing Sys., Inc.,* 630 F.Supp. 162, 164–65 (M.D.Ala.1986); *see also Ellis v. General Motors Acceptance Corp.,* 160 F.3d 703, 708 (11th Cir.1998).[24]

Therefore, in light of the foregoing, the court finds that Congress intended to place the increased burden of inquiring into the legitimacy of the lending practices engaged in by the original lender upon the assign-ees of HOEPA loans. In so doing, Congress sought to "halt the flow of capital" to original lenders who engaged in predatory lending practices harmful to consumers by providing for assignee liability under HOEPA. S.Rep. No. 103–169, at 28 (1994), *reprinted in* 1994 U.S.C.C.A.N. 1881,

---

22. With regard to non-HOEPA trans-actions, an assignee is liable only for viola-tions that are "apparent on the face of the disclosure statement." 15 U.S.C. § 1641(a). Therefore, the primary effect of section 1641(d)(1) is to render assignees of HOEPA loans liable for truth-in-lending violations regardless of whether they were apparent on the face of the loan document. Congress, however, did limit assignee liability by pro-viding that an assignee could escape liabili-ty upon establishing "by a preponderance of the evidence, that a reasonable person exercising ordinary due diligence, could not determine, based on the documentation re-quired by this subchapter, the itemization of the amount financed, and other disclo-sure disbursements that the mortgage was a [HOEPA] mortgage referred to in section 1602(aa) of this title." Moreover, Congress included a provision limiting the amount of damages a plaintiff could obtain in an ac-tion founded upon 15 U.S.C. § 1641(d)(1).

24. In *Ellis,* the Eleventh Circuit ad-dressed the scope of assignee liability under section 1641(a) of TILA. Examining section 433.2 in light of section 1641(a)'s mandate that violations be "apparent on the face of the disclosure statement," the *Ellis* court found that, although the FTC's "Holder Rule" empowers plaintiffs to raise affirma-tive claims and defenses against assignees, plaintiffs bringing claims which fall under 1641(a) are nevertheless limited by that section's requirement that violations be ap-parent on the face of the disclosure docu-ment. Therefore, while rejecting the plain-tiffs' claims against the assignee on the grounds that plaintiffs could not satisfy sec-tion 1641(a), the Eleventh Circuit implicitly recognized that the FTC's "Holder Rule" does more than simply eliminate the holder-in-due-course defense.

1912. Such an approach was intended to encourage investors in the secondary market for HOEPA loans to more carefully scrutinize the backgrounds and qualifications of those with whom they choose to do business. Moreover, Congress' approach allocates to the assignee the cost associated with the misconduct of the original lender in such instances where the assignee fails to inquire into or otherwise discover the deceptive and unlawful practices engaged in by the original lender.[25] It is against this backdrop that the court finds that section 1641(d)(1) provides plaintiffs with the affirmative right to assert claims against RFC based solely upon MCR's independent and allegedly unlawful conduct in connection with the issuance of plaintiffs' loans. * * *

* * *

Notes

1. Other cases have followed the reasoning in the Bryant case, to the effect that the assignee of a HOEPA loan is subject to all claims and defenses of the debtor, unless the assignee can show that a reasonable person exercising due diligence could not have determined, based on the loan documentation, that the loan was a HOEPA loan. 15 U.S.C. § 1641(d)(1). *See, e.g.*, Cooper v. First Government Mortgage, 238 F. Supp. 2d 50 (D.D.C. 2002); In re Rodrigues, 278 B.R. 683 (D.R.I. 2002). In the *Cooper* case itself, the question whether the loan was covered by HOEPA turned out to be too close to call on summary judgment.

2. Although HOEPA was passed in 1994, it did not include many subprime loans until the Federal Reserve Board lowered the "points" and expanded the "fees" triggers effective in 2002. 12 C.F.R. § 226.32(a), 66 Fed. Reg. 65604 (Dec. 20, 2001). Thus, many mortgage loans that were just under the HOEPA triggers were not subject to the extended assignee liability.

3. The subprime market in secondary mortgage loans has been marked by predatory practices, and yet the large financial institutions and investors who provide the capital for the unscrupulous lenders appear to have been protected from liability, despite the apparent intentions of Congress in the HOEPA assignee liability provisions. As one commentator put it:

> While some have claimed that the FTC Holder in Due Course Rule and other changes have effectively eliminated the importance or effects of negotiability, instead, the detrimental effects of negotiability, driven from their traditional home in consumer purchase contracts, have alighted in the area of home equity loans secured by residential property. Where loans once sat mostly undisturbed in the portfolios of their lenders, preventing the holder in due course doctrine from causing harm

---

25. Congress was, however, concerned with the burdens it was placing on assignees of HOEPA loans. In conjunction with providing for a limitation on damages, Congress also sought to ensure that purchasers of HOEPA loans on the secondary market were given notice of their potential liability. As a result, "[a]ny person who sells or otherwise assigns a [n] [HOEPA mortgage] shall include a prominent notice of potential liability ...." 15 U.S.C. § 1641(d)(4). Even so, it is clear Congress deemed assignees of HOEPA loans to be in the best position to absorb or recover the loss associated with the predatory lending practices of original lenders.

by ensuring that few new holders ever received the loans, now new secondary markets for loans cause the near instantaneous creation of a multitude of new holders of loans claiming status as bona fide purchasers. Chief among the changes in these secondary markets is the process of securitization of loans that has come to dominate the residential mortgage industry. Through securitization, investors have been able to channel huge sums of money into the lending industry, purchasing the beneficial interest in the loans produced. While they have often benefited from the high interest loans produced by predatory lenders, these investors have been too protected from bearing the risk of loss caused by the predatory nature of those loans.

Kurt Eggert, Held Up in Due Course: Predatory Lending, Securitization, and the Holder in Due Course Doctrine, 35 Creighton L. Rev. 503, 534–35 (2002).

4.   The FTC Rule applies only to credit sales of goods or services, and thus does not apply to most first mortgage residential real estate transactions. In the typical home purchase and mortgage transaction, the buyer approaches the lender directly, rather than obtaining credit from a seller who negotiates the paper to the lender. Thus, lender liability issues in real estate purchase transactions usually involve direct loans, rather than assignments or negotiable instruments.

There may well be interlocking relationships between the real estate seller and the lender. For instance, in a landmark California case, Connor v. Great Western Sav. & Loan Ass'n, 69 Cal.2d 850, 73 Cal.Rptr. 369, 447 P.2d 609 (1968), the financing institution was heavily involved in a disastrous development project in which residences were severely damaged due to poor construction decisions. Here, the savings and loan, Great Western, "became much more than a lender content to lend money at interest on the security of real property. It became an active participant in a home construction enterprise. * * *" 447 P.2d at 616. Great Western purchased land ahead of construction and "warehoused" it for the developer's later purchase at a substantial profit to the lender. It actively reviewed plans and specifications, suggested selling prices, held a right of first refusal to supply mortgage loans to purchasers, and received fees from the developer for every purchaser obtaining financing. Id. A divided California Supreme Court, in a majority opinion by Chief Justice Traynor, held that under these circumstances the lender would be liable to the purchasers of the defective homes for negligence in failing to correct the obvious structural problems. Id.

Despite the authority of a Traynor opinion, the decision in Connor has not been well received. The California legislature and the legislatures in many other states have enacted statutes protecting lenders from liability where they act solely as financing agencies. One authority has warned that "[t]he potential for lender liability under a Connor theory is real. Even though the case has been frequently distinguished, its theory has been occasionally applied to impose liability on financial institutions who operate outside the scope of normal lending activity." G. Nelson & D. Whitman, Real Estate Finance Law 12.11, at 930 (2d ed. 1985).

4.   CREDIT CARD ISSUER LIABILITY FOR DEFECTIVE GOODS

Credit cards like Visa, Master Card, Discover Card and American Express, involve at least three parties: the bank (or other company) as card issuer, the consumer as cardholder, and the merchant who honors the card. In the early 1970s it was a very controversial question whether a consumer could justifiably refuse to pay the card issuer if the merchant supplied defective goods or services in a credit card transaction. The legal question is a variation of the "holder in due course" issue, i.e., should the card issuer incur a vicarious liability for the merchant's defective performance.

Card issuers obviously preferred not to be liable for defective merchandise sold by the retailers who honored their cards, and waiver of defense clauses were common in credit card agreements. But in 1974 the Fair Credit Billing Act (Chapter 4 of the TIL Act) sharply curtailed the card issuers' ability to shield themselves from cardholder claims or defenses relating to transactions with participating merchants. See TILA 15 U.S.C. § 1666i; Reg. Z 12 C.F.R. § 226.12(c).

These special TILA provisions on card issuer liability for cardholder claims against merchants appear to complement the FTC Holder Rule provisions. This provision has been subject to much less controversy and has spawned very little litigation.

Problem 7–18

Similar facts to those in Problem 7–14, *supra*, Section C(2), Robbin Hood bought a used car from Dale, located in Hood's hometown, but this time Hood finances the $10,000 balance of the price on his Mastercard——credit card issued to him by Nottingham Bank. When Hood went to Dale and pointed out the car had been in a prior accident, Dale refused to take back the car. Hood made the same request a second time, but was again refused. Dale is on the verge of Bankruptcy.

When Dale refuses to take back the car, what can you safely advise Hood to do, under FCBA 15 U.S.C.A. §§ 1666 and 1666i? *See also*, Reg. Z 12 C.F.R. §§ 226.12(c), 226.13(a).

Notes

1.   What was the rationale for the $50 and 100 mile limitations in FCBA § 1666i? See Brandel & Leonard, Bank Charge Cards: New Cash or New Credit, 69 Mich.L.Rev. 1033 (1971).

2.   The exceptions built into FCBA by § 1666i by Congress have caused few practical problems. But for those who like theoretical puzzles, consider whether a consumer can withhold payment of his credit card bill in any of the following situations:

(a) He buys a defective set of cutlery from a company out-of-state (and more than 100 miles away) by responding to a flier included with his MasterCard monthly billing statement. See Reg. Z § 226.12(c)(3)(i), Note 26, at 6.

(b) He uses his VISA card to purchase a 10–speed bike at a local store, for $620. The bike's brakes lock, throwing him to the ground and breaking his arm. The bike is undamaged and can be adjusted at no cost.

Is a breach of warranty cause of action one which arises out of contract *and not* out of tort?

(c) He buys a ladder ($25) and three gallons of paint ($10 each) in order to paint his garage. The ladder breaks and the paint peels. See Reg. Z § 226.12(c).

Problem 7–19

Saul Brenner took his car to Kramer Auto Service for repairs. The repairs to be made were agreed upon and estimated to cost $25. When Brenner returned for the car, the bill read $51.02. Kramer had performed additional services, and, of course, demanded to be paid for them. Brenner objected that the extra services were not needed, but Kramer became obdurate and gave Brenner an option: either Brenner paid, or Kramer would keep possession of the car. Brenner paid by using his VISA card. What can Brenner do now to resolve this dispute? Complaining directly to the merchant is not likely to be effective; and if he has already paid, the burden of initiating litigation is on him. But, has he already paid? See Fair Credit Billing Act (CCPA) 15 U.S.C.A. §§ 1666, 1666i; Reg. Z § 226.12(c). If Brenner is a person who always pays within 30 days, how much of his VISA card account would you advise him to pay to avoid finance charges?

Can Brenner use 15 U.S.C.A. § 1666—that is, is this a "billing error" under FCBA? See Reg. Z § 226.13(a)(3). If not, should Brenner withhold the amount allowed under Reg. Z § 226.13(d)? Note that analysis of this issue requires comparison of the availability and overlap of Sections 1666 and 1666i, and of Reg. Z §§ 226.12 and 226.13. In particular, compare and contrast Reg. Z § 226.12(c)(1) and § 226.13(d)(3). Does Hood get positive rights from the regulations? Even if not supported by statutory language? See TILA, 15 U.S.C.A. § 1604.

CITIBANK (SOUTH DAKOTA), N.A. v. MINCKS

Missouri Court of Appeals, 2004.
135 S.W.3d 545.

JEFFREY W. BATES, JUDGE.

Citibank (South Dakota), N.A. ("Citibank") sued defendant Mary Mincks ("Mary") for breach of contract after Mary refused to make any further payments on her Citibank credit card account.[1] Mary defended on the ground that: (1) the only unpaid charges on the account related to merchandise which was never delivered by the merchant; and (2) since her Citibank credit card was used to order the merchandise, she was entitled to assert the defense of non-delivery against Citibank in its action to recover the balance due on her credit card account. After a bench trial, judgment was entered in Mary's favor. On appeal, Citibank

---

1. We will refer to Mary Mincks and her husband, Chuck Mincks, collectively as "the Mincks." We will refer to them individually by their first names. We do so for purposes of clarity and intend no disrespect.

argues that the trial court's judgment should be reversed because it was not supported by substantial evidence, and it was based on an erroneous application of the provisions of the Truth-in-Lending–Act, 15 U.S.C. 1601, *et seq*. We affirm.

I. STANDARD OF REVIEW

* * *

II. FACTUAL AND PROCEDURAL HISTORY

The facts in this case are relatively simple and virtually undisputed. The summary set forth below is a synthesis prepared from the pleadings, trial testimony and exhibits.

On September 18, 1999, Mary applied to have a credit card issued to her by Citibank. She filled out a document called a "Citibank Platinum Select Acceptance Form," which appears to be a typical application for personal credit. Nothing on the application indicates that credit was being sought by either a business or by an individual who intended to use the credit card for business purposes. The application listed Mary as the cardholder and showed her home address as the billing location. The form asked for the normal personal information (e.g., mother's maiden name, social security number, income) found in such personal applications. Mary applied for credit for herself, and she requested that her husband, Chuck, also be authorized to use her credit card account. * * *

Mary's application was accepted, and Citibank issued a credit card to her with an $8,000 line of credit. * * *

Between November 1999 and January 2000, Mary purchased a few additional items with her credit card and made several payments on her account. * * *

In February 2000, Chuck received a solicitation to order merchandise from Purchase Plus Buyers Group ("PPBG"). PPBG sold products like mailing cards, telephone cards and other similar items which could be used to promote a home business. After reviewing the solicitation, Chuck decided to order some high-definition, high-color postcards that he could use to contact potential customers for a home business that he had started about three months earlier. On February 24, 2000, Chuck placed an order with PPBG for 4,000 postcards. The order form was sent by fax from Lamar, Missouri, to PPBG's office in Westerville, Ohio. Chuck used Mary's Citibank credit card to pay the $7,600 purchase price for the postcards. The charge for this purchase first appeared on Mary's Citibank statement in March 2000.

Four weeks after placing the order, Chuck contacted PPBG by telephone to find out why he had not yet received the postcards. He was told that the merchandise was on backorder and would not be available for another month. Having no reason to doubt that explanation at the time, he waited another month. When he still had not received the postcards, he contacted PPBG again by telephone. The persons with whom he spoke were very positive and continued to assure him that he would receive the postcards in time. Thereafter, he called PPBG "innumerable times" by telephone, and PPBG personnel kept reiterating that he would ultimately receive the postcards he ordered. In mid-May 2000, Chuck first learned from PPBG that the type of postcards he ordered had been discontinued in December 1999, even though the product continued to be offered for sale until April 2000. On May 18, 2000, he faxed a letter to PPBG requesting that he be given some other type of product that he could use since the postcards he wanted were no longer available. He received no response. He faxed the same letter to PPBG's executive committee on July 13, 2000, and again received no response.

Around August 1, 2000, Chuck decided he was never going to receive the postcards he ordered from PPBG. On August 4, 2000, he faxed a written demand for a full refund to PPBG because the company had failed to deliver either the postcards or a satisfactory alternative product. He sent this fax because he still believed he could get a refund for the undelivered merchandise. This belief changed on September 1, 2000, when he received a fax from PPBG stating the company had ceased operations and permanently closed its doors that day. Chuck knew then he would not be able to get a refund from PPBG.

On September 28, 2000, the Mincks sent a letter to Citibank. In sum, the letter provided Citibank with the following information: (1) Chuck's $7,600 postcard order from PPBG had never been delivered; (2) the charge for this order first appeared on Mary's March 2000 statement; (3) the facts showing that Chuck had made a good faith effort to resolve the issue with PPBG were recounted with considerable specificity and detail; (4) PPBG committed a breach of contract and fraud by failing to deliver the ordered merchandise and by continuing to sell a discontinued product; and (5) the Mincks were invoking their rights under Regulation Z of the federal Truth-in-Lending–Act to have their account credited in the amount of $7,600 and to have this sum charged back to PPBG.

On October 9, 2000, Citibank responded in a letter sent to Mary. Citibank took the position that it was not able to assist the Mincks because it had not received their letter "within 60 days of the disputed charge." Citibank advised the Mincks to pursue the matter with the merchant or through some alternative means available to them.

After receiving the October 9, 2000, letter from Citibank, the Mincks continued to use Mary's credit card. They made a few additional purchases with the card, and they continued to make payments on the account. That changed in February 2002, when the Mincks stopped making any payments on the Citibank account. The outstanding account balance at this time was comprised solely of the remaining amount due for the undelivered postcards ordered from PPBG, plus accrued interest and late charges. Citibank continued to add interest charges, over credit limit fees, and late fees to Mary's credit card account until July 2002. As of that date, the outstanding account balance was $9,048.49.

On October 7, 2002, Citibank sued Mary for breach of contract and sought to recover the $9,048.49 then due, accrued interest at the rate of 24.99% per annum and a 15% attorney fee. * * * In Mary's answer, she specifically asserted non-delivery of the merchandise ordered from PPBG as a defense against Citibank's claim.

At trial, the sole dispute was whether Mary was entitled to assert PPBG's non-delivery as a defense against Citibank, which sought to recover the purchase price of the postcards as PPBG's assignee. Citibank argued that the non-delivery defense should not be permitted on two grounds. First, the PPBG postcard order, which was the only transaction at issue, was not within the scope of Regulation Z since this specific purchase was for a business or commercial purpose. Second, even if Regulation Z did apply, non-delivery of merchandise constitutes a "billing error" within the meaning of the regulation. According to Citibank, Mary lost the ability to assert non-delivery as a defense in this lawsuit because she did not give Citibank notice of this "billing error" within 60 days after the charge first appeared on her credit card statement. In response, Mary argued that Regulation Z imposed no time limit that precluded her from asserting non-delivery as a defense in Citibank's lawsuit against her, and she denied that this was a "billing error" within the meaning of the regulation. At the conclusion of the case, the trial court made the following ruling from the bench:

> I think that Reg. Z does apply, and I don't think this is a—a billing error. And I think that the provision of Reg. Z that allows the cardholder to assert any differences—any defenses that they could assert against the provider of the product is against the—the credit card company. Court's going to find the issues in favor of the Defendant and enter a judgment for the Defendant against the Plaintiff.

Judgment was entered in accordance with the trial court's pronouncement, and Citibank appealed.

III. DISCUSSION AND DECISION

Citibank's appeal presents two points for us to decide. Each point relied on is a rescript of the arguments Citibank made below.

Point I

In Citibank's first point, it contends the trial court erred in permitting Mary to assert PPBG's non-delivery as a defense in Citibank's breach of contract action. Specifically, Citibank argues that the trial court's judgment is not supported by substantial evidence and is based on a misapplication of the law because "Regulation Z" should not have been applied in this lawsuit, in that the PPBG transaction was primarily for a business or commercial purpose. * * *

* * *

In the case at bar, we * * * conclude that * * * the "overall purpose" test, * * * should be used when an open end consumer credit plan is involved. Under this test, the overall purpose of an account opened by a natural person must be considered. If the account was opened primarily for consumer purposes, the statutory and regulatory framework of the Truth-in-Lending-Act applies, even if the cardholder occasionally uses the card for a nonconsumer purchase.

We find support for this conclusion in the Official Staff Interpretations of Regulation Z. *See* Supplement I to part 226, 12 C.F.R. p. 357 (1–1–04 edition). The Official Staff Commentary dealing with 12 C.F.R. § 226.3 (exempt transactions) notes that a creditor must determine in each case whether the extension of credit "is primarily for an exempt purpose." Pt. 226, Supp. I p. 369. "Examples of business-purpose credit include:.... A business account used occasionally for consumer purposes. Examples of consumer-purpose credit include:.... A personal account used occasionally for business purposes." *Id.* Therefore, we disagree with Citibank's contention that the use of Mary's Citibank credit card account to purchase nonconsumer goods on one occasion prevents her from taking advantage of the Truth-in-Lending-Act's claims and defenses rule in this case.

Mary's Use of Non-delivery as a Defense Against Citibank Also Is Authorized by State Law

Even if we accepted Citibank's argument in Point I that the Truth-in-Lending-Act does not apply, our decision would not change. Like Ulysses' unfortunate sailors in *The Odyssey,* Citibank would successfully navigate past the Charybdis of federal law only to be devoured by the Scylla of state law.[10] Expressed in less metaphorical terms, the trial court's decision to enter judgment for Mary is still correct, based exclusively on Missouri common law and statutory principles. We must affirm the judgment under any reasonable theory supported by the evidence, even if the reasons advanced by the trial court are wrong or insufficient.

Citibank brought a breach of contract action against Mary for failing to pay her credit card account. The only unpaid charge on Mary's account was the PPBG purchase. As the petition expressly acknowledged, Citibank was suing Mary as PPBG's assignee.

"Missouri law is well-settled that an assignee acquires no greater rights than the assignor had at the time of the assignment." These common law principles compel the conclusion that any defense valid against PPBG is valid against its assignee, Citibank.

The same is true under Missouri statutory law. Article Nine of the Uniform Commercial Code describes a person obligated on an account as an "account debtor." Section 400.9–102(a)(3). Section 400.9–404(a)(1)

---

10. Homer, *The Odyssey,* Book XII (800 B.C.) (Samuel Butler trans.). A more homespun Homer from the Ozarks might describe Citibank's situation as being caught between a rock and a hard place.

states that the rights of an assignee of an account debtor are subject to "any defense or claim in recoupment arising from the transaction that gave rise to the contract...." The official Comment explains that this subsection of the statute "provides that an assignee generally takes an assignment subject to defenses and claims of an account debtor. Under subsection (a)(1), if the account debtor's defenses on an assigned claim arise from the transaction that gave rise to the contract with the assignor, it makes no difference whether the defense or claim accrues before or after the account debtor is notified of the assignment."[13] Therefore, without regard to the provisions of the federal Truth-in-Lending-Act, Missouri law gave Mary a common law and statutory right to assert any defense against Citibank that she could have asserted against its assignor, PPBG.

Assuming PPBG had sued Mary for breach of contract and sought to recover the cost of the postcards, would she have had a valid defense against that claim? We answer this question affirmatively because PPBG never delivered the merchandise for which Mary was charged. This defense is just as effective against Citibank as it would have been against PPBG.

Point II

Regardless of whether the trial court's decision is reviewed by using the federal Truth-in-Lending-Act or state law standards, the judgment is correct. The trial court committed no error by ruling in Mary's favor and denying Citibank any recovery on its action for breach of contract. Citibank's first point is denied.

In Citibank's second point, it contends the judgment is not supported by substantial evidence and is based on a misapplication of the law because, even if Regulation Z does apply, PPBG's non-delivery of the postcards constituted a "billing error" within the meaning of the regulation. Assuming that to be true, Citibank then argues Mary could not avoid responsibility for the PPBG purchase unless she gave Citibank notice of the error within 60 days after the charge first appeared on her credit card statement. According to Citibank, failure to invoke the billing error provisions of the Truth-in-Lending-Act prohibits a consumer from thereafter relying on the claims and defenses rule if he or she is sued on the debt by the creditor.

The relevant statutory and regulatory provisions of the Truth-in-Lending-Act dealing with billing errors are found in 15 U.S.C. § 1666 and 12 C.F.R. § 226.13. Hereinafter, we generically refer to the consumer protections contained in this statute and regulation as the "billing error rule." The billing error rule gives a consumer the right, upon proper written notice, to request correction of billing errors. The notice must be received within 60 days after the creditor has sent the consumer

---

13. Uniform Commercial Code Comment to § 400.9–404, 20C V.A.M.S. p. 524 (2003). Although comments to the Uniform Commercial Code do not have the same force as statutes enacted by the legislature, they provide persuasive assistance in interpreting U.C.C. provisions.

a statement reflecting a billing error. *See* 15 U.S.C. § 1666(a); 12 C.F.R.
§ 226.13(b). If the consumer properly invokes the billing error rule by
giving timely written notice, the creditor is required to investigate the
claim. 15 U.S.C. § 1666(a); 12 C.F.R. § 226.13(b) and (c). While the
investigation is pending, the consumer may withhold payment of the
disputed sum, and the creditor is prohibited from both collection and
adverse credit reporting activity. 15 U.S.C. § 1666(c); 12 C.F.R.
§ 226.13(d). As defined in 15 U.S.C. § 1666(b)(3) a billing error includes
"[a] reflection on a statement of goods or services ... not delivered to
the obligor or his designee in accordance with the agreement made at the
time of a transaction." Essentially the same definition of a billing error
is found in 12 C.F.R. § 226.13(a)(3).

The trial court concluded that PPBG's failure to deliver the postcards did not constitute a "billing error" within the meaning of 15
U.S.C. § 1666 and 12 C.F.R. § 226.13. We interpret this decision to be a
rejection of Citibank's position that the 60 day time limit for giving
written notice began running in March 2000 when the PPBG charge
first appeared on Mary's statement because the Mincks did not know,
during any portion of this 60 day period, that they would never receive
the postcards, an acceptable substitute product, or a refund from PPBG.
In order to dispose of Citibank's second point on appeal, however, it is
unnecessary for us to decide whether this ruling was in error. Assuming
PPBG's non-delivery of the postcards did constitute a "billing error"
within the meaning of the Truth-in-Lending-Act, Mary still was entitled
to invoke the claims and defenses rule in 15 U.S.C. § 1666i and 12
C.F.R. § 226.12(c). This statute and regulation are stand-alone provisions that operate independently of 15 U.S.C. § 1666 and 12 C.F.R.
§ 226.13, which give a consumer separate and distinct rights and remedies when seeking to correct a billing error. We find support for our
conclusion through a textual analysis of 15 U.S.C. § 1666 and an
examination of the Official Staff Interpretations of Regulation Z.

The only obligation imposed upon a consumer by 15 U.S.C. § 1666 is
the transmittal of an adequate written notice to the creditor within 60
days after receiving a statement containing a billing error. Once the
billing error process is properly initiated, the consumer may withhold
payment of the disputed sum and obtain an abatement of collection and
adverse reporting activity while the creditor investigates the issue.
Nothing in the statute affirmatively imposes any penalty on the consumer for failing to take advantage of the benefits of this statute. * * *

In contrast, the statute does affirmatively impose a penalty upon *a
creditor* that ignores the provisions of this statute. This conclusion
follows from 15 U.S.C. § 1666(e), which states:

(e) Effect of noncompliance with requirements by creditor

Any creditor who fails to comply with the requirements of this
section or section 1666a of this title forfeits any right to collect from
the obligor the amount indicated by the obligor under paragraph (2)
of subsection (a) of this section, and any finance charges thereon,

except that the amount required to be forfeited under this subsection may not exceed $50.

Thus, § 1666 only affects the amount of the debt in the event of a creditor's noncompliance with the statute. When this occurs, however, the creditor may still sue on the debt if there is a remaining balance due after subtracting the $50 forfeiture sum. If we were to accept Citibank's argument, it would mean that a consumer who failed to utilize this billing error statute—through ignorance, inadvertence, or purposeful action—would completely forfeit his right to contest the debt owed in a collection lawsuit. The creditor, on the other hand, could knowingly and willfully ignore its responsibilities under this statute and only be penalized a maximum of $50. In our view, this interpretation of the statute leads to an absurd result and turns topsy-turvy our duty to liberally construe the Truth-in-Lending-Act in a consumer's favor. Again, we decline to do so.

Our construction of how the billing error rule operates also is supported by the Official Staff Interpretations of Regulation Z. * * * The Official Staff Commentary for 12 C.F.R. § 226.12 states, in pertinent part:

> *12(c) Right of cardholder to assert claims or defenses against card issuer.*
>
> 1. *Relationship to § 226.13.* The § 226.12(c) credit card "holder in due course" provision deals with the consumer's right to assert against the card issuer a claim or defense concerning property or services purchased with a credit card, if the merchant has been unwilling to resolve the dispute. Even though certain merchandise disputes, such as non-delivery of goods, may also constitute "billing errors" under § 226.13, that section operates independently of § 226.12(c). The cardholder whose asserted billing error involves undelivered goods may institute the error resolution procedures of § 266.13; but whether or not the cardholder has done so, the cardholder may assert claims or defenses under § 226.12(c). Conversely, the consumer may pay a disputed balance and thus have no further right to assert claims and defenses, but still may assert a billing error if notice of that billing error is given in the proper time and manner. An assertion that a particular transaction resulted from unauthorized use of the card could also be both a "defense" and a billing error.

See Pt. 226, Supp. I p. 419. Thus, the Federal Reserve Board recognizes that the claims and defenses rule operates independently of the billing error rule. As the Board's analysis of the proper relationship between these two different rules and their respective remedies is not demonstrably irrational, we accept it as dispositive here.

For all of the foregoing reasons, we reject Citibank's argument that a consumer's failure to give a creditor timely notice of a billing error precludes the consumer from later invoking the claim and defense provisions of 15 U.S.C. § 1666i and 12 C.F.R. § 226.12(c) if the creditor sues on the debt. Citibank's second point is denied.

IV. CONCLUSION

Mary was entitled to assert non-delivery as a valid defense against Citibank in its action for breach of contract. The use of this non-delivery defense was authorized both by the Truth-in-Lending–Act and by state law. Furthermore, the use of this defense was not precluded by the billing error rule found in the Truth-in-Lending–Act. Therefore, the trial court ruled correctly when it denied Citibank any recovery and entered judgment in Mary's favor. The judgment is affirmed.

PARRISH and SHRUM, JJ., Concur.

Notes

1. Why would the Mincks agree to pay $7,600 for 4,000 postcards? Apparently the merchant in this case, Purchase Plus Buyers Group, Inc., was selling more than just postcards. They were alleged to be operating an illegal pyramid scheme in which participants would receive rewards for recruiting new participants. *See* Beaumont v. Citibank (S. Dak.) N.A., 2002 WL 87682 (S.D.N.Y. 2002). PPBG went bankrupt shortly after the Ohio Attorney General filed suit against them in August, 2000.

2. What test did the court apply to determine that the postcard purchase was covered under the TILA? Why wasn't this considered an exempt commercial transaction?

3. Can the same issue (i.e., non-delivery of goods), constitute both a "billing error" under 15 U.S.C. § 1666 and a claim or defense against the card issuer under 16 U.S.C. § 1666i? Does the consumer have to comply with the time limits for reporting a billing error to preserve their right to raise a claim or defense under § 1666i?

4. The Mincks raised their claims against PPBG as a defense in Citibank's suit against them for nonpayment. Could they have raised the same claim as plaintiffs in an independent suit against Citibank? *See* Beaumont v. Citibank (S. Dak.) N.A., 2002 WL 483431 (S.D.N.Y. 2002). What if their claim had been for fraud rather than breach of contract? *See* Citibank (S. Dak.) N.A. v. Kessler, 2004 WL 795689 (Ohio Ct. App. 2004).

Postscript

The doctrine of negotiability, and the cutting off of issuers' defenses, originated at a time when promissory notes and drafts were expected to circulate widely through many unknown hands before payment. By 1975, when the FTC issued the Holder Rule, this circulation pattern had changed radically. At that time, promissory notes were issued by a consumer-maker to a retailer-payee, and then the paper was sold once to a financer-endorsee, who held it until it was fully paid off. For paper with such limited circulation, the FTC Rule made sense; the FTC Statement of Basis and Purpose clearly indicates that this typical limited circulation pattern is an underlying assumption of the Holder Rule.

What are the costs of industry compliance? To date, the Federal Trade Commission has not done a study on the economic effects of the "Holder" Rule. In the late 1980's, the Commission decided not to extend the Holder Rule to creditors, stating, "the record contains little evidence of consumer injury occurring after the Holder Rule became effective and little evidence to suggest that creditor participation in cutting off consumers' claims is prevalent. Accordingly, the Commission has decided to terminate the Holder II proceeding without issuing an amended rule." 53 Fed. Reg. 44456 (1988). Furthermore, in the FTC's 1992 review of the Holder Rule, the Commission concluded no changes were needed: "The Notice attracted limited public interest, and no participation at all by any "small entity" that claimed to be negatively impacted by the Rule." 57 Fed. Reg. 28, 814 (June 29, 1992).

However, in the 1980s the banks developed a "secondary market" in consumer notes, whereby a bundle of 1000 or more notes would be sold by one financer to another. (A similar secondary market had been developed in the 1970s for bundles of home mortgages and promissory notes.) Thus, the notes signed by consumers now may have a new and different circulation pattern—from consumer-maker to retailer-payee to financer #1–endorsee to financer #2 to financer #3 and so on * * *. And, perhaps most important, this entire secondary market developed *after* the FTC Holder Rule, and originated using non-negotiable consumer paper.

Despite the dire predictions regarding the drying up of consumer credit due to the regulatory innovations of the 20th century, such as the Holder in Due Course Rule, the ECOA, the FCRA and the TILA, the market for consumer credit has apparently reached new heights in the 21st century. Credit card debt is at an all time high, and the subprime market is booming (see *infra* Chapter 9, on predatory lending). Have the regulations "worked"? Does that indicate that negotiability and cutting-off of defenses is in fact less important than it was thought to be? Or have creditors worked out loopholes, such as securitizations of consumer credit and insulation from liability for TILA creditors? Will mandatory arbitration clauses in consumer credit contracts prove to be yet another way for creditors to "cut-off" consumers' claims and defenses by depriving them of the right to go to court, file a class action or obtain statutory damages? (*see infra* chapter 10, on enforcement).

Chapter 8

ABUSIVE COLLECTION PRACTICES

SECTION A.   FOUNDATION

Most of this chapter focuses on what might be called "informal" collection practices creditors use to collect consumer debts. These are primarily processes a creditor might use before going to court. Here, too, we introduce the larger social and economic arena in which debtor defaults occur. Later the chapter explores creditor attempts to seize collateral.

1. COLLECTION TACTICS

The goal in debt collection is to collect the debt at the lowest possible cost. Litigation is sometimes a helpful avenue, but because of its cost, litigation is often unattractive and sometimes pointless. For example, in Clomon v. Jackson, *infra*, where the debt was $9.42, the cost of litigation would have substantially exceeded any possible recovery. Accordingly, debt collectors in such situations must use other means. That may mean working with debtors in a respectful manner to encourage them to pay. See Saul Hansell, Spending It; We Like You. We Care About You. Now Pay Up, N.Y. Times, Jan. 26, 1997. But not always, as you will see from the following materials.

Often debtors who do not pay debts lack the resources to meet all their obligations, but have enough funds to pay some debts. In such circumstances, a firm collecting debts may attempt to persuade the consumer to put its debt at the head of the line for payment by exerting "unwelcome pressure." If the pressure makes the debtor sufficiently uncomfortable, the debtor may indeed pay the firm's debt instead of some other debt. Consequently, the materials in this chapter concern the use of harassment as a collection tool, and in particular, on the line between permissible and impermissible unwelcome pressure.

The pressure often begins with letters. Sophisticated debt collection operations may employ computers, as in *Clomon*, to print form letters and envelopes, insert the letters into the envelopes, and mail the letters according to a predetermined schedule and all without human interven-

619

tion. If letters do not persuade the debtor to pay, the debt collector may turn to telephone calls or other measures.

As you read the following material, think about the different concerns of the collector and the debtor. For example, as some of the materials *infra* demonstrate, most consumers who do not pay have understandable reasons (loss of job, sudden medical emergency, etc.). Do you think a debt collector is likely to be sympathetic to these problems? Also consider the various collection tactics described below. Do you think a consumer would be likely to consider them as harassment? Would a creditor have a different view?

DALY, "HOW COLLECTION AGENCIES FORCE YOU OUT OF DEBT"

Village Voice, May 2, 1977.
Reprinted in the Fair Debt Collection Practices Act Hearings,
Subcommittee on Consumer Affairs, U.S. Senate
Committee on Banking, Housing and Urban Affairs.

95th Cong., 1st Sess., May 12–13, 1977, pp. 711–14.

Billy Maxwell of Riverdale was unemployed, two months in arrears with his rent, and three payments behind on his car loan. Last month, he saw a help-wanted ad for "investigators" who "like good money." The following morning, Maxwell put on a suit and hopped the subway to a downtown Brooklyn collection agency.

"It can be boring," the president of the company told Maxwell at the end of the 10–minute interview. "But, once you pick up the basics, there's plenty of room for innovation. We get half of what we collect as profit. The point is to get the money." A framed emblem certifying the firm's membership in the American Collectors Association hung behind the executive's desk. Of the $7 billion of consumer credit granted in New York City in 1975, over $27.2 million was referred to ACA members for collection. The ACA's code of operations calls on members to "show due consideration for the misfortunes of consumers in debt" and "do everything reasonable to assist the consumer in the solution of any financial problems he may have."

* * *

"Eric Tibbetts," the man [at the next desk] said, holding out his hand to Maxwell, "I'll be the one who breaks you in." Tibbetts tossed a blue folder onto Maxwell's desk. Maxwell's first case was a seven-year-old finance-company account.

"We'll start you with renewals," Tibbetts said. "In this business, the two most important things to know about the guy are his phone number and where he works. You already got both. This account kicked around the finance company's own collection office until it got on the far side of the statute of limitations. You got to call the guy up and tell him to send in a dollar as a gesture of good faith. He makes any partial payment, the debt's active again. Ask for a post-dated check. We deposit it early, it comes back. Then we can call the guy and tell him that he's going to jail for passing a bad check unless he pays the full amount."

Maxwell dialed the phone number scrawled on the outside of the folder.

"I don't talk to no debt men," the debtor said, hanging up. Maxwell dialed again. There was no answer.

"You should keep trying," Tibbetts said when Maxwell asked for advice. "But, since it's your first day, we'll teach the guy a lesson." Tibbetts grabbed the yellow pages. In 10 minutes, he ordered seven pizzas, 14 Chinese dinners, 100 roses, a team of carpet cleaners, and three masseurs sent to the debtor's house.

"Maybe you should just sit tight and watch me for a few days," Tibbetts said, opening another blue folder and reaching for his telephone. "We'll do the bank gag."

"Hello," Tibbetts said in a high-pitched voice. "Mrs. Engelman? This is Mr. Waters at Flatbush Federal Savings. This week we are offering free checking to new depositors. Are you interested? Oh, you already bank at the Dime. Thank you very much."

"Now we know where she banks," Tibbetts said to Maxwell. "I'll wait a week so she won't make the connection. Then I'll call and tell her that I know she can pay her bill because she's got an account at the Dime Savings Bank. Sometimes it's good to also call the bank and say you're with Master Charge and you're doing a credit check. They'll give you the account number. If you know that, you can really put people on the edge."

"Let's skip-trace this fella", Tibbetts said, grabbing a delinquent department-store account. The debtor, Charles Evans, had run up a $438 bill before he moved to a new address and switched his telephone to an unlisted number. Tibbetts dialed the Board of Education.

"Hello," Tibbetts said. "This is Dr. Williams at Kings County Hospital. We have a young girl here named Chimira Evans. She's been hit by a car. Do you have an emergency number for her parents?" Fifteen minutes later, when he had Evan's new phone number, Tibbetts dialed 518–471–8111.

"This is central name and address," Tibbetts said to Maxwell. "You give them a number and they give you the name and address it's listed to."

Tibbetts moved on to another "skipper," Herman Kahn. A copy of a credit application provided Tibbetts with the phone number of Kahn's parents.

"This is Willie, Herman's friend from high school," Tibbetts said to Kahn's mother. "Could you tell me how to get hold of him?" Tibbetts wrote Kahn's new address on the back of a post card stamped "Interstate Delivery Service Notice to Deliver."

"The mother didn't have the guy's number," Tibbetts explained to Maxwell, "He'll call the number on the delivery notice. The girl over in the corner takes those calls. She'll say that she's having trouble locating the package and ask the guy to leave a number where she can call him back."

"Now we'll do a social security case," Tibbetts smiled. "This one's a retiree. We're not legally allowed to touch any federal money. So, with the people on social security or welfare, you got to scare them into paying," Tibbetts called the pensioner and introduced himself as "Mr. Rath of the Social Security Administration in Washington."

"Of course you know," Tibbetts said in a nasal tone, "that you are responsible for meeting your debts and obligations if you wish to continue receiving benefits."

Before breaking for lunch, Tibbetts called up a woman on welfare and threatened to instruct the Department of Social Services to classify her as "an unfit mother who can't pay her bills" and place her children in a foster home.

"Isn't some of this stuff illegal?" Maxwell asked Tibbetts over lunch at Zum Zum. Tibbetts laughed. According to Section 601 of the New York State General Business Law, it is a misdemeanor for debt collectors to make phone calls that "abuse or harass debtors," or claim or threaten "to enforce a right with knowledge or reason to know that the right does not exist," including garnishment of salaries. The law also forbids: Impersonation of "any state representative"; any attempt to collect fees "unless legally done"; disclosure of "a debtor's reputation of credit worthiness with knowledge or reason to know that the information is false"; communication "of the nature of a consumer claim to the debtor's employer prior to obtaining final judgment against the debtor"; and use of "communication which simulates in any manner legal or judicial process or gives appearance of being authorized, issued, or approved by a government, governmental agency, or attorney of law when it is not."

"Of course it's illegal," Tibbetts said.

After lunch, Tibbetts gave Maxwell a phone number. "Call every 15 minutes," he said. "Just lower your voice and say that time is getting short and they'll have to pay hundreds of dollars in court costs if they don't cough up." Tibbetts dialed the home number of a new account. He introduced himself as "Mr. Star of the Social Security Administration" to the woman who answered the phone, and said he was "checking to make sure that our records were correct with regard to your husband's employment." Tibbetts wrote down the name of the husband's employer and reached for a directory.

"Do you know that you're employing a deadbeat?" Tibbetts asked the employer a few minutes later.

* * *

Notes

1. Why do debt collectors resort to abuse? Wouldn't it be easier, not to mention less risky, simply to use one of the many legal remedies?

2. Would you expect a creditor collecting her own debts or a professional debt collector to be more likely to use abusive techniques? Why?

3. Should courts or legislatures consider the reasons a debtor defaulted when structuring rules to regulate creditor conduct? For example, should the law permit more coercive or harassing collection methods when the debtor is a real "deadbeat," and prohibit aggressive collection methods when the debtor lost her job or had a sudden illness?

4. The testimony above preceded enactment of the federal Fair Debt Collection Practices Act (FDCPA), discussed at considerable length below. As for whether the FDCPA has made a difference, see the testimony immediately following, provided fifteen years after enactment of the FDCPA:

STATEMENT OF RICHARD BELL, FORMER DEBT COLLECTOR

Hearings on the Fair Debt Collection Practices Act Before the
U.S. House Subcom. On Consumer Protection of the
Com. on Banking and Housing (Sept. 10, 1992).

* * * I was a bill collector for over a decade. I started working shortly after the 1977 Federal Fair Debt Collection Practices Act was enacted. * * * [T]he Nation's bill collectors religiously ignore these laws. * * *

I worked for over 19 different agencies. At some I held management positions or trained new collectors. * * *

While I worked in Texas, 90 to 95 of my accounts, the consumers were out of the State of Texas. Texas has no licensing for bill collectors. That is probably one reason why creditors from all over the country use collectors from States with little regulation or enforcement.

What tactics did I witness that were used to collect bills? The same tactics, gentlemen, that are going on all over the country at this very moment. Initially, when you get a file from a creditor showing someone owes them money, you call the consumer. Nine times out of 10 the phone number is provided by the creditor.

If you cannot get hold of the consumer, they call the references in the file. They frighten them into divulging the whereabouts of the consumer. Parents always know where the kids are. You might say, I am with the investigations unit of Waller County. We are investigating a gang of thieves. By the way, if that stereo that is missing is in your home, you may be aiding and abetting a crime. I do not know, but your son has been implicated. Like I say, I don't have all the information, but this is urgent. Have him call me right away.

In that example I just gave I violated State and Federal laws in several different ways. However, if you read the notes on the consumers' file in my office and in offices across this country it will merely say that I called and left a message or something of that nature. When I would receive a phone call on my personal line, I would answer the phone, "Investigations or Law Office or Legal Department," and so forth. When I get a call back I would say Mr. Smith, you live at 500 Elm Street, don't you? A creditor of yours has placed your account with a collection agency. The agency has forwarded me the affidavit requesting criminal investigations, as well as capital gains tax fraud. Charges will be filed according to Federal and State codes. The bond has not been set yet. The warrants have not been issued. At this point, I believe the client is willing to forgo this procedure providing you are prepared to send the balance of your account by Western Union or overnight delivery to the collection agency.

If I receive a call by 1700 hours tomorrow and find out you have paid this bill, I will go to the courthouse and have the judge sign a stay of execution order and your criminal record will be expunged, Mr. Smith.

For the record, Mr. Smith, what is the plate number on your vehicle? I need that in the event you intend to skip out this evening.

Let me give you your case number. It is 91564301. Your parents can be implicated in this as well, or anyone else for that matter, if they have aided you in any way with reference to this crime. Do you understand? Would you prefer to have your parents wire the money from their credit card this evening so you *can* have a better sleep?

The trick the bill collectors have mastered is sounding helpful, yet threatening at the same time.

If the consumer, after being given the above talk does not pay or pays less than the amount demanded or does not pay by Western Union or Federal Express post-dated checks regardless of the consumer's condition or reasons provided, the tactics used would be severely intensified.

Each bill collector has a crisscross directory. Armed with this and the consumer's address, the phone numbers of the consumers' neighbors are at their disposal. Collectors are able to use some of their favorite tricks like the block party. A block party is where the collector contacts handfuls of neighbors close to or far away from the consumer, depending how mad the collector is. Block parties are often held for consumers who hang up on bill collectors. Their neighbors are told something to the effect of: Your neighbor is suspected of receiving stolen merchandise. Excuse me, you are not a member of Crime Watch, are you? Well, your neighbor, Fred Smith, may be gone by the time we get there. I wonder if you could go to his house and ask him to call us. We think he has some of the following possessions in his house, and we name a few consumer items bought.

When the neighbors are contacted they are told the consumer is under criminal investigation. On average 5 to 15 members would be invited to the block party.

A variant to the block party is the office party, where the collector dials every number on the rotary system similar to the consumer's and reaches the extensions of fellow employees. The coworkers are told about the consumers' bills, legal problems, or status as a thief.

The industry is riddled with an assortment of valued and classic intimidation tactics. They use verbal assaults that they feel they can impose upon consumers. Standard operating procedure has been developed. For instance, if Hispanics were on the line and that individual was only offering partial payment of his bill or was not returning phone calls, more than likely out of fright, he would be told Immigration will deport him and everyone in his family unless he can come up with the money. This can be validated by indicating that the INS is on the other line. Then one of my coworkers would pose as an immigration officer. If we were impersonating a sheriff, marshal, or the IRS, we would just hand the phone to a collector sitting next to us. This is a version of cross-pitching.

I wish to spare the subcommittee from hearing the ethnic slurs commonly used alongside threats of deportation, but ethnic and racial slurs, as well as profanity are commonly used.

The bill collector's standard operating procedure manual is an unwritten textbook on intimidation techniques providing the most effective techniques to collect bills. It told how best to collect from women, elderly, and minorities. These groups were perceived to be easy prey. The philosophy is that the more trouble he creates in the consumer's family, the quicker the bill will be paid.

For instance, we will tell kids that their father was having an affair. Of course, we will play parents off the same way by saying the bill was for a motel room.

The standard operating procedure described above was passed down by collectors. Management told me to emulate the collectors. They were the same ones making the most money. These were passed along to others. Often the method of training used was placing a novice next to an expert. After a few days of watching, the new employee would be given client files and employees were initially and periodically given tests on the Federal Fair Debt Collection Practices Act in the larger shops. It often focused on loopholes rather than the spirit of the law. However, taking a test or not taking a test did not matter. There was widespread cheating on the test with answers often yelled out from across the room, a carnival like atmosphere.

Once the new collector was put on the phone, he or she would be told to ignore the law and get the money in any way possible. The test was used as a smokescreen to keep investigators at bay.

Whenever a consumer complains, debt collection agencies simply deny they ever do anything wrong. They alter their files to support their positions, accuse the consumer of lying, accusing the consumer of cursing, breaking promises the consumer never made, accuse the consumer of failing to return telephone calls, refusing to pay, threatening the collection agency itself and, in general, tell any lie conceivable to convince State and Federal officials that their agency is innocent.

Collectors are expert liars and to catch them is very, very difficult. Collectors use every conceivable lie to avoid the consequences of their action. They and their management, most of whom are or were bill collectors, are so used to lying that it doesn't bother them at all to alter records, misrepresent facts, or lie under oath. They even convince consumers not to file complaints. I know it, I have seen it done.

As a consumer advocate I hear it every week. When the attorney general writes the collection agency indicating that a certain collector has broken the law, a common agency response is that the collector has been fired or left the company. Oftentimes the collector does not leave the agency at all, but changes his alias. This is not a difficult task since most bill collectors, if not all, have between one to five aliases. Agencies are not going to let the profitable employees go.

Each bill collector tries to outdo the other. It is a sick game. But the real sickness is not only that the sleazier the collector the more respected he is in the office. Even worse, collector's brutality is financially rewarded. This is an industry that attracts social misfits and even perhaps sociopaths. Quite a few members of the industry are ex-convicts themselves.

After repeated phone calls, the consumer at a certain point realizes that the nightmare will not go away, that the bill collector will not ever give up. Like a hunter, collectors are trained to know what the hysterical crying on the other end means. It is at that point the collectors know the consumers are totally helpless and totally submissive to all demands and threats. It is at that very moment that the speaker phone is cut on for our peers to hear. They cheer while he is on. It becomes a feeding frenzy, each collector trying to outdo the other to show how mean he can be. It is a badge of honor to get someone to cry and put it on the speakerphone, whether they are men, women, or children; management and/or owners of agencies participate in this outrageous, sadistic behavior on occasion. * * *

I must admit, while I was working I had scores of consumers on the phone saying they would file charges with the FTC or the attorney general's office. And they also talked to my managers. My coworkers and managers would lie for me. In fact. our managers knew we were working hard if we got an occasional FTC or attorney general or even a verbal consumer complaint. The one or two written complaints I received were lied about. Management already did. My computer screen and my files which were constantly doctored clearly showed I never did anything wrong. Yet. with all the conversations I have had, which is at least a quarter of a million and all the unbelievable conduct I have witnessed, you would be surprised at the number of complaints concerning misbehavior.

Members of the subcommittee, to the best of my recollection, there was only one or two written complaints lodged against me. These were complaints filed with the attorney general of the State of Texas. The Federal Trade Commission to my best knowledge, never received a compliant about me. If they did, I was never told. * * *

One of the biggest myths projected to government or the public is that people who don't pay their bills are deadbeats. Approximately 96% to 98% of consumers truly want to pay their bills. Every consumer tries to work out something with their collector, some form of payment by the month. This is not profitable for the collector or the agency. Collectors are only interested in immediate payment in full. In reality only two to four percent of the industry's accounts are deadbeats. The only true deadbeats are credit card thieves, who knowingly give false information on every aspect of their-credit application and run up charges with the intent of skipping out on such charges. It could take as long as a week or months, if ever, to find these true 'deadbeats.' Therefore it is more advantageous to call consumers who have provided correct information and collect from them in five minutes. * * *

2. UNDERSTANDING DEBTOR DEFAULT

Law students tend to get a somewhat jaded view of reality. In law school courses, by studying appellate cases, we tend to concentrate on transactions that have broken down. It is easy to forget that most transactions do not break down, and most of the time lawyers are not needed at all. This is as true in the consumer credit area as any other area. Almost all consumers pay their debts on time. According to Federal Reserve Board data, as of the first quarter of 2005, fewer than three percent of consumer loans from federally-chartered commercial banks were in default. See http://www.federalreserve.gov/releases/chargeoff/delallsa.htm. Similarly, a relatively recent report about credit card debt states that 87% of American consumers pay their credit card bills promptly. Paul Bannister, *25 Fascinating Facts About Personal Debt,* Bankrate.com, available at http://www.bankrate.com/brm/news/debt/debt guide2004/debt-trivial.asp (Sept. 20, 2004).

This chapter, though, focuses on the small minority of consumers whose debts go into collection—something that about 11% of Americans will experience with respect to credit card debt at some point in their lives, according to the Bannister article cited just above. The question of why and under what circumstances that happens is a fascinating issue that also has public policy implications: for example, if most debtors willfully fail to pay debts, the law might give debt collectors more latitude to engage in the practices described above, but if defaults are generally seen as beyond consumers' control, the law might impose greater restraints on collectors. The answer to that question, unfortunately, is less clear than we might like. An extensive study conducted over thirty years ago found that most serious consumer defaults were caused by factors that should earn defaulting debtors pity, rather than abuse. See David Caplovitz, Consumers in Trouble: A Study of Debtors in Default (1974). Thus, nearly half of the debtors in the study had experienced a loss of income, often because of a job loss. Another group defaulted because of illness while still others attributed their defaults to marital problems. About a fifth of the defaulting debtors cited creditor fraud as a reason. But Caplovitz later concluded that the reasons for defaults had changed. In 1974, he had found that a quarter of those defaulting did so because they had assumed more debt than they could pay off; by 1989, in Caplovitz's view, this group made up an "overwhelming majority" of defaulting debtors. Caplovitz blamed both "credit card junkies," as he called them, and the banks that had lent to them for the defaults. See David Caplovitz, Credit Card Mania in America and Personal Bankruptcy, Paper for Conference on Unemployment and Consumer Debts in Europe (Hamburg, 1989).

Not all investigators agree with Caplovitz' later theories on the source of consumer credit problems:

T. SULLIVAN, E. WARREN, & J. WESTBROOK, AS WE FORGIVE OUR DEBTORS

187–88, 332 (Oxford, 1989).*

We were unsuccessful in our efforts to predict credit and debt using indicators such as income, prestige, job tenure, chapter, and joint filing for our various "junkie" groups. For example, although we know from Table 10.2 that job tenure varies among these groups, it was not a significant predictor of credit card debt. While we can identify small numbers of debtors who are heavily burdened with debt, we conclude that in many respects they resemble the other debtors.

* * * Credit card debt is a substantial portion of what typical, wage-earning consumers carry into bankruptcy, but its impact is different from what we had anticipated. The stereotypical debtors with a special weakness for credit card debts are represented, but their number is small. Out of 1202 cases, we could find only 23 debtors (less than 2%) who met all three criteria indicating abuse: high credit card debt/income ratio, high proportion of unsecured debt in credit cards, and in the top 15% of the absolute amount of credit card debt carried into bankruptcy. Other potential abusers do not meet these criteria, although they might on some normative scales be abusers in every sense of the word. On the other hand, even among the 23 debtors, including the Voelkers and Tony Allegro, there might be debtors whose tales would make us pause before we branded them abusers.

Even when we use a broader classification of abuse, looking at debtors who meet only one or two of the tests, the data in the files introduce ambiguities. A large fraction of the debtors with staggering debt/income ratios had serious income interruptions during the years before bankruptcy, suggesting that a downturn in income rather than an upswing in discretionary spending accounted for their financial circumstances. But an almost equal number of debtors with high debt/income ratios had stable incomes; they had amassed huge credit card debts on the basis of incomes far too low to repay them.

* * *

The analysis of credit card debt, for example, reveals a substantial group (about 15% of the wage earners) who owe more than half a year's income in credit card debt alone. These cases break down into two parts: those who ran up huge debts compared to existing income and those for whom income dropped or was interrupted, making their debts insupportable.

The cases in which a debtor had stable income and managed to amass credit card debts in excess of half a year's income surely represent some clear abuses. But any fingerpointing has to go both ways. Credit card issuers were willing to give out the fifth, sixth, or seventh bank card and to approve charges after debtors already owed short-term debt so large that they could not possibly pay the interest, much less the principal. * * *

Notes

1. In a later study, Sullivan, Warren and Westbrook asked debtors in bankruptcy to provide the reasons for their bankruptcy. Two-thirds identified job issues as a reason; more than a fifth mentioned family troubles; and nearly a fifth described medical problems. Teresa A. Sullivan, Elizabeth Warren & Jay Lawrence Westbrook, The Fragile Middle Class; Americans in Debt 15 16 (2000). See also Elizabeth Warren & Amelia Warren Tyagi, The Two Income Trap 81 (2003) ("Nearly nine out of ten families with children cite just three reasons for their bankruptcies: job loss, family breakup, and medical problems. All the other reasons combined—acts of God, called up for military service, personal profligacy, and so on—account for just 13 percent of families in bankruptcy."); Ian Domowitz & Robert L. Sartain, Determinants of the Consumer Bankruptcy Decision, 54 J. Finance 403, 404 (1999) (health problems are the "most important factor in assessing the impact of household conditions" while "the largest single contribution to bankruptcy at the margin is credit card debt relative to income."). Do consumer misperceptions, credit card marketing or fee structures contribute to defaults? See Jason J. Kilborn, Behavioral Economics, Overindebtedness & Comparative Consumer Bankruptcy: Searching for Causes and Evaluating Solutions, 22 Emory Bankr. Dev. J. 13 (2005) (suggesting that people become overextended because they are overconfident about their ability to repay debts, underestimate the risk of borrowing too much, overvalue immediate gratification, and heavily discount future costs); Oren Bar–Gill, Seduction by Plastic, 98 Nw. U. L. Rev. 1373 (2004); Creola Johnson, Maxed Out College Students: A Call to Limit Credit Card Solicitations on College Campuses, 8 N.Y.U. J. Legis. & Pub. Pol'y 191 (2005). A very different reason for why people file for bankruptcy was offered in the testimony of Kenneth H. Beine, President, Shoreline Credit Union appearing on behalf of the Credit Union National Assoc. before the Senate Judiciary Comm. in Hearings on S.256,

the Bankruptcy Abuse Prevention and Consumer Protection Act of 2005 (Feb. 10, 2005):

> In one case, a couple in their mid-twenties decided that they wanted a "clean slate" prior to getting married. They ran up credit card purchases. One prepaid on an auto loan with us to have the cosigner released. (Both were employed full-time.) They both then filed for Chapter 7. My credit union's share of their version of financial planning was a write-off of almost $3,000 in credit card debt plus another couple of hundred dollars on the disposal of the auto.

2. The studies described in note one focus on those who file for a discharge of debts in bankruptcy. By contrast, Caplovitz's work dealt with those who merely default on one or more credit obligations, and who may have been considered sufficiently judgmentworthy to be worth suing. The latter is a very different group of people, and a group that is more relevant to any analysis of debt collection efforts. (From a creditor's point of view, it is the difference between a car with one or more flat tires and one which is "totalled."). Your authors have been unable to find any serious attempts to update the original Caplovitz study since 1974 so we are compelled either to continue to use those findings or to replace them with speculations and anecdotal data.

SECTION B.   CONTROLS ON COLLECTION ABUSES UNDER THE COMMON LAW AND THE FAIR DEBT COLLECTION PRACTICES ACT

Prefatory Note

The law of debt collection is found in a variety of sources. In 1977, Congress enacted the Fair Debt Collection Practices Act (FDCPA), codified as Title VIII of the Consumer Credit Protection Act (CCPA), 15 U.S.C. § 1692 et seq., and appearing in the Statutory Supplement. The FDCPA imposes a number of restrictions on debt collectors. Three of its sections forbid inappropriate debt collection in broad terms and then list more specific prohibitions. Thus, § 1692d bars harassing, oppressive and abusive conduct, and provides instances of such conduct in six subparagraphs; § 1692e proscribes false, deceptive, or misleading representations in debt collection, and then contains 16 subparagraphs listing examples of false representations; and § 1692f forbids any unfair or unconscionable means to collect debts and itemizes prohibited practices in eight subparagraphs. Each section explicitly provides that the list of outlawed practices is not exhaustive. The statute, in § 1692g, also requires debt collectors to offer to validate the debt, a topic that will be explored in Section C, below. Finally, the FDCPA limits debt collection communications in §§ 1692b and 1692c.

Despite its broad protections for consumer-debtors, the FDCPA is subject to a significant limit: it generally applies only to third party collectors, and governs collection efforts by the original creditors only in rare situations. In other words, collection tactics by original lenders are largely unaffected by this statute. Thus, the FDCPA probably affects only a small portion—perhaps 10%—of collection activity. Nevertheless, the FDCPA merits your careful attention for two reasons. First, even a small portion of collection activity represents an enormous amount; though precise figures are hard to come by, consultant Kaulkin Ginsberg Co. estimated that external debt collectors handled $135 billion of debt in the year 2000, David Milstead, Making Good on Bad Debt: Golden–Based Narex Uses Computer Models to Improve Collections, Denver Rocky Mountain News, May 20, 2002 at 6B, while a debt collector trade association representative put the 1999 figure at more than $216 billion with approximately $30.4 billion recovered. Statement of Rozanne M. Andersen, General Counsel and Senior Vice President, Legal and Governmental Affairs, ACA International, Before the U.S. House of Rep., Com. on Ways and Means, Subcom. on Oversight (May 13, 2003). The FTC receives more complaints about third-party debt collectors than about any other industry. See Federal Trade Commission, Annual Report 2004: Fair Debt Collection Practices Act 3 (2004) (hereinafter 2004 FTC Report). Second, as will be discussed below, the FDCPA applies to many of the attorneys who collect debts on behalf of their clients. The FDCPA contains numerous easily violated technical rules, as more than a few lawyers have discovered to their regret. In short, the FDCPA is both a trap for collection attorneys and a help for consumer attorneys and their clients.

Debt collection efforts that do not fall within the purview of the FDCPA may nonetheless violate other rules. The Federal Trade Commission may use its powers under the Federal Trade Commission Act to proceed against debt collectors. But most regulation of internal debt collection activities occurs at the state level. Many states have enacted their own debt collection statutes. A list may be found in Appendix 13A of Dee Pridgen, Consumer Credit and the Law (2006). Some states that lack debt collection statutes have applied little FTC acts to the debt collection context. See, e.g., State ex rel. Miller v. Midwest Service Bureau of Topeka, Inc., 229 Kan. 322, 623 P.2d 1343 (1981). In addition, common law tort claims may offer aid to distressed debtors. As the following cases show, different causes of action are available in different states. Is there any similarity in the analyses of the courts, even though different causes of action are involved? Any similarity in criteria used?

Problem 8–1

Your client, Daniel Default, bought goods from Charlie Cheerful using Charlie's private label credit card. There has been a dispute about the quality of the goods and whether Charlie should repair or replace them under the warranty; meanwhile, Dan has refused to make the payments called for in the credit card agreement. Yesterday, Charlie tried to telephone Dan at work, but the call was routed to the personnel manager of Dan's employer. The personnel manager stated that it was their normal policy not to allow personal telephone calls to employees during working hours. Charlie explained that he had tried to call Dan at home unsuccessfully, and that it was "necessary to contact Mr. Default at work to clear up an outstanding account." When the personnel manager still refused to permit the call to go through, Charlie called Dan a "deadbeat" and expressed the hope that the employer would discharge Dan if the debt was not paid.

(a) The employer did not in fact discharge Dan, but relations with his superiors at work "feel strained." Does Dan have a successful cause of action either for damages or to restrain such future conduct? Does it matter whether there was in fact a breach of warranty? See Jones v. U.S. Child Support Recovery, *infra*; Harrison v. Humble Oil & Refining Co., 264 F.Supp. 89 (D.S.C. 1967).

(b) Would your answers change if Charlie were collecting a debt owed to a third party? See FDCPA § 1692c.

JONES v. U.S. CHILD SUPPORT RECOVERY

United States District Court, District of Utah, 1997.
961 F.Supp. 1518.

BENSON, District Judge.

This matter is before the court on defendants United States Child Support Recovery's and Zandra L. Perkins' (collectively "Defendants") motion for summary judgment on Plaintiff Kathleen Francis Jones' third, and only remaining, cause of action, invasion of privacy. * * *

BACKGROUND

In 1993 Plaintiff and Clyde David Fritch divorced by a Decree of Divorce ("Decree") issued by the Superior Court of California. Under the Decree, Mr. Fritch was awarded primary physical custody of John Lawrence Fritch, the natural son of Plaintiff and Mr. Fritch. Plaintiff was ordered to pay $468.00 per month in child support. A short time later, after the Plaintiff had missed approximately three payments, Mr. Fritch retained Defendants to collect the child support.

On November 17, 1993 Defendants wrote Plaintiff informing her that she was $1,285.00 in arrears and requesting payment. In response, Plaintiff admitted her delinquency and asked Defendants for the opportunity to make payments on her child support debt. Defendants denied the request and demanded payment in full. A series of contacts and telephone calls ensued in the following weeks.

Plaintiff allegedly became very upset and emotionally distraught because of the words and tone of Defendants' proddings to pay the money. For example, in telephone messages left for Plaintiff, Defendants' statements included the following:

Kathleen, what kind of mother are you? ... [A] real mother would bend over backward to see that the child was supported.... It, it just appalls me.... How do you look at yourself in the mirror.... We work with literally thousands of people and I've never worked with a mother, and I use that term loosely, like you.... Very sad. You're a pitiful mother.

. . . .

Well, Kathleen, Christmas is here. Your son is still, uh, waiting for his child support. You're out, uh, spending it on who knows what. Definitely not him. I, uh, would think that that would spoil, uh, most real mother's Christmas, but, uh, I don't know that it bothers you too much.... Really a sad situation when we come across a, uh, mother like you, Kathleen.... Why don't you start acting like a mother and get your child support paid.

After repeated telephone messages and conversations failed to achieve the desired result, Defendants escalated their efforts by sending a "Wanted" poster to Plaintiff's employer, Silicon Systems; the Plaintiff's mother, Geraldine McQuaid; and the Plaintiff's siblings, Donna Prudence and Larry McQuaid. The poster referred to Plaintiff as a "Dead Beat Parent" with a "well-paying job" whose "own flesh and blood" "wishes his mother cared about him to send the child support which the court ordered her to contribute for his care."

DISCUSSION

As an initial matter, the court addresses the tort of publicity given to private life. The elements of this tort are 1) publicity; 2) disclosure of private facts (considered highly offensive to the reasonable person); 3) absence of waiver or privilege; 4) emotional distress and embarrassment or shame and humiliation; and 5) the disclosure is not a matter of legitimate public concern. Restatement (Second) of Torts § 652D. "Publicity," unlike the element of "publication" in a defamation case, requires that the information disclosed has or is substantially likely to become general knowledge to the public at large. * * * Examples would include newspapers, magazines, handbills to a large number of people or a statement made to a large audience. Restatement (Second) of Torts § 652D cmt. a.

In this case, although the Defendants threatened to disseminate the Wanted poster to the public at large, in fact the poster was only delivered to Plaintiff's employer and a few close relatives. This distribution of private information to a handful of people is insufficient to meet the element of publicity required for this tort. The court grants Defendants' motion for summary judgment as to the claim of publicity given to private matters.

The tort of intrusion upon seclusion is slightly different than the tort of publicity given to private matters. "To establish an invasion of privacy claim of intrusion upon seclusion, a complaining party must prove by a preponderance of the evidence that an intentional substantial intrusion, physically or otherwise, upon the solitude or seclusion of the complaining party ... would be highly offensive to the reasonable person." *Turner v. General Adjustment Bureau. Inc.,* 832 P.2d 62, 67 (Utah.Ct.App.1992) (citing Restatement (Second) of Torts § 652B & cmt.

d). The question in the instant case is whether the Defendants' actions substantially intruded upon Plaintiff's private life in a way that would be highly offensive to the reasonable person. The Restatement defines this tort as follows:

> § 652B.　　Intrusion upon Seclusion
>
> One who intentionally intrudes, physically or otherwise, upon the solitude or seclusion of another or his private affairs or concerns, is subject to liability to the other for invasion of his privacy, if the intrusion would be highly offensive to a reasonable person.

Restatement (Second) of Torts § 652B. Comment a explains:

> The form of invasion of privacy covered by this Section does not depend upon any publicity given to the person whose interest is invaded or to his affairs. It consists solely of an intentional interference with his interest in solitude or seclusion, either as to his person or as to his private affairs or concerns, of a kind that would be highly offensive to a reasonable man.

Comment d states:

> There is likewise no liability unless the interference with the plaintiff's seclusion is a substantial one, of a kind that would be highly offensive to the ordinary reasonable man, as the result of conduct to which the reasonable man would strongly object. Thus there is no liability for knocking at the plaintiff's door, or calling him to the telephone on one occasion or even two or three, to demand payment of a debt. It is only when the telephone calls are repeated with such persistence and frequency as to amount to a course of hounding the plaintiff, that becomes a substantial burden to his existence, that his privacy is invaded.

The court must view both the nature (quality) as well as the pattern (quantity) of the Defendants' actions. *Household Finance Corp. v. Bridge,* 252 Md. 531, 250 A.2d 878, 884 (1969) ("the communication, if not of such frequency as to constitute harassment, has been of such a nature as to possess a vicious quality"). In both *Trammell v. Citizens News Co., Inc.,* 285 Ky. 529, 148 S.W.2d 708 (1941), and *Norris v. Moskin Stores. Inc.,* 272 Ala. 174, 132 So.2d 321 (Ala.1961), the courts found that the nature (not the pattern) of the creditor's actions was so unreasonable, that a claim of invasion of privacy (i.e. intrusion upon seclusion) was warranted. At other times the court makes the same determination by looking at the overall pattern (not the nature) of the defendant's actions. *Household Finance,* 250 A.2d at 885; *Rugg v. McCarty,* 173 Colo. 170, 476 P.2d 753, 755 (1970); *see also Lewis v. Physicians and Dentists Credit Bureau. Inc.,* 27 Wash.2d 267, 177 P.2d 896, 899 (1947) ("A creditor or an assignee has a right to urge payment of a just debt, and to threaten to resort to proper legal procedure to enforce such payment."). In cases of debt collection, courts may also focus on plaintiff's behavior toward the debt collector. *See Munley v. ISC Financial House Inc.,* 584 P.2d 1336, 1340 (Okla.1978) (creditors are allowed more intrusive activity when a debtor refuses to communicate with them).

In the instant case, Plaintiff asserts that not only is the "Wanted" Poster by itself highly offensive to the reasonable person and substantially intrusive into her private life, but also that the overall actions and repeated phone calls of the Defendants were highly offensive as well. Because this case originates out of Defendants' efforts to collect a debt, the court finds the Supreme Court of Alabama's language applicable:

> The mere efforts of a creditor ... to collect a debt cannot without more be considered a wrongful and actionable intrusion. A creditor has and must have the right to take reasonable action to pursue his debtor and collect his debt. But the right to pursue the debtor is not a license to outrage the debtor. *Norris,* 132 So.2d at 323 (three telephone calls suggesting an illicit relationship with the debtor to members of the debtor's family constituted actionable invasion of the debtor's right of privacy).

In view of the content of these telephone calls, messages, and "Wanted" poster, the court holds that a jury could reasonably find that Defendants' actions invaded the solitude and private life of the Plaintiff in a manner that would be highly offensive to a reasonable person. * * *

The final issue is whether Plaintiff can maintain a cause of action for intrusion upon seclusion without alleging and proving special damages. * * * In general, however, courts appear to uniformly recognize that there is no specific standard for measuring damages of personal injury claims and that the jury is particularly well-suited for this type of case-by-case determination. More specifically, the Utah Court of Appeals quoted with approval, "The fact that damages resulting from an invasion of the right of privacy cannot be measured by a pecuniary standard is not a bar to recovery." *Turner,* 832 P.2d at 67 n. 6 (quoting *Fairfield,* 291 P.2d at 198). *Turner* further noted that "[o]nce a party establishes a cause of action for invasion of privacy, that party recovers for mental distress damages proved, if such damages are the kind that normally result from such an invasion." *Id.* (quoting Restatement (Second) of Torts § 652H(b)). * * * In light of the above cases, the Restatement, and general agreement among authorities that proof of special damages is not required for an invasion of privacy claim, the court concludes that Plaintiff's failure to allege special damages is not fatal to her invasion of privacy claim.

Defendants nevertheless contend that (1) Plaintiff should not be allowed to collect damages in her invasion of privacy claim without providing proof of damages as the court required in Plaintiff's intentional infliction of emotional distress claim; and (2) leaving a decision to the jury without proof of damages opens the door to an arbitrary award of damages. Neither contention is persuasive.

An intentional infliction of emotional distress claim requires a different standard of proof than an invasion of privacy claim. An intentional infliction of emotional distress claim requires evidence of "an actual and proximate causal link between the tortious conduct and the emotional distress." *White v. Blackburn,* 787 P.2d 1315, 1317 (Utah App.1990). This is because the tort has not been committed unless emotional distress has in fact occurred. Conversely, an invasion of privacy tort occurs when a person's privacy is invaded in a manner that "would be highly offensive to the ordinary man," regardless of actual emotional distress. *Machleder v. Diaz,* 618 F.Supp. 1367, 1370–71 (D.C.N.Y., 1985), *aff'd in part. rev'd on other grounds,* 801 F.2d 46 (2d Cir.1986); *See Gonzales,* 555 S.W.2d at 221–222 ("Damages for mental suffering are recoverable without the necessity of showing actual physical injury in a case of willful invasion of the right of privacy.").

Second, there is a pragmatic reason for the differing standards between the two torts. Intentional infliction of emotional distress is designed to compensate individuals who suffer damages due to the intentional acts of another. The proof of actual damages is therefore necessary to establish that the infliction actually caused a cognizable injury. Invasion of privacy, on the other hand, is intended to prevent invasions into the private matters of individuals' lives. The Restatement states:

> a. A cause of action for invasion of privacy, in any of its four forms, entitles the plaintiff to recover damages for the harm to the particular element of his privacy that is invaded. Thus one who suffers an intrusion upon his solitude or seclusion, under § 652B, may recover damages for the deprivation of his seclusion....
>
> b. The plaintiff may also recover damages for emotional distress or personal humiliation that he proves to have been actually suffered by him, if it is of a kind that normally results from such an invasion and it is normal and reasonable in its extent....

Restatement (Second) of Torts § 652H cmt. a-b.

Based on the evidence presented, the court holds that (1) there are genuine issues of material fact to be considered by the jury in determining whether Defendants' actions were substantially intrusive and highly offensive; (2) Defendants are not entitled to a public record defense; and (3) Plaintiff can maintain a cause of action for intrusion upon seclusion without alleging and proving special damages.

CONCLUSION

For the reasons set forth above, IT IS HEREBY ORDERED that Defendant's Motion for Summary Judgment is GRANTED as to Plaintiff's publicity given to private matters claim and DENIED as to Plaintiff's intrusion upon seclusion claim.

Notes

1. In Pachowitz v. Ledoux, 265 Wis.2d 631, 648, 666 N.W.2d 88 (App. 2003), the court held that the publicity element of an invasion of privacy claim can be satisfied by disclosure of private information to one person or to

a small group depending "upon the particular facts of the case and the nature of plaintiff's relationship to the audience who received the information."

2. Another invasion of privacy tort that is sometimes helpful in debt collection cases is the false light tort. Would a claim under that theory have succeeded in *Jones*?

Problem 8–2

(a) Your client, Ed Easy, also bought goods (including a crib and other baby furniture for his newborn child) from Charlie Cheerful on Charlie's private label credit card, and has not made any payments since six months ago. At that time Ed became unemployed. During that six months Charlie has called Ed about two or three times a week. The calls may come at any time from 9 A.M. to 11 P.M.

When the calls began, Ed explained that he was unemployed and had no extra funds with which to make payments. Charlie advised him to cut back further his standard of living so as to have funds left over from his unemployment check with which to make payments. When Ed refused to do this, Charlie called him a "cheat" and a "deadbeat" and said he "was just trying to beat his bills." Later, when Ed pleaded again that his unemployment was the real problem, Charlie suggested that he was not trying hard enough. "If you can't get a job, I can get one for you—digging ditches." Ed then stated that he was disabled, and could not dig ditches. Charlie replied that he thought Ed was "lying;" and even if he was not, he could find a job if he really tried.

Since then, the level of dialogue has gone downhill. Ed describes their content as mostly descriptions of new employment opportunities (none of them suitable for Ed) and Charlie's references to how Ed's credit rating will be destroyed and how the furniture will be repossessed (Charlie has a security interest in it). Three weeks ago Charlie told Ed that he was giving Ed 48 hours to pay the debt and that if Ed didn't, Charlie would proceed with any necessary lawful action. Two weeks ago Ed received a pamphlet in the mail—"How to Prepare Your Furniture for Repossession." Ed describes Charlie's tone of voice as "very rough" and his language as "obnoxious" and "nasty." Does Ed have a successful cause of action either for damages or to restrain such conduct in the future? Cf. Houston–American Life Ins. Co. v. Tate, 358 S.W.2d 645 (Tex.Civ.App. 1962). Would Charlie be protected from either the damage award or the injunction by the First Amendment materials in Chapter 1?

Would it matter whether Ed had a defense to payment—such as breach of warranty? In other words, is a creditor with a legitimate debt privileged to be more obnoxious than a creditor with a clouded or disputed claim? See Keele v. Wexler, 149 F.3d 589, 594 (7th Cir. 1998).

Should it matter whether Ed suffers only mental anguish from Charlie's conduct, or also suffers physical injury? The Texas Courts wrestled with this problem over a long period of time while developing the tort of "unreasonable collection practices." See Harned v. E–Z Finance Co., 151 Tex. 641, 254 S.W.2d 81 (1953); Wright v. E–Z Finance

Co., 267 S.W.2d 602 (Tex.Civ.App.1954). If such a dichotomy were insisted upon how would headaches or loss of sleep be classified?

(b) Would your answers change if Charlie were a debt collector collecting a debt owed to a third party? See FDCPA §§ 1692c, 1692d; 1692e, respectively; Clomon v. Jackson *infra*. What advice would you give Ed to stop Charlie's calls?

Problem 8–3

Sally Consumer owned a small dog, Rover, which was injured when it was struck by a car. She took Rover to Dr. Zorba, a local veterinarian, and Rover recovered while in the doctor's care. Dr. Zorba was fussy about his fees, however, and he demanded cash before he would release Rover. Sally offered to work out a payment schedule, but Zorba refused. Instead, he threatened to "do away with your dog" unless he got cash. Has he committed a tort?

CAPUTO v. PROFESSIONAL RECOVERY SERVICES, INC.

United States District Court, District of Kansas, 2003.
261 F.Supp.2d 1249.

CROW, SENIOR DISTRICT JUDGE.

The case comes before the court on the defendants' motion for summary judgment on plaintiff's claim[of] outrage. * * *

The plaintiff Michael D. Caputo filed this action against the defendant John P. Marzulli, a debt collector, and the defendant Professional Recovery Services, Inc. ("PRS"), the collection agency employing Marzulli, alleging * * *the state law torts of fraud and outrage. These claims arise entirely from one telephone message and four subsequent telephone conversations occurring in January and February of 2000. These calls were made concerning the defendants' efforts to collect on a credit card debt incurred by Caputo when he purchased a Honda tractor mower sometime before 1996. * * *

[The court quoted a transcript of the parties' taped conversations:]

Mr. Santos ("Marzulli"): ... And I'm talking about every creditor that you show in a credit report, how are you going to sit in front of a judge and explain to a judge that there was income due to you being a disabled vet. (pp. 7–8).

Mr. Santos: ... And basically a judge is not going to listen to the fact of you know, your disabled, correct. "Okay? There's income coming in." (p. 9).

Mr. Santos: Because if you're disabled, you're taking clients' money without any intention of repaying it back it's a federal offense.

Mr. Caputo: Well, then get me on it. All right?

Mr. Santos: Michael—

Mr. Caputo: You're threatening me, and I don't like it.

Mr. Santos: Michael, you've got 24 hours to have your attorney's name and number who is going to represent you. If not, we'll go ahead and recommend it to you in court. Do you understand me, Mike?

Mr. Caputo: Well, you know—

Mr. Santos: You want to play hardball, we can play hardball here in my firm.

Mr. Caputo: Sure.

Mr. Santos: Okay? But don't act like it's fine and dandy when you just stole $3,500 from my client's money with no intention of repaying it back.

Mr. Caputo: How are you saying I stole this because I was disabled?

Mr. Santos: Mike, you have no intentions, read the law book, Mike. You have willfully defrauded my clients a federal offense. You understand that?

Mr. Caputo: And how so?

Mr. Santos: How so, because haven't paid a dime for it, Mike. Neither have done to the other creditors, and a judge is going to see that. I'll make sure he sees it. Okay?

Mr. Caputo: Uh-huh.

Mr. Santos: You're not going to pay a dime to this account? I will make sure, okay, that we do an active litigation research we'll place a lien on everything you got. You understand me?

Mr. Caputo: Well, you said you've already done that.

Mr. Santos: I didn't say we did it, we're going to. And I'll make sure I send off your case tonight. You've got 24 hours to contact me for your audit tomorrow, Mike.

Mr. Caputo: Well, that doesn't make sense. Hello? Hello? (pp. 11–13). * * *

INTENTIONAL INFLICTION OF EMOTIONAL DISTRESS

To establish a claim of intentional infliction of emotional distress under Kansas law, a plaintiff must demonstrate four elements: (1) the conduct of defendant must be intentional or in reckless disregard of plaintiff; (2) the conduct must be extreme and outrageous; (3) there must be a causal connection between defendant's conduct and plaintiff's mental distress; and (4) plaintiff's mental distress must be extreme and severe. Conduct is not extreme and outrageous unless a civilized society would regard it as exceeding the bounds of decency or utterly intolerable. " 'The classic test is that liability may be found to exist when the recitation of the facts to an average citizen would arouse resentment against the actor and lead that citizen to spontaneously exclaim, Outrageous!' " *Mai v. Williams Indus., Inc.*, 899 F.Supp. 536, 542 (D.Kan.

1995) (quoting *Fusaro v. First Family Mortgage Corp., Inc.*, 257 Kan. 794, 805, 897 P.2d 123, 131 (1995)). Liability also depends on clearing two threshold determinations by the court that "the defendant's conduct may reasonably be regarded as so extreme and outrageous as to permit recovery; and . . . [that] the emotional distress suffered by plaintiff is in such extreme degree the law must intervene because the distress inflicted is so severe that no reasonable person should be expected to endure it." *Roberts v. Saylor*, 230 Kan. 289, 292–93, 637 P.2d 1175 (1981).

The Kansas Supreme Court has recognized that a "debtor impliedly consents for the creditor to take reasonable steps to pursue payment even though it may result in actual, though not actionable, invasion of privacy" and that creditors "must be given some latitude to pursue reasonable methods of collecting debts even though such methods often might result in some inconvenience or embarrassment to the debtor." *Dawson v. Associates Financial Services Co.*, 215 Kan. 814, 820, 821, 529 P.2d 104 (1974). "Nonetheless, methods of collecting debts which might be reasonable in some circumstances, might also be regarded as outrageous in others where it is known that the debtor is particularly susceptible to emotional distress due to a disease such as multiple sclerosis." 215 Kan. at 825, 529 P.2d 104. The Kansas Supreme Court in *Dawson* was persuaded that this tort should extend to debtor/creditor relationships when the creditor engages in extreme and outrageous conduct that a reasonable person would consider highly offensive and that causes severe emotional distress to the debtor.

Looking at the substance of the first two telephone calls and construing them in the light most favorable to the plaintiff, the court believes that a reasonable person could conclude that Mr. Marzulli's comments exceeded the bounds of decency and were utterly intolerable. Early in the first telephone call, Mr. Marzulli referred to the income that the plaintiff was receiving as disabled veteran and remarked that a judge would require him to explain how that income was being spent without considering his disability. Also in the first call, Mr. Marzulli spoke of the plaintiff's situation as implicating criminal conduct and charges:

> And secondly, I don't know if you know what the charge of upping in the State of Kansas it is willfully defrauding my client, which is called stealing, a federal offense-O.K. (p. 8). * * *

In the second telephone call when the plaintiff asked Mr. Marzulli about the fraud charges, Mr. Marzulli did not clear up any confusion about his statements but rather said, "Well, that were the charges that the attorneys wanted to go and proceed." *Id.* at 17. When the plaintiff asked if the attorneys were still talking about fraud charges, Mr. Marzulli answered, "Well, here's-I had spoken to the attorneys today. If you initially were between $3 and $400. We can get you out of the legal fee. If not, we have no other choice but go ahead and recommend you for summons." *Id.* at 18. Later, the conversation became more heated:

> **Mr. Caputo**: I have never committed fraud in my life. So if your attorneys want to do that because I can't talk to my attorney in their time schedule go, do.
>
> **Mr. Santos ("Marzulli")**: You've got federal taxes and state tax liens, Mike. You're a habitual debtor, Mike.
>
> **Mr. Caputo**: Do it.
>
> **Mr. Santos**: Why don't you take responsibility and be a man to try to get these things resolved?
>
> **Mr. Caputo**: Are you telling me I'm not a man?
>
> **Mr. Santos**: I'm telling you to resolve your debts, Mike, in accordance of your state.
>
> **Mr. Caputo**: Well, you made a comment.
>
> **Mr. Santos**: I made a comment. Yes, I did. I took-you know, if you want to be an adult and a responsibility of the legal and binding contract that you signed with every creditor out there, Mike, okay? Because, I'll make sure that every other creditor gets and knows that you will be recommended and be taken to court. If they want to do it also, then guess what, Mike? You'll have about 10 charge-offs on your account, No. 1, and you're going to have 10 civil judgments against you. You want to go that route, we can play hardball here.

Id. at pp. 27–28. Accusing the debtor of federal offenses, impliedly threatening to initiate criminal charges, personally attacking the debtor's manhood and maturity, threatening lawsuits and liens on all property, and threatening to tell all other creditors about his situation, all of which was said during two telephone calls, exceed the bounds of reasonable debt collection methods and could reasonably be termed extreme and outrageous conduct in the context of this case. As reflected in the conversations, Marzulli understood and assumed that the plaintiff was a disabled veteran whose only apparent source of income was disability benefits. While Marzulli may not have known or chose not to learn the nature of the plaintiff's disability, he should have known it was so serious as to preclude the [plaintiff] from working and to entitle the plaintiff to benefits. In addition, Marzulli attempted to exploit the plaintiff's disability by using it as a premise to his accusation that the plaintiff criminally defrauded his client and by chiding the plaintiff that his disability would not protect him in court. An average citizen hearing of these facts could be aroused to exclaim, Outrageous!

The plaintiff has retained the services of a psychologist who will testify that these threatening collection calls caused a marked reaction and deterioration in the plaintiff because he is "psychologically vulnerable and fragile." (Dk. 107, Herbert Shriver Dep. Ex. 1, p. 6). Subjectively, the plaintiff's "personal security has been threatened; resulting in increased isolation, depression, regression to a pre-treatment status." *Id.* The psychologist points to the objective indicators in the medical record that substantiate this severe emotional distress: "increased therapy, self isolation (in the woods), planning his own death, subsequent change in medication as well as his psychologists' assessment of this patients regressed paranoid states following the altercation." *Id.* This expert witness opines that "[t]his situation has caused Mr. Caputo a significant amount of added and needless suffering." *Id.* Such evidence is sufficient to create a genuine issue of material fact as to whether the plaintiff suffered severe emotional distress as a result of these collection calls. This is not the proceeding for parsing the plaintiff's medical records, drawing inferences about the presence of other stressors in the plaintiff's life, comparing the effect of other stressors with the effect of the collection calls, and doubting that a reasonable person would consider the plaintiff's emotional distress to be severe. The defendants' efforts in this regard are not persuasive in showing they are entitled to summary judgment.

HAMILTON v. FORD MOTOR CREDIT CO.

Court of Special Appeals of Maryland, 1986.
66 Md.App. 46, 502 A.2d 1057.

BLOOM, JUDGE.

Ford Motor Credit Company (FMCC) repossessed a motor vehicle that had been purchased by Sharon Marie Hamilton and her mother, Verna Hamilton, and financed through an installment sales contract that was assigned to FMCC. Because of FMCC's conduct before and after repossessing the vehicle, a jury in the Circuit Court for Baltimore County awarded the Hamiltons verdicts totalling $64,757.20 against FMCC and one of its employees, Bernard Alaimo. Judge John F. Fader, II, who had presided over the trial, granted a judgment N.O.V. with respect to one of the Hamilton's claims, reducing the verdict total to $12,206.20. Both Sharon and Verna appealed. FMCC and Alaimo cross-appealed, contending that the remaining verdicts resulted from errors committed by the trial judge.

* * *

We reject all of the contentions of error made by appellants and cross-appellant and affirm the judgment of the circuit court.

FACTS

On November 27, 1979, Sharon Hamilton and her mother, Verna Hamilton, purchased a Ford Courier truck from Al Packer Ford in Baltimore City. They executed a Maryland Automobile Retail Installment contract, which Sharon signed as buyer and Verna signed as co-buyer. The truck was purchased for Sharon's use and was titled in her name. The total purchase price was $9095.36 with monthly payments of $165.32. The contract was immediately assigned to FMCC.

In late 1980 or early 1981 Sharon drove to Florida to visit friends and to investigate the possibilities of working or attending school there. She was involved in an accident; the truck was damaged, and she sustained fractures of cervical vertebrae. She returned to Baltimore in

March 1981, leaving the truck in Florida. Verna told an agent of FMCC about the accident and informed him that Sharon would be out of work for a while. FMCC granted the Hamiltons an extension of one month on the truck payments.

In the spring of 1981, the Hamiltons fell behind in their payments. Sharon was only working part time and largely on a volunteer basis, while Verna was devoting most of her time to caring for her husband, who had suffered a heart attack and a stroke in 1980 and was terminally ill, requiring not only the care of Verna, a trained nurse, but other family members, as well, to meet many of his basic needs. Verna and her husband received social security benefits.

FMCC representatives began calling Verna persistently to demand payment, although Verna contends that she repeatedly told them that Sharon was injured and unable to work, that her husband was ill, and that she was financially unable to make the payments. FMCC and Alaimo, however, contend that they did not learn of the condition of Verna's husband until sometime in September of 1981, shortly before the truck was repossessed.

Although various FMCC representatives telephoned Verna, the majority of the calls were made by appellee Bernard Alaimo, who had apparently been assigned the role of principal antagonist. All parties agree that Alaimo was rude and hostile to Verna when he called and that his rudeness and abruptness increased with time. He telephoned at all hours of the day and into the early evening, sometimes several times a week. After a while, he stopped introducing himself when Verna answered the phone and merely began his calls with a demand for payment. One of Verna's neighbors received several calls for Verna, though no messages were left. In the fall of 1981, Alaimo called one evening after 10:00 p.m., awakening Verna from a sound sleep. He shouted at her and, referring to Sharon's earlier assurances that she was seeking employment and would make payment soon, said, "How could you have raised such a liar? I'll be seeing you in court." On another occasion he threatened to ruin Verna's credit.

Verna's daughter Mary and another witness testified that Verna was visibly upset by these calls. Mary took a number of calls herself and once asked FMCC to stop calling because her father was ill and the calls would awaken him and upset Verna. Verna testified that she began to have considerable difficulty sleeping. She claimed that FMCC's persistence was the cause of that condition, but there was other evidence to the effect that for several years she had suffered urinary incontinence that caused her to get up several times each night. It is clear, nevertheless, that Verna was extremely agitated, as were other members of her family. She felt harassed and abused. * * *

The vehicle was finally repossessed in Florida on November 16, 1981. * * *

In February 1984, Sharon and her mother brought suit against FMCC and Alaimo in the Circuit Court for Baltimore County. * * * In

Count Five, Verna sued FMCC and Alaimo for intentional infliction of emotional distress* * * The jury found for Verna on her claim for intentional infliction of emotional distress, awarding her $1.00 in compensatory damages and $52,500.00 punitive damages against FMCC and $50.00 punitive damages against Alaimo.

Judge Fader subsequently granted defendants' motion for judgment N.O.V. as to the count for intentional infliction of emotional distress on the basis that plaintiffs had failed to present sufficient proof to justify recovery on that cause of action. * * *

The tort of intentional infliction of emotional distress has only recently found recognition in this State, initially by the Court of Appeals in *Harris v. Jones*, 281 Md. 560, 380 A.2d 611, *aff'g Jones v. Harris*, 35 Md.App. 556, 371 A.2d 1104 (1977). * * * *Harris*, adopting the reasoning of the Supreme Court of Virginia in *Womack v. Eldridge*, 215 Va. 338, 210 S.E.2d 145 (1974), held that there are "four elements which must coalesce to impose liability for intentional infliction of emotional distress * * * " Those elements are:

(1) The conduct must be intentional or reckless;

(2) The conduct must be extreme and outrageous;

(3) There must be a causal connection between the wrongful conduct and the emotional distress;

(4) The emotional distress must be severe.

* * *

The evidence which the Hamiltons presented consisted of a wide array of objectionable and harassing conduct. There were persistent phone calls, one allegedly late at night. There were repeated calls even after Verna insisted she did not know where the truck was and that she was in no financial condition to pay. There were threats to sue, threats to ruin the Hamiltons' credit, and threats to attach Verna's house and property. There were incorrect assertions that Florida law applied. There was Verna's already strained emotional state due to her husband's illness, Sharon's injuries, and her own difficulty in sleeping, all of which Verna contends appellees knew.

Yet even considering all of the evidence in the light most favorable to appellants, which we must do when reviewing the entry of a judgment notwithstanding the verdict, we conclude that the four elements set out in *Harris* were not met. We focus particularly on the second and fourth elements. The second requirement is that the conduct be extreme and outrageous. Appellees' conduct was unquestionably rude, insensitive, callous, and in poor taste. It was not, however, extreme and outrageous. To satisfy that element, conduct must completely violate human dignity. "[E]xtreme and outrageous conduct exists only if 'the average member of the community must regard the defendant's conduct * * * as being a complete denial of the plaintiff's dignity as a person.' " *Dick v. Mercantile–Safe*, 63 Md. App. at 276, 492 A.2d 674, quoting *Alsteen v. Gehl*, 21

Wis.2d 349, 124 N.W.2d 312, 318 (1963). The conduct must strike to the very core of one's being, threatening to shatter the frame upon which one's emotional fabric is hung.

Appellees' acts were examples of bad taste and poor judgment in connection with the collection of a lawful debt but did not amount to intentional infliction of emotional distress. Creditors have the right to insist on payment of just debts and may threaten legal proceedings. Appellees' persistent attempts to extract payment were unquestionably offensive to appellants, but as Professor Calvert Magruder observed, " 'Against a large part of the frictions and irritations and clashing of temperaments incident to participation in community life, a certain toughening of the mental hide is a better protection than the law could ever be.' " *Harris,* 281 Md. at 568, 380 A.2d 611, quoting 49 Harv.L. Rev. 1033, 1035 (1936). Moreover, appellees were not so much unopposed invaders of Verna's psyche as they were combatants against Verna for the collection of payments. It appears that she did not meekly endure the telephone calls but responded in a hostile fashion herself, speaking loudly and hanging up on occasion, generating the "thrust and parry" this court observed in *Dick.*

Verna also failed to demonstrate that her emotional distress was severe. She produced evidence that she was upset, that she had difficulty sleeping, and that she was embarrassed. To sustain an action for intentional infliction of emotional distress, however, one must suffer an emotional response so acute that no reasonable person could be expected to endure it. One must be unable to function, one must be unable to tend to necessary matters. Verna simply produced no evidence that she could not function or tend to her everyday affairs. The tale of her frustration and anguish was not one of pain so acute that no reasonable person could be expected to endure. The absence of such evidence by itself was fatal to her claim.

Verna's emotional response to appellees' conduct was no more severe than that of the plaintiff in *Harris,* which the Court found to be an insufficient basis for recovery. Harris was humiliated; his nervous condition aggravated and his speech impediment worsened; he had to see a physician; and he felt " 'like going into a hole and hide [sic].' " Although Verna's distress was keen and apparently genuine, it was not disabling. Her ego was bruised and her dignity was bent, but neither was destroyed.

Appellants attempt to distinguish this case from *Harris* and its progeny that involved employer/employee relationships by arguing that an employee must expect to endure more abusive conduct by virtue of his subordinate position. This argument has no persuasive merit. Conduct that would qualify as extreme and outrageous when committed by a creditor should not have to be accepted from an employer. Moreover, *Dick v. Mercantile–Safe, supra,* dealt specifically with the relationship between debtor and creditor. We drew no distinction in that case between an employment relationship and a credit arrangement, and we find none here. In developing the tort of intentional infliction of emotional distress, whatever the relationship between the parties, recovery will be meted out sparingly, its balm reserved for those wounds that are truly severe and incapable of healing themselves.

Notes

1. Can *Caputo* and *Hamilton* be reconciled? How?

2. Would the activities of the witnesses who testified in the Congressional hearings on the FDCPA, reproduced at the beginning of the chapter be tortious?

3. Are the privacy theories really any different from that of intentional infliction of emotional distress? Is the explanation of the differences offered in *Jones* convincing? If the theories are basically the same, can you reconcile the cases? Was the conduct in *Jones* any worse than in *Hamilton?*

4. Courts have sometimes applied yet other tort theories in debt collection cases. See, e.g., Duty v. General Finance Co., 154 Tex. 16, 273 S.W.2d 64 (1954) (unreasonable collection efforts). As a practical matter, however, the types of facts the plaintiff needs to prove to establish a claim are similar for each theory. Do you see any advantage in using one theory or another? Are the courts better off applying existing common law claims to debt collection or would it be preferable to fashion a new tort confined to debt collection? How would the elements of such a tort differ from the existing common law claims?

5. According to the 2004 FTC Report at 4, the Commission received 8,559 complaints from consumers alleging that collectors called them repeatedly or continuously in 2003 and 5,650 complaints that collectors used obscene, profane or otherwise abusive language. These figures probably do not accurately portray the scope of the problem: the numbers may be overinclusive because some consumers may perceive harassment where a more neutral observer would not, and they may be underinclusive because many consumers do not report their victimization to the FTC.

CLOMON v. JACKSON

United States Court of Appeals, Second Circuit, 1993.
988 F.2d 1314.

José A. Cabranes, District Judge:

Philip D. Jackson appeals from a judgment of the United States District Court for the District of Connecticut (Peter C. Dorsey, Judge) granting summary judgment against him in an action for damages under the Fair Debt Collection Practices Act ("FDCPA"), 15 U.S.C. §§ 1692–1692o. The district court held that Jackson violated the FDCPA when he authorized the sending of debt collection letters bearing his name and a facsimile of his signature without first reviewing the collection letters or the files of the persons to whom the letters were sent. We affirm.

BACKGROUND

The appellant, Philip D. Jackson, is an attorney employed on a part-time basis as general counsel for a debt collection agency, NCB Collection Services ("NCB"). The agency collects debts on behalf of American Family Publishers ("AFP"), an organization engaged in the business of selling magazine subscriptions. This case arises out of an attempt by NCB to collect a debt of $9.42 allegedly owed to AFP by the appellee, Christ Clomon.

NCB issues debt collection letters on behalf of AFP to approximately one million debtors each year through a computerized mass-mailing system. Under this system, AFP provides NCB with computer tapes containing information about delinquent accounts. NCB then transfers this information from the tapes to its own computer system, which inserts each debtor's name, address, account number, and balance due into a form letter requesting payment of the debt. The computer system then causes each letter to be printed, folded, and inserted into a window envelope for mailing. If a debtor does not respond to the initial collection letter, the computer automatically produces and mails additional letters according to a predetermined schedule. The collection agency maintains a program for assessing the reliability of its computer data, but no employee of the agency reviews the file of any individual debtor until the debtor responds to the agency's demands for payment.

Clomon received a series of six form letters from NCB regarding her $9.42 debt to AFP. The first of these letters was sent on a form bearing the logo of NCB and the name of "Althea Thomas, Account Supervisor." The remaining five letters were sent on letterhead containing the following words in the top margin:

P.D. Jackson, G.C. Offices of General Counsel

Attorney-at-Law 336 Atlantic Avenue

East Rockaway, N.Y. 11518

In addition, each of these letters bore the following signature line:

P.D. JACKSON, ATTORNEY AT LAW

GENERAL COUNSEL

NCB COLLECTION SERVICES

The information in the letterhead and at the signature line was accurate, at least in a literal sense. Jackson is indeed an attorney, admitted to practice in the State of New York. He is employed as general counsel of NCB Collection Services, albeit on a part-time basis, for which he receives an annual salary of approximately $24,000. The address of NCB Collection Services in New York State is 336 Atlantic Avenue, East Rockaway, New York 11518. The letters were not, however, actually signed by Jackson or by any other person: each letter bore a mechanically reproduced facsimile of the signature of "P.D. Jackson."

The letters "signed" by Jackson were delivered to Clomon over a period of more than two months, from March 1991 to early June of that year. The letters contained a variety of threatening statements in an apparent effort to induce Clomon to pay the amount she owed. The following statements are representative of the letters' contents:

> You have 30 days before we take any additional steps deemed appropriate regarding your outstanding balance....
>
> . . . .
>
> Based on information made available to us, we must recommend that your creditor proceed with such further action as the circumstances may indicate to dispose of this outstanding balance.
>
> . . . .
>
> After NCB reviews your collection file and previous correspondence sent you, I am suggesting we take the appropriate measures provided under the law to further implement the collection of your seriously past due account.
>
> . . . .
>
> Your account was referred to us with instructions to pursue this matter to the furthest extent we deem appropriate.
>
> . . . .
>
> Acting as General Counsel for NCB Collection Services, I have told them that they can lawfully undertake collection activity to collect your debt....
>
> . . . .
>
> Accordingly, the disposition of your account has been scheduled for immediate review and/or further action as deemed appropriate.
>
> . . . .
>
> Because of your failure to make any effort to pay your lawful debt ... we may find it necessary to recommend to your creditor that appropriate action be taken to satisfy the debt.

Jackson asserts, and Clomon does not dispute, that he personally approved the form letters used by NCB and that he also approved the procedures according to which those letters were sent. Jackson acknowledges, however, that he did not have any direct personal involvement in the mailing of letters to Clomon (or to any other debtor): he never reviewed Clomon's file; he never reviewed or signed any letter that was sent in his name to Clomon; he never gave advice to AFP about how to address particular circumstances of Clomon's case; and he never received any instructions from AFP about what steps to take against Clomon. In short, Jackson never considered the particular circumstances of Clomon's case prior to the mailing of the letters and he never participated personally in the mailing.

In a complaint filed on September 23, 1991, Clomon alleged that Jackson had violated the FDCPA in authorizing NCB to issue the collection letters that she received. The district court denied Jackson's motion for judgment on the pleadings on May 4, 1992. While that motion was still pending, the parties submitted cross-motions for summary judgment. The district court issued a written ruling granting summary judgment for Clomon on May 11, 1992. The court then granted, over objection, Clomon's motion for the maximum statutory damages of $1000. The court found no actual damages. On appeal, Jackson contends that the district court erred (1) in finding that his conduct violated 15 U.S.C. § 1692e, (2) in awarding statutory damages in the amount of $1,000, and (3) in denying his motion for judgment on the pleadings.

Discussion

A.   Ruling on Cross–Motions for Summary Judgment

The FDCPA establishes a general prohibition against the use of "false, deceptive, or misleading representation or means in connection with the collection of any debt." 15 U.S.C. § 1692e. The sixteen subsections of § 1692e set forth a non-exhaustive list of practices that fall within this ban. These subsections include:

> (3) The false representation or implication that any individual is an attorney or that any communication is from an attorney.
>
> . . . .
>
> (10) The use of any false representation or deceptive means to collect or attempt to collect any debt or to obtain information concerning a consumer.

Id. Because the list in the sixteen subsections is non-exhaustive, a debt collection practice can be a "false, deceptive, or misleading" practice in violation of § 1692e even if it does not fall within any of the subsections of § 1692e. A single violation of § 1692e is sufficient to establish civil liability under the FDCPA. *See* 15 U.S.C. § 1692k (establishing civil liability for "any debt collector who fails to comply with any provision of this subchapter").

1.   The "Least Sophisticated Consumer" Standard

The most widely accepted test for determining whether a collection letter violates § 1692e is an objective standard based on the "least sophisticated consumer." This standard has also been adopted by all federal appellate courts that have considered the issue. We now adopt the least-sophisticated consumer standard for application in cases under § 1692e. In doing so, however, we examine in some detail the purposes served by this standard as well as the extent of the liability that it creates.

The basic purpose of the least-sophisticated-consumer standard is to ensure that the FDCPA protects all consumers, the gullible as well as the shrewd. This standard is consistent with the norms that courts have traditionally applied in consumer-protection law. More than fifty years ago, the Supreme Court noted that

> [t]he fact that a false statement may be obviously false to those who are trained and experienced does not change its character, nor take

away its power to deceive others less experienced. There is no duty resting upon a citizen to suspect the honesty of those with whom he transacts business. Laws are made to protect the trusting as well as the suspicious.

Federal Trade Commission v. Standard Education Society, 302 U.S. 112, 116, 58 S.Ct. 113, 115, 82 L.Ed. 141 (1937) (finding encyclopedia-selling scheme in violation of Federal Trade Commission Act). We subsequently sounded the same theme in our consumer-protection cases, holding that the Federal Trade Commission Act ("FTC Act"), 15 U.S.C. § 41 *et seq.,* was not made " 'for the protection of experts, but for the public—that vast multitude which includes the ignorant, the unthinking and the credulous.' " *Charles of the Ritz Distributors Corp. v. Federal Trade Commission,* 143 F.2d 676, 679 (2d Cir.1944), quoting *Florence Manufacturing Co. v. J.C. Dowd & Co.,* 178 F. 73, 75 (2d Cir.1910). This basic principle of consumer-protection law took on its modern formulation several years later, when we held that "[i]n evaluating the tendency of language to deceive, the [Federal Trade] Commission should look not to the most sophisticated readers but rather to the least." *Exposition Press, Inc. v. Federal Trade Commission,* 295 F.2d 869, 872 (2d Cir.1961). In recent years, as courts have incorporated the jurisprudence of the FTC Act into their interpretations of the FDCPA, the language of *Exposition Press* has gradually evolved into what we now know as the least-sophisticated-consumer standard. *See, e.g., Jeter,* 760 F.2d at 1174–75; *Baker,* 677 F.2d at 778.

To serve the purposes of the consumer-protection laws, courts have attempted to articulate a standard for evaluating deceptiveness that does not rely on assumptions about the "average" or "normal" consumer. This effort is grounded, quite sensibly, in the assumption that consumers of below-average sophistication or intelligence are especially vulnerable to fraudulent schemes. The least-sophisticated-consumer standard protects these consumers in a variety of ways. First, courts have held that collection notices violate the FDCPA if the notices contain language that "overshadows" or "contradicts" other language that informs consumers of their rights. *See Graziano,* 950 F.2d at 111 (notice of right to respond within thirty days is not effectively communicated when presented in conjunction with contradictory demand for payment within ten days). In addition, courts have found collection notices misleading where they employ formats or typefaces which tend to obscure important information that appears in the notice. *See Baker,* 677 F.2d at 778 (required information must be "large enough to be easily read and sufficiently prominent to be noticed"). Finally, courts have held that collection notices can be deceptive if they are open to more than one reasonable interpretation, at least one of which is inaccurate. *See Dutton v. Wolhar,* 809 F.Supp. 1130, 1141 (D.Del.1992) ("least sophisticated debtor is not charged with gleaning the more subtle of the two interpretations" of collection notice).

It should be emphasized that in crafting a norm that protects the naive and the credulous the courts have carefully preserved the concept of reasonableness. *See Rosa v. Gaynor,* 784 F.Supp. 1, 3 (D.Conn.1989) (FDCPA "does not extend to every bizarre or idiosyncratic interpretation" of a collection notice but "does reach a reasonable interpretation of a notice by even the least sophisticated"). Indeed, courts have consistently applied the least-sophisticated-consumer standard in a manner that protects debt collectors against liability for unreasonable misinterpretations of collection notices. One court has held, for example, that collection notices are not deceptive simply because certain essential information is conveyed implicitly rather than explicitly. *See Transworld Systems,* 953 F.2d at 1028–29 (collection notice that does not expressly inform debtors of right to contest portion of debt is not misleading, because that right is "implicit" in right to challenge entire debt). Other courts have held that even the "least sophisticated consumer" can be presumed to possess a rudimentary amount of information about the world and a willingness to read a collection notice with some care. *See Johnson,* 799 F.Supp. at 1306–07 (finding that "even the least sophisticated debtor knows that a 'Revenue Department' may be part of a department store or other commercial creditor just as it may be a governmental body"); *Gaetano v. Payco of Wisconsin, Inc.,* 774 F.Supp. 1404, 1411 (D.Conn.1990) (approving collection notice even though required disclosures were printed only on the back of the notice, since language on the front directed consumers to read the reverse).

We do not, of course, have occasion here to adopt other courts' interpretations of the least-sophisticated-consumer standard. But the existence of this substantial body of law demonstrates that the least-sophisticated-consumer standard effectively serves its dual purpose: it (1) ensures the protection of all consumers, even the naive and the trusting, against deceptive debt collection practices, and (2) protects debt collectors against liability for bizarre or idiosyncratic interpretations of collection notices.

2. *Violation of Section 1692e*

In the proceedings below, the district court based its decision to grant summary judgment on its determination that Jackson had violated subsection (3) of § 1692e. The court determined that Jackson violated subsection (3) when he approved collection letters which falsely implied that he had been retained for the purpose of collecting a particular person's debt. Jackson now contends that the court erred in holding that such conduct violated subsection (3). Specifically, Jackson insists that the letters at issue here complied with subsection (3) because they accurately state that he is an attorney and that the letters are from him. He also argues that the letters' overstatement of the degree of an attorney's involvement in individual debtors' cases does not violate subsection (3) or any other provision of § 1692e. We find these arguments unpersuasive.

At the outset, it should be emphasized that the use of *any* false, deceptive, or misleading representation in a collection letter violates § 1692e—regardless of whether the representation in question violates a particular subsection of that provision. *See* 15 U.S.C. § 1692e (specifying certain prohibited acts "[w]ithout limiting the general application of the foregoing" language). Given the broad sweep of this provision, it would be possible to uphold the district court's decision to grant summary judgment for the plaintiff even if the facts did not establish a violation of subsection (3). We find, however, that the district court properly concluded that the record establishes a violation of subsection (3). We note that the record also establishes a violation of subsection (10) and of the general ban in § 1692e.

First, the use of Jackson's letterhead and signature on the collection letters was sufficient to give the least sophisticated consumer the impression that the letters were communications from an attorney. This impression was false and misleading because in fact Jackson did not review each debtor's file; he did not determine when particular letters should be sent; he did not approve the sending of particular letters based upon the recommendations of others; and he did not see particular letters before they were sent—indeed, he did not even know the identities of the persons to whom the letters were issued. In short, the fact that Jackson played virtually no day-to-day role in the debt collection process supports the conclusion that the collection letters were not "from" Jackson in any meaningful sense of that word. Consequently, the facts of this case establish a violation of subsection (3) of § 1692e. *See Masuda v. Thomas Richards & Co.,* 759 F.Supp. 1456, 1460–61 (C.D.Cal. 1991) (finding violation of subsection (3) where collection letter falsely implied that attorney had personally reviewed debtor's file); *cf. Anthes v. Transworld Systems, Inc.,* 765 F.Supp. 162, 166–67 (D.Del.1991) (finding no violation of subsection (3) where collection letter was sent directly from attorney's office and attorney reviewed information provided by debt collection agency "to independently determine whether one of his letters should be sent").

We also note that the language used in the collection letters was sufficient to cause the least sophisticated consumer to believe that Jackson himself had considered individual debtors' files and had made judgments about how to collect individual debts. The letters stated that Jackson was "suggesting" certain measures be taken "to further implement the collection of your seriously past due account"; that Jackson had received "instructions" from his client "to pursue this matter to the furthest extent we deem appropriate"; that Jackson had "told" his client that it could "lawfully undertake collection activity to collect your debt"; and that Jackson had "scheduled" Clomon's debt for "immediate review and/or further action as deemed appropriate." In short, the collection letters would have led many consumers, and certainly the least sophisticated consumer, to believe that an attorney had personally considered the debtor's case before the letters were sent. This language was false or misleading because, as noted above, Jackson played virtually no day-to-day role in the debt collection process—and certainly did not engage in any discussion with NCB or AFP about how to collect Clomon's debt. Consequently, the facts of this case establish a violation of subsection

(10) of § 1692e. *See Pipiles v. Credit Bureau of Lockport, Inc.*, 886 F.2d 22, 25–26 (2d Cir.1989) (finding violation of subsection (10) where collection letter falsely implied that some action would be taken); *see also Gaetano*, 774 F.Supp. at 1415 (finding violation of subsection (10) where defendant attempted to collect a debt when prohibited from doing so by state law).

In sum, the facts of this case provide ample grounds for the district court's conclusion that Jackson violated § 1692e. It is clear that Jackson's conduct constituted a violation of subsection (3), which prohibits the false representation that a collection letter is a "communication ... from an attorney." The record also establishes that Jackson's conduct constituted a violation of subsection (10), which prohibits "[t]he use of any false representation or deceptive means to collect" a debt from a consumer. Finally, we note that the misrepresentations contained in these letters could also be characterized as violations of the general ban in § 1692e on the use of any "false, deceptive, or misleading representation or means in connection with the collection of any debt."

In reaching this conclusion, we are mindful of the appellant's concern regarding the economic necessity of mass mailing in the debt collection industry. It is apparent that mass mailing may sometimes be the only feasible means of contacting a large number of delinquent debtors, particularly when many of those debtors owe relatively small sums. But it is also true that the FDCPA sets boundaries within which debt collectors must operate. No mass mailing technique is permissible— regardless of how effective it might be—if that technique constitutes a false, deceptive, or misleading communication. As we have found here, the use of an attorney's signature on a collection letter implies that the letter is "from" the attorney who signed it; it implies, in other words, that the attorney directly controlled or supervised the process through which the letter was sent. We have also found here that the use of an attorney's signature implies—at least in the absence of language to the contrary—that the attorney signing the letter formed an opinion about how to manage the case of the debtor to whom the letter was sent. In a mass mailing, these implications are frequently false: the attorney whose signature is used might play no role either in sending the letters or in determining who should receive them. For this reason, there will be few, if any, cases in which a mass-produced collection letter bearing the facsimile of an attorney's signature will comply with the restrictions imposed by § 1692e.

B.   *Ruling on Motion for "Additional Damages"*

The FDCPA provides that "any debt collector who fails to comply with any provision of this subchapter with respect to any person" is liable to such person. 15 U.S.C. § 1692k. The statute further provides that upon a finding of liability a court may award an individual plaintiff actual damages in compensation for the harm suffered as a result of the violation, "additional damages" not to exceed $1,000, and reasonable costs and attorney's fees. *See* 15 U.S.C. § 1692k(a)(1)-(3). In this case,

Clomon requested no actual damages and the district court awarded none. The court did, however, grant Clomon's motion for $1,000 in "additional damages." The court also awarded Clomon $2,975 for attorney's fees and $120 for costs. On appeal, Jackson objects only to the award of "additional damages."

The decision on whether to award "additional damages" and on the size of any such award is committed to the sound discretion of the district court. * * *The district court must, however, consider the frequency and persistence of noncompliance by the debt collector, the nature of such noncompliance, the extent to which such noncompliance was intentional, and other relevant factors in deciding the amount of any "additional damages" awarded. *See* 15 U.S.C. § 1692k(b).

In sum, we find sufficient grounds for the district court's conclusion that Jackson knew or should have known that these collection letters violated § 1692e. For that reason, the court's decision to award statutory damages of $1,000 was amply justified. * * *

Notes

1.   Does it make sense to use the "least sophisticated consumer" standard under the FDCPA when the FTC no longer uses that standard in interpreting the Federal Trade Commission Act? See Chapter One, *supra.*

2.   In Gammon v. GC Services Ltd. Partnership, 27 F.3d 1254 (7th Cir. 1994), the court wrote:

It strikes us virtually impossible to analyze a debt collection letter based on the reasonable interpretations of the least sophisticated consumer. Literally, the least sophisticated consumer is not merely "below average," he is the very last rung on the sophistication ladder. Stated another way, he is the single most unsophisticated consumer who exists. Even assuming that he would be willing to do so, such a consumer would likely not be able to read a collection notice with care (or at all), let alone interpret it in a reasonable fashion. Courts which use the "least sophisticated consumer" test, however, routinely blend in the element of reasonableness. [citing *Clomon*]

In maintaining the principles behind the enactment of the FDCPA, we believe a simpler and less confusing formulation of a standard designed to protect those consumers of below-average sophistication or intelligence should be adopted. Thus, we will use the term, "unsophisticated," instead of the phrase, "least sophisticated," to describe the hypothetical consumer whose reasonable perceptions will be used to determine if collection messages are deceptive or misleading. We reiterate that an unsophisticated consumer standard protects the consumer who is uninformed, naive, or trusting, yet it admits an objective element of reasonableness. The reasonableness element in turn shields complying debt collectors from liability for unrealistic or peculiar interpretations of collection letters.

How, if at all, is the *Gammon* test different from the *Clomon* standard? In Avila v. Rubin, 84 F.3d 222, 227 (7th Cir. 1996), the court observed that there isn't "much of a practical difference in application." In that case, why did the Seventh Circuit create a different test? See Elwin Griffith, The Fair Debt Collection Practices Act—Reconciling the Interests of Consumers and Debt Collectors, 28 Hofstra L. Rev. 1, 17 (1999). In a later decision, the Seventh Circuit explained that the unsophisticated debtor standard assumes "that statements are not confusing or misleading unless a significant fraction of the population would be similarly misled." Veach v. Sheeks, 316 F.3d 690 (7th Cir. 2003).

3. How should the parties prove that something would mislead the least sophisticated consumer? In Durkin v. Equifax Check Services, Inc., 406 F.3d 410, 415 (7th Cir. 2005), the court explained:

> [W]hen the letter itself does not plainly reveal that it would be confusing to a significant fraction of the population, the plaintiff must come forward with evidence beyond the letter and beyond his own self-serving assertions that the letter is confusing in order to create a genuine issue of material fact for trial. We have repeatedly indicated that this need for additional evidence (frequently referred to as "extrinsic evidence") might be met through the use of a carefully designed and conducted consumer survey. Also, we have suggested that an appropriate expert witness might suffice.

Is it realistic to expect consumers to pay for the cost of a survey or expert witness?

4. Under § 1692l, the FTC has authority to enforce the FDCPA. Even prior to the enactment of the FDCPA, the FTC often prosecuted people who used abusive debt collection practices by using its authority under the FTC Act. See 15 U.S.C.A. § 45; In re National Account Systems, Inc., 89 F.T.C. 282 (1977). As *Clomon* indicates, consumers may also bring private claims under § 1692k and may collect statutory damages of up to $1,000. Would Jackson's malpractice insurance have covered his liability? Courts have generally limited plaintiffs to $1,000 per case, not $1,000 per violation of the FDCPA. See, e.g., Wright v. Finance Service of Norwalk, Inc., 22 F.3d 647 (6th Cir. 1994) (en banc); Harper v. Better Business Services, Inc., 961 F.2d 1561 (11th Cir. 1992). Would it make sense to bring each violation as a separate case and then move to have the cases consolidated? How would you expect a court to deal with this tactic? The statute also authorizes courts to award successful plaintiffs attorneys' fees.

Problem 8–4

In 1985, Myron Newby was treated at Swedish Hospital in Seattle. Myron and his wife, Nada, signed a note to the hospital for $23.35. In 1987, the Newbys moved to Alaska, where Mr. Newby died in 1989. Later that year, Nada Newby found work at Presbyterian Hospital in Palmer, Alaska, as a cook. Merritt Long was a professional debt collector in Palmer. He was also on the Board of Trustees of Presbyterian Hospital. As a debt collector, he had received an assignment of the debt the Newbys owed to Swedish Hospital. Long contacted Nada Newby and told her that if she did not make arrangements to pay the Swedish bill, it would mean her job. He also presented Nada Newby's case to the Board of Presbyterian Hospital, and the Board passed a resolution which required Nada to pay her debt to Swedish Hospital within 30 days or be dismissed from the staff of Presbyterian Hospital. Thirty days later, Nada Newby was fired. Does she have a case against either Long or Presbyterian Hospital? On what theory?

SECTION C.   SPECIAL ISSUES ARISING UNDER THE FDCPA (LAWYERS BE-WARE: LIABILITY LIES AHEAD)

As has already become apparent, the FDCPA made the law of debt collection far more complex. While some of its prohibitions have analogs in common law, other provisions were novel. This section explores issues arising under the FDCPA that would not arise at common law. First, the section examines the scope of the FDCPA. The FDCPA applies only to debt collectors collecting debts, and so it is necessary to look at the definitions of those terms. Next the section takes up some of the technical rules the FDCPA imposes on debt collectors: specifically, the validation requirement and the so-called "Miranda warning." Later this section turns to particular issues for lawyer-debt collectors—though the role of lawyers is a theme running through the entire section.

1.   THE MEANING OF "DEBT COLLECTOR" AND "DEBT"

The FDCPA's definition of debt collector, in FDCPA § 1692a(6), is limited to external debt collectors and creditors who, while collecting debts, use a name other than their own which suggests a third person is collecting the debt. See Kempf v. Famous Barr Co., 676 F.Supp. 937 (E.D.Mo. 1988). But not all external debt collectors are included: only those businesses which have as their principal purpose debt collection or those who regularly collect debts owed to another come within the statute. Application of the definition is usually fairly straightforward because most businesses that collect debts for others clearly satisfy the statutory threshold of doing so "regularly." Lawyers, however, are different. While some lawyers devote a significant amount of time to debt collection, and so would easily qualify as debt collectors, others have a more varied practice which includes a small amount of collection work, making the issue a line-drawing exercise. This problem did not arise until 1986 because the FDCPA as originally written expressly excluded attorneys from its coverage. Congress deleted the exclusion for lawyers after some attorneys advertised that they could collect debts without complying with the strictures of the FDCPA. Attorneys continued to argue that the FDCPA did not apply to lawyers whose debt collection efforts were confined to litigation, and the FTC Staff agreed, but the Supreme Court rejected that view in Heintz v. Jenkins, 514 U.S. 291, 115 S.Ct. 1489, 131 L.Ed.2d 395 (1995). Consequently, attorneys whose practices—whether limited to litigation or not—include enough collection work to make them "debt collectors" must now comply with the FDCPA. Does it matter to an attorney whether she is covered under the

FDCPA? What would an ethical and honest attorney have to do differently?

SCHROYER v. FRANKEL

United States Court of Appeals, Sixth Circuit, 1999.
197 F.3d 1170.

CLAY, CIRCUIT JUDGE.

[Kenneth Frankel, an attorney who had practiced law for twenty-two years and who was employed by Gerald M. Smith Co., L.P.A., a professional corporation engaged in the practice of law under the fictitious name of Smith & Smith, was retained by Michael Williams of Alexander's Sewer & Plumbing Company ("ASAP") in connection with state court litigation between ASAP and Michael and Gail Schroyer. The Schroyers subsequently sued Frankel and his law firm in federal court, alleging violations of the FDCPA.] * * * Plaintiffs filed a motion for partial summary judgment, but the district court denied the motion for partial summary judgment on the grounds that there was a genuine issue of material fact as to whether Defendants were "debt collectors" under the FDCPA. After a bench trial, the district court ruled in favor of Defendants and dismissed Plaintiffs' claims.

In doing so, the district court found that Smith & Smith handled fifty to seventy-five debt collection cases annually, that debt collection comprised less than two percent of the firm's overall practice, and that the firm did not hire any paralegals or other non-attorneys nor use any computer programs for debt collection purposes. The district court further found that Frankel handled 389 cases in one year, that twenty-nine, or 7.4%, of these cases were debt collection cases, and that his debt collection cases came from business clients he represented in matters not involving debt collection. The district court further noted the absence of evidence that Defendants handled debt collection for a major client on an ongoing basis, and the absence of evidence as to the total fees collected by Defendants in debt collection cases. On the basis of these findings, the district court determined that Defendants were neither "debt collectors" under the FDCPA or "suppliers" under the OCSPA, and concluded that defensive collateral estoppel partially precluded Gail's claims. * * *

II

The FDCPA defines "debt collector" as "any person who uses any instrumentality of interstate commerce or the mails in any business the principal purpose of which is the collection of any debts, or who regularly collects or attempts to collect, directly or indirectly, debts owed or due or asserted to be owed or due another." 15 U.S.C. § 1692a(6) (1994). * * *

When interpreting the FDCPA, we begin with the language of the statute itself since the intent of Congress is "best determined by the statutory language it chooses." *Sedima, S.P.R.L. v. Imrex,* 473 U.S. 479, 495 n. 13, 105 S.Ct. 3275 (1985). In so doing, this Court must consider the language and design of the statute as a whole as well as the specific provision at issue. The term "regularly" means "[a]t fixed and certain intervals, regular in point of time. In accordance with some consistent or periodical rule of practice." Black's Law Dictionary 1286 (6th ed.1990). The term "regular" means "[u]sual, customary, normal or general. . . . Antonym of 'casual' or 'occasional.' " *Id.* at 1285. These definitions suggest that an individual or entity must have more than an "occasional" involvement with debt collection activities to qualify as a "debt collector" under the FDCPA. Furthermore, considering § 1692a(6) as a whole, it is clear that Congress intended the "principal purpose" prong to differ from the "regularly" prong of its definition of "debt collector." *See Garrett v. Derbes*, 110 F.3d 317, 318 (5th Cir.1997) (per curiam). Thus, one "may regularly render debt collection services, even if these services are not a principal purpose of his business." *Id.* As another court has explained, "the word 'regular' is not synonymous with the word 'substantial.' Debt collection services may be rendered 'regularly' even though these services may amount to a small fraction of the firm's total activity." *Stojanovski v. Strobl & Manoogian, P.C.*, 783 F.Supp. 319, 322 (E.D.Mich.1992). Under this interpretation of "regular" or "regularly," an attorney may be a "debt collector" under the FDCPA even when the ratio of his debt collection efforts to other legal efforts is small. *Id.*

Ordinary interpretations of the words "regular" and "regularly" fail to delineate the amount of debt collection activity required for this Court to find an attorney a "debt collector" under the FDCPA. When the language of a provision is ambiguous, we look to the legislative history of the statute in question to ascertain its confines. In its enactment of the FDCPA, Congress intended that "[t]he requirement that debt collection be done 'regularly' would exclude a person who collects a debt for another in an isolated instance, but would include those who collect for others in the regular course of business." S.Rep. No. 95–382, *reprinted in* 1977 U.S.C.C.A.N. 1695, 1697–98. Assuming "that attorneys were only incidentally involved in debt collection activities," H.R.Rep. No. 99–405, *reprinted in* 1986 U.S.C.C.A.N. 1752, 1759, Congress originally retained in the statute an exception for attorneys collecting debts on behalf of clients. *See* Fair Debt Collection Practices Act of 1977, Pub.L. No. 95–109, § 803, 91 Stat. 874 (1977).

In the years that followed, Congress discovered that more attorneys were engaging in debt collection practices than non-attorneys. *See* H.R.Rep. No. 99–405, *reprinted in* 1986 U.S.C.C.A.N. 1752, 1752 (observing that by 1985, 5,000 attorneys were engaged in the debt collection industry, as compared to 4,500 lay debt collection firms). Congress also learned that many attorneys advertised their exemption from the FDCPA to solicit creditors. *See* H.R.Rep. No. 99–405, *reprinted in* 1986 U.S.C.C.A.N. 1752, 1756. In response to these findings, Congress repealed the attorney exemption in 1986. This repeal changed the FDCPA so that "any attorney who is in the business of collecting debts will be regarded by the Act as a debt collector." H.R.Rep. No. 99–405, *reprinted in* 1986 U.S.C.C.A.N. 1752, 1753.

Plaintiffs argue that in revoking the attorney exemption, Congress intended for the FDCPA to apply to any attorney who collects debts in the regular course of business, even if he does so as an incidental part of his regular practice of law. To support this assertion, Plaintiffs cite *Crossley v. Lieberman*, which notes the following analysis of Congress' intent:

> Both the legislative history of this amendment and the case law regarding similar provisions in the Federal Consumer Credit Protection Act demonstrates [sic] that any attorney who engages in collection activities more than a handful of times per year must comply with the FDCPA. Both sides in the floor debate conceded that the amendment would make the act apply not only to those lawyers who have collection practices but also to those who collect on an occasional basis and the small law firm which collects debts incidentally to the general practice of law.

868 F.2d 566, 569 (3d Cir.1989) (quoting R. Hobbs, *Attorneys Must Now Comply With Fair Debt Collection Law*, Pa. J.L. Rptr., Nov. 21, 1987, at 3). While the commentary cited in *Crossley* bolsters Plaintiffs' position, we find it unpersuasive.

As a preliminary matter, we observe that the question of whether the defendant "regularly" collected debts was not actually before the *Crossley* court. Setting that aside, the legislative history hardly makes clear that attorneys who collect debts occasionally and small firms that collect debts incidentally to their general law practices are "debt collectors" under the FDCPA. The House Report accompanying the 1986 amendment to the FDCPA explained that Congress revoked the attorney exemption because its assumption that attorneys were only incidentally involved in debt collection no longer rang true, stating: "[i]n recent years, a large number of law firms have gone into specialized debt collection, and many of these firms use persons full time to collect debts. Repeal of the exemption will require these firms to comply with the same standards of conduct as lay debt collection firms." H.R.Rep. No. 99–405, *reprinted in* 1986 U.S.C.C.A.N. 1752, 1759. Elsewhere the House Report expresses its concern about the entry of attorneys into the "debt collection industry," and "the proliferation of attorney debt-collection firms." *Id.* at 1754, 1756. Moreover, the House Report repeatedly identifies attorneys "in the business of" collecting debts as the target of its legislation. *See id.* at 1753, 1754.

Drawing from this legislative history, we believe it reveals that for a court to find that an attorney or law firm "regularly" collects debts for purposes of the FDCPA, a plaintiff must show that the attorney or law firm collects debts as a matter of course for its clients or for some clients, or collects debts as a substantial, but not principal, part of his or its general law practice. Such an interpretation actuates the apparent purpose of Congress in creating attorney liability under the FDCPA:

"[w]hile attorneys who are considered competitors of traditional debt collection companies should be covered under the Act, a firm whose debt collection activity does not approximate that of a traditional collection agency should not be suable under the act." *White*, 23 F.Supp.2d at 276. In identifying such attorneys, other courts have relied upon a variety of factors, including the volume of the attorney's collection activities, the frequent use of a particular debt collection document or letter, and whether there exists a steady relationship between the attorney and the collection agency or creditor he represented. Courts have considered what portion of the overall caseload debt collection cases constitute, and what percentage of revenues derive from debt collection activities. Some have maintained that even where debt collection takes up a minor portion of a law practice, "debt collector" liability may lie where the defendant has an "ongoing relationship" with a client whose activities substantially involve debt collection. *See Stojanovski*, 783 F.Supp. at 322.

Applying these principles to the undisputed factual findings in this case, we believe Plaintiffs failed to prove that Defendants "regularly" collect debts so as to constitute "debt collectors" under the FDCPA. The district court found that only two percent of Smith & Smith's overall practices consisted of debt collection cases, and that the firm did not employ individuals full-time for the purpose of collecting debts. The district court further found that only 7.4%, 29 of 389 cases annually, of Frankel's overall practice consisted of debt collection cases, and that in the majority of his debt collection cases, he represented debtors—implying that Frankel was not competing with lay debt collectors. Moreover, the district court found that Frankel represented a number of business clients who were the source of his twenty-nine debt collection cases.

Finally, the court observed that Plaintiffs failed to offer evidence showing that fees generated or collected by Smith & Smith or Frankel from debt collection activities constituted a great portion of overall revenues, and failed to offer proof that Smith & Smith or Frankel handled debt collection cases as part of an ongoing relationship with a major creditor or business client with substantial debts for collection. While these facts do support the inference that it was not unusual for Defendants to perform debt collection work, or that their debt collection work occurred in more than an isolated instance, we believe it does not support a claim that Defendants were "in the business" of debt collection, that they were in the "debt collection" industry, or that Smith & Smith was a "debt collection firm." Rather, the facts establish that Defendants' debt collection activities were incidental to, and not relied upon or anticipated in, their practice of law, and that therefore they should not be held liable as "debt collectors" under the FDCPA. Accordingly, we hold that the district court did not err in ruling in Defendants' favor and in dismissing Plaintiffs' FDCPA claims against Defendants.
* * *

Notes

1. Assume for the moment that Frankel's 29 debt collection cases were undertaken on behalf of creditors. Can you argue that something done 29 times per year—or more often than every other week, on average—is not done "regularly"? Is the court right to focus on the proportion of Frankel's practice that consisted of collection matters? Suppose an attorney who had no other business had handled Frankel's 29 collection cases. That attorney's practice would consist entirely of collection matters. Would that qualify her as a debt collector under the court's reasoning? Goldstein v. Hutton, Ingram, Yuzek, Gainen, Carroll & Bertolotti, 374 F.3d 56, 61, 62–63 (2d Cir. 2004) involved a law firm that had derived $5,000 in revenues from sending 145 collection notices in the year preceding the litigation, amounting to 0.05% of its $10,000,000 revenue over that period. The district court had granted summary judgment on the ground that the firm was not a debt collector, but the Court of Appeals vacated the judgment, commenting that "if the volume of a person's debt collection services is great enough, it is irrelevant that these services only amount to a small fraction of his total business activity; the person still renders them 'regularly.'

2. In Silva v. Mid Atlantic Management Corp., 277 F.Supp.2d 460 (E.D.Pa. 2003), the court, citing Schroyer, found a law firm to be a "debt collector" when the firm had handled approximately ten debt collection matters per year for several years, representing less than one percent of the firm's gross revenues. Are the cases consistent?

3. Why should some lawyers be subject to the FDCPA but not others? For that matter, why should external debt collectors have to comply with the FDCPA but not a creditor collecting its own debts? Would you advise a client to handle debt collection matters in-house to avoid application of the FDCPA? If so, is it desirable for federal law to encourage the use of in-house debt collectors rather than external debt collectors? Why?

4. Is the creditor liable for the debt collector's violations of the FDCPA? Courts have generally answered in the negative. See, e.g., Caron v. Charles E. Maxwell, P.C., 48 F.Supp.2d 932 (D.Ariz. 1999). Nevertheless, while the creditor would not be liable under the FDCPA, at least one court has held that a creditor can be liable at common law for negligently selecting and supervising a debt collector. See Colorado Capital v. Owens, 227 F.R.D. 181 (E.D.N.Y. 2005).

5. Are employees of debt collection agencies also considered debt collectors, and therefore subject to suit under the FDCPA? For a positive answer, see the FTC Staff Commentary, § 803(6).1. But debt-collecting employees of creditors are excluded from the definition of debt collector under FDCPA § 1692a(6)(A).

Problem 8–5

Union, a telegram company, provides a service to numerous debt collectors. When debt collectors do not have a phone number for a debtor but do have an address, Union will send a letter to the address stating that the debtor has a telegram waiting and must call Union to obtain it.

When the debtor calls, Union uses its caller-ID system to obtain the debtor's number. Mary received such a telegram from Union, called Union, and subsequently received a series of calls on her unlisted phone number from a debt collector. Does Mary have a claim against Union? Is Union a debt collector? See Romine v. Diversified Collection Services, 155 F.3d 1142 (9th Cir. 1998).

Problem 8–6

Your client, Julia, is delinquent in her child support payments. Her ex-husband has hired Cassandra Collections and they are picketing outside her home with signs reading "Deadbeat Mom." Does this violate the FDCPA? See FDCPA § 1692a(5); Mabe v. G.C. Serv., 32 F.3d 86 (4th Cir. 1994).

Problem 8–7

Dolores purchased a pet from Pet Emporium, paying with a check. The check was dishonored because Dolores's account was overdrawn. When Emporium's debt collector, MacNair, attempted to collect from Dolores on the check, MacNair charged a $25 service fee. Dolores claims that the service fee violates the FDCPA because no state statute provides for collection of such a fee, nor did Emporium notify customers that a fee would be charged for dishonored checks. MacNair defends on the ground that its conduct is not within the FDCPA on the theory that because taking a check is not an extension of credit, a check does not create a debt. Is MacNair right? See FDCPA § 1692f; compare Bass v. Stolper, Koritzinsky, Brewster & Neider, S.C., 111 F.3d 1322 (7th Cir. 1997) with Krevsky v. Equifax Check Services, Inc., 85 F.Supp.2d 479 (M.D.Pa. 2000). Would it make a difference if Emporium had posted a sign stating that a $25 service fee would be charged for bounced checks? Would Emporium have to prove that the consumer had seen the sign? Would it make a difference if MacNair had sent Dolores a letter on the letterhead of the local district attorney's office headed "Official Notice" and stating "The DA's Office has received a report stating that you have violated the Penal Code by passing a worthless check. A conviction under this statute may result in a jail sentence. You may avoid a court appearance if you agree to enroll in our check restitution program, take our class on financial accountability, and make full restitution, including payment of $200 in applicable administrative costs and fees." The letter also contains all required notices. See FDCPA § 1692p.

2. SOME TECHNICAL ISSUES UNDER THE FDCPA, INCLUD-ING VALIDATION AND THE "MIRANDA WARNING"

The FDCPA is filled with technical rules that have generated considerable confusion and its frequent byproduct: litigation. See, e.g., FDCAP § 1692i (special venue rules for debt collection suits). This subsection focuses particularly on two of the most important technical requirements of the FDCPA, the validation requirement, and the so-called "Miranda warning."

Problem 8–8

Bagman, a debt collector, sent as the following letter to Abbott:

Dear Ms. Abbott:

Our records show you owe our client, Quality Supplies, a debt of $1,000 (the amount of the unpaid principal balance) plus accumulated interest, and I am attempting to collect that debt. **IF THIS ACCOUNT IS PAID WITHIN THE NEXT 10 DAYS IT WILL NOT BE RECORDED IN OUR MASTER FILE AS AN UNPAID COLLECTION ITEM.** *A GOOD CREDIT RATING IS YOUR MOST VALUABLE ASSET.*

Beneath this notice, in a typeface one-third the size of the large print above, appeared the following:

Federal law gives you thirty days after the date of this letter to dispute the validity of the debt. If you don't dispute it within that period, I'll assume that it's valid. If you do dispute it—by notifying me in writing to that effect—I will, as required by the law, obtain and mail to you proof of the debt. And if, within the same period, you request in writing the name and address of your original creditor, if the original creditor is different from the current creditor (Quality Supplies), I will furnish you with that information too.

The law does not require me to wait until the end of the thirty-day period before suing you to collect this debt. If, however, you request proof of the debt or the name and address of the original creditor within the thirty-day period that begins with your receipt of this letter, the law requires me to suspend my efforts (through litigation or otherwise) to collect the debt until I mail the requested information to you.

Assuming that Bagman and Abbott had previously not had any contact, has Bagman violated the FDCPA? See FDCPA §§ 1692g; 1692e(11); Swanson v. Southern Oregon Credit Service, Inc., 869 F.2d 1222 (9th Cir. 1988); Miller v. McCalla, Raymer, Padrick, Cobb, Nichols, and Clark, L.L.C., 214 F.3d 872 (7th Cir. 2000); Adams v. Law Offices of Stuckert & Yates, 926 F.Supp. 521 (E.D.Pa. 1996); Dikeman v. National Educators, Inc., 81 F.3d 949 (10th Cir. 1996). Would Abbott have a claim against Bagman at common law?

Notes

1. Will a validation notice on the back of the debt collector's letter satisfy the statutory requirement in the absence of a reference to the notice on the front of the letter? For answers before Congress added the last sentence to § 1692g(b), compare Ost v. Collection Bureau, Inc., 493 F.Supp. 701 (D.N.D. 1980) (no) with Blackwell v. Professional Business Serv., 526 F.Supp. 535 (N.D. Ga. 1981) (yes).

2. Would a debt collector prefer that the consumer focus on the validation notice or the remainder of the letter? Does the statute require the

validation notice to be clear and conspicuous? If not, why shouldn't debt collectors be able to print the notice in tiny print?

3. Does the statute require the last sentence in the notice in the problem above? If not, would you advise a client to omit the sentence?

4. Because the FDCPA is a strict liability statute, the fact that a violation is unintentional is usually irrelevant. See Russell v. Equifax A.R.S., 74 F.3d 30 (2d Cir. 1996). The statute does provide, however, that debt collectors will not be liable for unintentional violations resulting from bona fide errors "notwithstanding the maintenance of procedures reasonably adopted to avoid any such error." FDCPA § 1692k(c). Courts have generally construed this provision narrowly. See Dee Pridgen, Consumer Credit and the Law § 13:33 (2006). Is the defense available for errors of law? See Johnson v. Riddle, 443 F.3d 723 (10th Cir. 2006).

Problem 8–9

Sally Bones, an attorney who frequently brings collection cases, recently served a summons and complaint in such a case against Frank Fubster. About two weeks later Fubster counterclaimed on the ground that Bones had not complied with FDCPA § 1692g. Bones in fact has not provided Fubster with a validation notice because she has not communicated with Fubster other than to have him served. Has Bones violated the FDCPA? If not, when should Bones supply the validation notice?

Notes

1. Could Bones have attached the validation notice to her summons? If so, might the summons and complaint overshadow the validation notice? See In re Martinez, 266 B.R. 523 (B.S.D.Fla.), *aff'd*, 271 B.R. 696 (S.D.Fla. 2001), *aff'd* 311 F.3d 1272 (11th Cir. 2002) (initial communication consisted of 16 pages; summons made up first two pages, followed by two-page lis pendens, and three-page complaint; validation notice appeared on eighth page). In many courts, the summons and complaint direct the defendant to respond in less than thirty days. Would attaching a validation to a summons and complaint in such a court generate any problems for Bones? See Kafele v. Lerner, Sampson & Rothfuss, L.P.A., 2005 WL 1379107 (S.D.Ohio 2005). If so, what should Bones do?

2. Isn't filing a summons and complaint with the court clerk a communication to a third party regarding a debt, and therefore a violation of FDCPA § 1692c?

3. The FDCPA has occasionally collided with other statutes, as reflected in Romea v. Heiberger & Assoc., 163 F.3d 111 (2d Cir. 1998), a case involving New York's summary eviction proceeding. New York permits landlords to bring such proceedings only after giving the tenant a written demand that the tenant pay back rent; the New York statute requires that the landlord wait at least three days after providing notice before commencing suit. *Romea* held that the demand letter was a communication within the meaning of the FDCPA and so the letter must comply with the validation requirement—which creates problems because of the conflict between the 30 days provided by the FDCPA and the three-day period specified by the New

York statute. A New York state court saw the matter differently. See Barstow Road Owners, Inc. v. Billing, 179 Misc.2d 958, 687 N.Y.S.2d 845 (Dist. Ct. 1998). Is there a way to avoid the conflict between the statutes?

Problem 8–10

Bagman is trying to collect a debt owed by Bertha. Bagman has a phone number at which he suspects Bertha can be reached, but no other contact information. He does not know whether Bertha shares the number with others. He has called the number several times, but has hung up upon getting an answering machine. He asks you how to proceed. Should he (a) continue hanging up if he gets the answering machine; or (b) leave a message; and (c) if he leaves a message, how should he identify himself? See Foti v. NCO Financial Systems, Inc., 424 F.Supp.2d 643 (S.D.N.Y. 2006); Hosseinzadeh v. M.R.S. Associates, Inc., 387 F.Supp.2d 1104 (C.D.Cal. 2005).

Problem 8–11

After receiving a phone call from Dickens Debt Collectors demanding payment of a debt owed to Bleak House, Copperfield sent a letter to Dickens demanding that Dickens cease further communication with him. A few weeks later, Copperfield received a call from Heep Debt Collections seeking to collect the same debt. Apparently Dickens had sold the debt to Heep. Copperfield sent a similar letter to Heep, only to receive a phone call about the same debt a month later from Uriah Debt Collections, which had purchased the debt from Heep. Does Copperfield have a claim against any of the debt collectors? See § 1692c(c). Would your answer be the same if Copperfield had sent Dickens a note disputing the validity of the debt and Dickens had failed to obtain verification? Would you advise a client to dispute the validity of a debt you know the client actually incurred?

Problem 8–12

Local Credit Bureau is both a credit reporting agency and a debt collection agency. As part of its debt collection activity, it writes collection letters to defaulting debtors on company stationery which contains its full name in the letterhead. It also uses pre-printed envelopes which contain the company name in the upper left corner and the words "Priority Letter." In light of FDCPA §§ 1692e(16) and 1692f(8), respectively, would you advise Local to continue this practice? See Goswami v. American Collections Enterprise, Inc., 377 F.3d 488 (5th Cir.), rehearing denied, 395 F.3d 225 (5th Cir. 2004), cert. denied, 126 S.Ct. 331 (2005).

3. SPECIAL COLLECTION ISSUES FOR LAWYERS

Not only are lawyers subject to the FDCPA, and state law rules governing collections for that matter, but lawyers are also restrained by the profession's ethical rules. See A.B.A. Model Rules of Professional Conduct (2002):

Rule 4.4 In representing a client, a lawyer shall not use means that have no substantial purpose other than to embarrass, delay, or burden a third person, or use methods of obtaining evidence that violate the legal rights of such a person.

Lawyers have on occasion been disciplined for violating ethical rules when collecting debts. See, e.g., In re Lehrman, 193 A.D.2d 211, 602 N.Y.S.2d 698 (2d Dept.), leave to appeal denied, 82 N.Y.2d 663, 632 N.E.2d 461, 610 N.Y.S.2d 151 (1993) (attorney suspended for two years). But the Model Rules are not congruent with the FDCPA. In effect the FDCPA imposes an additional set of obligations upon attorneys who meet the requirements for being "debt collectors."

Problem 8–13

Ace Debt Collectors is a nationwide debt collection agency with offices in every state. In each of its offices it maintains copies of "attorney letters." These letters were prepared by an attorney and are on the attorney's letterhead, but they are unsigned. The office manager in each of Ace's offices decides in each case when and whether the letter should be sent, and fills in the form letter with the name and address of the particular debtor involved, the amount of the debt, and the name of the client/creditor. The content of the letter resembles the letters used in Clomon v. Jackson, *supra*.

> a. Does use of these letters violate the FDCPA? See FDCPA §§ 1692e, 1692j, respectively; Clomon v. Jackson, *supra*; Boyd v. Wexler, *infra*. If so, who is liable?

> b. Is it ethical for an attorney to allow her name to be used in this manner? Doesn't the lawyer have some obligation to investigate the facts of each case? See In re Scheck, 171 A.D.2d 33, 574 N.Y.S.2d 372 (2d Dept. 1991).

> c. Who is the attorney's client? If the attorney has contact exclusively with Ace, is she authorized to represent the individual creditors?

Notes

1. Why would Ace want to use attorney letters rather than letters on its own letterhead?

2. The process of selling attorney letters to a debt collection agency is known as "flat-rating."

BOYD v. WEXLER

United States Court of Appeals, Seventh Circuit, 2001.
275 F.3d 642, cert. denied, 537 U.S. 883, 123 S.Ct. 106, 154 L.Ed.2d 141 (2002).

POSNER, CIRCUIT JUDGE.

This appeal from the grant of summary judgment to the defendant, a lawyer named Norman Wexler, presents questions regarding both the meaning of the Fair Debt Collection Practices Act, 15 U.S.C. §§ 1692 *et seq.*, and the minimum showing required to defeat a motion for summary judgment.

The Act forbids a debt collector, which Wexler is conceded to be, to "use any false, deceptive, or misleading representation or means in connection with the collection of any debt," 15 U.S.C. § 1692e, including "the false representation or implication that any individual is an attorney or that any communication is from an attorney." 15 U.S.C. § 1692e(3). A lawyer who merely rents his letterhead to a collection agency violates the Act, 15 U.S.C. § 1692j(a), for in such a case the lawyer is allowing the collection agency to impersonate him. The significance of such impersonation is that a debtor who receives a dunning letter signed by a lawyer will think that a lawyer reviewed the claim and determined that it had at least colorable merit; so if no lawyer did review the claim, the debtor will have been deceived and the purpose of the Act therefore thwarted. Similarly, a lawyer who, like Wexler, is a debt collector violates section 1692e(3) (and also section 1692e(10), which forbids "the use of any false representation or deceptive means to collect or attempt to collect any debt") if he sends a dunning letter that he has not reviewed, since his lawyer's letterhead then falsely implies that he has reviewed the creditor's claim.

The plaintiffs received dunning letters signed "Wexler & Wexler," the name under which the defendant practices law. The suit charges that no lawyer in fact reviewed the claims made in the letters before they were mailed. The defendant moved for summary judgment and supported the motion with his affidavit. The affidavit states that a lawyer reviews every individual file before the initial collection letter (the letters to the plaintiffs were initial, not follow-up, letters) is sent, that he himself reviewed the plaintiffs' files before approving the sending of collection letters to them, and that in every collection case handled by his office a lawyer "reviews each and every document in the client's file to insure the correctness of the data and the claim, paying strict attention to the various statutes of limitation which may apply . . . [and] to make sure that we comply with state requirements, such as the need for actual presence in the state, a collection agency license or a license to practice law in the state." If the lawyer approves the claim, a form letter is prepared "for review and approval [by him] before [it is] allowed to go into the mail." If "after reviewing the case file . . . the attorney is unable to verify that the client is making a valid claim, the case is pulled out and discussed with our client."

So far, so good. But pretrial discovery revealed that in a recent eight-and-a-half-month period Wexler's firm sent out 439,606 pieces of mail, which according to the deposition testimony of one of the firm's lawyers consisted overwhelmingly of collection letters. That is an average of 51,718 a month. So Wexler's firm must be large—but no, it turns out to have only three lawyers, although it has 45 other employees. Of the three lawyers, two, including the defendant, appear to be engaged in managing the firm and all three engage in normal litigation activities (Wexler's affidavit states that his firm "routinely engages in litigation with regards [sic] to collection matters"), leaving little time for them to be reviewing the routine collection activity that generates the vast bulk of the mailings. In addition, Wexler is constantly changing the form letter. We are amused (though we doubt the recipients were) by one of the variants, which Wexler dropped after being sued on account of it: "YOU ARE ABOUT TO BE TREATED IN A MANNER THAT WILL CAUSE YOU TO THINK TWICE BEFORE YOU WRITE ANOTHER WORTHLESS CHECK. OUR CLIENT HAS INSTRUCTED THAT WE NOTIFY YOU THAT YOU ARE GOING TO BE SUED UNLESS RE-PAYMENT IS FORTHCOMING AT ONCE." *Keele v. Wexler,* 149 F.3d 589, 591 (7th Cir.1998).

Suppose that each of the three lawyers in Wexler's firm devotes four hours a day to reviewing collection files and authorizing the mailing of dunning letters and that the process of review and authorization takes an average of 15 minutes per file. That comes to 16 collection letters a day per lawyer, which is fewer than 50 collection letters a day for all three lawyers or, assuming a five-day work week, fewer than 1,000 letters a month for the entire firm—if it is really true that each lawyer follows the review and authorization procedure set forth in Wexler's affidavit. To say the least, it is difficult to see how the firm could send out *fifty times* that number of letters yet still have a lawyer review the file and the letter in every one.

And it gets worse. The volume of mail sent by the firm varies from week to week, and in one particularly busy week in June 2000 the firm sent out 23,342 pieces of mail—93 times the maximum number consistent with 15–minute review. What is more, Wexler stated at his deposition that he personally is responsible for reviewing most of the collection letters; if he reviewed all of them himself, the estimate of 93 times the maximum consistent with 15–minute review would soar to 279 times. Our 15–minute estimate may be too high, but it could be cut in three, or for that matter in 15, without explaining the volume of collection letters.

The district judge, in explaining why despite this evidence he grant-ed summary judgment for Wexler, characterized Wexler's affidavit as "uncontradicted and unrefuted." This characterization was possible only because the judge gave no weight at all to the volume of mail, stating that "mathematical inferences about the volume of letters sent are not probative of [Wexler's] state of mind." State of mind is not the issue. The issue is credibility, the truthfulness of the affidavit; Wexler might think he reviewed the two plaintiffs' files carefully yet be mistaken. Circumstantial evidence can create an issue of credibility. Suppose a witness testifies that he saw a person draw a gun, but there is evidence that a truck was blocking the witness's line of sight. This would be circumstantial evidence that created an issue of the witness's credibility (though not necessarily of his state of mind—he might have *thought* he saw a gun, but have been mistaken). And so it is here. Wexler's testimony was made incredible, or at least highly implausible, by the evidence of the volume of mail, especially when that evidence is viewed against the background of his testimony that he personally reviewed the plaintiffs' files. The letters to the two plaintiffs were mailed in February and March 2000, respectively. They are very short form letters seeking unexceptional amounts of money; there is nothing memorable about them. Wexler gave his deposition in September, almost six months later—by which time, if his affidavit can be believed, close to 100,000 additional collection matters had passed through his hands. The volume of mail not only undermines Wexler's affidavit, but is evidence from which a reasonable jury could infer that the letters to the plaintiffs were not in fact reviewed by Wexler or any other lawyer.

Wexler argues that the plaintiffs did not conduct enough discovery, that they should have broken down the 439,606 figure into initial collection letters, follow-up collection letters, and noncollection mailings (such as receipts), and should have further broken down the figure for initial collection letters between bounced-check matters, requiring minimal lawyer review, and other matters, requiring more review. We do not agree that the plaintiffs had to do this in order to create a genuine issue of material fact regarding the defendant's compliance with the Fair Debt Collection Practices Act. Remember that there is testimony by one of the firm's lawyers that the overwhelming bulk of the mailings consist of collection letters. Granted that some of them are follow-up collection letters, which require less review than initial collection letters, and bounced-check collection letters, which also may require less review than other collection letters, we do not see how these facts could be thought to put a big dent in our 15–minute estimate, which is the sort of estimate that a reasonable jury might make and from which damaging inferences concerning the veracity of Wexler's affidavit and the review of the dunning letters sent the plaintiffs by his firm arise.

Before a follow-up letter can be responsibly approved by a lawyer, he must inspect the file to determine that there has been no partial payment or other response from the debtor, and, if interest on the debt is sought by the creditor, to determine how much interest is owing. This can be a complicated calculation. In the case of a bounced-check follow-up letter, if statutory penalties are sought the lawyer must determine whether the grace period for making good on such a check has expired. See 810 ILCS 5/3–806. No doubt the initial review of a bounced-check matter takes little time, but it is hard to believe that bounced checks are so common that they could account for the bulk of these enormous mailings.

An illuminating omission from the defendant's evidence is any indication of how often, if ever, his review of a collection file leads him to refuse to approve a dunning letter and to take the matter up with the client. If this happens often, it would bolster his claim to be engaged in a process of meaningful review of clients' referrals—but it would also dramatize how little time he has to review collection files, since refusal of a referral and ensuing discussion with the client about the refusal must take more than 15 minutes. One of the other lawyers in the firm acknowledged at his deposition that "we get cases all the time where individuals claim that their checks were stolen and that there were forgeries,'' and he said that in each of those cases the firm would follow up, for example by sending the debtor a forgery affidavit to fill out. A lawyer would have to review the affidavit to determine whether to send a follow-up letter to the affiant.

A further difficulty with the defendant's argument that an unknown fraction of the letters are follow-up rather than initial collection letters is that in a deposition given in a similar case just a few months before his affidavit in this case, Wexler stated that if the debtor doesn't pay up after receiving the initial collection letter, the firm forthwith institutes legal proceedings unless the debtor has either died or declared bankruptcy. If this is true (it can't be—it is unbelievable that Wexler's firm would be authorized by the client to file suit no matter how trivial the amount of the unpaid debt—but he can hardly gain a forensic benefit from making an incredible admission), there are few follow-up letters and an enormous number of legal proceedings. Those proceedings would leave the lawyers with no time to review what must be a colossal number of files.

The most practical, intuitive, and readily applied criterion for granting summary judgment is whether, if the evidence gathered in discovery were the evidence presented at trial, the party moving for summary judgment (Wexler) would be entitled to judgment as a matter of law because no reasonable jury could render a verdict for the opposing party (the two plaintiffs). A reasonable jury could infer from the evidence as we have summarized it that the defendant violated the Fair Debt Collection Practices Act by rubber stamping his clients' demands for payment, thus misrepresenting to the recipients of his dunning letters that a lawyer had made a minimally responsible determination that there was probable cause to believe that the recipient actually owed the amount claimed by the creditor. A reasonable jury informed of the size of the firm and the duties of the three lawyers, which leave them little time for review of collection files, informed also of the circumstances from which an estimate can be made of the time that it takes a lawyer to review such a file with sufficient care to be able to make a responsible professional judgment that a legally collectible debt is owing, and informed finally of the enormous mass of mailings, most apparently of collection letters, in relation to the number and available time of Wexler's tiny legal staff, could rationally conclude that Wexler's claim to have reviewed these plaintiffs' files was false, that he had not reviewed them (nor had any other lawyer), and therefore that he had violated the Act. These inferences are not certain, because no matter how perfunctory the firm's normal review of creditor files and dunning letters, it is always possible that Wexler for obscure reasons did actually review these two plaintiffs' files. But certainty of winning at trial is obviously not a precondition to getting a trial.

We need not determine in this case the minimum amount of lawyer review required to avoid misleading the debtor into thinking that a lawyer has made a responsible professional judgment about the existence of a legally enforceable debt. No reported decisions address that issue and it may not have to be resolved in this case. For if the jury believes the plaintiffs, Wexler gave their dunning letters no review at all, while if it believes Wexler, he gave it more than enough review. We say "more than enough" because the Act can be complied with by delegation of part of the review process to a paralegal or even to a computer program, see *Avila v. Rubin, supra,* 84 F.3d at 229–30; ABA Model Rule of Professional Conduct 5.3 (materially identical to Illinois Rule of Professional Conduct 5.3), provided the ultimate professional judgment concerning the existence of a valid debt is reserved to the lawyer. "An attorney's signature implies the attorney has formed a professional judgment about the debtor's case." *Avila v. Rubin, supra,* 84 F.3d at 229; see ABA Model Rule of Professional Conduct Rule 5.5(b) and comment 1 (materially identical to Illinois Rule of Professional Conduct 5.5(b)). In an age of specialization, professionals are not to be criticized for identifying subroutines that paraprofessionals can adequately perform under a professional's supervision. But Wexler does not argue that he has delegated some of the review tasks (for example, ascertaining whether the amount of the claim submitted by the client is the same as the amount that appears on the form letter prepared by the nonlawyer collection agents whom Wexler employs) to nonlawyers; he argues that he performs all these tasks himself, implying that if he is not telling the truth, no one performs them. We can leave for a future case the determination of the point at which delegation is so extensive or review so perfunctory that the lawyer's supposed authorship of the dunning letter becomes a deception, not because there was no review but because it was too meager to be meaningful. We are not suggesting a 15–minute minimum; we used that assumption merely to illustrate that a rational jury might find, given the volume of mail, that it was unlikely that Wexler had actually reviewed the plaintiffs' files before authorizing dunning letters to be sent to them.

REVERSED.

Notes

1. Suppose a client transmits electronically to an attorney a spreadsheet showing the name, account number and contact information of each debtor; the date each debt was incurred; the amount of each debt together with accumulated interest and other charges; a statement that the debt has not been paid; and a description of the client's efforts to collect the debt (which would tend to be similar for similar debts). A paralegal verifies that the debtor is not in bankruptcy proceedings and that the statute of limitations has not expired and adds that information to the spreadsheet. The attorney reads each entry in the spreadsheet and confirms that the information is not inconsistent or incomplete. See Miller v. Wolpoff & Abramson, L.L.P., 321 F.3d 292 (2d Cir.), cert. denied, 540 U.S. 823, 124 S.Ct. 153, 157 L.Ed.2d 44 (2003). Would that satisfy the attorney's obligation? If not, what more should the attorney do? How long would reading such entries take? Would it take fifteen minutes, or would fifteen seconds be closer to the truth? Both Boyd and Clomon refer to the "file." What more would (or

should) the file contain? One commentator has suggested that attorneys err on the side of doing too much and that they document what they do. See Steven Wechsler, Professional Responsibility, 54 Syracuse L. Rev. 1299, 1335–36 (2004). Would that increase the cost of attorney involvement to the point where creditors would be better off forgoing attorney letters? The same commentator interprets *Miller,* cited just above, as suggesting that it would be enough if the lawyer looked over the debtor's contract, credit report, and full payment history. As for whether it would violate the FCRA for the creditor's attorney to read the consumer's current credit report, see Chapter Four. Would reviewing the credit report help determine whether the debtor owed the money, or only whether the debtor was defaulting on other obligations?

2. Suppose Wexler's letter had conspicuously stated "this office represents the above named creditor in the collection of your debt. At this time, no attorney with this firm has personally reviewed the particular circumstances of your account." Suppose also that the letter did not suggest in any way that an attorney had reviewed the account or was otherwise involved in the matter. Would such a letter sent on attorney letterhead and with the firm's name printed as a signature block violate the FDCPA? See Greco v. Trauner, Cohen & Thomas, L.L.P., 412 F.3d 360 (2d Cir. 2005).

3. Did Wexler behave unethically? See United States v. Central Adjustment Bureau, 667 F.Supp. 370 (N.D. Tex. 1986), *aff'd in pertinent part,* 823 F.2d 880 (5th Cir. 1987); ABA Formal Opinion 253 (June 1943), Opinions on Professional Ethics (Amer. Bar. Found.] 560 (1967); Los Angeles County Bar Association Opinion No. 338 (Sept. 27, 1973).

Problem 8–14

FFC referred Cindy Ann Kimber's account to attorney Sally Bones for collection after the statute of limitations had expired. Bones sent a letter threatening suit if Kimber did not pay, and after receiving no response, filed suit. Kimber's lawyer got the suit dismissed because the statute of limitations had run. Kimber then sued Bones, arguing that Bones violated the FDCPA by threatening to sue and then suing on a consumer debt which was time-barred.

a. Bones argues that there is no violation because the statute of limitations is an affirmative defense which is waived if not raised by a defendant debtor, and therefore she should not be penalized for filing a time-barred suit. What result?

b. Is it ethical for an attorney knowingly to file a suit on a claim which is barred by the statute of limitations? Does it matter that the defendant is a consumer who is not likely to know this, and who may in fact respond to the suit by paying all or part of the debt?

c. Given that the statute of limitations must usually be raised as an affirmative defense, is it ethical for an attorney *not* to file a time-barred suit?

d. Would an attempt to collect the debt without a threat of litigation violate the FDCPA? See Freyermuth v. Credit Bureau Services, Inc., 248 F.3d 767 (8th Cir. 2001).

SECTION D.   FORECLOSING ON SECURITY

Up to now, this chapter has focused on informal debt collection efforts. Yet creditors who have taken a security interest in property have another option: repossession. When the debtor defaults under the security agreement, the creditor's remedies are spelled out in Article 9 of the Uniform Commercial Code (UCC). These remedies are supplemented in many states by special consumer statutes. In this book we will not repeat all of the material typically studied in courses in Secured Transactions and the like, such as the rules for taking and perfecting a security interest. (If you need review, James J. White & Robert S. Summers, Uniform Commercial Code (5th ed. 2000) would be a good place to start.) Instead, we will focus on issues which commonly arise in consumer cases, particularly those involving automobiles.

1.   REPOSSESSION—WHEN?

Although Article 9 prescribes both the debtor's and creditor's rights after default, it does not define the term "default." Instead, the events which constitute default in a particular transaction are left to the parties to define in the security agreement under § 9–601. Of course, in consumer cases, this means that the creditor will dictate the terms of default. Nonpayment is the most common term, and the most common cause, of default. The typical consumer security agreement will also list other events of default, including such things as failure to insure the collateral, moving the collateral out of the state, and allowing other liens to attach.

Beyond this, the security agreement often contains an acceleration clause coupled with a so-called "insecurity" clause. Under an insecurity clause, a creditor may declare a default and accelerate the obligation when it "deems itself insecure," even though the consumer might still be current on her payments. UCC § 1–310 provides that a creditor has the power to deem itself insecure "only if that party in good faith believes that the prospect of payment or performance is impaired." Section 1–310 imposes the burden of establishing lack of good faith on the consumer. Under § 1–201(b)(20), the relevant standard of good faith is "honesty in fact and the observance of reasonable commercial standards of fair dealing." Some states impose additional protections. See, e.g., N.Y. Pers. Prop. L. § 403.2 ("No contract or obligation shall contain any provision by which . . . (b) In the absence of the buyer's default, the holder may, arbitrarily and without reasonable cause, accelerate the maturity of any part or all of the amount owing thereunder."). How significant are these protections? What justification must a creditor show before it can exercise an insecurity clause?

Problem 8–15

On June 3, Blaine purchased an automobile from Calhoun Chevrolet Co., financing it through GMAC. The credit contract included a security interest on the car and required Blaine to make a payment on the third day of each month, maintain casualty insurance on the car, and notify GMAC of any change of address. On June 4, Old Reliable Insurance Co., after reviewing Blaine's driving record, cancelled all insurance on the car. Blaine has not obtained substitute insurance. On July 1, Blaine moved from the address listed on the contract to another apartment across the street. Blaine was so busy moving that he forgot to mail the payment check until July 3. It was not delivered to GMAC until July 5.

Which, if any, of the above facts constitute a default which will allow repossession under UCC § 9–609? Cf. Pierce v. Leasing International, Inc., 142 Ga.App. 371, 235 S.E.2d 752 (1977). Which, if any, of the above facts constitute a serious threat to the creditor's security? Does the consumer have any protection under the UCC against precipitous acceleration or repossession?

Problem 8–16

Again Blaine purchased a car and then financed it through GMAC. The credit contract stated that "There shall be a default hereunder if creditor has reasonable cause to believe that the car is in danger of misuse or confiscation, and creditor may then repossess the car." Two months later, Blaine was arrested and charged with "criminal possession of a controlled substance." The police said the car was used to transport narcotics and threatened to confiscate it. Before conviction, trial, or even indictment, GMAC notified Blaine that it felt its security interest was in jeopardy and sought repossession. The car was released to GMAC. Does Blaine have any action to recover possession of the car? What if he is subsequently acquitted? Cf. Blaine v. General Motors Acceptance Corp., 82 Misc.2d 653, 370 N.Y.S.2d 323 (1975).

Notes

1. U3C § 5.109 provides that "An agreement ... with respect to default on the part of the consumer is enforceable only to the extent that (1) the consumer fails to make a [required] payment ... or (2) the prospect of payment, performance, or realization of collateral is significantly impaired...." How, if at all, would the answers to the foregoing problems be affected by the U3C provision? Would you support adoption of a similar provision in your state?

2. Should consumers have a right to cure a default? If so, under what circumstances? See U3C §§ 5.110, 5.111.

3. Suppose a consumer repeatedly missed payments on a car loan and the creditor consistently allowed the consumer to bring the account up to date. The consumer again misses a payment, and the creditor repossesses the car. Has the creditor waived its right to declare a default by its past conduct? What if the agreement contained a term providing that acceptance of late payments did not constitute such a waiver? See Battista v. Savings Bank of Baltimore, 67 Md.App. 257, 507 A.2d 203 (App. 1986).

2. REPOSSESSION—HOW?

When the debtor defaults, the creditor ordinarily has the right to repossess the collateral. The creditor may do this through self-help, without going to court, as long as the repossession can be done without breaching the peace. See UCC § 9–609(b)(2), though the creditor may also employ judicial process under § 9–609(b)(1). If you were a creditor, would you prefer self-help or judicial process? Why? In consumer cases, the type of collateral most likely to be repossessed is the automobile. Naturally, confrontations and other problems sometime occur. What are the rights and responsibilities of the parties when this occurs?

WILLIAMS v. FORD MOTOR CREDIT CO.

United States Court of Appeals, Eighth Circuit, 1982.
674 F.2d 717.

BENSON, CHIEF JUDGE.

In this diversity action brought by Cathy A. Williams to recover damages for conversion arising out of an alleged wrongful repossession of an automobile, Williams appeals from a judgment notwithstanding the verdict entered on motion of defendant Ford Motor Credit Company (FMCC). In the same case, FMCC appeals a directed verdict in favor of third party defendant S & S Recovery, Inc. (S & S) on FMCC's third party claim for indemnification. We affirm the judgment n.o.v. FMCC's appeal is thereby rendered moot.

In July, 1975, David Williams, husband of plaintiff Cathy Williams, purchased a Ford Mustang from an Oklahoma Ford dealer. Although David Williams executed the sales contract, security agreement, and loan papers, title to the car was in the name of both David and Cathy Williams. The car was financed through the Ford dealer, who in turn assigned the paper to FMCC. Cathy and David Williams were divorced in 1977. The divorce court granted Cathy title to the automobile and required David to continue to make payments to FMCC for eighteen months. David defaulted on the payments and signed a voluntary repossession authorization for FMCC. Cathy Williams was informed of the delinquency and responded that she was trying to get her former husband David to make the payments. There is no evidence of any agreement between her and FMCC. Pursuant to an agreement with FMCC, S & S was directed to repossess the automobile.

On December 1, 1977, at approximately 4:30 a.m., Cathy Williams was awakened by a noise outside her house trailer in Van Buren, Arkansas. She saw that a wrecker truck with two men in it had hooked up to the Ford Mustang and started to tow it away. She went outside and hollered at them. The truck stopped. She then told them that the car was hers and asked them what they were doing. One of the men, later identified as Don Sappington, president of S & S Recovery, Inc., informed her that he was repossessing the vehicle on behalf of FMCC. Williams explained that she had been attempting to bring the past due payments up to date and informed Sappington that the car contained personal items which did not even belong to her. Sappington got out of the truck, retrieved the items from the car, and handed them to her. Without further complaint from Williams, Sappington returned to the truck and drove off, car in tow. At trial, Williams testified that Sappington was polite throughout their encounter and did not make any threats toward her or do anything which caused her to fear any physical harm. The automobile had been parked in an unenclosed driveway which plaintiff shared with a neighbor. The neighbor was awakened by the wrecker backing into the driveway, but did not come out. After the wrecker drove off, Williams returned to her house trailer and called the police, reporting her car as stolen. Later, Williams commenced this action.

The case was tried to a jury which awarded her $5,000.00 in damages. FMCC moved for judgment notwithstanding the verdict, but the district court, on Williams' motion, ordered a nonsuit without prejudice to refile in state court. On FMCC's appeal, this court reversed and remanded with directions to the district court to rule on the motion for judgment notwithstanding the verdict. The district court entered judgment notwithstanding the verdict for FMCC, and this appeal followed.

Article 9 of the Uniform Commercial Code (UCC) which Arkansas has adopted and codified as Ark.Stat.Ann. § 85–9–503 (Supp.1981), provides in pertinent part:

> Unless otherwise agreed, a secured party has on default the right to take possession of the collateral. In taking possession, a secured party may proceed without judicial process if this can be done without breach of the peace. * * *

In *Ford Motor Credit Co. v. Herring,* 27 U.C.C.Rep. 1448, 267 Ark. 201, 589 S.W.2d 584, 586 (1979), which involved an alleged conversion arising out of a repossession, the Supreme Court of Arkansas cited Section 85–9–503 and referred to its previous holdings as follows:

> In pre-code cases, we have sustained a finding of conversion only where force, or threats of force, or risk of invoking violence, accompanied the repossession. *Manhattan Credit Co., Inc. v. Brewer,* 232 Ark. 976, 341 S.W.2d 765 (1961); *Kensinger Acceptance Corp. v. Davis,* 223 Ark. 942, 269 S.W.2d 792 (1954).

The thrust of Williams' argument on appeal is that the repossession was accomplished by the risk of invoking violence. The district judge who presided at the trial commented on her theory in his memorandum opinion:

> Mrs. Williams herself admitted that the men who repossessed her automobile were very polite and complied with her requests. The evidence does not reveal that they performed any act which was oppressive, threatening or tended to cause physical violence. Unlike the situation presented in *Manhattan Credit Co. v. Brewer, supra,* it was not shown that Mrs. Williams would have been forced to resort to physical violence to stop the men from leaving with her automobile.

In the pre-Code case *Manhattan Credit Co. v. Brewer,* 232 Ark. 976, 341 S.W.2d 765 (1961), the court held that a breach of peace occurred when the debtor and her husband confronted the creditor's agent during the act of repossession and clearly objected to the repossession, 341 S.W.2d at 767–68. In *Manhattan,* the court examined holdings of earlier cases in which repossessions were deemed to have been accomplished without any breach of the peace, *id.* In particular, the Supreme Court of Arkansas discussed the case of *Rutledge v. Universal C.I.T. Credit Corp.,* 218 Ark. 510, 237 S.W.2d 469 (1951). In *Rutledge,* the court found no breach of the peace when the repossessor acquired keys to the automobile, confronted the debtor and his wife, informed them he was going to take the car, and immediately proceeded to do so. As the *Rutledge* court explained and the *Manhattan* court reiterated, a breach of the peace did not occur when the "Appellant [debtor-possessor] did not give his permission but he did not object." *Manhattan, supra,* 341 S.W.2d at 767–68; *Rutledge, supra,* 237 S.W.2d at 470.

We have read the transcript of the trial. There is no material dispute in the evidence, and the district court has correctly summarized it. Cathy Williams did not raise an objection to the taking, and the repossession was accomplished without any incident which might tend to provoke violence.

Appellees deserve something less than commendation for the taking during the night time sleeping hours, but it is clear that viewing the facts in the light most favorable to Williams, the taking was a legal repossession under the laws of the State of Arkansas. The evidence does not support the verdict of the jury. FMCC is entitled to judgment notwithstanding the verdict.

The judgment notwithstanding the verdict is affirmed.

Heaney, Circuit Judge, dissenting.

The only issue is whether the repossession of appellant's automobile constituted a breach of the peace by creating a "risk of invoking violence." *See Ford Motor Credit Co. v. Herring,* 267 Ark. 201, 589 S.W.2d 584, 586 (1979). The trial jury found that it did and awarded $5,000 for conversion. Because that determination was in my view a reasonable one, I dissent from the Court's decision to overturn it.

Cathy Williams was a single parent living with her two small children in a trailer home in Van Buren, Arkansas. On December 1, 1977, at approximately 4:30 a.m., she was awakened by noises in her driveway. She went into the night to investigate and discovered a wrecker and its crew in the process of towing away her car. According to the trial court, "she ran outside to stop them * * * but she made no *strenuous* protests to their actions." (Emphasis added.) In fact, the wrecker crew stepped between her and the car when she sought to retrieve personal items from inside it, although the men retrieved some of the items for her. The commotion created by the incident awakened neighbors in the vicinity.

Facing the wrecker crew in the dead of night, Cathy Williams did everything she could to stop them, short of introducing physical force to meet the presence of the crew. The confrontation did not result in violence only because Ms. Williams did not take such steps and was otherwise powerless to stop the crew.

The controlling law is the UCC, which authorizes self-help repossession only when such is done "without breach of the peace * * *." The majority recognizes that one important policy consideration underlying this restriction is to discourage "extrajudicial acts by citizens when those acts are fraught with the likelihood of resulting violence." Despite this, the majority holds that no reasonable jury could find that the confrontation in Cathy Williams' driveway at 4:30 a.m. created a risk of violence. I cannot agree. At a minimum, the largely undisputed facts created a jury question. The jury found a breach of the peace and this Court has no sound, much less compelling, reason to overturn that determination.

Indeed, I would think that sound application of the self-help limitation might require a directed verdict in favor of Ms. Williams, but certainly not against her. If a "night raid" is conducted without detection and confrontation, then, of course, there could be no breach of the peace. But where the invasion is detected and a confrontation ensues, the repossessor should be under a duty to retreat and turn to judicial process. The alternative which the majority embraces is to allow a repossessor to proceed following confrontation unless and until violence results in fact. Such a rule invites tragic consequences which the law should seek to prevent, not to encourage. I would reverse the trial court and reinstate the jury's verdict.

Notes

1. "Breach of the peace" has been left to the courts to define, and there are hundreds of cases. In consumer cases, the courts have routinely held that unauthorized entry into the debtor's residence or closed garage is a breach of the peace. Compare U3C § 5.112. By the same token, repossessions from the debtor's yard or driveway are usually allowed, absent any confrontation, despite the technical trespass. What should be the result if the creditor takes the car from an open garage or a carport?

2. Doesn't the majority opinion in *Williams* encourage debtors to use violence to try to prevent their cars from being repossessed? Suppose Cathy Williams had called you for advice before the repo men drove off with her car. What would you have said to her? Can you ethically advise a client to commit a breach of the peace? If not, can you ethically advise a client to protest a repossession? Conversely, what would you advise a repo person to do if the debtor showed up during the repossession?

3. Suppose a creditor breaches the peace in the course of a repossession. What consequences might ensue?

Problem 8–17

Bill Bones bought an airplane and financed it by borrowing from Friendly Finance Co. Bones gave Friendly a security interest in the airplane, but defaulted on his payments under the security agreement. Alert, an employee of Friendly, located the airplane in a hangar at the Boise Municipal Airport. Without notice to Bones, Alert opened the hangar door, "hot-wired" the ignition switch of the airplane, started the engine, took off from the Boise airport without clearance from the tower, and flew it to Oklahoma City, where it was resold.

Was the repossession in violation of UCC § 9–609? If it was, what is Bones' remedy? Does UCC § 9–625 apply? Does it preempt other possible remedies, such as tort recoveries?

Problem 8–18

Daniel Default bought on credit from Charlie Cheerful three rooms of furniture for his three room apartment. He failed to make any of the payments due. After four months, Charlie "picked" the lock to Dan's apartment, entered the apartment and removed all of the furniture. Dan's landlord discovered Charlie's actions during the repossession and called the police, but they never arrived. The landlord listened further and finally determined the motives behind Charlie's actions. He did not object, but merely asked that Charlie leave the door locked when through. Charlie did.

When Dan returned to his apartment, he objected greatly, and would like to pursue "any legal remedies available." Could you help him? Cf. Cherno v. Bank of Babylon, 54 Misc.2d 277, 282 N.Y.S.2d 114 (1967), aff'd, 29 A.D.2d 767, 288 N.Y.S.2d 862 (2d Dept. 1968).

Would it make any difference if the credit contract had the following clause: "In the event of default, Bank is authorized to repossess the collateral and to enter any premises where the collateral may be located and take the same with or without legal process."

Notes

1. When only a "technical" trespass has been involved, the courts have usually not found any breach of the peace, on a variety of grounds. See, e.g. Reno v. GMAC, 378 So.2d 1103, 27 UCC Rep.Serv. 1452 (Ala.1979); Raffa v. Dania Bank, 321 So.2d 83 (Fla.App.1975).

2. When self-help repossession requires entrance into a residence, courts have been quick to find a breach of the peace whenever the repossession occurs without the informed consent of the debtor. See, e.g., Girard v. Anderson, 219 Iowa 142, 257 N.W. 400 (1934).

3. "The law recognizes that personal property taken as a mortgage security, because of its transitory nature can be easily lost, strayed, converted or stolen. Realty can not stray, be converted, or stolen; hence the law of merchant recognizes the necessity of sanctioning summary methods of seizure to call in chattel mortgages. Were it otherwise, any system of credit extended upon chattels as security would be imperiled, and perhaps break down. Cautious lenders would decline to lend on so insecure a collateral; hence, we have the principal that immediately on default, the chattels are the property of the mortgagee to seize as the provisions direct, and no other

or further notice is required except as the chattel mortgage, itself, covenants." Goodman v. Schulman, 144 Misc. 512, 258 N.Y.S. 681 at 683 (1932).

4.   Is there something troublesome about creditors using self-help repossession? Should repossession require legal process? That was the approach taken by the Model Consumer Credit Act. See § 7.202. Would that increase the cost of repossession? If so, would that make the taking of security interests less useful to creditors? How might that affect the cost of credit and the behavior of creditors? See William Whitford & Harold Laufer, The Impact of Denying Self–Help Repossession of Automobiles: A Case Study of the Wisconsin Consumer Act, 1975 Wis.L.Rev. 607.

5.   Starter interrupt devices require drivers to enter a code into a vehicle before the car will start. The code changes each month and lenders provide the new code to the driver as each monthly payment is received. Would the refusal of a lender to provide a borrower with the code constitute a repossession? If so, would it breach the peace? See generally Thomas B. Hudson & Daniel J. Laudicina, The Emerging Law of Starter Interrupt Devices, 61 Bus. Law. 843 (2006).

Problem 8–19

David Default has been out of work for months and has missed several car payments on his loan from Charlie Cheerful. Recently he received a letter offering him a job interview with a company Default had never heard of. Default was told to report for the interview to an office suite in a local office building. The building, which has a parking lot in the rear, was not accessible by mass transit. Default drove to the building in his car, parked in the lot, walked to the front of the building and entered the office suite. He was ushered into a windowless office and told to await the interviewer there. Fifteen minutes later, a woman entered, handed Default an envelope, and instructed Default not to open it until after she left the office. Default did so. The envelope contained a letter explaining that Default's car had been repossessed by Cheerful and that in fact there would be no job interview. The letter asked Default to exit the building peacefully. Does Default have any recourse against Cheerful? See Cox v. Galigher Motor Sales Co., 158 W.Va. 685, 213 S.E.2d 475 (1975).

Chapter 9

PREDATORY LENDING
(INCLUDING PRICING ISSUES)

SECTION A.   FOUNDATION

The practices addressed in this chapter vary considerably, but all raise a fundamental question: to what extent should the law protect borrowers by barring them from entering into certain types of lending arrangements or at least requiring disclosures. As you will discover, the answer to that question differs depending on the practice involved and who is answering the question. The chapter opens with a discussion of the ancient problem of usury and how usury regulation fares today. It next turns, in order, to Congress's response to predatory lending, state initiatives, and the reaction of federal administrative agencies to those state initiatives. After that, the chapter explores a number of specific predatory lending problems, including unfair contract terms, yield-spread premiums, payday lending, and credit insurance.

SECTION B.   PERHAPS THE OLDEST
FORM OF PREDATORY LENDING
REGULATION: USURY LAWS

The doctrine of usury and the regulation of interest rates by the state can be traced several thousand years. In fact, Western society has seen very few historical periods in which interest rates were left to the free market.

Earliest societies. Lending, including consumer lending at interest, is far older than coinage or even writing. Primitive pastoral societies are known to have engaged in loan transactions involving working capital (grain, tools, etc.) as well as consumer goods (food, clothing, etc.). The earliest literate societies often adopted written laws, typically derived from ancient custom, which contained provisions regulating interest. For example, several rules on lending practices are contained in the Biblical texts of the Hebrew laws. Exodus 22:25 says: "If you lend money to any of my people with you who is poor, you shall not be to him as a creditor, and you shall not exact interest from him."

Biblical texts are not the only sources of early written laws. Surviving records from the Sumerian period, about 3000 B.C., show many commercial loans with interest. Around 1800 B.C., the Babylonian king Hammurabi created a legal code which contained many rules on lending, including the earliest surviving law establishing interest rate ceilings. Interest was permitted, but was limited to 33⅓% on loans of grain and 20% on loans of silver. These rates reflect customary levels during this period.

Greece and Rome. In early Greece, there were no interest rate ceilings. Rates were controlled entirely by the market. This apparently worked; commercial rates in Athens dropped from the range of 16% to 18% in the fifth century B.C. to about 6% to 10% in the first and second centuries. However, at the same time (as is true today), rates for consumer loans were much higher, typically around 36%.

In Rome, laws regulating credit and setting maximum interest rates appeared as early as the fifth century B.C. in the famous Twelve Tables (c. 443 B.C.). The Twelve Tables reduced the prevailing rates by setting the limit at 8⅓%. The limit was raised in the first century B.C. to 12%, where it remained until Rome was sacked in 410 A.D. Of course, actual rates during these periods could be lower than the legal limit.

The Christian Influence. The early Christian church not only condemned what we would call "usury," or excessive interest, but also any form of interest. As a result, and because of the strong church influence over civil authorities, usury was generally prohibited during the Middle Ages. In fact, in 800 Charlemagne made interest illegal throughout the Empire. This prohibition remained in effect through the 12th or 13th century.

English law. During the Middle Ages, England followed the pattern established in Europe; interest was prohibited by both church law and civil law. This pattern remained right up to the end of the 15th century. A statute in 1487, for example, declared void all contracts providing for interest. A half century later, however, attitudes had changed, and in 1545, a law was passed which allowed interest of up to 10%. Later, the maximum legal rate was lowered to 5%. 12 Anne.Stat. 2, c. 16 (1713). This latter statute was the forerunner of modern American statutes. England repealed its usury laws in 1854, while their American offspring remained.

Today, there are no general usury ceilings in England, although there may be mechanisms to deal with extremely oppressive lending practices. Under the Consumer Credit Act of 1974, the court can interfere in certain consumer transactions if the rate of return is so exorbitant as to be "extortionate." There are no numerical guidelines or presumptions, however, and courts must decide cases on an individual basis.

The American experience. The American colonies basically followed the English model. Massachusetts adopted a usury law (at 8%) in 1641, and during the 17th and 18th centuries, the other colonies and

states followed suit and adopted usury ceilings of their own. Rates varied
from 5% to 8%, although the most common limit was 6%. Massachusetts
also became the first state to follow the English pattern to the end; it
repealed its general usury law in 1867. Only a few other states followed
suit. By the turn of the 20th century, a few Western states allowed
interest at rates of 10% or 12%, but usury ceilings in most states
remained at 6%.

The Twentieth Century. The low usury ceilings prevalent at the
turn of the century simply did not allow for profitable legal lending to
consumers. This left the consumer market largely to illegal lenders. In
fact, during this period, loan sharks were probably the most common
source of small-scale consumer credit. Two processes developed to circumvent these price ceilings: one for lender credit and the other for
seller credit.

Regulation of Lender Credit. The standard approach by most
states was to enact numerous exceptions to their general usury statutes
which permitted various forms of cash credit that could not otherwise
have been accommodated. These exceptions opened up *legal* alternatives
to the unregulated *illegal* lending that flourished in America in the late
1800s and early 1900s in spite of the usury laws.

As always throughout history, a group of cleverly structured financial transactions appeared which legitimate lenders could use to get
around the usury laws. In the consumer area, one of the most important
was the so-called Morris plan loan. These were created in 1910 (by a
lawyer named Arthur Morris), and operated through Morris Plan Banks,
also known as industrial banks. Under these plans, a lump-sum, single-
payment loan was made for a definite period, say a year, at the highest
lawful rate. At the same time, but as a separate transaction, the
consumer would agree to make monthly or weekly deposits into a special
account at the bank. These deposits would be made during the entire
term of the loan transaction, and their total always equaled the amount
needed to pay off the original loan (plus interest). The overall effect was
to create an installment loan at effective rates nearly double the usury
ceiling. Morris plan loans are still available in about half the states, but
modern banking and usury laws have diminished their importance.

Small loan or consumer finance companies are also basically products of the 20th century. The major impetus for their development came
from studies produced by the Russell Sage Foundation between 1905 and
1908. These studies concluded that the best way to deal with the loan
shark problem was to raise the usury limits high enough so that
legitimate lenders would enter the market. This led to the Uniform
Small Loan Act in 1916, and all states (except Arkansas) ultimately
enacted some sort of small loan act. These acts were seen as exceptions
to the general usury laws. They all required consumer lenders to obtain
licenses, and in exchange they allowed small consumer loans to be made
at much higher rates.

In one sense, small loan acts helped to establish a pattern that came to dominate early Twentieth Century rate regulation legislation. Such legislation is often sponsored by the credit industry. This may seem surprising at first, but it should be less so if the matter is viewed historically. Each segment of the lending industry has often sponsored its own laws, usually seeking special treatment or exceptions to the general usury limits. One result of this activity is that the lending industry is highly fragmented; many segments do not directly compete with each other. These divisions reflect differences in the markets which lenders have carved out for themselves, sometimes encouraged by the various exceptions and special rules found in the usury laws. Banks, for example, are rarely regulated by the same laws (usury or otherwise) as are small loan companies, and the two rarely compete directly for their respective shares of the consumer loan market. In fact, each type of lender often has its own regulatory statute, interest rate ceilings, restrictions on required and permissible contract provisions, and licensing requirements. By the mid–20th century, so many exceptions and special rules had appeared that it sometimes seemed that as many transactions were excluded as were governed by the general usury laws. Of course, most of the excluded transactions are subject to statutes, including interest rate ceilings, of their own. Today, the most descriptive characteristics of state usury laws are probably complexity and disarray. In part, of course, this hodge-podge reflects the general lack of uniformity in the law of consumer credit which we have seen throughout this book. Yet, in large part, it also reflects the historical pattern of the usury laws.

Regulation of Seller Credit—The Time–Price Doctrine. The most remarkable division within the credit market is between lenders of money and credit sellers of goods, a division which was produced by the time-price doctrine.

> Essentially, this was a legal principle permitting a seller of goods and services freely to establish two prices, a cash price and a time, or credit, price. Under common law the differential was not considered interest subject to general usury statutes. So, sales credit—credit extended in conjunction with the sale of merchandise—became exempt from general usury statutes which facilitated its growth. Since 1935 many states have enacted legislation limiting the time-price differential on the credit sale of motor vehicles and other consumer goods as well as on revolving credit. NCCF Report, at 93 (1972).

Throughout history, creditors have always been on the lookout for ways to restructure their lending transactions into forms which were not affected by the usury laws. The judicially developed "time-price doctrine," for example, exempted credit sales from usury laws, and this prompted many creditors to create artificial sales to take advantage of this rule. However, such attempts to reshape the transaction to avoid application of the usury laws is little different from attempts during the Middle Ages to recast loan transactions in the form of partnerships or annuities. These devices permitted a profitable rate of return without running afoul of prohibitions against interest on loans.

Creditors today are not much different; new devices constantly appear which attempt to avoid the effects of usury or other restrictive laws. Recent examples include rent-to-own contracts and payday loans. As legislatures and courts catch up to these newer devices, no doubt others will appear. But perhaps the greatest aid to lenders seeking to avoid usury laws in recent decades has come from federal interventions.

Federal Developments. In recent decades, court decisions, statutes, and regulatory initiatives have greatly reduced the significance of state usury laws. During the late 1970s and early 1980s, inflation, high operating costs, and competition for the depositor's dollar made it difficult for creditors to offer consumer credit within the constraints of state usury laws. Banks were often reluctant to make auto loans, for example, or to extend credit card lines at rates of 18%, when their "prime" rates for commercial customers were over 20%. One result was pressure on law-makers to ease usury limits. In 1980, Congress enacted the Depository Institutions Deregulation and Monetary Control Act ("DIDMCA"), Pub. L. No. 96–221, 94 Stat. 161, codified in various sections of titles 12 and 15 U.S.C. DIDMCA largely preempts state usury laws covering loans for residential real property secured by first mortgages. 12 U.S.C. § 1735f–7. DIDMCA's impact is somewhat diminished by a provision that permitted states to opt out of its preemption, an invitation a number of states accepted. Two years later, Congress passed the Alternative Mortgage Transaction Parity Act ("AMTPA"), 12 U.S.C. § 3801 et seq., which preempted state laws limiting certain terms in mortgages, such as negative amortization clauses, variable rate loans and balloon payments (though Congress's enactment of HOEPA in 1994, to be discussed *infra*, limited AMTPA's effect as to high-cost loans). More recently, the Office of the Comptroller of the Currency (OCC) issued regulations which preempt state interest rate regulation as to national banks. See, e.g., 12 C.F.R. § 34.4(a)(12). These statutes and regulations have combined to limit dramatically the power of states to regulate interest rates and fees in mortgages. And not only mortgages: some lenders responded by conditioning their approval of non-real estate loans, such as car loans, upon consumers granting a mortgage on their homes, thereby enabling the lender to ignore state usury limits as to non-real estate loans as well. See Smith v. Fidelity Consumer Discount Co., 898 F.2d 907 (3d Cir. 1990).

Court decisions have also eroded the power of the states. The National Bank Act has long permitted national banks to charge the interest rate allowed other lenders in the bank's home state; that is, the state identified in the bank's organization certificate as the location where its operations are to take place. 12 U.S.C. § 85. In 1978, the Supreme Court interpreted this statute to allow national banks to do so even when the borrower lives in a state with lower usury limits. Marquette v. First of Omaha Service Corp., 439 U.S. 299, 99 S.Ct. 540, 58 L.Ed.2d 534 (1978). This power of "exportation" extends not only to interest rates but also to other charges, including late fees. See Smiley v. Citibank (South Dakota) N.A., 517 U.S. 735, 116 S.Ct. 1730, 135 L.Ed.2d 25 (1996). Federal courts have also allowed state-chartered lenders that are federally-insured to "export" rates. See Greenwood Trust v. Massachusetts, 971 F.2d 818 (1st Cir. 1992), cert. denied, 506 U.S. 1052, 113 S.Ct. 974, 122 L.Ed.2d 129 (1993). Similarly, the OCC takes the position that operating subsidiaries of national banks may export interest rates to the same extent as their parents. OCC Letter No. 968 (Feb. 12, 2003).

Federally-chartered lenders responded to these initiatives by moving to states which do not limit interest rates and exporting the laws of those states to the localities where their borrowers reside. Meanwhile, some state legislatures, in an effort to attract jobs and other benefits from having large national lending operations located in their states, raised or repealed usury limits. See, e.g. S.D. Codified Laws § 54–3–1.1. Other states provided for "parity," which is to say that they allowed state-chartered lenders to charge interest rates as high as federal institutions. See, e.g., Tenn. Code Ann. § 45–4–602(a)(2). The effect of these developments is illustrated by Wiseman v. State Bank & Trust, 313 Ark. 289, 854 S.W.2d 725 (1993). The Wisemans, residents of Arkansas, wished to buy a car from an Arkansas car dealer. The dealer provided the Wisemans with an application for financing which the dealer had obtained from State Bank. While State Bank was a subsidiary of an Arkansas company, its charter address and principal place of business were in Oklahoma. After the dealer faxed the Wisemans' completed application to the State Bank office in Oklahoma, a State Bank employee telephoned the Arkansas dealer from Oklahoma to report that the loan application had been approved. The Wisemans returned to the dealership in Arkansas and executed the loan agreement, which provided that Oklahoma law governed the transaction. The dealer then forwarded the agreement to the bank in Oklahoma, where the bank executed the agreement in turn. Though the parties agreed that the agreement would have violated the Arkansas usury limits, the court ruled that Oklahoma law, which allowed higher interest rates, applied. As *Wiseman* demonstrates, even states with strict usury limits are rarely able to apply them to transactions involving their citizens. Though state usury laws continue to govern transactions that cannot easily be conducted from other states, one commentator has concluded that most state usury laws are no more than a *trompe L'oeil*—an illusion. James J. White, The Usury Trompe l'Oeil, 51 S.C. L. Rev. 445 (2000). Another critic has amplified upon this theme:

> * * * the expanded Exportation Doctrine dramatically undermines the efficacy of the nonuniform state statutes that theoretically provide the foundation for consumer credit regulation. Virtually any lender interested in establishing a nationwide consumer credit program can get access to a depository institution charter, either through a subsidiary nonbank bank or unitary thrift, or through a contractual relationship with a depository institution. Once such a lender has access to a depository institution charter, almost no state

consumer credit law is going to pose any serious obstacle to its consumer credit operations. It can choose the jurisdiction from which its loans will be "made." If it chooses a jurisdiction with little or no meaningful restrictions, it can "export" that nonrestrictive regulatory regime to its customers in all other states, even residents of states with more restrictive laws. * * *

* * * The "location" of a bank, for purposes of the Exportation Doctrine, is a matter of choice, rather than a limitation. A bank can choose to "locate" its credit card bank subsidiary in South Dakota, book its loans out of its branch in South Dakota, or even designate South Dakota as the charter address of its Internet bank subsidiary. Each choice permits the bank to use the Exportation Doctrine to disregard any interest rate legislation of any other state, regardless of that bank's actual, physical location in any of those other states.

As a consequence, the Exportation Doctrine offers the myriad lenders within its orbit of beneficiaries an extraordinary type of preemption power. It is, in essence, an entirely elective preemption power. The lenders using it have virtually limitless power to choose the regulatory scheme that will preempt all other state interest rate laws. If the chosen regulatory scheme is one of deregulation, the lender can preempt all other state laws with a lack of regulation. This phenomenon gives states such as South Dakota and Delaware incentive to engage in a "race to the bottom" of consumer credit regulatory schemes, in order to attract consumer lending operations to their states. If a lender chooses such a state as its "location" for purposes of exportation, individual state attempts to curb predatory lending are largely irrelevant.

As a practical matter, this extreme elasticity of the concept of "location" in the Exportation Doctrine significantly diminishes the efficacy of state predatory lending laws. A lender's actual, physical presence in any one state does not trump the authority of that lender, through the Exportation Doctrine, to "choose" a different, deregulated state as its "location" for purposes of exportation. * * *

Elizabeth R. Schiltz, The Amazing, Elastic, Ever–Expanding Exportation Doctrine and its Effect on Predatory Lending Regulation, 88 Minn. L. Rev. 518, 618–20 (2004).* What then, is left for state usury and predatory lending laws to regulate?

The Future of Usury Regulation. While the future of usury regulation remains unclear, perhaps Congress gave a hint of its inclinations when it enacted 10 U.S.C. § 987, which bars lenders from charging soldiers and their dependents an APR greater than 36% in consumer loans other than mortgages and certain purchase money loans. Whether this statute will lead to additional restraints on interest rate charges, or whether it will be *sui generis*—or even repealed—remains to be seen. Can you think of a reason why Congress would impose special rules on

* Copyright Minnesota Law Review. Reprinted with permission.

those lending to soldiers? A clue appears in the subsection on payday loans below. What impact will the statute have on the willingness of lenders to lend to soldiers? Would you expect a lender to lend to a soldier if it could lend the same money to a civilian at a higher interest rate?

Problem 9–1

You are counsel for a group that advocates consumer rights. A bill is currently before the legislature in your state which would abolish interest rate ceilings for all consumer loans. The group has asked you to testify on this bill and to take a strong pro-consumer stand and to make any other points you feel are relevant. Will you testify in favor of or against the bill? Why? What will you say?

Note

The foregoing summary of the history of usury describes the shifts that have occurred in usury regulation. Perhaps the following brief excerpt will help students understand the ideological differences that in part propelled the shifts:

NATIONAL COMMISSION ON CONSUMER FINANCE (NCCF) REPORT

91–94 (1972).

Basically, there are two conflicting views on how to assure reasonable rates for consumer credit transactions. Some support "free rates," arguing that prices of credit should be established by the market unhindered by direct government interference. Others support "decreed rates," opting for price ceilings on consumer credit. Spokesmen for the two viewpoints are both numerous and dedicated. Economist Dr. Milton Friedman leaves no doubt as to his position:

> * * * I know of no economist of any standing * * * who has favored a legal limit on the rate of interest that borrowers could pay or lenders receive—though there must have been some * * *. Bentham's explanation of the "mischief of the anti-usurious laws" is also as valid today as when he wrote that these laws preclude "many people, altogether, from the getting the money they stand in need of, to answer their respective exigencies." For still others, they render "the terms so much the worse ... While, out of loving-kindness, or whatsoever other motive, the law precludes a man from borrowing, upon terms which it deems too disadvantageous, it does not preclude him from selling, upon any terms, howsoever disadvantageous." His conclusion: "The sole tendency of the law is to heap distress upon distress."

But economist Leon Keyserling does not agree:

> I find it deplorable that we feel bound to set an 18 percent interest rate ceiling for these people, which is three times the rate at which (as I have cited) a powerful corporation can borrow money on bonds

while many of our greatest corporations finance themselves and do not have interest costs of large significance. I think the ceiling should be very much lower * * * I am not going to take the position that even 12 percent is a conscionable interest rate for the kind of people borrowing money for these kinds of purposes. They ought to be able to borrow for much less, even if this requires new public programs.

These differing viewpoints have existed for centuries.

SECTION C.   GENERAL PREDATORY LENDING STATUTES

1.   THE PROBLEM

Over time, three different markets have evolved in mortgage lending. Prime borrowers tend to be middle-class and have good credit records. Subprime borrowers typically have blemished credit records and are charged higher rates than those in the prime market. Finally, the predatory market is a subset of the subprime market. See Elizabeth Renuart, An Overview of the Predatory Lending Process, 15 Housing Pol'y Debate 467, 474–76 (2004). The phrase "predatory lending" may evoke thoughts of loan sharks, but it has come to refer to a number of lending practices that take undue advantage of consumer borrowers. As might be expected, there is considerable debate about exactly which practices—and therefore which loans—can be described as predatory. To make matters even more complicated, the legal response to predatory lending is still evolving. There is no common law tort of "predatory lending," though, as you will see, some common law claims have been pressed into service against predatory loans. Certain practices violate longstanding statutory prohibitions, including some that you have already studied, and legislatures and regulatory agencies have fashioned new rules to prohibit other practices. Some of these legal responses have raised preemption issues that have at their root a jurisdictional dispute over which level of government should regulate which lenders. As you read through the materials that follow, consider how the legal system ought to respond to the problem of predatory lending, and whether its response thus far has been effective.

The following testimony, taken by the U.S. Senate Committee on Banking, Housing, and Urban Affairs on July 26, 2001 during a hearing titled "Predatory Mortgage Lending: The Problem, Impact and Responses," may shed some light on the types of practices considered predatory:

Testimony of Ms. Mary Podelco

* * * I live in Montgomery, West Virginia. I grew up in West Virginia and went through the sixth grade. I moved to Indiana where my husband and I worked in factories. I had four children with my husband of 19 years and was widowed for the first time in 1967. After I was

widowed the first time, I moved back to West Virginia and worked as a waitress, paid all my bills and rent in cash. When I remarried in 1987, my husband Richard and I were very proud that we were finally able to purchase our own small home. He worked as a maintenance worker and passed away in June 1994. I became the sole owner. In July, 1994, I paid off the $19,000 owed on the home from the insurance from my husband's death. Before my husband's death I had never had a checking account or a credit card. I had always paid my bills in cash and tried to be an upstanding, responsible citizen. I do not drive and never owned a car.

In 1995 I received a letter from Beneficial Finance offering to lend me money to do home improvements. I thought it was a good idea to put some new windows and a new heating system in my home. I signed a loan with Beneficial in May of 1995. This was the beginning of my troubles. My monthly income at that time was $458 from Social Security and my payments were more than half of this. They took a loan on my house of about $11,921. First flip: The very next month, Beneficial talked me into refinancing the home loan for $16,256. I did not understand that every time I did a new loan, I was being charged a bunch of fees.

Second flip: I began getting calls from people trying to refinance my mortgage all hours of the day and night. I received a letter from United Companies Lending telling me that I could save money by paying off the Beneficial loan. On September 28, 1995, I signed papers in their office; more fees were added and the loan went to $24,300 at an interest rate of 13.5%.

Third flip: Just a few months later I received a letter from Beneficial telling me I could save money by paying off United and going back to Beneficial. The loan was about $26,000. On December 14, 1995, according to the papers, Beneficial paid off United again charging me more fees and costs.

Fourth flip: In February of 1996, Beneficial advised me that it was time for me to refinance again. The loan papers show that I was charged a finance charge of $18,192 plus other fees and an interest rate of 14%. By the end of February, I had had five different loans in ten months. I didn't understand that they were adding a lot of charges each time.

Fifth flip: After that I was called by Equity One by telephone to refinance the loan. On May 28, 1996, I signed papers with Equity One in Beckley, West Virginia. The new loan paid off the Beneficial loan (which was for sixty months) and replaced it with a loan for $28,850 for 180 months which I understand increased my total loan from $45,000 to over $64,000. I got $21.70 cash out of the loan. My monthly payments were set at $355.58. They charged me closing costs of over $1,100.

Sixth flip: Then on June 13, Equity One suggested that I needed another loan to pay off a side debt and they loaned me $1,960 at over 26% interest. Monthly payments were $79.00. This loan brought my monthly payments to Equity One to over $434 a month. My monthly income at that time was $470. I really couldn't make the payments. My granddaughter had a monthly income from SSI but by law I cannot use her money for my benefit.

Seventh flip: Then on August 13, Equity One started me on another loan. I was later told that Equity One was acting as a broker for an out of state lender—Cityscape. This new loan was all arranged through the Equity One office to "help me" by lowering my payments. This loan included $2,770 in new fees and costs. There were a whole lot of papers with this Cityscape loan that I didn't understand. The payments were still too much.

Foreclosure: I missed my first payment when my brother died in December 1996. Cityscape said they wouldn't take any late payment from me unless I made up for the missed payment. I couldn't do it. Later in 1997, I lost my home to foreclosure by Cityscape. I now understand that these lenders pushed me into loans I couldn't pay. Adding all of these fees and costs each time caused me to lose my home, a home that I owned free and clear shortly after my husband died.

Testimony of Mr. Paul Satriano

* * * For the last eight years, I've been an auditor, working with numbers every day; I'm now an accounts payable clerk for Holiday Inn, making $11.75 an hour. Before that, I worked twelve years as a steelworker at NorthStar Steel in St. Paul, where I worked all along the line—loading, melting, and forming the steel—and as a crane operator. While I was there I was a member of the Steel Workers executive board and of our negotiating committee before back problems forced me to switch jobs. My wife, Mary Lee, works as a customer service representative for a delivery company, making $12.16 an hour. We both work full-time, and one of our daughters and her kids, our grandchildren, live with us in the house.

Our house was built by my wife's dad in 1947; it's the house she grew up in. In the spring of '98, my wife and I took out a mortgage with Norwest Bank to buy out her sisters on the house, so we would own it ourselves. Interest rates were falling, so we refinanced to a lower rate in February '99 with Bank One. Then a few months later we took out a second mortgage with The Money Store to replace the house's original windows. Our monthly payments were $791 on the first mortgage with Bank One and $166 on the second mortgage, and we never had problems with those loans or were late on those payments.

A few years ago, we dealt with Beneficial for the first time when we refinanced our car loan. We lowered the payments by spreading them out. They were very friendly, and everything seemed fine with the loan. Then they started sending us letter after letter telling us how we could get up to $35,000 in cash. We had some credit card bills totaling about $7,000—none of which we were behind on, but which we wanted to pay off—and so eventually we called them back.

We told the Beneficial representative that we wanted to pay off our credit card bills, and she convinced us that what we should do was consolidate our first and second mortgages with them.

Instead, we ended up with a loan that did not pay off most of our credit card bill, but that did cost us $10,000 in fees, plus almost $5,000 in credit insurance, and which had a higher total interest rate than we had before, and making a couple hundred dollars more in total monthly payments on our debt. We lost 15,000 dollars in equity in our home. And now we are locked into our new higher interest rate and higher payments—both because the loan has a five-year prepayment penalty for about $6,000, and because we now owe more than our house is worth, and no one will refinance us.

A few hours before we were supposed to go in to sign the closing papers, Beneficial faxed us the first written information on the loan we ever received. The paper they sent said our house was worth $106,000, and that that would be the maximum amount of the loan. It laid out what that 106,000 would pay—and none of it was points or fees to Beneficial.

When Mary Lee and I went in for the closing, they went through all the actual paperwork so fast it was like a barker in a circus. You put your money down to see the two-headed boy even though there isn't one. It was over in less than half an hour.

During the closing, the branch manager said they weren't able to pay off all our credit cards with this loan, but that they would try and add the unpaid amount to our car loan. The loan we got actually not only does not pay off the big credit card bill that was the reason we wanted the loan in the first place. It also does not pay off all of the bills listed on the sheet they faxed us.

When we got home we found a letter waiting for us saying that the change to our car loan to include the credit card debt had been denied. When we complained within the three-day rescission period, the manager made us think he could fix that for us. By the time he told us he couldn't, the three-day rescission period had already expired, and we were stuck in the loan.

At the closing, Beneficial made us feel like if we didn't get credit insurance we couldn't get the loan. So they added $4,900 dollars to our loan amount for that. After talking with someone from ACORN earlier this year, I realized that we could demand a refund on the unused part of the premium. We did, and when we got the $4,500 back we used it ourselves to pay off around $4,500 of our $7,000 in credit card debt. But of course, we'll be paying interest on that extra $4,900 until we pay off our loan.

They didn't say anything about this at the closing, but Beneficial also charged us 7.4 percent of the loan amount as so-called discount points—that's close to $8,900 on top of the usual third party fees—which were another $1,100.

We only really started to realize this when we got our first statement. It wasn't till then that we understood that our loan amount was over $119,000 dollars.

Also, the offer sheet Household sent us said our payments would be $1,168 a month—which was already more than we were paying before. Actually, we pay them $1,222 a month. We also have to pay another $49 dollars a month on the bills the Beneficial offer sheet said would be paid off on our loan, but was not.

Despite those discount points and our history of not a single late mortgage payment, Beneficial charged us an interest rate of nearly 12%. Bank rates were below 8% at the time.

Later, we began looking around to see if we could get a better rate elsewhere. We called Beneficial to find out the pay-off amount. It was only then we learned that the loan included a five-year prepayment penalty for around $6,000. They had never told us about any prepayment penalty. In fact, even without the prepay, I've learned that we are just stuck in this loan, because we owe more than the value of our house—so no one will make us a new one.

Our loan also contains a mandatory arbitration clause, which says we can't take Household to court.

After we sent in a complaint to the Minnesota Commerce Department, we got a call from Lisa Segara in the Household President's office. She said she would have a district manager call us about fixing any problems with our loan. When the district manager never called, we called Lisa again and she gave us his direct number. We called him and he said everything was ok with our paperwork and that there was nothing he could do.

So we're left with a loan amount much higher than the value of our home, higher payments, more debt staked against our house, a higher interest rate than before, and they paid off only a fraction of our credit card debt, which was the original reason we refinanced. Plus a prepayment penalty. And Beneficial is protected from legal action by the mandatory arbitration clause.

My wife and I have faced some difficult times this year, and the financial stress caused by this loan really has made things worse. In January, one of my sisters died. My wife and I went in for a share of the funeral and then had to pay another $500 to fix the car's brakes when they went out on the drive back from New Jersey. Then just recently my daughter-in-law died. Now Mary Lee and I are trying to help out our son with his three kids.

Even without a predatory loan, we'd be in a little bit of a tough spot financially with all of that, but we wouldn't be in as deep hole as we're in now. For the first time this month we weren't able to make our mortgage payment. I wrote Beneficial a letter telling them this, and now I'm expecting a late fee. When things are tight, as they are, it's pretty frightening to owe more money every month, without having gained anything from it, and pretty frightening to have more than $250 dollars of what we owe every month staked against our home. * * *

A lot's been said about how the most vulnerable are especially targeted, and I think that's true. But I think I've got a decent understanding of finances—like I said, I deal with it every day at my job—yet I got taken by a predatory loan. The basic problem is that when you sit down at that closing table, the lender just knows more than you do. You expect more or less honest dealing, like you've had on past loans, or other things. And with predatory loans, that's just not what happens. * * *

Note on Predatory Lending and Existing Law

Throughout this course, you have studied laws designed to prevent the types of conduct described in the foregoing testimony, such as the Truth in Lending Act. Wasn't TILA intended to insure that consumers were properly informed of credit terms? Have high-cost lenders found a way around TILA? See Christopher L. Peterson, Taming the Sharks: Towards a Cure for the High–Cost Credit Market 128–29, 291 (2004) (TILA "inadvertently facilitated the high-cost credit boom of the past twenty years, destroying the financial lives of millions of Americans. The irony is this: 'Truth' in Lending has become a collective lie."); Gian Ho & Anthony Pennington–Cross, The Impact of Local Predatory Lending Laws 7 (Fed. Reserve Bank of St. Louis Working Paper 2005–049B 2005) ("If borrowers actually read all the documents required by law at the time of closing it would take all day. Moreover, many of the documents are written in a manner that is difficult for non-lawyers to understand.... [T]he seller, buyer, and/or refinancer rely on the representations and interpretations of closing agents.... This makes it possible for unscrupulous agents to take advantage of that information gap."); Lauren E. Willis, Decisionmaking and the Limits of Disclosure: The Problem of Predatory Lending, Part I: Price, 65 Md. L. Rev. 707 (2006):

> The disclosures do not help a significant segment of consumers to price shop, because these consumers do not understand the disclosures, do not make use of the disclosures to price shop, and even misinterpret the price information provided in the disclosures.... the disclosures themselves may create an information overload and may cause the borrower to focus on less important dimensions of the decision. The disclosures give the veneer of legality to the transaction, falsely assuring some borrowers that they are more protected in the transaction than they are. Lenders, courts, and the borrowers themselves are more likely to blame the borrower for obtaining an overpriced loan, and to exonerate the seller of the loan, because the borrower received the disclosures.

Perhaps the following testimony, taken during a hearing before the Senate Special Committee on Aging on March 16, 1998, titled "Equity Predators: Stripping, Flipping and Packing Their Way to Profits," from a former employee of a predatory lender using a pseudonym will help explain how predatory lending can occur.

Testimony of Mr. "Jim Dough"

Finance companies try to do business with blue-collar workers, people who haven't gone to college, older people who are on fixed incomes, non English-speaking people and people who have significant equity in their homes. In fact, my perfect customer would be an uneducated widow who is on a fixed income—hopefully from her deceased husband's pension and social security—who has her house paid off, is living off of credit cards, but having a difficult time keeping up her payments, and who must make a car payment in addition to her credit card payments.

* * *

* * * [W]e were trained to sell the monthly "savings," that is, how much less per month the customer would be paying if we flipped the loan. In reality, the "savings" that we were trained to sell to customers were just an illusion. The uneducated customer would jump for the "savings," thinking that he would have more money to buy other things.

What the customer wouldn't figure out and what we wouldn't tell him is that he would be paying for a longer period of time and in the end would pay a whole lot more.

* * *

* * * We were instructed and expected to flip as many loans as possible. * * *

* * * Delinquent customers made good flipping candidates because we could put additional pressure on them. We were instructed to tell those customers that they could either bring their account balance current or refinance their loan. We knew that these customers would almost always agree to refinance because they didn't have the money to pay on their current loan and did not want the finance company to institute foreclosure or collection proceedings.

* * *

* * * The practice is to charge the maximum number of points legally permissible for each loan and each flip, regardless of how recently the prior loan that was being refinanced had been made. The finance companies I worked for had no limits on how frequently a loan could be flipped, and we were not required to rebate any point income on loans that were flipped.

* * *

We attempted to pack insurance during our very first pitch to a new customer. * * *The sales pitch would be substantially similar to the following: "Mr. Smith, in reviewing your loan application, I see that you have a lot of credit card payments. What if I could save you $550 a month through consolidating your debt into one loan?" I was taught that the most effective way to sell insurance was to always include insurance products in [the] quote without telling the customer that my monthly quote included insurance. * * *

* * * [I]f the customer did not express interest in my initial quote, I could eliminate one insurance product (without telling the customer that I was doing this) and give a quote for an even larger monthly savings. For example, if the customer rejected my pitch to save him $550 a month, I would eliminate one insurance product and respond "Suppose I could save you $600 per month?" Usually, the more naive the customer, the more insurance I would pack on the loan before I made the initial monthly payment quote. * * *

* * *

* * * [C]ustomers were not aware, until closing (if at all), that the loan included insurance. Once the customer indicated that we could schedule a closing regarding the loan proposed in the telephone solicitation, we merely presented the loan documents with insurance included, even though insurance had not been discussed previously. Through their training and experience, finance company employees know that customers are often desperate for the money, and usually will not object to the insurance once the loan reaches closing. If customers objected to the insurance at closing, we would add more pressure by telling them that if they wanted the loan without insurance, it would be necessary to re-do their loan documents and the closing would need to be rescheduled for a later date. That was a half-truth. We could re-do the loan documents in a few minutes. It wasn't really necessary to reschedule the closing for a later date, but we knew that customers would be more likely to cave-in and accept the insurance if they thought that they couldn't get the money that day. In my experience, this was usually enough to persuade the customers to go through with the closing and take the insurance.

* * *

* * * [T]he pressure to produce loan volume and insurance sales is so great that on many occasions, I've seen finance company employees commit forgery on a massive scale. These employees have forged everything from insurance forms, RESPA documents, income verification forms, and even entire loan files.

* * *

Our entire sale is built on confusion. Blue-collar workers tend to be less educated. I know I am being very stereotypical, but they are the more unsophisticated. They can be confused in the loan closings, and they look to us as professionals * * * they are more trusting toward us.

* * *

Senator Breaux: * * * Is it not required by Federal regulation or State regulation that that information be clearly presented to the customer—that if you keep your loan, here is what you pay and what you finish with, and if you refinance with us, here is how long it is going to take you, and here is how much you are going to pay—in simple English?

Mr. Dough: It is written in simple English, and it is on all the loan documents, but I can get around any figure on any loan sheet.

* * *

Senator Breaux: On the packing question, requiring them to buy credit life and life insurance and other insurance in order to get the loan, is there any requirement in the law that would spell out whether insurance was needed, and if so, how much is necessary, or is pretty much an open-ended situation.

Mr. Dough: There are requirements saying that you must tell the customer, with and without insurance, the loan payments, the total of the loan. In the paperwork, it shows that it is optional, and you have the questionnaire, but again, that is just like all the other figures. The customers believe what I tell them.

Senator Breaux: Was it a common practice, in other words, to insinuate to the customer that you would not make the loan without insurance?

Mr. Dough: Yes, you would insinuate that. You would tell them the importance of having the insurance on there.

Senator Breaux: Was that part of a disclosure form that was given to the customer that was lost in the pages and pages on information?

Mr. Dough: Yes, it got lost, but if a customer is backing out of the insurance, then you just delay the loan until he agrees to take it. There are laws saying that I have to disclose the information. There is no law saying in what time period I have to do a loan.

Notes

1. If you were counseling Ms. Podelco and Mr. Satriano, what would you advise them to do? Would they have a claim against the lenders? On what theory?

2. Is the problem of predatory lending one that the legal system can fix? Should fix? If so, how? By enacting new laws? Increasing enforcement of existing laws? Or would we be better off providing credit counseling to those most likely to be victims of predatory lending? See N.C. Gen. stat. § 24–1.1E(c)(1), reprinted in the Statutory Supplement (mandating counseling for borrowers of high-cost loans); Debra Pogrund Stark, Unmasking the Predatory Loan in Sheep's Clothing: A Legislative Proposal, 21 Harv. BlackLetter L.J. 129 (2005). As for the effectiveness of such counseling, see Abdighani Hirad & Peter M. Zorn, A Little Knowledge is a Good Thing: Empirical Evidence of the Effectiveness of Pre–Purchase Homeownership Counseling 2 (2001) ("counseling can be effective in reducing mortgage delinquency.... borrowers receiving counseling through individual programs experience a 34 percent reduction in delinquency rates."); Gregory Elliehausen, E. Christopher Lundquist & Michael E. Staten, The Impact of Credit Counseling on

Subsequent Borrower Credit Usage and Payment Behavior 31 ("one-on-one credit counseling has a positive impact on borrower behavior over an extended period."). Is providing more general instruction in financial matters to consumers (perhaps in high school) the answer? See GAO, Consumer Protection Federal and State Agencies Face Challenges in Combating Predatory Lending 6 (2004) ("consumer education is hampered by the complexity of mortgage transactions and the difficulty of reaching the target audience.") (hereinafter, GAO Report). Should consumers be obliged to consult lawyers before taking out loans secured by their homes? What would that do to the cost of borrowing?

3. How much does predatory lending cost consumers? One attempt to answer that question concluded that equity stripping (that is, the charging of excessive fees and adding them to the loan to "strip" equity from the home, as appeared to happen to Ms. Podelco) and rate-risk disparities (the charging of greater interest rates than the borrower's credit record justifies) alone cost $9.1 billion in 2001. See the Eric Stein, Quantifying the Economic Cost of Predatory Lending 2–3. (2001).

4. Predatory lending is sometimes associated with home improvements. Frequently the lender will refer the consumer to the contractor and disburse the funds directly to the contractor; often the contractor's work is shoddy.

KATHLEEN C. ENGEL & PATRICIA A. McCOY, A TALE OF THREE MARKETS: THE LAW AND ECONOMICS OF PREDATORY LENDING

80 Texas Law Review 1255, 1270–87 (2002).*

[T]he pathologies that epitomize predatory lending are the product of market failures in the subprime mortgage market. * * * [C]hanges in the financial services market have altered the conventional home-mortgage market and given rise to predatory lending. In particular, we argue that today's home-mortgage market is replete with information asymmetries that predatory lenders have exploited to the detriment of borrowers who are disconnected from the credit market. * * *

C. MARKET FAILURES AND PREDATORY LENDING

* * *

1. Information Asymmetries: Opportunities for Predatory Lenders and Brokers. * * *

Lenders and brokers have extensive knowledge about the credit market and mortgage products. In contrast, the typical victims of predatory lenders are unsophisticated about their options. Many were historically excluded from the home-mortgage market because of credit rationing and discrimination. They may need credit but not be aware that they are eligible for loans. Many do not know that there are less expensive sources of credit. And when lenders and brokers give these borrowers estimates and loan documents, the borrowers may not be able to comprehend the information. Predatory brokers and lenders take advantage of these information asymmetries and induce borrowers to commit to predatory loans. * * *

2. Taking Advantage of Information Asymmetries: Locating and Marketing Predatory Loans to Disconnected Borrowers.—

a. Identifying Communities and People to Target.—In order to exploit these information asymmetries, predatory lenders need to identify people who are disconnected from the credit economy and therefore unlikely or unable to engage in comparison shopping. The people most likely to meet these criteria are [Lower– and Middle–Income] LMI people of color who, because of credit rationing, discrimination, and other social forces, have not had experience with legitimate lenders. It is relatively easy for predatory lenders to identify these potential borrowers. They can use Home Mortgage Disclosure Act (HMDA) data to identify areas of cities in which there is minimal or no lending activity by prime lenders. They can also use census data to find neighborhoods with high percentages of people of color and LMI residents. * * *

* * * [P]redatory lenders procure information that enables them to identify specific individuals with equity in their homes and pressing needs for money. They can search registries of deeds to identify homeowners who do not have mortgages or who are close to paying off their mortgages. From the local tax office, they can learn of homeowners who have outstanding taxes and, therefore, may need money. From municipal offices, they can identify homeowners who have been cited for housing-code violations and thus may be in need of home-repair loans. They can drive through neighborhoods and identify homes with sagging porches, aged roofs, and peeling paint.

b. Predatory Lenders' Marketing Tools. * * *

Predatory lenders exercise market power by persuading borrowers to proceed to closing before their competitors knock on the door. To accomplish this, predatory lenders have a host of marketing tools at their disposal. Some lenders resort to out-and-out fraud. Other, more sophisticated lenders make truthful disclosures as required by law, but use a variety of hard-sell tactics. Many of these hard-sell tactics capitalize on LMI borrowers' lack of experience with this new breed of lenders and their complex products.

Predatory lenders pressure naïve borrowers to commit to loans under the pretext that their opportunity to borrow will soon vanish. The coup de grâce lies in persuading customers to sign their loan applications; once they have signed the applications, customers have a strong psychological urge to justify their decisions, rather than second-guess them. In the end, the borrowers commit to the loans, grateful for the lenders' personal service and willingness to loan them money.

c. Predatory Lenders' Products.—* * * Predatory lenders take advantage of the borrowers' lack of sophistication and lack of access to financial advice and insert loan terms that are not transparent and that would not be acceptable to more experienced borrowers.

* * *

In contrast to prime-mortgage lenders, predatory lenders rarely make plain-vanilla, fixed-rate loans with easily understood payment terms. Most predatory loans contain terms that require borrowers to make difficult probabilistic computations about the likelihood and magnitude of future market events that are entirely outside their control. For example, predatory loans often feature adjustable-rate mortgages (ARMs) whose interest rates and, therefore, monthly payments fluctuate. In order for borrowers to predict their monthly mortgage payments in any rigorous way, they would have to calculate the probability of changes in interest rates for each period over the life of the loan, and determine how the projected changes in the interest rates would affect their monthly payments. Introductory teaser rates, which are also common in predatory loans, exacerbate matters by masking true interest rates and lulling loan applicants into a false sense of security about their ability to repay. Predicting interest-rate movements confounds even the brightest financial analysts. Thus, the prevalence of adjustable-rate mortgages in predatory loans makes it difficult for borrowers to predict their ability to meet their monthly payments with any confidence.

* * *

Lenders who sell loans on the secondary market often use brokers to market their products. These brokers have little incentive to ensure that borrowers are creditworthy because they do not bear the risk of loss in the event of default. Brokers do, however, have an incentive to deceive lenders regarding borrowers' ability to pay. This is because lenders typically compensate brokers only for loans that the lenders approve, based on the interest rate and the size of the loans. For example, predatory brokers may write loans with very high interest rates that borrowers cannot afford and then falsify borrowers' credit histories to indicate to the lenders that the borrowers have the financial wherewithal to meet their loan obligations. * * *

Notes

1. Would some of the loan terms described above be legitimate? For example, can higher interest rates be explained by the greater risk in lending to those who are more likely to default? Similarly, consider the prepayment penalties which troubled Mr. Satriano. When lenders issue loans, they incur administrative and other costs which they normally expect to recover over the lifetime of the loan through interest payments and the like. When borrowers repay loans prematurely, they cut off the ability of the lender to recover those costs, unless the loan carries a prepayment penalty. In addition, the lender will incur costs in reinvesting the principal. Prohibitions on

prepayment penalties might cause lenders to raise interest rates to recover their costs. Would that be helpful to the borrowers who never prepay? But does that explain why predatory loans are more likely to carry such prepayment penalties than prime loans? Why would lenders need to impose prepayment penalties to recoup their costs in making subprime loans, but not prime loans?

2. Is the solution to the problem of predatory lending to increase lending requirements under the Community Reinvestment Act, discussed in Chapter Four? See Robert E. Litan, Unintended Consequences: The Risk of Premature State Regulation of Predatory Lending 3 (2003).

3. According to a report by the Government Accounting Office, "[w]hile there are no comprehensive data, government officials and consumer advocacy organizations have reported that elderly consumers have been disproportionately targeted and victimized by predatory lenders." GAO Report at 7. Why might the elderly be favored targets?

Note on the Definition of Predatory Lending

Defining predatory lending is more than just an academic exercise. See Michele Heller & Rob Gar, Gramm Takes Stand Against Predator Bills, Am. Banker, Aug. 24, 2000, at 1 (quoting Senator Phil Gramm as remarking: "As the regulators themselves admit, there is no definition of predatory lending," he said. "I don't know how we can hope to address the problem before we have decided what it is."). The absence of an accepted definition also makes it difficult to collect empirical evidence about the scope of the problem. The General Accounting Office has described predatory lending as "an umbrella term that is generally used to describe cases in which a broker or originating lender takes unfair advantage of a borrower, often through deception, fraud or manipulation, to make a loan that contains terms that are disadvantageous to the borrower." GAO Report at 18. One problem with that description is that it has an "I know it when I see it" quality. Kathleen C. Engel & Patricia A. McCoy, in their article A Tale of Three Markets: The Law and Economics of Predatory Lending, 80 Tex. L. Rev. 1255, 1260 (2002) defined predatory lending as:

> a syndrome of abusive loan terms or practices that involve one or more of the following five problems:
>
> (1) loans structured to result in seriously disproportionate net harm to borrowers,
>
> (2) harmful rent seeking,
>
> (3) loans involving fraud or deceptive practices,
>
> (4) other forms of lack of transparency in loans that are not actionable as fraud, and
>
> (5) loans that require borrowers to waive meaningful legal redress.

Does that capture the problems suggested by the testimony, above? Is it specific enough to be useful? See also American Financial Serv. Assn. v. Cleveland, 159 Ohio App.3d 489, 492, 824 N.E.2d 553, 555 (2004) (" "Predatory lending" can be defined as the practice of deceptive mortgage lending where a lender charges fees and interest that are greater than the risk presented by the borrower."); Robert E. Litan, A Prudent Approach to Preventing "Predatory" Lending 6 (2001) ("predatory loans are those that would not have been made in more competitive markets and where borrowers are more fully informed about the credit alternatives available to them."). Some have suggested that lengthy debates over the definition of predatory lending are pointless. See Christopher L. Peterson, Federalism and Predatory Lending: Unmasking the Regulatory Agenda, 78 Temp. L.Rev. 1, 12 (2005) ("A working definition of predatory lending has been the subject of more debate than it deserves, owing partly to the reluctance of key policymakers to admit that a problem exists.... Predatory lenders take more from borrowers than they are rightly entitled to. What is difficult to define is not predatory lending, but rather, the ethically acceptable commercial practices that demarcate entitlement."); Joint U.S. Department of Housing and Urban Development and U.S. Department of the Treasury Task Force on Predatory Lending Report, Curbing Predatory Lending (2000) (hereinafter, Curbing Predatory Lending) ("Any list of predatory practices is destined to be incomplete because bad actors are constantly developing new abusive practices, sometimes to evade new government regulation.").

While satisfactory definitions of predatory lending may be hard to come by, examples of predatory lending are more common. The testimony reprinted above illustrates several common predatory practices. Ms. Podelco testified as to flipping, equity-stripping, and asset-based lending. Flipping refers to the practice of frequent refinancings; the resulting fees often result in stripping the consumer of equity in the property. Asset-based lending consists of lending based on the value of collateral rather than the consumer's ability to repay. Because the consumer's income is not enough to permit her to make the loan payments, such loans generally end in foreclosure. Mr. Satriano mentioned credit insurance, which will be the subject of a separate subsection below. As Mr. Dough's testimony demonstrates, predatory lenders sometimes "pack" loans with additional charges for such items to increase both the amount the consumer owes and the equity stripped from the property. Prepayment penalties and mortgages that exceed the value of the property lock consumers into the loan, and mandatory arbitration prevents the bringing of class actions which might make litigation more economical. High interest rates and points and fees are also typical of predatory loans. Perhaps the overarching theme is that the consumer agrees to a poor deal, one that is likely to be more expensive than the best deal she could have obtained. Here are some other practices which some consider predatory and that are sometimes addressed in predatory lending regulation:

A. Balloon payment provisions. A balloon payment is a payment, usually scheduled at the end of a loan obligation, which is abnormally large when compared to the other payments. Balloons have the effect of making the early payments smaller than they would otherwise be, and this enables many consumers to make payments on loans they could not otherwise afford. It also leaves many consumers unprepared to make the final balloon payment, and refinancing—with new fees and reduced equity—is a typical result. Are balloon payments a problem the law should address in some way?

If so, how? The U3C represents one statutory approach to this problem. See §§ 2.308 and 3.308. See also the discussion of HOEPA, below.

B. Negative Amortization. This occurs when the consumer's payments are not large enough to cover all the interest, so that the unpaid interest is added to the principal. The result is that over time the borrower owes more than he originally borrowed, making it harder to pay off the loan.

C. Steering Those Who Could Qualify for Prime Loans to Subprime Lenders. The result of this practice is that borrowers pay more for loans than necessary. It is discussed more fully in the immediately following note.

D. Yield-spread premiums. This practice was also discussed in Chapter Four. Lenders provide a "buy-rate" (that is, the minimum interest rate at which they will provide the loan to the particular borrower) to the broker, who then charges the borrower a higher interest rate (the "mark-up"). The lender and the broker may share the markup. It will be treated in a separate subsection below.

Would any of these practices violate any of the rules that you have studied thus far in this course?

Note on Subprime Lending

Subprime loans need not be predatory, and in fact they usually are not. But predatory loans are necessarily subprime, even if the borrowers would have qualified for a prime loan. Like predatory lending, definitions of subprime lending vary. The phrase itself seems not to have existed before the 1990s, though subprime lenders—known by other names, such as "consumer finance companies"—have been around since at least the 19th century. See SMR Research Corp., The Subprime Lending Industry and Allegations of Predatory Practices 5 (2000). Perhaps, as its name implies, subprime lending is best defined by what it is not: prime lending. According to the Comptroller of the Currency, subprime borrowers typically have at least one of the following characteristics: a credit score below 661; a debt-to-income ratio of greater than 49%; a bankruptcy in the last five years; at least one 60–day delinquency, judgment, foreclosure, repossession, or chargeoff in the last two years; or at least two 30–day delinquencies in the last year. OCC Bulletin 2001–6.

Subprime loans are higher-priced than prime loans. One study found that the interest rate on subprime loans averaged three points higher than on prime loans, though some subprime loans carried a much higher interest rate. See John C. Weicher, The Home Equity Lending Industry: Refinancing Mortgages for Borrowers with Impaired Credit 16 (1997). In theory, that is because subprime borrowers present a greater risk of default and so the lender is compensated for assuming a greater risk. See Curbing Predatory Lending at 34–35 ("From January 1998 through September 1999, delinquency rates (total loans past due) in the subprime market averaged 13.5 percent and foreclosure rates averaged 2.6 percent. In contrast, for prime mortgages, over the same period, delinquency rates averaged 2.8 percent and foreclosure rates averaged 0.24 percent. . . ."). Others have attributed the higher fees at least in part to the fact that subprime loans tend to be for smaller amounts than prime loans, and so lenders must charge higher fees per dollar loaned to recover their costs, Robert E. Litan, Unintended Consequences: The Risk of Premature State Regulation of Predatory Lending 7 (2003), and to higher originating and servicing costs for subprime loans. See Weicher, supra, at 17; OCC Working Paper, Economic Issues in Predatory Lending at 4 (2003).

The demographics of subprime borrowers appear to differ from those of prime borrowers. Several studies have reported that subprime borrowers are more likely to be people of color, female, elderly, lower income, less well educated, less financially sophisticated, less likely to search for better credit terms, more likely to live in lower and moderate income census tracts, or some combination of the foregoing. See, e.g, Howard Lax, Michael Manti, Paul Raca & Peter Zorn, Subprime Lending: An Investigation of Economic Efficiency, 15 Housing Pol'y Debate 533 (2004) (hereinafter, "Lax Study"); National Community Reinvestment Coalition, Fair Lending Disparities by Race, Income, and Gender in All Metropolitan Areas in America (2005); Paul S. Calem, Kevin Gillen & Susan Wachter, The Neighborhood Distribution of Subprime Mortgage Lending, 29 J. Real Est. Fin. & Econ. 393 (2004); Binyamin Appelbaum & Ted Mellnik, *The Hard Truth in Lending,* Charlotte Observer, Aug. 28, 2005 ("Blacks who bought homes in communities across America last year were four times as likely as whites to get high interest rates for mortgage loans, according to an Observer analysis of records from 25 of the nation's largest lenders.") (hereinafter, "Observer Study"). Studies have found that even when controlling for income, people of color are more likely to pay higher rates than whites are. See ACORN, Predatory Lending in America 3 (2004) (depending on income, African–Americans and Latinos were 1.4 to 3.7 times more likely than whites of similar income to receive a subprime loan when purchasing a home); Daniel Immergluck & Marti Wiles, Two Steps Back: The Dual Mortgage Market, Predatory Lending, and the Undoing of Community Development 19–28 (1999); Observer Study. Indeed, a HUD study concluded that even homeowners in high-income African–American neighborhoods are twice as likely to have subprime loans as those in low-income white neighborhoods. U.S. Dept. of Housing & Urban Development, Unequal Burden: Income & Racial Disparities in Subprime Lending in America 3 (2000). See also Observer Study ("blacks with incomes above $100,000 a year were charged high rates more often than whites with incomes below $40,000."). But see Robert B. Avery, Glenn B. Canner & Robert E. Cook, New Information Reported Under HMDA and Its Application in Fair Lending Enforcement, Fed. Reserve Bull. 344, 384–85 (2005) (hereinafter 2005 Fed. Study) ("there is little evidence of systematic differences in pricing when borrowers are distinguished by sex.").

There has been considerable discussion about whether some subprime borrowers could have had access to the prime market with its lower rates. See, e.g. Marsha J. Courchane, Brian J. Surette & Peter M. Zorn, Subprime Borrowers: Mortgage Transitions and Outcomes, 29 J. Real Est. Fin. & Econ. 365, 381 (2004) (concluding that some borrowers "may inappropriately receive subprime mortgages, because search behavior and other demographic factors including adverse life events, age, and Hispanic ethnicity also contribute to explaining whether borrowers receive prime or subprime mortgages" and noting also that "typical mortgage underwriting criteria are most important in explaining whether borrowers obtain prime or subprime mortgages"). Some believe that potential prime borrowers are occasionally "steered" to subprime lenders. See Michael S. Barr, Credit Where It Counts: The Community Reinvestment Act and Its Critics, 80 N.Y.U.L. Rev. 513, 556 (2005). This debate has been fueled by claims that not all subprime loans carry a greater risk of default. See Mike Hudson and E. Scott Reckard, More Homeowners With Good Credit Getting Stuck With Higher–Rate Loans, L.A. Times, Oct. 24, 2005; Remarks by Franklin D. Raines, Chairman & CEO, Fannie Mae, available at http://www.fanniemae.com (Oct. 11, 2000) ("we estimate that about half of the A-minus borrowers out there could qualify for conventional Fannie Mae financing and save a lot of money."). The Lax study found that the greater risks incurred by subprime lenders do not fully explain the higher prices they charge. See also Center for Community Change, Risk or Race? Racial Disparities and the Subprime Refinance Market 75 (2002) (risk does not fully explain racial differences in subprime lending). On the other hand, a Federal Reserve Board study of HMDA data on subprime loans, after noting differences in the incidence of higher-priced loans to different races, found that "more than two-thirds of the aggregate difference in the incidence of higher-priced lending between black and non-Hispanic white borrowers can be explained by differences in the groups' distributions of income, loan amounts, other borrower-related characteristics included in the HMDA data, and the choice of lender." When the Fed combined the HMDA data with additional data, even more of the differences were explained. 2005 Fed. Study at 393.

Subprime lending has become a big business, increasing seven-fold in the eight years from 1994 to 2002. See Remarks by Federal Reserve Board Governor Edward M. Gramlich at the Texas Assoc. of Bank Counsel 27th Annual Convention (Oct. 9, 2003), available at http://www.federalreserve. gov/boarddocs/speeches/2003/20031009/default.htm. It now represents more than ten percent of the mortgage market. Amy Crew Cutts & Robert Van Order, On the Economics of Subprime Lending, Freddie Mac Working Paper #04–01 1 (2004). Several factors have been credited with leading to the substantial increases in subprime lending. One of these was the development of securitization, a process in which lenders package many home loans into securities backed by the loans as collateral. The lenders then sell these securities to others in the secondary market, and can use the money received to make still more loans. A second factor was increased federal incentives to lend to lower income borrowers, as exemplified by the Community Reinvestment Act, discussed in Chapter Four. A third factor was new federal statutes, such as the Depository Institutions Deregulation and Monetary Control Act of 1980 and the Alternative Mortgage Transactions Parity Act of 1982 that gave lenders more flexibility in the types of mortgage products they were able to offer lenders. See generally Kathleen C. Engel & Patricia A. McCoy, A Tale of Three Markets: The Law and Economics of Predatory Lending, 80 Tex. L. Rev. 1255, 1260 (2002).

Notes

1.   Would ECOA present any problems for subprime lenders? Should it?

2.   The Lax Study reported at 555 that a quarter of subprime borrowers did not search for rates at all, compared with only 11% of prime borrowers. Is that a problem that law-makers should attempt to address? If so, how?

3. Lenders are more likely to foreclose on subprime loans than prime loans. That is, of course, at least in part because subprime loans carry a greater risk of default than prime loans. But what about predatory loans? Predatory lenders who strip equity from homeowners might prefer defaults so they can foreclose on the home. When the authors of one study examined the terms of a sample of subprime mortgages in foreclosure in one county, they found that nearly two-thirds exhibited predatory characteristics. Richard D. Stock, Predation in the Sub–Prime Lending Market: Montgomery County 6 (2001).

4. If an obligor on a predatory loan has a defense to payment—a subject addressed below—would the obligor be able to assert it against someone who had purchased the loan on the secondary market? Think back to the materials on holder in due course in Chapter Seven. When legislatures and the FTC abrogated the holder in due course defense, did they do so for mortgages?

5. Is any law violated by charging a higher interest rate or more in points and fees than is justified by the borrower's credit-worthiness? Or by steering a consumer who would qualify for a prime loan to a subprime loan? See GAO Report at 35. If not, should legislatures enact such a law?

6. As you read the following decision, ask yourself what it tells you about the extent to which existing laws protect those who borrow from predatory lenders. Try not to let the procedural posture distract you from that question.

UNITED COMPANIES LENDING CORPORATION v. SARGEANT

United States District Court, District of Massachusetts, 1998.
20 F.Supp.2d 192.

YOUNG, DISTRICT JUDGE.

This case comes before the Court as a case stated. That is, the parties have stipulated to all material facts and it remains for this Court to review the record, draw such inferences as are reasonable and, applying the governing law, enter such judgment as may be appropriate.
* * *

I. BACKGROUND

United Companies Lending Corporation ("United") makes, sells, and services refinancing, first lien residential mortgage loans which are used primarily for debt consolidation, home improvement, or major household purchases. United is licensed to do business in Massachusetts as a mortgage lender. United operates in the subprime market making loans to consumers who have a higher credit risk than borrowers in the prime market. * * *

Subprime loans have higher securitization costs associated with the sale of these loans on the private secondary market compared to loans in the prime market because they are "nonconforming" loans. United loans are also sold "with recourse" in the event of a default by the borrower.

As a result of these terms, the risk to the lender on a subprime loan is substantially higher than on a prime loan. "Due to the higher risks and costs associated with subprime loans, the total cost of such loans to the borrower—as reflected in the Annual Percentage Rate ("APR")—is generally higher than the cost of loans by traditional lenders such as banks. Such costs typically include interest, origination fees or 'points' and other fees associated with the closing of the loan."

Daisy Sargeant ("Sargeant") is the owner of a New England triple-decker in Dorchester, Massachusetts. She resides on the second floor and rents out the first floor and third floor apartments for $600.00 per month each. Desiring to make improvements to the interior and the exterior of the house, she responded to an advertisement in the *Boston Herald* regarding the availability of loans. She contacted the toll-free number in the advertisement and received a mortgage application. The advertisement was placed by a California-based mortgage broker, John P. McIntyre ("McIntyre"). McIntyre referred Sargeant's name to David Richard ("Richard"), a United mortgage loan originator located at the Warwick, Rhode Island office. Richard contacted Sargeant. Richard is the United agent with whom Sargeant dealt in obtaining the mortgage loan at issue.

On August 9, 1995, Sargeant completed the loan application and executed disclosure documents related to the loan. Sargeant was classified as a "C" borrower by United. On August 29, 1995, United approved Sargeant's loan. A title search disclosed an undischarged mortgage on the property, however, as well as unpaid real estate taxes. United states that McIntyre negotiated with the lien holder who agreed to accept $5000 as payment in full. United reapproved the loan, and the closing was held in Warwick, Rhode Island, on September 29, 1995.

Sargeant thus obtained a loan from United for $134,700. The mortgage had an adjustable interest rate with an initial rate of interest of 10.99%. The loan provided that the rate could be adjusted upward one percent every six months with a maximum interest rate of 16.99%. The initial annual percentage rate charged on the mortgage was 13.556%. The loan proceeds were disbursed as follows: $15,681 was applied to the home improvements upon their completion; $4,910 was applied to pay off credit card debt; and $93,000 was applied to two prior mortgages on her residence. According to the settlement statement, Sargeant was assessed a brokerage fee payable to United in the sum of $13,461.40. United claims that this entry is incorrect and that the $13,461.40 was paid to United as an origination fee or "points." Sargeant was also charged a broker's fee in the amount of $4,150 made payable to McIntyre. Her total closing costs and fees equaled $23,029.87. Her initial mortgage payments were $1,281. Her previous mortgage payments were $956 per month.

Sargeant fell behind in the repayment of her loan and United initiated foreclosure proceedings against her. Sargeant then filed a consumer complaint with the Consumer Protection and Antitrust Division of the Massachusetts Attorney General's Office.

After the filing of this Complaint, the Attorney General, on behalf of the Commonwealth of Massachusetts, commenced an action against United in the Massachusetts Superior Court sitting in and for the county of Suffolk seeking, *inter alia,* to enjoin United 1) from making any mortgage loans in violation of Mass. Gen. Laws ch. 184, § 17D and the Mortgage Brokers and Mortgage Lenders Regulations of the Attorney General, 940 C.M.R. § 8.00 *et seq.,* and 2) from making any mortgage loans in violation of Mass. Gen. Laws ch. 183, § 63. A preliminary injunction issued in that case on January 24, 1997, prohibiting United from taking any further action in foreclosing on Sargeant's property and requiring it to notify the Commonwealth thirty days prior to a foreclosure sale on any other residential property.

At this point, United went forum shopping. It commenced this defendant class action suit against Daisy Sargeant and all persons similarly situated, seeking a declaratory judgment that 940 C.M.R. § 8.06(6) is void and unenforceable, that the mortgage loan origination fee or points charged to Sargeant were lawful and proper, and that a judgment of default against Sargeant on the mortgage note was therefore appropriate. Sargeant counterclaimed, asking for a declaration that the mortgage transaction was an unfair or deceptive act because it was unconscionable pursuant to 940 C.M.R. § 8.06(6), and that rescission of the mortgage loan is therefore permissible.

* * *

The federal action thus went forward, the parties falling to with a will, promptly filing cross motions for summary judgment and, after a case management conference, a joint statement of facts on which the case can be decided. * * *

II. Discussion

Pursuant to his authority under the Massachusetts General Laws, the Attorney General has the authority to make rules and regulations interpreting what acts or practices by mortgage lenders and brokers are unfair or deceptive and, therefore, illegal under Mass. Gen. Laws ch. 93A, § 2(a). *See* Mass. Gen. Laws ch. 93A, § 2(c). * * *

Regulation 8.06(6) ("the Regulation"), which became effective August 1, 1992, states that: It is an unfair or deceptive practice for a mortgage broker or lender to procure or negotiate for a borrower a mortgage loan with rates or terms which *significantly deviate from industry-wide standards* or which are *otherwise unconscionable.* (emphasis added). * * *

E. *Default on the Promissory Note*

United seeks damages for Sargeant's breach of contract. Sargeant counterclaims that she may rescind the mortgage because United's conduct in the mortgage transaction was unconscionable. In support of this claim of unconscionability, Sargeant argues that 1) the origination fee was above the industry standard of 3 to 5 points; [and] 2) the fees paid by Sargeant were grossly disproportionate to the value received * * *

Unconscionability

Sargeant avers that the points charged are unconscionable because they substantially deviate from the industry-wide standard. To establish the industry-wide standard for subprime loans, Sargeant offers the Affidavit of Eric C. Dupont, Deputy Commissioner for Consumer Compliance for the Division of Banks of the Commonwealth of Massachusetts, and an Affidavit from Stephanie Benig, volunteer extern at the Office of the Attorney General of the Commonwealth of Massachusetts. *See* Ex. 48 & 49. Both of these affidavits have been submitted by the Attorney General in its suit against United in Massachusetts Superior Court. Sargeant argues that these affidavits establish that the industry-wide standard for the number of points to charge in a subprime loan transaction is two or three points with five points representing the outer limit. The Benig Affidavit shows the subprime mortgage lenders offering an interest rate similar to United charged no more than five points. United offers no contrary evidence. As this is a case stated, this Court may draw all reasonable inferences. This Court concludes that Sargeant has established by a fair preponderance of the evidence that the charging of ten points on a subprime mortgage with an interest rate of 10.99 percent substantially deviates from industry-wide practice. United's conduct thus violates Mass. Gen. Laws ch. 93A, § 2(a).

The fact that this conduct constitutes an unfair or deceptive practice, however, does not mean that this conduct was unconscionable.

a. *Substantive Unconscionability*

1) Disparity Between Fees and Value

Sargeant avers that the terms of the loan are substantively unconscionable given the gross disparity in the value she received in comparison to the consideration given by her. "Gross disparity in the values exchanged is an important factor to be considered in determining whether a contract is unconscionable." *Waters*, 412 Mass. at 69, 587 N.E.2d 231.

Sargeant's loan initially closed on August 28, 1995, but was canceled because United was unable to record its mortgage in first priority position due to the existence of a mortgage to Foremost Services Company. Sargeant was not making any payments on this obligation nor had Foremost commenced any foreclosure proceedings. Upon learning of this title problem, United avers that it enlisted the services of McIntyre who negotiated an agreement with Foremost to settle this obligation for a payment of $5000. The loan was restructured, in light of this other mortgage, with different terms on the consolidation of Sargeant's credit card debt. Under the initial proposal, $9826 was to be applied to pay off six out of her eight cards. Under the second loan, none of her credit card debt was paid off and only $4910 was applied to pay down three credit cards. In its request for loan approval dated September 22, 1995, the originator wrote "Customer will benefit by paying off all debt and saving $350 per month and completing desired home improvements. United will benefit by acquiring st [sic] position on a well maintained property." This statement mischaracterizes the value or benefit obtained for Sargeant in the transaction. Prior to obtaining the loan, Sargeant owned a three-family home with an appraised value of $159,000 encumbered by mortgages totaling $93,000. She had unsecured consumer debt of $14,963. After entering into the mortgage loan with United, her home was subject to a $134,700 mortgage. The equity value in her home had declined from $56,000 to $24,300 and $4,910 of previously unsecured consumer debt was now secured debt. The amount of the loan allocated for home improvements, which was the reason for Sargeant's application for loan from United, was only $15,681.92.

United argues that Sargeant obtained substantial value in the transaction because she received a discharge of the lien on her house held by Foremost Services Company, her desired home improvements, and a lower monthly debt payment. United's explanation glosses over the resulting financial ramifications of this loan transaction, namely the increase in secured debt beyond the amount of the home improvement loan. Moreover, the decrease in overall monthly total debt offered by United was not fixed. As the mortgage had a variable interest rate, the amount of Sargeant's monthly debt payment would not remain constant. Prior to the loan, her monthly credit card payments were $569 and her monthly mortgage payment was $956.00. Her total monthly debt payment was $1525. Following the execution of the loan, her monthly credit card payments were $236 and her initial monthly mortgage payment was $1281. Her total monthly payment initially was $1517, but would eventually rise to $1620. Do these terms "drive too hard a bargain"?

* * *

b.   Procedural Unconscionability

* * *

2) Failure to Follow Disclosure Requirements

According to the evidentiary record, United provided Sargeant with a Good Faith Estimate of Settlement Costs which listed the origination fee as ten percent with an estimated cost of $13,750.00. Sargeant signed this document on August 9, 1995, the date on which the initial loan application was completed. Moreover, on the same date Sargeant signed a Receipt of Disclosure Information form indicating her receipt of the disclosure information required by Mass. Gen. Laws ch. 184, § 17D. Thus the prior disclosure required by Massachusetts laws in order to charge points has been satisfied. *See* Mass. Gen. Laws ch. 183, § 63.

* * *

CONCLUSION

1. For the reasons stated herein, this Court declares that the Regulation is valid and enforceable.

2. The origination fee charged by United constituted an unfair and deceptive trade practice as the points charged substantially deviated from industry-wide practice in Massachusetts. Therefore, Sargeant is entitled to actual damages of $13,461.40 plus interest. * * *

3. Upon reflection, as the question of unconscionability is a close one, the matter is a fact-specific expression of Massachusetts common law, and an equally just ground of decision between these particular parties is available, this Court refrains from expressing an opinion on the issue of unconscionability. While the question could readily be decided by a Justice of the Massachusetts Superior Court, I am hesitant as a federal judge to declare Massachusetts common law in the absence of some decisional guidance. Nor is the question of sufficient significance to warrant certification pursuant to Massachusetts Supreme Judicial Court Rule 3:03.

A court sitting in equity, however, is necessarily empowered to do complete justice as between the parties. Here, Daisy Sargeant initiated neither the state nor the federal action. She only filed a consumer complaint with the Massachusetts Attorney General who, appreciating the seriousness of the matter, filed suit on behalf of all the citizens of the Commonwealth in the Massachusetts Superior Court. It was United who went forum shopping, and named Sargeant as the representative of the defendant class in the federal court. The Attorney General chose not to litigate here and Sargeant was thus left to fend for herself, ultimately vindicating the Attorney General's regulation generally as well as successfully rebuking the application of United's attempted unfair and deceptive acts to her. While she is entitled to her attorney's fees in prosecuting her counterclaim under Chapter 93A, this cannot adequately compensate her for alone bearing the full burden of this complex litigation. The Court also notes that her success will inure to the benefit of all others similarly situated through the offensive use of collateral estoppel against United. Finally, it is well within a court's equitable powers to reward a named class representative in successful class action litigation. The Court therefore awards Sargeant an opportunity similar to, albeit not as complete as, recission. Should Sargeant, within six months of the date of this order, tender to United the outstanding principal (not interest) due on the loan as of the date of this order as well as interest thereon at the contract rate from this date, the mortgage shall be discharged and the mortgage note satisfied.

Notes

1. Why didn't Sargeant sue under TILA?

2. Are existing laws sufficient to solve the problem of predatory lending? After all, United was found to have violated a state UDAP statute and

the plaintiff was able to obtain rescission. Is litigation after the fact on a case-by-case basis the best way to handle predatory lending? Would it be hard for consumers to find lawyers willing to represent them in such cases? Sargeant's attorneys took the case on a pro bono basis, but the court later awarded them $83,115 in attorney's fees. United Companies Lending Corp. v. Sargeant, 32 F.Supp.2d 21 (D.Mass. 1999).

3. Was United's conduct unconscionable? Was the deal here so terrible? Initially Sargeant's monthly payments declined by eight dollars, though later they would increase. In exchange for that, she received more than $15,000 to spend on home improvements.

4. How useful is unconscionability against predatory lending? Note that the unconscionability doctrine does not provide for attorney's fees.

5. Given the disclosures mandated by TILA, RESPA, and Massachusetts law, wasn't Ms. Sargeant apprised of the terms of the transaction? Then how could the court find the transaction to be unfair and deceptive? Would any other predatory lending practices violate a UDAP statute? If so, which ones? The FTC has charged a number of lenders with committing unfair and deceptive predatory lending practices. See, e.g., F.T.C. v. Citigroup, complaint available at http://www.ftc.gov/os/2001/03/citigroupcmp.pdf.

6. In Chedick v. Nash, 151 F.3d 1077 (D.C.Cir. 1998), the court ruled that a claim for fraudulent misrepresentation would lie against a lender who entered into a mortgage intending to prevent the borrower from repaying the loan so that the lender could foreclose on the property. The borrower claimed, among other things, that the lender repeatedly miscalculated her monthly payments, a practice it had allegedly employed with other borrowers after which it had foreclosed on their homes. The court also found that the evidence supported the jury's finding that the lender's overstatement of the amount due, its improper accounting, and the resulting frustration of the borrower's efforts to pay down the mortgage breached the lender's duty to act in good faith.

2. HOEPA

Congress enacted the Home Ownership and Equity Protection Act of 1994 ("HOEPA"), 15 U.S.C. § 1639, to address predatory lending. HOEPA is incorporated into TILA and the Federal Reserve Board has in turn amended Regulation Z and the Commentary to implement the statute. See Reg. Z, §§ 226.32, 226.34. The statute, which applies only to loans secured by the borrower's principal dwelling, works on a trigger principle: it can be triggered by either a high APR—an APR exceeding by more than ten percentage points (the Board has in Regulation Z, § 226.32(a)(1)(i), lowered this to eight percentage points for first lien mortgages) the yield on certain treasury securities—or by high points and fees—if the total of points and fees exceeds both eight percent of the credit extended and a certain amount, adjusted for inflation (in 2005 it was $510). § 1602(aa).

HOEPA loans are treated differently from conventional loans in several respects. First, they are subject to additional disclosure requirements. For example, at least three days before consummation, the lender must conspicuously disclose to the borrower the APR and the amount of the monthly payments. § 1639(a), (b). Recall that for non-HOEPA loans, the disclosures can come later. The lender must also warn the borrower that "You could lose your home, and any money you have put into it, if you do not meet your obligations under the loan." § 1639(a)(1)(B).

Second, HOEPA loans are not permitted to contain certain onerous loan terms. Among these prohibited terms: HOEPA loans are not allowed to impose prepayment penalties, subject to certain exceptions, § 1639(c); balloon payments are prohibited in loans of less than five years duration, § 1639(e); and negative amortization is prohibited. § 1639(f). In addition, lenders cannot engage in a "pattern or practice of extending credit to consumers in [HOEPA loans] based on the consumers' collateral without regard to the consumers' repayment ability, including the consumers' current and expected income, current obligations and employment." § 1639(h). The regulations also bar a lender from refinancing a HOEPA loan through another HOEPA loan within one year of the original loan unless the refinancing "is in the borrower's interest." Reg. Z, § 226.34(a)(3). This provision does not, however, prevent a creditor from refinancing a HOEPA loan extended by another lender.

Notes

1.   Nearly all of the loans entered into by Ms. Podelco and Mr. Satriano were extended while HOEPA was in effect. Wouldn't HOEPA's provisions governing refinancing of loans and the making of loans based on the borrower's collateral rather than the borrower's ability to repay have prevented the making of the loans to Ms. Podelco? Yet HOEPA did not protect the consumers, nor was it helpful to Ms. Sargeant in *United Companies.* Why not?

2.   Why does HOEPA focus on the extension of loans based on collateral rather than the borrower's ability to repay? If borrowers cannot repay a loan, what happens to the collateral? How easy would it be for a consumer to show that a lender has a "pattern or practice" of making loans without regard to the consumer's ability to repay?

3.   Are the HOEPA triggers too high? See Curbing Predatory Lending at 85 ("evidence suggests that due to the high thresholds that a loan must exceed in order for HOEPA to apply, very few consumers in the subprime market benefit from the law's provisions. Anecdotal evidence ... also suggests that abuses often occur in loans just below the HOEPA triggers...."). According to the 2004 HMDA data, only 0.003% of all home-secured refinance or home improvement loans originated that year were subject to HOEPA (though that figure may exclude some HOEPA loans that are issued by institutions not covered by HMDA). Robert B. Avery, Glenn B. Canner & Robert E. Cook, New Information Reported Under HMDA and Its Application in Fair Lending Enforcement, Fed. Reserve Bull. 344, 371–72 (2005). Support for the view that lenders just below the HOEPA triggers use terms prohibited in HOEPA loans is found in a study that reported balloon

payments and pre-payment penalties more common in loans with high interest rates—but not high enough to fall under HOEPA—than in loans carrying lower interest rates. Richard D. Stock, Predation in the Sub–Prime Lending Market: Montgomery County 10, 11 (2001). Is anything wrong with lenders employing such terms in non-HOEPA loans?

4. If TILA's and RESPA's disclosure provisions have not solved the problems, why did Congress think additional disclosures would? Does the answer have something to do with the timing of the disclosures? If so, why not change the timing of the required disclosures under TILA and RESPA?

5. Why is HOEPA limited to mortgage loans? Why shouldn't it apply to car loans, say?

6. How marketable do you think HOEPA loans are in the secondary market? Many large purchasers in the secondary market refuse to buy HOEPA loans. If HOEPA loans are difficult to sell, how eager do you think lenders are to make such loans?

7. What effect has HOEPA had on the availability of subprime credit? Before the Federal Reserve Board adopted regulations lowering the APR trigger for HOEPA coverage, a banking industry association predicted that the regulation would drive legitimate lenders from the subprime market. See Sandra Fleishman, Fed Favors Tougher Loan Rules; Abuses in Subprime Lending Are Targeted, Wash. Post, Dec. 14, 2000 at E01. In fact, subprime lending appears to have increased substantially since the regulations went into effect, though it is impossible to know whether the increase would have been greater still in their absence. See, e.g., Subprime Lenders Shatter Records in '03 and Get Set for More in '04, Inside B & C Lending, Feb. 9, 2004 at 1.

8. To what extent are lenders complying with HOEPA's disclosure requirements? See In re Jackson, 245 B.R. 23, 32 (Bankr. E.D. Pa. 2000) (omitting HOEPA disclosure "appears to be a prevalent practice in the industry.").

9. Consumers suing for HOEPA violations may recover, in addition to the normal remedies for TILA violations, "an amount equal to the sum of all finance charges and fees paid by the consumer, unless the creditor demonstrates that the failure to comply is not material." 15 U.S.C. § 1640(a)(4).

Problem 9–2

Grin's Bank wishes to enter the subprime mortgage lending market but does not want to comply with HOEPA. Because it believes it will experience a greater risk of default on such loans, Grin's concludes that to make the profit it wants to make without charging an APR that exceeds the HOEPA interest rate threshold, it must recover the equivalent of nine percent of the loan amount in points and fees. It asks you how to structure its loans to accomplish that without becoming subject to HOEPA. Would you advise Grin's to:

(A) Provide open-end credit rather than closed-end credit? See TILA § 1602(aa)(1); Reg. Z § 226.34(b).

(B) Limit its lending to purchase money security interests to finance the purchase of homes? See TILA § 1602(w), (aa)(1).

(C) Charge the nine percent in points and fees but permit that sum to be financed in the loan itself? See Short v. Wells Fargo Bank Minnesota, N.A., *infra*.

(D) Accept that if it charges nine percent of the loan in points and fees it must provide the HOEPA disclosures?

SHORT v. WELLS FARGO BANK MINNESOTA, N.A

United States District Court, S.D. West Virginia, 2005.
401 F.Supp.2d 549.

Chambers, District Judge.

Pending is a motion for summary judgment brought by defendants Countrywide Home Loans, Inc. (hereinafter "Countrywide") and Wells Fargo Bank Minnesota, N.A. (hereinafter "Wells Fargo") pursuant to Rule 56 of the Federal Rules of Civil Procedure. For the reasons set forth below, the motion is GRANTED in part and DENIED in part.

I

On April 15, 2005, the plaintiff Michael L. Short filed an eight count amended complaint against defendants Wells Fargo; Countrywide; Tri–State Title, Inc. (hereinafter "Tri–State"); Bonnie Sue Fleming (hereinafter "Fleming"); and Douglas M. Legg (hereinafter "Legg"). The plaintiff has named defendants Wells Fargo and Countrywide in six of the eight counts in his amended complaint. Specifically, defendants Wells Fargo and Countrywide are named in Count I for violating the Truth in Lending Act (hereinafter "TILA"). * * *

The amended complaint alleges the following facts: In April of 2000, the plaintiff spoke to a loan officer for Delta Funding and applied for a mortgage loan to refinance his home. On June 2, 2000, a man called the plaintiff at approximately 11:00 P.M. The man told the plaintiff that he had the loan documents for closing plaintiff's loan and asked for permission to come by plaintiff's residence to close the loan. At approximately 1:45 A.M., the man showed up at plaintiff's residence and presented a large stack of papers, directing him where to initial and sign. From plaintiff's review of the Deed of Trust, he asserts that the man was Legg. Plaintiff was approached again a few weeks later by a different man in a car and asked to sign additional papers. Plaintiff was never provided any copies of the loan documents he signed nor was he given any explanation of their content at the closing.

* * *

III

A

[The court explained that whether Wells Fargo is liable depends on whether the loan is a HOEPA loan.] * * * [T]he defendants argue that plaintiff's loan is not a high cost loan under HOEPA and is not subject to any special protections under the statute because the plaintiff did not pay any points or fees at or before closing. Specifically, defendants contend that 15 U.S.C. § 1602(aa) provides that TILA protection only applies if the total points and fees payable by the consumer at or before closing satisfy a certain threshold amount and that the fees and costs associated with the loan at issue here were financed. As the plaintiff paid nothing at closing, the defendants argue that his loan is not a high cost loan as defined by the statute and that he is not entitled to HOEPA protection. In support of this assertion, defendants point to *Terry v. Community Bank of Northern Virginia,* 255 F.Supp.2d 811, 817 (W.D.Tenn., 2003); *Nunn v. IMC Mortgage Company,* 308 B.R. 150 (2004); and *Collins v. Countrywide Home Loans, et. al.,* 310 B.R. 299 (2004).

In his surreply, the plaintiff argues that the holding in *Terry* is wrong because it would remove ninety-five percent of all brokered loans from HOEPA coverage, and he urges the Court to hold that financed fees are in essence fees paid at closing by the consumer satisfying § 1602(aa) and triggering HOEPA protection. In support of this assertion, he points to the Official Staff Commentary of the Federal Reserve Board concerning § 226.32(b)(1)(ii) and to *Cunningham v. EquiCredit Corp. of Ill.,* 256 F.Supp.2d 785 (N.D.Ill.2003).

* * *

In order for a mortgage loan to be considered a HOEPA loan and qualify for its protection, it must satisfy the criteria outlined in 15 U.S.C. § 1602(aa). Section 1602(aa) provides, in pertinent part, as follows:

A mortgage referred to in this subsection means a consumer credit transaction that is secured by the consumer's principal dwelling, other than a residential mortgage transaction, a reverse mortgage transaction, or a transaction under an open end credit plan, if—

. . .

(B) the total points and fees payable by the consumer at or before closing will exceed the greater of—

(i) 8 percent of the total loan amount; or

(ii) $400.

15 U.S.C. § 1602(aa). *See also*12 C.F.R. § 226.32(a)(1)(ii).

Regulation Z, 12 C.F.R. § 226.1, *et seq.,* which implements TILA and HOEPA, defines points and fees as including the following:

(1) For purposes of paragraph (a)(1)(ii) of this section, *points and fees* means:

(i) All items required to be disclosed under § 226.4(a) and 226.4(b), except interest or the time-price differential;

(ii) All compensation paid to mortgage brokers;

(iii) All items listed in § 226.4(c)(7) (other than amounts held for future payment of taxes) unless the charge is reasonable, the creditor receives no direct or indirect compensation in connection with the charge, and the charge is not paid to an affiliate of the creditor; and

(iv) Premiums or other charges for credit life, accident, health, or loss-of-income insurance, or debt-cancellation coverage (whether or not the debt-cancellation coverage is insurance under applicable law) that provides for cancellation of all or part of the consumer's liability in the event of the loss of life, health, or income or in the case of accident, written in connection with the credit transaction.

12 C.F.R. § 226.32(b)(1) (2005). With regard to § 226.32(b)(1)(ii), the Federal Reserve Board's Official Staff Interpretation provides:

1. *Mortgage broker fees.* In determining "points and fees" for purposes of this section, compensation paid by a consumer to a mortgage broker (directly or through the creditor for delivery to the broker) is included in the calculation whether or not the amount is disclosed as a finance charge. Mortgage broker fees that are not paid by the consumer are not included. Mortgage broker fees already included in the calculation as financed charges under section 226.32(b)(1)(I) need not be counted again under section 226.32(b)(1)(ii).

12 C.F.R. Pt. 226, Supp. I, ¶ 32(b)(1)(ii) (2005).

* * *

The issue at hand in the instant case is whether plaintiff qualifies as a holder of a high cost HOEPA loan. In resolving this issue, the defendants argue that the Court should employ the statutory interpretation of 15 U.S.C. § 1602(aa) as outlined in *Terry*. In response, the plaintiff argues that the holding in *Terry* is wrong and that the broker fees should be considered paid at closing pursuant to the Federal Reserve Board's Official Staff Interpretation of § 226.32(b)(1)(ii) and the holding in *Cunningham*.

The following cases support the defendants position: In *Terry*, the plaintiffs refinanced their existing mortgage home equity loan in 1999. * * *

DISTRICT JUDGE DONALD held:

Title 15 U.S.C. § 1602(aa)(1) plainly states that unless a mortgage satisfies § 1602(aa)(1)(A), the loan qualifies for TILA protections only if "the total points and fees payable by the consumer at or before closing" meet a certain threshold amount. 15 U.S.C. § 1602(aa)(1)(B) (emphasis added). There have been no allegation that Plaintiffs' loans are covered by § 1602(aa)(1)(A). Thus, for RFC to be liable, Plaintiffs must meet the criteria stated in § 1602(aa)(1)(B).

Black's Law Dictionary defines "payable" as follows:

> Capable of being paid; suitable to be paid; admitting or demanding payment; justly due; legally enforceable. A sum of money is said to be payable when a person is under an obligation to pay it. Payable may therefore signify an obligation to pay at a future time, but, when used without qualification, [the] term normally means that the debt is payable at once, as opposed to owing.

Black's Law Dictionary 1016 (6th ed.1979) (emphasis added). Under this definition, even if the time for payment of points and fees on a "high cost" loan was unspecified, the points and fees would be "payable at once," as opposed to over the course of a loan. However, Congress specifically qualified the term "payable" with a time certain—i.e. the points and fees must be payable "at or before closing." 15 U.S.C. § 1602(aa)(1)(B). There is nothing ambiguous about the language of § 1602(aa)(1)(B) which lends to another interpretation of this statute. Accordingly, the Court finds that a mortgage qualifies for TILA protections only where the mortgagor is required to pay certain points and fees at or before closing of a loan, not over the course of the loan.

Terry, 255 F.Supp.2d at 816–17 (footnote omitted). Based upon the above reasoning, Judge Donald held that plaintiff's loan did not qualify as a high cost HOEPA loan because plaintiff had paid nothing at closing.

* * *

In the case *sub judice,* the plaintiff testified that he wanted $2,000.00 to $4,000.00 over the payoff on his first mortgage in order to payoff some small bills and to take a weekend trip. The settlement statement indicates that the principal amount of plaintiff's loan was $35,000.00. In the section labeled "Gross Amount Due From Borrower," it indicates that settlement charges to borrower were $6,724.99, that the plaintiff owed $17,610.86 on his first mortgage and $118.09 on his second mortgage. The statement also indicated that the plaintiff received $10,546.06 in cash. On the second page of the settlement statement, there is a list of settlement charges that are characterized as "PAID FROM BORROWER'S FUNDS AT SETTLEMENT." The charges are as follows: Four Seasons received $475.00 for an appraisal. Delta Funding Corporation received $495.00 for processing the loan, $76.00 for tax services and $20.00 for flood certification. Equity South Mortgage received $2,950.00 for brokerage services. State Farm Insurance received $150.49 for providing hazard insurance. Tri–State Title, Inc. received $150.00 for closing the loan, $50.00 for courier service, $430.00 for title examination, $25.00 for fax service and $25.00 for wire service. Bonnie S. Fleming, Esq. received $65.00 for document preparation. First American Title Insurance Company received $135.00 for providing title insurance. Recording fees were $30.50. Lowes/MCCBG received $536.00. Bank First received two payments, one for $463.00 and another for $649.00.

Unlike the facts in *Terry,* here the second page of the plaintiff's settlement statement indicates that the fees were paid from borrower's funds at settlement. Thus, on its face the lender acknowledged that the fees were paid by the plaintiff. * * * In the instant case, it appears from the settlement statement that $6,724.99 in settlement charges were paid out of the $35,000.00 loaned to the plaintiff. Thus, whether plaintiff would have received that amount at his closing as well as $10,546.06 and then had the responsibility of individually paying the various service providers for obtaining his loan or whether that amount was disbursed to the service providers on his behalf is immaterial because both processes result in the same outcome. As the lender acknowledged in the settlement statement that the fees were paid by the borrower, and as the $6,724.99 in settlement charges were paid out of the $35,000.00 loaned rather than added to the principal, the Court finds that a reasonable jury could find that the settlement charges were paid by the plaintiff at the closing of his loan. As there is a genuine issue of material fact, the Court denies summary judgment.

Next, the Court must examine which settlement charges count in the calculation of whether HOEPA protection is triggered. In order to trigger HOEPA in this case, the total points and fees must exceed 8% of $35,000.00 or $2,800.00. Pursuant to 12 C.F.R. § 226.32(b)(1)(ii), the broker fee of $2,950.00 would count in the calculation. Pursuant to 12 C.F.R. § 226.32(b)(1)(iii), the following would also count in the calculation: $430.00 title examination fee, $65.00 document preparation fee, $135.00 title insurance fee, $475.00 appraisal fee, 495.00 processing fee, $76.00 tax service fee and $20.00 flood certification fee. The total for the above counted fees is $4,646.00 or 13% of the loan. As the points and fees paid by the plaintiff at closing clearly exceed the 8% trigger, the Court holds that a reasonable jury could conclude that the plaintiff is entitled to HOEPA protection (elimination of the holder-in-due-course defense) and that Wells Fargo, as assignee, is subject to all claims and defenses, whether under TILA or other law, that could be raised against Delta Funding Corporation. As there is a genuine issue of material fact, the motion to dismiss Wells Fargo from Counts I and II is denied.

Although the facts in this case make it unnecessary for the Court at the summary judgment stage to further interpret the phrase "payable by the consumer at or before closing" in 15 U.S.C. § 1602(aa), nevertheless, this Court finds the interpretation of that phrase by Judge Donald * * * to be inapposite to the meaning Congress intended. Instead, the term "payable" should be interpreted as meaning "legally enforceable" or "obligation to pay." Moreover, it appears from the Federal Reserve Board's Official Staff Interpretation of 12 C.F.R. § 226.32(b)(1)(ii) that fees paid to a mortgage broker directly or indirectly are included in the calculation of fees and points. The Court notes that neither Judge Donald in *Terry* nor Judge McKeague in *Mourer* acknowledged this interpretation by the Federal Reserve Board, whose responsibility it is to interpret and implement TILA. Finally, while TILA is highly technical, it is a remedial statute. *See Pfennig v. Household Credit Services, Inc.,* 286 F.3d 340, 344 (6th Cir.2002). It was designed to protect consumers like the plaintiff here, not more sophisticated lending and financial institutions, who are able to control the structure of the loan transaction.

Congress did not use the term "paid" in § 1602(aa), instead, it used the term "payable" which looks to the fact that the consumer bears the cost of those fees at the time of closing, not whether those fees were financed, paid separately or deducted from the loan proceeds. Given the statute's remedial purpose, the Court believes that to allow lenders and financial institutions to manipulate the payment of points and fees in these transactions to avoid triggering the HOEPA protections is unfair and defeats the purpose of the law. Accordingly, this Court agrees with the plaintiff that *Terry* and its progeny have been wrongly decided.

* * *

IV

On the basis of the foregoing, it is hereby ORDERED that defendants' motion for summary judgment with regard to Wells Fargo is DENIED on Counts I, II and VIII of the amended complaint * * *.

Problem 9–3

Grin's has decided to make loans that are subject to HOEPA. It would like to know if HOEPA would bar it from any of the following practices:

A. Grin's would like to provide loans to consumers who already have mortgages but need to borrow more. Rather than extending loans only for the additional amount needed, Grin's would like to replace the earlier loan with a new, larger loan at a higher interest rate.

B. May Grin's refinance HOEPA loans into new HOEPA loans within one year of extending the earlier loan, but lend an additional $5,000 to the consumer or extend the term in which the borrower can repay the loans by five years if it also charges additional fees in connection with the refinancing? See Reg. Z § 226.34(a)(3).

C. May Grin's refinance HOEPA loans into new HOEPA loans for borrowers every thirteen months?

D. May Grin's charge a late fee of $100 and raise the interest rate by one percent every time a payment is late? See Reg. Z § 226.32(d)(4).

E. May Grin's use loans that provide for a balloon payment after five years? See Reg. Z § 226.32(d)(1).

Problem 9–4

An originator of subprime loans, RB Finance ("RBF"), has offered to sell Grin's a number of subprime loans in the secondary market. The loan documents and related documents do not contain any information suggesting that the loans are HOEPA loans, nor is there a TILA violation apparent on the face of the loans. Nevertheless, Grin's has heard rumors that RBF is a predatory lender and fears RBF may have inadvertently triggered application of HOEPA. Would Grin's take any risk in purchasing the loans? See TILA § 1641(d); Bryant v. Mortgage Capital Resource Corp., in Chapter Seven, *supra*. Would Grin's be liable if RBF had violated ECOA in connection with the loans, but the violation was not apparent on the face of the documents though it could have been discovered by an appropriate investigation? See 15 U.S.C. § 1691a(e); 12 CFR 202.2(1); *In re* Barber, 266 B.R. 309 (Bkrtcy.E.D.Pa. 2001).

3. STATE STATUTES

Dissatisfaction with HOEPA has led many states and municipalities to enact their own predatory lending laws. The first such statute, enacted by North Carolina in 1999, appears in the Statutory Supplement. Like HOEPA, the state statutes generally work on a trigger principle, though the state triggers are often lower than HOEPA's. The North Carolina statute uses the same APR trigger as HOEPA but a lower trigger for points and fees. Some states have adopted a lower APR trigger, see, e.g., 815 Ill. Comp. Stat. 137/10 (6%), while others use the same triggers as HOEPA, but impose additional limits on loan terms. See e.g. Fla. Stat. Ann. 494.00791 (rules on late fees). The state statutes also vary in what they prohibit; some of the variations are mentioned below.

Critics charge that the state statutes impair the ability of subprime borrowers to obtain non-predatory loans. Not surprisingly, others see things differently. This debate has sparked considerable study of the effect of the North Carolina statute on the subprime market. Some have attempted to determine—and disagreed over—whether lenders have responded to the statute by withdrawing from the North Carolina subprime market. Compare Erick Bergquist, Industry Hits Back on Lending Abuse Laws; State Rules Drive Countrywide Out of N.C. Subprime Market, Am. Banker, Jan. 26, 2001; David Boraks, B of A: Subprime Lending is Not Worth the Trouble, Am. Banker, Aug. 16, 2001, with North Carolina Office of the Commissioner of Banks, Joseph A. Smith, Jr., Mortgage Lending Act Report (Sept. 23, 2003), available at http://www.nccob.org/NR/rdonlyres/40198467–C64E–4630–9469–674C3B 21AA8F/0/MLAReporttoGovernor.pdf ("The number of mortgage lenders and brokers operating in North Carolina today is essentially the same as it was prior to the enactment of [the predatory lending statute]."); Keith Ernst, John Farris & Eric Stein, North Carolina's Subprime Home Loan Market After Predatory Lending Reform iii-iv (2002) (no major subprime lender left North Carolina after enactment of the statute) (hereinafter Ernst, Farris & Stein Study); Lenders Will Try to Pin Down Effects of NC Mortgage Law, Inside B&C Lending, March 5, 2001, at 3 (top subprime lenders continue to offer full array of products in North Carolina with little or no rate variations; while some companies have left market, the statute may not have been the cause). See also Morgan Stanley, Channel Check: Surprisingly Strong Subprime Growth (2002) (telephone survey of branch managers of lenders found that tougher predatory lending laws, including North Carolina's did not hurt growth).

Analysts also examined Home Mortgage Disclosure Act and other data for signs that subprime lending had dried up. The Ernst, Farris & Stein Study concluded that by one measure, "North Carolina was the sixth most active state for subprime lending in 2000 ..." and the statute's restraints on certain terms had saved borrowers more than $100 million. *Id.* at iii-iv. Another study of a database of 3.3 million subprime loans for the period 1998–2002 concluded that after passage of the North Carolina law, "the subprime market behaved essentially as the law intended: There was a reduction in predatory loans but no change in the cost of subprime credit or reduction in access to credit for high-risk borrowers." Roberto G. Quercia, Michael A. Stegman & Walter R. Davis, The Impact of North Carolina's Anti–Predatory Lending Law: A Descriptive Assessment 1 (2003). The authors also reported that loans to borrowers with credit scores under 589 increased by nearly one-third after the law became effective. *Id.* at 17. But other observers concluded that the law impaired the ability of borrowers to obtain subprime loans. See Gregory Elliehausen & Michael Staten, Regulation of Suprime Mortgage Products: An Analysis of North Carolina's Predatory Lending Law 29 J. Real Estate Fin. & Econ. 411, 412 (2004) ("creditors appear to have sharply restricted lending to higher-risk customers in North Carolina—but not to customers in neighboring states nor to lower risk customers in North Carolina—after passage of the law. The findings support the hypothesis that creditors rationed lending to the highest risk customers in response to the higher costs imposed by the North Carolina anti-predatory lending statute."); Keith D. Harvey & Peter J. Nigro, Do Predatory Lending Laws Influence Mortgage Lending? An Analysis of the North Carolina Predatory Lending Law, 29 J. Real Estate Fin. & Econ. 435, 453 (2004) (relying on HMDA data to conclude that "the volumes of both subprime mortgage applications and originations declined significantly in North Carolina compared with ... four other Southeastern states...." The authors also noted that a steeper decline in non-bank subprime lending as opposed to bank subprime lending might indicate a decline in predatory lending practices.); Remarks by John D. Hawke, Jr. Comptroller of the Currency Before the Federalist Society, July 24, 2003, at 6 ("Based on OCC's analysis, among the mainstream group of subprime borrowers—those with FICO scores between 580 and 660—mortgage loan originations dropped a stunning 30 percent in the 18 months after the North Carolina law was passed."). Some of these studies criticize the methodologies employed by others.

Social scientists have also studied the impact of other predatory lending laws. See Keith D. Harvey & Peter J. Nigro, How Do Predatory Lending Laws Influence Mortgage Lending in Urban Areas? A Tale of Two Cities, 23 J. Real Estate Res. 479 (2003) (after Philadelphia and Chicago enacted predatory lending laws, both cities experienced significant declines in subprime mortgage lending; the authors speculate that some of the loans, but not all, that would otherwise have been entered into would have been predatory); Robert F. DeMong, The Impact of the New Jersey Home Ownership Security Act of 2002 (2004) (industry-sponsored survey of NJ subprime lenders and mortgage brokers found drop in subprime lending); Gregory Elliehausen, Michael E. Staten, & Jevgenijs Steinbuks, The Effects of State Predatory Lending Laws on the Availability of Subprime Mortgage Credit iii (2006) (Study's "findings suggest that the more restrictive state predatory mortgage lending laws reduced availability of regulated high-cost subprime mortgage credit."). If predatory lending laws reduce the availability of subprime lending, does that necessarily mean the laws are unsound?

Notes

1. Does the North Carolina statute seem like a better solution to the problem of predatory lending than HOEPA? Why or why not? Would it have prevented the abuses described by Ms. Podelco and Mr. Satriano in their testimony or protected Ms. Sargeant in *United Companies*?

2. North Carolina has also passed a statute providing for licensing and oversight of mortgage brokers. See N.C. Gen. Stat. §§ 53–243.01 et seq. For the argument that the licensing statute is a more effective weapon against predatory lending than the predatory lending statute, see Donald C. Lampe, Wrong From the Start? North Carolina's "Predatory Lending" Law and the Practice vs. Product Debate, 7 Chap. L. Rev. 135, 144 (2004).

3. Some states have prohibited brokers from steering borrowers to higher-cost loans than the borrower's credit history would justify. See Cal. Fin. Code § 4973(l)(1). Does the North Carolina statute address this problem? Should North Carolina have included a requirement for advance disclosures similar to HOEPA's requirement?

4. Given that subprime loans tend to average only three percentage points higher interest rates than prime loans, does it make sense for the APR triggers for application of predatory lending statutes to be as high as they are? Is there a cost to making them lower?

5. Critics of predatory lending legislation claim that such statutes are unnecessary and expensive. They argue that "virtually all of the practices complained of are already against federal law." See Robert E. Litan, A Prudent Approach to Preventing "Predatory" Lending 2 (2001) (calling for increased enforcement of existing laws). Is that statement borne out by the materials you have already studied?

6. According to a 2004 article by the North Carolina Commissioner of Banks, the counseling provision of the statute had been used only "a dozen times." The Commissioner suggested that lenders had stopped offering loans that triggered application of the statute, but reported anecdotal evidence that some borrowers who had received the counseling ended up not entering into the loans. See Joseph A. Smith, Jr., Financial Literacy, Regulation and Consumer Welfare, 8 N.C. Banking Inst. 77, 91 (2004).

Problem 9–5

What advice would you give Grin's in Problem 9–2 if it desired to make high cost loans in North Carolina? Would any of the approaches that worked in Problem 9–2 avoid application of the North Carolina statute? As we will see in the next subsection, preemption by federal regulatory agencies might offer Grin's a way to avoid application of the North Carolina statute, but short of that, what other options does Grin's have?

Problem 9–6

Assuming that Grin's makes loans subject to the North Carolina statute, can it employ the practices described in Problem 9–3, supra?

Note on State Statutes and Assignee Liability

Does the North Carolina statute have a provision, like HOEPA's, subjecting assignees to borrowers' defenses? Should it? See Kurt Eggert, Held Up in Due Course: Predatory Lending, Securitization, and the Holder in Due Course Doctrine, 35 Creighton L. Rev. 503 (2002); Siddhartha Venkatesan, Abrogating the Holder in Due Course Doctrine in Subprime Mortgage Transactions to More Effectively Police Predatory Lending, 7 N.Y.U.J. Legis. & Pub. Pol'y 177 (2003). In 2002, Georgia enacted such a statute. Ga. Code Ann. § 7–6A–1 et seq. In response to this provision as well as to others appearing to subject lenders and assignees to unlimited and uncertain liability, bond-rating agencies decided that they could not rate many of the home loans issued in Georgia. The lack of a rating prevented lenders from selling the loans on the secondary market, which led some lenders to curtail their mortgage lending in Georgia. See Georgia Fair Lending Act: The Unintended Consequences (2003). Georgia's legislature subsequently amended the statute to limit assignee liability, among other changes, and the rating agencies resumed rating Georgian home loans. See Baher Azmy, Squaring the Predatory Lending Circle: A Case for States as Laboratories of Experimentation, 57 Fla. L. Rev. 295, 374–75 (2005). Some other states also subject assignees to borrower defenses in certain circumstances. See, e.g., 815 ILCS 137/135(d)(1). New York permits borrowers to assert claims and defenses only when the assignee sues the borrower to foreclose or collect on a loan in default for more than sixty days. N.Y. Banking Law § 6–l(13).

Has the market made assignee liability provisions unnecessary? Purchasers in the secondary market typically undertake a "due diligence" review of the loans they purchase to insure that the loans are safe investments. This process may reveal that loans are predatory, and some purchasers will refuse to buy them for that reason—though others decline to buy only because of characteristics that would make the loan too risky. See GAO Report at 77.

4. PREEMPTION

The variation in state predatory lending laws may create problems for national lenders or purchasers in the secondary market that wish to operate across state lines. Some federal regulators have responded by announcing that state predatory lending laws are preempted as to federally-regulated institutions. This subsection explores some of the resulting issues.

One such federal regulator is the Office of Thrift Supervision ("OTS"), which has jurisdiction over nationally-chartered thrifts, or savings banks, and their subsidiaries. The OTS interprets the statutes authorizing it to promulgate lending regulations as permitting its regulations to "occupy the field" of lending rules; in its view, therefore, states cannot impose their own rules, including predatory lending rules, on thrifts. See 12 C.F.R. § 545.2 (OTS has "plenary and exclusive authority . . . to regulate all aspects of the operations of Federal savings associations. . . . This exercise of the Office's authority is preemptive of any state law purporting to address the subject of the operations of a Federal savings association."). See also 12 C.F.R. § 560.2. The OTS has issued a number of letters stating that the predatory lending statutes of specifically-named states are preempted as to the institutions it regulates. See e.g., OTS Op. Chief Counsel, P–2003–6 (Sept. 2, 2003) (New Mexico statute); OTS Op. Chief Counsel, P–2003–5 (July 22, 2003) (New Jersey); OTS Op. Chief Counsel, P–2003–2 (Jan. 30, 2003) (New York); OTS Op. Chief Counsel, P–2003–1 (Jan. 21, 2003) (Georgia statute). The National Credit Union Administration ("NCUA") also appears to have concluded that at least some provisions in state predatory lending laws are preempted as to federally-chartered credit unions. See NCUA Legal Op. Letter 00–0827 (Mar. 2, 2001) (addressing NY banking regulations), available at http://www.ncua.gov/RegulationsOpinionsLaws/opinion _letters/2000/00–0827.html; NCUA Legal Op. Letter 02—649 (July 29, 2002) (addressing Georgia statute), available at http://www.ncua.gov/ RegulationsOpinionsLaws/opinion_letters/2002/02–0649.html.

In 2004, the Office of the Comptroller of the Currency ("OCC") promulgated a number of regulations preempting state law, including 12 C.F.R. §§ 34.3, 34.4, 7.4000, 7.4007, 7.4008, and 7.4009, which appear in the Statutory Supplement.

Notes

1. In a statement explaining the regulations and its approach to predatory lending, titled Bank Activities and Operations; Real Estate Lending and Appraisals, 69 Fed. Reg. 1904, 1908, 1913, 1914 (Jan. 13, 2004), the OCC stated:

> When national banks are unable to operate under uniform, consistent, and predictable standards, their business suffers, which negatively affects their safety and soundness. The application of multiple, often unpredictable, different state or local restrictions and requirements prevents them from operating in the manner authorized under Federal law, is costly and burdensome, interferes with their ability to plan their business and manage their risks, and subjects them to uncertain liabilities and potential exposure. In some cases, this deters them from making certain products available in certain jurisdictions. * * *

> The OCC shares the view of the commenters [on the then-proposed regulation] that predatory and abusive lending practices are inconsistent with national objectives of encouraging home ownership and community

revitalization, and can be devastating to individuals, families, and communities. We will not tolerate such practices by national banks and their operating subsidiaries. Our Advisory Letters on predatory lending, our pioneering enforcement positions resulting in substantial restitution to affected consumers, and the anti-predatory lending standards adopted in this final rule reflect our commitment that national banks operate pursuant to high standards of integrity in all respects. The provisions of this final rule, clarifying that certain state laws are not applicable to national banks' operations, do not undermine the application of these standards to all national banks, for the protection of all national bank customers—wherever they are located. * * *

Indeed, several practices that we identify as abusive in our Advisory Letters—such as equity stripping, loan flipping, and the refinancing of special subsidized mortgage loans that originally contained terms favorable to the borrower—generally can be found to be unfair or deceptive practices that violate the FTC Act. * * *

Other than ... isolated incidences of abusive practices that have triggered the OCC's aggressive supervisory response, evidence that national banks are engaged in predatory lending practices is scant. Based on the absence of such information—from third parties, our consumer complaint database, and our supervisory process—we have no reason to believe that such practices are occurring in the national banking system to any significant degree.

In an earlier document described as a work in progress to stimulate discussion, the OCC expressed the view that "There is a good deal of empirical evidence to suggest that anti-predatory statutes impede the flow of mortgage credit especially to low income and higher-risk borrowers, and any reductions in predatory abuses resulting from these measures is probably achieved at the expense of many legitimate loans." OCC Working Paper, Economic Issues in Predatory Lending 20 (2003). This Paper also observed that anti-predatory lending laws can retard the sale of loans in the secondary market.

2. Because the OCC is empowered to enforce section five of the FTC Act as to national banks, 12 U.S.C. § 1818(b), its statement that predatory practices may violate that statute is of particular significance to banks. OCC Advisory Letter 2003–2, Guidelines for National Banks to Guard Against Predatory and Abusive Lending Practices (Feb. 21, 2003), available at http://www.occ.treas.gov/ftp/advisory/2003–2.doc, notes that "it is generally necessary to consider the totality of the circumstances to assess whether a loan is predatory."

3. How important is the OCC's preemption of state predatory lending laws, given the OCC's observation that national banks appear not to engage in predatory lending? Another OCC regulation, codified at 12 C.F.R. § 7.4006, extends its preemption rules to operating subsidiaries of national banks. Courts have upheld the authority of the OCC to issue this regulation. See Wachovia Bank v. Watters, 431 F.3d 556 (6th Cir. 2005), cert. granted sub nom. Watters v. Wachovia Bank, N.A., ___ U.S. ___, 126 S.Ct. 2900, 165 L.Ed.2d 915 (2006); Wells Fargo Bank N.A. v. Boutris, 419 F.3d 949 (9th Cir. 2005); Wachovia Bank, N.A. v. Burke, 414 F.3d 305 (2d Cir. 2005). *Burke*

involved an institution that had previously been licensed by the Connecticut Banking Commissioner, but four days after being examined by the Commissioner, the institution reportedly notified the Commissioner that it would become a subsidiary of a national bank, thereby excusing it from compliance with Connecticut licensing laws. See O. Dudley Gilbert, Update on State and Banking Law and Regulations, 58 Consumer Fin. L. Q. Rep. 18, 23 (2004). One critic claims that national bank operating subsidiaries originated nearly a quarter of total subprime loans in 2003. See Baher Azmy, Squaring the Predatory Lending Circle: A Case for States as Laboratories of Experimentation, 57 Fla. L. Rev. 295, 359 (2005). See also Arthur E. Wilmarth, Jr., The OCC's Preemption Rules Exceed the Agency's Authority and Present a Serious Threat to the Dual Banking System and Consumer Protection, 23 Ann. Rev. Banking & Fin. L. 225, 314–15 (2004) ("most of the largest subprime mortgage lenders are nonbank affiliates of major bank holding companies.... a number of [national bank subsidiaries] have produced serious allegations of abusive lending practices."). Preemption of state law as to nonbank subsidiaries is particularly significant because such subsidiaries are not routinely examined by federal regulators. GAO Report at 49, 51–53. Federal preemption may also have an impact on application of state predatory lending laws to state lenders. Some state predatory lending laws provide that to the extent application of the laws is preempted as to federal institutions, the statutes are also preempted as to state-chartered institutions. See, e.g., Ga. Code Ann., § 7–6A–12; Declaratory Ruling by David G. Sorrell, Commissioner, Georgia Dept. of Banking & Fin., Aug. 5, 2003 (Ga. State Lending Law no longer applicable to state banks). The Georgia statute, however, does not extend the preemption to independent mortgage brokers. Except as to mortgage brokers, is anything left of the Georgia statute? Why would a state legislature limit its statute in such a way? In 2003, one lender obtained a federal charter for more than 300 of its offices around the country, stating that it wished to "operate under a uniform federal system of regulation." Liz Moyers, In Brief: OTS Approves Thrift Charter for Chase, Am. Banker, Dec. 4, 2003 at 18. Does that explain the Georgia statute?

4. Professor Azmy argues, at 301–02 in the article cited in the preceding note, that preemption of state predatory lending laws is unwise:

> Regulatory responses—or "experiments"—to predatory lending are particularly appropriate at the state or local level because: (i) the problem is both immature and difficult to define; (ii) its economic and social costs on borrowers are hard to isolate or evaluate; and (iii) the positive or negative effects of any particularly regulatory strategy are thereby hard to quantify abstractly or in isolation; rather, they require empirical assessment. As a result, the recent efforts by federal regulators to preempt some aspects of state predatory lending legislation and emerging congressional attempts to more broadly preempt this legislation are at a minimum premature, and they may even be counterproductive.*

5. The OCC Rules have also drawn criticism from state law enforcement officials. See, e.g., Statement by Attorney General Eliot Spitzer Regarding Preemption of State Consumer Protection Laws, Jan. 6, 2004, available at http://www.oag.state.ny.us/press/2004/jan/jan07a_04.html (call-

---

* Reprinted with permission.

ing the OCC rules "shamefully bad public policy," and noting that all fifty attorneys general had opposed the rules on the ground "that OCC devotes the vast majority of its time and resources to monitoring the safety and soundness of financial institutions, and does not have the states' experience, expertise, resources or record in addressing consumer protection issues."). According to the GAO Report at 43, issued in January 2004, no formal enforcement actions related to predatory mortgage lending had been taken by OTS, the Federal Reserve Board, or NCUA while the OCC had taken only one such formal enforcement action. Regulators had, however, acted informally on a number of occasions.

6. Another vigorous attack on the actions of federal regulators in this area appears in Christopher L. Peterson, Federalism and Predatory Lending: Unmasking the Deregulatory Agenda, 78 Temp. L.Rev. 1, 8 (2005):

> [T]oday's advocates of exclusive federal power over predatory lending policy care less for the niceties of balance or power, nor even for the benefits of uniform regulation, than they do for the covert protection of a powerful industry that profits, either directly or indirectly, from predatory lending.... current efforts to preempt state law have little or nothing to do with federalism in general or uniformity in particular, but are, in fact, simply efforts to deregulate.

7. What impact would the OCC regulation have on the practices described in Ms. Podelco's and Mr. Satriano's testimony, or in the *United Companies* case?

8. The question of whether federal regulators have the power to preempt state law, as opposed to the wisdom of preemption or its effects, seems better left to a course in banking law, though it is worth noting that early decisions have upheld the OCC's preemption powers. See Office of the Comptroller of the Currency v. Spitzer, 396 F.Supp.2d 383 (S.D.N.Y. 2005); Abel v. Keybank USA, 313 F.Supp.2d 720 (N.D.Oh. 2004). That question is addressed in a number of the publications cited in this section, as well as Marcel C. Duhamel, Predatory Lending and National Banks: The New Visitorial Powers, Preemption and Predatory Lending Regulations, 121 Banking L.J. 455 (2004). You should also understand that while the issue of preemption arises in these materials in connection with predatory lending statutes, many other state laws are said to be preempted by federal regulations.

9. Does federal preemption make the state predatory lending statutes irrelevant? If so, is that good? Would you feel the same way if federal legislation was more protective of consumers and state legislation was more protective of lenders?

Problem 9–7

Grin's is a national bank making non-HOEPA loans in North Carolina that exceed the threshold for points and fees required to trigger application of the North Carolina predatory lending statute. Grin's would like to know whether it can engage in the practices described supra in Problem 9–3.

SECTION D. SPECIAL PREDATORY LENDING ISSUES

1. THE FTC AND UNFAIR CONTRACT TERMS

In 1985, the Federal Trade Commission adopted its Trade Regulation Rule on Credit Practices, 16 C.F.R. Part 444 (reprinted in the Statutory Supplement) barring certain unfair contract terms. Several of these are treated in this subsection. In reviewing the materials that follow, consider what the FTC's role should be in addressing predatory lending issues—not just the issues raised in this subsection, but also the issues raised in the other subsections of this chapter. Why has the FTC played so limited a part in addressing the practices described in this chapter?

a. *Blanket Security Interests*

It was once standard practice for small loan companies to take so-called "blanket" security interests in a consumer's household goods as collateral for a consumer loan. Under these arrangements, a creditor could seize a defaulting consumer's furniture even for transactions in which the collateral was completely unrelated to the purpose of the loan. In 1985, however, blanket security interests were essentially abolished by the Credit Practices Rule. Section 444.2(a)(4) of that rule makes it an unfair act or practice under the FTC Act for a lender or retail installment seller to take or receive from a consumer any obligation that "constitutes or contains a non-possessory security interest in household goods other than a purchase money security interest."

The Credit Practices Rule was first proposed in 1975, and it was the subject of intense debate for a decade. In 1980, the staff of the FTC's Bureau of Consumer Protection issued a lengthy report on the then-proposed rule. The following excerpt should help you understand the reason for the rule.

CREDIT PRACTICES, STAFF REPORT AND RECOMMENDATION ON PROPOSED TRADE REGULATION RULE

192–228 (1980).

In return for the credit they receive consumers are often required to give their creditors a security interest in the property they own at the time credit is extended or may obtain after the credit transaction is consummated. * * * Loans secured by non-possessory liens on debtor's household goods and personal effects [have become] increasingly common. Between 1900 and the present, the use of security interests has become standard business practice in the consumer credit market.

Specifically at issue in this proceeding are two kinds of security interests affecting consumers' property. The first is a broadly cast lien on all of a consumer's household goods taken in connection with a loan.

The second is the reservation of a security interest in specific property which is not the subject of a credit sale as additional security for the sale. Both forms of security interest give rise to a right to seize property from a consumer, inflicting a substantial forfeiture on the consumer. They also equip a creditor with a capacity to threaten the consumer with extreme deprivation to induce the consumer to acquiesce to the creditor's demands, whether or not the demands are reasonable.

* * *

The practice of securing consumer loans with a blanket security interest in household goods (HHG) appears to be almost universal, based on this record. * * *

* * *

* * * [T]he record reflects instances where co-signors as well as the primary debtor are impelled to pledge all of their household goods when they guarantee the loan of another. In such cases, the co-signor receives no consideration for a pledge of all of his or her personal property.

* * *

The vast majority of industry witnesses conceded that household goods have little, if any, economic value to creditors. Their value is psychological. * * * When consumers run into difficulty, the blanket security interest in household goods enables a creditor to threaten the consumer with the loss of all personal property located in the home.

* * *

[T]he National Consumer Law Center found that non-purchase money security interests were the single most common basis for threats and harassment of consumers of all of the creditors' remedies surveyed.

> The abuse occurred in 77% of the cases studied, and injury resulted just as frequently. Anxiety was the most common, followed by disruption of household finances and other delinquency. Costly financings were reported in 40% of the instances, and distinct out-of-pocket expenses were reported 30% of the time and payment of the [sic] disputed debt as often (31%). Unreasonable settlements, and abandonment of bona fide defenses all occurred 25%, if not more frequently. Loss of job time and marital instability each occurred 20% of the time.

> In summary, three out of every four cases involving a delinquent account secured by non-purchase money collateral lead to harassment; and in two of every four situations, injury results.

The findings of the National Consumer Law Center Survey are borne out by the testimony received in this proceeding.

* * *

While seizure of household goods is rare, when it occurs it may have devastating consequences. It may occur in the context of divorce, where a wife finds herself financially devastated and deprived of her personal belongings, or without baby furniture, or a refrigerator. Repossessed furniture may be taken to the dump or auctioned for a tiny fraction of its replacement value. For the debtor, the replacement value is a true measure of the cost of the repossession. This fact was acknowledged by the industry as well as by consumer witnesses. Thus, seizure often means the infliction of a cost which is grossly disproportionate to the benefit obtained. This is particularly true of cross-collateral clauses where a debtor faces the loss of many purchases for the failure to pay for one.

In the context of seizure, the disproportionate impact of blanket security interests thus becomes all the more apparent. Debtors lose property which is of great value to them and little value to the creditor. While creditors are entitled to payment, such security interests offer little economic return to creditors at great economic and social cost.

FTC CREDIT PRACTICES RULE STATEMENT OF BASIS AND PURPOSE AND REGULATORY ANALYSIS

49 Fed.Reg. 7740, 7744 (March 1, 1984).

* * *

In consumer credit transactions, the rights and duties of the parties are defined by standard-form contracts, over most of which there is no bargaining. The economic exigencies of extending credit to large numbers of consumers each day make standardization a necessity. The issue, however, is whether the contents of these standard form contracts are a product of market forces.

Although market forces undoubtedly influence the remedies included in standard form contracts, several factors indicate that competition will not necessarily produce optimal contracts. Consumers have limited incentives to search out better remedial provisions in credit contracts. The substantive similarities of contracts from different creditors mean that search is less likely to reveal a different alternative. Because remedies are relevant only in the event of default, and default is relatively infrequent, consumers reasonably concentrate their search on such factors as interest rates and payment terms. Searching for credit contracts is also difficult, because contracts are written in obscure technical language, do not use standardized terminology, and may not be provided before the transaction is consummated. Individual creditors have little incentive to provide better terms and explain their benefits to consumers, because a costly education effort would be required with all creditors sharing the benefits. Moreover, such a campaign might differentially attract relatively high risk borrowers.

For these reasons, the Commission concludes that consumers cannot reasonably avoid the remedial provisions themselves. Nor can consumers, having signed a contract, avoid the harsh consequences of remedies by avoiding default. When default occurs, it is most often a response to events such as unemployment or illness that are not within the borrower's control. Thus, consumers cannot reasonably avoid the substantial injury these creditor remedies may inflict.

* * *

Note

Students may be familiar from their course in contracts with Williams v. Walker–Thomas Furniture Co., 350 F.2d 445 (D.C. Cir. 1965), a trail-blazing case on the unconscionability doctrine. The case dealt with a contract clause that kept a balance due on all items a consumer had purchased from Walker–Thomas on credit until the consumer paid off the full indebtedness. That clause, combined with Walker–Thomas's practice of taking a security interest in items sold on credit, meant that as long as a consumer still owed money to Walker–Thomas, Walker–Thomas could threaten to repossess all the items it had sold the consumer. The court remanded the case to the lower court for a determination as to whether the contract term in question was unconscionable. Would the Credit Practices Rule bar the term? Does it help the consumer establish that the furniture store's conduct was unconscionable or otherwise violated state law? Would the U3C? See §§ 3.302 and 3.303. The principal argument against decisions like *Williams* is that, without such clauses, lenders may be unwilling to lend to poorer consumers, restricting credit to them unduly. Who is better able to resolve this kind of an issue, a court, a legislature, or a regulatory agency?

Problem 9–8

On February 1, Ms. Williams purchased a refrigerator on credit from Walker–Thomas, the contract to be paid over a three year period. On June 1, Ms. Williams sought to buy a DVD player on credit from Walker–Thomas. The credit manager said he would approve the DVD player contract if he had additional collateral. Ms. Williams offered to put up, as collateral, all her currently-owned furniture and appliances, including her equity in the refrigerator.

(a) What collateral can Walker–Thomas safely take under the U3C? Could it use a term that kept a balance due on all items until the consumer paid off the full indebtedness? See §§ 3.301–3.303.

(b) What can it safely take under the FTC Credit Practices Rule? Are cross-collateral clauses prohibited by the rule?

Notes

1. The rule does not directly prohibit blanket security interests in household goods, yet that is its effect. Why? Does the FTC have the authority to amend state law by abolishing certain types of security interests? If not, does it have the authority to accomplish the same thing through the back door of unfair trade practices? The validity of the Credit Practices rule was upheld in American Financial Services Ass'n v. FTC, 767 F.2d 957

(D.C.Cir.1985), cert. denied 475 U.S. 1011, 106 S.Ct. 1185, 89 L.Ed.2d 301 (1986). Note also that the FTC's rule technically applies only to those lending institutions within the regulatory jurisdiction of the FTC, such as small loan companies and retail sellers. Before the rule went into effect, small loan companies were the principal users of blanket security interests. However, the Federal Reserve Board has also adopted a credit practices rule which is nearly identical to the FTC rule and which applies to banks, institutions beyond the reach of the FTC. See 12 C.F.R. Part 227.

2. Why should purchase money security interests in household goods continue to be allowed? If furniture loses its value almost the minute the consumer gets it home, wouldn't any attempt to repossesses it have to be for reasons other than economic ones? Is a creditor who repossesses furniture ever likely to recoup the entire debt? If a consumer buys but doesn't pay for a new sofa, is she likely to be surprised when the creditor comes to take it back? Is she likely to be surprised when the same creditor wants to take the refrigerator as well? Does this help explain the rule? Why does the Rule treat goods previously sold by the same creditor and not yet paid off differently from goods previously sold by other creditors?

3. Notice that the FTC rule does not prevent nonpossessory security interests in things like electronic entertainment equipment, jewelry, and works of art. Why? Is it because these items may be considered to be luxuries? If so, is it proper for the FTC to decide which property is "luxury" property? Is it because these items are more likely to maintain their value than ordinary household furniture?

4. Several states also restrict or prohibit non-purchase money security interests in household goods. Some retail installment sales acts, for example, restrict sellers to security in either the goods sold or closely related goods. U3C § 3.301 is of this type. In addition to statutory approaches, at least one state court has held that blanket household goods security interests were unconscionable. State v. Avco Financial Services of New York, 70 A.D.2d 859, 418 N.Y.S.2d 52 (1979). This ruling was reversed on appeal, however, on procedural grounds. State v. Avco Financial Services of New York, 50 N.Y.2d 383, 429 N.Y.S.2d 181, 406 N.E.2d 1075 (1980). With the FTC rule in effect, will these state law restrictions continue to have any viability?

5. Are rules restricting security unduly paternalistic? Don't they amount to a restriction on the alienability of the consumer's property? A provision in a private contract such as a security agreement, for example, which purported to restrict the debtor's ability to sell or grant a security interest in particular property would almost certainly be unenforceable. See UCC § 9–401(b). Why should the FTC or a state legislature be able to tell consumers what they may or may not do with their own property?

6. Why should the law limit what a consumer can offer as security? After all, it *is* the consumer's property; can't she do anything she wants to with her own assets? Some limitations seem to be easily accepted—e.g., prohibiting the taking of "a pound of flesh" or the proverbial "first-born child"—without a great deal of analysis. But other types of security demand more analysis. Consumers may be asked to put up as security for loans their automobiles, shares of stock, furniture, works of art, the family jewels, or

any other property they own. They may also be asked to put up property they do not yet own, through after acquired property clauses, or their future wages, through wage assignments, or even the assets of third parties, through surety or "co-signer" arrangements.

b. Other Forms of "Security"

1. Wage assignments

A wage assignment, as the name suggests, is a device under which consumers assign their future earnings to their creditors. Traditionally, wage assignments were taken at the time credit was extended, but most often the creditor treated them as fall-back security and did not exercise his rights under the assignment until after a default. At that time, the creditor would simply notify the consumer's employer to begin paying all or a portion of the consumer's wages directly to the creditor. Nearly all wage assignments were irrevocable.

As you can imagine, wage assignments are a particularly harsh form of security. By the mid–1980s, over half the states had severely restricted their use or outlawed them altogether. U3C § 3.305 is typical. In addition, the FTC Credit Practices Rule outlaws certain forms of irrevocable wage assignments. See § 444.2(a)(3). In its original draft, this rule matched most state laws on the subject and outlawed all forms of wage assignments. As finally adopted, however, the rule incorporates several exceptions. It now permits irrevocable "payroll deduction plans." What is the difference between irrevocable wage assignments and a "payroll deduction plan"?

2. Co-signers

A creditor can add a substantial measure of contractual security to a consumer transaction by requiring a co-signer—a spouse, parent, friend or relative whose creditworthiness compensates for any weaknesses in the debtor's own. Over the years, many observers of the consumer credit industry felt that unpaid co-signers such as parents and rich uncles did not really understand the nature of their obligation. For example, many believed that the creditor must sue the principal debtor before suing the co-signer. In most cases, this is not true. The co-signer is liable in his capacity as maker of the note, and the creditor may ordinarily come after the parent without bothering about the broke kid. See UCC § 3–419.

Because of concern about widespread misunderstanding of co-signer obligations, the FTC included in its Credit Practices Rule a provision which requires a special disclosure to consumer co-signers. See § 444.3. The U3C contains a similar provision. See § 3.208. Do you think this disclosure will cause many potential co-signers to refuse to sign? Do you think it will help them better understand their obligations?

Note

What accounts for the different treatment of these two types of non-property security? That is, why are wage assignments regulated substantively by being outlawed or severely restricted, while co-signer obligations are regulated solely through disclosure? Does this make sense? Do you think co-signers should be outlawed? (Would you have made it to law school without one?).

2. YIELD–SPREAD PREMIUMS

SCHUETZ v. BANC ONE MORTGAGE CORPORATION

United States Court of Appeals, Ninth Circuit, 2002.
292 F.3d 1004, cert. denied 537 U.S. 1171, 123 S.Ct. 994, 154 L.Ed.2d 913 (2003).

RYMER, CIRCUIT JUDGE.

This appeal requires us to decide whether yield spread premiums, which are fees paid by mortgage lenders to mortgage brokers that are based on the difference between the interest rate at which the broker originates the loan and the par, or market rate offered by the lender, are lawful under the Real Estate Settlement Procedures Act (RESPA), 12 U.S.C. § 2601 *et seq.* (West 2001). RESPA prohibits the giving or receiving of fees for referral as part of a real estate settlement service but permits fees that are paid for facilities actually furnished or services actually performed in the making of a loan. RESPA, § 8(a), (c)(2); 12 U.S.C. § 2607(a), (c)(2).

Bettina J. Scheutz obtained a federally related mortgage loan from Banc One Mortgage Corporation through a mortgage broker, Home Mortgage Financial Corporation. She paid Home Mortgage direct fees and Banc One paid it a yield spread premium. She brought a class action challenging the yield spread premium payment as contrary to § 8(a).

We do not write on a clean slate in deciding whether the yield spread premium was a referral, because the Department of Housing and Urban Development (HUD), which is charged with enforcing RESPA, has prescribed a test for determining the propriety of a yield spread premium payment. It asks whether services were actually performed for the total compensation paid to the mortgage broker, and whether that compensation is reasonably related to the services provided. The district court deferred to this test, correctly we believe, and declined to certify a class of borrowers for lack of a common question of fact. It then granted summary judgment in favor of Banc One on Scheutz's claim that its payment of the yield spread premium was really for a referral of business by Home Mortgage. The court concluded that the broker performed services that contributed to the transaction, and that Home Mortgage's total compensation (of which the yield spread premium was a part) was reasonably related to the services provided. We agree with these rulings.

As we have jurisdiction, 28 U.S.C. § 1291, we affirm.

I

When Schuetz found a house that she wanted to buy in the Sun Lakes Country Club development in Sun Lakes, Arizona, she hired Home Mortgage Financial Corporation, a mortgage broker, to arrange a loan. Mortgage brokers are intermediaries who bring borrower and lender together. Borrowers typically approach the mortgage settlement process with a variety of individual characteristics and needs, including their credit rating, income, sensitivity to interest rate variations, and preference for paying charges up front or spreading them out in the form of a higher interest rate. Brokers furnish numerous services to consumers;[1] in Schuetz's case, Home Mortgage analyzed her income and debt, explained the loan process and loan products available to her, collected her financial information, obtained a credit report on her behalf, secured an appraisal, prepared her loan package, and submitted it to Banc One. Mortgage brokers are compensated in several ways for their services. Compensation from the borrower to the broker is a direct fee, while money that the borrower pays the lender and the lender pays the broker is an indirect fee. Because lending institutions such as Banc One offer intermediaries options in structuring their compensation, brokers in effect determine their own compensation for any particular transaction by choosing the combination of loan characteristics and prices to offer a consumer.

A broker selects a loan product from among the various loans offered by the lending institutions with which it maintains a relation-

---

1. These services were first catalogued in a HUD letter to the Independent Bankers Association of America, dated February 14, 1995, and were listed again in HUD's Statement of Policy 1999–1. They include:

(a) Taking information from the borrower and filling out the application;

(b) Analyzing the prospective borrower's income and debt and pre-qualifying the prospective borrower to determine the maximum mortgage that the prospective borrower can afford;

(c) Educating the prospective borrower in the home buying and financing process, advising the borrower about the different types of loan products available, and demonstrating how closing costs and monthly payments could vary under each product;

(d) Collecting financial information (tax returns, bank statements) and other related documents that are part of the application process;

(e) Initiating/ordering VOEs (verifications of employment) and VODs (verifications of deposit);

(f) Initiating/ordering requests for mortgage and other loan verifications;

(g) Initiating/ordering appraisals;

(h) Initiating/ordering inspections or engineering reports;

(i) Providing disclosures (truth in lending, good faith estimate, others) to the borrower;

(j) Assisting the borrower in understanding and clearing credit problems;

(k) Maintaining regular contact with the borrower, realtors, lender, between application and closing ... and gather any additional needed information ...;

(l) Ordering legal documents;

(m) Determining whether the property was located in a flood zone ...; and

(n) Participating in the loan closing.

Real Estate Settlement Procedures Act (RESPA) Statement of Policy 1999–1 Regarding Lender Payments to Mortgage Brokers, 64 Fed.Reg. 10080, 10085 (March 1, 1999) (footnotes omitted).

ship. According to Home Mortgage, loans are selected based on the lender's service, turnaround time, ability to make the required funds available, reputation in the community, level of professionalism, reputation with the banking department, competitive rates, underwriting flexibility, and the availability of products.

Home Mortgage obtained Schuetz a 30–year loan in the principal amount of $68,000 with a 7.5% interest rate from Banc One, which is a wholesale lender. This was above Banc One's par rate. "Par rate" refers to the rate at which the lender will fund 100% of a loan with no premiums or discounts to the broker. For each loan product, Banc One estimates the secondary market value of a model loan and derives a "par" price (taking into account its own costs and return requirements) that it uses in developing rate sheets for brokers. If the interest rate on a particular loan exceeds the rate assumed by Banc One's par price model, Banc One will pay the broker a "yield spread premium" equal to the value of the additional interest.

A yield spread premium, or "YSP," is a lump sum paid by a lender to a broker at closing when the loan originated by the broker bears an above-par interest rate. As HUD has explained it:

> Payments to brokers by lenders, characterized as yield spread premiums, are based on the interest rate and points of the loan entered into as compared to the par rate offered by the lender to the mortgage broker for that particular loan (e.g., a loan of 8% and no points where the par rate is 7.50% will command a greater premium for the broker than a loan with a par rate of 7.75% and no points). In determining the price of a loan, mortgage brokers rely on rate quotes issued by lenders, sometimes several times a day. When a lender agrees to purchase a loan from a broker, the broker receives the then applicable pricing for the loan based on the difference between the rate reflected in the rate quote and the rate of the loan entered into by the borrower. . . .

> Lender payments to mortgage brokers may reduce the up-front costs to consumers. This allows consumers to obtain loans without paying direct fees themselves. Where a broker is not compensated by the consumer through a direct fee, or is partially compensated through a direct fee, the interest rate of the loan is increased to compensate the broker or the fee is added to principal. In any of the compensation methods described, all costs are ultimately paid by the consumer, whether through direct fees or through the interest rate.

1999 Statement of Policy, 64 Fed.Reg. at 10081 (footnotes omitted).

In this case, Schuetz paid her broker direct fees of $1,661.00, consisting of $688.00 for loan origination, $688.00 for loan discount, and $285.00 for processing. Banc One also paid Home Mortgage a yield spread premium of $516.00. This payment was identified on Schuetz's HUD–1 Settlement Statement as "Mortgage Broker fee to Home Mortgage from BANC ONE."

Scheutz sued Banc One on behalf of a class of borrowers whose loan settlements included a yield spread premium payment, claiming that the YSP violates RESPA because it is a kickback for referral of a federally related mortgage loan. She sought class certification, which the district court denied. It concluded that the issue on which this litigation would turn is whether the yield spread premiums paid by Banc One are compensation for facilities or services actually performed, and decided that this issue was too fact intensive to be resolved on a class-wide basis. * * *

Cross-motions for summary judgment resulted in judgment for Banc One. The district court held that HUD's 1999 Statement of Policy guided the outcome because Congress authorized HUD to promulgate rules and regulations to implement RESPA, and to interpret the statute. Applying HUD's test for legality of yield spread premium payments, the court found it undisputed that compensable services were performed by Home Mortgage and that they were worth what the broker was paid. Accordingly, the court concluded that no RESPA violation occurred.

Schuetz appeals both orders.

II

In a nutshell, Schuetz contends that the direct fees which she paid fully compensated Home Mortgage for the services it performed and that the yield spread premium paid by Banc One, which was not tied to-or in exchange for-any particular services, is necessarily a fee for referral. In her view, HUD and the district court got the liability test wrong, and the Eleventh Circuit got it right in *Culpepper v. Irwin Mortgage Corp.*, 253 F.3d 1324 (11th Cir.2001). Banc One counters that HUD's test is binding and that courts must defer to it.

The backdrop is cumbersome but important.

A

Congress enacted RESPA in 1974 to protect home buyers from inflated prices in the home purchasing process. It sought to increase the supply of information available to mortgage consumers about the cost of home loans in advance of settlement, and to eliminate abusive practices such as kickbacks, referral fees, and unearned fees. To accomplish the first purpose, the Act requires lenders to provide borrowers with a statement identifying all settlement charges on a standardized form, commonly known as a "HUD–1," 12 U.S.C. § 2603 (West 2001), and with an information booklet prepared by HUD that counsels borrowers on how mortgage transactions work and how to recognize inflated charges. Id. at § 2604.

Sections 8(a) and 8(c)(2) are the provisions primarily at issue in this case. Section 8(a) prohibits fees for referrals. It provides: "No person shall give and no person shall accept any fee, kickback, or thing of value pursuant to any agreement or understanding, oral or otherwise, that business incident to or a part of a real estate settlement service involving a federally related mortgage loan shall be referred to any person." 12 U.S.C. § 2607(a). Section 8(c)(2) provides: "Nothing in this section shall be construed as prohibiting ... the payment to any person of a bona fide salary or compensation or other payment for goods or facilities actually furnished or for services actually performed...." *Id.* § 2607(c)(2).

HUD is the administrative agency charged with enforcing RESPA. It is authorized by statute to prescribe rules and regulations, and to make interpretations of RESPA. 12 U.S.C. § 2617(a). HUD has issued regulations pursuant to this authority. *See* "Regulation X," 24 C.F.R. § 3500.1 *et seq.* Section 3500.14 pertains to kickbacks and unearned fees that are prohibited by § 8 of the statute. This regulation proscribes referral fees, 24 C.F.R. § 3500.14(b),[4] and defines a "referral" as "any oral or written action ... which has the effect of affirmatively influencing the selection by any person of a provider of a settlement service or business incident to or part of a settlement service when such person will pay for such settlement service or business incident thereto or pay a charge attributable in whole or in part to such settlement service or business." *Id.* at § 3500.14(f)(1). The regulations also implement § 8(c)(2) of the Act by providing that "[a] payment to any person of a *bona fide* salary or compensation or other payment for goods or facilities actually furnished or for services actually performed" is permissible. *Id.* at § 3500.14(g)(1)(iv).

Sections 8(a) and (c)(2) of RESPA generated a considerable amount of litigation. In light of the legal uncertainty about lender payments to mortgage brokers for services performed, Congress directed HUD to address the issue within 90 days of October 21, 1998 (the date on which the Department's 1999 appropriations bill was enacted).

Meanwhile, the Eleventh Circuit Court of Appeals rendered its first opinion in the *Culpepper* litigation. *Culpepper v. Inland Mortgage Corp. (Culpepper I),* 132 F.3d 692 (11th Cir.1998). The Culpeppers had obtained a federally insured home mortgage from Inland Mortgage Corporation through their mortgage broker at an interest rate of 7.5%. Unbeknownst to them, this was over Inland's par rate and carried a yield spread premium of $1,263.61 even though Inland would have made

---

4. Section 3500.14(b) provides:

No person shall give and no person shall accept any fee, kickback or other thing of value pursuant to any agreement or understanding, oral or otherwise, that business incident to or part of a settlement service involving a federally related mortgage loan shall be referred to any person. Any referral of a settlement service is not a compensable service, except as set forth in § 3500.14(g)(1). A business entity (whether or not in an affiliate relationship) may not pay any other business entity or the employees of any other business entity for the referral of settlement service business.

24 C.F.R. § 3500.14(b). Subsection (e) further provides:

An agreement or understanding for the referral of business incident to or part of a settlement service need not be written or verbalized but may be established by a practice, pattern or course of conduct. When a thing of value is received repeatedly and is connected in any way with the volume or value of the business referred, the receipt of the thing of value is evidence that it is made pursuant to an agreement or understanding for the referral of business.

Id. at § 3500.14(e).

the same loan at 7.25% with a YSP of only $97.20. They challenged the yield spread premium on the footing that it was not tied to services but to the size and interest rate of their loan. The court agreed that the only service for which the YSP was compensation was the "service" of referring an above par loan to the lender, which RESPA does not permit.

HUD issued a Statement of Policy March 1, 1999 after consulting industry groups, federal agencies, consumer groups and other interested parties. 1999 Statement of Policy, 64 Fed.Reg. at 10084. The heart of HUD's position is that lender payments to mortgage brokers are not illegal per se; yield spread premium payments may be legal (or illegal) in individual cases or classes of transactions. *Id.* Accordingly, the Policy Statement prescribes the following test:

> In determining whether a payment from a lender to a mortgage broker is permissible under Section 8 of RESPA, the first question is whether goods or facilities were actually furnished or services were actually performed for the compensation paid. The fact that goods or facilities have been actually furnished or that services have been actually performed by the mortgage broker does not by itself make the payment legal. The second question is whether the payments are reasonably related to the value of the goods or facilities that were actually furnished or services that were actually performed.

> In applying this test, HUD believes that total compensation should be scrutinized to assure that it is reasonably related to goods, facilities, or services furnished or performed to determine whether it is legal under RESPA. Total compensation to a broker includes direct origination and other fees paid by the borrower, indirect fees, including those that are derived from the interest rate paid by the borrower, or a combination of some or all. The Department considers that higher interest rates alone cannot justify higher total fees to mortgage brokers. All fees will be scrutinized as part of total compensation to determine that total compensation is reasonably related to the goods or facilities actually furnished or services actually performed. HUD believes that total compensation should be carefully considered in relation to price structures and practices in similar transactions and in similar markets.

Id.

After HUD's 1999 Policy Statement was issued, Inland (by then known as Irwin) appealed certification of a class of borrowers on whose loans it had paid a yield spread premium to the mortgage broker. *Culpepper v. Irwin Mortgage Corp. (Culpepper III),* 253 F.3d 1324 (11th Cir.2001). Irwin argued that the Policy Statement overruled *Culpepper I's* interpretation of § 8(a). The court rejected that argument, as well as the lender's contention that the legality of a YSP payment could only be determined loan transaction by loan transaction. It held that the test for § 8 liability is not whether the broker performed *some* services, but whether the YSP is payment *for* those services. Otherwise, the Policy Statement's requirement that payment be "for compensation paid" would not be met; the result would be inconsistent with § 8(c) because the preposition "for" connotes an exchange and the word "fee" implies a money-services exchange to be within § 8(c); and it would permit payments under the guise of § 8(c) that § 8(a) plainly prohibits.

HUD then issued another Statement of Policy "to eliminate any ambiguity concerning the Department's position with respect to those lender payments to mortgage brokers characterized as yield spread premiums ... as a result of questions raised by ... Culpepper v. Irwin Mortgage Corp." Real Estate Settlement Procedures Act Statement of Policy 2001–1: Clarification of Statement of Policy 1999–1 Regarding Lender Payments to Mortgage Brokers, and Guidance Concerning Unearned Fees Under Section 8(b), 66 Fed.Reg. 53052 (October 18, 2001). The 2001 Statement explicitly rejects *Culpepper's* interpretation, and reiterates the position taken in the 1999 Statement—that yield spread premiums are not per se legal or illegal and that this turns on meeting the requirements of its two-prong test.

The 2001 Statement indicates that under the first prong, "it is necessary to look at each transaction individually, including examining all of the goods or facilities provided or services performed by the broker in the transaction, whether the goods, facilities or services are paid for by the borrower, the lender, or partly by both." *Id.* at 53055. It further states that a yield spread premium may not be presumed to be a referral fee based solely on the fact that the lender makes such a payment to a broker. *Id.* The 2001 Statement notes that yield spread premiums are by definition derived from the interest rate and that this, by itself, does not indicate whether a particular YSP is a payment for facilities actually furnished or services actually performed. *Id.* HUD also makes clear that the first part of its test does not contemplate identifying or allocating which facilities, goods or services are performed for the lender or for the borrower as all of them inure to the benefit of both. *Id.* In addition, the 2001 Statement advises that the list of services provided in the 1999 Statement, while not exhaustive, is still accurate, and that compensation for them may be paid either by the borrower or the lender or partly by both. However, "[c]ompensable services for the first part of the test do not include referrals or no, nominal, or duplicative work." *Id.*

The 2001 Statement essentially repeats the considerations that HUD set out in the 1999 Statement for resolving the second, or reasonableness, part of the test. In sum, the pivotal question is whether a mortgage broker's total compensation is reasonable. Total compensation includes fees paid by a borrower and any yield spread premium paid by a lender, not simply the yield spread premium alone. *Id.* Total compensation to the broker must be reasonably related to the total value of goods or facilities provided or services performed; "simply delivering a loan with a higher interest rate is not a compensable service." *Id.* And payments must be commensurate with the amount normally charged for similar services in similar transactions in similar markets. *Id.*

Finally, by way of background, the district court in this case rejected *Culpepper's* interpretation and granted *Chevron*-style deference to HUD's 1999 Policy Statement. The 2001 clarification was not issued until after briefing had begun on appeal. However, we have heard from both parties on its impact and turn now to their arguments.

B

Schuetz urges us not to defer for a number of reasons. As she sees it, HUD's liability test permits what the statute prohibits by necessarily including the illegal referral fee in the "reasonableness of total compensation" analysis. In addition, the HUD test was adopted without "notice and comment" rulemaking, and a mere policy statement cannot have the same force and effect. Beyond this, in Schuetz's view, HUD rewrote § 8(c)(2) by eliminating the words "for" and "actually" ("for goods or facilities actually furnished or for services actually performed") in clarifying that total compensation should be "reasonably related to the goods, facilities or services furnished or performed." She posits that this also makes the 2001 Statement inconsistent with the regulations, the 1999 Statement, and with opinion letters sent by HUD's general counsel in 2000 to Congressman Bruce Vento and Senator Richard Shelby which indicated that the facilities or services must have been performed in exchange for compensation paid to the broker. Similarly, Schuetz submits, HUD's clarification is internally inconsistent in its application of § 8(c)(2)'s language in that for purposes of § 8(a) it adopts a "total compensation/reasonableness" test but requires a quid pro quo showing for purposes of § 8(b)'s prohibition on splitting fees. 2001 Policy Statement, 66 Fed.Reg. at 53054–55. Finally, she maintains that HUD lacked authority to correct the Eleventh Circuit's interpretation of a federal statute that is, in any event, not ambiguous.

We are not persuaded. First, *Chevron* deference is due even though HUD's Policy Statements are not the result of formal rulemaking or adjudication. "[T]he fact that the Agency previously reached its interpretation through means less formal than 'notice and comment' rulemaking does not automatically deprive that interpretation of the judicial deference otherwise its due." *Barnhart v. Walton,* 535 U.S. 212, 122 S.Ct. 1265, 1271–72, 152 L.Ed.2d 330 (2002); *United States v. Mead Corp.,* 533 U.S. 218, 121 S.Ct. 2164, 2173, 150 L.Ed.2d 292 (2001) ("[T]he want of that [notice-and-comment] procedure . . . does not decide the case, for we have sometimes found reasons for *Chevron* deference even when no such administrative formality was required and none was afforded."). Here, RESPA authorizes HUD to interpret the statute, 12 U.S.C. § 2617(a), and HUD's regulations indicate that a "statement of policy" published in the Federal Register constitutes "a rule, regulation or interpretation" for purposes of RESPA. 24 C.F.R. § 3500.4(a)(1)(ii). Both policy statements are published in the Federal Register. Nothing suggests that the more formal process of notice and comment was short-circuited for any reason other than Congress's directive to issue the 1999 Statement of Policy within 90 days. Indeed, both policy statements comport with

Congressional intent to provide a safe harbor for good faith compliance with HUD rules, regulations, and interpretations. 12 U.S.C. § 2617(a), (b). Schuetz relies on *Christensen v. Harris County,* 529 U.S. 576, 587, 120 S.Ct. 1655, 146 L.Ed.2d 621 (2000), in which an informal opinion letter failed to pass muster, but HUD's policy statements are different because Congress authorized the Department to interpret RESPA, HUD has responsibility for enforcing the statute, and it has expertise in the home mortgage lending industry. *See Barnhart,* 535 U.S. 212, at ___, 122 S.Ct. 1265, 1271–72, 152 L.Ed.2d 330, ___.

We must first determine whether the language of § 8(c)(2) "unambiguously forbids [HUD's] interpretation." *Barnhart,* 535 U.S. 212, at ___, 122 S.Ct. 1265, 1269–70, 152 L.Ed.2d 330. It does not. Schuetz's argument is premised on the assumption that "payment for" can only be interpreted as protecting payments *offered in exchange* for" services rendered. This language, however, is equally capable of supporting HUD's 2001 interpretation, which would read § 8(c)(2) as protecting payments "used as compensation for" services performed. Therefore, we turn to the question of "whether the interpretation for other reasons, exceeds the bounds of the permissible." *Id.* Whether or not HUD's interpretation is preferable, we cannot say that it is impermissible. The Eighth Circuit has recently so held, and we agree with its reasoning. *Glover v. Standard Federal Bank,* 2002 WL 432992, 283 F.3d 953 (8th Cir. March 21, 2002).

The HUD test focuses on whether compensable services of the sort identified in the 1999 Statement are provided, and if they are, then on whether the total compensation (without regard to whether it comes from the borrower, the lender, or both) is reasonably related to the services provided. This is consistent with the general intent of Congress in enacting RESPA, which is to foster home ownership. By allowing lenders to pay mortgage brokers yield spread premiums, prospective homeowners with a dearth of cash at the time of settlement can front less money and pay for some of their mortgage broker's services over time. Nor is HUD's test inconsistent with the prohibition on fees for referral; § 8 can reasonably be construed as only prohibiting payments that are for nothing else than the referral of business. HUD's test prevents this, too, for the first prong requires actual performance of compensable services. By the same token, the second prong requires that the total compensation, including the YSP if it is a component, be in the ball park. If it isn't, then regardless of whether there is a YSP or the YSP is high or low, an illegal referral may be inferred.

Neither is the 2001 Statement inconsistent with HUD's prior communications. It carries forward the same principles articulated in the 1999 Statement, and we do not read the 2001 Statement as backing off the 1999 position that services must still actually have been performed for the compensation paid. Likewise, we do not see any conflict between the regulations and the Policy Statement. Schuetz contends that § 3500.14(e), which describes how an "agreement or understanding" for referral of business can be proved, adopts a different test for proving liability, but we do not agree. That section pertains to one element of § 8(a) but does not say anything about § 8(c)(2) or its intersection with § 8(a). Similarly, no fatal inconsistency exists on account of two informal letters that HUD's general counsel sent to members of Congress; regardless of how their language may be construed, they are not binding (nor may they be relied upon) in any event.

HUD's 2001 Statement of Policy is not internally inconsistent by virtue of how it treats the same language in § 8(c) for purposes of § 8(a) and (b). The Statement explains that § 8(b) prohibits any fee "in excess of the reasonable value of goods and services provided or the services actually performed." 66 Fed.Reg. at 53059. Regardless, to the extent that there is any difference in treatment, § 8(a) and (b) contain distinct prohibitions. Section 8(a) relates to referrals and § 8(b) to fee-splitting. Whereas a yield spread premium involves compensation from lender and borrower for loan origination, the charges that § 8(b) addresses involve a single payment split among settlement service providers.

Finally, HUD has not exceeded its area of expertise. Congress asked for its policy on the legality of yield spread premium payments. The 1999 Policy Statement and its clarification in 2001 respond to that query, concern administration of real estate settlement that is clearly within HUD's province, and interpret a complex statute that HUD enforces.

For these reasons, we agree with the district court that deference is due the HUD policy statements.

C

Having resolved that the two-prong test contained in HUD's 2001 Statement of Policy provides the appropriate standard of liability for yield spread premiums under RESPA, we apply that test to Schuetz's case. With respect to the first prong, there is substantial evidence that Schuetz's mortgage broker provided her a host of compensable goods, facilities, and services. There is no evidence to the contrary. Under the second prong, the record demonstrates that Home Financial offered Schuetz the best interest rate it could based upon her situation, the rates available at the time, and its need to be compensated. It would not have originated her loan only for the direct fees that she personally paid up front. The evidence shows that the broker's total compensation, including direct as well as indirect fees, was consistent with local practice and reasonably related to the value that Home Financial contributed to Schuetz's transaction. Schuetz offered no evidence to the contrary, and none to show that her broker's services weren't worth what it was paid. In these circumstances, the district court correctly concluded that payment of the yield spread premium did not violate § 8.

III

It follows that the district court did not abuse its discretion in denying class certification. Yield spread premiums are not illegal per se, so whether they amount to a prohibited referral in any particular case depends upon the services provided by the broker and the total compensation paid for those services. This necessarily means that individual issues predominate, and that a class action is not superior.

KLEINFELD, CIRCUIT JUDGE, dissenting:

I agree with the Eleventh Circuit [decision in *Culpepper III*] and respectfully dissent.

The problem with treating the "yield spread premium" as payment for services rendered *to the borrower,* to be evaluated for reasonableness in each individual case, is that the relationship between the amount of the premium and the value of the services is entirely fortuitous. Because the yield spread premium is calculated purely by the extent to which the borrower's interest rate is above par, sometimes it will be what the broker's services are worth, but only by chance. It's like a stopped clock that shows the right time twice a day, but the clock doesn't measure the time, and the yield spread premium doesn't measure the value of services. Indeed, the higher the interest rate the broker's client pays, the bigger the yield spread premium the broker gets. This makes the premium tend to be inversely proportional to the value of the services to the borrower. Whether the amount approximates the value of services for Schuetz or not, she should have been allowed to go forward with her class action, because it is precisely the fortuitousness that makes the yield spread premium violate RESPA.

RESPA prohibits "kickbacks" by lenders to mortgage brokers. I see the phrase "yield spread premium" as an obfuscatory way of avoiding calling a kickback a kickback. A kickback is "a usually secret rebate of part of a purchase price ... to the one who directed or influenced the purchaser to buy from such seller."[2] It is a payment by a third party to an agent to act on behalf of the third party rather than the principal. The home buyer hires a mortgage broker to shop for a good loan for her, but the broker takes $500 from a lender to steer the buyer to the lender, if the buyer can be persuaded to sign a loan with interest above par. This is how the "yield spread premium" is calculated. The measure has nothing to do with how much work the broker does. Instead, it is based on one thing: how far above par the interest rate is.

Conceivably, the yield spread premium could be good policy to promote home ownership, as HUD and the majority suggest. The theory would be that some home buyers might not be able to get their loans if they have to pay the broker's reasonable fee up front for doing all the work of putting them together with a lender, and the "yield spread premium" lets them roll the fee into the financing and pay it over the term of their mortgage, perhaps twenty or thirty years. But Congress is no more bound by the "law and economics" school than by "Mr. Herbert Spencer's Social Statics."

There are several problems with vindicating the yield spread premium on this theory that the yield spread premium is a means of, in

2. Webster's Third New International Dictionary (1981).

practical economic effect, financing closing costs. One is that Congress didn't enact it. It prohibited kick-backs whether they work out as good economics or not. The second is that the record doesn't support it. No evidence has been shown to us that the yield spread premium offsets foregone closing costs. Schuetz was charged closing costs anyway, and it was not demonstrated that they should have been higher to compensate the broker, or that the yield spread premium capitalized the value of any inadequacy of the closing costs she paid compared to the value of the broker's services.

Third, Congress may have been right to reject kickbacks as a matter of economics. The yield spread premium doesn't necessarily roll over the amount of the broker's reasonable fee into the loan and capitalize that portion of the fee as the yield spread premium fee paid by the lender to the broker. The HUD test merely requires that the resulting closing costs be "reasonably related to the value of the goods or facilities that were actually furnished or services that were actually performed," but this does not require that the yield spread premium be subtracted from the closing costs, so the borrower may not actually benefit from the increase in her interest rate. Few but the most alert and aggressive borrowers are likely to spot the obscure "yield spread premium" charge on their closing statement, obtain and comprehend an accurate and coherent explanation from the broker's employee of what it means, and leave in a huff if they don't want to pay the extra interest. Both its obscurity of meaning and its relative size, perhaps a few hundred dollars, of closing costs in the thousands, on a five or six figure loan, may give Congress a reason to protect buyers from it.

It is tempting to defer to HUD anyway because of its expertise, but I do not think we can properly defer to HUD's interpretation. First, the yield spread premium is a kickback, and kickbacks are expressly prohibited by the statute, which says that "[n]o person shall give and no person shall accept any ... kickback." That express language cannot be interpreted away. RESPA does create several exceptions to its expansive reach, including the most arguably applicable: an exception for "(1) the payment of a fee ... (C) by a lender to its duly appointed agent for services actually performed in the making of a loan." As discussed above, the yield spread premium has no relation to the services actually performed by the mortgage broker. The yield spread premium is not within RESPA's explicit exceptions.

Congress did give the HUD Secretary the power to exempt:

> such other payments or classes of payments or other transfers as are specified in regulations prescribed by the Secretary, after consultation with the Attorney General, the Secretary of Veterans Affairs, the Federal Home Loan Bank Board, the Federal Deposit Insurance Corporation, the Board of Governors of the Federal Reserve System, and the Secretary of Agriculture.

Thus, when a conference committee told HUD to decide whether yield spread premiums were consistent with RESPA, HUD should have followed the procedure prescribed by the statute. It did not. The interpretations it promulgated were not regulations. Moreover, the Secretary did not consult with the other executive offices, such as the Secretary of Veterans Affairs, with whom the statute required consultation. HUD did not properly exempt yield spread premiums under RESPA.

RESPA also creates a safe harbor. It states that

> (a) The Secretary is authorized to prescribe such rules and regulations, to make such interpretations, and to grant such reasonable exemptions for classes of transactions, as may be necessary to achieve the purposes of this Act.

> (b) No provision of this Act ... shall apply to any act done or omitted in good faith in conformity with any rule, regulation, or interpretation thereof by the Secretary or the Attorney General ....

Where a defendant relied on HUD's rule, regulation, or interpretation of RESPA, he or she would not be liable. There is no rule or regulation at issue here. Assuming HUD's 1999 and 2001 interpretations could provide safe harbors for subsequent yield spread premium charges, they could not here, because Schuetz closed on her mortgage and Banc One received its kickback in 1997. Because Banc One could not have relied on the then-nonexistent interpretations, it cannot claim a safe harbor under the statute.

The majority relies on *Barnhart v. Walton* and *United States v. Mead Corp.* for the proposition that "the fact that the Agency previously reached its interpretation through means less formal than 'notice and comment' rulemaking does not automatically deprive that interpretation of the judicial deference otherwise its due." However, where the statute is unambiguous, and the intent of Congress is clear, as it is here—"[n]o person shall give and no person shall accept any ... kickback"—there is no occasion for *Chevron* deference, and we need not reach the question of whether HUD's policy statements are formal enough to merit *Chevron* deference in the absence of notice and comment rulemaking.

Notes

1. The same panel of the Eleventh Circuit that had decided *Culpepper III* declined to follow it in Heimmermann v. First Union Mortg. Corp., 305 F.3d 1257 (11th Cir. 2002), cert. denied, 539 U.S. 970, 123 S.Ct. 2641, 156 L.Ed.2d 675 (2003), concluding that it had in effect been overruled by the 2001 HUD Policy Statement.

2. A study based on data obtained through discovery in a case in which one of the study's authors served as an expert witness found that mortgage brokers obtained $1046 on average more compensation through yield-spread premiums than they would have received in the absence of the premiums. Howell E. Jackson & Jeremy Berry, Kickbacks or Compensation: The Case of Yield Spread Premiums (unpublished manuscript available at http://www. law.harvard.edu/faculty/hjackson/pdfs/january_draft.pdf and to be published as Howell E. Jackson, Jeremy Berry & Laurie Burlingame, Kickbacks or

Compensation: The Case of Yield Spread Premiums,—Annual Review of Banking—(forthcoming). The authors also concluded that 75% of the money consumers spend on yield-spread premiums goes only to enrich mortgage brokers while consumers receive value equivalent to the remaining 25%. Finally, the study found that African–Americans pay $474 more per loan than whites and Hispanics pay $580 more per loan.

3. Are mortgage brokers who receive a percentage of the loan payments any different from real estate brokers who receive a percentage of the selling price, or for that matter, lawyers who receive a contingency fee?

4. Do mortgage brokers have an incentive to arrange higher priced mortgages so that they receive a larger fee? If so, is the problem cured by the disclosure of the yield-spread premium to the consumer at the time of closing, as described in *Schuetz*? Notice that among the fees Schuetz paid the broker directly was $688 for a loan discount, and that the broker secured for Schuetz an above-par loan; that is, a loan at a higher interest rate than the lender was willing to provide to Schuetz. Did Schuetz get what she paid for? If not, how can you explain the court's decision? Does the incentive to steer consumers to higher-priced loans explain why some borrowers who could qualify for prime loans instead end up with subprime loans?

5. Do HOEPA and the North Carolina statute address the problem of yield-spread premiums?

6. As will be discussed in Chapter Ten, the cost of litigating consumer rights often exceeds the available damages. One way of dealing with that problem is to bring consumer cases as class actions, which has the effect of spreading the cost of litigation over many claims, thereby making the bringing of the case more affordable. Does the HUD test lend itself to class action treatment? See Elliot Klayman, Yield Spread Premiums, Illegal Referrals, and the Real Estate Settlement Procedures Act: Blurred Vision, 32 Real Es. L. J. 222 (2003). If not, what will be the impact of the HUD test?

7. Should yield-spread premiums count against the points and fee trigger for high-cost loan statutes? Courts have generally answered in the negative. See, e.g., In re Mourer, 309 B.R. 502 (W.D.Mich. 2004) (HOEPA); Wolski v. Fremont Investment & Loan, 127 Cal.App.4th 347, 25 Cal.Rptr.3d 500 (4th Dist. 2005) (California statute). Are these decisions consistent with 12 C.F.R. § 226.32(b)(1)(ii) (points and fees include "All compensation paid to mortgage brokers") or the *Short* case, *supra*?

8. The current RESPA regulations require the yield-spread premium to be disclosed in a box labeled "P.O.C." 12 C.F.R. § 3500.7(a)(2). Is that likely to be meaningful to consumers? In 2002, HUD proposed amendments to its RESPA regulations that would have changed the disclosure on the RESPA Good Faith Estimate to increase the likelihood that borrowers would understand if they are paying yield-spread premiums, how much those premiums would be, and what alternatives for paying mortgage brokers exist. 67 Fed. Reg. 49,134 (2002). Would this proposal have solved the problem of yield-spread premiums? By contrast, a Texas statute, V.T.C.A. Finance Code § 348.301, provides that "no person acquiring or assigning a retail installment contract, or any balance under a contract, has any duty to disclose to any other person the terms on which a contract or balance under a contract

is acquired, including any discount or difference between the rates, charges, or balance under the contract and the rates, charges, or balance acquired.''

Problem 9–9

Rufus, while purchasing a car from Yax Motors, inquired about financing. Yax explained that it had an arrangement with Moon Lending under which Moon would extend loans to qualified Yax customers at the lowest rates Moon offered. After excusing himself to confer with Moon representatives, Yax returned and stated that the best rate Moon could offer Rufus was 13.5%. Rufus accepted, signed the papers, and drove the car home. Later, Rufus learned that Moon had quoted Yax a rate of 11.25% and that Yax had added 2.25% to the quote to arrive at the 13.5% rate. Can you identify any causes of action Rufus could assert against Yax? If so, are they likely to be successful? See Beaudreau v. Larry Hill Pontiac/Oldsmobile/GMC, Inc., 160 S.W.3d 874 (Tenn.Ct.App. 2004).

Note

Some states have limited the amount of the dealer's markup in automobile financing. See, e.g., La. Rev. Stat. Ann. § 32:1261(2)(k) (limiting markup to three percent). Is that approach desirable?

3. PAYDAY LOANS

Problem 9–10

(a) Last year, Eric visited Slim Check Cashing to obtain $300 with which to purchase much-needed clothing for his children. He wrote out a check to Slim in the amount of $405, and received $300 in exchange. Slim said that the $105 difference represented a service fee. Slim also told Eric that he would not cash the $405 check for thirty days, explaining that when the thirty days were up, Eric would have the choice of (1) doing nothing, in which case Slim would deposit the $405 check; (2) paying Slim $405, in which case Slim would return the $405 check to Eric; or (3) paying Slim $105 in cash, in which case Slim would hold off on depositing the original $405 check for another thirty days and the cycle would start over again. Slim also had Eric sign an agreement providing that if one of Eric's checks was dishonored, Eric would pay Slim a 20% returned check fee. The agreement also stated that Eric acknowledged that Slim did not make loans or charge interest and that Slim merely deferred its presentment of the check for collection. The transaction did not involve any other documents. In each of the next seven months, Eric elected to pay the $105 in cash, and roll the transaction over. From time to time, at Slim's request, Eric substituted a newer check in the amount of $405. After eight months and $840 in service charges, Eric failed to pay Slim, and Slim deposited the check, which was promptly dishonored for insufficient funds. Slim then wrote Eric threatening criminal prosecution unless Eric paid $405, plus the returned check fee of $81. Does Eric have any claims against Slim or defenses to payment? See Turner v. E–Z Check Cashing of Cookeville, TN, Inc., 35 F.Supp.2d 1042 (M.D.Tenn. 1999).

(b) Would it make a difference if Slim also provided Eric a gift certificate in the amount of $105, usable only at a catalog company? The catalog states that the company accepts only mail orders and does not have a telephone number or web site for placing orders. The catalog does not identify an address to which orders may be sent or contain an order form or any other ordering information. See Cashback Catalog Sales, Inc. v. Price, 102 F.Supp.2d 1375 (S.D.Ga. 2000).

(c) Would it make a difference if Slim and Eric entered into a sale and leaseback arrangement under which Eric sold Slim for $300 a television set Eric already owned and then Slim leased it back to Eric for a one-time rental payment of $405?

Notes

1.   The type of transaction described in the preceding problem is known as payday lending, because consumers often arrange for the check casher to deposit the check on their payday. You may recall the discussion of payday lending in Chapter Two. If the service fee in the problem had been expressed as an APR, it would have exceeded 400%. One study of payday lenders found an average APR of 470% and a range of 182 to 910%. Consumer Federation of America & U.S. Public Interest Research Group, Rent–A–Bank Payday Lending: How Banks Help Payday Lenders Evade State Consumer Protections 3 (2001) (hereinafter, CFA/USPIRG Report). See also Paul Chessin, Borrowing from Peter to Pay Paul: A Statistical Analysis of Colorado's Deferred Deposit Loan Act, 83 Denv. U. L. Rev. 387 (2005) (study of payday loans in Colorado found average APR of 391%) (hereinafter, Chessin Study).

2.   Given its high cost, why would consumers use payday lending? It is clear that many do; the CFA/USPIRG Report described "explosive growth" in payday lending. CFA/USPIRG Report at 4. More than half the respondents to a survey stated that their most important reason for borrowing from a payday lender as opposed to other sources was the quick and easy process for securing the loan. Gregory Elliehausen & Edward C. Lawrence, Payday Advance Credit in America: An Analysis of Customer Demand 51–52 (2001). Is it possible that borrowers are not aware of the expense of payday lending? Elliehausen & Lawrence found that most payday borrowers know the finance charge for their most recent advance but few remember the APR. *Id*. at 50. In a survey of Columbus, Ohio-area payday lenders, 32% of the lenders denied that their loans had an APR; 18% of the lenders reported that they did not know the APR; and 14% claimed that the finance charge was the APR. See Creola Johnson, Payday Loans: Shrewd Business or Predatory Lending? 87 Minn. L. Rev. 1, 38 (2002). While most of the lenders in that study posted the fee schedule, few of the postings reported the APR. *Id*. at 40. Is that a violation of TILA? See also Gregory Elliehausen, Consumer's Use of High–Price Credit Products: Do They Know What They are Doing? 34 (Indiana State Univ. Networks Fin. Inst. Working paper 2006–WP–02 2006) ("Customers are largely satisfied with their decisions and generally do not believe that they have insufficient information. . . . The decision to use high-

price credit typically is a result of the consumer's situation rather than a lack of knowledge or information."). Is the cost of payday lending excessive in light of the expenses lenders bear? Compare Mark Flannery & Katherine Samolyk, Payday Lending: Do the Costs Justify the Price? FDIC Center for Financial Research Working Paper No. 2005–09 21 (2005) ("To a great extent, the 'high' APRs implied by payday loan fees can be justified by the fixed costs of keeping stores open and the relatively high default losses suffered on these loans.") with Chessin Study at 408 (finding charge-off rate for payday loans comparable to commercial banks' charge-off rates on consumer loans).

3.   Though payday lending has existed in one form or another since the Nineteenth Century, see Christopher L. Peterson, Taming The Sharks: Towards a Cure for the High–Cost Credit Market 10 (2004), it probably surfaced in its current form in the early 1990s.

4.   Might the transaction described in the problem violate RICO? See 18 U.S.C.A. § 1962(b) ("It shall be unlawful for any person through a pattern of racketeering activity or through collection of an unlawful debt to acquire or maintain, directly or indirectly, any interest in or control of any enterprise which is engaged in, or the activities of which affect, interstate or foreign commerce."); 18 U.S.C.A. § 1961(6) (" "unlawful debt" means a debt . . . (B) which was incurred in connection with . . . the business of lending money or a thing of value at a rate usurious under State or Federal law, where the usurious rate is at least twice the enforceable rate."); Hamilton v. York, 987 F.Supp. 953 (E.D.Ky. 1997).

5.   State legislatures have responded to payday lending in various ways. While some states have enacted statutes that authorize and regulate payday lending, see, e.g. Miss.Code Ann. 75 67 501 et seq., others prohibit them, often by enacting interest rate ceilings that make payday loans uneconomic, see, e.g. N.Y. Penal L. §§ 190.40, 190.42. Still other states do not limit the interest rate at all, see, e.g., Del. Code Ann. Tit. 5, § 2229, while others impose interest rate limits that seem reasonable—until you realize that they may apply to loans extended for two weeks. See, e.g., Ala.Code § 5–18A–12(a) (17.5%). Some of the states that permit payday loans limit the amount of the loan. See, e.g. Mo. Rev. Stat. § 408.500 ($500). What are the justifications for these different approaches? Could payday lenders avoid application of state laws by affiliating with national banks? How would you expect federal regulators to respond to such affiliations? Should payday lending be regulated at the federal level, state level, or both?

6.   Some states have limited the number of times a consumer can rollover a loan. See, e.g., Ky. Rev. Stat. Ann. § 368.100(15); Fla. Stat. Ann. § 560.404(18). Why would rollovers be more objectionable to policy-makers than initial loans? One study of the costs of payday lending concluded that payday borrowers who repeatedly rolled over loans spent $3.4 billion annually on payday lending fees. Keith Ernst, John Farris & Uriah King, Quantifying the Economic Cost of Predatory Payday Lending 2 (2004). The study also found that 91% of payday lenders' revenues derive from consumers who make five or more payday loans per year and more than half their revenues

comes from borrowers with 13 or more such loans per year. *Id.* at 5. How might payday lenders evade statutory restrictions on payday rollovers?

7. Should payday borrowers be subject to criminal prosecutions for dishonored checks? Some states have answered in the negative. See, e.g., Ky. Rev. Stat. Ann. § 368.100(17) (requiring payday lenders to post sign reading "No person who enters into a post-dated check or deferred deposit check transaction with this business establishment will be prosecuted or convicted of writing cold checks or of theft by deception under the provisions of KRS 514.040.").

8. Many payday lenders are located near military bases. According to one estimate, more than a quarter of military households have patronized payday lending services. Diana B. Henriques, Lenders at the Gate: Debtors in the Barracks; Seeking Quick Loans, Soldiers Race Into High–Interest Traps, N.Y.Times, Dec. 7, 2004 at A1. See also Steven M. Graves & Christopher L. Peterson, Predatory Lending and the Military: The Law and Geography of "Payday" Loans in Military Towns, 66 Ohio St. L.J. 653, 659 (2005) ("We conclude that (1) there is irrefutable geographic evidence demonstrating that payday lenders are actively and aggressively targeting U.S. military personnel and (2) all state legal strategies except for aggressive criminal prosecution of usury laws have been ineffective in deterring this commercial behavior."). Partly in response, in 2006 Congress enacted 10 U.S.C. § 987, which bars those lending to soldiers and their dependents from taking a check as security for an obligation or charging an APR greater than 36% in consumer loans. What would you advise soldiers to do if they are not able to obtain payday loans but need credit?

9. Title loans are a cousin to payday loans. In a typical arrangement, the borrower provides the lender a security interest in the borrower's car, and surrenders the title to the lender in exchange for a short-term loan at a high rate. For example, in Wisconsin Auto Title Loans, Inc. v. Jones, 290 Wis.2d 514, 714 N.W.2d 155, 160, 161 (2006), the court explained that "The loan agreement calls for a single payment of $1,197.08, . . . which includes the original $800 loan amount, $243.08 of finance charges, and the $154 the borrower borrowed from Wisconsin Auto Title Loans to pay Wisconsin Auto Title Loans' fees. Wisconsin Auto Title Loans represents in its loan agreement that the annual percentage rate for the finance charge is 300%." Are consumers adequately protected in these transactions by the TILA disclosures? If not, what additional protections would be desirable? The court also noted:

> The loan agreement also includes a single printed page entitled **RE-MINDER TO BORROWER,** including seven reminders. The seventh reminder states as follows: "**Please note, this is a higher interest loan. You should go to another source if you have the ability to borrow at a rate of interest below 25 percent per month or 300 percent APR**." * * * At the bottom of this REMINDER is a place for a borrower to sign, indicating that he had read the reminder, understood its contents, and understood that unless he paid the amount due he was placing continued ownership of his automobile at risk. The borrower signed the reminder. [bold in original]

4. CREDIT INSURANCE

LEMELLEDO v. BENEFICIAL MANAGEMENT CORP. OF AMERICA

Superior Court of New Jersey, Appellate Division, 1996.
289 N.J.Super. 489, 674 A.2d 582, aff'd 150 N.J. 255, 696 A.2d 546 (1997).

ARNOLD M. STEIN, J.A.D.

Plaintiff Jeanne C. Lemelledo filed a class action against defendants Beneficial Management Corp. of America and Beneficial New Jersey, Inc., (collectively "Beneficial") claiming Beneficial violated the Consumer Fraud Act, the Consumer Loan Act and the criminal usury statute. Lemelledo also alleged breach of contract, conversion and common law fraud. The Law Division judge granted Beneficial's motion to dismiss the Consumer Fraud Act and usury counts for failure to state a claim upon which relief can be granted.

We reverse the dismissal of the Consumer Fraud count and affirm the dismissal of the usury count.

On this motion to dismiss for failure to state a claim, we examine the legal sufficiency of the facts alleged in the complaint. We accept all facts alleged by plaintiff as true, giving plaintiff "the benefit of all inferences that may be drawn from those facts." *Feinberg v. New Jersey Dep't of Environmental Protection*, 137 N.J. 126, 129, 644 A.2d 593 (1994).

Beneficial Management Corp. of America and Beneficial New Jersey, Inc. are subsidiaries of Beneficial Corp., a financial services company specializing in consumer loans. Beneficial sells credit insurance policies in conjunction with its loans. There are four basic types of credit insurance: credit life, credit disability, credit property and loss of income. If the borrower defaults, a credit insurance policy will pay the lender the outstanding balance of the loan.

Plaintiff alleges Beneficial engages in "loan packing," a practice by which lenders sell credit insurance policies along with consumer loans through the use of deceptive or coercive marketing practices. Her complaint asserts that credit insurance offers little or no benefit to borrowers, but primarily protects creditors. In addition, creditors have other financial incentives for selling the insurance, as they may receive commissions as high as 50% of the premium cost. Because the premiums are usually added to the principal of the loan, creditors also receive more interest income.

Plaintiff alleges credit insurance is often marketed through a "captive insurer," an insurance company affiliated with or owned by the creditor. Beneficial Wesco, The Central National Life Insurance Company of Omaha, and the First Central National Life Insurance Company of New York are three subsidiaries of Beneficial Corp. that sell credit insurance. In 1993, $80.7 million in credit insurance premiums were written through Beneficial's insurance subsidiaries and $11.6 million through non-affiliated insurance companies.

Plaintiff challenges the manner in which Beneficial sells credit insurance policies. She alleges that the typical Beneficial customers are individuals lacking established credit who cannot obtain a loan elsewhere. These individuals often have no knowledge of lending practices and are desperate for money. Beneficial allegedly takes advantage of this vulnerability by misrepresenting the purpose of credit insurance and failing to disclose its hidden benefits for the lender. According to plaintiff, borrowers are given a "negative option" to buy the insurance, since all loans are packaged with credit insurance even if the borrower does not request it.

When the borrower arrives at the loan office to pick up the check, he or she is presented loan documents already filled out to include credit insurance. This makes it appear that the insurance is necessary to obtain the loan. If the borrower questions or objects to the unrequested insurance, the salesperson implies that the borrower will not be given the loan proceeds at that time, but will have to return later. Plaintiff alleges that Beneficial uses these hard sell tactics to exploit the borrower's reluctance to walk away from the loan.

Plaintiff claims she was a victim of Beneficial's coercive tactics. On July 19, 1992, she applied for a $2000 loan from Beneficial to pay for her daughter's college tuition. The application form required her to list, among other things, personal property and household goods. After she was told that her loan was approved, plaintiff returned to Beneficial's office expecting to be issued a $2,000 check. Instead, she was given a form entitled "Disclosure of Credit Costs," to which pre-completed forms for credit life insurance, disability insurance, and personal property insurance were attached. She was also given a Certificate of Insurance for credit life and disability insurance from The Central National Life Insurance Company of Omaha, a Beneficial subsidiary, and a personal property insurance policy from the American Centennial Insurance Company, an unaffiliated company.

The disclosure form identified the "amount financed" as $2,538.47. It identified $335.28 as "Amount Paid to Others on Your Behalf," representing the insurance premiums, and $2,203.19 as "Amount Given to You Directly by Us." The loan was to be repaid in 36 monthly installments of $105 at a 28% annual percentage rate. The form also stated that plaintiff's loan was "secured" by "certain" unidentified "household items." Plaintiff was not told that federal regulations prohibit Beneficial from taking security interests in certain household and personal items. 16 *C.F.R.* 444.2(a)(4).

Plaintiff claims she never requested any insurance, nor did Beneficial employees discuss the purpose of or need for insurance before giving her the forms. Plaintiff does not know why she was given $203.19 more than the $2,000 she requested.

Plaintiff prepaid the $2,203.19 shortly after obtaining the loan. Beneficial then sent her four coupons for $100 each, representing the insurance premiums and accrued interest. Plaintiff made two payments but refused to pay anything more. Beneficial sued to recover the two remaining payments but then voluntarily dismissed the case. Plaintiff's lawsuit followed.

The Consumer Fraud Act, *N.J.S.A.* 56:8–1 *et seq.,* provides:

> The act, use or employment by any person of any unconscionable commercial practice, deception, fraud, false pretense, false promise, misrepresentation, or the knowing, concealment, suppression, or omission of any material fact with intent that others rely upon such concealment, suppression or omission, in connection with the sale or advertisement of any merchandise or real estate, or with the subsequent performance of such person as aforesaid, whether or not any person has in fact been misled, deceived or damaged thereby, is declared to be an unlawful practice....

[*N.J.S.A.* 56:8–2.]

We reject Beneficial's argument that it is exempt from the Consumer Fraud Act because it is a highly regulated business.

As Beneficial concedes, it is subject to a myriad of statutory schemes and regulations administered by both the Department of Insurance and the Department of Banking.

Although it is not an insurance company, Beneficial is a licensed insurance producer pursuant to the New Jersey Insurance Producer Licensing Act, *N.J.S.A.* 17:22A–1 to –36, which permits it to sell credit insurance. Its sale of credit insurance subjects it to the Insurance Trade Practices Act, *N.J.S.A.* 17B:30–1 to –22, which "regulate[s] trade practices in the business of life insurance, health insurance, and annuities"; and arguably to the Credit Life and Health Insurance Act, *N.J.S.A.* 17B:29–1 to –13, which defines and regulates the terms of credit insurance. These statutory schemes subject Beneficial to the jurisdiction of the Department of Insurance. Although it is not a bank, Beneficial makes consumer loans and is subject to the Consumer Loan Act, *N.J.S.A.* 17:10–1 to –21. The Act subjects Beneficial to the jurisdiction of the Department of Banking. Beneficial is therefore already subject to the jurisdiction of at least two administrative agencies.

* * *

The regulations do not wholly encompass the acts alleged in the complaint. Plaintiff alleges that she and other consumers have been victimized by unscrupulous or fraudulent marketing practices, precisely the type of acts the Consumer Fraud Act prohibits. Beneficial cannot rely on the "fortuitous circumstance" of being subject to various insurance and banking regulations to circumvent the Consumer Fraud Act on a "loan packing" claim.

Finally, we reject Beneficial's argument that the Consumer Fraud Act does not apply to the making of loans.

We affirm the dismissal of plaintiff's usury claim. We reject plaintiff's argument that the commissions earned by Beneficial on its sale of credit insurance should be considered interest for the purpose of New Jersey's usury laws. In *Sherman v. Citibank (South Dakota)*, 143 *N.J.* 35, 45, 668 *A.*2d 1036 (1995), the New Jersey Supreme Court held that the definition of interest under the National Bank Act referred only to the periodic interest rate, and not to late fees and other charges associated with a loan. The Court also noted that New Jersey rejects such an expansive definition of interest:

> New Jersey's banking statutes also reflect the basic understanding that the notion of interest was conceived and continues to be defined as specific percentage rates, rather than discrete charges, such as late fees, which are not directly related to borrowing money.

[*Id.* at 61, 668 *A.*2d 1036.]

The Court cited *N.J.S.A.* 17:13A–2(g), which excludes credit life insurance premiums from its definition of interest, as well as various other statutes distinguishing discrete charges from interest "by either authorizing or prohibiting certain lending institutions from making such charges." *Ibid.* As section 17:10–14.1(c) of the Consumer Loan Act expressly permits lenders to retain commissions on the sale of insurance policies in connection with loans, those commissions cannot be included in the definition of interest. *N.J.S.A.* 17:10–14.1(c). The Law Division judge therefore properly dismissed plaintiff's usury claim.

The dismissal of the Consumer Fraud Act claim is reversed and the dismissal of the usury claim is affirmed.

Notes

1.   Credit insurance may insure the life of the debtor or provide him with disability, accident, health, or even unemployment insurance. It may also insure the collateral for the loan against fire, accident or other hazards.

In all forms of credit insurance, the consumer debtor is the insured, and the creditor is the beneficiary. Policies are normally written in group form, with the creditor acting as policyholder. The creditor in turn normally issues a certificate to the consumer reflecting his enrollment in the group policy. The creditor also arranges the insurance and pays the premium to the insurance company, but this cost is universally passed on to each individual consumer.

2.   The loan involved in the principal case was a college loan. If you are financing your education through loans, do you have credit insurance? If so, how much thought did you give to whether you need credit insurance? Did you shop around for the insurance, or did you simply follow the lender's recommendation? Do you recall signing a form that said that the credit insurance is not required? Did you read the form before signing it? How sure are you of your answers? Surveys typically find that some consumers who

purchased credit insurance think they did not while others who declined the insurance believe they purchased it. See, e.g., John M. Barron & Michael E. Staten, Credit Insurance: Rhetoric and Reality 1–3 (1994) (more than a quarter made one mistake or the other).

3. Credit insurance is big business. Each year, consumers spend about $6 *billion* to insure their debts. Consumer Federation of America & Center for Economic Justice, Credit Insurance Overcharges Hit $2.5 Billion Annually 1 (2001) (hereinafter CFA/CEJ Report). It is also a highly profitable business.

4. Credit insurance is regulated in all states by statute and administrative regulations. In most states, the relevant statute is a version of the model act promulgated by the National Association of Insurance Commissioners (NAIC), "the NAIC Model Bill to Provide for the Regulation of Credit Life Insurance and Credit Accident and Health Insurance" (hereafter, the NAIC Model Act). U3C states, of course, use the U3C; Article 4 of the U3C applies to credit insurance. Administrative regulations commonly set maximum rates and the like. In light of what you are reading in this chapter, how effective has all this regulation been? According to the CFA/CEJ Report, about half the state insurance regulators fail to enforce state consumer protection laws as to credit insurers.

5. The premium rates for credit insurance are very high. The National Association of Insurance Commissioners has adopted a 60% loss ratio as a *goal* to be striven for. See NAIC Model Regulation for Short Term Credit Life and Accident and Health Insurance (Minimum Requirements) § 5(1) (1981). (That means for each $1.00 of premiums paid in, 60 cents are paid out in losses while 40 cents can be kept by the insurer for administrative expenses and profits.) Many experts believe that 75% or 80% would be a more appropriate level, and that loss ratios below this level produce windfall profits. Nevertheless, many states permit lower loss ratios; indeed according to the CFA/CEJ Report, overall loss ratios in 2000 were below 35%. See also Consumers Union & Center for Economic Justice, Credit Insurance: The $2 Billion A Year Rip–Off ii (1999) ("Overall, less than 39 cents on the premium dollar was paid out in claims on behalf of consumers."). The CFA/CEJ Report concludes that consumers paid $2.5 billion more in premiums than they would have if the industry had used the suggested NAIC goal of 60%.

6. Direct regulation of premium rates and coverages is always the prerogative of the state insurance commissioner. Otherwise, the treatment of credit insurance in consumer legislation has been equivocal. Both the U3C and the Truth in Lending Act exclude premiums from the finance charge if the coverage is not required and is specifically assented to, or, in the case of property insurance, could be obtained elsewhere. See U3C § 2.501(2); Reg. Z § 226.4(d)(1) and (2). The U3C's only attempt to control excessive premiums is in § 4.203(2) which directs the state insurance commissioner to disapprove rate schedules which are "unreasonable in relation to the benefits provided."

7. Pursuant to provisions enacted in the 1999 Gramm–Leach–Bliley Act, federal agencies published regulations requiring depository institutions (i.e., institutions, such as banks, that accept customer deposits) to disclose conspicuously in readily understandable language that lenders may not

condition loans on the consumer's purchase of credit insurance. 65 Fed. Reg. 75,822 (Dec. 4, 2000). The regulations are codified at several points in the Code of Federal Regulations; one version may be found at 12 C.F.R. § 208.84. The disclosure must be made both in writing and orally, and the consumer must acknowledge in writing its receipt. Banks are also barred from engaging in practices that would lead a consumer to believe that loans are conditioned on the purchase of insurance. 12 C.F.R. § 208.83. In addition, the regulations provide that certain persons who make referrals to credit insurers may "receive[] no more than a one-time, nominal fee of a fixed dollar amount for each referral that does not depend on whether the referral results in a transaction." 12 C.F.R. § 208.85(b). Would these regulations have been helpful to Lemelledo?

8.   There is a long history of abuses in credit insurance terms. The insurance has been written for greater amounts or longer durations than the credit extension it secures. Upon refinancing or consolidation ("flipping"), the old insurance may not be cancelled (providing double coverage) or unearned premiums may not be rebated. Valid claims may not be paid. As the principal case demonstrates (and as the testimony by Messrs. Satriano and Dough implies), the consumer's acquiescence in accepting insurance may be voluntary in form only—creditor suggestions are at least subtly coercive. But not everyone shares the view that creditors pressure borrowers to buy credit insurance. The Barron & Staten study, cited in note 2 *supra*, concluded that "marketing/coercion alone accounts for a maximum of 3.4 percent of credit life insurance sales." Id. at 1–5.

9.   Creditors receive many benefits when a debtor buys credit insurance. First, they become beneficiaries on an insurance policy paid for by the consumer, thereby increasing the likelihood that the underlying debt is paid off. Second, as in *Lemelledo*, they may generate more income for a captive insurer. Third, if the insurance premiums are financed, the creditor will obtain additional interest payments. Fourth, and perhaps most important, they get to collect a commission for selling the policy; as noted in *Lemelledo*, this commission may represent 50% of the premium. The effect of this practice is to make creditors look for insurance companies who charge the highest rates for the same coverage, because their commissions will be higher. This turns the normal market forces upside down. According to classic economic theory, competition is supposed to drive prices down. Here, competition drives prices up in a practice that has become known as "reverse competition." These practices are widespread and widely tolerated. Is it legal for a lender to be the debtor's creditor, his insurance broker, and the beneficiary of his credit insurance—all at the same time? Such circumstances would seem to create both fiduciary relationships and conflicting interests. These issues are addressed more fully in the following case.

SPEARS v. COLONIAL BANK OF ALABAMA

Supreme Court of Alabama, 1987.
514 So.2d 814.

Per Curiam.

This case originated as a class action against Colonial Bank of Alabama and Colonial Banc Corporation (both hereinafter referred to as

"Colonial Bank"), and Jim Burke Buick, Inc. ("Jim Burke"), for alleged violations of the Alabama Mini–Code (Code 1975, § 5–19–1, *et seq.*); for alleged improper credit of insurance premium refunds; and for alleged conversion. The named plaintiffs, Kennie J. Spears and Handy Wilson, Jr., sought to represent a class of all individuals who had purchased automobiles from Jim Burke, the purchases of which, along with premium payments for credit life and credit disability insurance, were financed by Colonial Bank.

The plaintiffs allege that Jim Burke required them to purchase credit life and disability insurance in order to purchase the automobiles, and that the price of this insurance exceeded the premium charged by the insurance company, all in violation of § 5–19–20. In essence, they contend that Jim Burke's receipt of a commission of 50 percent of the premium from each sale of credit insurance was in violation of the Mini–Code.

* * *

Colonial Bank and Jim Burke filed motions for summary judgment on each of the plaintiffs' claims and a motion to dismiss all class-action claims. The circuit court entered two separate orders on the defendants' motions.

The first order dealt with only one issue: "Whether or not Jim Burke Buick was entitled to charge or receive a commission on the credit life insurance, credit disability insurance, and property insurance it sold to the named Plaintiffs in conjunction with loans the named Plaintiffs obtained from the Defendants."

The trial court ruled that § 5–19–1, *et seq.*, does not "prohibit car dealers or other companies making loans covered by such sections from receiving commissions on the various types of insurance allowable under § 5–19–20, so long as all other provisions of those sections are met."

The court held that the premiums charged to the named plaintiffs were within the amounts allowed by the applicable statutes, rules, and regulations. It found, therefore, that Colonial Bank and Jim Burke were entitled to summary judgment on this theory of the plaintiffs' claims. The court also found that Colonial Bank's and Jim Burke's motions to dismiss all class-action claims were due to be granted, because the only issue supportive of the class certification was decided adversely to the plaintiffs by summary judgment.

* * *

We hold that the trial court did not err in its determination that § 5–19–20(a) does not prohibit Jim Burke, as a creditor, from receiving a commission on its sale of insurance to the plaintiffs, as debtors.

Jim Burke had arrangements with various insurers, whereby, for every policy sold to its customers, it would remit the entire premium to the insurer.[3] Thereafter, for each credit life and disability policy sold, the insurer would compensate Jim Burke by payment of a sum equal to 50 percent of the premium costs, a payment which plaintiffs contend is more correctly characterized as an illegal kickback, rather than a commission. They contend that § 5–19–20(a) prohibits a creditor from charging more than the actual coverage costs, and that only 50 percent of the premium actually paid represented the full amount charged by the insurer.

Colonial Bank states, and the record bears out, that, while its loans to the plaintiffs included the premium payments, it did not receive a commission. Jim Burke argues that the Mini–Code, and regulations promulgated pursuant thereto, permit receipt of a commission on the sale of credit insurance. It contends that the plaintiffs' definition of "premium," which would exclude commissions made thereon, is strained. Further, Jim Burke points out that § 5–19–21 provides that an "administrator is authorized and empowered to make such reasonable rules and regulations as may be necessary for the execution and enforcement of the provisions of this chapter," and that the insurer and Jim Burke relied on these rules and regulations in setting rates for credit insurance.

The plaintiffs urge us to consider this case in light of the underlying tenor of the Mini–Code, which is that of consumer protection. The plaintiffs' premise is correct. *Derico v. Duncan,* 410 So.2d 27, 31 (Ala. 1982) ("the provisions of Code 1975, § 5–19–1, *et seq.,* 'Consumer Finance,' known collectively as the Mini–Code, are regulatory in nature and are for the protection of the public, specifically, the consumer/debtor"). Thus, construction of the statute in this case must be made with the protection of the consumer in mind.

Section 5–19–20 provides, in pertinent part:

"(a) With respect to any credit transaction, the creditor shall not require any insurance other than insurance against loss of or damage to any property in which the creditor is given a security interest or insurance insuring the lien of the creditor on the property which is collateral for said transaction. Credit life and disability insurance may be offered and, if accepted, may be provided by the creditor. *The charge to the debtor for any insurance shall not exceed the premium charged by the insurer.* Insurance with respect to any credit transaction shall not exceed the approximate amount and term of the credit." (Emphasis added.)

The key to this Court's consideration of whether § 5–19–20 was violated is a determination of the meaning of "premium." There being no definition of "premium" in the Mini–Code, we look to the case law. In *Reid v. United Security Life Ins. Co.,* 290 Ala. 253, 256, 275 So.2d 680

---

3. All life insurance procured by Jim Burke on behalf of its customers was placed with one company, Volunteer State Life Insurance Company, while two companies, MIC and Autry Insurance Agency, handled the property insurance of Jim Burke's customers.

(1973), the Court defined "premium" as "the amount paid to the insurer by the insured for the insurance," and the Court added, " 'Premium' has been defined as the sum which the insured is required to pay, and in its proper and accepted sense it means the amount paid to the company as consideration for insurance." Thus, because it is a cost of procuring the insurance, a premium may include the commission paid to the seller of the insurance.

The Alabama State Banking Department has promulgated rules and regulations establishing and authorizing the maximum single premium rates for credit life insurance and credit disability insurance. The superintendent of banks of the state banking department is empowered to make such rules and regulations as are reasonably necessary for the execution and enforcement of the provisions of the Mini–Code, pursuant to § 5–19–21. All parties agree that the premiums charged to the plaintiffs for the various insurance coverages were within the lawful maximum rates established by the state banking department.

Because the premiums charged to the plaintiffs, as debtors, were within the maximum lawful rates, there has been no cognizable violation of the Mini–Code, nor of the rules and regulations promulgated pursuant thereto. Absent any evidence to support the claim that § 5–19–20(a) was violated, we find no error requiring reversal of the defendants' summary judgment on the payment-of-commissions issue. Thus, it is axiomatic that the trial court did not err in granting the defendants' motions to deny class certification on this theory of the plaintiffs' claims.

Affirmed.

MADDOX, ALMON, SHORES, ADAMS and STEAGALL, JJ., concur.

JONES, J., concurs specially.

BEATTY, J., recused.

JONES, JUSTICE (concurring specially).

I concur in the opinion affirming the summary judgment on the plaintiffs' claims based on the defendants' alleged violations of the Mini–Code. I write separately to express my concern that we may have overly narrowed the intended scope of the trial court's ruling.

* * *

The plaintiffs' arguments as to the problems inherent in the sale of credit insurance are well taken. The fact that the creditor is allowed compensation under the language of § 5–19–20 results in a clear probability of expensive credit insurance for the consumer. As pointed out in Fonseca, *Handling Consumer Credit Cases* § 12:10, pp. 494–99 (1986), because insurers compete against each other to place their business with creditors, the creditor is in a position to choose the insurer that offers it the highest compensation for every dollar of insurance sold. "Since Consumer has no voice in determining these rates, and since he is a non-shopping 'captive' in the sense that the sale of insurance will only come up as an incidental matter after the credit transaction is completed, the premium rate has been set high by 'reverse competition.' " *Fonseca,* at 495–96.

These observations notwithstanding, however, Jim Burke's liability, if any, under general agency law, can only be determined once its status as an insurance "agent" or as an insurance "broker" is ascertained.

* * *

Generally, agents and brokers have been distinguished by the fact that an insurance agent is "one employed by an insurance company to solicit risks and effect insurance," while a broker "is one who acts as a middleman between [the] insured and the company; one who solicits contracts from the public under no employment from any special company, but [who,] having secured an order[,] places the insurance with the company selected by [the] insured, or, in the absence of any selection by him, with the company selected by such broker." 44 C.J.S. *Insurance* § 136, at 797 (1945).

The question of whether a person is an insurance agent or is a broker is generally determined by his acts. But categorizing the creditor that procures credit insurance for its customers, primarily to protect the *creditor* from loss, is not so easily done. The creditor that procures such insurance presents a unique situation.

* * *

[The] description of "broker" aptly describes an entity in Jim Burke's unique position. Clearly, the bargaining power of potentially thousands of customers each year puts Jim Burke in a situation where it can obtain the "most favorable terms from competing [insurance] companies." While brokers generally seek to obtain the most favorable terms for their *clients,* the *creditor*/broker uses the competition between insurance companies to obtain the highest compensation for *itself.* This "reverse competition" results in a high premium rate for the consumer because he has no voice in determining rates, but obtains insurance only as an incident to the purchase of retail merchandise.

Notes

1.   Regardless of whether it is an insurance broker or an agent, doesn't Jim Burke owe its customer good faith, loyalty, and a duty to exercise reasonable skill, care, and diligence to protect the customer's interests? If Jim Burke is a broker, it is clear that the insured (consumer) is its principal, and is owed such duties. That should ordinarily include advice as to the price of insurance, and the availability of any less expensive comparable insurance. Do you believe that Jim Burke did any of that? Should an insurance agent owe any less duty to the purchaser of the insurance?

Would a cause of action based on breach of fiduciary duty provide an avenue for recovery by plaintiffs? Do state UDAP statutes offer any help?

2.   Is there a problem with a creditor persuading its borrowers to purchase credit insurance from a subsidiary as in *Lemelledo?*

3. In First United Bank of Poplarville v. Reid, 612 So.2d 1131, 1138 (Miss. 1992), the court, citing Justice Jones's concurrence in *Spears*, wrote: "We hold that those who would offer to procure [credit] insurance and enjoy commissions for their service owe as much candor and good faith as any other insurance agent." But in Strong v. First Family Financial Services, Inc., 202 F.Supp.2d 536 (S.D.Miss. 2002), the court held that this duty was satisfied by providing the consumers with the terms of the insurance policy and a statement that the loan did not require purchase of credit insurance. The court also rejected the claim that the relationship of lender-borrower by itself gives rise to a fiduciary duty relating to the selection of credit insurance.

4. In some states, most notably Arkansas, excessive credit insurance costs have been held to be disguised interest and to violate the usury laws. See, e.g., Robinson v. Rebsamen Ford, Inc., 258 Ark. 935, 530 S.W.2d 660 (1975). How would you go about calculating what portion of an insurance premium was "excessive" and therefore usurious?

5. Evaluate the provisions of Article 4 of the U3C on insurance. They do not set maximum premiums or loss ratios, nor do they prohibit the payment of "commissions" or "experience rebates" to the creditor who sells the insurance. § 4.107. The U3C also contains special unconscionability guidelines. § 4.106. Are these sufficient safeguards against reverse competition and excessive premiums? Against deceptive sales techniques?

6. What is the solution to the problem of credit insurance and reverse competition? Should creditors who tie-in insurance sales be charged with a "fiduciary" responsibility with respect to that insurance, since they are acting ostensibly on the consumer debtor's behalf and for his protection? What are the implications of this notion? Could the creditor still earn commissions on insurance sales? Alternatively, would it make sense for credit insurance premiums to be included as part of the finance charge for disclosure (TIL) and rate ceiling purposes? Wouldn't this discourage over-pricing? Or would it be preferable to require creditors to include within the finance charge that portion of the insurance premium they get to keep? Robert Sable, then-executive director of the National Consumer Law Center, has stated that the problem of high cost in credit insurance could be solved if creditors were simply prohibited from imposing a separate charge for insurance in consumer credit contracts. "By prohibiting a separate charge, nearly every problem in credit life insurance would disappear." Credit Life Insurance: Hearing before the Subcommittee on Antitrust, Monopoly, and Business Rights of the Committee on the Judiciary, United States Senate, 96th Cong., 1st Sess., serial no. 96–44, at 57 (1979). How can this be so? Is the remedy to the abuses of the credit insurance industry really that simple?

7. Are HOEPA loans subject to special credit insurance regulation? Should they be? Do credit insurance premiums count against HOEPA's points and fees trigger? See Reg. Z, 12 C.F.R. § 226.32(b)(1)(iv). What about the North Carolina statute? See § 24–1.1E(a)(5)(b)(ii), (c)(3)(c). Is single-premium credit insurance more troublesome than the type of credit insurance paid for on a monthly basis? Why? Would purchasers of single-premium credit insurance be more likely than those who pay monthly premiums to add the cost of the premium to the amount they're borrowing, and end up

paying extra interest? Many purchasers in the secondary market no longer buy loans for which single-premium credit insurance was sold and numerous lenders no longer sell it.

8.   When an insured loan is paid off prematurely, the insurer may still possess unearned premiums, something that is especially likely with single-premium credit insurance. Would a borrower have a claim against an insurer that did not refund the unearned premiums to the borrower? See U3C § 4.108; NAIC Model Act § 8(B) (requiring prompt refund). Would you expect a consumer to know if she had unearned premiums due?

Problem 9–11

You have just graduated from law school and are getting ready to buy a car. You are trying to decide whether credit insurance is a good idea, assuming you can obtain it from the least expensive insurer rather than the most expensive insurer. Assume that your loan will be in the amount of $10,000 for four years. Should you insure the loan? Why? In whose favor are the actuarial odds on this insurance? Under what circumstances would it make sense for a consumer to buy credit insurance?

Problem 9–12

Upon graduation from Law School, you have taken a job with your state's insurance commissioner. The office has received complaints that Bagshot Credit Insurance has denied several credit insurance claims because the claimants were ineligible for credit insurance. The eligibility guidelines were provided to the claimants in advance and they were in fact ineligible for the insurance (based on pre-existing medical conditions and the like). The claimants had paid the premiums for periods ranging from several months to a year before they made their claim and were not aware of their ineligibility, though they knew of the underlying condition which rendered them ineligible. Upon discovering that the claimants were ineligible, Bagshot promptly refunded their premiums in accordance with a term in the policy providing that Bagshot has the right to cancel the policy as to ineligible claimants as long as it returns their premiums. Is anything wrong with this practice? Is there anything you can do about it?

Note

Credit insurance is an example of a common phenomenon in consumer transactions: the tied sale. Often businesses make substantial profits by selling "add-ons" like credit insurance. For example, appliance sellers may find the sale of service contracts very profitable, while auto dealers may make tidy sums from the sale of rust proofing. Consumer advocates sometimes complain that these tied products are not worth what consumers pay for them. Is this a problem that is best addressed by regulation? If so, how?

Note on Debt Cancellation Contracts

If you have a credit card or have taken out certain other types of loans, you may have received a solicitation to enter into a debt cancellation contract (DCC) or debt suspension agreement (DSA). Under these contracts, the credit card issuer promises for a fee to waive or suspend (depending on whether the agreement provides for cancellation or suspension) the consumer's obligation to make payments upon the occurrence of certain events, such as the consumer's disability, being laid off, etc. One difference between credit insurance on the one hand, and DCCs and DSAs on the other, is that with credit insurance the consumer contracts with a third-party insurer while with DCCs and DSAs the consumer contracts directly with the lender (though as noted in *Lemelledo*, third party credit insurers are sometimes affiliated with lenders and to make matters more complicated, lenders may look to credit insurers to administer their DCC and DSA programs). As a result, strictly speaking DCCs and DSAs are not insurance, which matters because insurance is normally regulated by states. Consequently, there is authority that debt cancellation contracts issued by federal banks are not subject to state regulation, see First Nat'l Bank of Eastern Arkansas v. Taylor, 907 F.2d 775 (8th Cir.), *cert. denied*, 498 U.S. 972, 111 S.Ct. 442, 112 L.Ed.2d 425 (1990); 12 C.F.R. § 37.1(c). National banks tend to prefer national regulation of their products over regulation by individual states for a number of reasons, including that complying with the rules of different states may increase compliance costs. Federal banking regulators such as the OCC have jurisdiction over DCCs and DSAs entered into by federal banks, while state banking regulators have jurisdiction over state banks offering DCCs and DSAs. In 2003, the OCC promulgated regulations governing DCCs and DSAs. See 12 C.F.R. Parts 7 and 37. The regulations authorize national banks to enter into DSSs and DSAs and to charge fees for doing so—but the OCC rules do not regulate the fees and, unlike the NAIC rules for credit insurance, do not establish a goal for loss ratios. The regulations require banks offering DCC's and DSA's to make certain disclosures, such as the amount of the fees and that the product is optional. They also bar misleading practices. When it adopted the regulations, the OCC explained:

> Many commenters urged that the OCC regulate the amount of fees banks can charge for DCCs and DSAs. The premise of a number of these comments was the assertion that DCCs and DSAs are substitute products for credit insurance. These commenters contended that the market for DCCs is analogous to the market for credit insurance, which is characterized by "reverse competition." * * *

> For several reasons, we decline [this suggestion]. First, as the *Taylor* court explained, DCCs and DSAs are distinct from credit insurance as a matter of law. Moreover, we see no evidence that the market for DCCs and DSAs suffers from the same flaws as the commenters assert prevail in the credit insurance market. Issuers of DCCs and DSAs do not compete to enlist independent, third-party sellers to place their product. Instead, every national bank that issues DCCs or DSAs is its *own* seller because these products are provided in conjunction with loans that the bank itself makes. Commenters provided no evidence of impairment in the market for DCCs and DSAs, but instead relied on concerns regarding distortions and abuses in the credit insurance market. Thus, we cannot conclude that the strongest reason given by the commenters in support of fee regulation—dysfunction in the market that disclosures are inadequate to overcome—is present in the market for DCCs and

DSAs. Moreover, as the rule's express prohibition on tying makes clear, the choice of purchasing the product is left exclusively to the customer. We have concluded, therefore, that a regulatory approach that includes price controls as a primary component is not warranted.

OCC, Debt Cancellation Contracts and Debt Suspension Agreements, 67 Fed. Reg. 58962, 58964 (Sept. 19, 2002). Some states have adopted similar rules governing DCCs and DSAs issued by state lenders. See, e.g., N.Y.S. Banking Dept., Guidelines for Debt Cancellation Contracts and Debt Suspension Agreements (2004), available at http://www.banking.state.ny.us/il040401a. htm. Do you think the regulations are adequate? If not, what more is needed? Would you counsel a lender to offer credit insurance or a DCC to its borrowers? Which is more likely to be profitable for the lender? See Center for Economic Justice, The Impact of Debt Cancellation Contracts on State Insurance Regulation 27 (2003) (estimating that loss ratio for DSA is "generally in the 3% to 5% range."); Frederick W. Stakelbeck, Jr. & Anne Stanley, Debt Cancellation Contracts and Debt Suspension Agreements: Consumer Products Raise Industry Interest—Part I, CCCRA Compliance Corner CC3, CC5 (Fed. Res. Bank of Phil. 3rd Quarter 2004), available at http://www.phil.frb.org/src/srcinsights/srcinsights/CC3Q04.pdf (loss ratios generally between 30% and 40%). Which is better from the consumer's perspective?

SECTION E.   PERSPECTIVES

The goal of most predatory lending regulation is to eliminate abusive practices without driving up the cost of legitimate loans to the point that borrowers are unable to obtain loans. HOEPA, state legislation, and the OCC rules all represent attempts to achieve this goal. Numerous other solutions to the problem have been proposed. Thus, some scholars have argued that the solution is to transplant the "suitability" requirement of investment law to the lending context, so that subprime borrowers would have a claim against lenders who made unsuitable loans to them. See Kathleen C. Engel & Patricia A. McCoy, A Tale of Three Markets: The Law and Economics of Predatory Lending, 80 Tex. L. Rev. 1255, 1318 (2002); Daniel S. Ehrenberg, If the Loan Doesn't Fit, Don't Take It: Applying the Suitability Doctrine to the Mortgage Industry to Eliminate Predatory Lending, 10 J. Affordable Housing 117 (2001). This suggestion has, however, been criticized on the ground that it misconceives the relationship between broker and borrower and might impair the issuance of subprime loans. See Abraham B. Putney, Rules, Standards, and Suitability: Finding the Correct Approach to Predatory Lending, 71 Fordham L. Rev. 2101 (2003) (calling instead for more sophisticated trigger system). Christopher L. Peterson has called for the transplantation of a different concept—informed consent, from the practice of medicine—so that the focus of disclosure statutes like TILA would shift from providing notices which might not be read to verifying that borrowers genuinely understand the transaction they are entering into. Christopher L. Peterson, Taming the Sharks: Towards a Cure for the High–Cost Credit Market (2004). Professor Peterson has also proposed that the required disclosures include the APR on comparable loans offered by other lenders to those with the same credit score and in the same area as the borrower. *Id*. at 304–05. Still another commentator, noting that few, if any, laws are directed at protecting the elderly from predatory lenders even though the elderly are disproportionately victimized by such lenders, has suggested that older consumers be able to record an instrument that would limit the terms of loans they could obtain at a later date. See Kurt Eggert, Lashed to the Mast and Crying for Help: How Self–Limitation of Autonomy Can Protect Elders From Predatory Lending, 36 Loy. L.A.L. Rev. 693 (2003). Another critic calls for simplifying and standardizing home loans, dramatically simplifying the disclosures, and a centralized auction process in which lenders would compete to lend to a particular borrower. Lauren E. Willis, Decisionmaking and the Limits of Disclosure: The Problem of Predatory Lending, Part I: Price, 65 Md. L. Rev. 707 (2006). Curbing Predatory Lending contains dozens of recommendations including changes in TILA, RESPA, and increasing consumer financial education. Others have made other reform suggestions, some of which are reflected in the preceding pages. The problem of predatory lending, in its present form is a relatively young one, and so it should not be surprising that the legal system's response to it is still evolving. Your authors believe that we have not yet seen the legal system's final answer to the problem.

Problem 9–13

You are a legislative assistant for a member of the United States Senate. The Senator's state contains many victims of predatory lenders. It also contains many borrowers in the subprime market who will not be able to purchase housing unless lenders are willing to lend in the subprime market. Finally, several nonbank subsidiaries of national banks make subprime loans in the state, but have threatened to stop doing so if they are subject to expensive and stringent predatory regulation. Your Senator asks you for a recommendation as to what position to take on predatory lending legislation. Among the pending proposals are the following:

A.   Bar federal regulatory agencies from preempting state predatory lending statutes.

B.   Enact a North Carolina-like statute as federal law;

C.   Appropriate more money for financial education; and

D.   Oppose any new legislation on the matter.

What position would you recommend on each of these? Would you recommend any other measures?

Chapter 10

PRIVATE ENFORCEMENT OF CONSUMER RIGHTS

———

None of the substantive measures discussed in the preceding pages can be very helpful to the public unless they can readily be enforced. In fact, many of the early consumer protection statutes failed to provide such enforcement. More recent statutes are more likely to have effective enforcement provisions, and this development has created a subspecialty within consumer protection: the development of appropriate enforcement mechanisms. Some enforcement issues are specific to particular statutes or doctrines, and in many cases those issues have been addressed within the pertinent substantive chapters. But other enforcement issues are relevant to many substantive rights, and so are better treated in a separate chapter limited to enforcement. Those issues appear in this chapter.

How can a statute be unenforceable? One obvious method is to provide no enforcement mechanism at all, but this happens rarely. A more usual method is to place no sanction on the violator, other than a duty to return any ill-gotten gains when caught. In practice, the FTC did this for years. A less obvious method is to provide *only* a criminal law sanction, and require that it be enforced by an official who is not usually involved in criminal proceedings. At the state level, Small Loan Acts frequently have this as their only sanction. At the federal level, Title III of the CCPA, which restricts creditor garnishment of wages, is an example. Other methods include limiting the persons who can seek enforcement (perhaps to regulators only, as with some provisions of the FCRA) or to limit the enforcement mechanisms (to cease and desist orders only, or to fines only, or to restitution only, etc.).

Even claims for which the law provides an enforcement mechanism may be unenforceable for economic reasons. In one sense, the idea of using $20,000 in total resources to resolve a $100 dispute seems silly—unless it is *your* $100. Nevertheless, one primary contact of most people with the court system is the resolution of such small disputes, and its failure to resolve such disputes, despite the cost, would be a subtle poison, reducing general satisfaction with the legal system. A recurring theme within this chapter will be the enforcement of claims when the amounts at issue are less than the cost of litigation. This chapter explores several different solutions to that problem, most notably class actions and providing attorney's fees.

Another enforcement issue may be created when businesses insert terms in their customer contracts requiring that any disputes be submitted to arbitration. These agreements may also impose other restraints on the enforceability of consumer rights, such as barring the use of class actions. The issues generated by such agreements will be treated in Section C.

When consumers are unable to bring private claims to enforce their rights—perhaps because the statute creating the right does not provide for private enforcement or because a private claim would be uneconomic—the consumer's only recourse is to complain to a public enforcement agency. Under what circumstances would you advise a client to complain to a public agency?

SECTION A. HOW DO DISSATISFIED CONSUMERS BEHAVE?

Prefatory Note

This section concerns the practical problems faced by consumers as they attempt to resolve disputes over consumer goods and services. For instance, you have a car (or a $50 telephone answering machine) which doesn't run "right" and the dealer isn't being cooperative. It is not the kind of problem which will bankrupt you, but it is continually annoying. It is also often not of sufficient economic value to bring to an attorney, unless she is part of a pre-paid legal system. However, whether attorneys are involved or not, consumer complaint resolution is an important part of the total legal system. What are appropriate responses? Are any of them effective?

Usually, the first consumer response is to complain to the merchant directly to seek repair or a refund (although a surprising number of consumers simply suffer their losses silently). In a majority of cases, unless the consumer has dealt with a deliberate rip-off artist, this will obtain some relief, but can sometimes require the consumer to conduct complex personal negotiations.

A second step may be to seek help from an industry-sponsored informal dispute resolution mechanism. The oldest of these is the Better Business Bureau (BBB) program. In the 1980s, most car manufacturers began to offer such programs, spurred on by state lemon laws which required or encouraged consumers to pursue this option before claiming a refund or replacement vehicle in court. Some state governments have also set up their own consumer dispute resolution systems. Over time, many businesses have concluded that arbitration better serves their interests than the legal system, and so have added clauses to their standard consumer agreements requiring arbitration.

Some consumers eventually use the legal system for dispute resolution, either by choice or because they are sued. A few can use the shield of unconscionability, but a sword would be more useful. Statutes like the Truth-in-Lending Act and the Magnuson–Moss Warranty Act provide some weapons for consumers on the attack, such as statutory damages and attorney's fees.

BEST AND ANDREASON, "CONSUMER RESPONSE TO UNSATISFACTORY PURCHASES: A SURVEY OF PERCEIVING DEFECTS, VOICING COMPLAINTS, AND OBTAINING REDRESS"

11 Law & Soc.Rev. 701, 728–29 (1977).*

At the problem perception stage, individuals of low socioeconomic status notice fewer problems. Similarly, low household interest in consumer affairs is linked to low problem perception rates. For all households, simple manifest problems are perceived more strongly than judgmental problems. And almost all consumers are reluctant to acknowledge that they have suffered more than an average amount of trouble with purchases.

At the complaint voicing stage, buyers suppress complaints concerning about two-thirds of the problems they perceive. Not all suppressed complaints are associated with complete inaction. In some instances, buyers may exit [that is, refuse to buy from the seller or manufacturer again]; however, these exit actions do not serve to compensate the buyer for the loss incurred nor to inform the appropriate business about its failure. Buyers do present roughly one-third of perceived problems to complaint processors, but these do not accurately represent the full range of consumer problems. Compared with perceived problems, voiced complaints overrepresent problems that are simple, that involve high cost, and that are experienced by high socioeconomic status households. The data show, too, that third parties deal with only a small segment of the problems people perceive and the complaints people voice. This provides an illustration of Stewart Macaulay's thesis in a consumer setting, although it may be more accurate to say that only a small number of cases reach third parties than to say that involvement of third parties is particularly likely to occur in certain kinds of cases. Because of the pattern of third-party use, businesses are able to impose their own unreviewed standards for decision-making on almost all the complaint cases they handle.

The data on response to complaints show that overall, somewhat more than half are resolved to the satisfaction of consumers. Complaints concerning services do not produce as many favorable outcomes as those concerning products, and there is a similar disparity between complaints about judgmental and manifest problems.

Buyers thus provide business with a subsidy in the form of up to a two-thirds discount on requests for redress, and many voiced complaints are not resolved to the buyer's satisfaction. Perhaps our society is so organized that it can easily tolerate the existence of many unresolved grievances. On the other hand, feelings of powerlessness in the marketplace may contribute to social distress.

Note

There are numerous surveys in this field, with, predictably, a wide variety of results. See, e.g., Rex H. Warland, Robert O. Herrmann, and Jane Willits, Dissatisfied Consumers: Who Gets Upset and Who Takes Action, 9 J. Consumer Affairs 148 (1975) (of 458 dissatisfied consumers, about half either did nothing, complained to family or friends, or resolved not to buy product in future while remaining consumers contacted lawyer, government official, or Better Business Bureau). Indeed, the Journal of Consumer Satisfaction, Dissatisfaction, and Complaining Behavior is devoted to the subject. Why would dissatisfied consumers not seek redress? What implications, if any, does the reticence of consumers have for manufacturers and sellers of products, consumer advocates, and the marketplace in general?

Problem 10–1

Yesterday, while making a rare visit to a particular neighborhood about half an hour from your home, you bought a personal CD player for about $30 at a store. The next day you discovered that the player doesn't work. What will you do? Would you behave differently if the CD player worked but when you took it out of the packaging you didn't like its appearance? Would you behave differently if it were a built-in CD player in your car?

Problem 10–2

Saul Brenner took his car to Kramer Auto Service for repairs. The repairs to be made were agreed upon and estimated to cost $25. When Brenner returned for the car, the bill read $51.02. Kramer had performed additional services and, of course, demanded to be paid for them. Brenner objected that the extra services were not needed, but Kramer became obdurate and gave Brenner an option: either Brenner paid, or Kramer would keep possession of the car. Brenner paid by using his VISA card. What can Brenner do now to resolve this dispute? Complaining directly to the merchant is not likely to be effective; and if he has already paid, the burden of initiating litigation is on him. But does Brenner have a self-help remedy under Federal statutes? Under Federal regulations? See Fair Credit Billing Act (CCPA) §§ 1666, 1666i; Reg. Z §§ 226.12(c)(1), 226.12(c). If Brenner is a person who always pays within 30 days, how much of his VISA card account billing would you advise him to pay to avoid finance charges?

SECTION B.   APPROACHES TO MAKE DISPUTE RESOLUTION MORE AFFORDABLE FOR CONSUMERS

Prefatory Note

The great expense of litigation creates problems even in cases in which substantial damages are sought. But individual consumer complaints are rarely for large sums. Consequently, many consumer cases are not worth bringing because any victory would be pyrrhic. Policy-makers have attempted numerous solutions to this problem. Some solutions attempt to increase the benefits of victory; thus, some statutes provide for statutory damages or attorney's fees or both (e.g., FDCPA § 1692k) while at both common law and under some statutory claims, consumers may obtain punitive damages (e.g., ECOA § 1691d). Another solution, the class action, is intended to spread the cost of litigation over many claims, thus reducing the cost borne by any individual plaintiff. Still other solutions—notably small claims courts and arbitration—attempt to reduce the cost of litigation. This section explores two of these mechanisms: attorney's fees and class actions. The following section takes up arbitration. As you read through the materials that follow, consider whether they achieve the goal of offering enough assurance that meritorious cases will be affordable to make consumers and their attorneys willing to undertake consumer litigation. Are the costs of these mechanisms—including costs incurred by defendants—too great to justify their use? Do businesses benefit from these mechanisms?

1.   ATTORNEY'S FEES IN INDIVIDUAL CLAIMS

We have seen that consumer protection statutes often include a provision for the award of attorney's fees for the successful consumer plaintiff as a means of opening the court system to consumers with relatively small claims. See, e.g., TILA § 1640(a)(3); Magnuson–Moss Act § 2310(d)(2). Most state little FTC Acts and lemon laws also provide for the award of attorney's fees. However, some state laws may provide that fees are available to the "prevailing party," thus placing the unwary consumer in danger of having to pay his adversary's legal fees if he should lose the case. See, e.g., Dillree v. Devoe, 223 Mont. 47, 724 P.2d 171 (1986).

Attorney fee provisions have apparently succeeded in encouraging consumers to go to court with their grievances, judging from the number of reported cases. However, there may be some traps for the unwary attorney. Consider the following.

Problem 10–3

Buck N. Ham bought an entertainment system for $1,500 on credit from Constant Co., but defaulted in his payments on it because it became inoperable during the warranty period and Constant refused to repair it. Constant dunned him for the late payments, using their standard 30, 60 and 90 day letters. Then Constant brought an action to recover the unpaid balance and stated they might later garnish his wages. This so frightened Buck that he sought counsel from a local attorney, May D. Marion. He brought with him all papers relating to the action and transaction, including a TILA Disclosure Statement. After some study, Marion spotted several material violations of TILA and assured Buck that his troubles were over. They would counterclaim under TILA, get the statutory damages for Buck; and Constant would be required to pay Marion's fee. They would also counterclaim for breach of warranty, but since that would require an expensive trial it could be dropped in return for the TILA recoveries. Thus, the procedure would cost Buck nothing. Marion filed the appropriate pleadings and then received a call from Constant's attorney suggesting "a wash"—a settlement in which Constant would dismiss its complaint and Buck would dismiss the TILA counterclaim and release any claim for attorney's fees for Marion.

The settlement offer is a good deal for Buck, but not for Marion. If the litigation proceeds, Buck's recovery is not likely to grow, but Marion's recovery will grow from $0 to a substantial fee.

(A) What should Marion do now in advising Buck?

(B) What should she do next time such a case walks into her office?

Notes on "Independent" Claims for Attorney's Fees under TILA

1. In James v. Home Construction Company, 689 F.2d 1357 (11th Cir. 1982), the court found that an attorney could have standing to pursue her independent claim for attorney's fees after settlement of a TILA case. In *James,* attorney Diana Hicks represented Roscoe James in a TILA action for rescission and damages. The case was successfully settled, but the issue of fees for Ms. Hicks was left open. After the district court dismissed the case with prejudice pursuant to the settlement, Hicks petitioned the court for award of attorney's fees. The district court held that a TILA plaintiff's attorney did not have standing to seek fees after settlement of the case-in-chief. The Court of Appeals for the Eleventh Circuit reversed.

The Court of Appeals said in part:

Section 1640(a)(3) of the Truth-in-Lending Act creates a legal right to a fee award in a successful action for rescission. The fact that a plaintiff prevails through settlement should not weaken this claim to fees. Contrary to dicta in Smith v. South Side Loan Co., 567 F.2d 306, 307 (5th Cir.1978), suggesting that attorney's fees are the right of the party suing, we find that it is the attorney who is entitled to fee awards in a TILA case, not the client. * * *

* * * The key to the inquiry is the intent of the legislature. One of the congressional goals underlying TILA was the creation of a system of private attorneys general who could effectively enforce the Act without government intervention. The award of attorney's fees, as a practical matter, is a critical and integral part of this plan. In order to effectuate this scheme, attorneys who bring TILA cases should be secure in their

expectation of fees from a successful action, and should be able to pursue their right to fees in federal court. If settlement of a TILA case precluded the plaintiff's attorney from seeking a fee award, nothing would prevent indigent clients, who have no financial interest in statutory fee awards, from freely bargaining them away without personal detriment. Such a result would enable creditors who have violated the Act to escape liability for attorney's fees; such a practice would thwart both the statute's private enforcement scheme and its remedial objectives. Congress could not have intended such a result. We therefore find that the Truth-in-Lending Act creates a right of action for attorneys to seek fee awards after settlement of the plaintiff's claim.

2.   In Freeman v. B & B Associates, 790 F.2d 145 (D.C.Cir. 1986), on the other hand, the attorney did not fare so well. Plaintiffs had received a loan from B & B Associates with a grossly understated rate of interest. They sued under the Truth in Lending Act for rescission, penalties and attorney's fees. The plaintiffs accepted an offer of judgment which granted rescission but specifically excluded all liability for attorney's fees. The district court held that the plaintiffs' attorney, David Fox, had an independent cause of action for legal fees under TILA. The District of Columbia Court of Appeals reversed.

The Court of Appeals opinion said, in part:

While we are sensitive to the concerns underlying the District Court's opinion and the Eleventh Circuit's holding in *James,* we do not think they support the creation of an attorney's independent right of action under TILA for fees. The District Court is correct that a major congressional goal behind TILA was the creation of a system of private enforcement. The court's analysis, however, ignores the fact that Congress specified how this remedial purpose was to be effectuated. The words of the statute show that Congress chose to create its system of private enforcement by giving borrowers access to a source of funds with which to compensate an attorney.

The words of section 1640 unambiguously vest the right to recover attorney's fees in the client rather than in the attorney. Section 1640 states that "any creditor who fails to comply with any (disclosure) requirement * * * with respect to any person is liable *to such person* in an amount equal to * * * the costs of the action, together with a reasonable attorney's fee as determined by the court." 15 U.S.C. § 1640(a) (emphasis supplied). In other words, under the statute the creditor is liable for attorney's fees to the person to whom the creditor failed to make the required TILA disclosures, i.e., to the borrower. We find nothing in the words of the statute suggesting any right to fees in an attorney which is independent and separate from the right of the borrower-client to collect attorneys' fees.

Because we find that section 1640 clearly places the right of action for attorneys' fees in the borrower, we will not ignore the words of the statute in pursuit of some disembodied congressional purpose. While the language of TILA "should be construed liberally in light of its broadly remedial purpose," * * * this does not mean that a court may interpret

TILA to encompass any policy that increases the total number of TILA suits brought. * * *

We also regard the District Court's reliance on *James v. Home Construction Company* as misplaced. *James* involved an attorney's standing to pursue his client's claim for attorneys' fees under TILA. *James* is silent on the question of an attorney's right of action where the client has expressly waived any claim to attorneys' fees. * * *

3.   In Zeisler v. Neese, 24 F.3d 1000, 1001 (7th Cir. 1994), the Seventh Circuit sided with *Freeman*. The court responded to the concern expressed in James that plaintiffs would broker settlements directly with defendants which did not provide for attorney's fees by noting "the offsetting danger that the lawyer's insistence on his fee might block settlements advantageous to plaintiffs."

4.   Can *Freeman* and *Zeisler* be reconciled with *James*? Which view has the better reasoning? Would either approach help May D. Marion in the preceding problem? If you were a defendant in a TILA case, and you thought you could work out a settlement with the plaintiff, wouldn't you always condition the settlement on an agreement of no attorney's fees? How can plaintiff's attorneys prevent such settlements?

Note on Calculating Attorney's Fees

Cases on the calculation of attorneys' fees in consumer protection cases appear with unrelenting frequency in the pages of the appellate reports. Given the "bread and butter" nature of the issue to the practicing bar, this should not be terribly surprising.

The basic issues dealt with by the courts in these cases include:

— Should the attorney fee award be proportionate to the size of the plaintiff's judgment, or should it be based on an hourly fee?

— How should the court handle a case which involves some claims that are subject to a statutory fee award, and some that are not?

— Should there be attorney's fees for appellate work?

— How can the court protect against excessive claims for hours spent on frivolous legal arguments?

— How much of a free hand should the trial court have in determining the amount of attorney's fees?

— What if the consumer wins on some claims but loses on others? How do you tell if the consumer prevailed when the consumer did not recover the full amount sought?

The answers to these questions will of course often hinge on the precise wording of the relevant statutory provision, but there are issues that appear to be common to all attorney's fees cases. Consider the following as a small sampling of the caselaw.

Problem 10–4

Same facts as in Problem 10–3, but this time there is no settlement offer. The case goes to trial and Buck wins a modest judgment ($300 for breach of warranty, and $100 for the TILA violation). Marion, however, had to put in a considerable amount of time researching and trying the case, as well as fending off the various pretrial discovery and other motions filed by Constant. She requests $40,000 in legal fees based on the time expended defending Buck's rights—200 hours at $200 per hour.

If you were the judge, how would you rule on Marion's request? What criteria would you use? What further information would you require?

Problem 10–5

Robin Hood bought a used car from Dale Dodge Dealers. Dale gave Hood a "Limited Warranty" under the Magnuson–Moss Warranty Act and the car had several defects in breach of that warranty. Dale refused to fix the defects, so Hood consults you. You are aware of the provisions of Magnuson–Moss under which a court "may" allow recovery of a successful plaintiff's attorney's fees from a warrantor. How would you analyze this fact situation to determine whether to accept Hood as a client, and whether to litigate this case if necessary?

Consider the information that you can obtain at the initial interview with Hood, and the imponderables remaining at that point, at which time you must decide whether to accept the case. Do the Magnuson–Moss provisions on plaintiff's attorney's fees assure aggrieved consumers that they will obtain legal representation easily and reliably? Should they?

HANKS v. PANDOLFO

Superior Court of Connecticut, Appellate Session, 1982.
38 Conn.Supp. 447, 450 A.2d 1167.

COVELLO, JUDGE.

On April 2, 1979, the plaintiffs brought suit claiming damages caused by the defendant's sale of a dented refrigerator. * * * [T]he complaint alleged (1) false, misleading and deceptive representations by the defendant; (2) breach of express and implied warranties; (3) delivery of a defective appliance (a refrigerator with a two foot dent); (4) violation of the Retail Installment Sales Financing Act; (5) two violations of the federal Consumer Product Warranties Act; and (6) unfair trade practices. The plaintiffs claimed damages and attorney's fees payable to the New Haven Legal Assistance Association, Inc. The plaintiffs were willing throughout the proceedings to settle the matter for $900 plus $750 attorney's fees.

Examination of the record discloses entry of numerous pleadings. Together with this state of the pleadings, the court had before it counsel's affidavit that she had expended twenty-five and one-quarter hours on the file plus three hours spent in drafting the application and supporting memorandum. She also submitted a claim with supporting affidavits that the fair value of her services was $100 per hour. The counsel fees claimed were $2825. The court awarded $450.

The summary judgment as to liability resolved only the fifth and sixth counts of the amended complaint in favor of the plaintiffs. These counts dealt exclusively with alleged violations of the federal Consumer Product Warranties Act. 15 U.S.C. §§ 2301 through 2312. Since the fundamental principle is "that every litigant must bear his own expenses of litigation except as otherwise provided by statute"; Peterson v. Norwalk, 152 Conn. 77, 80, 203 A.2d 294 (1964); this claim for attorney's fees must be dealt with solely within the context of the language contained in that statute.

The federal Consumer Product Warranties Act provides that "(i)f a consumer finally prevails in any action brought under paragraph (1) of this subsection, he may be allowed by the court to recover as part of the judgment a sum equal to the aggregate amount of cost and expenses (*including attorneys' fees based on actual time expended*) determined by the court to have been reasonably incurred by the plaintiff for or in connection with the commencement and prosecution of such action, *unless the court in its discretion shall determine that such an award of attorneys' fees would be inappropriate*." (Emphasis added.)

The provision makes four points clear. First, the use of the permissive language "may" instead of the mandatory language "shall" connotes a clear option of the court to allow or not to allow the recovery of costs whether they be attorney's fees or otherwise.

Second, if the court allows attorney's fees, such fees may be based on actual time expended. Thus, if the court elects to do so, it may totally exclude otherwise relevant considerations and base its fee calculation solely on the time expended, a procedure which presumably would not otherwise be permissible absent the specific language contained in this statute.

Third, whatever method of calculation is used, the costs must be "reasonably incurred."

Finally, the use of the mandatory language "shall" in the last phrase of the provision connotes that a determination must be made that an award of attorney's fees is or is not appropriate. The plain meaning of the language "in its discretion" contained in this phrase, when read together with the other language of the subsection, permits the court to exercise its judgment (1) to award no attorney's fees, or (2) to award attorney's fees based on time only, or (3) to award attorney's fees pursuant to its discretion. Whatever its content, a decision must be made on the issue of counsel fees.

In its articulated memorandum of decision, the trial court accepted as proved the claim that twenty-five and one-quarter hours were expended in pursuing the plaintiffs' claim. The court further found that this amount of time bore a reasonable relationship to the pleadings filed and that the attorney involved was unquestionably well qualified. The court concluded that these factors were outweighed, however, "by the nature of the litigation and the amount involved therein."

The action was initially to recover damages for the sale and delivery of a dented refrigerator. The plaintiffs indicated from the very beginning that the perceived value of the case was $900 plus attorney's fees. Under these circumstances, it is not unreasonable for the court to conclude that these factors outweighed the other relevant considerations bearing on the issue of attorney's fees.

"A court has few duties of a more delicate nature than that of fixing counsel fees. The degree of delicacy increases when the matter becomes one of review on appeal. The principle of law, which is easy to state but difficult at times to apply, is that only in the case of clear abuse of discretion by the trier may we interfere." Hoenig v. Lubetkin, 137 Conn. 516, 525, 79 A.2d 278 (1951). Such is not the case here. There is no error.

STEIGER v. J.S. BUILDERS, INC.

Appellate Court of Connecticut, 1995.
39 Conn.App. 32, 663 A.2d 432.

LANDAU, JUDGE.

The plaintiffs, Dennis Steiger and Carol Steiger, appeal from the judgment of the trial court, rendered after a bench trial, in their favor. They claim that (1) the trial court's award of damages is against the weight of evidence and contrary to law, and (2) the trial court applied the incorrect standard in calculating the award of attorney's fees pursuant to the contract and the Connecticut Unfair Trade Practices Act (CUTPA), General Statutes § 42–110a et seq. We reverse the judgment in part.

This matter pertains to a contract entered into by the plaintiffs for the purchase of land and construction of a house. In September, 1987, the plaintiffs filed an eleven count complaint against J.S. Builders, Inc., Blue Spruce Developers, Inc., Tradewind Developers, Inc., John I. Slezak, Louisette Slezak and Susan Moreau. In their complaint, the plaintiffs alleged breach of contract, breach of warranties and a violation of CUTPA and asked the court, inter alia, to pierce the corporate veil and to award damages and attorney's fees pursuant to CUTPA.

Subsequently, the trial court entered defaults against each defendant. The court conducted a hearing in damages, at the conclusion of which it found the defendants to be liable for damages suffered by the plaintiffs in the amount of $26,142.83. The court also found that John I. Slezak had violated CUTPA and awarded $7500 in attorney's fees.

* * *

The plaintiffs next claim that the trial court applied the wrong standard in calculating the award of attorney's fees pursuant to both the contract and CUTPA. We agree.

In its memorandum of decision, the trial court found that "the conduct of the defendant John Slezak clearly was contrary to public policy and was deceptive re: using an unlicensed plumber and that CUTPA has been violated. The plaintiffs' claim for attorney's fees against the corporate and individual defendants Slezak and Moreau was for $22,000 plus costs. On the basis of the cases noted above [*Hernandez v. Monterey Village Associates Ltd. Partnership,* 24 Conn.App. 514, 517 n. 3, 589 A.2d 888 (1991), and *Johnson v. Georgia Highway Express, Inc.,* 488 F.2d 714, 717–19 (5th Cir.1974)], this is clearly not warranted and would equal the damages the court is allowing [$26,142.83]. *There must be some reasonable relationship to the end result and the attorney's fees.* The court allows $7500 for attorney's fees as against these defendants." (Emphasis added.)

The trial court has discretion whether to award attorney's fees under CUTPA and " 'the exercise of such discretion will not ordinarily be interfered with on appeal unless the abuse is manifest or injustice appears to have been done.' " *Nielsen v. Wisniewski,* 32 Conn.App. 133, 138, 628 A.2d 25 (1993). The issue here, however, is not whether attorney's fees and costs could be or should have been awarded within the discretion of the trial court, but rather, whether the court applied the correct standard in setting the amount of attorney's fees. After determining that John Slezak had violated CUTPA, the trial court found evidence of attorney's fees against "the corporate and individual defendants Slezak and Moreau" in the amount of $22,000 plus costs. It awarded only $7500, however, clearly disallowing the remainder on the rationale that the larger award "would equal the damages the court is allowing" and that "there must be some reasonable relationship to the end result and attorney's fees." * * *

* * *

In *Johnson v. Georgia Highway Express, Inc.,* supra, 488 F.2d at 715, the question before the Fifth Circuit Court of Appeals concerned the adequacy of attorney's fees awarded by the District Court in an " 'across-the-board' action to remedy employment discrimination" pursuant to Title VII of the Civil Rights Act of 1964, 42 U.S.C. § 2000e et seq. The Circuit Court of Appeals set out twelve guidelines for the District Court to consider on remand in setting reasonable attorney's fees: (1) the time and labor required; (2) the novelty and difficulty of the questions; (3) the skill requisite to perform the legal service properly; (4) the preclusion of other employment by the attorney due to acceptance of the case; (5) the customary fee for similar work in the community; (6) whether the fee is fixed or contingent; (7) time limitations imposed by the client or the circumstances; (8) the amount involved and the results obtained; (9) the experience, reputation and ability of the attorneys; (10) the "undesirability" of the case; (11) the nature and length of the professional relationship with the client; and (12) awards in similar cases. Id. at 717–19.

As under CUTPA, a District Court has discretion under Title VII to award the prevailing party reasonable attorney's fees. 42 U.S.C. § 2000e–5(k). Mindful that the purpose of Title VII "is to effectuate the congressional policy against racial discrimination''; id. at 716; the Court of Appeals in *Johnson* noted that the guidelines are an attempt ''to enable litigants to obtain competent counsel worthy of a contest with the caliber of counsel available to their opposition and to fairly place the economical burden of Title VII litigation.'' Id. at 719.

The guidelines set forth in *Johnson* for calculating reasonable attorney's fees are appropriate in CUTPA litigation because, similar to Title VII, ''CUTPA seeks to create a climate in which private litigants help to enforce the ban on unfair or deceptive trade practices or acts.'' *Hinchliffe v. American Motors Corp.*, 184 Conn. 607, 618, 440 A.2d 810 (1981). Our review of whether the trial court correctly applied the guidelines and set a reasonable award of attorney's fees is limited to a consideration of whether the court abused its discretion. *Johnson v. Georgia Highway Express, Inc.*, supra, 488 F.2d at 717.

In this case, the trial court focused on only one of the twelve enunciated guidelines—the reasonableness of the relationship between the award of attorney's fees and the award of damages. We conclude that the trial court abused its discretion in seizing from the full panoply merely one guideline, to the exclusion and disregard of the others. To interpret the attorney's fees provision of CUTPA so narrowly would render insignificant the legislative intent—it would neither enhance the private CUTPA remedy, nor serve to encourage private CUTPA litigation. The judgment is reversed only as to the award of attorney's fees and costs and the case is remanded for a hearing to determine, consistent with this opinion, the amount of attorney's fees and costs that the plaintiffs may recover.

Notes

1. Can the two cases be reconciled? If not, which takes the better approach?

2. On remand, the lower court in Steiger awarded $10,000 in attorney's fees. Steiger v. J.S. Builders, 1996 WL 218689 (Conn.Super. 1996). Was the increase in the fee worth incurring the burden and expense of the appeal?

3. Suppose you represented the defendant in a Magnuson–Moss Act case before Judge Covello, the author of the *Hanks* decision. What impact, if any would *Hanks* have on your strategy? Similarly, what impact will *Hanks* have on the willingness of attorneys to represent plaintiffs in such cases and what will that do to enforcement of the Magnuson–Moss Act?

4. Does it make sense to spend more on plaintiff's attorney's fees than the plaintiff recovers? What impact does it have on the public's opinion of lawyers when lawyers receive more in fees than their clients recover? Should the legal profession care? Does it have a choice?

5. The attorney's fee-shifting provisions common in consumer statutes and considered in this subsection are an exception to the normal ''American Rule'' that litigants bear their own attorney's fees. By contrast, the ''British

Rule" requires the loser in litigation to pay the attorney's fees of the winner. Thus, fee-shifting statutes of the sort common in consumer litigation—in which losing defendants pay the fees of victorious consumer-plaintiffs—represent a hybrid of the two systems. How might the different systems affect the incentives to bring or defend a suit, or to settle a suit once brought?

Problem 10–6

Fleur D. Lee bought an automobile from Muck Motors. Muck gave Fleur a "Limited Warranty" under the Magnuson–Moss Warranty Act, and the car had several defects, in breach of that warranty. Muck refused to fix the defects, and so Fleur went to the Legal Aid Society for help. At Legal Aid, Dart N. Yan was assigned as her attorney, and Fleur was charged nothing for his services. Dart first contacted Muck, but they still refused to fix the defects, so Dart sued Muck, on Fleur's behalf, for damages both under the UCC and under Magnuson–Moss and won. Fleur was awarded $1,000, the amount established for fixing the car's defects.

Dart then applied for an award of his attorney's fees in the case. He established that he had spent 200 hours of his time on the case and that attorneys in private practice with his same credentials were paid $200 per hour. Thus, Dart sought a total of $40,000 under 15 U.S.C.A. § 2310(d)(2).

Muck makes three points: (1) Fleur did not have to pay anything to Legal Aid or to Dart. They are supported by donations from the public. Thus, Muck contends that the fee of plaintiff's attorney is $0. Since the court only "may" (not "shall") award fees to a successful consumer, any award to Dart would be "unconscionable." (2) Muck does some quick calculations, based on Dart's salary, and states that 200 hours of his time cost Legal Aid only $6,000. It further says that any award greater than $6,000 would be "unconscionable." (3) Muck also contends that, since only $1,000 was in issue, an award of $40,000, or even $4,000, as attorney's fees would be disproportionate to the amount at issue, and therefore "unconscionable."

In determining awards of attorneys' fees under § 2310(d)(2), are any of the above theories persuasive? See Sellers v. Wollman, 510 F.2d 119 (5th Cir. 1975). Is this an appropriate circumstance for use of the unconscionability doctrine?

Query: Should statutory attorney's fees be awarded to attorneys who are representing themselves as consumer plaintiffs? Why or why not? See White v. Arlen Realty & Devel. Corp., 614 F.2d 387 (4th Cir.), cert. denied, 447 U.S. 923, 100 S.Ct. 3016, 65 L.Ed.2d 1116 (1980); Kurz v. Chase Manhattan Bank USA, NA., 324 F.Supp.2d 444 (S.D.N.Y. 2004).

2. CLASS ACTIONS

Prefatory Note

In many consumer cases, in which the amount an individual would obtain in a judgment is not enough to offset the cost of bringing litigation, the same case brought as a class action would generate a sufficient recovery to pay for the cost of litigation and more. As the Supreme Court has explained:

> The policy at the very core of the class action mechanism is to overcome the problem that small recoveries do not provide the incentive for an individual to bring a solo action prosecuting his or her rights. A class action solves this problem by aggregating the relatively paltry potential recoveries into something worth someone's (usually an attorney's) labor.

Amchem Prods., Inc. v. Windson, 521 U.S. 591, 617, 117 S.Ct. 2231, 138 L.Ed.2d 689 (1997) (quoting Mace v. Van Ru Credit Corp., 109 F.3d 338, 344 (7th Cir. 1997)); see also Phillips Petroleum Co. v. Shutts, 472 U.S. 797, 809, 105 S.Ct. 2965, 86 L.Ed.2d 628 (1985) ("Class actions ... permit the plaintiffs to pool claims which would be uneconomical to litigate individually."). Consequently, the critical factor in determining whether some disputes are litigated is whether the case warrants class action treatment. That is why some consumer class actions settle immediately after a class is certified or are voluntarily dismissed after a certification motion is denied. Are there non-economic reasons why a lawyer might prefer to bring a claim as a class action?

It is not the purpose of this subsection to examine all aspects of class actions, for that would be a course in itself. In addition, many students will be familiar from procedure courses with the standard requirements of class actions laid out by Federal Rule of Civil Procedure 23 and similar state laws: the class is so numerous that joinder of all members is impracticable; there are common questions of law and fact; and the class representatives can fairly and adequately represent the interests of the class and their claims or defenses are typical of the claims or defenses of the class. Other requirements, depending on the particular type of class action brought, can include that questions of law or fact predominate over questions affecting only individual members; that a class action is superior to other available methods for the fair and efficient adjudication of the controversy; and the case is manageable as a class action. The purpose of this subsection is to focus on a few issues involving consumer class actions that students are unlikely to encounter in procedure courses but that are particularly relevant for this course.

Problem 10–7

You are employed by Neighborhood Legal Services. Your client, John Little, bought a car from William Scarlet and signed a negotiable promissory note promising to pay $7200 over a four year period. The note did not have the FTC required legend (see supra Chapter Seven). Scarlet negotiated the note to Tuck Trust Company.

One week after the sale and negotiation, the transmission fell out of the car. The car had a new car warranty which was breached by this occurrence, but Scarlet refused to repair or replace the transmission of the car, saying something about owner misuse of the car. Tuck is insisting on payment of installments on the note, regardless of the breach of warranty, alleging that it is a holder in due course of a negotiable instrument. You also have another client, Alan Dale (on another matter), who has recently bought a car from Scarlet, and signed a negotiable promissory note which did not have the FTC required legend. There has been no breach of warranty on this car yet.

You wish to bring a class action against Scarlet or Tuck for any or all of the violations you have found. Can you successfully do it? For what violation(s)? What remedies can you obtain for the class? Redress for aggrieved consumers? Injunction against future violations? Penalties due to past violations? Would it be desirable to bring the case as a class action? Recall that in federal court, in most class actions, the plaintiff is obliged to bear the sometimes considerable expense of notifying class members of the pendency of the law suit. See Fed.R.Civ.Pro. 23(c); Eisen v. Carlisle & Jacquelin, 417 U.S. 156, 94 S.Ct. 2140, 40 L.Ed.2d 732 (1974).

Will it matter whether you are in state or federal court? Should it matter? Do you have a choice?

Notes

1. Why would any consumer undertake to underwrite notice expenses where the recovery will be quite small? Is the practical effect of the notice rules to protect class members, to protect class action defendants, or to protect judges from working too hard?

2. In addition to meeting the prerequisites of Rule 23, Magnuson–Moss class actions in federal court must also meet stringent statutory prerequisites. The total amount in controversy must be at least $50,000 (with individual claims of at least $25), and there must be at least 100 named plaintiffs. Magnuson–Moss Act § 110(d)(3), 15 U.S.C.A. § 2301(d)(3). Even a class that initially meets this requirement may be decertified if upon discovery or motions for summary judgment or dismissal, it becomes necessary to dismiss the actions of some of the named plaintiffs, and the number drops to below the required 100. *See* Abraham v. Volkswagen of America, Inc., 795 F.2d 238 (2d Cir.1986).

3. Given that Magnuson–Moss incorporates state warranty law by reference, and given that warranty laws vary from state to state (notwithstanding the Uniform Commercial Code), how likely is it that a multi-state Magnuson–Moss class action will be able to fulfill the requirement of the predominance of a common question of law? Also, will Magnuson–Moss class actions be plagued by the issue of individual factual differences, as are class actions alleging fraud? See Feinstein v. Firestone Tire & Rubber Co., 535 F.Supp. 595 (S.D.N.Y.1982) (no class action allowed because an alleged tire defect did not affect each car in the same way).

4. The federal Class Action Fairness Act of 2005 ("CAFA"), Pub. L. No. 109–2, was enacted in response to a perception that certain state courts were unduly generous to class action plaintiffs, with the result that plaintiffs brought a disproportionate number of class actions in those courts. CAFA addressed this by significantly expanding federal jurisdiction over class actions. Specifically, CAFA extends federal diversity jurisdiction over class actions to include cases in which plaintiffs' claims as an aggregate exceed $5

million and any plaintiff is from a different state than any defendant (so-called "minimal diversity"). 28 U.S.C. § 1332(d). CAFA also makes it easier to remove class actions filed in state court. See 28 USCA § 1453. In certain cases federal courts have discretion to decline to exercise jurisdiction and in other situations they must decline to hear the case. Early reports on CAFA indicate that it has increased the number of state-law diversity class action cases heard in and removed to federal court. See Thomas E. Willging & Emery G. Lee III, The Impact of the Class Action Fairness Act of 2006: Second Interim Report to the Judicial Conference Advisory Committee on Civil Rules (2006).

GREISZ v. HOUSEHOLD BANK (ILLINOIS), N.A.

United States Court of Appeals, Seventh Circuit, 1999.
176 F.3d 1012.

Posner, Chief Judge.

This is a suit under the Truth in Lending Act, 15 U.S.C. §§ 1601 *et seq.*, against Household Bank, with supplemental claims (28 U.S.C. § 1367) under Illinois law (the Consumer Fraud and Deceptive Business Practices Act, 815 ILCS 505, and the Uniform Deceptive Trade Practices Act, 815 ILCS 510) against both the bank and the Golden Seal Heating & Air Conditioning company. The district judge refused to certify the suit as a class action and later dismissed the entire suit. The appeal challenges these rulings.

The principal ground on which the district court denied class certification was the proved incapacity of the lawyer for the class, Joseph A. Longo, to litigate a class action. The class action is a valuable economizing device, especially when there is a multiplicity of small claims, but it is also pregnant with well-documented possibilities for abuse. The smaller the individual claim, the less incentive the claimant has to police the class lawyer's conduct, and the greater the danger, therefore, that the lawyer will pursue the suit for his own benefit rather than for the benefit of the class. The lawyer for a plaintiff class has not only an impaired incentive to be the faithful agent of his (nominal) principal, but also the potential to do great harm both to the defendant because of the cost of defending against a class action and to the members of the class because of the preclusive effect of a judgment for the defendant on the rights of those class members who have not opted out of the class action. That is why Fed.R.Civ.P. 23(a)(4), which requires the judge to determine whether the class representative (that is, the named plaintiff) will fairly and adequately protect the interests of the class, has been interpreted to require the judge also to assess the class lawyer's competence before certifying a suit to proceed as a class action. *General Telephone Co. v. Falcon*, 457 U.S. 147, 157–58 n. 13, 102 S.Ct. 2364, 72 L.Ed.2d 740 (1982)

Mr. Longo's extensive but inept and wholly unsuccessful efforts to conduct class actions have drawn unusually pointed criticisms from Illinois state judges. In one case the judge called the complaint drafted by Longo (which had already been amended four times) the "lousiest complaint I've ever read" in twenty years on the bench, and added that "I wouldn't want to be in a class action where you were representing the Plaintiff." Longo has several times sought to file Truth in Lending class actions with his own relatives as the named plaintiffs, which is of course improper. E.g., *Susman v. Lincoln American Corp.,* 561 F.2d 86, 95 (7th Cir.1977). He has filed untimely appeals, failed to protect the right of clients to opt out of doomed class actions, engaged in flagrant forum shopping, made exorbitant settlement demands, filed frivolous motions, displayed a lack of familiarity with procedural rules—and in the end always lost. In *Urso v. United States,* 72 F.3d 59 (7th Cir.1995), we criticized him on multiple grounds, while in *Estate of Henry, by Henry v. Folk,* 285 Ill.App.3d 262, 220 Ill.Dec. 831, 674 N.E.2d 102, 103 (1996), the court noted that he had attempted to serve process on a saloon by leaving a copy of the summons with one of the saloon's customers. In one of his class actions, he sent a nonlawyer to appear in his stead at oral argument, and in the same case he filed a motion to jail the opposing counsel for nonexistent discovery abuses. Acting as his own lawyer in a consumer-protection case, the field of his claimed expertise, he not only lost the case but was sanctioned for his incompetent handling of the litigation. See *Longo v. AAA–Michigan,* 201 Ill.App.3d 543, 155 Ill.Dec. 450, 569 N.E.2d 927 (1990); *Longo v. Michel,* 1993 WL 476967 (6th Cir.1993) (per curiam); *Longo v. Glime,* 1991 WL 32356 (6th Cir.1991) (per curiam). We are about to see that he has sacrificed the interests of the named plaintiff in this case to his desire to keep the case going in the forlorn hope that it might somehow, someday fly as a class action. Given Longo's track record, the district judge was clearly right to refuse to let the suit proceed as a class action.

* * *

Note

Was Mr. Longo's behavior ethical?

Note on TILA and FDCPA Class Actions

The original version of the Truth in Lending Act simply provided for civil liability, but made no special mention of class actions. This resulted in a range of opinion in the courts as to the availability of the class action device in TILA cases. The combination of the $100 minimum penalty damages available to each class member for each violation, plus the availability of attorney's fees meant that a TILA class action could result in a staggering liability for creditors who commit disclosure violations replicated with hundreds of thousands of customers.

In the landmark case of Ratner v. Chemical Bank New York Trust Co., 54 F.R.D. 412 (S.D.N.Y.1972), United States District Judge Frankel denied class certification in a TILA case because the potential $13 million award (130,000 credit card holders each receiving the $100 minimum penalty) "would be a horrendous, possibly annihilating punishment, unrelated to any damage to the purported class or to any benefit to defendant, for what is at most a technical and debatable violation of the Truth in Lending Act." Other courts followed Judge Frankel's lead, and TILA class actions were becoming scarce.

Congress responded to the situation in 1974 by limiting liability in TILA class actions to the lesser of $100,000 (raised to $500,000 in 1976) or 1% of the creditor's net worth. TILA § 130(a)(2)(B), 15 U.S.C.A. § 1640(a)(2)(B). The amendment eliminated the potential for devastating liability, thus encouraging the judicial certification of more TILA class actions. The 1980 TILA Simplification Act added language to the effect that the class action liability ceiling applied not only to a single class action, but also to any "series of class action suits arising out of the same failure to comply by the same creditor." Id. The Fair Debt Collection Practices Act contains a similar provision. See FDCPA § 1692k(a)(2)(B).

Notes

1. How should courts proceed in cases in which class action defendants might face annihilating damages but the statute under which the case is brought does not contain a provision like that of TILA or the FDCPA? Compare ESI Ergonomic Solutions, LLC v. United Artists Theatre Circuit, Inc., 203 Ariz. 94, 50 P.3d 844 (Ariz.App. 2002) (in deciding whether class action is superior method for adjudicating case brought under Telephone Consumer Protection Act, court should not consider fact that class might recover "annihilating damages" of $45 million to $135 million) with *In re* Trans Union Corp. Privacy Litigation, 211 F.R.D. 328 (N.D.Ill. 2002), appeal dismissed by Albert v. Trans Union Corp., 346 F.3d 734 (7th Cir. 2003) (taking into account potential for $19 billion in statutory damages in concluding that class action is not superior method for adjudicating Fair Credit Reporting Act case). If courts refuse to certify classes in meritorious cases because of the potential for "annihilating damages," and the cases cannot be brought economically except as class actions, what remedy do injured plaintiffs have?

2. Theoretically, the cap on damages in class actions means that individual plaintiffs are less well off in class actions because they could recover greater damages in individual actions. As a practical matter, however, few plaintiffs, if any, would bring such cases as individual suits and so they are better off in class actions based on the cliché that half a loaf is better than none. Courts have been willing to certify classes notwithstanding the theoretical problem as long as the individual plaintiffs have the opportunity to opt out of the class and bring an individual claim. See Sarafin v. Sears, Roebuck & Co., Inc., 73 F.R.D. 585 (D.C.Ill. 1977). But what about the named class representatives? They represent the class—which is at least as burdensome as bringing an individual action—but if their damages are capped, are they not worse off than if they had brought the case as an individual suit? On the other hand, if their damages are not capped, would they be able to represent the class fairly and adequately? See Brame v. Ray Bills Finance Corp., 85 F.R.D. 568 (N.D.N.Y. 1979). Is it ethical for an attorney to recommend to a client that the case be brought as a class action

when doing so reduces the client's recovery? Would the ethical problem be cured if no attorney is willing to bring the case except as a class action?

3.   Is the cap on damages a good solution to the problem of annihilating damages? Is the *Ratner* approach of not certifying a class at all preferable? Is there another solution?

Problem 10–8

A trial court determined that a furniture retailer's TILA disclosure statement violated the statute. Since this was a class action against a corporation whose net worth was approximately $150 million, the trial court awarded the then-maximum $100,000 class recovery. The class was composed of 700 credit customers of one of the retailer's 48 stores. On appeal, should this damage award be modified? See Barber v. Kimbrell's, Inc., 577 F.2d 216 (4th Cir.), cert. denied, 439 U.S. 934, 99 S.Ct. 329, 58 L.Ed.2d 330 (1978).

Should the court consider the fact that it is theoretically possible for customers of the other 47 stores (which used the same forms, and thereby committed the same violation) to bring 47 other class actions for 47 additional awards? Should the court therefore allow an award of only 1/48 of $100,000? Or 1/48 of $1.5 million? Or, should the court delay any award until the one-year TILA statute of limitations has run, and then consider only actual class actions brought? How helpful is the statute in answering these questions?

Problem 10–9

(a) Assume a large and wealthy bank supplies non-conforming TILA disclosure statements to dozens of small local retail stores. The bank regularly discounts the consumer paper for which these forms are used. The retail stores are all thinly-capitalized shoestring operations. Their combined "net worth" is about $100,000. The bank on the other hand has a net worth of $5.7 billion. What is the maximum liability of the bank for all the violations in its forms, if the customers from those stores bring a class action? $1,000? $500,000?

(b) What law governs the class action certification if the action is brought in state court?

Problem 10–10

You are a judge. Last year you certified a class in a case against Icy Refrigerators, Inc.: plaintiffs claim that the bottom shelf in the refrigerator door was designed defectively and consequently broke prematurely, reducing the capacity of the refrigerators. The class consists of all those who bought Icy Refrigerators in the last three years. Lawyers for Icy and the plaintiff class have now reached a settlement and have asked for your approval. The settlement provides that the 100,000 class members will receive non-transferable coupons good for $100 off a full-size Icy refrigerator. The coupons, which cannot be combined with other discounts, may be redeemed any time within the next two years upon submission of a two-page notarized form. The lawyers describe the settlement as a win-win deal. They claim that the consumers will receive a benefit worth $100 while the cost to Icy will be about $50 per coupon because Icy will have economies of scale in manufacturing the refrigerators. While Icy is willing to settle the case on these terms, it also claims that the refrigerators are not defective and that if the case proceeded to trial, Icy would prevail and consequently the plaintiffs would not recover any damages. Plaintiffs' attorneys have also filed a petition for a substantial fee, arguing that because the total value of redeemable coupons is $10 million, they have secured a significant victory for their clients in a case that the plaintiffs might in fact lose if it were to be litigated. You provide notice to the class of the proposed settlement and hold a hearing; no unnamed member of the plaintiff class submits comments. Will you approve the settlement? If not, what modifications would make you approve the settlement?

Notes

1. CAFA also addresses coupon settlements in 28 U.S.C. § 1712, which provides that to the extent attorney's fees are attributable to the award of coupons, the fees must be contingent on the value of the coupons actually redeemed rather than the value issued. Any other attorney's fees must be determined based on time reasonably spent working on the case. Under the statute, a court may not approve a coupon settlement unless it determines that the settlement is fair, reasonable, and adequate for class members—though since Fed.R.Civ.Pro. 23(e)(1)(C) already provided that settlements must be fair, reasonable, and adequate, that does not represent a substantive change.

2. Some coupon settlements have elicited few takers. In Buchet v. ITT Consumer Financial Corp., 858 F.Supp. 944 (D.Minn. 1994), the court described the redemption rate of four previous coupon offers as having ranged from .002% to .110%. What implications does this have for the value of coupon settlements? Does this explain CAFA?

3. Coupon settlements have been much criticized in the legal and popular media. See, e.g., the collection of articles in 18 Geo. J. Legal Ethics No. 4 (2005) (including transcripts from an FTC Workshop titled "Protecting Consumer Interests in Class Actions"); Trisha L. Howard, Lawyers Profit Most in Suit, Defendant Says; Attorney's Take is Reported to be 10 Times That of Plaintiffs; Lawyers for Firm That Sued Says Clients Got More Than Stated, St. Louis Post–Dispatch, Mar. 31, 2004 at A1 (plaintiffs' class action lawyers claimed class included about 29 million people, but only 92,000 made claims, collecting $8.4 million, while lawyers were paid $84.5 million); Christopher R. Leslie, A Market–Based Approach to Coupon Settlements in Antitrust and Consumer Class Action Litigation, 49 UCLA L.Rev. 991, 996 (2002) ("coupon settlements neither adequately compensate most class members nor deter future misconduct by defendants."). But they also have their defenders. For example, the CEO and President of a company that provides a secondary market in coupons, buying them from consumers and selling them to others, including consumers, explain:

> Coupon settlements benefit class members when the coupon's face value exceeds the class member's claim and the discount coupon is used to

purchase the defendant's product or service. If the coupon is transferable and a vibrant secondary market exists, the class member benefits when he sells his coupon for more than his underlying claim. Defendants accept coupon settlements because they pay only when a sale is made, spreading their liability over time while ridding themselves of risky litigation. Class counsel benefits because they get paid to deliver justice to their class in cases that are complex and often difficult to prosecute.

James Tharin & Brian Blockovich, Coupons and the Class Action Fairness Act, 18 Geo. J. Legal Ethics 1443, 1445 (2005). Similarly, the National Association of Consumer Advocates' Class Action Guidelines conclude that "rare instances do exist where [coupon settlements] may be appropriate or add value to a settlement that otherwise could not be obtained for a class" such as cases in which the main goal of the litigation is to obtain injunctive relief.

4. Is CAFA's attempt to reform coupon settlements the best solution to the problem? Texas Rule of Civil Procedure 42(i) provides: "If any portion of the benefits recovered for the class are in the form of coupons or other noncash common benefits, the attorney fees awarded in the action must be in cash and noncash amounts in the same proportion as the recovery for the class." See also V.T.C.A., Civil Practice & Remedies Code § 26.003(b). Is that preferable to CAFA's approach? Compare Lisa M. Mezzetti & Whitney R. Case, The Coupon Can Be the Ticket: The Use of "Coupon" and Other Non–Monetary Redress in Class Action Settlements, 18 Geo. J. Legal Ethics 1431, 1435 (2005) (the authors, who suggest a minimum pay-out requirement would be a better solution, write that "the coupons cannot pay the attorney's employees' salaries or electricity for the office.") with Christopher R. Leslie, A Market–Based Approach to Coupon Settlements in Antitrust and Consumer Class Action Litigation, 49 UCLA L.Rev. 991, 997, 1094 (2002) ("judges can create proper incentives for class counsel to insure that settlement coupons are marketable by requiring that class counsel be paid in the same currency as class members.... If settlement coupons are so worthless that attorneys will not bring litigation if paid in coupons, then why pay attorneys millions of dollars in cash to negotiate settlements in which their clients receive these same coupons?"). How should the attorney be paid in cases in Texas in which the court enters an injunction or provides declarative relief?

Note on Class Representation

In any type of consumer protection class action, what if the named plaintiffs' claims are fully satisfied pending the litigation? Will they be able adequately to represent the interests of the class? Consider the following.

KAGAN v. GIBRALTAR SAVINGS AND LOAN ASSOCIATION

Supreme Court of California, 1984.
200 Cal.Rptr. 38, 35 Cal.3d 582, 676 P.2d 1060.

REYNOSO, JUSTICE.

May a consumer who notifies a prospective defendant of class grievances under the Consumer Legal Remedies Act and informally obtains individual relief, subsequently bring a class action for damages on behalf of herself and as a representative of the class against the prospective defendant?

Plaintiff Eleanor M. Kagan brought this action individually and as a representative of a class against the Gibraltar Savings and Loan Association (Gibraltar) and various "Doe" defendants. She alleges that Gibraltar engaged in deceptive practices proscribed by the Consumer Legal Remedies Act in falsely advertising that customers would not be charged management fees in connection with Individual Retirement Accounts. Upon a motion by Gibraltar that the action lacked merit, the trial court determined that since the threatened fee had not been deducted from plaintiff's account she "ha(d) not suffered any injury or sustained any damage cognizable under the Consumer Legal Remedies Act." Accordingly, the trial court entered judgment in favor of Gibraltar.

Plaintiff contends that the Consumer Legal Remedies Act (Civ. Code, § 1750 et seq.) does not permit a prospective defendant to "pick off" prospective class representatives by offering them individual relief not made available to the entire class. As will appear below, we agree.

* * *

[Ms. Kagan opened an Individual Retirement Account with Gibraltar in April of 1979, in response to Gibraltar's promotional brochure promising "No commissions. No establishment fees. No management fees." Kagan was outraged when Gibraltar informed her by letter in November of 1979] that all IRAs would be charged a $7.50 "trustee fee." On June 2, 1980, Ms. Kagan and her husband (who had also been charged a fee) sent a demand letter to Gibraltar asserting that Gibraltar's conduct was prohibited by the California Consumer Legal Remedies Act (California Civil Code Section 1770), and demanding that the amounts deducted from their accounts be restored and that the false advertising cease. They threatened to sue if relief was not granted within 30 days.]

In a letter dated June 24, 1980, within the prescribed 30–day period, Gibraltar promised to remove and discard from its branch offices the disputed promotional brochures, advised that no trustee fees had been deducted from plaintiff's account, and by check reimbursed plaintiff's husband the $15 in trustee fees which had been charged his account for the years 1979 and 1980.

On July 31, 1980, plaintiff filed the instant class action, on behalf of herself and those other persons who had been induced to establish IRA accounts through Gibraltar's alleged false advertising and misrepresentations. The complaint sought actual damages for the deducted fees, declaratory and injunctive relief preventing future deductions, $5 million in punitive damages and reasonable attorneys' fees and costs.

* * *

Gibraltar contends that since the contested fee was not deducted from plaintiff's account, she no longer "suffers any damage" as required for bringing an individual action under section 1780. Therefore, Gibraltar argues, plaintiff is also precluded from bringing a class action under section 1781, which is expressly limited to "(a)ny consumer entitled to bring an action under Section 1780."

We agree that a consumer who has notified a prospective defendant of an individual grievance and has obtained his or her requested relief cannot subsequently bring either an individual or class action under the Act. However, this is not simply because the consumer no longer "suffers any damage" but because the prospective defendant has remedied the contested practices. Similarly, a prospective defendant receiving notice of a grievance which affects a class of consumers can avert a subsequent class action only by remedying the contested practices as to all affected consumers. The critical inquiry for determining whether a prospective defendant may be subject to an individual or class action is therefore whether the prospective defendant has made all remedies appropriate to the notice which it has received.

The demand letter sent Gibraltar by plaintiff and her husband requested that the "amounts deducted from their accounts for management fees be restored to their accounts, together with interest thereon." It also demanded that Gibraltar "cease its misleading and false advertising practices" and "rectif(y) * * * (its) misconduct in falsely advertising its services, as well as conditioning the conferral of an economic benefit on a contingency which will occur subsequent to the consummation of a transaction." These demands put Gibraltar on notice that its alleged violations of section 1770 affected individuals in addition to plaintiff and her husband, and possibly a broad class of consumers. This notice was formalized by the December 19, 1979, letter from plaintiff's husband to the president of Gibraltar in which he stated: "I believe Gibraltar could be guilty of a major consumer fraud if it attempts to retroactively impose trustee fees." This letter also stated that the intended charge "conflicts with both written and oral representations which were made to myself, my wife and other IRA depositors" and that Gibraltar's oral representation that the fee provision in the agreement would not be operative was presumably "conveyed to anyone else who may have noticed the provision."

As these letters, taken together, put Gibraltar on notice that its alleged violations of section 1770 affected a class of consumers, Gibraltar was under an affirmative obligation to meet the conditions set forth in section 1782, subdivision (c) in order to avert a class action. There is no evidence to indicate that Gibraltar made an effort to meet any of these conditions. Gibraltar did not seek to identify consumers similarly situated to plaintiff, or notify such consumers that it would provide them relief upon their request. Nor did Gibraltar demonstrate that it had provided requested relief to any similarly situated consumers or that it would cease from engaging in the challenged conduct within a reasonable time. Gibraltar made no mention of stopping any of its allegedly false advertising other than withdrawing its promotional brochures. Nor did Gibraltar indicate that it would require its employees to stop making the allegedly misleading oral representations. Additionally, assuming plaintiff's husband is a member of the purported class of IRA depositors fraudulently induced to open IRAs with Gibraltar, Gibraltar's reimbursement to him of the $15 which it acknowledged deducting from his 1979 and 1980 accounts did not include any compensation for the requested interest thereon.

As Gibraltar did not meet the conditions of section 1782, subdivision (c) in response to notification of its alleged class violations of section 1770, a class action for damages pursuant to section 1781, subdivision (a) may lie. * * *

* * *

Gibraltar further asserts that permitting plaintiff to bring a class action is contrary to the well recognized rule that a class representative be a member of the class which she purports to represent * * *, in this case the putative class of persons, induced to establish IRA accounts through Gibraltar's alleged misrepresentations concerning the imposition of fees, whose accounts were actually debited the trustee fee. This argument ignores the clear legislative intent that prospective defendants under the Act not avert a class action by exempting or "picking off" prospective plaintiffs one-by-one through the provision of individual remedies.

Those responsible for drafting the Act specifically sought to preclude such "picking off" of prospective class action plaintiffs:

> "The most important point in connection with the settlement of class actions is that settlement with the named plaintiffs will not preclude them from further prosecuting the action on behalf of the remaining members of the class. Note that section 1782(c) precludes the further maintenance of the action only if *all* the described conditions are shown to exist. Those conditions require settlement with all reasonably identifiable members of the class. The term 'maintained' in section 1782(c) was deliberately and carefully chosen just as the term 'commenced' was deliberately avoided. *The intent was to make certain that a person can commence a class action 30 days after he has made a demand on behalf of the class even if the merchant has offered to settle his particular claim in accordance with section 1782(b).* An action so commenced may not be maintained, however, if the conditions for settlement with the class have been met. It is evident that construction of section 1782(c) so as to preclude a person from maintaining any action if his particular claim had been settled would destroy class actions under the statute. That most certainly was not the intent of the legislature." (Emphasis added.)

(Reed, Legislating For The Consumer: An Insider's Analysis Of The Consumers Legal Remedies Act (1971) 2 Pacific L.J. 1, 19.)

* * *

We now hold only that Gibraltar's exemption of plaintiff from the imposition of the trustee fee does not render her unfit per se to represent the class. In determining whether plaintiff's claims are typical of those of the class, and whether plaintiff can fairly and adequately protect the class she seeks to represent, the trial court on remand

> "may take into account that the named plaintiff( ) (has) already obtained (her) individual benefits from the action; plaintiffs who have nothing at stake often will not devote sufficient energy to the prosecution of the action; further, the receipt of benefits by the named plaintiffs may sometimes create a conflict of interest between the class and its would-be representatives. * * *

We do note that plaintiff's claims appear to be typical of those of the putative class, and that the tenacity with which plaintiff has thus far pursued this matter is indicative that she has those qualities necessary to fairly and adequately protect the interests of that class. Moreover, plaintiff's demonstrated energy in pursuing this matter would appear to advance the primary purposes for maintaining a class action, by " 'eliminat(ing) the possibility of repetitious litigation and provid(ing) small claimants with a method of obtaining redress for claims which would otherwise be too small to warrant individual litigation.' " (Richmond v. Dart Industries, Inc. (1981) 29 Cal.3d 462, 469, 174 Cal.Rptr. 515, 629 P.2d 23, quoting Eisen v. Carlisle & Jacquelin (2d Cir.1968) 391 F.2d 555, 560.)

* * *

Problem 10–11

In Illinois, in order to maintain a class action, the court must find:

(1) the class is so numerous that joinder of all members would be impracticable;

(2) there are questions of fact or law common to the class which predominate over any questions affecting only individual members;

(3) the representative party will fairly and adequately protect the interests of the class; and

(4) a class action is an appropriate method for the fair and efficient adjudication of the controversy.

735 ILCS 5/2–801.

In a class action suit filed in Illinois, Hungry Hanna alleged that the defendant, Harvey's, had advertised and sold "roast beef" sandwiches which in fact were simulated roast beef and not the real thing. Hanna alleged that such advertising violated the Illinois Deceptive Practices Act. The sole remedy under this Act is an injunction that may be granted to a person "likely to be damaged by a deceptive trade practice of another." 815 ILCS 510/3. The proposed class consisted of all Illinois residents who had purchased simulated roast beef sandwiches from Harvey's within the past three years.

Harvey's opposed the class certification on the basis that the class was unmanageable and that Hanna, the only named plaintiff, could not be granted relief under the Deceptive Practices Act because she was not "likely to be damaged" since she clearly is aware that Harvey's uses simulated roast beef. How would you rule if you were the judge in this case and why? Cf. Hayna v. Arby's, Inc., 99 Ill.App.3d 700, 55 Ill.Dec. 1, 425 N.E.2d 1174 (1981); Brooks v. Midas–International Corp., 47 Ill. App.3d 266, 5 Ill.Dec. 492, 361 N.E.2d 815 (1977); Hockley v. Hargitt, 82 Wash.2d 337, 510 P.2d 1123 (1973).

Attorney's Fees in Class Actions

Prefatory Note

The subsection on attorney's fees, *supra,* focused on fee awards under statutes that require defendants to pay the attorney's fees of prevailing plaintiffs. Those statutes are, of course, also relevant to attorney's fees awards in class actions. But some successful class actions are brought under statutes and common law doctrines that do not provide for fee-shifting. In such cases, courts normally award the plaintiffs' attorneys some portion of the funds recovered for the class, on the theory that the attorneys would not have provided their service without compensation. In both these so-called "common fund cases" and fee-shifting cases, courts must develop criteria for determining the amounts of fees. To what extent do the two different types of cases call for different treatment of fees? Two leading approaches to setting fees are (1) the percentage of recovery method—a sort of contingent fee arrangement under which the attorneys receive a percentage of the amount won by the class—and (2) the lodestar method. The lodestar is calculated by multiplying the total number of hours reasonably expended on the case by a reasonable hourly rate of compensation. In determining what is reasonable for the hourly rate, the court may consider the attorney's usual hourly rate, the level of skill required by the particular litigation, judicially imposed time limits, the attorney's reputation, and the undesirability of the case.

IN RE GENERAL MOTORS CORP. PICK–UP TRUCK FUEL TANK PRODUCTS LIABILITY LITIGATION

United States Court of Appeals, Third Circuit, 1995.
55 F.3d 768, cert. denied, 516 U.S. 824, 116 S.Ct. 88, 133 L.Ed.2d 45 (1995).

BECKER, CIRCUIT JUDGE:

[This was a multi-state products liability action. After the district court had certified a class, approved a coupon settlement, and awarded attorney's fees, some members of the class appealed. The Court of Appeals found that the settlement was not fair and reasonable.]

(1) Class Action Attorneys' Fees Theory and Structure

Beyond their ethical obligations to their clients, class attorneys, purporting to represent a class, also owe the entire class a fiduciary duty once the class complaint is filed. *See* 2 NEWBERG & CONTE § 11.65, at 11–183. The large fees garnered by some class lawyers can create the impression of an ethical violation since it may appear that the lawyer has an economic stake in their clients' case. But class actions cannot be analyzed in the same framework as conventional bipolar litigation. Because of the collective action problems associated with cases where individual claims are relatively small, *see* 7A CHARLES A. WRIGHT, ARTHUR R. MILLER & MARY KAY KANE, *Federal Practice and Procedure* § 1754, at 49, and the social desirability of many class suits (the private enforcement model), *id.* at 51, large attorneys' fees serve to motivate capable counsel to undertake these actions. Thus, large fee awards standing alone do not suffice to show that the representation was inadequate or unethical. These allowances generally reflect the realization that the lawyer represents numerous individuals with somewhat varying interests, not acceptance of a situation where the lawyer's personal interests trump the interests of the entire class.

Some commentators blame the system of compensating class action lawyers in a manner that fails to confront fully the differences between class action litigation and classical bipolar litigation for creating incentives that diverge markedly and predictably from their clients' interests. The leading critic is Professor Coffee. *See* John C. Coffee, Jr., *Understanding the Plaintiff's Attorney: The Implications of Economic Theory For Private Enforcement of Law Through Class and Derivative Actions,* 86 COLUM.L.REV. 669, 671–72 (1986) (noting that critics "have argued that the legal rules governing the private attorney general have created misincentives that unnecessarily frustrate the utility of private enforcement. These critics have focused chiefly on the conflicts that arise between the interests of these attorneys and their clients in class and derivative actions. . . .") [hereinafter *Understanding the Plaintiff's Attorney*]; *id.* at 677 ("Ultimately, the most persuasive account of why class actions frequently produce unsatisfactory results is the hypothesis that such actions are uniquely vulnerable to collusive settlements that benefit plaintiff's attorneys rather than their clients."); John C. Coffee, *Rescuing the Private Attorney General: Why the Model of the Lawyer As Bounty Hunter Is Not Working,* 42 MD.L.REV. 215 (1983); John C. Coffee, *The Unfaithful Champion: The Plaintiff as Monitor in Shareholder Litigation* 48 LAW & CONTEMP. PROBS. 5 (Summer 1985); Kevin M. Clermont & John D. Currivan, *Improving on the Contingent Fee,* 63 CORNELL L.REV. 529 (1978); Murray L. Schwartz & Daniel J.B. Mitchell, *An Economic Analysis of the Contingency Fee in Personal–Injury Litigation,* 22 STAN.L.REV. 1125 (1970).

Economic models have shown how conventional methods of calculating class action fee awards give class counsel incentives to act earlier than their clients would deem optimal. *See* Coffee, *Understanding the Plaintiff's Attorney,* 86 COLUM.L.REV. at 688. Because, under a percentage of recovery award mechanism, the attorneys will only enjoy a relatively small portion of whatever incremental award they can extract from the defendant, the defendant can pressure the plaintiffs' attorney into early settlement by threatening to expend large sums on dilatory tactics that would run the expenses up beyond what plaintiffs' attorneys can expect to profit. *Id.* at 690. Rather than presenting a possible solution, the lodestar method seemingly exacerbates the problem of cheap settlement by divorcing the fee award from the settlement's size, since plaintiffs' attorneys have no incentive to take the risk on a trial for a potentially larger award to the class where their own fees will not necessarily reflect the greater risk taken at trial. *See also id.* at 718 (discussing how lodestar method may create structural collusion).

Coffee also blames the principal-agent problem endemic to class actions for creating a situation where the defendants and plaintiffs can collusively settle litigation in a manner that is adverse to the class's interest: "At its worst, the settlement process may amount to a covert exchange of a cheap settlement for a high award of attorney's fees. Although courts have long recognized this danger and have developed some procedural safeguards intended to prevent collusive settlements, these reforms are far from adequate to the task." *Id.* at 714 n. 121 (citing cases). A number of commentators have identified settlements that afford only nonpecuniary relief to the class as prime suspects of these cheap settlements. *See* Coffee, *Understanding The Plaintiff's Attorney,* 86 COLUM.L.REV. at 716 n. 129; Jonathan R. Macey & Geoffrey P. Miller, *The Plaintiffs' Attorneys Role in Class Action and Derivative Litigation: Economic Analysis and Recommendations for Reform,* 58 U.CHI.L.REV. 1, 45 n. 10 (1991); Nancy Morawetz, *Bargaining, Class Representation, and Fairness,* 54 OHIO ST.L.J. 1, 5 n. 40 (1993).

While courts may fail to appreciate adequately the distinction between conventional bipolar litigation and class actions in many respects, they may over-emphasize these differences in other respects. To be sure, courts will be willing to award fees in class actions that would appear extraordinary and arguably improper in conventional litigation. Nevertheless, some of the critiques based on ethical or collusive concerns remain instructive. Although subsequent versions seem to avoid a discussion, the Manual for Complex Litigation (First) acknowledged the potential for attorney-class conflict. It condemned fees that are paid separate and apart from the settlement funds paid to the class because amounts "paid by the defendant(s) are properly part of the settlement funds and should be known and disclosed at the time the fairness of the settlement is considered." MCL 1st § 1.46.

One court has noted that the "effect of such an arrangement [where the counsel fees are not resolved and the details not included in the class notice] may be to cause counsel for the plaintiffs to be more interested in the amount to be paid as fees than in the amount to be paid to the plaintiffs." *In re General Motors Corp. Engine Interchange,* 594 F.2d at 1131. Commentators have also noted how, where there is an absence of objectors, courts lack the independently-derived information about the merits to oppose proposed settlements. *See* Coffee, *Understanding the Plaintiff's Attorney*, 86 COLUM.L.REV. at 714 n. 131. Of course, by endorsing a practice where the class is, for practical purposes, deprived of information concerning the fees, courts foster a situation where there will be fewer objectors.

(2) The Stewardship of Counsel Here

A number of factors militate against the conclusion that the class's interests were sufficiently pursued here. First, the settlement arguably did not maximize the class members' interests. Every owner received a coupon whose value could only be realized by purchasing a new truck. Significant obstacles existed to the development of a secondary market in the transfer certificates given that the transfer restrictions and the certificates' limited lifespan minimize the value of the transfer option. Second, class counsel effected a settlement that would yield very substantial rewards to them after what, in comparison to the $9.5 million fee, was little work.

* * *

The French and Young objectors also contest the district court's award of attorneys' fees. (Orders dated Dec. 20, 1993, 1993 WL 533155 and Feb. 2, 1994, 1994 WL 30301.) The court initially awarded fees without an independent review of the agreement, explaining its refusal to review the award: "[The fee agreement] is a matter of contract between the parties, rather than a statutory fee case, ... and payment of the fees will have no impact on the class members...." Subsequently, on February 2, 1994, the court issued an "amplification" of its prior ruling, which justified the award under both the lodestar and the percentage of recovery methods. Class counsel maintain that the objectors lack standing to contest the agreement made between GM and themselves, and that the objectors waived their right to appeal the award by not raising their objections below. Although our disposition of the certification and settlement approval issues obviates the need for a review of the fee award at this stage (and moots the waiver question), we highlight some of the primary issues in analyzing the appropriateness of a particular fee agreement for the district court on remand (in the event that the record is expanded, the class certified, and the settlement approved).

At the outset, we note that a thorough judicial review of fee applications is required in all class action settlements. The district court did not accommodate practical realities here when, rationalizing its initial refusal to review the fee, it stated that the fee award was "to be paid by General Motors Corporation and will in no way reduce the recovery to any of the settlement class members." Indeed, this court has recognized that "a defendant is interested only in disposing of the total claim asserted against it; ... the allocation between the class payment and the attorneys' fees is of little or no interest to the defense." *Prandini v. National Tea Co.*, 557 F.2d 1015, 1020 (3d Cir.1977); 2

NEWBERG & CONTE § 11.09 (purpose of judicial review is to police abuses even where defendant pays plaintiff's fees). In light of these realities, class counsel's argument that objectors have no standing to contest the fee arrangement is patently meritless: the fee agreement clearly does impact their interests, as it is, for practical purposes, a constructive common fund.

Moreover, as discussed at length in the adequacy of representation section, *see* Part V.B.3 *supra,* the divergence in financial incentives present here creates the "danger ... that the lawyers might urge a class settlement at a low figure or on a less-than-optimal basis in exchange for red-carpet treatment for fees," *Weinberger v. Great Northern Nekoosa Corp.,* 925 F.2d 518, 524 (1st Cir.1991). *See also Prandini,* 557 F.2d at 1020 ("When the statute provides that a fee is to be paid as a separate item, the conflict between client and attorney may not be as apparent.... It is often present nonetheless."). This generates an especially acute need for close judicial scrutiny of fee arrangements that implicate this concern. *See In re Agent Orange Prod. Liab. Litig.,* 818 F.2d 216, 224 (2d Cir.1987) ("The test to be applied is whether, at the time a fee sharing agreement is reached, class counsel are placed in a position that might endanger the fair representation of their clients and whether they will be compensated on some basis other than for legal services performed."); *Piambino v. Bailey,* 757 F.2d at 1139 ("Because of the potential for a collusive settlement, a sellout of a highly meritorious claim, or a settlement that ignores the interests of minority classes members, the district judge has a heavy duty to ensure that ... the fee awarded plaintiffs' counsel is entirely appropriate."). We have previously acknowledged that the potential for conflict between the class and its counsel is not limited to situations meeting the strict definitions of a common fund.

As we have also explained in this opinion, courts must be especially vigilant in searching for the possibility of collusion in pre-certification settlements. *See* Part IV.E *supra.* In addition, the court's oversight task is considerably complicated by the fact that these attorney-class conflicts are often difficult to discern in the class action context, "where full disclosure and consent are many times difficult and frequently impractical to obtain." *Agent Orange,* 818 F.2d at 224 (citations omitted). Finally, we emphasize that the court's oversight function serves not only to detect instances of "the actual abuse [that potential attorney-class conflicts] may cause, but also [the] potential public misunderstandings they may cultivate in regard to the interests of class counsel." *Agent Orange,* 818 F.2d at 225 (citing *Susman v. Lincoln American Corp.,* 561 F.2d 86, 95 (7th Cir.1977), and *Prandini v. National Tea Co.,* 557 F.2d 1015, 1017 (3d Cir.1977)); *see also Grinnell I,* 495 F.2d at 469; MODEL CODE OF PROFESSIONAL RESPONSIBILITY Canon 9 (1975). On remand, therefore, the district court must be alert to the presence in the fee agreement of any actual abuse or appearance of abuse capable of creating a public misunderstanding.

Having emphasized the necessity for judicial review of fee awards in all class action settlements, we will briefly clarify some principles of fee approval for the district court to apply on remand if it certifies a class and approves a settlement.

Because the district court purported to use both the lodestar and the percentage-of-recovery methods, the actual grounds for its approval of the fee are not entirely clear. Although it is sensible for a court to use a second method of fee approval to cross check its conclusion under the first method, we believe that each method has distinct advantages for certain kinds of actions, which will make one of the methods more appropriate as a primary basis for determining the fee. Here, for the reasons that follow, the court should probably use the percentage-of-recovery rather than the lodestar method as the primary determinant, although the ultimate choice of methodology will rest within the district court's sound discretion.

The lodestar and the percentage of recovery methods each have distinct attributes suiting them to particular types of cases. *See Task Force,* 108 F.R.D. at 250–53. Ordinarily, a court making or approving a fee award should determine what sort of action the court is adjudicating and then primarily rely on the corresponding method of awarding fees (though there is, as we have noted, an advantage to using the alternative method to double check the fee).[40]

Courts generally regard the lodestar method, which uses the number of hours reasonably expended as its starting point, as the appropriate method in statutory fee shifting cases. Because the lodestar award is decoupled from the class recovery, the lodestar assures counsel undertaking socially beneficial litigation (as legislatively identified by the statutory fee shifting provision) an adequate fee irrespective of the monetary value of the final relief achieved for the class.

This de-coupling has the added benefit of avoiding subjective evaluations of the monetary worth of the intangible rights often litigated in civil rights actions. Outside the pure statutory fee case, the lodestar rationale has appeal where as here, the nature of the settlement evades the precise evaluation needed for the percentage of recovery method. The lodestar method has the added benefit of resembling modes of fee determination in conventional bipolar litigation. On the other hand, the lodestar method has been criticized as giving class counsel the incentive to delay settlement in order to run up fees while still failing to align the interests of the class and its counsel, and for not rewarding counsel incrementally for undertaking the risk of going to trial. *See* Coffee, *Understanding the Plaintiff's Attorney,* 86 COLUM.L.REV. at 691.

Courts use the percentage of recovery method in common fund cases on the theory that the class would be unjustly enriched if it did not

---

40. For example, a court can use the lodestar method to confirm that a percentage of recovery amount does not award counsel an exorbitent hourly rate; similarly, the percentage of recovery method can be used to assure that counsel's fee does not dwarf class recovery.

compensate the counsel responsible for generating the valuable fund bestowed on the class. *See Task Force,* 108 F.R.D. at 250. Because these cases are not presumed to serve the public interest (as evidenced by the lack of a fee statute), there is no social policy reason that demands an adequate fee. Instead, the court apportions the fund between the class and its counsel in a manner that rewards counsel for success and penalizes it for failure. Courts have relied on "common fund" principles and the inherent management powers of the court to award fees to lead counsel in cases that do not actually generate a common fund. *See, e.g., In re Air Crash Disaster at Florida Everglades,* 549 F.2d 1006 (5th Cir.1977) (using common fund principles in settlement of consolidated cases). The rationale behind the percentage of recovery method also applies in situations where, although the parties claim that the fee and settlement are independent, they actually come from the same source.

We believe that this case presents a situation more closely aligned with the common fund paradigm than the statutory fee paradigm. Although class counsel and GM contend (and the district court believed) that the fee was a separate agreement, thus superficially resembling the separate awards in statutory fee cases, private agreements to structure artificially separate fee and settlement arrangements cannot transform what is in economic reality a common fund situation into a statutory fee shifting case. Certainly, the court may select the lodestar method in some non-statutory fee cases where it can calculate the relevant parameters (hours expended and hourly rate) more easily than it can determine a suitable percentage to award. But the court must vigilantly guard against the lodestar's potential to exacerbate the misalignment of the attorneys' and the class's interests. *See* Coffee, *Understanding the Plaintiff's Attorney,* 86 COLUM.L.REV. at 717.

In this case, the fee clearly was not made pursuant to a statute; therefore no legislatively endorsed policy favors assuring counsel an adequate fee. And the settlement, though difficult to value, did not award the even more hard-to-value intangible rights that could in some limited circumstances justify using the lodestar method. In sum, although this case presents a hybrid, we believe that it more closely resembles a common fund case.

At all events, to the extent that the district court relied on the lodestar method, it erred by applying a multiplier. In the lodestar section of its analysis, the district court calculated the multiplier needed to apply to the simple lodestar result, $3,158,182, to obtain the requested amount, $9,500,000. After estimating the multiplier to be between 2.5 and 3, the court proceeded with a "contingent nature of the success" analysis of the multiplier's appropriateness from *Lindy. See Lindy Bros. Builders Inc., v. American Radiator & Standard Sanitary Corp.,* 540 F.2d 102, 116–17 (3d Cir.1976). The Supreme Court, however, has rejected the use of multipliers to enhance the lodestar's hourly rate amount. *See City of Burlington v. Dague,* 505 U.S. at ___, 112 S.Ct. at 2638. Notwithstanding this clear Supreme Court precedent, GM's counsel failed to apprise the district court about *Dague* even though its pertinence was patent.

To the extent that the district court construed the fee agreement as a common fund, its analysis also appears to misapprehend key aspects of the percentage of recovery method. In common fund cases, a district judge can award attorneys' fees as a percentage of the fund recovered. *See Blum v. Stenson,* 465 U.S. 886, 900 n. 16, 104 S.Ct. 1541 n. 16, 79 L.Ed.2d 891 (1984); *In re Smithkline Beckman Corp. Secur. Litig.,* 751 F.Supp. 525 (E.D.Pa.1990). One court has noted that the fee awards have ranged from nineteen percent to forty-five percent of the settlement fund. *Id.* at 533. Here, the district court summarily asserted that, although it could not value the settlement precisely, "whatever method is used in computing the ultimate value of the settlement, the attorneys' fees sought in this action will constitute an extremely small percentage of the total value and will be minute compared to the aforesaid 19–45% range." (Feb. 2, 1994 Order, 1994 WL 30301 at *4.)

Given our skepticism of the settlement's value generally and of Simonsen's estimates in particular (*see supra* discussion on settlement fairness), we are much less sanguine that the $9,500,000 fee actually constitutes an acceptable percentage of the class recovery. On the current record, we are constrained to reject that conclusion. At the very least, the district court on remand needs to make some reasonable assessment of the settlement's value and determine the precise percentage represented by the attorneys' fees. The problem, however, is not simple, for arguably, any settlement based on the award of certificates would provide too speculative a value on which to base a fee award. (*See Task Force,* 108 F.R.D. at 250–53 (discussing the preferability of the lodestar method for civil rights actions where the difficulty of valuing injunctive relief complicates the calculation of a fee using the percentage method.))

On remand, the district court might wish to examine the fee primarily under the percentage of recovery scheme. If so, the court will need to determine a precise valuation of the settlement on which to base its award. The court may however, as a check, want to use the lodestar method to assure that the precise percentage awarded does not create an unreasonable hourly fee.

* * *

[Judge Gibson's concurrence is omitted.]

Notes

1. There is considerable divergence among the federal circuits about the best way to determine fees in common fund class actions. See, e.g., Swedish Hosp. Corp. v. Shalala, 1 F.3d 1261, 1271 (D.C. Cir. 1993) ("percentage-of-the-fund method is the appropriate mechanism for determining the attorney fees award in common fund cases."); Strong v. BellSouth Telecommunications, Inc., 137 F.3d 844 (5th Cir. 1998) (Fifth Circuit uses

lodestar method to assess fees in class actions); Goldberger v. Integrated Resources, Inc., 209 F.3d 43 (2d Cir. 2000) ("both the lodestar and the percentage of the fund methods are available to district judges in calculating attorneys' fees in common fund cases. Of course, no matter which method is chosen, district courts should continue to be guided by the traditional criteria in determining a reasonable common fund fee, including: '(1) the time and labor expended by counsel; (2) the magnitude and complexities of the litigation; (3) the risk of the litigation . . . ; (4) the quality of representation; (5) the requested fee in relation to the settlement; and (6) public policy considerations.' "). On the other hand, the lodestar approach is preferred in fee-shifting cases. See Blanchard v. Bergeron, 489 U.S. 87, 94, 109 S.Ct. 939, 945, 103 L.Ed.2d 67 (1989) (lodestar approach is the centerpiece of attorney's fee awards). What accounts for the difference?

2. To what extent does the different approach matter? See Vaughn R. Walker & Ben Horwich, The Ethical Imperative of a Lodestar Cross–Check: Judicial Misgivings About "Reasonable Percentage" Fees in Common Fund Cases, 18 Geo. J. Legal Ethics 1453, 1468 (2005) (reporting preliminary results of study that "Percentage-based fee awards are about 28% larger than lodestar-based fee awards, and fee awards are about 20% larger when class counsel's hours are not reported."); Theodore Eisenberg & Geoffrey P. Miller, Attorney Fees in Class Action Settlements: An Empirical Study, 1 J. Empirical Leg. Studies 27, 28–29, 76–77 (2004) (the level of the client's recovery is "by far the most important determinant of the attorney fee amount" under both fee-shifting statutory awards and common fund awards, even when courts use lodestar calculation; fees in fee-shifting cases are significantly higher percentage of class recovery than fees in common fund cases).

3. After the court issued the decision in the principal case, the parties submitted a similar settlement to a state court in Louisiana, where a parallel case had been filed earlier. The Louisiana court approved the restructured settlement, and the federal courts declined to intervene on procedural grounds. See In re General Motors Corp. Pick–Up Truck Fuel Tank Products Liability Litigation, 134 F.3d 133 (3d Cir. 1998).

4. In one widely reported settlement, a bank agreed to recalculate its escrow formula which resulted in its issuing consumers refunds of up to $8.76. The bank then deducted a larger amount—in at least one case, $91.33—from many of its customers' accounts to cover plaintiffs' attorney's fees. See Kamilewicz v. Bank of Boston Corp., 92 F.3d 506 (7th Cir.), *rehearing denied*, 100 F.3d 1348 (7th Cir. 1996), *cert. denied*, 520 U.S. 1204, 117 S.Ct. 1569, 137 L.Ed.2d 714 (1997); Joe Stephens, Coupons Create Cash for Lawyers; Class Action 'Paper' Settlements Mean Little to Individual Plaintiffs, Wash. Post, Nov. 14, 1999 at A01. Congress responded in CAFA by enacting 28 U.S.C. § 1713, which bars settlements in which class members pay so much to class counsel that the members suffer a net loss, unless the court finds that nonmonetary benefits to the class substantially outweigh the monetary loss.

5. As noted in the principal case, the Supreme Court in *Burlington*, limited the use of multipliers in fee-shifting cases. Nevertheless, some courts

continue to approve the use of multipliers in common fund cases. See, e.g, *Goldberger*, cited in note one, *supra*.

6.   How should an attorney representing a plaintiff class proceed during a settlement conference when the defendant indicates that it wants to discuss simultaneously the claims of the class and attorney's fees? Would the attorney for the class face a conflict of interest in discussing both simultaneously? Would it matter to the defendant whether the attorney received a larger or smaller share of the total amount paid by the defendant?

Problem 10–12

Howard Helpful is a young attorney with a storefront office and a general practice. When Ima Victim consulted him because she was being pestered by Friendly Finance Co., he discovered an error in Friendly's Truth in Lending disclosure statement. Howard filed a class action under the Truth in Lending Act, which Friendly's attorneys resisted vigorously. After two years, the judge decided that there had been an unintentional, short-duration violation of TILA, and enjoined any further violations. She further decided that, since the violation was in the printed language of the form and no member of the class had read that printing, no member of the class had suffered actual damage and no member would recover monetary damages.

Howard then sought attorney's fees under TILA § 130(a)(3). Since the violation he had discovered was novel, he had worked long and hard on the case. He sought compensation for 500 hours at $100 per hour with a contingency factor multiplier of 1.5, because his theory of the case was entirely original, for a total of $75,000. The judge humphed, said that ordinarily she would permit only 15% of the total recovery as reasonable attorney's fees, but that would be $0, so she would allow Howard "the minimum recovery" of $100.

Howard is appealing the case on several grounds, including the attorney fee award. What are the arguments on appeal, and who should win? Should a rational legal system pay $75,000 to resolve a dispute in which no one has been hurt?

Problem 10–13

After the case described in the preceding problem was resolved, some clients asked Howard to represent them in a class action based on a state common law invasion of privacy tort under which defendants need not pay the attorney's fees of prevailing plaintiffs. The clients had earlier invited several other lawyers to represent them in the matter, but the lawyers refused because they felt the case was unlikely to succeed. Howard took the case on, conceived an imaginative theory, and recovered a judgment of $20 million for the class on summary judgment. The case required 500 hours of Howard's time. Howard has now filed an application for fees, seeking 20% of the recovery, or $4 million. How should the court rule on Howard's fee application? Is Howard's request ethical? See ABA Model Rule of Professional Conduct 1.5 ("A lawyer shall not ... charge, or collect an unreasonable fee....").

SECTION C.   ARBITRATION

1.   PRE–DISPUTE ARBITRATION TERMS AND THEIR IM-PACT ON ENFORCEMENT OF CONSUMER CLAIMS

Preliminary Note

The parties to a dispute are always free to agree on arbitration instead of litigation, and many disputants have decided to submit their disagreements to arbitration after a controversy has arisen. But this subsection addresses something slightly different. Many businesses today include in their customer contracts a term providing that any disputes will be resolved in arbitration. Why do you think businesses insert such provisions in their agreements?

The enforceability of pre-dispute arbitration agreements is itself often a subject of dispute. The Federal Arbitration Act ("FAA"), which applies to arbitration agreements "evidencing a transaction involving [interstate] commerce" allows challenges to arbitration agreements "upon such grounds as exist at law or in equity for the revocation of any contract." 9 U.S.C. § 2. See also Allied–Bruce Terminix Companies, Inc. v. Dobson, 513 U.S. 265, 271, 115 S.Ct. 834, 838, 130 L.Ed.2d 753 (1995) (FAA is intended to put arbitration agreements "upon the same footing as other contracts"); Doctor's Associates, Inc. v. Casarotto, 517 U.S. 681, 116 S.Ct. 1652, 134 L.Ed.2d 902 (1996) (FAA preempts Montana law declaring an arbitration clause unenforceable unless "[n]otice that [the] contract is subject to arbitration" is "typed in underlined capital letters on the first page of the contract."). For criticism of the Supreme Court's approach to arbitration, see Jean R. Sternlight, Panacea or Corportate Tool? Debunking the Supreme Court's Preference for Binding Arbitration, 74 Wash.U.L.Q. 637 (1996). On what grounds may arbitration clauses be attacked? Would a consumer prefer litigation or arbitration?

Problem 10–14

Your client, Jesse, recently defaulted on a debt to the Mustard Department Store, which is incorporated under the laws of another state and has its principal place of business in that state. Shortly afterwards, Mustard took out a full-page advertisement in the local paper listing 300 consumers from your state, including Jesse, who had defaulted on debts to Mustard. Mustard's conduct does not violate the Fair Debt Collection Practices Act (do you see why?), but it is probably tortious under the laws of your state. Accordingly, Jesse has retained you to bring suit against Mustard. Because of the cost of litigation and the fact that no fee-shifting statute applies, you have determined that it makes economic sense to bring the case only if you can bring it as a class action. Jesse cannot afford to pay you because he has serious financial problems, which is why he defaulted on the debt in the first place. Accordingly, you filed a complaint and moved to have a class certified. Mustard timely moved to dismiss the complaint on the ground that the lengthy standard term loan agreement signed by Jesse and the other putative members of the class provided for binding arbitration by Lucky Arbitration. After receiving the motion, you review Lucky Arbitration's rules, which were not provided to Jesse at the time he signed the agreement. The rules provide for a filing fee of $150; that Mustard bears the cost of the first day of the arbitrator's time; and that thereafter the parties split the cost of the arbitrator's time. The rules also bar bringing matters as class actions.

(a) How should the motion be resolved? See Green Tree Financial Corp.-Alabama v. Randolph; Ting v. AT&T, *infra.*

(b) Would it make a difference if the arbitration agreement provided that the arbitration is to take place in Mustard's home city, which happens to be 1,000 miles away?

(c) Would it make a difference if the arbitration agreement applied only to claims brought by the consumer?

GREEN TREE FINANCIAL CORP.-ALABAMA v. RANDOLPH

Supreme Court of the United States, 2000.
531 U.S. 79, 121 S.Ct. 513, 148 L.Ed.2d 373.

CHIEF JUSTICE REHNQUIST delivered the opinion of the Court.

In this case we first address whether an order compelling arbitration and dismissing a party's underlying claims is a "final decision with respect to an arbitration" within the meaning of § 16(a)(3) of the Federal Arbitration Act, 9 U.S.C. § 16(a)(3), and thus is immediately appealable pursuant to that Act. Because we decide that question in the affirmative, we also address the question whether an arbitration agreement that does not mention arbitration costs and fees is unenforceable because it fails to affirmatively protect a party from potentially steep arbitration costs. We conclude that an arbitration agreement's silence with respect to such matters does not render the agreement unenforceable.

I

Respondent Larketta Randolph purchased a mobile home from Better Cents Home Builders, Inc., in Opelika, Alabama. She financed this purchase through petitioners Green Tree Financial Corporation and its wholly owned subsidiary, Green Tree Financial Corp.-Alabama. Petitioners' Manufactured Home Retail Installment Contract and Security Agreement required that Randolph buy Vendor's Single Interest insurance, which protects the vendor or lienholder against the costs of repossession in the event of default. The agreement also provided that all disputes arising from, or relating to, the contract, whether arising under case law or statutory law, would be resolved by binding arbitration.[1]

---

1. The arbitration provision states in pertinent part: "All disputes, claims, or controversies arising from or relating to this Contract or the relationships which result from this Contract, or the validity of this arbitration clause or the entire contract, shall be resolved by binding arbitration by one arbitrator selected by Assignee

Randolph later sued petitioners, alleging that they violated the Truth in Lending Act (TILA), 15 U.S.C. § 1601 *et seq.*, by failing to disclose as a finance charge the Vendor's Single Interest insurance requirement. She later amended her complaint to add a claim that petitioners violated the Equal Credit Opportunity Act, 15 U.S.C. §§ 1691–1691f, by requiring her to arbitrate her statutory causes of action. She brought this action on behalf of a similarly situated class. In lieu of an answer, petitioners filed a motion to compel arbitration, to stay the action, or, in the alternative, to dismiss. The District Court granted petitioners' motion to compel arbitration, denied the motion to stay, and dismissed Randolph's claims with prejudice. The District Court also denied her request to certify a class. She requested reconsideration, asserting that she lacked the resources to arbitrate, and as a result, would have to forgo her claims against petitioners. The District Court denied reconsideration. Randolph appealed.

The Court of Appeals for the Eleventh Circuit first held that it had jurisdiction to review the District Court's order because that order was a final decision. 178 F.3d 1149 (1999). * * *

The court then determined that the arbitration agreement failed to provide the minimum guarantees that respondent could vindicate her statutory rights under the TILA. Critical to this determination was the court's observation that the arbitration agreement was silent with respect to payment of filing fees, arbitrators' costs, and other arbitration expenses. On that basis, the court held that the agreement to arbitrate posed a risk that respondent's ability to vindicate her statutory rights would be undone by "steep" arbitration costs, and therefore was unenforceable. We granted certiorari, and we now affirm the Court of Appeals with respect to the first conclusion, and reverse it with respect to the second.

II

[The Court held that the district court's decision was immediately appealable.]

with consent of Buyer(s). This arbitration Contract is made pursuant to a transaction in interstate commerce, and shall be governed by the Federal Arbitration Act at 9 U.S.C. Section 1. Judgment upon the award rendered may be entered in any court having jurisdiction. The parties agree and understand that they choose arbitration instead of litigation to resolve disputes. The parties understand that they have a right or opportunity to litigate disputes through a court, but that they prefer to resolve their disputes through arbitration, except as provided herein. THE PARTIES VOLUNTARILY AND KNOWINGLY WAIVE ANY RIGHT THEY HAVE TO A JURY TRIAL EITHER PURSUANT TO ARBITRATION UNDER THIS CLAUSE OR PURSUANT TO A COURT ACTION BY ASSIGNEE (AS PROVIDED HEREIN). The parties agree and understand that all disputes arising under case law, statutory law, and all other laws, including, but not limited to, all contract, tort, and property disputes, will be subject to binding arbitration in accord with this Contract. The parties agree and understand that the arbitrator shall have all powers provided by the law and the Contract."

III

We now turn to the question whether Randolph's agreement to arbitrate is unenforceable because it says nothing about the costs of arbitration, and thus fails to provide her protection from potentially substantial costs of pursuing her federal statutory claims in the arbitral forum. Section 2 of the FAA provides that "[a] written provision in any maritime transaction or a contract evidencing a transaction involving commerce to settle by arbitration a controversy thereafter arising out of such contract ... shall be valid, irrevocable, and enforceable, save upon such grounds as exist at law or in equity for the revocation of any contract." 9 U.S.C. § 2. In considering whether respondent's agreement to arbitrate is unenforceable, we are mindful of the FAA's purpose "to reverse the longstanding judicial hostility to arbitration agreements ... and to place arbitration agreements upon the same footing as other contracts." *Gilmer v. Interstate/Johnson Lane Corp.*, 500 U.S. 20, 24, 111 S.Ct. 1647, 114 L.Ed.2d 26 (1991).

In light of that purpose, we have recognized that federal statutory claims can be appropriately resolved through arbitration, and we have enforced agreements to arbitrate that involve such claims. We have likewise rejected generalized attacks on arbitration that rest on "suspicion of arbitration as a method of weakening the protections afforded in the substantive law to would-be complainants." *Rodriguez de Quijas, supra,* at 481, 109 S.Ct. 1917. These cases demonstrate that even claims arising under a statute designed to further important social policies may be arbitrated because " 'so long as the prospective litigant effectively may vindicate [his or her] statutory cause of action in the arbitral forum,' " the statute serves its functions. See *Gilmer, supra,* at 28, 111 S.Ct. 1647 (quoting *Mitsubishi, supra,* at 637, 105 S.Ct. 3346).

In determining whether statutory claims may be arbitrated, we first ask whether the parties agreed to submit their claims to arbitration, and then ask whether Congress has evinced an intention to preclude a waiver of judicial remedies for the statutory rights at issue. See *Gilmer, supra,* at 26, 111 S.Ct. 1647; *Mitsubishi, supra,* at 628, 105 S.Ct. 3346. In this case, it is undisputed that the parties agreed to arbitrate all claims relating to their contract, including claims involving statutory rights. Nor does Randolph contend that the TILA evinces an intention to preclude a waiver of judicial remedies. She contends instead that the arbitration agreement's silence with respect to costs and fees creates a "risk" that she will be required to bear prohibitive arbitration costs if she pursues her claims in an arbitral forum, and thereby forces her to forgo any claims she may have against petitioners. Therefore, she argues, she is unable to vindicate her statutory rights in arbitration.

It may well be that the existence of large arbitration costs could preclude a litigant such as Randolph from effectively vindicating her federal statutory rights in the arbitral forum. But the record does not show that Randolph will bear such costs if she goes to arbitration.

Indeed, it contains hardly any information on the matter.[6] As the Court of Appeals recognized, "we lack ... information about how claimants fare under Green Tree's arbitration clause." 178 F.3d, at 1158. The record reveals only the arbitration agreement's silence on the subject, and that fact alone is plainly insufficient to render it unenforceable. The "risk" that Randolph will be saddled with prohibitive costs is too speculative to justify the invalidation of an arbitration agreement.

To invalidate the agreement on that basis would undermine the "liberal federal policy favoring arbitration agreements." *Moses H. Cone Memorial Hospital,* 460 U.S., at 24, 103 S.Ct. 927. It would also conflict with our prior holdings that the party resisting arbitration bears the burden of proving that the claims at issue are unsuitable for arbitration. See *Gilmer, supra,* at 26, 111 S.Ct. 1647; *McMahon, supra,* at 227, 107 S.Ct. 2332. We have held that the party seeking to avoid arbitration bears the burden of establishing that Congress intended to preclude arbitration of the statutory claims at issue. See *Gilmer, supra; McMahon, supra.* Similarly, we believe that where, as here, a party seeks to invalidate an arbitration agreement on the ground that arbitration would be prohibitively expensive, that party bears the burden of showing the likelihood of incurring such costs. Randolph did not meet that burden. How detailed the showing of prohibitive expense must be before the party seeking arbitration must come forward with contrary evidence is a matter we need not discuss; for in this case neither during discovery nor when the case was presented on the merits was there any timely showing at all on the point. The Court of Appeals therefore erred in deciding that the arbitration agreement's silence with respect to costs and fees rendered it unenforceable.[7]

---

6. In Randolph's motion for reconsideration in the District Court, she asserted that "[a]rbitration costs are high" and that she did not have the resources to arbitrate. But she failed to support this assertion. She first acknowledged that petitioners had not designated a particular arbitration association or arbitrator to resolve their dispute. Her subsequent discussion of costs relied entirely on unfounded assumptions. She stated that "[f]or the purposes of this discussion, we will assume filing with the [American Arbitration Association], the filing fee is $500 for claims under $10,000 and this does not include the cost of the arbitrator or administrative fees." Randolph relied on, and attached as an exhibit, what appears to be informational material from the American Arbitration Association that does not discuss the amount of filing fees. She then noted: "[The American Arbitration Association] further cites $700 per day as the average arbitrator's fee." For this proposition she cited an article in the Daily Labor Report, February 15, 1996, published by the Bureau of National Affairs, entitled Labor Lawyers at ABA Session Debate Role of American Arbitration Association. Plain-

tiff's Motion for Reconsideration, Record Doc. No. 53, pp. 8–9. The article contains a stray statement by an association executive that the average arbitral fee is $700 per day. Randolph plainly failed to make any factual showing that the American Arbitration Association would conduct the arbitration, or that, if it did, she would be charged the filing fee or arbitrator's fee that she identified. These unsupported statements provide no basis on which to ascertain the actual costs and fees to which she would be subject in arbitration.

In this Court, Randolph's brief lists fees incurred in cases involving other arbitrations as reflected in opinions of other Courts of Appeals, while petitioners' counsel states that arbitration fees are frequently waived by petitioners. None of this information affords a sufficient basis for concluding that Randolph would in fact have incurred substantial costs in the event her claim went to arbitration.

7. We decline to reach respondent's argument that we may affirm the Court of Appeals' conclusion that the arbitration

The judgment of the Court of Appeals is affirmed in part and reversed in part.

JUSTICE GINSBURG, with whom JUSTICE STEVENS and JUSTICE SOUTER join, and with whom JUSTICE BREYER joins as to Parts I and III, concurring in part and dissenting in part.

I

I join Part II of the Court's opinion, which holds that the District Court's order, dismissing all the claims before it, was a "final," and therefore immediately appealable, decision. On the matter the Court airs in Part III, to this page—allocation of the costs of arbitration—I would not rule definitively. Instead, I would vacate the Eleventh Circuit's decision, which dispositively declared the arbitration clause unenforceable, and remand the case for closer consideration of the arbitral forum's accessibility.

II

The Court today deals with a "who pays" question, specifically, who pays for the arbitral forum. The Court holds that Larketta Randolph bears the burden of demonstrating that the arbitral forum is financially inaccessible to her. Essentially, the Court requires a party, situated as Randolph is, either to submit to arbitration without knowing who will pay for the forum or to demonstrate up front that the costs, if imposed on her, will be prohibitive. As I see it, the case in its current posture is not ripe for such a disposition.

The Court recognizes that "the existence of large arbitration costs could preclude a litigant such as Randolph from effectively vindicating her federal statutory rights in the arbitral forum.". But, the Court next determines, "the party resisting arbitration bears the burden of proving that the claims at issue are unsuitable for arbitration" and "Randolph did not meet that burden." In so ruling, the Court blends two discrete inquiries: First, is the arbitral forum *adequate* to adjudicate the claims at issue; second, is that forum *accessible* to the party resisting arbitration.

Our past decisions deal with the first question, the *adequacy* of the arbitral forum to adjudicate various statutory claims. See, *e.g., Gilmer v. Interstate/Johnson Lane Corp.,* 500 U.S. 20, 111 S.Ct. 1647, 114 L.Ed.2d 26 (1991) (Age Discrimination in Employment Act claims are amenable to arbitration); *Shearson/American Express Inc. v. McMahon,* 482 U.S. 220, 107 S.Ct. 2332, 96 L.Ed.2d 185 (1987) (Claims under Racketeer Influenced and Corrupt Organizations Act and Securities Exchange Act are amenable to arbitration). These decisions hold that the party resisting arbitration bears the burden of establishing the inadequacy of the arbitral forum for adjudication of claims of a particular genre. See

agreement is unenforceable on the alternative ground that the agreement precludes respondent from bringing her claims under the TILA as a class action. See Brief for Respondent 39–48. The Court of Appeals did not pass on this question, and we need not decide here issues not decided below.

Gilmer, 500 U.S., at 26, 111 S.Ct. 1647; *McMahon,* 482 U.S., at 227, 107 S.Ct. 2332. It does not follow like the night the day, however, that the party resisting arbitration should also bear the burden of showing that the arbitral forum would be financially inaccessible to her.

The arbitration agreement at issue is contained in a form contract drawn by a commercial party and presented to an individual consumer on a take-it-or-leave-it basis. The case on which the Court dominantly relies, *Gilmer,* also involved a nonnegotiated arbitration clause. But the "who pays" question presented in this case did not arise in *Gilmer.* Under the rules that governed in *Gilmer*—those of the New York Stock Exchange—it was the standard practice for securities industry parties, arbitrating employment disputes, to pay all of the arbitrators' fees. See *Cole v. Burns Int'l Security Servs.,* 105 F.3d 1465, 1483 (C.A.D.C.1997). Regarding that practice, the Court of Appeals for the District of Columbia Circuit recently commented:

> "[I]n *Gilmer,* the Supreme Court endorsed a system of arbitration in which employees are not required to pay for the arbitrator assigned to hear their statutory claims. There is no reason to think that the Court would have approved arbitration in the absence of this arrangement. Indeed, we are unaware of any situation in American jurisprudence in which a beneficiary of a federal statute has been required to pay for the services of the judge assigned to hear her or his case." *Id.,* at 1484.

III

The form contract in this case provides no indication of the rules under which arbitration will proceed or the costs a consumer is likely to incur in arbitration. Green Tree, drafter of the contract, could have filled the void by specifying, for instance, that arbitration would be governed by the rules of the American Arbitration Association (AAA). Under the AAA's Consumer Arbitration Rules, consumers in small-claims arbitration incur no filing fee and pay only $125 of the total fees charged by the arbitrator. All other fees and costs are to be paid by the business party. Other national arbitration organizations have developed similar models for fair cost and fee allocation. It may be that in this case, as in *Gilmer,* there is a standard practice on arbitrators' fees and expenses, one that fills the blank space in the arbitration agreement. Counsel for Green Tree offered a hint in that direction. See Tr. of Oral Arg. 26 ("Green Tree does pay [arbitration] costs in a lot of instances. . . ."). But there is no reliable indication in this record that Randolph's claim will be arbitrated under any consumer-protective fee arrangement.

As a repeat player in the arbitration required by its form contract, Green Tree has superior information about the cost to consumers of pursuing arbitration. Cf. *Raleigh v. Illinois Dept. of Revenue,* 530 U.S. 15, 21, 120 S.Ct. 1951, 147 L.Ed.2d 13 (2000) ("the very fact that the burden of proof has often been placed on the taxpayer [to disprove tax liability] . . . reflects several compelling rationales . . . [including] the taxpayer's readier access to the relevant information"); 9 J. Wigmore, Evidence § 2486 (J. Chadbourn rev. ed.1981) (where fairness so requires, burden of proof of a particular fact may be assigned to "party who presumably has peculiar means of knowledge" of the fact); Restatement (Second) of Contracts § 206 (1979) ("In choosing among the reasonable meanings of . . . [an] agreement or a term thereof, that meaning is generally preferred which operates against the [drafting] party. . . ."). In these circumstances, it is hardly clear that Randolph should bear the burden of demonstrating up front the arbitral forum's inaccessibility, or that she should be required to submit to arbitration without knowing how much it will cost her.

As I see it, the Court has reached out prematurely to resolve the matter in the lender's favor. If Green Tree's practice under the form contract with retail installment sales purchasers resembles that of the employer in *Gilmer,* Randolph would be insulated from prohibitive costs. And if the arbitral forum were in this case financially accessible to Randolph, there would be no occasion to reach the decision today rendered by the Court. Before writing a term into the form contract, as the District of Columbia Circuit did, see *Cole,* 105 F.3d, at 1485,[3] or leaving cost allocation initially to each arbitrator, as the Court does, I would remand for clarification of Green Tree's practice.

The Court's opinion, if I comprehend it correctly, does not prevent Randolph from returning to court, postarbitration, if she then has a complaint about cost allocation. If that is so, the issue reduces to when, not whether, she can be spared from payment of excessive costs. Neither certainty nor judicial economy is served by leaving that issue unsettled until the end of the line.

For the reasons stated, I dissent from the Court's reversal of the Eleventh Circuit's decision on the cost question. I would instead vacate and remand for further consideration of the accessibility of the arbitral forum to Randolph.

Notes

1. On remand, the Eleventh Circuit held that the arbitration term was enforceable even if it prevented the plaintiff from bringing the case as a class action. Randolph v. Green Tree Financial Corp.—Alabama, 244 F.3d 814 (11th Cir. 2001).

2. What impact will the principal case have on enforcement of TILA and other consumer protection legislation?

3. The Court's decision does not state how a consumer might show that a claim cannot be effectively vindicated because of the cost of arbitration. Lower courts have disagreed over the criteria to be used. Some have

---

3. The court interpreted a form contract to arbitrate employment disputes, silent as to costs, to require the employer "to pay all of the arbitrator's fees necessary for a full and fair resolution of [the discharged employee's] statutory claims." 105 F.3d, at 1485.

focused on the cost of arbitration and the financial circumstances of the particular consumer. See Camacho v. Holiday Homes, Inc., 167 F.Supp.2d 892 (W.D.Va. 2001) (plaintiff's financial circumstances did not permit her to pay for arbitration when arbitration rules required fee of $2,000 to proceed to evidentiary hearing plus parties would each bear half of arbitrator's expenses and fees, which typically range between $100 and $300 per hour); In re Hicks, 285 B.R. 317 (B.W.D.Okla. 2002) (cost of arbitration proceedings after first day to be borne by non-prevailing party and so might make arbitration inaccessible). Others have concentrated more on the cost of arbitration relative to litigation. See Torrance v. Aames Funding Corp., 242 F.Supp.2d 862 (D.Or. 2002) ("Requiring payment of arbitrator's fees, as opposed to reasonable costs, is not permitted as a condition of arbitration."); Ball v. SFX Broadcasting, Inc., 165 F.Supp.2d 230, 240 (N.D.N.Y. 2001) (employment case). Still others have melded these criteria. Thus, in Bradford v. Rockwell Semiconductor Systems, Inc., 238 F.3d 549, 556 (4th Cir. 2001), another employment case, the court established the following test:

> [T]he appropriate inquiry is one that evaluates whether the arbitral forum in a particular case is an adequate and accessible substitute to litigation, i.e., a case-by-case analysis that focuses, among other things, upon the claimant's ability to pay the arbitration fees and costs, the expected cost differential between arbitration and litigation in court, and whether that cost differential is so substantial as to deter the bringing of claims * * *

Might the cost of case-by-case litigation on the issue, as distinct from a bright-line rule, itself discourage litigants from challenging arbitration agreements, and thus effectively vindicating their rights? The attorneys representing the plaintiffs in Ting v. AT & T, *infra*, reportedly spent more than 2,000 hours on the case even before the appeal. See Jean R. Sternlight & Elizabeth J. Jensen, Using Arbitration to Eliminate Consumer Class Actions: Efficient Business Practice or Unconscionable Abuse? 67 Law & Contemp. Probs. 75, 100 (2004) (speculating that high cost of litigation prevents bringing of meritorious attacks on arbitration terms).

4. In determining if the cost of arbitration is prohibitive, is the cost of the good or service that is the arbitration's subject relevant? Brower v. Gateway 2000, 246 A.D.2d 246, 676 N.Y.S.2d 569, 570 (1st Dept. 1998), involved arbitration over a personal computer. The arbitration rules required payment of an advance fee of $4,000; of that fee, $2,000 was nonrefundable even if the consumer prevailed. Given the cost of personal computers, would it make sense for a consumer to file for arbitration?

5. When should a court determine that the cost of arbitration is prohibitive? In an employment case, one court decided that courts should compare the likely costs of arbitration to the likely costs of litigation at the beginning of the proceeding. See Cooper v. MRM Investment Co., 367 F.3d 493, 511 (2004) ("The issue is whether *the terms of the arbitration agreement itself* would deter a substantial number of similarly situated employees from bringing their claims in the arbitral forum.") (emphasis in original). Other courts have also approved the use of predictions of the cost. See, e.g. Morrison v. Circuit City Stores, Inc., 317 F.3d 646, 662–63 (6th Cir. 2003) (employment case in which court explained that "the *post hoc* judicial review

approach places plaintiffs in a kind of 'Catch–22.' They cannot claim, in advance of arbitration, that the risk of incurring arbitration costs would deter them from arbitrating their claims because they do not know what the costs will be, but if they arbitrate and actually incur costs, they cannot then argue that the costs deterred them because they have already arbitrated their claims."); Phillips v. Associates Home Equity Serv., Inc., 179 F.Supp.2d 840, 847 (N.D.Ill. 2001). How reliable are these estimates given that they come at the very outset of the proceedings and necessarily include a guess as to the length of the proceeding and perhaps also the arbitrator's hourly rate? By contrast, another court held in an employment case that the employee can satisfy the burden of showing that the cost of a provision obliging the loser to pay for the arbitration is prohibitive only at the end of the arbitration proceeding. See Musnick v. King Motor Co., 325 F.3d 1255 (11th Cir. 2003).

6. Some courts have dealt with the problem of costly arbitration by obliging the business to pay for it even though the arbitration clause required the consumer to bear some of the expense, see Smith v. Beneficial Ohio, Inc., 284 F.Supp.2d 875 (S.D.Ohio 2003) (arbitration clause contained severability provision), or ordering the consumer to comply with an arbitration agreement when the business has offered to bear the cost. See Livingston v. Associates Finance, Inc., 339 F.3d 553 (7th Cir. 2003); Large v. Conseco Finance Servicing Corp., 292 F.3d 49 (1st Cir. 2002). Does this amount to rewriting the parties' agreement? What empowers courts to do so?

7. Would a business be better off inserting information about arbitration costs in its standard contract, referring to rules that specify costs, or omitting cost information altogether? See R. Brian Tipton, Allocating the Costs of Arbitrating Statutory Claims Under the Federal Arbitration Act: An Unresolved Issue, 26 Am. J. Trial Advocacy 325 (2002).

8. Do consumers understand what they give up when they agree to arbitration? See Jean R. Sternlight, Panacea or Corportate Tool? Debunking the Supreme Court's Preference for Binding Arbitration, 74 Wash.U.L.Q. 637, 675 (1996) ("even a consumer who reads the clause might well lack the legal sophistication to understand its significance, perhaps not recognizing that appeals from arbitration are virtually unwinnable and that little or no discovery may be made available in an arbitration proceeding."). What alternatives would they have if they did understand?

9. Do consumers benefit when businesses save money from arbitration? As for the savings for businesses, see Stephen J. Ware, Paying the Price of Process: Judicial Regulation of Consumer Arbitration Agreements, 2001 J. Disp. Resol. 89:

> First, arbitration does away with juries and, for that reason, is commonly thought to reduce the likelihood of high damages awards against businesses. Second, arbitration's confidentiality "lessens the risk of adverse publicity" about a business and its disputes. Third, arbitration can resolve disputes "according to a nationally uniform set of procedures," thus saving interstate businesses the costs of adapting to different procedural rules in different states. Fourth, arbitration's finality (near absence of appellate review) saves businesses the costs of appeals.

Fifth, arbitration can eliminate the possibility of class actions against businesses. Sixth, arbitration can deter claims against businesses by requiring consumer-plaintiffs to pay arbitrator fees, as well as filing fees that exceed the filing fees in litigation. Seventh, arbitration can reduce the amount of discovery available to consumer-plaintiffs, thus reducing the amount of time and money businesses must spend on the discovery process and also making it harder for consumers to prove their claims.

Professor Ware argues that when businesses reduce their dispute-resolution costs, they are able to pass the savings along to consumers in the form of lower prices. Cf. Stiles v. Home Cable Concepts, Inc., 994 F.Supp. 1410 (M.D. Ala. 1998) (lender reduced interest rate by 2% for consumers who agreed to arbitration). Accordingly, in Professor Ware's view, to the extent lawmakers impair the ability of businesses to obtain these advantages, they increase consumer prices. Should that have an impact on the willingness of courts to sustain challenges to arbitration clauses? Similarly, should courts considering whether the cost of arbitration makes it unaffordable take into account the savings streamlined arbitration procedures may provide? See Bradford v. Rockwell Semiconductor Systems, Inc., 238 F.3d 549, 556 (4th Cir. 2001) ("we fail to see how a claimant could be deterred from pursuing his statutory rights in arbitration simply by the fact that his fees would be paid to the arbitrator where the overall cost of arbitration is otherwise equal to or less than the cost of litigation in court."). Might consumers be better off if some procedures—such as discovery—are not streamlined?

10.   Are consumers better off in other ways with arbitration? See Eric J. Mogilnicki & Kirk D. Jensen, Arbitration and Unconscionability, 19 Ga. St.U.L.Rev.761, 766–67 (2003) ("Arbitration is more convenient than litigation. . . . Arbitration is also faster than litigation. . . . Arbitration is also less expensive than litigation."); Ernst & Young, Outcomes of Arbitration: An Empirical Study of Consumer Lending Cases 2, 15 (2004) (study of consumer arbitrations found that consumers prevailed in 55% of arbitrations and reached satisfactory settlement or dismissed case in additional 24% of cases; the authors concluded that the study "appear[s] to refute claims that the arbitration process is biased towards the business."). Cf. Michael Delikat & Morris M. Kleiner, An Empirical Study of Dispute Resolution Mechanisms: Where Do Plaintiffs Better Vindicate Their Rights? 58–JAN Disp. Resol.J. 56 (2003–2004) (study finds that claimants in employment cases have higher success rate in arbitration than in cases litigated in federal court).

11.   The right to a jury trial is rooted in the Seventh Amendment to the Constitution. Have courts been sufficiently protective of this right in enforcing arbitration terms? Compare Jean R. Sternlight, Mandatory Binding Arbitration and the Demise of the Seventh Amendment Right to a Jury Trial, 16 Ohio St. J. on Disp. Resol. 669 (2001) (giving a negative answer) with Stephen J. Ware, Arbitration Clauses, Jury–Waiver Clauses, and Other Contractual Waivers of Constitutional Rights, 67–SPG Law & Contemp. Probs. 167 (2004) (giving a positive answer).

TING v. AT&T

United States Court of Appeals, Ninth Circuit, 2003.
319 F.3d 1126, cert. denied, 540 U.S. 811, 124 S.Ct. 53, 157 L.Ed.2d 24 (2003).

TASHIMA, CIRCUIT JUDGE:

Darcy Ting, individually and on behalf of all others similarly situated, and Consumer Action, a non-profit membership organization, both as private attorneys general, brought suit against AT&T, alleging that AT&T's Consumer Services Agreement ("CSA") violates California's Consumer Legal Remedies Act and that state's Unfair Practices Act by barring customers from, among other things, pursuing claims against AT&T on a classwide basis. Finding the CSA unconscionable and in violation of California public policy, the district court issued a permanent injunction against enforcement of sections 4 and 7 of the CSA. *See Ting v. AT&T,* 182 F.Supp.2d 902 (N.D.Cal.2002). AT & T appeals on the ground that the application of California's consumer protection laws is preempted by the Federal Communications Act and the Federal Arbitration Act. We have jurisdiction pursuant to 28 U.S.C. § 1291, and we affirm in part and reverse in part.

BACKGROUND

* * *

[AT&T began replacing its published tariffs with a Customer Service Agreement ("CSA") in California in 2000.] * * * AT&T's CSA included a series of provisions designed to limit customers' rights and remedies in the event of a dispute with AT&T. These provisions are contained in sections 4 and 7 of the CSA and are collectively known as the "Legal Remedies Provisions." Section 4 limits AT&T's liability for claims other than negligence to the amount of charges for service during the affected period and precludes liability for punitive, reliance, special, and consequential damages. Section 7(a) mandates binding arbitration and bans all class-wide dispute resolution.[4] The CSA also contains a secrecy provision for all arbitration proceedings and requires consumers to bring all claims within a two-year limitations period.

---

4. Section 7, captioned "Dispute Resolution," sets forth procedures for resolving customer disputes. In approximately eight-point font (replicated below), section 7(a) provides in part:

THIS SECTION PROVIDES FOR RESOLUTION OF DISPUTES THROUGH FINAL AND BINDING ARBITRATION BEFORE A NEUTRAL ARBITRATOR INSTEAD OF IN A COURT BY A JUDGE OR JURY OR THROUGH A CLASS ACTION. YOU CONTINUE TO HAVE CERTAIN RIGHTS TO OBTAIN RELIEF FROM A FEDERAL OR STATE REGULATORY AGENCY.

NO DISPUTE MAY BE JOINED WITH ANOTHER LAWSUIT, OR IN AN ARBITRATION WITH A DISPUTE OF ANY OTHER PERSON, OR RESOLVED ON A CLASS WIDE BASIS. THE ARBITRATOR MAY NOT AWARD DAMAGES THAT ARE NOT EXPRESSLY AUTHORIZED BY THIS AGREEMENT AND MAY NOT AWARD PUNITIVE DAMAGES OR ATTORNEYS' FEES UNLESS SUCH DAMAGES ARE EXPRESSLY AUTHORIZED BY A STATUTE. YOU AND AT & T BOTH WAIVE ANY CLAIMS FOR AN AWARD OF DAMAGES THAT ARE EXCLUDED UNDER THIS AGREEMENT.

Before presenting the CSA to its customers, AT&T conducted extensive market research designed to predict how consumers would react to the CSA, which AT & T planned to mail with a cover letter and a set of frequently asked questions. AT&T's cover letter stated in bold text **"[P]lease be assured that your AT & T service or billing will not change under the AT&T Consumer Services Agreement; there's nothing you need to do."** AT&T's market study concluded that most customers "would stop reading and discard the letter" after reading this disclaimer. AT&T did not change the substance of the letter as a result of its market research—indeed, internal AT & T documents indicate that the letter was specifically intended to make customers less alert to the details of the CSA.

AT&T mailed the CSA in two separate mailings. To approximately 18 million of its residential, long-distance customers, AT&T included the materials in the envelope that contained the customer's monthly bill. No statement regarding the new agreement appeared on the outside of the envelope. To its remaining 42 million residential, long-distance customers, AT&T mailed the CSA and other materials in a separate envelope marked, "ATTENTION: Important information concerning your AT&T service enclosed." According to AT&T's research, only 25 percent of its customers were likely to open the separate mailing, approximately 10 percent would not even look at it, and only 30 percent would actually read the entire contract.

Sometime in July 2001, plaintiff Ting received, opened, and read the mailing from AT&T. Like most of AT&T's customers, she was not aware of AT&T's obligation under mandatory detariffing to forge contracts with its residential customers and was not expecting a contract from AT&T. The CSA and letter advised customers that by continuing to use or to pay for AT&T's service, the customer was accepting the terms of the CSA through the so-called "negative option". The second paragraph of the CSA itself provided that, in the event a customer did not wish to be bound by the CSA, the customer could call a toll-free number and cancel his or her AT&T service. The cover letter advised customers that the CSA described AT&T's "new binding arbitration process, which used an objective third party rather than a jury for resolving any disputes that may arise." The letter never mentioned the word "contract," but instead spoke of "providing information" to customers. Finally, the CSA did not include a provision informing customers that federal law would govern its relationship with AT&T, but instead included an express New York state law choice-of-law provision.

Plaintiffs Ting and Consumer Action brought a state-court class action against AT&T for declaratory and injunctive relief, alleging that the Legal Remedies Provisions violate California's consumer protection and contract laws. AT&T argued that it had satisfied California's contract-formation requirements as required in the Second Report and Order, 11 F.C.C.R. 20,730, at ¶ 77, and that in any event, plaintiffs' substantive challenges to the lawfulness of the CSA were preempted by the Communications Act. After concluding that the Legal Remedies

Provisions violated California's public policy and unconscionability law, the district court concluded that neither § 201(b) nor § 202(a) of the 1934 Act preempted state law in the detariffed environment because Congress removed the filing requirement with the intention of ending the preemptive regime of the filed rate doctrine.

* * *

DISCUSSION

* * *

II. California Law

We next consider AT & T's claim that even if federal law does not preempt Ting's state law challenges, California law does not render the Legal Remedies Provisions unenforceable. The district court enjoined sections 4 and 7 of the CSA on two grounds. First, the district court held that the CSA's two-year limitations period for bringing claims, as well as the bar on class actions, were unenforceable under the anti-waiver provisions of the CLRA. Next, the district court concluded that four aspects of sections 4 and 7 of the CSA were procedurally and substantively unconscionable.

A. Consumer Legal Remedies Act

[The court held that the CLRA does not invalidate the CSA's arbitration provision.]

B. Unconscionability

In California, a contract or clause is unenforceable if it is both procedurally and substantively unconscionable. *See Armendariz v. Found. Health Psychcare Servs., Inc.*, 24 Cal.4th 83, 99 Cal.Rptr.2d 745, 6 P.3d 669, 690 (2000); *Circuit City v. Adams*, 279 F.3d 889, 893 (9th Cir.2002) (citing *Stirlen v. Supercuts, Inc.*, 51 Cal.App.4th 1519, 60 Cal.Rptr.2d 138, 145 (1997)). Pursuant to *Armendariz*, courts apply a sliding scale: "the more substantively oppressive the contract term, the less evidence of procedural unconscionability is required to come to the conclusion that the term is unenforceable, and vice versa." 99 Cal. Rptr.2d 745, 6 P.3d at 690; *Soltani v. W. & S. Life Ins. Co.*, 258 F.3d 1038, 1042 (9th Cir.2001).

1. Procedural Unconscionability

A contract is procedurally unconscionable if it is a contract of adhesion, *i.e.*, a standardized contract, drafted by the party of superior bargaining strength, that relegates to the subscribing party only the opportunity to adhere to the contract or reject it. *Armendariz*, 99 Cal.Rptr.2d 745, 6 P.3d at 690 (citing *Neal v. State Farm Ins. Co.*, 188 Cal.App.2d 690, 10 Cal.Rptr. 781 (1961)); *see also Circuit City*, 279 F.3d at 893; *Flores v. Transamerica HomeFirst, Inc.*, 93 Cal.App.4th 846, 113 Cal.Rptr.2d 376, 382 (2001) ("A finding of a contract of adhesion is essentially a finding of procedural unconscionability."). In finding the CSA procedurally unconscionable, the district court emphasized that, after drafting the agreement, AT&T imposed the CSA on its customers without opportunity for negotiation, modification, or waiver. We agree. AT&T mailed the CSA in an envelope that few customers realized contained a contract, and offered its terms on a take-it-or-leave-it basis. *Cf. Flores,* 93 Cal.App.4th at 853–54 (holding that generic arbitration clauses contained in loan agreement and deed of trust constituted a contract of adhesion because offered without opportunity for negotiation).

AT&T responds that the district court ignored the fact that the third largest carrier, Verizon, had no arbitration agreement in their contract and that consumers therefore had the option of rejecting AT&T's CSA and switching to a competitor. Even if this is the case, and even assuming such alternatives matter under California law, *see Armendariz,* 99 Cal.Rptr.2d 745, 6 P.3d at 691 (rejecting contention that availability of alternative sources of supply affects the procedural unconscionability analysis), it nonetheless fails to overcome the district court's well-founded conclusion that the CSA is a procedurally unconscionable contract. *See Szetela v. Discover Bank,* 97 Cal.App.4th 1094, 118 Cal. Rptr.2d 862, 867 (2002) ("Szetela received the amendment to the Cardholder Agreement in a bill stuffer.... His only option, if he did not wish to accept the amendment, was to close his account. [This] establishes the necessary element of procedural unconscionability."). Indeed, if customers complained about the arbitration provision, AT&T responded with a letter informing them that "all other major long distance carriers have included an arbitration provision in their services agreement." Consequently, if consumers had meaningful choices, AT&T intentionally dissuaded its own customers from seeking them. *See Flores,* 93 Cal.App.4th at 853 (finding procedural unconscionability in part because "HomeFirst's representative told plaintiffs that HomeFirst was the only company in California offering reverse mortgages, thereby indicating that plaintiffs had no real choice of alternate lenders").

2. *Substantive Unconscionability*

Substantive unconscionability focuses on the one-sidedness of the contract terms. *Armendariz,* 99 Cal.Rptr.2d 745, 6 P.3d at 690; *Flores,* 93 Cal.App.4th at 854. Where an arbitration agreement is concerned, the agreement is unconscionable unless the arbitration remedy contains a "modicum of bilaterality." *Armendariz,* 99 Cal.Rptr.2d 745, 6 P.3d at 692. "Although parties are free to contract for asymmetrical remedies and arbitration clauses of varying scope ... the doctrine of unconscionability limits the extent to which a stronger party may, through a contract of adhesion, impose the arbitration forum on the weaker party without accepting that forum for itself." *Id.* In determining whether an arbitration agreement is sufficiently bilateral, courts assessing California law look beyond facial neutrality and examine the actual effects of the challenged provision. *See Acorn v. Household Int'l, Inc.,* 211 F.Supp.2d 1160, 1172 (N.D.Cal.2002); *Szetela,* 118 Cal.Rptr.2d at 868.

The district court declared unconscionable four aspects of the CSA: (1) the bar on class actions, (2) the arbitration fee scheme, (3) the secrecy provision, and (4) the limitation on willful misconduct.[13]

a.   Class Action Provision

In *Szetela,* 97 Cal.App.4th 1094, 118 Cal.Rptr.2d 862, the California Court of Appeal recently considered the conscionability of a class action ban in a contract of adhesion. *Id.* at 867. The court stated that "[a]lthough styled as a mutual prohibition on representative or class actions, it is difficult to envision the circumstances under which the provision might negatively impact [defendant] Discover [Card], because credit card companies typically do not sue their customers in class-action lawsuits." *Id.* Given the actual effects of the provision, the court found the class action ban "manifest[ly] one-sided[ ]" and therefore substantively unconscionable. *Id.*

The district court below adopted similar reasoning, as have most other courts to consider the issue. *See Luna v. Household Fin. Corp. III,* 2002 WL 31487425, *9 (W.D.Wash. Nov.4, 2002); *Acorn,* 211 F.Supp.2d at 1172; *Mandel v. Household Bank,* 105 Cal.App.4th 75, 129 Cal.Rptr.2d 380, 2003 WL 57282, at *4 (2003) (applying Nevada law); *Mercuro v. Superior Court,* 96 Cal.App.4th 167, 116 Cal.Rptr.2d 671, 678 (2002) (arbitration forum, though equally applicable to both parties, relevant to finding of unconscionability because "repeat player effect" rendered provision disadvantageous to weaker party). It is not only difficult to imagine AT & T bringing a class action against its own customers, but AT & T fails to allege that it has ever or would ever do so. Instead, it raises a number of alternative challenges to the district court's holding. However, because "bilaterality" is a requirement in all California arbitration agreements, *see Armendariz,* 6 P.3d at 692; *Circuit City,* 279 F.3d at 893, we affirm the district court's conclusion that the class-action ban violates California's unconscionability law.

b.   Fee–Splitting Scheme

The CSA requires customers to split the arbitrator's fees with AT & T. In enjoining the provision as unconscionable, the district found that while the majority of complainants would be handled satisfactorily either by customer service representatives or subsidized arbitration, some complainants would hypothetically face prohibitive arbitration costs, effectively deterring them from vindicating their statutory rights.

In *Circuit City,* 279 F.3d 889, we recently applied California law in declaring a similar fee-splitting scheme unenforceable. *Id.* at 894. That case is indistinguishable from the one at bench. Here, the scheme is unconscionable because it imposes on some consumers costs greater than

---

13.   AT&T subsequently amended the CSA to eliminate the language limiting its liability for willful misconduct. AT&T also re-wrote the confidentiality provision. On appeal, AT&T challenges the district court's judgment enjoining the provisions on the sole ground that the court erred in not rewriting the provisions. Yet the district court reasonably concluded that because the Legal Remedies Provisions were so "permeated with unconscionability and illegality," they could not as a whole be saved or reformed. The court did not abuse its discretion in so concluding.

those a complainant would bear if he or she would file the same complaint in court. * * *

Our decision is also consistent with the FAA. AT & T contends that the district court "singled out" arbitration agreements for special treatment by declaring the provision unconscionable simply because it would require customers to share some of the costs. However, parties that agree to arbitrate statutory claims still are entitled to basic procedural and remedial protections so that they can effectively realize their statutory rights. *Circuit City,* 279 F.3d at 895 (citing *Gilmer v. Interstate/Johnson Lane Corp.,* 500 U.S. 20, 111 S.Ct. 1647, 114 L.Ed.2d 26 (1991)); *Cole,* 105 F.3d at 1482. Among these protections is the assurance that an individual need not "pay either unreasonable costs or any arbitrators' fees *or* expenses as a condition of access to the arbitration forum." *Cole,* 105 F.3d at 1482 (emphasis in the original) (listing five basic requirements that arbitration forum must meet). Additionally, because unconscionability is a defense to contracts generally and does not single out arbitration agreements for special scrutiny, it may be raised consistent with § 2 of the FAA. *Doctor's Assocs.,* 517 U.S. at 688, 116 S.Ct. 1652.

c. Confidentiality Provision

The CSA's confidentiality provision requires "[a]ny arbitration [to] remain confidential." Although facially neutral, confidentiality provisions usually favor companies over individuals. In *Cole,* 105 F.3d 1465, the D.C. Circuit recognized that because companies continually arbitrate the same claims, the arbitration process tends to favor the company. *Id.* at 1476. Yet because of plaintiffs' lawyers and arbitration appointing agencies like the AAA, who can scrutinize arbitration awards and accumulate a body of knowledge on a particular company, the court discounted the likelihood of any harm occurring from the "repeat player" effect. *Id.* at 1486. We conclude, however, that if the company succeeds in imposing a gag order, plaintiffs are unable to mitigate the advantages inherent in being a repeat player. This is particularly harmful here, because the contract at issue affects seven million Californians. Thus, AT&T has placed itself in a far superior legal posture by ensuring that none of its potential opponents have access to precedent while, at the same time, AT&T accumulates a wealth of knowledge on how to negotiate the terms of its own unilaterally crafted contract. Further, the unavailability of arbitral decisions may prevent potential plaintiffs from obtaining the information needed to build a case of intentional misconduct or unlawful discrimination against AT&T. For these reasons, we hold that the district court did not err in finding the secrecy provision unconscionable.

* * *

CONCLUSION

In sum, we affirm the district court's conclusion that the Legal Remedies Provisions are unenforceable as unconscionable under California law, the application of which is not preempted by §§ 201(b) and 202(a) of the Federal Communications Act. The FAA preempts the CLRA's anti-waiver provision. We therefore reverse the district court's conclusion that the CLRA renders void the CSA's class action ban and two-year limitations period. Because the district court did not find the two-year limitations period unconscionable, this aspect of the CSA is revived. The other provisions remain unenforceable as originally drafted. We, of course, do not rule on the legality of any changes to the CSA since the district court's decision.

Notes

1. In Green Tree Financial Corp. v. Bazzle, 539 U.S. 444, 123 S.Ct. 2402, 156 L.Ed.2d 414 (2003), a plurality of the Court ruled that when an arbitration clause does not bar class-wide arbitration, the decision of whether to permit the arbitration to proceed as a class action is left to the arbitrator as a matter of interpretation of the parties' contract. The arbitrator in *Bazzle* reportedly later decided that the arbitration agreements permitted class-wide arbitration. Scott L. Nelson, Bazzle, Class Actions, and Arbitration: An Unfinished Story in Tenth Annual Consumer Financial Services Litigation Institute (Practising law Institute 2005). After *Bazzle*, if you were counsel to a business that included an arbitration clause in its customer agreements identical to the one used in *Randolph*, what advice would you offer your client? The *Bazzle* plurality did not specifically address whether a term banning class actions would be enforceable, but some commentators have predicted that the Supreme Court would enforce such a ban. See Alan S. Kaplinsky & Mark J. Levin, Arbitration Update: Green Tree Financial Corp v. Bazzle—Dazzle for Green Tree, Fizzle for Practitioners, 59 Bus. Law. 165, 1272 (2004).

2. What is left of the *Ting* court's statements that the class action ban is unconscionable after the *Bazzle* decision? As for the precedential value of the *Bazzle* plurality opinion, compare Employers Ins. Co. of Wausau v. Century Indem. Co., 443 F.3d 573 (7th Cir. 2006) with Pedcor Management Co. v. Nations Personnel of Texas, Inc., 343 F.3d 355 (5th Cir. 2003). Courts upholding class action bans include Jenkins v. First Am. Cash Advance of Ga., LLC, 400 F.3d 868 (11th Cir.), rehearing and rehearing en banc denied, 143 Fed. Appx. 311 (11th Cir. 2005), cert. denied, ___ U.S. ___, 126 S.Ct. 1457, 164 L.Ed.2d 132 (2006); Livingston v. Associates Fin., Inc., 339 F.3d 553 (7th Cir. 2003); Iberia Credit Bureau, Inc. v. Cingular Wireless, 379 F.3d 159 (5th Cir. 2004). Why do you suppose they reach a different conclusion from *Ting*? Courts finding such clauses unconscionable at least in some circumstances include Leonard v. Terminix International Co., LLP, 854 So.2d 529 (Ala. 2003); Discover Bank v. Superior Court, 36 Cal.4th 148, 30 Cal.Rptr.3d 76, 113 P.3d 1100 (2005); Kinkel v. Cingular Wireless, LLC, 357 Ill.App.3d 556, 293 Ill.Dec. 502, 828 N.E.2d 812 (2005), aff'd, Kinkel v. Cingular Wireless LLC, 223 Ill.2d 1, 306 Ill.Dec. 157, 857 N.E.2d 250 (2006). Can firms use choice-of-law provisions to insure that challenges to class action bans will be rejected? See Discover Bank v. Superior Court, 134 Cal.App.4th 886, 36 Cal.Rptr.3d 456 (2005) (on remand from California Supreme Court's decision invalidating class action waiver in consumer

arbitration contract, the Court of Appeals relied on a Delaware choice-of-law clause, among other things, to conclude that Delaware law applied and that Delaware would enforce the class action waiver). In determining whether a ban on class-wide arbitration is unconscionable, would it matter whether consumers have other opportunities to seek vindication of their rights, such as involving regulators or suing in small claims courts? See *Iberia, supra* (noting that state regulators could pursue restitution for injured consumers). Would a contract term banning the use of class actions in court litigation be enforceable? If not, why should the same term be given effect in arbitration?

3. Among the organizations providing arbitration services are the American Arbitration Association ("AAA"), Judicial Arbitration and Mediation Services ("JAMS") and the National Arbitration Forum. AAA and JAMS have adopted class action procedures which can be found at http://www.adr.org/sp.asp?id=21936 and http://www.jamsadr.com/rules/class _action.asp, respectively. In November, 2004, JAMS announced that it would not enforce class action preclusion clauses in arbitrations, but in March 2005 it issued a press release, available at http://www.jamsadr.com/press/show _release.asp?id=198, stating that it was withdrawing its policy. In the meantime, several credit card issuers had reportedly deleted JAMS from their list of arbitration providers. See Erick Bergquist, JAMS Backs Down on Class–Action Arbitration, Am. Banker, March 11, 2005 at 1. The initial JAMS decision is criticized in Kirk D. Jensen, Can Financial Institutions be Required to Arbitrate on a Class–Wide Basis Notwithstanding Provisions that Prohibit Class Arbitration? 122 Banking L. J. 328 (2005) (arguing that arbitrators cannot impose arbitral class action when parties' agreement bans class actions). For a review of the fees of these organizations, see Mark E. Budnitz, The High Cost of Mandatory Consumer Arbitration, 67 Law & Contemp. Probs. 133 (2004).

4. Do courts have an interest in the enforceability of class action bans in arbitration contracts?

5. Are consumers helped by class action bans? Consider the following:

It is practically beyond dispute that a prohibition against class arbitration is an essential part of the arbitration agreement from the institution's perspective. One of the reasons financial institutions and other businesses incorporate arbitration agreements into their consumer contracts is to shield themselves from frivolous class action litigation. Given the stakes often involved, the certification of a class—even when the claims are wholly without merit—creates massive pressure on a company to settle. * * * There is also good reason to believe that a prohibition on class arbitration is essential to an arbitration agreement from a consumer's perspective. Class treatment inevitably delays the resolution of a claim in arbitration. Such delays may harm consumers—particularly working families and seniors—who cannot afford to wait longer for resolution of their claims. In addition, the less formal procedures in arbitration, which are designed for and work well in individual arbitrations, may raise concerns about whether the rights of absent class members are sufficiently protected. Furthermore, consumers who have been promised that they will not be part of a class arbitration might ignore, in reliance on that promise, notices from an arbitrator and opportunities to opt out of any class, reasonably believing that any arbitration award will not be binding on or have preclusive effect regarding them. From a consumer's perspective, a provision that facilitates quick and efficient resolution of claims while simultaneously protecting the consumer's due process rights surely is essential to the arbitration agreement.

Kirk D. Jensen, Can Financial Institutions be Required to Arbitrate on a Class–Wide Basis Notwithstanding Provisions that Prohibit Class Arbitration? 122 Banking L. J. 328, 340–41 (2005).* See also Christopher R. Drahozal, "Unfair" Arbitration Clauses, 2001 U.Ill.L.Rev. 695, 754 ("class actions too often may not achieve their theoretical benefits.").

6. Can *Ting* be reconciled with Hill v. Gateway in Chapter Three *supra*?

7. Are contracts that oblige consumers but not complaining businesses to submit to arbitration unconscionable? Compare Anderson v. Delta Funding Corp., 316 F. Supp. 2d 554, 566–67 (N.D. Ohio 2004) (lack of mutuality does not render clause unconscionable if underlying agreement supported by consideration) with Iberia Credit Bureau, Inc. v. Cingular Wireless, 379 F.3d 159 (5th Cir. 2004) (unconscionable) and Wisconsin Auto Title Loans, Inc. v. Jones, 290 Wis.2d 514, 714 N.W.2d 155 (2006) (unconscionable).

8. For a case disagreeing with *Ting* about the enforceability of a confidentiality clause in an arbitration agreement, see Iberia Credit Bureau, Inc. v. Cingular Wireless LLC, 379 F.3d 159, 175–76 (5th Cir. 2004).

9. Can forum selection clauses in arbitration agreements render the term unconscionable? Compare Patterson v. ITT Consumer Fin. Corp., 14 Cal.App.4th 1659, 18 Cal.Rptr.2d 563 (1993), cert. denied, 510 U.S. 1176, 114 S.Ct. 1217, 127 L.Ed.2d 563 (1994) (clause providing for arbitration in Minneapolis, Minnesota unconscionable when transaction occurred in San Francisco, California. and involved small claims); and Comb v. PayPal, Inc., 218 F.Supp.2d 1165 (N.D.Ca. 2002) with Doctor's Associates, Inc. v. Hamilton, 150 F.3d 157 (2d Cir. 1998), cert. denied, 525 U.S. 1103, 119 S.Ct. 867, 142 L.Ed.2d 769 (1999) (clause in franchise agreement that required New Jersey franchisee to arbitrate in Connecticut not unconscionable). Should the rules for enforcing forum selection clauses in arbitration agreements differ from the rules for enforcing such clauses in contracts that do not provide for arbitration? A leading case, Carnival Cruise Lines, Inc. v. Shute, 499 U.S. 585, 111 S.Ct. 1522, 113 L.Ed.2d 622 (1991), provides that forum selection clauses are enforceable as long as they are reasonable and not fundamentally unfair, even if they appear in an adhesion contract. Is the different treatment accorded forum selection clauses in arbitration and litigation an example of judicial hostility to arbitration? See Susan Randall, Judicial Attitudes Toward Arbitration and the Resurgence of Unconscionability, 52 Buff. L. Rev. 185 (2004) (arguing courts are quicker to find arbitration clauses unconscionable than other terms). Cf. Jeffrey W. Stempel, Arbitration, Unconscionability, and Equilibrium: The Return of Unconscionability Analysis as a Counterweight to Arbitration Formalism, 19 Ohio St. J. on Disp. Resol. 757, 766, 859 (2004) (arguing that lower courts have

* Reprinted with permission.

"gradually reacted [to the Supreme Court's arbitration rulings] in a manner designed to achieve greater equilibrium between drafters and nondrafters of arbitration terms" by using the unconscionability doctrine to " 'tap[] the brakes' on arbitration rather than allowing contractual proponents of arbitration clause to accelerate to the degree that might have been initially suggested by the Court's cheerleading for arbitration."). For the argument that courts in California and the Ninth Circuit are using unconscionability as a vehicle for their hostility towards arbitration, see Michael G. McGuinness & Adam J. Karr, California's "Unique" Approach to Arbitration: Why This Road Less Traveled Will Make All the Difference on the Issue of Preemption Under the Federal Arbitration Act, 2005 J. Disp. Resol. 61.

10. Why do courts use both the effective vindication test and the unconscionability doctrine to invalidate arbitration clauses? They seem to overlap, do they not?

11. The repeat-player problem mentioned by the *Ting* court in connection with the confidentiality clause has other ramifications as well. Arbitrators and providers of arbitration services can continue providing their services only if selected by the parties. Businesses are unlikely to select arbitrators who persistently rule for consumers. What impact do you think that would have on arbitrators? Compare Richard M. Alderman, Pre–Dispute Mandatory Arbitration in Consumer Contracts: A Call for Reform, 38 Hous. L. Rev. 1237 (2001) ("even though anecdotal, the evidence seems to support the conclusion that, consciously or not, arbitrators tend to favor the repeat-player whose continued business is essential for their financial success.") with Robert Alexander Schwartz, Can Arbitration Do More for Consumers? The TILA Class Action Reconsidered, 78 N.Y.U.L.Rev. 809, 823 (2003) ("Even if complainants are not repeat players, their attorneys likely will be. It would seem, then, that arbitrators' economic self-interest would lead them to craft an arbitration process that is efficient and accessible, so that complainants—and plaintiffs' attorneys specializing in these kinds of disputes—would actually use it.") and Christopher R. Drahozal, "Unfair" Arbitration Clauses, 2001 U.Ill.L.Rev. 695, 769 ("arbitration institutions have a strong incentive to enhance the fairness of the process in order to assure users that their arbitration awards will be enforceable.").

12. Is it possible to write an arbitration clause that can survive a challenge before even the most critical court? See Christopher A. Taravella, John C. Tracy, Kathleen Moran, An Annotated Arbitration Clause, 56 Consumer Fin. L.Q.Rep. 263 (2002). If so, is it just a matter of time before all challenges to arbitration fail? If so, what impact will arbitration clauses have on the use of class actions in consumer disputes and the viability of litigation under such consumer protection statutes as TILA? See Myriam Gilles, Opting Out of Liability: The Forthcoming, Near–Total Demise of the Modern Class Action, 104 Mich. L. Rev. 373 (2005). Would the demise of the class action be a bad thing for consumers? If so, how can it be prevented? Critics of consumer class actions claim that governmental agencies are better suited to enforcing consumer rights than private attorneys general and that attorneys use class actions abusively to extort large settlements, thereby driving up costs for other consumers. See Alan S. Kaplinsky, The Use of Pre–Dispute Arbitration Agreements by Consumer Financial Services Pro-

viders in the Eleventh Annual Consumer Financial Services Litigation Inst. (PLI 2006).

13. Is it ethical for attorneys to counsel their business clients to include arbitration clauses in contracts with consumers? If it is in the business's best interest to add such terms to their agreements, is it ethical for the attorney not to so counsel the client? Compare Paul D. Carrington, Unconscionable Lawyers, 19 Ga. St.U.L.Rev. 361 (2002) (questioning ethics of lawyers who advise business clients to include arbitration terms in consumer contracts) with Eric J. Mogilnicki & Kirk D. Jensen, Arbitration and Unconscionability, 19 Ga. St.U.L.Rev.761 (2003) ("lawyers not only act ethically when they advise clients regarding arbitration provisions, but would be remiss if they failed to do so."). How would you advise your business clients in such circumstances? Would you include an arbitration clause in your retainer agreement? Why or why not? Would that be in the best interests of your clients?

14. Suppose a consumer claims that a contract containing an arbitration clause is void because the contract itself violates criminal laws. Must an arbitrator decide whether the contract is void, or can a court resolve the issue? In Buckeye Check Cashing, Inc. v. Cardegna, 546 U.S. 440, 126 S.Ct. 1204, 163 L.Ed.2d 1038 (2006), consumers sought to have a court decide whether a contract that allegedly violated criminal usury laws was void, arguing that if the contract itself was illegal, its provisions—including the arbitration clause—should not be enforceable. The Supreme Court disagreed, ruling that questions as to the enforceability of the entire contract, as distinct from the arbitration clause itself, must be submitted to an arbitrator.

15. In 2006, Congress enacted 10 U.S.C. § 987, which bars the enforceability of arbitration terms in loans to soldiers and their dependents. Why should soldiers be treated differently from civilians in this regard? Writing on the Consumer Law and Policy Blog at http://pubcit.typepad.com/clpblog/2006/09/defense_departm.html, attorney Paul Bland asked "If Congress recognizes that binding mandatory arbitration provisions are unfair as applied to all members of the military who deal with lenders, how does that jibe with the assertion often made that binding arbitration is fairer, cheaper, and better for other consumers who deal with lenders?" How would you respond to Bland?

Problem 10–15

You are an arbitrator in the case of Digg v. Dela Services Inc. Digg, whose claim does not involve a large sum, has moved to have a class certified. The parties' contract—Dela's standard agreement, which provides for arbitration—does not mention class actions, nor do the arbitration rules governing the proceeding. Dela opposes the motion. You believe that if the case were proceeding in court, it would satisfy the requirements for a class action. Who decides the motion? If the motion is properly addressed to you, would you grant it? Would you face an ethical problem in doing so? See Lawrence Young, Hot Topics for Consumer Class Actions in Tenth Annual Consumer Financial Services Litigation

Institute (Practising Law Institute 2005). Do you see any practical problems in granting the motion?

Problem 10–16

You operate an arbitration service. All of your business comes because of lenders that have designated your service as the arbitrator in their consumer lending contracts. Recently, however, one of the lenders, without explanation, amended its contracts to switch to a different arbitration provider, Smith Arbitrators. You are concerned because your service will not survive if the other lenders designating your service were also to switch to other providers. Accordingly, you are comparing your service to Smith's to see if you can identify strategies which would enable you to retain your existing business and perhaps expand it. Among the things you have noticed:

1. You employ as arbitrators some lawyers who formerly represented consumers and other lawyers who formerly represented lenders (though they do not arbitrate disputes involving their former clients). Smith employs only lawyers who formerly represented lenders.

2. Your arbitration rules do not require losing plaintiffs to reimburse prevailing defendants for their attorney's fees while Smith's rules do so provide.

3. Your arbitration rules permit the use of class actions while Smith's rules bar their use.

4. Your arbitration rules permit arbitrators to write opinions while Smith's forbid the use of written opinions.

What changes will you make as a result of your examination? What impact will they have on the fair adjudication of disputes? Does all this have an effect on your view about whether arbitration clauses should be enforceable?

Problem 10–17

Darnay has discovered that an identity thief impersonated him, obtained a credit card from Grin's Bank, incurred $20,000 in debt, and disappeared. The Grin's credit card agreement contains a binding arbitration clause and Grin's commences an arbitration proceeding against Darnay to collect the debt. What should Darnay do? Is Darnay bound by the arbitration clause? Who decides that question—in other words, who decides whether the agreement was signed by the real Darnay or an identity thief? Would the arbitrator have a conflict of interest in deciding the issue?

Problem 10–18

You are a legislative assistant to a state legislator who is troubled about pre-dispute arbitration clauses in lending agreements. The lenders in question are all from out of state. The legislator asks you to prepare a proposal which would enable consumers to avoid arbitration (perhaps by making pre-dispute arbitration clauses unlawful or by giving consumers an opportunity to opt out of arbitration agreements at the time they enter into the contract), or failing that, which would require sufficient notice to enable consumers to understand what they were giving up when they enter into agreements containing arbitration clauses, or, if that is not possible, enable aggrieved consumers to bring arbitral class actions to the same extent that they could if they were proceeding in court. What will you advise the legislator?

Problem 10–19

You are a legislative assistant to a United States Senator who is troubled about pre-dispute arbitration clauses in lending agreements. The legislator asks you to prepare a proposal which would enable consumers to avoid arbitration (perhaps by making pre-dispute arbitration clauses unlawful or by giving consumers an opportunity to opt out of arbitration agreements at the time they enter into the contract), or failing that, which would require sufficient notice to enable consumers to understand what they were giving up when they enter into agreements containing arbitration clauses, or, if that is not possible, enable aggrieved consumers to bring arbitral class actions to the same extent that they could if they were proceeding in court. What will you advise the Senator?

2. ARBITRATION AND THE MAGNUSON–MOSS ACT

WALTON v. ROSE MOBILE HOMES LLC

United States Court of Appeals, Fifth Circuit, 2002.
298 F.3d 470.

E. Grady Jolly, Circuit Judge:

Defendant–Appellant Southern Energy Homes, Inc. appeals the district court's denial of its motion to compel arbitration of the Waltons' claim for breach of express written warranty under the Magnuson–Moss Warranty Act, 15 U.S.C. §§ 2301–12 (1994). For the following reasons, we REVERSE and REMAND.

I

In January 1999, Plaintiffs–Appellees Thomas and Le'Ellen Walton ("the Waltons") purchased a mobile home manufactured by Defendant–Appellant Southern Energy Homes, Inc. ("Southern Energy") from a retail seller, Rose Mobile Homes ("Rose"). Southern Energy issued the Waltons a one-year manufacturer's warranty against defects in materials and workmanship. This warranty contained an arbitration provision requiring the Waltons to submit any claims under the warranty to binding arbitration.[1]

---

1. The sales contract also contained a binding arbitration provision that stated: "[A]ny controversy or claim ... arising out of or relating to this Contract or any agreements or instruments relating to or delivered in connection with this Contract ...

The Waltons discovered a variety of defects in their mobile home. They requested repairs from both Southern Energy and Rose on numerous occasions, but these repairs never were completed to the Waltons' satisfaction. Consequently, in October 1999, the Waltons revoked their acceptance of the mobile home by letter.

In December 1999, the Waltons filed suit against Southern Energy and Rose in the Circuit Court of Kemper County, Mississippi, alleging negligence, breach of contract, breach of express and implied warranties, and violation of the Magnuson–Moss Warranty Act (the "MMWA"). The defendants removed the case to federal district court pursuant to 28 U.S.C. § 1331, 28 U.S.C. § 1332, and the MMWA's jurisdictional provision, 15 U.S.C. § 2310(d).

Both Southern Energy and Rose filed motions to compel arbitration of the Waltons' claims. They contended that the arbitration provisions in the warranty and sales contracts and the separate "Binding Arbitration Agreement" signed by Thomas Walton at the time of sale are valid and enforceable under the Federal Arbitration Act (the "FAA") with respect to all of the Waltons' claims. In response, the Waltons argued that the MMWA precludes the enforcement of binding arbitration provisions contained in express written warranties. The Waltons maintained that, because of this statutory prohibition, neither their warranty claims under the MMWA nor their related state law claims are subject to compulsory arbitration. A federal magistrate judge agreed with the Waltons and denied Southern Energy and Rose's motions to compel arbitration with respect to all of the Waltons' claims.

Upon review of the magistrate judge's order, the district court agreed with the magistrate judge's conclusion that the MMWA precludes Southern Energy (the warrantor) from requiring the Waltons to submit their written warranty claims to binding arbitration. Contrary to the magistrate judge's conclusion, however, the district court compelled arbitration of the Waltons' claims that did not arise under the MMWA. Thus, the district court ordered the Waltons to submit their negligence, breach of contract and breach of implied warranty claims to arbitration. Southern Energy now appeals the district court's denial of its motion to compel arbitration of the Waltons' MMWA claim.

II

We review a district court's grant or denial of a motion to compel arbitration de novo. *Webb v. Investacorp, Inc.,* 89 F.3d 252, 257 (5th Cir.1996). We have determined that a two-step inquiry governs the adjudication of motions to compel arbitration under the FAA: "The first

shall ... be determined by arbitration, reference, or trial by a judge as provided below. A controversy involving only a single claimant, or claimants who are related or asserting claims arising from a single transaction, shall be determined by arbitration [pursuant to the Federal Arbitration Act]." Separate and apart from the warranty and the sales contract, Thomas Walton also signed a "Binding Arbitration Agreement" at the time of sale. This agreement stated: "All disputes ... resulting from or arising out of the design, manufacture, warranty or repair of the manufactured home ... will be submitted to BINDING ARBITRATION [pursuant to the Federal Arbitration Act]."

step is to determine whether the parties agreed to arbitrate the dispute in question.... The second step is to determine whether legal constraints external to the parties' agreement foreclosed the arbitration of those claims." *Id.* at 257–58 (internal citations and quotations omitted). Because neither party disputes that the warranty contains a valid arbitration agreement that encompasses the Waltons' breach of express warranty claim, we focus our attention on the second step of the *Webb* inquiry: whether the MMWA presents a legal constraint that forecloses arbitration of the express warranty claim.

We first consider the background and dictates of the Federal Arbitration Act, and then of the Magnuson–Moss Warranty Act.

A

* * *

In order to overcome [the] presumption in favor of arbitration, the party opposing arbitration bears the burden of demonstrating that "Congress intended to preclude a waiver of judicial remedies for the statutory rights at issue." *Id.* (citing *Mitsubishi Motors Corp. v. Soler Chrysler–Plymouth, Inc.,* 473 U.S. 614, 628, 105 S.Ct. 3346, 87 L.Ed.2d 444 (1985)). Courts consider three factors in determining whether Congress intended to preclude application of the FAA to a particular statutory right: (1) the statute's text; (2) its legislative history; and (3) whether there is "an inherent conflict between arbitration and the statute's underlying purposes." *Id.*

In every case the Supreme Court has considered involving a statutory right that does not explicitly preclude arbitration, it has upheld the application of the FAA. This includes cases falling under the Age Discrimination in Employment Act, Sherman Act, Racketeer Influenced and Corrupt Organization Act, Securities Act of 1933, Securities Exchange Act of 1934, and the Truth in Lending Act.

We now turn to the provisions of the Magnuson–Moss Warranty Act ("MMWA"). * * *

* * * The MMWA also permits warrantors to establish "informal dispute settlement procedures" for breach of written warranty claims, and to require consumers to resort to such procedures before bringing a civil action.[12] *Id.* § 2310(a). While the term "informal dispute settlement procedure" is not defined anywhere in the text of the Act, the Federal Trade Commission (the "FTC") is instructed to "prescribe rules setting forth minimum requirements for any informal dispute settlement procedure which is incorporated into the terms of a written warranty." *Id.* § 2310(a)(2). If a warrantor establishes an informal dispute settlement

---

12. The provisions of the MMWA governing informal dispute settlement procedures appear to be applicable only to claims brought pursuant to written warranties. *See* 15 U.S.C. § 2310(a)(2) (1994) ("The Commission shall prescribe rules setting forth minimum requirements for any informal dispute settlement procedure which is incorporated into the terms of a *written* warranty to which any provision of this chapter applies.") (emphasis added).

procedure in accordance with the FTC rules, the warrantor is permitted to include language in the warranty requiring consumers to resort to this procedure "before pursuing any legal remedy" under the Act. *Id.* § 2310(a)(3)(C). The FTC has adopted a regulation stating that informal dispute settlement procedures under the MMWA cannot be legally binding on any person. *See* 16 C.F.R. § 703.5(j). The FTC therefore has found that written warranties cannot require binding arbitration. 40 Fed. Reg. 60168, 60211 (1975) ("[T]here is nothing in the Rule which precludes the use of any other remedies by the parties following a Mechanism decision. . . . However, reference within the written warranty to any binding, non-judicial remedy is prohibited by the Rule and the Act.") Thus, according to the FTC's interpretation, binding arbitration is simply impermissible under the MMWA.

III

When we review an agency's construction of a statute that it administers, we must defer to that agency's interpretation of the statute if: (1) Congress has not spoken directly to the issue; and (2) the agency's interpretation "is based on a permissible construction of the statute." *Chevron U.S.A., Inc. v. Natural Resources Defense Council, Inc.,* 467 U.S. 837, 843, 104 S.Ct. 2778, 81 L.Ed.2d 694 (1984). "The judiciary is the final authority on issues of statutory construction and must reject administrative constructions which are contrary to clear congressional intent. . . . If a court, employing traditional tools of statutory construction, ascertains that Congress had an intention on the precise question at issue, that intention is the law and must be given effect." *Id.* at 843 n. 9, 104 S.Ct. 2778.

There is no doubt that Congress has expressed a clear intention in favor of arbitration for contractual claims. *See* 9 U.S.C. § 2. We therefore must determine if Congress expressed any contrary intent with respect to such claims arising under the MMWA.

A

Under *McMahon,* in order to determine if Congress intended to preclude arbitration of a statutory claim, we consider the statute's text, its legislative history, and its purpose. *McMahon,* 482 U.S. at 226, 107 S.Ct. 2332. The text of the MMWA does not specifically address binding arbitration, nor does it specifically allow the FTC to decide whether to permit or to ban binding arbitration. Although the MMWA allows warrantors to require that consumers use "informal dispute settlement procedures" before filing a suit in court, and allows the FTC to establish rules governing these procedures, it does not define "informal dispute settlement procedure." However, the MMWA does make clear that these are to be used *before* filing a claim in court. Yet binding arbitration generally is understood to be a *substitute* for filing a lawsuit, not a prerequisite. *See Mitsubishi Motors Corp. v. Soler Chrysler–Plymouth, Inc.,* 473 U.S. 614, 628, 105 S.Ct. 3346, 87 L.Ed.2d 444 (1985) ("By agreeing to arbitrate a statutory claim, a party does not forgo the substantive rights afforded by the statute; it only submits to their resolution in an arbitral, rather than a judicial, forum.").

In *Gilmer v. Interstate/Johnson Lane Corp.*, 500 U.S. 20, 111 S.Ct. 1647, 114 L.Ed.2d 26 (1991), the Court held that the Age Discrimination in Employment Act ("ADEA") does not preclude compulsory arbitration of ADEA claims, even though the ADEA allows the EEOC to pursue " 'informal methods of conciliation, conference, and persuasion.' " *Id.* at 29, 111 S.Ct. 1647 (quoting 29 U.S.C. § 626(b)). Therefore the availability of informal methods of settling a dispute plainly does not itself preclude the availability of arbitration. Further, the fact that the MMWA creates a judicial forum for MMWA claims is insufficient evidence of congressional intent to preclude application of the FAA. *See McMahon*, 482 U.S. at 227, 107 S.Ct. 2332 (finding that a provision of the Securities Exchange Act stating that "[t]he district courts of the United States . . . shall have exclusive jurisdiction of violations of this title or the rules and regulations thereunder, and of all suits in equity and actions at law brought to enforce any liability or duty created by this title" did not preclude application of the FAA to claims brought under the statute) (quoting 15 U.S.C. § 78aa); *Gilmer*, 500 U.S. at 29, 111 S.Ct. 1647 (rejecting the argument that compulsory arbitration under the ADEA is improper because the statute provides claimants with a judicial forum); *Matsushita Elec. Indus. Co. v. Epstein*, 516 U.S. 367, 385, 116 S.Ct. 873, 134 L.Ed.2d 6 (1996) ("[A] statute conferring exclusive federal jurisdiction for a certain class of claims does not necessarily require resolution of those claims in a federal court."). In short, the availability of a judicial forum is no basis for precluding arbitration of claims under the MMWA.

We also note that binding arbitration is not normally considered to be an "informal dispute settlement procedure," and it therefore seems to fall outside the bounds of the MMWA and of the FTC's power to prescribe regulations. We thus conclude that the text of the MMWA does not evince a congressional intent to prevent the use of binding arbitration.

B

We next consider the legislative history of the MMWA. The legislative history does not specifically discuss the availability of arbitration, nor does it define or shed light on the meaning of "informal dispute settlement procedure." The legislative history does indicate that such procedures were meant to be non-binding. For example, the House Report on the MMWA states that "[a]n adverse decision in any informal dispute settlement procedure would not be a bar to a civil action on the warranty involved in the proceeding. . . ." H.R. Rep. No. 93–1107 (1974), *reprinted in* 1974 U.S.C.C.A.N. 7702, 7723. The Conference Committee report also indicates that if a consumer chooses not to pursue an informal dispute settlement procedure, a consumer can still pursue "all alternative avenues of redress." S. Conf. Rep. No. 93–1408 (1974), *reprinted in* 1974 U.S.C.C.A.N. 7755, 7758. However, there is still no evidence that Congress intended binding arbitration to be considered an informal dispute settlement procedure. Therefore the fact that any informal dispute settlement procedure must be non-binding, does not imply that Congress meant to preclude binding arbitration, which is of a different nature. The legislative history's reference to "civil action" neither explicitly includes nor precludes binding arbitration. However, the reference to "informal dispute settlement procedure" seemingly precludes binding arbitration from its scope, as binding arbitration is not normally considered an informal procedure. Binding arbitration simply is not part of these reports. These passages therefore do not support an assertion that Congress intended to preclude binding arbitration.

Additionally, the Conference Committee Report states that the legislation requires "provision [by the warrantor] for governmental or consumer participation in internal or other private dispute settlement procedures...." *Id.* Again, this does not indicate an intent to preclude binding arbitration. It simply requires that the consumer (or perhaps the government) participate in the informal procedures established by the warrantor. The Committee cannot have had in mind binding arbitration in its comments, as the government does not normally participate in private binding arbitration procedures. Again, these congressional reports do not demonstrate that Congress intended for binding arbitration to be included within the scope of these informal dispute settlement procedures, nor that it intended to preclude binding arbitration under the MMWA.

* * *

* * * [W]e must conclude that the legislative history here does not evidence a congressional intent to preclude arbitration of MMWA claims.

C

Finally, we examine the purposes of the MMWA, and whether there is an inherent conflict between the MMWA and the FAA. We know that the MMWA was enacted in order to "improve the adequacy of information available to consumers, prevent deception, and improve competition in the marketing of consumer products." 15 U.S.C. § 2302(a). The House Report on the MMWA states that "[t]he purpose of this legislation is (1) to make warranties on consumer products more readily understood and enforceable, (2) to provide the Federal Trade Commission (FTC) with means of better protecting consumers and (3) to authorize appropriations for the operations of the FTC for fiscal years 1975, 1976, and 1977." We do not see any inherent conflict between arbitration and these purposes. Consumers can still vindicate their rights under warranties in an arbitral forum. Warranties can provide adequate and truthful information to consumers, while also requiring binding arbitration. Arbitration is not inherently unfair to consumers. *See Allied–Bruce Terminix Cos. v. Dobson,* 513 U.S. 265, 280, 115 S.Ct. 834, 130 L.Ed.2d 753 (1995) ("Congress, when enacting the [FAA], had the needs of consumers ... in mind.") Although the legislative history of the MMWA expresses a concern with the unequal bargaining power of consumers, *see* S. Rep. No. 93–151, at 22–23 (1973), a perception of unequal bargaining power is not enough to unilaterally hold arbitration agreements unenforceable. *See Gilmer,* 500 U.S. at 33, 111 S.Ct. 1647. Of course, courts can consider individual claims of fraud or unconscionability in arbitration agreements as they would in any other contract. *See id.* We thus can find no inherent conflict between the MMWA and the FAA.

We therefore hold that the text, legislative history, and purpose of the MMWA do not evince a congressional intent to bar arbitration of MMWA written warranty claims. The clear congressional intent in favor of enforcing valid arbitration agreements controls in this case.[15] The Waltons signed a valid binding arbitration agreement, and they must arbitrate their MMWA claims.

IV

We recognize that some courts have found that the MMWA precludes binding arbitration, and that a number of courts have agreed with us.[16] We have found no other federal appellate opinions on point, outside of the Eleventh Circuit. Those cases that have found arbitration to be precluded have relied, at least in part, on the fact that the MMWA provides consumer access to a judicial forum. However, as discussed in Part III.A, this is not evidence of an intent to prohibit arbitration of a statutory claim.

Some of those cases also rely on the FTC regulations to determine congressional intent, and note that the regulations state that consumers

15. We note again, as we stated in Part II.B, that the MMWA requires consumers to submit to informal dispute settlement procedures for breach of written warranty claims, if the warrantor has established such procedures, before filing a civil action. *See* 15 U.S.C. § 2310(a)(3). Our holding in no way conflicts with this provision.

16. Compare Parkerson v. Smith, 817 So.2d 529, 2002 WL 358678, * 3 (Miss.) (en banc) (not yet released for permanent publication) (MMWA precludes arbitration, as it was enacted more recently than the FAA and is more specific; relying on Waverlee Homes, infra, the MMWA's provision of a judicial forum, and the FTC regulations under the MMWA); Browne v. Kline Tysons Imports, Inc., 190 F.Supp.2d 827 (E.D.Va. 2002) (claims under MMWA based on written warranties not subject to binding arbitration because Congress intended to allow consumers to adjudicate such claims in court); Yeomans v. Homes of Legend, Inc., 2001 WL 237313 (M.D.Ala.) (finding that Congress intended to preclude binding arbitration of express and written warranty claims under the MMWA; relying on the reasoning in Waverlee Homes, infra, which states in part that arbitration is precluded because the MMWA grants access to a judicial forum); Pitchford v. Oakwood Mobile

Homes, Inc., 124 F.Supp.2d 958, 962–65 (W.D.Va.2000) (relying largely on FTC's regulations finding binding arbitration to be impermissible and on the MMWA's grant of access to a judicial forum to find that the MMWA precludes binding arbitration of disputes over written warranties); Raesly v. Grand Housing, Inc., 105 F.Supp.2d 562, 573 (S.D.Miss.2000) (finding that MMWA precludes binding arbitration of written warranty claims, relying on Waverlee Homes); Wilson v. Waverlee Homes, Inc., 954 F.Supp. 1530, 1532 (M.D.Ala.1997) (MMWA precludes binding arbitration of MMWA claims, in part because it provides access to a judicial forum and because the FTC regulations have so interpreted it), with In re American Homestar of Lancaster, Inc., 50 S.W.3d 480, 490 (Tex.2001) (MMWA's text, legislative history, and purpose do not preclude binding arbitration); Results Oriented, Inc. v. Crawford, 245 Ga. App. 432, 538 S.E.2d 73, 79–81 (2000) (MMWA does not preclude arbitration of express and implied warranty claims, unless arbitration clause is unconscionable), aff'd as Crawford v. Results Oriented, Inc., 273 Ga. 884, 548 S.E.2d 342 (2000); Southern Energy Homes, Inc. v. Ard, 772 So.2d 1131, 1135 (Ala.2000) (holding arbitration provisions of a written warranty to be binding).

should have full access to the courts and that informal dispute mechanisms should be non-binding. For example, in *Wilson v. Waverlee Homes, Inc.,* 954 F.Supp. 1530, 1537–39 (M.D.Ala.1997), *aff'd,* 127 F.3d 40 (11th Cir.1997) (table op.), the court held that the MMWA precludes binding arbitration of MMWA claims. The court relied on: (1) the MMWA's provision of access to a judicial forum; (2) the fact that informal dispute settlement mechanisms are a prerequisite to suit; (3) the FTC regulations which reflect the MMWA's "command" that consumers should have access to the courts; and (4) the history of the FTC regulations which prohibit binding arbitration. *Id.; see also Yeomans v. Homes of Legend, Inc.,* 2001 WL 237313 (M.D.Ala.) (expressly adopting the reasoning and result in *Wilson*). *But see Richardson v. Palm Harbor Homes, Inc.,* 254 F.3d 1321 (11th Cir.2001) (predispute arbitration agreement not rendered unenforceable by MMWA with respect to breach of oral express warranty claim under the Alabama Uniform Commercial Code). Again, the provision of access to a judicial forum is not evidence of intent to prevent the use of arbitration. Further, it is improper to use the FTC regulations themselves to determine congressional intent here. As noted previously, we must consider the statute's text, legislative history, and whether its purpose conflicts with another statute, to determine congressional intent. An agency's regulations, promulgated pursuant to a statute, are not part of this test. It is only after considering these three factors and determining that Congress's intent is ambiguous, that we would then proceed to consider the FTC's regulations and whether they are a permissible interpretation of the statute, per *Chevron*. We would not, in any case, use the regulations themselves to determine congressional intent.

V

We hold that the MMWA does not preclude binding arbitration of claims pursuant to a valid binding arbitration agreement, which the courts must enforce pursuant to the FAA. The Waltons are bound to arbitrate their claims. We REVERSE the judgment of the district court and REMAND for entry of judgment in accordance with this opinion.

KING, CHIEF JUDGE, dissenting:

The case before us is, in essence, a classic *Chevron* case. The text of the MMWA contains a conspicuous and significant ambiguity: the Act can be read to prohibit the use of binding arbitration agreements in written warranties, or it can be read not to address the enforceability of binding arbitration clauses in written warranties, in which case the FAA's presumption of arbitrability would likely be applicable. The FTC—the agency to which Congress entrusted the task of implementing and elaborating the provisions of the MMWA—has interpreted the MMWA to preclude the enforcement of binding arbitration clauses in written warranties governed by the Act. We are bound to defer to the FTC's interpretation of the Act unless (1) Congress has "directly spoken to the precise question at issue" or (2) the FTC's construction of the statute is unreasonable. *Chevron U.S.A., Inc. v. Natural Res. Defense*

Council, Inc., 467 U.S. 837, 842–43, 104 S.Ct. 2778, 81 L.Ed.2d 694 (1984). While the majority apparently concedes that the text of the Act is ambiguous and that the legislative history is unilluminating, the majority nonetheless concludes that we must reject the FTC's interpretation under the first prong of *Chevron* because Congress has unambiguously stated that binding arbitration clauses in written warranties governed by the MMWA are enforceable. Because I find no such clear indicia of congressional intent, and because I conclude that the Commission's interpretation of the MMWA is reasonable and entitled to judicial deference, I respectfully dissent.

I. *The FTC's Regulatory Construction of § 2310*

* * *

As the majority correctly recognizes, we are required to defer to the FTC's construction of the MMWA unless: (1) Congress has directly spoken to the precise question at issue, or (2) the FTC's construction is unreasonable. *Chevron,* 467 U.S. at 842–43, 104 S.Ct. 2778. The majority reaches only the first of these inquiries, finding that Congress has unambiguously stated that binding arbitration clauses are enforceable in written warranties governed by the MMWA. Because I cannot agree with this conclusion, I address both prongs of the *Chevron* inquiry in turn.

II. *Has Congress Directly Spoken to the Precise Question at Issue?*

Despite its acknowledgment that neither the text nor the legislative history of the MMWA clearly indicates whether the "informal dispute settlement procedures" provided for in § 2310 are intended to be the exclusive alternative to litigation available for breach of written warranty claims under the Act, the majority nonetheless finds that Congress has "directly spoken to the precise question at issue." Initially, the majority points to the fact that, fifty years prior to the passage of the MMWA, Congress expressed a general policy favoring arbitration of contractual claims in a different statute. The majority apparently finds that this general policy expressed in the FAA is indicative of Congress's intent in enacting the MMWA.

* * *

As the Supreme Court has consistently recognized, the presumption of arbitrability established by the FAA is not absolute and "may be overridden by a contrary congressional command" in the statute creating the right at issue. *Shearson/Am. Express Inc. v. McMahon,* 482 U.S. 220, 226, 107 S.Ct. 2332, 96 L.Ed.2d 185 (1987); *see also Gilmer v. Interstate/Johnson Lane Corp.,* 500 U.S. 20, 26, 111 S.Ct. 1647, 114 L.Ed.2d 26 (1991). The question in the instant case is whether the informal dispute settlement mechanism provisions in § 2310 of the MMWA express such a contrary congressional command. The majority, however, concludes that Congress did not intend to express such a command *in the MMWA,* based on indicia of congressional intent expressed *in the FAA.* Such circular logic is unpersuasive: the presumption of arbitrability becomes relevant *after* it is established that there is no contrary congressional command. It is inappropriate to apply the presumption in ascertaining whether the statute in question contains such a command.

The majority further argues that Congress could not possibly have intended for § 2310's provisions regarding "informal dispute settlement procedures" to govern arbitration proceedings because "binding arbitration is not normally thought of as an informal procedure." Unlike the majority, I am extremely hesitant to conclude that Congress has directly addressed an apparent statutory ambiguity based on a judicial assumption about what a term "normally" means. In addition, even assuming the majority's understanding of the generally accepted meaning of "informal procedures" was persuasive indicia of Congress's intent in enacting the MMWA, it is not at all clear that the majority's conclusion that arbitration "is not normally thought of as an informal procedure" accurately reflects how "arbitration" was perceived at the time of the MMWA's enactment in 1974. As numerous commentators have recognized, the formality of arbitration proceedings has increased notably in the latter half of the twentieth century, particularly in the period since the Supreme Court "revitalized" the FAA by clarifying its applicability to statutory claims in the late 1980s. * * * Moreover, even today, arbitration undoubtedly constitutes a more "informal" procedure than litigation. Thus, to categorize arbitration as "formal" or "informal" largely begs the question of the appropriate basis of comparison. Under these circumstances, even if the majority is correct that most people would characterize arbitration as a "formal" procedure at this point in time, this perception hardly provides conclusive evidence that the 1974 Congress did not intend to address arbitration proceedings in enacting MMWA provisions governing "informal dispute resolution proceedings."

Neither the text of § 2310 nor the statutory context of this provision conclusively indicates whether § 2310 applies to arbitration proceedings (i.e., whether § 2310–governed "informal dispute settlement procedures" are intended to be the *exclusive* alternative to litigation under the Act). While the legislative history contains some indication that Congress did intend for § 2310 procedures to be the exclusive non-judicial forum available under the Act, these indicia are not sufficiently illuminating that the legislative history can be deemed conclusive regarding congressional intent. Moreover, there are no subsequent congressional enactments addressing written warranties that clarify this issue. Under these circumstances, there is no basis for this court to conclude that Congress has "directly spoken to the precise question at issue."

Because I conclude that Congress has not directly spoken to the question we face today, I find it is necessary to reach the second prong of the *Chevron* inquiry—namely, whether the Commission's interpretation of § 2310 is based on a permissible construction of the statute.

III.   *Is the FTC's Interpretation of the MMWA Unreasonable?*

Because Congress has "delegated authority to the agency generally to make rules carrying the force of law," *United States v. Mead Corp.,*

533 U.S. 218, 121 S.Ct. 2164, 2171, 150 L.Ed.2d 292 (2001), we are required to defer to the Commission's construction of the statute unless that interpretation is unreasonable. *Chevron,* 467 U.S. at 843, 104 S.Ct. 2778. Southern Energy argues that the FTC's interpretation is unreasonable because the regulations indicate that the Commission's rationale for concluding that the MMWA prohibits binding arbitration provisions in written warranties was its determination that such provisions are "deceptive since . . . the Act gives state and federal courts jurisdiction over suits for breach of warranty and service contract." 16 C.F.R. § 700.8 (2001). Pointing to the Supreme Court's holding that a mere statutory grant of jurisdiction to federal or state courts does not preclude enforcement of a mandatory arbitration provision under the FAA, *see, e.g., Gilmer,* 500 U.S. at 29, 111 S.Ct. 1647; *McMahon,* 482 U.S. at 227, 107 S.Ct. 2332, Southern Energy argues that deference to the FTC regulations is inappropriate because the Commission's interpretation of the MMWA is not based on a permissible construction of the statute. Two state supreme courts have found this reasoning persuasive in determining that the FTC's regulations do not preclude the enforceability of binding arbitration agreements in written warranties. *See In re Am. Homestar of Lancaster, Inc.,* 50 S.W.3d 480, 491 (Tex.2001) (noting that while it would normally be appropriate to accord *Chevron* deference to the FTC's interpretation of the statute it administers, no such deference is owed to the regulation precluding binding arbitration agreements under the MMWA because "the Supreme Court . . . has rejected arguments similar to those upon which the FTC relies to conclude the statute prohibits binding arbitration"); *Southern Energy Homes, Inc. v. Ard,* 772 So.2d 1131, 1135 (Ala.2000) (explicitly adopting Justice See's dissent in *Southern Energy Homes, Inc. v. Lee,* 732 So.2d 994, 1010 (Ala.1999), which reasoned that "[a]lthough reasonable deference is due an interpretation of a statute by an agency charged with administering that statute, no such deference is due when the Supreme Court has expressly rejected the rationale on which the agency interpretation is based").

While the FTC's interpretive regulations do suggest that the Commission's construction of the statute was partially based on its reading of the statute's jurisdictional provision, the materials accompanying the FTC's promulgation of its legislative regulations (the appropriate focus of our *Chevron* inquiry) signal that the Commission had a number of permissible reasons for reading the statute as it did. According to the Federal Register commentary accompanying the FTC's promulgation of its legislative regulations, the Commission based its determination that Congress intended to preclude enforcement of binding arbitration clauses in written warranties on two factors: (1) the Commission's reading of a staff report of the House Interstate and Foreign Commerce Committee's Subcommittee on Commerce and Finance; and (2) the Commission's concern that such arbitration provisions would inadequately protect the interests of consumers. *See* 40 Fed. Reg. 60167, 60210 (Dec. 31, 1975). Initially, the Commission apparently read portions of the legislative history of the MMWA (specifically, the subcommittee staff report) to signal Congress's intent that dispute resolution mechanisms established pursuant to the Act would not be legally binding. While it is not possible to confirm the validity of this reading of the subcommittee staff report, such resources are certainly a permissible basis for an agency's conclusions regarding congressional intent, as the reasonableness of an agency's construction of a statute is often assessed in light of the legislative history. *See, e.g., Chevron,* 467 U.S. at 862–64, 104 S.Ct. 2778; *Babbitt v. Sweet Home Chapter of Cmtys. for a Great Or.,* 515 U.S. 687, 704–08, 115 S.Ct. 2407, 132 L.Ed.2d 597 (1995).

The Commission's second expressed motive for precluding binding arbitration agreements in written warranties is its concern that such binding arbitration agreements inadequately protect consumers. As a general rule, this court is obliged to defer to the FTC's expertise regarding the most appropriate way to effect the MMWA's consumer protection goals. * * *

While the majority purports not to reach the second prong of *Chevron*, the majority espouses an additional argument against the Commission's construction of § 2310 that appears to be more directly relevant to the inquiry under the second *Chevron* prong (i.e., whether the Commission's interpretation of the MMWA is reasonable) than under the first *Chevron* prong. Specifically, the majority contends that the agency's construction of § 2310 is unreasonable because it is inconsistent with the Supreme Court's opinion in *Gilmer*. In *Gilmer*, the Court considered whether an employee's claim under the Age Discrimination in Employment Act (ADEA), 29 U.S.C. § 621 *et seq.* (1994), should be submitted to compulsory arbitration pursuant to an arbitration agreement in the employee's securities registration application. The employee argued that Congress intended to preclude application of the FAA to claims under the ADEA, suggesting that under the third prong of the *McMahon* test, there is an "inherent conflict" between arbitration and the ADEA's underlying purpose. *Gilmer,* 500 U.S. at 26–27, 111 S.Ct. 1647. The employee relied in part upon an ADEA provision requiring the EEOC to "promptly seek to eliminate any alleged unlawful practice by informal methods of conciliation, conference, and persuasion" upon receipt of a charge of discrimination. 29 U.S.C. § 626(d) (1994). The employee apparently argued, *inter alia,* that this provision signaled Congress's intent to have the EEOC involved in any judicial or non-judicial resolution of statutory claims, thus precluding enforcement of a binding arbitration provision that would resolve disputes without EEOC involvement because this alternative would "undermine the role of the EEOC." *Gilmer,* 500 U.S. at 28, 111 S.Ct. 1647. The Court rejected this argument, concluding that "nothing in the ADEA indicates that Congress intended that the EEOC be involved in all employment disputes" and that "the mere involvement of an administrative agency in the enforcement of a statute is not sufficient to preclude arbitration." *Id.* at 28–29, 111 S.Ct. 1647.

The majority reads *Gilmer* to hold, as a broad proposition, that express provision in a statute for out-of-court dispute resolution does not preclude application of the FAA. However, I find the *Gilmer* Court's discussion of the EEOC's participation in "informal methods of conciliation, conference, and persuasion" to be too far afield from the facts of the instant case to be dispositive.

Initially, it merits notice that the position advanced by the Waltons in the instant case is materially different from the position advanced by the employee in *Gilmer*. The Waltons ask this court to defer to an administrative agency's regulatory interpretation that Congress intended for a statute to preclude binding arbitration, not to read a prohibition of binding arbitration into a statute and its regulations based on concerns about impermissibly diminishing the role of the agency. Moreover, the language of the statutory provision at issue in *Gilmer* is materially different from the language in the MMWA at issue in this case. The ADEA's admonishment that the EEOC should attempt to engage in "conciliation, conference, and persuasion" with the employer upon receipt of an employment discrimination charge cannot be read to speak to the availability of binding arbitration in the same way as a statutory provision that, by its terms, addresses "any informal dispute settlement procedure" provided for in a written warranty. Indeed, it is clear that Congress did not attribute the same meaning to the two phrases. Unlike the MMWA, the ADEA contains no statutory language instructing the regulatory agency to promulgate procedures and regulations governing "conciliation, conference, and persuasion" under the ADEA. Moreover, the EEOC regulations contain no detailed alternative dispute resolution procedures akin to those contained in the FTC's MMWA regulations, suggesting that the EEOC did not read the "conciliation, conference, and persuasion" language in the ADEA to constitute a congressional delegation of authority to regulate alternative dispute resolution mechanisms under the Act. Under these circumstances, the FTC's construction of the MMWA cannot be deemed "unreasonable" based on a perceived inconsistency with the Court's reasoning in *Gilmer*. *Gilmer* is simply inapposite.

As none of the arguments advanced by Southern Energy or the majority convincingly demonstrates that the FTC's construction of § 2310 is unreasonable, this court is required to defer to the FTC's interpretation of the statute. Moreover, there are a number of compelling independent reasons why the FTC regulations at issue in the instant case are entitled to particular deference from this court.

Initially, it merits notice that the FTC's legislative regulations constitute a *contemporaneous* regulatory interpretation of the MMWA. An administrative interpretation "has peculiar weight when it involves a contemporaneous construction of a statute by the [persons] charged with the responsibility of setting its machinery in motion, of making the parts work efficiently and smoothly while they are yet untried and new." *Zenith Radio Corp. v. United States*, 437 U.S. 443, 450, 98 S.Ct. 2441, 57 L.Ed.2d 337 (1978) (alteration in original) (quoting *Norwegian Nitrogen Prods. Co. v. United States,* 288 U.S. 294, 315, 53 S.Ct. 350, 77 L.Ed. 796 (1933)). Similarly, this court should accord particular deference to the

FTC's regulatory interpretation of the MMWA because the regulations represent a longstanding, consistent interpretation of the statute. While agency interpretations that are revised over time are certainly entitled to *Chevron* deference, *see Rust v. Sullivan,* 500 U.S. 173, 186, 111 S.Ct. 1759, 114 L.Ed.2d 233 (1991), longstanding and consistent agency interpretations carry special weight. *See NLRB v. Bell Aerospace Co. Div. Textron Inc.,* 416 U.S. 267, 274–75, 94 S.Ct. 1757, 40 L.Ed.2d 134 (1974) ("[A] court may accord great weight to the longstanding interpretation placed on a statute by an agency charged with its administration."); *see also Smiley,* 517 U.S. at 740, 116 S.Ct. 1730 (noting that, while antiquity is not a condition of validity under the second prong of *Chevron,* "agency interpretations that are of long standing come before us with a certain credential of reasonableness, since it is rare that error would long persist"). Such a "credential of reasonableness" appears to be particularly warranted in the instant case, where the agency has recently reconsidered and reaffirmed its longstanding, consistent interpretation of the statute through a notice-and-comment regulatory review proceeding.

Finally, while the legislative history of the MMWA does not contain any specific discussion of the availability of arbitration, there is some indirect indication in the legislative history that Congress intended for internal dispute settlement mechanisms governed by § 2310 to be the exclusive alternative to litigation available under the Act, thus confirming the validity of the reading espoused by the FTC and the Waltons. Language in the report of the Senate Committee on Commerce is particularly enlightening. The general description of the legislation contained in that report describes the bill's remedial provisions as follows:

> If a supplier fails to honor his warranty or service contract promises, the consumer can avail himself of *certain specified remedies.* If that supplier has provided a bona fide informal dispute settlement mechanism by which disputes between suppliers and consumers are to be resolved, then the consumer would utilize the informal dispute settlement mechanism before pursuing other avenues of redress. *If a supplier does not have an informal dispute settlement mechanism for resolving consumer complaints,* or if the consumer is not satisfied with the results obtained in any informal dispute settlement proceeding, *the consumer can pursue his legal remedies in a court of competent jurisdiction,* provided that he has afforded the supplier a reasonable opportunity to cure the breach.

S. Rep. No. 93–151, at 2–3 (1973) (emphasis added). This passage suggests that Congress intended for the MMWA to authorize only the specific remedial mechanisms mentioned in the Act. This language also implies that litigation, not arbitration, is the "other avenue[ ] of redress" available to the consumer if the warrantor has not established an informal dispute settlement mechanism or if the consumer is unsatisfied with the results of that proceeding.

The same conclusion is suggested in the report's subsequent, more detailed analysis of the MMWA's remedial provisions. This portion of the report states: "[Section 2310] spells out the remedies available to the purchaser of consumer products. A purchaser can utilize informal dispute settlement procedures established by suppliers or, having afforded a supplier a reasonable opportunity to cure, may resort to formal adversary proceedings with reasonable attorney's fees available if successful in the litigation." *Id.* at 22–23. This passage suggests that litigation (not arbitration) is the "formal adversary proceeding" contemplated by the Act for a consumer who is dissatisfied with the warrantor's attempt to cure or with any informal dispute settlement procedure that the warrantor has established.

Language in the Conference Committee report provides further confirmation that Congress intended § 2310–compliant procedures to be the exclusive method of non-judicial dispute resolution available under the Act. The Conference Committee report states:

> It should be recognized ... that provision for governmental or consumer participation in *internal or other private dispute settlement procedures* under the bill is required by this legislation. Consequently warranties providing that consumers must first resort to informal dispute settlement procedures before initiating a suit are contrary to the intent of the legislation where there is no provision for governmental or specific consumer participation in the procedure or where the procedure is otherwise unfair.

S. Conf. Rep. No. 93–1408 (1974), *reprinted in* 1974 U.S.C.C.A.N. 7755, 7758 (emphasis added). This passage is enlightening for two reasons. First, it equates the term "informal dispute settlement procedure" as used in the Act with a more general definition (i.e., "internal or other private dispute settlement procedure"), thus suggesting that Congress intended for the term "informal dispute settlement procedure" to be read broadly. In addition, by specifically indicating that any procedure that does not comply with the statutory requirement for consumer or governmental participation is "contrary to the intent of the legislation," this passage suggests that § 2310 was intended to govern all forms of alternative dispute resolution provided for in a written warranty.

These passages from the Conference Committee report and the Senate report reinforce the Commission's interpretation that Congress intended for § 2310 (and, thus, the FTC's implementing regulations) to govern all non-judicial forms of dispute resolution included in the terms of written warranties. Thus, while the legislative history of the MMWA may not be sufficient by itself to establish Congress's intent to preclude application of the FAA to claims for breach of written warranty under the MMWA, these materials provide added support for the "reasonableness" of the Commission's interpretation.

Accordingly, because I find that Congress has not "directly spoken to the precise question" whether binding arbitration clauses in written warranties governed by the MMWA are enforceable, and because the FTC's construction of the statute is eminently reasonable, I would defer to the Commission's expertise and affirm the district court's judgment refusing to compel arbitration of the Waltons' written warranty claims. I dissent.

Notes

1. In accord with the principal case is Davis v. Southern Energy Homes, Inc., 305 F.3d 1268, 1270 (11th Cir.), reh. and reh. en banc denied, 54 Fed.Appx. 687 (11th Cir. 2002), cert. denied, 538 U.S. 945, 123 S.Ct. 1633, 155 L.Ed.2d 486 (2003); Pack v. Damon Corp., 320 F.Supp.2d 545 (E.D.Mich. 2004), rev'd on other grounds, 434 F.3d 810 (6th Cir. 2006). But see Rickard v. Teynor's Homes, Inc., 279 F.Supp.2d 910 (N.D.Ohio 2003). The principal case is criticized forcefully in Andrew P. Lamis, The New Age of Artificial Legal Reasoning as Reflected in the Judicial Treatment of the Magnuson–Moss Act and the Federal Arbitration Act, 15 Loy. Consumer L. Rev. 173, 234 (2003), in which the author asks why Congress would go to the trouble of specifying procedures, to be amplified upon by the FTC, for non-binding arbitration under Magnuson–Moss, and leave binding arbitration largely unfettered: "This interpretation renders the Magnuson–Moss Act absurd. If Congress was so keenly interested in making the non-binding alternative dispute resolution procedures it was legislating entirely fair, then surely it must have had at least as great a concern in ensuring that every step of a binding alternative dispute resolution mechanism was also fair."

2. How would you counsel a manufacturer that had established an informal non-binding arbitration procedure in accordance with the FTC's regulations after *Walton*? If you were an FTC commissioner, would you vote to uphold the regulation rejected in the principal case?

3. Would an arbitration clause barring the award of attorney's fees govern an arbitration under the Magnuson–Moss Act, given that the Act provides for attorney's fees in § 2310(d)(2)?

4. A number of automobile manufacturers established informal non-binding arbitration programs pursuant to the Magnuson–Moss Act and the FTC's regulations thereunder, for the purpose of addressing lemon law grievances. The following problems raise issues under these programs.

Problem 10–20

Robin Hood bought a new car in New York from Dale Dodge Dealers and received a one year "Limited Warranty" from Chrysler under Magnuson–Moss. The sale was also subject to New York's "Lemon Law" which appears in the Statutory Supplement.

After 30 days, the clutch in the new car failed to operate properly. Hood took the car to Dale, who "repaired" the clutch. Although the clutch operated properly when it left the dealership that day, it failed again within 10 days. Dale "repaired" again, but it failed for a third time five days later. Dale "repaired" it a third and a fourth time, but it failed a fifth time 15 days later. Hood had the car towed to the dealership once again.

At this point, Dale began to believe something serious was wrong, so it called Chrysler to ask for instructions. The Chrysler representative told Dale that clutches were not covered by Chrysler's Limited Warranty, and that the Dealership Service Manual stated that point very clearly. The Chrysler representative stated that she did not care what Dale did with, or to, Hood's car, but that Chrysler would not pay for any of it— and also would not reimburse Dale for past services provided to Hood for the failed clutch.

Dale then contacted Hood and explained that clutches are not covered by Chrysler warranties, so that any repairs would be at his expense. Dale also explained that past services had been at Dale's expense, and that all the bills ($600) from the three prior repair attempts would have to be paid before Hood could get his car back. To date, Hood has not done so, and Dale still has possession of the car.

Hood has tried to negotiate with Dale and with the Chrysler representative, but they have made no adjustment in their demands. Meanwhile, he is walking. He visited your office to seek legal counsel, and you advised him of the informal arbitration program sponsored by Chrysler. Since this was a low-budget case, you suggested that Hood might well want to try arbitration first, because it would involve no attorney fees. At that time, you were aware that the Chrysler arbitration program did not meet FTC Guidelines under Magnuson–Moss, but that did not seem critical.

Hood took your advice and filed a proper complaint with the Chrysler arbitration program. He then prepared his case and asked for an arbitration hearing. He was granted the hearing.

On the morning of the hearing, he overheard the arbitrator, William Scarlet, and the Chrysler representative talking to each other. It was obvious that the Chrysler representative had previously appeared before Scarlet at least six times, and had previously handled at least 100 arbitrations. The Chrysler representative had also brought an experienced mechanic with her to be an "expert witness" on Chrysler's behalf. Finally, Scarlet thanked the Chrysler representative for Chrysler's reimbursement to Scarlet of Scarlet's travel expenses of $150. Hood knows where Scarlet lives, and it is about 10 miles from the hearing site.

After overhearing this conversation, Hood becomes concerned and calls you for advice.

(a) Hood states that he has not yet signed any paper which binds him to arbitrate. He now wants to "walk away" from the arbitration process, and use the courts instead. Can he do that? Is there any requirement that he arbitrate before going to court? Does he have any other alternatives?

(b) If Hood continues the arbitration process, and the arbitrator rules against him, can he still pursue his legal remedies in court or otherwise? If he later sues in court, will the arbitration findings and decision be admissible against him? Will they be binding on the court?

(c) Would you advise Hood to continue the arbitration process or not? Does it seem unreasonably biased against him? Why, or why not?

(d) If Hood's primary concern arises from Scarlet's statements, can Hood ask Scarlet to disqualify himself due to Chrysler's payments or previous association with Chrysler's representative? If so, what is the likelihood that Scarlet's replacement will create an improvement in these aspects?

Problem 10–21

Same facts as Problem 10–20. This time, however, you are the arbitrator, and Hood has continued the arbitration process. Hood presented evidence that Dale tried to fix the clutch four times, and failed four times. He wants to cancel the sale and get his money back. He also presented evidence of his cost of renting a substitute car from Hertz while Dale kept possession of his new car.

The Chrysler representative has presented evidence that Chrysler has never considered the clutch to be a "covered item" under the "Limited Warranty", that the Dealership Service Manual has so stated for the past 25 years, and that it has been a custom of Chrysler, continuously and rigorously, not to pay for any clutch repairs. Chrysler defends this practice on the ground that clutches are easily abused and that after a failure it is impossible to determine whether that failure was caused by a defect or driver abuse, and therefore any failure of a clutch is considered a product of driver abuse. The "expert witness" testifies that all of the above is true.

You, as arbitrator, must now decide this dispute.

(a) Must you follow state law? For example, must you follow all the warranty rules established by UCC Article 2, including its definitions of what is warranted (UCC §§ 2–313, 2–315), and its notification requirements (UCC § 2–607)? More importantly, must you follow the same rules on burden of proof of a defect that a court should use, and insist that Hood prove what was wrong with the clutch, rather than merely assert that it failed?

(b) Must you follow state law, revisited. For example, if the clutch has failed to be repaired 4 times, and you find that the clutch problem is due to manufacturer's defect and not driver abuse, must you order a "buy-back"? Or, can you limit your order to a requirement that Chrysler provide Hood with a replacement equivalent car? Or install a replacement clutch? Or pay the bill of an independent mechanic to replace the clutch?

Note on State–Sponsored Dispute Resolution Mechanisms

State-sponsored dispute resolution mechanisms provide an alternative in some states to the mechanisms provided under the auspices of the manufacturer. For instance, the New York Lemon Law gives consumers the option of submitting their claims to an independent arbitrator approved by the attorney general, in lieu of the manufacturer's arbitration procedure. Manufacturers are required to submit to the state-sponsored binding arbitration if the consumer elects this procedure. Unlike the manufacturer proceeding, the state-sponsored program is binding on both parties. N.Y. McKinney's General Business Law. § 198–a(k).

Why do you suppose the New York and other state legislatures felt it necessary to set up an independent arbitration procedure?

*

Index

References are to Pages

---

†